2007
U.S. Master™
Accounting
Guide

John C. Wisdom, MBA, CPA
James R. Hasselback, Ph.D.

CCH
a Wolters Kluwer business

Preface

Practicing accountants can understand the value of collecting information from authoritative sources and organizing it for fingertip reference. Many clients do not understand the time it can take to research what is perceived to be a simple question, and so the *2007 U.S. Master™ Accounting Guide* is offered to provide quick answers in an efficient and inexpensive way. The book also features facts and examples that serve as memory joggers and aids in the day-to-day duties requiring the special knowledge of the accounting profession.

The *2007 U.S. Master Accounting Guide* is organized into nine primary chapters and one supporting chapter. The primary chapters include: Accounting Journal Entries, Accounting Principles, Business Entities, Business Valuation, Government Programs, Financial Analysis, Investments, Taxation and Human Resources. The Directories chapter supports the first nine.

The most common feature in the book is a simple heading or lead sentence followed by important bullet point items. When more technical information, such as Internal Revenue Code highlights, is desired, the treatment becomes more detailed.

The broad subjects in the book are an excellent representation of subjects the accountant must deal with on a day-to-day basis. Within these broad subjects, the book covers a selection of concepts and issues. Individual topics are treated as independently as possible so that the reader is not required to go back and forth between pages, chapters and sections. Since the work is geared to practicing accountants, most sections are very direct, and little time is spent actually teaching concepts.

Here's a quick chapter-by-chapter summary:

ACCOUNTING JOURNAL ENTRIES

This chapter consists of sample journal entries and related calculations. Many of the journal entries may seem rather basic, but some have little wrinkles that are worth a second look. Breeze through the entries now and refer to them when you are working on your own entries.

ACCOUNTING PRINCIPLES

This chapter offers a quick reference digest of accounting principles. New GAAP changes occur every year that create new rules and affect existing ones as well. This digest chapter offers the busy accountant a quick refresher on the most frequently encountered rules.

BUSINESS ENTITIES

Quick memory-joggers on various business entities make up this chapter. This chapter is very selective in coverage, and highlighted, but hot topics, such as franchises and LLCs, are covered at great length.

BUSINESS VALUATION

Valuation methods are discussed in very concise terms. Concepts are covered in rapid succession and essential how-to information is provided in checklists and worksheets. The business valuation process is clearly explained.

GOVERNMENT PROGRAMS

This section keys in on Medicare and Social Security. It offers a concise explanation of the two programs and their coverage.

FINANCIAL ANALYSIS

Practicing accountants are often seen as the one person in their clients' circle of professionals who knows the most about finance. This section provides concentrated coverage of financial formulas, sample calculations, helpful tables and much more.

INVESTMENTS

Clients like to talk about investments, so the accountant must be aware of important investment principles and have a good working knowledge of investment strategies. This section offers condensed coverage of these issues, along with tables, formulas, calculations and more.

TAXATION

Accountants have used CCH's *U.S. Master Tax Guide*® for over 75 years. The Taxation chapter does not attempt to condense or digest what is already in the *U.S. Master Tax Guide;* rather, it supplements it with selected information on key issues.

HUMAN RESOURCES

Key facts are presented that relate to human resources, with special attention given to independent contractors, immigration, withholding and various employment law issues.

DIRECTORIES

These helpful directories provide the phone numbers and addresses of accounting groups and federal and state government offices. Internet addresses are also included.

John C. Wisdom, MBA, CPA

James R. Hasselback, Ph.D.

April 2007

About the Authors

John C. Wisdom is a Certified Public Accountant practicing in Dallas, Texas. He is the author of several popular books on accounting, tax and business issues. Mr. Wisdom received an MBA from the University of Alabama and is a Registered Representative and Registered Investment Advisor. He has over 25 years of practice experience and is frequently called on to speak at seminars and educational programs. He has taught college accounting courses and also worked for data processing and manufacturing firms. Mr. Wisdom is a member of the American Institute of Certified Public Accountants, the Texas Society of CPAs and the Texas Association of Advisors.

James R. Hasselback is the Mary Ball Washington Eminent Scholar at the University of West Florida. He previously taught at Florida State University for 27 years. He regularly conducts continuing education seminars for tax practitioners. He is co-author and technical editor of several federal taxation textbooks as well as the author of numerous articles published in accounting and academic journals. He is also well known as the editor of the *Hasselback Accounting Faculty Directory* and numerous other faculty directories. Professor Hasselback is a member of the American Accounting Association and the American Taxation Association, and has a Ph.D. in Accounting from Michigan State University.

Acknowledgments

We would like to acknowledge the efforts of many professional colleagues who helped to revitalize and update the *2007 U. S. Master™ Accounting Guide*. Our readers know the ambitious scope of the work and it takes special expertise in many areas to properly cover the topics. Many CCH editors contributed to the project in areas of their expertise. John Strzelecki, Senior Editor of the CCH PAYROLL MANAGEMENT GUIDE, updated our withholding materials. Geraldine Szuberla, Senior Health Law Editor, updated the Medicare and Medicaid coverage. Dem Hopkins, Senior Editor of the CCH LIMITED LIABILITY COMPANY GUIDE; Donna Flanagan, Senior Editor of the CCH S CORPORATIONS GUIDE; and Tom Cody, Senior Editor of CCH PARTNERSHIP TAX PLANNING AND PRACTICE, updated our chapter on business entities.

We also received help from some of CCH's top authors. William Hubbartt, President of Hubbartt Associates, updated much of the human resources materials. Mr. Hubbartt has published several books on HR issues including performance appraisal, work groups, and employee handbook construction. His latest venture is in privacy law. Bill Jarnagin, author of CCH's *U.S. Master GAAP Guide,* updated the accounting journal entries and principles chapters. Professor Jarnagin of Wichita State University has been one of the top GAAP experts in the United States for over 20 years. Alan Campbell updated the Social Security coverage and the Small Business Administration information. Mr. Campbell is the co-author of *Tax Strategies for the Self-Employed* and the revision editor of the *CCH Financial and Estate Planning Guide.*

We would like to thank you, our fellow accounting professionals throughout the country, who have bought this book. We hope it will help you every day and we look forward to your comments and criticisms.

Table of Contents

Chapter 1: Accounting Journal Entries

Accounts Receivable: Assignment	¶ 101
Accounts Receivable: Bad Debts	¶ 103
Acquisitions of Assets by Exchange	¶ 104
Business Combination (SFAS No. 141)	¶ 105
Bonds	¶ 107
Asset Retirement Obligations (SFAS No. 143 and 146 and FASB Interpretation No. 47)	¶ 108
Cash Flow Statement	¶ 109
Construction Contracts—Long Term	¶ 111
Cost of Goods Manufactured Schedule	¶ 113
Depreciation and Impairment	¶ 115
Accounting Changes and Error Corrections	¶ 116
Direct Costing	¶ 117
Discontinued Segments (SFAS No. 144)	¶ 119
Derivatives and Financial Instruments	¶ 120
Dividends	¶ 121
Earnings Per Share	¶ 123
Expenses	¶ 125
Franchise	¶ 126
Income	¶ 127
Incorporation	¶ 129
Insurance—Cash Surrender Value of Life Insurance	¶ 130
Inventory	¶ 131
Interest Capitalized	¶ 133
Investments	¶ 137
Losses	¶ 139
Lease	¶ 140
Notes	¶ 141
Pension Plan and Postretirement Plans	¶ 142
Retained Earnings	¶ 143
Revenue Recognition	¶ 144
Stock	¶ 145
Taxes	¶ 146
Treasury Stock	¶ 147
Troubled Debt Restructuring	¶ 148
Product Costing	¶ 149

Chapter 2: Accounting Principles

Accounting Changes and Error Corrections	¶ 201
Accounting Policies	¶ 202
Business Combinations	¶ 203
Cash Flow Statement	¶ 204
Changing Prices	¶ 205
Consolidated Financial Statements	¶ 206
Contingencies	¶ 207
Contributions Received and Contributions Made for Both Profit and Nonprofit Entities	¶ 209
Convertible Debt and Debt with Warrants	¶ 210
Current Assets and Current Liabilities	¶ 211
Debt Extinguishment	¶ 213
Transfer and Servicing of Financial Assets	¶ 214
Deferred Compensation Contracts	¶ 215
Depreciation	¶ 217
Derivative Instruments and Hedging Activities	¶ 218
Development Stage Company	¶ 219
Earnings Per Share	¶ 221
Equity Method Investment	¶ 222
Financial Instruments	¶ 223
Impairment of a Loan—Income Recognition and Disclosures—Accounting by Creditors	¶ 225
Impairment of Long-Lived Assets and for Long-Lived Assets to Be Disposed	¶ 227
Income Taxes	¶ 229
Installment Method of Accounting	¶ 230
Intangible Assets	¶ 231
Interest Capitalized	¶ 233
Interest on Receivables and Payables	¶ 235
Interim Financial Reporting	¶ 237
Inventory	¶ 239
Investments in Debt and Equity Securities	¶ 241
Investments Held by Not-For-Profit Organizations	¶ 243
Investment Tax Credit	¶ 245
Leases	¶ 247
Long-Term Construction Contracts	¶ 249
Mortgage Banking Activities and Accounting for Mortgage Servicing	¶ 251
Non-Monetary Transactions	¶ 253
Offsetting of Amounts Related to Certain Contracts and Offsetting of Amounts Related to Certain Repurchase and Reverse Repurchase Agreements (See ¶ 211)	¶ 255
Pension Plans	¶ 257
Postretirement Benefits	¶ 259
Product Financing Arrangements	¶ 261

Property Taxes—Real .... ¶ 263
Quasi-Reorganizations .... ¶ 265
Real Estate Time-Sharing .... ¶ 266
Related Party Transactions .... ¶ 269
Research and Development .... ¶ 271
Results of Operations .... ¶ 273
Revenue Recognition .... ¶ 275
Segment Reporting .... ¶ 277
Stockholder's Equity .... ¶ 279
Share-Based Payments .... ¶ 283
Troubled Debt Restructuring .... ¶ 285
Unconditional Purchase Obligations .... ¶ 289
Asset Retirement Obligations and Exit Activity Cost .... ¶ 290
Fair Value Accounting .... ¶ 295

Chapter 3: Business Entities

Buying-Selling Business .... ¶ 301
Choice of Entity .... ¶ 303
Corporations .... ¶ 305
Partnerships .... ¶ 307
Limited Liability Company .... ¶ 309
Sole Proprietorship .... ¶ 311
S Corporation .... ¶ 313
Franchising .... ¶ 317

Chapter 4: Business Valuation

Business Valuation Concepts .... ¶ 401
Valuation of Financial Data .... ¶ 403
Valuation of Non-Financial Considerations .... ¶ 404
Valuation Methods .... ¶ 405
Valuation Process .... ¶ 406

Chapter 5: Government Programs

Small Business Administration .... ¶ 501
Social Security—SSI, Supplemental Security Income .... ¶ 502
Disability and Social Security .... ¶ 503
Retirement Benefits and Social Security .... ¶ 505
"Survivors (Life) Insurance" from Social Security .... ¶ 507
Social Security System—Medicare .... ¶ 509
Social Security Administration: Internet Services .... ¶ 510
Social Security System Statistical Tables .... ¶ 511

Chapter 6: Financial Analysis

Accounts Payable .... ¶ 601

Accounts Receivable . . . . ¶ 602
Bond Value . . . . ¶ 603
Bonus . . . . ¶ 605
Breakeven . . . . ¶ 607
Cash . . . . ¶ 609
Cash Flow . . . . ¶ 611
Common Dollars . . . . ¶ 613
Common Size Statements—Horizontal vs. Vertical Analysis . . . . . . ¶ 614
Cost of Capital . . . . ¶ 615
Credit Cards . . . . ¶ 616
Dates . . . . ¶ 617
Debt . . . . ¶ 619
Depletion . . . . ¶ 621
Depreciation . . . . ¶ 623
Earnings Per Share . . . . ¶ 625
Employee Stock Ownership Plan . . . . ¶ 627
Factorial . . . . ¶ 629
Financial Analysis . . . . ¶ 631
Future Value . . . . ¶ 632
Growth . . . . ¶ 633
Indexes . . . . ¶ 634
Interest—Simple . . . . ¶ 635
Interest—Compound . . . . ¶ 637
Inventory . . . . ¶ 639
Investment . . . . ¶ 641
Lease . . . . ¶ 643
Leverage . . . . ¶ 644
Line of Credit Versus Accounts Payable Extension . . . . ¶ 645
Marginal Analysis . . . . ¶ 646
Margin of Safety . . . . ¶ 647
Opportunity Cost Analysis . . . . ¶ 648
Mortgage . . . . ¶ 649
Present Value . . . . ¶ 651
Probability and Expected Value . . . . ¶ 653
Product Pricing . . . . ¶ 654
Profit . . . . ¶ 655
Pricing . . . . ¶ 656
Profitability Index . . . . ¶ 657
Business Profit Triangle . . . . ¶ 658
Projection . . . . ¶ 659
Random Numbers . . . . ¶ 661
Ratios . . . . ¶ 663
Refinancing . . . . ¶ 665
Return on Investment . . . . ¶ 667
Rule of 78 Factors . . . . ¶ 669
Sales . . . . ¶ 671

Sales Tax . . . . ¶ 673
Standard Costs . . . . ¶ 674
Statistics . . . . ¶ 675
Stock Rights . . . . ¶ 676
Sum of Series of Payments . . . . ¶ 677
Sunk Cost Analysis . . . . ¶ 678
Tax Annualized . . . . ¶ 679
Trends . . . . ¶ 681
Vehicle Business Use — Cash vs. Loan vs. Lease . . . . ¶ 682
Venture Capital . . . . ¶ 683
Wages . . . . ¶ 685
Wasting Asset . . . . ¶ 687
Working Capital . . . . ¶ 688
Yield . . . . ¶ 689
Tables . . . . ¶ 691
Loans . . . . ¶ 693

Chapter 7: Investments

Basics and Risk . . . . ¶ 701
College Funding—Monthly Investment Required . . . . ¶ 703
Dollar Cost Averaging . . . . ¶ 705
Estate Planning . . . . ¶ 707
Investment Mix . . . . ¶ 709
Price/Earnings Ratio—Projected for Given Periods for Given
    Projected Annual Growth Rates . . . . ¶ 713
Retirement . . . . ¶ 715
Annuities . . . . ¶ 717
Bonds . . . . ¶ 719
Insurance . . . . ¶ 721
Mutual Funds . . . . ¶ 723
Property . . . . ¶ 724
Securities . . . . ¶ 725
Unit Investment Trusts . . . . ¶ 727

Chapter 8: Taxation

2006 Change Highlights and Other Significant Issues . . . . ¶ 801
Business Tax Issues . . . . ¶ 802
Estate and Other Taxes . . . . ¶ 805
Gains and Losses—Business, Capital, and Depreciation . . . . ¶ 807
Gains and Losses—Passive Activity . . . . ¶ 809
Individual Returns—Tables . . . . ¶ 811
Penalties Tables . . . . ¶ 813
Record Retention Requirements . . . . ¶ 815
Internal Revenue Service . . . . ¶ 817
Tax Audits—Substantiation of Expenses . . . . ¶ 821

Chapter 9: Human Resources

Employee Benefits	¶ 903
Hiring	¶ 904
Wages and Withholding	¶ 907
Labor and Employment Laws	¶ 908
Discrimination Law	¶ 909
Enforcement Procedures	¶ 911
Fair Labor Standards Act	¶ 912
The Fair Labor Standards Act—Equal Pay	¶ 913
Ergonomics	¶ 914
Health Insurance Benefits	¶ 915
Immigration Reform and Control Act of 1986	¶ 917
Personal Responsibility and Work Opportunity Reconciliation Act (PRWORA) of 1996	¶ 918
Independent Contractor Status	¶ 919
Employment of Foreign Workers	¶ 920
Retirement Considerations	¶ 922
Retirement Plans	¶ 923
Retirement Account Distribution Rules	¶ 924

Chapter 10: Directories

Accounting Organizations Directory	¶ 1001
Federal Government Resources Directory	¶ 1002
State Agencies and Departments of Revenue	¶ 1003

Index

Index	Pg. 1271

Chapter 1
Accounting Journal Entries

¶ 101 ACCOUNTS RECEIVABLE: ASSIGNMENT

.01 Basic Assignment

ABC Co. assigns A/R $20,000 to Financing Inc. in exchange for $17,000 cash. Interest of 1% per month is charged on the outstanding balance of the obligation. Collections on Accounts Receivable are to be remitted to Financing Inc. on a monthly basis; $1,000 is collected during the first month.

Recording on ABC's Books:

Accounts receivable assigned	$20,000	
Accounts receivable		$20,000
Cash	$17,000	
Note payable—Financing Inc.		$17,000
Cash	$1,000	
Accounts receivable assigned		$1,000
Note payable—Financing Inc.	$830	
Interest expense (.01 × $17,000)	$170	
Cash		$1,000

Balance Sheet Presentation

A/R assigned (net) ($20,000 – $1,000)	$19,000
Less: N/P on A/R assigned ($17,000 – $830)	$16,170
Equity in A/R assigned	$2,830

¶ 103 ACCOUNTS RECEIVABLE: BAD DEBTS

.01 Basic Entry Data for Estimating and Recording Bad Debts Expense and Uncollectible Receivables

Beginning balances:	
Accounts receivable	$50,000
Allowance for uncollectible accounts	(1,200)
Accounts receivable, net	$48,800
Transactions during the period:	
Credit sales	$35,000
Collections on credit sales	$45,000
Accounts written off as uncollectible	$1,000

	Total	0-30	31-60	61-90	Over 90
Accounts receivable at end of period	$39,000	= $22,000	$8,000	$6,000	$3,000
Estimated % uncollectible		3%	5%	20%	40%
Estimated amount uncollectible	$3,460	= $660	$400	$1,200	$1,200

.03 Percentage-of-Sales Method

The following is the method of estimating and recording bad debt expense and uncollectible receivables using the Percentage-of-Sales Method

Assume 4% of credit sales

Bad debt expense ($35,000 × .04)	$1,400	
Allowance for uncollectible accounts		$1,400

.04 Percentage-of-Outstanding-Receivables Method

Simple percentage—Assume 5% of accounts receivable balance is uncollectible

Desired balance in allowance account, (.05 × $39,000) =	$1,950
Current balance	$200
Bad debts expense to be recognized	$1,750

Bad debts expense	$1,750	
Allowance for uncollectible accounts		$1,750

Aging method:

Desired balance (Cr)	$3,460
Current balance (Cr)	$200
Bad debts expense to be recognized	$3,260

Aged accounts receivable:

Bad debts expense	$3,260	
Allowance for uncollectible accounts		$3,260

.06 Bad Debt Write-Off

Allowance for uncollectible accounts	$1,000	
Accounts receivable—Joe Doe		$1,000

.07 Bad Debts Collections—Reestablishing Account Previously Written Off

Accounts receivable—Joe Doe	$1,000	
Allowance for uncollectible accounts		$1,000
Cash	$1,000	
Accounts receivable—Joe Doe		$1,000

¶ 104 ACQUISITIONS OF ASSETS BY EXCHANGE

A company exchanges inventory with a recorded amount of $20,000 for other inventory with a current selling price of $30,000. The exchange transaction is made to facilitate sales to customers.

| Inventory | $20,000 | |
| Inventory | | $20,000 |

Assume in the preceding transaction that the current selling price of the inventory received is $15,000.

Inventory	$15,000	
Loss on nonmonetary exchange	$5,000	
Inventory		$20,000

A company exchanges land with a recorded amount of $100,000 for land with a fair value of $125,000. The exchange transaction has commercial substance.

Land	$125,000	
Land		$100,000
Gain on nonmonetary exchange		$25,000

Nonmonetary Transactions (APB29 & SFAS 153)

Company exchanged a used delivery truck that cost $12,000 and had accumulated depreciation of $9,000 and received in exchange a newer delivery truck with an FMV of $13,000 and $3,000 cash. Assume the transaction lacks commercial substance.

Book value of old asset ($12,000 – $9,000) = $3,000

Portion Sold =

Book Value — Book Value × [Cash Received / (Cash Received + FMV of New Asset)]

= $3,000 — ($12,000 × $9,000) × [$3,000 / ($3,000 + $13,000)]

= $3,000 × ($3,000 / $16,000)

= $2437

Cash	$3,000	
Accumulated Depreciation—Old Delivery Truck	9,000	
New Delivery Truck	2,437	
Gain on Sale of Delivery Truck		$2,437
Old Delivery Truck		$12,000

Gain on sale of old asset = Cash received less portion of BV sold.

Cash received	$3,000
Proportion of BV sold	– 563
Gain on disposal	$2,437

If the cost of the used delivery truck had been $26,500, the loss realized would be calculated as follows:

Cash	$3,000	
Accumulated Depreciation—Old Delivery Truck	9,000	
New Delivery Truck	13,000	
Loss on Exchange of Delivery Truck	1,500	
Old Delivery Truck		$26,500

The loss realized is calculated as follows:

Cash Received	$3,000
FMV of New Delivery Truck	13,000
Total Amount Received	$16,000
Less: Book Value of Old Delivery Truck ($26,500 – $9,000)	17,500
Loss Realized	(1,500)

¶ 105 BUSINESS COMBINATION (SFAS NO. 141)

.01 Pooling of Interests Method Eliminated

All business combinations must be accounted for using the purchase method. The FASB has eliminated the pooling-of-interests method when accounting for business combinations. Goodwill will be created when the purchase price of the combination exceeds the fair value of the assets less any liabilities assumed in the transaction. When the purchase price is less than the fair value of the net assets (assets -liabilities purchased), negative goodwill is created. Negative goodwill is first used to reduce specific assets acquired on a pro rata basis. If the specific assets are reduced to zero, any remaining negative goodwill is reported as an extraordinary gain. In addition, SFAS No. 147 states that the business combination standard also applies to the acquisition of financial institutions meeting the definition of a business combination.

.03 Business Combination to Recognize Goodwill

On March 1, 20X1, Company A paid $250,000 for all the issued and outstanding common stock of Company B in a transaction properly accounted for as a purchase.

Partial Balance Sheet of Company B:

Cash	$50,000
Inventory	120,000
Property and equipment	110,000
accumulated depreciation	(65,000)
Liabilities	(55,000)

On March 1, 20X1, the inventory of Company B had a fair market value of $105,000 and the property and equipment (net of depreciation) had a fair market value of $45,000.

Goodwill to be Recognized on Purchase:

Purchase price		$250,000
Less fair value of assets acquired:		
Cash	$50,000	
Inventory	105,000	
Property and equipment, net	$45,000	
Liabilities	(55,000)	
Fair value of net assets	$145,000	
Times percentage acquired	× 100%	(145,000)
Goodwill to be recognized		$105,000

Goodwill is not amortized but is tested for impairment using the provisions of SFAS No. 142. Assume goodwill impairment of $20,000 for 20X1. The following entry is required:

Goodwill Impairment	$20,000	
Goodwill		$20,000

FASB Interpretation No. 46 covers the consolidation of variable interest entities. See ¶ 206 for more details about this concept.

¶ 107 BONDS

.01 Recording Bond Issue

Company A issued 5-year bonds on 1-1-X1 with face amount of $100,000 and stated interest of 6% payable semiannually. The bonds were priced to yield 8%.

Cash*	$91,889	
Bond discount (to balance)	$8,111	
Bonds payable		$100,000

*To Calculate Cash to be Received:

Present value of principal payment [$100,000 × .67556 (PV of 1 for 10 periods at 4%)]	= $67,556
Present value of periodic interest payments [$100,000 × 6% / 2) × 8.11090 (PV of an ordinary annuity of 1 for 10 periods at 4%)]	= 24,333
Cash to be received from issuance of the bonds	$91,889

Period	Cash Interest Payment[1]	Interest Expense[2]	Discount Amortization[3]	Unamortized Discount[4]	Carrying Value[5]
Issue				$8,111	$91,889
6/30/X1	3,000	$3,676	$676	7,435	92,565
12/31/X1	3,000	3,703	703	6,732	93,268
6/30/X2	3,000	3,731	731	6,001	93,999
12/31/X2	3,000	3,760	760	5,241	94,759

[1] $100,000 × .06 / 2 = $3,000, to pay semiannually
[2] Prior carrying value × .08 / 2
[3] Interest expense minus interest payment
[4] Prior unamortized discount minus discount amortization
[5] Carrying value plus amortization

6/30/X1:

Interest Expense	$3,676	
Discount on Bonds Payable		$676
Cash		$3,000

12/31/X1

Interest Expense	$3,703	
Discount on Bonds Payable		$703
Cash		$3,000

6/30/X2

Interest Expense	$3,731	
Discount on Bonds Payable		$731
Cash		$3,000

12/31/X2

Interest Expense	$3,760	
Discount on Bonds Payable		$760
Cash		$3,000

.03 Long-Term Investments in Debt Security—Bond Purchase

A 9%, $1,000 bond issued on June 1, 20X1 is purchased at par on September 1. Interest dates are June 1 and December 1.

Investment in bonds	$1,000.00	
Interest receivable ($1,000 × 3/12 × .09)	$22.50	
Cash		$1,022.50
To record receipt of the interest proceeds on December 1:		
Cash ($1,000 × 6/12 × .09)	$45.00	
Interest receivable		22.50
Interest income		$22.50

.04 Premium or Discount—Bond Purchased

Bond premiums or discounts are not recorded separately, but at the net purchase amount of the investment. The premium or discount is amortized from the acquisition date to the maturity date. The following illustrates a 9%, $10,000 bond purchased on 6/30 to mature in 10 years paying semiannual interest on 6/30 and 12/31. Current market yield is 10% annually.

Semiannual interest payment to be received ($10,000 × .09 × 6/12)		$450
Present value factor for an ordinary annuity (5%, 20 periods) =	× 12.46221	
Present value of future interest payments		$5,608
Maturity (face) amount to be received	$10,000	
Present value factor for a single amount (5%, 20 periods) =	× .37689	
Present value of the maturity amount		$3,769
Present value of the bonds		$9,377

Bond investment	$9,377	
Cash		$9,377

.05 Interest Income and Discount Amortization of Bond

Straight-Line Method

Cash ($10,000 × .045)	$450	
Bond Investment ($10,000 – $9,377) / 20	$31	
Interest income		$481

Interest Method

Cash ($10,000 × .045)	$450	
Bond investment (to balance)	$19	
Interest income ($9,377 × .05)		$469

Bond Interest Accrued

Assume corporation's Fiscal Year End = 4/30

Straight-Line Method

Accrued interest receivable ($10,000 × .09 × 4/6)	$300	
Bond investment ($31 × 4/6)	$21	
Interest income		$321

Interest Method

Accrued interest receivable ($10,000 × .09 × 4/12)	$300	
Bond investment (to balance)	$13	
Interest income ($9,377 × .10 × 4/12)		$313

.07 Bond Retirement Before Maturity

On Jan. 1, 20X1, Corporation A issued $200,000 of 6% ten-year bonds at 104. Corporation A records amortization using the straight-line method.

On Dec. 31, 20X6, Corporation A repurchased $150,000 of the bonds in the open market at 98, the FMV. Interest and amortization for 20X6 has been recorded. The retirement is recorded as follows:

To compute gain/loss on bond retirement:

Original carrying amount ($200,000 × 104%)		$208,000
Premium to be amortized ($208,000 – 200,000)	$8,000	
Amortization [($8,000 / 10) × 6 yrs.]	– 4,800	3,200
Carrying value of bonds, 12/31/X6		$204,800
Percent of bonds retired 150,000 / 200,000		×.75
Carrying amount of retired bonds		$153,600
Purchase price ($150,000 × 98%)		147,000
Gain on bond retirement		$6,600

Bonds payable ($200,000 × .75)	$150,000	
Bond premium ($4,800 × .75)	$3,600	
Cash ($150,000 × .98)		$147,000
Gain on bond retirement (to balance)		$6,600

.09 Sale of Bond Investment

A company purchased on 6/30/X1 $10,000 face value of bonds for $9,377 on 6/30. The bonds mature in 10 years and pay semiannual interest on 6/30 and 12/31. The stated rate on the bonds is 9%, but the market rate at the time of the purchase was 10%. The discount is being amortized using the straight line method.

To compute the carrying amount of the bonds

Original purchase price, June 30, 20X4		$9,377
Plus discount amortization: Through June 30, 20X4 ($31 × 6 semiannual periods)		186
July 1 to Sept. 30, 20X4 ($31 × 3/6)		16
Carrying value of bonds		$9,579

On Sept. 30, 20X4, Company sold $10,000 bond investments for $9,500 which included interest accrued on the bonds. Company amortized the original discount on the bonds under the straight-line method.

Cash	$9,500	
Loss on Sale of Bonds	$304	
Interest Income		$225
Bond Investment		$9,579
Proceeds received		$9,500
Less: amount attributable to accrued interest ($10,000 × .09 × 3/12)		225
Sale price of bonds		$9,275
Carrying amount of bonds		(9,579)
Loss on sale of bonds		$(304)

.11 Convertible Bonds

To record conversion of bonds on issuer books if:

- Face value of bonds = $100,000

- Carrying value = $106,000

- Convertible into 1,000 shares of $80 per common

- Common stock has Fair Market Value of $85/share

Book Value Method

Bonds payable	$100,000	
Bond premium ($106, 000 – $100,000)	$6,000	
Common stock (1,000 × $80 par value)		$80,000
Additional paid-in capital (to balance)		$26,000

Market Value Method

Bonds payable	$100,000	
Bond premium ($106,000 – $100,000)	$6,000	
Common stock (1,000 × $80 par value)		$80,000
Additional paid-in capital [1,000 × ($85 FMV – $80 PV)]		$5,000
Gain on conversion ($106,000 – (1, 000 × $85 FMV))		$21,000

.13 Bond Issued with Detachable Stock Warrants

- One hundred, $1,000 9% bonds were sold at 102 with one detachable stock purchase warrant for each bond.

- Fair Market Value of bond without warrant = 97

- Each warrant entitles holder to purchase 20 shares of common, par value $20, at $25 per share.

Cash proceeds [(100 × $1,000) × 102%]	$102,000
Allocation to bonds (100 × $1,000 × 97%)	$97,000
Allocation to warrants	$5,000
Bond discount ($100,000 – $97,000) =	$3,000

Journal Entry for Issuance of Debt

Borrower

Cash	$102,000	
Bond discount	$3,000	
Bonds payable		$100,000
Stock warrants		$5,000

Investor (Net)

Bond investment	$97,000	
Stock warrants	$5,000	
Cash		$102,000

Assume 25 of the 100 stock purchase warrants are exercised:

Borrower

Cash (500 × $25)	$12,500	
Stock warrants ($5,000 × 25 / 100)	$1,250	
Common stock (500 × $20)		$10,000
Add'l. paid-in capital to balance		$3,750

Investor

Investment in common stock (500 × $27.50)	$13,750	
Stock warrants ($5,000 × 25 / 100)		$1,250
Cash (500 × $25)		$12,500

¶ 108 ASSET RETIREMENT OBLIGATIONS (SFAS NO. 143 AND 146 AND FASB INTERPRETATION NO. 47)

Liabilities must be established for costs related to the retirement of long-lived assets. A liability is reported for an amount equal to the fair value of the liability in the accounting period that the liability is incurred and the long-lived asset is increased for an equal amount. The liability is increased for passage of time and the increase in the liability is charged to accretion expense using the interest method. The increase in the long-lived asset is depreciated over the estimated life of the increase. Journals to reflect asset retirement obligations are:

Long-lived Asset	XXXXX	
Liability for Asset Retirement		XXXXX
To record the asset retirement liability		

Accretion Expense	XXX	
Liability for Asset Retirement		XXX
To record accretion expense		

Depreciation Expense	XXX	
Accumulated Depreciation		XXX
To record depreciation of asset retirement liability		

¶ 109 CASH FLOW STATEMENT

Statement of Cash Flows For the Year Ended December 31, 20X1

Statement of Cash Flows (SFAS-95)

.01 Direct Method

The direct method reflects the gross amounts of cash receipts and cash payments from operating activities. The gross amount of cash receipts from operating activities less the gross amount of cash payments from operating activities equals the net cash provided by or used in the period arising from operating activities.

Statements of Cash Flows for the Year Ended December 31, 20X1 Increase (Decrease) in Cash and Cash Equivalents

Cash Flows from Operating Activities:		
Cash received from customers	$217,000	
Cash paid for inventory	(125,000)	
Cash paid for general and administrative expense	(42,000)	
Interest paid	(9,100)	
Income taxes paid	(2,000)	
Net cash provided (used) by operating activities		$38,900
Cash Flows from Investing Activities:		
Proceeds from sale of land	$25,000	
Proceeds from sale of marketable equity securities	10,000	
Purchase of equipment for cash	(30,000)	
Net cash provided (used) in investing activities		5,000
Cash Flows from Financing Activities:		
Dividends paid	$(6,000)	
Proceeds from issuance of bonds payable	50,000	
Net cash provided by financing activities		44,000
Net increase in cash and cash equivalents		$87,900
Cash and cash equivalents at beginning of year		25,000
Cash and cash equivalents at end of year		$112,900

Reconciliation of Net Income to Net Cash Provided by Operating Activities:

Net income		$50,000
Adjustments to reconcile net income to net cash provided by operating activities:		
Depreciation	$1,500	
Bond discount amortization	200	
Deferred income taxes	400	
Loss on sale of marketable equity securities	800	
Gain on sale of land	(12,000)	
Equity in earnings of equity method invested in excess of cash dividends	(5,000)	
Decrease in net accounts receivable	15,000	
Increase in net inventory	(18,000)	
Increase in accounts payable	4,000	
Increase in income taxes payable	2,000	
Total adjustments		$(11,100)
Net cash provided (used) by operating activities		$38,900

.03 Indirect Method

The indirect method starts with net income and then adjusts that amount for non-cash changes to determine the net cash flow from operations.

U.S.A. Company Statement of Cash Flows For the Year Ended December 31, 20X1 Increase (Decrease) in Cash and Cash Equivalents

Cash Flows from Operating Activities:		
Net income		$50,000
Adjustments to reconcile income to cash provided by operating activities:		
Depreciation	$1,500	
Bond discount amortization	200	
Deferred Income taxes	400	
Loss on sale of marketable equity securities	800	
Gain on sale of land	(12,000)	
Equity in earnings of equity method investee in excess of cash dividends	(5,000)	
Decrease in net accounts receivable	15,000	
Increase in inventory	(18,000)	
Increase in accounts payable	4,000	
Increase in income taxes payable	2,000	
Total adjustments		(11,100)
Net cash provided by operating activities		$38,900
Cash Flows from Investing Activities:		
Proceeds from sale of land	$25,000	
Proceeds from sale of marketable equity securities	10,000	
Purchase of equipment for cash	(30,000)	
Net cash provided (used) in investing activities		5,000

Cash Flows from Financing Activities:		
Dividend paid	$(6,000)	
Proceeds from issuance of bonds payable	50,000	
Net cash provided (used) by financing activities		44,000
Net increase in cash and cash equivalents		$87,900
Cash and cash equivalents at beginning of year		25,000
Cash and cash equivalents at end of year		$112,900

Note: For the indirect method SFAS-95 requires separate presentation of changes in inventory, receivables, and payables relating to operating activities.

¶ 111 CONSTRUCTION CONTRACTS—LONG TERM

.01 Percent-of-Completion Method

Construction company contracted to build a $3,500,000 building to be completed in 3 years.

Date	Estimated Total Cost of Project	Costs Incurred During Year
20X1	$2,000,000	$1,300,000
20X2	$2,900,000	$1,100,000

Year	Costs Incurred	Cumulative Costs	Total Expected Cost	Revenue Recognized	Profit (Loss)
1	$1,300,000	$1,300,000	$2,000,000	$2,275,000	$975,000
2	1,100,000	2,400,000	2,900,000	621,552	(478,448)
3	500,000	2,900,000	2,900,000	603,448	103,448
Totals	$2,900,000	2,900,000	2,900,000	$3,500,000	$600,000

Current income =

$$\left[\left(\frac{\text{Cost to date}}{\text{Estd. total cost}}\right)\times\left(\text{Total estd. Contract income}\right)\right]-\left(\text{income recognized to date}\right)$$

$$19X1=\left(\frac{\$1,300,000}{\$2,000,000}\right)\times(\$3,500,000-\$2,000,000)$$

$$= \$975,000$$

$$19X2=\left[\left(\frac{\$2,400,000}{\$2,900,000}\right)\ (\$3,500,000-\$2,900,000)\right]-\$975,000$$

$$= \$(478,448)\,\text{Loss}$$

Note: Total estimated contract income = contract price - estimated total cost
Assume in Year 1 that progress billings on the long-term construction contract are
$300,000 and collections are $200,000

Entries for Percentage of Completion for Year 1

Recording of Construction Cost

Construction in Progress	$1,300,000	
Cash, Payables, etc.		$1,300,000

Recording of Billing in Progress

Receivable for Progress Billings	$ 300,000	
Billings in Progress		$ 300,000

Recording of Collections of Billings

Cash	$200,000	
Receivable for Progress Billings		$200,000

Recording of Profit and Revenue from Contract

Construction in Progress	$975,000	
Construction Cost	$1,300,000	
Contract Revenue		$2,275,000

¶ 113 COST OF GOODS MANUFACTURED SCHEDULE

.01 Normal Format

Cost of Goods Manufactured Schedule—Normal Format

USA Co.

For Year Ended Dec. 31, 20X1

Beginning work-in-process:			$75,000
Plus current manufacturing costs:			
Direct materials:			
Beginning inventory	$ 25,000		
Purchases	125,000		
Materials available for use	$150,000		
Less ending inventory	(32,000)		
Total direct materials used		$118,000	
Direct labor		75,000	
Manufacturing overhead:			
Indirect material	$15,000		
Indirect labor	16,000		
Other Mfg overhead costs	4,000	35,000	
Manufacturing cost incurred			228,000
Total mfg. costs incurred			$303,000
Less ending work-in-process			(30,000)
Cost of goods manufactured			$ 273,000

.03 Alternative Format

Cost of Goods Manufactured Schedule—Alternative Format

USA Co.

For Year Ended Dec. 31, 20X1

Direct materials:			
Beginning inventory	$25,000		
Purchases	125,000		
Material available	$150,000		
Less ending inventory	(32,000)		
Total direct materials		$118,000	
Direct labor		75,000	
Manufacturing overhead:			
Indirect material	$15,000		
Indirect labor	16,000		
Miscellaneous	4,000	35,000	

Total manufacturing cost incurred	
Beginning work-in-process	$75,000
Total manufacturing cost	303,000
Less ending work-in-process	$(30,000)
Cost of goods manufactured	$273,000

¶ 115 DEPRECIATION AND IMPAIRMENT

.01 Financial vs. Tax

Differences between taxable income and pretax financial income

Assumes no salvage value

Cost = 12,000 straight-line, 5 years   Cost = 12,000 MACRS-3 years

Year	Depreciation for Financial Reporting	Cost × Rate		Depreciation for Tax Purposes	Difference
19X1	$2,400	12,000 × .3333 =		$4,000	$(1,600)
19X2	$2,400	12,000 × .4445 =		$5,334	$(2,934)
19X3	$2,400	12,000 × .1481 =		$1,777	$623
19X4	$2,400	12,000 × .0741 =		$889	$1,511
19X5	$2,400			0	$2,400
	$12,000			$12,000	$0

Future Difference Between Financial and Tax Depreciation

Future	**20X2**	**20X3**	**20X4**	**20X5**	**Total**
(deductible) amount	$(2,934)	$623	$1,511	$2,400	$204
Future	**20X3**	**20X4**	**20X5**	**Total**	
(deductible) amount	$623	$1,511	$2,400	$3,138	
Future	**20X4**	**20X5**	**Total**		
(deductible) amount	$1,511	$2,400	$2,515		
Future	**20X5**	**Total**			
(deductible) amount	$2,400	$2,400			

At the end of 20X5, no temporary difference exists because the asset is fully depreciated for both financial statements and tax purposes.

.03 Fractional-Year Calculation

Use proportional expense based on number of months asset was used.

Assume cost = $1,200. Depreciate over 3 years by sum-of-years digits.

Assumes no salvage value

Assumes bought 1/1/X1

Year	Full Year Depreciation	Months Held/12	Fractional Year Depreciation Totals
1	$1,200 × 3/6 = $600	12/12	= $600
2	$1,200 × 2/6 = $400	12/12	= $400

Year	Full Year Depreciation	Months Held/12	Fractional Year Depreciation Totals
3	$1,200 × 1/6 = $200	6/12 sold 7/1/X3	= $100
		Total depreciation	= $1,100

Computation of Loss on Disposal:

Historical cost	$1,200
Accumulated depreciation	(1,100)
Book value	$100
Sales price	65
Loss on disposal	$(35)

Journal Entry for Disposal

Cash	$65	
Accumulated Depreciation	$1,100	
Loss on Disposal of Asset	$35	
Equipment		$1,200

.05 Composite Depreciation Method

Calculated as total of individual depreciation amounts expressed as a percentage of the total cost of all the assets.

Asset Class	Asset Cost	-	Salvage Value	=	Estimated Depreciation Basis	÷	Useful Life	= ST Line Depreciation
X	$100,000		$15,000		$85,000		8	$10,625
Y	50,000		5,000		45,000		6	7,500
Z	20,000		2,000		18,000		6	3,000
	$170,000		$22,000		$148,000			$21,125

Composite life ($148,000 / $21,125) = 7 years

Composite depreciation rate ($21,125 / $170,000) = 12.43%

Annual composite depreciation = ($170,000 × .1243) = $21,131

Additions are debited to asset group at cost.

Retirements are recorded as:

Debit to cash or receivable for the consideration received

Balance is debited to accumulated depreciation

Credit to the asset account

.07 Declining Balance

Double Declining Balance Depreciation

Depreciation = (Cost – Accumulated Depreciation) × 200% / years of useful life

¶115.05

For declining balance depreciation other than double declining balance, substitute the appropriate percentage for 200%. For example, 150% declining balance depreciation is computed as follows:

Depreciation = (Cost – Accumulated Depreciation) × 150% / years of useful life

Note that salvage value is not relevant for declining balance depreciation except that any tentative depreciation deduction may not cause the book value of the asset to go below its salvage value. If the tentative depreciation deduction would cause the book value of the asset to go below its salvage value, then the depreciation deduction is limited to the amount that will cause the book value of the asset to equal its salvage value.

Example:

Cost $25,000

Salvage $5,000

Useful Life 12 Years

What is the depreciation expense for year 3 using double declining balance depreciation?

Year 1: $25,000 × 200% / 12 = $4,167
Year 2: ($25,000 – 4,167) × 200% / 12 = $3,472
Year 3: ($25,000 – 4,167 – 3,472) × 200% / 12 = $2,894

.08 Impairment (SFAS 144 and 147)

A long-lived asset should be tested for impairment when circumstances indicate that the carrying amount of the asset may not be recovered. If gross future cash flows from the lowest level for which identifiable cash flows can be identified independent of other cash flows for the asset or asset group are less than the carrying amount of the asset, fair value of the asset is then compared to the carrying value of the asset. If fair value is less than carrying value, an impairment loss is reported for the difference. In addition, SFAS No. 147 states that the impairment rules also apply to intangible assets in the form of long-term customer relationships, other than servicing assets. Assume that cash flows are less than the carrying amount of Asset A and the fair value and carrying value of Asset A are $100,000 and $80,000, respectively. The impairment loss is $20,000 ($100,000 – $80,000). The journal entry is:

Loss From Asset Impairment	$20,000	
Asset A		$20,000

¶ 116 ACCOUNTING CHANGES AND ERROR CORRECTIONS

.01 Changes in Accounting Principle

Assume XYZ Company changed inventory methods from average cost to first-in-first-out (FIFO) in 20X5. If FIFO had been used in all years prior to 20X5, income and inventory would have been higher by $200,000. Entry for 20X5 for the change in accounting principle is as follows:

Inventory	$200,000	
Retained Earnings		$200,000

.02 Changes in Accounting Estimate

On January 1, 20X2, XYZ Company purchased equipment at a cost of $200,000 with a useful life of 10 years. The company uses straight-line depreciation. In the fourth year of life of the asset (after three years of depreciation), new information indicated that the useful life of the equipment should have been 8 years instead of 10 years. There is no entry to report the change in useful life since a change in accounting estimate is reported in a prospective manner; however, there is a normal adjusting entry for depreciation for 20X5 that reflects the change in the annual depreciation amount.

Depreciation Expense	$28,000	
Accumulated Depreciation		$28,000

$200,000 cost/10 year useful life = $20,000 annual depreciation for 20X2–20X4 × 3 years = $60,000. $200,000 cost – $60,000 depreciation = $140,000 new carrying value/5 (8 revised life – 3 years of depreciation) year remaining useful life = $28,000. Prior year's depreciation was $20,000 per year and new annual depreciation is $28,000 per year.

.03 Error Corrections

In 20X4, XYZ Company understated salary expense by $100,000 and the additional $100,000 salary expense was reported in 20X5 when the salary was paid resulting in an overstatement of salary expense in 20X5. The error was discovered by XYZ prior to the issuance of the 20X5 financial statements. The entry to correct this error in 20X5 is:

Retained Earnings	$100,000	
Salary Expense		$100,000

¶ 117 DIRECT COSTING

.01 Definition

Direct costing (variable costing) is an inventory costing method where direct materials, direct labor, and variable manufacturing overhead are treated as inventoriable costs, while fixed manufacturing overhead is treated as a period cost and expensed currently in the income statement. Direct costing is not acceptable for external financial reporting and income tax reporting.

.03 Direct vs. Absorption Costing

Accounting For Fixed Manufacturing Overhead

Direct costing—The costs to be inventoried include only the variable manufacturing costs. Fixed manufacturing overhead is treated as a period cost—and is expensed with selling and administrative costs.

Direct Costing	
Direct materials	$XXX
Direct labor	XXX
Variable manufacturing overhead	XXX
Product cost	$XXX

Absorption costing—Inventoried costs include all the manufacturing costs, both variable and fixed.

¶116.02

Absorption Costing

Direct labor	$XXX
Direct materials	XXX
Fixed manufacturing overhead	XXX
Variable manufacturing overhead	XXX
Product cost	$XXX

Facts:

	20X1	20X2
Inventory Beginning Balance	0 units	1,000 units
Production	5,000	4,000
Available for Sale	5,000	5,000
Less: Units Sold	4,000	3,000
Ending Balance	1,000 units	2,000 units

Facts:

	20X1	20X2
Sales ($4 / unit)	$16,000	$12,000
Variable mfg. Cost ($0.50 / unit)	2,500	2,000
Fixed mfg. Cost	4,000	4,000
Variable Selling and administration ($0.40 / unit)	1,600	1,200
Fixed Selling and administration	5,000	6,000

Income Statement 20X1

Absorption Costing:

Sales		$16,000
Beginning Inventory	$0	
Variable Mfg Costs:		
$0.50 × 5,000	2,500	
Fixed Mfg. Costs	4,000	
Cost of Goods Available	$6,500	
Less: Ending Inventory [0.50 + ($4,000 / 5,000)] × 1,000	1,300	
Cost of Goods Sold		5,200
Gross Margin		$10,800
Selling and Administrative Expenses:		
Variable ($0.40 × 4,000)	$1,600	
Fixed	5,000	6,600
Net Income		$4,200

Direct Costing:

Sales		$16,000
Beginning Inventory	$0	

Variable Mfg Costs:		
$0.50 × 5,000	2,500	
Variable Cost of Goods Available	$2,500	
Less: Ending Inventory ($0.50 × 1,000)	500	
Variable Cost of Goods Sold	$2,000	
Variable Selling and Administrative ($0.40 × 4,000)	1,600	
Total Variable Costs		3,600
Contribution Margin		$12,400
Fixed Mfg. Costs	$4,000	
Fixed Selling and Administrative	5,000	
Total Fixed Costs		9,000
Net Income		$3,400

Difference in Net Income: $4,200 – $3,400 = $800

Reconciliation of Net Income

Fixed Costs Charged to Income Under Absorption Costing	$0.80 × $4,000 = $3,200
Fixed Costs Charged to Income Under Direct Costing	4,000
Difference	$800

Income Statement 20X2

Absorption Costing:

Sales		$12,000
Beginning Inventory [$0.50 + ($4,000 / 5,000)] × 1,000	$1,300	
Variable Mfg Costs:		
$0.50 × $4,000	2,000	
Fixed Mfg. Costs	4,000	
Cost of Goods Available	$7,300	
Less: Ending Inventory [$0.50 + ($4,000 / 4,000)] × 2,000	3,000	
Cost of Goods Sold		4,300
Gross Margin		$7,700
Selling and Administrative Expenses:		
Variable ($0.40 × 3,000)	$1,200	
Fixed	6,000	7,200
Net Income		$500

Direct Costing:

Sales		$12,000
Beginning Inventory ($0.50 × 1,000)	$500	

¶117.03

Variable Mfg Costs:		
$0.50 × 4,000	2,000	
Variable Cost of Goods Available	$2,500	
Less: Ending Inventory ($0.50 × 2,000)	1,000	
Variable Cost of Goods Sold	$1,500	
Variable Selling and Administrative ($0.40 × 3,000)	1,200	
Total Variable Costs		2,700
Contribution Margin		$9,300
Fixed Mfg. Costs	$4,000	
Fixed Selling and Administrative	6,000	
Total Fixed Costs		10,000
Net Loss		($700)

Difference in Net Income: $500 – (–$700) = $1,200
Reconciliation of Net Income
Fixed Costs Charged to Income Under Absorption Costing:

From Beginning Inventory $0.80 × 1,000 =	$800
Current Period Costs $1.00 × 2,000 =	2,000
Total Fixed Costs Charged to Income Under Absorption Costing	$2,800
Fixed Costs Charged to Income Under Direct Costing	4,000
Difference	$1,200

¶ 119 DISCONTINUED SEGMENTS (SFAS NO. 144)

.01 Income Presentation for Discontinued Segments

Statement No. 144 changed the accounting for discontinued operations and requires companies to determine if the disposition or expected disposition is a component of a business and if the disposition of the component will eliminate its cash flows and operations from the continuing operations of the entire enterprise and after the transaction, the entity will not have a significant involvement in the component's operations. The results of operations and any gain or loss expected on the disposition must be included in a separate section of the income statement in the year of the expected disposition and for all prior years presented with the gain or loss on disposition separately disclosed.

Loss from operations of discontinued Component X (including loss on disposal of $XXXXX)	$(XXXXXX)	
Income tax benefit	XXXXX	
Loss on discontinued operations		$(XXXXXX)

¶ 120 DERIVATIVES AND FINANCIAL INSTRUMENTS

SFAS No. 133 as amended by Statement Nos. 137, 138, 149, and 150 cover the accounting and reporting requirements for derivatives and financial instruments. The journal entries cover derivatives not classified as a hedges, cash flow hedges, and fair value hedges.

.01 Derivative Not Classified as a Hedge

ABC Company enters into gold futures contracts and had a loss of $50,000 for the year.

Loss on Derivative Contract	$50,000	
Derivative Instrument—Gold Contract		$50,000

.02 Derivative Classified as a Cash Flow Hedge

XYZ Company has 200,000 bushels of soybeans in inventory that is held for resale. The Company enters into a futures contract for the soybean inventory and had a loss from the futures contract of $60,000 for the year.

Loss on Futures Contract—Other Comprehensive Income	$60,000	
Derivative Instrument—Futures Contract		$60,000

.03 Derivative Classified as a Fair Value Hedge

Z Company has a fixed rate debt and enters into an interest rate swap agreement by swapping the fixed rate stream for a variable rate stream of interest payments. The Company had loss from the interest rate swap of $200,000 for the year.

Loss on Interest Rate Swap	$200,000	
Interest Rate Swap		$200,000
Notes Payable	$200,000	
Gain from Adjustment of Debt to Fair Value		$200,000

Statement No. 150 covers classification of financial instruments that have characteristics of both debt and equity. See ¶ 223 for details about such instruments.

¶ 121 DIVIDENDS

.01 Cash Dividends

Date of declaration		
Retained earnings—dividends	XX	
Dividends payable		XX
Date of record—No journal entry is required.		
Date of payment		
Dividends payable	XX	
Cash		XX

.03 Property Dividends

When fair market value of securities is $3,000 at date of declaration, Company A transfers to shareholder debt securities which cost $1,800 by declaring a property dividend.

Date of declaration:		
Retained earnings—dividends	$3,000	
Property dividends payable		$3,000
Investment in marketable securities	$1,200	
Gain on invest. in marketable securities		$1,200
At date of payment:		
Property dividends payable	$3,000	
Investment in marketable securities		$3,000

.04 Liquidating Dividends

These are dividends distributed in excess of retained earnings and represent a return of capital rather than from profits.

Date of declaration:		
Paid-in capital in excess of par	XX	
Dividends payable		XX
On date of payment:		
Dividends payable	XX	
Cash		XX

¶ 123 EARNINGS PER SHARE

.01 Weighted Average Shares Outstanding

Facts: Corp. has 500,000 shares of common stock issued and outstanding on January 1, 20X1.

On June 1, 20X6, 100,000 shares are reacquired as treasury stock.

On Oct. 1, 20X6, 75,000 shares are issued for cash.

	Transactions	Balance
Jan		500,000
Feb		500,000
March		500,000
April		500,000
May		500,000
June	(100,000)	400,000
July		400,000
August		400,000
Sept		400,000
Oct	75,000	475,000
Nov		475,000
Dec		475,000
		5,525,000
Average / 12		460,417

The weighted average number of shares outstanding for the year ended December 31, 20X1 is as follows:

Common stock outstanding at beginning of year	500,000
Shares reacquired weighted (100,000 × 7/12 of a yr.)	(58,333
Shares reissued (75,000 × 3/12 of a yr.)	18,750
Weighted average shares outstanding	460,417

.03 Retroactive Adjustments for Stock Splits, Dividends, Reverse Splits

Facts: Corp. has 100,000 shares of CS outstanding at January 1, 20X5.

On Oct. 1, 20X5, 5,000 additional shares are issued for cash.

On June 30, 20X6, a 20% stock dividend is declared.

On May 31, 20X7, a 2-for-1 stock split occurs.

The weighted average number of common shares outstanding for the periods ended December 31, 20X5, 20X6, and 20X7 is computed as follows.

Part 1

	20X5	20X6	20X7
Common stock outstanding at beginning of yr.	100,000	105,000	126,000
Sale of additional shares	5,000		
20% dividend		21,000	
2-for-1 split			126,000
Common stock actually outstanding	105,000	126,000	252,000

Part 2

	20X5	20X6	20X7
CS outstanding at beginning of yr.	100,000	105,000	126,000
Sales of additional shares			
(5,000 × 3/12 of a year) % stock dividend:	1,250		
(101,250 × 20%)	20,250		
(105,000 × 20%)		21,000	
2-for-1 split (100% increase)	121,500	126,000	126,000
Weighted average CS outstanding for EPS computation	243,000	252,000	252,000

Simple Capital Structure

$$\text{Adjusted EPS fraction} = \frac{\text{NI - PS dividends}}{\text{Weighted avg. CS outstaning} \pm \text{Retroactive adjustments}}$$

.05 Basic Earnings Per Share (BEPS)

$$\text{BEPS} = \frac{\text{Income From Continuing Operations - Preferred Dividends}}{\text{Weighted Average Number of Shares Outstanding}}$$

Facts: A company had income of $800,000 for the year ended December 31, 20X1 and 2000 shares of cumulative preferred stock requiring a dividend of $4 per share or $8000 per year (2000 shares X $4). Each share of preferred stock is convertible into two shares of common stock. Weighted average number of shares for 20X1 are 200,000.

Basic Earnings Per Share

$$\frac{\$800,000 - \$8000}{200,000} = \$3.96$$

.06 Diluted Earnings Per Share (DEPS)

$$DEPS = \frac{\text{Income - Preferred Dividends + Any Adjustments For Dilutive Securities}}{\text{Weighted Average Number of Shares Outstanding + Any Adjustments For Dilutive Securities (such as options, convertible securities and contingent agreements)}}$$

Facts: A company had income of $800,000 for the year ended December 31, 20X1 and 2000 shares of cumulative preferred stock requiring a dividend of $4 per share or $8000 per year (2000 shares x $4). Each share of preferred stock is convertible into two shares of common stock. Weighted average number of shares for 20X1 are 200,000. Throughout 20X1, 200,000 options were outstanding to purchase 50,000 common shares at $50 per share. Average market price for 20X1 was $75.

Diluted earnings per share is computed as follows:

Options—Treasury stock method is used which assumes that the options are dilutive if the average market price exceeds the option price ($75 compared to $50). In addition, it assumes that all options are exercised at the beginning of the year or later if issued later, and all proceeds from exercise of the options are used to repurchase shares at the average market price. The difference between shares issued upon assumed exercise of the options and the number repurchased is used as the incremental shares in the EPS computation.

Convertible preferred stock—If converted method is used which assumes that the preferred stock is converted at the beginning of the year or later if issued later. Any preferred dividends deducted are added back to net income and the number of common shares is added to the weighted average number of shares outstanding if the preferred stock is dilutive. The preferred stock is dilutive if the assumed conversion of the preferred stock decreases earnings per share.

Weighted average shares outstanding during period		200,000
Shares from assumed option exercise	50,000	
Assumed treasury shares purchased ($2,500,000 / $75)	(33,333)	
Shares included in weighted average outstanding		16,667
Number of common shares from conversion of convertible preferred stock (2,000 X 2 shares)		4,000
Total shares		220,667

Since the 2,000 shares of preferred stock are assumed to be converted to common shares, the $8,000 in preferred dividends deducted are added back to net income when computed diluted earnings per share.

Diluted Earnings Per Share

$$\frac{\$800,000 - \$8000 + \$8,000}{220,667} = \$3.63$$

.07 Diluted Earnings per Share—Antidilution

Facts: Corp. has 80,000 common shares outstanding throughout year.

Also outstanding were 200 shares of preferred stock requiring a dividend of 4 per share. Each share of preferred stock is convertible into two shares of common stock.

Net income was $55,000.

$$\text{Basic earnings per share} = \frac{\$55,000 \text{ Net income} - \$800 \text{ PS dividend}}{80,000 \text{ Common stock outstanding}} = \$.678$$

> **Note:** Preferred stock is assumed not converted because the effect would be antidilutive:

$$\frac{55,000}{80,000 \text{ CS Outstanding} + 400 \text{ Assumed PS conversion}} = \$.684$$

¶ 125 EXPENSES

.01 Accrued Expenses

An accrued expense is an expense incurred but not yet paid in cash.

Expense	XX	
Payable		XX

.03 Prepaid Expenses

Prepaid expenses are recognized when incurred.

The following illustrates the purchase of a 3 year insurance policy for $75,000. The fiscal year end is 6/X1.

March 1, 20X1

Prepaid insurance	$75,000	
Cash		$75,000

June 2X1

Insurance expense (1)	$8,333.33	
Prepaid insurance		$8,333.33

(1) Premium paid	$75,000
Number of months	÷36
Monthly insurance fiscal yr.	$2,083.33
Months in current fiscal yr.	× 4
	$8,333.33

Balance Sheet Presentation

Current Assets

Prepaid insurance (12 mos. × $2,083.33) = $25,000

Non-current assets

Prepaid insurance (20 mos. × $2,083.33) = $41,667

¶ 126 FRANCHISE

.01 Franchise Fee Revenue

Franchise Fee $20,000 with $1,000 paid down at signing of franchise agreement.

Balance of fee is due over 5 years.

Continuing franchise fee is 2% of gross revenues per year

$145,000 Revenue for 20X2, $155,000 Revenue for 20X3

The $20,000 franchise fee is for service the franchisor will perform equally over years 1 and 2.

Year 1: 20X1		
Franchise fee receivable	$19,000	
Cash	$1,000	
Unearned franchise fee revenue		$20,000
Year 2: 20X2		
Unearned franchise fee revenue	$10,000	
Franchise fee revenue		$10,000
Cash ($19,000 / 5)	$3,800	
Franchise fee receivable		$3,800
Cash ($145,000 × 2%)	$2,900	
Franchise fee revenue		$2,900
Year 3: 20X3		
Cash ($19,000 / 5)	$3,800	
Franchise fee receivable		$3,800
Cash ($155,000 × 2%)	$3,100	
Franchise fee revenue		$3,100

.02 Franchise Fee Revenue and Expenses

Transfer of funds from Franchisee to Franchisor.

Cash	$200,000	
Deferred Initial Franchise Fee (Liability on balance sheet of Franchisor until related services have been substantially performed.)		$200,000

Direct and indirect costs incurred by Franchisor during 20X1. Indirect costs incurred are expensed. Direct costs incurred are deferred until revenue relating to those agreements is recognized.

Prepaid Franchise Costs (Deferred)	$6,000	
Administrative Expenses	$2,000	
Cash		$8,000

Initial services offered by Franchisor are substantially completed and recognized as income:

Deferred Initial Franchise Fee	$200,000	
Initial Franchise Fee Revenue		$200,000

Deferred direct costs are charged to expense when the revenue is recognized.

Franchise Expense	$6,000	
Prepaid Franchise Costs		$6,000

Three-percent continuing franchise fee of 300,000 gross revenue is recognized.

Receivable from Franchisee, Inc.	$9,000	
Franchise Fee Revenue		$9,000

.03 Franchise Fee Revenue and Expenses

Facts:

Franchisee paid $400,000 to Franchisor as an initial franchise fee.

A continuing franchise fee of four percent of gross revenues is required per year.

Discounted purchase of first year's supplies & inventory = $10,000.

Franchise fee costs:

Land	$50,000
Buildings	150,000
Equipment	20,000
Signs & Fixtures	8,000
	$228,000

Allocation of the initial franchise fee:

Land	$50,000
Building	150,000
Equipment	20,000
Signs & Fixtures	8,000
Deferred Fee—Product Supplies/ Inventory	10,000
Total	$238,000

Compute allocation of franchise fee:

Total Initial Franchise Fee	$400,000
Total Allocation	238,000
Initial Franchise Fee	$162,000

Receipt of initial franchise fee by franchisor:

Cash		$400,000
Land	$50,000	
Building	150,000	
Equipment	20,000	
Signs & fixtures	8,000	

Deferred Fee—Product Supplies/Inventory	10,000	238,000
Deferred Initial Franchise Fee		$162,000

Revenue associated with the initial franchise fee upon completion of initial services recorded by franchisor:

Deferred Initial Franchise Fee	$162,000	
Initial Franchise Fee Revenue		$162,000

Earned franchise fee for year one for franchisor.

Receivable from Franchisee, Inc.	$19,000	
Franchise Fee Revenue		$19,000
(Gross sales × fee % $475,000 × .04)		

Franchisor estimated that Franchisee would realize 8,500 in benefits under the discounted purchase agreement during 20X1.

Deferred Fee-Product Supplies/Inventory	$8,500	
Sales		$8,500

¶ 127 INCOME

.01 Deferred Revenues

As in a subscription business

For income billed and collected in cash, but not yet earned.

Accounts Receivable	XX	
Unearned revenues		XX
Cash	XX	
Accounts Receivable		XX
When revenues are earned, the following is made:		
Unearned revenues (liability account)	XX	
Revenue		XX

.03 Financial Income vs. Tax Income

Corporation has pretax financial income of $50,000. The following differences exist between financial income and taxable income:

- Goodwill (amortization) = $1,500.
- Financial depreciation = $2,500, tax depreciation = $1,000.
- Excess of installment sales revenue over cash received is $8,000
- Excess of accrued warranty expense over amounts paid to satisfy warranties during the year is $3,000.
- Interest on investments in tax-exempt securities = $1,200.
- Fines and penalties = $800.

Permanent Differences vs. Temporary Differences		
Financial income		$50,000

Permanent differences:

• Nondeductible fines and penalties	$2,300
• Tax-exempt interest	(1,200)
Permanent differences	$1,100
Income after permanent differences	$51,100

Temporary differences from:

• Excess of depreciation per tax return	$(1,500)
• Excess of book installment revenue	(8,000)
• Excess of book warranty expense	3,000
Temporary differences	(6,500)
Taxable income	$44,600

Current Taxes

Taxable income	$44,600
Current tax rates (assumed = .25)	×.25
Income taxes currently payable	$11,150

Deferred Taxes

Net future taxable amount (from temporary differences) = ($3,000) + $8,000 + $1,500 =	$6,500
Future tax rate (.25)	× 25%
Deferred tax liability at end of year	$1,625

To Record Current Income Taxes

Income tax expenses (to balance)	$12,775	
Income taxes payable ($44,600 × 25%)		$11,150
Deferred tax liability		$1,625

.05 Income from Continuing Operations

Using Multiple Step Format

Sales revenue	$550,000
Less: sale returns and allowances	(25,000)
Net sales	$525,000

Cost of goods sold:

Beginning inventory		$200,000
Purchases	$480,000	
Less: Purchase returns/allowances	(15,000)	$465,000
Net purchases		$665,000
Freight-in		10,000

Goods available for sale	$675,000	
Less: Ending inventory	(210,000)	
Total cost of goods sold		465,000
Gross margin		$60,000

Operating expenses:

Marketing	$18,000	
General & administrative	32,000	$50,000
Income from operations		$10,000

Other revenues:

Interest and dividends	$1,500	
Gain on sale of assets	2,500	$4,000

Other expenses:

Interest	$1,200		
Loss on sale of investments	800	(2,000)	2,000
Income before income taxes and extraordinary items			$12,000
Provision for income taxes			1,800
Income before extraordinary items			$10,200

Extraordinary Item:

Loss due to flood (less tax benefit of $450)	(2,550)
Net income	$7,650

Using Single Step Format

Revenues:

Income before extraordinary items

Sales (less returns and allowances of $25,000)	$525,000
Interest and dividends	1,500
Gain on sale of assets	2,500
Total revenues	$529,000

Expenses:

Cost of goods sold	$465,000
Marketing	18,000
General & administrative	32,000
Interest	1,200

Loss on sale of investments	800
Income before income taxes and extraordinary items	$12,000
Provision for income taxes	(1,800)
Income before extraordinary items	$10,200
Extraordinary item:	
Loss due to flood (less tax benefit of $450)	(2,500)
Net income	$7,650

¶ 129 INCORPORATION

.01 Incorporation of Sole Proprietorship

Facts:

- Fair market value of other current assets is $18,000
- Equipment is appraised at $33,000

Sole Proprietorship Balance Sheet, as of 12/31/X1

Cash	$ 8,000
Other current assets	15,000
Equipment	35,000
Less, accumulated depreciation	(5,000)
Total assets	$53,000
Liabilities	$9,000
Capital owner	44,000
Total liabilities and equity	$53,000

Journal entry to incorporate new business exchanging assets for 1,000 shares at 1 par.

Cash	$8,000	
Current assets	$18,000	
Equipment	$33,000	
Liabilities		$9,000
Common Stock ($1.00 par × 1,000)		$1,000
Additional paid-in capital to balance		$ 49,000

¶ 130 INSURANCE—CASH SURRENDER VALUE OF LIFE INSURANCE

.01 Insurable Interest

Corporation is owner and sole beneficiary of a $400,000 life insurance policy on its chief executive officer. Annual premium is $18,000. The policy is starting its third year.

The cash value, in year three, increases $25 per thousand.

Life insurance expense-officers	$8,000
(Income statement as expense)	

¶129.01

Cash surrender value—life insurance policy (400 × $25)	$10,000	
(Balance sheet as asset)		
Cash		$18,000

¶ 131 INVENTORY

.01 Lower-of-Cost-or-Market

Inventory value calculated on an item-by-item basis

Cost   Market

Net Realizable Value

Cost (A)	Replacement Cost (B)	Selling Price (C)	Cost of Completing (D)	(C - D) Ceiling Maximum (E)	Normal Profit (F)	(E - F) Floor Minimum (G)	Market:[1] Limited by Floor &Ceiling (H)	Lower of[2] Cost or Market (I)
13.00	17.00	21.00	1.00	20.00	5.00	15.00	15.00	13.00
12.00	13.00	24.00	4.00	20.00	6.00	14.00	14.00	12.00
17.00	16.00	20.00	5.00	15.00	3.00	12.00	15.00	15.00

[1] Column (B) value, but not to exceed column (E), or not to be below column (G)
[2] Lower of column (A) or (H)

.03 Periodic Inventory System

ABC company illustrative data:

Beginning inventory = $15,000

Purchases = $85,000

Sales = $95,000

Ending inventory physical count = $25,000

Purchases	$85,000	
Cash or accounts payable		$85,000

To record acquisition of inventory goods.

Cash or accounts receivable	$95,000	
Sales		$95,000

To record sales.

Ending inventory (per physical count)	$25,000	
CGS (to balance)	$75,000	
Beginning inventory		$15,000
Purchases		$85,000

.05 Perpetual Inventory System

Inventory	$85,000	
Cash or accounts payable		$85,000

To record purchase of inventory goods.

Cash or accounts receivable	$95,000	
Sales		$95,000

Cost of goods sold	$75,000	
Inventory		$75,000

To record the sale of inventory items.

CGS is recorded at the time the inventory is sold.

.07 FIFO

First-in, First-out

	Units	Unit Cost	Total Cost
Beginning inventory	200	$6	$1,200
Purchase, 2/12/X1	100	7	700
Purchase, 6/15/X1	50	8	400
Goods available for sale	350		2,300
Ending inventory	150 [1]		1,100 [2]
Cost of goods sold	200		1,200

[1] Determined by physical count of inventory.
[2] Ending inventory:

6/15/X1 layer 50 @ $8 =	$400
2/12/X1 layer 100 @ $7 =	$700
Ending Inventory 20X1	$1,100

.09 Dollar Value LIFO

Allocation of inventory costs is based on dollar value of inventory rather than physical units.

Given Ending Inventory — **Compute**

Year	Item	Quantity	@[1]	Base Yr. Amt.	Current Year Amount	Price Index Curr/ Base
20X0 (base)	A	8,000	$2.00	16,000	16,000	
	B	4,000	$3.00	12,000	12,000	
20X0 Total				28,000	28,000	= 1.00
20X1	A	9,000	$2.25	18,000	20,250	
	B	5,000	3.25	15,000	16,250	
20X1 Total				33,000	36,500	= 1.11
20X2	A	11,000	$2.50	22,000	27,500	
	B	6,000	$3.50	18,000	21,000	
20X2 Total				40,000	48,500	= 1.21
20X3	A	7,000	[2]	14,000	[2]	
	B	4,500	[2]	13,500	[2]	
20X3				27,500		

---

[1] These may be weighted average purchase prices during a specific year
[2] No index computed due to inventory liquidation

Valuation of ending inventory, 20X1—20X3:

	20X1	20X2	20X3
Base year	$36,000	$36,000	$36,000
20X1 layer (5,000[3] × 1.11)	5,550	5,550	
20X1 layer, partially liquidated in 20X3 ($500 × 1.11)			(555)
20X2 layer ($7,000[4] × 1.21)	0	8,470	0
20X3 (no new layers added)	0	0	0
Valuation, ending inventory	$41,550	$50,020	$35,445

Increase in inventory, at base year prices

[3] 20X1 layer = 5,000 = (33,000 − 28,000)
[4] 20X2 layer = 7,000 = (40,000 − 33,000)

.11 Average Inventory Method

Purchases

	Unit	Unit Cost	Extended
3/15/X1	5,000	$4.00	$20,000
7/1/X1	10,000	4.50	45,000
9/15/X1	8,000	4.25	34,000
Goods available for sale	23,000		$99,000
Goods available for sale			23,000
Sales:			
7/1/X1		4,000	
9/15/X1		+ 2,000	
		6,000	
Ending inventory in units			17,000
Weighted average cost per unit ($99,000 / $23,000)			× $4.30
Ending inventory			73,100

.13 Gross Margin Method

Sales for the period	$200,000
GM ratio is 22%	
GM ratio × sales (22% × $200,000)	$44,000
Cost of goods sold	$156,000
Goods available for sale (from inventory and purchases)	$200,000
Cost of goods sold	156,000
Estimated ending inventory	$44,000

.15 Retail Method

Data:

	Cost	Retail
Merchandise Inventory		
January 1, 20X1	$175,000	$250,000
Purchases, net	600,000	750,000
Markups, net		20,000
Markdowns, net		50,000
Sales, net		900,000

Inventory value:

Weighted average using lower of cost or market

	Cost	Retail
Beginning inventory	$175,000	$250,000
Purchases, net	600,000	750,000
Markup, net	0	20,000
Weighted average/lower of cost or market	$775,000	$1,020,000

Retailed ratio = 775,000 / 1,020,000 = 76%

Less: Sales, net	($900,000)
Markdowns, net	(50,000)
Ending inventory at retail	$70,000

Ending inventory at cost: ($70,000 × .76) = $53,200

.17 LIFO Retail Method

	Cost	Retail
Beginning inventory	$175,000	$250,000
Inventory: cost/retail ratio (175,000 / 250,000) = 70%		
Purchases, net	600,000	750,000
Purchases cost/retail ratio = 600,000 / 750,000 = 80%		
Markups, net		20,000
Markdowns, net		(50,000)
Goods available for sale		$970,000
Less: Sales, net		(900,000)
Ending inventory at retail		$70,000

Inventory Layer	Ending Inventory At Retail	Cost/Retail Ratio	Ending Inventory At Cost
Beginning	$70,000	70%	$49,000
Purchases	0	80%	0
	$70,000		$49,000

¶ 133 INTEREST CAPITALIZED

.01 Assets Constructed for Self-Use

Firm borrowed $150,000 to finance construction of new equipment. The loan was to be repaid in five equal payments of $39,570, which includes interest of 10%. The equipment will be depreciated using the straight-line method over an estimated useful life of 12 years. Proceeds borrowed were invested in short-term liquid assets, yielding 8% interest income, until the construction would actually begin.

Note: Interest cost to capitalize (SFAS34) is the interest cost incurred during the acquisition period that could have been avoided if the asset had not been made.

If a specific interest rate is associated with the asset, use that rate. If not, then use a weighted average of rates applicable to other borrowings.

Cost of completed asset:

Total materials, labor, overhead, etc.	$150,000
Capitalized interest cost (applied to average accumulated expenditures)	
$[0 + 150,000) / 2] \times .10$	7,500
Capitalized cost of asset	$157,500

Interest expense, year 1:	
Total interest cost incurred $(150,000 \times .10)$	$15,000
Less capitalized interest cost	7,500
Interest expense	$7,500

Depreciation expense, year 2:	
Capitalized cost of asset	$157,500
Estimated useful life	÷ 12
Depreciation expense	$13,125

¶ 137 INVESTMENTS

.01 Marketable Equity Securities

Current Portfolio		MES Portfolio, 12/31/X1	
Cost	FMV	Cost	FMV
$700	$1,200	$700	$ 1, 000

Marketable equity securities (1,000 FMV) 700

Show at cost, because cost is lower than FMV at beginning or year end.

MES Portfolio, 1/1/X1		MES Portfolio, 12/31/X1	
Cost	FMV	Cost	FMV
$700	$1,100	$700	$600

Unrealized loss on current MES (I/S)	$100	
Valuation allowance for current MES (B/S)		$100

To recognize unrealized loss, because FMV at year end is less than cost.

Marketable equity securities	$700	
Less valuation allowance	($100)	$600

To present on B/S at year end

MES Portfolio, 1/1/X1		MES Portfolio, 12/31/X1	
Cost	FMV	Cost	FMV
$900	$600	$1,000	$800

Unrealized loss on current MES	$300	
Valuation allowance		$300

Valuation allowance for current MES	$100	
Recovery of unrealized loss on MES		$100

To bring valuation allowance from ($300) to ($200)

Marketable equity securities	$1,000	
Less valuation allowance	($200)	$800

To present at year end on B/S

MES Portfolio, 1/1/X1		MES Portfolio, 12/31/X1	
Cost	FMV	Cost	FMV
$800	$600	$1,200	$1,200

Unrealized loss on current MES	$200	
Valuation allowance		$200

Valuation allowance for current MES	$200	
Recovery of unrealized loss on MES		$200
To bring valuation account at year end back to zero		
Marketable equity securities ($1,200 FMV)		$1,200

To present at year end, shown at cost

Noncurrent Portfolio

MES Portfolio, 1/1/X1		MES Portfolio, 12/31/X1	
Cost	FMV	Cost	FMV
$700	$1,200	$700	$1,000

Marketable equity securities ($1,200 FMV) 700

To present at year end on B/S

MES Portfolio, 1/1/X1		MES Portfolio, 12/31/X1	
Cost	FMV	Cost	FMV
$700	$1,100	$700	$600

Unrealized loss on noncurrent MES		$100	
Valuation allowance for noncurrent MES			$100

To present at year end on B/S

Marketable equity securities	$700	
Less valuation allowance	($100)	$600

To present at year end on B/S at year end

MES Portfolio, 1/1/X1		MES Portfolio, 12/31/X1	
Cost	FMV	Cost	FMV
$900	$600	$1,000	$800

Unrealized loss on noncurrent MES		$300	
Valuation allowance for noncurrent MES			$300
Valuation allowance for noncurrent MES		$100	
Unrealized loss on noncurrent MES			$100

To record at year end

Marketable equity securities	$1,000	
Less valuation allowance	($200)	$800

To present on B/S at year end

MES Portfolio, 1/1/X1		MES Portfolio, 12/31/X1	
Cost	FMV	Cost	FMV
$800	$600	$1,100	$1,200

Valuation allowance for noncurrent MES		$200	
Unrealized loss on noncurrent MES			$200
Unrealized loss on noncurrent MES		$200	
Valuation allowance			$200

Marketable equity securities ($1,200 FMV) 1,100

To present at year end on B/S

Example of company's marketable equity security portfolio:

		Cost		Market	
Security	No. Shares	$ Per Share	Total	$ Per Share	Total
ABC	100	$6	$600	$8	$800
XYZ	300	10	3,000	12	3,600
Aggregate			$3,600		$4,400

Current Portfolio

Purchased 10 shares of BCD @ $5/share.

MES portfolio, C (10 × $5)	$50	
Cash		$50

¶137.01

Sold 30 shares of ABC @ $9/share.

Cash (30 × $9)	$270	
MES portfolio, XYZ (30 × $6)		$180
Realized gain on sale		$90

Sold 10 shares of XYZ @ $12/share.

Cash (10 × $12)	$120	
MES portfolio, XYZ (10 × $10)		$100
Realized gain on sale		$20

Sold 5 shares of BCD @ $3/share.

Cash (5 × $3)	$15	
Realized loss on sale	$10	
MES portfolio, BCD (5 × $5)		$25

The market values of the securities at year-end are as follows: ABC, $9/share; XYZ, $13/share; BCD, $6/share.

Security	No. Shares	Cost $ Per Share	Total	Market $ Per Share	Total
ABC	70	$6	$420	$9	$630
XYZ	290	10	2,900	13	3,770
BCD	5	5	25	6	30
			$3,345		$4,430

Year end balance sheet will show:

Marketable equity securities ($4,430 FMV)	$3,345

.03 Equity Method For Long Term Investment

Company A acquires 25% of company B's outstanding common stock for $50,000.

Company B's Owner Equity	
Common stock ($1 par)	$20,000
Additional paid-in capital	10,000
Retained earnings	25,000
Book value of net assets	$55,000

Record acquisition of 25% interest in B's common stock outstanding (5,000 shares).

Investment in B	$50,000	
Cash		$50,000

Record A's share of B's net income for 19X1.

Investment in B (25% × $22,000)	$5,500	
Investment income		$5,500

Reduce the investment in B for amortization of purchased goodwill.

Investment income (1)	$2,417	
Investment in B		$2,417

(1) Detailed as follows:

Purchased price of B's common stock		$50,000
Co. B's owner's equity (net assets)	$55,000	
% Interest acquired	×.25	
Book value of investment		13,750
Excess of cost over book value		$36,250
Amortized over 15 years = Divided by 15		÷15
Periodic amortization		$2,417

To adjust income and the investment account for Co. A's share of intercompany unrealized profits.

Investment income (1)	$300	
Investment in B		$300

Company A received 1,500 ($6,000 × 25%) in dividends from Company B. The journal entry on Company A's books would be as follows:

Cash	$1,500	
Investment in B		$1,500

(1) Detailed as follows:

B's profit on sale of inventory to A	$5,000
Sale price of inventory to A	÷25,000
B's gross margin ratio	.20
A's ending inventory	× 6,000
B's recorded profit on A's ending inventory	$1,200
A's percentage ownership in B	×.25
A's share of unrealized intercompany profit	$300

If B sold 2,000 additional shares of common stock.

Prior to Sale-Computation of Book Value of Common Stock

Common stock (1 par)		$20,000
Additional paid-in capital		10,000
Beg. Retained Earnings		$25,000
Net income - year 1		22,000
Dividends - year 1	(6,000)	41,000
Total stockholders' equity, Co. B		$71,000
Total common shares outstanding		÷20,000
Book value per common share		$3.55

Computation of Co. A's change in Additional Paid-In-Capital

		For Stock Sold at	
Common stock			
Sale price	$5.00	$2.25	$2.55
Co. B owner's equity prior to sale	$71,000	$71,000	$71,000
2000 shares sold ($1 par)	2,000	2,000	2,000
Additional paid-in capital			
2,000 × 4.00 =	8,000		
2,000 × 2.25 =		4,500	
2,000 × 2.55 =			5,100
B owner's equity subsequent to sale	$81,000	$77,500	$78,100
A % ownership subsequent to sale (5,000 shares / (20,000 + 2,000 shares)	×.2272	.2272	.2272
A interest subsequent to sale	$18,403	$17,608	$17,744
Co. A interest prior to sale	17,744	17,744	17,744
Change in paid-in capital	$659	$(136)	$0

For shares sold for $5.00		
Investment in Co. B	$665	
Additional paid-in capital		$665

For shares sold for $2.25		
Additional paid-in capital	$130	
Investment in Co. B		$130

For shares sold at $2.25 which equals book value new only to show ownership change from 25% to 22.72%. If ownership drops below 20%, change to cost method of accounting for investment.

¶ 139 LOSSES

.01 Operating Loss Tax Effects During an Interim Period

Provision for Taxes or Benefits

Quarter	Estimated Quarter	Income Cumulative	Estimated Tax Rate	Current Period	Prior Period	Cumulative
1	($5,000)	($5,000)	25%	($1,250)	—	($1,250)
2	15,000	10,000	25%	3,750	(1,250)	2,500
3	20,000	30,000	25%	5,000	2,500	7,500
4	25,000	55,000	25%	6,250	7,500	13,750

Recognize tax effects of losses only when realization is assured.

.03 Losses Recognized in Later Periods

Tax effects of losses incurred in early interim periods may be recognized in later interim periods of a fiscal year if their realization later becomes assured.

Provision for Taxes or Benefits

Quarter	Estimated Quarter	Income Cumulative	Estimated Tax Rate	Current Period	Prior Period	Cumulative
1	($5,000)	($5,000)	25%	—	—	—
2	15,000	10,000	25%	2,500	—	2,500
3	20,000	30,000	25%	5,000	2,500	7,500
4	25,000	55,000	25%	6,250	7,500	13,750

.05 Losses Recognized in Periods-Cumulative Benefit

Provision for Taxes or Benefits

Quarter	Estimated Quarter	Income Cumulative	Estimated Tax Rate	Current Period	Prior Period	Cumulative
1	$15,000	$15,000	25%	$3,750		$3,750
2	(20,000)	(5,000)	25%	(5,000)	3,750	(1,250)
3	(25,000)	(30,000)	25%	(5,000)[1]	(1,250)	(6,250)
Est. Inc. 4	10,000	(20,000)	25%	—	(6,250)	(6,250)

[1] quarter cumulative $5,000-quarter loss 25,000 = ($20,000) × .25 = $5,000
Given: A company has an operating loss of $20,000 for the fiscal year. The maximum cumulative tax benefit which can be recognized in any interim period is $6,250, assuming a 25% tax rate.

¶ 140 LEASE

.01 Operating Lease

Facts:

- Corporation rents machine for 1 year only for $12,000 payable in advance.
- FMV = $35,000
- estimated useful life = 5 years
- there is no bargain purchase price
- there is no ownership transfer
- corporation is on calendar year

Lessor Company

July 1, 20X1

Cash	$12,000	
Unearned rental revenue		$12,000

Dec. 31, 20X1

Unearned rental revenue ($12,000 × 6/12)	$6,000	
Rent revenue		$6,000

June 30, 20X2

Unearned rental revenue	$6,000	
Rent revenue ($12,000 × 6/12)		$6,000

Lessee Company

July 1, 20X1

Prepaid rent	$12,000	
Cash		$12,000

Dec. 31, 20X1		
Rental expense		
($12,000 × 6/12)	$6,000	
Prepaid rent		$6,000
June 30, 20X2		
Rental expense	$6,000	
Prepaid rent (12,000 × 6/12)		$6,000

.02 Capital Leases

Facts:

- Corporation leases machine for 5 years on January 1, 20X1 for $12,000 per year payable at the end of the year
- Both the incremental borrowing rate and the rate implicit in the lease are 10%
- The cost and fair value of the equipment are equal at $45,489
- Present value of the lease payments is $45,489
- There is no transfer or ownership and no bargain purchase option
- All risk transfer tests are met by the lessor
- The corporation has a December 31 year end
- Straight-line deprecation is used for similar owned property

Lessee

Lease is a capital lease because it meets the 75% rule—lease term is 75% or more of the life of the property (5 year lease / 5 year life = 100%). Asset and obligation are reported at the smaller of the fair value of the property of $45,489 or the present value of $45,489.

January 1, 20X1

Leased Asset Under Capital Lease	$45,489	
Obligation Under Capital Lease		$45,489

December 31, 20X1

Interest Expense	$4,549	
Obligation Under Capital Lease	$7,451	
Cash		$12,000
$45,489 × 10% = $4,549		
Deprecation Expense - Leased Asset	$9,098	
Leased Asset Under Capital Lease		$9,098
$45,489 / 5 years = $9,098		

December 31, 20X2

Interest Expense	$3,804	
Obligation Under Capital Lease	$8,196	
Cash		$12,000
$45,489 - $7,451 = $38,038 × 10% = $3,804		
Deprecation Expense - Leased Asset	$9,098	
Leased Asset Under Capital Lease		$9,098
$45,489 / 5 years = $9,098		

¶140.02

December 31, 20X3

Interest Expense	$2,984	
Obligation Under Capital Lease	$9,016	
Cash		$12,000

$38,038 - $8,196 = $29,842 × 10% = $2,984

Deprecation Expense - Leased Asset	$9,098	
Leased Asset Under Capital Lease		$9,098

$45,489 / 5 years = $9,098

December 31, 20X4

Interest Expense	$2,083	
Obligation Under Capital Lease	$9,917	
Cash		$12,000

$29,842 - $9,016 = $20,826 × 10% = $2,083

Deprecation Expense - Leased Asset	$9,098	
Leased Asset Under Capital Lease		$9,098

$45,489 / 5 years = $9,098

December 31, 20X5

Interest Expense	$1,091	
Obligation Under Capital Lease	$10,909	
Cash		$12,000

$20,826 - $9,917 = $10,909 × 10% = $1,091

Deprecation Expense - Leased Asset	$9,097	
Leased Asset Under Capital Lease		$9,097

$45,489 / 5 years = $9,097

Lessor

Lease is a capital lease because it meets the 75% rule—1 term is 75% or more of the life of the property (5 year lease / 5 year life = 100%) and both risk transfer tests. The lease is a direct financing lease since both fair value and cost are the same. Interest income reported by the lessor is the same as the interest expense reported by the lessee since both the incremental borrowing rate and the implicit rate are the same.

January 1, 20X1

Lease Receivable	$60,000	
Unearned Income		$14,511
Machine		$45,489

December 31, 20X1

Cash	$12,000	
Lease Receivable		$12,000
Unearned Income	$4,549	
Income from Capital Lease		$4,549

December 31, 20X2

Cash	$12,000	
Lease Receivable		$12,000

¶140.02

| Unearned Income | $ 3,804 | |
| Income from Capital Lease | | $ 3,804 |

December 31, 20X3

Cash	$12,000	
Lease Receivable		$12,000
Unearned Income	$2,984	
Income from Capital Lease		$2,984

December 31, 20X4

Cash	$12,000	
Lease Receivable		$12,000
Unearned Income	$2,083	
Income from Capital Lease		$2,083

December 31, 20X5

Cash	$12,000	
Lease Receivable		$12,000
Unearned Income	$1,091	
Income from Capital Lease		$1,091

.03 Capital Lease—Sale and Lease Back

Facts:

- Corporation sells equipment and leases back
- Book value = $140,000
- Fair market value = $155,000
- Lease rental = $40,889 / year, due at year end
- Lease period = 5 years
- Estimated useful life = 5 years
- Depreciation = straight line
- Implicit interest rate = 10%

Cash	$155,000	
Equipment (net)		$140,000
Deferred gain		$15,000
Leased equipment under capital lease	$155,000	
Obligation under capital lease		$155,000
Interest expense (10% × 155,000)	$15,500	
Obligation under capital lease ($40,889 - $15,500)	$ 25,389	
Cash		$40,889
Amortization expense on leased Equipment ($155,000 / 5)	$31,000	
Accumulated amortization		$31,000
Deferred gain ($15,000 / 5)	$3,000	
Amortization expense on leased equipment		$3,000

Note: Entire gain/loss should be recognized at point of sale if seller-lessee retains only a minor portion of remaining use of property.

¶ 141 NOTES

.01 Long-Term Notes Payable

A company acquires a logo for a 4 year noninterest-bearing $10,000 note. Neither the logo nor the note has a ready market.

The prevailing rate of interest is 10%.

To record the logo and the note:

Logo	$6,830	
Discount on note payable (to balance)	$3,170	
Note payable		$10,000

(PV = $10,000 × present value Interest factor (n = 4, i = 10%) = $10,000 × .68301 = $6,830)

To record at year-end payment of note and interest expense:

20X1:

Interest expense	$683	
[$10,000 - $3,170) × .10]		
Discount on note payable		$683

20X2:

Interest expense	$751	
[$10,000 – $3,170 + $683) × .10]		
Discount on note payable		$751

20X3:

Interest expense	$826	
[$10,000 – $2,487 + $751) × .10]		
Discount on note payable		$826

20X4:

Interest expense	$910	
[$10,000 – $1,736 + $826) × .10]		
Discount on note payable		$910
Note payable	$10,000	
Cash		$10,000

.03 Non-Interest Bearing Notes

Company A borrowed $13,761 on June 30, 20X1, and signed a noninterest-bearing note agreeing to repay $15,000 in one year. The implicit interest rate that equates $13,761 with $15,000 is 9%. The entries required for this transaction are as follows:

June 30, 20X1

Cash	$13,761	
Discount on notes payable	$1,239	
Notes payable, short-term		$15,000

Dec. 31, 20X1

Interest expense ($13,761 × 9% × 6/12)	$619	
Discount on notes payable		$619

June 30, 20X2

Notes payable, short-term	$15,000	
Interest expense ($13,761 × 9% × 6/12)	$620	
Discount on notes payable		$620
Cash		$15,000

.05 Interest Bearing—Notes Payable

Company A borrows $15,000 at 9% interest on March 30, 20X1. Principal plus interest is due in one year. The company has a calendar year end.

Cash	$15,000	
Notes payable, short-term		$15,000
To record interest expense on December 31, 20X1		
Interest expense ($15,000 × .09 × 9/12)	$1,013	
Accrued Interest payable		$1,013

On March 30, 20X1, company A records the payment of the note plus interest as follows:

Notes payable, short-term	$15,000	
Accrued interest payable	$1,013	
Interest expense ($15,000 × .09 × 3/12)	$337	
Cash		$16,350

.06 Liabilities—Estimated

Product warranty example:

To record the liability at the point of sale.

To record estimated warranty expense

Warranty expense	XX	
Estimated warranty liability		XX

To record actual warranty expenditures:

Estimated warranty liability	XX	
Cash or other assets		XX

To record liability at the end of year:

- No entry is made at the date of sale:
- Any *direct costs* for servicing customer claims:

Warranty expense	XX	
cash and/or		XX
assets		XX

- At end of year, an estimate of the year's warranty liability is made based on past experience and current estimates. Any shortage between the estimate and the actual amounts previously charged to warranty expenses is booked.

¶141.05

The following example illustrates:

Warranty expenses should be recognized at the time of sale in accordance with the matching principle.

Product A was first introduced as a new product in 20X1. Thus, no balance exists in its Warranty Liability account at the beginning of 20X1. Sales and actual warranty expenditures for product A with a 3-year warranty are as follows:

	Product A Sales	Actual Warranty Expenditures	Estimated Warranty Costs as Percent of Sales	Estimated Warranty Cost
20X1	$250,000	$4,000	3%	$7,500
20X2	$375,000	$12,000	4%	$15,000
20X3	$425,000	$18,500	4%	$17,000

Journal entries for the warranty expense and warranty payments for 20X1 - 20X3 are as follows:

20X1

Warranty Expense	$7,500	
Warranty Liability		$7,500
Warranty Liability	$4,000	
Cash, Payable, Etc.		$4,000

20X2

Warranty Expense	$15,000	
Warranty Liability		$15,000
Warranty Liability	$12,000	
Cash, Payable, Etc.		$12,000

20X3

Warranty Expense	$17,000	
Warranty Liability		$17,000
Warranty Liability	$18,500	
Cash, Payable, Etc.		$18,500

The adjusted balance in the warranty liability account at the end of 20X3 is $5,500 ($15,000 + $7,500 + $17,000 – $4,000 – $12,000 – $18,500).

.07 Present Value of Note

To Determine Present Value of Note

On January 1, 20X1, Company Y received a $20,000 note in exchange for equipment sold. The stated rate of interest was 6%, payable yearly on December 31. The prevailing interest rate at the time of the exchange was determined to be 10%. The note matures on December 31, 20X5.

$20,000 × .06 = $1,200 interest per year

Present Value of Note

PV = $20,000 (.62092) + $1,200 (3.79079) = $16,967

Discount Amortization

Date	Interest Income 10%	Interest Payment 6%	Discount Amortized	Carrying Value
1/1 /X1	—	—	—	$16,967
12/31/X1	$1,697	$1,200	$497	17,464
12/31/X2	1,746	1,200	546	18,010
12/31/X3	1,801	1,200	601	18,611
12/31/X4	1,861	1,200	661	19,272
12/31/X5	1,927	1,200	727	20,000

1/1/X1			
Notes receivable		$20,000	
Disc. on N/R			$3,033
Equipment			$16,967
(assume no gain or loss)			
12/31/X1			
Cash		$1,200	
Disc. on N/R		$497	
Interest income			$1,697
12/31/X5			
Cash		$1,200	
Disc. on N/R		$727	
Interest income			$1,927
Cash		$20,000	
N/R			$20,000

.09 Present Value of Note With Interest

A company acquires a logo for a $10,000, 4 year note.

The note specifies annual interest payments of 6%. This rate is considered unreasonably low based on the current market rate of 10%. To record the logo and the note:

Logo	$8,732	
Discount on note payable (to balance)	$1,268	
Note payable		$10,000

Present value of principal:

= $10,000 × Present value factor of $10,000 × .68301 = $6,830

(n = 4; i = .10)

Present value of interest payments:

= ($10,000 × .06) × present value of annuity (n = 4; 1 = .10)

= ($10,000 × .06) × (3.16987) = $1,902

Present value of note

= $6,830 + $1,902 = $8,732

To record at year-end the payment of the note and interest expense:

20X1:

Interest expense		
[(10,000 – $1,268) × .10]	$873	
Cash ($10,000 × .06)		$600
Discount on note payable (to balance)		$273

20X2:

Interest expense		
[(10,000 – $1,268 + $273) × .10]	$901	
Cash ($10,000 × .06)		$600
Discount on note payable (to balance)		$301

20X3:

Interest expense		
[(10,000 – $995 + $301) × .10]	$930	
Cash ($10,000 × .06)		$600
Discount on note payable (to balance)		$330

20X4:

Interest expense		
[(10,000 – $694 + $330) × .10]	$964	
Cash ($10,000 × .06)		$600
Discount on note payable (to balance)		$364
Note payable	$10,000	
Cash		$10,000

.11 Discount of Note

Discounting or Sale of Note to Third Party for Immediate Cash

Assume XYZ Company has a $5,000, 3 month, 8% interest-bearing note; 1 month after acquiring the note, XYZ Company decides to discount it at a bank that charges a 10% discount rate.

Determining accrued interest:

$5,000 × 8% × 1/12 = $33.33

Proceeds to be received upon discounting:

Proceeds = Maturity value - Discount charged by bank

Maturity value:		
Face Amount		$5,000
Interest (5,000 × .08 × 3/12)		100
		$5,100
Interest cost: (5,100 × .10 × 2/12)		85
Proceeds from discounting		$5,015
Discounting of N/R:		
Cash	$5,015.00	

Interest expense	$18.33	
Interest income		$33.33
N/R discounted		$5,000.00

Repayment of note by maker:		
N/R discounted	$5,000.00	
N/R		$5,000.00

Default by maker on note discounted "with recourse"		
N/R overdue	$5,100.00	
Cash		$5,100.00
N/R discounted	$5,000.00	
N/R		$5,000.00

.12 Liabilities Related to Exit Cost Activities (SFAS 146)

A company decides to stop operations in 60 days at a specific location which will require the termination of 200 employees. The company agrees to pay each employee $10,000 at the date of termination for a total cost to the company of $2,000,000. A liability should be reported at fair value in the accounting period that the information is communicated to the employees. Assuming no significant difference between the $2,000,000 payment and the present value of the $2,000,000, the $2,000,000 amount is assumed to be fair value. The following entry is required:

Exit activity cost	$2,000,000	
Liability for exit cost activity		$2,000,000

.13 Liabilities Related to Guarantees (SFAS Interpretation 45)

In the accounting period that a guarantee is provided, a liability should be reported by a guarantor for an amount equal to the fair value of the guarantee. When a liability is reported for a guarantee using SFAS 5, the initial liability reported under SFAS Interpretation No. 45 is the larger of the amount under Interpretation No. 45 or SFAS No. 5. The other side of the liability entry depends on the circumstances of the guarantee. To illustrate the entry, assume that the fair value of a guarantee under Interpretation No. 45 is $20,000 (the premium to be paid for the guarantee), and there is no liability required under SFAS No. 5.

Receivable of Premium on Guarantee	$20,000	
Liability for Guarantee		$20,000

¶ 142 PENSION AND POSTRETIREMENT PLANS

.01 Defined Benefit Pension Plan

A defined benefit pension plan is one where the method of determining future benefit is defined (such as the pension benefit payment will be equal to 80 percent of the average of the three highest years of salary in the last five years of employment). Pension expense for a specific accounting period is determined using six possible components (every company may not have all of the components). Assume the following defined pension benefit expense information for a specific accounting period. A company had the following annual pension information: (1) an actuarial loss increased by $600 during

¶141.12

the accounting period, (2) contribution to the pension trust was $800, and (3) pension cost was as follows:

Service cost	$1,600
Interest cost	1,200
Expected return on plan assets	(400)
Amortization of prior service cost	280
Amortization of net actuarial loss	320
Amortization of transitional obligation	80
Total pension cost	$3,080

Journal entry for annual pension expense:

Pension expense	$3,080	
Other comprehensive income—prior service cost		$280
Other comprehensive income—actuarial gain		320
Other comprehensive income—transitional obligation		80
Cash		800
Pension liability		1,600
Other comprehensive income—actuarial loss	600	
Pension liability		600

SFAS 158 amends defined benefit pension plan rules and requires an entity to report any pension plan assets and liabilities for over funded and under funded pension plans and to record any unamortized pension plan items. Assume a company had the following over funded pension plan items at the date of adoption of SFAS 158.

Projected benefit obligation	$5,000,000
Fair value of plan assets	6,000,000
Unrecognized actuarial gain	700,000
Unrecognized prior service cost	200,000
Transitional asset	500,000

Journal entry for adoption of SFAS 158 for an over funded pension plan:

Pension asset	$1,000,000	
Accumulated other comprehensive income—prior service cost	200,000	
Accumulated other comprehensive income—actuarial gain		$700,000
Accumulated other comprehensive income—transitional asset		500,000

Assume a company had the following under funded pension plan items at the date of adoption of SFAS 158.

Projected benefit obligation	$5,000,000
Fair value of plan assets	4,000,000
Unrecognized actuarial loss	400,000
Unrecognized prior service cost	300,000
Transitional obligation	300,000

Journal entry for adoption of SFAS 158 for under funded pension plan:

Accumulated other comprehensive income— prior service cost	$300,000	
Accumulated other comprehensive income— actuarial loss	400,000	
Accumulated other comprehensive income— transitional obligation	300,000	
Pension liability		$1,000,000

.02 Defined Contribution Pension Plan

A defined contribution pension plan is one where the amount of the contribution to the plan is defined (such as a company will pay into a plan 8 percent of the annualized salary of the employee). Pension cost for the accounting period is equal to the percentage paid times the specified base.

Annual entry to record pension cost assuming that a company pays 10 percent of annual salaries and annual salaries are $10,000,000. Annual pension cost is $1,000,000 ($10,000,000 × 10%).

Pension Cost	$1,000,000	
Cash		$1,000,000

.03 Defined Benefit Postretirement Plan

A defined benefit postretirement plan is one in which the method of determining future benefit is defined. Postretirement expense for a specific accounting period is determined using six possible components (every company may not have all of the components). Assume the following defined benefit postretirement benefit expense information for a specific accounting period. A company had the following annual postretirement information: (1) an actuarial loss increased by $1,200 during the accounting period, (2) contribution to the postretirement trust was $1,600, and (3) postretirement cost was as follows:

Service cost	$3,200
Interest cost	2,400
Expected return on plan assets	(800)
Amortization of prior service cost	560
Amortization of net actuarial (gain)	(640)
Amortization of transitional obligation	160
Total postretirement cost	$4,880

Journal entry for annual postretirement expense:

Postretirement expense	$4,880	
Other comprehensive income—actuarial gain	640	
Other comprehensive income—prior service cost		$560
Other comprehensive income— transitional obligation		160
Cash		1,600
Postretirement liability		3,200
Other comprehensive income—actuarial loss	1,200	
Postretirement liability		1,200

SFAS 158 amends defined benefit postretirement plan rules and requires an entity to report any postretirement plan assets and liabilities for over funded and under funded postretirement plans and to record any unamortized postretirement plan items. Assume a company had the following under funded postretirement plan items at the date of adoption of SFAS 158.

Accumulated postretirement benefit obligation	$10,000,000
Fair value of plan assets	8,000,000
Unrecognized actuarial loss	800,000
Unrecognized prior service cost	600,000
Transitional obligation	600,000

Journal entry for adoption of SFAS 158 for under funded postretirement plan:

Accumulated other comprehensive income— prior service cost	$600,000	
Accumulated other comprehensive income— actuarial loss	800,000	
Accumulated other comprehensive income— transitional obligation	600,000	
Postretirement liability		$2,000,000

.04 Defined Contribution Postretirement Plan

A defined contribution postretirement plan is one in which the amount of the contribution to the plan is defined. Postretirement cost for the accounting period is equal to the percentage paid times the specified base. The annual entry to record postretirement cost is calculated assuming a company pays eight percent of annual salaries and annual salaries are $20,000,000. Annual postretirement cost is $20,000,000 × 8% = $1,600,000.

Postretirement cost	$1,600,000	
Cash		$1,600,000

SFAS No. 132 (Revised), as amended by SFAS No. 158, covers all disclosure requirements for all types of pension and postretirement plans. See ¶ 259 for details about the required disclosures.

¶ 143 RETAINED EARNINGS

.01 Appropriated Retained Earnings

Retained Earnings Not Available for Dividends

Retained earnings	XX	
Appropriated RE—plant construction (to appropriate for construction)		XX

APB10 requires disclosures in the separate accounts of retained earnings.

Do not include:

- Gifts of property
- Gains from treasury stock transactions

Statement of Changes in Retained Earnings

Retained earnings, Jan. 1, 20X1,		XXX
+/− Prior period adjustments		XXX

Retained earnings, Jan. 1, 20X1, as adjusted	XXX
+ Net income (– loss)	XXX
– Dividends declared	(XXX)
Retained earnings, Dec. 31. 20X1	XXX

Research and Development Costs

Jan. 2:

	Cost
Purchase of general purpose lab equipment (7 year life)	$35,000
Machine to be used exclusively for research on project a (7 year life)	$25,000

Feb. 1:

Purchase of misc. lab supplies for several projects.	$3,500
Purchase of materials to be used on Project A.	$4,500

March 31:

Purchase of building (estimated useful life, 15 years)	$250,000

Direct labor costs of 55,000 were incurred on various R & D projects.

Overhead costs of $4500 were appropriately allocated to R & D activities.

All materials purchased for Project A and general purpose supplies of $800 were used up during the year.

The company's R & D expense for the year is:

Building ($250,000 / 15 years)	$16,667
General purpose lab equipment ($35,000 / 7 years)	5,000
Machine to be used exclusively on Project A	25,000
Materials for Project A	4,500
Misc. lab supplies (portion used for project A)	800
Direct labor	55,000
Overhead allocated to R and D	4,500
Total R & D expense	$111,467

¶ 144 REVENUE RECOGNITION

.01 Cost Recovery Method

APB10 states that the cost recovery method is not acceptable for financial purposes, except under exceptional circumstances where collectibility of proceeds is doubtful.

Sand Pit Company sold one of its pits (pit 1) with a net book value of $200,000 for $350,000. Payment was to be at $100,000 per year with no interest with the final payment of $150,000 in the last year.

Year	Amount Collected	Unrecovered Cost (20X0: 200,000)	Deferred Profit	Recognized Profit
			Dr/Cr	Cr.
20X1	$100,000	$100,000	($150,000)	0
20X2	$100,000	0	(150,000)	0
20X3	$150,000	0	0	(150,000)

20X1:

Cash	$100,000	
Notes receivable	$250,000	
Sand pit 1 (net)		$200,000
Deferred profit		$150,000

20X2:

Cash	$100,000	
Notes receivable		$100,000

20X3:

Cash	$150,000	
Deferred profit	$150,000	
Recognized profit		$150,000
Notes receivable		$150,000

.03 Franchise Fee Revenue (SFAS 45)

Franchisor sold to new franchisee an outlet for $200,000.
Payment is as follows:

> $100,000 down
> $50,000 due in 1 year
> $50,000 due in 2 years
> The market rate of interest is 8%.

The franchisor will receive 10% of gross sales each year.
Franchisee had $250,000 in gross sales for the year.

Initial franchise fee:		
Down payment	$100,000	
PV of installments ($50,000 × 1.78326)	89,163	$189,163
% of gross sales (.10 × 250,000)		25,000
Interest income (.08 × $89,163)		7,133
		$221,296

¶ 145 STOCK

.01 Issuance of Capital Stock

Cash Consideration Given for Stock

Assume 200 shares of $20 par value common stock are sold for $25 per share.

To record the stock issue:

Cash (200 × $25)	$5,000	
Common stock (200 × $20)		$4,000
Paid in capital in excess of par-common		$1,000

.03 Issues Pursuant to Subscription

Company A received subscriptions for 10,000 shares of $20 par value common stock at $25 per share. The company requires an initial payment of 10% of the subscription price.

Date of subscription contract		
Cash (10,000 × $25 × 10%)	$25,000	
Subscriptions receivable (10,000 × $25 × 90%)	$225,000	
Common stock subscribed (10,000 × $20)		$200,000
Paid in capital in excess of par (10,000 × 5)		$50,000
Cash receipt and issuance of stock:		
Cash	$225,000	
Subscriptions receivable		$225,000
Common Stock subscribed	$200,000	
Common Stock		$200,000

.05 Issuing Stock for Property Other Than Cash

Assets	XX	At Fair Market Value of stock unless not known. Then use FMV of Assets.
Common stock	XX	At Par Value
Paid in capital in excess of par	XX	To Balance

.06 Stock Dividends

Stock Dividends

For small stock dividends (less than 20% - 25%)

Retained earnings	XX	At Fair Market Value
Common stock	XX	At Par Value
Paid in capital in excess of par	XX	To Balance

For large stock dividends where dividend is greater than 20% - 25%, only capitalize the par value.

Retained earnings	XX	At Par Value
Common stock	XX	Par Value

Corporation declares a 6% stock dividend on its 1,000,000 shares of outstanding 10 par common stock

5,000,000 of common stock is authorized.

Stock is selling for $35 per share on the date of declaration.

Total stock dividend (6% of 1,000,000)	60,000 shares
Value of 60,000 shares @ $35 per share (Fair market value)	$2,100,000

¶145.03

On Date of declaration:

Retained earnings	$2,100,000	
Stock dividend to be distributed (60,000 × $10)		$600,000
Paid-in capital in excess of par		$1,500,000

On Date of Distribution:

Stock dividend to be distributed (Temporary Account)	$600,000	
Common stock (60,000 × $10)		$600,000

.07 Stock Split

Increase the shares and reduce the par value.

Corp. A declares a 2 for 1 stock split on common stock in order to increase trading of the stock on the open market.

Prior to the split the corporation had 200,000 shares of $10 par value common stock issued and outstanding.

Common stock (par $10; 200,000 shares outstanding)	$2,000,000	
Common stock (par $10 / 2; 200,000 × 2 shares outstanding)		$2,000,000

Memo: 2 for 1 stock split—

Par value $10 to $5

Stock outstanding—200,000 shares to 400,000 shares

.09 Stock Options

Share options are granted to an employee to purchase 1,000 shares of $1 par value common stock at $10 per share on January 1, 20X4. The selling price of the stock on the date of grant is $10. The fair value of the share options on the date of grant is $5 using an appropriate valuation model. All of the options vest at the end of two years. The service period is two years. The share options are not considered incentive options for tax purposes and the tax rate is 40 percent. There were no forfeitures of the options. The share options were all exercised December 31, 20X6 when the market price of the stock was $25. The Company has a December 31 year end.

December 31, 20X4—Amortization of Annual Compensation Cost

Compensation cost	$2,500	
Paid-In-Capital—share options		$2,500

1,000 share options × $5 fair value = $5,000/2 year service period = $2,500.

Deferred tax asset	$1,000	
Deferred tax benefit		$1,000

$2,500 compensation cost × 40% tax rate = $1,000.

December 31, 20X5—Amortization of Annual Compensation Cost

Compensation cost	$2,500	
Paid-In-Capital—share options		$2,500

1,000 share options × $5 fair value = $5,000/2 year service period = $2,500.

Deferred tax asset	$1,000	
Deferred tax benefit		$1,000

$2,500 compensation cost × 40% tax rate = $1,000.

December 31, 20X6—Exercise of Share Options

Exercise of options:

Cash	$10,000	
Paid-In-Capital—share options	$5,000	
Common stock		$1,000
Paid-In-Capital in excess of par		$14,000

1,000 shares × $10 option price.
$5,000 = $2,500 + $2,500.
1,000 shares × $1 par value = $1,000.
$15,000 – $1,000 common stock = $14,000.

Reversal of deferred tax asset:

Deferred tax expense	$2,000	
Deferred tax asset		$2,000

Recognition of tax benefit from deductible compensation expense at date of exercise:

Taxes payable	$6,000	
Tax expense		$2,000
Additional paid-in-capital		$4,000

$25 market price on date of exercise – $10 option price = $15 × 1,000 share options = $15,000 × 40% = $6,000.
$15,000 – $5,000 total compensation cost = $10,000 × 40% = $4,000.

.11 Stock Warrants

Assume that a company issues 100,000 of bonds at face value (100 bonds) for an issue price of 102,000 (1,020 each). Each bond has 10 detachable warrants. Each warrant is redeemable for 1 share of 15 par common stock at an exercise price of 75. After issuance, the bonds without the warrants have a fair market value of 1,010 each, and the warrants without the bonds have a fair market value of 3 each.

$$\text{Value Assigned to Bonds} = \frac{\$1,010 \times 100}{(\$1,010 \times 100) + (\$3 \times 10 \times 100)} \times \$102,000$$

$$= \frac{\$101,000}{\$101,000 + \$3,000} \times \$102,000$$

$$= \frac{\$101,000}{\$104,000} \times \$102,000 = \$99.058$$

$$\text{Value Assigned to Warrants} = \frac{\$3 \times 10 \times 100}{(\$1,010 \times 100) + (\$3 \times 10 \times 100)} \times \$102,000$$

$$= \frac{\$3,000}{\$104,000 + \$2,000} \times \$102,000$$

$$= \frac{\$3,000}{\$104,000} \times \$102,000 = \$2,942$$

Cash	$102,000	
Discount on Bonds Payable ($100,000 – $99,058)	$942	
Bonds Payable		$100,000
Stock Warrants		$2,942

The journal entry to record the redemption of 100 warrants at the exercise price of $75 is as follows:

Cash (100 × $75)	$7,500	
Stock Warrants (100 / 1,000) × $2,942	$294	
Common Stock (100 × $15)		$1,500
Paid in Capital in Excess of Par (to balance)		$6,294

¶ 146 TAXES

.01 Tax Rate Change or Tax Law Change

Corporation began operations in 20X1. At year end the Corporation had the following cumulative temporary differences:

- The reported amount of installment receivables was in excess of the tax basis of those receivables which will result in future taxable amounts of 14,000 (8,000 for 20X3 and $6,000 for 20X4).

- An estimated litigation liability was 4,000. The liability was expected to be paid in 20X4. There was no provision made for this for tax purposes.

Tax Rates

20X1	25%
20X2 and later years	27%

Taxable income for 20X1 was $25,000.

Pretax financial income for 20X1 was $45,000.

Future Years

Deferred Tax Liability	20X3	20X4
Future taxable amounts	$8,000	$6,000

Future deductible amounts		(4,000)	
Net future taxable amounts		$4,000	$6,000
Enacted tax rate		× 27%	× 27%
Total deferred tax liability	$2,700 =	$1,080	$1,620

The journal entry to record income taxes for 20X1:

Income tax expense (to balance)	$8,950	
Deferred tax liability ($1,080 + $1,620)		$2,700
Income taxes payable ($25,000 × 25%)		$6,250

During 20X2, a new tax rate of 30% was enacted.

Other temporary difference facts remain the same.

Taxable income for 20X2 was $27,000.

Pretax financial income was $32,000.

The deferred tax previously provided is to be adjusted downward or upward to reflect the new rate.

Deferred schedule if new tax rate had been known:

Future Years

		20X3	20X4
Deferred Tax Liability			
Future taxable amounts		$8,000	$6,000
Future deductible amounts		(4,000)	
Net future taxable amounts		4,000	6,000
Enacted tax rate		× 30%	× 30%
Total deferred tax liability	$3,000 =	$1,200	$1,800
Current tax liability schedule		$3,000	
Prior tax liability schedule		2,700	
Deferred tax liability increase		$300	

Journal entries related to income taxes for 20X2:

Income tax expense	$300	
Deferred tax liability		$300
Income tax expense	$8,100	
Income taxes payable ($27,000 × 30%)		$8,100

Comparative income statement:		20X1		20X2
Income before income taxes		$45,000		$32,000
Income tax expense:				
Current	$6,250		$8,100	
Deferred	2,700	8,950	300	8,400
Net income		$36,050		$23,600

.02 Uncertain Tax Positions

To illustrate journal entries related to uncertain tax positions, assume that an entity expensed $2,000,000 of estimated costs related to ground water pollution issues. The company did not expect to pay the $2,000,000 until later years, however, subsequently, the entity entered into a transaction that accelerated the payment and deducted the $2,000,000 on the tax return. The entity's tax rate is 40 percent. The accelerated payments did not meet the more likely than not criteria specified by Interpretation 48, and the company expects to have an underpayment of taxes. In addition, the entity expects to pay interest on the underpayment of taxes of $70,000 and a penalty of $85,000.

Deferred tax asset	$800,000	
Income taxes payable		$800,000
$2,000,000 × 40% = $800,000		
Interest expense	70,000	
Interest payable		70,000
Penalty for tax underpayment	85,000	
Liability for tax underpayment		85,000

¶ 147 TREASURY STOCK

.01 Cost vs. Par Value

Original issue: 2,000 shares of $10 par value common stock at $25 per share.

Cost Method

Cash (2,000 × $25)	$50,000	
Common stock (2,000 × $10)		$20,000
Paid in capital in excess of par (2,000 × ($25 – $10))		$30,000

Acquisition of 100 shares at $30 share:

Treasury stock	$3,000	
Cash (100 × $30)		$3,000

Original issue: 2000 shares of $10 par value common stock at $25 per share.

Par Value Method

Cash (2,000 × $25)	$50,000	
Common stock (2,000 × $10)		$20,000
Paid in capital in excess of par (2,000 × ($25 – $10))		$30,000

Acquisition of 100 shares at 40 per share:

Treasury stock (100 × $10)	$1,000	
Paid in capital in excess of par (100 × ($25 – $10))	$1,500	
Retained earnings (to balance)	$1,500	
Cash		$4,000

Cost Method

Acquisition of 125 shares at $20 per share:

Treasury stock	$2,500	
Cash		$2,500

Reissuance of 25 shares at $32 per share (FIFO):

Cash (25 × $32)	$800	
Treasury stock (25 × $20)		$500
Paid-in capital, Treasury stock		$300

Reissuance of 25 shares at $20 per share (FIFO):

Cash (25 × $20)	$500	
Treasury stock (25 × $20)		$500

Par Value Method

Acquisition of 125 shares at $20 per share:

Treasury stock (125 × $10)	$1,250	
Paid in capital in excess of par 125 shares at (25 – $10)	$1,875	
Cash		$2,500
Paid-in capital, treasury stock		$625

Reissuance of 25 shares at $32 per share:

Cash (25 × $32)	$800	
Treasury stock (25 × $10)		$250
Add'l. paid in capital		$550

Reissuance of 25 shares at $20 per share:

Cash (25 × $20)	$500	
Paid-in capital, treasury stock (25 × $10)		$250
Treasury stock (25 × $10)		$250

Retire 100 shares of $10 par value stock originally issued for $15/share:

Cost Method

Retired 100 shares at $20 per share:

Common stock (100 × $10)	$1,000	
Paid in capital in excess of par (100 × ($15 – $10))	$500	
Retained earnings (to balance)	$500	
Treasury stock (100 × $20)		$2,000

¶ 148 TROUBLED DEBT RESTRUCTURING

.01 Discharge

On January 1, 20X1, Company A, borrowed $200,000 from Finance Corp. at 8% interest, payable annually on Dec. 31.

On April 1, 20X2, Company A and Finance Corp. reached an agreement where the entire obligation would be discharged by the transfer of undeveloped land valued at

¶148.01

$80,000 purchased by Company A in 20X0 for $65,000 and Company A preferred stock with a fair value of $35,000.

Restructure for Debtor

Note payable	$200,000	
Accrued interest $200,000 × (.08 × 12/12) + $200,000 × (.08 × 3/12)	$20,000	
Ordinary gain on disposal of land (to balance)		$15,000
Land		$65,000
Preferred stock		$35,000
Extraordinary gain on debt restructuring [$220,000 – ($80,000 + $35,000)]		$105,000

Restructure for Creditor

Land	$80,000	
Investment in company A stock	$35,000	
Ordinary loss on settlement of receivable (to balance)	$105,000	
Notes receivable, with accrued interest		$220,000

.03 Modification of Terms

Assume finance company agrees to

- reduce the amount of the obligation from $200,000 to $150,000
- lower the interest rate from 10% to 8%
- postpone payment of principal from Dec 20X1 until December 31, 20X4.

Finance will reduce the recorded amount of the note receivable to $206,000 and recognize an ordinary loss of $14,000.

Company A will reduce the amount of its obligation to $206,000 and recognize a $14,000 extraordinary gain.

Interest for year 1 ($200,000 × .10)	20,000
Interest for years 20X2 thorough 20X4 ($12,000[1] × 3)	36,000
Principal	150,000
New Obligation	$206,000
Less original obligation with interest ($200,000 + $20,000)	– 220,000
Extraordinary gain	$14,000

[1] New interest for each year = $150,000 × .08

¶ 149 PRODUCT COSTING

.01 Process Costing

Flow of Units

Beginning units + units begun = units transferred out + ending inventory

Facts:

- All material for product is added at beginning of production process.

- Conversion takes place continuously throughout the process.
- FIFO cost flow is assumed
- Beginning Inventory = 400 units (1/2 complete)
  - Beginning Inventory material costs = $400
  - Beginning Inventory conversion cost = $600
- During the period 600 units were started.
  - Material costs for the period = $800
  - Conversion costs for the period = $2,000
- Ending Inventory = 300 units (1/2 complete).

Physical flow in units:	Physical Flow
Beginning WIP (1/2 complete)	400
Units started	600
Units to account for	1,000
Units completed (1,000 – 300)	700
Ending WIP (1/2 complete)	300
Units accounted for	1,000

Equivalent units of production	Equivalent Units Materials	Conversion Costs
Units completed	700	700
Ending WIP (1/2 complete)	300	150
Weighted average equivalent units	1,000	850
Beginning WIP × 1/2% complete	(400)	(200)
FIFO Equivalent units	600	650

Material is added to process all at one time and is 100% complete when added.

Total costs	Beginning WIP	Current Costs	Total Costs
Materials	$400	$800	$1,200
Conversion costs	600	2,000	2,600
Total costs to account for	$1000	$2,800	$3,800

Equivalent unit cost	Current Costs	FIFO EU Divisor	Equivalent Unit Cost
Materials	$800	$600	$1.33
Conversion costs	2,000	650	3.08
Total current costs	$2,800		$4.41

Allocation of total costs between work-in-process and finished goods.

Total Costs

Total costs	$3,800	
Ending WIP	861	[(300 × $1.33) + (150 × $3.08)]
Cost of finished goods	$2,939	

¶149.01

Allocation of Costs to Product

	Total Costs	Beginning WIP	Current Cost	EU Divisor	Equivalent Unit Cost
Materials	1,200	400	800	600	1.33
Conversion costs	2,600	600	2,000	650	3.08
Total costs to account for	3,800	1,000	2,800		4.41
Goods completed		$2,939			
Ending WIP		861			
Total costs accounted for		$3,800			

.02 Manufacturing—Material Requirement Planning

The following ratios can be used by management to focus on the performance regarding manufacturing requirements.

$$\text{Quality performance} = \frac{\text{number of units accepted}}{\text{number of units delivered}}$$

$$\text{Order execution} = \frac{\text{number of orders completed on schedule}}{\text{total number of orders completed}}$$

$$\text{Material nonavailability} = \frac{\text{number of items short}}{\text{number of items shown in inventory records}}$$

$$\text{Delivery performance} = \frac{\text{number of orders received on time}}{\text{number of orders scheduled to be received (on time)}}$$

.03 Job-Order—Product Costing

Overhead Rate

$$\text{Overhead rate} = \frac{\text{Total Budgeted Overhead}}{\text{Total Labor Hours}}$$

Facts:

1)	Sales (all through A/R)	$500,000
2)	Cost of goods sold	270,000
3)	Materials Issued for production (all direct)	150,000
4)	Materials and supplies (purchased through A/P)	21,000
5)	Unused materials returned to storage	4,000
6)	Supplies issued to production departments	20,000
7)	Direct labor	175,000
8)	Indirect labor	25,000
9)	Depreciation—plant and equipment	15,000
10)	Other Factory overhead incurred	20,000
11)	Overhead applied (45% of direct labor cost)	$78,750
12)	Cost of completed production	$220,000

Journal Entries

1)	Accounts receivable		$500,000	
	Sales			$500,000
2)	Cost of goods sold		$270,000	
	Finished goods control			$270,000
3)	Work-in-process control		$150,000	
	Stores control			$150,000
4)	Stores control		$21,000	
	Accounts payable			$21,000
5)	Stores control		$4,000	
	Work-in-process control			$4,000
6)	Factory overhead control		$20,000	
	Stores control			$20,000
7)	Work-in-process control		$175,000	
8)	Factory overhead control		$25,000	
	Accrued factory payroll			$200,000
9)	Factory overhead control		$15,000	
	Accumulated depreciation			$15,000
10)	Factory overhead control		$20,000	
	A/P, cash, etc.			$20,000
11)	Work-in-process control		$78,750	
	Factory overhead applied			$78,750
12)	Finished goods control		$220,000	
	Work-in-process			$220,000

Factory Overhead Applied		Factory Overhead Control	
	78,750(11)	(6) 20,000	
		(8) 25,000	
		(9) 15,000	
		(10) 20,000	
	78,750	80,000	

To close overhead accounts to COGS :

Factory overhead applied		$78,750	
Cost of goods sold		$1,250	
Factory overhead control			$80,000

Burden Factor—Normal Burden Factor (By Job Cost Method)

Normal Burden Factor

$$= \frac{\text{Fixed expenses and variable expenses at nomal capacity}}{\text{Normal capacity of units}}$$

Example: What is the burden factor given the following data at normal capacity?

Fixed expenses = $75,000

Variable expenses = $35,000

Normal units = 55,000

.07 Equivalent Units of Production

Equivalent Units of Production

= number of units transferred to next dept.

– (% completion of beg. of year work in progress)

× (units in beg. of year work in progress)

– (% completion of end of year work in progress)

× (units in end work in progress)

The FIFO method is used to compute equivalent units. The other possible method is the weighted average method.

Example: Data from company records

	Beginning of year	End of year
% complete	75%	25%
Number of units in progress	10,000	25,000

Production records showed 150,000 units transferred to the next department. What were the equivalent number of units?

Equivalent units of production = 150,000 – (.75) × (10,000) – (.25) × (25,000) = 136,250 units

.09 Quantity Variance (Standard Cost)

Quantity Variance

= Standard price × (actual quantity - standard quantity)

Example: Determine the quantity variance based on the following records.

Bill of materials calls for a quantity of 3 of part B at a standard price of .50 each.

Order quantity is 6,200.

Actual units produced 2,000.

Quantity variance = ($.50) (6,200 – (2,000 × 3)) = $100U

Price Variance (standard cost)

Price variance = actual quantity × (actual price - standard price)

Example: Standard price for part A = $.65

Purchasing bought 6,000 of part A for $.70

What is the price variance?

Price variance = 6,000 (.70 – .65) = $300U

Direct Labor Wage Variance (standard cost)

= actual direct labor hours × (actual wage rate - standard wage rate)

Example: What is the labor wage rate variance given the following data:

	Wage Rate	Direct Labor Hours
Standard	$8.50	225
Actual	$9.50	235

D.L. wage variance = 235 ($9.50 – $8.50) = $235U

Direct Labor Efficiency variance (Standard Cost)

D.L. eff variance = standard wage rate × (actual time - standard time)

Example: Given data in previous example, compute the direct labor efficiency variation.

D.L. eff variance = $8.50 (235 – 225) = $85.00U

.11 Volume Variance (By Job Cost)

Volume Variance

$$= \text{(attained capacity)} \times \frac{\text{variable expense at normal capacity}}{\text{normal capacity units}}$$

+ Fixed expenses at normal capacity
– Attained capacity (normal burden rate)

Given the following data, complete the volume variance for Dept. D.

Budgeted expenses at normal capacity:

    Variable = $35,000
    Fixed = $75,000
Normal burden rate = $2.00
Normal unit capacity = 55,000 hours
Attained unit capacity = 50,000 hours
Manufacturing expense per general ledger = $125,000

$$\text{Volume variance} = (50{,}000)\ \frac{\$35{,}000}{55{,}000} + \$75{,}000 - 50{,}000\ (\$2.00) = \$6{,}818\ U$$

Budget Variance (By job cost)

= actual manufacturing expense

$$- \text{(Attained capacity)}\ \frac{\text{Variable expense at normal capacity}}{\text{normal capacity units}}$$

– Fixed expenses at normal capacity

Example: See previous example data

$$\text{Budget variance} = \$125{,}000 - (50{,}000)\ \frac{\$35{,}000}{55{,}000}\ \$75{,}000 = \$18{,}182\ U$$

Chapter 2
Accounting Principles

¶ 201 ACCOUNTING CHANGES AND ERROR CORRECTIONS
SFAS 111 & 154, SFAS Interpretation 1

Changes

- Accounting principle.
- Accounting estimate.
- Reporting entity.
- Correction of error in previous statement is not an accounting change.

Accounting Principles

- Changing from one acceptable principle or method to another acceptable principle or method.
- Do not make accounting change for a single transaction.
- Consistency in the financials should be the pervasive principle.
- Change may result from the issuance of a new accounting principle if GAAP hierarchy is followed.
- Change may result from the justifiable use of a preferable alternative accounting principle. Entity must justify this type of change.
- Not a change in accounting principle:
  - Principle adopted for first time on new or previously immaterial events.
  - Change from unacceptable to acceptable accounting practice—this is correction of an error.
  - Principle modified because events are different in substance.
- Examples of changes that are accounting principle changes:
  - Change in inventory pricing method, LIFO to FIFO, etc.
  - Change between percentage completion or completed contract.
  - Change in composition of cost elements of labor, material and overhead.
  - Change to or from full cost in oil and gas industry.
  - Change in method of revenue recognition.

Reporting Change in Accounting Principle

- A change in accounting principle is reported in a retrospective manner using only direct impacts and related tax impacts of the change.
- When indirect impacts are actually incurred, the indirect impacts should be reported in the accounting period of the change.
- The following process is used to account for a change in principle:

— Report in appropriate assets and liabilities the cumulative effect of the change in the first accounting period presented for periods prior to the accounting periods presented.

— Adjust beginning retained earnings (or other appropriate accounts) for an offsetting amount that was reported in the assets and liabilities in the same accounting period that assets and liabilities were adjusted.

— Adjust the financial statements of each accounting period presented as if the new accounting principle had been applied during that accounting period (period-specific impact of the change).

• When the cumulative effect of the change can be determined but the period-specific impact cannot be computed, the following accounting is required:

— Adjust the appropriate assets and liabilities in the first accounting period presented where the change can be applied.

— Adjust beginning retained earnings (or other appropriate accounts) for an offsetting amount that was reported in the assets and liabilities in the same accounting period that assets and liabilities were adjusted.

• When the cumulative effect of the change in principle cannot be determined, the following accounting is appropriate:

— Account for at the earliest date possible in a prospective manner.

— Example includes a change in inventory methods to LIFO.

• If one of the following is met, it is assumed that an entity cannot apply the change in accounting principle retrospectively (impracticability concept):

— The entity cannot apply the retrospectively approach after making every reasonable effort.

— Application of the retrospectively method requires assumptions about the intent of management of the entity that cannot be verified on an independent basis.

— The entity cannot determine, on an objective basis, information about estimates that is required to apply the retrospective method.

• A change in accounting principle made in an interim period is reported the same as a change made in an annual period.

— The impracticability concept, noted above, cannot be applied to prechange interim accounting periods of the year of change.

— The change in principle must be applied at the beginning of the next accounting period when it is impracticable to apply the change to prechange interim periods.

— When a change is made in the fourth quarter and is not included in a separate fourth quarter or annual report in accordance with APB Opinion No. 28, provide the above disclosures required for annual reports.

• The following disclosures are required for a change in accounting principle:

— Reason and nature of the change.

— Method of application of the change including (1) description of retrospectively adjusted prior period information, (2) impact of the change on selected income items and assets and liability items, (3) cumulative effect on beginning retained earning and net assets of earliest accounting period presented, and the alternative method used when the impracticability concept is applied to at least some prior accounting periods.

— The amount, related earnings per share and description of indirect impacts when recognized, and, when possible, the impact and related earnings per share for each prior accounting period.

— When a change in principle does not have a material impact in the period of change but is anticipated to have a material impact in future accounting periods, the preceding disclosures should be reported in the accounting period of the change in principle.

— When interim period financial information is reported in the year of change in principle and the interim period information is presented subsequent to the date of change, disclose the impact of the change on selected income, other performance indicators, related earnings per share information.

Change in Accounting Estimate

- Examples—allowance for bad debt, provisions for warranty.
- Change in estimated life of asset or salvage value is a change in accounting estimate.
- A change in depreciation methods, such as a change from straight-line to the sum-of-year's digits, is a change in accounting estimate affected by a change in principle.
- Any change in estimate effected by a change in principle must be justified the same as if it is a change in accounting principle.

Reporting Change in Accounting Estimate

- Do not restate prior period statements.
- Report in period of change and/or future periods.
- If change affects future periods, disclose:
  - Effect on income before extraordinary items.
  - Net income.
  - Impact on per share information.
  - If appropriate, changes in net assets or other indicators of performance.
- Present disclose requirements for both changes in accounting estimates and changes in accounting principles when a change is a change in estimate effected by a change in principle.
- If the change in estimate does not have a material impact in the accounting period of the change but is expected to have a material impact in future accounting periods, provide a description of the change in the accounting period of the change.

Change in Reporting Entity

- A change that results in a different reporting group such as a change in the specific subsidiaries included in a set of consolidated financial statements.

- Restate the financial statements of all prior accounting periods presented as if the new reporting group had been used in all accounting periods presented (retrospective application).
- Retrospective application should be used for prior interim accounting periods, except for interest capitalization under FASB Statement No. 58.
- Disclose for accounting periods presented the nature, reason for the change and the impact of the new reporting group on income before extraordinary items, net income, other comprehensive income, other appropriate income titles and related earnings per share.
- If the change in reporting entity does not have a material impact in the accounting period of the change but is expected to have a material impact in future accounting periods, the nature and reason for the change should be disclosed in the accounting period of the change.

Error Corrections

- An error is a mathematical mistake, GAAP application mistake, misuse of facts or oversight of facts that results in a recognition, measurement, presentation or disclosure error.
- A change from an unacceptable GAAP standard to a GAAP standard.
- An error correction is accounted for as a prior period adjustment by restating the financial statements of all prior accounting periods presented.
- The cumulative effect of the error correction is accounted for as a direct adjustment to beginning retained earnings and reflected in the carrying amounts of the affected assets and/or liabilities for periods prior to the accounting periods presented.
- For each prior accounting period presented, the financial statements should be adjusted to correct the impact of the error for that specific accounting period.
- Disclosures include the following:
  — description of the nature of the error and statements that financial statements of prior periods have been restated for the error.
  — impact of each line item in the financial statements and any per-share impact for each accounting period that is presented.
  — for the earliest period presented, disclose the cumulative impact of the change on retained earnings, other equity accounts or net assets.
  — provide disclosures required by Paragraph 26 of APB No. 9 related to prior-period adjustments.

¶ 202 ACCOUNTING POLICIES
APB 22

- Nonprofit entities also should disclose significant accounting policies.
- Need not be followed for "unaudited or internal use only" reports.
- Report:
  — Preferably report as first footnote to financial statements under caption "Summary of Significant Accounting Policies."
  — Do not duplicate information if reported elsewhere.

- Disclose:
  - — Unusual applications or uses of GAAP.
  - — A selection from existing acceptable GAAP alternatives.
  - — Areas peculiar to a specific industry.
- Examples of disclosures of accounting policies:
  - — Patents, trademarks.
  - — Goodwill.
  - — Inventory valuation methods.
  - — Earnings per share—EPS disclosures are required by SFAS 128.
  - — Pension plan highlights.
  - — Fixed assets and depreciation methods.

¶ 203 BUSINESS COMBINATIONS
SFAS 141 & 147, FASB Technical Bulletin 85-5 & 85-6 and Interpretation Nos. 9 & 21

Business Combination
- A transaction where an enterprise acquires the net assets of a business or acquires an equity interest that leads to control.
- A transaction where one company is buying another, a purchase transaction, with one company designated as the acquiring company and the other company the acquired company.
- The pooling-of-interest method of accounting for a business combination is no longer acceptable; only the purchase method can be used.

Purchase Method
- If assets are exchanged, record at cost based on the most clear evidence of fair market value of property acquired or given up.
- If purchased by cash, record at the amount disbursed.
- If purchased by issuance of stock, record at the fair market value of the stock issued after certain adjustments.
- Liabilities assumed are recorded at present value of amount that will eventually be paid.
- Any part of purchase price not assignable to specifically identifiable tangible and intangible assets, less liabilities assumed, shall be recorded as goodwill.
- Interpretation No. 9 states that the net-spread method is not appropriate in the valuation of assets and liabilities required in a business combination of savings and loans.
- Interpretation No. 21 states that the classification of a lease acquired in a business combination should not be changed unless the lease is modified in the business combination.
- Allocate total cost of purchase to individual assets:
  - — Based on fair value at date of acquisition.
  - — Any excess goes to goodwill.

- If fair values of net assets exceed cost, reduce certain assets proportionately, and if reduced to zero, the remaining amount (negative goodwill) is accounted for as an extraordinary gain and reporting net of tax in the income statement.
- Purchase method includes direct costs of acquisition.
- Contingent assets and liabilities—allocate portion to contingencies:
  - If fair value cannot be determined during allocation period.
  - If it is probable that contingency existed at purchase date.
  - The amount can be reasonably estimated.
  - Include contingency in the allocation based on fair value if fair value can be determined during allocation period.
- For purchase acquisition of pension plans:
  - Excess of projected benefit obligation over plan assets are recognized as a liability.
  - Excess of plan assets over projected benefits are recognized as an asset.
  - Eliminate any preexisting unrecognized net gain or loss, unrecognized prior service cost, unrecognized net obligation or net asset that existed.
  - Account for the acquisition of all or part of a financial institution using the purchase method in accordance with Statement No. 141 if the acquisition meets the definition of a business combination.
  - Account for the acquisition of a financial institution that does not meet the definition of a business combination using SFAS No. 141, Paragraphs 4-8.
- Disclosures:
  - Description and name of the company acquired and the percent of voting equity securities acquired.
  - Describe factors that require a purchase price such that goodwill is recognized and the major reason for the acquisition.
  - Time period for which income from the entity acquired is included in the income of the combined company.
  - Cost of the entity acquired, equity interest issued, value allocated to shares or interest issued to effect the combination and how the value was determined.
  - An abbreviated balance sheet of the acquired entity with amounts allocated to each major asset and liability caption at acquisition date.
  - Any contingency specified in the agreement and the required accounting requirement if the contingency occurs.
  - Acquisition amount and write off of purchased research and development assets in the accounting period and the location of such write offs in the income statement.
  - Reason for any allocation of purchase price that has not been finalized at the end of the accounting period and the amount and nature of any material

adjustments to the allocation processes that occurred in subsequent accounting periods.

— Additional disclosures are required when amounts assigned to goodwill and intangible assets are material relative to the cost of the entity (See Paragraph 52).

— Additional disclosures are required for immaterial business combinations that are material in total.

— Selected pro forma disclosures are required for combinations of public companies that is material individually or in total.

¶ 204 CASH FLOW STATEMENT
SFAS 95, SFAS 102, & SFAS 104

Form of Statement
- Shows net cash effect provided or used by enterprise.
  — Operating activities.
  — Investing activities.
  — Financing activities.
- Contains an explanation of change during the period.
- Cash flow per share is prohibited.

Investing Activities
- Include collecting and making loans.
- Acquiring and disposing of debt or equity instruments.

Financing Activities
- Borrowing and repaying amounts borrowed.
- Obtaining and paying for other resources obtained for creditors.

Operating Activities
- All other events not classified as investing or financing.
- Generally, these activities involve producing and delivering goods with the related sales and payables.
- Net income to net cash flow must be reconciled.

Cash Flow from Operations
- Direct method is preferable:
  — Reflects gross amounts.
  — Net cash is equal to difference between gross cash receipts and gross cash payments.
- Indirect method:
  — Reflects net income and adjustments necessary to reconcile net income to cash for the period.
  — Net cash is determined by making adjustments to recognize net income of the period to the amount of net cash of the period.

- Direct method presentation:
  - Cash collected from customers.
  - Dividends and interest received.
  - Cash paid to suppliers of goods.
  - Other operating receipts.
  - Any other cash payments such as interest, taxes, etc.
- Indirect method presentation:
  - Recognize net income to net cash flow.
  - Adjust for deferrals, accruals, changes in inventory, accounts receivable, accounts payable, etc.
  - Disclose amount of cash paid for income taxes and interest expense.

Exemption for Certain Employee Benefit Plans
- According to SFAS 102, defined benefit plans that present their financial information in accordance with SFAS 35 are exempt from the provisions of SFAS 95.

Exemption for Certain Investment Companies
- Investment type entities that are subject to the registration and regulatory requirements of the Investment Company Act of 1940 are exempt from providing cash flow statements if:
  - Materially all their assets are highly liquid.
  - Substantially all the investments are carried at market value.
  - The entity provides a statement of changes in net assets.
  - The enterprise had little or no debt.

¶ 205 CHANGING PRICES
SFAS 89
- Neither price level accounting nor current value accounting are required in financial reporting.
- FASB 89 encourages disclosures but does not require them.
- FASB 89 superseded all pronouncements relating to changing prices and financial reporting.
- SFAS No. 139 replaces the definition of motion picture films as currently used in Statement No. 89.

¶ 206 CONSOLIDATED FINANCIAL STATEMENTS
ARB 51 SFAS 94 & Interpretation 46 (Revised)
- Must be used where parent company owns over 50 percent of a subsidiary, unless parent does not have control or control is temporary.
- If subsidiary year-end is within 3 months of parents, it's acceptable to use subsidiary's fiscal year-end statement.
- Financial statements are combined.

Variable Interests

- Variable interest entities are subject to consolidation when either of the following three conditions are met:
  - The entity cannot finance activities without additional subordinated financial help using the total equity investment at risk (expected losses from the entity are not less than the equity investment at risk).
  - Generally, if the equity at risk is less than 10 percent of the total assets of the entity, additional subordinated debt would be required to finance the activities of the entity. However, this rule may be overcome by providing appropriate evidence.
  - The group holders of the investment at risk lack any of the following: (1) unable, through voting or other rights, to make decisions, directly or indirectly about the entity's activities, (2) unable to absorb losses of the entity, and (3) the right to receive residual returns.
  - The holders of equity investment at risk's economic interest and voting rights are not proportionate and the entity's activities are conducted for or involved with voting interests that are disproportionately small.
- Entities that meet the preceding requirements are considered variable interest entities (VIE) and the holders of interest in the entities are holders of variable interests.
- A variable interest holder that absorbs a majority of the expected losses, a majority of the expected residual interests, or both is considered the primary beneficiary.
  - If one variable interest holder absorbs a majority of the expected losses and another holder absorbs a majority of the expected residual interest, the holder that absorbs a majority of the losses is considered the primary beneficiary.
  - Expected losses are the expected negative variability in the fair value of net assets, excluding variable interests, and expected residual interests are the positive variations.
- The primary beneficiary is the party that consolidates the variable interest entity when it is subject to consolidation.
- The primary beneficiary should report the assets, liabilities, and noncontrolling interest of the consolidated variable interest entity at fair value, except for entities under common control and assets and liabilities consolidated soon after transfer from the primary beneficiary.
- The assets newly consolidated should be adjusted on a pro-rata basis (as if it were a business combination under Statement No. 141) for any excess of the sum of the consolidated assets and any reported amounts of assets transferred by the primary beneficiary to the variable interest entity over the following: (a) consideration paid using fair value, (b) reported amounts of prior held interests, and (c) fair value of liabilities and noncontrolling interest newly consolidated. If the excess is reversed, report the excess as goodwill if the variable interest is classified as a business and as an extraordinary loss if the variable interest is not classified as a business.

- The primary beneficiary generally should use the provisions of ARB No. 51 to account for the variable interest entity subsequent to initial consolidation.
- Disclosures required by the primary beneficiary include:
  — Size, purpose, nature, and activities of the entity classified as a variable interest entity.
  — Classification and amount of variable interest assets used as collateral for obligations of the VIE.
  — When there is no recourse to the general credit of the primary beneficiary, indicate that fact in the disclosures.
- Disclosures required by a party not considered a primary beneficiary but with a significant variable interest.
  — Beginning and nature of involvement with the VIE.
  — Size, purpose, nature, and activities of the entity classified as a variable interest entity.
- Other disclosures are required for specific situations.

Intercompany Transactions

- Sales and purchases gross amounts are eliminated on the consolidated work papers.
  — Includes advances from affiliates.
  — Accounts receivable and accounts payable.
  — Notes receivable and notes payable.
  — Interest receivable and payable.
- All unrealized intercompany profits in inventory must be eliminated.

The following adjustments should be made: P = Parent S = Subsidiary

Retained Earnings	XXX	
Inventory-Balance Sheet		XXX
Adjust the income statement as follows:		
Sales - S	XXX	
(To eliminate intercompany sales and purchases)		
Purchase-P		XXX
Consolidated Retained Earnings	XXX	
(To reverse prior year consolidated adjustments)		
Cost of Goods Sold		XXX
Cost of Goods Sold	XXX	
(To eliminate intercompany profit in ending inventory)		
Inventory-Ending		XXX

Unrealized profits in long-lived assets between parent and subsidiary should be eliminated.

Gain on Machine Sale	XXX	
(To eliminate intercompany profit)		
Machine		XXX

Accumulated Depreciation	XXX	
(To reverse depreciation)		
Depreciation Expense		XXX

2nd Year

Retained Earnings	XXX	
(To eliminate intercompany Machinery profit and prior year's sale)		
Accumulated Depreciation	XXX	
(To eliminate depreciation expense and depreciation expense on prior year's sale)		
Retained Earnings		XXX
Depreciation Expense		XXX

This continues until asset is disposed of or retired.

¶ 207 CONTINGENCIES
SFAS 5, 118 & SFAS Interpretation Nos. 14 & 45

- Contingency is a transaction, event, set of circumstances for which the future outcome is uncertain.
  - Loss contingency may result in a reduction of an asset or an incurrence of a liability.
  - Gain contingency may result in an increase in an asset or reduction of a liability.
- Examples include litigation, warranties, bad debts, possible expropriations, and guarantees.
- The following items are excluded:
  - Stock issued to employees.
  - Deferred compensation.
  - Employment related costs (i.e., insurance, vacation pay, disability, etc.).
- Loss contingencies are accounted for as follows:
  - Accrue with loss or expense when the loss is probable and the amount can be estimated. When only a range can be estimated, the lower end of the range should be used as the loss.
  - Disclose when the loss is reasonably possible or when the loss is probable but an amount cannot be estimated.
  - Do nothing when the loss is remote, except for all forms (both direct and indirect) of guarantees which are disclosed.
- A guarantor should recognize a liability for a guarantee at the inception of the guarantee equal to the fair value of the guarantee.
- When a guarantor is required to report a liability for the anticipated loss from a guarantee under the provisions of SFAS No. 5, the liability reported for the guarantee is the larger of the amount computed as the fair value of the guarantee or the liability computed under Statement No. 5 provisions.

- Loss contingencies that occur after the balance sheet date, but are know prior to issuance date, may have to be disclosed if professional judgment deems necessary.

- Gain contingencies are recognized only when realized and should be disclosed in such a way as to not mislead the readers of the financial statements.

- Disclosures of contingencies include the nature and range of loss or a statement that the loss cannot be estimated.

- Disclosure of non-insured property is suggested.

Treatment of Certain Loss Contingencies

Contingency Losses Relative to:	Typically Accrued	Accrual Possible	Accrual Unnecessary	Disclose	Not Disclosed
1. Collectibility of receivables	X			X	
2. Obligations related to product warranties and product defects and customers premiums	X			X	
3. Threat of expropriation		X		X	
4. Litigation, claims and assessments		X		X	
5. Guarantees of indebtedness of others		X		X	
6. Obligations of commercial banks under standby letters of credit		X		X	
7. Guarantees to repurchase receivables that have been sold		X		X	
8. Risk of loss or damage of enterprise property			X	X	
9. Catastrophe losses of property and casualty insurance companies			X	X	
10. General or unspecified business risks			X		X

Source: CCH U.S. Master GAAP Guide

¶ 209 CONTRIBUTIONS RECEIVED AND CONTRIBUTIONS MADE FOR BOTH PROFIT AND NONPROFIT ENTITIES
SFAS Nos. 116 & 136

Paragraph 5 of SFAS No. 116 defines a contribution as a transfer that meets the following three conditions:

- A nonreciprocal transfer (one-way transfer) of either cash, or other assets or liability settlement that is considered unconditional;

- The entity making or receiving the transfer is not acting as an owner of the enterprise; and

- The transfer is voluntarily made.

Contributions Received

- Contributions received can be divided into (1) contributions in the form of works of art, (2) contributions in the form of services, contribution of assets or contributions that result in a reduction of liabilities.

- When works of art are received as a contribution, an enterprise is not required to recognize the contribution if the following three conditions are met.

— The contribution is not used for financial gain, but is held for education purposes, public exhibition, or public service research.

— The assets from the contribution are preserved, protected, cared for and never encumbered.

— The entity has a policy requiring that if the assets are sold, the proceeds from the sale will be used to acquire other collection assets.

- If the preceding three conditions are not met, the enterprise must capitalize the assets and recognize revenue equal to fair market value of the assets received.

- A contribution in the form of services should be recognized if one of the following two conditions is met:

— Nonfinancial assets are created or enhanced from the contributed services.

— The contributed services received require special skills, the persons contributing the services have the required skills and if the skills were not donated, the enterprise would have to pay for the services.

- If one of the preceding requirements is met, the enterprise must recognize the contributed services by debiting an expense and crediting a revenue or gain for fair value of the services received.

- If neither of the preceding conditions are met, the contributed services are not recognized.

- When contributions of cash, other assets or settlement of liabilities are received, the enterprise should record the contribution received equal to fair market value:

— When an asset is received, debit the asset and credit revenue or gain.

— When settlement of a liability is received, debit the liability and credit revenue or gain.

Contributions Made

- An unconditional promise to pay is a promise that is dependent upon time passage or demand by the entity receiving the promise.

— The promise should be recorded by debiting contribution expense and a liability for an amount equal to the present value of the future cash flows.

— The future cash flows should be discounted using an interest rate equivalent to the risk involved.

- A conditional promise to give is a promise that is dependent upon a future event that is uncertain and is specified.

— Recognize when the promise becomes conditional.

- When a contribution is made by transferring assets or providing services, fair value should be sued to record the contribution.

— If assets are transferred, contribution expense should be debited for fair value, and the asset should be credited for its cost or carrying value.

— Any difference between the cost or carrying value of the asset and fair market value is recognized as a gain or loss.

¶209

Transfer of Assets to Non-Profit Organization (SFAS No. 136)

- Specifies the accounting and reporting requirements for donor (party or organization making the contribution), non-profit organization (recipient organization which is either a non-profit organization or a charitable trust) and beneficiary (party receiving the assets from the recipient organization when assets are transferred to the non-profit organization by the donor and the non-profit organization agrees to transfer the assets to a beneficiary.

- Donor accounts for the transfer as an asset, the non-profit organization accounts for the transfer as a liability and the beneficiary records no transaction in the following situations:
  - The donor keeps the right to redirect the transferred assets to another beneficiary.
  - The transfer of assets is based on a conditional promise or the transfer can be revoked or be repaid to the donor.
  - The non-profit organization is controlled by the donor and an unaffiliated beneficiary is specified.
  - The beneficiary is the donor or an affiliate of the donor and the transaction does not qualify as an equity transaction under the provisions of Paragraph 18.

- Donor or an affiliate of the donor is the beneficiary and the transfer meets all requirements of Paragraph 18 for an equity transaction.
  - Donor debits either an interest in the assets transferred if the donor is the beneficiary or an equity transaction if an affiliate is the beneficiary and credits an asset or liability in both situations.
  - Non-profit organization debits an asset for the receipt of the transfer and credits either a liability, if the donor is the beneficiary or an equity transaction, if the beneficiary is an affiliate of the donor.
  - Beneficiary makes no entry when the donor is the beneficiary except for the original donor entry, and when the beneficiary is an affiliate of the donor, the beneficiary debits interest in the transferred assets and credits equity transaction.

- Non-profit organization has variance power (power to redirect the use of the transferred assets).
  - Donor debits an expense and credits an asset or liability.
  - Non-profit organization debits asset and credits contribution revenue
  - Beneficiary has no entry.

- Non-profit organization does not have variance power and the non-profit organization and the beneficiary are financially interrelated in accordance with Paragraph 13 of SFAS No. 136.
  - Donor debts an expense and credits an asset or a liability.
  - Non-profit organization debits asset and credits contribution revenue.
  - Beneficiary debits an interest in the transferred assets and credits a change in interest in the non-profit organization.

- Non-profit organization does not have variance power and the non-profit organization and the beneficiary are not financially interrelated and the transferred asset is either cash or another financial asset.
  - Donor debits an expense and credits an asset or liability.
  - Non-profit organization debits an asset and credits a liability.
  - Beneficiary debits receivable and credits contribution revenue.
- Non-profit organization does not have variance power and the non-profit organization and the beneficiary are not financially interrelated and the transferred asset is a nonfinancial asset.
  - Donor debits an expense and credits an asset or liability.
  - Non-profit organization has no entry.
  - Beneficiary debits receivable and credits contribution revenue.
- The following disclosures are required when the donor is a non-profit organization and the beneficiary of the assets transferred to the recipient organization is the donor or an affiliate of the donor.
  - Identification of the recipient organization.
  - Terms of variance power if it was granted to the recipient organization.
  - Terms of distribution to the donor beneficiary or affiliate.
  - Amounts reported for the transfer in the statement of financial position and an indication of whether the transfer was reported as an interest in net assets or some other asset designation.
- When a non-profit organization discloses a ratio of fundraising expenses to the amount of funds actually raised, the organization must disclose how the ratio was computed.
- SFAS No. 136 is effective for fiscal years beginning after December 15, 1999, except for the provisions of Paragraph 12.

¶ 210 CONVERTIBLE DEBT AND DEBT WITH WARRANTS
APB 14 & SFAS 84

Convertible Debt Is Convertible into Common Stock

- Interest rate is usually lower than on an equivalent but non-convertible issue.
- The debt is usually callable.
- The conversion price does not change, unless specified in the initial agreement.
- The debt is usually subordinate to the issuer's non-convertible debt.
- The initial conversion price is greater than the market value of the underlying security.

Issuance of Convertible Debt or Debt with Nondetachable Warrants

- All of the price goes to the debt issue—the conversion option receives no value.
  - Credit security at par.
  - Show cash received.
  - Discount on premium is residual amount.

Example: Corporation issues $10,000 of convertible bonds at 97% of par value.

Cash	9,700	
Discount on bonds	300	
Bonds		10,000

Issuance of Debt with Detachable Warrants

- Selling price of the debt with warrants is divided between the debt (debt issue) and equity (the warrants).
  - Selling price is divided using the relative fair values of each security trading separately if the value of each trading separately are known.
  - If the fair value of only one of the security's trading separately is know, give that value to that security and what is left over goes to the other security. For example, if the fair value of the warrants trading without the debt is know and the value of the debt trading without the warrants is unknown, the fair value of the warrants is given to the warrants and the remaining part of the selling price of the package is allocated to the debt.

Conversion of Debt with Separate Conversion Feature

- When separate conversion feature (i.e., detachable stock purchase warrant) is exercised and converted, no gain or loss is recognized on the conversion. It is accounted for as an equity transaction.
- The amount previously credited to Paid in Capital is debited, cash is debited. Par value of stock and Paid in Capital is credited.

Inseparable Conversion Feature

- Entire security must be surrendered.
- If converted into stock with original conversion terms, no gain or loss is recognized, assuming book value method is used.
- Debt is retired and equity is issued.

Example:

12% convertible bonds payable	XXX	
Unamortized bond premium	XXX	
Common stock (at par)		XXX
PIC in excess of par		XXX

Induced Conversions of Debt SFAS 84

- Original conversion's terms are changed to induce holder to convert.
- SFAS 84 applies only to induced conversions that are offered for a limited period of time.
- Debtor does not recognize gain or loss on the amount under original conversion terms, but fair value of equity securities or other consideration paid which exceeds the amount originally required for conversion is recognized as an ordinary expense when the indirect offer is accepted by the bondholder.
- Incremental consideration may be calculated as difference between fair value of securities required to be issued under original terms and fair value that is actually issued.

¶ 211 CURRENT ASSETS AND CURRENT LIABILITIES
ARB 43, 1A & 3A, SFAS 6, 43 & 78, SFAS Interpretation 8, Interpretation 39, & Interpretation 41

Operating Cycle

- Average time from cash out to cash back through the normal firm's operations—cash expensed for materials and labor into inventory. Inventory sold and converted into accounts receivable and finally collected.
- One year is used as basis to classify assets as current when operating cycle is less than a year.
- If operating cycle is longer than one year, the longer cycle is used.

Current Assets

- Assets that are expected to be realized in cash, sold, or consumed during the normal operating cycle.
- Cash—all forms, inventory, accounts receivable, prepaid expenses.

Current Liabilities

- Liabilities whose liquidation is expected to require use of current assets or creation of other current liabilities and which are due within one year or normal operating cycle, whichever is longer and will be paid by something classified as current (current asset or current liability).
- Accounts payable, accrued wages, short-term notes, current maturing portion of long-term debt, prepayments such as advance payments for services, or deferred revenues.

Assets and Liabilities Offset

- Unacceptable unless a legal right of offset exists.
- Report net amount in the financials.
- Right of offset of a debtor is legal right by contract or otherwise to discharge part or all of a debt against an amount owed to the debtor by another party.
  - Amount must be determinable.
  - Debtor intends to offset.
  - Debtor's right to offset is enforceable by law.
  - Debtor has legal right to offset.

FIN 39 as modified by FIN 41 extends the general principle of allowing offsets to conditional amounts recognized for contracts where the amount depends on future interest rates, future exchange rates, etc. The following four criteria must be met for the right of offset to exist (see ¶ 255).

- The reporting party has the right to offset the receivable and payable.
- Each party owes the other party specific amounts.
- The right to offset is enforceable by law.
- The reporting party intends to offset.

FIN 41 allows, but does not require an enterprise to offset receivables and payables related to repurchase and reverse repurchase agreements when certain conditions are met.

Working Capital

- Indicates the relative liquidity of the enterprise.
- Excess of current assets over current liabilities.

Accounts Receivable

- Show at net realizable value.
  - Gross amount of receivable less allowance for uncollectable amount.
- Direct write-off method is not acceptable for GAAP.
  - Recognizes bad debt expense when a specific account is determined to be uncollectable.
  - This does not match against related sale and overstates accounts receivable balance.

Allowance Method

- Bad debts are estimated as a percent of ending accounts receivable or percent of sales.
- Finance charges or unearned interest is deducted from the related receivable.

Life Insurance

- Account for the amount that can be realized by the owner of the policy as of the date of its financial statement.
- Generally, this amount is the cash surrender value.
- If the intention is to cash in the policy in one year, then show cash value as a current asset.
- If there is no intention of cashing in the policy, then show cash value as a non-current investment.
- Insurance expense is difference in premiums paid and increase in cash surrender value.

Disclosures—Examples

- Notes and accounts receivable from officers and employees.
- Description of accounting policies.
- Method of valuing current marketable securities.
- Inventory valuation methods.
- Restrictions on current assets.

Current Obligations Expected To Be Refinanced

- If a company intends to refinance current obligations and can demonstrate the ability to refinance on a long-term basis, they should be reclassified into non-current.
  - Prior to the issuance of the financials the company must have entered into a qualifying agreement that enables it to refinance.

— Could also have a post-balance sheet issuance of long-term securities with the expressed purpose of using the proceeds to pay the debt when due.

Compensated Absences

- Absences such as holidays, vacation, illness, etc.
- If the employer expects to pay for such absences then a liability for the estimated probable future payments should be accrued if:
  — It is probable the compensation will be paid.
  — The amount can be estimated reasonably.
  — The employee's right to receive vests or accumulates.
  — The right to receive is attributable to services already performed SFAS 43 (Accounting for Compensated Absences).

Does not apply to:

- Stock options issued to employees.
- Postretirement benefits.
- Severance or termination pay.
- Sick pay benefits, fringe benefits.
- Disability pay or group insurance.

¶ 213 DEBT EXTINGUISHMENT
APB 26, SFAS 127, 140, & 145, Technical Bulletin 80-1 & 84-4

Overview

- Reacquisition of debt prior to the debt's maturity date.
- Gain or loss is difference between total reacquisition cost of the debt and the net carrying amount of the debt at extinguishment.
- SFAS 76 was superceded by SFAS 125.

And SFAS No. 125 has been superseded by SFAS No. 140. Statement No. 140 covers extinguishments of liabilities. An in-substance defeasance is no longer allowed as an extinguishment of debt. Liabilities are extinguished and should be derecognized by the debtor in the following situations (Paragraph 16):

- The debtor has paid the creditor and the debtor is relieved of obligation. Payments by the debtor may include cash, goods or services, other financial assets, and acquisition of outstanding debt whether cancelled or carried as treasury debt.
- Legal release of primary obligation of the debtor.

Extinguishment Forms

- There is no difference in accounting for debt extinguishment by:
  — Exchange of stock for debt.
  — Cash purchase.
  — Exchange of debt for debt.
  — Or, any other method.
- Reacquisition price includes the total amount paid to extinguish the debt.

— If achieved by exchange of securities, the reacquisition price is the present value of the securities being issued.

- Net carrying amount of debt is amount due at maturity adjusted for any unamortized discount or premium or other legal costs of issuance.

- In-substance defeasance including an instantaneous in-substance defeasance is prohibited. Instantaneous in-substance is where an enterprise borrows at one interest rate and at about the same time invests in other securities that yield a different interest rate.

Date of Extinguishment

- On date debtor pays or exchanges the debt.

- On date debtor is legally released as the primary obligor.

Gain or Loss

- Recognized immediately in current year's net income.

- Classify the gain or loss using the provisions of APB Opinion No 30.

- Gains or losses on extinguishment should not be amortized over future periods.

- The recorded value of the new debt should not be adjusted from any amount of the old debt.

Disclosure

- Description of any in-substance defeasance and related outstanding debt amounts at the balance sheet date from such extinguishments occurring before the effective date of Statement No. 125, as superseded by SFAS 140.

¶ 214 TRANSFER AND SERVICING OF FINANCIAL ASSETS
SFAS 140, 155, & 156

Control Criteria of SFAS No. 140

The following are conditions required when the transferor has surrendered control over transferred assets and the assets transferred are to be accounted for as a sale (Paragraph 9):

- The transferred assets have been isolated and are beyond the reach of the transferor and its creditors.

- The transferee, or the holder of a beneficial interest when the transferee is a special purpose entity (SPE), may exchange or pledge the assets or interest with no constraints other than trivial benefit to the transferor.

- Effective control over the assets transferred is not maintained by the transferor through one of the following:

  — Inability of the transferor to unilaterally cause the holder of the assets to return specified assets, except for cleanup calls.

  — No agreement that both obligate and require the transferor to redeem or repurchase the transferred assets prior to maturity.

Accounting for Transferred Assets

- When transferred assets are accounted for as a sale, the following accounting is appropriate for the transferor (Paragraph 11 of SFAS No. 140 & Paragraph 4(d) of SFAS No. 156).
  - All assets sold should be derecognized
  - Report all assets received and all liabilities incurred as proceeds from the sale at fair value, if practicable, otherwise apply alternative measures.
  - Examples include cash, call or put options, forward commitments, servicing assets, and servicing liabilities.
  - Report any gain or loss on the sale in the income statement.
- When a transfer of an asset does not meet the requirements for a sale, the following accounting is required by both the transferor and transferee (Paragraph 12 of SFAS No. 140).
  - Treat the transfer as a secured borrowing coupled with a pledge of collateral.
- The transferor should apply the following accounting for any transfer of financial assets (Paragraph 10 of SFAS No. 140 & Paragraph 4(c) of SFAS No. 156).
  - All servicing assets and servicing liabilities that require recognition under SFAS No. 140 should be initially measured and reported at fair value, if practicable (see ¶ 295 and SFAS No. 157 for new requirements on how to measure fair value).
  - Use relative fair value on the transfer date as a basis for allocating the carrying amount between any assets that the transferor continues to hold and the assets sold.
  - Report in the balance sheet any interest that the transferor continues to hold in assets transferred. Include in this amount any of the following, if appropriate: beneficial interests related to assets transferred to SPEs in a securitization and undivided interest.
- The transferee should report assets received and liabilities incurred at fair value.

Initial Recognition of Servicing Assets and Servicing Liabilities (Paragraph 13 of SFAS No. 156)

- Obligation to service financial assets should be reported as a servicing asset or servicing liability under any of the following conditions:
  - Transfer of financial assets meets sale accounting requirements.
  - Transfer of financial assets to a qualifying SPE in a guaranteed mortgage securitization where the resulting securities retained by the transferor are classified as trading or available-for-sale securities using the provisions of SFAS No. 115.
  - A servicing obligation acquired or assumed that is unrelated to a servicer's financial asset or consolidated affiliates.
- Servicing assets or liabilities should initially be measured at fair value (see ¶ 295 and SFAS No. 157 for fair value measurements).
- An entity may report servicing assets or liabilities separately or combine with the asset that is being serviced when there is a transfer of financial assets to a

qualifying SPE in a guaranteed mortgage securitization where the resulting securities retained by the transferor are classified as held-to-maturity securities using the provisions of SFAS No. 115.

Subsequent Accounting of Servicing Assets and Servicing Liabilities (Paragraphs 13A & 13B of SFAS No. 156)

- Each class servicing assets or servicing liabilities are measured using either the fair value measurement method or the amortization method.

  — *Fair value measurement method*—Each reporting date, the assets or liabilities are measured at fair value, and changes in fair value are reported as part of earnings in the accounting period of the change.

  — *Amortization method*—Servicing assets or servicing liabilities are amortized in proportion to and over the time period of the net servicing income or loss. In addition, at each reporting date, the assets or liabilities should be tested for impairment or obligation increase using fair value.

- The fair value or amortization method is applied separately to each class of servicing assets or servicing liabilities.

- Servicing assets and servicing liabilities where the fair value method is used should be reported in the financial statements separately from the servicing assets and servicing liabilities for which the amortization method was used.

Disclosure Requirements (Paragraph 17 of SFAS No. 140 & Paragraph 4(h) of SFAS No. 156)

- Disclose the following for all servicing assets and servicing liabilities (Paragraph 17(e)):

  — The basis management used for determining classes of servicing assets and liabilities.

  — Describe risks associated with servicing assets and liabilities and indicate any instruments used to reduce the impact of fair value changes on the income statement.

  — Amount of servicing fees earned and the location of the presentation of such fees in the income statement. Information should be reported for each period that an income statement is presented and include contractually specified fees, late fees, and ancillary fees.

- Disclose the following for servicing assets and servicing liabilities that use the fair value method for subsequent measurements (Paragraph 17(f)):

  — Disclose the activity in the balance of each class of servicing assets and servicing liabilities including items such as the following:

    - Location of the changes in fair value reported in the income statement.

    - Beginning and ending balances in the servicing assets and servicing liabilities.

    - Dispositions and additions.

    - Fair value changes from changes in inputs, assumptions, and other fair value changes and a description of the other fair value changes.

    - Impact of other changes related to the balance and describe the changes.

¶214

— Describe the valuation methods or techniques or models used to determine fair value of the servicing assets and liabilities.

- Disclose the following for servicing assets and servicing liabilities that use the amortization method for subsequent measurements (Paragraph 17(g)):

— Disclose the activity in the balance of each class of servicing assets and servicing liabilities including items such as the following:

- Location of the changes in carrying amounts reported in the income statement.

- Beginning and ending balances in the servicing assets and servicing liabilities.

- Dispositions and additions.

- Amortization, impairments classified as other than temporary, and application of the valuation allowance.

- Impact of other changes related to the balance and describe the changes.

— If practicable, beginning and ending fair values for each class of servicing assets and servicing liabilities.

— Describe the valuation methods, techniques, or models used to determine fair value of the servicing assets and liabilities.

— Activity in the impairment valuation allowance by class of servicing assets.

— Characteristics of risk related to underlying financial assets used in stratification of servicing assets when applying impairment requirements.

- Disclose the following by each major asset type for securitized financial assets where the transfer is accounted for as a sale (Paragraph 17 (f)):

— Accounting policies used to measure any retained interest.

— The important assumptions used when determining the retained interest fair value at time of securitization.

— Attributes of the securitizations and any gain or loss from the sale.

— If not reported in the financial statements or related footnote disclosures, the cash flows between the transferor and the securitization special purpose entity.

- Disclose the following by each major asset type at the latest balance sheet date for retained interest in financial assets that have been securitized (Paragraph 17 (g)):

— Accounting policies used to measure any retained interest and method for fair value determination.

— The important assumptions used when subsequently determining fair value of the retained interest.

— A test of sensitivity analysis that indicates the hypothetical impact of two or more adverse variations from fair value levels determined using each key assumption (indicated above) independently of the other assumptions.

— The limitations, methodology and objectives used in the sensitivity analysis.

¶214

— Disclose the following for managed securitized assets and other managed financial assets:

— In the balance sheet at the end of the accounting period report outstanding principal balance, amount derecognized, amount that continues to be reported in each group, delinquencies, and net credit losses.

— The FASB encourages disclosures of average balances during the accounting period.

- Disclose the following for collateral (Paragraph 17(a)):

— Policy for collateral requirements related to repurchase agreements or transactions related to security lending.

— Classification and carrying amount of assets pledged as collateral when the pledged assets have not been separately reclassified in the balance sheet.

— Disclose the following about accepted collateral that can be resold or pledged for each date that a balance sheet is presented:

— Fair value of the collateral.

— Amount of collateral sold or repledged.

— Information about the collateral's source and use.

- Other disclosures (Paragraphs 17(c)&(d)).

— Describe the items and why fair value cannot be estimated in transfers of financial assets where an entity is not able to estimate fair values.

— Describe the nature and restrictions on assets that are segregated for the purpose of satisfying scheduled payments on specific obligations.

¶ 215 DEFERRED COMPENSATION CONTRACTS
APB 12, Paragraphs 6-8

Summary

- Account on an individual accrual basis for each employee.
- Liability is determined by terms of individual contract.
- The periodic accrual must total no less than the present value of the benefits provided for in the contract.
- If contract contains benefits payable for life, total liability should be based on life expectancy or estimated cost of an annuity contract that would provide sufficient funds to pay the benefits.

Postretirement Benefits

- These are now covered by SFAS 106.

¶ 217 DEPRECIATION
ARB 43, APB 6 & 12 & SFAS 93

Basic Principle of Depreciation

- To match revenue and expenses for long-lived assets.

Basis of Assets

- Cost plus normal expenses of readying an asset for use should be capitalized.

- Razing and renewal costs of structures on land (net of salvage) are added to the cost of land.
- Land is never depreciated.
- Write-up of fixed assets to market value is prohibited.
- Write-down of fixed assets is required for any impairment of value in accordance with SFAS 121.
- Expenditures that increase the capacity of operating efficiency, if material, are added to cost.

Salvage Value

- If minimal, ignore.
- Use estimate of amount that will be realized at end of useful life.

Estimated Useful Life

- May differ from company to company.

Self-Constructed Fixed Assets

- Capitalize all direct costs.
- Interest cost may or may not be included.
- Fixed deferred costs should not be included.

Depreciation Methods

$$\text{Straight Line Depreciation} = \frac{\text{cost} - \text{salvage}}{\text{estimated useful life}}$$

Sum of the Years' Digits

- Provides for higher depreciation in earlier years.
- Denominator is sum of years' digits.
- Sum of years' digits = (number of years).
- Numerator—the digit of the highest year becomes the first numerator.

Example of 4 years

$$\text{Depreciation (year 1)} = (\text{cost less salvage}) \frac{4}{\frac{4(4+1)}{2}}$$

$$\text{Depreciation (year 2)} = (\text{cost less salvage}) \frac{3}{\frac{4(4+1)}{2}}$$

Units of Production

- Expressed in rate per unit or per hour.
- Relates depreciation to estimated production capacity.
- Use where usage of the asset varies considerably from period to period.

$$\text{Rate per unit} = \frac{\text{Cost less salvage}}{\text{Estimated units or hours}}$$

Declining Balance

- Meets requirement of being systematic and rational.
- Provides higher depreciation in early years where the expected higher productivity for revenue earning is expected and provides lower depreciation in later years where productivity decreases and maintenance increases.
- No allowance is made for salvage.
-
  $$\text{Depreciation straight line \% rate} = \frac{1}{\text{Life}}$$

- Apply a factor, i.e., 1.25, 1.50, 2.00, to the straight line rate.
- Apply the determined rate to the remaining book value each year.

Cost Recovery Method

- Sunk cost theory.
- All cost is recovered before any gain is recognized.

Retirement Depreciation

- Original cost is carried on books.
- Replacement cost is charged to expense in the period the replacement occurs.

Present Value Depreciation

- Depreciation is computed so that return on investment on the asset remains constant over the period.

Depletion

- Estimate in units the total amount of natural resources.
- The estimate of total recoverable units is divided into the total cost to give depletion rate per unit.
- Depletion = (rate per unit) × (number of units estimated in the year).

Disclosures

- Balances of major classes of depreciable assets.
- Accumulated depreciation by major classes.
- Depreciation expense for the period.
- Methods used in computing depreciation.

¶ 218 DERIVATIVE INSTRUMENTS AND HEDGING ACTIVITIES
SFAS Nos. 133, 137, 138, 149, & 155

SFAS 133 applies to all entities and establishes standards for derivative instruments and hedging activities. SFAS No. 137 defers the effective date of SFAS No. 133 one year to all fiscal quarters of fiscal years beginning after June 15, 2000. These rules should not be applied retroactively to financial statements of prior periods.

- Derivative instrument is a financial instrument or other contract that meets all of the following criteria:

  — Has one or more underlyings.

  — Has one or more settlement provisions or notional amounts.

  — Has no initial investment or an initial investment that is lower than required for similar contracts.

  — Permits or requires net settlement.

- Derivative instruments are recorded as assets or liabilities and reported at fair value in the financial statements.

- Derivatives are divided into non-hedge derivatives and hedged derivatives. Hedged derivatives are divided into fair value hedges, cash flow hedges, and hedges related to foreign activities.

- Non-hedged derivatives are accounted for at fair value and changes in fair value are reported in the income statement in the period of the change.

- Fair value hedges hedge risk associated with the exposure to possible changes in an asset or liability's fair value as a result of fix terms and are reported at fair value.

  — May be hedges of existing assets, liabilities or firm commitments.

  — Changes in the value of highly effective fair value hedges are reported in income in the period of the change.

  — Changes in the value of the hedged item are used to adjust the hedged item and are reported as a component of income.

- Cash flow hedges risk associated with the exposure to possible changes in anticipated cash flows from potential increases or decreases in prices or interest rates:

  — Reported at fair value.

  — May be hedges of existing assets, liabilities or forecasted transactions.

  — Changes in fair value of the effective part of the hedge is reported as a component of other comprehensive income.

  — Changes in the value of the hedged item are not reported as an adjustment to the hedged item.

- Hedges of net investments in foreign operations hedge the gains and losses from the translation of foreign subsidiary financial statements.

  — The hedge may be accomplished by either a derivative or non-derivative instrument.

  — Changes in the fair value of the effective part of the hedge is reported as a component of other comprehensive income.

- Changes in the value of hedges that are ineffective as a hedge are reported as a component of income in the income statement.

- SFAS No. 138 amends Statement No. 133 in the following areas:

— Issues related to normal purchases and normal sales.

— Definition of interest rate risk is changed to a benchmark interest rate.

— Issues concerning foreign-currency denominated assets and liabilities.

— Issues related to intercompany derivatives.

— Issues related to the derivative implementation guide.

- SFAS No. 149 amends Statement No. 133 in the following areas:

— Loan commitments under SFAS No. 65.

  - the issuer of a loan commitment relative to mortgage loan origination as covered by Paragraph 21 of Statement No. 65 should account for the commitment as a derivative instrument.

— Clarification of the initial net investment for classification of an instrument as a derivative.

— Clarification of regular way security trades.

— Clarification of normal purchases and normal sales.

— Clarification of when the following are not subject to the provisions of Statement No. 133.

  - financial guarantee contracts

  - investments in life insurance

  - selected investment contracts

  - loan commitments

— Clarification of when an embedded derivative is not clearly and closely related to the host contract.

— Clarification of issues related to firm commitments.

— Clarification of certain issues related to fair value and cash flow hedges.

— Specifies reporting requirements for derivative cash flows that have a financing element.

— Clarification of issues related to when items are readily convertible to cash.

— Specifies when power purchase or sales agreements related to electricity are accounted for as normal purchases and sales.

— Specifies when forward purchase or sales of when-issued securities are excluded from the requirements of Statement No. 133 and defines a capacity contact as used in the Statement.

— Specifies amendments to other standards related to cash flow issues as specified by FASB Concept Statement No. 7.

— Clarification of other issues related to derivative instruments.

- SFAS No. 155 amends Statement No. 133 in the following areas:

— The exception scope of Paragraph 14 is met for allocation of part of the cash flows from a specific debt issue when the allocation is considered reasonable compensation to a servicer of the instrument or for stripping the instrument.

— The exception scope is not met if the allocation is for a guarantee or other purposes in excess of reasonable compensation (Paragraph 14).

— Interest in securitized financial assets not specified in Paragraph 14 of Statement No. 133 should be reviewed to determine if the interest is an embedded derivative requiring separation from the host contract or a free standing derivative (Paragraph 14A).

— Credit risk concentration where one financial instrument is subordinated to another financial instrument is not classified as an embedded derivative.

— An interest in securitized financial assets and liabilities is classified as an embedded derivative when changes in the credit worthiness of the interest results in cash flow changes (Paragraph 14B).

— A hybrid financial instrument that is required by Statement No. 133 to be divided into a host contract and a derivative may be reported at fair value if an entity irrevocably elects to measure the entire instrument at fair value (see ¶ 295 and SFAS 157 for new fair value measurement requirements). Changes in fair value in subsequent accounting periods are reported in income (Paragraph 16).

¶ 219 DEVELOPMENT STAGE COMPANY
SFAS 7 & Interpretation No. 7

Definition

• A company in which principal operations have not commenced or have only generated a minimum amount of revenue.

• The company has devoted most of its activities toward establishing a new business.

Accounting

• Issue financials in conformity to GAAP.

• Interpretation No. 7 indicates that changes in accounting principles in a development stage enterprise included in consolidated financial statements of an operating enterprise generally are reflected in the consolidated statements that include the development stage enterprise.

Disclosures

• Losses accumulated should be described as "deficit accumulated during development stage."

• For comparative income statements, also provide a cumulative total of all periods.

• Stockholder's equity should show:

— Date and number of shares issued for cash.

— Non-cash share issuance providing description of nature of the consideration and basis for its valuation.

— Must disclose that company is in development stage.

• Financials should indicate that this is a development stage company and describe proposed business activities.

• Indicate the first year in which the company is no longer in the development stage.

¶ 221 EARNINGS PER SHARE
SFAS 128

SFAS No. 128, Earnings per Share for financials issued for periods ending after 12/15/97, supersedes APB 15, SFAS 21 & 85.

Overview

- New rules replace primary/fully diluted share computations with simpler basic/diluted calculations.
- Eliminates the Primary EPS and requires dual presentation of basic and diluted EPS on face of income statement for all entities with complex capital structures and requires a reconciliation of numerator and denominator of basic EPS computation to the numerator and denominator of the EPS computation.
  - A company is classified as a complex structure, rather than simple, if it has "potential" shares of common stock outstanding.
  - "Potential" shares are items such as warrants, options, convertible preferred stock, and convertible bonds.
- Treasury stock repurchases are no longer limited to 20 percent of outstanding stock, but are unrestricted.
- Treasury stock repurchases will be valued at average market value only.
- Diluted EPS will no longer be restricted to 10 years, but will have no time limitations. Disclosure of potential dilution will always be required.
- The determination of common stock equivalents for primary EPS is eliminated.

Basic Earnings Per Share

(Net Income - Preferred Stock Dividends) / Weighted Average Number of Shares Outstanding

Where, Weighted Average Number of Shares Outstanding = number of shares × time period

> **Example:** 500,000 shares are outstanding for 4 months, then another 500,000 shares are issued.

Net income = $800,000

Preferred Dividend = $160,000

Weighted Average Number of Shares Outstanding

$= (500,000 \times 4/12) + [(500,000 + 500,000) \times 8/12]$

$= 166,667 + 666,666.6 = 833,334$

Basic Earning Per Share = ($800,000 – $160,000) / 833,334 = $.77

Treasury Stock Method

Diluted EPS

(Net income - Preferred stock dividends) / (Weighted Average No. of shares + Incremental shares)

Incremental Shares = shares required for conversion shares purchased from proceeds

Example: Company has 100,000 stock options outstanding convertible into 100,000 shares of stock.

Exercise price = $30.

The company's average market value is $45.

Since the exercise price is less than average market price, the hypothetical exercise of these options would dilute EPS.

Net income equals $4,000,000.

Current outstanding shares equals 1,000,000

Incremental Shares = 100,000 – [($30 × 100,000 Options) / $45 Average Market Price]

= 100,000 – 66,666 = 33,333

Diluted EPS = (4,000,000 – 0) / (1,000,000 + 33,333) = $3.87 Share

If-Converted Method—For Company with Dilutive Shares of Preferred Stock

Basic EPS

(Net Income - Preferred Stock Dividends) / (Weighted Avg. No. of Shares of Common Stock)

Diluted EPS

(Net Income - Preferred Stock Dividends + Dividend Savings) / (Weighted Avg. No. of Shares of Common Stock + Extra Shares from Conversion)

Example: Illustration of potential earnings dilution that may arise from outstanding preferred stock

Company net income = $800,000

Shares outstanding = 100,000

Convertible preferred stock = 20,000 shares of 8%, $100 par value, preferred stock which is convertible into common stock on a one-to-one basis.

Basic EPS = ($800,000 – 160,000) / 100,000 = $6.40

Diluted EPS = ($800,000 –160,000 + 160,000) / (100,000 + 20,000) = $6.67

Since $6.67 is greater than $6.40, the preferred stock is anti-dilutive and would not be used in the computation.

If-Converted Method—For a Company with Convertible Bonds

$$\text{Diluted EPS} = \frac{\text{Net Income} - \text{Preferred Stock Dividends} + \text{After-Tax Interest Savings}}{\text{Weighted Average Shares} + \text{Additional Shares}}$$

Example: Illustration of potential Earnings Dilution that may arise for a company with outstanding convertible bonds.

Company net income = $800,000

Shares outstanding = 100,000

Marginal tax rate = 34%

1,000 convertible outstanding bonds at 8%, with $1,000 par value, convertible to common at five-to-one basis.

Basic EPS = ($800,000 – 0) / 100,000 = $8.00/Share

$$\text{Diluted EPS} = \frac{(\$800,000 - 0) + (1,000 - \$1,000 - .08) - (1 - .34)}{100,000 + (1,000 - 5)}$$

$$= \frac{\$800,000 + 80,000 - .66}{100,000 + 5,000}$$

$$= \$852,800/105,000 = \$8.12$$

Since $8.12 is not less than $8.00, the convertible bonds are not dilutive.

¶ 222 EQUITY METHOD INVESTMENT
APB 18, FIN 35, EITF 98-13

- If investment in common stock (or voting preferred stock) of a corporation gives the investor the ability to exercise significant influence over the operating and financial policies of the investee, then the equity method is appropriate to include in the results of operations of the investor, the investee's share of the net income or loss.
- Include the proportionate share of net income of the investee for periods subsequent to acquisition.
- Any dividends received are treated as adjustments to the investment amount.
- The equity method is appropriate for investments greater than 20% and less than 50%.
  - However, the presumptions of significant influence may be overcome by sufficient evidence.
- Record original investment at cost.
- Reduce the investment by dividends received.
- Show the investor's share of earnings or losses as a single amount in the income statement.
- Eliminate intercompany profits.
- Account for capital transactions as if the entities were consolidated.
- Difference between equity in net assets and the investment is amortized over period of remaining life of the assets.
- A long-term loss in the value of the investment should be recognized by the investor.
- When the investor sells the stock investment, gain or loss is recognized equal to the difference between the selling price and the carrying amount of the investment at the time of the sale.
- Do not decrease the basis in the investment below zero. Subsequently resume the equity method after net income exceeds the investor's share of net losses not recognized during the period of discontinuance, unless advances have been

guaranteed by investor company. EITF 98-13 provides additional accounting requirements in some situations.

¶ 223 FINANCIAL INSTRUMENTS
SFAS 107 & 150 (Also see ¶ 218)

Reporting Standards of SFAS 107

- Fair value is the amount which instruments could be exchanged in a transaction between willing parties other than a forced liquidation or sale.
- Disclosures required in estimating fair value of financial instruments:
  - An entity should disclose fair value of financial instruments where estimates are practicable, including the method and assumptions used.
  - Quoted market prices are preferred; consider exchange market, dealer market, brokered market, and principal to principal market.
  - In estimating fair value of deposit liabilities, do not take into account core deposits of intangibles.
  - If an estimate is not practicable, provide all pertinent information regarding the instrument.

Reporting Standards of SFAS No. 150

- Statement No. 150 specifies the classification and measurement of certain freestanding financial instruments with characteristics of both equity and liabilities.
- Statement No. 150 does not apply to the following:
  - Obligations accounted for using the provisions of SFAS No. 123 (Revised) or AICPA SOP 93-6.
  - Measurement guidance and timing of recognition of instruments used as contingent consideration under SFAS No. 141.
  - Features embedded in a financial instrument that is not accounted entirely accounted for as a derivative.
- The following three categories of financial instruments are covered by the Statement:
  - Mandatorily redeemable financial instruments.
    - Unconditional obligation where the instrument must be redeemed by the issuer using an asset transfer on a specific date(s) or upon the occurrence of an event that is certain.
    - Classify as a liability unless redemption is required only upon termination or liquidation of the enterprise.
    - Examples include mandatorily redeemable preferred stock, trust-preferred shares, and stock that will be redeemed upon death of holder.
  - Requirements to repurchase equity shares of the issuer by asset transfer:
    - Classify as a liability (sometimes an asset) if, at inception, the financial instrument (excluding outstanding shares) includes a requirement to repurchase equity shares of the issuer or is indexed to such a require-

ment and assets are required or may be required to be transferred to settled the obligation.

- Examples include written put options or forward purchase contracts requiring net cash or physical settlement.

— Requirements to issue variable number of shares.

- Includes a financial instrument (excluding outstanding shares) with an unconditional or conditional obligation to issue a variable number of shares to settle the obligation.

- Classify as a liability (sometimes an asset) if, at inception, the instrument's monetary value is based on one of the following items.

  - Fixed monetary amount known at the inception of the instrument.

  - Variations related to something other than fair value of the shares of the issuer.

  - Variations that are inversely related to fair value changes in equity shares of the issuer.

  - Example is receipt of $200,000 with a promise to pay in a number of shares equal to $220,000 at a specified future date.

- Instruments covered by Statement No. 150 should be included in the liability section of the balance sheet and should not be presented in a separate section between liabilities and equity.

- Measurement of instruments covered by SFAS No. 150.

  — Mandatorily redeemable financial instruments—fair value.

  — Forward contracts with physical settlement by a repurchase of shares in exchange of cash—fair value adjusted for any rights, privileges, or consideration.

  — Forward contracts with physical settlement by a repurchase of share exchange of cash and mandatorily redeemable instruments.

    - Fixed settlement date and fixed amount—present value of amount at settlement.

    - Variable settlement date or variable amount—amount of cash that would be paid on the reporting date and any required adjustments subsequent to reporting date reported as interest costs.

  — Other instruments—fair value.

  — Subsequent measurements should be accordance with SFAS No. 133 if instrument is covered by Statement No. 133 or fair value if not covered by SFAS No. 133 or other statements.

- Several disclosures are required by Statement No. 150.

¶223

¶ 225 IMPAIRMENT OF A LOAN—INCOME RECOGNITION AND DISCLOSURES—ACCOUNTING BY CREDITORS
SFAS 114 & 118

Loan defined as "a contractual right to receive money on demand or on fixed or determinable dates that is recognized as an asset in the creditor's statement of financial position."

Income Measurement

SFAS 118 amends SFAS 114 to indicate that guidance is not provided concerning how a creditor should recognize, measure, or display interest income on an impaired loan.

Recognition of Impairment

A loan is impaired when it is probable that a creditor will be unable to collect all amounts due, including principle and interest, according to the contractual terms and schedules of the loan agreement. A loan is not considered impaired if there is merely an insignificant delay or shortfall and the creditor expects to collect all amounts due.

Measurement of Impairment

This requires judgment and estimation. Measurement may be on a loan-by-loan or an aggregate basis.

- Impairment generally is based on the present value of expected future cash flows discounted at the loan's effective interest rate. The present value amount, based on estimated future cash, is discounted at the loan's effective interest rate.
- Estimated costs to sell, on a discounted basis may be a factor.
- If the measurement of the impaired loan is less than the recorded investment in the loan, the creditor shall recognize the impairment by creating or adjusting a valuation allowance with a corresponding charge to bad-debt expense.

Disclosures

- The average recorded investment in the impaired loans during each period.
- The total recorded investment in the impaired loan at the end of each period.
- The creditor's policy for recognizing interest income on impaired loans.
- Selected information about the allowance for losses account related to the impaired investment.
- Amount of interest income related to the impaired investment.
- Amount of the investment for which an allowance for losses has been established and amount for which no allowance has been established.
- Amount of interest income on a cash basis related to the impaired loans, if possible.

¶ 227 IMPAIRMENT OF LONG-LIVED ASSETS AND FOR LONG-LIVED ASSETS TO BE DISPOSED
SFAS 144 & 147

The following long-lived assets are excluded:

- Goodwill.

- Intangible assets not being amortized.
- Customer affiliations of a long-term nature.
- Servicing rights.
- Financial instruments.
- Deferred tax assets.
- Cost of policy acquisitions that are deferred.
- Unproven oil and gas properties using successful efforts.
- Long-lived assets covered by SFAS Nos. 50, 63, 86, and 90.

Long-Lived Assets Held for Disposition

- Assets meeting certain requirements are classified as held for sale and are reported in the statement of financial position at the lower of fair value less the cost to sell (adjusted fair value) or carrying amount.
- Fair value is the price received or paid on the date of measurement between participants in the market place when an asset is sold or a liability is transferred in an orderly transaction (the exit price) (see ¶ 295).
- SFAS 157 should now be used to determine the amount of fair value.
- If the adjusted fair value is less than the carrying amount of the asset, a loss is reported for an amount equal to the difference between the adjusted fair value, the carrying amount, and the related asset is written down to equal the adjusted fair value.
- The loss is reported before tax in the income statement as part of income from continuing operations.
- If fair market value or expected costs of disposition require adjustments prior to actual asset disposition, the carrying value of the asset should be increased, but not in excess of the cumulative losses, or decreased and a gain or loss reported.

Long-Lived Assets Held for Use

- Situations or circumstances may indicate that the carrying value of long-lived assets held and used may not be recoverable.
- Such assets should be tested for possible impairment.
- The long-lived assets should be placed in asset groups using the lowest level of assets that generate independent cash flows.
- Cash flows for each group are estimated on a gross cash flow basis and the carrying amount of the asset is compared to the undiscounted future cash flows.
- If the undiscounted cash flows are less than the carrying amount of the asset, the asset or asset group must be tested further for impairment.
- If the fair value of the asset or group is less than the related carrying value, an impairment loss is reported for the difference, the asset is reduced by the amount of the loss and a new cost basis is established for the asset.
- Depreciation expense should be based on the new cost basis and the asset should be depreciated over its remaining useful life.
- The asset should not be increased if the impairment loss is recovered in future accounting periods.

- Impairment loss is reported before tax in the income statement as part of income from continuing operations.

- SFAS No. 139 amends Statement No. 121 (superseded by SFAS No. 144) relative to impairment of motion picture films. All references to SFAS No. 53 are deleted and replaced with AICPA Statement of Position (SOP) 00-2.

- Intangible assets composed of long-term customer-relationships, other than servicing assets, resulting from the acquisition of a financial institution are covered by the provisions of Statement No. 144.

- Any impairment loss related to long-term customer relationships should be reported in the accounting period when the impairment criteria are first applied and *do not* classify any impairment loss as a change in accounting principle where the cumulative effect is reported.

¶ 229 INCOME TAXES
SFAS 109, APB 10 par 6, 7, APB 23, & Interpretations 18 & 48

SFAS 109 requires entities to account for income taxes using the asset/liability method, or the deferred method. The deferred method places emphasis on the valuation of current and deferred tax assets and liabilities.

The amount of income tax expense recognized for a current period (is equal to the payable or refundable) plus or minus the change in aggregate deferred tax assets and liabilities.

Income tax effects of all revenues, expenses, gains, losses, etc. that create differences between tax bases of assets and liabilities are required to be recognized.

The emphasis is on the balance sheet. The principles are:

- Recognize a deferred asset or liability for the estimated future tax effects of temporary differences (operating loss carryforwards and tax credit carryforwards).

- Measure current and deferred tax assets and liabilities based on provisions of enacted tax laws.

- If necessary, reduce the amount of any deferred tax assets by a valuation allowance based on available evidence.

Temporary Differences

- Deferred tax assets and liabilities from temporary differences are based on the assumption the assets and liabilities in a company's balance sheet will eventually be realized or settled at their recorded amounts.

- Revenues or gains that are taxable before they are recognized in accounting income.

- Revenues or gains taxable after being recognized in accounting income.

- Expenses or losses deductible after being recognized in accounting income.

- Expenses or losses deductible before being recognized in accounting income.

- Direct adjustments to assets and liabilities that cause a difference between the tax and book basis of the asset or liability.

- A taxable temporary difference is one that will result in the payment of income taxes in the future when the temporary differences reverse.
- A deductible temporary difference is one that will result in reduced income taxes in future years when the temporary difference reverses.
- The amount of temporary differences is computed using the provisions of FASB Interpretation 48 (see the discussion of Interpretation 48 in the discussion of income tax uncertainty).

Examples of Taxable Temporary Differences

- Depreciable assets.
- Installment sales.

Examples of Deductable Temporary Differences

- Accounts receivable allowance for bad debts.
- Litigation liabilities.
- Warranty liabilities.
- Revenue received in advance.

Computation of Deferred Assets and Liabilities

- Determine amounts of existing temporary differences and the amount of each type of operating loss and tax credit carryforward and its remaining term.
- Measure the deferred tax asset and liability for taxable and deductible temporary differences using the applicable tax rate.
- Measure deferred taxes for interim accounting periods using the estimated annual effective tax rate.
- Provide statement showing measurement of defined tax asset based on deductible temporary differences and operating loss carry forwards.
- Determine deferred tax assets for each type of tax credit carryforward.
- Reduce deferred tax assets by a valuation allowance if it is more likely than not that some or all of the deferred tax assets will not be realized.

Do the following steps at the end of each accounting period to calculate the amount of the valuation allowance.

- Determine the amount of the deferral tax asset recognized on each deductible temporary difference on each operating loss and tax credit carryforward. Do not offset these by the deferred tax liability on taxable temporary differences.
- Assess the sources of future taxable income which may be available to recognize the deductible differences and carryforwards.
  - Future taxable income exclusive of reversing differences.
  - Future reversals of existing taxable temporary differences.
- Based on available evidence, make a judgment concerning the realizability of the deferred tax asset.
- Record the amount of the valuation allowance, or change in the valuation allowance.

Example:

Income tax expense	XXX
Allowance to reduce deferred tax asset to lower receivable value	XXX

- The applicable tax rate is the currently enacted rate expected to apply to the income in the periods in which the deferred tax asset or liability is expected to be settled or realized based on the current tax law.
- Disclosure of net deferred tax liability or asset:
  — The total of all deferred tax liabilities for taxable temporary differences.
  — The total valuation allowance recognized for deferred tax assets.
  — The total of all deferred tax assets for deductible temporary differences and loss and tax credit carryforwards.
- Disclosure of significant components of income tax expense related to continuing operations:
  — Investment tax credit.
  — Current tax expense.
  — Deferred tax expense.
  — Tax benefits of operating loss carryforwards.
- Disclosures for when deferred taxes are not recognized:
  — Description of types of temporary differences and events that would cause those temporary differences to become taxable.
  — The cumulative amount of the temporary differences.
  — Differences related to investments in foreign subsidiaries.

Income Tax Uncertainty (FASB Interpretation No. 48)

- All tax positions accounted for using the provisions of SFAS 109 are covered by Interpretation 48.
- Temporary differences under SFAS 109 are computed using the provisions of Interpretation 48.
- A tax position is a position taken by an entity in a past tax return or a position expected to be taken in a future tax return that impacts the computation of current or deferred tax assets and/or liabilities and may include the following:
  — Not filing a tax return.
  — Income shift or allocation between jurisdictions.
  — Not reporting income in tax return.
  — Classifying a transaction as tax exempt.
- An entity should report the impact of a tax position in the financial statements when it is more likely than not that the tax position will be sustained.
  — More likely than not is more than 50 percent.
  — When making a decision assume that the tax position will be examined by the appropriate taxing authority and will be reviewed based on the technical merits of the position.

— Each tax position should be evaluated individually without consideration of other tax positions.

- A tax position meeting the requirements for recognition should be reported at the largest amount that is greater than a 50-percent likelihood of being realized considering amounts and probabilities of outcomes.

- A tax position that has been recognized should be removed or derecognized when it no longer meets the more than likely requirement.

- Recognition, derecognition, or measurement change that result from changes in judgment in accounting periods subsequent to initial consideration should be considered in the accounting period of change as a discrete item.

- Interest should be reported for underpayment of taxes on the difference between the amount reported per tax return and the amount recognized under Interpretation 48 by applying the appropriate statutory tax rate to the difference. The interest can be either classified as income tax expense or interest expense.

- Recognize an expense for any penalties in the accounting period that the tax position is taken. The penalty expense can be classified as income tax expense or put in a separate expense category.

- Report an unrecognized tax benefit in the financial statements as a current liability when payments will be made within one year of the normal operating cycle or a reduction in an operating loss carry forward or tax refund, where appropriate, for the difference between the amount reported on the tax return and the amount computed using Interpretation 48.

- Temporary differences may result from changes in the tax bases of assets or liabilities when applying the provisions of Interpretation 48.

- The following disclosures are required by Interpretation 48:

  — The policy for classifying interest and penalties.

  — Reconcile the beginning and ending balance of the unrecognized tax benefit account using a tabular format and include as a minimum the following:

    - As a result of tax positions taken during the current accounting period, disclose the increases or decreases in the unrecognized tax benefit using gross amounts.

    - As a result of tax positions taken during prior accounting periods, disclose the increases or decreases in the unrecognized tax benefit using gross amounts.

    - Decrease in the unrecognized tax position from settlement during the accounting period with the taxing authority and from lapse of statute of limitations.

  — Impact on the effective tax rate if unrecognized tax benefits were recognized.

  — Amount of interest and penalties reported in the balance sheet and statement of operations.

  — Report the following for unrecognized tax benefits where it is reasonably possible that the benefits will significantly change over the next 12 months:

    - Nature of the uncertainty and the event that could occur within one year that causes the change.

¶229

- Estimate the range of the change or state that an estimate could not be made.
— Describe the tax years that are still subject to examination.

¶ 230 INSTALLMENT METHOD OF ACCOUNTING
APB 10, PAR 12, ARB 43, Chapter IA

Prohibited

- Accounting for sales by using an installment method of accounting is prohibited except in exceptional circumstances where collectability cannot be assured or reasonably estimated.
- Doubtfulness of collectability might be caused by length of extended collection period.

Cost Recovery Method

- Used where cost is undeterminable.
- All cost is recovered before any gain is recognized.
- Once all cost is recovered, all collections are recognized as revenue.

Installment Sales Method

- Each payment is recorded as part recovery of cost and part recovery of profit.
- Ratio of recovery is same ratio that existed in original sales applied to each dollar received.
- Ratio is gross profit % as income and cost, % as recovery of property.

¶ 231 INTANGIBLE ASSETS
SFAS 142 & 147

Overview

- Long-lived assets such as legal rights or competitive advantages.
- May be purchased or internally developed, except goodwill. Goodwill must be purchased.
- Record initially at fair value.
- Goodwill is recorded at amount equal to the excess of the purchase price of the entity over the fair value of the assets less the liabilities assumed.
- Intangible asset with a finite life should be amortized over its estimated useful life using the method that would best reflect the pattern of use of the asset. The useful life is determined by using the time period that an intangible is estimated to contribute directly or indirectly to the entity's future cash flows.
- Intangible asset with an indefinite life is not amortized but is tested for impairment at least on an annual basis and more frequently if circumstances warrant more frequent testing using the provisions of Statement No. 142.
- Goodwill is not amortized but tested for impairment using the provisions of Statement No. 142.
  — Other than straight line is allowed if another systematic method is more appropriate.

- The carrying value of an unidentifiable intangible asset acquired in a business combination previously accounted for using the provisions of Statement No. 72 should be reclassified as goodwill and accounted for prospectively using Statement No. 142.

- Any unidentifiable intangible asset reclassified as goodwill should be tested for impairment using Statement No. 142 and any adjustment should be reported as a change in accounting principle using Paragraph 56 of Statement No. 142.

- The following transitional disclosures are required for reclassified goodwill: (1) carrying amount of reclassified goodwill, (2) impact on income from the restatement for each restated accounting period, and (3) adjustments related to goodwill impairment from the reclassified goodwill.

Disclosure

— Goodwill is shown as a separate line item in the balance sheet.

— Goodwill impairment losses are reported as the last item in income from continuing operations.

— Intangible assets are shown as line item in the balance sheet.

— Intangible asset impairment losses and amortization expense are reported in the income statement as a line item in income from continuing operations.

— Intangible assets requiring amortization report: amount assigned, significant residual value, and weighted-average amortization period (Paragraph 44(a)).

— Intangibles not subject to amortization report: total amount assigned to intangibles and amount assigned to major intangible asset classes (Paragraph 44(b)).

— Acquired research and development assets should report: amount acquired, amount written off, and location in the income statement where amounts written off are reported.

— For intangible assets that require amortization: gross carrying amount, accumulated amortization, total amortization expense, and expected total amortization expense for each of the next five years subsequent to the current accounting period (Paragraph 45(a)).

— For intangibles not subject to amortization report: total carrying amount for intangibles and carrying amount for major intangible asset classes (Paragraph 45(b)).

— Report the following changes in goodwill: total amount of acquired goodwill, total amount of losses reported from impairment, and goodwill reported in a gain or loss from disposition of part or all of a reporting unit (Paragraph 45(c)).

— Disclose any significant goodwill allocation changes involving reportable segments and other disclosures related to segments (Paragraph 45(c)).

— Amount of goodwill not allocated to reporting units and reason it has not been allocated (Paragraph 45 (c)).

— When intangible asset impairment loss is reported report: facts and circumstances causing the impairment and describe the impaired intangible, method used to calculate fair value, amount of impairment loss, caption where the loss is reported in the income statement or statement of activities, and operating segment where loss is reported (Paragraph 46).

— When goodwill impairment loss is reported show: facts and circumstances causing the impairment, method used to calculate fair value of the related reporting unit, amount of impairment loss, and if appropriate, the fact and reason that the loss is estimated and is not final and adjustments made to the original estimate in subsequent accounting periods (Paragraph 47).

¶ 233 INTEREST CAPITALIZED
SFAS 34, 42, & 62

Overview

- In certain conditions, interest costs should be capitalized as part of the acquisition cost of an asset.
- Before interest costs can be capitalized, expenditures must have been made for the qualifying asset, providing an investment base on which to compute interest, activities that are required to get the asset ready for its intended use must actually be in progress, and interest must have been incurred (8).
- Capitalize only interest costs incurred during the acquisition period (the time it takes to get an asset ready for use).
  - Capitalization period begins with first expenditure for the asset and ends when asset is substantially complete and ready for use.
  - The usual materiality tests should be applied to determine if capitalization is required.
- Capitalization of interest is required for:
  - Assets for company's own use.
  - Assets for sale in the ordinary course of business, but not for inventories that are routinely produced in large quantities.
- Do not capitalize interest for:
  - Completed assets.
  - Assets not used in the earnings process of the business.

Interest Amount

- Cannot exceed total interest cost.
  - Determine average accumulated expenditures.
  - Weight by time each expenditure is outstanding.
- Compute weighted average interest rate.
- Interest cost is average accumulated expenditure times appropriate interest rate.

¶ 235 INTEREST ON RECEIVABLES AND PAYABLES
APB 21

Excluded from APB 21

- Security of retainage deposits.
- Lending institution transactions.

- Parent and subsidiary transactions.
- Where interest rate is determined by a governmental agency.
- Arising in ordinary business due in less than one year.

Record

- Record at present value if:
  — Interest rate is not stated.
  — Interest rate is unreasonable.
- Interest stated on a note is presumed to be fair and adequate unless evidence indicates otherwise.

Discount or Premium Amortization

- Discount or pension is difference between present value and face amount of the receivable or payable.
- Amortize the discount or premium over the life of the note.
- The discount or premium is deducted from the related asset or liability on the balance sheet.
- Do not classify discounts or premiums as deferred charges or credits.

Disclosure

- Description of asset or payable.
- Effective interest rate.
- Face amount of note.

¶ 237 INTERIM FINANCIAL REPORTING
APB 28, SFAS 132 (Revised)(Also see ¶ 259), SFAS 148 (Also see ¶ 201) & Interpretation No. 18

Overview

- Interim financials are financials issued at intervals of less than a year, i.e., monthly, quarterly.
- GAAP procedures are applicable to interim financials with some modifications.
- Measure deferred taxes for interim accounting periods using the estimated annual effective tax rate.

Expenses and Costs

- Those that benefit more than one period should be properly allocated to periods affected.
- Companies should make disclosures regarding seasonal revenue variations.
- Unusual and infrequent transactions should be reported separately.
- Interim reports should not contain arbitrary amounts of costs or expenses.

Inventories

- Companies using the gross profit method to value inventories should disclose that fact.
- Temporary market declines need not be recognized.

— Other than temporary inventory losses from market declines should be shown on income statement, and subsequent gains should be recognized in later periods as they occur, but not when they exceed prior losses recognized.

- Inventory computed by standard costing should be the same as those used at year-end.

Publicly Traded Company's Interim Minimum Information

- Basic and diluted earnings per share data.
- Material seasonal variations.
- Income statement gross revenues, net income, provision for taxes and extraordinary items.
- Material changes in financial position.
- Changes in accounting principles or estimates.
- Gains and losses from discontinued operations and unusual and infrequent items.
- Contingent items.
- Significant changes in tax provisions or estimates.

Pension Disclosures Under Statement No. 132 (Revised)

- The following disclosures are required by public companies in interim reports:
  — Amount of benefit costs showing specific components of the costs.
  — Amount of employer contributions paid and estimated to be paid for the accounting period, if different from prior disclosures.
- The following disclosures are required by nonpublic companies in interim reports:
  — Amount of employer contributions paid and estimated to be paid for the accounting period, if different from prior disclosures.

¶ 239 INVENTORY
ARB 43, SFAS 151 & 153, FASB Interpretation 1

Overview

- Inventory excludes assets subject to depreciation.
- Excessive inventories not expected to be used or sold in current operating cycle should be classified as non-current.
- The major objective in valuing inventory is to match revenue and costs.
- Periodic system:
  — Inventory is determined by a physical count at a specified date.
  — Net change between beginning and ending inventory is cost of goods sold.
- Perpetual system:
  — Inventory records are maintained and currently updated requiring posting of individual transactions.
  — Periodic physical checks are made to reconcile perpetual records to actual.

Title

- The firm must have legal title to the goods to include the amount in inventory.
- Title passes based on conditions as explicitly agreed to by parties involved.
- If no agreed conditions exist, title passes when seller completes his performance with reference to physical delivery of goods.
- If contract requires delivery at destination, title passes when goods are delivered at the destination.

Inventory Costs

- Inventory is assumed to be stated at cost.
- Cost is price paid or consideration given.
- Cost is the sum of direct and indirect expenditures.
  - Selling expenses are not to be included.
  - The exclusion of all overhead is unacceptable.
- Cost may be written down to allow for obsolescence, physical deterioration, etc., as a loss for the current period.
- Variable production overhead should be allocated to inventory cost based on actual production facility use.
- Fixed production overhead should be allocated to inventory cost based on the production facility's normal capacity.
- Normal capacity is the expected production of a facility considered under normal circumstances over a period of time.
- Unallocated overhead is reported as an expense in the accounting period incurred.
- Abnormal freight, handling costs, and spoilage is accounted for as a current change and not as part of inventory cost.

Lower of Cost or Market

- Market means current replacement cost limited as:
  - Maximum—cannot exceed the estimated selling price less any costs of completion or disposal—prevents a loss in future periods.
  - Minimum is the maximum less an allowance for normal profit—prevents any future periods from realizing any more than a normal profit.
- Apply to a single item, category or total inventory.
- Use the method that most clearly reflects periodic income.
- Purpose of writedown is to reflect fairly the income of the period.
- Consistency of valuation must be maintained.
- Exceptions are allowed:
  - If costs are difficult to maintain.
  - Immediate marketable quoted prices exist, e.g., precious metals having a fixed determinable monetary value.

¶239

Cost Methods

- Method used should most clearly reflect income.
- Specific identification method tracks specific item from purchase to sale.
- Standard costs:
  - Acceptable if physical inventories are periodically taken with variances closed to cost of goods sold.
- FIFO—assures that costs should be charged against income in the order in which they occurred.
- LIFO—provides that latest inventory costs are charged to income.
  - Layers are maintained year by year.
  - If ending inventory is greater than beginning inventory, an additional layer is created.
  - If ending inventory is less than beginning inventory, then LIFO layers may be used up. When a LIFO layer is used up, any new LIFO layer is priced at the cost of the year in which it is created.
  - SEC reporting of LIFO requires current replacement value of the LIFO inventory at each balance sheet date and the effects of the results of operations for any reduction of a LIFO layer.
- Dollar-value LIFO.
  - Base year inventory is priced in dollars with base index of 100.
  - Subsequent years are priced with price index applied times ending inventory at base-year prices.
- Weighted average method:
  - Charges against income an average of the number of units acquired at each price level.
  - Total inventory value is the average price applied to the ending inventory.
- Moving average:
  - Use with perpetual inventory.
  - The ending inventory is costed at the last moving average unit cost for the period.
- Retail inventory method—calculates a ratio of cost to retail and applies this to ending inventory at retail to compute the cost.

Firm Purchase Commitments

- Losses are measured in the same manner as inventory losses and, if material, should be disclosed separately.

Disclosures

- Description of accounting principles used.
- Specifics peculiar to a specific industry.
- Method of costing inventory.
- Classifications of inventory.
- If inconsistency occurs:

— Nature of change.

— The effect on income, if material.

Inventory

Inventory—Nonmonetary Exchange

- A reciprocal transfer is considered an exchange only if the party transferring the nonmonetary assets has no continuing involvement in the asset.
- Inventory received is reported at recorded amount of asset given up, after reduction for any impairment in value of the inventory surrendered when one or more of the following are met:
  - Fair value cannot be determined within reasonable limits.
  - Transaction is for the purpose of facilitation of sales to customers.
  - Transaction lacks commercial substance. The nonmonetary exchange has commercial substance when one of the following is achieved:
    - Future cash flows are anticipated to change significantly, or
    - The entity-specific value of the assets given up as compared to the assets received is significantly different.
- No gain is recognized.
- New inventory exchanged is recorded at book value of inventory surrendered.

Inventory—Accounting Change

- Show cumulative effect of change, except for change to or from LIFO.

Inventory—Intercompany Profits

- All intercompany profits are to be eliminated for consolidated financial statements.

Inventory—Research and Development

- Supplies used in R & D should be charged against expense unless they clearly have an alternate use, or can be used in future R & D projects.
- The carrying value of the inventory consumed should be charged to R & D expense.

Inventory of Discontinued Segments

- Write down to net realizable value.
- Include as part of gain/loss recognized on disposal of discontinued segment.

Inventory—Business Combinations

- Purchase:
  - Work in process—net realizable value less a reasonable profit.
  - Finished goods—net realizable value less a reasonable profit.
  - Raw materials—current replacement cost.

Inventory and Interim Financials

- Generally, apply same methods and principles as used for annual statements.

¶239

- Estimated gross profit method is acceptable if periodic physical inventories are taken to adjust the gross profit percent used.

- Inventory losses from market declines, if not temporary, should be recognized up to the extent of recognized losses.

- Standard costs are acceptable.

¶ 241 INVESTMENTS IN DEBT AND EQUITY SECURITIES
SFAS 115

SFAS No. 115 supersedes SFAS No. 12 and FASB Interpretation Nos. 11, 12, 13, and 16. Statement No. 115 specifies the accounting and reporting requirements for all debt securities and for equity securities with fair values that can be readily determined carried on the cost method.

- A debt security under SFAS No. 115 is a security for which the entity is the debtor, and the counterparty to the security is the creditor.

- An equity security is a security that meets one of the following conditions:

  — Represents an interest in the ownership of an entity,

  — Represents a right of disposition of an interest in the ownership of an entity at an amount that is either fixed or can be determined, or

  — Represents a right of acquisition of an interest in the ownership of an entity at an amount that is either fixed or can be determined.

- Debt and equity securities are divided into trading, available-for-sale and held-to-maturity.

- Trading securities:

  — Securities held for resale in the near future.

  — Reported in the statement of financial position at fair market value.

  — Changes in fair value of the securities is reported as a component of income.

- Available-for-sale securities:

  — Securities not classified as trading or held-to-maturity.

  — Reported in the statement of financial position at fair market value.

  — When fair value is less than cost a loss is reported in the period of change and included as a component of other comprehensive income.

  — When a decline in fair value below cost is other than temporary, a loss is reported in the income statement and a new cost basis is established for the security.

  — When fair value exceeds cost a gain is reported in the period of change and included as a component of other comprehensive income.

- Held-to-maturity securities:

  — Securities where the company has the intent and ability to hold the securities until maturity.

  — Only includes debt securities.

  — Reported at amortized cost in the statement of financial position.

— No gains or losses are reported for changes in fair value, except for losses resulting from permanent declines in value.

Financial Statement Requirements

Investments in trading securities should be classified in a statement of financial position as current assets, and investments classified as held-to-maturity or available-for-sale should be classified based on when an entity expects to turn an investment into cash.

Disclosure requirements for available-for-sale securites:

- Unrealized holding gains on a gross basis included in accumulated other comprehensive income.
- Unrealized holding losses on a gross basis included in accumulated other comprehensive income.
- Fair market value on an aggregate basis.

Disclosure requirements for held-to-maturity securities:

- Unrecognized gross holding gains and holding losses.
- Fair value on an aggregate basis.
- Carrying amount on a net basis.
- Gross gains and losses reported in accumulated other comprehensive income as a result of the provisions of SFAS No. 133.

Amortized cost and fair market value for:

- Debt maturing in one year or less.
- Debt maturing in more than one year and not more than five years.
- Debt maturing in more than five years and not more than ten years.
- Debt maturing in more than ten years.

Disclose the following information from the sale or transfer of securities from the held-to-maturity category:

- Realized gain or loss.
- Unrealized gain or loss.
- Amortized cost.
- Circumstances causing the sale or transfer.

The following information is required for investments in available-for-sale securities:

- Gross realized gains and losses from sales.
- Proceeds from sales.
- Gross gains and losses from transfers to the trading category.
- Changes in the unrealized holdings gain or loss included in accumulated other comprehensive income.

The following should be disclosed:

- Cost flow method used when computing the gain or loss from the sale of investments.
- Amount of gains and losses from trading securities that are still on books as of the balance sheet date.

¶241

¶ 243 INVESTMENTS HELD BY NOT-FOR-PROFIT ORGANIZATIONS
SFAS No. 124

SFAS No. 124 specifies the accounting and reporting requirements for all debt securities and for most equity securities for which fair values can be easily determined that are held by not-for-profit organizations.

A debt security under SFAS No. 124 is a security that represents a creditor relationship with an enterprise. Examples of debt securities include: corporate bonds, debt convertible into other securities, preferred stock that is redeemable, and securities of the U.S. Treasury.

An equity security is a security that meets one of the following conditions: the security represents an interest in the ownership of an entity; the security represents a right of disposition of an interest in the ownership of an entity at an amount that is either fixed or can be determined; or the security represents a right of acquisition of an interest in the ownership of an entity at an amount that is either fixed or can be determined.

SFAS 124 applies to equity securities accounted for under the cost method, i.e., to those signifying ownership interest of less than 20 percent and absence of significant influence over the operating policies of the investee company. SFAS 124 does apply to equity securities where fair value can be easily determined.

Debt and equity securities covered by SFAS No. 124 are reported in the statement of financial position at fair market value, and changes in value are reported as gains and losses.

The investment may be classified as an endowment fund that is donor restricted because of donor stipulations and requirements. Gains and losses from changes in the value of the investment are subject to the restrictions stipulated by the donor.

In some cases, losses from endowment funds that are donor restricted reduce the funds below levels required by legal or donor stipulations or requirements. In such cases, subsequent gains that reinstate asset fair value to specified amounts are accounted for as an increase in net assets classified as unrestricted.

Investment income related to restricted investments increases net assets that are either permanently or temporarily restricted, depending on the type of restriction.

Disclose

- Nature and carrying amount of investments, on either a group or individual basis, that have a market risk concentration considered significant.
- The investment carrying amount.
- The basis used for ascertaining investment carrying amount.
- When investments that are not classified as financial instruments are reported on a fair value basis, the assumptions and methods used for estimating fair value.
- The amount of deficiencies, on an aggregate basis, for endowment funds that are donor restricted, when asset fair values are below stipulated levels.
- The elements of return on investment.

- A reconciliation of amounts in the statement of activities with the return on investment.
- A description of the policy for determining the amount of the investment return.

¶ 245 INVESTMENT TAX CREDIT
APB 2 & 4, SFAS 109

Methods

- Treating investment credit as a direct contribution to capital is irrational and unacceptable because it bypasses the income statement.
- Deferral method—to amortize investment credit to net income over the productive life of the acquired property.
- Flow-through method (preferred method):
  — To treat credit as a reduction of tax expense in year credit arises.
  — The amount of ITC used in a year reduces the amount of income tax expense currently payable for the year, and thereby reduces income tax expense. The ITC flows into income.
- Once a method is selected, it should be applied consistently from year to year. However, FASB No. 154 allows for a change in principle.

Disclosure of ITC

- Show as deduction from corresponding asset, or
- Show as a deferred credit.
- Disclose method followed and amounts for the ITC.

¶ 247 LEASES
SFAS 13, 22, 23, 27, 28, 29, 91, & 98
FASB Interpretations 19, 23, 24, 26, & 27
Technical Bulletin 79-10, -12, -14, -16, -17 & -18, 85-3, 86-2, & 88-1

Lease Defined

- An agreement that conveys the right to use assets for a stated period.

Substance vs. Form

- Substance over form should prevail regarding ownership of property.
- If, at inception of lease, it meets one or more of the following criteria, it should be classified as ownership by the lessee:
  — By end of lease term, ownership is transferred to lessee.
  — The lease contains a bargain purchase price.
  — The lease term is 75% or more of the estimated remaining useful life of the asset.
  — The present value of the minimum lease payments is 90% or more of the fair value of the leased property.
- Classification of lease by lessors:
  — If any of the above four criteria are met and:
  — Collection of the minimum lease payments is reasonably predictable, and

— No important uncertainties exist for unreimburseable costs yet to be incurred by the lessor under the lease.

Capital Lease Highlights

- Transfers substantially all the benefits and risks of ownership of the property to the lessee.
- The lessee records a capital lease as an asset with a corresponding liability.
- Lessee records asset and obligation at smaller of fair value or the present value of the minimum lease payments.
- Use the smaller of the following to compute present value, if both rates are known:
  — The lessor's implicit rate of interest.
  — The lessee's incremental borrowing rate.
- Lessor computes present value of minimum lease payments using interest rate implicit in the lease that results in a present value equal to the fair value.
- Amortization of a capital lease asset is done using the lessee's normal depreciation methods.
- The interest method is used to produce a constant rate of interest on the remaining lease liability—portion of each lease payment is allocated to interest, and the balance applied to reduce the principal.
- If lessee term changes, adjust present values to the revised agreement using the original interest rate.
- If lessee lease payments change, adjust present values of asset and liability values. Use original interest rate.
- If lessee lease change is to an operating lease, eliminate asset/liability and record gain/loss.
- New lease, renewal, or extension for lessee:
  — For capital lease, make adjustment for difference between original and new present values, using the original interest rate.
  — For operating lease, continue to account for as a capital lease until end of its term, classify renewal or extension as operating lease.
- Termination of capital lease—lessee eliminates asset/liability and records gain/loss.
- Fair values, such as appraisals and estimated replacement costs, may be used to estimate fair value when determining lease classification related to part of a building when there are no sales of similar property.

Disclose for Lessee

- Gross asset.
- Minimum future lease payments.
- Total contingent rentals actually incurred for each period for which an income statement is presented.
- Minimum sublease income.

¶247

Sales Type Lease

- Dealer's or manufacturer's profit or loss results to lessor.

- Substantially all benefits and risks of ownership are transferred to the lessee.

- The minimum lease payments must be reasonably predictable of collection.

- No important uncertainties must exist regarding costs to be incurred by the lessor under the terms of the lease.

- Discount lessor's gross investment to present value with rate implicit in the lease. The sales price of the property is equal to the present value of MLP, which may or may not be different from the gross investment.

- Cost of property plus initial direct cost to consummate the sale (i.e., legal fees) less the present value of the unguaranteed residual value is charged to expenses against the sale.

- Difference in lessor's gross investment in the lease and present value of gross investments is unearned income, which is amortized to income over the life of the lease. Sales price may or may not be the present value of the gross investment.

Direct Financing Lease

- Same as sales type, but no dealer's or manufacturer's profit results.

- Lessor's gross investment in lease is sum of lessor's minimum lease payments less any executory costs and profit thereon to be paid to the lessor and any unguaranteed residual value accruing to the benefit of the lessor.

- Offset loan organization fees and direct loan origination costs with resulting amount deferred and recognized over the life of the loan as an adjustment to the yield on the loan.

- Unearned income is difference between lessor's gross investment and the cost of the leased property. This is amortized over the lease term by the interest method.

- The unearned income is recorded on balance sheet as deduction from gross investment, resulting in net investment in the lease. Any unamortized Initial Direct Costs would have to be considered when computing the net investment.

Disclosure for Lessor for Sales Type and Direct Financing

- Schedule of minimum lease payments for next 5 years.

- Schedule of components of net investment in lease:

  — Unearned income.

  — Contingent rentals.

  — Future minimum lease payments.

  — Executory costs.

  — Unguaranteed residual values accruing to the benefit of the lessor.

  — Allowance for uncollectables.

¶247

Disclose for Lessee for Operating Lease
- Minimum future rental payments.
- Minimum sublease income.
- Schedule of total rental expense.
- Description of lessee's leasing arrangements.

Operating Lease—Lessor
- Lessor's contingent rental income is accrued in the period in which it arises.
- Increasing rental payments—lessor amortizes the total rental income over the lease on a straight line basis.
- Lease incentives for lessor—recognize as a reduction of rental revenue on a straight line basis over the life of the lease.

Disclosure for Lessors on Operating Lease
- Schedule of property.
- Schedule of future minimum rentals for next five years.
- Amount of contingent rentals income in income.
- Description of lessor's leasing arrangements.

¶ 249 LONG-TERM CONSTRUCTION CONTRACTS
ARB 45

Percentage of Completion
- Revenues are recognized when the earnings process is complete and an exchange has taken place. The percentage of completion method is an exception to this principle.
- Purpose is to recognize income currently rather than irregularly as contracts are completed. This method recognizes income as costs are incurred on the contract.
- Disadvantage is its reliance on estimates of total costs.
- Estimated loss is recognized in current period. Any previous gross profit reported in prior years must be deducted from the loss.
- Method—Recognize income by determining the percent of estimated total income that incurred costs-to-date bear to total estimated costs.

Completed Contract
- Recognizes income only at substantial completion of the contract.
- Substantially complete means remaining costs are insignificant.
- Advantage is that there are no estimates to income.
- Disadvantage is that current performance is not reflected in income.
- Costs-billings of uncompleted contracts in excess of related billings-costs.
  - Excess of accumulated costs over related billings is shown on balance sheet as current asset.
  - Excess of accumulated billings over related costs are shown as current liability.

Construction in progress-B/S	XXX	
Cash or liability-B/S		XXX
Accounts receivable-B/S	XXX	
Advance billings-B/S		XXX
Cash-B/S	XXX	
Accounts receivable-B/S		XXX

The above continues until final year, where: gross profit = contract price – total costs

Advance billings-B/S	XXX	
Construction in progress-B/S		XXX
Realized gross profit (I/S)		XXX

¶ 251 MORTGAGE BANKING ACTIVITIES AND ACCOUNTING FOR MORTGAGE SERVICING
SFAS 65, SFAS 122, & SFAS 134

Mortgage banking industry: This pronouncement is very limited in scope and will have little meaning to those outside the industry. A mortgage banking institution may hold mortgage-backed securities or mortgage loans for sale or as a long-term investment. The appropriate accounting depends upon whether the loan will be sold or held.

Mortgage-backed securities should be categorized as trading securities and classified as current a ssets and carried at fair value if the securities: are held for sale and relate to the activities of the mortgage banking business (SFAS No. 115, Paragraph 128).

Mortgage loans that are for sale should be recorded using the lower of cost or market rule. Market value is determined by reference to the nature of the loan or security.

- Interest retained in mortgage-backed securities after securitization should be classified using the provisions of SFAS No. 115.

- When an entity enters into a commitment to sell the securities prior to or during the securitization, the retained securities should be classified as trading securities.

Financial Reporting and Disclosures

A mortgage banking entity is required to report mortgage loans held for sale in a separate category from those loans held as long-term investments. Disclose the method used to determine lower of cost or market. When amounts are capitalized in connection with rights to service loans, the following should be disclosed:

- Current period capitalization, along with the method and amount of amortization for the current period.

- Fair value of amounts capitalized, along with the assumptions and methods for computing fair value.

¶ 253 NON-MONETARY TRANSACTIONS
APB 29, SFAS No. 151 & FASB Interpretation 30

Non-Monetary Defined

- Business transactions involving the exchange or transfer of non-monetary assets or liabilities which are not fixed in terms of currency.
- A reciprocal transfer is considered an exchange only if the party transferring the nonmonetary assets has no continuing involvement in the asset.

Method

- Account for the transfer of the non-monetary asset or liability based on the fair value of whichever (item received or given up) is more clearly evident.
- If fair value is not determinable, use the recorded book values of the asset.
- An asset received in a nonmonetary exchange is reported at the recorded amount of the asset given up (instead of fair value), after reduction for any impairment in value of the asset surrendered when one or more of the following are met:
  — Fair value cannot be determined within reasonable limits.
  — Transaction is for the purpose of facilitation of sales to customers.
  — Transaction lacks commercial substance. The nonmonetary exchange has commercial substance when one of the following is achieved:
    - Future cash flows are anticipated to change significantly, or
    - The entity-specific value of the assets given up as compared to the assets received is significantly different.
- When determining if commercial substance is achieved, tax cash flows are not used in the determination if the cash flows arise exclusively as a result of the tax business purpose being used for achieving a specified result from financial reporting.
  — If transaction results in a loss, the entire loss on the exchange should be recognized.
  — On receiving monetary consideration, recognize realized gain to the extent that the monetary amount exceeds a proportionate share of the recorded amount of the asset relinquished.
  — On paying monetary consideration, record the cost of the nonmonetary asset received at the amount of the nonmonetary asset surrendered, plus the amount of the monetary consideration paid. Do not recognize gain on the exchange.
- If over 25% or more of the fair value of the exchange, then account for as a monetary transaction. All gain should then be recognized. (Source: EITF 86-29)

Formula for Recognition of Gains and Losses

- Gain/loss = fair market value – book value of asset surrendered.
- Recognized gain if the above conditions for reporting at book value are not met.
- If conditions for book value reporting are met, recognize gains as follows:
  — No boot = no gain recognized

— Boot given = no gain recognized

— Boot received

$$\text{Gain recognized} = \text{gain} \times \frac{\text{Cash received}}{\text{Cash received} + \text{fair market value of asset received}}$$

¶ 255 OFFSETTING OF AMOUNTS RELATED TO CERTAIN CONTRACTS AND OFFSETTING OF AMOUNTS RELATED TO CERTAIN REPURCHASE AND REVERSE REPURCHASE AGREEMENTS (SEE ¶ 211)
FASB Interpretation No. 39 & FASB Interpretation No. 41

This is commonly referred to as a right of setoff. A right of setoff exists when the debtor has the legal right to release or eliminate an obligation owed to a counterparty by offsetting that obligation with an obligation owed to the debtor by the same counterparty.

Assets and liabilities can be offset when four conditions are met.

- Two entities to the transaction each owe the other amounts that can be determined.
- The entity has the intent to offset assets and liabilities.
- The entity preparing the financial statements has the right to offset receivables against payables.
- The right of offset legally can be enforced.

If all of the preceding four conditions are met, the debtor can offset related assets and liabilities and report the net amount in the statement of financial position. However, if any one of the conditions is not met, the enterprise cannot offset assets and liabilities.

FASB Interpretation No. 41 modifies FASB Interpretation No. 39 and allows offsetting of receivables and payables in repurchase and reverse repurchase arrangements in specific situations. A repurchase arrangement is a sale of a security (collateralized borrowing) to another party with an agreement to buy back the security in the future. The arrangement will specify either a future date or specific repurchase price. The specified repurchase price is the payable to be recognized by the entity. A reverse repurchase agreement is the purchase of a security from another party with an agreement to sell the security back to the party in the future.

An entity may elect to offset the payable and receivable in repurchase and reverse repurchase arrangements when certain conditions are met.

First, the repurchase and reverse repurchase agreements must be with the same counterparty, and second, both agreements must have the same settlement date. Next, a master netting arrangement must be used for both agreements. The fourth condition states that a book entry system is used for the securities that support the two agreements. The next requirement, that a specified transfer system be used for settling both agreements, means that appropriate banking arrangements be available where only the net amount due is required as a cash settlement for transferred securities at the end of each day, assuming that the counterparties transfer securities, as required under the agreement. The last requirement states that the same account will be used by the entity to pay cash under the repurchase agreement and to receive cash under the reverse repurchase agreement. If all six requirements are met, the entity may elect, but is not required, to offset the payable under the repurchase agreement and the receivables under the reverse repurchase agreement. The method selected by the entity should be applied on a consistent basis.

¶ 257 PENSION PLANS
SFAS 87, SFAS 106, SFAS 112, SFAS 132 (Revised), SFAS 135, & SFAS 158

Overview

- Assets of a pension plan are usually kept in a trust account completely segregated from the firm's assets.

- Employer contributions are made and invested in bonds, stocks, real estate, etc.

- Pension plans that are not effectively restricted for the payment of pension benefits or segregated in a separate account are not considered pension plans under GAAP.

- SFAS No. 35 specifies the accounting and reporting requirements for preparation of pension plan financial statements. SFAS No. 75 deferred the application of SFAS No. 35 to pension plans of state and local governmental units. SFAS No. 135 rescinds the requirements of SFAS No. 75.

- SFAS No. 87, as amended, covers both defined contribution and defined benefit pension plans.

Defined Contribution Pension Plan

- Net periodic pension cost is the amount of contributions in an accounting period to the individual's account that performed services during the accounting period.

- Annual pension cost is generally determined as a percentage of annual employee salary.

- Employee future benefits from the plan are based on the contributions to the plan and earnings on the plan assets.

Defined Benefit Pension Plan

- Plan is based on a pension benefit formula determining the amount of benefit the employee will receive upon retirement.

- Actuarial assumptions are used to calculate the estimated cost of pension plan benefits.

- Each assumption must reflect the best estimate for that particular assumption.

- The following terms are important when accounting for defined benefit pension plans:

  — *Service cost*—present value on an actuarial basis of benefits provided to employees for services performed during a specific accounting period.

  — *Interest cost*—the increase in the projected benefit obligation from the passage of time. Interest cost is computed by applying the assumed discount rate used in the computation of present value of pension plan items to the beginning of period projected benefit obligation.

— *Projected benefit obligation*—present value on an actuarial basis of the total cost of all employee benefits as of a specific date. Includes vested and nonvested benefits and the impact of future salary levels, when appropriate.

— *Expected return*—the expected increase or decrease in the fair value of plan assets during an accounting period. Expected return is computed by applying the expected long-term rate of return on plan assets to the beginning of period market-related value of pension plan assets.

— *Market-related value of plan assets*—fair value of the plan assets or a computed amount for fair value that allows changes in fair value to be recognized over future years instead of the current year.

— *Fair value of plan assets*— the price received or paid on the date of measurement between participants in the market place when an asset is sold or a liability is transferred in an orderly transaction (the exit price) (see ¶ 295 and SFAS 157 for more details on fair value measurements).

— *Unrecognized prior service cost*—retroactive granting of pension benefits to employees as a result of a plan amendment or initiation of a new plan.

- Included in other comprehensive income.
- Amortized to pension cost over future accounting periods.

— *Unrecognized net gain/loss*—the amount of the actuarial gain or loss which is computed as the difference between the estimated and actual projected benefit obligation and the difference between the estimated and actual fair value of plan assets.

- Included in other comprehensive income.
- The beginning of year gain or loss in excess of 10 percent of the larger of the beginning of year projected benefit obligation or market-related value of plan assets is subject to amortization.
- Amortized excess gain or loss to pension cost over future accounting periods using the remaining service life of the active employee group.

— *Unrecognized net obligation or net asset at date of initial application of SFAS No. 87*—the amount of the net obligation or asset is computed at the date of transition to SFAS No. 87 as the difference between the projected benefit obligation and the fair value of plan assets adjusted for any existing balance sheet account.

- Net obligation is the excess of the projected obligation over the fair value of plan assets after any required balance sheet adjustment.
- Net asset is the excess of the fair value of plan assets over the projected benefit obligation after any required balance sheet adjustment.
- Included in other comprehensive income.
- Amortized to pension cost over future accounting periods using the remaining service life of the active employee group.
- If the remaining service life is less than 15 years, a 15-year time may be elected for the amortization.

— *Funded status of pension plan*—difference between the projected benefit obligation and the fair value of plan assets on a specific date.

— *Pension asset or liability*—represents the pension balance sheet account reported in company financial statements.

- Annual pension cost is composed of the following elements:

  — *Service cost*—added in the computation.

  — *Interest cost*—added in the computation.

  — *Expected return*—added in the computation if a gain and deducted if a loss.

  — *Amortization of unrecognized prior service cost*—added in the computation if an increase in the pension obligation or deducted if a decrease in the pension obligation.

  — *Amortization of unrecognized net gain or loss*—added in the computation if a loss and deducted if a gain.

  — *Amortization of unrecognized net obligation or net asset*—added in the computation if an obligation and deducted if a net asset.

- Pension journal entry

  — Debit pension expense for the amount of the annual pension cost computation.

  — Debit other comprehensive income as a reclassification entry for amortization of any unamortized items included in pension cost that were credits in accumulated other comprehensive income (such as unamortized actuarial gains).

  — Debit other comprehensive income for the addition of any new unamortized items that require a debit entry (such as the increase in an actuarial loss).

  — Credit other comprehensive income as a reclassification entry for amortization of any unamortized items included in pension cost that were debits in accumulated other comprehensive income (such as unamortized actuarial losses).

  — Credit other comprehensive income for the addition of any new unamortized items that require a credit entry (such as the increase in an actuarial gain).

  — Credit cash for contributions to the pension trust.

  — Credit or debit a pension asset or liability for the difference.

- Pension example—ABC Company had the following annual pension information: (1) an actuarial loss increased by $300 during the accounting period, (2) contributions to the pension trust were $400, and (3) pension cost was as follows:

Service cost	$800
Interest cost	600
Expected return on plan assets	(200)
Amortization of prior service cost	140
Amortization of net actuarial (gain)	(160)
Amortization of transitional obligation	40
Total pension cost	$1,220

¶257

Journal entry:

Pension expense	1,220	
Other comprehensive income—actuarial gain	160	
Other comprehensive income—prior service cost		140
Other comprehensive income—transitional obligation		40
Cash		400
Pension liability		800
Other comprehensive income—actuarial loss	300	
Pension liability		300

- Pension accounting changes required by SFAS No. 158.
  - Report a pension asset or liability for over funded and under funded pension plans.
    - Aggregate all over funded pension plans to determine amount of the pension asset. Pension asset is equal to the excess of the fair value of the pension assets over the projected benefit obligation, after adjustment for any balance sheet account.
    - Aggregate all under funded pension plans to determine amount of the pension liability. Pension liability is equal to the excess of the projected benefit obligation over the fair value of the plan assets, after adjustment for any balance sheet account.
  - Include any unamortized prior service cost, actuarial gains and losses, and transitional assets or obligations as part of accumulated other comprehensive income on the date of transition to SFAS No. 158.
  - Record as part of other comprehensive income any prior service cost and actuarial gains and losses generated during the accounting period and not used in the annual computation of pension cost.
  - Report any amortization of prior service cost, actuarial gains and losses, and transitional assets or obligations in other comprehensive income as a reclassification adjustment when the items have been included in accumulated other comprehensive income.
  - Deferred taxes should be computed where appropriate.
  - Classify pension assets and liabilities as current, long term, or a combination of current and long-term depending on the situation.
  - Measurement date for pension plans is the date of the statement of financial position with limited exceptions.
  - SFAS No. 158 provides guidance on selecting the assumed discount rate to use in the pension plan present value computations.

¶ 259 POSTRETIREMENT BENEFITS
SFAS 106, 112, 132 (revised), & 158

Postemployment and Postretirement Benefits Other Than Pensions

- Changes in the obligations for postretirement benefits and the value of plan assets are recognized systematically over future periods.

¶259

- The recognized consequences of events and transactions affecting a postretirement benefit plan are reported as a single amount in the employer's financial statements.

- Plan assets segregated and restricted for the payment of postretirement benefits offset the accumulated postretirement benefit obligations for the amounts in the financials.

- Postemployment benefits are benefits paid after employment and before retirement and include items such as health care, life insurance, worker compensation and disability payments.

  — Accrue a liability if the conditions for accrual under either SFAS Nos. 5 or 43 are met.

  — Expense in the period incurred if SFAS Nos. 5 or 43 are not met.

Accounting Requirements

- Postretirement benefits are a form of deferred compensation to be accounted for as part of the employee's total compensation package.

- A deferred compensation plan is one that establishes an amount of compensation to be paid in future periods.

- Employers should account for postretirement benefits on the accrual basis.

- The employer should use reasonable estimates.

- The plan should cover employees in general, rather than selected individuals.

- SFAS 106 states that an employer incurs a liability to be accounted for, if it promises to pay benefits.

- The employer has to make assumptions to account for the accrual amount regarding the time value of money, expected long-term rate of return on plan assets, and future compensation levels.

- After the postretirement benefits obligation is determined, an equal amount of that obligation is attributed to each year of service in the attribution period.

- SFAS No. 106, as amended, covers both defined contribution and defined benefit postretirement plans.

Defined Contribution Postretirement Plan

- Net periodic postretirement cost is the amount of contributions in an accounting period to the individual's account that performed services during the accounting period.

- Employee future benefits from the plan are based on the contributions to the plan and earnings on the plan assets.

Defined Benefit Postretirement Plan

- Plan is based on a postretirement benefit formula determining the amount of benefit the employee will receive upon retirement.

- Actuarial assumptions are used to calculate the estimated cost of the postretirement plan benefits.

- Each assumption must reflect the best estimate for that particular assumption.

- The following terms are important when accounting for defined benefit postretirement plans:

  — *Service cost*—present value on an actuarial basis of benefits provided to employees for services performed during a specific accounting period.

  — *Interest cost*—the increase in the accumulated benefit obligation from the passage of time. Interest cost is computed by applying the assumed discount rate used in the computation of present value of postretirement plan items to the beginning of period accumulated benefit obligation.

  — *Accumulated postretirement benefit obligation*—present value on an actuarial basis of the total cost of all employee benefits as of a specific date. The accumulated postretirement benefit obligation is a percentage of the expected postretirement benefit obligation.

  — *Expected return*—the expected increase or decrease in the fair value of plan assets during an accounting period. Expected return is computed by applying the expected long-term rate of return on plan assets to the beginning of period market-related value of pension plan assets.

  — *Market-related value of plan assets*—fair value of the plan assets or a computed amount for fair value that allows changes in fair value to be recognized over future years instead of the current year.

  — *Fair value of plan assets*— the price received or paid on the date of measurement between participants in the market place when an asset is sold or a liability is transferred in an orderly transaction (the exit price) (see ¶ 295 and SFAS 157 for more details on fair value measurements).

  — *Unrecognized prior service cost*—retroactive granting of postretirement benefits to employees as a result of a plan amendment or initiation of a new plan.
    - Included in other comprehensive income.
    - Amortized to postretirement cost over future accounting periods to full eligibility.

  — *Unrecognized net gain/loss*—the amount of the actuarial gain or loss which is computed as the difference between the estimated and actual postretirement accumulated benefit obligation and the difference between the estimated and actual fair value of plan assets.
    - Included in other comprehensive income.
    - The beginning of year gain or loss in excess of 10 percent of the larger of the beginning of year accumulated postretirement benefit obligation or market-related value of plan assets is subject to amortization.
    - Recognize immediately or amortize excess gain or loss to postretirement cost over future accounting periods using the remaining service years of the active employee group.

  — *Unrecognized net obligation or net asset at date of initial application of SFAS No. 106*—the amount of the net obligation or asset is computed at the date of transition to SFAS No. 106 as the difference between the accumulated postretirement benefit obligation and the fair value of plan assets adjusted for any existing balance sheet account.

¶259

- Net obligation is the excess of the accumulated postretirement benefit obligation over the fair value of plan assets after any required balance sheet adjustment.
- Net asset is the excess of the fair value of plan assets over the accumulated postretirement benefit obligation after any required balance sheet adjustment.
- Included in other comprehensive income.
- Recognize immediately or amortize to postretirement cost over future accounting periods using the remaining service life of the active employee group.
- If the remaining service life is less than 20 years, a 20-year time may be elected for the amortization.

— *Funded status of postretirement plan*—difference between the accumulated postretirement benefit obligation and the fair value of plan assets on a specific date.

— *Postretirement asset or liability*—represents the postretirement balance sheet account reported in company financial statements.

- Annual postretirement cost is composed of the following elements:

— *Service cost*—added in the computation.

— *Interest cost*—added in the computation.

— *Expected return*—added in the computation if a gain and deducted if a loss.

— *Amortization of unrecognized prior service cost*—added in the computation if an increase in the postretirement obligation or deducted if a decrease in the postretirement obligation.

— *Amortization of unrecognized net gain or loss*—added in the computation if a loss and deducted if a gain.

— *Amortization of unrecognized net obligation or net asset*—added in the computation if an obligation and deducted if a net asset.

- Postretirement journal entry

— Debit postretirement expense for the amount of the annual postretirement cost computation.

— Debit other comprehensive income as a reclassification entry for amortization of any unamortized items included in postretirement cost that were credits in accumulated other comprehensive income (such as unamortized actuarial gains).

— Debit other comprehensive income for the addition of any new unamortized items that require a debit entry (such as the increase in an actuarial loss).

— Credit other comprehensive income as a reclassification entry for amortization of any unamortized items included in postretirement cost that were debits in accumulated other comprehensive income (such as unamortized actuarial losses).

— Credit other comprehensive income for the addition of any new unamortized items that require a credit entry (such as the increase in an actuarial gain).

¶259

— Credit cash for contributions to the postretirement trust.

— Credit or debit a postretirement asset or liability for the difference.

- Postretirement example—XYZ Company had the following annual postretirement information: (1) prior service cost, which increased the accumulated postretirement obligation, increased by $200 during the accounting period, (2) contributions to the postretirement trust were $250, and (3) postretirement cost for the year were as follows:

Service cost	$500
Interest cost	300
Expected return on plan assets	(150)
Amortization of prior service cost	80
Amortization of net actuarial loss	100
Amortization of transitional obligation	30
Total postretirement cost	$860

Journal entry:

Postretirement expense	860	
Other comprehensive income—prior service cost		80
Other comprehensive income—actuarial loss		100
Other comprehensive income—transitional obligation		30
Cash		250
Postretirement liability		400
Other comprehensive income—prior service cost	200	
Postretirement liability		200

- Postretirement accounting changes required by SFAS No. 158.

— Report a postretirement asset or liability for over funded and under funded postretirement plans.

- Aggregate all over funded postretirement plans to determine amount of the postretirement asset. Postretirement asset is equal to the excess of the fair value of the postretirement asset over the accumulated postretirement benefit obligation, after adjustment for any balance sheet account.

- Aggregate all under funded postretirement plans to determine amount of the postretirement liability. Postretirement liability is equal to the excess of the accumulated postretirement benefit obligation over the fair value of the plan assets, after adjustment for any balance sheet account.

— Include any unamortized prior service cost, actuarial gains and losses, and transitional assets or obligations as part of accumulated other comprehensive income on the date of transition to SFAS No. 158.

— Record as part of other comprehensive income any prior service cost and actuarial gains and losses generated during the accounting period and not used in the annual computation of postretirement cost.

— Report any amortization of prior service cost, actuarial gains and losses, and transitional assets or obligations in other comprehensive income as a reclassification adjustment when the items previously have been included in accumulated other comprehensive income.

— Deferred taxes should be computed where appropriate.

— Classify postretirement assets and liabilities as current, long term, or a combination of current and long-term depending on the situation.

— Measurement date for postretirement plans is the date of the statement of financial position with limited exceptions.

— SFAS No. 158 provides guidance on selecting the assumed discount rate to use in the postretirement plan present value computations.

• Accounting for settling a postretirement obligation.

— The maximum gain or loss to be recognized in income is the unrecognized gain or loss plus any unrecognized transition asset.

• When entire obligation is settled:

— If a gain, the amount of gain first reduces any unrecognized transition obligation, then excess gain is recognized in income.

— If a loss, then recognize the full loss in income.

• When partial amount of obligation is settled:

— Recognize in income a pro rata portion of gain or loss as if the entire obligation were settled. The pro rata portion equals the percentage by which the partial settlement reduces the accumulated postretirement benefits obligation.

• Accounting for plan curtailment:

— A curtailment is an event that significantly changes the accrual amounts. For example, discontinuation of a segment of the employer's business.

• Gain or loss in curtailment:

— Employer recognizes as a loss the appropriate remaining balance amount of unrecognized prior service cost.

— Employer recognizes gain or loss from the change in the accumulated postretirement benefit obligation.

• Curtailment resulting from termination of employees:

— Loss consists of the portion of the remaining unrecognized prior service cost attributable to the previously estimated number of remaining future years of service of all terminated employees, plus

— The portion of the remaining unrecognized transition obligation attributable to the previously estimated number of remaining future years of service, but only of the terminated employees who were participants in the plan at the date of transition to SFAS 106.

• Curtailment resulting from terminating accrual of additional benefits for future services—the curtailment loss consists of the pro rata amount of the remaining unrecognized prior service cost, plus the pro rata amount of the remaining unrecognized transition obligation.

• Net gain is recognized in income when affected employees terminate.

- Net loss is recognized in income when it is probable that a curtailment will occur and the net effect is reasonably estimated.

Pensions and Other Postretirement Benefits—Employers' Disclosures

- SFAS No. 132 (Revised), as amended by SFAS 158, amends SFAS Nos. 87, 88, 106, and 132 and specifies the disclosure requirements for both pension and postretirement plans.
- SFAS No. 132 (Revised) suggests combined formats for presentation of pension and other postretirement benefits, but reported in separate columns.
- SFAS No. 132 (Revised) specifies disclosures for both public and non-public companies with reduced disclosures for non-public companies.
- The following general disclosures are required for public companies:
  - Amount of pension and postretirement cost divided into specified categories of costs.
  - Beginning and ending projected benefit obligation (for pensions) and accumulated benefit obligation (for postretirement) reconciled using specified pension or postretirement items.
  - Funded status of the pension and postretirement plan showing separately the amount of assets, current liabilities, and noncurrent liabilities recognized in the balance sheet.
  - Various rate information such as weighted average discount rates, long-term rate of return on assets, and compensation rates, where appropriate.
  - Pension and postretirement amounts reported in the income statements and balance sheets.
  - Beginning and ending fair value of plan assets reconciled showing separately specific items that cause the assets of pension and postretirement plans to change during the accounting period.
  - The accumulated benefit obligation for defined benefit pension plans.
  - Disclosures about plan assets including the following information:
    - The percentage of fair value held by each category of assets on the measurement date.
    - Investment policies and strategies described in narrative form.
    - Describe the basis, in narrative form, of determining the assumptions used in the long-term rate of return on plan assets.
    - Any other asset information that might be useful in understanding risk related to the assets and the expected long-term rate of return.
  - Benefits anticipated to be paid for each of the next five years and aggregate amount of benefits expected to be paid over the subsequent five years.
  - An estimate of the contributions to be paid over the next year.
  - For each income statement, separately disclose the following items included in other comprehensive income during the accounting period: increase or decrease in prior service cost and the net gain or loss.

— For each income statement, the amount of the reclassification adjustments related to the recognition of prior service cost, net gain or losses, and transitional assets or obligations.

— For each annual balance sheet presented, disclose separately the prior service cost, net gain or loss, and transitional asset or obligation included in accumulated other comprehensive income not included as a component or pension or postretirement cost.

— For the fiscal year that follows the most recent balance sheet presentation, disclose separately the prior service cost, net gain or loss, and transitional asset or obligation included in accumulated other comprehensive income that will be reported as a component of pension or postretirement cost over that next fiscal year.

— For the 12-month or operating cycle, whichever is longer, subsequent to the most recent financial statement date, report both the amount and timing of any plan assets anticipated to be returned to the entity.

— Assumptions used to determine the net benefit cost and benefit obligation.

— Next year's assumed health care cost trend rate, direction, and pattern of change in rate ultimate rate when such rate would be achieved and the impact of a one percentage point increase and decrease in such a rate.

— Specific employer and related party information.

— Alternative amortization methods, if any, used for prior service cost and unrecognized gains and losses.

— Substantive commitments, if any, used for determining the benefit obligation.

— Information about special and contractual termination benefits.

— Other relevant information about changes in obligations or plan assets not apparent in the required disclosures.

• The following general disclosures are required for non-public companies but in less detail than required for public companies:

— Amount of pension and postretirement cost.

— Fair value of plan assets, obligation balance and funded status.

— Amount of benefit payments and contributions by employers and participants.

— Various rate information such as weighted average discount rates, long-term rate of return on assets, and compensation rates, where appropriate.

— Pension and postretirement amounts reported in the income statements and balance sheets.

— Disclosures about plan assets including the following information:

  • The percentage of fair value held by each category of assets on the measurement date.

  • Investment policies and strategies described in narrative form.

  • Describe the basis, in narrative form, of determining the assumptions used in the long-term rate of return on plan assets.

¶259

- Any other asset information that might be useful in understanding risk related to the assets and the expected long-term rate of return.
— The accumulated benefit obligation for defined benefit pension plans.
— Benefits anticipated to be paid for each of the next five years and aggregate amount of benefits expected to be paid over the subsequent five years.
— An estimate of the contributions to be paid over the next year.
— For each income statement, separately disclose the following items included in other comprehensive income during the accounting period: increase or decrease in prior service cost and the net gain or loss.
— For each income statement, the amount of the reclassification adjustments related to the recognition of prior service cost, net gain or losses, and transitional assets or obligations.
— For each annual balance sheet presented, disclose separately the prior service cost, net gain or loss, and transitional asset or obligation included in accumulated other comprehensive income not included as a component or pension or postretirement cost.
— For the fiscal year that follows the most recent balance sheet presentation, disclose separately the prior service cost, net gain or loss, and transitional asset or obligation included in accumulated other comprehensive income that will be reported as a component of pension or postretirement cost over that next fiscal year.
— For the 12-month or operating cycle, whichever is longer, subsequent to the most recent financial statement date, report both the amount and timing of any plan assets anticipated to be returned to the entity.
— Next year's assumed health care cost trend rate, direction, and pattern of change in rate ultimate rate when such rate would be achieved.
— Specific employer and related party information.
— Assumptions used to determine the net benefit cost and benefit obligation.
— Nature and impact of nonroutine situations considered significant in nature, such as curtailments, amendments, and settlements.
- The following disclosures are required for defined contribution plans:
— Amount of cost reported for pension plans and for postretirement plans reported separately from defined benefit information.
— Describe the nature and impact of significant changes, if any, impacting comparability.
- The following disclosures are required for multiemployer plans:
— Amount of contributions to such plans.
— Describe the nature and impact of significant changes, if any, impacting comparability.

¶ 261 PRODUCT FINANCING ARRANGEMENTS
SFAS 49

- This is an arrangement where an enterprise sells and agrees to repurchase inventory at a purchase price equal to the original sale price plus carrying and financing cost. The substance of a product financing arrangement is that of a financing arrangement and not a sale.

- Accounting for product financing arrangements:
  - No sale is recorded and the product remains an asset.
  - A liability is recorded in the amount of proceeds received from the other entity.
  - If another entity buys a product for a sponsor's benefit and the sponsor agrees to buy the product in a related arrangement back from the other entity, an asset and the related liability are recorded by the sponsor at the time the other entity acquires the product.
  - The difference between the regular product cost the sponsor would have paid if there was no product financing arrangement and the cost the sponsor actually pays under the terms of the agreement is accounted for by the sponsor as financing and holding costs.

¶ 263 PROPERTY TAXES—REAL
ARB 43, Chapter 10A

- Legal liability accrues on the date the taxes are assessed.
- If exact amount is unknown, a reasonable estimate must be made.
- Classify as a current liability.
- Apply monthly accruals over the fiscal period.
- When prior period exact amount is known, make adjustment in current income.

¶ 265 QUASI-REORGANIZATIONS
ARB 43 & 46

- A corporate readjustment that eliminates the deficit in retained earnings.
- A quasi-reorganization is an acceptable alternative to legal bankruptcy.
- A new basis of accountability is established.
- Assets are adjusted up or down to their fair values.
- Stockholder's equity is adjusted so that retained earnings have a zero balance.
  - Retained earnings deficit is charged either to paid in capital or
  - To donated capital contributed.
  - A business might reduce its stock par value of the existing capital stock and transfer the excess to PIC (Paid in Capital), which makes available more equity to apply to retained earnings.
- A new retained earnings account is established and dated for 10 years.

¶ 266 REAL ESTATE TIME-SHARING
SFAS 66, 152 & Interpretation No. 43

- Transactions classified as real estate time-sharing are accounted for as nonretail land sales.
- SFAS No. 66 covers the accounting requirements for nonretail land sales.

¶266

- SFAS No. 66 covers sales of real estate with integral equipment or property improvements.
- Nonretail sale is accounting for at the time of sale using the full accrual method when the following are met:
  — Profit can be determined.
  — The earnings process is nearly complete.
- The full accrual method should be applied when all of the following are met:
  — The sale has been completed.
  — Any initial or continuing investment by the buyer is adequate to indicate a commitment by the buyer to pay for the nonretail property.
  — The receivable of the seller is not subject to subordination in the future.
  — The normal risks and rewards of ownership have been transferred to the buyer and there is no continuing involvement in the property by the seller.
- When the sale of nonretail real estate does not meet the requirements for recognition of sales on the full accrual basis, another method specified by SFAS No. 66 should be used depending on the circumstances of the transaction.
- AICPA SOP 04-2 provides additional guidelines when accounting for real-estate timing sharing transactions.

¶ 269 RELATED PARTY TRANSACTIONS
SFAS 57

Overview

- Related party is one who can exercise significant control over the management or operating policies of the other party.
- Significant related party transactions should be disclosed.
  — The detail disclosed must be sufficient for the user of the financials to be able to understand the related party transactions.
- Disclose the nature of the material related party relationship.
  — Description.
  — Effects of any change in terms.
  — Effects on operating results that would differ if there were no control relationship.
  — Receivables or payables to related parties.

¶ 271 RESEARCH AND DEVELOPMENT
SFAS 2, 68 & 86, FASB Interpretation 4 & 6

Research and Development Rules

- Research is planned effort to discover new information.
- Development is the method of creating or improving the product.
  — Does not include normal improvements in existing operations.
  — Does not include market research.

— Does not include general and administrative expenses not directly related to R & D activities.

- R & D activities are expensed when incurred.

— This includes General & Administrative directly related to R & D.

- Machinery, equipment and facilities which have alternate future uses are capitalized and depreciated.

- Disclose the amount of R & D charged to expense for the period.

- Research and development arrangements under SFAS No. 68 may be accounted for as a borrowing when the arrangement requires the repayment of funds advanced to the entity doing the research. If a liability is recorded for the funds advanced, research and development expense should be recorded as incurred.

Computer Software

- SFAS 86 covers software purchased or developed to be sold or marketed by the enterprise.

- SFAS 86 does not cover software produced under a contractual arrangement or created for internal use.

- Treat all costs establishing the technological feasibility as R & D costs and expense when incurred.

- After technological feasibility has been established, all computer costs should be capitalized and then amortized.

— Capitalization of computer software costs shall be discontinued when the computer software is available to be sold or marketed.

Technological Feasibility

- Is established when all activities have been completed that substantiate that the computer software meets the design specifications.

- Completes the design work.

- Successfully tests the model.

Disclosure

- Disclose the amount of unamortized computer software costs included in each balance sheet date.

- Disclose amount expended.

¶ 273 RESULTS OF OPERATIONS
APB 9 & 30, SFAS 130 & 144

- GAAP requires the presentation of income using the all-inclusive concept.

— All items, except dividends, prior period adjustments, and capital transactions, should be included in computing net income if it affects net increases in owner's equity.

— Excluded from net income are certain foreign currency adjustments and changes in the value of equity and debt instruments.

— Investment companies, insurance companies and certain nonprofit companies need not comply with APB 9.

- Extraordinary items are disclosed separately in the income statement, net of any related tax effect.

  Examples of extraordinary items:

  — Gains on restructuring payables regarding troubled debt restructurings.

  — Most expropriations of property.

  — Most casualty gains or losses.

  — Gains or losses on debt extinguishments.

- Discontinued operations is disclosed separately.

  — Only a component of an enterprise with operations and cash flows distinguished both operatically and financially from the cash flows and operations of the rest of the entity can be considered a discontinued operation.

  — The disposition or expected disposition of a component is treated as a discontinued operations when: (1) cash flows and operations have been or will be eliminated from the continuing operations of the entire entity as a result of the transaction, and (2) there will be no significant continuing involvement in the component by the enterprise.

  — Include the results of operations and any gain or loss on the disposition in a separate section of the income statement in the accounting period that the disposition occurs and is expected to occur for the current period and all prior periods presented, net of tax.

  — The gain or loss expected on the disposition must either be reported on the face of the income statement or in related footnotes.

  — Component asset and liabilities cannot be offset but should be separately reported by major class either on the face of the statements or in related footnotes.

  — Disclosures should include description of the circumstances and facts that lead to the anticipated disposal, the anticipated manner and timing of the disposition, the carrying amounts of assets and liabilities of the disposition by major class, if not presented separately on the face of the financial statements, the loss or gain reported for the write down to fair value or recovery of losses computed using the provisions of Paragraph 37 of Statement No. 144, and the location of the gain or loss on the income statement if not separately reported on the face of the statement, amount of revenue and pretax profit reported in discontinued operations, if appropriate, and the segment where the assets and liabilities are reported in accordance with SFAS No. 131, if appropriate.

- Prior period adjustments:

  — The correction of an error in a prior period.

- Unusual or infrequent items:

  — A material item, not considered extraordinary, but separately reported as a component of continuing operations.

- Interim period adjustments:

  — Any adjustments of prior periods are made to the first interim period of the current year.

  — Adjustments to other periods are made to the interim period affected.

¶273

Net Income Presentation per APB 30

Income (loss) from continuing operations before provision for federal taxes	$ XXX
Provision for federal taxes	–XXX
Income (loss) from continuing operations	XXX

Discontinued Operations:

Loss from operations of discontinued Component A (including loss on disposal of $XXX)	$(XXX)
Income tax benefit	XX
Loss on discontinued operations	$(XXX)
Net income before extraordinary items (net of tax of $____)	XXX
Extraordinary items (net of taxes of $____)	XXX
Net Income	$XXX

SFAS-130 Reporting Comprehensive Income

- SFAS-130 requires the presentation of comprehensive income and its components in the financial statements and applies to all entities that provide a complete set of financials. It does not apply to Not-for-Profit entities that must follow SFAS 117.
- Comprehensive income includes all forms of income. Other comprehensive income includes revenues, expenses, gains, losses, etc. that are in comprehensive income but not in net income according to GAAP. Detailed information should be provided. In other words, after net income is computed, present other comprehensive income items such as unrealized holding gains, foreign currency translations, etc.
- Display formats of Financial Income statement.
  - Display in a traditional Income statement with the elements of other comprehensive income extending the statement.
  - Display in a traditional Income statement. Display a second Income statement that begins with net income and includes the elements of other comprehensive income.
  - Display in another financial statement such as the statement of equity.
- Equity Section of Statement of Financial Position.

Net income is closed to retained earnings. Other comprehensive income is similarly closed to a separate account titled Accumulated Other Comprehensive Income. Disclosure of the details is made on the face of the financial statement.

¶ 275 REVENUE RECOGNITION
SFAS 48

Recognized

- Revenue is recognized when the earnings process is complete and an exchange has taken place.
  - The earnings process is not complete until collection of the sales price is reasonably assured.

Revenue Recognition if Right of Return Exists

If all of the following conditions exist, revenue shall be recognized on sales for which a right of return exists:

- The price is determinable.
- The seller has received full payment, or the buyer's indebtedness is not contingent on the resale of the merchandise.
- Physical destruction of the merchandise would not change the buyer's obligation to the seller.
- No obligations exist for the seller to help the buyer resell the merchandise.
- The buyer is real.
- A reasonable estimate can be made of the amount of future returns.
- If one or more of the conditions are not met, revenue cannot be recognized until the right of return privilege has substantially expired. Seller should do one of the following:
  - Refrain for now from recording transaction of sale on the books.
  - Record as debt to deferred accounts receivable and a credit to deferred revenue.
  - Treat sale as a consignment.

¶ 277 SEGMENT REPORTING
SFAS 131

SFAS-131 Disclosures About Segments of an Enterprise and Related Information

- SFAS-131 replaces SFAS 14, 18, 21, 24 & 30 for financials whose fiscal years begin after 12/15/97. It does not apply to nonpublic business enterprises, not-for-profit enterprises, or parent-subsidiary situations. Operating segments are components of the business that has revenues and expenses, whose operation results can be segmented and reviewed by chief decision makers and for which discrete financial information is available.
- Generally, information provided is a disaggregation of the entity's consolidated financial statements.
- A reportable segment is one where one of the following is net:
  - Its revenue is 10% or more of all the enterprise's industry segments.
  - Its operating profit or loss is 10% or greater of the total of all the enterprise's industry segments that had operating profits and the total of all the enterprise's industry segments that had operating losses.
  - Its assets are 10% or more of the company's combined assets.
  - Quantitative criterion is that the identifiable segment must constitute at least 75% of the total consolidated revenue.
  - Also have a Number 10 test.

- Generally the segment should continue to be presented to provide for comparablility between years. The entire enterprise should provide information on its products, major customers, and geographical areas.
  — Products. Show Revenues from external customers for each product.
  — Geographical Area. Show revenues attributable to the company's country, all foreign countries, and individual foreign countries if material in amount.
  — Major Customers. Revenues from a single customer that accounts for 10% or more in revenue.
- Disclosure of segment information covers:
  — Segment profit or loss and assets.
  — Reconciliation of segment information to enterprise totals.
  — Interim period information.
  — General information.
- General Information:
  — Definition regarding types of products or services used for the basis for revenues from each segment. Factors used to identify the reportable segments.
- Segment profit or loss and assets.
  The following is required for each segment:
  — Interest revenue, interest expense, depreciation, extraordinary items, revenues from customers, revenues from other operating segments, income tax consequences, equity method income recognized, unusual items, and other significant non-cash items (Profit and loss elements depend on what profit and loss items are used in the assessment process).
- Reconciliation of segment information to enterprise totals.
  — In reconciling the segments to the company totals, all significant items must be separately identified.
- Interim period information:
  — Provide abbreviated segment information in interim financials. Disclose revenue from external customers and intersegmental. Disclose segment profit or loss. Disclose any material changes. Disclose reconciliation to company total.

¶ 279 STOCKHOLDER'S EQUITY
ARB 43 Chap IA, Chap IB, Chap 7B, APB 6, 10 & 12 & SFAS 129

Composition of Stockholders Equity

- Legal capital:
  — Defined by state law.
  — The amount of capital that must be retained by a corporation for the protection of its creditors.
  — Disclose changes in capital stock, paid in capital, retained earnings and treasury stock.

— Disclose capital stock by class, number of shares authorized, issued, and outstanding, stock option information, and any unused voting rights.

— Disclose appropriated and unappropriated retained earnings.

- Paid in capital:

  — Stockholder's equity that is not classified as legal capital, minority interests or retained earnings.

  — May result from excess of par on capital stock, donated assets, capital created by quasi-reorganization, and sale of treasury stock.

- Minority interests:

  — Under the parent company theory, minority interests are not considered a part of stockholder's equity and are disclosed on the consolidated balance sheet between the liability and stockholder's equity section.

- Retained earnings:

  — Should be disclosed by appropriated and unappropriated amounts.

- Treasury stock:

  — Stock which is reacquired by the company.

  — Treasury stock is similar to authorized but unissued capital stock.

  — Treasury stock should not be classified as an asset.

- Cost method:

  — Each acquisition of stock is accounted for at cost.

  — Upon resale, the initial cost is credited, with difference to paid in capital.

- Equity or par value method—The treasury stock is debited only for the par value, with difference to paid in capital.

SFAS 129 Disclosure of Information about Capital Structure

- SFAS 129 applies to all entities. The disclosure requirements pertain to securities, liquidation preference of preferred stock, and redeemable stock.

- Redeemable Stock:

  — For 5 years after the latest Balance Sheet date, the firm must disclose the amount of redemption requirements for all issues of stock where the redemption price and dates are fixed.

- Information about Securities:

  — Information about rights and privileges of outstanding securities must be provided in the financial statements. Examples are: The number of shares issued upon conversion, participating rights, call prices and dates, voting rights, dividend and liquidation preferences, etc.

- Liquidation Preference of Preferred Stock:

  — SFAS 129 requires the disclosure regarding the preference in involuntary liquidation that is in excess of the security's par value. It should be presented as an aggregate amount in the equity section and not on a per-share basis.

¶279

¶ 283 SHARE-BASED PAYMENTS
SFAS 123 (Revised)

SFAS No. 123 (Revised) supersedes SFAS No. 123 and APB Opinion No. 25 and amends or supersedes other standards related to stock compensation plans. SFAS No. 123 specifies the accounting and reporting requirements for share-based payments including share-based payments to both employees and nonemployees. The statement requires share-based payments to be measured at fair value. Compensation expense from share-based arrangements with employees is recognized over the requisite service period.

.01 Share-Based Payments Provided to Nonemployees

- Goods or services received by issuing share-based payments are reported when the goods or services are received.
- A liability or equity should be increased for the share-based payment.
- The related costs should be reported when the services are consumed or when the goods are disposed of or consumed.
- The share-based payments should be reported at the fair value of the goods or services received or the fair value of the share-based payment, whichever is more clearly determinable.
- SFAS No. 123 (Revised) does not provide guidance as to what measurement date to use when determining fair value, but suggests using the provisions of EITF No. 96-18 to determine the date to use for fair value determination.

.02 Share-Based Payments Provided to Employees

- A share purchase plan meeting the following conditions is considered a non-compensatory stock plan and no compensation expense is reported.
  — One of the following conditions is met:
    - The terms of the agreement are equivalent to the terms available for all stock holders of the same class of stock.
    - The discount allowed on the purchase is 5 percent or less of the market price of the stock.
  — Only limited employment qualification are required to participate in the plan on an equitable basis.
  — There are no option features associated with the plan other than as noted below:
    - A short period of time (not greater than 31 days) is allowed to enroll in the plan subsequent to the fixed date of the plan.
    - Price of the stock is based on the market price of the stock on the date of purchase.
    - Employees may cancel prior to purchase date and receive a refund.
- Share-based transactions with employees that are compensation transactions are accounted for as follows:
  — Cost of services measured at the fair value of the equity instrument given or the liabilities settled.

- — Amount related to employee service is net of the amount that the employee pays.
- — Example: The amount related to employee service is $60 when an employee pays $10 at the date of grant for an option with a fair value at the date of grant of $70.
- Share-based awards to employees when the award is classified as equity.
  - — Estimate fair value at the date of grant of equity instruments that are to be issued when the required service has been provided and any other required conditions are satisfied.
  - — Estimate is based on share price and other factors such as expected volatility of the stock and transferability of the share-based awards.
    - The market price of options with the same or similar terms should be used to measure fair value of equity share options or similar instruments, if available.
    - If an observable market price of similar options is not available, fair value should be computed using valuation techniques, such as option pricing models.
    - Historical volatility of an acceptable industry index should be used to estimate fair value when fair value cannot be determined.
  - — Compensation cost (fair value) of the share-based awards is amortized over the required service.
  - — The service period may be stated or implied in the agreement.
- Share-based awards to employees when the award is classified as a liability.
  - — Share-based awards classified as liabilities should be measured using the same procedures discussed above for equity awards.
  - — Measurement date for liability awards is the settlement date.
  - — Liability awards requires initial measurement at the date of grant and remeasurement at each reporting date until settlement.
  - — Compensation cost each accounting period reflects the change in the fair value of the instrument.
- Disclosures for share-based awards.
  - — Nature and terms of the arrangement and the impact on shareholders.
  - — Impact of compensation cost on the income statement.
  - — Method used to estimate the fair value of equity instruments provided or the goods or services received.
  - — The cash flow impact from share-based payment arrangements.

¶ 285 TROUBLED DEBT RESTRUCTURING
SFAS 15, 114 & 118

Defined

- Troubled debt restructuring is where a creditor allows the debtor certain concessions. Examples are:

¶285

— Modification of payment terms of stated interest, maturity, reduction of face amount, or accrued interest.

— Creditor receives an equity interest in the debtor.

— Creditor accepts other assets as payment, or a third party receivable as payment.

- Early extinguishment of debt arising from troubled debt restructuring does not include:

— Employment-related agreements.

— A debtor's failure to pay accounts payable or collect accounts receivable that do not involve a restructure agreement.

— Changes in lease agreements.

Types of Restructuring

- Transfer of assets in full settlement.
- Modification of terms of the debt.
- Granting equity interest in full settlement.
- Partial settlement and modification of terms.

Transfer of Assets

- Debtor recognizes gain in the excess of the debt over the fair value of the asset.
- Gain/loss is recognized in net income of current period. Gain on restructuring is an extraordinary item for the debtor.
- Fair value determined using SFAS No. 157.

Modification of Terms

- If new total future payments are less than the carrying amount of the debt, the carrying amount should be reduced with the difference recognized as a gain by the debtor.
- Any time future payments might exceed the carrying amount, the debtor recognizes no gain.

Transfer of Equity Interest

- Differences between fair value of equity interest and amount of liability is gain/loss.
- Gain/loss is included in net income of current period.
- Gain is extraordinary item for the debtor and loss is part of income from continuing operations for the creditor.

Disclosure

- Description of terms of each restructuring.
- Gain and related tax effects.
- Gain/loss on asset transfer.
- Per share data on gain or restructuring.

Creditor's Accounting on Debt Restructure

- Receipt of equity or assets as payment:

— Record at fair value.

— Excess of the receivable over the fair value of the asset or equity received is recognized as a loss.

- Modification of terms:

  — Account for prospectively.

  — SFAS 114 requires that the present value of the future cash receipts be computed and compared to the receivable. If the present value of cash is less than the receivable, recognize impairment by adjusting or establishing an allowance account.

Creditor Disclosure

- Receivable amount.
- Interest that would have been earned if not restructured.
- Interest income included in net income on restructured receivables and policy for income recognition.
- Selected information about allowance for losses.
- Obligations, if any, to lend money to debtors when restructuring is a modification of terms.

¶ 289 UNCONDITIONAL PURCHASE OBLIGATIONS
SFAS 47

- An unconditional purchase obligation is when one party is required to pay for a future delivery of goods or services at a specified price.

  — SFAS 47 is primarily directed to take-or-pay contracts where a buyer agrees to pay certain periodic amounts for certain services or products (This could also be Through-Put contracts).

- Disclosure of unrecorded unconditional purchase obligations

  — Description and nature of contract

  — SFAS 47 encourages the disclosure of the present value of the total determinable amount for each of the succeeding five years.

  — Description of any variable components

  — The amounts actually purchased as reflected in the income statement

  — Fixed part for the current year and each of the next five years

¶ 290 ASSET RETIREMENT OBLIGATIONS AND EXIT ACTIVITY COST
SFAS No. 143 & 146 and FASB Interpretation No. 47

Accounting For Asset Retirement Obligations

- An asset retirement obligation is reported for costs related to the retirement of long-lived assets.
- A conditional asset retirement obligation is an asset retirement obligation where the timing and/or method of settlement are contingent on some future event that the company may or may not control.

- An asset retirement liability is reported for an amount equal to the fair value of the liability in the accounting period that the liability is incurred.

- An asset retirement obligation should be reported in the accounting period that sufficient information is available to estimate the liability when sufficient information is unavailable in the accounting period that the liability is incurred.

- A company should report a liability for a conditional asset retirement obligation when the fair value of the liability can be estimated.

- Fair value of the asset retirement obligation should be determined using SFAS No. 143, as amended by SFAS No. 157.

- The related long-lived asset is increased by the amount reported for the liability.

- The asset retirement liability is increased each accounting period for the passage of time (accretion).

- The increase in the liability is computed using the interest method and the increase is charged to accretion expense.

- The increase in the long-lived asset is depreciated over the useful life of the increase.

Disclosures

- Description of the asset retirement obligation and the related long-lived asset.

- Fair value of legally restricted assets used for the purpose of settling obligations related to asset retirements.

- Reconcile beginning and ending balances of the asset retirement obligation when significant changes occur in one or more of the following items: accretion expense, settlement of liabilities, liabilities incurred, and estimated cash flow revisions.

- The fact and reasons that fair value could not be reasonable estimated when fair value is not reported for asset retirement obligations.

Accounting for Exit or Disposal Activity Cost

- Includes costs related to an exit activity such as termination benefits, contract termination costs other than capital leases, facility consolidation, or employee relocation costs.

- Does not apply to situations under Statement No. 143.

- Report a liability at fair value in the accounting period when the liability is incurred, except one-time termination benefits incurred over time.

- A liability is assumed to be incurred in the accounting period when the definition of a liability has been met.

- Costs related to exit or disposal activities are reported in the income statement as a component of income from continuing operations before tax, if the activity does not relate to a discontinued operation.

- When the heading "income from operations" is reported, exit costs should be included in such headings.

- Exit costs related to discontinued operations are reported as part of the discontinued operation.

Disclosures For Exit Activity

- The exit or disposal activity should be described.
- Report the following for each major type of exit cost.
  — The amount incurred in the current accounting period, amount anticipated to be incurred, and cumulative amount incurred to date.
  — Reconcile beginning and ending exit liability balances and report the following separately: (1) changes in costs incurred and charged to expense, (2) costs paid or settled, and (3) any liability adjustment with explanation.
- Report line item in income statement where the exit costs are reported.
- Report the fact and reasons why fair value is not reported when an exit liability is not reported because fair value cannot be determined.
- Report the following for each reportable segment: (1) total costs expected to be incurred, (2) amount incurred in current accounting period, (3) cumulative cost to date, and (4) any liability adjustment with explanation.

¶ 295 FAIR VALUE ACCOUNTING
SFAS 157

Application of SFAS 157

- Provides a fair value definition.
- Specifies how fair value should be measured.
- Expands fair value disclosures.
- Applies to fair value requirements of other standards, unless exempt.

Fair Value Measurements (Paragraphs 5-10)

- Fair value is the price received or paid on the date of measurement between participants in the market place when an asset is sold or a liability is transferred in an orderly transaction (the exit price).
  — Fair value is based on the specific attributes of the asset or liability such as condition, location, and restrictions.
  — Fair value is impacted by whether the asset or liability is an individual asset (standalone) or liability or a group of assets or liabilities and this determines its unit of account (what is being measured).
  — An orderly transaction assumes sufficient exposure to the market prior to the date of measurement to allow for adequate marketing of the asset or liability (not a forced liquidation).
  — Fair value is determined assuming that the asset is sold or liability is transferred in the principal market, or if the principal market is unavailable, the most advantageous market.
    • Principal market is the market with the greatest activity and most volume.
    • Most advantageous market is one in which the price for the asset is maximized and the amount to transfer the liability is minimized.
    • Price in the principal market excludes transactions costs, except for costs to transport the asset or liability to the principal market.

— Participants in the market are the sellers and buyers in the principal or most advantageous market meeting the following conditions:

- Parties unrelated to the reporting entity.
- Parties are knowledgeable about the transaction and the asset or liability.
- Willing and able to transact for the asset or liability.

Application of Fair Value Measurement to Assets and Liabilities (Paragraphs 12–17)

- Fair value assumes the highest and best use of the asset (in-use or in-exchange).
  - In-use of the asset should be used if the use of the asset provides the maximum benefit. Fair value is determined as the price that would be received assuming that the asset is used in connection with the other existing assets of the reporting entity.
  - In-exchange use of the asset assumes that the asset provides the maximum benefit as an individual asset (standalone). Fair value is the price that would be received by the seller from the sale of the asset by itself.
- Fair value for the transfer of a liability assumes a transfer of the liability on the date of measurement, and risk related to nonperformance and liability to the counterparty does not change as a result of the transfer. Nonperformance risk, which includes credit risk, is the risk related to failure to fulfill the obligation.
- When an asset or liability is initially acquired or assumed, the entry price (price paid to acquire the asset or assume the liability) and the exit price are generally the same and that price represents the fair value of the asset or liability. However, a reporting entity should be aware that in some cases, at initial acquisition, the entry price and exit price may be different, and in such situations, the entry price does not represent fair value.

Techniques Used to Measure Fair Value (Paragraphs 18–21)

- Techniques used to measure fair value:
  - *Market approach*—uses market transactions of identical or comparable assets or liabilities to compute fair value.
  - *Income approach*—uses present value of future amounts, such as cash flow or earnings, to compute fair value, such as present value methods, option pricing models, or excess earnings models.
  - *Cost approach*—uses a current replacement cost concept based on service capacity to compute fair value.
- Either single or multiple valuation techniques can be used depending on the situation.
- Consistently apply the valuation techniques, and any changes in the methods should be accounted for as a change in estimate using the provisions of SFAS No. 154.
- When measuring fair value, observable inputs or unobservable inputs may be used. However, use of observable inputs should be maximized, and use of unobservable inputs should be minimized. Observable inputs use assumptions

¶295

independent of the reporting entity, and unobservable inputs are assumptions developed by the reporting entity.

Hierarchy for Fair Value (Paragraphs 22–31)

- When measuring fair value, the reporting entity must prioritize inputs used in the valuation techniques into the following three categories:

  — *Level 1 inputs (highest priority inputs)*—quoted market prices found in active markets for assets and liabilities that are identical and that are available on the measurement date. Active markets are markets with transactions that have sufficient volume and frequency to provide proper pricing information.

  — *Level 2 inputs*—direct or indirect observable inputs, excluding quoted market prices. Observable inputs should be for the full term of the contract for contractual assets and liabilities.

  — *Level 3 inputs (lowest priority inputs)*—unobservable inputs are used to measure fair value. Should be used when observable inputs are unavailable.

Disclosure Requirements (Paragraphs 32–35)

- Separately disclose at each interim and annual accounting period the following items for each major category of assets and liabilities in which fair value is measured on a recurring basis (the use of the word *earnings* or *income statement* in the following disclosures also refers to similar measurements or statements such as changes in net assets and statement of activities).

  — Measurements of fair value on the date of the financial statements (reporting date).

  — The level, separately reported, within the fair value hierarchy (Level 1, Level 2, or Level 3) used in the measurement process.

  — When Level 3 inputs are used in the measurement process, reconcile the beginning and ending balance of fair value and separately report the following:

    - Total realized and unrealized gains and losses, segregation of gains and losses reported in the income statement, and the location of the gains and losses in the income statement.

    - Sales, purchases, settlements, and issuances reported on a net basis.

    - Level 3 transfers (both in and out).

  — Unrealized gains and losses reported in the income statement related to assets and liabilities still held by the entity on the financial statement date, and location of such gains and losses in the income statement.

  — Valuation methods used and any changes in valuation methods used to determine fair value for annual accounting periods.

- Separately disclose at each interim and annual accounting period the following items for each major category of assets and liabilities in which fair value is measured on a nonrecurring basis (the use of the word *earnings* or *income statement* in the following disclosures also refers to similar measurements or statements such as changes in net assets and statement of activities).

— Measurements of fair value during the accounting period and the reasons the measurements were made.

— The level, separately reported, within the fair value hierarchy (Level 1, Level 2, or Level 3) used in the measurement process.

— When Level 3 inputs are used in the measurement process, describe the inputs and information used for the input development.

— Valuation methods used and any changes in valuation methods used to determine fair value for annual accounting periods, and discuss any changes made in valuation methods for prior accounting periods used in the measurement of assets and liabilities that are similar in nature.

- A tabular format should be used when disclosing quantitative information.

- The FASB encourages all entities to report fair value disclosures required by SFAS No. 157 with fair value disclosures of other accounting standards.

Chapter 3
Business Entities

Buying and Selling a Business . . . . ¶ 301
Business Entities Selection . . . . ¶ 303-317

BUYING AND SELLING A BUSINESS
¶ 301 BUYING-SELLING BUSINESS

Preparations
- Keep accurate financial statements.
- Have three to five years' worth of business valuations performed by professional outside consultants.
- Provide audited or reviewed financial statements for three to five years before a contemplated sale.
- Prepare a sales strategy.
- Choose a professional business broker.
- Prepare a list of likely buyers from personal contacts such as customers, suppliers, and competitors.
- Prepare realistic sales and earnings projections.
- Be flexible when discussing financing terms.

Financing Considerations
- Purpose of the loan.
- Type of capital sought.
- Total amount required.
- Estimated capital needed to operate until business generates sufficient cash—estimated time frame for this.
- Principal sources of available capital.
- Estimated reserve funds needed for unexpected expenses.
- Estimated funds for shortfall.
- Amount down.
- The term.
- Annual interest rate.
- Periodic payment amount.
- Frequency of payment.

Stock vs. Asset Purchase

In a Stock Purchase
- The new owners step into the shoes of the previous owners.
- The bases of the assets and the liabilities remain the same.
- The new owners just continue the existing corporation.
- The new owners inherit any contingent liabilities.

In an Asset Purchase

- The original business is discontinued.
- A new business is formed.
- The buyer can choose which assets to purchase.
- The business's contingent liabilities don't carry forward to the new owner.
- The assets typically get a step-up in basis in the hands of the new buyer.
- In the purchase of a business, for asset acquisitions occurring after January 5, 2000, the allocation must be made among the following assets in proportion to (but not more than) their fair market value on the purchase date in the following order:
    - 1) Certificates of deposit, U.S. Government securities, foreign currency, and actively traded personal property, including stock and securities.
    - 2) Accounts receivable, mortgages, and credit card receivables that arose in the ordinary course of business.
    - 3) Property of a kind that would properly be included in inventory if on hand at the end of the tax year and properly held by the taxpayer primarily for sale to customers in the ordinary course of business.
    - 4) All other assets except Section 197 intangibles, goodwill, and going concern value.
    - 5) Section 197 intangibles except goodwill and going concern value.
    - 6) Goodwill and going concern value (whether or not they qualify as Section 197 intangibles).

Negotiation Elements in a Buy-Sell Agreement

- Seller name.
- Buyer name.
- Purchase price.
- Items not free from encumbrances.
- The sales price allocation.
    - Inventory
    - Accounts receivable
    - Furniture and fixtures
    - Equipment
    - Leasehold improvements
    - Vehicles
    - Intellectual property rights (patents, etc.)
    - Covenants not to compete
    - Repayment for future services
    - Goodwill
- Closing time, date, and place.

¶301

- Indemnification and "hold harmless" clauses.
- How disputes shall be arbitrated.

BUSINESS ENTITIES SELECTION

¶ 303 CHOICE OF ENTITY

.01 Choice of Entity Chart

Characteristic	C Corp	S Corp	Proprietorship	General Partnership	Limited Liability Company
Centralization of authority	Yes	Yes	Yes	No	No
Ease of creation of entity	No	No	Yes	Yes	No
Ease of division through subsidiaries	Yes	Yes	No	No	No
Limited personal liability	Yes	Yes	No	No	Yes
Ease of ownership transferability	Yes	Yes	No	No	No
Income taxed to owner	No	Yes	Yes	Yes	Usually*
Ease of operation of entity	Yes	Yes	Yes	Yes	Yes
Personal holding company income tax	Yes	No	No	No	No
Underpayment of estimated taxes penalty	Yes	Yes	Yes	No	No
Ease of changing tax year	Yes	No	No	No	No
Second tax on distributions to owners	Yes	No	No	No	No**
Organization expense deductions	Yes	Yes	No	Yes	Yes
Losses available to offset owner's income	No	Yes	Yes	Yes	Yes
Charitable contributions deduction (limited)	Yes	No	No	No	No
Accumulated earnings tax	Yes	No	No	No	No
Income adjusted for reasonable salary	Yes	Yes	No	No	No
Indefinite life—continuity of existence	Yes	Yes	No	No	No***

* An LLC may elect to be taxed as a corporation.
** Note: This tax would apply if the LLC elected to be taxed as a C corporation.
*** Most state statutes allow an LLC duration to be perpetual.

.02 Entity Considerations

Most businesses are not structured solely according to what makes the most business sense. Tax considerations are extremely important as well. The entity form that a business venture assumes has a great impact on its treatment under federal, state, local, and (in some cases) foreign tax laws.

There are several entity types in which businesses are operated:

Sole proprietorships are individuals who generally do not use a particular business form and thus individual tax rates apply: 10, 15, 25, 28, 33, or 35 percent, depending on the level of income. The maximum tax rate on the net capital gain for individuals is currently 15 percent.

Sole proprietors are subject to the alternative minimum tax (AMT). AMT for a tax year is the excess of the sole proprietor's tentative minimum tax over his or her regular tax. Form 6251 must be used by individuals to compute the AMT. The tentative minimum tax is the sum of 26 percent of the first $175,000 (or $87,500, in the case of married taxpayers filing separately) of alternative minimum taxable income (AMTI) in excess of the applicable exemption amount and 28 percent of any additional AMTI. The tentative minimum tax of the noncorporate taxpayer is then reduced by the alternative minimum tax foreign tax credit.

C corporations are entities separate from their shareholders. C corporations compute and pay taxes based on their own operations, with no reference to the income or losses of the shareholders. The shareholders generally are not liable for any debts of the corporation beyond the value of their investments. Even though a corporation pays taxes on its income, the shareholders must also pay a tax on any dividends paid to them out of any after-tax corporate profits.

Corporate tax rates are as follows: (1) on the first $50,000 of income: 15 percent; (2) on $50,001-$75,000: 25 percent; (3) on $75,000-$10 million: 34 percent; (4) over $10 million: 35 percent. The 34-percent rate is phased out by an additional five-percent rate on income between $100,000 and $335,000. The 35-percent rate is phased out by an additional three-percent rate on income over $15 million. The additional tax under the three-percent add-on is limited to $100,000. The effect of the added rates is to impose a flat 35-percent rate on corporations whose taxable incomes exceed $18.33 million and a flat 34-percent rate on corporations whose taxable incomes exceed $335,000, but are $10 million or less.

A corporation is taxed on net capital gain at the regular tax rates, including the additional phase-out rates for high-income corporations. Although the corporate alternative tax on net capital gain is limited to 35 percent, this limitation applies only in tax years in which the regular corporate tax exceeds 35 percent, excluding the additional phase-out rates.

In addition to the regular corporate income tax, an alternative minimum tax (AMT) may be imposed on a corporation having tax preference items. Corporations must use Form 4626 to compute the tax. The tentative minimum tax for the tax year is 20 percent of the excess of the alternative minimum taxable income (AMTI) over the AMTI exemption amount, reduced by the alternative minimum tax foreign tax credit.

If the corporation is *not* a "small corporation" exempt from the AMT (as explained below), file Form 4626 if:

- The corporation's taxable income or loss before the net operating loss (NOL) deduction plus its adjustments and preferences total more than $40,000 or, if smaller, its allowable exemption amount, or

- The corporation claims any general business credit, the qualified electric vehicle credit, the nonconventional source fuel credit, or the credit for prior year minimum tax.

Small Corporation Exemption

A corporation is treated as a small corporation exempt from the AMT for its tax year, if that year is the corporation's first tax year in existence, or

1. It was treated as a small corporation exempt from the AMT for prior tax years beginning after 1997, and

2. Its average annual gross receipts for the three-tax-year period ending before its current tax year did not exceed $7.5 million ($5 million if the corporation had only one prior tax year).

Hybrid C corporations are basically C corporations, but they do not have all of the rights and attributes of regular C corporations. Frequently, these corporations are taxed at the maximum *individual* tax rate. Examples of these hybrid C corporations include the following:

- *Personal holding companies.* A "personal holding company" is any corporation (with specific exceptions) if (1) at least 60 percent of adjusted ordinary gross income for the tax year is personal holding company income, and (2) at any time during the last half of the tax year, more than 50 percent in value of its outstanding stock is owned, directly or indirectly, by or for not more than five individuals.

- *Personal service corporations.* A "personal service corporation" is subject to rules and limitations not ordinarily imposed upon a C corporation. A personal service corporation is a corporation the principal activity of which is the performance of personal services substantially performed by owner-employees. An "owner-employee" is any employee who owns a specified amount of stock in the corporation, after taking into account the ownership attribution rules. Specific rules and limitations are imposed, or not, depending upon how the term "personal service corporation" is defined for that rule or limitation. Generally, the differences in the definition relate to the amount of stock an employee must own to be characterized as an owner-employee. One set of rules and limitations defines an owner-employee as an employee who owns (directly or indirectly) *any* stock in the corporation (minimal ownership personal service corporation). Another set of rules and limitations defines an owner-employee as an employee who (directly or indirectly) owns more than 10 percent of the stock (10-percent ownership personal service corporation). A final set of rules and limitations defines an owner-employee as an employee who owns more than five percent of the corporation's stock (five-percent ownership personal service corporation).

- *Qualified personal service corporations.* A "qualified personal service corporation" is exempt from the general prohibition against use of the cash method of accounting by corporations. In addition, a qualified personal service corporation is not entitled to utilize the graduated tax rates available to other corporations. A qualified personal service corporation is taxed at a flat rate of 35 percent on taxable income. A corporation is a qualified personal service corporation if it meets *both* of the following tests:

— Substantially all of the corporation's activities involve the performance of services in the fields of health, law, engineering, architecture, accounting, actuarial science, performing arts, or consulting, and

— At least 95 percent of the corporation's stock, by value, is owned, directly or indirectly, by (1) employees performing the services, (2) retired employees who had performed the services listed above, (3) any estate of the employee or retiree described above, or (4) any person who acquired the stock of the

¶303.02

corporation as a result of the death of an employee or retiree (but only for the two-year period beginning on the date of the employee's or retiree's death).

- **Professional corporations.** Professional persons may incorporate under state law to engage in the practice of their profession. The income is treated as earned by the corporation for tax purposes. State laws generally authorize professionals to operate in the corporate form under specially tailored corporation statutes, provided various conditions are met. Typical statutes force the professional to use his or her name as the corporation's name, be the sole shareholder, and have no power to contract away malpractice liability. In addition, professional corporations may be subject to the provisions limiting tax avoidance by personal service corporations. Professional corporations are also subject to rules governing the use of the cash, rather than the accrual, method of accounting for income and loss.

S corporations are special corporations that exist primarily for federal tax purposes. The shareholders have the same protection from liability as shareholders of a C corporation. However, the S corporation passes through most of its income and loss items to the shareholders. Each shareholder is subject to his or her own individual tax rate. S corporations are not directly subject to the AMT. Any S corporation AMT adjustments and preferences are passed through to the shareholders.

Trusts are usually formed to protect assets for a child or other dependent. Beneficiary trusts are often used for business purposes. The donors of the trust place business assets "in trust," and the trust operates a business or owns an investment. This form generally provides limited liability for the donors and beneficiaries. Trusts pay the same tax rates (15, 25, 28, 33, 35 percent) that apply to individuals, except that the "brackets" are computed differently. The maximum tax rate on the net capital gain of trusts is 28 percent. Trusts are also subject to the AMT.

Partnerships are entities that serve generally as *pass-through* conduits for their partners. Partnerships typically take one of the following forms:

- **General partnerships.** All of the partners of a general partnership are entitled to participate in the operation of the business, and all are liable for the full amount of any portion of the partnership's debts (under the concept called "joint and several liability"). The general partnership generally does not compute or pay taxes. Rather, its income and loss attributes generally *"pass through"* to the partners. Thus, the tax rate of each partner depends upon his or her own level of income.

- **Limited partnerships.** Limited partnerships are partnerships that have two classes of partner: one or more general partners who run the business operations and are fully liable for any partnership debts, and limited partners who are discouraged by law from running the partnership's business and are liable only for the amount they invested in the partnership, unless they become too active in partnership affairs. As with a general partnership, income and loss generally pass through to the partners. These partnerships are taxed the same as other partnerships. Limited partnerships are not directly subject to the AMT.

- **Publicly traded partnerships.** Publicly traded partnerships that derive less than 90 percent of their gross income from qualifying passive income sources (such as interest, dividends, real property rents, gain from the disposition of real property, mining and natural resource income, and gain from the disposition of capital assets or property held for the production of such income) are treated as corporations. A publicly traded partnership (PTP) is a partnership with interests traded on an established securities market or readily tradable on a secondary market (or its substantial equivalent). The passive activity loss rules are applied separately to each publicly traded partnership not treated as a corporation. As a result, a passive activity loss from one publicly traded partnership cannot be used to offset passive income from any other publicly traded partnership. A 10-year grandfather rule exempted certain existing parnterhips from corporate treatment. The Taxpayer Relief Act of 1997 allowed grandfathered publicly traded partnerships to elect to continue their partnership status if they agreed to pay an annual 3.5-percent tax on any income from active businesses. Other requirements exist as well.

Limited liability companies are entities that resemble both limited partnerships and corporations. They provide limited liability to members but also permit members to conduct the business affairs of the limited liability company (LLC). An LLC that does not elect to be taxed as an association (C corporation) does not compute or pay taxes, but passes tax items through to members. Thus, each member is subject to his or her own tax rate. LLCs are not directly subject to the AMT.

Entity Classification Regulations

The "check-the-box" business entity classification regulations (Reg. § 301.7701-1 through Reg. § 301.7701-3) greatly simplify the entity classification process.

Reg. § 301.7701-1 provides the step-by-step analysis used in determining a business organization's federal tax classification. The first step in the process is to determine whether there is even a separate entity for federal tax purposes. Whether an organization is treated as an entity for federal tax purposes is a matter of federal tax law. Certain joint undertakings that are not considered to be entities under local law may nonetheless constitute separate entities for federal tax purposes. And, in contrast, not all entities formed under local law are recognized as separate entities for federal tax purposes.

If an organization is recognized as a separate entity for federal tax purposes, it must then be determined whether the entity is a trust or a business entity. (Note, however, that specific Code sections may provide for special treatment; *i.e.*, see the Real Estate Mortgage Investment Conduit rules under Code Sec. 860A(a).) The regulations provide that a trust can be distinguished from a business entity in that a trust generally does not have associates or an objective to carry on a business for profit.

Reg. § 301.7701-2 clarifies that those business entities that are classified as "corporations" for federal tax purposes include not only corporations denominated as such under applicable law, but also associations, joint-stock companies, insurance companies, certain banking organizations, certain State organizations, organizations that are taxable as corporations under a provision of the Code other than Code Sec. 7701(a)(3), and certain organizations formed under the laws of a foreign jurisdiction (including a U.S. possession, territory or commonwealth). The regulation specifically includes a number of foreign *per se* corporations.

Any business entity not required to be treated as a corporation for federal tax purposes may choose its classification under Reg. § 301.7701-3. This regulation provides that such

¶303.02

an "eligible entity" with at least two members can be classified as either a partnership or as an association. In general, an "eligible entity" with only a single member can be classified as an association or can be disregarded as an entity separate from its owner.

In order to provide most eligible entities with the classification that they would likely choose without requiring them to affirmatively file an election, the final regulations provide default classification rules that aim to match the taxpayers' expectations (thus reducing the number of elections that will actually be needed).

The regulations adopt a passthrough default for domestic entities under which a newly formed eligible entity will be classified as a partnership if it has at least two members, or will be disregarded as an entity separate from its owner if it has but a single owner.

An eligible entity may affirmatively elect its classification on Form 8832, Entity Classification Election. An election will not be accepted unless it includes all of the required information, including the entity's taxpayer identifying number. This election must be signed by (1) each member of the entity or (2) any officer, manager, or member of the entity who is authorized to make the election and who represents to having such authorization under penalties of perjury.

If the election is made by all of the members pursuant to (1) above, each person who is an owner at the time that the election is made must consent to the election. If the election is made pursuant to (2) above, the determination of whether a person is actually authorized to make an election is based on local law. Thus, the election can be made by anyone authorized to act on behalf of the entity. This authority provides taxpayers with a great deal of flexibility in complying with the election requirements.

However, if the election is to be effective for any period prior to the date that it is filed, each person who was an owner between the date that the election is to be effective and the date that the election is filed, and who is not an owner at the time that the election is filed, must also consent to the election.

Although the classification election must be made at the beginning of the tax year, taxpayers can specify the date on which an election will be effective, provided that date is not more than 75 days prior to the date on which the election is filed and not more than 12 months after the date the election was filed. If a taxpayer specifies an effective date more than 75 days prior to the date on which the election is filed, the election will be effective 75 days prior to the date on which the election was filed. If a taxpayer specifies an effective date more than 12 months from the filing date, the election will be effective 12 months after the date the election was filed.

Protective elections where there is uncertainty about an entity's status as a business entity are not prohibited under the regulations.

Although, the regulations limit the ability of an entity to make multiple classification elections by prohibiting more than one election to change an entity's classification during any sixty month period. When there has been a substantial change in ownership of the entity the final regulations permit the IRS to waive the application of the sixty month limitation by letter ruling. However, a waiver will not be granted unless there has been more than a fifty- percent ownership change. The sixty-month limitation only applies to a change in classification by election; the limitation does not apply if the organization's business is actually transferred to another entity.

¶303.02

An electing entity and its direct or indirect owners must attach a copy of the entity's election to their federal tax returns. However, the failure of one owner to attach a copy of the election to the owner's return will not void an otherwise valid election. But such a failure to attach the election form to a federal tax or information return may give rise to penalties against the non-filing party. Other applicable penalties may also apply to parties who file federal tax or information returns inconsistent with the entity's election.

Note, finally, that a change in classification, no matter how achieved, will have certain reportable tax consequences. For example, if an organization classified as an association elects to be classified as a partnership, the organization and its owners must recognize any gain under the rules applicable to the liquidation of a corporation.

¶ 305 CORPORATIONS

.01 Advantages and Disadvantages

Advantages

- Separate legal entity.
- Outside capital easier to raise.
- Continuous existence.
- Limited personal liability.
- Specialized management.
- Possible tax advantages, such as employee benefit plans, stock options plans, stock rights, etc.
- Ownership easily transferable.
- Code Sec. 1244 stock allows ordinary loss.

Disadvantages

- Organizational costs.
- State charter restrictions.
- Government regulations—Securities and Exchange Commission.
- Double taxation—on corporation and again on distributions of dividends to shareholders.
- Extensive record-keeping necessary.
- Constructive dividend problems for owner of closely held corporation.
- Out-of-state registrations.
- Potential stockholder loan abuse.
- Requirements of meetings and minutes.

.03 Checklist for Incorporation

Topic	Party Responsible			Date Completed
	Owner	Accountant	Attorney	
Choose corporate name	___	___	___	___
Establish beginning target date	___	___	___	___
Choose corporate officers	___	___	___	___
Choose corporate directors	___	___	___	___

| | **Party Responsible** | | | |
Topic	Owner	Accountant	Attorney	Date Completed
Select accountant	___	___	___	___
Select attorney	___	___	___	___
Assign a statutory agent	___	___	___	___
Select bank and loan officers	___	___	___	___
Negotiate financing arrangements	___	___	___	___
Choose insurance agent	___	___	___	___
Draft Articles of Incorporation	___	___	___	___
Issue Code Sec. 1244 stock	___	___	___	___
Apply for "assumed name" certificate	___	___	___	___
Establish corporate seal	___	___	___	___
Complete stock register details	___	___	___	___
Establish debt-to-equity ratio	___	___	___	___
Establish corporate records	___	___	___	___
—Stock register's certificates	___	___	___	___
—Issue stock certificates	___	___	___	___
Establish employment agreements	___	___	___	___
Adopt plans for stock redemptions	___	___	___	___
Establish buy-sell agreements	___	___	___	___
Set up meeting to elect officers, select transfer agents, and adopt bylaws	___	___	___	___
File Form SS-4 for federal ID number	___	___	___	___
File for S corp status (if desired)	___	___	___	___
Establish licenses needed	___	___	___	___
Establish employee benefits	___	___	___	___
Determine officers' salaries	___	___	___	___
Obtain completed Forms W-4	___	___	___	___
Establish checking account	___	___	___	___
Determine assets to be contributed and liabilities to be charged to corporation	___	___	___	___
Choose accounting method	___	___	___	___
Determine insurance needs	___	___	___	___
Provide accident and health plans	___	___	___	___
Provide group-term life	___	___	___	___
Establish auto benefits requirements	___	___	___	___
Set up workers' compensation file	___	___	___	___
Set up key persons' death benefits	___	___	___	___
Set up file for unemployment coverage	___	___	___	___
Determine wage continuation plans or medical reimbursement plans	___	___	___	___
Develop chart of accounts	___	___	___	___
Keep detailed minutes	___	___	___	___
Establish employee benefits	___	___	___	___

.05 Transfer to Corporation

Tax-Free Exchange of Property for Corporate Stock

Code Sec. 351 allows contributions to the corporation to be tax free to the contributing shareholder provided three conditions are met:

1. Property is transferred to the corporation.
2. Stock is received.
3. Contributing shareholders receive 80-percent control of the corporation.

To be in control of a corporation, the investors must own, immediately after the exchange, at least 80 percent of the total combined voting power of all classes of stock entitled to vote and at least 80 percent of the outstanding shares of each class of nonvoting stock. (Code Sec. 368(c))

The term "property" does not include services rendered or to be rendered to the issuing corporation. Therefore, stock received for services is income to the recipient.

Transfer of Property for Corporate Stock with Assumption of Liabilities

If the corporation assumes the taxpayer's liabilities or if the property is taken subject to a liability, the transfer generally will not be treated as if the taxpayer received money or other property. There are two exceptions to this treatment:

1. If the liabilities the corporation assumes are more than the taxpayer's adjusted basis in the property exchanged, gain is recognized up to the amount of the excess. However, if the liabilities assumed would give rise to a deduction when paid, such as a trade account payable or interest, no gain is recognized.
2. If there is no good business reason for the corporation to assume the taxpayer's liabilities or if the taxpayer's main purpose in the exchange is to avoid federal income tax, the assumption will be treated as if the taxpayer received money in the amount of the liabilities. (Source: IRS Publication 544)

.07 Corporate Tax

Corporate Tax Rates

- 15 percent of the taxable income that does not exceed $50,000;
- 25 percent of the taxable income that exceeds $50,000, but does not exceed $75,000;
- 34 percent of the taxable income that exceeds $75,000, but does not exceed $100,000; and
- 35 percent of the taxable income that exceeds $10,000,000.

For taxable income in excess of $100,000 for any tax year, increase tax determined above by the lesser of:

- Five percent of such excess, or
- $11,750. (Code Sec. 11(b)(1))

Personal Service Corporation Tax Rate

The amount of the tax imposed on the taxable income of a qualified personal service corporation is 35 percent of the taxable income. (Code Sec. 11(b)(2))

Estimated Corporate Income Tax

Every corporation whose tax is expected to be $500 or more is required to make estimated tax payments. These must be deposited with an authorized financial institution or a Federal Reserve Bank. Each deposit must be accompanied by a federal tax deposit coupon and deposited according to the instructions in the coupon book.

Estimated Corporate Tax Deposit Due Dates

Required Installment	15th Day of Month
1st	4th month
2nd	6th month
3rd	9th month
4th	12th month

Amended Estimated Tax

If, after figuring and making payments of estimated tax, a corporation determines that its tax will be substantially larger or smaller than originally estimated, it should refigure the tax before the next installment to determine the amount of its remaining installment payments.

Example: A calendar-year corporation determined that its federal income tax for 20X1 would be $800,000. Accordingly, it pays $200,000 (25% of $800,000) of estimated tax by April 15, 20X1, and another $200,000 by June 15, 20X1. At the end of August 20X1, a recalculation shows that its 20X1 tax is expected to be $1,000,000. Assuming that there is no later change in the estimated tax, the estimated tax installments for September and December are computed as follows:

Estimated tax required to be paid by 9/15/20X1 (75% of $1,000,000)	$750,000
Less payments made in April and June	400,000
Payment due in September	$350,000
Payment due in December (25% of $1,000,000) . . .	$250,000

.09 Dividend Distributions

Taxable Status of Distribution

The part of a distribution from either current or accumulated earnings and profits is a dividend. The part of the distribution that is more than the earnings and profits must be used first to reduce the adjusted basis of the stock in the hands of the stockholder. Any amount that exceeds the adjusted basis of the stock held by the stockholder is treated as gain from the sale or exchange of property (usually a capital gain).

Whether a distribution is a taxable dividend to the stockholders, is applied against and used to reduce the adjusted basis of their stock, or is treated as gain from the sale of property depends upon whether the amount of the distribution is more than:

- Earnings and profits for the tax year in which the distribution was made (figured as of the close of that year without reduction for any distribution made during the year), plus
- Accumulated earnings and profits since February 28, 1913.

The amount of current earnings and profits at the time of the distribution does not necessarily determine whether the distribution is a taxable dividend.

¶305.09

If there is a deficit in earnings and profits for the tax year in which the distribution was made, the taxable status of the distribution depends upon the amount of accumulated earnings and profits. In determining accumulated earnings and profits, the deficit in earnings and profits for the current year is prorated to the dates of distribution.

Example (1): Corp C, a calendar year corporation, had accumulated earnings and profits of $40,000 as of January 1, 20X1, the beginning of its tax year. Corp C had an operating loss of $50,000 for the first 6 months of 20X1, but had earnings and profits of $5,000 for 20X1. A distribution of $15,000 was made to the stockholders on July 1, 20X1. The entire distribution is an ordinary dividend, of which $5,000 is considered as being paid from 20X1 earnings and profits and $10,000 is considered paid out of accumulated earnings and profits.

Example (2): Assume the same facts as in Example 1, except that the corporation had a deficit in earnings and profits (E & P) of $55,000 for 20X1. To figure the available earnings and profits, the deficit is prorated to the date of the distribution as follows:

Accumulated E & P – 1/1/X1	$40,000
E & P deficit for 20X1, prorated to date of distribution – 7/1/X1 (1/2 × $55,000)	(27,500)
E & P available – 7/1/X1	$12,500
Distribution – 7/1/X1 – taxable as a dividend	(12,500)
E & P deficit – 7/1/X1 – 12/31/X1	(27,500)
Accumulated E & P – 12/31/X1	$(27,500)

(Source: IRS Publication 542)

.11 Section 1244 Stock

Section 1244 stock is stock issued by a qualifying small business corporation. Its purpose is to allow the stockholders to deduct a loss from the worthlessness of the stock or a loss from a sale or exchange of the stock as an ordinary loss instead of as a capital loss. The maximum loss allowed in one year is $50,000 on a single return, and $100,000 for taxpayers filing jointly. The stock need not be held jointly to qualify for the $100,000 ordinary deduction.

"Section 1244 Stock" Defined

The term "section 1244 stock" means stock in a domestic corporation if:

- At the time the stock was issued, such corporation was a small business corporation;

- The stock was issued by such corporation for money or property other than stock and securities; and

- Such corporation, during the period of its five most recent tax years ending before the date the loss on such stock was sustained, derived more than 50 percent of its aggregate gross receipts from sources other than royalties, rents, dividends, interests, annuities, and sales or exchanges of stocks or securities. (Code Sec. 1244(c)(1))

¶305.11

Common Stock Requirement

Only common stock, either voting or nonvoting, in a domestic corporation may qualify as section 1244 stock. Neither securities of the corporation convertible into common stock nor common stock convertible into other securities of the corporation is treated as common stock. An increase in the basis of outstanding stock as a result of a contribution to capital is not treated as an issuance of stock under section 1244. (Reg. § 1.1244(c)-1(b))

Loss on Small Business Stock Treated as Ordinary Loss

In the case of an individual, a loss on section 1244 stock issued to the individual or to a partnership, which would be treated as a loss from the sale or exchange of a capital asset, is treated as an ordinary loss. (Code Sec. 1244 (a)) Such a loss is allowed as a deduction from gross income in arriving at adjusted gross income. (Reg. § 1.1244(a)-1(a))

Taxpayers Entitled to Ordinary Loss

Who is entitled:

- An individual sustaining the loss to whom the stock was issued by a small business corporation; or
- An individual who was a partner in a partnership at the time the partnership acquired the stock in an issuance from a small business corporation and whose distributive share of partnership items reflects the loss sustained by the partnership.

A corporation, trust, or estate is not entitled to ordinary loss treatment under section 1244, regardless of how the stock was acquired. An individual who acquires stock from a shareholder by purchase, gift, devise, or in any other manner is not entitled to an ordinary loss under section 1244 with respect to this stock. (Reg. § 1.1244(a)-1(b))

Maximum Loss Amount for Any Tax Year

For any tax year, the aggregate amount treated by the taxpayer as an ordinary loss cannot exceed:

- $50,000; or
- $100,000 in the case of a husband and wife filing a joint return. (Code Sec. 1244 (b))

Any amount of loss in excess of the applicable limitation is treated as loss from the sale or exchange of a capital asset. (Reg. § 1.1244(b)-1)

Stock Must Be Issued for Money or Other Property

Stock issued for services rendered or to be rendered to or for the benefit of the issuing corporation does not qualify as section 1244 stock.

Stock issued in consideration for the cancellation of indebtedness of the corporation is considered issued in exchange for money or other property unless such indebtedness is evidenced by a security or arises out of the performance of personal services. (Reg. § 1.1244(c)-1(d))

¶305.11

Section 1244 Stock and Gross Receipts Requirement

Stock will not qualify under section 1244 if 50 percent or more of the gross receipts of the corporation, for the period consisting of the five most recent tax years of the corporation ending before the date the loss on such stock is sustained by the shareholders, were derived from royalties, rents, dividends, interest, annuities, and sales or exchanges of stock or securities. (Reg. § 1.1244(c)-1(e))

"Small Business Corporation" Defined

A corporation will be treated as a small business corporation if the aggregate amount of money and other property received by the corporation for stock, as a contribution to capital and as paid-in surplus, does not exceed $1,000,000. (Code Sec. 1244(c)(3))

Increases in Basis of Section 1244 Stock

In computing the amount of the loss on stock, any increase in the basis of such stock is treated as allocable to stock which is not section 1244 stock. (Code Sec. 1244(d)(1)(B))

Records to Be Kept

In order to substantiate an ordinary loss deduction claimed by its shareholders, the corporation should maintain records showing the following:

- Financial statements of the corporation, such as its income tax returns, that identify the source of the gross receipts of the corporation for the period consisting of the five most recent tax years of the corporation or, if the corporation has not been in existence for five tax years, for the period of the corporation's existence;

- The money value and the basis in the hands of the corporation of other property received for its stock, as a contribution to capital and as paid-in surplus;

- If the consideration received is property, the basis in the hands of the shareholder and the fair market value of the property when received by the corporation;

- The persons to whom stock was issued, the date of issuance to those persons, and a description of the amount and type of consideration received from each; and

- Information relating to any tax-free stock dividend made with respect to section 1244 stock and any reorganization in which stock is transferred by the corporation in exchange for section 1244 stock. (Reg. § 1.1244(e)-(1)(a))

A person who owns section 1244 stock in a corporation is required to maintain records sufficient to distinguish such stock from any other stock he or she may own in the corporation. (Reg. § 1.1244(e)-1(b))

Constructive Ownership of Stock

An individual is considered to be the owner of the stock owned, directly or indirectly, by or for:

- His or her spouse (other than a spouse who is legally separated from the individual under a decree of divorce or separate maintenance); and

- His or her children, grandchildren, or parents. (Code Sec. 318)

A legally adopted child of an individual is treated as a child of such individual by blood. (Code Sec. 318)

If 50 percent or more in value of the stock in a corporation is owned, directly or indirectly, by or for any person, such corporation is considered to be the owner of the stock owned, directly or indirectly, by or for such person. (Code Sec. 318)

Stock owned, directly or indirectly, by or for a partner or a beneficiary of an estate is considered as owned by the partnership or estate. (Code Sec. 318)

¶ 307 PARTNERSHIPS

.01 Definition

A partnership is created when persons join together with the intent to conduct unincorporated venture and share profits. Intent is determined from facts and circumstances, including division of profits and losses, ownership of capital, conduct of parties, and written agreement. Under the check-the-box selection rules, an entity generally can elect to be treated as a partnership for federal income tax purposes. However, the IRS recently has proposed new regulations that would prevent, in limited circumstances, the use of entity classification changes made to alter a taxpayer's federal tax consequences.

A partnership may elect to be treated as a partnership or as an association. A partnership includes any business entity that has at least two members and that is not classified as a corporation. A business entity with a single owner and that is not required to be classified as a corporation may decide between two options. First, the entity may elect to be classified as an association. Alternatively, it may elect to have the organization disregarded as an entity separate from its owner. In the latter case, the business activity is treated for federal tax purposes in the same manner as if it were conducted as a sole proprietorship, branch, or division of the organization's owner. These elective classification rules have no effect on an organization's ability to elect to be excluded from the rules governing partnership taxation. Accordingly, an organization that is classified as a partnership under the check-the-box regulations still may elect to be excluded from the rules on partnership taxation.

For taxpayers not subject to those rules, a partnership includes a syndicate, group, pool, joint venture, or other unincorporated organization that is not a corporation, trust, or estate, through or by means of which any business, financial operation, or venture is carried on. An arrangement's treatment for tax purposes does not depend on its treatment under state law.

.03 Partnership Attributes

Liability of Owners

- General partner: Unlimited.
- Limited partner: Amount of capital contribution.

Management

- General partnership: Not centralized; all general partners usually participate.
- Limited partnership: Centralized; only general partners may participate; limited partners are prohibited from participating in control.

Continuity of Life

- Generally for a specific or agreed-upon term.

¶307.01

- The death, withdrawal, insolvency, or legal disability of a general partner may terminate the partnership.

Transferability of Interest

Generally subject to partners' approval. Limited partners may freely assign.

Ease of Formation

Few formal restrictions; small amount of expense. Limited partnership required to file a Certificate of Limited Partnership. Formation of a limited partnership and syndication costs can be expensive.

Availability of Outside Capital or Financing

Normally limited to capital contributions, loans from partners, and bank loans.

Liquidation of Entity

Ordinarily, agreement among partners will cause liquidation of the partnership, unless the partnership agreement provides otherwise.

Classes of Ownership Interest

Different classes of limited partners and general partners can exist.

Taxation of Income

Partners taxed on their share of income, regardless of distributions. Losses may be deducted by partners to the extent of basis.

Allocation of Income, Deductions, and Credits

In accordance with the partnership agreement, as long as there is substantial economic effect (i.e. special allocations).

Distribution of Earnings Subsequent to Year End

No tax consequences unless cash, unrealized receivables, and inventory exceed partner's adjusted basis.

Limitation on Deductibility of Losses:

Deductible by the partner to the extent of the partnership basis under and subject to the at-risk rules. Nondeductible losses may be carried over indefinitely to future years. Passive losses subject to special rules.

.05 Checklist for Partnership Set-Up

- Define partnership purpose and term.
- Determine how amendments to partnership agreement should be made.
- Determine restrictions to be placed on partners in dealing with the partnership or outside parties.
- Establish methodology for arbitration of disputes.
- Proposed sale-of-interest per buy-sell agreements.
- Establish if non-compete agreements are required.
- Establish how partnership changes will be handled upon death of a partner.
- Determine method for expulsion of partners.

¶**307.05**

- Determine methods for admission of new partners.
- Determine partners' authority for incurring indebtedness.
- Determine business purpose, place of business, capital contributions, profit and loss sharing ratios of partner.
- Determine any restrictions on partner's authority with third parties.
- Detail initial property contributions of each partner.
- Determine partners.
- Analyze the problem of nepotism.
- Detail management authority of each partner.
- Choose beginning date.
- Determine if each partner's work is to be full-time or part-time.
- Determine partnership name.
- Obtain all proper numbers—SS-4 form for federal identification number, sales tax, state unemployment, and other state identification numbers.
- Detail how draws will be taken.
- Determine the ratio in which draws will be made.
- Detail how guaranteed payments will be made to partners.
- Determine dates and procedures for distributions of profits.
- Choose accrual or cash accounting methods.
- Apply for assumed name certificate.
- Select accountant.
- Select loan officer.
- Select attorney.
- Select insurance agent.
- Implement insurance provisions—life, disability, major medical, and liability.
- Determine place for keeping partnership records.
- Establish times when periodic partnership meetings will be held.
- Establish majority rule or quorum rule for voting purposes.
- Discuss in detail how reimbursed expenses incurred by partners will be handled.
- Discuss and determine plan for addition of new partners.
- Discuss and determine plan for partial or total disability of partners.
- Discuss and determine plan for permanent withdrawal.
- Discuss and determine plan for retirement, early retirement, and death.
- Establish mechanics for expulsion for cause.
- Discuss and determine plan for bankruptcy or insolvency of a partner.
- Discuss and determine plan for payment for past services rendered.
- Discuss and determine plan for partial liquidation of partnership interest.

¶307.05

.07 Basis of Partner's Interest

The adjusted basis of a partner's interest in a partnership is:

- Increased by the sum of the partner's distributive share for the tax year and prior tax years of:
  - — Taxable income of the partnership.
  - — Income of the partnership exempt from income.
  - — The excess of the deductions for depletion over the basis of the property subject to depletion.
- Decreased (but not below zero) by distributions of the partnership by the sum of the partner's distributive share for the tax year and prior tax years of:
  - — Losses of the partnership.
  - — Expenditures of the partnership not deductible in computing its tax income and not properly chargeable to capital account. (Code Sec. 705(a))

Year in Which Partnership Income Is Includible

In computing the tax income of a partner for a tax year, the inclusions are based on the income, gain, loss, deduction, or credit of the partnership for any tax year of the partnership ending within or with the tax year of the partner. (Code Sec. 706(a))

Tax Year

Partnership treated as taxpayer—the tax year of a partnership is determined as though the partnership were a taxpayer.

A partnership must use its required tax year. If the partners that own a majority of the capital and profits interests in the partnership have the same tax year, the partnership's required tax year is the same year as that used by these partners. If partners who own the majority of interests do not use the same year, the partnership is required to use the tax year used by all its principal partners. If neither the majority nor principal partners use the same tax year, the partnership is required to use the year that results in the least aggregate deferral of income to its partners. These required tax year rules do not apply if the partnership: establishes that it has a business purpose for a different year; or elects a tax year that does not defer income for more than three months and makes estimated tax payments for the deferral period.

.09 Partnership Distributions

Recognition of Gain

Where money is distributed by a partnership to a partner, no gain is recognized to the partner except to the extent that the amount of money distributed exceeds the adjusted basis of the partner's interest in the partnership immediately before the distribution. This rule is applicable both to current distributions (i.e., distributions other than in liquidation of an entire interest) and to distributions in liquidation of a partner's entire interest in a partnership. Thus, if a partner with a basis for his interest of $10,000 receives a distribution in cash of $8,000 and property with a fair market value of $3,000, no gain is recognized to the partner. If $11,000 in cash were distributed, gain would be recognized to the extent of $1,000. For these purposes, marketable securities are treated as cash. (Reg. § 1.731-2) No gain is recognized to a distributee partner with respect to a distribution of property (other than money) until the partner sells or otherwise disposes of such property. (Reg. § 1.731-1(a)(1)(i))

Advances or drawings of money or property against a partner's distributive share of income is treated as current distributions made on the last day of the partnership tax year with respect to such partner. (Reg. § 1.731-1(a)(1)(ii))

Recognition of Loss

Loss is recognized to a partner only upon liquidation of the partner's entire interest in the partnership, and only if the property distributed to the partner consists solely of money, unrealized receivables, and inventory items. Loss is recognized to the distributee partner in such cases to the extent of the excess of the adjusted basis of such partner's interest in the partnership at the time of the distribution over the sum of:

- Any money distributed to the partner; and

- The basis to the distributee, as determined under Code Sec. 732, of any unrealized receivables and inventory items that are distributed to the partner. (Reg. § 1.731-1(a)(2))

.11 Partnership—Unrealized Receivables and Substantially Appreciated Inventory

Gain or loss on the disposition by a distributee partner of unrealized receivables is considered as ordinary income or as ordinary loss. Thus, if the sale proceeds exceed the partner's basis, ordinary income will result; if the sales proceeds are less than the partner's basis, an ordinary loss will result.

Gain or loss on the sale or exchange by a distributee partner of inventory items distributed by a partnership is, if sold or exchanged within five years from the date of distribution, be considered as ordinary income or as ordinary loss. (Code Sec. 735(a))

Any gain realized or loss sustained by a partner on a sale or exchange or other disposition of unrealized receivables received by the partner in a distribution from a partnership is considered gain or loss from the sale or exchange of property other than a capital asset. (Reg. § 1.735-1(a)(1))

Inventory Items

Any gain realized or loss sustained by a partner on a sale or exchange of appreciated inventory items received in a distribution from a partnership is considered gain or loss from the sale or exchange of property other than a capital asset if such inventory items are sold or exchanged within five years from the date of the distribution by the partnership. (Reg. § 1.735-1(a)(2))

Distributions of inventory made in exchange for all or a part of a partner's interest in other partnership property, including money, are governed by the "substantially appreciated" rule. Thus, gain from such distributions are taxed as ordinary income if the fair market value exceeds 120 percent of the partnership's adjusted basis of the inventory. The 120-percent test is applied to the total of all partnership inventory items, not to specific items or groups of items. (Reg. § 1.751-1(d))

¶307.11

Inventory Items That Have Appreciated in Value

Example: Assume that Taxpayer A sold his 1/3 interest in your partnership. The partnership used the accrual method, had no liabilities, and had the following assets:

	Adjusted Basis	Fair Market Value Assets
Cash	$10,000	$10,000
Accounts receivable	5,000	2,500
Trade notes receivable	2,000	2,100
Merchandise on hand	4,000	9,500
Land	80,000	100,000
Total Assets	$101,000	$124,100

The inventory items—the accounts receivable, trade notes receivable, and merchandise—had a total adjusted basis of $11,000 and a fair market value of $14,100. Taxpayer A realized ordinary income to the extent that the amount received for his interest in the inventory items exceeded his basis in them. If the amount received for the interest in the other assets exceeded the basis of his interest, he would realize a gain to that extent. (IRS Publication 541)

Taxpayer A would also realize ordinary income if he were to receive a distribution from the partnership for his interest, other than his proportionate share of inventory items, because the inventory is "substantially appreciated." The fair market value of the inventory items exceeds 120 percent of their basis.

Inventory Items Held More than Five Years

If a partner sells inventory items being held for more than five years, the type of gain or loss depends on how they are being used on the date sold. The gain or loss is capital gain or loss if the property is a capital asset in the partner's hands at the time sold. (Code Sec. 735(a)(2))

Installment Method—Gain or Loss on Unrealized Receivables and Substantially Appreciated Inventory

A taxpayer that sells his interest in a partnership with unrealized receivables and appreciated inventory is treated as constructively selling his share of those items. IRS states that he is not allowed to use the installment method to report his gain on this sale regarding these items. The installment sale cannot be used to report gain from the sale of inventoriable personal property. (Rev Rul 89-108, 1989-2 CB 100; Notice 2000-26, 2001 CB 954)

Sale, Exchange, Transfer of Partnership Interest—Recognition and Character of Gain or Loss on Sale or Exchange

In the case of a sale or exchange of an interest in a partnership, gain or loss is recognized to the transferor partner. Such gain or loss is considered as gain or loss from the sale or exchange of a capital asset, except as otherwise provided in Code Sec. 751 (relating to unrealized receivables and inventory items which have appreciated in value). (Code Sec. 741)

.13 Partner's Liabilities

Increase in Partner's Liabilities

Any increase in a partner's share of the liabilities of a partnership or any increase in a partner's individual liabilities by reason of the assumption by such partner of partnership liabilities is considered as a contribution of money by such partner to the partnership. (Code Sec. 752(a))

Decrease in Partner's Liabilities

Any decrease in a partner's share of the liabilities of a partnership or any decrease in a partner's individual liabilities by reason of the assumption by the partnership of such individual liabilities is considered as a distribution of money to the partner by the partnership. (Code Sec. 752(b))

.15 Partnership Liabilities

The IRS has issued regulations defining the term "liability" under Code Sec. 752 and prescribing rules designed to prevent taxpayers from manipulating the liability rules to create artificial losses when a partnership assumes a partner's obligations. The new Code Sec. 752 regulations describe two types of liabilities: "section 1.752-1 liabilities" and "section 1.752-7 liabilities" and are applicable to certain liability transfers occurring on or after June 24, 2003.

An obligation is a "section 1.752-1 liability" to the extent that it:

(1) creates or increases the basis of any of the obligor's assets, including cash;

(2) gives rise to an immediate deduction to the obligor; or

(3) gives rise to an expense that is not deductible in computing the obligor's taxable income and is not properly chargeable to capital. (Reg. § 1.752-1(a)(4)(i))

All obligations that do not meet the definition of section 1.752-1 liabilities obligations are section 1.752-7 liabilities. (Reg. § 1.752-1(a)(4)(ii))

A partner must immediately reduce his basis in the partnership when a section 1.752-1 liability is transferred by the partner and assumed by the partnership. However, a partner does not reduce the outside basis of the section 1.752-7 liability partner upon the partnership's assumption of the section 1.752-7 liability. If the partnership satisfies the section 1.752-7 liability while the section 1.752-7 liability partner is a partner in the partnership, then the deduction with respect to the portion of the section 1.752-7 liability assumed by the partnership from the section 1.752-7 liability partner (the built-in loss associated with the section 1.752-7 liability) is allocated to the section 1.752-7 liability partner, reducing the partner's outside basis. (Reg. § 1.752-7(c))

If, instead, one of the three events occur that separate the section 1.752-7 liability partner from the section 1.752-7 liability, then the section 1.752-7 liability partner's outside basis is reduced at that time. These events are:

(1) a disposition (or partial disposition) of the partnership interest by the section 1.752-7 liability partner (Reg. § 1.752-7(e)),

(2) a liquidation of the section 1.752-7 liability partner's partnership interest (Reg. § 1.752-7(f)),

(3) the assumption (or partial assumption) of the section 1.752-7 liability by a partner other than the section 1.752-7 liability partner (Reg. § 1.752-7(g)).

¶307.13

Partnership Recourse Liabilities

A partnership liability is a recourse liability to the extent that any partner bears the economic risk of loss for that liability, and a partner's share of any recourse liability of the partnership equals the portion, if any, of the economic risk of loss for such liability that is borne by such partner. (Reg. § 1.752-1(a))

Generally, a partner bears the economic risk of loss for a partnership liability to the extent that the partner (or person related to the partner) would be obligated to make a payment to the creditor or a contribution to the partnership with respect to a partnership liability (and would not be entitled to be reimbursed for such contribution or payment by another partner, a person related to another partner or the partnership) if all of the partnership's liabilities were due and payable in full, all of the partnership's assets (including money) were worthless, the partnership disposed of all of its assets in a fully taxable transaction for no consideration (other than relief from certain liabilities), and the partnership allocated its items of income, gain, loss, deduction, and credit for the year among the partners and liquidated the partners' interests in the partnership. (Reg. § 1.752-2)

The determination of the extent to which a partner (or a related person) has an obligation to make a payment is based on the facts and circumstances at the time of the determination. All statutory and contractual obligations relating to the partnership liability are taken into account including: contractual obligations outside the partnership agreement (such as guarantees, indemnifications, reimbursement agreements); obligations to the partnership that are imposed by the partnership agreement, including the obligation to make a capital contribution and to restore a deficit capital account upon liquidation of the partnership; and payment imposed by state law. (Reg. § 1.752-2(b)(3))

Partnership Non-Recourse Liabilities

Non-Recourse Liability Defined

A liability of a partnership is a non-recourse liability of the partnership to the extent, but only to the extent, that no partner bears the economic risk of loss for such liability. (Reg. § 1.752-1(a)(2))

Partner's Share of Non-Recourse Liabilities

A partner's share of the non-recourse liabilities of a partnership is equal to the sum of:

- The partner's share of partnership minimum gain;
- The amount of any taxable gain that would be allocated to the partner in connection with a revaluation of partnership property if the partnership disposed of (in a taxable transaction) all partnership property subject to one or more non-recourse liabilities of the partnership in full satisfaction of such liabilities and for no other consideration; and
- The partner's proportionate share of the excess non-recourse liabilities of the partnership. (Reg. § 1.752-3)

.17 Partnership Changes

Termination

A partnership terminates when the operations of the partnership are discontinued and no part of any business, financial operation, or venture of the partnership continues to be carried on by any of its partners in a partnership. A partnership is considered as terminated only if:

- No part of any business, financial operation, or venture of the partnership continues to be carried on by any of its partners in a partnership; or
- Within a 12-month period, there is a sale or exchange of 50 percent or more of the total interest in partnership capital and profits. (Reg. § 1.708-1(b))

Merger or Consolidation

In the case of the merger or consolidation of two or more partnerships, the resulting partnership is considered the continuation of any merging or consolidating partnership whose members own an interest of more than 50 percent in the capital and profits of the resulting partnership. (Code Sec. 708(6)(2)(A))

Death of Partner in Two-Member Partnership

Upon the death of one partner in a two-member partnership, the partnership is not considered as terminated if the estate or other successor-in-interest of the deceased partner continues to share in the profits or losses of the partnership business. (Reg. § 1.708-1(b)(1)(i))

Formation

Owners' Equity Accounts

Cash	XX	
Asset (FMV)	XX	
Capital, A		XX
Capital, D		XX

Profit and Loss Division for Ending Capital Balances

Assume:

- All partners are to receive interest of eight percent on beginning capital balances.
- Partner B is to receive a $5,000 annual salary and Partner C an $8,000 annual salary.
- Beginning capital—

Partner A	$25,000
Partner B	$65,000
Partner C	$55,000

- The remaining income is to be divided—

Partner A	30%
Partner B	30%
Partner C	40%

If partnership income is $35,000, what is the ending capital balance of each partner at year end?

	Total	Partner A	Partner B	Partner C
Beginning capital	$145,000	$25,000	$65,000	$55,000
8% Interest	11,600	2,000	5,200	4,400
Salaries	13,000	0	5,000	8,000
Division of remaining NI (35,000 – (11,600 + 13,000))	10,400	3,120	3,120	4,160
Ending capital	$180,000	$30,120	$78,320	$71,560

Admission of New Partner

New Partner Purchases Interest from Old Partner

Capital, A (old partner)	XX	
Capital, D (new partner)		XX

Note that the price paid for the entire interest by the new partner to the old partner does not affect the partnership's books.

One Partner Purchases Interest of Other Partner

Given:

Partner A capital = $35,000

Partner B capital = $25,000

Partner C capital = $10,000

Journal entry on the partnership books is recorded as follows:

If partner A buys partner B's interest for $27,000—

Partner B capita	$25,000	
Partner A capital		$25,000

New Partner Admitted

Admission by Investment of Additional Assets—Bonus Method

No Bonus Recognized

Given:

Partner A capital = $55,000

Partner B capital = $45,000

Income and losses are shared equally (50 percent). Partner C is granted a 1/3 interest in the partnership in exchange for $50,000.

Total value with new partner C=	$55,000
	+ 45,000
	+ 50,000
	$150,000

Cash (or other assets)	$50,000 DR	
Partner C capital (1/3 × $150,000)		$50,000 CR

Bonus to Old Partners

Facts as above, except partner C invests $75,000 for a 1/3 interest. The partnership records admissions of new partners under the *bonus* method.

Total value with new partner C=		$55,000
		+ 45,000
		+ 75,000
		$175,000

Cash	$75,000	
Partner A capital (75,000 – 58,333) ×.50		$8,334
Partner B capital (75,000 – 58,333) ×.50		$8,334
Partner C capital (175,000 × 1/3)		$58,333

Bonus Granted to New Partner

Facts as above, except person C is to contribute only $45,000 in exchange for 1/3 ownership interest.

Cash	$47,000
Partner A capital (49,000 – 47,000) ×.50	$1,000
Partner B capital (49,000 – 47,000) ×.50	$1,000
Partner C capital (147,000 ×1/3)	$49,000

Total value with new partner C=	$55,000
	+ $45,000
	+ $47,000
	$147,000

Admission by Investment of Additional Assets—Goodwill Method

Goodwill Attributable to Old Partners

Facts as above, except person C contributes and is credited with $55,000 for a 1/3 interest.

$55,000 / (1/3) = $165,000 Implied Total

Actual capital = $55,000 + $45,000 + $55,000 = $155,000

$165,000	Implied Total
–155,000	Actual Total
$ 10,000	

Goodwill	$10,000	
Partner A capital		$5,000
Partner B capital		$5,000
Cash	$55,000	
Partner C capital		$55,000

Goodwill Attributable to New Partner

Facts as above except that person C invests $35,000 for a 1/3 interest.

Partner A + Partner B = 2/3 interest

$55,000 + $45,000 = 2/3 x

¶307.17

($55,000 + $45,000) × 3/2 = x

$150,000 = x

Therefore, 1/3x = $50,000

Cash	$35,000	
Goodwill	$15,000	
Partner C capital		$50,000

.19 Partnership Liquidation

Lump-Sum Distribution

The partnership is to be liquidated and excess cash is to be distributed to the partners on the following basis.

ABC Partnership Balance Sheet

Cash	$45,000	Liabilities	$25,000
Other Assets	125,000	Capital:	
		A (35%) (P/L ratio)	$35,000
Total Assets	$170,000	B (40%) (P/L ratio)	$65,000
		C (25%) (P/L ratio)	$45,000
		Total Liabilities and Capital	$170,000

The following is a schedule showing the liquidation of assets and distribution of proceeds to creditors and partners:

Description	Cash	Assets	Liabs.	A(35%)	B(40%)	C(25%)

ABC Partnership Liquidation of Assets Schedule

Capital	Cash	Assets	Liabs.	A(35%)	B(40%)	C(25%)
Balances before realization	$45,000	$125,000	$25,000	$35,000	$65,000	$45,000
Sale of assets at loss of $115,000	10,000	(125,000)		(40,250)	(46,000)	(28,750)
Balances after realization	55,000	0	25,000	(5,250)	19,000	16,250
Payment of liabilities	(25,000)		25,000			
Balances	30,000		0	(5,250)	(19,000)	16,250
Distribution of A's deficit				5,250		
B = (40/(40 + 25)) × 5252 =					(3,231)	
C = (25(40 + 25) × 525 =						(2,019)
Balances				0	15,769	14,231
Distribution of cash	(30,000)				(15,769)	(14,231)
	$0				$0	$0

Installment Distributions

Facts same as example above, except assets are disbursed as follows:

Cost of disposal = $3,000

ABC Partnership Liquidation of Assets Schedule

Date	BV	Sale Price	(Loss)
Sept. 30	$75,000	$3,000	$(72,000)
Oct. 10	30,000	3,000	(27,000)
Dec. 15	20,000	4,000	(16,000)
	$125,000	$10,000	$(115,000)

ABC Partnership Liquidation Schedule

Description	Cash	Assets	Liabs.	A(35%)	B(40%)	C(25%)
Bal. before realization	$45,000	$125,000	$25,000	$35,000	$65,000	$45,000
Sept. 30 sale	3,000	(75,000)		(25,200)	(28,800)	(18,000)
Balance	48,000	50,000	25,000	9,800	36,200	27,000
Liabs. paid	(25,000)		(25,000)			
Balance	23,000	50,000	$0	9,800	36,200	27,000
Cash dist.(1)	(20,000)	50,000		0	(9,615)	(10,385)
Balance	3,000	50,000		9,800	26,585	16,615
Oct. 10 sale	3,000	(30,000)		(9,450)	(10,800)	(6,750)
Balance	6,000	20,000		350	15,785	9,865
Cash dist.(2)	(3,000)			0	(1,845)	(1,153)
Balance	3,000	20,000		350	13,940	8,712
Dec. 15 sale	4,000	(20,000)		(5,600)	(6,400)	(4,000)
Balance	7,000			(5,200)	7,540	4,712
Payment of liquidation costs	(3,000)			(1,050)	(1,200)	(750)
Balance	4,000		$0	(6,300)	6,340	3,962
Allocation of debit bal.				6,300	(3,877)	(2,423)
Balance	4,000			$0	2,463	1,539
Cash dist.	(4,000)				(2,463)	(1,539)
	$0				$0	$0

ABC Partnership Schedule of Safe Cash Distribution

Capital Balances

Date	Description	A(35%)	B(40%)	C(25%)	Total(100%)
Sept. 30	Acct. balance following sale of assets and payment of liabilities	$9,800	$36,200	$27,000	$73,000
	Estimated cost of disposal	(1,050)	(1,200)	(750)	(3,000)
	Balance	8,750	35,000	26,250	70,000
	Maximum loss possible	(17,500)	(20,000)	(12,500)	(50,000)
	Balance	(8,750))	15,000	13,750	20,000
	Allocation of debit balance	8,750	(5,385)	(3,365))	
	Sale cash dist.	0	$9,615	$10,385	$20,000

¶307.19

Date	Description	A(35%)	B(40%)	C(25%)	Total(100%)
Oct. 10	Acct. balance following sale of fixed assets	$350	$15,785	$9,865	$26,000
	Max. loss possible, (Incl. $3000 est. exp.)	(8,050)	(9,200)	(5,750)	(23,000)
	Balance	7,700	6,585	4,115	3,000
	Allocation of debit balance	7,700	(4,738)	(2,962)	
	Safe cash distribution	$0	$1,845	$1,153	$3,000

¶ 309 LIMITED LIABILITY COMPANY

.01 Overview

A limited liability company (LLC) is a hybrid entity that combines the most favorable features of both partnerships and corporations. The big advantage to an LLC is that none of the members are personally liable for the obligations of the LLC. Similar to a corporation, the LLC shields the assets of the owners and investors from liability claims. Generally, an LLC is a pass-through entity which passes its losses or profits through to its members. Unless electing otherwise, a multi-member LLC is treated as a partnership for tax purposes. However, an LLC may be taxed as a corporation if it elects to under the check-the-box regulations. An LLC is allowed to use the cash method of accounting. The IRS has held that the conversion from a limited partnership to an LLC does not cause the termination of the partnership or cause gain or loss to be recognized. An LLC member's tax basis in his or her interest in the LLC includes the member's share of the LLC's liabilities. This may provide for a larger basis for the pass-through of losses. State tax treatment of LLCs is not consistent, but varies from state to state. However, in most states, the state tax classification follows the federal classification. A few states require an LLC to file a state corporate income tax return regardless of the LLC's classification for federal income tax purposes. LLCs may be allowed under state laws to make disproportionate distributions. All states have adopted statutes allowing for LLCs. The LLC statutes of each state spell out what is required in the articles of organization and any applicable operating agreement.

LLC as a Partnership or Corporation

Prior to 1997, to be treated as a partnership, the LLC must have had more partnership characteristics than corporate characteristics.

"Check-the-Box" Regulations

The so-called "check-the-box" regulations, Reg. § 301.7701-1 through -3, replaced these rules with ones that are simple and elective. Final Reg. § 301.7701-3 provides that any eligible business entity that is not required to be treated as a corporation for federal tax purposes can be classified as either an association or a partnership. Under the check-the-box regulations, a multi-member LLC that does not affirmatively elect to be taxed as a corporation will be taxed as a partnership. (See also ¶ 303.02)

Partnership Reorganized as an LLC

Under Code Sec. 708, a general partnership may reorganize as an LLC without any recognition of gain or loss by the members. The LLC will be considered to be a continuation of the partnership. The conversion into the LLC will not result in a termination of the partnership (Rev. Rul. 95-37). Generally, all partnership attributes such as basis, capital interest, and flow-through items carry over to the LLC.

Although federal tax treatment is relatively clear, the law governing conversions to an LLC vary among the different states.

In Rev. Rul. 2001-61, the IRS determined that if a partnership becomes a disregarded entity (*i.e.*, is reduced to one purported partner), and it opts to calculate, report, and pay employment tax obligations under its own name, the entity is required to retain the employee identification number (EIN) it had used as a partnership. In addition, if an entity's federal tax classification changes to a partnership, the partnership should retain the EIN it had used as a disregarded entity.

Comparison with Partnerships

An LLC is a separate legal entity that has full powers to conduct business in its own name. All states allow single-member LLCs. For federal tax purposes, a single-member LLC is treated as a disregarded entity unless the member affirmatively elects to be taxed as a corporation under the check-the-box rules. An LLC that is owned solely by a husband and wife as community property under the laws of a state, a foreign country, or a possession of the United States may also be recognized as a disregarded entity by the IRS (Rev. Proc. 2002-69). An LLC may either be managed by its members or by appointed or elected managers. Like a partnership, the properly structured LLC, with two or more members, is a pass-through entity. An LLC differs from a general partnership in that none of its members are personally liable for the LLC's debts. The LLC also shields the assets of its owners and investors from personal liability claims.

Comparison with S Corporation

LLCs are not subject to the many restrictions applicable to S corporations. An LLC is not limited by the number of shareholders and types of shareholders. An LLC member's tax basis includes his or her share of the LLC's liabilities. However, the at-risk rules may limit the deduction of losses. LLCs are also exempt from the annual meeting requirements.

¶ 311 SOLE PROPRIETORSHIP

.01 Definition

A sole proprietorship is a business owned and controlled by one person exclusively. No other parties are involved with the ownership.

.03 Advantages vs. Disadvantages

Advantages

- Informality of operations
- Low start-up costs
- Owner controls
- Offers most freedom from regulation
- Requires minimal working capital
- All profits are taxed to owner

Disadvantages

- Sole proprietor has unlimited personal liability

¶311.01

- Difficult to raise capital
- Lack of continuity upon death
- Limited by individual's talents
- Sole proprietor often is involved in too many areas

.05 Checklist for Proprietorship Start-Up

Topic	Party Responsible			
	Owner	Accountant	Attorney	Date Completed
Choose business name	___	___	___	___
File Federal SS-4 form	___	___	___	___
Select accountant	___	___	___	___
Select attorney	___	___	___	___
Select loan officer	___	___	___	___
Apply for sales tax ID number	___	___	___	___
Apply for state unemployment number	___	___	___	___
Select insurance agent	___	___	___	___
Provide for insurance needs	___	___	___	___
Secure worker's compensation insurance	___	___	___	___
File for assumed name certificate	___	___	___	___
Apply for any licenses needed	___	___	___	___
Establish bank accounts	___	___	___	___
Prepare financial goals	___	___	___	___
Prepare intermediate goals	___	___	___	___
Prepare current year budget	___	___	___	___
Establish loan/equity arrangements	___	___	___	___
Purchase of assets	___	___	___	___
Develop personnel manual	___	___	___	___
Set up job descriptions	___	___	___	___
Set up internal accounting controls	___	___	___	___
Develop internal forms	___	___	___	___
Develop business procedure manual	___	___	___	___
Prepare tax projections	___	___	___	___
Make payroll tax deposits	___	___	___	___

.07 Proprietorship Formation

Owner's Equity Account

Cash	XX	
Assets (FMV)	XX	
Capital		XX

.09 Liquidation of Proprietorship

Liquidation Schedule	Cash	Assets	Liabs.	Capital for A
Balances before realization	$45,000	$125,000	$25,000	$145,000
Sale of assets at loss of $115,000	$10,000	125,000		(115,000)
Balances after realization	55,000	0	25,000	30,000

Liquidation Schedule	Cash	Assets	Liabs.	Capital for A
Payment of liabilities	(25,000)		(25,000)	
Balances	30,000		0	30,000
Distribution of cash	(30,000)			(30,000)
	$0			$0

¶ 313 S CORPORATION

.01 Definition

An S corporation is a corporation that has made a tax election to have the income or losses passed through to the individual owners. The S corporation is similar to a partnership in that it is a conduit for ordinary gains and losses, charitable contributions, dividends received, tax-exempt interest, and capital gains and losses.

.03 Advantages and Disadvantages

Advantages

S corporations are exempt from the corporate alternate minimum tax. Also, S corporations are exempt from double taxation on liquidating sales and distributions.

Disadvantages

A disadvantage of the S corporation is that it is subject to some forms of taxation. The S corporation may be subject to the built-in gains tax, the tax on net passive investment income, the tax on LIFO recapture, and the general business tax recapture.

Other disadvantages could be the 100-stockholder limit, the one class of stock requirement, and the fact that none of the shareholders can be corporations, partnerships, or nonresident aliens.

.05 Tax Treatment of Shareholders

Gross Income of a Shareholder

Income includes the shareholder's *pro rata* share of the gross income of the corporation. (Code Sec. 1366(c))

Pass-Through of Items to Shareholders

Each shareholder is required to take into account the shareholder's *pro rata* share of the corporation's:

- Items of income (including tax-exempt income), loss, deduction or credit, the separate treatment of which could affect the liability for tax of any shareholder; and
- Nonseparately computed income or loss. (Code Sec. 1366(a)(1))

Character of Items Passed Through

The character of any item is determined as if such item were realized directly from the source from which realized by the corporation or incurred in the same manner as incurred by the corporation. (Code Sec. 1366(b))

¶313.01

Shareholder Basis Adjustments

Increase in Basis of Stock

The basis of a shareholder's stock in an electing small business corporation is increased by the amount required to be included in the gross income of such shareholder, but only to the extent to which such amount is actually included in the shareholder's gross income on the shareholder's income tax return, increased or decreased by any adjustment of such amount in any redetermination of the shareholder's tax liability. (Reg. § 1.1367-1)

A shareholder's basis is also increased for the allocable share of any income that is not includible in determining income or loss. Such items would include municipal interest and the proceeds of life insurance policies. Shareholders' basis is not increased by foreign debt that is exempt from income.

The effect of this is the same as if, on the last day of the corporation's tax year, such amount had actually been distributed as a dividend and then reinvested by such shareholder. This increase in basis will affect only those shares of stock of the electing small business corporation which the shareholder owned at the end of the corporation's tax year and is apportioned in equal amounts to each such share. The increase is effective as of such last day and survives a termination of the corporation's election. (Reg. § 1.1367-1)

Decrease in Basis

The basis of each shareholder's stock in an S corporation is decreased for any period (but not below zero) by the sum of the following items determined with respect to the shareholder for such period:

- Items of loss and deduction;
- Any nonseparately computed loss;
- Distributions by the corporation which were not includible in the income of the shareholder (by reason of Code Sec.1368 regarding distributions);
- Any expense of the corporation not deductible in computing its taxable income and not properly chargeable to capital account; and
- The amount of the shareholder's deduction for depletion for any oil and gas property held by the S corporation to the extent such deduction does not exceed the proportionate share of the adjusted basis of such property allocated to such shareholder. (Code Sec. 1367(a)(2))

Note that in the case of a charitable contribution of property by an S corporation in tax years 2006 and 2007, the Code Sec. 1367(a) decrease in the basis of a shareholder's S corporation's stock will be equal to the shareholder's *pro rata* share of the adjusted basis in the donated property. (Code Sec. 1367(a)(2))

The basis of a shareholder's stock in an electing small business corporation is reduced by an amount equal to his or her portion of the corporation's net operating loss for any tax year attributable to such stock. However, the basis of such stock is not to be reduced below zero. (Reg. § 1.1367-1(c))

If, for any tax year, the amount of items of loss, any non-separately computed loss, and any nondeductible corporate expense exceed the amount which reduces the shareholder's basis to zero, then such excess shall be applied to reduce (but not below zero) the shareholder's basis in any indebtedness of the S corporation to the shareholder. (Code Sec. 1367(b)(2)(A))

Restoration of Basis After Reduction

If there is a reduction in the shareholder's basis in the indebtedness of an S corporation to a shareholder, any net increase for any subsequent tax year is applied to restore such reduction in debt basis before any of it may be used to increase the shareholder's basis in the stock of the S corporation. (Code Sec. 1367(b)(2)(B))

Amount of Reduction in Basis of Individual Shares

The amount of the reduction in the basis of each share of stock is that portion of the shareholder's *pro rata* share of the corporation's net operating loss which is attributable to each such share. (Reg. § 1.1367-1(c)(3))

Fringe Benefits

Partnership Rules to Apply for Fringe Benefit Purposes

For purposes of applying the provisions regarding S corporations which relate to employee fringe benefits:

- The S corporation is treated as a partnership, and
- Any two-percent-plus shareholder of the S corporation is treated as a partner of such partnership. (Code Sec. 1372(a))

.07 Electing Small Business Trusts

The establishment of an "electing small business trust" (ESBT) as a permissible S corporation shareholder enables the trustee of such a multiple-beneficiary trust to accumulate or distribute income to one or more income beneficiaries of this trust funded with S corporation stock. Permitting a trustee to meet the changing needs of several beneficiaries simultaneously by "spraying" and "sprinkling" the income generated by the stock grants broader estate planning opportunities to related S corporation shareholders. These opportunities would be otherwise unavailable, even through the use of multiple qualified Subchapter S trusts.

In order to qualify as an ESBT, all of the potential current income beneficiaries of the trust must be individuals or estates eligible to be S corporation shareholders, except that charitable organizations may hold contingent remainder interests. Furthermore, all of the interests in the trust must be acquired by reason of gift or bequest. No interest in the trust can be acquired by purchase. Finally, the trust must elect to be treated as an ESBT. (Code Sec. 1361(e))

For purposes of the 100-shareholder limitation, each potential current income beneficiary of the trust is counted as a shareholder. A potential current income beneficiary is any person, with respect to the applicable period, who is entitled to, or, at the discretion of any person, may receive, a distribution from the principal or income of the trust. (Reg. § 1.1361-1(m))

The portion of the trust that consists of stock in one or more S corporations is treated as a separate trust only for purposes of computing the federal income tax attributable to the S corporation stock held by the trust. The income from this portion of the trust is taxed at the highest rate for estates and trusts (35 percent on ordinary income and at the special long-term capital gain rates), and includes: (1) the items of income, loss or deduction allocated to the trust as an S corporation shareholder under the rules of Subchapter S; (2) gain or loss from the sale of the S corporation stock; and (3) any state or local income taxes and administrative expenses of the trust properly allocable to the S corporation stock. Otherwise, allowable capital losses are permitted only to the extent that they offset capital gains. (Code Sec. 641(c))

.08 Tax-Exempt Organization as Shareholder

An organization described in Code Sec. 401(a) or Code Sec. 501(c)(3) and exempt from taxation under Code Sec. 501(a) is an eligible S corporation shareholder. However, all items of income and loss of the S corporation, regardless of the source or nature of the income, will flow through to the qualified tax-exempt shareholder as unrelated business taxable income. Furthermore, any gain or loss on the sale or other disposition of the S corporation stock by the tax-exempt shareholder will also be treated as unrelated business taxable income, even if such would constitute passive income to the S corporation itself. However the unrelated business income rules do not apply to an employee stock ownership plan that is an S corporation shareholder. (Code Sec. 404(a)(9)(C), Code Sec. 512(e), and Code Sec. 1361(c)(6); and Code Sec. 170(e)(1), Code Sec. 404(k)(1), Code Sec. 1361(b)(1)(B) and Code Sec. 1361(e)(1)(A)(i))

.09 Certain Financial Institutions Are Eligible Corporations

In tax years beginning after December 31, 1996, a bank (as defined in Code Sec. 581) will be an eligible small business corporation unless such institution uses a reserve method of accounting for bad debts. Thus, a large bank (as defined by Code Sec. 585(c)(2)) that meets all of the usual Subchapter S eligibility requirements may elect to be treated as an S corporation. An otherwise qualified small bank may elect S corporation status if it uses the specific charge-off method of Code Sec. 166 to account for its bad debts. (Code Sec. 1361(b)(2)(A))

Note that bank or depository institution holding companies can now elect S corporation status despite the fact that IRAs or Roth IRAs owned stock in the bank or depository institution as of October 22, 2004.

.11 S Corporation Permitted to Hold C or Qualified S Corporate Subsidiaries

An S corporation is permitted to own 80 percent or more of the stock of a C corporation or 100 percent of a "qualified Subchapter S subsidiary."

However, unlike any of its C corporation subsidiaries, the S corporation parent will not be eligible to file a consolidated return with its subsidiary C corporations.

Of some import, note that, under the law, the dividends received by an S corporation from a qualified C corporation subsidiary will not be treated as passive investment income for purposes of the Code Sec. 1375 passive investment income penalty tax and the potential loss of S corporation status under Code Sec. 1362(d)(3) to the extent that the dividends are attributable to accumulated earnings and profits derived from the active conduct of a trade or business. Consequently, an investment in a corporate subsidiary conducting an active trade or business is now an option in combating an S corporation's passive investment income problem (i.e., where an S corporation has accumulated earnings and profits and has generated passive investment income exceeding 25 percent of its gross receipts).

An S corporation will also be permitted to own a qualified Subchapter S subsidiary (QSub). The term "qualified Subchapter S subsidiary" includes any domestic corporation that is not an ineligible corporation (i.e., a corporation that would be eligible to be an S corporation if its stock were owned directly by the shareholders of its parent S corporation) and is 100 percent owned by an S corporation parent which elects to treat this entity as a QSub. Pursuant to the election, the QSub is not treated as a separate corporation, and all of its assets, liabilities, and items of income, deduction, and credit are treated as the assets, liabilities, and items of income, deduction, and credit of the parent S corporation. Effectively, this election treats the subsidiary as if it were a division, resulting in flow-through tax treatment of all of the items. However, all of the assets of the parent-subsidiary group will remain subject to the built-in gains tax. (See Code Sec. 1361(b)(3), Code Sec. 1362(d)(3)(E) and Code Sec. 1504(b)(8); and amended Code Sec. 1361(b)(2) and Code Sec. 1361(c)(6))

.13 S Corporation Overview

Election of Status

- File Form 2553.
- All shareholders must consent and sign (includes spouses in community property state(s)).
- File within 2½ months of current tax year.
- After 2½ months, election is valid for following year.

Automatic Relief for Late S Corporation Elections Under Revenue Procedures 2003-43 and 97-48

If the election is late, relief is provided under Rev. Proc. 2003-43 which allows the S corporation to file Form 2553 even though the due date has passed. Relief under Rev. Proc. 2003-43 is available only if:

(a) on the first day that the entity desired to be an S corporation, it fails to qualify as an S corporation solely because of the failure to file Form 2553 on a timely basis;

(b) less than 24 months have passed since the original due date of election under Subchapter S;

(c) the entity has reasonable cause for its failure to make the timely S election; and

(d) either:

 (i) the entity has not yet filed a tax return for the first year in which it intended to be an S corporation, and the entity meets all of the following criteria:

 - The entity files the application for relief no later than six months after the due date of the tax return (excluding extensions) that covers the first year for which the S election was intended to be effective.

 - All taxpayers whose tax liability or tax return would be affected by the S election (i.e., the shareholders) have reported their share of the corporation's income, consistent with the S election on all affected returns for the year for which the S election was intended.

OR

    (ii) the entity has already filed a tax return (as an S corporation) for the first year in which the election was intended (even though it had not yet filed the election form), and the entity meets all of the following criteria:

- The return was filed within six months of its original due date (excluding extensions).

- All taxpayers whose tax liability or tax return would be affected by the S election (i.e., the shareholders) have reported their share of the corporation's income, consistent with the S election on all affected returns for the year for which the election was intended, as well as for any subsequent year.

No user fee is required.

To obtain relief under Rev. Proc. 2003-43, "FILED PURSUANT TO REV. PROC. 2003-43" should be written or typed at the top of page 1 of Form 2553 when it is filed. The entity must also attach a statement explaining the reason for its failure to file a timely S election. The Form 2553 must be signed by an officer of the corporation authorized to sign and all persons who were shareholders at any time during the period that began on the first day of the tax year for which the election is to be effective and ends on the day the election is made. The completed Form 2553 must include the following material:

    (a) Statements from all shareholders during the period between the date the S corporation election was to have become effective and the date the completed election was filed that they have reported their income (on all affected returns) consistent with the S corporation election for the year the election should have been made and for all subsequent years; and

    (b) A dated declaration signed by an officer of the corporation authorized to sign which states: "Under penalties of perjury, I declare that, to the best of my knowledge and belief, the facts presented in support of this election are true, correct, and complete."

Automatic relief is available under Rev Proc. 97-48 if all of the following conditions are met: The corporation fails to qualify as an S corporation solely because the Form 2553 (Election by a Small Business Corporation) was not filed timely; the corporation and all of its shareholders reported their income consistent with S corporation status for the year the S corporation election should have been made, and for every subsequent tax year (if any); at least six months have elapsed since the date on which the corporation filed its tax return for the first year the corporation intended to be an S corporation; and neither the corporation or any of its shareholders was notified by the Internal Revenue Service of any problem regarding the S corporation status within six months of the date on which the Form 1120S for the first year was timely filed.

The corporation must file with the applicable service center (or district director if under examination) a completed Form 2553, signed by an officer of the corporation authorized to sign and all persons who were shareholders at any time during the period that the corporation intended to be an S corporation. The Form 2553 must state at the top of the document "FILED PURSUANT TO REV. PROC. 97-48." Attached to the Form 2553 must be a dated declaration signed by an officer of the corporation authorized to sign and all persons who were shareholders at any time during the period that the corporation intended to be an S corporation attesting (but, in the case of a shareholder, only with respect to that shareholder) that: the corporation and shareholder reported their income (on all affected returns) consistent with S corporation status for the year the S corporation election should have been made, and for every subsequent tax year; and "Under penalties of perjury, to the best of my knowledge and belief, the facts presented in support of this election are true, correct, and complete."

Tax Year

- The year should end on December 31.
- The year can end on any other period for which the corporation establishes a business purpose to the satisfaction of the Secretary of Treasury.
- The year may also be elected under Code Sec. 444.
- A 52-53 week tax year ending with reference to the required tax year or a tax year elected under Code Sec. 444 is also an option. (Reg. § 1.1378-1)

Taxes

- An S corporation is not subject to the corporate income tax. The tax attributed passes through to the individual.

Small Business Corporation Requirements

- Can have only one class of stock.
- Cannot have a nonresident alien as a shareholder.
- Must be a domestic corporation.
- Must have no more than 100 shareholders.
  - A husband and wife are treated as one shareholder. All qualifying members of a family who hold S corporation stock are automatically treated as one shareholder of the S corporation when counting the number of shareholders.
  - Estate of a family member is now treated as a member of the family for purposes of determining the number of shareholders.
- Straight debt shall not be treated as a second class of stock.
  - Interest rates must not be contingent on profits.
  - The debt must be nonconvertible into stock.

Tax Treatment of Shareholder

- Shareholder receives *pro rata* share of income and loss computed on daily basis of stock ownership and nonseparately computed income or loss.
- The "character" of the item passes through to the shareholder.
- Losses cannot exceed:
  - The shareholder's adjusted basis of stock, plus
  - The shareholder's adjusted basis of indebtedness to the shareholder.
- Disallowed losses are allowed indefinite carryovers.

Shareholders' Basis

- Basis is increased by:
  - Amount included in income, plus
  - Non-separately computed income.

¶313.13

- Basis is decreased by:
  - — Distributions which were not includible in shareholder's income.
  - — Any non-separately computed loss.
  - — Items of loss and deductions.
  - — Any corporate expense not deductible in computing its taxable income.

Reduction to Basis

- Reduction to stock basis shall not be below zero.
- Any excess is applied to reduce the shareholder's basis in any indebtedness of the S corporation to the shareholder.
- Any increase in subsequent year is applied to restore the indebtedness reduction before any may be used to increase the shareholder's stock basis.
- Reduction in basis of stock is effective at the close of the corporation's tax year.

Distributions

- For S corporation having no earnings and profits.
  - — The distribution is not included in income if it does not exceed the adjusted basis of the stock.
  - — Any amount in excess of basis is treated as gain from the sale or exchange of property.

Fringe Benefits

- For these purposes, the S corporation shall be treated as a partnership.
- Any two-percent-or-more shareholder shall be treated as if the shareholder were a partner of the partnership.

Termination of S Status

- Inadvertent termination.
  - — Such as exceeding 100 shareholders or other definitional requirements.
  - — Cannot re-elect until after fifth tax year.
- Termination by revocation.
  - — May be revoked for any tax year.
  - — More than one-half of shareholders of shares owned must consent.
- Revocation where passive income exceeds 25 percent of gross receipts for three consecutive years (corporation must have also earnings and profits).
  - — The election terminates automatically.
  - — Effective on first day of first tax year after third consecutive tax year of above.
  - — Passive income is from rents, royalties, dividends, and interest, etc.

¶313.13

¶ 317 FRANCHISING

.01 Franchising Overview

Franchising is a form of licensing by which the owner (the franchisor) of a product, service, or method obtains distribution through affiliated dealers (the franchisees). The holder of the right is often given exclusive access to a defined geographical area. The International Franchise Association, the major trade association in the field, defines franchising as "a continuing relationship in which the franchisor provides a licensed privilege to do business, plus assistance in organizing, training, merchandising, and management in return for a consideration from the franchise." The product, method, or service being marketed is identified by a brand name, and the franchisor maintains control over the marketing methods employed. In many cases the operation resembles that of a large chain, with trademarks, uniform symbols, equipment, storefronts, and standardized services, or products, and maintains uniform practices as outlined in the franchise agreement.

In a way, the franchisee is not his or her own boss, because in order to maintain the distinctiveness and uniformity of the service and to insure that the operations of each outlet will reflect favorably on the organization as a whole to protect and build its goodwill, the franchisor usually exercises some degree of continuing control over the operations of franchisees and requires them to meet stipulated standards of quality. The extent of such control varies. In some cases, a franchisee is required to conduct every step of the operation in strict conformity with a manual furnished by the franchisor— and this may be desirable. In return, the individual franchisee can share in the goodwill built up by all other outlets which bear the same name.

.03 Investing in a Franchise

The risk of buying a franchise is usually greater than the risk of buying individual stock. When stock is bought, the investor relies on the business skills of the company that issued the stock. An individual who buys a franchise relies not only on the business skills of the franchisor, but also on his own business aptitude and experience. If the investor gives up a good job to purchase and operate a franchise, that person will obviously have a lot more to lose than the financial investment if the franchise does not work out.

Risk Protection Actions in Investing in a Franchise

- Investigating the franchise.
- Studying disclosure statements.
- Checking out the disclosures.
- Questioning earnings claims.
- Obtaining professional advice.
- Knowing a franchisee's legal rights.

Protection by Knowing Legal Rights

A franchisee has the following rights:

- The right to receive a disclosure statement at the first personal meeting with a representative of the franchisor to discuss the purchase of a franchise, but in no event less than 10 business days before signing a franchise, or related agreement, or before paying any money in connection with purchase of a franchise;

- The right to receive documentation stating the basis and assumptions for any earnings claims that are made at the time the claims are made; but in no event less than 10 business days before signing a franchise, or related agreement, or before paying any money in connection with the purchase of a franchise. If an earnings claim is made in advertising, the franchisee/investor has the right to receive the required documentation at the first personal meeting with a representative of the franchisor;

- The right to receive sample copies of the franchisor's standard franchise and related agreements at the same time as receipt of the disclosure statement and the right to receive the final agreements to be signed at least five business days before the signing date;

- The right to receive any refunds promised by the franchisor, subject to any conditions, or limitations on that right which have been disclosed by the franchisor; and

- The right not to be misled by oral or written representations made by the franchisor, or its representatives that are inconsistent with the disclosures made in the disclosure statement.

.05 Code of Ethics (International Franchise Association)

Preface

The International Franchise Association Code of Ethics is intended to establish a framework for the implementation of best practices in the franchise relationships of IFA members. The Code represents the ideals to which all IFA members agree to subscribe in their franchise relationships. The Code is one component of the IFA's self-regulation program, which also includes the IFA Ombudsman and revisions to the IFA bylaws that will streamline the enforcement mechanism for the Code. The Code is not intended to anticipate the solution to every challenge that may arise in a franchise relationship, but rather to provide a set of core values that are the basis for the resolution of the challenges that may arise in franchise relationships. Also the Code is not intended to establish standards to be applied by third parties, such as the courts, but to create a framework under which IFA and its members will govern themselves. The IFA's members believe that adherence to the values expressed in the IFA Code will result in healthy, productive, and mutually beneficial franchise relationships. The Code, like franchising, is dynamic and may be revised to reflect the most current developments in structuring and maintaining franchise relationships.

Trust, Truth and Honesty

Foundations of Franchising. Every franchise relationship is founded on the mutual commitment of both parties to fulfill their obligations under the franchise agreement. Each party will fulfill its obligations, will act consistent with the interests of the brand and will not act so as to harm the brand and system. This willing interdependence between franchisors and franchisees, and the trust and honesty upon which it is founded, has made franchising a worldwide success as a strategy for business growth.

Honesty embodies openness, candor, and truthfulness. Franchisees and franchisors commit to sharing ideas and information and to face challenges in clear and direct terms. IFA members will be sincere in word, act, and character—reputable and without deception.

The public image and reputation of the franchise system is one of its most valuable and enduring assets. A positive image and reputation will create value for franchisors and franchisees, attract investment in existing and new outlets from franchisees and from new franchise operators, help capture additional market share and enhance consumer loyalty and satisfaction. This can only be achieved with trust, truth, and honesty between franchisors and franchisees.

Mutual Respect and Reward

Winning Together, As a Team. The success of franchise systems depends upon both franchisors and franchisees attaining their goals. The IFA's members believe that franchisors cannot be successful unless their franchisees are also successful, and conversely, that franchisees will not succeed unless their franchisor is also successful. IFA members believe that a franchise system should be committed to help its franchisees succeed, and that such efforts are likely to create value for the system and attract new investment in the system.

IFA's members are committed to showing respect and consideration for each other and to those with whom they do business. Mutual respect includes recognizing and honoring extraordinary achievement and exemplary commitment to the system. IFA members believe that franchisors and franchisees share the responsibility for improving their franchise system in a manner that rewards both franchisors and franchisees.

Open and Frequent Communication

Successful franchise systems thrive on it. IFA's members believe that franchising is a unique form of business relationship. Nowhere else in the world does there exist a business relationship that embodies such a significant degree of mutual interdependence. IFA members believe that to be successful, this unique relationship requires continual and effective communication between franchisees and franchisors.

IFA's members recognize that misunderstanding and loss of trust and consensus on the direction of a franchise system can develop when franchisors and franchisees fail to communicate effectively. Effective communication requires openness, candor, and trust and is an integral component of a successful franchise system. Effective communication is an essential predicate for consensus and collaboration, the resolution of differences, progress, and innovation.

To foster franchising as a unique and enormously successful relationship, IFA's members commit to establishing and maintaining programs that promote effective communication within franchise systems. These programs should be widely publicized within systems, available to all members of the franchise system and should facilitate frequent dialogue within franchise systems. IFA members are encouraged to also utilize the IFA Ombudsman to assist in enhancing communication and collaboration about issues affecting the franchise system.

Obey the Law

A responsibility to preserve the promise of franchising. IFA's members enthusiastically support full compliance with, and vigorous enforcement of, all applicable federal and state franchise regulations. This commitment is fundamental to enhancing and safeguarding the business environment for franchising. IFA's members believe that the information provided during the presale disclosure process is the cornerstone of a positive business climate for franchising, and is the basis for successful and mutually beneficial franchise relationships.

Conflict Resolution

IFA's members are realistic about franchise relationships, and recognize that from time to time disputes will arise in those relationships. IFA's members are committed to the amicable and prompt resolution of these disputes. IFA members believe that franchise systems should establish a method for internal dispute resolution and should publicize and encourage use of such dispute resolution mechanisms. For these reasons, the IFA has created the IFA Ombudsman program, an independent third-party who can assist franchisors and franchisees by facilitating dialogue to avoid disputes and to work together to resolve disputes. The IFA also strongly recommends the use of the National Franchise Mediation Program (NFMP) when a more structured mediation service is needed to help resolve differences.

Support of IFA and the Member Code of Ethics

Franchisees and franchisors have a responsibility to voice their concerns and offer suggestions on how the Code and the International Franchise Association can best meet the needs of its members. Franchisors and franchisees commit to supporting and promoting the initiatives of the IFA and advocating adherence to the letter and spirit of the Member Code of Ethics. Members who feel that another member has violated the Code in their U.S. operations may file a formal written complaint with the President of the IFA.

.07 Evaluating a Franchise—Considerations and Resources

Franchisee

- Did your lawyer approve the franchise contract you are considering after the lawyer studied it paragraph by paragraph?
- Does the franchise call upon you to take any steps which are, according to your lawyer, unwise or illegal in your state, county, or city?
- Does the franchise give you an exclusive territory for the length of the franchise or can the franchisor sell a second or third franchise in your territory?
- Is the franchisor connected in any way with any other franchise company handling similar merchandise or services?
- If the answer to the last question is "yes," what is your protection against the second franchisor organization?
- Under what circumstances can you terminate the franchise contract, and at what cost to you, if you decide for any reason at all that you wish to cancel it?
- If you sell your franchise, will you be compensated for your goodwill or will the goodwill you have built into the business be lost to you?
- Discuss with other franchisees—how successful is franchise? What kind of treatment from franchisor?
- How many years has the firm offering you a franchise been in operation?

- Has it a reputation for honesty and fair dealing among the local firms holding its franchise?
- Has the franchisor shown you any certified figures indicating exact net profits of one or more going firms which you personally checked yourself with the franchisee?
- Will the firm assist you with:
  — A management training program?
  — An employee training program?
  — A public relations program?
  — Capital?
  — Credit?
  — Cooperation?
  — Advertising?
  — Merchandising ideas?
- Will the firm help you find a good location for your new business?
- Is the franchising firm adequately financed so that it can carry out its stated plan of financial assistance and expansion?
- Is the franchisor a one-person company or a corporation with an experienced management trained in depth (so that there will always be an experienced person at its head)?
- Exactly what can the franchisor do for you that you cannot do for yourself?
- Has the franchisor investigated you carefully enough to assure itself that you can successfully operate one of its franchises at a profit both to it and to you?
- Does your state have a law regulating the sale of franchises, and has the franchisor complied with that law?

International Franchise Association

The International Franchise Association (IFA) is a nonprofit trade association that represents more than 800 franchisors, speaks on behalf of franchising, provides services to member companies and those interested in franchising, sets standards of business practice, serves as a medium for the exchange of experience and expertise, and offers educational programs for top executives and managers. The IFA is highly selective in its membership. Full members are granted the use of the IFA logo in their advertising.

The IFA's executive offices are located at 1350 New York Avenue, N.W., Suite 900, Washington, D.C. 20005, (202) 628-8000.

.09 Franchising in the Economy

Franchising represents the small entrepreneur's best chance to compete with giant companies that dominate the marketplace. Without franchising, thousands of business persons would never have had the opportunity of owning their own businesses and never have felt the immense satisfaction of being a part of the free enterprise system. Franchisees enjoy the use of trade names, marketing expertise, acquisition of a distinctive business appearance, standardization of products and services, training, and advertising support from the parent organization.

¶317.09

Product and Trade Name Franchising

Product and trade name franchising began in the United States as an independent sales relationship between supplier and dealer in which the dealer acquired some of the identity of the supplier. Franchised dealers concentrate on one company's product line and to some extent identify their business with that company. Typical of this segment are automobile and truck dealers, gasoline service stations, and soft drink bottlers. Together they dominate the franchise field.

Business Format Franchising

Business format franchising is characterized by an ongoing business relationship between franchisor and franchisee that includes not only the product or service and the trademark, but the entire business concept itself—a marketing strategy and plan, operating manuals and standards, quality control, and a continuing process of assistance and guidance. Restaurants, nonfood retailing, personal and business services, rental services, real estate services, and a long list of other service businesses fall into the category of business format franchising.

.11 Key Issues for Potential Franchisors

Franchise Factors to Consider Before Entering into a Franchise Agreement

Perform Due Diligence before purchasing a franchise. Check out the franchise company thoroughly. Visit some operating franchisee sites if possible.

The Franchisor

- How many franchises have been sold to date?
- How many have failed and why did they fail?
- Is the territory exclusive or not? What are the territorial rights?
- How many new franchises are planned for the next year?
- What types of meetings/conventions for franchisees are available, etc?
- What approval is needed and what limitations exist if you decide to sell the franchise?
- What type of financing is available?
- What type of site-selection is available
- What franchisee training are available?
- Length of time franchisor has been in business.
- Reputation to public of franchisor.
- Financial strength of franchise.
- Are financial summaries available regarding other franchises operating?
- Number of franchises now operating.
- Is experienced, trained management assistance available and satisfactory?
- Does franchisor have protectable trademarks, copyrights, or patents?
- What location protection is afforded?
- Does franchisor have an acceptable Dun and Bradstreet credit rating?
- Is financial assistance available?

- What are advertising requirements?
- Are royalty fees acceptable?
- Are operating standards acceptable?
- Is freedom of operation satisfactory?
- Is franchise fee acceptable?
- Are the prices from the franchisor competitive?
- Must the product be bought exclusively from the franchisor?
- In what other locations does this product sell?
- Is the product of solid quality?
- What will be the product's demand in the near future?
- Is it easy to use?
- Does the product's future compare favorably with that of competing products?
- Is it safe?
- Is product or service customarily a "repeat buy" or "one time buy"?
- Does the product have good customer acceptance?
- Is the product or service priced competitively for local market?
- Is the product a fad or a staple?
- Is the product seasonal?

Ask Other Franchisees

- How would you do it if you could do it again?
- If you have questions, is the parent company helpful and timely in the assistance?
- Are there continuing innovations in product, service, etc.?
- What is your main criticism of the franchise?
- What is your main compliment regarding the franchise?
- Have your expectations been met?
- Was the site selection and franchisee training adequate?
- When did you reach your break-even point?

The Franchise Contract

- Is the contract complete?
- Is the agreement beneficial to both parties?
- Does the contract appear legal in all respects?
- Does your lawyer approve of the content of the contract?
- What are the renewal terms of the contract?
- Is the contract too prohibitive?
- How are royalties computed?
- What is the requirement for advertising?

¶317.11

- Does contract interfere in any way with other financial assistance that might be required?
- Can one return merchandise for credit?
- Are there required purchases?
- Can the franchisor easily terminate the agreement?
- Is the franchise fee appropriate and reasonable?
- Is there territory protection?
- Is the selling market open or restricted?
- Are there minimum sales quotas?
- Are the continuing royalties reasonable?

The Franchise Market
- What is the existing level of competition in the local area?
- What is the short-term population trend?
- What is the per capita income trend projection?
- Are the territory boundaries clearly defined?

The Franchisee
- Has a business plan been prepared?
- Is there adequate equity capital?
- Are financing sources arranged as needed?
- Has there been an analysis of the franchise cost compared with that of starting one's own business?
- Are the contract's operational procedures acceptable?
- Is one prepared to operate with less independence?
- Can the start-up time required be supported?
- Does a long-lasting relationship with this franchisor appear satisfactory?

.13 Legal Issues in Franchising

Franchise Disclosure Statement

Pursuant to 16 CFR 436.1 et seq., a Trade Regulation Rule of the Federal Trade Commission regarding Disclosure Requirements and Prohibitions Concerning Franchising and Business Opportunity Ventures, the following information is set forth on (name of franchisor) for your examination:

- Identifying information as to franchisor.
- Business experience of franchisor's directors and executive officers.
- Business experience of the franchisor.
- Litigation history.
- Bankruptcy history.
- Description of franchise.
- Initial funds required to be paid by a franchisee.
- Recurring funds required to be paid by a franchisee.

¶317.13

- Affiliated persons the franchisee is required or advised to do business with by the franchisor.

- Obligations to purchase.

- Revenues received by the franchisor in consideration of purchase by a franchisee.

- Financing arrangements.

- Restriction of sales.

- Personal participation required of the franchisee in the operation of the franchise.

- Termination, cancellation, and renewal of the franchise.

- Statistical information concerning the number of franchises (and company-owned outlets).

- Site selection.

- Training program.

- Public figure involvement in the franchise.

- Financial information concerning the franchisor.

Chapter 4
Business Valuation

Business Valuation Concepts .... ¶ 401
Valuation of Financial Data .... ¶ 403
Valuation of Non-Financial Considerations .... ¶ 404
Valuation Methods .... ¶ 405
Valuation Process .... ¶ 406

¶ 401 BUSINESS VALUATION CONCEPTS

.01 Introduction

Business valuation presents some very unique problems. There is no one formula for valuing a business. This chapter will present the various factors that enter into the valuation process. Valuation of a business becomes important for many different reasons. The taxpayer may need to know the value of a business for (1) income tax charitable contributions, (2) gift taxes, (3) estate taxes, (4) corporation recapitalization, (5) ownership changes within the present owners, (6) sales to outside investors, and (7) for external financing purposes. So, there is no single figure that is absolutely correct. Business valuation is an inexact science. It is an educated guess at best. Although quantitative in calculations, it is still a very subjective process where there are many occasions to exercise personal judgment throughout the entire process.

.02 Glossary

Accounts Payable Turnover—Accounts payable outstanding divided by the daily purchases of goods and supplies. Days purchased outstanding equals accounts payable times 365 divided by annual purchases.

Accounts Receivable Turnover—The average number of days a company's A/R is outstanding.

Formula: Collection Period = Accounts receivable times 365 divided by annual credit sales.

Accountant's Method—A valuation method used by accountants in the allocation of a purchase price for a business. Goodwill arises when the total purchase price for a business exceeds the acquired company's net worth—the total costs of assets acquired less any liabilities that are assumed in the purchase.

Activity Ratios—Ratios measuring how well the business is using its available financial resources. How well the firm is being managed, the better it uses its resources, the more profitable it will be and the less capital it will need.

Adjusted Book Value—A valuation that uses a formula based on book value that incorporates adjustments to certain asset accounts, such as inventory, plant, and equipment.

Aesthetic Value—The intangible enhancement of value of an asset or asset group as a result of aesthetic factors or considerations.

Amenity Value—Value that results from benefits enjoyed by the owner, that are not in the form of money.

Amortize—To liquidate on an installment basis; an amortized loan means the principal amount of the loan is repaid in installments during the life of the loan.

Appraisal—A valuation in which the stock value is set by a disinterested party, generally a majority of the stockholders must approve the appraiser. The process or act of estimating value.

Assessed Value—Value established by governmental authorities as basis for taxation of property ownership.

Book Value—The accounting value of an asset. For assets, the capitalized cost of an asset less accumulated depreciation or amortization as it appears on the books of account of the firm. The difference between total assets and total liabilities of an enterprise as they appear on the balance sheet.

Book Value Per Share—Stockholder's equity divided by the total number of common shares outstanding.

Business Appraiser—A person who by education, training, and experience makes an appraisal of a business or its assets or intangible assets.

Business Cycle—Alternating periods of growth and decline in overall economic activity that are of varying duration and intensity.

Business Risk—Risk inherent in a firm's operations.

Business Valuation—The process of arriving at an opinion or estimate of the value of a business enterprise.

Capital—All equity plus long-term debt.

Capital Asset—An asset with a life, generally, of more than one year which is not bought, sold, or used in the ordinary course of business.

Capital Surplus—The amount, over and above par value, paid by an investor to the issuer for stock on original issue.

Capitalization—Capitalization equals the total amount of all long-term capital. Generally, this includes preferred stock, common stock, retained earnings, and long-term debt. Process converting income into value.

Capitalization Factor—Any divisor or multiple used to convert income into value.

Capitalization of Income—Estimating the present investment value of a property by reducing future cash inflows to present worth.

Capitalization Rate—A discount rate used to determine the present value of a series of future cash flows. Also called the "reciprocal of the P/E ratio."

Cash Flow—Cash generated over a period through normal business operations—primarily net income plus noncash expenditures such as depreciation and amortization.

Comparable Sales Method—Used to value a business, this analyzes the actual sales of stock in comparable companies, recent offers to purchase the company, and actual recent sales of stock in the company being valued.

Comparative Balance Sheet—A balance sheet showing comparisons between current and prior periods to illustrate changes between periods.

Comparative Income Statement—A statement of profit and loss comparing current period with previous periods to illustrate changes between periods.

Compound Interest—An interest rate that is applicable when interest in succeeding periods is earned on the principal plus accumulated interest of prior periods.

Contributory Value—The increment of value that an improvement or addition adds to an asset.

Compounding—The arithmetic process of determining the final value of a sum or series of sums when compound interest is applied.

Cost of Capital—Discount rate that should be used in the capital budgeting process.

Cost of Purchase Method—A valuation method that uses the *cost to obtain* the asset in question.

Cost Savings Method—A valuation method that uses the *cost savings* result from an asset.

Cost to Create Method—A valuation method that uses an asset based on the *cost to duplicate* it.

Debenture—A long-term debt obligation that is not secured by any specific collateral. The debenture holder has a claim on any assets the business owns that are not already pledged as collateral, just as any other creditor in an unsecured position.

Debt-to-Equity Ratio—Total liabilities divided by total stockholders' equity. Measures the degree of leverage of a company.

Discounted Earnings—Projects future earnings and capitalizes this income stream by calculating the present value.

Discount Rate—Discounted earnings. The discounted future earnings method takes the present value of projected future earnings by applying an appropriate discount rate. A rate of return used to convert a monetary sum into present value.

Earning Power—The earning power of a business is calculated by multiplying its operating profit margin times its asset turnover.

Earnings per Share—The net income after payment of all preferred stock dividends divided by the total number of common shares outstanding.

EBIT—Earnings before interest and taxes.

Economic Net Worth—A valuation method that adjusts the assets to reflect higher market or replacement values.

Economic Life—The period over which property may be used profitably.

Equity Capital—The capital of a business that has been furnished by the stockholders as ownership, as opposed to borrowed capital, furnished by the corporate creditors.

Excess Value—Value over and above market value.

Fair Market Value—The price that would generally be agreed upon by a willing seller and a willing buyer, where both have reasonable knowledge of the facts.

Fixed Price—A valuation among several owners used to set an initial arbitrary price, usually leaving room for revision. Commonly used to value stock in buy-sell agreements.

Funding—The conversion of short-term debt into long-term debt.

Going Concern—The concept that a business is in operation and expects to continue in operation.

Going Concern Value—Value of a business considered as an operating enterprise rather than as merely a collection of assets and liabilities.

Goodwill—The "intangible" aspects of a business. This can include patents, trademarks, customer lists, reputation, history, and arrangements with suppliers—elements that contributed to a business's success and worth but are not recorded in the financial statements.

Gross Profit Margin—The company's gross profit as a percent of sales; basically, its profit after deducting the cost of goods sold.

Growth Ratios—Ratios that indicate the company's compounded annual growth rates; usually of sales or earnings.

Hurdle Rate—The minimum acceptable rate of return on a project; if the expected rate of return is below the hurdle rate, the project is not accepted.

Hypothecation—Pledging securities to secure a debt instrument.

Intangible Assets—Assets carried on a company's balance sheet that are not physical or material in nature. Common intangible assets are goodwill, copyrights, patents, franchises, and deferred financing costs.

Internal Rate of Return—The net present value of all cash inflows and outflows. IRR determines the percent such that the discount rate of these flows will equate to zero.

Intrinsic Value—The value which is justified by the facts, as distinguished from the asset's current market value.

Investment—Funds "put" into the business. Includes equity as well as long-term debt.

Investment Value—The value that arises from its presumed ability to produce a profit or return on investment for its owners.

IRS Fair Market Value—"Price at which property would change hands . . . between a willing buyer and willing seller . . . neither being under any compulsion . . . both having knowledge of relevant facts . . . ."

IRS Method—A valuation method that the IRS will apply. It is based on the concept that the existence of goodwill creates an excess rate of return in a business. The method is designed to isolate excess returns and then value it.

Leverage Ratios—They indicate the degree of debt capital rather than equity capital, indicating the amount of financial risk in a business.

Liquidity—The measure of the firm's ability to meet maturing obligations. The ability of a company to pay its debt obligations as they become due. It is generally measured by a company's net working capital level, current ratio, net quick position, net quick ratio, and cash ratio.

Liquidation Value—A valuation that does not assume an ongoing business. It assumes that the business ceases operation, sells all assets, and pays all liabilities. The remainder goes to the owners. This approach gives the absolute bottom price for the company.

Liquidity Ratios—Ratios that measure a company's ability to meet its current maturing obligations; the ability to convert assets into cash to pay liabilities.

Majority—Ownership position greater than 50 percent of the voting interest in a firm.

Marketability—The ability to sell in an established market.

Marketability Discount—An amount deducted from an equity interest to reflect lack of marketability.

Minority—Ownership position less than 50 percent of the voting interest in a firm.

Minority Discount—The adjustment, to reflect lack of control, from a proportionate share of the value in the equity of a firm.

Mortgage Value—Value of an asset for mortgage borrowing purposes.

Multiple of Earnings—A valuation in which net profits for recent periods can be averaged and then capitalized at a certain rate. The result is then divided by the number of outstanding shares giving a value per share.

Net Assets—Assets less liabilities.

Net Book Value—Total assets less total depreciation.

Net Present Value Method—An analysis tool for comparing investment alternatives by computing the net present values of their expected cash inflows and outflows using a specified discount rate.

Non-identifiable Intangible Value—Synonym for "goodwill value."

Note—A written promise to unconditionally pay a certain sum of money at a certain time—whether on a demand basis or at some specified future time.

Nuisance Value—The price that would probably be paid for the avoidance of or relief from, an objectionable condition or situation.

Overcapitalization—When a corporation's earnings are not large enough to yield a fair return on the amount of invested capital.

Paid-In Capital—The sum that has actually been received by the corporation in consideration for its stock.

Paper Profit—Appreciation that is not realized until the property is sold.

Payback Method—An analysis that computes the amount of time required to recover an investment through the net cash flow it generates. Its weakness is that no allowance is made for the present value of the cash inflows and outflows.

Payback Period—An analysis tool that determines the amount of time required to recover an investment through the net cash flow it generates. No allowances are made for the present value of these cash inflows and outflows.

Point—A percent of some principal sum. Discounts and loan origination charges are frequently expressed as points or percentages of the amount of the borrowing.

Potential Value—Value that is dependent on the actual occurrence of stated possibilities or probabilities.

Present Value—The value today of future cash flows in or out, discounted at a certain discount rate.

Price Earnings Ratio—The market value of a company expressed as a multiple of its earnings.

Prime Rate—The lowest rate of interest commercial banks charge their preferred customers.

Prospectus—A formal document describing securities to be issued. The minimum content of a prospectus is prescribed by federal and state laws. The document is intended to disclose enough valid information on the company so the prospective purchaser of the securities is well informed.

Qualitative Analysis—Rather than analyzing only numbers, this takes into effect non-financial aspects, such as management, customer relations, distribution channels, quality of products, etc.

Quantitative Analysis—Any analysis that involves numbers, such as return rates, book values, earnings per share, etc.

Rate of Return—An amount expected on an investment, as a percentage of that investment.

Real Value—Synonym for "market value."

Recapitalizing—When there is a change in the overall composition of the debt and equity structure of a business. A rearrangement of the capital structures recapitalization involves the conversion of debt securities to equity securities. It usually occurs because of financial problems. Other common recapitalizations are stock splits and stock dividends.

Replacement Cost New—The current cost of a similar new item having similar equivalent features as the item being appraised.

Replacement Value—The company's assets measured as if they had been purchased in today's market. Because of inflation, replacement value generally exceeds book value.

Reproduction Cost New—The current cost of an identical new item.

Required Rate of Return—The required rate of return the market requires in order to attract money with similar risks and characteristics.

Return on Investment—Earnings before interest and taxes / (Equity + Long-Term Debt).

Scrap Value—The value in event of sale for removal and reclamation of the material(s) of which the article is composed.

Special Purpose Value—Value of an item as related to its use for a special purpose.

Stabilized Value—A value figure or estimate that excludes consideration of transitory conditions.

Subjective Value—Value as related primarily or substantially to a state of mind.

Tangible Assets—Those assets carried on a company's balance sheet that have a specific value and are physical in nature. Common tangible assets are cash, inventory, equipment, buildings, and land.

Tangible Book Value—A valuation set at the corporation's last balance sheet. It is the book value of the business, total assets less total liabilities adjusted for any intangibles, such as goodwill.

Taxable Value—"Assessed value."

Term Loan—Where a lender lends a certain amount of money for a certain period.

Thinly Capitalized—A company with a small equity investment by its founding stockholders. This results in high leverage—a great deal of debt in relation to stockholders' equity.

Total Rate of Return—Total financial benefit investor receives divided by investment.

Total Return—The total financial benefit the investor expects to receive.

Trading on the Equity—If a corporation is able to earn more on its borrowed money than it pays for use of that money, it is said to be trading on its equity.

Treasury Bills—Short-term obligations of the United States Government.

Treasury Bonds—Long-term obligations of the United States Government.

Treasury Stock—Stock lawfully issued by a corporation, paid for in full and repurchased by the issuing firm.

Trend Analysis—Analysis of successive financial data stressing the changes in items between periods.

Utility Value—"Value in use."

Value—The true "worth" of an item according to some standard of worth.

Value in Place—Value of an asset that is already installed and ready for use.

Working Capital—The excess of current assets over current liabilities is net working capital.

Yield—The rate of return on an investment.

.03 Definition of Value

The definition of value depends on the *purpose* of the valuation.

The terms appraisal and valuation are synonymous when it comes to federal, estate, or gift tax purposes. Internal Revenue Code Section 170 (related to charitable contributions) is the IRS's closest definition of a qualified appraiser. There is no legal barrier to entry into the field of valuations. An appraiser should be qualified to make the appraisal, must hold himself out to the public as such, and must understand that he or she may be subjected to penalties for false or fraudulent overvaluation statements. The term "qualified appraiser" means an appraiser qualified to make appraisals of the type of property donated. Not qualified is: the taxpayer, a party to the transaction in which the taxpayer acquired the property, the donee or any person employed by any of the foregoing persons, or related to any of the foregoing persons. To the extent provided in the regulations, any person whose relationship to the taxpayer would cause a reasonable person to question the independence of such appraiser.

.05 Purposes of Valuation

Buy-sell agreements. Between Partners—Between others for inheritance tax purposes.

Valuation decisions affecting income taxes. Business transfers—Inheritance—Gifts—Preparing estate and gift returns.

Personal financial statements. For preparing personal financial statements the AICPA makes closely held business valuations mandatory.

Sale of an asset. A sale of only a part of a business may be the valuation concern.

¶401.05

Business reorganization. For insolvent companies—Through court order—Through bankruptcy laws.

Financing. Through debt—Through equity—For the purpose of new credit sources—For the purpose of expanded credit.

Acquisitions. Absorbing other companies.

Spin-offs. Valuations for stock purposes of the part of the company separating, as well as the remaining parent, must be made.

Selling out. Usually one of the most important and critical decisions of the owner—May arrive unexpectedly due to death of key person—Potential buyer approaches "out of the blue."

Going public. A price must be determined when a company decides to sell its securities to the public. The stock's basis becomes critical to the owner for income tax purposes.

Family planning. Continual transfers throughout life of stock to family members. As the firm continues to grow, fixed valuations may minimize estate taxes.

Charitable contributions. Gifts to charity of business stock seek a high valuation for deductible purposes. Non-cash properties in excess of $5,000 must be certified and signed on Form 8283 of the tax return.

Business insurance. Keyperson life insurance is important in providing for the continuity of the business, buyout provisions, payment of taxes, etc.—Insurance claims regarding loss of business value.

Employee transactions. (Such as stock options) Employee stock ownership plans (ESOP) where contributed stock to the plan is deductible to the company—Profit sharing plans—Where minority stockholders request that the business purchase their stock—Development of a gift program of business property.

Divorce settlements.

Litigation support services.

.07 Business Appraisal

A business appraisal involves most or all of the following steps:

- A clear statement of the purpose for which the appraisal is to be performed.
- An exact definition of just what is to be appraised.
- Study of external conditions affecting the value of the business (such as competition) and future outlook for the business itself and for the industry of which it is a part.
- Detailed analysis of the business, including study of past and recent financial statements, and interviews with the owner(s) and other persons who are familiar with the business, etc.
- Analysis of all pertinent information collected to arrive at an estimate of the value of the business.
- Preparation of a written appraisal report.

.09 Determination of Value

Principal factors include: Reputation, management, marketability, labor force, history of past sales, customer base, vendor relations, product line, market share, etc. Most feel that the dominant ingredient is the firm's stream of future earnings.

It is the business's potential income that mostly determines value. Therefore, emphasis is often shifted from the Balance Sheet to the Income Statement's projections of future earnings. Typically, these future earnings are discounted back to a present value; valuation, then, requires a quantified forecast of future benefits.

.11 Factors to Be Addressed in Business Valuations

Gross revenues. The small owner will constantly seek to minimize taxes, through techniques of travel and entertainment, salary, benefits, etc. Service businesses tend to focus valuation on some multiple of gross revenues.

Cash flow. Cash flow analysis may be very proper for companies that have holdings, such as real estate, which may provide a better measure of incremental value. Cash flow may be defined in numerous ways.

Assets. Provide the means of producing earnings power.

Earnings. Define which definition of earnings is being accounted for (i.e., net income, EBIT, etc.) For the most pessimistic figure, use prior ax returns.

.13 Valuation Steps, Method Choice, and Pitfalls

Steps in Valuing a Business

- Determine the reason for the valuation.
- Determine what data concerning the business is presently available.
- Identify the potential seller's alternatives.
- Seek to gain a complete understanding of the business to be valued. Make inquiries concerning the nature of the business.
- Determine key dates:
  — Determine the date when the report is needed.
  — Determine the date of the valuation.
  — Determine the fiscal year-end of the business.
- Identify the potential buyer's alternatives.
- Determine benchmark values.
- Evaluate the alternative methods to be used.
- Establish the values.

Choosing a Valuation Method

- Determine if an enforceable agreement exists.
- Determine if recognized industry formulas exist.
- Use earning approaches, unless not appropriate.
- Use asset approaches, unless not appropriate.
- Use cash flow approaches.

Valuation Errors to Avoid

- Failure to consider adequately all major factors that have a bearing on the value.
- Committing oneself too early to a value without having all the facts.
- Failure to take into account correctly the purpose of the valuation.
- Using improper capitalization rates for the income flow being analyzed.
- Failure to substantiate the appraisal effectively and rationally.
- Failure to be objective.
- Failure to gather the facts carefully and deliberately.
- Failure to provide an analysis with an orderly and logical deduction process using appropriate valuation methods.

.15 Value of Hindsight

The value of hindsight should take into account subsequent events when:

- The only way to reach a valuation is to work backwards from a subsequent event.
- Hindsight provides real evidence of real conditions that existed at the valuation date, but were not known at the date when the financials were prepared.
- Subsequent facts support the valuations projections and estimates.
- The valuation is weighted on subjective forecasts.

.17 Validity of Conventional Valuation Techniques

With respect to Revenue Ruling 59-60, the IRS is basically focusing on three primary valuation methods—Adjusted Book Value, Dividend Yield, and Capitalization of Earnings. Typically, the valuator will use some variations of these and apply a weighing technique to summarize. But what about the validity of the "conventional" valuation techniques?

Difficulties with Conventional Approaches

In using the earnings approach, the valuator, without being able to identify comparable firms, will have difficulty developing a reliable and defensible discount rate for the Earnings Capitalization approach.

- Stock and earnings data is often not reported in a format that allows for useful and clean comparisons.
- For small firms, the intangible qualities are often significantly important factors in the valuation process. These intangibles are specific to the particular business at hand.
- Small firms lack internal controls for separation of cash handling and accounting functions. This provides little assurance on self-prepared financials.
- Many small firms lack a reasonable length of history of operations.
- Too often there are inadequate accounting records which do not provide critical data which is needed to develop reasonable estimates.

.19 Valuation and Comparables

The search for comparable corporations must be extensive and exhaustive. The practitioner needs to consider companies of similar size, capital structure, stability, leverage,

age, growth, product, markets, type of entity, dividends, ratios, and operating performance. It is generally agreed that finding comparables can at best only provide an *initial* guideline for valuation. The goal is the "right" valuation, and comparables may not be the correct solution. "Forced" comparables that are not truly comparable may do more harm than good.

Regarding comparables, Revenue Ruling 59-60 says: " . . . in valuing unlisted securities, the value of the stock or the securities of corporations engaged in the same or similar line of business which are listed on an exchange should be taken into consideration along with all other factors. An important consideration is that the corporations to be used for comparisons have capital stocks which are actively traded by the public. In accordance with Section 2031(b) of the Code, stocks listed on an exchange are listed first. If sufficient comparable companies whose stocks are listed on an exchange cannot be found, other comparable companies which have stocks actively traded on the over-the-counter market also may be used. The essential factor is that, whether the stocks are sold on an exchange or over-the-counter, there is evidence of an active, free, public market for the stock as of the valuation date. In selecting the corporations for comparative purposes, care should be taken to use only comparable companies. Although the only restrictive requirement as to comparable corporations specified in the statute is that their lines of business be the same or similar, it is obvious, nevertheless, that consideration must be given to other relevant factors in order that the most valid comparison possible will be obtained. For illustration, a corporation having one or more issues or preferred stock, bonds, or debentures in addition to its common stock should not be considered to be directly comparable to one having only common stock outstanding. In like manner, a company with a declining business and decreasing market is not comparable to one with a record of "current progress and market expansion."

Size: The size differential makes invalid comparisons of listed companies with closely held ones.

Similarity: Finding similar companies is not an exact science but rather a discretionary and judgmental call.

Geographical Considerations: Questions must be asked like—Would a business with similar characteristics in Miami sell for the same price as one in North Dakota or as one in California?

.21 Valuation Differences

Entity Type

- Though not universally true, the small, one-person business is often found as a non-incorporated entity.
- Partnerships may have different capital-contributing arrangements as well as profit-sharing ratios.
- Smaller corporations typically have one class of voting common stock.
- S corporations have no provision for federal taxes, since the earnings are passed through to the shareholders.
- For the reasons above, pre-tax earnings will require the least amount of adjustments to financials between different entity types. This also removes the problem of different tax rates among individuals, etc.

¶401.21

Financial Statements

- Sometimes small companies hardly have invoices, vouchers, or check stubs.
- Smaller companies may sometimes have review statements, compilations, or sometimes only tax returns.
- With large corporations, there is available information such as stockholders' reports, K-1's, and Q-1's. Large corporations typically have audited financial statements.
- The underlying analysis is that smaller companies often lack financials that have much assurance associated with them.

Owner Compensation

The financials should be adjusted to reflect "fair wages" to the owners. The small sole practitioner or partnership must give consideration to draws to allow for proper comparability. For the larger company, this will appear as salary. Few small companies compensate the owners on what their services are truly worth. Often it is the owner who is the last to be paid. The small company usually only pays based on its unencumbered cash funds, where the larger corporation will typically pay what the market requires.

Owner/Manager

For a small business, the owner usually "is" the business. Its successes or failures are due to the individual's efforts. How much of this can be passed to the new owners? Will profit contributing factors persist under the new ownership? For larger corporations, absentee ownership is possible. Many decisions are committee-driven, with numerous individuals having their share of responsibility. Profit-contributing factors are usually in place and can continue under new ownership.

Capital Structure

Only outstanding capital stock is a consideration in valuation. Treasury stock is subtracted in determining the book value on common.

Cash vs. Accrual

Conversion between cash and accrual is necessitated for proper comparison purposes. Large corporations, generally because of GAAP, will prepare their financials on an accrual basis. Small companies typically prepare their statements on a cash or tax preparation basis.

.23 Concerns Regarding Lack of Marketability

Investors would prefer any business interest that is liquid versus illiquid. A rough rule of thumb may be that the majority of companies will typically fall in a 35 to 45 percent discount range due to lack of marketability. Restricted stock must be tracked by the valuator to find the differences in price compared with open market transactions of the same stock on the same date.

.25 Periods of Uncertainty and Valuation

Any future projection represents a period of uncertainty. The more subjective the valuator's estimates are, the more uncertain will be the results. Estimates need to be made throughout the valuation process. Trends should be compared over the years within the same company, with competing companies in the industry and with industry norms.

.27 Debt and Firm Value

From an investor's standpoint, the value of a firm is its net cash returns to the investor divided by his or her required rate of return. The investor's required rate of return is his or her opportunity rate, given an accepted level of inherent risk. It is the investor's cost of capital.

Suppose an investor requires a 15 percent rate of return, earnings are to grow at five percent and the firm is expected to generate net cash flows of $75,000/year. The value of the firm would compute as:

Firm Value

$$\text{Value} = \frac{\text{Net Cash Flows}}{\text{Cost of Capital - Annual Growth}} = \frac{\text{Return on Capital}}{\text{Required Rate of Return}}$$

$$= \frac{75,000}{.15-.05} = \$750,000$$

Too much debt will increase the firm's risk. The investor's cost of capital can decline by introducing debt to the firm. This debt will affect the firm's value.

The Effect of Debt on the Firm's Net Cash Flows

For firm (A) with 100 percent equity capital (assume cash flows = EBIT)

— Net cash flow = cash flow × (1 – tax rate)

— All cash flows belong to the equity owners.

For firm (B) with debt and equity

— Net Cash Flow = Cash flow × (1 – tax rate) + (interest × tax rate *)

* (Add back to cash flow tax savings due to interest expense)

The net cash flow of a leveraged firm (B) is greater than a non-leveraged firm (A) by the interest tax shield. The interest flows belong to the debt holder, with the remainder going to the equity owners.

Value of Leveraged Firm

$$\text{Value} = \frac{\text{Increased Net Cash Flows}}{\text{Cost of Capital}} = \text{Increased Value}$$

Debt has increased the potential net cash flows by the interest tax shield.

The Debt Effect

When debt is introduced into the firm's capital structure, the average cost of capital declines. The cost of debt is less than the cost of equity. The cost of debt is tax deductible, which further reduces the true cost of debt. When the overall cost of capital declines, the effect on the firm is to increase its value. The cash flows are capitalized at a lower rate, which increases the firm's value.

Debt Effect

$$Value = \frac{Net\ Cash\ Flows}{Lowest\ Cost\ of\ Capital} = Increased\ Value$$

The Effect of Risk Due to Debt on Firm Value

The debt effect will continue as long as the debt/equity ratio is acceptable. As the risk exposure of the firm increases, finally the cost of equity and debt will also increase. The cost of debt increases because lenders will charge higher rates. At an excessive level of debt, the market will perceive the increased use of debt to be so risky that it increases the probability of the firm's bankruptcy. At that point, the average cost of capital will increase because of the perceived increase in risk to the firm. Then the increased costs of capital will cause the value of the firm to decline.

.29 Capitalization Rate Defined

The capitalization rate is composed of two elements: the discount rate, which considers the time value of money, and the assumption that future cash flows will grow at a constant annual rate. It is also thought of as the rate of return that could be obtained by investing in similar vehicles of similar risk. It is the rate that converts a future income stream into a value.

The Process Called Capitalization

To capitalize net income of $20,000 a year at 20% is saying, "What is the value of a future stream of income of $20,000 a year, to perpetuity, discounted at 20 percent?"

$$\frac{\$20,000}{.20} = \$100,000$$

.31 Valuation Problems of Discounting

Revenue Ruling 59-60 States

Determining the proper discount rate is one of the most difficult areas of valuation. Important factors are type of business, risk involved, and earnings stability or lack of stability.

.33 Valuation and Risk

Characteristics of Risk in Valuations

The degree of uncertainty with respect to the realization of expected future returns or estimated capitalization rates to apply must be considered. Management is generally regarded as the key element of risk.

Some characteristics:

- Regional or locally controlled economy.
- Generally undercapitalized with high leverage.

- Reliance on few customers.
- Reliance on few suppliers and the related uncertainty of supplies.
- Often controlled by the personalities of a few owners.
- Often lack of management depth.

Wide Range—The more the practitioner calculates a *large* range around the "best estimate," the more risky and uncertain will be the company's valuation.

Adjusting for Risk

- Raise the discount rate to be applied. A company with a highly uncertain projection of future earnings will have a lower present value than a company with a more consistent expected earnings forecast.
- Reduce future estimates of earnings to a level of confidence-assured values.

Lowest Business Value

- Apply higher discount rate to a conservative estimate of future earnings to determine the lowest business value.

.35 Reasonable Compensation

In valuing a business to determine normalized earnings, careful attention should be given to the owner's compensation. With respect to small corporations, is this amount reasonable? For sole proprietors and partnerships, a reasonable compensation needs to be reflected in the earnings. Typically, the valuator looks to what the industry is currently paying.

Reg. Sec. 1.162-7: Compensation for Personal Services

(a) There may be included among the ordinary and necessary expenses paid or incurred in carrying on any trade or business a reasonable allowance for salaries or other compensation for personal services actually rendered. The test of deductibility in the case of compensation payments is whether they are reasonable and are, in fact, payments purely for services.

(b) (1) Any amount paid in the form of compensation, but not in fact as the purchase price of services, is not deductible. An ostensible salary paid by a corporation may be a distribution of a dividend on stock. If in such a case the salaries are in excess of those ordinarily paid for similar services and the excessive payments correspond or bear a close relationship to the stockholding of the officers or employees, it would seem likely that the salaries are not paid wholly for services rendered, but that the excessive payments are a distribution of earnings upon the stock.

(2) The form or method of fixing compensation is not decisive as to deductibility. Generally speaking, if contingent compensation is paid pursuant to a fee bargain between the employer and the individual, made before the services are rendered and not influenced by any consideration on the part of the employer other than that of securing on fair and advantageous terms the services of the individual, it should be allowed as a deduction even though, in the actual working out of the contract, it may prove to be greater than the amount which would ordinarily be paid.

¶401.35

(3) In any event, the allowance for the compensation paid may not exceed what is reasonable under all the circumstances. In general, it is just to assume that reasonable and true compensation is only such amount as would ordinarily be paid for like services by like enterprises under like circumstances. The circumstances to be taken into consideration are those existing at the date when the contract for services was made, not those existing at the date when the contract is questioned.

¶ 403 VALUATION OF FINANCIAL DATA

.01 Adjusting Financial Statements

Income Statement Adjustments

The valuator is seeking to normalize income from its effects by decisions of management that may be purely tax-driven or unique to the company. Annual Net Income must be adjusted to remove non-recurring or unusual items.

Common Adjustments

Related-party transactions:

- Below market rental expense
- Sales of autos, etc.
- Working capital loans at below-market rates

Unusual, Non-operating Income

- Settlements of lawsuits
- Loss on discontinued operations
- Interest income from excessive invested cash
- Sale of major operating assets
- Sale of investment assets

Excessive Benefits

- Excessive office salaries and bonuses
- Excessive fringes—autos, club dues, travel and entertainment, etc
- Family members on payroll

Consistent Data Necessary

Data must be consistent. The valuator must not "mix before tax" data with "after tax" data. Differing tax rates in the valuation process should be given consideration. If specific parties to the buy/sell arrangement can be identified, the valuator of the company should take into account the respective tax rates of each party. This is especially true in analyzing comparables. To analyze and compare the trend analysis, the financial statements must be truly comparable. If there has been a major reclassification of accounting changes, these must be standardized. For example, prior statements may have had all salary under general and administrative expenses, but later year statements more properly divided out direct labor into the cost of goods section. This resulted in a more accurate gross profit margin. Without reclassifying the earlier statements direct labor into COGS, a distorted view of gross profit would appear, and incorrect conclusions might be drawn regarding the trend of gross profit.

¶403.01

.03 Balance Sheet Analysis

Current Assets

Cash

Confirm the type of account, the amount, and reconcile the bank statement.

Accounts Receivable

Those receivables with high realization risk should be identified, such as receivables emanating from loose agreements with customers arising from a push-to-sell type policy. Adjust the accounts receivable for uncollectability. Discount the receivables for bad debts by individually analyzing each customer account or discount by analyzing the preceding five years as a weighted percent of the outstanding receivables balance at year-end.

Inventory

Verify the quantity by physical count. Items not to be sold should be clearly segregated. Identify inventory that is not sellable. Verify the quantity and unit price extensions. Adjust inventory for scrap, obsolescence, or slow moving items. Value inventory at its net realizable value. Analyze inventory for various accounting methods used, such as FIFO (use FIFO-LCM), LIFO (use balance sheet value plus LIFO reserve), weighted average, lower of cost or market, market value, etc. The turnover for each major inventory category by departments should be ascertained. A low turnover may indicate overstocking in the product line, inefficiency in marketing or obsolescence of the inventory. Too high a turnover rate may indicate inadequate inventory levels, which may result in loss of sales. What cost has been capitalized into the inventory? Has the firm in recent years switched inventory methods? What was the purpose? What was the economic reason or reality for changing inventory valuation methods? Did it result in illusionary earnings growth?

Difficulties in Inventory Analysis

A change in inventory methods that increases the profits creates illusionary profits. What is the normal inventory level? What is the actual current inventory? How is the inventory broken down? Finished goods, work in process, raw materials? What is the inventory's condition? New, obsolete, or damaged? Is any inventory on consignment? What percentage? Who is it consigned to? Who is it consigned from? Are there significant fourth quarter adjustments that materially affect the valuation of inventory and cost of goods? Technologically oriented inventory items? Inventory valuation that is very dependent on internally developed records. Sudden write-offs of inventory?

Inventory Work in Process

Labor and overhead should be valued at standard costs. Raw materials are valued at replacement cost.

Non-current Assets Considerations

Firms carry assets at historical cost, often purchased years before. Depreciation is based on historical costs generally controlled by tax laws as to the net amount. What would a new owner have to pay if he were to purchase similar assets in the marketplace today?

Fixed Assets

The Balance Sheet does not tell the historical age of the assets. Are they old and outdated? What types of depreciation have been applied? Is it accelerated or is it reasonable to the estimated life of the asset? Are they new and modern? Do the assets have charges for labor, overhead, and interest in their value? Obtain depreciation schedules. Make actual physical inspection of the assets. Determine if all assets are properly reflected in the schedules. Are installation costs reflected in the depreciation schedules? Is sales tax properly included? Determine if the assets were purchased new or used. Was there a trade-in that is reflected in the current value? Contact suppliers for market value information of similar equipment with similar features. Consider replacement cost and liquidation value to obtain a range. For forced liquidation price, contact auction houses that deal with dissolution of businesses. Have replacement of obsolete fixed assets been made by new and more efficient equipment? Have necessary repairs and maintenance on existing equipment been done? What is the aging condition of each major asset category? What is the replacement cost of each category's component part? What is the trend of fixed asset acquisitions to total gross assets?

Prepaid Expenses

Are there items included in prepaid expenses that should have been expensed? Do these typically exist, such as deposits or prepaid rent?

Real Estate

Obtain independent written real estate appraisals and then apply an averaging convention to estimate a final value. Use qualified individuals certified by recognized appraisal institutes.

Non-Current Assets Replacement Cost

Determine today's replacement cost. Estimate the useful life of the asset. Estimate the remaining life of the asset. Multiply the replacement cost times the remaining life ratio (remaining life divided by useful life) to determine an estimated cash value for today. Analyze each asset by considering its age, utility original cost (if purchased new or used), and current book value.

Intangible Assets

Intangible assets are those items that add to the value of the business. They generally cannot be sold separately and apart from the business. The balance sheet shows no monetary value for characteristics which may represent the most important aspects of the business such as customer lists, goodwill, reputation, vendor relationships, production expertise, physical "retail" location, patents, trademarks, and copyrights.

Lease Rights

Leases also have value if the lessee has the right to sublease. The lease has value if its lease has no provision for inflationary adjustments and increases for taxes and insurance. The lease value is the present value of all potential savings and benefits to be passed on to the new tenant; if any option periods are available on the current lease. These rental terms have value if the new lessee would have to pay higher rates than those currently being paid and if the new lessee desires to retain the present location. Is the present location suitable for the new owner? Is the lease assignable? Can it be subleased? Have valuable leasehold improvements been made?

¶403.03

Goodwill

Goodwill is the element that allows the company to generate a higher return than expected solely from the assets or the amount attributable to the return on the capital investment. It is the element that tends to bring customers back to the business. Goodwill includes items such as licenses, secret formulas or processes, designs, drawings, contractual type relationships, such as franchises, customer lists, mailing lists, subscriber lists, customer base, and relations such as retention, reputation from things like historic promotion efforts, patents, copyrights, and publication rights.

Goodwill Valuation Process Using Return on Assets and Capitalized Excess Earnings Method

This method values goodwill by comparison with other companies in the industry. This method is a modification of that detailed by Rev. Rul. 68-609.

Determine Tangible Assets

- Apply average industry return rate to tangible assets.
- Subtract industry's return on assets from the company's earnings.
- Capitalize the excess earnings.
- Add the capitalized goodwill value to the firm's tangible net worth at market.

Goodwill—Capitalized Value Method

Goodwill (capitalized method)

$$\frac{\text{(Annual future earnings) - ((Fair market value) x (Normal industry rate of return))}}{\text{Capitalization rate of excess earnings}}$$

Current Liabilities

Estimated liabilities for future costs and losses should be viewed with skepticism. Are reserved provisions understated or overstated? Do these provisions conform to the reality of the situation? Current debt should be valued at face value. What are the details concerning the accounts payable by major suppliers? To whom payable, amount, aging, any specific circumstances? Analyze accrued expenses payable. What is detail of this item? What is included? Are there payables to be purchased? Are all federal and state taxes current? Analyze and detail which debts will be taken as part of the purchase. Analyze and consider contingent liabilities. Are there accrued or past wages that should be paid? What liabilities or contingencies exist in connection with product warranty? Are there any existing claims that are currently detailed? Long-term debt should be valued at its present value. Use the local area's prime rate and discount to the valuation date.

Non-Current Liabilities

- How has the company financed its growth? Through debt? Through equity?
- Track and analyze debt to equity ratios.
- Restate non-current debt into its present values by using the company's current borrowing rate.

¶403.03

Purchase Cost Method

- Used to value a specific intangible asset by comparing today's cost versus the historical cost.
- Obtain today's cost to purchase the asset.
- Subtract from today's cost the adjusted cost *basis* of the historical cost. This cost basis may be an adjusted cost.

Savings of Cost Method

- Used to value a specific intangible method that produces a cost savings, such as a manufacturing process that saves on materials, labor, overhead, rework, etc.
- Estimate expected annual savings.
- Determine number of years this is appropriate.
- Apply present value of ordinary annuity factor to convert to today's dollars.

.05 Income Statement Analysis

The income statement provides little information on the following valuation factors: projected sales, product sales mix, wholesale and retail prices, cost of goods sold mix, competition, trends in marketplace, etc.

Gross Income

What is the compounded annual growth percent of gross income?

Returns and allowances:

- Due to one or a few problem clients.
- Due to poor credit policies.
- Accepting high-risk clients.

Cost of Goods Sold

Attention should be given to companies where they have valued their inventory with the LIFO method. The cost of goods should be converted back to the FIFO or at least to a real cost value. Basically, take the beginning inventory and add back the LIFO reserve. Then take the ending inventory and add back the LIFO reserve. This converts the cost of the goods to the First-In First-Out basis. The valuator needs to analyze year-end adjustments. Owners may have had a prosperous year and become very aggressive in writing down inventory or markdowns or slow moving items to avoid paying excessive income tax or property tax. One way to recognize such adjustments is to analyze income statements for several years.

Gross Profit

The amount of gross profit tells the valuator the initial worth of the firm.

General and Administrative

For the small business, the general and administrative area often can represent discretionary costs. Many costs, such as rent, may be considered fixed costs. Areas such as advertising and promotion should be compared to industry norms. Has this business over-funded in these areas? The owner's salary should be compared against industry norms.

Net Income

What is the compounded annual growth rate of net income? Determine why growth is what it is. Appropriate adjustments must be made to each year of operation in looking at the net income of the firm being valuated. Future earnings and projections can be given a sharper focus by examining the past earnings as they are adjusted properly. Is there income from non-operating assets such as portfolio income, dividends, and interest income that would not be sold and carried to the new owners? Analyze the earning trends of the net income. Have the trends been erratic? Average? Have they been rising? Have they been falling? Should the later years be weighted? The reasons for changes should be investigated thoroughly. Are the owners' fringe benefits excessive? Are they hidden inside of other areas? With respect to the type of depreciation methods used, are they very aggressive? Are they tax related? Are they high? Are the lives of the assets reasonable? What about inventory in the cost of goods section? Is it LIFO-reserve based? Has inventory been tremendously understated over the years and the net income understated due to the LIFO valuation of inventory? Have there been extraordinary items such as sale of land or equipment which do not represent normal business operations? Were there unusual years of profits or unusual years of loss due to some unfortunate or one time unique circumstance that does not indicate a recurring trend?

Cash Flow

In analyzing cash flow, the valuator should compute the ratio of cash flow to net income. A high ratio will indicate good earnings quality since net income is backed up by cash. The ratios of cash expenses to total expenses and cash revenue to total revenue should be determined. High ratios are indicative of better earnings quality.

Working Capital

Net working capital consists of the firm's current assets minus current liabilities. Analyze the firm's working capital structure over recent periods to obtain a feel for its current position. What is the direction of key items, such as accounts receivable, inventory, and equipment? Have payables grown out of proportion? Are taxes rising? Is there a sense of worsening liquidity? Have there been large inventory buildups? Has there been lower inventory turnover? Has the business over-purchased equipment items?

Analysis of the Stability and Quality of Earnings

"Quality of earnings" refers to the stability of income. The earnings quality relates to the nature of currently reported results. The valuator must analyze the earnings quality in regard to different degrees. In analyzing the stability and quality of earnings, the net income that's reported is only the beginning point. Watch for non-normal and erratic income statement elements. Firms with poor internal controls or high instances of previous accounting errors often have unreliable financial reporting systems. There may exist a lack of management honesty, resulting in attempts to cover up low quality products.

Analyzing the Income Statement

The company's policies should be compared with industry standards. How do the company's accounting policies compare with those of the industry? Are they considerably more liberal? Or are they normal to the industry? Do the accounting principals and estimates used reflect the underlying financial reality concerning the firm and the industry?

Analysis of the income statement also means referring to the economics of the industry in which the firm operates. Has the company recently made any major accounting changes in its computations of net income? Is the industry seasonal in nature? What is the nature of the product demand? What is the nature of the cost? Does the reporting of net income over recent years really reflect the way management wants it presented? Is there an artificial shifting of net income from one period to the other? This could be analyzed by the net income to gross sales ratio.

Evaluating the Financial Situation of the Firm

Stable elements of income and expenses should be separated from those that appear random and erratic. Operating income and non-operating income should be clearly separated from non-operating sources of income, separate franchise income, dividends, interest, royalties, or rental income. Earnings derived from recurring transactions will result in higher quality earnings than those resulting from isolated transactions. Abnormal and erratic income elements, such as a sale of administrative offices, collections from life insurance policies, casualty losses, sale of real property, etc., should be separated from the normal operations of the company in evaluating the net income figure.

What is the stability of the revenue base? Is it vulnerable to external factors? Does the company have sales in diversified industries? Is the company geographically diversified? Lack of diversification may make it more susceptible to economic downturns in specific areas.

Projections and Forecasts

The greater the length of time the forecast covers, the greater the risk of error. Some forecasts may be very reliable, such as during periods of relatively stable business conditions. The valuator should seek to obtain the most reliable data available and document the process of preparing the evaluator projections. To what degree are the historical numbers, say on gross sales, accurate? How is the evaluator developing the forecast? By interviews with or reference to the sales force? Top executives? Consumers? U.S. economic indicators? Most valuators believe the past five years should be given consideration. The period must be representative.

How long a period should the forecast cover? The valuator must consider the reasonable ability of management to continue its internal operation. Mathematical techniques exist to forecast with some precision, but real world factors, changes in the economy or industry market and other economic factors make such projections questionable.

.07 Financial Ratios

Compute and Analyze Key Ratios

The following ratios should be considered in a valuation:

Income ratios. Measure management's effectiveness by returns generated.

Working capital ratios. Measure various relationships relating to factors of the firm's current assets.

Liquidity ratios. Measure the firm's ability to meet maturing short-term obligations. This ratio focuses the firm's ability to convert assets into cash to pay liabilities.

Profitability ratios. Indicate how profitably the firm is being managed.

Coverage ratios. Measure the company's earnings ability to cover, for example, interest and debt service.

Limitations of Ratios

Ratios analyze the relationship between two or more variables. In most cases, they are simply one number divided by another. Limit the ratios to those relevant to the valuation. Realize that there are often weak standards for industry comparisons (numbers based possibly on small, unrepresentative samples). Define the ratios clearly so they will not be misinterpreted. Analyze the ratio considering its component parts. Provide enough ratios for conclusions to be drawn.

Ratio Interpretation

Ratios are useful for comparisons of the business with relative company size, with specific industries, and concerning variances from industry standards.

Ratios allow the valuator to make valid comparisons between the firm being valuated and others in the industry. Select only the ratios appropriate to the valuation. In comparing ratios to industry standards, the proper comparative source must be used. Ratios provide a continuing analysis of a company's performance. Ratios help identify a firm's financial strengths and weaknesses. Ratios should never be a substitute for sound judgment. Similar ratios may often be defined differently. Ratio analysis may help identify financial data markedly different from industry averages. Use ratios for period-to-period comparisons; it is good practice to compare several periods of ratios. Trends are the key elements for analysis. Ratio analysis may point out potential advantages of the subject firm for opportunities. In calculating ratios, consistent treatment must be applied from period to period. Conclusions or recommendations concerning the ratios must be drawn in light of the various assumptions applied to the ratios.

Liquidity Ratios

The liquidity of a firm is the ability to meet short-term maturing obligations. Liquidity ratio analysis points toward any weaknesses in the financial strength of the firm. It focuses on the size and relationship of the firm's current assets to its current liabilities.

Current Ratio

$$\frac{\text{Current Assets}}{\text{Current Liabilities}}$$

The current ratio is the most commonly used measure of short-term solvency. It indicates the amount of coverage the current assets can provide to meet the claims for short-term liabilities. The current ratio indicates the amount of this cash flow "buffer." The integral parts of the current ratio should be analyzed carefully. A company that has a higher percentage of current assets in unencumbered cash is more liquid than a company with the same ratio but with a higher percentage in other assets. The current ratio may be improved by the reduction of short-term debt or additional long-term debt or conversion of fixed assets into current assets.

Sales to Receivables

$$\frac{\text{Total Credit Sales}}{\text{Average Net Account Receivabes}}$$

The sales/receivables ratio measures the efficiency of management in applying credit policies and collection procedures. The greater the number of days, the more slowly sales are converted to cash. A higher sales/receivables ratio may indicate that management is not emphasizing the collection process.

Average Collection Period or Days to Receivable

$$\frac{365 \text{ x Accounts Receivable}}{\text{Annual Net Credit Sales}}$$

The days to receivable ratio (or average collection period) represents the average length of time from sale to cash receipt. This ratio points out trends in management of credit terms. This ratio reveals the efficiency in collecting receivables.

Inventory Turnover

$$\frac{\text{Cost of Goods Sold}}{\text{Average Inventory}}$$

The inventory turnover ratio measures the number of times the average inventory is sold during an annual period. This ratio is a measure of management expertise. If management invests too heavily in inventory, the firm may be carrying too much debt and its related high interest cost. A high ratio could be the result of inadequate inventory stock-out levels; the problem of lost customers due to stock-outs must be carefully considered. A lower inventory turnover ratio might imply inventory over-buying or an accumulation of unsalable or slow turning items.

Profitability Ratios

Profitability ratios show how profitably the firm is being managed. These ratios provide an analysis of the overall effectiveness of management by analyzing various profits generated on sales.

Gross Profit

$$\frac{\text{Gross profit}}{\text{Net Sales}}$$

Gross profit is net sales minus the cost of goods sold. This ratio indicates the overall margin obtained on all items sold.

Net Income to Tangible Net Worth

$$\frac{\text{Earnings after Taxes}}{\text{Tangible Net Worth}}$$

This ratio indicates the profitability of the firm's investment. It indicates the average amount earned by each dollar invested in the business. A consistently profitable net profit ratio indicates the results of management's policies over long-term periods.

Net Income to Sales

$$\frac{\text{Net Income}}{\text{Net Sales}}$$

This ratio is commonly referred to as the net income percentage or the net income after-tax ratio. It is the bottom-line overall measure of the firm's profitability. This ratio should be analyzed by considering the total volume of sales for the period.

Earning Power

The earnings power formula measures the company's ability to earn money.

Earnings Power

$$= \text{Asset Turnover} \times \text{Operating Profit Margin}$$

Where:

$$\text{Asset turnover} = \frac{\text{Sales}}{\text{Operating Assets}}$$

The asset turnover ratio indicates how effectively the firm's operating assets (cash, A/R, inventory) are being utilized.

Where:

Operating Profit Margin

$$\text{Operating Profit Margin} = \frac{\text{Net Income From Operations}}{\text{Total Sales}}$$

This ratio indicates how much is earned on each dollar of sales.

Coverage Ratios

Coverage ratios measure the firm's earnings ability to cover items such as interest. Coverage ratios analyze Earnings Before Interest and Taxes (EBIT) and the company's ability to cover items such as common stock dividends, debt amortization, and interest expense.

Total Fixed Charge Coverage Ratio

$$\frac{\text{Earnings Before Interest and Taxes}}{(\text{Fixed Obligations}) + \text{Interest}}$$

This ratio indicates the amount that the firm's earnings can decline yet still provide coverage of its debt requirements. The total fixed charge coverage ratio indicates the number of times the company's earnings can cover interest plus any contractual fixed obligations such as debt reductions, rent, lease payments, etc.

Times Interest Earned

$$\frac{\text{Earnings Before Interest and Taxes}}{\text{Total Interest}}$$

The times interest earned ratio analyzes leverage financing. It determines for the relationship between earnings and interest charges. The ratio indicates the ability of the firm to cover its interest charges.

Total Interest Coverage

$$\frac{\text{Earnings Before Interest and Taxes}}{\text{Principl Payments} + \text{Total Interest}}$$

This ratio analyzes the principal periodic repayments which are just as mandatory as interest payments. This ratio indicates to the purchaser the firm's cash flow available for debt service.

Income Ratios

These ratios measure management's effectiveness in generating returns. Income ratios indicate how efficiently management has performed on various functions of the business, providing a broad knowledge of management's efficiency.

Net Sales to Tangible Net Worth

$$\frac{\text{Net Sales}}{\text{Tangible Net Worth}}$$

Tangible net worth equals owner's equity less intangible assets. This ratio indicates the relationship to investment and sales.

Sales to Total Operating Assets

$$\frac{\text{Net Sales}}{\text{Total Operating Assets}}$$

Total assets, less intangible assets and less long-term investments equal total operating assets. This ratio provides an analysis of overall returns for investment in operating assets. This ratio indicates the effectiveness that asset expansion provides in generating increased sales.

Operating Ratio

$$\frac{\text{Operating Income}}{\text{Net Sales}}$$

This ratio indicates profits generated in the normal conduct of business operations. It excludes items such as interest on non-current debt, income taxes, extraordinary items, etc. The operating income is the income derived from ordinary business operations.

¶403.07

Operating Expense Ratio

$$\frac{\text{Total Operating Expenses}}{\text{Net Sales}}$$

This ratio reflects management's ability to adjust expense items to changes in sales volume. Total operating expenses include all normal expenses associated with operations.

Working Capital Ratios

These ratios measure the various relationships of the firm's working capital.

Inventory to Working Capital

$$\frac{\text{Average Inventory}}{\text{Working Capital}}$$

This ratio indicates the amount of risk that could arise from a decline in the value of the firm's inventory. It indicates any inventory overstocking problems.

Working Capital Turnover

$$\frac{\text{Net Sales}}{\text{Working Capital}}$$

This ratio provides the number of times that coverage sales occur to each working capital. It indicates if the enterprise is too heavily invested in fixed or slow assets.

Current Asset Turnover

$$\frac{\text{Cost of Goods Sold} + \text{Expenses} + \text{Interest} + \text{Taxes}}{\text{Average Current Assets}}$$

This ratio analyzes trends in the profitability of the firm's current assets. This rate indicates the number of times current assets are used in covering operating costs.

Current Liabilities to Inventory

$$\frac{\text{Current Liabilities}}{\text{Inventory}}$$

This ratio measures the extent to which a firm relies on sales of inventory to meet current obligations.

Long-Term Debt to Net Working Capital

$$\frac{\text{Long Term Debt}}{\text{Net Working Capital}}$$

Long-term debt generally consists of obligations due more than one year.

¶403.07

Current Debt to Net Worth

$$\frac{\text{Current Liabilities}}{\text{Tangible Net Worth}}$$

This ratio indicates the financial condition of the firm by comparing its debt to its equity. The firm's tangible net worth consists of its common stock, preferred stock, and retained earnings less its intangible assets (i.e., goodwill, patents, and organizational expenses, etc).

.09 Real Estate Valuation

Approaches

- The Income Capitalization Approach—used for shopping malls, office towers, apartment blocks, etc.
- The Comparable Sales Approach—used for appraisals of dwellings and similar type properties.
- The Cost Approach—used most often in new construction and specialized properties.

The Income Capitalization Approach

$$\text{Indicated Value} = \frac{\text{Income Stream}}{\text{Capitalization Rate}}$$

This technique looks at income-producing properties such as rental income. These properties include theaters, airports, commercial parking garages, hotels, etc.

The Comparison Approach

The valuator should research factors such as physical similarity, encumbrances, dates, location, type of property, motivation, etc. Generally, the sales date is of primary importance, and should be near the effective date of the valuation property. Location should be carefully analyzed. For example, a small distance can remove the property from a prime downtown area. Convenience and noise are factors of consideration. Physical similarity includes terrain, building area, floor plan, and physical condition. The valuator, using this method, is researching records for nearby, similar properties which have recently sold. The analysis should include offers to buy, refusals, and asking prices. Real estate listings should generally be discounted because of their "retail" inflated prices. The comparable property's prices are then reduced to a common denominator such as cost per square foot.

The Cost Approach

This method establishes the value by determining the hypothetical cost to replicate the building. This cost is adjusted downward for deterioration and obsolescence of the appraised building. The market value of the vacant land is added to this value. The land value is estimated as if the property were vacant. It should be appraised as though available for its most productive use. The size of the site should be considered. Any excess land should be appraised separately.

¶403.09

¶ 404 VALUATION OF NON-FINANCIAL CONSIDERATIONS

.01 Management, Stockholders, and Market

Management—Organization

- Obtain details on directors and officers such as length of service, age, education, compensation, fringes, deferred compensation plans, and other benefits.

Management Relationships

- Are there any strong differences of opinion?
- What is the relationship among upper and middle management?
- Do separate departments cooperate willingly and effectively with each other?

Labor

- What type labor turnover does the company have in the labor force?
- What type labor turnover does the company have with key management?
- What is the total number of employees?
- Provide for general breakdown between various functions of production and office personnel.
- Is the company unionized? If so, how often are there strikes and work stoppages?
- Are the company's wages and personnel policies competitive?
- Are written personnel policies and procedures available?

Management and Labor Force Turnover

- Loss of key personnel.
- What is the average turnover of management?
- How long has the key management been there?

Analyzing the Labor Force

- How will turnover affect the value of the business and future profitability?
- Is turnover of the labor force average or above industry norm?
- Determine the reasons for turnover.

Competition

- Who are the major competitors?
- What is the firm's relative position?
- Who are the potential customers?

Ownership

- Is the entity a sole proprietor, partnership, or corporation?
- List current owners.
- Are there buy-sell agreements?

Product

- Describe major products.
- Define company's major business and the major market in which it operates.

- How does company's product differ from competition?
- What is unique about any specific products of the company?
- How does the company's gross profit margin compare with competitors?
- How does the company's product pricing compare with major competitors?
- Become familiar with the industry in which the business operates.

Product Line

- What are the principal products or services of the business?
- What is the length of time each major product has been sold?
- Are any of the products proprietary?
- What is the nature of agreements between the suppliers regarding these products?
- What other products or services could be produced from existing facilities?

Market

- What are the principal applications for each major product?
- Define the principal market in which the business operates.
- What is the future outlook for growth or lack of growth in these markets?

Industry Outlook

- What is the industry's technology?
- What is the level of competition?
- Is the industry expanding or declining?
- Is the company in a rapidly changing technological industry?
- Is the company labor intensive?
- Is the industry, in general, expanding or declining?

Marketing Distribution

- What is the distribution channel?
- Is the marketing aggressive and skillful?
- Who is responsible for marketing research?
- Who is responsible for advertising?
- Is there a direct-selling organization?

Customers

- Break down the sales geographically.
- What portion of the total sales volume does each of these customers represent?
- What major potential customers might be secured for the business?

Sales and Distribution

- What type of discount or sales terms are offered?
- What are their credit policies? What are their policies concerning returns and allowances?

¶404.01

- In what manner does the company sell—through their own sales force or through manufacturing representatives?
- Is the company's compensation of sales force characteristic to the industry?
- Do they use sales branches?
- Does the company operate nationwide or just in a certain geographically defined area?

.03 Company History, Manufacturing, and Facilities

Historical Information to Obtain

- Date company was started.
- Basic information on corporate charter, by-laws, minutes, state incorporated in, etc.
- Main line of business.
- Who are the present owners?
- How long has it been owned by the present owners?
- What is the firm's basic attitude toward government agencies?
- How is the business regarded by its customers, employees, competitors, community, and suppliers?
- How is the business regarded by its bank?

Manufacturing

- What is the production cycle?
- What type of quality assurance does the company have?
- Does the company have assembly-type operations or does it manufacture from raw materials?
- What types of materials are required to manufacture the product?
- What type of stability does the company have with suppliers?
- What type of safety record does the company have?

Physical Facilities

- What is the square footage, cost, and location of company facilities?
- Will there be any problems if expansion is needed soon?
- Which facilities are owned and which are leased?
- Is insurance adequately attained and maintained?
- Obtain a complete list of physical facilities and equipment available.
- Is real estate owned or leased?
  - If owned, what is the present value?
  - When was the appraisal made?
  - By whom was the appraisal made?

¶ 405 VALUATION METHODS

.01 Conventional Valuation Technique

Most of the following are accepted conventional valuation methods or versions thereof. The final valuation method rests with the experience of the valuator. These worksheets are designed to provide a mechanical step-by-step worksheet approach. Listed below are the accepted conventional valuation methods per Rev. Rul. 59-60.

Asset Derived

- Liquidation Value.
- Adjusted Book Value.
- Book Value.

Revenue or Income Derived

- Excess Earnings.
- Gross Revenue.
- Capitalized Earnings.
- Discounted Cash Flow.
- Discounted Future Earnings.

Market Derived

- Rules of Thumb.
- Price Earnings Multiple.
- Comparable Sales.

These accepted conventional valuation methods per Rev. Rul. 59-60 are discussed below.

.03 Asset Valuation

Asset valuation techniques are more objective in nature than are earnings approaches. They are generally used for firms such as holding companies or retail companies comprised mostly of inventories.

Advantages and Characteristics

- They are easy for the average person to understand.
- The value of assets lies in their ability to generate future earnings.
- Generally book value, because of its ready availability, is the starting point with asset approaches.
- Adjustments to the book values often depend on the availability of data.
- Asset approaches are more relevant when assets are of a highly liquid nature, such as accounts receivable or contracts.
- Asset approaches are popular because they can be more readily verified than can earnings projections.
- Non-operating assets should be valued separately from operating activities and added to the capitalized earnings value.

¶405.01

Disadvantages

Some businesses require significant investments yet only return marginal profits. These businesses may well be overstated if based solely on assets. Some businesses can earn substantial profits on a small asset base.

Balance Sheet Book Value

Book value is the assets' historical cost less any depreciation. The shorter the time span that the company has owned the asset, the closer is its value to current market value.

Advantage

It is readily available in the financial statement.

Disadvantage

Inventory methods, such as LIFO, FIFO, lower of cost or market, weighted average, writedown, etc., may give little indication of their true market value. Real property showing historic purchase cost may be far different from current market. Intangible assets, such as goodwill, are not even booked unless acquired by purchase, yet a firm's customer base and reputation may be one of its most important assets. Intangible assets are usually not an accurate measure of the firm's value because the assets reflect the historical cost of the assets less depreciation, which may be regulated by tax rules which have nothing to do with economic reality.

Adjusted Book Value Method

This method is like the tangible book value method, but adjusts for certain assets. Typical adjustments are placing fair value on inventory, real property, equipment, and accounts receivable. Use the firm's most recent Balance Sheet. Do not become too bogged down in detail.

Use:

- For a new business.
- For a sole proprietor who is disabled or has died.
- Where the firm has minor ascertainable intangible value—intangibles such as goodwill, covenants not to compete.
- Where the earnings are unstable.
- For a business where the earnings are highly speculative.
- Where recent economic conditions prevent the earnings from portraying a true picture of the firm.

Disadvantage

Does not provide consideration of "above normal" earnings.

Adjusted Book Value Worksheet

$ Current Assets	_____
+ Non-current Assets	_____
= Total of Current and Non-current Assets	_____
Less: Total Liabilities	_____
Equals: Adjusted Net Worth	_____
+ / – Adjusted for Intangibles:	_____
Goodwill, etc.	_____
= Adjusted Book Value	_____

Replacement Value

Determine today's replacement cost on an asset-by-asset basis. What is the total amount of money that it would take to replace or reproduce the assets or the systems of the business being valued? Use for a company that has unique property like land or a physical plant that is operating.

Replacement Value Worksheet

Current Balance Sheet

Adjustment	Adjusted Asset	Replacement Value
Current Assets:		
Cash	_____	_____
Accounts Receivable	_____	_____
Inventory	_____	_____
Prepaid Expenses	_____	_____
Total Current Assets	_____	_____
Fixed Assets:		
Property and Equipment	_____	_____
Buildings	_____	_____
Land	_____	_____
Less: Accum. Depr.	_____	_____
Total Fixed Assets	_____	_____
Other Assets	_____	_____
Total Assets	_____	_____

Liquidation Value

This method determines the bottom value for a business. This method can be used for a going concern company to establish a starting point or base value for the tangible assets. This method does not assume an on-going concern, but rather, that the business ceases operations, sells its assets, and pays its debts.

Apply a cents-on-the-dollar or percent-on-liquidation approach to all assets. Subtract liabilities. Answer is Net Liquidation Value.

For percent of liquidation values consider:

- Analysis of the allowance for bad debts
- Salability of assets
- Obtain current replacement prices from vendors for similar assets with similar features in similar situations.
- Accounts Receivable
- General or specialized equipment
- Inventory and raw materials are more salable than work in progress.
- Give careful consideration to replacement cost of inventory. Was a physical count taken? Allow for obsolescence and scrap.
- Real property may have value in excess of 100 percent of the book value shown.
- Assets should be excluded that will be retained by the owner.

Liabilities

- Current liabilities are taken at book value.

¶405.03

- Non-current liabilities should be deducted at the firm's discounted present value using the company's borrowing rate.

- Liabilities should be adjusted for any that will be retained by the owner.

Liquidation Value Method Worksheet

Assets:	Book Value $	Expected % on Liquidation	Adjusted Value $
Cash			
Accounts Receivable			
Inventory			
Equipment			
Furniture and Fixtures			
Land			
Other			
Liquidation Asset Value Total			
Less: Liabilities (to be paid)			
Liquidation Value of Firm			

Adjusted Liquidation Value

Focuses strictly on the operating assets of the business. This method should be used for a firm that will be substantially changed in form, a firm whose interests are to strictly transfer the assets, a firm with a short history of operations, and a firm that will be relocated after purchase.

For fixed assets:

- Determine replacement cost (medium value).

- Determine forced liquidation sell value (lowest value).

- Determine acquisition cost of assets if purchased new (high value).

- Weight fixed assets generally with emphasis on replacement cost.

- Add adjusted inventory (adjusted for slow moving, obsolete, etc).

- Add intangibles.

- Adjusted current assets (adjusted accounts receivable, cash, etc).

- Weight the above four factors.

Adjusted Liquidation Value Worksheet

	New	Replacement	Forced Liquidation
I. Fixed Assets:			
Furniture and fixtures			
Equipment			
Transportation			
Leasehold			
Land			

¶405.03

	New	Replacement	Forced Liquidation
Other:	_____	_____	_____
= Totals	_____	_____	_____
× Weights Assigned	_____	_____	_____
= Weighted Values	_____	_____	_____
Total of New + Replacement + Forced Liquidation			_____
Divided by totals of weights			_____ /
Weighted Fixed Assets			_____

	Adjusted Value	×	Weights	=	Weighted Value
I. Fixed Assets	_____	×	_____	= $	_____
II. Inventory	_____	×	_____	= $	_____
III. Current Assets	_____	×	_____	= $	_____
IV. Intangibles	_____	×	_____	= $	_____
Total	_____			= $	_____
Divided by totals of weights				/	_____
Adjusted Liquidation Value				= $	_____

Tangible Book Value Worksheet

Total Assets	_____
Less: Total Liabilities	_____
= Net Worth	_____
Adjusted for:	
- Goodwill	_____
- Deferred Costs	_____
= Tangible Net Worth	_____

Tangible Market Net Worth

Restate book values of tangible assets into current market or replacement values related to their true economic worth. Use and restate only operating assets. Subtract liabilities and intangibles such as goodwill, trademarks, patents, copyrights, etc. The result equals Tangible Market Net Worth.

Tangible Market Net Worth Worksheet

Market	Current Balance	Market Value	Excess over Cost
Assets:			
Current	_____	_____	_____
Non-current	_____	_____	_____
Other Assets	_____	_____	_____
Other:	_____	_____	_____
Total	_____	_____	_____
Market Value in Excess of Book Value			
Less: Liabilities			_____
= Adjusted Market Net Worth			_____
Less: Intangibles			_____
Tangible Market Net Worth			_____

¶405.03

.05 Revenue Methods

Earnings methods are generally considered to be of a more subjective nature than asset methods which are considered more objective. Most valuators generally agree that earnings approach is superior in most valuation situations. The estimate of future flows is necessitated with these flows being discounted to present values. Income Statement flows are more subjective in their approach. Typically, future flows are projected based on the recent history of the firm. However, the past does not necessarily project the future.

Revenue Method Considerations

The practitioner should analyze three to five years of past income statements to identify trends to help in predicting future performance. A weighted averaging convention should be applied to these flows to give more significance to recent periods. Sophisticated mathematical techniques are available for projections, but may not be warranted given the often-times limited data, uncertainties in the raw data, and the assumptions on which the techniques are based. The factor most important to the prediction of future performance is the analysis of the historical financial performance. These income factors are intrinsic to the business itself. It's the character of the business. Income methods recognize the importance of earnings as a contributing factor to value. Secondary considerations are external factors such as inflation, market conditions, competition, etc.

Gross Revenues

Capitalization of gross revenues implicitly assumes that a given level of gross revenues will generate a certain level of earnings. The approach assumes a consistent relationship between gross revenues and profits. Gross revenue capitalization is frequently used in valuations for service businesses, since they are less dependent on major assets such as machinery or inventories in generating their profits. Use gross revenue capitalization on multiples to obtain "quick" rough range values. Use gross revenue methods when other data is not available or inadequate.

Advantages

This method eliminates numerous adjustments to the income statement that are often required. It is simple and easy to compute. Gross revenues are easily defined and quick to obtain. It is generally easier to verify than Net Income.

Disadvantages

Gross revenue data sometimes is not available. Often their simplicity brings about misuse through trying to oversimplify complex situations. The consistent relationship between revenues and profits may not hold for different businesses in different industries.

Divide the gross revenue by an appropriate capitalization rate or multiply the gross revenue by an appropriate gross revenue multiplier.

Gross Revenue Valuation Formula

$$\text{Valuation} = \frac{\text{Gross Revenue}}{\text{Capitalization Rate}}$$

Discounted Cash Flow

Cash flow may be defined as: Net income plus depreciation, net income plus non-cash expenses, and net income less principal repayments. (As defined in the Statement of Cash Flows by operating, financing, and investing activities.)

Many feel that cash flow is a valid criterion for valuations because it is with cash returns that the investment will be paid off. Cash flow will vary considerably from "GAAP" profits. Thus, cash flow analyzes the capacity of the business to meet its obligations. These cash flows are discounted to present value with a rate that allows for business and economic risks. Use the area's prime rate plus an adjustment for risk.

Use discounted cash flow methods for:

- A business established solely to fulfill a specific contract or project.
- An investor who sets a specific time frame in which he or she wishes to have the investment returned and money expended today for a future cash inflow.
- Companies that have insignificant assets, such as for service companies or for mergers.
- Start-up companies where cash flow is of most significance.

Discount Rate vs. Capitalization Rate

The discount rate will be higher than a capitalization rate used in other methods. This is because the capitalization rate allows for a built-in estimate of earnings growth. With the discounted method, these future estimates are reflected in the forecasts.

Process

- Estimate cash flow, listing the most recent period first.
- Estimate the liquidation value of the assets.
- Determine the liabilities for inclusion.
- From the present value of the cash flows, add the liquidation asset value and subtract the liabilities.

The discount rate is the desired rate of return an investor requires considering competing investments and assumed risk. Or, what amount invested today (the present value amount), when growing at the required rate, will provide the required sum. Or, it can be thought of as the present value of the projected future income streams.

Cash Flow Discounted Worksheet

Present Value Factor = _____ % (Choose appropriate present value rate)

(Cash Flow) Period Ending	Cash Flow $	Projected 10%	15%	20%	25%	30%	Discounted Present Value Factors 35% at	____%
_____	_____	.909	.869	.833	.800	.769	.741	_____
_____	_____	.826	.756	.694	.640	.591	.549	_____
_____	_____	.751	.657	.579	.512	.455	.406	_____
_____	_____	.683	.572	.482	.410	.350	.301	_____

		Projected					Discounted Present Value Factors		
(Cash Flow)									
Period Ending	Cash Flow $	10%	15%	20%	25%	30%	35% at	___%	
_____	_____	.621	.497	.402	.328	.269	.223	_____	
_____	_____	.564	.432	.335	.262	.207	.165	_____	

Total Projected _____   Total Discounted Cash Flows _____

Add: Liquidation Value of Assets + _____

Less: Liabilities _____

Estimated Business Value _____

Dividend Capacity Capitalization

The dividend-paying capacity, not the dividends actually paid, is the more important concern, per Rev. Rul. 59-60. The dividend capacity method is generally not appropriate for small firms because they strip their profits with a large year-end bonus. It is also inappropriate for small firms which must retain maximum profits to meet debt requirements. Use when valuing larger, closely held companies. Use when the owners are not the company management and receive profit distributions rather than substantial salaries.

Step 1—Refer to dividend yields on comparable publicly traded companies that were actually paid.

Step 2—Determine the average dividend yield:

Average Dividend Yield

$$\frac{\text{Annual Dividends}}{\text{Market Price per Share}}$$

Step 3—Analyze the dividend-paying capacity of the business being valued, as on a $X per share basis.

Step 4—Capitalize the value by dividing the dividend-paying capacity of $X per share in Step 3 by the average dividend yield in Step 2.

Disadvantages

Difficulty in developing dividend-paying capacity of the firm being valued. Difficulty in finding truly comparable companies.

Capitalized Earnings

The capitalized earnings approach is intended to compare the firm's earnings with others in the same industry. Convert a single earnings figure into an indication of value by multiplying that earnings by an appropriate factor or dividing by an appropriate rate.

Income Stream to Be Capitalized

Consider the purpose of the valuation. Consider the availability of reliable data for a small sole proprietor who often keeps inadequate records. Possibly the tax return Schedule C is the best indicator of income factors for the small business.

¶405.05

Capitalization Rate

Obtain industry rates of net income to equity over appropriate five-year period. The chosen rate must be appropriate to the defined income stream. Consider the facts and circumstances peculiar to the business. The practitioner often must use his or her experience and best judgment to determine the appropriate rate.

Capitalization Rate as Percentage of Stockholder's Equity Based on Industry Returns

	Ratio of Income to Equity %	×	Weights	=	Weighted
(Current)			5		
			4		
			3		
			2		
			1		

15 Weighted Total _____

+15 _____

Weighted Average Ratio of Income = _____

$$\text{Capitalization Rate} = \frac{\text{Weighted Average Ratio of Income}}{\text{Equity}} =$$

$$\text{Value} = \frac{\text{Earnings or Income Flow}}{\text{Capitalization Rate}}$$

Excess Earnings Method

The excess earnings method is similar to the capitalized earnings approach. It divides earnings into expected earnings and excess earnings.

Determine Net Tangible Asset Value

- Determine adjusted net income; deduct an allowance from earnings for sole proprietorship's or partnership's salary.

- Determine a percentage rate of return on the net tangible assets.

- Multiply net tangible assets by above rate.

- Subtract from normalized earnings. This equals the excess earnings or the amount considered above a fair return on the net tangible assets.

- Capitalize only the excess earnings.

Disadvantages

Determining a fair return for the industry is difficult. The IRS feels the method results in improper appraisals. Rates applied to tangibles are arbitrary and have no foundation according to the IRS. The excess earnings method was developed by the Treasury Department in 1920 in Appeal and Review Memorandum (A.R.M) 34 as a method of valuing intangible assets of a business for purposes of determining income tax bases.

¶405.05

Excess Earning Method Worksheet

I. Net Tangible Asset Value (Do not include intangibles)

	Current Value	Adjusted Value (Fair Market Value)
Current Assets	_____	_____
+ Non-current Assets	_____	_____
Less: Liabilities	_____	_____
= Adjusted Tangible Net Asset		_____
% Rate of return a buyer could earn invested elsewhere with similar risk	×	_____
Expected Earnings: Earnings attributable to Net Tangible Assets	=	_____

II. Determine Excess Earnings

Adjusted Net Income		_____
Less: Expected earnings	−	_____
= Excess Earnings	=	_____

III. Estimated Value of Intangibles

Adjusted Tangible Net Assets		_____
Number of years factor	×	_____
(5 = Well Established)		
(3 = Moderate)		
(1 = Young Firm)		
Intangibles Value:		_____

IV. Total Estimated Value

Adjusted Tangible Net Assets		_____
Intangible Value	+	_____
Total Value	=	_____

Discounted Future Earnings (DFE) Method

A theory that a business's value equals its cash flows discounted to present value. Analyze current and past Net Income. Project future Net Income. Discount the future flows to present value.

Disadvantages

Small business owners generally seek to minimize Net Income in order to minimize taxes. Small business future income projections are by nature very speculative. This is the most difficult aspect of the DFE method. The IRS considers it too speculative.

Formula:

Discounted Future Earnings

$$\text{Present Value} = \frac{\text{Net Income in nth year}}{(1+\text{Discount Rate})^n}$$

Where n = the nth year

Future Earnings Projection

Complete Net Income Projection

- Project the number of years that can be reliably projected, and capitalize the final year as follows:

$$\text{Capitalized Value} = \frac{\text{Net Income}}{\text{Discount Rate}}$$

- Take present value of each period, including final capitalized period.

- Choose appropriate capitalization rate for denominator.

- Consider a lower capitalization rate to compensate for inherent risk in forecasting accurate future flows.

- If the year-to-year percentage increases in projected earnings are greater than the discount rate, then the present value of each increment also increases.

Discounted Future Earnings Method Worksheet

Projected net income = Method A

Net Income: Optimistic _____   Moderate _____   Pessimistic _____
Discount Rate: Optimistic _____   Moderate _____   Pessimistic _____

Period Ending: _____   _____   _____
Proj. Net Income: _____   _____   _____

Discount %   × _____   _____
PV of Net Inc.   = _____   _____
    = Total present Value of Net Income
    = $_____ = Firm's value from earnings.

Summary—Weighted Averaging Technique

	Optimistic	Moderate	Pessimistic
Indicated Firm Value:	_____	_____	_____
× Weights	× 1	× 3	× 1
	(_____	_____	_____)/5
= Projected Firm Value			= _____

Projected Net Income Defined As

1. Net income after taxes

2. Net income before taxes

3. Earnings before interest and taxes

¶405.05

.07 Market Derived

Comparable Sales Method

Steps in seeking comparable companies for valuation purposes:

- Determine proper Standard Industrial Classification (SIC) for the company.
- Consult financial directories such as Securities and Exchange Commission's (SEC's) "Directory of Companies Required to File Annual Reports."
- Obtain annual report data.
- Synthesize the data into form for comparable analysis.
- Eliminate corporations which dictate lack of comparability.
- Develop the values of the comparable companies; consult directories such as Standard & Poor's Stock Guide.
- Determine earnings per share.
- Determine average price per share.
- Compute Price/Earnings ratio.
- Compute the average P/E ratios of all the comparable companies.
- Apply the average P/E ratio to the earnings per share of the company being valuated.

Price/Earnings Multiples

Price/earnings multiples of comparable public companies are used. The P/E multiple is the price of a company's share of common stock divided by its earnings per share. The factors reflected in the P/E ratio are the company's earnings, stability, profitability, and growth.

Step 1: Obtain five or more P/E ratios of comparable companies. Obtain the P/E ratios for publicly traded companies whose businesses are similar to the company being valued. Sources: Standard & Poor's Stock Guide, The Wall Street Journal, etc.

Step 2: Compute this average P/E multiple.

Step 3: Multiply the normalized adjusted net income of the company being valued by the average P/E multiple of Step 2.

Disadvantages

Comparing the P/E multiples of dissimilar chosen companies amounts to comparing apples and oranges, i.e., comparing a publicly traded company to an illiquid closely held company.

Market values fluctuate often based on market conditions such as supply and demand or unique market situations that have no apparent relationship to the true value of the particular business.

Usually, the buyer of the closely held business is seeking to take an active part in management. Such an investment in a public company would not provide this opportunity. The buyer's reasons for purchasing closely held stock vs. public stock are totally different, and totally different prices would be applied.

¶405.07

Price/Earnings Multiple Worksheet

	Aggressive	Most Likely	Conservative
After tax adjusted net income	$ _____	_____	_____
Average P/E Ratios of comparable companies	× _____	_____	_____
= Estimated Value	= _____	_____	_____

Fair Market to Net Book Value

Use when the asset base is of greater significance than the earnings ability. Use when future earnings are difficult to estimate.

Fair Market to Net Book Value Steps

- Obtain for 5 or more comparable companies the market value of their stock.
- Obtain for the same companies their book values.
- Divide Step 1 values by those in Step 2 to obtain a market-to-book-value ratio.
- Multiply the ratio in Step 3 by the book value net worth.

Fair Market to Net Book Value

Company	Fair Market Value of Stock	Net Book Value per Share
_____	_____	_____
_____	_____	_____
_____	_____	_____
_____	_____	_____

Ratio = Market / Book Value	_____ =	=	
Book Value Net Worth of Company		×	_____
Estimated Total Value		=	_____

Formula Method

The formula method computes a firm's value by adding values computed by the adjusted book value method (tangibles) and a modern version of Rev. Rul. 68-609 (intangibles).

Under the Formula Method

Earnings = Adjusted taxable income (normalized income for extraordinary items) plus officers' compensation.

Weighted averages are suggested but not required. Industry percent of Net Income to revenues is used because most reporting industry statistics have these data readily available.

Adjustments to initial intangible value may be items such as: minority interests, death of owner, disability of owner, industry trends, etc.

Formula Method

Compute Firm's Earnings

Taxable Income	Adjustments +/−	Adjusted Taxable = Income	Officer's Compensation +	Earnings =
_____	_____	_____	_____	_____
_____	_____	_____	_____	_____
_____	_____	_____	_____	_____

Compute Normal Earnings to Industry Averages

Industry % Income to Revenues	Firm's Gross × Revenues	Normal Earnings =
_____ %	$ _____	$ _____
_____ %	$ _____	$ _____
_____ %	$ _____	$ _____

Compute and Weight Excess Earnings

Firm's Earnings	Normal − Earnings	Excess = Earnings	× Weights	Weighted = Earnings
_____	_____	_____	_____	_____
_____	_____	_____	_____	_____
_____	_____	_____	_____	_____
			Total	_____
				/ by Weights

Weighted Average Excess Earnings   _____

/ Capitalization Rate   _____

= Initial Tangible Value   _____

+/− Adjustments   _____

= Final Intangible Value   _____

+ Adjusted Book Value (for tangibles)   _____

Total Formula Business Value   _____

Quick Methods of Valuation

There are often appropriate times when the valuator provides only a rough value to the business owner concerning the enterprise. The person may simply press for a rough range, only wishing to have this information for formulating future plans such as when to sell for retirement, etc.

Business Value

$$\text{Value} = \frac{\text{Profit from Business}}{\text{Rate of Return on Investment}}$$

Going Concern Value

$$\text{Value} = \frac{\text{Income}}{\text{Capitalization Rate}}$$

¶405.07

Capitalized Net Worth

$$\text{Value} = \frac{\text{Net Worth}}{\text{Capitalization Rate}}$$

Book Value per Share

This ratio is a good indicator for a small company that does not have its shares listed on an exchange. It's used as a simple measure for the investment in the company.

Book Value per Share = (Total Assets of Business – Total Debt of Business) / Number of outstanding common shares

Intrinsic Value of Share of Stock

Formula 1
Value per share of Stock = Anticipated Earnings per Share / Capitalization Rate

Formula 2
Value per share of Stock = Anticipated Earnings per Share × Price Earnings Ratio

Given the following data, what is the expected Value per share of Stock?

EPS = $6.50

Expected EPS = $6.85

Capitalization Rate = 8%

Price Earnings Ratio = 12.5

Formula 1

Value per share of Stock   = $6.85 / .08
                                   = $85.63

Formula 2

Value per share of Stock   = $6.85 × 12.5
                                   = $85.63

Dividend Payout Valuation of Price of Stock per Share

Dividend Payout Valuation of Price of Stock per Share =

$$\frac{(1-\text{Income Tax Rate})(\text{Dividend Payout Rate})(\text{Rate of Return on Assets})}{(\text{Value of Total Assets} / \#\text{ of Common Shares outstanding})}$$
$$\overline{\text{Discount Rate} - [(1-\text{Income Tax Rate})(\text{Retention Rate on Earnings})(\text{Rate of Return on Assets})]}$$

Given the following data, what is the Dividend Payout Valuation of Price of Stock per Share?

Income Tax Rate = .25

Dividend Payout Rate = .30

Rate of Return on Assets = .25

¶405.07

Value of Total Assets = $150,000

# of Common Shares Outstanding = 10,000

Discount Rate = .08

Retention Rate on Earnings = .35

Dividend Payout Valuation of Price of Stock per Share =

$$\frac{(1-.25)\,(.30)\,(.25)\,(\$150{,}000\,/\,10{,}000)}{.08 - [(1-.25)\,(.35)\,(.25)]}$$

$$= \frac{.84375}{.0144}$$

$$= 58.59$$

Going Concern Value of Leveraged Firm

Use to valuate the worth of a firm's acquisition of another firm and how much debt the potential acquisition can sustain.

Going Concern Value of Leveraged Firm

$$\text{Value} = \frac{\text{EBIT (1- tax rate)}}{\text{After Tax Discount Rate}} + (\text{tax rate}) \times \left(\begin{array}{c} \text{total amount} \\ \text{of debt} \end{array} \right)$$

Value of Leveraged Firm

Value of Leveraged Firm =
[((Earnings before Interest & Taxes) × (1 – Income Tax Rate)) /
After-Tax Discount Rate for Unleveraged Firm] + (Income Tax Rate × Total Debt)

Where:

After-Tax Discount Rate for Unleveraged Firm = [(Earnings before Interest and Taxes × (1– Income Tax Rate)) / Number of Outstanding Common Shares] / (Value of Unleveraged Firm / Number of Outstanding Common Shares)

Given the following data, what is the value of the leveraged firm?

Earnings before Interest and Taxes = $900,000

Income Tax Rate = .31

Total Debt = $300,000

Number of Outstanding Common Shares = 100,000

Value of Unleveraged Firm = $7,000,000

After-Tax Discount Rate for Unleveraged Firm = [($900,000 × (1– .31)) / 100,000] / ($7,000,000 / 100,000) = 8.87%

Value of Leveraged Firm = [(($900,000) × (1 – .31)) / .0887] + (.31 × $300,000)

= $7,094.127

General Small Business Formula

$$\text{Value} = (.80 \cdot \text{Inventory}) + \frac{(\text{Leasehold improvements} + \text{equipment})}{2}$$

$$+ \frac{(\text{Net Income}^1 + \text{Net Income}^2 + \text{Net Income}^3)}{3}$$

Where[1] = Net income 1 year ago.

Where[2] = Net income 2 years ago.

Where[3] = Net income 3 years ago.

Equity and Capitalized Earnings Value

Use the formula for a quick starting business valuation for a lender, partner, spouse, investor, etc. This formula will provide a business valuation by averaging (dividing by 2) the value of the equity and the capitalized earnings. The tangible equity value is doubled (or by some other multiple that is appropriate) to reflect that a consistently profitable business will be valued higher than low-risk bonds. Equity investments are expected to return higher rates than fixed income investments to reflect the greater risk.

Equity and Capitalized Earnings Value =

$$\frac{[\ 2\ \times [\ (\text{Stockholder's Equity} - \text{Intangible Assets}\ ) + \ (\text{Net Income Before Taxes \& Interest}\ /\ \text{Capitalized Rate})\ ]\ ]}{2}$$

Price Earnings Ratio for Valuation

Expected Price Earnings Ratio =
(Expected Retention Ratio – 1) + [(Current Price Earnings Ratio) ×
((1 + Discount Rate) / (1 + Expected Growth Rate of Earnings per Share))]

Given the following data, what is the Price Earnings Ratio for Valuation?

Expected Retention Ratio = 33%

Current Price Earnings Ratio = 12

Discount Rate = 10%

Expected Growth Rate of Earnings per Share = 5%

Expected Price Earnings Ratio = (.33– 1) + [(12) × ((1 + .10) / (1 + .05))] = 11.90

.09 Payback Analysis

Payback Method

It highlights how quickly cash will return. The payback method computes the time required for estimated future cash flows to equal the purchase price. Adjust Net Income by adding back depreciation.

¶405.09

Disadvantages

Doesn't recognize time value of money and doesn't take into account returns beyond the payback period.

Formula: Payback years = Purchase price / Yearly cash flow return

Payback Method Worksheet

	Payback Years =	Purchase Price/	Yearly Cash Flow
Pessimistic	_____	/ _____	_____
Moderate	_____	_____	_____
Optimistic	_____	_____	

	Payback Years		Weights
Pessimistic	_____	× 1 =	_____
Moderate	_____	× 3 =	_____
Optimistic	_____	× 1 =	_____
Weighted Years Total	=	_____ /5	
Expected Years	=	_____	

.10 Ability to Pay Method

This method is similar to the discounted cash flow method, but does not discount the cash flow to present values. It's a first quick look valuation. The ability to pay method provides a very simple valuation to determine if the buyer has the ability to pay for the purchased business. If the company can't pay for itself over a reasonable time, then it's a bad investment and a bad price, no matter what the purchase price is.

Advantages

- Good if buying the business solely for its income flow
- Good for negotiating a seller's unrealistic high value back to a reasonable level

Disadvantages

- Very simplistic method that ignores many considerations
- Bases value almost totally on assumed future sales prediction

Ability to Pay Method Process

- Predict normalized, realistic future sales per year
- Multiply by net income profit the percent that is reasonable or a weighted average of the last 3-5 years
- Interest: Add back to the net income the prior interest and subtract the new expected interest on the new expected purchase price loan. This number will be fine tuned and recalculated when you arrive at a more exact purchase price.
- Depreciation: Normalize the current net income by adding back the prior year depreciation and subtracting the new stepped up basis of the assets from the purchase.
- After determining the average net income expected, add back the new depreciation and new interest to obtain the cash flow from the income statement.

Example: Ability to Pay Valuation Method

	$640,000	Projected expected sales
×	.05	Net income profit % expected
=	$32,000	Net income expected
+	2,000	Interest expense prior year
−	2,000	Interest expense current projection
+	3,000	Depreciation prior year
−	4,000	Depreciation current projection
=	31,000	Taxable net income
−	4,000	Income taxes
=	27,000	Average net income expected
+	4,000	Depreciation current projection
+	2,000	Interest expense current projection
=	33,000	Net cash flow from income statement
−	3,000	Annual capital expenditures expected
=	30,000	Net cash flow before debt service
−	6,000	Investor/lender safety cushion requirement (20% to 40%)
=	24,000	Net annual cash flow available for debt service
×	5	Negotiated years to pay to obtain purchase price (5 assumed for example)
=	$120,000	Ability to pay purchase price

¶ 406 VALUATION PROCESS

.01 Gathering the Facts

Key Steps in Valuations

- The facts and unique circumstances of each case must be evaluated.
- There are no "set" formulas or rules that can be applied to all cases.
- There is usually not a "quick fix" answer.
- The valuation of a business is an art rather than a science, requiring interpretation, analysis, and value judgments.
- A good appraiser must transpose useful data into proper valuation procedures.
- The most significant aspect in the appraisal process is the selection of the appropriate valuation technique.
- Reasonableness must be applied to the valuation conclusion.
- Use several methods to estimate the value.
- Be prepared to justify which methods were chosen.
- Be prepared to justify why alternate methods were not appropriate.

Steps in Valuing a Business

- Determine the reason for the valuation.
- Determine what data concerning the business is presently available.
- Identify the potential seller's alternatives, if a sale situation exists.
- Identify the potential buyer's alternatives.
- Determine benchmark values.
- Evaluate the alternative methods to be used.
- Establish the values.
- Seek a complete understanding of the business to be valued.
- Make inquiries concerning the nature of the business.
- Determine key dates.
  - Determine the date when the report is needed.
  - Determine the date of the valuation. A valuation of the business in prior periods will preclude any physical observations.
  - Determine the fiscal year-end of the business. If the valuation is to coincide with the fiscal-year end (FYE) of the firm, then financial information will be more readily available.

Preference Steps in Choosing a Valuation Method

- Determine if enforceable agreement exists.
- Determine if recognized industry formulas exist.
- Use Earning approaches, unless not appropriate.
- Use Asset approaches, unless not appropriate.
- Use Cash Flow approaches.

Documents and Information Checklist Financials

- Previous five years of FYE financials.
- Review interim statements for end of year adjustments.
- Review federal tax returns.
- Corporate records.
  - Articles of incorporation.
  - By-laws.
  - Minute Book.
- Financial schedules.
- Inventory lists.
- Officer compensation detail.
- Schedule of dividends paid.
- Off balance sheet assets or liabilities.
- Key person life insurance.
- Aged accounts receivables.
- Aged accounts payables.

- Stockholder loans.
- Depreciation schedules.
- Stock transactions.
- Customer information.
- Supplier information.
- Order backlog.
- Projections and budgets.
- Real and personal property values.
  — Copies of real and personal property tax assessments.
  — Insurance appraisals.
  — Copies of any independent appraisals, such as piecemeal equipment.
  — Appraisals.
  — Contractual obligations.
  — Equipment leasing contracts.
  — Loan agreements.
  — Franchise or distributorship agreements; Customer contracts/agreements.
  — Supplier contracts/agreements.
  — Employment agreements.
  — Non-competition agreements.
  — Patents, copyrights.

Financial Analysis Checklist

- Compute current and quick ratios, debt-to-equity ratios, and cash flow statements.
- Analyze firm's basic liquidity and turnovers, such as accounts receivable and inventory turnover.
- Analyze accounts receivable aging schedule, accounts payable aging schedule, and sales-to-net-working-capital ratio.
- Verify cash balances.
- Determine minimum/maximum cash balances throughout year.
- If company has marketable securities, obtain current market value.
- Review any notes receivable.
- Analyze inventory such as scrap, obsolete stock, or slow moving items.
- Determine projections of income and cash flow needs.
- Determine likelihood of future sales and profits and their financing needs.
- Review any pension or profit sharing plans.
- Do comparatives on income statements.
- Pay particular attention to cost of goods and gross profit margin.
- Analyze inventory accounting methods, such as LIFO, FIFO, and weighted moving average.

¶406.01

- Obtain company's tax returns.
- Obtain personal financial statements on principal stockholders.
- Analyze current liabilities.
- Age accounts payable.
- Obtain details regarding bank debts or other loans such as interest, term, and collateral. Review the loan agreements. Do same for long-term debt.
- Determine if there are any contingent liabilities. List and detail.
- Reconcile differences between financials and tax returns.
- Reconcile retained earnings from year to year.
- Determine what level of assurance the financials are, such as audits, reviews, or compilations.
- For balance sheet information, compute financials for the last five years; review financial statements.
- Obtain details on fixed assets, date of purchase, cost, accumulated depreciation, and current replacement value.
- Obtain independent market appraisals on large fixed assets, real property, machinery, and equipment.
- Analyze prepaid expenses and deferred charges.

.03 Minimum Valuation Standards

The following is a valuation procedure checklist based on highlights from various revenue rulings (mostly Rev. Rul. 59-60). Fair market value is the price in which property would change hands between a willing buyer and seller. Fair market value is unique to each set of facts at hand. Common sense must be applied. Uncertainty of future income will decrease the property's value by increasing the risk of loss of these earnings.

Valuations should be done in accordance with the Internal Revenue Code and regulations.

Factors to be considered:

- Business nature and history.
- Industry and economic outlook.
- Book value of stock.
- Sales of stock and size of block of stock to be valued.
  - Comparable company's stock values.
- Analysis of risk related to firm.
- Study firm's Income Statement history comparables—suggests previous five years.
- Provide and clarify any notes to financials—prediction of future earnings emphasizing past history.
  - Business quality of earnings.
  - Earnings capacity.
  - Intangibles.

- Dividend paying capacity, not dividends actually paid.
- Presence of goodwill rests on excess of net earnings over industry's fair return.
- Stock sales of comparable companies should be investigated to determine if they represent transactions at arm's length or forced or distressed sales.
- Different weights should be accorded to various factors. Assets may be the most important criterion in some cases, while earnings should receive primary consideration in other cases.
- Capitalization rates must be appropriate (this is one of the most difficult values to determine). Wide variations will be found over companies in the same industry.
- No useful purpose is accomplished by taking an average of various applicable computed factors.
- The formula approach may be used in determining the fair market value of intangible assets only if there is no better basis available.

Highlights of Appraisal Standards

In Developing the Appraisal

- Define the purpose and intended use of the appraisal.
- Identify any limiting conditions.
- Date the appraisal.
- Consider all major factors that have an influence on value.
- Indicate if assets are appraised independently or as parts of a going concern.
- Understand and correctly employ recognized methods and techniques necessary for a credible appraisal.
- Do not commit a substantial error of omission.
- Do not render appraisal services in a negligent or careless manner.
- Consider if the appraisal is based on majority or minority interests.
- Select the appropriate technique for the appraisal.
- Analyze and collect data concerning:
  — Prices, terms, and conditions affecting similar businesses.
  — Physical conditions, remaining life, and obsolescence considerations.
  — History and nature of business.
  — Economic and industry conditions.
  — Past, current, and future business prospects.
  — Sales of similar firms and similar stock sales.
- Select the appropriate valuation methods.
- Consider and reconcile the quality and quantity of data.
- Disclose pertinent information.

In Creating the Appraisal Report

Communication of the appraisal report:

- Set forth the appraisal in a clear and accurate manner.

¶406.03

- Provide sufficient information for understandability.
- Disclose any limiting condition or extraordinary assumption that may directly affect the value.
- The appraisal report should:
  - — Specify the date of appraisal and date of appraisal report.
  - — Describe scope of appraisal.
  - — Detail assumptions and any limiting conditions.
  - — Set forth procedures used and supporting reasoning.
  - — Describe the business being appraised.
  - — Define the value to be estimated.
  - — Certify.
  - — Include responsible party's signed transmittal.

.05 Combination Valuation Methods

Many believe that a combination of several valuation methods is generally the preferred way of valuing businesses. This is the method often employed by the courts and most often used by the IRS in practice. The combination of various valuation methods for a final conclusion should usually not be done by a simple averaging of the methods used. A pure averaging convention should only be applied when the range of values is reasonably tight and consistent with one another. The relevance of each valuation method must be carefully assessed for its validity. Each relevant fact and circumstance should be considered.

Averaging Conventions

Typically, different weights can be applied to the different valuation approaches used based on the practitioner's desire to stress the results of the different valuation approaches. The obvious weakness is determining what weights should be assigned to each valuation method. The concept of applying averaging conventions is to minimize the defects in any method and to assure that no single valuation method is determinative. Zeroing in on a range gives the valuator a better feeling of assurance concerning his or her values. These weights are dependent on the judgment of the practitioner in the final analysis. The weighting should be derived considering the reliability and availability of the data and the conceptual soundness of the valuation approaches.

The Weighted Approach

Valuation Method Used	Weight ×	Value	Weighted = Value
_____	_____	_____	_____
_____	_____	_____	_____
_____	_____	_____	_____
_____	1.00	_____	_____
	Total Weighted Value		_____
	Less Discount =		_____
	Indicated Value =		_____

The Modal Approach

Choosing the final valuation by the modal technique is to simply array the values from the lowest to the highest. Then concentrate on the middle ranges that show a more tight, consistent value.

Example: Method

A	B	C	D	E	F	G
$206,000	$267,000	$452,000	$468,000	$471,000	$479,000	$513,000

The valuator should focus on values C, D, E, F, concluding that the range of $452,000 to $479,000 is best indicative of the firm's value. A final choice may be computed with a simple averaging:

$$\text{Indicated Value} = \frac{\$452,000 + \$468,000 + \$471,000 + \$479,000}{4} = \$467,500$$

.07 Report Presentation

Principals on Preparing the Valuation Report

- Conclude the report with one or two major points. If too many points are emphasized, the reader may overlook the major points. The reader should not have to stop and analyze what the valuator meant or do further research to verify the conclusion.
- Present the report in clear terms the reader will understand. Minimize technical jargon.
- Clearly define what assumptions were used.
- Provide the report in a clear and readable format.
- Don't expect the reader to sort out the important points. The valuator must provide this in a clear, summary format.
- Keep the report brief, with summary information, but provide sufficient detail to support all computation and conclusions.
- Consider visual charts to assist the reader in understandability.

Presentational Errors to Avoid

- Reports that provide reams and reams of computer-generated data.
- Failure to state why certain valuation methods were considered as most appropriate and others were not.
- Failure to present the analysis in a clear and logical manner.
- Failure to provide signature of the appraiser.
- Failure to provide name of appraising firm.
- Failure to provide minimum detail in the valuation section of the report.

Written Presentation Guidelines

Cover Letter

- Discuss the purpose of the valuation.
- Discuss the valuation methods used.

- Provide statement limiting responsibility for data or reports provided by others and for subsequent events.
- State the valuator did not audit or review data used in the valuation.
- Sign and date cover letter.

Valuation Report

- Identify the business being valued.
- Specify the valuation date.
- Provide data on intangibles. Detail how valued.
- Provide summary conclusions in a simple and readable format.
- Provide general information about the firm, history, management, and operations.
- Identify information relied on for the valuation.
- State the purpose of the valuation and its intended use.
- Provide data on tangibles and detail how valued.

Valuation Approach

- Justify the valuation methods that were chosen.

Years Selected

- Justify the years which were selected for the analysis.
- Why were those periods covered?
- Why were other periods not covered?
- Were they representative years?

Financial Adjustments

- Justify the adjustments to the financial statements and the rationale for each adjustment.
- Outside statistics or surveys should be included in the report where appropriate.
- Specify what weighting techniques were used and why.
- Provide all necessary supporting documents, statistics, authorities, articles, analyses, etc.
- Be ready to explain and defend conclusions reached.
- State independence of valuators.
- Provide a conclusion on the value or range of values.

Sample Valuation Engagement Letter

The letter should state the terms of the agreement, the purpose of the valuation, the degree of responsibility taken, the methodology to be used for the valuation, and the fees and payment schedule.

Sample Valuation Engagement Letter

John C. Wisdom, CPA
2915 LBJ Freeway
Dallas, Texas 75234
November 1, 20XX

Mr. John Smith, President
USA Manufacturers, Inc.
140 Main Street
Dallas, Texas 75231

Dear Sir:

This letter confirms the terms of our engagement and the nature of services to be provided. I will prepare a valuation of USA Manufacturers, Inc. as of December 20XX for use in negotiating the sale of the company. The final valuation will present a range of values after considering various financial and non-financial factors pertinent to the valuation at hand. I will rely on information submitted by the management of Manufacturers, Inc. as being materially true, correct, and complete.

If necessary and pertinent to the valuation process, I will compile an earnings forecast and summaries of significant forecast assumptions and accounting policies as of December 31, 20XX, and for the five years ending December 31, 20XX, based on the information and representations provided by the management of Manufacturers, Inc. I will seek to make any necessary adjustments to the financials which I deem as appropriate to clearly reflect the financials and provide for normalized earnings required for this evaluation. All assumptions and adjustments will be clearly substantiated. I will not express any form of assurance on the likelihood of achieving the forecast or on the reasonableness of the underlying assumptions and representations.

Any schedules used throughout the analysis will be presented as an integral part of the valuation report and are not intended to be used separately. The earnings forecast is management's estimate of the most probable financial situation for the forecast period. It is based on management's assumptions, reflecting the most likely set of conditions and the most likely course of action. Some assumptions inevitably will not materialize and unanticipated events and circumstances may occur; therefore, the actual results achieved during the forecast period will vary from the forecast, and the variations may be material. The valuation report will contain a statement to that effect.

I have no responsibility to update my report for events and circumstances occurring after the date of the valuation report. The total fee for these services will be $_____. Payment will be _____ percent on execution of this agreement and the balance on submission of the report. Please indicate your approval of this valuation by signature. Upon proper receipt of this engagement letter and down payment, execution of my services shall begin.

Sincerely,
John C. Wisdom, CPA

Acknowledged by:
John Smith, President
USA Manufacturers, Inc.

Date:

¶406.07

Sample Valuation Report Cover Letter

John C. Wisdom, CPA
2915 LBJ Freeway
Dallas, Texas 75234
January 12, 20XX

Mr. John Smith, President
USA Manufacturers, Inc.
140 Main Street
Dallas, Texas 75231

Dear Mr. Smith:

I have prepared a valuation report of USA Manufacturers, Inc. as of December 31, 20XX. I have made my valuation using a combination approach. I performed various procedures on certain data necessary for the preparation of the valuation, namely, adjusted book value, gross revenues, valuation review by cost justification, and discounted future earnings.

I have based the valuation of USA Manufacturers, Inc. on the most probable quantitative valuation. The range presented for the valuation was developed by using the general weighted approach.

Management provided to me the pertinent financial historicals as well as basic future assumptions. After performing limited analytical review procedures, the data was used in preparing the valuation report.

Had performance of an examination of the underlying financial statements of Manufacturers, Inc. in accordance with generally accepted auditing standards been made, significant matters that would alter the amounts used in the preparation of the valuation might have come to my attention. I have no responsibility as to the financial information provided me by management.

I take no responsibility for updating this report to reflect events and circumstances occurring after the date of the valuation.

Sincerely,

John C. Wisdom, CPA

Chapter 5
Government Programs

Small Business Administration . . . . ¶ 501
Social Security—SSI, Supplemental Security Income . . . . ¶ 502
Disability and Social Security . . . . ¶ 503
Retirement Benefits and Social Security . . . . ¶ 505
"Survivors (Life) Insurance" from Social Security . . . . ¶ 507
Social Security System—Medicare . . . . ¶ 509
Social Security Administration: Internet Services . . . . ¶ 510
Social Security System Statistical Tables . . . . ¶ 511

¶ 501 SMALL BUSINESS ADMINISTRATION

The U.S. Small Business Administration (SBA) was established in 1953. The SBA provides a great deal of information helpful to small businesses and their advisors on the SBA's website: *www.sba.gov*. The SBA helps small businesses with many programs that provide financial, technical, and management assistance. The SBA has offices in every state, the District of Columbia, Guam, and Puerto Rico. In addition, the SBA works with thousands of lending, educational, and training institutions. Of all of the SBA programs, SBA loan programs will be of the most interest to many small business advisors.

.01 SBA Decision Considerations

Repayment ability from cash flow, good character, management capability, collateral, and owner's equity contribution are important considerations in SBA approval. Individuals who own 20 percent or more of the business and other owners who hold key management positions must guarantee SBA loans personally.

Eligibility

The following four factors generally determine eligibility for SBA loans:

1. Type of Businesses Eligible

Most businesses are eligible but applicant businesses must operate for profit, do business in the United States or its possessions, have reasonable owner equity to invest, and use other financial resources first—including personal assets.

2. Size of Businesses Eligible

An eligible small business is defined as one that is independently owned and operated and not dominant in its field of operation. The Small Business Act also states the definition of small business varies from industry to industry. SBA size standards define the maximum size of an eligible small business:

Retail and service—$6.5 to $32.5 million in average annual sales or receipts over three years, depending on the type of business.

Construction—$12 to $28.5 million in average annual sales or receipts over three years.

Wholesale—not more than 100 employees.

Manufacturing—generally not more than 500 employees, but in a few cases, up to 1,500 employees. Some manufacturing companies are subject to a size standard of 750 or 1,000 employees.

Mining—mining industries, other than mining services, are subject to a size standard of 500 employees.

3. Use of Loans

Loan proceeds must be used for business purposes such as the purchase of real estate to house the business operations; construction, renovation or leasehold improvements; acquisition of furniture, fixtures, machinery, and equipment; purchase of inventory; and, working capital. A business may use the loan proceeds to refinance existing debt that does not have reasonable terms and conditions. A borrower may use the loan proceeds to purchase an existing business.

A business may not use the proceeds of SBA loans to refinance existing debt where the lender is likely to sustain a loss. In addition, a business may not use the loan proceeds to finance a partial change of business ownership or a change in ownership that will not help the business. A business may not use the loan proceeds to reimburse any owner for loans or repayments of temporary injections of equity capital pending the receipt of the loan proceeds. Further, a business may not use the loan proceeds to pay any trust fund taxes owed to the federal government or to any state. The business should be holding the taxes withheld from employees in trust for the government. Finally, a general restriction is that the business may not use the loan proceeds for a non-sound business purpose.

4. Special Circumstances

Franchises are eligible except when the franchisor has excessive control over the business.

Recreational facilities and clubs are eligible provided the facilities are open to the general public or in membership only clubs and membership is not restricted for any particular group.

Farms and agricultural businesses are eligible, but applicants should first explore Farm Service Agency (FSA) programs.

Fishing vessels are eligible, but those seeking funds for the construction or reconditioning of vessels with a cargo capacity of five tons or more must first request financing from the National Marine Fisheries Service.

Medical facilities, such as hospitals, clinics, emergency outpatient facilities, and medical and dental laboratories are eligible. Properly licensed convalescent and nursing homes are eligible if services exceed those of room and board.

Eligible Passive Company (EPC), which is an entity that does not engage in regular business activity but leases real or personal property to operating companies, is eligible if the EPC uses the loan proceeds to acquire, lease, or improve the property it leases. The EPC must comply with certain conditions (13 CFR Sec. 120.111).

Change of ownership. Loans for this purpose are eligible provided the business benefits from the change. In most cases, this benefit should be seen in promoting the sound development of the business or, perhaps, in preserving its existence. Loans cannot be made when proceeds would enable a borrower to purchase: (a) part of a business in which it has no present interest or (b) part of an interest of a present and continuing owner. Loans to effect a change of ownership among members of the same family are discouraged.

Aliens are eligible; however, status possessed, e.g., resident, lawful temporary resident, etc., is considered in determining the degree of risk relating to the continuity of the applicant's business. The borrower may offset the excessive risk by providing full collateral.

Probation or parole applications will not be accepted from firms where one of those required to submit a personal history statement is currently incarcerated, on parole, or on probation; is a defendant in a criminal proceeding; or whose probation or parole is lifted expressly because it prohibits an SBA loan.

Ineligible Businesses:

Businesses engaged in illegal activities, loan packaging, speculation, multi sales distribution, gambling, investment or lending, or where the owner is on parole are not eligible along with the following specific types of businesses:

- Real estate investment and other speculative activities
- Lending activities
- Pyramid sales plans
- Illegal activities
- Gambling activities
- Charitable, religious, or certain other nonprofit institutions

.02 Loan Amounts, Rates, and Fees

Loan Amounts

Loan amounts vary by program. The maximum loan amount is $2 million. The maximum amount the SBA can guaranty is generally $1.5 million. Small loans of $150,000 or less carry a maximum guaranty of 85 percent, and loans more than $150,000 carry a maximum guaranty of 75 percent. SBAExpress loans have a maximum guaranty of 50 percent. The Export Working Capital Loan Program has a maximum guaranty of 90 percent up to a guaranteed amount of $1 million.

Interest Rates

Interest rates are negotiated between the borrower and the lender but are subject to SBA maximums, which are pegged to the prime rate.

Interest rates may be fixed or variable. Fixed rate loans of $50,000 or more must not exceed prime plus two and one-quarter percent (2.25%) if the maturity is less than seven (7) years, and prime plus two and three-quarters percent (2.75%) if the maturity is seven (7) years or more.

For loans of less than $25,000, the maximum interest rate must not exceed prime plus four and one-quarter percent (4.25%) if the maturity is less than seven years and prime plus four and three-quarters percent (4.75%) if the maturity is seven years or more; for loans between $25,000 and $50,000, maximum rates must not exceed prime plus three and one-quarter percent (3.25%) if the maturity is less than seven years and prime plus three and three-quarters percent (3.75%) if the maturity is seven years or more.

¶501.02

Variable rate loans may be pegged to either the lowest prime rate or the SBA optional peg rate. The optional peg rate is a weighted average of rates the federal government pays for loans with maturities similar to the average SBA loan. It is calculated quarterly and published in the "Federal Register."

The lender and the borrower negotiate the amount of the spread, which will be added to the base rate. An adjustment period is selected which will identify the frequency at which the note rate will change. It must be no more often than monthly and must be consistent, (e.g., monthly, quarterly, semiannually, annually or any other defined, consistent period).

Fees Associated with SBA Loans

The SBA charges lenders a guaranty and a servicing fee for each loan approved. These fees can be passed on to the borrower once the lender has paid them. The fees shown here apply to loans approved on or after December 8, 2004. When the loan amount is $150,000 or less, the guaranty fee will be two percent of the guaranteed portion. Lenders are permitted to retain 25 percent of this fee. For loans more than $150,000 to $700,000, a three percent guaranty fee will be charged. For loans more than $700,000, a 3.5 percent guaranty fee will be charged. For loans of more than $1 million, an additional guaranty fee of 0.25 percent applies to the portion of the loan in excess of $1 million. Also, all loans will be subject to a 25 basis point (0.25%) annualized servicing fee, which is applied to the outstanding balance of SBA's guaranteed portion of the loan. For loans approved on or after October 1, 2004, the annual servicing fee is 0.5 percent of the outstanding balance of the guaranteed portion of the loan. For loans approved on or after October 1, 2005, the annual servicing fee is 0.545 percent of the outstanding balance of the guaranteed portion of the loan. For loans approved on or after October 1, 2006, the annual servicing fee is 0.55 percent of the outstanding balance of the guaranteed portion of the loan. Processing fees, origination fees, application fees, points, brokerage fees, bonus points, and other fees are prohibited. The only time a commitment fee may be charged is for a loan made under the Export Working Capital Loan Program.

Prepayment

Effective for all loans where the applications were received by the lender on or after December 22, 2000, a new prepayment charge paid by the borrower to SBA ("subsidy recoupment fee") has been added for those loans that meet the following criteria:

    a. Have a maturity of 15 years or more where the borrower is prepaying voluntarily;

    b. The prepayment amount exceeds 25 percent of the outstanding balance of the loan; *and*

    c. The prepayment is made within the first three years after the date of the first disbursement (not approval) of the loan proceeds.

The prepayment fee calculation is as follows:

    a. During the first year after disbursement, five percent of the amount of the prepayment;

    b. During the second year after disbursement, three percent of the amount of the prepayment; or

    c. During the third year after disbursement, one percent of the amount of the prepayment.

¶501.02

Maximum Loan Maturities

The maximum loan term for which the SBA will guarantee the loan is 25 years for real estate and equipment loans and generally seven years for working capital loans. The SBA allows a term of up to 10 years for working capital loans where the longer term is necessary to ensure repayment. The maximum maturity for loans used to finance fixed assets, except real estate, is the economic life of the assets, not to exceed 25 years.

The maximum loan maturity is 25 years for the acquisition of land and buildings or the refinancing of debt incurred in their acquisition. If business premises are to be constructed or significantly renovated, the 25-year maximum maturity is in addition to the time required to complete the construction or renovation. Significant renovation is construction of at least one-third of the current value of the property.

If the borrower uses the loan proceeds for a combination of purposes, the maximum maturity may be a weighted average of the applicable maturities, which allows level payments. Alternatively, the monthly loan payment can be the sum of equal monthly installments on the allowable maturities for each purpose. This treatment requires higher payments during the initial term of the loan.

.03 SBA Loan Guaranty Program

The 7(a) Loan Guaranty Program is one of SBA's primary lending programs and provides loans through private-sector lenders to small businesses unable to secure financing on reasonable terms through normal lending channels. The SBA guarantees the loans.

Types of Loans Under the Program

SBA LowDoc. Designed to increase the availability of funds under $150,000 and stream-line/expedite the loan review process.

SBAExpress. Designed to increase the capital available to businesses seeking loans up to $350,000.

SBA Export Express. SBA Export *Express* combines the SBA's small business lending assistance with its technical assistance programs to help small businesses that have traditionally had difficulty in obtaining adequate export financing. SBA Export *Express* helps small businesses that have exporting potential but need funds to buy or produce goods, and/or to provide services, for export. Loan proceeds may be used for most business purposes, including expansion, equipment purchases, working capital, inventory or real estate acquisitions. The pilot program is available throughout the country and is expected to run through September 30, 2005. No further information about a possible termination date is available on the SBA's website. However, the program is apparently still available.

Home and Personal Property Disaster Loans. This program provides loans to individuals who are victims of a disaster in a declared disaster area. The disaster victim does not have to own a business to qualify.

CAPLines. An umbrella program to help small businesses meet their short-term and cyclical working capital needs with five separate programs.

¶501.03

International Trade. If the business is preparing to engage in or is already engaged in international trade, or is adversely affected by competition from imports, the International Trade Loan Program is designed for this purpose.

Export Working Capital. Designed to provide short-term working capital to exporters in a combined effort of the SBA and the Export-Import Bank.

Pollution Control. Designed to provide loan guaranties to eligible small business for the financing of the planning, design, or installation of a pollution control facility.

DELTA. Defense Loan and Technical Assistance is a joint SBA and DOD effort to provide financial and technical assistance to defense-dependent small firms adversely affected by cutbacks in defense.

Qualified Employee Trusts. Designed to provide financial assistance to Employee Stock Ownership Plans.

Prequalification Loan Program. This program uses intermediaries to assist prospective borrowers in developing viable loan application packages and securing loans. Once the loan package is assembled, it is submitted to the SBA for expedited consideration; a decision is usually made within three days. If the application is approved, the SBA issues a letter of prequalification stating the SBA's intent to guaranty the loan. The intermediary, usually a Small Business Development Center, then helps the borrower locate a lender offering the most competitive rates.

Community Express. This is a pilot SBA loan program that was developed in collaboration with the National Community Reinvestment Coalition (NCRC) and its member organizations. Under the pilot, which will initially be limited to selected NCRC lenders, an SBA *Express* like program will be offered to pre-designated geographic areas serving mostly New Markets small businesses. The program will also include technical and management assistance, which is designed to help increase the loan applicant's chances of success. The maximum loan amount is $250,000.

CAIP Loan Program. The United States Community Adjustment and Investment Program was created to help communities that suffered job losses due to changing trade patterns with Mexico and Canada following the North American Free Trade Agreement (NAFTA). The CAIP works with the SBA in both their 7(a) Loan Guarantee Program and 504 Program to reduce borrower costs and increase the availability of these proven business assistance programs.

Military Reservist Economic Injury Disaster Loans. These loans provide funds to an eligible small business to meet its ordinary and necessary operating expenses that it could have met, had an essential employee not been called to active duty in his or her role as a military reservist. The maximum interest rate on these loans is four percent.

.04 Other SBA Loan Programs

Microloan, a 7(m) Loan Program

This program works through non-profit community-based intermediaries to provide small loans up to $35,000. The maximum loan term is six years.

Certified Development Company (504 Loan) Program

The 504 Certified Development Company (CDC) Program provides growing businesses with long-term, fixed-rate financing for major fixed assets, such as land, buildings, machinery, or equipment for expansion or modernization. A Certified Development Company is a nonprofit corporation set up to contribute to the economic development of its community or region. CDCs work with the SBA and private-sector lenders to provide financing to small businesses.

.05 Survey of Selected SBA Programs

Small Business Investment Company Program

Licensed and regulated by the SBA, SBICs are privately owned and managed investment firms that make capital available to small businesses through investments or loans. Most SBICs are profit-motivated businesses whose incentive is to share in the success of a small business. In addition to equity capital and long-term loans, SBICs provide debt-equity investments and management assistance.

New Markets Venture Capital Program

The New Markets Venture Capital (NMVC) Program is a developmental venture capital program designed to promote economic development and the creation of wealth and job opportunities in low-income geographic areas and among individuals living in such areas.

The Business Development Program

The Business Development Program (8(a) Program) is a business development program that provide entrepreneurs and contractors assistance in understanding, preparation, negotiation, and assistance in competing for federal government contract awards. The 8(a) program is growing in its assistance to small businesses owned by socially and economically disadvantaged firms.

SCORE

Service Corps of Retired Executives (SCORE), are locally-chartered volunteer organizations funded by SBA, which provide free, expert, problem-solving assistance to small businesses.

Women's Business Center

The SBA's Office of Women's Business Ownership promotes the growth of women-owned businesses through programs that address business training and technical assistance, and provide access to credit and capital, federal contracts, and international trade opportunities.

Small Business Development Center Program

Small Business Development Center (SBDC) Program provides one-stop management assistance to current and prospective small business owners. The program is a cooperative effort of the private sector, the educational community and federal, state and local governments to provide information and guidance in central and easily accessible branch locations. There are nearly 1,000 SBDC service locations in the United States, Puerto Rico, U.S. Virgin Islands, Guam, and American Samoa. In each state there is a lead organization that sponsors the SBDC and manages the program. The lead organization coordinates program services offered to small businesses through a network of subcenters and satellite locations in each state. Subcenters are located at colleges, universities, community colleges, vocational schools, chambers of commerce and economic development corporations.

Subcontracting Assistance Program

Promotes use of small businesses by major prime contractors. Commercial Marketing Representatives (CMRs) concentrate on large businesses that have contracts in excess of $500,000 and identify small business sources to satisfy specific needs of the prime contractor.

Certificate of Competency Program (COC)

COC helps small businesses secure Federal contacts by providing an appeal process to low-bidder firms denied government contracts for a perceived lack of ability or financial resources to perform the work.

PRO-Net

PRO-Net is an electronic gateway of procurement information for and about small businesses. PRO-Net is an Internet-based database of information on small, disadvantaged, 8(a), and women-owned businesses. It is free to federal and state government agencies as well as prime and other contractors seeking small business contractors, subcontractors, and/or partnership opportunities. On January 1, 2004, PRO-Net and the Department of Defense's Central Contractor Registration (CCR) became an integrated database of small businesses that want to do business with the government. CCR assumed all of PRO-Net's search capabilities and functions. For more information, please consult the following websites: *http://www.ccr.gov* and *http://pro-net.sba.gov*.

Small Business Innovation Reasearch (SBIR) Program

The Small Business Innovation Research Program helps to carry out the mission of the Office of Technology to strengthen and expand competitiveness of small business high technology research and development businesses in the federal environment.

Disaster Assistance Loan Program

This loan program is the primary federally funded, disaster assistance loan program for funding long-range recovery for private sector, nonagricultural disaster victims.

Small Business Technology Transfer (STTR)

This program requires each small firm competing for an R&D project to collaborate with a nonprofit research institution. It is a joint venture from the initial proposal to the project's completion, and is administered by the SBA Office of Technology.

HUBZone Empowerment Contracting Program

The HUBZone Empowerment Contracting Program provides federal contracting opportunities for qualified small businesses located in distressed areas.

¶ 502 SOCIAL SECURITY—SSI, SUPPLEMENTAL SECURITY INCOME

The Supplemental Security Income program is an assistance source of last resort for those age 65 or older, blind, or disabled with little income and financial resources. About 7 million (as of September 2006) aged, blind, and disabled individuals receive SSI payments for the basic necessities of food, clothing, and shelter. SSI is a means-tested program. Legislation and court decisions have made the SSI program very complex.

The Social Security Act of 1935 created not only the Social Security program, but it also established two Federal-State grant programs: Old-Age Assistance and Aid to the Blind.

The Federal Government paid half the cost of State benefits to the needy, aged, and blind. Aid to the Permanently and Totally Disabled was added in 1950. States varied widely in their eligibility criteria, financial capacity, and willingness to provide support. So effective January 1974, Congress replaced the State-administered programs with the Federally administered SSI program, which required a uniform Federal benefit and uniform eligibility standards. Benefits are financed from general revenues, and some states supplement the Federal benefit.

.03 Eligibility Criteria

An individual must be at least age 65, blind, or disabled. In addition, the individual must be a United States citizen or an eligible noncitizen and reside in the United States. The individual must not be absent from the United States for more than 30 days. An individual also must meet income and resource limits.

Income

In 2007, an individual cannot be eligible for Federal SSI benefits if he or she has countable income of more than the Federal benefit rate of $623 a month ($934 for a couple). The amount of a person's income is used to determine both eligibility for, and the amount of, that person's benefit.

SSI law defines four kinds of income: (1) earned income, (2) unearned income, (3) in-kind income, and (4) deemed income. Earned income consists of wages, salaries, net income from self-employment, and certain royalties and honoraria. Unearned income is any income other than earned income, such as Social Security benefits, pensions, state disability payments, unemployment benefits, interest income, and cash gifts from friends and relatives. In-kind income is food or shelter received free of charge or for less than its fair market value. Deemed income is the part of the income of the applicant's spouse with whom the applicant lives, parent(s) with whom the applicant lives, or the applicant's sponsor (if the applicant is an alien), which the Social Security Administration uses to compute the SSI benefit amount.

The amount of income a person can have each month and still get SSI depends partly on where that individual lives. State income limits can be checked through the Social Security Administration at 1-800-772-1213. Individuals who are deaf or hard of hearing may call the Social Security Administration's TTY number at 1-800-325-0778.

SSA does not count all income in determining eligibility. For example, these items do not count:

- The first $20 of most income received in a month
- The first $65 of earnings and one-half of earnings over $65 received in a month
- The value of food stamps
- Income tax refunds
- Home energy assistance
- Assistance based on need funded by a state or local government
- Small amounts of income received irregularly or infrequently
- Interest or dividends earned on countable resources or resources excluded under other federal laws (effective July 1, 2004)

- Grants, scholarships, fellowships or gifts used for tuition and educational expenses (effective June 1, 2004)
- Food or shelter based on need provided by nonprofit agencies
- Loans received in cash or in-kind that must be repaid
- Money someone else spends to pay for items other than food or shelter
- Income set aside under a Plan to Achieve Self-Support (PASS)
- Earnings up to $1,460 per month to a maximum of $5,910 per year (effective January 2006) for a student under age 22
- Gifts of clothing
- The value of impairment-related work expenses for items or services that a disabled person needs in order to work
- The value of work expenses that a blind person incurs in order to work
- Disaster assistance
- Certain exclusions on Indian trust fund payments paid to American Indians who are members of a federally recognized tribe

Resources

In 2007, the resources of an individual cannot exceed $2,000 or, in the case of an individual with an eligible spouse living in the same household, $3,000. SSI regulations define a resource as cash or other liquid assets or any real or personal property that an individual (or spouse) owns and could convert to cash to be used for his or her basic needs.

SSA does not count everything an individual owns in determining eligibility. For example, these items do not count:

- Home lived in and the land it is on.
- Household goods and personal property.
- One wedding ring and one engagement ring.
- Life insurance policies with a face value of $1,500 or less.
- Car—generally an auto does not count.
- Burial plots.
- Retroactive SSI or Social Security benefits for up to nine months after the individual receives them (including payments received in installments).
- Up to $1,500 in burial funds and up to $1,500 in burial funds for a spouse.
- Property essential to self-support.
- Resources that a blind or disabled person needs for an approved plan for achieving self-support.
- Money saved in an Individual Development Account (IDA).
- Support and maintenance assistance and home energy assistance that the SSA does not count as income.
- Cash received for medical or social services that the SSA does not count as income is not a resource for one month except for cash reimbursement of

expenses already paid for by the individual is counted under the regular income and resources rules.

- State or local relocation assistance payments do not count for nine months.
- Crime victim's assistance does not count for nine months.
- Earned income tax credit payments do not count for nine months.
- Grants, scholarships, fellowships or gifts used for tuition and educational expenses (for nine months after the month of receipt, effective June 1, 2004).
- Dedicated accounts for disabled or blind children.
- Disaster relief assistance that the SSA does not count as income.
- Cash received for the purpose of replacing an excluded resource (*e.g.*, a car) that is lost, damaged, or stolen.
- Child tax credit payments do not count for nine months.
- Certain trusts.

In certain situations, other people (e.g., parents and spouses) are expected to share financial responsibility for the individual. In such cases, the income and resources of these people are considered in determining the person's eligibility and payment amount. This process is called deeming. If married, SSA looks at the income of the spouse and the things he or she owns. If under 18, the parents' income and possessions may be considered. In the case of a sponsored alien, the income and possessions of the sponsor may be considered.

Living Arrangements

Individuals' monthly SSI benefit amounts are also affected by their living arrangements. SSI benefits for individuals in nursing homes in which more than half the bill is paid by Medicaid whose expected stay is for more than 90 days are reduced to not more than $30 per month. Generally, benefits also are reduced when individuals move from their own household into the household of another person and that person provides food and/or shelter.

Redeterminations

While nonmedical eligibility determinations are made at the time an initial application is filed, SSA field office staff also conduct periodic reviews, called redeterminations, to determine whether the beneficiary remains eligible and to determine the correct benefit amount. SSI beneficiaries are required to report significant events that may affect their benefit eligibility or monthly payment amounts, including changes in income, resources, marital status, or living arrangements. SSA must then verify the accuracy of information provided by a beneficiary.

.05 SSI Disability

Eligibility for SSI disability benefits requires that an individual must be unable to engage in any substantial gainful activity because of an impairment that is expected to last at least 12 months or to result in death. Eligibility for SSI based on blindness requires that a person's corrected vision may not be better than 20/200 or that a person have a limited visual field in the better eye so that the person has a contraction of peripheral visual fields to 10 degrees from the point of fixation or the widest diameter of the visual field subtends an angle of 20 degrees or less with the best correction. The

State-administered, Federally funded Disability Determination Services (DDSs) make disability determinations for SSA based on Social Security regulations and guidelines. After an individual becomes eligible for disability benefits, SSA periodically conducts continuing disability reviews to determine whether a beneficiary has medically recovered and is no longer considered disabled. In such a case, the beneficiary is no longer eligible for benefits.

Children as well as adults can get benefits because of disability. A disabled child is one who suffers from an impairment that results in marked and severe functional limitations that is expected to last 12 months or result in death.

.07 Deeming

Income and resources of people responsible for an eligible individual must be considered in determining the eligibility and payment for the SSI recipient. This concept is called deeming.

Four types of deeming situations may exist:

1. From an ineligible spouse to an eligible individual both living in the same household—the income and resources of the ineligible spouse are deemed to be available to the eligible individual. Deeming can also apply when the eligible individual is not in the same household as the ineligible spouse if the absence is temporary or the ineligible spouse is absent from the household due solely to a duty assignment as a member of the armed forces on active duty.

2. From a parent to a child under age 18. A child under age 18 is subject to deeming from a natural or adoptive parent or from a stepparent living in the same household.

3. From a sponsor to an alien. The income and resources of a sponsor and the sponsor's living-with spouse are deemed to an alien for three years after an alien is admitted for permanent residence. Deeming applies whether or not the alien lives in the sponsor's household. Sponsor-to-alien deeming does not apply in the following situations:

   - The alien has been granted asylum by the Attorney General; or
   - The alien is residing in the U.S. under color of law and has not been admitted for permanent residence; or
   - The alien filed for SSI prior to October 1, 1980; or
   - The alien is sponsored by an organization; or
   - The alien becomes blind or disabled after admission for permanent residence. (In this last case, deeming applies up until the month disability or blindness begins.)

4. From an essential person to an eligible qualified individual. An eligible qualified individual with an essential person in the household receives an amount of SSI which is increased by an increment for the essential person. All of the essential person's income is deemed to the qualified individual.

.09 Those Living in a Public or Private Institution

People who live in city or county rest homes, halfway houses, or other public institutions usually cannot get SSI checks or may receive a maximum benefit of $30 per month. But there are some exceptions. A person who lives in a publicly operated community residence which serves no more than 16 people may get SSI. A person who lives in a public institution mainly to attend approved educational or job training that will help get a job may get SSI. If a person is living in a public emergency shelter for the homeless, he or she may be able to get SSI checks. An individual in a public or private institution where Medicaid is paying more than half the cost of care may get a small SSI check.

.10 Signing Up for SSI

Call 1-800-772-1213 for an appointment with a Social Security representative. An individual who is deaf or hard of hearing may call the SSA's TTY line at 1-800-325-0778.

Information to Provide

- Social Security card or a record of Social Security number.
- Birth certificate or other proof of age.
- Information about the home, such as mortgage or lease, and landlord's name.
- Payroll slips, bank statements, and other information about income and work expenses.
- If signing up for disability, medical reports and the names, addresses, and telephone numbers of physicians, hospitals, and clinics seen.
- If applying as a disabled child or on behalf of a disabled child, the contact information of teachers and other caregivers.
- Proof of U.S. citizenship or eligible noncitizen status.
- Proof of resources such as bank statements, life insurance policies, disability income insurance policies, certificates of deposit, title or registration of vehicles, and deeds or tax appraisal statements for real estate owned other than the applicant's residence.
- Work history including job titles, duties, dates worked, and names of employers.
- Proof of living arrangements such as rent receipts, property tax bill, or deed, and names, dates of birth, and Social Security numbers for all household members.

Social Security Benefits and SSI

SSA also pays Social Security benefits to people who have worked long enough under Social Security. An individual may be able to receive both Social Security and SSI benefits if the Social Security benefit is low. Social Security pays retirement benefits, disability benefits, and survivors' benefits.

.11 Continuing Disability Reviews

SSA conducts continuing disability reviews (CDRs), approximately every three years to determine whether beneficiaries of disability benefits have medically improved so that they are no longer considered disabled and no longer eligible for benefits. The SSA also redetermines eligibility for children at least one month before the child turns age 18.

In addition the CDRs already conducted by SSA, the Personal Responsibility and Work Opportunity Reconciliation Act of 1996 requires SSA to conduct:

- CDRs within one year of birth on all children who are eligible because of their low birth weight;

- CDRs at least once every three years on all SSI childhood beneficiaries whose impairments are considered likely to improve; and,
- Medical redeterminations (using the adult disability standard) on all SSI childhood beneficiaries within 1 year after reaching age 18.

Prior to 1993, all CDRs were conducted as full medical reviews. SSA developed statistical profiles for estimating the likelihood of medical improvement based on beneficiary information and if a profile indicates a relatively low likelihood of medical improvement, SSA uses a CDR mailer; when the profile indicates a relatively high or medium likelihood of medical improvement, SSA uses a full medical CDR.

.13 SSI Program Fraud

Fraud and abuse in the SSI program generally involve individuals who file false claims, make false statements or deliberately conceal information affecting initial or continuing eligibility for benefits. SSI program fraud falls within three broad categories:

- Fraudulently claiming residency in the United States in order to receive SSI benefits;
- Collaborating with individuals to help them fraudulently obtain disability benefits; and
- Intentionally failing to comply with reporting requirements by withholding information about earnings, bank accounts, living arrangements, settlements, etc., to obtain or continue SSI eligibility.

The SSA's Office of the Inspector General has an online fraud reporting form that is available at the SSA's website www.ssa.gov/oig/hotline. A fraud reporting hotline is also available between 10:00 a.m. and 4:00 p.m. Eastern Time. The number is 1-800-269-0271 or TTY 1-866-501-2101 for the deaf or hard of hearing. The fax number is 410-597-0118. Fraud may also be reported by mail. The address is Social Security Fraud Hotline, P.O. Box 17768, Baltimore, MD 21235.

.15 Debt Collection

SSA currently makes use of the following debt collection tools that are authorized by law: benefit offset, cross-program recovery repayment agreement, and tax refund offset.

Benefit Offset

Collection is relatively easy from overpaid beneficiaries who remain on the SSI rolls because SSA withholds a portion of the monthly benefit and eventually recovers the entire overpayment. The Social Security Act limits withholdings to 10 percent of debtors' monthly income until the debt is collected. If the debtor can demonstrate that a 10-percent withholding would be a financial burden, SSA can use a lower rate.

Cross-Program Recovery

Individuals who receive an SSI overpayment who are no longer receiving SSI benefits, but who *are* receiving old-age, survivors, or disability payments under Title II or special benefits paid to certain WWII veterans under Title VIII, may be subject to recovery of the overpayment by recoupment through offset of their Title II or Title VIII benefit. No more than 10 percent of the total monthly payment may be withheld for this purpose unless the overpaid individual requests a different amount or had willfully misrepresented or concealed material information in connection with the offset.

¶502.13

Repayment Agreements

Collecting debt from persons who are no longer receiving SSI benefits is difficult and costly. SSA negotiates installment agreements with former beneficiaries who choose to repay by installment and locate former beneficiaries who fail to respond to SSA's overpayment notice.

Tax Refund Offset

If an individual is eligible for a Federal tax refund, the amount of outstanding SSI debt is recovered directly from the tax refund before any refund is sent to the individual. Debtors can avoid the tax refund offset by fully refunding the debt or by establishing an installment agreement.

Credit Bureau Reporting

If an individual does not pay his or her debt, the SSA may issue a negative report to a credit bureau. This possibility acts as an incentive for people to pay their debts.

Administrative Wage Garnishments

The SSA may collect debts by garnishing the wages of people with delinquent debts.

¶ 503 DISABILITY AND SOCIAL SECURITY

SSA pays disability benefits under two programs. The Supplemental Security Income Program (SSI) which was discussed at ¶ 502 and the Social Security disability insurance program discussed here. The medical requirements for disability payments are the same under both programs and the same process determines a person's disability. Eligibility for Social Security disability is based on prior work under Social Security.

.01 Disability Eligibility

"Disability" Defined

It's important to understand how Social Security defines "disability" because different programs have different bases for determining disability. Some programs may pay for partial disability or for short-term disability. Social Security does not. Disability under Social Security is based on inability to work. An individual will be considered disabled if unable to do any kind of work for which that person is suited, and only if inability to work is also expected to last for at least a year or to result in death. Benefits continue as long as an individual remains disabled.

Who Can Get Social Security Disability Benefits

A person can receive Social Security disability benefits at any age. If an individual is receiving disability benefits at full retirement age, they become retirement benefits, although the amount remains the same. Certain family members may also qualify for benefits on a person's record. They include:

- An unmarried son or daughter, including a stepchild, adopted child, or, in some cases, a grandchild. The child must be under 18 or under 19 if in high school full time.

- An unmarried son or daughter, 18 or older, or who has a disability that started before 22. (If a disabled child under 18 is receiving benefits as a dependent of a retired, deceased, or disabled worker, someone should contact Social Security to have his or her checks continued at 18 on the basis of disability.)

- A spouse who is 62 or older.
- A spouse at any age if he or she is caring for the insured individual's child who is under 16 or disabled and also receiving checks.

Certain family members may qualify for disability benefits if an insured individual should die. They include:

- A disabled widow or widower age 50 or older who meets the Social Security's disability requirement. The disabling impairment must have started before age 60 and within seven years of the latest of the following dates: (1) the month the worker died, (2) the last month the disabled widow or widower was entitled to mother's or father's benefits on the worker's record, or (3) the month a previous entitlement to benefits for the disabled widow or widower ended because the disability ended.
- A diabled ex-wife or ex-husband who is 50 or older of the marriage lasted 10 years or longer.

Disability Benefits for People with HIV Infection

People with HIV infection or AIDS may also qualify for disability benefits when they are no longer able to work or when they must severely limit the amount of work they do because of the disease. A person diagnosed with AIDS who is not working generally qualifies for disability benefits. Some people with HIV infection that has not progressed to AIDS may be just as severely disabled as a person with AIDS, and therefore just as likely to qualify for disability.

Dependents' Benefits

Social Security dependents benefits are payable to children under 18 (under 19 if in elementary or high school, full time) if a parent is receiving retirement or disability benefits or is deceased. These benefits may also be paid to children 18 or older who were disabled before age 22. Benefits will continue into their adult years as long as they remain disabled.

How Much Work is Required for Social Security Disability Benefits

To qualify for Social Security disability benefits, an individual must meet the "recent work" test and the "duration of work" test. A person earns up to a maximum of four credits per year. The amount of earnings required for a credit increases each year as general wage levels rise. Family members who qualify for benefits on an insured individual's work record do not need work credits. The number of work credits needed for disability benefits depends on a person's age when that person becomes disabled. Generally, a person who becomes disabled at age 31 or older needs 20 credits earned in the last 10 years. Applicants who become disabled before age 31 need fewer credits.

To meet the "recent work" test, the applicant must have worked the number of years indicated below based on the applicant's age.

If an Individual Becomes Disabled	Years of Work Needed
In or before the quarter in which the individual turns age 24	1.5 years in the 3 years ending with the quarter that the disability began
In the quarter after the individual turns age 24 but before the quarter in which the individual turns age 31	Worked for half the years after turning age 21 and ending with the quarter in which the disability began
In the quarter in which the individual turns age 31 or later	Worked for 5 years out of the 10-year period ending with the quarter in which the disability began

¶503.01

To meet the "duration of work" test, the applicant must have worked a certain number of years based on the age of the individual at the time the disability began. The following table shows examples of the years of work needed to satisfy the "duration of work" test.

Examples of Work Needed to Satisfy the "Duration of Work" Test

If an Individual Becomes Disabled	Years of Work Required
Before age 28	1.5
Age 30	2
Age 34	3
Age 38	4
Age 42	5
Age 44	5.5
Age 46	6
Age 48	6.5
Age 50	7
Age 52	7.5
Age 54	8
Age 56	8.5
Age 58	9
Age 60	9.5

.03 Disability Program Processes

Signing Up for Disability

As soon as they become disabled, individuals should apply online at www.socialsecurity.gov or call 1-800-772-1213 to schedule an appointment to file a disability claim at the local Social Security office or for a Social Security representative to take the application over the telephone. Individuals who are deaf or hard of hearing may call the TTY line at 1-800-325-0778 between 7:00 a.m. and 7:00 p.m., Monday through Friday. An individual may also apply for disability benefits online at www.socialsecurity.gov/applyfordisability. Individuals may also file by mail. However, Social Security disability benefits will not begin until the sixth full month of disability. This "waiting period" begins with the first full month after the onset of disability. The claims process for disability benefits is generally longer than for other types of Social Security benefits. The process usually takes three to five months. It takes longer to obtain medical information and to assess the nature of the disability in terms of ability to work. Information needed:

- The Social Security number and proof of age for each person applying for payments. This includes one's spouse and children, if they are applying for benefits.

- Checking or savings account number.

- Name, address, and phone number of a person whom the SSA can contact if they are not able to contact the applicant.

- An original or certified copy of the applicant's birth certificate or baptismal certificate.
- If the applicant served in the military, the original or certified copy of discharge papers for all periods of active duty.
- Names, addresses, and phone numbers of physicians, hospitals, clinics, and institutions that provided treatment and dates of treatment along with patient ID numbers and dates seen.
- Names of all medications being taken.
- Laboratory and test results.
- A summary of where the applicant worked and the kind of work performed for the 15 years before the applicant became unable to work.
- A copy of the applicant's W-2 Form (Wage and Tax Statement), or if self-employed, the federal tax return for the past year.
- Dates of any prior marriages if the spouse is applying.
- If the applicant was born in a foreign country, proof of U.S. citizenship or legal residency.
- Medical records in the applicant's possession.
- Worker's compensation information, including date of injury, claim number, and proof of payment amounts.

Where applicable, original documents or copies certified by the issuing offices are required.

Who Decides if the Applicant is Disabled

After the application is complete, the Social Security office will review it to see if the applicant meets the requirements of the law. These include such factors as whether the individual has worked long enough and recently enough to qualify for disability benefits, applicant's age, and, if the applicant is applying for benefits as a family member, the applicant's relationship to the worker. The office will then send the application to the Disability Determination Services (DDS) office in the applicant's state. This state agency will decide whether the applicant is disabled under the Social Security law. In the DDS office, a team consisting of a physician (or psychologist) and a disability evaluation specialist will consider all the facts in the case and decide if the individual is disabled. They will first make every reasonable effort to get medical evidence from the applicant's physicians and from hospitals, clinics, or institutions. The government pays a reasonable charge for any medical reports that it needs and requests.

Medical Information

On the medical report forms, physicians or other sources are asked for a medical history of the applicant's condition: what is wrong and when it began; how the condition limits activities; what the medical tests have shown; and what treatment has been provided. They are also asked for information about the applicant's ability to do work-related activities, such as walking, sitting, lifting, and carrying. They are not asked to decide whether the applicant is disabled. Additional medical information may be needed before the DDS team can decide the case. If it is not available from current medical sources, the applicant may be asked to take a special examination called a "consultative examination." The applicant's physician or the medical facility where treatment has been provided is the preferred source to perform this examination. Social Security will pay for the examination or any other additional medical tests one may need, and for certain travel expenses related to it. The rules in the Social Security law for determining disability differ from those in other government and private programs. However, a decision made by another agency and the medical reports it obtains may be considered in determining whether the individual is disabled under Social Security rules. Once a decision on a claim is reached, the applicant will receive a written notice from the Social Security Administration. If the claim is approved, the notice will show the amount of benefit and when payments start. If it is not approved, the notice will explain why and explain how to appeal.

How SSA Determines Disability

SSA disability determination is a step-by-step process involving five questions.

1. Is the applicant working? If yes, and earnings average more than $900 a month in 2007, the applicant generally cannot be considered disabled.

2. Is the condition "severe"? Impairments must interfere with basic work-related activities for the claim to be considered further.

3. Is the condition found in the list of disabling conditions? The state agency maintains a list of medical conditions that are so severe they automatically mean an individual is disabled. If the condition is not on the list, the state agency has to determine if it is of equal severity to a medical condition on the list. If it is, the claim is approved. If it is not, the state agency goes to the next step.

4. Can the applicant do the work done previously? If the condition is severe, but not at the same or equal severity as a medical condition on the list, then the state agency must determine if it interferes with a person's ability to do the work done previously. If it does not, the claim will be denied. If it does, the claim will be considered further.

5. Can the applicant do any other type of work? If the individual cannot do the work done previously, the state agency then looks to see if the person can do any other type of work. The state agency considers age, education, past work experience, and transferable skills. If the applicant cannot do any other kind of work, the claim will be approved. If one can, the claim will be denied.

Rules for Blind Persons

The Social Security disability program has special rules for blind persons. If an individual qualifies, that person may receive benefits either on the basis of blindness or on the basis of disability. An individual is considered blind under Social Security rules if vision cannot be corrected to better than 20/200 in the better eye, or if the visual field is 20 degrees or less, even with a corrective lens. If blind, an individual can earn up to $1,500 a month in 2007 without becoming disqualified for disability benefits on the basis of engaging in substantial gainful activity. If blind, an individual should file for disability even if working regularly and earnings are too high to receive disability benefits. That is because an individual might be eligible for a disability "freeze." This means that future benefits, which are figured on average earnings over an individual's working life, will not be reduced because of relatively lower earnings in those years when that person is blind.

.05 Disability Appeals

If Claim is Denied

There are four levels of appeal. If the applicant disagrees with the decision at one level, he or she may appeal to the next level. The applicant has 60 days from the receipt of the letter from SSA to file a written appeal. The SSA assumes that the applicant receives the letter from the SSA five days after the date on the letter unless the applicant can show that it was received later.

Reconsideration

Four Levels of Appeal

1. Reconsideration—File is reviewed by persons other than those who made the original decision.

2. Hearing—Application can be made for a hearing before an administrative law judge. If appealing a decision that the individual is no longer medically disabled, that person may also request that SSA continue benefits while waiting for a decision.

3. Appeals Council—The Appeals Council will review a case if it feels that there is an issue that the judge did not address. If it denies an individual's review, or a person otherwise disagrees with its decision, that person may appeal to a federal district court.

4. United States District Court—The notice of the Appeals Council's decision will inform the applicant how to appeal to a federal district court.

.06 Disability Benefits—Post Approval

When Claim is Approved

First Check

Once a decision is made that an applicant is disabled, that person will receive his or her first Social Security disability check dating back to the sixth full month from the onset of disability.

How Much Will Social Security Provide

The amount of monthly disability benefits is based on lifetime average earnings covered by Social Security. An estimate of disability benefits can be obtained by calling or visiting a Social Security office. SSA sends a form that can be used to get a Social Security Statement. A person may transmit a request for a Social Security Statement using an online form available at the SSA's website. The SSA will mail the Social Security Statement within four weeks of the request.

How Other Payments Affect Benefits

Eligibility for other government benefits can affect the amount of one's Social Security disability benefits.

Other Disability Benefits

Social Security benefits may be affected if a person is also eligible for workers' compensation (including black lung) or for disability benefits from certain federal, state, local government, civil service, or military disability programs. Total combined payments to an individual and his or her family from Social Security and any of these other programs generally cannot exceed 80 percent of that individual's average current earnings before becoming disabled.

Government Pension Offset

If a person is a disabled widow or widower or the spouse of a disabled worker, a "government pension offset" may reduce his or her Social Security payment. The offset applies if the individual becomes eligible for a federal, state, or local government pension based on the individual's own work not covered by Social Security. The amount of a Social Security spouse's benefit may be reduced by two-thirds of the amount of that individual's government pension. There are several exceptions to the government pension offset rule.

Pension from Work Not Covered by Social Security

If a person becomes disabled and entitled to a Social Security disability benefit and also receives a monthly pension based on work not covered by Social Security, that person's disability payment will be smaller than normal. That is because SSA uses a different formula to figure the Social Security benefit of people who get other public pensions. This rule is called the windfall elimination provision.

Benefits May Be Taxed

A relatively small number of people may have to pay federal income taxes on their Social Security benefits. This usually happens only if total income is high. At the end of the year, an individual will receive a Social Security Benefit Statement (Form 1099-SSA) showing the amount of benefits received. The statement is to be used for completing the individual's federal income tax return if any benefits are subject to tax.

Obtaining Medicare if Disabled

An individual is automatically enrolled in Medicare after two years from the month he or she is entitled to receive disability benefits, not the month when he or she receives the first disability check.

Reviewing One's Disability

Benefits continue as long as an individual is disabled, but an individual's case will be reviewed periodically to see if that peson is still disabled. The frequency of the review depends on the expectation of recovery.

- If medical improvement is "expected," a case will normally be reviewed within 6 to 18 months.
- If medical improvement is "possible," a case will normally be reviewed about every three years.
- If medical improvement is "not expected," a case may be reviewed about once every five to seven years.

What Can Cause Benefits to Stop

There are two things that can cause SSA to decide that someone is no longer disabled and to stop benefits. Benefits will stop if an individual works at a level considered "substantial." In 2007, average earnings over $900 a month ($1,500 a month for blind individuals) are considered substantial. Disability benefits would also stop if SSA decides that a medical condition has improved to the point that the individual is no longer disabled. An individual must promptly report any improvement in condition, return to work, and certain other events as long as that person is receiving benefits.

Benefits While Working

There are a number of special rules that provide cash benefits and Medicare for those who attempt to work. SSA calls these rules "work incentives."

Work Incentives Rules

For those receiving Social Security disability benefits, the following rules are among the work incentives that apply:

- Trial Work Period for Nine Months (not necessarily consecutive)—an individual may earn as much as possible without affecting benefits. (The nine months of work must fall within a five-year period before the trial work period can end.) In 2007, a trial work month is any month in which an individual earns more than $640. After the trial work period ends, work is evaluated to see if it is "substantial." In 2007, if earnings do not average more than $900 a month, benefits will generally continue. If earnings do average more than $900 a month, benefits will continue for a three-month grace period before they stop.

- Extended Period of Eligibility—For 36 months after a successful trial work period, if still disabled, an individual will be eligible to receive a monthly benefit without a new application for any month in 2007 in which earnings drop below $900 ($1,500 if blind).

- Deductions for Impairment-Related Expenses—Work expenses related to disability will be discounted in figuring whether earnings constitute substantial work.

- Expedited Reinstatement—After benefits stop because earnings are substantial, the individual has five years to ask the SSA to start benefits again if the individual is unable to continue working because of the disability. A new disability application is not necessary, and the individual does not have to wait for benefits to begin again while the individual's medical condition is reviewed.

- Medicare Continuation—Medicare coverage will continue for at least 93 months beyond the nine-month trial work period. If Medicare coverage stops because of work, an individual may purchase it for a monthly premium.

Ticket to Work and Work Incentive Improvement Act of 1999

Since 2001, disability beneficiaries under both Title II (SSDI) and Title XVI (SSI) have more options for obtaining rehabilitation and vocational services. Under this voluntary program, beneficiaries may receive a ticket that may be redeemed at an employment network that will work with the individual to develop a vocational goal and provide services and supports necessary to accomplish that goal. An employment network may include state vocational rehabilitation agencies as well as private and other public providers. Maximus, Inc. is a private company that works with the Social Security Administration in managing the Ticket Program. For more information on the Ticket Program, call Maximus, Inc. toll free at 1-866-968-7842 (TTY 1-866-833-2967).

¶ 505 RETIREMENT BENEFITS AND SOCIAL SECURITY

.01 Basics and Decisions

How Do People Qualify for Retirement Benefits?

Those who work and pay Social Security taxes earn Social Security credits. Most people earn four credits per year. The number of credits needed to get retirement benefits depends on date of birth. Individuals born in 1929 or later need 40 credits (10 years of work). People born before 1929 need fewer than 40 credits (39 credits if born in 1928; 38 credits if born in 1927; etc.). For individuals who stop working before having enough credits to qualify for benefits, earned credits remain on their Social Security record. Most people will earn many more credits than needed to qualify for Social Security. These extra credits do not increase the Social Security benefit. However, the income earned while working will increase the benefit.

How Much Will the Retirement Benefit Be?

The benefit amount is based on an individual's earnings averaged over most of that person's working career. Higher lifetime earnings result in higher benefits. The benefit amount also is affected by age at the time an individual starts receiving benefits.

Personalized Benefit Estimate

Social Security will provide a personalized benefit estimate upon request. Call the toll-free telephone number 1-800-772-1213 to ask for a Request for Social Security Statement. SSA will send a simple form to complete and return. Forms are available from SSA on the Internet at *http://www.ssa.gov*. A benefit calculator is also available on the SSA website.

Normal Retirement Age

Until recently, individuals had to wait until age 65 to claim a retirement benefit in order to receive the full benefit amount, without any reductions for early retirement. However, this "normal retirement age" is now increasing to age 67 over a 22-year period and affects people born January 2, 1938, and later. The first group of affected retirees reached age 62 in 2000. For these individuals, who reached age 65 in 2005, normal retirement age is 65 and 6 months. In the following table, which shows how the age of normal retirement will rise, note that individuals born on January 1 of any given year are deemed to have reached retirement age on the day before and therefore are subject to normal retirement age for the prior year.

Age to Receive Full Social Security Benefits

If one's date of birth is:	Normal retirement age is:
Before 1/2/1938	65
1/2/1938 - 1/1/1939	65 and 2 months
1/2/1939 - 1/1/1940	65 and 4 months
1/2/1940 - 1/1/1941	65 and 6 months
1/2/1941 - 1/1/1942	65 and 8 months
1/2/1942 - 1/1/1943	65 and 10 months
1/2/1943 - 1/1/1955	66
1/2/1955 - 1/1/1956	66 and 2 months
1/2/1956 - 1/1/1957	66 and 4 months
1/2/1957 - 1/1/1958	66 and 6 months

If one's date of birth is:	Normal retirement age is:
1/2/1958 - 1/1/1959	66 and 8 months
1/2/1959 - 1/1/1960	66 and 10 months
1/2/1960 and later	67

Early Retirement

An individual can start to receive Social Security benefits as early as age 62, but the benefit amount received will be less than a full retirement benefit. By taking early retirement, benefits will be reduced based on the number of months a person will receive checks before reaching full retirement age. Individuals reaching retirement age (age 62) at any time between 2006 and 2016 must delay retirement until age 66 in order to receive a full retirement benefit. For individuals reaching age 62 at any time between 2006 and 2016 and retiring early, the reduction for starting Social Security retirement benefits at age 62 is 25.00 percent. The percentage reduction is 0.520 percent per month for each month before normal retirement age for people born in 1943-1954.

Delayed Retirement

Those who decide to continue working full-time beyond full retirement age can increase Social Security benefits in two ways:

- By adding a year of high earnings to one's Social Security record, higher lifetime earnings may result in higher benefits.

- In addition, an individual's benefit will be increased by a certain percentage by delaying retirement. These increases will be added in automatically from the time an individual reaches normal retirement age until that individual starts taking benefits, or reaches age 70. The percentage varies depending on date of birth.

Chart of Increases for Delayed Retirement

If one's date of birth is:	The credit for each month one delays retirement is:
1/2/1933 - 1/1/1935	11/24 of 1%
1/2/1935 - 1/1/1937	1/2 of 1%
1/2/1937 - 1/1/1939	13/24 of 1%
1/2/1939 - 1/1/1941	7/12 of 1%
1/2/1941 - 1/1/1943	5/8 of 1%
After 1/1/1943	2/3 of 1%

If born in 1943 or later, SSA will add an extra 8 ($12 \times 2/3 \times 1\%$) percent to an individual's benefit for each year that person delays signing up for Social Security beyond normal retirement age up to age 70.

Interaction of Delayed Retirement Credit and Actuarily Reduced Benefit Amounts

The following table shows the effect of early retirement versus delayed retirement on the percentage of PIA received as a benefit. The chart also shows how these percentages differ as a result of the increase in normal retirement age from age 65 to age 67.

¶505.01

Normal Retirement Age and Delayed Retirement Credits

(Increases in Normal Retirement Age and Delayed Retirement Credits with Resulting Benefit as a Percentage of Primary Insurance Amount (PIA), Payable at Selected Ages for Persons Reaching Age 62 in Each Year 1986 and Later)

Year of birth	Normal retirement age (NRA)	Credit for each year of delayed retirement after NRA (%)	Benefit, as a percentage of PIA, beginning at age—				
			62	65	66	67	70
1924	65	3	80	100	103	106	115
1925	65	3 1/2	80	100	103 1/2	107	117 1/2
1926	65	3 /12	80	100	103 /12	107	117 1/2
1927	65	4	80	100	104	108	120
1928	65	4	80	100	104	108	120
1929	65	4 1/2	80	100	104 1/2	109	122 1/2
1930	65	4 1/2	80	100	104 1/2	109	122 1/2
1931	65	5	80	100	105	110	125
1932	65	5	80	100	105	110	125
1933	65	5 1/2	80	100	105 1/2	111	127 1/2
1934	65	5 1/2	80	100	105 1/2	111	127 1/2
1935	65	6	80	100	106	112	130
1936	65	6	80	100	106	112	130
1937	65	6 1/2	80	100	106 1/2	113	132 1/2
1938	65, 2 mo.	6 1/2	79 1/6	98 8/9	105 5/12	111 11/12	131 5/12
1939	65, 4 mo.	7	78 1/3	97 7/9	104 2/3	111 2/3	132 2/3
1940	65, 6 mo.	7	77 1/2	96 2/3	103 1/2	110 1/2	131 1/2
1941	65, 8 mo.	7 1/2	76 2/3	95 5/9	102 1/2	110	132 1/2
1942	65, 10 mo.	7 1/2	75 5/6	94 4/9	101 1/4	108 3/4	131 1/4
1943-54	66	8	75	93 1/3	100	108	132
1955	66, 2 mo.	8	74 1/6	92 2/9	98 8/9	106 2/3	130 2/3
1956	66, 4 mo.	8	73 1/3	91 1/9	97 7/9	105 1/3	129 1/3
1957	66, 6 mo.	8	72 1/2	90	96 2/3	104	128
1958	66, 8 mo.	8	71 2/3	88 8/9	95 5/9	102 2/3	126 2/3
1959	66, 10 mo.	8	70 5/6	87 7/9	94 4/9	101 1/3	125 1/3
1960 and later	67	8	70	86 2/3	93 1/3	100	124

Choosing Retirement Date

In some cases, a choice of a retirement month could mean additional benefits. It may be an advantage to have Social Security benefits start in January, even if an individual does not plan to retire until later in the year. Depending on earnings and benefit amount, it may be possible to start collecting benefits even while continuing to work. Under current rules, many people can receive the most benefits possible with an application that is effective in January.

¶505.01

When to Start Receiving Social Security Benefits

An individual who has earned 40 quarters (or 10 years) of Social Security coverage can start receiving Social Security retirement benefits at age 62. For individuals born in 1943 through 1954, the full retirement benefits are available at age 66. If an individual born in those years claims Social Security retirement benefits at age 62, the benefits are reduced by 25.00 percent. If the individual retires after age 62 but before full retirement age, the benefits are reduced by a factor of 0.520 percent per month for the number of months before full retirement age.

Assume that John Abel was born in 1945. He wants to retire in 2007 instead of waiting until he attains full retirement age of 66 in 2011. Assume that his primary insurance amount (PIA) based on his earnings is $1,300 per month. If he retires at age 62, his benefits will be $975 ($1,300 × 75%) per month. If he retires in 2008 at age 63, his benefits will be reduced by 18.72 percent (0.520% per month × 36 months). Therefore, his benefits will be reduced by $243.36 ($1,300 × 18.72%) to $1,056.64 ($1,300 − $243.36).

Assume that Jean Brown was born in 1945. She wants to retire in 2007 instead of waiting until she attains full retirement age of 66 in 2011. Assume that her primary insurance amount (PIA) based on her earnings is $1,200 per month. If she retires at age 62, her benefits will be $900 ($1,200 × 75%) per month. By the time she attains full retirement age in 2011, she will have received $43,200 ($900 × 48) in Social Security benefits (disregarding cost of living adjustments). A period of 144 months or 12 years ($43,200 / $300 per month) would be required before the additional $300 per month she could have received by waiting the four years to full retirement age equals the $43,200 she received by beginning benefits four years before full retirement age. These calculations ignore cost of living adjustments in the Social Security benefits and the time value of money.

Social Security and Family Benefits

If an individual is receiving retirement benefits, some members of that individual's family also can receive benefits. Here is a list of those who can also receive benefits:

- Wife or husband age 62 or older.
- Wife or husband under age 62, if she or he is taking care of a beneficiary's child, who is receiving Social Security benefits, until the child is age 16.
- A divorced spouse can receive benefits at 62, whether or not the former spouse receives them. Their marriage must have lasted 10 years or more. The former spouse must be at least 62, unmarried, and not entitled to a higher Social Security benefit on his or her own record.
- Unmarried children up to age 18.
- Unmarried children age 18-19, if they are full-time elementary or secondary school students.
- Unmarried children over age 18, if they are severely disabled before age 22 and who continue to be disabled.

How Much Can a Spouse and Children Get?

The full benefit for a spouse is one-half of the retired worker's full benefit. If a spouse takes benefits before normal retirement age, the benefits will be reduced. However, a

¶505.01

spouse who is taking care of a child who is under 16 or disabled gets full (50 percent) benefits, regardless of age. If each person is eligible for his or her own retirement benefits and for benefits as a spouse, he or she gets the higher amount. If an individual has children eligible for Social Security, each will receive up to one-half of an individual's full benefit. But there is a limit to the amount of money that can be paid to a family. If the total benefits due spouse and children exceed this limit, their benefits will be reduced proportionately.

How to Sign Up for Social Security?

Before payments can start, an individual must apply for them. An individual can apply for benefits by telephone, via the Internet as described below, or by going to any Social Security office. Depending on circumstances, an individual will need some or all of the documents below.

Information Needed

- Proof of U.S. citizenship or lawful alien status if the applicant was not born in the U.S.
- Social Security number.
- Birth certificate.
- W-2 forms or self-employment tax return for last year.
- Military discharge papers if one had military service.
- Spouse's birth certificate and Social Security number if he or she is applying for benefits.
- Children's birth certificates and Social Security numbers, if applying for children's benefits.
- Checking or savings account information, if direct deposit is wanted.

Individuals need to submit original documents or copies certified by the issuing office. These can be mailed or taken to the Social Security Office. SSA will make photocopies and return the documents.

Social Security Now Offers Internet Retirement Insurance Benefits at www.ssa.gov, SSA's Website

- Individuals may go to *www.ssa.gov/applytoretire* to start the online application process.
- To use this service, people must be 61 years and 9 months or older and plan to start receiving retirement benefits within 4 months. They must also reside in the United States or one of its territories, and agree to receive their benefits by direct deposit. Individuals who are currently receiving Social Security benefits or have already applied for retirement benefits with a Social Security office will not be able to use the online service.
- Answers to six screening questions will determine whether or not a person can proceed and file for retirement benefits over the Internet. Those who meet the conditions are presented with information describing the application process and then move on to the actual application.
- The answers provided on the screens are used by SSA to make an entitlement determination on an individual's claim for Social Security Retirement Benefits.

¶505.01

- Upon completion of the online application, a person's application is electronically signed and sent to SSA. Alternatively, an individual may print the application, sign it, and mail or bring it to the address provided by SSA.

Along with the signed application, applicants must also submit any applicable documentation needed to process their claim, such as:

- Birth certificate.
- W-2 forms or self-employment tax return for last year.
- Military discharge papers (if there is military service).

A Claim Confirmation Number is provided to every applicant. This verifies that the online information was successfully transmitted to SSA and can be used to verify the status of a person's claim.

Right to Appeal

If a person disagrees with a decision made on a claim, that person may ask the Social Security Administration to reconsider it. If still not satisfied, there are other steps that can be taken after the reconsideration. Individuals can be represented by an attorney or other qualified person of choice.

.03 Working and Receiving Social Security Benefits

Earnings Limits and Work Under Senior Citizen Freedom to Work Act of 2000

Before 2000, individuals could continue to work and get full retirement benefits as long as their earnings were under certain limits. The dollar limits were referred to as the retirement earning test amount. This applied to those who retired after reaching the normal retirement age (but, who had not reached an upper limit) as well as those who retired prior to reaching normal retirement age. The earnings limit was not applicable to those over the upper age limit, which was 70 years of age. For those who retired prior to normal retirement age, the limits were more strict than for those who retired after normal retirement age.

Normal retirement age is age 65 for those born before 1938, and it is gradually increasing to age 67 (see the "Age at Which Full Benefits Are Payable" table that follows this discussion).

Under the Senior Citizen Freedom to Work Act of 2000, the retirement earnings test no longer applies to those above the normal retirement age. Social Security withholds benefits *only* when earnings exceed a certain level *and* the beneficiary is under the normal retirement age.

One of two exempt amounts applies, depending on the year a beneficiary attains the normal retirement age. For those reaching the normal retirement age in the current year, the exempt amount is higher than the one used for those who are not reaching normal retirement age in the current year. This amount, however, only applied to amounts earned during the taxable year prior to the month in which full retirement age is attained.

For those working and receiving retirement benefits *who reach the normal retirement age in 2007*, one dollar in Social Security benefits for each *three dollars* above the limit is withheld for those months prior to attaining the normal retirement age. The annual limit that applies to these individuals is $34,440 or $2,870 per month.

¶505.03

For those working and receiving retirement benefits *who are under the normal retirement age throughout all of 2007*, one dollar in Social Security benefits for each *two dollars* above the limit is withheld. The annual limit that applies to these individuals is $12,960 or $1,080 per month.

Increases in the annual exempt amounts are triggered by annual cost-of-living adjustments and new exempt amounts are published in the Federal Register on or before November 1 of the year preceding the calendar year in which they are to become effective.

The First Year of Retirement

A special rule applies to an individual's earnings for one year, usually the first year of retirement. Under this rule, a person can receive a full Social Security check for any month that person is "retired," regardless of yearly earnings. A person's earnings must be under a monthly limit. If self-employed, the services performed in the person's business are taken into consideration as well.

.04 Taxation of Benefits

Reporting Earnings

If a person earns more than the earnings limit and receives some benefits from Social Security, that person must complete an Annual Report of Earnings. In this report, the exact earnings for the previous year are provided and an estimate is made for the current year. Those at or above normal retirement age (all year) do not have to fill out a report. The Annual Report of Earnings must be sent by April 15 of the following year. There is a substantial penalty for not filing this report on time.

In 1997, SSA changed its regulations for reports due on or after April 15, 1997, to allow Form W-2 (and Schedule SE for self-employed persons) as the report of earnings the law requires. However, because earnings for income tax purposes and earnings for annual earnings test purposes are not always equivalent, some beneficiaries will still need to file additional information with the Social Security Administration. Under the earnings test, wages are counted for the year in which services are performed, while under IRS regulations, wages are reported on forms W-2 for the year in which they are paid. Thus, if the W-2 or self-employment income tax form shows wages or earnings that were earned in a year prior to the year for which the form is filed, e.g., deferred compensation, a beneficiary will need to report to the Social Security Administration the correct amount of earnings for the year for which the report is made in order to insure that the correct amount of earnings is recorded for that year. An official form for these reports no longer exists; however, the report may be made to the Administration in person, by telephone, or in writing.

Other circumstances where a beneficiary may still need to provide the Administration with additional information include the following:

- The year in which the monthly earnings test applies (frequently the year of retirement), monthly earnings information will need to be provided;

- The beneficiary earned wages above the exempt amount and also had a net loss from self-employment;

- Wages are reported on a W-2 that are also included on a self-employment tax return (e.g. members of the clergy and certain employees of religious institutions);
- Earnings are reported on a fiscal year basis which is not the calendar year;
- The beneficiary had federal agricultural program payments or income from carry-over crops that is included on the self-employment tax return; and,
- The beneficiary estimated earnings over the exempt amount and some benefits were withheld, but there were no earnings for the year, i.e., no wages reported, no self-employment.

A beneficiary who does not separately notify the Administration and report the correct amount of earnings when one or more of these circumstances is present may risk an erroneous reduction in benefits under the earnings test.

Pensions from Work Not Covered by Social Security

Individuals who receive pensions from work where they paid Social Security taxes will not have their Social Security benefits reduced. However, pensions from work not covered by Social Security—for example, the federal civil service or some state or local government employment—may offset or lower their Social Security benefit by two-thirds of the pension amount. The public pension offset does not apply to persons entitled only to old-age or disability benefits, or to child or parent beneficiaries. Thus, affected beneficiaries include spouses, widow(er)s, divorced spouses, surviving divorced spouses, mothers, or fathers receiving a pension based on non-covered employment. However, several exceptions apply to the rule.

Social Security Credits

Social Security credits are earned by working in a job covered by Social Security. Up to a maximum of four credits can be earned for each year. The amount of covered earnings needed to earn one credit are as follows for the years indicated:

2007	$1,000
2006	970
2005	920
2004	900
2003	890
2002	870
2001	830
2000	780
1999	740
1998	700
1997	670
1996	640
1995	630
1994	620
1993	590
1992	570
1991	540
1990	520
1989	500

1988	470
1987	460
1986	440
1985	410

Domestic Employees

If a person works as a domestic employee in a private household and receives $1,500 or more in 2007, these wages are covered by Social Security.

Household service performed by anyone under age 18 is not considered employment for FICA purposes unless it is the individual's prinicpal occupation.

Also, note that all cash remuneration for domestic service is counted as earnings for purposes of the retirement test even though it fails to meet the $1,500 threshold.

Self-Employment

If a person is self-employed, the self-employment income is covered by Social Security if there is net profit of $400 or more in a year. Even if the actual net earnings are less than $400, the self-employment income may count for Social Security if the taxpayer uses an optional method for reporting net earnings.

A $400 floor exists on paying self-employment tax after the deduction under Code Sec. 1402(a)(12) for the unadjusted net earnings for self-employment times half the self-employment tax rate. Thus, the adjusted earnings from self-employment are 92.35% of the unadjusted net earnings from self-employment [100% − (15.3% × ½)]. Thus, the unadjusted earnings from self-employment must be $433 or greater ($400 / .9235) for the taxpayer to have a self-employment tax liability. However, even if a person has to pay self-employment tax, he or she still needs $1,000 of adjusted self-employment income in 2007 to receive a credit toward Social Security.

Retirement Credits Needed to be Fully Insured—For Workers Reaching Age 62 in

Year	Credits Needed
1984	33
1985	34
1986	35
1987	36
1988	37
1989	38
1990	39
1991 or later	40

Retirement Benefits May Be Taxable

Part of Social Security benefits may be taxable for some individuals. The test is whether the individual's modified adjusted gross income plus 50 percent of the Social Security benefits exceeds a base amount.

Modified adjusted gross income is the sum of the individual's adjusted gross income plus any tax-exempt interest received. Modified adjusted gross income is adjusted gross income calculated without including any Social Security or equivalent railroad retirement benefits and without subtracting the following from gross income:

¶505.04

- The interest exclusion that applies to savings bonds used to finance education.
- The exclusion from an employee's income of amounts paid under an adoption assistance program of the employer.
- The deduction for qualified U.S. production activities income.
- The deduction that applies to interest on qualified educational loans.
- The deduction for qualified tuition and related higher education expenses, for tax years beginning after December 31, 2001, and before January 1, 2008.
- The foreign earned income exclusion and the foreign housing exclusion or deduction.
- The exclusion of income from U.S. possessions.
- The exclusion of income from Puerto Rico by bona fide residents of Puerto Rico.

The base amount is $25,000 for an individual, $32,000 for a couple filing jointly, and zero for a couple filing separately if they lived together any part of the year. The amount of benefits subject to tax will be the smaller of:

- One-half the benefits, or
- One-half the amount of combined income (adjusted gross income, plus nontaxable interest plus one-half of total benefits) in excess of the base amount.

After 1993, provisional income that exceeds the adjusted base amount, must include an additional amount of benefit in gross income. The adjusted base amount is $44,000 for married taxpayers filing jointly, zero for married persons not filing jointly, and $34,000 for other individuals. If a taxpayer has provisional income, above the adjusted base amount, then gross income includes the lesser of 85% of the taxpayer's Social Security benefit, or the sum of 85% of the excess of the taxpayer's provisional income over the applicable new threshold amount plus the smaller of one-half of the taxpayer's Social Security benefit or $4,500 ($6,000 for taxpayers filing jointly).

Retirement Amount Benefits—Social Security

Benefits will replace a proportion of preretirement earnings, the exact amount depending on the worker's level of earnings. Benefits replace about 40 percent of an average wage earner's income after retirement. Most people will need 70-80 percent of the income they received during their working years to have a comfortable retirement. They must rely on income from pension plans, IRAs, and savings and investments to provide the additional income.

Events that Call for Social Security Contact

Social Security benefits must be applied for. The Social Security Administration should be contacted if an individual is:

- Unable to work because of an illness or injury that is expected to last a year or longer.
- Age 62 or older and plans to retire.
- Within three months of normal retirement age, even if not planning to retire.
- Someone in the immediate family dies.
- Someone in the immediate family suffers permanent kidney failure.
- Age 65 or older, blind, or disabled with limited income and resources, in order to apply for supplemental security income (SSI).

.05 Retirement Benefits—Tables

Wages—Maximum Wages Covered By Social Security

Annual Maximum	For Each Year
$3,000	1937 through 1950
$3,600	1951 through 1954
$4,200	1955 through 1958
$4,800	1959 through 1965
$6,000	1966 and 1967
$7,800	1968 through 1971
$9,000	1972
$10,800	1973
$13,200	1974
$14,100	1975
$15,300	1976
$16,500	1977
$17,700	1978
$22,900	1979
$25,900	1980
$29,700	1981
$32,400	1982
$35,700	1983
$37,800	1984
$39,600	1985
$39,600	1985
$42,000	1986
$43,800	1987
$45,000	1988
$48,000	1989
$51,300	1990
$53,400	1991
$55,500	1992
$57,600	1993
$60,600	1994
$61,200	1995
$62,700	1996
$65,400	1997
$68,400	1998
$72,600	1999
$76,200	2000
$80,400	2001
$84,900	2002
$87,000	2003
$87,900	2004
$90,000	2005
$94,200	2006
$97,500	2007

National Average Wage Index

The national average wage index for 2005 is $36,952.94—the latest available amount in the national average wage indexing series. This series is used to index the earnings of individuals for benefit computation purposes. It is also used to index several amounts that are important to the operation of the OASDI program.

National Average Wage Indexing Series (1955-2005)

Year	$Amount	Year	$Amount	Year	$Amount
1955	3,301.44	1975	8,630.92	1995	24,705.66
1956	3,532.36	1976	9,226.48	1996	25,913.90
1957	3,641.72	1977	9,779.44	1997	27,426.00
1958	3,673.80	1978	10,556.03	1998	28,861.44
1959	3,855.80	1979	11,479.46	1999	30,469.84
1960	4,007.12	1980	12,513.46	2000	32,154.82
1961	4,086.76	1981	13,773.10	2001	32,921.92
1962	4,291.40	1982	14,531.34	2002	33,252.09
1963	4,396.64	1983	15,239.24	2003	34,064.95
1964	4,576.32	1984	16,135.07	2004	35,648.55
1965	4,658.72	1985	16,822.51	2005	36,952.94
1966	4,938.36	1986	17,321.82		
1967	5,213.44	1987	18,426.51		
1968	5,571.76	1988	19,334.04		
1969	5,893.76	1989	20,099.55		
1970	6,186.24	1990	21,027.98		
1971	6,497.08	1991	21,811.60		
1972	7,133.80	1992	22,935.42		
1973	7,580.16	1993	23,132.67		
1974	8,030.76	1994	23,753.53		

When indexing an individual's earnings for benefit computation purposes, one must first determine the first year of eligibility for benefits. For retirement, eligibility is at age 62. If a person retires at age 62 in 2007, for example, then 2007 is the person's first year of eligibility. An individual's earnings are always indexed to the average wage level two years prior to the year of first eligibility, i.e., two years prior to the year age 62 is attained. Thus, a person retiring at age 62 in 2007 would have benefits indexed to the average wage index for 2005, or $36,952.94. Earnings in a year before 2005 would be multiplied by the ratio of $36,952.94 to the average wage index for that year. Earnings at 2005 or later would be taken at face value.

Benefit Tables for Workers with Maximum Earnings

Maximum earnings are defined as equal to the OASDI contribution and benefit base.

The Average Indexed Monthly Earnings (AIME) is calculated on the basis of such earnings. Retirement at age 62 means at exact age 62 and 1 month. Such early retirement results in a monthly benefit that is reduced from the Primary Insurance Amount (PIA). Retirement at age 65 means at exact age 65 and 0 months. For retirement in 2003 and later, the monthly benefit is reduced for early retirement.

Worker with Steady, Maximum Earnings Since Age 22

Year	Retirement at age 62 AIME	Monthly PIA	Benefit	Retirement at age 65 AIME	Monthly PIA	Benefit
1987	2,205	827.70	666	2,009	798.20	798
1988	2,311	858.40	691	2,139	838.60	838
1989	2,490	917.60	739	2,287	899.60	899
1990	2,648	968.30	780	2,417	975.00	975
1991	2,792	1,012.50	815	2,531	1,022.90	1,022
1992	2,978	1,067.70	860	2,716	1,088.70	1,088
1993	3,154	1,117.00	899	2,878	1,128.80	1,128
1994	3,384	1,185.00	954	3,024	1,147.50	1,147
1995	3,493	1,207.40	972	3,219	1,199.10	1,199
1996	3,657	1,249.90	1,006	3,402	1,248.90	1,248
1997	3,877	1,311.40	1,056	3,634	1,326.60	1,326
1998	4,144	1,387.00	1,117	3,750	1,342.80	1,342
1999	4,463	1,479.60	1,191	3,296	1,373.10	1,373
2000	4,775	1,568.50	1,248	4,161	1,433.90	1,433
2001	5,126	1,669.00	1,314	4,440	1,536.70	1,538
2002	5,499	1,875.20	1,382	4,770	1,765.80	1,660
2003	5,729	1,831.80	1,412	5,099	1,741.10	1,721
2004	5,892	1,865.80	1,422	5,457	1,800.60	1,784
2005	6,137	1,926.60	1,452	5,827	1,800.10	1,874
2006	6,515	2,030.00	1,530	6,058	1,961.50	1,961
2007	6,852	2,119.20	1,598	6,229	2,025.75	1,998

¶ 507 "SURVIVORS (LIFE) INSURANCE" FROM SOCIAL SECURITY

Part of Social Security taxes an individual pays goes toward survivors insurance. In fact, the value of the survivors insurance under Social Security is probably more than the value of an individual's commercial life insurance. When someone who has worked and paid into Social Security dies, survivor benefits can be paid to certain family members. These include widows, widowers, children, and dependent parents, and surviving divorced spouses in certain circumstances. Right now, 98 out of every 100 children could get benefits if a working parent should die.

There is also a special one-time payment of $255 that can be made to one's spouse or minor children if they meet certain requirements.

.01 Basics

Survivor Benefit Amounts

How much survivor benefits a family can get from Social Security, again, depends on the insured worker's average lifetime earnings. Basically, that means the higher the earnings, the higher the benefits will be. For an estimate of the Social Security survivors benefits that could be paid to a family, individuals can request a Social Security Statement online, by telephone, or in person at a Social Security Administration office.

The amount of survivor benefits is a percentage of the deceased's basic Social Security benefit. The percentage depends on the beneficiary's age and the type of benefit that person is eligible for. Here are the most typical situations.

- Widow or widower at full retirement age or older—100 percent.

- Widow or widower age 60 to month before month in which full retirement age is attained—71.5 to 99 percent.

- Widow any age with a child under age 16—75 percent.

- Children disabled or under age 18 (under age 19 if still in elementary or secondary school)—75 percent.

For Those Already Getting Social Security Benefits

Those getting benefits as a wife or husband on their spouse's record when he or she dies, should report the death to Social Security which will change their payments to survivors benefits. For those getting benefits on their own record, they will need to complete an application to get survivors benefits. Individuals can check with Social Security to see if they can get more as a widow or widower. SSA will need to see the spouse's death certificate to process a claim. Benefits for any children will automatically be changed to survivors benefits after the death is reported.

Age to Receive Full Retirement Benefit for Widow(er)s

A widow(er) may receive unreduced widow(er)'s benefits beginning with the month the widow or widower reaches the age shown below:

If one's date of birth is:	Full retirement age is:
Before 1/1/1940	65
1/2/1940 - 1/1/1941	65 and 2 months
1/2/1941 - 1/1/1942	65 and 4 months
1/2/1942 - 1/1/1943	65 and 6 months
1/2/1943 - 1/1/1944	65 and 8 months
1/2/1944 - 1/1/1945	65 and 10 months
1/2/1945 - 1/1/1957	66
1/2/1957 - 1/1/1958	66 and 2 months
1/2/1958 - 1/1/1959	66 and 4 months
1/2/1959 - 1/1/1960	66 and 6 months
1/2/1960 - 1/1/1961	66 and 8 months
1/2/1961 - 1/1/1962	66 and 10 months
1/2/1962 and later	67

Maximum Family Benefits

There is a limit to the amount of money that can be paid to a surviving spouse and other family members each month. The limit varies, but is generally equal to about 150 to 180 percent of the deceased's benefit rate. If the sum of the benefits payable to the family members is greater than this limit, the benefits will be reduced proportionately.

How Work May Affect Survivor Benefits

For those who receive Social Security survivors benefits, the amount of benefits may be affected by earnings from work. Survivor beneficiaries can receive all their Social Security benefits in a year if earnings do not go over certain limits, which are the same as the limits for retirees under the earnings test. (*See* ¶ 505.03) Earnings will affect only the worker's survivors benefits, not the benefits of other family members.

Remarrying

In general, individuals may not receive survivors benefits if they remarry. But, remarriage after 60 (50 if disabled) will not prevent benefit payments. And, those who remarry at 62 or older may receive benefits on the record of their new spouse if such benefits are higher.

¶ 509 SOCIAL SECURITY SYSTEM—MEDICARE

.01 Highlights for 2007

The Centers for Medicare and Medicaid Services (CMS) is the agency within the federal Department of Health and Human Services that administers Medicare.

Prescription Drug Coverage

The Medicare Modernization Act of 2003 required CMS to establish a voluntary prescription drug benefit under a new Part D of the Medicare Act. Beneficiaries entitled to Part A and enrolled in Part B, enrollees in Medicare Advantage plans, and enrollees in Medicare Savings Account plans are eligible individuals for the prescription drug benefit. Eligible individuals have access to at least two prescription drug plans (PDPs) in their region.

Under the drug benefit eligible individuals must be able to choose from at least two PDPs in their region, either a standard coverage plan or an alternative coverage plan with actuarially equivalent benefits. In 2007, standard coverage has a $265 deductible and a 25 percent coinsurance for costs between $266 and $2400. Beneficiaries pay 100 percent of prescription drug costs between $2401 and $5,451.25 for the year, which is $3850 out of their own pockets. The gap period when beneficiaries pay 100 percent of their costs is sometimes called the "doughnut hole." Once the out-of-pocket threshold is met, beneficiaries will pay $2.15 for a generic version (preferred multi-source drugs) and $5.35 for a brand name version (nonpreferred drugs) or five percent of the cost of a drug, whichever is greater.

In general, coverage for the new prescription drug benefit is provided through private PDPs that offer drug-only coverage, or through Medicare Advantage (MA) plans that offer integrated prescription drug and health care coverage (MA-PD plans). PDPs must offer a basic drug benefit. MA-PD plans must offer either a basic benefit or broader coverage for no additional cost.

Subsidies are established for deductibles, premiums, and cost-sharing for low-income individuals with incomes below 150 percent of the federal poverty line. Eligibility determinations will be made by state Medicaid plans.

Medicare Advantage Drug Coverage

A Medicare Advantage organization that offers an MA plan in an area must offer at least one MA plan that includes prescription drug coverage that matches the coverage under Medicare Part D. An MA enrollee enrolled in a plan that provides prescription drug coverage (MA-PD) must obtain drug coverage through the plan; the MA enrollee may not enroll in a standard prescription drug plan (PDP) under Part D.

Preventive Care

Medicare coverage of an initial preventive physical examination (IPPE), also called the "Welcome to Medicare" physical, became effective January 1, 2005, subject to deductible and beneficiary cost-sharing. A covered IPPE is performed no later than six months after the individual's initial coverage date under Part B. This benefit is available only to beneficiaries whose Part B coverage began on or after January 1, 2005.

The IPPE includes a measurement of height, weight, and blood pressure, a screening EKG, a review of the individual's medical and social history, and a review of the individual's potential (risk factors) for depression, functional ability, and level of safety with the goal of health promotion and disease detection. It also includes education, counseling, and referral with respect to screening and preventive services currently covered under Medicare Part B, which include cardiovascular screening blood tests and diabetes screening tests.

Beneficiary Premiums and Copayments

Most individuals do not pay a monthly Part A premium because they or their spouses have 40 or more quarters of Medicare-covered employment. The Part A premium in 2007 is $226 per month for those with 30–39 quarters of Medicare-covered employment and $410 per month for those with fewer than 30 quarters of Medicare-covered employment.

An additional 10 percent is added to these premiums when enrollment takes place more than 12 months after a person's initial enrollment period for Health Insurance (Part A) benefits. In that case, the premium for those with 30–39 quarters of covered employment is $248.60 and for those with fewer than 30 quarters, $451 per month.

The Part A deductible is $992 per spell of illness in 2007. There is a per-day copayment charge for inpatient hospital stays of more than 60 days in the same spell of illness. In 2007, the copayment is $248 per day for the 61st through the 90th day of an inpatient hospital stay, and if lifetime reserve days are used, the copayment is $496 per day.

The Part B deductible increased in 2007 to $131. There are some items and services for which no deductible or copayment is charged, most notably clinical diagnostic laboratory tests paid under a federally approved fee schedule, home health services (except for durable medical equipment and osteoporosis drugs), transplant surgery services for kidney donors, pneumococcal pneumonia and influenza vaccine, mammograms, and pap smears and pelvic exams.

For 2007, the standard Part B premium is $93.50 per month. Beginning in 2007, Medicare beneficiaries with incomes over $80,000 for an individual (or $160,000 for a married couple) will pay a higher premium on a sliding scale. Previously, Medicare beneficiaries who elected to participate in Part B paid the same premium regardless of their income.

.02 Medicare Basics

The Medicare program is a federal health insurance program for people 65 or older and certain disabled people. It is administered by the Centers for Medicare and Medicaid Services (CMS) of the U.S. Department of Health and Human Services. Social Security Administration offices across the country take applications for Medicare and provide general information about the program.

The Four Parts of Medicare

The Medicare program initially offered two kinds of benefits, which continue to be available. Hospital Insurance (Part A) helps pay for inpatient hospital care, inpatient care in a rehabilitation or a skilled nursing facility, home health care, and hospice care. Supplemental Medical Insurance (Part B) helps pay for physicians' services, outpatient hospital services, durable medical equipment, and a number of other medical services and supplies not covered by the Hospital Insurance part of Medicare.

Part C is the managed care option for delivery of services called the Medicare Advantage program, and Part D is the Voluntary Prescription Drug Benefit Program.

Part A has deductibles and coinsurance, but most people do not pay premiums for Part A. Part B has premiums, deductibles, and coinsurance amounts that the insured must pay personally or through coverage by another insurance plan. Part B premiums and Part A deductible and coinsurance amounts are set each year based on formulas established by law.

Medicare Advantage Program

Medicare Part C, originally called Medicare+Choice, was added in 1999 for Medicare beneficiaries who are entitled to Part A and enrolled in Part B. The Medicare Modernization Act of 2003 changed the name of the benefit program to "Medicare Advantage." Instead of obtaining health benefits through the traditional "fee-for-service" program—which pays health care providers for the services they provide at a rate that does not vary based on the services that are provided, and does not restrict a beneficiary's choice of provider—these beneficiaries may choose a Medicare Advantage managed care plan. When a beneficiary chooses coverage under a Medicare Advantage managed care plan, the payments Medicare makes under its contract with that plan replace the amounts Medicare otherwise would have paid under Parts A and B. In addition, the beneficiary's monthly plan premium is equal to the Part B premium otherwise paid to Medicare.

A beneficiary's choice of provider is restricted to the providers that contract with the managed care plan.

Those Eligible for Medicare Hospital Insurance (Part A)

Generally, persons age 65 and older are entitled to premium-free Medicare Part A benefits, based on their own or their spouse's employment. An individual can receive premium-free Medicare Part A if 65 or older and any of these three statements is true:

- The person receives benefits under the Social Security or Railroad Retirement system.

- The person could receive benefits under Social Security or the Railroad Retirement system but has not filed for them.
- His or her spouse had Medicare-covered government employment.

If under 65, a person can get premium-free Medicare Part A benefits if that person has been a disabled beneficiary under Social Security or the Railroad Retirement Board for more than 24 months (one month for patients with amyotrophic lateral sclerosis (ALS)). Certain government employees and certain members of their families can also get Medicare when they are disabled for a prescribed period of time. A person may be able to get premium-free Medicare Part A benefits if that person receives continuing dialysis for permanent kidney failure or he or she has had a kidney transplant.

Those Eligible for Medicare Medical Insurance (Part B)

Any person who can get premium-free Medicare Part A benefits based on work as described above can enroll for Part B, pay the monthly Part B premiums, and get Part B benefits. In addition, most United States residents age 65 or over can enroll in Part B.

Buying Medicare Part A and Part B

If an individual or spouse does not have enough work credits to be able to get Medicare Part A benefits and that individual is 65 or over, he or she may be able to buy Medicare Parts A and B—or just Medicare Part B—by paying monthly premiums. Also, an individual may be able to buy Medicare Parts A and B if disabled and has lost premium-free Part A solely because that individual is working.

Assistance for Low-Income Beneficiaries

Federal law requires that state Medicaid programs pay Medicare costs for certain elderly and disabled people with low incomes and very limited resources. There are four categories of assistance: QMB, SLMB, QI and QDWI.

Qualified Medicare Beneficiaries (QMB)—General Requirements

- The person must be entitled to Medicare Hospital Insurance (Part A).
- The person's monthly income must be at or below the federal poverty level plus $20 ($827 in 2006 in all states except Alaska and Hawaii).
- The person cannot have resources such as bank accounts or stocks and bonds worth more than approximately $4,000 for an individual or $6,000 for a couple. A person's personal home, automobile, burial plot, furniture, jewelry, or life insurance is not counted, unless those items are of extraordinary value.

If an individual qualifies as a QMB, the Medicare premiums, deductibles, and coinsurance will be covered by the state medical assistance (Medicaid) program.

Specified Low-Income Medicare Beneficiaries (SLMB)

There is a program for certain low-income Medicare beneficiaries whose income is above the level to qualify as a QMB, but whose income is between 100 and 120 percent of the national poverty guidelines (less than $980 monthly income in 2006). If an individual qualifies as an SLMB, Medicaid will pay the Medicare Part B premium only.

Qualifying Individual (QI)

A QI is entitled to Medicare Part A, income at least 120 percent FPL but less than 135 percent FPL (between $980 and $1,103 monthly income in 2006), and resources that do not exceed twice the SSI limit ($4,000 for an individual, and $6,000 for a couple) and not otherwise eligible for Medicaid benefits. Medicaid will pay the Part B minimum.

Qualified Disabled and Working Individual (QDWI)

A QDWI has lost Medicare Part A benefits due to return to work, but is eligible to enroll in and purchase Medicare Part A. The individual must have an income of 200 percent FPL ($1634 a month in 2006) and resources that do not exceed twice the SSI limit ($4,000 for an individual, and $6,000 for a couple) and not otherwise eligible for Medicaid benefits. Medicaid will pay the Part A premium.

Medicare Administrative Contractors

The federal government contracts with private insurance organizations and carriers to process claims and make Medicare payments. These Medicare Administrative Contractors (MACs) handle inpatient and outpatient claims submitted on an individual's behalf by hospitals, skilled nursing facilities, home health agencies, hospices, and other providers of services. Between 2005 and 2011, CMS is conducting open competitions to replace existing carrier and intermediaries with MACs that will have access to centralized data, rather than data maintained by carriers or intermediaries.

Quality Improvement Organizations

Quality Improvement Organizations (QIOs), formerly called Peer Review Organizations, are groups of practicing physicians and other health care professionals paid by the federal government to review the care given to Medicare patients. Each state has a QIO that decides, for Medicare payment purposes, whether care is reasonable, necessary, and provided in the most appropriate setting. QIOs also decide whether care meets the standards of quality generally accepted by the medical profession. QIOs have the authority to deny payments if care is not medically necessary or not delivered in the most appropriate setting. QIOs investigate individual patient complaints about the quality of care and respond to requests for review of notices of noncoverage issued by hospitals to beneficiaries and requests for reconsideration of QIO decisions by beneficiaries, physicians, and hospitals.

Beneficiary Complaints

QIOs are responsible for reviewing beneficiary complaints about the quality of care provided by inpatient hospitals, hospital outpatient departments and hospital emergency rooms; skilled nursing facilities; home health agencies; ambulatory surgical centers; and certain health maintenance organizations.

.03 Medicare Part C, the Medicare Advantage Program

Medicare Advantage (MA) plans are prepaid managed care plans, usually coordinated care plans such as health maintenance organizations (HMOs), preferred provider organizations (PPOs), or private fee-for-service plans, that contract with Medicare to provide Part A and Part B services to enrollees.

Enrollment in Medicare Advantage Plans

Most Medicare beneficiaries are eligible to enroll in MA plans. These plans cannot screen applicants to decide if they are healthy, or delay coverage for pre-existing conditions. The only enrollment criteria for Medicare MAs are as follows:

¶509.03

- A person must be entitled to Part A unless he or she was enrolled in certain MAs on December 31, 1998.
- A person must be enrolled in Medicare Part B and continue to pay the Part B premiums.
- A person must live in the plan's service area.
- A person cannot have permanent kidney failure prior to enrollment.

Enrollment may be made during the initial enrollment period (when the beneficiary is first eligible for Medicare), during the annual coordinated election period (from November 15th through December 31st), or during the annual general enrollment period from January 1 to March 31 of the year. These periods are described below.

Disenrolling from a Medicare Managed Care Plan

MA plans have contracts with Medicare. All plans with Medicare contracts have an advertised open enrollment period at least once a year. Once a person joins, he or she may stay with the plan as long as it continues to contract with Medicare. Individuals may return to regular Medicare at any time.

Summary

An MA plan may take one of the following forms:

(1) A coordinated care plan, which includes plans offered by HMOs, provider-sponsored organizations (PSOs), PPOs, or religious and fraternal benefit societies.

(2) A private fee-for-service plan, which is a plan that pays providers of services at a rate determined by the plan on a fee-for-service basis without placing the provider at financial risk; does not vary the rates for a provider based on the utilization of that provider's services; and does not restrict enrollees' choices among providers.

(3) A combination of a medical savings account (MSA) plan and a contribution into the MSA by CMS.

Initial Election of New Enrollees

When they become eligible for Medicare, individuals have a choice, called an "initial election," between fee-for-service Medicare coverage and enrollment in a Medicare Advantage plan in their area. Information must be sent to newly eligible beneficiaries no later than 30 days before their initial enrollment period.

Newly eligible beneficiaries who do not choose a Medicare Advantage plan will be treated as though they selected the fee-for-service option.

The coverage choice that a beneficiary makes during initial election will take effect on the date on which the individual becomes entitled to benefits under Part A, and enrolled under Part B.

Open Enrollment and Disenrollment

In order for an MA organization to accept an election, the individual must make the election during an election period. There are four types of election periods during which individuals may make elections. They are:

(1) The Annual Election Period (AEP);

¶509.03

(2) The Initial Coverage Election Period (ICEP);

(3) All Special Election Periods (SEP); and

(4) The Open Enrollment Period (OEP).

During the AEP, SEP, and OEP, individuals may enroll in and disenroll from MA plans, or may move between MA plans, or between an MA plan and Original Medicare. Individuals may elect to enroll in MA plans during an ICEP.

Unless a CMS-approved capacity limit applies, all MA organizations must accept elections into their MA plans (with the exception of MA MSA plans) during the AEP, an ICEP, and an SEP. When an MA plan is closed due to a capacity limit, the MA plan must remain closed to all prospective enrollees (with the exception of reserved vacancies) until the limit is lifted.

Annual Coordinated Election Period

The annual election period (AEP) occurs November 15 through December 31 of every year, but in 2005, the AEP was extended from November 15, 2005, through May 15, 2006.

At least 15 days before the beginning of the annual election period, Medicare must mail each eligible Medicare Advantage enrollee the following: (1) general coverage information, (2) a list of plans that are available to residents in the area, (3) plan comparisons, and (4) any other information that would help a beneficiary make an informed choice of healthcare plan.

An election or change of coverage made during an annual coordinated election period takes effect on the first day of the following year.

The **Initial Coverage Election Period (ICEP)** is the six-month period during which an individual newly eligible for MA may make an initial election to enroll in an MA plan. This period begins three months immediately before the individual's entitlement to *both* Medicare Part A and Part B

The **Special Election Period (SEP)** applies when an enrollee moves out of the area of his original plan or the plan is terminated. In the case of a permanent move, the SEP begins the month prior to the month of the individual's permanent move and continues during the month of the move and up to two months after the move. Other time periods apply to different situations.

The **Open Enrollment Period (OEP)** in 2006 allowed one OEP election from January 1st through June 30th. In *2007 and each year thereafter*, an MA eligible individual may make *one* MA OEP election from January 1st through March 31st.

Beneficiary Protections

Guaranteed Issue and Renewal

Under the law, organizations that participate in the Medicare Advantage program must accept, without restrictions, the beneficiaries who choose their health plans. If the health plan has a capacity limit, however, the plan may be allowed to limit the number of Medicare beneficiaries who enroll.

As a general rule, however, a Medicare Advantage organization cannot terminate a beneficiary's participation in a health plan unless:

- The beneficiary did not pay monthly premiums on time;

- The beneficiary's behavior has been disruptive; or
- The health plan has been terminated.

Comparable Benefits

A Medicare Advantage plan must provide enrolled beneficiaries with the same items and services that are available under Medicare Parts A and B. The plan may, at the beneficiary's option, provide supplemental health care benefits that are approved by Medicare.

Disclosure Requirements

Information about a Medicare Advantage plan's service area, benefits, access, out-of-area coverage, emergency coverage, supplemental benefits, prior authorization rules, grievance and appeal procedures, and quality assurance must be made available to beneficiaries in a clear, accurate, and standardized form. If so requested, a plan must provide information on the following:

- General and comparative plan coverage;
- Utilization and cost control procedures;
- The number of grievances, redeterminations, and appeals, and their disposition; and
- Summaries that describe the way that plan physicians are paid.

Quality Assurance

Medicare Advantage plans must ensure the quality of the health care that is provided to beneficiaries. The plans must arrange for outside review of care quality, community outreach, and beneficiary complaints.

Access to Services

A Medicare Advantage plan must ensure that:

- Beneficiaries receive prompt and continuous care;
- Medically necessary care is available 24 hours a day, seven days a week;
- Emergency out-of-network care is covered;
- Beneficiaries have adequate access to specialists; and
- Emergency services are covered without the necessity of prior authorization by a "gatekeeper" or a contractual agreement between the emergency care provider and the plan.

An "emergency medical condition" as defined by law presents acute symptoms that are so severe that a person without medical training could reasonably expect that, without medical attention, the condition could seriously jeopardize an individual's health or cause a serious impairment. This is called the "prudent layperson" standard.

Expanded Preventive Benefits

Medicare Part C established some new preventive benefits for beneficiaries while it increased and expanded others. These covered services include the following:

- Annual mammograms for female beneficiaries age 40 and over.

- Screening Pap smear and pelvic exam, which also includes a breast examination, once every three years, or annually for women at risk for cervical or vaginal cancer.
- Colorectal cancer screening tests.
- Bone density measurement for high-risk beneficiaries, and
- Annual prostate cancer screening examinations for men over age 50.
- Influenza and pneumococcal vaccinations.

Additional Part C Program Rules

Plan Service Area

A beneficiary will be able to choose a particular Medicare Advantage health plan so long as the plan serves the geographic area where the beneficiary lives. A plan may offer its enrolled beneficiaries the option of continuing their enrollment in the plan even if they move out of the plan service area, however, so long as they have reasonable access to the plan's full range of basic benefits with reasonable cost-sharing.

Special Rule for Hospital Stays

For individuals receiving inpatient hospital services when their new Medicare Advantage plan election becomes effective, payment for the hospital services will be made by the individual's prior health plan or by the Medicare fee-for-service plan, as the case may be, until the individual is discharged from the hospital.

Special Rule for Hospice Care

A Medicare Advantage plan must inform its enrolled Medicare beneficiaries whether a hospice program is located within the plan's service area, or the plan's common practice is to refer patients to hospices outside of the service area. If a Medicare Advantage plan enrollee receives care from a hospice program, payment will be made to that hospice program. Payment for other services for which the enrollee is eligible, however, will be made to the Medicare Advantage plan, or to the provider or supplier of the service. This payment arrangement applies whether or not the enrollee has elected hospice care or the services are related to the beneficiary's terminal illness.

Secondary Payer Rule

A Medicare Advantage organization may seek payment from insurers, employee health plans, or other "secondary payers."

Monthly Premiums

A beneficiary who is enrolled in a Medicare Advantage plan will be charged a monthly premium that equals the sum of the Medicare Advantage monthly basic premium and the monthly supplementary beneficiary premium, if any. The "monthly supplemental beneficiary premium" is the amount authorized to be charged for supplemental benefits or, in the case of an MSA or a fee-for-service plan, the amount that is filed with Medicare. Basic and supplementary beneficiary premiums may not vary among individuals who are enrolled in a Medicare Advantage plan.

Limits on Cost-Sharing

The total of a beneficiary's Medicare Advantage premiums, deductibles, and coinsurance for basic and additional benefits may not exceed what the beneficiary's total

¶509.03

deductibles and coinsurance would have been if the beneficiary received benefits under Part A and was enrolled in Part B. Similarly, if a Medicare Advantage plan provides a beneficiary with supplemental benefits, the total of the Medicare Advantage basic beneficiary premiums, deductibles, and coinsurance charged may not exceed the adjusted community rate for those benefits.

Excess Capitation Payments

Except in the case of an MSA, a Medicare Advantage plan must provide beneficiaries with additional benefits that are equal to any excess amount in a plan for a contract year. These extra benefits must be provided uniformly to all the enrollees in a plan area.

.05 Medicare and Other Insurance

Private Non-Medicare Contracts with Physicians

Medicare beneficiaries and their physicians may enter into private contracts that permit physicians to charge more than the Medicare program allows. A physician who enters into such a private contract is frozen out of the Medicare program for at least two years, but must nevertheless include certain clauses in the private contract that meet Medicare requirements. Dentists, optometrists, and podiatrists may also use these private contracts.

Medicare requires private contract rules to be in writing and signed by the patient before any services are provided. Certain patient notification clauses must be included. The contract may not be entered into at a time when the beneficiary is facing an emergency or urgent care situation.

Buying Health Insurance to Supplement Medicare

Medicare does not pay all medical expenses, nor most long-term care expenses. For this reason, many private insurance companies sell supplemental (Medigap) insurance as well as separate long-term care insurance. Medigap policies only work with the Original (fee-for-service) Medicare plan; they may not be sold to enrollees of managed care plans.

The Medigap program allows Medicare participating providers to file one claim that will be processed by both Medicare and the beneficiary's supplemental plan.

Open Enrollment Period for Medigap Policies

An open enrollment period for selecting Medigap policies guarantees that for six months immediately following the effective date of Medicare Part B coverage, people age 65 or older cannot be denied Medigap insurance or charged higher premiums because of health problems.

The Medigap policy in this open enrollment period may still exclude coverage for "preexisting conditions" during the first six months the policy is in effect. Pre-existing conditions are conditions that were either diagnosed or treated during the six-month period before the Medigap policy became effective.

If a beneficiary previously enrolled in a Medicare Advantage plan returns to Original Medicare, he or she may apply for a Medigap plan within 63 days after the Medicare Advantage coverage ends.

Medigap Policies Guaranteed

Four Medicare supplemental insurance policies, commonly called "Medigap" policies "A," "B," "C," and "F," must be issued to various classes of Medicare beneficiaries without a preexisting condition exclusion. These policies must be offered, without exclusion, for beneficiaries:

- Whose supplemental coverage under an employee welfare benefit plan terminates;

- Who disenroll from a Medicare Advantage plan for permissible reasons outside of an annual election period;

- Who disenroll from Medicare SELECT policies for permissible reasons outside of an annual election period;

- Whose enrollment in a Medigap policy is involuntarily terminated, for reasons including the insurer's bankruptcy, and there is no state law on continuation of coverage;

- Previously enrolled under a Medigap policy, who terminate enrollment to participate for the first time in a Medicare Advantage plan or Medicare SELECT policy and then terminate that enrollment during any permissible period within the first 12 months of enrollment; or

- Who enroll in a Medicare Advantage plan when they reach Medicare eligibility at age 65, but disenroll from the plan within 12 months.

Limits on Exclusions Due to Pre-Existing Conditions

Under certain circumstances, a beneficiary may not be excluded from enrollment in a Medigap policy based on a pre-existing condition during the six-month initial enrollment period. Such an exclusion is not allowed in the case of an individual who, on the date he or she applies for Medigap coverage, has had at least six months of "continuous coverage," as that term is defined by law. Individuals who have fewer than six months of continuous coverage are entitled to have the period of any pre-existing condition exclusion reduced by the amounts of the periods of coverage that they have accumulated.

High-Deductible or Out of Pocket Threshold Medigap Policies

Insurance companies are permitted to offer at least one Medigap policy, classified either as an "F" or a "J" plan, with a "high deductible" amount that has been set for calendar year 2007 at $1,860. This policy must pay 100 percent of the enrolled beneficiary's out-of-pocket expenses after the deductible is satisfied.

Effective January 1, 2006, there are two new Medigap policies that eliminate first-dollar coverage for most Medicare cost-sharing until an annual "out-of-pocket" limit has been reached. The 2007 out-of-pocket limits for Medigap Plans K and L are $4,140 and $2,070 respectively. Like all other Medigap policies designated Plans A–J, Plans K and L can only provide benefits that supplement benefits under Parts A and B of Original (fee-for-service) Medicare, which means they may not be sold to managed care plan enrollees. No Medigap policies sold after January 1, 2006, may provide any prescription drug coverage.

¶509.05

Medicare SELECT

Medicare SELECT refers to a type of Medigap Policy. It must meet all of the requirements that apply to a Medigap Policy, and it must be one of the prescribed benefit packages. The only difference is that a Medicare SELECT Policy may require you to use physicians and hospitals within its network, except in an emergency, in order for you to be eligible for full benefits. Because of this limitation, a Medicare SELECT Policy will generally have a lower premium than a regular Medigap Policy.

Employment-Related Retiree Coverage Instead of Medigap

Some retired people can get health coverage through their former employer or union. This health coverage may supplement Medicare, but it is not Medigap insurance and does not have to meet federal and state Medigap requirements. Retiree coverage is usually provided free or at a greatly reduced price and may be a good bargain, but the benefits may not be adequate to serve as a supplement to Medicare.

Medicare has special rules that apply to beneficiaries who have employer group health plan coverage through their current employment or the current employment of a spouse. Group health plans of employers with 20 or more employees are primary payers and Medicare is secondary payer for workers age 65 or older, and workers' spouses age 65 or older. Group health plans must offer these people the same health insurance benefits under the same conditions offered to younger workers and spouses.

Disabled and Under Age 65

Medicare is the secondary payer for certain disabled people who have premium-free Medicare Part A and are covered under their employer's health plan or the employer health plan of an employed family member. This secondary payer provision applies to group health plans of employers that employ 100 or more people. The secondary payer provision also applies to group health plans of employers with fewer than 100 employees if they are part of a multi-employer plan in which at least one employer has 100 or more employees.

Other Situations Where Medicare Is the Secondary Payer

If an individual has a work-related illness or injury, services provided as treatment of that illness or injury should be covered by workers' compensation or federal black lung benefits. Medicare is a secondary payer during a period (generally 30 months) for beneficiaries who have Medicare solely on the basis of permanent kidney failure, if they have employer group health plan coverage themselves or through a family member. Medicare also serves as the secondary payer in cases where no-fault insurance or liability insurance is available as the primary payer. Although Medicare benefits are secondary to benefits paid by liability insurers, Medicare may make a conditional payment if it receives a claim for services covered by liability insurance. In those cases, Medicare may pay the claim and when a liability settlement is reached, recover its conditional payment from the settlement amount.

If an individual has or can receive both Medicare and veterans benefits, that person may choose to get treatment under either program, but Medicare:

- Cannot pay for services received from Veterans Affairs (VA) hospitals or other VA facilities, except for certain emergency hospital services; and

¶509.05

- Generally cannot pay if the VA pays for VA-authorized services that a person gets in a non-VA hospital or from a non-VA physician.

.07 Medicare Coverage

Custodial Care

Medicare does not pay for custodial care when that is the only kind of care needed. Care is considered custodial when it is primarily for the purpose of helping a person with daily living or meeting personal needs and could be provided safely and reasonably by people without professional skills or training. Much of the care provided in nursing homes to people with chronic, long-term illnesses or disabilities is considered custodial care. Even in a participating hospital or skilled nursing facility, Medicare does not cover the stay if a patient needs only custodial care.

Care Not Reasonable and Necessary

Medicare does not pay for services that are not reasonable and necessary for the diagnosis or treatment of an illness or injury. These services include drugs or devices that have not been approved by the Food and Drug Administration (FDA); medical procedures and services performed using drugs or devices not approved by the FDA (some services are not covered by Medicare even when the FDA has approved the drug or device used); and services, including drugs or devices, not considered safe and effective because they are experimental or investigational.

Services Medicare Does Not Pay for as Required by Law

Medicare, by law, cannot pay for services performed by immediate relatives or members of your household and services paid for by another government program.

Limitation of Liability

Under Medicare law, Medicare patients will not be held responsible for payment of the cost of certain health care services for which they were denied Medicare payment if they did not know or could not reasonably be expected to know that the services were not covered by Medicare. This provision is called limitation of liability and is often referred to as a "waiver of liability." This protection from financial liability applies only when the care was denied because it was one of the following:

- Custodial care.
- Not "reasonable and necessary" under Medicare program standards for diagnosis or treatment.
- For home health services, the patient was not homebound or not receiving skilled nursing care on an intermittent basis.
- The only reason for the denial is that, in error, the patient was placed in a skilled nursing facility bed that was not approved by Medicare.

.09 Medicare Hospital Insurance (Part A)

Medicare Part A Helps Pay for Four Kinds of Medically Necessary Care

1) Inpatient hospital care.
2) Inpatient care in a skilled nursing facility following a hospital stay.
3) Home health care.
4) Hospice care.

Inpatient Hospital Services

Part A Medicare beneficiaries typically pay coinsurance amounts and deductibles and they face a lifetime limit of 190 days on inpatient psychiatric hospital services. The hospital insurance benefits program covers services provided to *inpatients* by qualified hospitals participating in the program for up to 90 days in any one *spell of illness*. Each beneficiary also has a lifetime reserve of 60 days of added coverage after the 90 days have been exhausted.

Ordinarily, for hospital services to be covered by Medicare, the hospital that provides the services must be participating in Medicare. However, in emergencies, services provided by nonparticipating hospitals are covered.

Inpatient Defined

An inpatient is a person who has been admitted to a hospital for occupancy for purposes of receiving inpatient hospital services. A person is an inpatient under Medicare if he or she is formally admitted as an inpatient with the expectation that an overnight stay and occupancy will be required. The patient is considered an inpatient even if it later develops that the patient is discharged or transferred to another hospital and does not use the hospital bed overnight.

Benefit Period Defined

The duration of inpatient hospital services and posthospital services in a skilled nursing facility is limited in accordance with the beginning or ending of a benefit period, also called a *spell of illness*. A benefit period is a period of consecutive days that begins the first day a patient is furnished inpatient hospital or extended care services by a qualified provider in a month for which the patient is entitled to Part A benefits. Generally, the spell of illness begins when covered inpatient emergency services are initially furnished to an entitled individual. The spell of illness ends with the close of a period of 60 consecutive days during which the patient was neither an inpatient of the hospital nor an inpatient of a skilled nursing facility.

The individual may be discharged from and readmitted to a hospital or skilled nursing facility several times during a spell of illness and still be in the same spell if 60 days have not elapsed between discharge and readmission. The stay need not be for related physical or mental conditions. Once a spell of illness has ended, the beneficiary's next admission to a qualified hospital or skilled nursing facility will constitute the beginning of a new spell of illness. As long as a person continues to be entitled to hospital insurance, there is no limit to the number of spells of illness covered. When the beneficiary begins a new spell of illness as a hospital inpatient, a new inpatient deductible must be paid.

Examples of How the Benefit Period Works

Example (1): Ms. Jones enters the hospital on January 5. She is discharged on January 15. She has used 10 days of her first benefit period. Ms. Jones is not hospitalized again until July 20. Since more than 60 days elapsed between her hospital stays, she begins a new benefit period, her Part A coverage is completely renewed, and she will again pay the hospital deductible.

Example (2): Ms. Smith enters the hospital on August 14. She is discharged on August 24. She also has used 10 days of her first benefit period. However, she is then readmitted to the hospital on September 20. Since fewer than 60 days elapsed between hospital stays, Ms. Smith is still in her first benefit period and will not be required to pay another hospital deductible. This means that the first day of her second admission is counted as the eleventh day of hospital care in that benefit period. Ms. Smith will not begin a new benefit period until she has been out of the hospital (and has not received any skilled care in a skilled nursing facility) for 60 consecutive days.

How Medicare Pays for Part A Services

Medicare Part A helps pay for most, but not all, of the services the Medicare patient receives in a hospital or skilled nursing facility or from a home health agency or hospice program. There are covered services and noncovered services under each kind of care. Covered services are services and supplies that Part A pays for. Hospitals, skilled nursing facilities, home health agencies and hospices are called "providers" under the Medicare Part A program. Providers submit their claims directly to Medicare—the Medicare patient cannot submit claims for his or her services. The provider will charge a patient for any part of the Part A deductible not met and any coinsurance payment owed. Providers cannot require a Medicare patient to make a deposit before being admitted for inpatient care that is or may be covered under Part A of Medicare. When a hospital, skilled nursing facility, home health agency, or hospice sends Medicare a Part A claim for payment, the patient gets a Medicare Summary Notice (MSN) that explains the decision Medicare made on the claim. This notice is not a bill.

Medicare Part A Payments

Medicare Part A services provided by most providers are now paid for under the Prospective Payment System. Payments are a fixed amount for each Medicare discharge, and the amount is based on the diagnosis-related group (DRG) into which a discharge is classified, regardless of the number of services received or the length of the patient's stay in the hospital. Under this system, all patient illnesses and injuries resulting in admission to a hospital are classified into groups termed DRGs. These groups are clinically coherent and relatively homogeneous with respect to the resources used by a hospital.

In the case of a few hospitals, payment for Part A services is made on a reasonable cost basis.

Hospital Inpatient Care Under Medicare

Medicare Part A helps pay for inpatient hospital care if all of the following four conditions are met:

1) A physician prescribes inpatient hospital care for treatment of the illness or injury.

2) The Medicare patient requires the kind of care that can be provided only in a hospital.

3) The hospital is participating in Medicare. (Under certain conditions, Medicare helps pay for emergency inpatient care received in a nonparticipating hospital.)

4) The Utilization Review Committee of the hospital, a Peer Review Organization or an intermediary does not disapprove the stay.

¶509.09

If these four conditions are met, Medicare will help pay for up to 90 days of medically necessary inpatient hospital care in each benefit period. During 2007, from the first day through the 60th day in a hospital during each benefit period, Part A pays for all covered services, except the first $992, the inpatient hospital deductible. The hospital may charge the deductible only for the first admission in each benefit period. If discharged and then readmitted before the benefit period ends, the patient does not have to pay the deductible again. From the 61st through the 90th day in a hospital during each benefit period, Part A pays for all covered services, except for a copayment of $248 a day for 2007. The hospital charges the patient the $248. The copayment is $496 per day for days 91-150 in 2007. Hospital reserve days (explained below) can help with expenses if the patient needs more than 90 days of inpatient hospital care in a benefit period. Medicare Part A does not pay for the services of physicians and certain other practitioners, even though one receives these services in a hospital. Instead, those services are covered under Medicare Part B.

Major Services Covered Under Part A for a Hospital Inpatient

- A semiprivate room (two to four beds in a room).
- All meals, including special diets.
- Regular nursing services.
- Costs of special care units, such as intensive care or coronary care units.
- Drugs furnished by the hospital during the stay.
- Blood transfusions furnished by the hospital during the stay (except for the first three pints of blood).
- Lab tests included in the hospital bill.
- X-rays and other radiology services, including radiation therapy, billed by the hospital.
- Medical supplies, such as casts, surgical dressings, and splints.
- Use of appliances, such as a wheelchair.
- Operating and recovery room costs.
- Rehabilitation services, such as physical therapy, occupational therapy, and speech pathology services.

Some Services Not Covered Under Part A for a Hospital Inpatient

- Personal convenience items requested, such as a telephone or television.
- Private duty nurses.
- Any extra charges for a private room, unless it is determined to be medically necessary.

Hospital Inpatient Reserve Days

Medicare helps pay for care in a hospital for up to 90 days in each benefit period. Medicare Part A also includes an extra 60 hospital days if a patient has a long illness and has to stay in the hospital for more than 90 days. These extra days are called reserve days. Each Medicare beneficiary has only 60 reserve days in his or her lifetime.

¶509.09

Care in a Psychiatric Hospital

Part A helps pay for no more than 190 days of inpatient care in a participating psychiatric hospital in a patient's lifetime. After a person has used these 190 days, Part A does not pay for any more inpatient care in a psychiatric hospital.

Care Outside the United States

Medicare generally does not pay for hospital or medical services outside the United States. (Puerto Rico, the U.S. Virgin Islands, Guam, American Samoa, and the Northern Mariana Islands are considered part of the United States.) There are rare emergency cases where Medicare can pay for care in Canada or Mexico.

Religious Nonmedical Health Care Institution

In the past, Medicare Part A helped pay for inpatient hospital and skilled nursing facility services received specifically in a participating Christian Science sanatorium. In 1997, Congress expanded this concept to include "religious nonmedical health care institutions," with respect to items and services ordinarily furnished by those institutions.

Skilled Nursing Facility Care

Medicare Part A can help pay for certain inpatient care in a Medicare-participating skilled nursing facility following a hospital stay. A person's condition must require daily skilled nursing or skilled rehabilitation services which, as a practical matter, can only be provided in a skilled nursing facility, and the skilled care received must be based on a physician's orders. The daily co-insurance for days 21 through 100 is $119 in 2006.

Medicare Payment Requirements for Skilled Nursing Facilities

Medicare Part A can help pay for care in a Medicare-participating skilled nursing facility if all of these five conditions are met:

1) The condition requires daily skilled nursing or skilled rehabilitation services which, as a practical matter, can only be provided in a skilled nursing facility.

2) The patient has been in a hospital at least three days in a row (not counting the day of discharge) before being admitted to a participating skilled nursing facility.

3) The patient is admitted to the facility within a short time (generally within 30 days) after leaving the hospital.

4) The care in the skilled nursing facility is for a condition that was treated in the hospital, or for a condition that arose while the patient was receiving care in the skilled nursing facility for a condition which was treated in the hospital.

5) A medical professional certifies that the patient needs and receives skilled nursing or skilled rehabilitation services on a daily basis.

Major Services Covered Under Part A in a Skilled Nursing Facility

- A semiprivate room (two to four beds in a room).
- All meals, including special diets furnished by the facility.
- Regular nursing services.
- Physical, occupational, and speech therapy.
- Drugs furnished by the facility during the stay.

¶509.09

- Blood transfusions furnished during the stay (except for the first three pints of blood).
- Medical supplies, such as splints and casts, furnished by the facility.
- Use of appliances, such as a wheelchair, furnished by the facility.

Some Services Not Covered Under Part A When in a Skilled Nursing Facility

- Personal convenience items that a person requests, such as a television.
- Private duty nurses.
- Any extra charges for a private room, unless it is determined to be medically necessary.

Home Health Care

Medicare pays for covered home health services furnished by a participating home health agency. A home health agency is a public or private agency that specializes in giving in-house skilled nursing services and other therapeutic services, such as physical therapy, in the home. Medicare pays for home health visits only if all four of the following conditions are met:

1) The care needed includes intermittent skilled nursing care, physical therapy, or speech therapy.
2) The patient is primarily confined to home (homebound).
3) The patient is under the care of a physician who determines the need for home health care and sets up a home health plan.
4) The home health agency providing services participates in Medicare.

After the first 100 visits, coverage for home health services shifts from Part A to Part B.

Home Health Services Covered by Medicare

- Part-time or intermittent skilled nursing care. (This means care that is provided on fewer than seven days each week or fewer than eight hours of each day for up to 21 consecutive days—or longer in exceptional circumstances.)
- Physical therapy.
- Speech therapy.

If a person needs intermittent skilled nursing care, or physical or speech therapy, Medicare also pays for:

- Occupational therapy.
- Part-time or intermittent services of home health aides.
- Medical social services.
- Medical supplies.
- Durable medical equipment (80 percent of approved amount).

Home Health Services Not Covered by Medicare

- 24-hour-a-day nursing care at home.
- Drugs and biologicals.
- Meals delivered to your home.
- Homemaker services.
- Blood transfusions.

¶509.09

Hospice Care

A hospice is a public agency or private organization that is primarily engaged in providing pain relief, symptom management and supportive services to terminally ill people. Hospice care is a special type of care for people who are terminally ill. It includes both home care and inpatient care, when needed, and a variety of services not otherwise covered under Medicare. Under the Medicare hospice benefit, Medicare pays for services every day and also permits a hospice to provide appropriate custodial care, including homemaker services and counseling. Medicare Part A helps pay for hospice care if all three of these conditions are met:

1) A physician certifies that the patient is terminally ill.

2) The patient chooses to receive care from a hospice instead of standard Medicare benefits for the terminal illness.

3) Care is provided by a Medicare-participating hospice program.

Special benefit periods apply to hospice care. Part A pays for two 90-day periods, followed by a 30-day period, and, when necessary, an extension period of indefinite duration. A beneficiary may disenroll from the hospice at any time and return to regular Medicare coverage.

Services Covered by Part A When Provided by a Hospice

- Nursing services.

- physicians' services.

- Drugs, including outpatient drugs for pain relief and symptom management.

- Physical therapy, occupational therapy and speech-language pathology.

- Home health aide and homemaker services.

- Medical social services.

- Medical supplies and appliances.

- Short-term inpatient care, including respite care.

- Counseling.

.11 Medicare Medical Insurance (Part B)

Medicare Part B helps pay for:

- Physicians' services.

- Outpatient hospital care.

- Diagnostic tests.

- Durable medical equipment.

- Ambulance services.

- Many other health services and supplies that are not covered by Medicare Part A.

Deductible and Coinsurance Amounts Under Part B

The Annual Deductible

A person must pay the first $131 in 2007 in approved charges for covered medical expenses. This is called the Medicare Part B annual deductible. The individual needs to meet this deductible only once during the year, and the deductible can be met by any combination of covered expenses.

The deductible increases each year by the same percentage applied to the Part B premium increase.

The Blood Deductible

One must pay any nonreplacement fees charged for the first three pints or units of blood and blood components used each year.

Coinsurance

After a person pays the annual deductible, that person will owe a share of the Medicare-approved amount for most services and supplies. This is called the coinsurance or copayment. Usually, the coinsurance is 20 percent of the Medicare-approved amount.

Physicians' Services Covered By Medicare Part B

Medicare Part B helps pay for covered services received from the physician in his or her office, in a hospital, in a skilled nursing facility, at home, or any other location.

Major Physicians' Services Covered by Medicare Part B

- Medical and surgical services, including anesthesia.
- Diagnostic tests and procedures that are part of treatment.
- Radiology and pathology services by physicians while an individual is a hospital inpatient or outpatient.
- Treatment of mental illness. (Medicare payments for treatment is limited.)
- Other services such as:
  — X-rays.
  — Services of your physician's office nurse.
  — Drugs and biologicals that are usually not self-administered by the patient.
  — Transfusions of blood and blood components.
  — Medical supplies.
  — Physical/occupational therapy and speech pathology services.

Some Physicians' Services Not Covered by Medicare Part B

- Routine physical examinations, and tests directly related to such examinations (except Pap smears, mammograms, and certain other preventive services or the "Welcome to Medicare" initial preventive exam).
- Most routine foot care and dental care.
- Examinations for prescribing or fitting eyeglasses or hearing aids.
- Immunizations (except influenza and pneumococcal pneumonia vaccinations, immunizations required because of an injury or immediate risk of infection, and hepatitis B for certain persons at risk).
- Cosmetic surgery, unless it is needed because of accidental injury or to improve the function of a malformed part of the body.

¶509.11

Dentists' Services

Medicare Part B generally does not pay for care in connection with the treatment, filling, removal, or replacement of teeth; root canal therapy; surgery for impacted teeth; or other surgical procedures involving the teeth or structures directly supporting the teeth. However, Medicare does help pay for services of a dentist in certain cases when the medical problem is more extensive than the teeth or structures directly supporting them.

Optometrists' Services

Medicare helps pay for some vision care services, including the services of an optometrist if the optometrist is legally authorized to perform those services by the state in which he or she performs them. However, Medicare will not pay for routine eye exams and usually will not pay for eyeglasses. (Medicare will pay for cataract spectacles, cataract contact lenses, or intraocular lenses that replace the natural lens of the eye after cataract surgery. Medicare will also pay for one pair of conventional eyeglasses or conventional contact lenses if necessary after cataract surgery with insertion of an intraocular lens.)

Outpatient Hospital Services

Major Outpatient Hospital Services Covered by Part B

- Services in an emergency room or outpatient clinic, including same-day surgery.
- Laboratory tests billed by the hospital.
- Mental health care in a partial hospitalization psychiatric program, if a physician certifies that inpatient treatment would be required without it.
- X-rays and other radiology services billed by the hospital.
- Medical supplies such as splints and casts.
- Drugs and biologicals that are usually not self-administered by the patient.
- Blood transfusions furnished to an outpatient.

Some Outpatient Hospital Services Not Covered by Part B

- Routine physical examinations and tests directly related to such examinations (except some prevention services).
- Eye or ear examinations to prescribe or fit eyeglasses or hearing aids.
- Immunizations (except influenza and pneumococcal pneumonia and hepatitis B vaccinations, immunizations required because of an injury or immediate risk of infection).
- Most routine foot care.

Other Services and Supplies Covered by Medicare

Ambulatory Surgical Services

An ambulatory surgical center is a facility that provides surgical services that do not require a hospital stay. Medicare Part B will pay for the use of an ambulatory surgical center for certain approved surgical procedures. However, by law, Medicare can only pay centers that have an agreement with Medicare to participate in the Medicare program.

Home Health Services

If a person has both Medicare Part A and Part B coverage, Part A pays for home health services for up to 100 visits. But Part B will pay for home health services after the first 100 visits or for all visits if a person does not have Part A.

Outpatient Physical and Occupational Therapy and Speech Pathology Services

Medicare Part B helps pay for medically necessary outpatient physical and occupational therapy or speech pathology services, if all the following three conditions are met:

1) The physician prescribes the service.
2) The physician or therapist sets up the plan of treatment.
3) The physician periodically reviews that plan.

There is an annual dollar limitation on the amount of therapy services covered, which changes each year.

Comprehensive Outpatient Rehabilitation Facility Services

Under certain circumstances, Medicare helps pay for outpatient services one receives from a Medicare-participating comprehensive outpatient rehabilitation facility (CORF). Covered services include physicians' services; physical, speech, occupational and respiratory therapies; counseling; and other related services.

Partial Hospitalization for Mental Health Treatment

Partial hospitalization (sometimes called day treatment) is a program of outpatient mental health care. Under certain conditions, Medicare Part B helps pay for these programs when provided by hospital outpatient departments or by community mental health centers.

Medicare Payments for Outpatient Treatment of Mental Illness

Medicare helps pay for outpatient mental health services received from professionals such as physicians, clinical psychologists, clinical social workers and other nonphysician practitioners. These professionals furnish services in various settings, for example, hospitals, comprehensive outpatient rehabilitation facilities, community mental health centers, and skilled nursing facilities.

Rural Health Clinic Services

Medicare Part B helps pay for services of physicians, nurse practitioners, physician assistants, nurse midwives, visiting nurses (under certain conditions), clinical psychologists, and clinical social workers funished by a rural health clinic.

Federally Qualified Health Center Services

Federally qualified health centers are located in both rural and urban areas, and any Medicare beneficiary may seek services at these centers. As part of the "federally qualified health center benefit," Medicare Part B helps pay for services of physicians, nurse practitioners, physician assistants, nurse midwives, visiting nurses (under certain conditions), clinical psychologists, and clinical social workers. Also, as part of the federally qualified health center benefit, Medicare helps pay for certain preventive health services.

¶509.11

Laboratory Services

All laboratories must be certified under the Clinical Laboratory Improvement Amendments to perform laboratory testing. Medicare Part B pays the full approved fee for covered clinical diagnostic tests provided by certified laboratories that are participating in Medicare. The laboratory can be independent, part of a hospital outpatient department or in a physician's office. The laboratory must accept assignment for the tests. It may not bill the Medicare patient for the tests.

Diagnostic Services

Medicare Part B helps pay for portable diagnostic X-ray services received at home or other locations if they are ordered by a physician and if they are provided by a Medicare-approved supplier.

Medicare Part B also helps pay for other diagnostic tests, including X-rays, that the physician orders to evaluate medical problems.

Pap Smear Screening

Medicare Part B helps pay once every two years for Pap smears to screen for cervical cancer. Medicare helps pay once every year for women at high risk. Medicare also pays for diagnostic Pap smears as needed when symptoms are present.

Prostate Tests

Prostate cancer screening tests are covered each year for men over 50.

Breast Cancer Screening (Mammography)

Medicare Part B helps pay for X-ray screenings for the detection of breast cancer, if they are provided by a Medicare-approved supplier. Medicare will help pay for mammogram screening once for women between age 35-39 and once every year for all women with Medicare who are age 40 or older. The usual Part B deductible is waived for these tests.

Radiation Therapy

Medicare Part B helps pay for outpatient radiation therapy given under the supervision of a physician.

Kidney Dialysis and Transplants

Medicare Part B helps pay for kidney dialysis and transplants.

Heart and Liver Transplants

Under certain limited conditions, Medicare Part B helps pay for heart, liver, and lung transplants in a Medicare-approved facility.

Ambulance Transportation

Medicare Part B helps pay for medically necessary ambulance transportation, including air ambulance, but only if:

- The ambulance, equipment and personnel meet Medicare requirements.
- Transportation provided in any other vehicle could endanger the patient's health.
- The trip is to the nearest capable facility.

¶509.11

Durable Medical Equipment

Medicare Part B helps pay for durable medical equipment, such as oxygen equipment, wheelchairs, and other medically necessary equipment that the physician prescribes for use at home. To be considered durable medical equipment, the equipment must be able to be used over again by other patients, must primarily serve a medical purpose, must not be useful to people who are not sick or injured, and must be appropriate for use in the patient's home. The equipment should be either purchased or rented, depending on which one is more economical.

Prosthetic Devices

Medicare Part B helps pay for prosthetic devices needed to replace an internal body organ. These include Medicare-approved corrective lenses needed after a cataract operation, ostomy bags and certain related supplies, and breast prostheses (including a surgical brassiere) after a mastectomy. Medicare also helps pay for artificial limbs and eyes, and for arm, leg, back, and neck braces. Medicare does not pay for orthopedic shoes, unless they are an integral part of leg braces and the cost is included in the charge for the braces. Medicare does not pay for dental plates or other dental devices.

Medical Supplies

Medicare Part B helps pay for surgical dressings, splints, and casts ordered by a physician in connection with medical treatment. This does not include adhesive tape, antiseptics, or other common first-aid supplies.

Drugs and Biologicals

Influenza and Pneumococcal Pneumonia Vaccine

Medicare Part B pays the full approved charges for influenza and pneumococcal pneumonia vaccine and its administration. Neither the annual deductible nor the 20 percent coinsurance applies to these services.

Hepatitis B Vaccine

Medicare Part B helps pay for hepatitis B vaccine administered to beneficiaries considered to be at high or intermediate risk of contracting the disease.

Hemophilia Clotting Factors

Medicare Part B helps pay for blood clotting factors and items related to their administration for hemophilia patients who are able to use them to control bleeding without medical or other supervision. The amount of clotting factors necessary to have on hand for a specific period is determined for each patient individually.

Blood

Medicare Part B helps pay for blood and blood components received as a hospital outpatient or as part of other services.

Antigens

Under certain circumstances, Medicare Part B helps pay for antigens prepared by a physician.

¶509.11

Immunosuppressive Drugs

Immunosuppressive drugs are often given to prevent rejection of transplanted organs. Medicare Part B helps pay for drugs used in immunosuppressive therapy for as long as needed after a Medicare-covered organ transplant is performed.

Epoetin Alfa

Medicare Part B helps pay for the drug Epoetin alfa (EPO) when used to treat Medicare beneficiaries with anemia related to chronic kidney failure, or related to use of AZT in HIV-positive beneficiaries or for other uses that a Medicare carrier finds medically appropriate. The EPO must be administered incident to the services of a physician in the office or in a hospital outpatient department. Part B also helps pay for EPO that is self-administered by home dialysis patients or administered by their caregivers.

Osteoporosis Drugs

Medicare covers injectable drugs approved for the treatment of bone fracture related to post-menopausal osteoporosis if (1) the drugs are administered by a home health agency, (2) the patient's attending physician certifies that the patient has suffered a bone fracture related to post menopausal osteoporosis and the patient is incapable of self-administering the drugs and the patient is confined to her home.

Oral Anti-Cancer and Anti-Emetic Drugs

Oral cancer chemotherapeutic drugs are covered, even when self-administered, if they contain the same active ingredients as intravenously administered anti-cancer drugs.

.15 Medicare Medical Insurance—Part B Payments

The Assignment Payment Method

Under the assignment method, the physician or supplier agrees to accept the amount approved by the Medicare carrier as total payment for covered services. Medicare usually pays 80 percent of the approved amount and the patient (or the patient's supplementary insurer) is responsible for the other 20 percent as a coinsurance.

Participating Physicians and Suppliers

Physicians and suppliers may sign agreements to become Medicare-participating. Medicare-participating physicians and suppliers have agreed in advance to accept assignment on all Medicare claims. Physicians and suppliers are given the opportunity to sign participation agreements each year. The names and addresses of Medicare-participating physicians and suppliers are listed (by geographic area) in the Medicare-Participating Physician/Supplier Directory (MEDPARD).

Many physicians and suppliers who do not take assignment on all claims may take assignment on some or most claims.

Some Physicians Do Not Accept Assignment

If a physician or supplier does not accept assignment, the patient must pay the physician or supplier directly and is usually responsible for the part of the bill that is more than the Medicare-approved amount. In this case, Medicare pays 80 percent of the approved amount, after subtracting any part of the $124 annual deductible not met. Even though a physician does not accept assignment, for most covered services, there are limits on the amount that he or she can actually charge. The most the physician can charge is 115 percent of what Medicare approves. Physicians who charge more than these limits must refund the excess charges to the patient and may be fined.

Special Rule for Physicians Performing Elective Surgery

Medicare law requires physicians who do not take assignment for elective surgery to give a written estimate of costs before the surgery if the total charge for the surgical procedure is $500 or more. If the physician does not give a written estimate, a patient is entitled to a refund of any amount paid him or her over the Medicare-approved amount.

Payment Examples

Three payment examples for the same service are shown below. Dr. A participates in the Medicare program and, therefore, accepts assignment on the claim. Drs. B and C do not participate and do not accept assignment. In all three examples, the beneficiary has already met the $131 (for 2007) deductible. Even though Dr. A's bill is not the lowest, the beneficiary pays the least for Dr. A's services. Also, even though Drs. B and C charge different amounts, the beneficiary pays the same amount because of the limiting charge.

Three Payment Examples
(Assuming the annual Part B deductible has been met)

	Physician's Bill	Medicare-Approved Amount*	Medicare Pays	Beneficiary Responsible For
Physician A accepts assignment	$480	$400	$320 (80% of approved amount)	$80 (20% of approved amount)
Physician B does not accept assignment and charges no more than the	$437	$380	$304 (80% of approved amount)	$133 (difference between the $437 actual charge—which is also the limiting charge— and Medicare Payment)
Physician C does not accept assignment and charges more than the limiting charge	$500	$380	$304 (80% of approved amount)	$133 (difference between the $437 limiting charge and Medicare Payment)

---

* The Medicare-approved amount is less for nonparticipating physicians than for participating physicians.

   Three states have laws that could further reduce your medical costs: Connecticut, Massachusetts, and Pennsylvania. Those who reside in these states should check with their state Department of Aging for details.

Participating Providers

Hospitals, skilled nursing facilities, home health agencies, hospices, comprehensive outpatient rehabilitation facilities, and providers of outpatient physical and occupational therapy and speech pathology services are all participating providers under Medicare Part B. They submit their claims to Medicare. The provider must accept the Medicare-approved amount as payment in full for covered services. The provider bills the patient only for any deductible and coinsurance amounts.

¶509.15

Medicare-Approved Amounts

Medicare Part B payments are based for the most part on Medicare fee schedule amounts. The fee schedule for physicians and certain suppliers lists payments for each Part B service and takes into account geographic variation in the cost of practice. The fee schedule amount is often less than the actual charges billed by physicians and suppliers. Part B usually pays 80 percent of the fee schedule amount, even if it is less than the actual charge. When a Part B claim is submitted, the carrier compares the actual charge shown on the claim with the fee schedule amount for that service. The Medicare-approved amount is the lower of the actual charge or the fee schedule amount.

Submitting Part B Claims

Physicians, Suppliers and Other Providers Must Submit Claims

Physicians, suppliers and other providers of Part B services are required to submit Medicare claims for their services; they cannot put the burden of claim submission on the patient. They must submit the claims within one year of providing the service or may be subject to certain penalties. (If a patient has other health insurance that should pay before Medicare, the patient can be required to submit these claims.)

How the Physician or Supplier Submits Claims

A physician or supplier must submit a form, called a CMS-1500, requesting that Medicare Part B payment be made for covered services. The physician or supplier completes the CMS-1500 form and sends it to the proper Medicare administrative contractor. Generally, physicians obtain a signature from the patient authorizing the submission of claims to Medicare.

When Enrolled in a Managed Care Plan

If a patient is enrolled in a managed care plan, a claim will seldom need to be submitted on the patient's behalf. Medicare pays the plan a set amount and the plan provides medical care. In most cases, the patient is required to receive all nonemergency care through the plan, or through arrangements it makes. However, if the patient gets an out-of-plan service, the claim should be submitted directly to the managed care plan.

Submitting Claims to the Railroad Retirement System

If a person gets Medicare under the Railroad Retirement system, the physician or supplier must submit claims to the Travelers Insurance Company office that serves that region.

Medicare Summary Notice

After the physician, provider, or supplier sends in a Part B claim, Medicare will send the patient a notice called "Medicare Summary Notice (MSN)" to communicate the decision on the claim. The MSN will also tell the patient how much Medicare will pay, how much the patient's obligation will be, and how much the physician or supplier is allowed to charge if assignment was not agreed to.

Filing Claims

In some cases, a patient may need to file a Medicare Part B claim. The claim should be sent to the Medicare administrative contractor (MAC) responsible for processing Medicare claims in the area.

Time Limits

Under the law, there are time limits for submitting Medicare Part B claims. For Medicare to make payments on claims, they must be sent within these time limits. Patients always have at least 15 months to submit claims.

Calling the Medicare Administrative Contractor

Most patients will communicate frequently with their Medicare administrative contractor (MAC), which will respond to their inquiries and problems. If a patient believes he or she has been charged more than the limiting charge by a physician and a dispute arises, the MAC should be contacted. If a physician refuses to submit a Part B Medicare claim for services believed to be covered, the MAC should be contacted. The MAC can also provide information on the status of a claim and answer many other questions.

Claims for a Person Who Has Died

When a Medicare beneficiary dies, the way Medicare pays Part B claims depends on whether the physician's or supplier's bill has been paid. (Any Part A payments due to the hospital, skilled nursing facility, home health agency or hospice will be made directly to the provider of services.) If the bill was paid by the patient or with funds from the patient's estate, Medicare's payment will be made either to the estate representative or to a surviving member of the patient's immediate family. If someone other than the patient paid the bill, payment may be made to that person. If the bill has not been paid and the physician or supplier does not accept assignment, the Medicare payment can be made to the person who has or assumes the legal obligation to pay the bill for the deceased patient.

Obtaining Medicare Coverage

If a person has Medicare premium-free Hospital Insurance but does not have Medicare Part B, that person can sign up for Part B during a general enrollment period. A general enrollment period is held January 1 through March 31 each year. Protection will begin July 1 of the year enrolled. If not enrolled during a general enrollment period, the monthly premium may be increased by 10 percent for each 12-month period the insured could have had Part B but was not enrolled.

Some people 65 or older have Medicare Medical Insurance (Part B), but do not meet the requirements for premium-free Part A. If an individual is in this category, Part A can be obtained by paying a monthly premium. This is called "premium hospital insurance." A person can sign up for premium Part A during a general enrollment period: January 1 through March 31 each year. If enrolled during a general enrollment period that begins more than one year after becoming eligible to buy Part A, the monthly premium may be 10 percent higher than the basic premium amount. Protection will begin July 1 of the year enrolled. If a person has been covered under a Medicare Advantage (MA) plan, that person can sign up for premium Part A at any time while in the MA plan and up to eight months after the MA plan coverage has ended. The premium penalty, if any, may be reduced because of the coverage under the MA plan.

Special Enrollment Period

If covered by an employer group health plan based on a spouse's current employment (not a plan for retired people and their spouses), a person may be able to delay enrollment in Medicare Medical Insurance (Part B) or premium Hospital Insurance

(Part A) without premium penalty and without waiting for a general enrollment period. Delayed enrollment without penalty or wait is usually available if an individual is covered by an employer group health plan at the time a person is first able to get Medicare.

In general, if a person is 65 or over, that person may enroll in Medicare Part B during the eight-month period beginning after the month:

- Spouse's current employment ends, or
- Coverage under the employer group health plan ends, whichever comes first

If disabled and covered by an employer group health plan, a person is also given a special enrollment period in certain circumstances. If covered under a group health plan based on current employment status when first able to get Medicare, a person may enroll in Medicare Part B during the eight-month period that begins the month after:

- When the employment status ends
- When the plan is no longer classifiable as a large group health plan (one that covers 100 or more employees), or
- When the plan coverage is terminated

Events That Can Change Medicare Protection

When Protection Ends for People 65 and Older

Medicare Hospital Insurance (Part A) based on a spouse's work record ends if the insured is divorced during the first 10 years of marriage.

Medicare Part B protection stops for nonpayment of premiums. If the insured cancels Part B and then later re-enrolls, that individual must wait for a general enrollment period (January 1 through March 31), and the enrollment may result in higher premiums. Protection will not begin until July 1 of the enrollment year.

If covered under an employer group health plan based on current employment, a person may be eligible for a special enrollment period, and the premium penalty may be decreased or waived. If buying Medicare Part A by paying monthly premiums, coverage will be lost if the person cancels Medicare Part B since people who buy Part A must enroll and pay the premium for Part B. A person is, however, allowed to cancel Part A coverage and still maintain Part B.

Protection Ends for Disabled

If a person has Medicare because of a disability, protection will end if that person recovers before reaching age 65. If the individual works, but is still disabled, premium-free Part A protection will continue for at least 48 months after beginning work. Part B will also continue for at least 48 months if the individual continues to pay premiums. If the individual continues to be disabled longer than 48 months after returning to work, and subsequently loses premium-free Part A coverage (and Part B) solely because of working status, the individual can buy Part A only or both Part A and B coverage.

If an individual has Medicare because of permanent kidney failure, protection will end 12 months after the month maintenance dialysis treatment stops or 36 months after the month of a kidney transplant.

.17 Appealing Medicare Decisions

Appealing Decisions Made by Providers of Part A Services

In many cases, the first written notice of noncoverage received will come from the provider of the services (for example, a hospital, skilled nursing facility, home health agency or hospice). This notice of noncoverage from the provider should explain why the provider believes Medicare will not pay for the services. This notice is not an official Medicare determination, but the insured can ask the provider to get an official Medicare determination. If the insured asks for an official Medicare determination, the provider must file a claim on that person's behalf to Medicare. Then the insured will receive a Medicare Summary Notice, which is the official Medicare determination. If a person still disagrees, that person can appeal by following the instructions on the Medicare Summary Notice.

Appealing Decisions Made by Quality Improvement Organizations (QIOs)

When an individual is admitted to a Medicare-participating hospital, that person will be given a notice called An Important Message From Medicare. The notice contains a brief description of QIOs, and the name, address and phone number of the QIO in the subject state. Also, it describes appeal rights. QIOs make determinations mainly about inpatient hospital care and ambulatory surgical center care. The QIOs decide whether care provided to Medicare patients is medically necessary, provided in the most appropriate setting, and is of good quality. When a person disagrees with a QIO decision about a case, that person can appeal by requesting a reconsideration. Then, if the individual disagrees with the QIO's reconsideration decision, and the amount remaining in question is $200 or more, he or she can request a hearing by an Administrative Law Judge (ALJ) within 60 days. ALJ decisions may be appealed to the Medicare Appeals Council (MAC) of the Departmental Appeals Board (DAB).

A beneficiary can request judicial review of ALJ or MAC decisions on the issue of medical necessity or appropriateness of setting if the amount of the denied services is $2,000 or more.

Appealing Decisions of Intermediaries on Part A Claims

Appeals of decisions on most other services covered under Medicare Part A (skilled nursing facility care, home health care, hospice services, and a few inpatient hospital matters not handled by QIOs) are handled by a qualified independent contractor (QIC). If the insured disagrees with the QIC's initial decision, that person has 60 days from the date the decision was received to request an appeal to an ALJ if the amount in dispute is at least $110. (Beginning in 2005, this amount may increase, based on the consumer price index.) ALJ hearings are currently performed by ALJs employed by the Office of Medicare Hearings and Appeals in the Department of Health and Human Services (HHS). Decisions of the Social Security Administration ALJ may be appealed to the HHS Departmental Appeals Board. Cases involving $1,130 in 2007 or more that are not settled at the HHS Departmental Appeals Board may be appealed to a federal district court. (The minimum amount in dispute is adjusted each year.)

Appealing Decisions Made by Carriers on Part B Claims

If an individual disagrees with Medicare's decision on a Part B claim, that person has the right to request a redetermination within four months (120 days) from the date of the decision. Then, if the individual disagrees with the contractor's final determination, and the amount remaining in question is $110 or more, that person has six months from the date of the determination to request a reconsideration by a QIC. A person may combine claims that have been reviewed or reopened—so long as all claims combined are at the proper level of appeal and the appeal for each claim combined is filed on time. If the individual disagrees with the QIC's decision, and the amount remaining in question is $110 or more, that person has 60 days from the date he or she receives the decision to request a hearing before an ALJ. The ALJ's decision may be appealed to the HHS Departmental Board and the DAB decision may be appealed to federal court.

Medicare Advantage Appeals

Plans have been required to:

- respond within 72 hours on appeals of care denials that could jeopardize life, health, or ability to regain maximum function;
- respond within 14 days for initial decisions on all other appeals of service denials, and within 30 days for reconsiderations of appeals;
- state the reasons for a denial in writing;
- use denial notice forms that describe beneficiary appeal rights;
- accept oral requests for expedited appeals;
- follow up verbal notifications in writing within two working days;
- grant automatically all physician requests for expedited appeals; and
- maintain logs and periodically report on requests for expedited appeals.

An MA organization must respond to an enrollee's grievance within *24 hours* if:

(1) The complaint involves an MA organization's decision to invoke an extension relating to an organization determination or reconsideration.

(2) The complaint involves an MA organization's refusal to grant an enrollee's request for an expedited organization determination or reconsideration.

All appeals rejected by plans are automatically forwarded to the independent appeals contractor for independent review, with no monetary threshold or other barrier. This independent contractor, called an independent review entity (IRE), is also required to act on expedited appeals within 72 hours, and within 14 days for all other service denials.

Beneficiaries have up to 60 days to appeal an IRE's decision involving at least $110 to an ALJ. There is no time limit on ALJ actions. Beneficiaries have up to 60 days to request a review of the ALJ decisions by the Health and Human Services Departmental Appeals Board.

(Source: U.S. Department of Health and Human Services, Centers for Medicare and Medicaid Services)

Beneficiary Information Resources

Medicare maintains a toll-free telephone number and an Internet site for Medicare Advantage inquiries and information. Current and newly eligible Medicare beneficiaries with questions about their new Medicare Advantage coverage options may obtain additional information by calling the Medicare Hotline at (800) 633-4227, or by accessing Medicare's Internet site at *www.medicare.gov*.

¶509.17

.19 Medicare Coverage Summary Chart
For People on Medicare-Hospital Insurance (Part A)

	2006	2007
For first 60 days in a hospital, patient pays	$952 deductible	$992 deductible
For 61st through 90th days in a hospital, patient pays	$238 daily co-pay	$248 daily co-pay
Beyond 90 days in a hospital, patient pays (for up to 60 more days)	$476 daily co-pay	$496 daily co-pay
For first 20 days in a skilled nursing facility, patient pays	$0	$0
For 21st through 100th days in a skilled nursing facility, patient pays	$119 daily co-pay	$124 daily co-pay

Medical Insurance (Part B)

	2006	2007**
Premium	$88.50 per month	$93.50 per month
Deductible*	$124 per year	$131 per year

* After the patient has paid the deductible, Part B pays for 80% of covered services. Effective January 1, 2006, the Part B annual deductible is indexed to the increase in the average cost of Part B services for aged beneficiaries.

** The Part B premium increase may not exceed the beneficiary's cost of living adjustment in their Social Security check.

Note: Some states may pay Medicare premiums and, in some cases, deductibles and other out-of-pocket medical expenses for those with little income or resources.

¶ 510 SOCIAL SECURITY ADMINISTRATION: INTERNET SERVICES

General Services

- Find out what Social Security benefits for which you can apply.
- Estimate your benefit amounts.
- Request a Social Security Statement.
- Apply for Social Security retirement, spouse's, or disability benefits.
- Begin or continue the Adult Disability and Work History Report.
- Continue the Online Appeal Disability Report.
- Check the status of your online application.
- Get the address of your local Social Security office.
- Get a form to request an original Social Security card or a replacement Social Security card.

Business Services for Employers

- Register for a Personal Identification Number (PIN) and password.
- Update registration information, change password, or deactivate PIN.
- Submit W-2 wage reports online.
- Check the status of your submissions.
- Receive confirmation of resubmitted wage reports.

Services for People Who Get Benefits

- Change your address or telephone number.
- Get a replacement Medicare card.
- Get a replacement Form 1099/1042S-Social Security Benefit Statement (not available for SSI).
- Request a Proof of Income letter (a letter that verifies Social Security benefits).
- Get a password.
- Block online and automated telephone access to your personal information.

¶ 511 SOCIAL SECURITY SYSTEM STATISTICAL TABLES

.01 Social Security Summary Table

2007 Social Security Information Summary

Tax rate:
Employee and employer each:

7.65 percent (6.20 percent—OASDI,
1.45 percent—HI)

Self-employed:
15.30 percent (12.40 percent—OASDI,
2.9 percent—HI)
OASDI—contribution and benefit base: $97,500

Limitation on earnings subject to HI tax was repealed, effective 1994.
Earnings required for a quarter of coverage:

$1,000

2007 Retirement test exempt earnings limits:

Under full retirement age: $12,960 annual, $1,080 monthly
Individuals attaining full retirement age in 2007: $34,440 annual, $2,870 monthly*

---

* Applies only to earnings in the months before attaining full retirement age.

.03 Social Security Financing Tables

Calendar OASDI Tax Rates (percent) for Employer and Employee, Each

Years	Wage Base*	Total	OASI	DI	HI
1986	$42,000	7.150	5.200	0.500	1.450
1987	43,800	7.150	5.200	0.500	1.450
1988	45,000	7.510	5.530	0.530	1.450
1989	48,000	7.510	5.530	0.530	1.450
1990	51,300	7.650	5.600	0.600	1.450
1991	53,400	7.650	5.600	0.600	1.450
1992	55,500	7.650	5.600	0.600	1.450
1993	57,600	7.650	5.600	0.600	1.450
1994	60,600	7.650	5.260	0.940	1.450
1995	61,200	7.650	5.260	0.940	1.450
1996	62,700	7.650	5.260	0.940	1.450
1997	65,400	7.650	5.350	0.850	1.450
1998	68,400	7.650	5.350	0.850	1.450
1999	72,600	7.650	5.350	0.850	1.450
2000	76,200	7.650	5.300	0.900	1.450
2001	80,400	7.650	5.300	0.900	1.450
2002	84,900	7.650	5.300	0.900	1.450
2003	87,000	7.650	5.300	0.900	1.450
2004	87,900	7.650	5.300	0.900	1.450
2005	90,000	7.650	5.300	0.900	1.450
2006	94,200	7.650	5.300	0.900	1.450
2007	97,500	7.650	5.300	0.900	1.450

* The maximum amount of taxable earnings for the hospital insurance (HI) program is the same as that for the old-age, survivors, and disability insurance (OASDI) program for 1966 through 1990. In 1991, 1992, and 1993, the maximum taxable earnings for the HI program were $125,000, $130,000, and $135,000, respectively. Beginning in 1994, no limit applies to earnings for purposes of the tax for the HI program. The OASDI portion of the tax is known as the Social Security tax, and the HI portion of the tax is known as the Medicare tax.

Payroll Tax Rates for Self-Employed Individuals, 1986 and Later

Year	OASI	DI	OASDI Combined	HI	OASDI and HI Combined
1986-87	10.4000	1.0000	11.4000	2.9000	14.3000 *
1988-89	11.0600	1.0600	12.1200	2.9000	15.0200 *
1990-93	11.2000	1.2000	12.4000	2.9000	15.3000
1994-96	10.5200	1.8800	12.4000	2.9000	15.3000
1997-99	10.7000	1.7000	12.4000	2.9000	15.3000
2000 and later	10.6000	1.8000	12.4000	2.9000	15.3000

* Excludes tax credit for the self-employed which was 2.7 percent in 1984, 2.3 percent in 1985, and 2.0 percent for the years 1986 through 1989.

.05 Exempt Earning Amounts Affecting Retirement Benefits Table

Retirement Test Exempt Amounts

Year	Under Age 65 (for yrs. 1990-99) Individuals not yet FRA in yrs. prior to attainment of FRA (for yrs. after 1999)*	Age 65 through 69 (for yrs. 1990-99) Individuals not yet FRA in year FRA is attained (for yrs. after 1999)*
1990	$6,840	$9,360
1991	7,080	9,720
1992	7,440	10,200
1993	7,680	10,560
1994	8,040	11,160
1995	8,160	11,280
1996	8,280	12,500
1997	8,640	13,500
1998	9,120	14,500
1999	9,600	15,500
2000	10,080	17,000 *
2001	10,680	25,000 *
2002	11,280	30,000 *
2003	11,520	30,720 *
2004	11,640	31,080 *
2005	12,000	31,800 *
2006	12,480	33,240 *
2007	12,960	34,440 *

---

* FRA = full retirement age. Beginning in 2000, the upper thresholds apply only to amounts earned during the taxable year prior to the month that full retirement age is attained. Since 2000, earnings for those who are at or above full retirement age are no longer subject to an earnings test.

Chapter 6
Financial Analysis

Financial Concepts and Analysis . . . . ¶ *601-689*
Tables . . . . ¶ *691*
Loans . . . . ¶ *693*

FINANCIAL CONCEPTS AND ANALYSIS

¶ 601 ACCOUNTS PAYABLE

.01 Accounts Payable Budget

Accounts Payable Budget Ending Balance = (Accounts Payable Beginning Balance) + (Purchases-Capital Assets + Purchases-COGS + Selling Expenses + Adminstrative Expenses + Other) – (Payments-Capital Assets + Payments – COGS + Payments Selling + Payments Adminstrative)

.02 Accounts Payable Estimated Disbursements

Estimated Cash Disbursements = (Accounts Payable Beginning Balance) + (Estimated Purchases of Materials + Estimated Labor Costs + Estimated General & Administrative Expenses + Estimated Manufacturing Overhead Costs + Estimated Selling & Marketing Costs) – (Accounts Payable Ending Balance)

¶ 602 ACCOUNTS RECEIVABLE

.01 Receivables—Interest on Receivables—Equivalent Interest Rate

Receivables should be carefully monitored to ensure they are turned into cash. Receivables should be thought of as their net amount—net of discounts, interest, returns, uncollectibles, and price allowances. When a company extends credit to a customer, there are more considerations than that of being just a sales tool. Receivables have related costs—order costs, parallel inventory ordering costs, etc. If the company allows discounts to encourage payment, it should consider the equivalent annual interest rate that the discount represents between the discount period and the net due date.

Annual Equivalent Interest Rate
(of trade discount)

(of trade discount)

$$\left[\begin{array}{c} \text{discount rate} \\ \text{on receivables} \end{array} \right] \times \left[\frac{360}{\text{net period - discount period}} \right]$$

Example: The company allows customers terms of 2/10 net 30. What does the 2% represent as an annual equivalent interest rate?

Annual equivalent interest rate =

Terms	Annual Equivalent Interest Rate
1% 10 days, net 30 days	18% per annum
1% 10 days, net 60 days	7.2% per annum
2% 10 days, net 30 days	36% per annum
2% 10 days, net 60 days	14.4% per annum
3% 10 days, net 30 days	54% per annum
4% 10 days, net 30 days	72% per annum
5% 10 days, net 30 days	90% per annum

.03 Receivables—Discounts

Pre-Discount Profits Versus Post-Discount Profits

A company might consider offering discounts to try to expand sales and encourage prompter payment, which provides for improved liquidity and greater profits. The company would like to discourage over-aged receivables that reduce profits due to attorney costs, court costs, specific handling of the accounts (follow-up calls, dunning letters, etc.), increased credit carrying charges, possible collection agency fees, and finally, eventual write-off to bad debt. But what discount should be offered? Will sales rise by any appreciable quantity to enhance profits? The following formula will determine estimated profits by offering discounts:

Profit (After New Credit Terms)

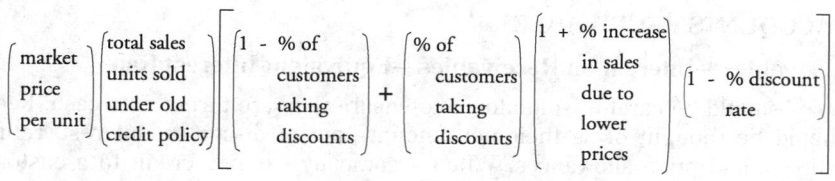

Costs will rise if prompt payments are not made, or are bad debts, or there are delinquent accounts. The formula can account for these factors by adjusting the estimates to some of the percentages.

> **Example:** What are the estimated profits arising from the new credit policy given the following data?

Current terms: net 30

New terms: 2/10, net 30%

Discount rate = 2%

¶602.03

Market price per unit = $15

Total sales of units sold under old credit policy = $3000

% of customers taking discounts = 80%

% increase in sales due to lower prices = 10%

Cost of good per unit = $10

Carrying cost of receivables per period = 1% per month

Portion of period during which receivables are carried for customers taking discounts = .33

Profit (after new credit terms) =

($15)(3000)[(1–.80)+(.80)(1+.10)(1 – .02)] – ($10)(300)[(1 – .80)(1 + .01) + (.80)(1 + .10)(1 +(.33)(.01))]

= $45,000 [(.20) + .8624] – $30,000 [(.202) + (.88)(1.0033)]

= $47,808 – 32,547

= $15,261

.05 Receivables—Days Sales Outstanding Ratio

The days sales outstanding (DSO) ratio reveals the extent to which receivables build up, or the effectiveness of management's collective policies. A DSO increasing value would indicate greater odds of not collecting on receivables. The ratio relates average daily sales per month to total accounts receivable to determine how many days sales are outstanding.

DSO

$$\frac{\text{accounts receivable balance}}{\frac{\text{monthly credit sales}}{30}}$$

Example: The DSO ratio computed from the following data may indicate concern regarding the aging of the account receivables.

Month	Monthly Credit Sales	Accounts Receivable Balance	DSO
J	$1800	$2500	2500/(1800/30) = 42
F	1500	2400	2400/(1500/30) = 48
M	1200	2000	2000/(1200/30) = 50

.07 Receivables—Days Sales Outstanding with Three-Month Moving Average

The Days Sales Outstanding ratio can be modified and smoothed by using a moving average. The following technique illustrates the smoothing on a quarterly basis. However, any period chosen by management can be appropriate for analysis. To keep the average moving, drop the 1st month of the series, add the current month, then divide by 90 days.

Monthly Month	Acct Rec Credit Sales	90-Day Moving Balance	3-Month Moving Average	Average DSO
J	1800	2500	-	-
F	1500	2400	-	-
M	1200	2000	50 (A)	40
A	1400	2200	46 (B)	47.8
M	1300	2100	43 (C)	48.8
J	1600	2300	48 (D)	47.9

(A) = (1800+1500+1200)/90 = 50
(B) = (1500+1200+1400)/90 = 46
(C) = (1200+1400+1300)/90 = 43
(D) = (1400+1300+1600)/90 = 48

.09 Receivables—Aging by Percentages

To help better spot trends, the aging of the accounts receivables can be presented in the format of percentages. Each line of the aging total should equal 100%.

> **Example:** Present the following accounts receivable data in the format of percentages.

Month	Total Accounts Receivable	Aging by $ 0 - 30	30 - 60	60 - 90	Over 90
J	50,000	$35,000	$81,000	$2,000	$51,000
F	52,000	40,000	3,200	1,000	7,800
M	58,000	45,000	2,000	600	10,400
A	71,000	48,600	6,000	2,200	14,200

Month	Total Accounts Receivable	0 - 30	30 - 60	60 - 90	Over 90
J	50,000	70 %	16 %	4 %	10 %
F	52,000	77	6	2	15
M	58,000	78	3	1	18
A	71,000	68	9	3	20

By only reviewing the dollar aging distribution chart, column 1 and column 4 seem to be growing, but so does the total receivables. However, by placing the receivables in a % format, we see that the current aged receivables remain rather steady, but the over-90 aged receivables have grown from 10% to 20% of the outstanding receivables.

.10 Receivables—Aging forward

The following illustrates the technique of aging receivables forward as well as by past due amounts. The aged future amounts show how soon an invoice will come due.

Receivables—Aging forward

Company	Total	Future 90	Future 60	Future 30	Current 0	Past Due 30	Past Due 60
XYZ Comp	$11,050	2400	3500	2500	800	1200	650
ABC Comp	$17,400	3500	2500	1800	1200	5200	3200
LMN Comp	$14,450	2500	3200	1850	2500	3200	1200
Totals	$42,900	8400	9200	6150	4500	9600	5050

Some of the purposes of aging receivables is to better understand the risks regarding collections and the associated cash flows associated with the receivables, its liquidity and reliability. Each month a new set of questions can be generated based on the data compiled. Proper reporting provides an early warning system. Negative trends can be promptly recognized and addressed. Comparisons to industry trends and statistics can be developed and compared. Such a schedule identifies current as well as past due amounts. The future accounts receivable column can predict cash flow. It shows sales terms per client in the future invoice column. Each column represents when a particular invoice is expected to be paid or how late the payment is in coming. Such a report also shows the concentrations between the customers. For instance, what percentage is the mix between the customers.

.11 Receivables—Percentage Uncollected (Relative)

Further detail is achieved in the following analysis by relating the aged receivable to the original sale that gave rise to the receivable. In other words, the receivables are apportioned in such a way that seasonal sales fluctuations, and year-to-year swings do not come into play.

$$\text{Percentage uncollected} = \frac{\text{Receivables in time period t}}{\text{Credit sales in time period t}}$$

For instance, if terms were net 30 days, then receivables in aging bracket 31-60 days old, relate to last month's sales. And the following month, in the aging bracket of 60-90, are only the receivables that relate to the 1st period's sales. The period for analysis could be any term. Assume the following table is constructed from the percentage of uncollected receivables based on an annual period.

Outstanding Receivables

Percentage uncollected relative to sales that gave rise to the receivable

Month	19x1 Current	19x - 1 1 year ago	19x - 2 2 years ago	19x - 3 3 years ago
J	98 %	22 %	8 %	3 %
F	96	25	10	8
M	97	20	5	2
A	99	28	4	1
M	96	32	8	4
J	98	20	6	1

.13 Receivables—Percentage Uncollected with Variance from Norm

An effective tool that improves on the above analysis is to create a device that provides for variances from a norm. A standard (norm) is established from which the uncollected percentages are subtracted. Assume in the table above, that the following standards (norms) are acceptable:

19x1 = 99%   19x - 1 = 25%   19x - 2 = 8%   19x- 3 = 4%

Then the variances from them are computed as shown in the following table:

Month	19x1 Current	19x - 1 1 year ago	19x - 2 2 years ago	19x - 3 3 years ago
	99 %	25 %	8 %	4 %
J	1 %(A)	3 %(C)	0 %	1 %
F	3 (B)	0 (D)	−2	−4
M	2	5	3	2
A	0	−3	4	3
M	4	−7	0	0
J	1	5	2	3

(A) = 99% − 98%
(B) = 99% − 96%
(C) = 25% − 22%
(D) = 25% − 25%

.14 Receivables—Non-Collection Cash Flow Requirement

When a customer never pays and the sale is never collected on, the company is out its profit, its fixed costs are not contributed to, and the variable costs have to be paid by the company on the product it made or sold. In a manner of speaking, it would have been better to not have made the sale in the first place, rather than to have "given" away the product. The company is out its direct product and labor costs. The following analysis illustrates the death trap of not collecting on a sale, and the difficult earning road back to different cash-flow breakeven points on the lost collection. For instance, if a company does not collect on a $500 sale, it is not just out the $500 of cash flow in, but consider how much more in sales the company has to generate to recover that lost $500 it will not receive. Assume the following:

Original Sale:

Sale	$500	100%
Direct material	300	60%
Direct labor	100	20%
Gross profit	100	20%
Fixed expenses	80	16%
Net income	20	4%

Sales needed to earn back the lost net income of $20.

In other words, how much in gross sales is needed to generate cash flow in to the company of $20.

Gross sales of $500 is needed by the company to cover this cash flow.

$20 / .04 = $500

Proof:

Sale	$500	100%
Direct material	300	60%
Direct labor	100	20%

Gross profit	100	20%
Fixed expenses	80	16%
Net income	20	4%

Sales needed to earn back the cost of fixed expenses of $80.

In other words, how much in gross sales is needed to generate cash flow in to the company of $80.

Gross sales of $2000 is needed by the company to cover this cash flow.

$80 / .04 = $2000

Proof:

Sale	$2000	100%
Direct material	1200	60%
Direct labor	400	20%
Gross profit	400	20%
Fixed expenses	320	16%
Net income	80	4%

Sales needed to earn back the cost of variable expenses of $400.

In other words, how much in gross sales is needed to generate cash flow in to the company of $400.

Gross sales of $10,000 is needed by the company to cover this cash flow.

$400 / .04 = $10,000

Proof:

Sale	$10000	100%
Direct material	6000	60%
Direct labor	2000	20%
Gross profit	2000	20%
Fixed expenses	1600	16%
Net income	400	4%

Sales needed to earn back the cost of all expenses of $480.

In other words, how much in gross sales is needed to generate cash flow in to the company of $480.

Gross sales of $12,000 is needed by the company to cover this cash flow.

$480 / .04 = $12,000

Proof:

Sale	$12000	100%
Direct material	7200	60%
Direct labor	2400	20%
Gross profit	2400	20%
Fixed expenses	1920	16%
Net income	480	4%

Sales needed to earn back the loss of gross income of $500.

In other words, how much in gross sales is needed to generate cash flow in to the company of $500.

Gross sales of $12,500 is needed by the company to cover this cash flow.

$500 / .04 = $12,500

Proof:

Sale	$12500	100%
Direct material	7500	60%
Direct labor	2500	20%
Gross profit	2500	20%
Fixed expenses	2000	16%
Net income	500	4%

.15 Receivables—Probability of Collection

When an account gets extremely past due, the firm needs to decide whether it should continue its collection efforts at the additional costs that will be incurred—either internally, or with an outside collection agency.

The summary rule regarding additional collection efforts is:

- If additional collection costs exceed the expected value of anticipated collections, then discontinue collection efforts and write the account off as bad debt.

The formula to compute expected value is:

$$\text{expected value} = (\text{probability of amount to be connected}) \times \left(\frac{\text{anticipated amount}}{\text{to be collected}} \right)$$

Even further, a probability distribution table may be constructed that represents management's best judgment regarding collection of the account. If the total expected value of all outcomes is less than the cost to collect, then the receivable should be written off.

Example: A company that has receivable of $1,000 that is 1 year old. Should $400 be spent to collect on the account? Assume a management determines the following:

Probability of Collection	Expected Value	Anticipated Amount To Be Collected
.10	$0	$0
.20	200	40
.40	300	120
.20	500	100
.05	700	35
.05	800	40
1.00	Total expected value =	335

Even if all possible outcomes could happen, the $335 it would expect to receive is less than the cost of $400 to collect the receivable. The receivable should be written off to bad debt.

.17 Receivables "Interest Cost" Due to Billing Delay

An analysis of the internal delay time between the sale and the invoicing of the product can show an undetected "interest" cost to the firm.

Billing Delay "Interest" Cost

Customer	$ Sales (1)	Sales Date (2)	Invoice Date (3)	Lag Time (days between sales and invoicing) (4)	Sales x Lag Time
ABC	20,000	02/01/XX	02/10/XX	9	$180,000
DEF	10,000	03/02/XX	02/12/XX	10	100,000
Totals	30,000 (5)				280,000

Weighted average of days time lag = (6)/(5) or 280,000/30,000 = 9.33 weighted days

Estimated annual interest rate = .08

Total sales invoices = 30,000

Sales (5) × Rate ×Weighted Avg. Days = Interest Cost

$30,000 × .08 × 9.33/365 = $61.35

Thus, delay in billing cost firm $61.35 per day on these two. When this cost is accumulated over many accounts over a period of time, it can become substantial.

¶ 603 BOND VALUE

.01 Bond Value—Approximate Yield to Maturity

Bond Value—Approximate Yield to Maturity

Bond Yield

$$\frac{\text{Average bond income}}{\text{Average cost}}$$

Bond at Discount

Where average bond income =

$$\text{annual coupon interest} + \frac{\text{Discount}}{\text{No. of years to maturity}}$$

Bond at Premium

Where average bond income =

$$\text{annual coupon interest} - \frac{\text{Premium}}{\text{No. of years to maturity}}$$

Average Cost

$$\frac{\text{Bond cost} + \text{maturity value}}{2}$$

Example: A 20 year, 8%, $1,000 bond is purchased at $1,040. What is the approximate yield to maturity?

$$\text{Average cost} = \frac{\$1,000 + \$ 1,040}{2} = \$1,020$$

$$\text{Income (bond at premium)} = (\$1,000)(.08) - \frac{\$40}{20} = \$78$$

$$\text{Yield} = \frac{\$78}{\$1.020} = .0765 \text{ or } 7.65\%$$

.03 Bond Value with Known Yield

(1) Present Value of Face Value of Bond

(Maturity Value) × (1 + Effective rate of interest)$^{(-\text{number of periods})}$

(2) Present Value of Series of Payments

(Nominal rate of interest) (Maturity Value) ×

$$\left[\frac{1 - (1 + \text{Effective rate of interest})^{(-\text{number of periods})}}{\text{Effective rate of interest}} \right]$$

(3) Bond value = (1) + (2) (above)

Example: $200,000 of 8%, 10 year bonds were issued by company A, with interest payable semiannually. The bonds were issued to yield 6%. Each bond has a face value of $1,000. How much did the company receive for each bond?

Solution

10 year bond at 6% annual yield = 3% semiannually for 20 periods. 10 year bond at 8% annual coupon interest = 4% semiannually for 20 periods.

PV of face value of bond = $(1,000)(1+.03)^{(-20)}$

Step One

Using the factor from table for present value of $1.00 at compound interest (see ¶ 691.07 for table)

= $1,000 (.5537)

= $553.70

Step Two

$$\text{Present value of series of payments} = (.04)(1,000) \times \left[\frac{1 - (1 + .03)^{(-20)}}{.30} \right]$$

Using the factor from table for present value of annuity of $1.00 per period (see ¶ 691.11 for table)

= (.04) (1,000) (14.8775) = $595.10

Step Three

Bond value = $553.70 + $595.10 = $1,148.80

¶ 605 BONUS

Given:

Bonus rate = 10%

Income before bonus and taxes = $125,000

Tax rate = 34%

.01 Bonus Based on Income Before Bonus and Taxes

$$
\begin{aligned}
\text{Bonus} &= \text{bonus rate} \times \text{income} \\
&= .10 \times \$125,000 \\
&= \underline{\$12,500}
\end{aligned}
$$

Bonus Based on Income After Bonus and Before Taxes

$$
\begin{aligned}
\text{Bonus (B)} &= \text{bonus rate} \times (\text{income} - \text{bonus}) \\
\text{B} &= .10 \times (\$125,000 - \text{B}) \\
1.10\text{B} &= \$12,500 \\
\text{B} &= \underline{\$12,500} \\
&\ \ 1.10 \\
\text{B} &= \underline{\$11,363.64}
\end{aligned}
$$

Bonus Based on Income After Taxes but Before Bonus

Bonus (B) = bonus rate × (income – taxes)

Taxes = tax rate × (income – bonus)

Substituting for Taxes in the Bonus Equation

B = bonus rate × {income – [tax rate (income – bonus)]}

B = .10 {$125,000 – [.34($125,000 – B)]}

B = $12,500 – $4,250 + .034B

.966B = $12,500 – $4,250

B = $8,540.37

Bonus Based on Income After Bonus and After Taxes

Bonus = bonus rate × (income – bonus – taxes)

Taxes = tax rate × (income – bonus)

Substituting for Taxes in the Bonus Equation

B = bonus rate × {income – bonus – [tax rate (income – bonus)]}

B = .10 {$125,000 – B – [.34($125,000 – B)]}

B = .10 {$125,000 – B – $42,500 + .34B}

B = $12,500 – .10B – $4,250 + .034B

1.066B = $12,500 – $4,250

B = $7,739.21

¶ 607 BREAKEVEN

The point where sales less variable expenses, less fixed expenses equals zero. The point at which revenue equals expenses.

.01 Breakeven Concepts

Breakeven Assumptions

- All the underlying assumptions are valid within a relevant range
- Assumes a straight line relationship
- Productive efficiency constant
- Over a relevant range, fixed expenses remain constant for all volume levels
- Variable expenses vary linearly with sales
- Costs are classified as either variable or fixed
- The sales mix remains constant
- A change in sales volume (over relevant range) will not affect the selling price per unit

Breakeven Usages

- Determines sales needed to obtain a specific profit level
- Determines realistic selling prices
- Used for projecting budgets

Breakeven Disadvantages

- Linear relationships often prove invalid in many cases
- Oversimplifies complex situations
- Separations into variable or fixed expenses are difficult
- Fixed and variable expenses don't remain fixed and variable
- Selling price rarely remains constant over a given range

Expenses are defined as:

- Variable expenses—change in direct proportion to the change in sales volume. Examples: direct labor and material
- Semi-variable expenses—change with sales volume, but not in direct proportion (linearly) to the volume changes. Examples: advertising and utilities
- Fixed expenses—remain constant as the sales volume changes. Examples: insurance, rent, etc.

Semi-variable expenses are classified as either fixed or variable depending on their nature over the range of analysis.

.03 Breakeven Point—in Dollars

The breakeven formula is derived from the income statement

Sales = variable expenses + fixed expenses + net income

or

Net income = sales – variable expenses – fixed expenses

Example:

Sales	$100
–Variable	–$60
–Fixed	–$40
0	0

or $S = V + F$ Where: S = Sales at breakeven point

         $S - V - F$ V = Variable expense

                                                       F = Fixed expenses

Breakeven Point—in Dollars

$$\frac{\text{Fixed expenses}}{\dfrac{\text{Sales} - \text{Variable Expense}}{\text{Sales}}}$$

Example:

$$\frac{\$40}{\dfrac{\$100 - \$60}{\$100}} = \$100$$

Breakeven—Percentage of Capacity

The breakeven formula stated as a percentage of capacity or the ratio of breakeven point to capacity is as follows.

Ratio of Breakeven Point to Capacity   =

$$\frac{\text{Total Fixed Expenses}}{[\,1 - (\text{Total Variable Cost}/\text{Total Sales})\,](\text{Capacity})}$$

Example: If sales were $100, then

Ratio of Breakeven Point to Capacity   = $\dfrac{\$40}{[1 - (\$60 \,/\, \$100)]\,(\$100)}$

                    = 100%

If sales were $200, then

Ratio of Breakeven Point to Capacity   = $\dfrac{\$40}{[1 - (\$120 \,/\, \$200)]\,(\$200)}$

                    = 50%

.05 Breakeven Point for Target Net Income — In Dollars

To obtain a given level of net income, the breakeven formula is modified to:

Breakeven Sales

$$\frac{\text{Fixed} + \text{Net Income}}{\dfrac{\text{Sales} - \text{Variable Expenses}}{\text{Sales}}}$$

Example: Net income desired = $10

$$\frac{\$40 + \$10}{\dfrac{\$100 - \$60}{\$100}} = \$125$$

Breakeven Point for Target Net Income—Additional Fixed Costs

Breakeven Point for Target Net Income—Additional Fixed Costs =

$$\frac{\text{Fixed} + \text{Net Income} + \text{Additional Fixed Cost}}{\dfrac{\text{Sales} - \text{Variable Expenses}}{\text{Sales}}}$$

Example: Suppose new plant expansion is proposed with new machinery. What is the new Breakeven Point given the following assumptions?

Sales = $100,000

Variable Costs = $60,000

Fixed Costs = $ 40,000

New equipment cost = $80,000

Estimated additional fixed costs = $45,000

After tax rate required on new equipment = 10%

Income tax rate = 25%

Target Net Income = $10,000

Breakeven Point for Target Net Income—Additional Fixed Costs =

$$\frac{\$40,000 + \$10,000 + \$45,000}{\dfrac{\$100,000 - \$60,000}{\$100,000}}$$

$$= \frac{\$95,000}{.40}$$

$$= \$237,500$$

Breakeven Point for Target Net Income—Additional Fixed Costs and Required After-Tax Rate of Return on New Equipment

Breakeven Point for Target Net Income—Additional Fixed Costs and Required After-Tax Rate of Return on New Equipment =

$$\frac{\text{Required After Tax Rate of Return} + \text{Fixed} + \text{Net Income} + \text{Additional Fixed Cost}}{\dfrac{\text{Sales} - \text{Variable Expenses}}{\text{Sales}}}$$

$$\frac{[\$80,000 \times (.10 \times (1 - .25))] \, \$40,000 + \$10,000 + \$45,000}{\dfrac{\$100,000 - \$60,000}{\$100,000}}$$

$$= \frac{\$6,000 + \$40,000 + \$10,000 + \$45,000}{\frac{\$100,000 - \$60,000}{\$100,000}}$$

$$= \$252,500$$

.06 Breakeven Point For Target Net Income After Tax—In Dollars

Breakeven sales (after taxes)

$$\frac{Fixed \quad + net\ income}{(1 - effective\ tax\ rate)}$$

$$\frac{Sales - variable}{\frac{expenses}{sales}}$$

Example: What is the required sales volume for a target income amount net of taxes, given the above data and an effective tax rate of 25%?

$$Breakeven\ sales = \frac{\$40 + \frac{\$10}{1 - .25}}{\frac{\$100 - \$60}{\$100}}$$

$$= \frac{\$53.33}{.40}$$

$$= \$133.33$$

Breakeven Point for Target Net Income—In Percent for Target Net Income

Breakeven Point for Target Net Income—in Percent for Target Net Income =

$$\frac{Total\ Fixed\ Expenses}{1 - [(Total\ Variable\ Cost\ /\ Total\ Sales) + Percent\ for\ Target\ Net\ Income]}$$

Example: Total Fixed Expenses = \$60,000 or 60% of Sales

Total Variable Cost = \$40,000

Total Sales = \$100,000

Percent for Target Net Income = 10%

If Net Income were to be 10% of Net Sales, what would be the Sales volume required?

Breakeven Point for Target Net Income—in Percent for Target Net Income =

$$\frac{\$40,000}{1 - [(\$60,000\ /\ \$100,000) + 10\%]}$$

Breakeven Point for Target Net Income —in Percent for Target Net Income = \$133,000

Proof:

Sales	= $133,000	100%
Variable	= $79,800	60%
Fixed	= $40,000	30%
Net Income	= $13,200	≈10%

.07 Breakeven Point—In Units

Breakeven Sales

$$\frac{\text{Fixed Expenses}}{\text{Unit sales price} - \text{Unit variable expenses}}$$

The breakeven point can be modified to show the number of units required to obtain a desired amount of net income.

Breakeven Sales For Target Net Income

$$\frac{\text{Fixed Expenses} + \text{Net Income}}{\text{Unit sales price} - \text{Unit variable expenses}}$$

.09 Breakeven Point for Cash Flow

Breakeven Cash Flow

$$\frac{\text{Fixed Expenses} - \text{Depreciation}}{\dfrac{\text{Sales} - \text{Variable Expenses}}{\text{Sales}}} = \frac{\text{Fixed Expenses} - \text{Depreciation}}{\text{Gross Profit Margin}}$$

Example: Monthly sales = $150,000

Monthly variable expenses = $110,000

Total fixed costs = $30,000 (which includes depreciation of $6,000)

What is the firm's monthly cash flow breakeven point?

Breakeven (Cash flow) =

$$\frac{\dfrac{\$30,000 \quad \$6,000}{\$150,000 \quad \$110,000}}{\$150,000} = \frac{\$24,000}{.267} = \$89,000$$

.11 Breakeven Point with Multiple Product Sales Mix

Breakeven with multiple sales mix =

$$\frac{\text{Fixed}}{\dfrac{\text{Sales} - (\text{weighted average gross margin})}{\text{Sales}}}$$

Where weighted average gross margin percentage = the sum of the gross margin % for each product as a % of sales.

Example of breakeven with multiple sales mix:

- Assume a pest control company provides services to residential and commercial customers.

¶607.07

- Assume sales mix = 1:1 or 50% to each.
- Gross sales = $350,000
- Gross Profit for residential = 45%
- Gross profit for commercial = 35%
- Fixed expenses = $130,000

What is breakeven point with 50/50 sales mix?

1. Compute weighted average gross profit:

	G/P		Sales Mix		
Residential	45%	×	50%	=	.225
Commercial	35%	×	50%	=	.175
				=	.40

2.

$$\frac{\text{Sales} - \text{Variable Costs}}{\text{Sales}} = \text{G/P}$$

3. Breakeven with sales mix
$$= \frac{\$129,000}{.40}$$

$$= \$322,500$$

Example 2:

Assume all variables stay the same except sales mix changes to higher profit margin as follows:

Sales mix =

Residential	–	60%
Commercial	–	40%

1. Compute weighted average gross profit:

	G/P		Sales Mix		
Residential	45%	×	60%	=	.27
Commercial	5%	×	40%	=	.14
				=	.44

2. Breakeven sales with sales mix
$$= \frac{\$129,000}{.44}$$

$$= \$293,182$$

Therefore, with same gross profit on each product/service, by shifting the sales mix to 10% more residentially, the breakeven can drop from $322,500 per year to $293,182.

Example 3:

Assume the sales mix shifts 10 percent toward the less profitable product/service. Assume all other factors remain the same as Example 1.

Sales Mix:

Residential	=	40%
Commercial	=	60%

¶607.11

1. Compute weighted average gross profit:

	G/P		Sales Mix		
Residential	45%	×	40%	=	.18
Commercial	35%	×	60%	=	.21
				=	.39

2. Breakeven Sales with sales mix

=	$129,000
	.39
=	$330,769

If sales mix were to shift toward lower gross product/service, breakeven increases from $322,500 to $330,769.

¶ 609 CASH

.01 Cash discounts

The following table shows annual interest equivalents of cash discounts based on various terms. Annualizing vendor terms into equivalent interest rates provides guidance regarding the true cost of purchasing. From this table, an analysis may be made of the "cost" of purchasing by foregoing cash discounts.

Goods sold on terms "2/10 net 30" means the purchaser is allowed a 2% discount if payment is received within 10 days of the invoice; otherwise the full amount is due in 30 days of the invoice date.

Goods sold on terms "2/10 net 60" means the purchaser is allowed a 2% discount if payment is received within 10 days of the invoice; otherwise the full amount is due in 60 days of the invoice date.

Formula for calculating the annual percentage rate, based on a 360-day year:

Annual Percentage Rate (360 Day Year)

$$\text{APR} = \frac{D}{(T - D)} \times \frac{360}{N}$$

Where: T is the total amount of the invoice

D is the dollar value of the discount

N is the number of days between the end of the discount period and the end of the net period.

If an invoice for $100 comes in marked "2/10, net 30," and the firm decides to pass up the discount and pay on the final day of the net period instead, it would be paying the following annual interest cost:

$$\frac{2}{98} \times \frac{360}{20} = .367 \text{ or } 36.7\%$$

If the invoice is marked "2/10, net 60," the annual rate for using that $98 for 50 extra days would be:

$$\frac{2}{98} \times \frac{360}{50} = .147 \text{ or } 14.7\%$$

Annual Rate Given Vendor Discounts (10-Day Discount Period)

Discount Rate	Net Period		Per Annum Rate	Net Period		Per Annum Rate
1%	Net	20	36.36%	Net	60	7.27%
2%	Net	20	73.47%	Net	60	14.69%
3%	Net	20	111.34%	Net	60	22.27%
4%	Net	20	150.00%	Net	60	30.00%
5%	Net	20	189.47%	Net	60	37.89%
6%	Net	20	229.79%	Net	60	45.96%
7%	Net	20	270.97%	Net	60	54.19%
8%	Net	20	313.04%	Net	60	62.61%
9%	Net	20	356.04%	Net	60	71.21%
10%	Net	20	400.00%	Net	60	80.00%
1%	Net	30	18.18%	Net	70	6.06%
2%	Net	30	36.73%	Net	70	12.24%
3%	Net	30	55.67%	Net	70	18.56%
4%	Net	30	75.00%	Net	70	25.00%
5%	Net	30	94.74%	Net	70	31.58%
6%	Net	30	114.89%	Net	70	38.30%
7%	Net	30	135.48%	Net	70	45.16%
8%	Net	30	156.52%	Net	70	52.17%
9%	Net	30	178.02%	Net	70	59.34%
10%	Net	30	200.00%	Net	70	66.67%
1%	Net	40	12.12%	Net	80	5.19%
2%	Net	40	24.49%	Net	80	10.50%
3%	Net	40	37.11%	Net	80	15.91%
4%	Net	40	50.00%	Net	80	21.43%
5%	Net	40	63.16%	Net	80	27.07%
6%	Net	40	76.60%	Net	80	32.83%
7%	Net	40	90.32%	Net	80	38.71%
8%	Net	40	104.35%	Net	80	44.72%
9%	Net	40	118.68%	Net	80	50.86%
10%	Net	40	133.33%	Net	80	57.14%
1%	Net	50	9.09%	Net	90	4.55%
2%	Net	50	18.37%	Net	90	9.18%
3%	Net	50	27.84%	Net	90	13.92%
4%	Net	50	37.50%	Net	90	18.75%
5%	Net	50	47.37%	Net	90	23.68%
6%	Net	50	57.45%	Net	90	28.72%
7%	Net	50	67.74%	Net	90	33.87%
8%	Net	50	78.26%	Net	90	39.13%
9%	Net	50	89.01%	Net	90	44.51%
10%	Net	50	100.00%	Net	90	50.00%

¶ 611 CASH FLOW

.01 Cash Flow Required to Purchase Fixed Assets

The cash flow related to asset purchases can be determined from the beginning and ending balances of the financial statements for fixed assets and accumulated depreciation, the book value of the assets sold, and the net income statement current period depreciation.

Cash Flow for Purchases of Fixed Assets

Balance Sheet

	Beginning Balance	Ending Balance
Fixed assets	_____	_____
Less: Accumulated depreciation	_____	_____
Net fixed assets	_____ (B)	_____ (A)
Net income statement current period depreciation		_____ (C)
Book value of assets sold		_____ (D)

Cash flow required to purchase fixed assets:

Ending net fixed assets		_____ (A)
– Beginning net fixed assets	–	_____ (B)
+ Current period depreciation	+	_____ (C)
+ Book value of assets sold	+	_____ (D)
= Cash flow to purchase fixed assets	=	_____

Example of Cash flow required to purchase fixed assets:

Assume the following:

Fixed assets purchased: $10,000 (This is the $10,000 cash flow usage we wish to compute)

Current period depreciation	$500(C)
Historical cost of fixed assets sold	$8,000
Accumulated depreciation of fixed assets sold	–$3,000
Book value of assets sold	$5,000(D)

Balance Sheet

	Beginning	Net Change	Ending
Fixed assets	$25,000	$2,000 DR	$27,000
Accumulated depreciation	(10,000)	2,500 DR	(7,500)
Net fixed assets	15,000(B)	4,500 DR	19,500(A)

Net change is analyzed as follows:

Net change

Fixed assets	$2,000 =	+10,000 fixed assets purchased	–8,000 historical cost of assets sold

Net change

Accum deprec	$2,500 =	– 500 current period depreciation	+ 3,000 accum deprec of fixed assets sold

Net change

Net fixed assets	$4,500=+10,000	–500 fixed assets purchased less current depreciation	–5,000 book value of assets sold

Cash flow for purchases of fixed assets:

Ending net fixed assets	$19,500 (A)
– Beginning net fixed assets	15,000 (B)
+ Current period depreciation	500 (C)
+ Book value of assets sold	5,000 (D)
= Cash flow for purchase of fixed assets	$10,000

.02 Cash Flow Need to Support Sales Growth

Use the following formula to analyze the cash needs to support a company's sales growth. This formula determines how much cash is needed for each additional dollar in sales. If a company is cash poor and does not have this in the bank, then it must turn to other sources to support this growth such as selling equity or borrowing. Although increased sales are nice and profits are nice, it is cash flow that is critical to survival. An increase in sales generally will mean less cash flow. This model is simplistic by design and errs on the *needs* side. For instance, it assumes that the increased costs are to be covered by payments rather than increased accounts payable, or lengthened payment terms. Its purpose is to provide a look-ahead planning tool.

Additional cash needed to support increase in sales =

[[(Sales × COGS %) + overhead] / 365] × [Average A/R collection period in days]

> *Example:* Annual increase in Sales = $100,000
>
> Gross Margin % = 32%　　　　　　　COGS % = 68%

Additional overhead required to support sales increase = $8,000

(composed of commission, support people, etc.)

Average A/R collection period = 60 days

Additional cash needed to support increase in sales =

[[($100,000 × 68 %) + $8,000] / 365] × [60] =$12,493

.03 Cash Management—Baumol Approach

The following model is similar in form to the Economic Order Quantity (EOQ) models relating to inventory. The concept, with cash management, is to estimate cash flows, maximize return on liquid assets, and minimize cash balances. The following formula seeks to aid in cash balance optimization. If a certain sum of cash is needed for a year, what would be the optimum "order size" of cash?

$$\text{Cash order size (optimum)} = \sqrt{\frac{(2)\,(\text{total cash needed})\,(\text{transaction cost to obtain cash})}{\text{cost of carrying cash inventory}}}$$

> *Example:* Assume management needs to raise an additional $2 million dollars next year by selling common stock. How much should be raised each time, and how many times should that occur next year given the following data?

Total cash needed	=	$2 million
Transaction cost to obtain cash	=	$20,000
Cost of carrying cash cost short-term	=	6% (the difference between the company's of capital and expected return on securities (12% – 6%)

$$\text{Cash order size (optimum)} = \sqrt{\frac{(2)\,(\$2{,}000{,}000)\,(\$20{,}000)}{.06}}$$

= $1,154,701

Approximately $1 million should be raised 2 times a year.

.05 Cash Management—Investment in Securities

When a firm has a short period of excess cash, it can invest in short-term marketable securities. The rate of return must exceed the transaction costs. Usually, the firm invests in U.S. Treasury bills. The following formula estimates the net return:

Net gain = (number of days funds are invested) (amount invested) (daily interest rate) + (expected capital gain on sale) – (per transaction costs)

.07 Cash Management—Miller-Orr Approach

The Miller-Orr Approach focuses on cash "in to" or "out of" marketable securities. It allows for random cash flows without reference to a specific time period. Management determines cash limits. The lower limit sets a target cash balance and when discretionary balances hit zero, it triggers a flow from securities into cash in order to restore this minimum level. When cash reaches a maximum level, the surplus funds are drained off to below the limit level and placed in income-yielding securities. Between these levels, cash balances change randomly without triggering any action. Lower and upper limits represent optimal balances. The probability that cash balances will swing in either direction is 50/50.

Cash desired level (target level) =

$$\sqrt[3]{\frac{3 \times \left(\begin{array}{c}\text{average transaction}\\\text{cost between securities}\\\text{and cash}\end{array}\right)\left(\begin{array}{c}\text{demand}\\\text{for}\\\text{cash}\end{array}\right)^{2}\left(\begin{array}{c}\text{number of}\\\text{operating cash}\\\text{transactions per day}\end{array}\right)}{4 \times \text{(daily interest rate)}}}$$

.09 Short-Term Cash Needs—Percent-of-Sales Forecast Method

Generally, if sales are to be increased, assets must also increase in some relationship to these sales. These increased sales will require additional investments in accounts receivable, inventory, and fixed assets. Increased growth and increased sales will be accompanied by an increase in assets to support those sales. Assume that similar percentage relationships will hold. Restate Balance Sheet items as a percentage of sales. This is true only for relatively short-term forecasting. Some financing needs will be absorbed by normal increases in liabilities, such as accounts payable, and short-term accruals.

Example:

- Restate Current Balance Sheet as % of Current Sales
- Do not restate Common Stock or Retained Earnings as they do not vary directly with sales relating to cash needs

Total Current Sales = $600,000

Net Income after taxes 20% (as % of total sales)

Projected sales = $950,000

BALANCE SHEET

Assets	Current	% of Current Sales	Liabilities	Current	% of Current Sales
Cash	$8000	1.33	Accounts Payable	$6500	1.08
Accounts Receivable	75000	12.5	Taxes	3000	.5
Inventory	65000	10.83	Accrual	5000	.83
Fixed Assets (net)	80000	13.33			
Total Assets (B)	37.99 %		Total Liabilities (C)	2.41 %	

Total assets as % of Current Sales	(B)	37.99%
Less: Natural Increase in Liabilities from Growth	(C)	2.41%
% of each sales dollar that must come from funds	=	35.58% (A)
Sales - Projected	$950,000	
Less: Current Sales	– 600,000	
Increase in Sales	= 350,000	
× Funding Needs Rate	(A) × .40	
Total Funding Requirements		= 140,000
Current Net Income	$600,000	
Net Income after Tax Rate	× 20%	
Net Income after Taxes		= – 120,000
Funds Needed from Outside Sources		= 20,000

.11 Cash Gap

Effective cash management is important to a company's bottom line. If sufficient operating cash is not available, then the cash gap must be financed. The longer that the cash gap term is, the higher is the financing cost, and the less is the overall company profit. Although most companies are controlled by industry practices, seasonal trends, geography, etc., effective cash management is still a must. A company must actively manage its cash gap to sustain profitable growth.

Cash Gap = Number of days between when a business pays for products/services and the receipt of cash from its customers for the products/services sold

or

Cash Gap = Inventory days on hand + receivables collection period - accounts payable period

or

Cash Gap = IDOH + RCP – APP

Visually, the cash gap time line looks like this:

(You purchase inventory, pay for it, sell it, and collect for it. The cash gap is the time from paying for inventory until the time the cash on the sold inventory is collected.)

The Cash Gap—Time Line:

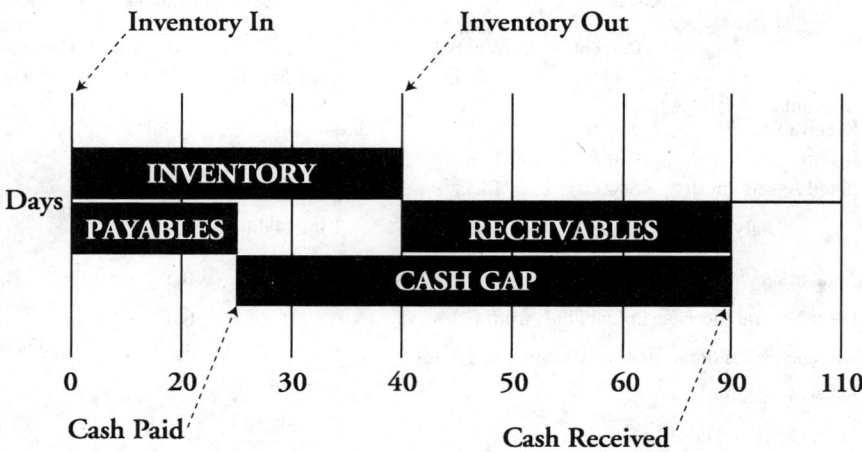

To Reduce the Cash Gap:

- Increase inventory turnover. Increasing inventory turnover will reduce the time that inventory is held.

- Decrease A/R collection period.

- Increase or lengthen accounts payable payment due period.

Growing companies must monitor carefully their cash gap, their sales growth and their profit margins, or they will encounter cash flow shortages.

A company that collects from customers up front, purchases inventory to order, and keeps no inventory on hand will have a negative cash gap.

If a cash gap is increasing in length of time, it should be a signal to management about potential cash flow problems.

If a company has sales growth and a growing cash gap, it can rapidly reach a point where cash outflow exceeds cash inflow. When cumulative cash outflows outpace cash inflows, the company can get into serious financial problems. Any additional sales growth will just drain cash out of the company. The faster the sales growth, the faster is the cash drained out. Additional sales growth will not improve the cash position. A company in this position must seek to reduce its cash gap. It should slow down its rate of growth and seek to increase its margins.

¶611.11

¶ 613 COMMON DOLLARS

.01 Converting Dollars to Common Dollars

Converting Dollars to Common Dollars

$$\text{Adjusted \$'s} = \text{current \$'s} \times \frac{\text{Current general price level index}}{\text{Index of price level of base year}}$$

Example (1): Depreciation is computed by straight line method of $12,000/year

Price level index during year of acquisition of asset = 30

Price level index during current year = 85

$$\text{Adjusted depreciation expense} = \$12,000 \times \frac{85}{30} = \underline{\$34,000}$$

Example (2): (Converting assets to common dollars):

Historical asset cost = $150,000

Current price level index = 85

Price level index at acquisition date = 30

$$\text{Adjusted asset cost} = \$150,000 \times \frac{85}{30} = \$425,000$$

.02 Common Size Analysis

In analyzing financial statements for trends, the absolute value of the number often does not readily indicate trends. Significant relationships are often not readily apparent. Common size analysis takes the absolute value of the numbers and restates them as a percentage of a base amount. Trends are then often made more apparent by the use of percentages. The following illustrates the trends in the Income statement by showing the absolute dollars with the corresponding common size percentages. One can then analyze the percentages for their relationships.

Category	20xx $	20xx %	20x1 $	20x1 %	20x2 $	20x2 %	20x3 $	20x3 %
Sales	20,000	100	25,000	1.25	27,500	1.38	28,250	.41
COGS	13,000	100	14,000	1.08	15,000	1.15	16,500	1.27
Gross Margin	7,000	100	11,000	1.57	12,500	1.79	11,750	1.68
Salary	5,000	100	6,000	1.20	7,500	1.50	8,500	1.70

¶ 614 COMMON SIZE STATEMENTS—HORIZONTAL VS. VERTICAL ANALYSIS

.01 Overview

Users of financial statements can gain clearer understanding of their numbers by using horizontal and vertical analysis of common size numbers. They can compare their own company's multi-periods within a single year, successive years, or with other companies. Such analysis will disclose relationships and trends in financial condition. Common size numbers are where numbers are expressed only in relative terms, where one number is divided by another. Relationships become more readily available for understanding when stated in relative terms.

Horizontal analysis indicates the increase/decrease in corresponding items on comparative financial statements. The current amount of each item is compared with the corresponding item on earlier statements. Each asset item is stated as a percentage of total assets, and each liability/equity item is stated as a percentage of total liabilities and equity. Vertical analysis is used to analyze the component parts to the total in a single statement. In vertical analysis of the income statement, each item is stated as a percent of total net sales. Multi-periods can then be compared to prior periods to study relationships.

.02 Benefits of Using Common Size Statements

Common size statements allow for the following. The ratios put data from past years for the company on the same playing field. Historical dollars are now equal to today's dollars, because we are not using dollars but ratios. It doesn't matter how historical the dollars are. It puts data from different companies on the same playing field, because relationships are being analyzed not absolute dollars. Ratios simplify further calculations. Ratios of ratios are computed in the same manner and compute to the same answer as ratios of dollars. However, changes between amounts will obtain different answers. In analyzing interrelationships of parts to whole, absolute dollar relationship and changes distorts real relationship changes; percent of totals and percent changes of percent show real relationships more accurately. Changes of horizontal analysis from x1 to x2 is simplified. Since it is already stated in percent, you simply subtract to obtain the increase/decrease amount.

.05 Common Size Statement—Illustration

Balance Sheet

	2001 $	2001 %	2002 $	2002 %	2003 $	2003 %
Cash	$5,000	10	20000	20	30000	24
A/R	10000	20	10000	10	15000	12
Inventory	20000	40	30000	30	35000	28
Equipment	15000	30	40000	40	45000	36
Total Assets	50000	100	100000	100	125000	100
Current Liab	15000	30	50000	50	60000	48
Non-Current L	25000	50	20000	20	30000	24
Common	5000	10	15000	15	15000	12
Retained Earn	5000	10	15000	15	20000	16
Total Liab&/Eq	50000	100	100000	100	125000	100

Ratios computed on ratios are equivalent to ratios computed on dollars.

Current ratio = Current Assets/ Current Liabilities

	2001	2002	2003
in %	30/30=1	30/50=60%	36/48=75%
in $	15/15=1	30/50=60%	45/60=75%

¶614.02

Debt Ratio = Total Debt / Total Assets

	2001	2002	2003
in %	80/100= 80%	70/100=70%	72/100=72%
in $	40/50=80%	70/100=70%	90/125=72%

Balance Sheet Analysis in Dollars

	Horizontal Change x2 /x1	Vertical Change x2 /Total x1
Cash	20000/5000 = 400%	20000/50000=40%
A/R	10000/10000=100%	10000/50000=20%
Inventory	30000 / 20000 = 150%	30000/20000=60%
Equipment	40000/15000 = 267%	40000/50000=80%
Total Assets	100000/50000=200%	100000/50000=200%
Current Liab	50000 / 15000=333%	50000 / 50000 =100%
Non-Current L	20000 / 50000 = 80%	20000 / 50000 = 100%
Common	15000 / 5000 = 300%	15000 / 50000 = 30%
Retained Earn	15000 / 5000 = 300%	15000 / 50000 = 30%
Total Liab&/Eq	100000/100000=100%	100000/100000=100%

	$ Change to parts (x2 -x1) / x1	$ Change to total (x2 -x1) / Total x1
Cash	(20000 – 5000) /5000 =300%	(20000 – 5000) / 50000 = 30%
A/R	(10000 – 10000) / 10000= 0	(10000 – 10000)/ 50000 =0%
Inventory	(30000 –20000) / 20000=50%	(30000 –20000) /50000 = 20%
Equipment	(40000 – 15000) / 15000 =167%	(40000 – 15000)/50000= 100%
Total Assets	(100000–50000)/50000=100%	(100000–50000)/50000=100%
Current Liab	(50000 – 15000) /15000 = 233%	(50000 – 15000) / 50000=70%
Non-Current L	(20000 – 25000) / 25000 =(20%)	(20000 – 25000)/50000=(10%)
Common	(15000 – 5000) / 25000 =20%	(15000 – 5000) / 50000=20%
Retained Earn	(15000 – 5000) / 25000 =20%	(15000 – 5000) / 50000=20%
Total Liab&/Eq	(100000–50000)/50000=100%	(100000–50000)/50000=100%

Balance Sheet Analysis in Percent

	Horizontal Change x2 /x1	Vertical Change x2 /Total x1
Cash	20/10 = 200%	20/100=20%
A/R	10/20=50%	10/100=10%
Inventory	30 / 40 = 75%	30/100=30%
Equipment	40/30 = 133%	40/100=40%
Total Assets	100/100=100%	100/100=100%
Current Liab	50 / 30=167%	50 / 100 =50%
Non-Current L	20 / 50= 80%	20 / 100 = 20%
Common	15 / 10 = 150%	15 / 100 = 15%

	Horizontal Change x2 /x1	Vertical Change x2 /Total x1
Retained Earn	15 / 10 = 150%	15 / 100 = 15%
Total Liab&/Eq	100/100=100%	100/100=100%

	$ Change to parts (x2 –x1) / x1	$ Change to total (x2 –x1) / Total x1
Cash	(20 –10) / 10 =100%	(20 – 10) / 100 = 10%
A/R	(10 – 20 / 20= (50)	(10 – 20)/ 100 =(10)%
Inventory	(30 –40) / 40=(25)%	(30 –40) /100 = (10)%
Equipment	(40 – 30) / 30 =33%	(40 – 30)/100= 10%
Total Assets	(100–100)/100=0%	(100–100)/100=0%
Current Liab	(50 – 30) / 30 = 67%	(50 – 30) / 100=20%
Non-Current L	(20 – 50) / 50 =(60%)	(20 – 50) / 100=(30%)
Common	(15 – 10) / 10 =20%	(15 – 10) / 100=5%
Retained Earn	(15 – 10) / 10 =20	(15 – 10) / 100=5%
Total Liab&/Eq	(100–100)/100=0	(100–100)/100=0%

.07 Observations

Cash. The change in cash from $5000 in 2001 to $20,000 in 2002 on a horizontal basis indicates a change of 400%, but vertically it's only a percent change of 20%, from a company's cash being 10% of total assets to 20%. So what appeared to be a huge increase in cash is really a small increase in relation to the parts of the whole.

Equipment. The change in equipment from $15,000 in 2001 to $40,000 in 2002 on a horizontal basis indicates a change of 267%, but vertically it's only a percent change of 40%, from a company's equipment being 30% of total assets to 40%. So what appeared to be a huge increase in equipment is really a small increase in relation to the parts of the whole.

One can review the following amounts and provide for numerous conclusions regarding the financials.

Balance Sheet Analysis in Dollars

	Horizontal Change x3 /x1	Vertical Change x3 /Total x1
Cash	30000/5000 = 600%	30000/50000=60%
A/R	15000/10000=150%	15000/50000=30
Inventory	35000 / 20000 = 140%	35000/50000=70%
Equipment	45000/15000 = 300%	45000/50000=90%
Total Assets	125000/50000=250%	125000/50000=250%
Current Liab	60000 / 15000=4003%	60000 / 50000 =120%
Non-Current L	30000 / 25000 = 120	3000 / 50000 = 60%
Common	15000 / 5000 = 300%	15000 / 50000 = 30%
Retained Earn	20000 / 5000 = 400%	20000 / 50000 = 40%
Total Liab&/Eq	125000/50000=250%	125000/50000=250%

	$ Change to parts (x3 -x1) / x1	$ Change to total (x3 -x1) / Total x1
Cash	(30000 –5000) /5000 =500%	(30000 – 5000) / 50000 = 50%
A/R	(15000 – 10000 / 10000= 30%	(15000 – 10000)/ 50000 =10%
Inventory	(35000 –20000) / 20000=75%	(30500 –20000) /50000 = 30%
Equipment	(45000 – 15000) / 15000 =200%	(45000 – 15000) / 50000= 60%
Total Assets	(125000–50000)/50000=150%	(125000–50000)/50000=150%
Current Liab	(60000 – 15000) /15000 = 300%	(60000 – 15000) / 50000=90%
Non-Current L	(30000 – 25000) / 25000 =20%	(30000 – 25000)/50000=10%
Common	(15000 – 5000) / 5000 =200%	(15000 – 5000) / 50000=20%
Retained Earn	(20000 – 5000) / 5000 =300%	(20000 – 5000) / 50000=30%
Total Liab&/Eq	(125000–50000)/50000=150%	(125000–50000)/50000=150%

Balance Sheet Analysis in Percent

	Horizontal Change x3 /x1	Vertical Change x3 /Total x1
Cash	24/10 = 240%	24/100=24%
A/R	12/20= 60%	12/100=12%
Inventory	28 / 40 = 70%	28/100=28%
Equipment	36/30 = 120%	36/100=36%
Total Assets	100/100=100%	100/100=100%
Current Liab	48 / 30=160%	48 / 100 =48%
Non-Current L	24 / 50= 48%	24 / 100 = 24%
Common	12 / 10 = 120%	12 / 100 = 12%
Retained Earn	16 / 10 = 160%	16 / 100 = 16%
Total Liab&/Eq	100/100=100%	100/100=100%

	$ Change to parts (x3 -x1) / x1	$ Change to total (x3 -x1) / Total x1
Cash	(24 –10) / 10 =140%	(24 – 10) / 100 = 14%
A/R	(12 – 20 / 20= (40)	(12 – 20)/ 100 =(8)%
Inventory	(28 –40) / 40=(30)%	(28 –40) /100 = (12)%
Equipment	(36 – 30) / 30 = 20%	(36 – 30)/100= 6%
Total Assets	(100–100)/100=0%	(100–100)/100=0%
Current Liab	(48 – 30) / 30 = 60%	(48 – 30) / 100=18%
Non-Current L	(24 – 50) / 50 =(52%)	(24 –50) / 100=(26%)
Common	(12 – 10) / 10 =20%	(12 – 10) / 100=2%
Retained Earn	(16 – 10) / 10 =60%	(16 – 10) / 100=67%
Total Liab&/Eq	(100–100)/100=0%	(100–100)/100=0%

¶ 615 COST OF CAPITAL

.01 Cost of Capital—Marginal Overall Cost for Company

The cost of capital is the mix of long-term debt and equity required to provide the
necessary funds for the operation and growth of the company. Management should use
a projected capital structure that represents the average of the company's needs over

the projected years—the marginal capital structure. The cost of capital for that mix of debt and equity that is anticipated to be used to raise the capital in the future is the marginal cost of capital.

What is the overall cost of Capital for a company given the following assumptions? The Company income tax rate is 25%.

Security	Capitalization	Rate Required Before Taxes by Investors	After-Tax Rate For Company	Cost of Capital For Company
Bonds	$75,000	10%	10% x (1 – 25%)	$5,625
Common Stock	$125,000	15%	15%	$18,750
	$200,000		Cost of Capital =	$24,375

Cost of Capital Percentage = $24,375 / $200,000 = 12.19%

.02 Financing—Debt

The approximate effective interest rate on long-term debt financing is defined as follows:

$$\text{Rate} = \frac{r \times F \times (1-t) + [(F-P)/(n-m)](1-t)}{(F+P)/2}$$

Where:

r = Coupon or contractual rate of interest

F = Face value of bond

t = Marginal tax rate on corporate income

P = Market price of bond

n = The original maturity of the bond issued

m = The number of periods elapsed since the bond was issued

(note: n – m = the number of additional periods that the bond will remain outstanding. Assumption is made that the company will not call the bond before maturity.)

> ***Example:*** The approximate effective interest rate of company issuing a long-term bond is calculated as follows, given the following data:
>
> Company just sold an 8%, 20 year $1,000 bond for $1,200.
>
> Marginal tax rate = 40%

$$\text{Rate} = \frac{(.08) \times (1,000)(1-.40) + [(1,000-1,200)/(20-0)](1-.40)}{(1,000 + 1,200)/2} = \frac{48 + (-6)}{1,100}$$

$$= .0382 = 3.82\%$$

.03 Financing—Preferred Stock

Financing the company with preferred stock is different from debt in that preferred dividends paid on stock is not deductible where interest on debt is. Secondly, preferred stock payments have no maturity dates, where debt instruments do. The price formula is the present value of a perpetuity of Fd dollars per period with r as the discount rate.

$$P = \frac{Fd}{r}$$

¶615.02

The effective cost of funds raised through preferred stock financing is then defined as:

$$r = \frac{Fd}{P}$$

Where:

P = Market price of preferred stock

F = Face or par value of preferred stockd

d= The contractual preferred dividend rate

r = The effective cost of preferred stock financing to the company

    Example: A company sells a 5.75%, $100 preferred stock for $98.

The effective rate of such financing is:

$$r = \frac{Fd}{P} = \frac{(\$100)(.0575)}{98} = 5.87\%$$

.05 Cost of Common Equity Under Static Conditions

A "static" company is one whose existing assets may be expected to generate a constant annual net income and the net worth is not expected to be augmented by future investments.

The following symbols are used for defining the cost of common equity formulas.

P = Current market price of common shares

P1 = Price at which new shares are sold

C = Cost of common equity

E = Expected earnings per share, assuming that current transactions were not undertaken

Y = Rate of return required by stockholders, assuming it is not affected by the current transaction

n0 = Number of existing shares

n1 = Number of new shares sold to existing stockholders

n2 = Number of new shares sold to new stockholders

.07 Cost of Common Equity for New Issue

The following formula defines the cost of common equity if the entire equity is bought by existing shareholders: Note that the cost of capital is unaffected by the discount at which the new shares are sold.

$$C = \frac{E}{P} \quad \text{where E= PxY} \quad C = \frac{P \times Y}{P}$$

Example 1 of cost of common equity: A static company owns assets that have an expectation of generating constant annual earnings of $6,000/year. There are 1,000 outstanding shares. The market price per share = $60. The rate of return required by shareholders is 10%. If all new shares are sold entirely to existing shareholders, the cost of common equity is as follows:

$$C = \frac{E}{P} = \frac{(\$60)(.10)}{\$60} = \frac{6}{60} = 10\%$$

.09 Cost of Common Equity Where Entire New Issue is Sold to New Shareholders

The following formula defines the cost of common equity if the entire equity issue is bought by new shareholders.

$$C = Y\frac{(P)}{P1}$$

Example 2 cost of common equity if the new shares are sold entirely to new stockholders: Facts are the same as in Example 1. What is the cost of common equity associated with the sale of 100 new shares at a price of \$45/share if the new shares are sold entirely to new stockholders?

$$C = .10\frac{(\$60)}{(\$45)} = 13\%$$

.11 Cost of Common Equity Where n1 Shares are Sold to Existing Shareholders and n2 Shares are Sold to New Shareholders

The following formula defines the cost of common equity if n1 shares are sold to existing shareholders and n2 shares are sold to new shareholders:

$$C = \frac{n0\ n2}{(n0+n1)(n1+n2)} \quad [Y]\frac{P}{P1} + \frac{(n0+n1\ x\ n2)(n1)}{(n0+n1)(n1+n2)}\ x\ [Y]$$

Example 3 of Cost of Common Equity if some sold to old stockholders and some sold to new stockholders: Facts are the same as in Examples 1 and 2. What is the cost of common equity if half of the shares are sold to old stockholders and half are sold to new shareholders?

$$C = \frac{(1,000)(50)}{(1,000+50)(50+50)}[.10]\frac{(60)}{(45)} + \frac{(1,000+50+50)(50)}{(1,000+50)(50+50)}[.10]$$

$$= \frac{50,000}{105,000}(.13) + \frac{55,000}{105,000}(.10)$$

$$= 11.43\%$$

.13 Cost of Common Equity Under Static Conditions—Net Cost

The three formulas above represent the gross cost of common equity, that is, the cost before the deduction of the costs of selling the new issue. To arrive at the net cost of common equity, multiply the gross cost by:

$$\frac{1}{1-e}$$

Where e = selling cost expressed as a percentage of the total capital raised.

.15 Cost of Common Equity with Pre-emptive Right

Usually existing stockholders of a firm have a premptive right to subscribe to new stock issues in proportion to their existing holdings.

The cost of common equity with preemptive rights is defined as follows:

$$C = \frac{n0\ n2}{(n0+n1)(n1+n2)}\ [Y]\frac{(P)}{(P1)} + \frac{n(n1\ P1 - n2\ RV)}{(n0+n1)(n1+n2)P1}[Y]$$

V = Value of one right defined as:

$$V = \frac{m - m1}{R + 1}$$

Where:

m = Share market price (on-right)

m1 = Subscription price

R = Subscription ratio

Example 4 of cost of common equity if current shareholders exercise their rights to subscribe to new shares: Facts are the same as in examples 1, 2 & 3 plus the present stockholders are given the right to subscribe to 100 new shares on a proportionate basis at a subscription price of $40. Since the current market price is $60 and R = 10 (1000 old shares/100 new shares) each right has a value as follows:

$$V = \frac{m - m1}{R + 1} = \frac{60 - 40}{10 + 1} = \$1.81$$

What is the cost of common equity if the current shareholders exercise their rights and subscribe to 100 new shares at $40 each:

$$C = \frac{(1,000)(50)}{(1,000+50)(50+50)}[.10]\frac{60}{40} + \frac{(1,000+50+50)[(50\text{x}40) - (50\text{x}10\text{x}1.81)]}{(1,000+50)(50+50)(40)}[.10]$$

$$C = \frac{50,000}{105,000}(.15) + \frac{1,100(2,000 - 905)(.10)}{105,000(40)} = 10.01\%$$

.17 Cost of Common Equity Under Simple Growth Conditions

A growth company requires expanding opportunities for profit. A growth company has specific opportunities to invest funds at a perpetual after-tax rate of return, r, that exceeds the rate of return required by stockholders, y. The following formula is based on an investment opportunities approach that states that the market price, P, of shares of a company is composed of the present value of the perpetual earnings on existing assets, plus the per share present value of excess profits arising from the company's ability to invest funds at rates of return above the rate required by stockholders. The cost of common equity is stated as a function of, y, the rate of return required by stockholders as follows:

$$y = \frac{E}{P} + \frac{Eb\,(m - 1)}{P}$$

Where:

r = the perpetual after-tax return per annum that the constant amount each year yields

E = the constant earnings per share on existing assets

b = the fraction of earnings retained

m = perpetual return of specific investment opportunity stated as a function of the rate of return required by stockholders

The price of the company's share would be defined as:

$$P = \frac{E}{y} + \frac{(bE)}{y} + \frac{(r-y)}{y}$$

Example: Company has 1,000 outstanding shares. Company is expected to generate constant perpetual earnings of $5,000/year. The company has opportunities to invest $2,500/year at a perpetual return that is 1.5 times the rate of return required by stockholders.

Therefore:

$$E = \frac{\$5,000}{1,000} = \$5 \quad \text{(constant earnings per share on existing assets)}$$

$$b = \frac{\$2,500}{5,000} = \$.5 \quad \text{(the fraction of earnings retained)}$$

m = 1. 5 (return stated as function of rate of return required by stockholders)

$$y = \frac{5}{P} + \frac{(5)(.5)(1.5-1)}{P}$$

$$y = \frac{5}{P} + \frac{1.25}{P}$$

$$y = \frac{6.25}{P}$$

If P = $25, then y =25%

If P =$50, then y =12.5%

If P =$75, then y = 8.33%

If P = $100, then y = 6.25%

For a growth company, the stockholder's capitaization rate is not measured simply by E/P, but E/P plus a factor that represents the growth potential of the company.

In summary, the stock's current earnings is E = $5,000/1,000 = $5 per share. If stock is selling at $25/share, which is 5 times the company's earnings, the investors are capitalizing the company's earnings at 25%, not 20% ($5/$25=20%).

¶615.17

If stock is selling at $50 per share, which is 10 times the company's earnings, the investors are capitalizing the company's earnings at 12.50%, not 10% ($5/$50=10%).

.19 Cost of Common Equity Under Exponential Growth

The following formula states that the capitalization rate for the company's earnings is equal to the current dividend yield plus the rate at which earnings, dividends, and re-investments are expected to *increase*.

Terms are defined as:

r = The perpetual after-tax return per annum that the constant amount each year yields

b = The fraction of earnings retained

1- b = The fraction of earnings paid out in dividends

E = The constant earnings per share on existing assets

(1- b)E = The per share dividends paid in year 1

Capitalization rate for the company's earnings:

$$y = \frac{(1-b)E}{P} + br$$

The price of the company's share would be defined as:

$$P = \frac{(1-b)E}{y - br}$$

Example: Company has 1,000 outstanding shares. Company is expected to generate constant perpetual earnings of $5,000 per year. The company has opportunities to invest $2,500 per year at a perpetual return that is 1.5 times the rate of return required by stockholders. Therefore:

E = $5 (constant earnings per share existing assets $5,000/$1,000)

b = .5 (the fraction of earnings retained $2,500/$5,000)

m = 1.5 (return stated as a function of a rate of return required by stockholders)

$$y = \frac{(1-b)E}{P} + br$$

$$\text{Where } r = \frac{Em}{P}$$

$$y = \frac{(1-b)E}{P} + \frac{bEm}{P}$$

$$y = \frac{(1 \quad .5)E}{P} + \frac{(.5)(5)(1.5)}{P}$$

$$y = \frac{5 + 2.5 = 3.75}{P}$$

Substituting values obtains:

$$P = \frac{6.25}{y}$$

and solving for y,

$$y = \frac{6.25}{P}$$

If P = \$25, then y = 25%

If P = \$50, then y = 12.5%

If P = \$75, then y = 8.3%

If P = \$100, then y = 6.25%

These capitalization rates are higher than a normal growth company, since, here, there is a *growing* re-investment opportunity for the company.

.20 Cost of Common Equity (Capital Asset Pricing Model)

The CAPM is an idealized concept of how financial markets price securities in relation to perceived risks and the related estimated of expected return. Accordingly an investor is rewarded with higher expected returns for assuming market related risks. This is an unavoidable risk associated with the movement of the market. The investor must estimate the future values of the risk-free risk, the stock's Beta (volatility or correlation of movement in relation to the market) and the expected return in the market. The formula for the estimated cost of equity for a company based on the CAPM is as follows:

Cost of Common Equity =
Risk-free rate + (stock's Beta × (expected return on the stock market as a whole – risk-free rate))

Example: Assume: Stock's Beta = 1.10   Risk-free rate = 6%

Expected return on the stock market as a whole = 15%

Cost of Common Equity   =   6% + (1.10 × (15% – 6%))

=   6% + (9.9%)

=   15.9%

.21 Cost of Capital—Real Estate Method

Cost of Capital

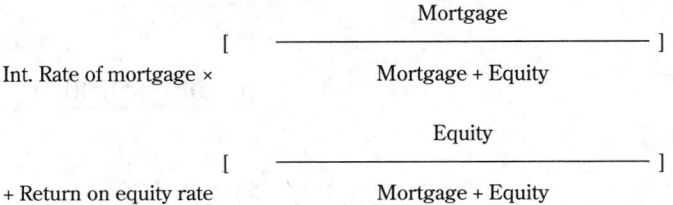

$$\text{Int. Rate of mortgage} \times \left[\frac{\text{Mortgage}}{\text{Mortgage} + \text{Equity}} \right]$$

$$+ \text{Return on equity rate} \left[\frac{\text{Equity}}{\text{Mortgage} + \text{Equity}} \right]$$

Example: What is the cost of capital where equity investors require a 10% return on investment? They will invest \$100,000 on property and obtain a mortgage for the balance of \$950,000 for 20 years at 8% interest.

$$\text{Cost of capital} = .08 \times \left(\frac{\$950,000}{950,000 + 100,000} \right) + .10 \times \left(\frac{\$100,000}{950,000 + 100,000} \right)$$

$$= (.08)(.9048) + (.10)(.0952)$$

$$= .07238 + .00952$$

$$= .08190 \text{ or } \underline{8.19\%}$$

.23 Cost of Capital—Weighted Average

Weighted Average Cost of Capital After Taxes

$$\left(\frac{\text{Interest}(1 - \text{tax rate}) + \text{dividends on common stock}}{\text{Market value of common stock} + \text{non-current liabilities}} \right)$$

$$+ \text{ Compared growth rate of share value} \times \left(\frac{\text{Market value of common stock}}{\text{Market value of common stock} + \text{non - current liabilities}} \right)$$

Example: What is the weighted average cost of capital given:

Non-current interest = 200,000

Non-current liabilities = 2,000,000

Corporate tax rate = 34%

Dividends = $75,000

Common shares outstanding = 800,000

Market value = $6/share

Shares have grown over recent period at 8%

Weighted average cost of capital after taxes

$$= \left(\frac{200,000(1 - .34) + 75,000}{4,800,000 + 2,000,000} \right) + (.08) \left(\frac{4,800,000}{4,800,000 + 2,000,000} \right)$$

$$= .0304 + .0565$$

$$= .0869 \text{ or } 8.69\%$$

¶ 616 Credit Cards

.01 Payment Amount

Given:

Credit card monthly purchase = $1050

Credit card annual rate charged on unpaid balance = 18%

Card minimum payment required this month = $50

How much interest is charged?

Solution:

Convert annual rate to monthly rate: 18% / 12 = 1.5%

$1050 Credit card balance
 – 50 Payment
_____

$1000 Unpaid balance
× 1.5% Monthly interest rate
_____

    $15 Interest charged to carry $1000 on credit card for one month

.02 Interest Rate

Given:

Credit card balance = $4000

$64 is interest owed on the monthly credit card balance

What is the monthly interest rate?

What is the annual interest rate?

Solution:

Monthly rate = $64 / $4000 = 1.6 % monthly

Annual rate = 1.6 × 12 = 19.2 %

¶ 617 DATES

.01 Accumulated Days in a Year

Number of Days Between Dates for Year

Month	Total Days	Accumulated Days
January	31	31
February	28*	59*
March	31	90*
April	30	120*
May	31	151*
June	30	181*
July	31	212*
August	31	243*
September	30	273*
October	31	304*
November	30	334*
December	31	365*

_____

* Add one day for leap years

.03 Number of Days Between Dates

The exact number of days between the corresponding dates of any two months is indicated on the line of the month of the beginning date, under the month of the later date.

Number of Days Between Dates To the Same Day of the Following:

	31 Jan.	28 Feb.	31 Mar.	30 Apr.	31 May	30 June	31 July	31 Aug.	30 Sept	31 Oct.	30 Nov.	31 Dec.
January	365	31	59	90	120	151	181	212	243	273	304	334
February	334	365	21	59	89	120	150	181	212	242	273	303
March	306	337	365	31	61	92	122	153	184	214	245	275
April	275	306	334	365	30	61	91	122	153	183	214	244
May	245	276	304	335	365	31	61	92	123	153	184	214
June	214	245	273	304	334	365	30	61	92	122	15	183
July	184	215	243	274	304	335	365	31	62	92	123	153
August	153	184	212	243	273	304	334	365	31	61	92	122
September	122	153	181	212	242	273	303	334	365	30	61	91
October	92	123	151	182	212	243	273	304	335	365	31	61
November	61	92	120	151	181	212	242	273	304	334	365	30
December	31	62	90	121	151	182	212	243	274	304	335	365

Note: If February 29 of a leap year is included in the period for which the exact number of days is being calculated from the table, add + 1 to the result obtained.

Example: A loan made on July 15 is repaid on September 18. For how many days should interest be calculated?

From table, from July 15 to September 15	= 62 days
Add, from September 15 to September 18	= 3 days
Total days	= 65 days

Example: Number of days from July 15 to September 13?

From table, from July 15 to September 15=	62 days
Subtract September 15 – September 13=	–2 days
Total days	= 60 days

Number of Days Between Dates (use only if time span crosses year)

= [365 (or 366 if leap year)]

+ [Cumulative days prior to terminal month + number of days in terminal month]

– [Cumulative days prior to commencement month + number of days in commencement month]

Example: How many days have elapsed from July 29, 19X1 to September 14, 19X2 (not a leap year)?

Number of days = 365 + (243 + 14) – (181 + 29) = 622 – 210 = 412

.05 Number of Full Months Between Dates

Number of full months = 12 (last full year – first full year + 1)

+ Number of full months in commencement year following commencement month

+ Number of full months in terminal year preceding terminal month.

Example: What is the number of full months between April 15, 1960 and August 18, 1990?

Number of full months = 12 (1989 – 1961 + 1) + 8 + 7 = 363

¶ 619 DEBT

.01 Cost of Debt

Simple cost of debt = Interest/Principal

After tax cost of debt = (Interest/Principal) (1 – tax rate)

Cost of Capital for a Bond

$$\frac{A + B + C}{D}$$

Where:

$$A = (1 - \text{income tax rate}) \times \text{Annual interest payments}$$

$$B = \frac{1}{\text{term of debt}} \left(\begin{array}{l} \text{gross price rec'd by borrower} \\ \text{-net proceeds from debt issue} \end{array} \right)$$

$$C = \frac{1}{\text{term of debt}} \left(\begin{array}{l} \text{face value of bond} \\ \text{-gross price rec'd by borrower} \end{array} \right)$$

$$D = \frac{\text{net proceeds from debt issue} + \text{face value of bond}}{2}$$

.03 After Tax Cost of Interest

Table at ¶ 691.01 illustrates the after-tax percentage cost of interest payments at various tax rates.

When interest is tax deductible, the higher the tax bracket, the lower the true cost of interest: After-tax rate of interest = (1 – marginal tax rate) × (interest rate)

Example: Annual interest rate = 12%

Taxpayer's marginal tax rate = 33%

After tax rate of interest = (1 – .33) × .12 = .0804 or 8.04%

.05 Cost of Debt After Inflation and Taxes

When making financing decisions, consider not just the interest rate, but also the after-tax interest rate and the effects of inflation. It is possible for inflation to reduce the real cost of debt below the after-tax cost of borrowing, and thus provide a "benefit" to the company from borrowing. Most feel that a 4% or 5% inflation rate is representative for recent time periods.

Note:

- The higher the firm's tax rate and/or inflation rate, the higher will be the firm's breakeven interest rate.
- The lower the corporation's effective tax rate, the higher the after-tax cost of debt.
- The higher the interest rate, the higher the after-tax cost of debt.
- Due to the effects of inflation, the borrower can realize a benefit by deducting interest costs and repaying principal with dollars that have less purchasing power than when borrowed.

After Inflation Cost of Debt

The cost of debt rate after inflation can be determined by subtracting the actual inflation rate from the after-tax interest rate.

After Inflation Cost of Debt Rate

(Interest rate × one's complement of tax rate) – inflation rate

> *Example:* Interest rate = 8%

Tax rate = 34%

Determine one's complement of tax rate = 1 – .34 = .66

Inflation rate = 5%

=(8% × (1–.34)) –5%

=5.28% – 5% = .28%

After-Tax Interest Rate

To convert the interest rate into an after tax rate, multiply the interest rate by one's complement of the tax rate (subtract the tax rate from the number 1).

> *Example:* Interest rate = 8%

Tax rate = 34%

One's complement of tax rate = 1 – .34 = .66

After-tax interest rate = 8% × .66 = <u>5.28%</u>

Breakeven Interest Rate

The firm's breakeven interest rate can be calculated taking into account the effects of the firm's marginal tax rate and inflation. The breakeven interest rate is the interest rate giving a real cost of debt of zero. This occurs when the purchasing power borrowed equals the purchasing power repaid. The higher the firm's tax rate and/or inflation rate, the higher will be the firm's breakeven interest rate.

Example of breakeven interest rate:

Inflation rate = 4%

Tax rate = 34%

$$I = \frac{R}{1-T}$$

$$I = \frac{4\%}{1-.34} = 6.06\%$$

Where:

R = Rate of Inflation

T = Tax Rate

I = Breakeven Interest Rate

Therefore, if the inflation rate is 4%, a firm in the 34% tax bracket can incur an interest cost of 6.06% and have no real cost of debt.

Tables at ¶ 691.01 show the breakeven point of borrowing, given different interest rates and different inflation assumptions. Negative numbers indicate a "benefit" of borrowing rather than a cost.

Referring to the portion of the table reproduced below, if a firm were in the 25% tax bracket, and inflation was 4%, then the firm has no real cost of debt if the interest rate charged is 5% or less.

Cost of Debt After Inflation and Taxes (Inflation Rate of 4.0 Percent)

Interest Rate	Tax Rate						
	0%	**15%**	**25%**	**28%**	**33%**	**34%**	**35%**
2%	-2.00%	-2.30%	-2.50%	-2.56%	-2.66%	-2.68%	-2.70%
3%	-1.00%	-1.45%	-1.75%	-1.84%	-1.99%	-2.02%	-2.05%
4%	0.00%	-0.60%	-1.00%	-1.12%	-1.32%	-1.36%	-1.40%
5%	1.00%	0.25%	-0.25%	-0.40%	-0.65%	-0.70%	-0.75%
6%	2.00%	1.10%	0.50%	0.32%	0.02%	-0.04%	-0.10%
7%	3.00%	1.95%	1.25%	1.04%	0.69%	0.62%	0.55%

See ¶691.01 for complete tables.

.06 Cost of Money

Overall Cost of Money by Loans, Receivables and Suppliers' Credit

Determine each source of capital and their related annual percentage rate from:

- Loans
- Suppliers' credit
- Receivable financing

Determine the fractional part from all sources to total. Calculate the before-tax and after-tax effects. Multiply the after-tax cost times the fractional then total the results.

Receivable Loan—Determine the rate of a loan against receivables:

Rate = "Service Charge × (Sales/Receivables)" + Loan Rate

¶619.06

Example: Bank will provide a loan with invoices as security for 10% with a 1% service charge. Total yearly sales are $970,000. Average Accounts Receivables are $65,000.

Rate   =   [.01 × (970,000 / 65,000)] + .10
    =   (.01 × 14.92) + .10
    =   24.9 %

Vendor Discounts—Determine the rate of not taking vendor discounts:

Rate = (Percent discount 5 365) / (Term – Discount Period)

 Example: 2/10 Net 30: Paid 40 days late

Rate   =   (.02 × 365) / (40 – 10)
    =   24.33%

Overall Cost of Money—Annual Analysis

(A)	(B)	(C)	(D)	(E)	(D × E)	(C × F)
Type of Credit	Total $	Fraction of Total	APR	Tax Rate	APR Net of Taxes	Fractional Rate Net of Taxes
Loan						
Loan						
Loan						
Loan						
Loan						
Lost						
Discounts by						
Vendor						
Vendor						
Vendor						
Vendor						
Vendor						
Receivable						
Loan						
	100%			Total Cost of Capital =		

.07 Debt Repayment—Amount Unknown—Annual Installment

The following formula defines the present value of a uniform series of annual payments where the amount of each payment is unknown.

Payment (annuity amount) =

$$\text{Principal} \left[\frac{\text{Annual interest rate } (1 + \text{annual interest rate})^{\text{term in years}}}{[1 + \text{annual interest rate}]^{\text{terms in years}} - 1} \right]$$

¶619.07

Example:

$$\text{Payment} = \$200,000 \left[\frac{.09\,(1+.09)^5}{[1+.09]^5 - 1} \right]$$

$$= \$200,000 \left[\frac{.09\,(1.5386)}{[1.5386] - 1} \right] = \$51,429.63]$$

Taxpayer A purchases land for $200,000 at 9% annual interest, to be paid annually for 5 years. What is the annual payment required to cover the principal plus interest?

Debt Repayment—Amount Unknown—Annual Installment (Alternate Formula)

$$\text{Payment} = \text{Principal} \left[\frac{\text{Annual Interest Rate}}{1 - (1/(1 + \text{Annual interest rate})^{\text{term in years}})} \right]$$

Example:

$$\text{Payment} = \$200,000 \left[\frac{.09}{1 - (1/(1 + .09))} \right]$$

$$= \$200,000\,[.09 / (1 - (1 / 1.5386))]$$
$$= \$200,000\,[.09 / .3501]$$
$$= \$51,413 \text{ (rounding difference)}$$

.09 Debt Repayment—Amount Unknown—Monthly Installments

The following formula defines the present value of a uniform series of monthly payments where the amount of each monthly payment is unknown.

Payment (annuity amount) =

$$\left[\frac{\dfrac{\text{Annual interest rate}}{12} \left[1 + \dfrac{\text{annual interest rate}}{12} \right]^{(12)(\text{term in years})}}{\left[1 + \dfrac{\text{Annual interest rate}}{12} \right]^{(12)(\text{terms in years})} - 1} \right]$$

Example: Corporation X wishes to purchase 2 autos for $35,000. Terms are:

Annual interest rate = 9%

Term of loan = 4 years

What will the monthly payments be to cover the principal plus interest?

¶619.09

$$\text{Payment (Monthly)} = \$35,000 = \left[\frac{\frac{.09}{12}\left[1+\frac{.09}{12}\right]^{12(4)}}{\left[1+\frac{.09}{12}\right]^{12(4)}-1} \right] =$$

$$\$35,000 \left[\frac{.0075(1.0075)^{48}}{(1.0075)^{(48)}-1} \right]$$

$$= \$870.98 \quad \$871$$

.11 Debt Repayment—Total Unknown with Given Monthly Installments

Use the following formula to determine the total cost when monthly payments are known.

Future value =

$$\text{Monthly payment}\left[\frac{1-[1+(\text{annual interest rate}/12]^{-(12)(\text{term in years})}}{\dfrac{\text{annual interest rate}}{12}} \right]$$

Example: Corporation X wishes to purchase two new autos. Management has determined that they can comfortably cash flow a payment of $870.98/month. The corporation's bank will provide a 4 year term note at 9%, repaid monthly. What is the total cost to the corporation X to purchase the two new vehicles?

$$\text{Future value} = \$870.98 \left[\frac{1-(1+.09)^{-(12)(4)}}{\dfrac{.09}{12}} \right]$$

$$= \$870.98 \left[\frac{1-(1.0075)^{-48}}{(.0075)} \right]$$

$$= \$870.98 \left[\frac{1-.6986}{.0075} \right]$$

$$= \$35,000$$

.13 Credit—Cost of Credit

A company's real cost of credit should be analyzed. When a company enters into a formal credit arrangement (loan, line of credit, etc.) with a bank, the borrowing costs may include compensating balances, interest charges, committment fees, etc. With such a credit analysis, various credit options demonstrate advantages or disadvantages on which terms are negotiated regarding money management alternatives. The following formulas determine the average available funds, dollar costs of credit, effective interest rates, and average borrowings that emphasize the real cost of credit.

Average available funds (on credit line) =

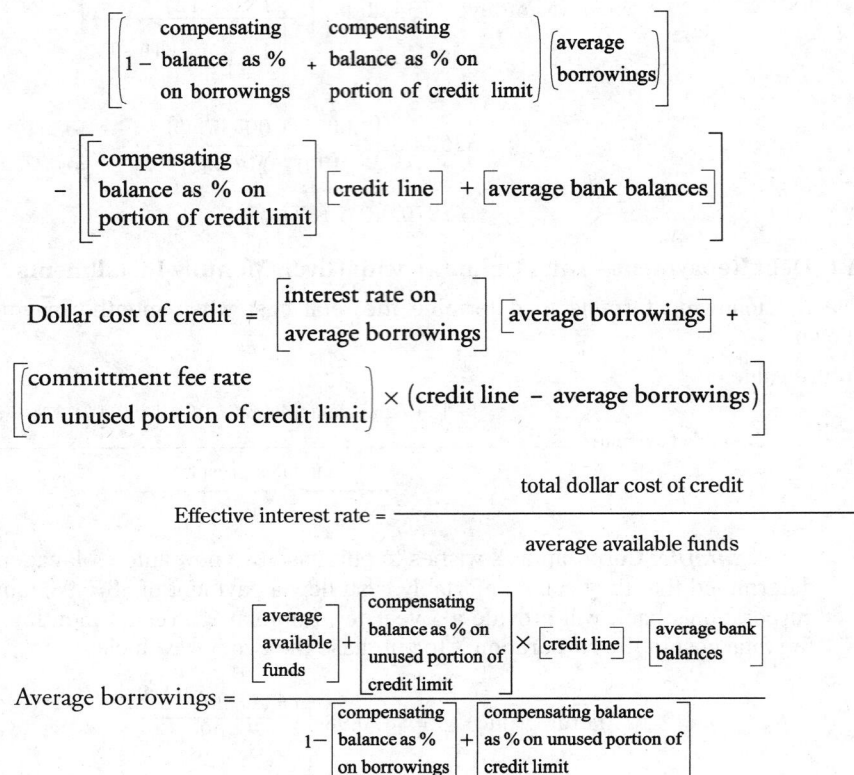

$$\text{Dollar cost of credit} = \begin{bmatrix} \text{interest rate on} \\ \text{average borrowings} \end{bmatrix} \begin{bmatrix} \text{average borrowings} \end{bmatrix} +$$

$$\begin{bmatrix} \text{committment fee rate} \\ \text{on unused portion of credit limit} \end{bmatrix} \times (\text{credit line} - \text{average borrowings})$$

$$\text{Effective interest rate} = \frac{\text{total dollar cost of credit}}{\text{average available funds}}$$

$$\text{Average borrowings} = \frac{\begin{bmatrix} \text{average} \\ \text{available} \\ \text{funds} \end{bmatrix} + \begin{bmatrix} \text{compensating} \\ \text{balance as \% on} \\ \text{unused portion of} \\ \text{credit limit} \end{bmatrix} \times \begin{bmatrix} \text{credit line} \end{bmatrix} - \begin{bmatrix} \text{average bank} \\ \text{balances} \end{bmatrix}}{1 - \begin{bmatrix} \text{compensating} \\ \text{balance as \%} \\ \text{on borrowings} \end{bmatrix} + \begin{bmatrix} \text{compensating balance} \\ \text{as \% on unused portion of} \\ \text{credit limit} \end{bmatrix}}$$

Example: Firm A has negotiated a line of credit for $3 million. What are the associated credit costs given the following data:

Committment fee rate on unused portion of credit limit	= .3%
Interest rate on average borrowings	= 8%
Average bank balances	= $50,000
Compensating balance as % on unused portion of credit limit	= 10%
Compensating balance against borrowed funds	= 15%
Average borrowings (owed past 12 months)	= $800,000

Average available funds
= [(1 –.15 + .10) ($800,000)] – (.10) ($3,000,000) + $50,000
= $760,000 – $300,000 + $50,000
= $510,000

Dollar cost of credit
= (.08) ($800,000) + (.003) ($3,000,000 – $800,000)
= $64,000 + $6,600
= $70,600

Effective interest rate = $\dfrac{\$70,600}{\$510,000}$ = 13.84%

$$\text{Average borrowings} = \frac{\$510,000 + (.10)(\$3,000,000) - (\$50,000)}{(1-.15+.10)} = \$800,000$$

.15 Credit—Target Liquidity

The following formula defines the desired liquidity position of a firm as consisting of cash, plus marketable securities, plus its credit line. The sales may be actual or projected sales. The credit line may be included or excluded from the formula. For smaller businesses, the liquidity is defined as cash, or cash plus near-cash assets.

$$\text{Target liquidity} = \frac{\text{desired cash balances + near cash assests + credit line sales}}{\text{sales}}$$

¶ 621 DEPLETION

.01 Depletion is the Systematic Writeoff of the Exhausting of Natural Resources

Depletion

$$\frac{\text{Cost - salvage}}{\text{Estimated total output in units}}(\text{current output})$$

Example: Given the following data, what is the annual depletion in year 3?

Cost = $4,000,000

Salvage = $0

Estimated total output in tons=20 million tons. 500 tons are sold in year 3.

Current output = 500,000

$$\text{Depletion} = \frac{\$4,000,000 - 0}{20,000,000}(500,000)$$

$$= \$100,000$$

.03 Estimated Production of a Wasting Asset

Estimated Reserve

$$\frac{(\text{Current year's production})(1-(\text{rate of decline})^{(\text{number of years})})}{1-(\text{rate of decline})}$$

Example: Oil well production is estimated to decrease at 25% per year.

Current year's production = 25,000 barrels.

After 5 years, the well will be abandoned as economically infeasible.

What is the estimated remaining production?

Rate of decline = (1 − decrease rate) = (1 − .25) = .75

$$\text{Estimated reserve} = \frac{25,000(1-(.75)^5)}{1-.75}$$

$$= 25,000 \frac{(1-.2373)}{1-.75} = \frac{19.068}{.25} = 76,270 \text{ (barrels)}$$

¶ 623 DEPRECIATION

.01 Composite Rate of Depreciation

Rate of Group

$$\frac{\text{Asset 1 deprec} + \text{asset 2 depec} + \text{asset 3 deprec}...}{\text{total cost of assets}}$$

$$= \frac{\dfrac{\text{Cost - salvage}}{\text{life}} + \dfrac{\text{Cost - salvage}}{\text{life}} + ...}{\text{total cost of assets}}$$

Depreciation = composite rate 3 total cost of all assets

Example: What is composite rate of depreciation for the following group?

	Cost	Salvage	Life
Asset 1	500	50	5
Asset 2	800	100	7
Asset 3	1,100	150	7
Asset 4	1,200	200	5
	3,600		

$$\text{Depreciation rates} = \frac{\dfrac{500-50}{5} + \dfrac{800-100}{7} + \dfrac{1,100-150}{7} + \dfrac{1,200-200}{5}}{3,600}$$

$$= \frac{90+100+136+200}{3,600}$$

$$= \frac{526}{3,600} = .1461 \text{ or } 14.61\%$$

If at year end the group of assets totalled $5,000, what is the depreciation expense for that year?

Depreciation (composite) = $5,000 × .1461 = $731

.02 Straight-Line Method of Depreciation

Straight-Line Depreciation

$$\frac{\text{cost - salvage}}{\text{life}}$$

Example: An asset cost $50,000. Its estimated life is 7 years. The estimated salvage is $8,000. What is the annual depreciation charge?

$$\text{Depreciation} = \frac{\$50,000 - \$8,000}{7} = \$6,000$$

.03 Straight Line with Maintenance

The following formula implies that the asset wears out at an even rate throughout its life. It does not encompass the time value of money. It requires an economic forecast of the assets' life. The economic life is not necessarily the same as service life or ownership life.

Annual Depreciation (straight line with maintenance) =

$$\frac{\text{(Original basis of asset – salvage)} + \text{Maint. costs during life of asset}}{\text{Economic life in years}}$$

Example: What is the annual depreciation cost given the following data:

Cost	= $50,000	total maintenance costs	= $12,000
Salvage	= $3,000	economic life	= 10 years

Annual Depreciation (straight line with maintenance) =

$$\frac{(\$50,000 - \$3,000) + \$12,000}{10} = \$5,900$$

.04 Capital Recovery

The following formula calculates the capital recovery depreciation, which is the annual payment to recover the asset's depreciation, if those funds had been available for alternate uses.

Capital recovery depreciation = [Original basis of asset-salvage]

$$\left[\frac{\text{interest rate} \times (1 + \text{interest rate})^{\text{economic life in years}}}{(1 + \text{interest rate})^{\text{economic life in years}} - 1}\right]$$

Example: Given the following data, what is the annual payment to recover the depreciation of the asset, plus an acceptable rate of return?

Cost of asset =	$50,000	Interest rate =	9%
Economic life =	10 years	Salvage =	$5,000

Capital recovery depreciation =

$$[\$50,000 - \$5,000]\left[\frac{.09(1+.09)^{10}}{(1+.09)^{10} - 1}\right] = (\$45,000)\frac{(.21306)}{1.3674} = \$7,012$$

Proof: Multiply the above result by the present value of an annuity.

$$= (\$7{,}012)\frac{(1-(1+.09)^{10}}{.09}$$

$$= (\$7{,}012)\frac{(1-.4224)}{.09}$$

$$= (\$7{,}012)\,(6.418)$$

Depreciation as Capital Recovery

The following table illustrates how a company that purchases an asset can recover its capital over the economic life and provides a return at a given interest rate on the outstanding investment. The "depreciation" of the asset represents capital recovery. This illustrates the use of a capital recovery factor, where the investor recovers his original investment, plus a 9% return. Assume the following data:

Cost of asset	=	$50,000
Economic life	=	10 years
Interest rate	=	9%

Compute the approximation that represents annual capital recovery for a 10 year period, with straight line depreciation, plus average annual interest of 9%.

Capital recovery (annual amount at 9% for 10 yr period)

= cost × capital recovery estimation factor

= $50,000 × .1558

= $7,790

Capital Recovery Table: Factor of 1

n	9%	10%	11%	12%
1	1.09000000	1.10000000	1.11000000	1.12000000
2	0.56846890	0.57619048	0.58393365	0.59169811
3	0.39505476	0.40211480	0.40921307	0.41634898
4	0.30866866	0.31547080	0.32232635	0.32923444
5	0.25709246	0.26379748	0.27057031	0.27740973
6	0.22291978	0.22960738	0.23637656	0.24322572
7	0.19869052	0.20540550	0.21221527	0.21911774
8	0.18067438	0.18744402	0.19432105	0.20130284
9	0.16679880	0.17364054	0.18060166	0.18767889
10	0.15582009	0.16274539	0.16980143	0.17698416
11	0.14694666	0.15396314	0.16112101	0.16841540
12	0.13965066	0.14676332	0.15402729	0.16143681
13	0.13356656	0.14077852	0.14815099	0.15567720
14	0.12843317	0.13574622	0.14322820	0.15087125
15	0.12405888	0.13147378	0.13906524	0.14682424
16	0.12029991	0.12781662	0.13551675	0.14339002
17	0.11704625	0.12466413	0.13247148	0.14045673
18	0.11421229	0.12193022	0.12984287	0.13793731
19	0.11173041	0.11954687	0.12756250	0.13576300
20	0.10954648	0.11745962	0.12557564	0.13387878
21	0.10761663	0.11562439	0.12383793	0.13224009

n	9%	10%	11%	12%
22	0.10590499	0.11400506	0.12231310	0.13081051
23	0.10438188	0.11257181	0.12097118	0.12955997
24	0.10302256	0.11129978	0.11978721	0.12846344
25	0.10180625	0.11016807	0.11874024	0.12749997

.05 Capital Recovery Factor—Estimation

The following formula approximates the capital recovery factor with straight line depreciation plus average annual interest, if the time frame is reasonably short.

Capital recovery factor

$$= \frac{1}{\text{economic life in years}} + \frac{\text{interest rate (economic life in yrs.} + 1)}{2 \text{ (economic life in years)}}$$

Example: Assume interest rate = 9 percent and economic life is 10 years.

$$\text{Capital recovery factor} = \frac{1}{10} + \frac{.09(10.+1)}{2(10)}$$
$$= .1 + .0495$$
$$= .1495$$

Note: The exact capital recovery factor = .1558

.06 Units of Production Method of Depreciation

Units of Production Depreciation

$$(\text{cost - salvage}) \times \left[\frac{\text{units produced this year}}{\text{total estimated units over life}} \right]$$

Example: Machine cost = $80,000

Estimated salvage = $7,500

Total number of units machine will produce = 600,000

Total number of units produced in year 2 = 35,000

$$\text{Depreciation (year 2)} = \$4,229 \; (\$80,000 - 7,500) \times \left[\frac{35,000}{600,000} \right] = \$4,229$$

.07 Sum of Years Digits Method of Depreciation

Sum of Years Depreciation

$$(\text{cost - salvage}) \times \left[\frac{\text{Life of asset} - \text{Number of years prior depreciation}}{\text{Sum of the years digits}} \right]$$

Note: Sum of years digits $= \left[\dfrac{\text{Life of asset} + 1}{2} \right] \times (\text{Life of asset})$

¶623.07

Example: Asset cost = $150,000

Estimated life = 10 years

Salvage = $15,000

What is the amount of depreciation in year 6?

$$\text{Sum of years digits } = \left(\frac{10+1}{2}\right)(10) = 55$$

$$\text{Depreciation (years 6)} = \left(\frac{10-5}{55}\right) \times (\$150,000 - 15,000)$$
$$= .0909 \times \$135,000$$
$$= \$12,272$$

.08 Sum of the Years Digits (Method 2)

Another form of the formula is as follows:

$$\text{Depreciation} = \left[\frac{2\,(\text{life of asset} - \text{year of depreciation} + 1)}{\text{life of asset}\,(\text{life of asset} + 1)}\right]\left[\text{cost} - \text{salvage}\right]$$

Example: Asset cost = $150,000

Estimated life = 10 years

Salvage = $15,000

What is the depreciation in year 6?

$$\text{Depreciation} = \left[\frac{2(10-6+1)}{10(10+1)}\right]\,(\$150,000 - \$15,000)$$

$$= \left[\frac{2(5)}{10(11)}\right]\,(\$135,000) = \$12,272$$

Sum of the Years Digits - Book Value at Year X

Book Value (at end of year 6) =

$$\left[\frac{(\text{life of asset} - \text{year x})[(\text{life of asset} - \text{year x}) + 1\,(\text{cost} - \text{salvage})]}{\text{life of asset}\,(\text{life of asset} + 1)}\right]\left[\text{salvage}\right]$$

Given the above data, what is the book value of the asset at the end of year 3?

Book Value (at end of year 3) =

$$= \left[\frac{(10-3)\,(10-3+1)\,(\$150,000 - \$15,000)}{10(10+1)}\right] + [\$15,000]$$

¶623.08

$$= \frac{(7)\,(8)\,(\$135{,}000)}{110} + \$15{,}000 = \$83{,}727$$

.09 200 Percent Declining Balance Method of Depreciation

200% Declining Balance Depreciation

$$2 \times \left[\frac{(\text{cost - salvage}) - \text{accumulated depreciation at beginning of year}}{\text{life}} \right]$$

Example: Cost of assets = $50,000

Salvage = $5,000

Estimated life = 7 years

Accum. deprec. at beginning of year = $1,500

$$\text{Depreciation} = 2 \left[\frac{(\$50{,}000 - 5{,}000) - \$1{,}500}{7} \right] = \$12{,}429$$

.10 Depreciation—Declining Balance Method

The declining balance method of depreciation applies a fixed rate to the net asset value. As the asset value declines the depreciation declines.

$$\text{Depreciation} = 1 - {}^{\text{life of asset}}\sqrt{\frac{\text{Salvage}}{\text{Cost of asset}}}$$

Example: Cost of asset = $150,000

Estimated life = 10 years

Salvage value = $15,000

What is the depreciation using the declining balance method?

$$\text{Depreciation (declining balance method)} = 1 - {}^{10}\sqrt{\frac{\$15{,}000}{\$150{,}000}}$$

$$= 1 - {}^{10}\sqrt{.10}$$

$$= 1 - .7943$$

$$= .2057 = 20.57\%$$

.11 Declining Balance Depreciation—Book Value at Year X

The following formula approximates the book value at year x using the declining balance depreciation method.

Book Value (at end of year x) =

$$\left[\text{Cost of asset} \right] \, {}^{\text{Life of asset}}\sqrt{\left[\frac{\text{salvage}}{\text{cost of asset}} \right]}^{\,\text{year x}}$$

Example: Cost of asset = $150,000

Estimated life = 10 years

Salvage value = $15,000

What is the book value of the asset at the end of year 6 using the declining balance depreciation method?

$$\text{Book value (at end of year 6)} = [\$150,000]\left(\sqrt[10]{\left[\frac{\$15,000}{\$150,000}\right]^6}\right)$$

$$= (\$150,000)\left(\sqrt[10]{.000001}\right)$$
$$= (\$150,000)\,(.2512)$$
$$= \$37,680$$

.12 200 Percent Declining Balance Method—Book Value at Year X

The following formula approximates the book value at year x using the 200% declining balance depreciation method.

$$\text{Book value (at end of year x)} = [\text{cost of asset}]\left[1 - \frac{2}{\text{life of asset}}\right]^{\text{year x}}$$

Example: Cost of asset = $50,000

Salvage = $5,000

What is the book value of the asset at the end of year 3 using the 200% declining balance method of depreciation?

Estimated life = 7 years

$$\text{Book value (at end of year 3)} = \left[(\$50,000)\ 1 - \frac{2}{7}\right]^3$$

$$= (\$50,000\,(.71429)^3)$$
$$= \$18,222$$

.13 200 Percent Declining Balance Method-Year to Switch to Straight Line

If an asset is continually depreciated using the 200% double declining method, each year will compute smaller and smaller amounts of depreciation. Theoretically, this can continue indefinitely. However, at the end of the economic life, there will be an undepreciated balance. By switching somewhere during the term to straight line, the balance can be easily depreciated to zero. The following formulas determine the beginning year to switch to straight line depreciation.

If economic life is odd number:

$$\text{Year to switch to st. line} = \frac{\text{Life of asset}}{2} + \frac{3}{2}$$

If economic life is even number:

$$\text{Year to switch to st. line} = \frac{\text{Life of asset}}{2} + 2$$

Example: Given the above data, in what year should the change to straight line be made?

$$\text{Year to switch to st. line (old)} = \frac{7}{2} + \frac{3}{2}$$

$$= \frac{10}{2} = 5$$

Switch at the beginning of year 5. Straight line depreciation should be made for year 5, 6, and 7.

.14 200 Percent Declining Balance Method—Accumulated—Depreciation Not Known

Use the following formula to calculate the annual depreciation for year x, where the accumulated depreciation is unknown.

Depreciation (200% declining balance at year x)

$$= \frac{2}{\text{life of asset}} \left[1 - \frac{2}{\text{life of asset}} \right]^{\text{year x - 1}} \left[\text{cost of asset} \right]$$

Example: Cost of asset = $50,000

Salvage = $5,000

Estimated life = 7 years

What is the 200 percent declining balance of depreciation for year 3?

$$\frac{2}{7} \left[1 - \frac{2}{7} \right]^{3-1} (\$50,000) = .2857(.5102)(\$50,000) = \$7,288$$

.15 Depreciation—Service Hours

The depreciation service hour method is based on the amount of time an asset functions. This method implies that an asset is serviceable as long as it can economically produce. The physical life of the asset is what the depreciation life is base on. Depreciation is stated as a function of useage of time, typically, per hour.

$$\text{Depreciation per hour} = \frac{(\text{Cost - salvage}) + \text{maintenance}}{\text{Estimated useful life in hours}}$$

Example: What is the rate of depreciation per hour given:

Cost= $50,000   Estimated useful life in hours= 200,000

Salvage=$5,000   Maintenance of estimated useful life= $7,000

$$\text{Depreciation per hour} = \frac{(\$50,000 - \$5,000) + \$7,000}{200,000} = \$.26$$

Service Hours—Book Value

Book value at end of x hours of use =

$$(\text{Cost} + \text{maintenance}) - \left[\frac{\text{cost} - \text{salvage} - \text{maintenance}}{\text{estimated useful life in hours}}\right] \times \left[\text{hours of use}\right]$$

Example: What is the book value of the asset above at the end of 52,000 hours of use?

Book value (at end of 52,000 hours)

$$= (\$50,000 + \$7,000) \quad \frac{\$50,000 \quad \$5,000 + \$7,000}{200,000} (52,000)$$

$$= (\$57,000) \quad (\$.26)(52,000)$$

$$= \$43,480$$

.16 Depreciation—Productive Output (per unit)

Instead of using any factor relating to time, the productive output depreciation method corresponds to depreciation charges per unit. Depreciation using the productive output method is defined as:

$$= \frac{(\text{cost} - \text{salvage}) + \text{maintenance}}{\text{estimated output in units}}$$

Example: Given the following data, what is the depreciation per unit of a cutting machine?

Cost = $50,000   Maintenance = $15,000

Salvage = $5,000   Estimated output in units = 800,000

$$\text{Depreciation per unit} = \frac{(\$50,000 - \$5,000) + \$15,000}{800,000} = \$.075$$

.17 Depreciation Tax Effect

The following illustrates the estimated tax savings and subsequent net cost to a business associated with depreciation expense write-off.

Gross Depreciation Deduction	$20,000
Employer Tax Rates:	
Federal Income tax rate	15%
State Income tax rate (deductible on Federal return)	2%

Depreciation deduction	$20,000
(Less) Tax savings	3,400
Net Cost to Business	16,600

.18 Accumulated Depreciation—Declining Balance Method

Accumulated Depreciation at End of Year

$$\text{Cost} \times \left[1 - \left(1 - \text{rate of depreciation} \right)^{(\text{number of years})} \right]$$

Example: What should the accumulated depreciation be at the end of year 3, using the declining balance method if the asset cost $15,000, has salvage value of $3,500, and the constant rate = .1429 (using IRS required years of 7, the constant rate is 1/7 = .1429)

Accumulated depreciation at end of year 3

$$= \$15,000 \left[1 - \left(1 - .1429 \right)^3 \right]$$
$$= \$15,000 \left[1 - (.6296) \right]$$
$$= \$5,556$$

.19 Accumulated Depreciation—Double Declining Balance Method

Accumulated Depreciation at End of Year

$$\left(\text{Cost Salvage} \right) \times \left[1 - \left(1 - \frac{2}{\text{life}} \right)^{(\text{number of years expired})} \right]$$

Example: Cost = $12,000

Salvage = $2,500

Life = 7 years

What is the accumulated depreciation at the end of year 3?

$$= (\$12,000 - 2,500) \times \left[1 - \left(1 - \left(\frac{2}{7} \right) \right)^3 \right]$$

$$= \$9,500 \times \left[1 - \left(1 - (.71422)^3 \right) \right]$$
$$= \$9,500 \times \left[1 - (.3645) \right]$$
$$= \$9,500 \times .6355$$
$$= \$6,037$$

.20 Accumulated Depreciation—Sum of Years Digits Method

Accumulated Depreciation at End of Year N

$$\left(\text{Cost} - \text{Salvage}\right)$$

$$\times \left[1 - \frac{\left(\text{Remaining life of asset}\left(\text{Remaining life of asset} + 1\right)\right)}{2 \times \left(\text{sum of years}\right)}\right]$$

Example: Asset Cost = $12,000

Salvage = $2,000

Life = 8 years

What is the balance in the accumulated depreciation account at the end of year 3?

Accumulated depreciation at end of year 3

$$= \left(\$12,000 - \$2,000\right) \times \left[1 - \frac{5\left(5 + 1\right)}{2\left(36\right)}\right]$$

$$= \$10,000 \times \left(1 - .4167\right)$$
$$= \$5,833$$

.21 Book Value At End of Specific Year

The above formula can be rearranged to derive the book value of the asset for any given year.

$$\text{Book Value (at end of year x)} = \left[\begin{array}{l}\text{original basis} + \text{maintenance cost} \\ \text{of asset during life of asset}\end{array}\right]$$

$$\left[\begin{array}{l}\text{original basis} - \text{salvage} + \text{maintenance cost} \\ \text{of asset during life of asset} \\ \hline \qquad\qquad \text{economic life in years}\end{array}\right] \times \left(\text{end of year x}\right)$$

Original basis of asset = $50,000

Maintenance cost = $12,000

Salvage = $3,000

Economic Life = 10 years

Given the data above, what is the book value of the asset at the end of year 3?

¶623.20

Book Value (at the end of year 3)

$$= \$50,000 + \$12,000 - \left[\frac{\$50,000 - \$3000 + \$12,000}{10}\right] \times 3$$

$$= \$62,000 - (\$59,000 / 10) \times 3$$
$$= \$62,000 - \$17,700$$
$$= \$44,300$$

¶ 625 EARNINGS PER SHARE

.01 Primary Earnings per Share (PEPS)

"If converted" method

Facts: Corp. had 300,000 shares of common stock outstanding during 19X1.

Net income for 19X1 was $800,000.

Also outstanding were $600,000, 8% interest, debentures convertible into 30,000 shares of common stock.

The debentures are common stock equivalents.

Tax rate is 25%.

Primary earnings per share is computed as follows:

Primary Earnings per Share

$$\frac{\text{net income} + \left[\text{debentures interest rate} \times (1 - \text{tax rate}) \times \text{debentures}\right]}{\text{common stock} + \text{common stock equivalents}}$$

$$\text{PEPS} = \frac{\$800,000 + \left[8\% \times (1 - .25) \times \$600,000\right]}{300,000 + 30,000}$$

$$= \frac{\$836,000}{330,000} = \$2.53$$

.03 Fully Diluted Earnings per Share

Facts: Corp. has 800,000 common shares outstanding throughout year.

Also outstanding were $5,000,000, 5% interest, debentures convertible into 200,000 common shares. The bonds were issued at face value with the average yield of Aa corporate bonds at 6%.

Corp. has $2,000,000 current net income.

Tax rate is 25%.

Because the bond yield is not less than 2/3 of the average yield of Aa corporate bonds (i.e., 5%/6% = .83) at the date of issuance, the convertible bonds are not CSEs and do not enter into the computation of FDEPS.

The PEPS and FDEPS computations are:

Primary Earnings per Share

$$\frac{\text{Net income}}{\text{common stock}}$$

$$\text{Primary earnings per share} = \frac{\$2,000,000}{800,000} = \underline{\$2.50}$$

Fully Diluted Earnings Per Share

$$\frac{\text{net income} + (\text{interest} - \text{tax})}{\text{common stock} + (\text{assumed bond conversion})}$$

$$\text{Fully diluted earnings per share} = \frac{\$2,000,000 + (\$250,000 - \$62,500)}{800,000 + 200,000} = \underline{\$2.19}$$

¶ 627 EMPLOYEE STOCK OWNERSHIP PLAN

.01 Value and Number of Shares

ESOP—Diluted Value per Share—Number of Shares Contributed

Diluted Value of Shares

$$\frac{\left(\text{Share value prior to dilution} \times \text{Number of primary shares outstanding}\right) - \text{Dollar of contribution to ESOP}}{\text{Number of primary shares outstanding}}$$

$$\text{Number of shares} = \frac{\text{Dollar of contribution to ESOP}}{\text{Diluted value of share}}$$

Example: Market value of current shares outstanding = \$45/share, and the company will contribute \$400,000 of new stock to the ESOP.

Current outstanding shares = 150,000.

What is the diluted value per share? How many new shares will be issued?

$$\text{Diluted value per share} = \frac{(\$45 \times 150,000) - \$400,000}{150,000} = \underline{\$42.33}$$

$$\text{Number of shares} = \frac{\$400,000}{\$42.33 \text{ per share}} = \underline{9,450}$$

¶ 629 FACTORIAL

Factorial is the number of different arrangements of all of the elements.

.01 Factorial

$$m! = m(m-1)(m-2)...(3)(2)(1)$$

(note: 0! = 1)

> ***Example:*** What is 6!
>
> | 6! | = | $6 \times 5 \times 4 \times 3 \times 2 \times 1$ |
> |---|---|---|
> | | = | $\frac{720}{}$ |

¶ 631 FINANCIAL ANALYSIS

.01 Management Analysis

Accounts Receivable—Collections

- Are credit policies reviewed periodically
- Do customers understand the firm's credit policies?
- Is credit insurance utilized?
- Is the invoice difficult to understand due to codes or acronyms?
- On collection calls, have the accounts receivable clerks take notes and document the situation with proper information that management can review and use to take proper action.
- Is analysis made of A/R by:
  - Credit limits
  - Volume of credit sales
  - Customer turnover
- Are new credit customers investigated adequately?
- Is there a credit manager?
- Are sales contracts written to permit recovery of collection fees?
- Have credit management policies been established?
- Are there established credit limits? Are they enforced?
- Is there a final review of accounts to attempt collection before writeoff?
- Are overdue accounts promptly followed up?

Accounts Receivable Controls

- Are there proper controls of accounts receivable that may reduce the need for borrowed funds?
- Does the A/R system provide for proper analysis; by customer; by aging?
- Are accounts receivable seasonal in nature?
- Are controls in place to safeguard assets?
- Are returns and allowances controlled properly?

Accounts Receivable Cash Flow—Maximizing

- Are major collection efforts spent on the largest balances?
- Can billing errors be reduced?
- Can invoicing be done more frequently?
- Are dunning notices used?
- Will cash discounts improve collectability?
- Can salesman commissions be paid when collections have been made?
- Are accounts receivable statements prepared to summarize invoices?
- Should receivables be factored?
- Consider converting A/R invoices into promissory notes at the 60-day aging period. This takes possible bad debts and turns them into current obligations. This may help eliminate confusion on a possible whole mess of invoices into just one promissory note. Seek to receive a personal guarantor signature on the promissory note which should also include agreement to pay attorney or collection fees if the promissory note is defaulted on.
- Generally, if the executive or owner will guarantee the payment, this provides a good indication of the confidence regarding their feelings about their company. If they refuse to sign, they may view their company as in trouble, and it may be time to turn the account over to a collection agency or attorney.
  - Will interest be charged on the note?
  - Can the note be discounted?

Accounts Payable Management

- Is a proper analysis regularly made of A/P concerning:
  - Aging, due dates, discounts?
- Is there a formal accounts payable policy?
- Are terms sought to:
  - Increase credit amounts?
  - Extend payment days?
- Are payments made at the maximum time due?
- Can some supplier payments safely be postponed?
- Are discounts timely taken?
- Do vendors supply products on a timely basis?
- Are vendors' supplies quality acceptable?
- Are lost discounts properly monitored?
- Are there excessive returns to vendors?
- Overall costs of ordering reduced by:
  - Ordering by phone?
  - Using FAX machines?
- Is larger storage required to support purchasing decisions?
- Should "number of vendors used" be reduced?

¶631.01

— Will this provide for better service or better quality?

— Can redesign of product reduce parts needed or eliminate outside purchases?

- Can "number of purchases made" be reduced?
  — Special packaging?
  — More reliable delivery?
  — Special delivery services?
  — Possible technical help?
  — Will this provide for better overall relations?

Accounts Payable—Maximizing Cash Retention

- Hold vendor payments to length of terms.
- Minimize discretionary purchases.
- Reduce or eliminate repayments of expenses.
- Strive for zero balance checking on non-interest bearing accounts.

Accounts Payable—Cash Disbursements

- Limit who can sign checks.
- Strive to make all payments by check.
- A check protector should be used to prevent alteration.
- Never pre-sign blank checks.
- A cash disbursement journal should be prepared in numerical order.
- Supporting documentation should be attached to the check.

Accounts Payable—Outsourcing

- Hiring outsiders to handle the A/P function can provide savings in many cases. The outsouce provider can create a synergistic relationship.
- A qualified outsources can bring a level of expertise that may not exist internally.
- Can improve service and reduce costs.
- Can provide for more efficient use of current human workforce.
- Provides processing at a fixed unit cost which allows for budgeting.
- This can be the entire function, or any part thereof. For instance, only the payments might be outsourced.
- The business continues to control what is paid, by requiring certain authorization over set $ limits, or that a purchase order be matched with the invoice and have appropriate departmental approval.
- Businesses should consider A/P outsourcing if:
  — Payable function is decentralized, which often results in duplicate activities.
  — Are there multiple systems?
  — Does company need to reduce staff?
  — There has been a sharp growth or decline
  — The payables process is antiquated, not streamlined.

Accounts Payable—Cost Savings on Outsourcing

- Handling costs eliminated
- Human handling costs reduced
- Postage eliminated
- Paper checks, etc. eliminated
- Printer costs eliminated
- Storage costs eliminated
- Lost/stop check costs eliminated
- Bank lock-box costs eliminated
- Other bank charges eliminated
- Delivery charges—none

Benchmarking

A technique used by management to improve internal performance by continually identifying and adapting outstanding practices and processes found inside and outside the organization.

A benchmark is an improvement goal. It can be used to raise a company's expectations in whatever area it is applied.

A benchmark is a better way of doing something without "reinventing the wheel."

A benchmark is designed to raise a company's expectations of its processes.

A benchmark to shoot for, can provide an exponential improvement in its cost structure or performance for the company.

Ratio Comparisons to Other Companies

Where to obtain benchmark ratios for comparisons:

- Industry groups
- Trade associations
- Prominent corporations often conduct surveys
- Workshops
- Seminars
- Regional groups
- Government statistical reports
- Risk Management Association (www.rmahq.org)

Cash Management

Cash Deposits—Accelerating

- Use banks that provide instant credit on charge cards.
- Use wire transfers to centralized bank from depository locations.
- Use minimum number of bank accounts.
- Use one centralized bank.

¶631.01

- Deposit earlier in the day.
- Deposits should be made daily.
- Independently prepared cash receipts journal should compare with the deposit slips.

Cash Management—Overall

- Maximize investment opportunities.
- Minimize borrowing costs.
- Hasten cash inflow-delay cash outflow.
- Provide for best sources of borrowings.

Cash Management—Implementation of Changes

- Develop an attitude in employees of cash efficiency.
- Implement as soon as possible changes that require the least effort.
- Focus on the techniques that will provide the most financial benefit.

Cash Management of Disbursements

- Seek to maximize terms and discounts with vendors.
- Use direct deposit of payroll.
- Pay by check to provide float time not available with wire transfers.
- Take vendor discounts.

Cash Management of Accounts Payable

- Use automated A/P system that lets the firm maximize the time to pay by taking discounts to end of vendor terms.
- Consider having salesman use credit cards rather than taking cash advances and consider mailing payments on Thursday or Friday to take advantage of weekend mail float.

Misappropriation

- The visibility of managers can help mimimize irregularities.
- Look for collusion among employees.
- Be aware of attitudes of an employee who may insist on total control of his job information, seldom takes time off from work, and does not allow other employees to do his work when absent.
- Provide for secret controls to monitor employees.

Debt Analysis

- Does the company adhere to the matching principle?
  - — Short-term debt for short-term needs
  - — Long-term debt for long-term needs
- Is the company's overall debt to equity ratio proper?
- What is the ratio of current debt to non-current debt?
- Is debt budgeted properly?
- Does the company plan to convert any debt into equity?

- Does the company have an adequate line of credit?
- Does the company have a debt reduction plan?
- Will there be adequate cash available to timely meet repayment needs?

Equity Management

- What is the composition of common stock among the shareholders?
- Are there preferred stock shareholders?
- Is the company overcapitalized or undercapitalized?
- Does the firm pay appropriate dividends?
- Are the firm's debt to equity ratios proper?
- Does the firm have plans to secure additional capital through equity financing?

Change

Here are some thoughts about change and today's business world.

- The only constant in today's business world is change.
- It's the reality in today's society of games companies play.
- Change is inevitable
- Change or fail.
- Be proactive to change or be reactive to problems of change.
- Companies that are slow to change might have financial problems.
- Most people hate change—the concept of change often brings fears.
- How fast or how slow should change take place?
- People will resist change—either actively or passively.
- Most people like things the way they are. They resist change.

Analysis by Nonfinancial Strategies

Management might consider "alternate" new measures of performance beyond the traditional accounting analysis. For financial statements, for example, management might consider the following examples of items to measure performance:

- The company's market share
- The company's price/earnings ratio
- The company's return on equity
- Customer satisfaction
- Employee satisfaction
- Shareholder satisfaction
- Cost reduction through improved manufacturing quality
- Rapid product development
- Lower inventory levels
- Reduce delivery time, etc.

Important questions to ask are:

- Which phenonmena to measure?

¶631.01

- What is the best definition of this phenomena?
- How can the performance criterion best be measured?
- Is this performance best for employees, lower, middle or senior managment?
- Can the performance be measured accurately and in a timely manner?
- Can the performance be measured precisely?
- Is the measure useful for decision making?

.03 Financial Analysis of Balance Sheet and Net Income

Balance Sheet Quality Analysis

- For fixed assets
  - What is age and condition of assets?
  - Carefully review specialized assets of a higher risk
  - Are assets technically obsolete?
  - How many inactive assets exist?
  - Are repairs and maintenance expense percentages becoming excessive?
  - Does the depreciation rate adequately reflect the decline in service potential of the asset?
- For inventory
  - Does the inventory percentage growth exceed the sales percentage growth?
  - Is inventory subject to political risks?
  - Does poor inventory turnover risk obsolescence?
  - Is inventory of a perishable nature?
  - Raw materials are of lower risk than are finished goods.
- Analyze assets by risk categories.
  - The more dollars in high risk categories, the lower is the firm's earnings quality.
- Specialized assets have higher risks than multi-purpose assets.
- Does the company have adequate cash?
  - Analyze the amount of cash available.
  - Analyze the ability to obtain financing.
  - Analyze cash flow from operations.
- For accounts receivables
  - Older receivables are higher risk.
  - Having a few large accounts is higher risk.
- Analyze trends in current liabilities.
- Analyze the firm's ability to meet long-term debt payments.

Financial Analysis of Earnings Quality—Net Income

- How much are accounting estimates used in preparing the income statement?
- Are accruals realistic?

- How stable have past earnings been?
- Is the firm constantly changing its accounting methods?
- Has management altered beyond realistic ranges discretionary costs such as advertising, entertainment, research, and management salary?
- How is depreciation accounted for?
- A firm that generates additional sales related to original sales has higher stability of income.
- Does the firm show a high gross profit percentage?
- What level of reports are issued? Compilation, review or audit?
- A company geographically diversified reduces vulnerability to economic downturns.
- A company with a single product line may indicate a higher risk.
- A company that sells staple items has a higher stability of income.
- A company that has numerous raw material sources is at lower risk.
- What is the availability of future financing sources?
- Has the company shown a solid growth rate?
- Companies with high fixed costs are higher risk.
- Is revenue being recognized properly as it is earned?

.04 Financial Analysis Reporting

- Consider streamlining financial reports used for management decisions.
- Most managers only need summarized financial data.
- Focus on key indicators.
- Focus less on details.
- Focus on exceptions reporting.
- Start with GAAP financials and "pick out" the important indicators for the company.
- Keep managers focused on the big picture and not bogged down in details.
- Provide reports that show trends and significant variances.
- Consider graphics—bar charts and pie charts.
- Consider summarizing the balance sheet and income statement with a key indicator statement that takes no more than one page.
- The art of designing a key indicator report is determining which indicators specific for the company are needed.

.05 Financial Difficulties

External Warning Signs

- Business population characteristics change
- Social and cultural changes
- Lack of credit availability
- Legal changes that adversely affect the industry

- Major competitive developments change structure of the marketplace
  — Such as the industry having an economic decline
  — Such as the industry having economic growth
- Product innovation causing obsolescence of production technology

Internal Warning Signals

- Management problems
- Increasing breakeven level required
- Poor product quality
- No business strategy
- Excessive advertising and marketing costs
- Poor management decisions
- Poor production utilization
- Insufficient internal controls
- No diversification
- Using too few suppliers
- Decrease in key ratios
- Number of overdrafts
- Bank balance trend declining
- Inadequate insurance coverage
- Reliance on few major customers

Short-Term Danger Signals

- Increased customer complaints
- Bank credit restrictions
- Crisis management
- Employee dissatisfaction growing
- Lack of financial information
- Employee absenteeism increase
- Difficulty in meeting payroll needs
- Payroll taxes increasing
- Penalties on payroll taxes
- Growing accounts payable
- Need for expanded sales to break even
- Lack of controlled planning
- Declining sales
- Continuous periods of losses
- Management problems
- Working capital reductions
- Cash shortages

Intermediate-Term Danger Signals

- Continuous bank overdrafts
- Profit margins declining
- Increasing levels of debt
- Declining sales
- Bad debts increasing
- Slowing inventory turns
- Decline in employees
- Lack of adequate internal controls
- Mismatching of long-term credit for short-term needs
- Increasing management problems
- Owners extending credit to firm
- Increasing overhead
- Troubled accounts payable terms
- Cost over-runs
- Unreliable financial information
- Accounts receivable collection difficulties
- Customer confidence decline
- Bank overdrafts

Long-Term Danger Signals

- Unclear chains of command
- Ineffective management
- Low employee morale
- Decrease in profit margins
- Accounts payable over 90 days
- Accounts receivable over 90 days
- Management by exception rather than by planning
- Bank overdrafts
- Declining sales
- Cash crises
- Little department interaction
- Major staff cutbacks
- Vendors requiring C.O.D. terms
- Payroll difficulties
- Drawing working capital
- Deteriorating or declining credibility
- Marketing problems

¶631.05

Mistakes Made by Businesses in Financial Crisis

- Failure to Build a Sufficient Cash Reserve
  - New borrowing, either secured or unsecured
  - Liquidating non-essential property
  - Retaining proceeds of accounts which would otherwise be turned over to the secured lender
  - Capital contributions
  - Sale of securities, etc.
- Providing or Increasing Collateral in Exchange for an Extension of Debt.
  - Provide additional collateral for the extension of new credit in an amount equal to or greater than the value of the collateral being offered.
- Misleading Creditors or Refusing to Communicate with Them
  - The dissemination of accurate and consistent financial information is a key in maintaining a good working relationship with creditors and in maximizing the opportunity for a successful reorganization.
- Misleading Employees.
  - Employees should be treated with respect should not be victims of inaccurate or misleading information.
- Letting go of Accounting Personnel.
  - Accounting personnel are indispensable during a financial crisis. It is the numbers that tell the story regarding the financial crisis.
- Failure to Timely Identify and Eliminate Sections of the Business.
  - Separate limbs of the company which drain more from the bottom line than they contribute must be dealt.
- Failure to Cut Overhead

Financial Difficulty Remedies

- Involve customers, bankers, vendors, employees and management in the financial turnaround goals.
- Acknowledge problems.
- Understand the danger signals.
- Take immediate action.
- Obtain accurate financial information.
- Understand that other problems are interrelated.
- Understand that management is responsible.
- Review revenue generating methods.
- Review cost cutting procedures.
- Review the company's strategic plan.
- Allow for flexibility in corporate objectives.
- Analyze the customer base for profitability.
- Analyze the products and markets for profitability.

- Prepare cash projections and cash flow reports and budgets.
- Consider:
  — Refinancing
  — Additional capitalization
  — Liquidation or sale
  — Reorganization under Chapter 11 or out of court restructuring
- Remove unnecessary, unproductive assets.

Financial Fraud Warning Signs

- Adverse legal circumstances confront company
- Company entered into one or a few specific transactions that materally affect financials
- Management has lied or been evasive to audit inquires.
- Management is considered highly unreasonable
- Management displays a hostile attitude toward auditors
- Management displays significant disrespect for regulatory bodies
- The company is subject to significant contractural commitments
- Management displays significant resentment of authority
- Management decisions are dominated by a single or concise group acting in concert
- Management diplays qualities of dishonesty
- The company entered into a significant number of acquistion transactions
- The company has excessive numbers of bank accounts with numerous transfer transactions
- The company is in a period of rapid growth
- Management is inexperienced
- Management places undue stress and demands on the auditors through fee structuring or unreasonable deadlines.
- Management has an aggressive attitude against financial reporting
- Management places undue emphasis on meeting projections or other targets
- Management engages in frequent disputes with auditors regarding accounting principles
- Management is unduly concerned over the need to maintain the company image.
- Accounting personnel exhibit inexperience in performing their tasks.
- The company's profitability is inconsistent relative to its industry.
- The company has numerous difficult to audit transactions.
- Management constantly takes undue risks.
- A significant portion of management's salary depends on meeting quantified targets.
- The company displays a weak internal control environment.

¶ 632 FUTURE VALUE

.01 Value n Periods from Now of $1 Received Today Using Tables

Table provides the value that $1.00 will grow to at the end of a given period at a specified interest rate.

The interest = APR (Annual Percentage Rate)

Factors are values of $1.00

> *Example:* How much will $10,000 grow to in 11 years at 4% APR?

From table Factor = 1.5394541

$10,000 × 1.53945.41 = $15,394.54 = Future Value

Future Value of $1 at End of Period

Period	Interest Rate						
	2%	3%	4%	5%	6%	7%	8%
6	1.12616242	1.19405230	1.26531902	1.34009564	1.41851911	1.50073035	1.58687432
7	1.14868567	1.22987387	1.31593178	1.40710042	1.50363026	1.60578148	1.71382427
8	1.17165938	1.26677008	1.36856905	1.47745544	1.59384807	1.71818618	1.85093021
9	1.19509257	1.30477318	1.42331181	1.55132822	1.68947896	1.83845921	1.99900463
10	1.21899442	1.34391638	1.48024428	1.62889463	1.79084770	1.96715136	2.15892500
11	1.24337431	1.38423387	1.53945406	1.71033936	1.89829856	2.10485195	2.33163900
12	1.26824179	1.42576089	1.60103222	1.79585633	2.01219647	2.25219159	2.51817012
13	1.29360663	1.46853371	1.66507351	1.88564914	2.13292826	2.40984500	2.71962373
14	1.31947876	1.51258972	1.73167645	1.97993160	2.26090396	2.57853415	2.93719362

See ¶ 691.09 for complete table.

.03 Future Value of Ordinary Annuity of $1 per period for n periods

> *Example:* A firm is estimated to have annual Adjusted Net Income of $100,000/year for 10 years. The interest growth rate to be applied is 12%. What is the future value of these 10 cash flows?
>
> - Locate interest column of 12% for rate.
> - Read down column to locate Term of 10 years.
> - Future value of Adjusted Net Income = $100,000 × 17.5487351 = $1,754,873.51

See ¶ 691.15 for complete table.

Future Value of Ordinary Annuity of $1 per Period

Period	Interest Rate					
	9%	10%	11%	12%	13%	14%
6	7.5233346	7.7156100	7.9128596	8.1151890	8.3227058	8.5355187
7	9.2004347	9.4871710	9.7832741	10.0890117	10.4046575	10.7304914
8	11.0284738	11.4358881	11.8594343	12.2996931	12.7572630	13.2327602
9	13.0210364	13.5794769	14.1639720	14.7756563	15.4157072	16.0853466
10	15.1929297	15.9374246	16.7220090	17.5487351	18.4197492	19.3372951
11	17.5602934	18.5311671	19.5614300	20.6545833	21.8143165	23.0445164
12	20.1407198	21.3842838	22.7131872	24.1331333	25.6501777	27.2707487
14	26.0191892	27.9749834	30.0949180	32.3926024	34.8827119	37.5810650

.05 Future Value of Ordinary Annuity Using Mathematical Formula

Value of Annuity After Fixed Number of Years

$$\left(\text{Amount per period}\right) \times \frac{\left(1 + \text{interest rate per period}\right)^{(\text{number of periods})} - 1}{\text{interest rate per period}}$$

Example: What is the value at the end of 5 years of an annuity of $5,000 per year with payments made at the end of each year for 5 years assuming an interest rate of 5% compounded annually?

$$\text{Amount of annuity (FV)} = \$5,000 \frac{\left(1 + .05\right)^5 - 1}{.05}$$

$$\frac{(1 + 5)^5 - 1}{.05} = 5.5256313$$

Thus, amount of annuity (FV) = ($5,000) (5.5256313) = $27,628

See ¶ 691.09 for Future Value of Ordinary Annuity tables.

.07 Future Value of Amount with Annual Investing and Compounding—Formula Method

Future value of annuity =

$$\text{Annual amount} \left[\frac{\left(1 + \text{annual interest rate}\right)^{\text{number of annual payments}} - 1}{\text{annual interest rate}} \right]$$

Example: Mr. X wishes to save and purchase his next car for cash. He feels he can invest $3,000 a year for the next 5 years in an investment strategy that will yield 9% compounded annually. The amount he saves will be added to his trade-in allowance to purchase the new vehicle. What will his portfolio be worth in 5 years given these facts?

$$\text{Future Value} = \$3,000 \left[\frac{((1 + .09)^5 - 1)}{.09} \right]$$

$$= \$3,000 \left[\frac{(1.5386)}{.09} \right] = \$17,953$$

.09 Future Value—Sinking Fund to Reach Target Amount

$$\text{Annuity amount} = \frac{\text{Target amount} \left[\dfrac{\text{interest rate}}{\text{term}} \right]}{\left[1 + \dfrac{\text{interest rate}}{\text{term}} \right] \text{term} - 1}$$

Taxpayer A had borrowed $10,000 that was due in one year. At the end of the 3rd month taxpayer A decided to make monthly deposits into an account which yields 9% com-

¶632.05

pounded monthly. What is the monthly deposit (annuity) amount needed to reach the target amount of $10,000?

$$\text{Annuity amount} = \frac{\$10,000 \, \dfrac{(.09)}{9}}{\left[1 + \dfrac{.09}{9}\right]^9 - 1} = \frac{100}{(1.0937) - 1} = \$1,067$$

Note: Term = 12 months – 3 months = 9 months

¶ 633 GROWTH

.01 Sustainable Growth Rate for Firm

The following formula calculates the maximum growth rate in sales that a firm can achieve in the future assuming financial statement relationships remain constant.

A firm growing too fast will put itself out of business. The firm must grow at the right pace and in the right way. How fast is fast enough? The firm should grow at a level of profitability that can sustain the business.

The concept of sustainable growth rate is the firm's maximum rate of growth given the firm's use of assets, desired debt ratio, dividend payout, and profitability. If the firm grows too fast, it can be profitable, but must expand out of additional borrowing. The model was developed by R.C. Higgins in "How Much Growth Can a Firm Afford?", Financial Management, Fall 1977.

$$\text{Sustainable growth rate} = \left[\frac{\text{Sales}}{\text{Beginning assets}} \times \frac{\text{Net income}}{\text{Sales}} \times \frac{1 + \text{Debt}}{\text{Equity}} \times \text{Earnings Retention Ratio}\right]$$

Where, earnings retention ratio = (1 – dividend payout)

$$\text{Required Earnings Retention Ratio} = \frac{\text{Target Sustainable Growth Rate}}{\left(\dfrac{\text{Sales}}{\text{Beginning assets}}\right)\left(\dfrac{\text{Net Income}}{\text{Sales}}\right)\left(\dfrac{1 + \text{Debt}}{\text{Equity}}\right)}$$

$$\text{Required Asset Utilization} = \frac{\text{Target SGR}}{\left(\dfrac{\text{Net Income}}{\text{Sales}}\right)\left(1 + \dfrac{\text{Debt}}{\text{Equity}}\right)\text{Earnings Retention Ratio}}$$

$$\text{Required Asset Utilization} = \frac{\text{Target SGRs}}{\left(\dfrac{\text{Sales}}{\text{Beginning assets}}\right)\left(1 + \dfrac{\text{Debt}}{\text{Equity}}\right)\text{Earnings Retention Ratio}}$$

Target Growth Rate

Target Growth Rate =

[(Net Income – Dividends) / Net Income] × (Total Assets / Equity) × (Net Income / Total Assets)

.02 Growth vs. Debt vs. the Business

- Profitable growth is not an accident but comes from proper planning and design.

- A company should not just seek excessive sales growth, or it may find itself in deeper debt, depending on its profit margins, etc.
- The company should strive for balanced growth in sales, profitability, and net worth.
- If the firm is growing too fast in sales, it may constantly need funds in excess of the profits it generates.
- Management is the key variable for company growth. Growth firms have mangement with planning ability, organization, and good relations with employees, customers, creditors, and the general public.

Growth vs. Profit vs. Debt

The following examples analyze the firm's growth in relation to its profit and related debt. A firm must maintain a reasonably consistent percentage of balance sheet accounts to gross sales to maintain those sales. For example, to generate twice as much in gross sales, an increase in the amount of inventory available is required.

In the following examples, the balancing account is the long-term debt. Note the effects on noncurrent liabilities given the different assumptions in the following examples.

Assume that assets stated as a percentage of sales for balance sheet assumptions are as follows:

Current assets = 35%

Fixed assets = 65%

Accounts payable = 30%

Current liabilities = 20%

Noncurrent liabilities = the "balancing account" (the account under analysis)

Income statement assumptions, as a percentage of gross sales, for a given sales volume are as follows:

Cost of goods sold = 65%

Operating expenses = 33%

Net income = 2%

Analysis of Growth vs. Profit vs. Debt
Example A—Sales Increase of 50% with 2% Net Income

Years		(1)	(2)	vs.	(1)	(2)	(3)	(4)	(5)
Balance Sheet									
Cur Asset	35%	$ 350	$ 525		$ 350	$ 393	$ 437	$ 481	$ 525
Fix Asset	65%	$ 650	$ 975		$ 650	$ 731	$ 812	$ 893	$ 975
Acct Pay	30%	$ 300	$ 450		$ 300	$ 337	$ 375	$ 412	$ 450
Cur Liab	20%	$ 200	$ 300		$ 200	$ 225	$ 250	$ 275	$ 300
Lg Liab**		$ 280	$ 500		$ 280	$ 320	$ 357	$ 392	$ 425
C/S—Cap		$ 100	$ 100		$ 100	$ 100	$ 100	$ 100	$ 100
R/E—Cap		$ 120	$ 150		$ 120	$ 142	$ 167	$ 195	$ 225

Years		(1)	(2)	vs.	(1)	(2)	(3)	(4)	(5)
Income Statement									
Sales									
(Increase)	50%	$1000	$1500		$1000	$1125	$1250	$1375	$1500
Cogs	65%	$ 650	$ 975		$ 650	$ 731	$ 812	$ 893	$ 975
Exp	33%	$ 330	$ 495		$ 330	$ 371	$ 412	$ 453	$ 495
N/I	2%	$ 20	$ 30		$ 20	$ 22	$ 25	$ 27	$ 30

** To Balance

Example A illustrates, given the above assumptions, the effects on noncurrent liabilities if the firm were to increase its sales by 50% over a given time period.

The first column illustrates sales growth over two periods (two years). The remaining five columns illustrate the same 50% sales growth but over five periods (five years).

Too rapid expansion puts the firm further into debt, while with slower controlled growth, the firm can reduce its debt by growing through its profits.

Analysis of Growth vs. Profit vs. Debt
Example B—Sales Increase of 50% with a 6% Net Income

Years		(1)	(2)	vs.	(1)	(2)	(3)	(4)	(5)
Balance Sheet									
Cur Asset	35%	$ 350	$ 525		$ 350	$ 393	$ 437	$ 481	$ 525
Fix Asset	65%	$ 650	$ 975		$ 650	$ 731	$ 812	$ 893	$ 975
Acct Pay	30%	$ 300	$ 450		$ 300	$ 337	$ 375	$ 412	$ 450
Cur Liab	20%	$ 200	$ 300		$ 200	$ 225	$ 250	$ 275	$ 300
Lg Liab**		$ 240	$ 400		$ 240	$ 235	$ 222	$ 202	$ 175
C/S—Cap		$ 100	$ 100		$ 100	$ 100	$ 100	$ 100	$ 100
R/E—Cap		$ 160	$ 250		$ 160	$ 227	$ 302	$ 385	$ 475
Income Statement									
Sales									
(Increase)	50%	$1000	$1500		$1000	$1125	$1250	$1375	$1500
Cogs	65%	$ 650	$ 975		$ 650	$ 731	$ 812	$ 893	$ 975
Exp	29%	$ 290	$ 435		$ 290	$ 326	$ 362	$ 398	$ 435
N/I	6%	$ 60	$ 90		$ 60	$ 67	$ 75	$ 82	$ 90

** To Balance

In example B, the net income is 6%. Fifty percent growth in two years by the firm increases the long-term liabilities from $240,000 to $400,000.

The same 50% increase over five years allows the firm to generate its growth through its profits and reduce its long-term debt from $240,000 to $175,000.

Analysis of Growth vs. Profit vs. Debt
Example C—Sales Increase of 30% with a 2% Net Income

Years		(1)	(2)	vs.	(1)	(2)	(3)	(4)	(5)
Balance Sheet									
Cur Asset	35%	$ 350	$ 455		$ 350	$ 376	$ 402	$ 428	$ 455
Fix Asset	65%	$ 650	$ 845		$ 650	$ 698	$ 747	$ 796	$ 845
Acct Pay	30%	$ 300	$ 390		$ 300	$ 322	$ 345	$ 367	$ 390
Cur Liab	20%	$ 200	$ 260		$ 200	$ 215	$ 230	$ 245	$ 260
Lg Liab**		$ 280	$ 404		$ 280	$ 296	$ 310	$ 323	$ 335
C/S—Cap		$ 100	$ 100		$ 100	$ 100	$ 100	$ 100	$ 100
R/E—Cap		$ 120	$ 146		$ 120	$ 141	$ 164	$ 189	$ 215
Income Statement									
Sales (Increase)	30%	$1000	$1300		$1000	$1075	$1150	$1225	$1300
Cogs	65%	$ 650	$ 845		$ 650	$ 698	$ 747	$ 796	$ 845
Exp	33%	$ 330	$ 429		$ 330	$ 354	$ 379	$ 404	$ 429
N/I	2%	$ 20	$ 26		$ 20	$ 21	$ 23	$ 24	$ 26

** To Balance

In example C, the firm increases its sales by 30%.

With the 2% net income, the long-term liabilities increase from $280,000 to $404,000 over a two-year period. Even with slower growth over five periods, the debt continues to grow to $335,000.

In continuing the above examples, it can be shown that when the firm, given the above assumptions, has a sales increase of 30% with 6% net income, it is able to *decrease* its long term debt to $105,000.

¶ 634 INDEXES

.01 Index Numbers

Data:

	Item 1		Item 2		Item 3	
	Price	Quantity	Price	Quantity	Price	Quantity
20x1	21	100	20	101	23	104
20x2	24	110	22	107	20	112
20x3	26	105	25	108	27	107

.03 Aggregative price index weighted with fixed weights

$$\text{Price index (for given year)} = \frac{(\text{price of item for year being computed})(\text{Fixed weight})}{(\text{Price of item in base year})(\text{Fixed weight})}$$

Example: Given the above data, what is the aggregative price index for 20x3 using 20x1 weights and 20x1 as a base?

$$I_{20x3} = \frac{(26)(100) + (25)(101) + (27)(104)}{(21)(100) + (20)(101) + (23)(104)}$$

$$= \frac{7933}{6512}$$

$$= 1.218$$

.05 Aggregative price index weighted with variable weights

$$\frac{\text{Index}}{\text{(for given year)}} = \frac{\text{(Price of item for year being computed)(Variable weight)}}{\text{(Price of item in base year)(Variable weight)}}$$

Example: Given the data above, what is the aggregative price index for 20×3 using variable weights and 20x1 as a base?

$$1_{20x3} = \frac{(26)(105) + (25)(108) + (27)(107)}{(21)(105) + (20)(108) + (23)(107)}$$

$$= \frac{8319}{6826}$$

$$= 1.219$$

.07 Price relative's arithmetic mean with fixed weights

$$\text{M (for a given year)} = \frac{\left(\dfrac{\text{Price of item in present period}}{\text{Price of item in base period}}\right) - \text{(Base period price) (Fixed quantity)}}{\text{(Base period price) (Fixed quantity)}}$$

Example: Given the data above, what is the price relative's arithmetic mean for 20x3 if 20x2 is the base year and 20x2 fixed weights are used?

$$M_{20x3} = \frac{\dfrac{26}{24} \times (24)(110) + \dfrac{25}{22} \times (22)(107) + \dfrac{27}{20} \times (22)(112)}{(24)(110) + (22)(107) + (20)(112)}$$

$$= \frac{2860 + 2675 + 3024}{2640 + 2354 + 2240}$$

$$= \frac{8559}{7234}$$

$$= 1.183$$

.09 Price relative's arithmetic mean with variable weights

$$\text{M (for a given period)} = \frac{\dfrac{\text{Price of item in present period}}{\text{Price of item in base period}} \times \text{(Price of item in present period)} \times \text{(Variable quantity)}}{\text{(Price of item in present period)} \times \text{(Variable quantity)}}$$

Example: Given the above data, what is the price relative's arithmetic mean for 20x3 if 20x2 is the base year and variable weights for 20x2 are employed?

$$M_{20x3} = \frac{\frac{26}{24} \times (26)(105) \ + \ \frac{25}{22} \times (25)(108) \ + \ \frac{27}{20} \times (27)(107)}{(26)(105) \ + \ (25)(108) \ + \ (27)(107)}$$

$$= \frac{2958 + 3068 + 3900}{2730 + 2700 + 2889}$$

$$= \frac{9926}{8319} = 1.193$$

¶ 635　INTEREST—SIMPLE

.01　Basic Concepts and Examples

Simple Interest

Interest = principal × rate × time

　　　Example: What is the total of simple interest on $1,800 for 90 days at 8% interest?

$$I = \$1,800 \times .08 \times 90 \ / \ 365 = \underline{\$35.51}$$

Note: Ordinary simple interest uses 360 days in the year.

Simple Interest—Growth of $1.00

Period	Interest Rate		
	18%	19%	20%
0	1.00	1.00	1.00
1	1.18	1.19	1.20
2	1.36	1.38	1.40
3	1.54	1.57	1.60
4	1.72	1.76	1.80
5	1.90	1.95	2.00
6	2.08	2.14	2.20
7	2.26	2.33	2.40
8	2.44	2.52	2.60
9	2.62	2.71	2.80
10	2.80	2.90	3.00
11	2.98	3.09	3.20
12	3.16	3.28	3.40
13	3.34	3.47	3.60
14	3.52	3.66	3.80

See ¶ 691.03 for complete tables

Example using table:

Value of $600 at 18% simple interest in 10 years.

What will $600 grow to in 10 years at 18% simple interest?

From table, locate 10 years at 18% simple interest.

$600 × 2.80 = $1,680

.03 Time Required to Yield a Sum of Simple Interest

Time Required to Yield a Sum of Simple Interest

$$\frac{I}{(P \times R)}$$

Where:

P = Principal

R = Interest rate

I = Interest

Example: What is the amount of time in years needed for $6,000 to yield $600 simple interest at 8%?

T = $600 / ($6,000 × .08) = 1.25 years, i.e., 15 months

Principal Needed to Obtain a Target Amount of Cash where C = net cash

$$P = \frac{C}{(1 - RT)}$$

Example: If $4,000 cash is required and the bank will discount a note for 90 days at 8%, what is principal amount of the note?

P = $4,000 / (1 - (.08 × 90 / 360)) = $4,081.63

.05 Banker's Rule

Banker's Rule

Uses ordinary simple interest based on 360 days/year when ordinary interest accrues for an exact number of days

$$\text{Repayment} = \text{principal} \times \left[1 + (\text{interest} \times \text{term})\right]$$

Example: Principal borrowed = $1,100

Interest rate = 12%

Term = 1 year + 45 days

$$\text{Repayment} = \$1,100 \times \left[1 + .12\left(1 + \frac{45}{360}\right)\right]$$

$$= \$1,248.50$$

.07 Modified Merchants Rule—Exact Simple Interest

Modified Merchants Rule—Exact Simple Interest

$$\text{Repayment} = \text{principal} \times \left[1 + \text{interest}\left(1 \text{ year} + \left(\frac{\text{days}}{365}\right)\right)\right]$$

.08 Present Value of Simple Interest Note

Present Value of Simple Interest Note

$$Pv = \frac{P \quad (1 + R \times T)}{(1 + R_1 \times T_1)}$$

$$Mv = P \times (1 + R \times T)$$

Where: Pv = Present Value

Mv = Maturity Value

R = Rate

T = Time

R_1 = Current interest rate

T_1 = Time remaining on note

Example: Note for $1,800 is dated Sept. 1 with ordinary simple interest of 8% for 90 days. Valuation date is Oct. 1 with current money rate at 7%. What is the maturity value of the note? What is the present value of the note?

$$Mv = P \times (1 + RT) = \$1,800 \quad (1 + .08(90 / 360)) = \$1,836$$

$$Pv = \$1,836 / (1 + (.07)(60 / 360)) = \$1,814.83$$

.09 Cash Proceeds on Discount of Ordinary Simple Interest Note

Cash Proceeds on Discount

$$\text{Cash Proceeds} = P \times (1 + RT) \times (1 - R_1 \times T_1)$$

Where: R_1 = Rate of discount by purchaser

T_1 = Time remaining on note

Example: Note is $1,800 for 8% for 90 days dated Aug 1. Note was discounted at bank on Aug 31 at 6%. What were the cash proceeds received?

$$\text{Cash proceeds} = \$1,800 \times (1 + .08 \times 90/360) \times (1 - (.06 \times 60/360))$$
$$= \$1,836 \times .99$$
$$= \$1,817.64$$

.10 Interest Rate Corresponding to Discount Rate

Interest Rate Corresponding to Discount Rate

$$i = \frac{\text{Discount rate}}{1 - (\text{time} \times \text{discount rate})}$$

Example: What is the actual rate of interest that the borrowers must pay if a bank discounts a 90 day note at 8%?

$$i = \frac{.08}{1 - (90/360 \times .08)} = .082 \text{ or } 8.2\%$$

.11 Interest—Simple Interest Method—Discount Paid Up Front

Interest discount = (Principal × Rate × Annual term) (simple)

Net proceeds = Principal – Interest discount

A company borrows $2,000 at 9% simple interest for 9 months, where interest is prepaid. What is the interest discount amount?

Discount   = $2,000 × .09 × 9/12
           = $135

What is the amount of net proceeds?

Net proceeds   = $2,000 – $135
                 = $1,865

Note: The true interest rate exceeds 9%, because only $1,865 is available for use and yet $135 interest was paid on it.

.12 Interest—Simple Interest Method—True Discount

Interest discount   = $\dfrac{\text{Amount due at end of term}}{1 + (\text{simple annual interest rate})(\text{term in years})}$

A company borrows $2,000 at 9% simple interest for 9 months, where interest is prepaid. What is the true interest discount amount?

$$\text{Discount (true)} = \frac{\$2,000}{1 + (.09)(9/12)} = \frac{\$2,000}{1.0675}$$

$$= \$1873.54$$

Net proceeds = $2,000 – $1,873.54 = $126.46

Proof: That borrower paid 9%:

1,873.54 × .09 × 9/12 = $126.46

Note: That discount and effective interest rates do not necessarily equate.

.13 Interest—Discount Rate Versus Effective Rate

If the discount rate is 9%, what is the effective rate on a 3-month loan discounted up-front?

Equate loan amount as $1

3 months = 3/12 = 1/4 of year

where r = effective rate

$$\$1 \ (1 - (.09)(1/4)) = \frac{\$1}{(1+(r)(1/4))}$$

$$1 - \frac{.09}{4} = \frac{4}{4+r}$$

Loan amount $\times$ (1 - (annual discount rate)(term in years)) $= \dfrac{\text{loan amount}}{(1 + (\text{effective rate})(\text{term in years}))}$

$$\frac{3.91}{4} = \frac{4}{4 + r}$$

$$3.91 \ (4 + r) = 4 \times 4$$

$$15.64 + 3.91r = 16$$

$$3.91r = 16 - 15.64$$

$$r = \frac{16 - 15.64}{3.91}$$

$$r = 9.2\%$$

.14 Interest—Discount of Promissory Note

A gave a note for $4,000 for 9 months at 8% interest to B. Three months later B discounted the note to C for 10%. What were the proceeds that B received?

Total simple interest = Principal $\times$ annual rate $\times$ term in years

Total simple interest = $4,000 $\times$ .08 $\times$ 9/12 = $240

Maturity value of note = $4,000 + $240 = $4,240

Discount = $4,240 $\times$ .10 $\times$ 6/12 = $212

(period of discount = 6 months)

(Note: Period of discount=(9 months – 3 months = 6 month, or stated as fraction of year = 6/12)

Proceeds to B = $4,240 – $212 = $4,028
Note: Proceeds to C = $4,240, cost = $4,028

Effective rate = (4,240/4,028 – 1)

= 5.26% for 6 months

= or 10.52% for annual rate (5.26 × 2)

Interest proceeds to B = $4,028 – $4,000 = $28

$28 / $4,000 = .7% for 3 months return

= 2.8% annual return (.7% × 4)

.15 Interest Rate Equivalent to Cash Discount Rate

Interest Rate Equivalent to Cash Discount Rate

$$i = \frac{\text{cash discount rate}}{1 - \text{cash discount rate}} \times \frac{360}{\text{days of credit} - \text{days in discount period}}$$

Example: Terms are 2/10 net 30. What is the effective rate of interest equivalent to the cash discount?

$$i = \frac{.02}{.98} \times \frac{360}{30 - 10} = .367 = 36.7\%$$

.16 Effective Interest Rate—Simple Formula

Use the following formula to calculate the effective interest rate being paid:

$$R = \left(\frac{\text{Interest}}{\text{Principal}}\right)\left(\frac{360}{\text{Days of Loan}}\right)$$

Example: Find the cost of a 60 day loan for $10,000 if the interest paid was $500.

$$R = \left(\frac{500}{10,000}\right) \times \left(\frac{360}{60}\right)$$

$$R = 30\%$$

Effective Rate—Fees

Fees reduce the amount borrowed and are another form of "interest" cost.

$$R = \frac{(\text{Interest} + \text{Fees})}{(\text{Principal} - \text{Fees})} \times \frac{(360)}{(\text{Days of Loan})}$$

Effective Rate—Compensating Balances

$$R = \left(\frac{\text{Interest}}{\text{Principal} - \text{Compensating Balance}}\right) \times \left(\frac{360}{\text{Days of Loan}}\right)$$

.17 Effective Interest Rate—Discount Loan

The interest payment is made at the beginning of the loan period. At maturity the borrower repays the principal.

$$R = \frac{\text{Interest}}{\text{Principal} - \text{Interest change}} \times \frac{360}{\text{Days of Loan}}$$

Annual Percentage Rate (APR)—Regular Payments

Use this formula to approximate the APR (Annual Percentage Rate) for short-term loans with regularly scheduled payments of equal amounts.

$$APR = \frac{200 \times \text{Total finance charge} \times \text{Number of payments per year}}{\text{Principal} \times (\text{total number of payments} + 1)}$$

Example: What is the approximate annual percentage rate where:

Principal = $2,000

Payments = monthly = 12/year

Term = 18 months

Total Finance Charge = $185.00

$$APR = \frac{200 \times 185 \times 12}{2,000 \times (18 + 1)} = \frac{444,000}{38,000} = 11.68\%$$

Interest—Total Finance Charge:

The following formula approximates the total finance charge for short-term loans with regularly scheduled payments of equal amounts.

$$\text{Total finance cost} = \frac{APR \times \text{principal} \times (\text{term} + 1)}{200 \times \text{number of payments per year}}$$

Example: What is the approximate total finance charge where

APR = 10%

Principal = $2,000

Term = 24 months

Payments are made monthly = 12/year

$$\text{Total finance cost} = \frac{10 \times 2,000 \times (24 + 1)}{200 \times 12} = \frac{500,000}{2,400} = \$208.33$$

.18 Effective Interest Rate—Residuary Method

When partial payments are made, the residuary method approximates the true interest rate. It applies payments, first to the unpaid loan balance and then to the interest cost.

Effective Interest Rate—Residuary Method

$$\frac{(2)(\text{No. of Payments in Year})(\text{Total \$ Amount of Interest Paid})}{(\text{Principal}(\text{No. of Interest Payments})) + 1 + (\text{Total \$ Amount of Interest Paid}(\text{No. of Interest Payments}))}$$

Example: What is the effective interest rate, given

Unpaid principal = $1,500

Total $ amount of interest paid = $150

Number of interest payments during year =2

Number of interest periods = 3

¶635.18

$$\text{Effective Interest Rate} = \frac{(2)(2)(\$150)}{\$1,500(3+1)+(\$150)(3-1)}$$

$$\frac{\$600}{\$6000 \quad \$300} = 10.53\%$$

.19 Effective Interest Rate—Direct Ratio Method

The direct ratio formula, developed by H. E. Stelson, is considered more accurate than the residuary method, due to the different weighting of each expression. Differences on small loans are negligible.

Effective Interest Rate =

$$\frac{(6)(\text{No. of payments during the year})(\text{total dollar amount of interest paid})}{(3)(\text{principal})(\text{no. of interest payments} + 1)}$$
$$+ (\text{total \$ amount of interest paid})(\text{no. of interest payments} - 1)$$

Example (1): Given the data in the residuary method, what is the effective interest rate using the direct ratio method?

$$\text{Effective interest rate (direct ratio method)} = \frac{6(2)(\$150)}{3(\$1,500)(3+1) + (\$150)(3-1)}$$
$$= \frac{\$1,800}{\$18,000 + \$300}$$
$$= 9.84\%$$

Example (2): A bank advertised new car loans at 6% interest. Mr. X, after trading in his auto, still needed to finance $4,000 from the bank, which they loaned at 6%, repayable in 24 equal monthly installments. How much did Mr. X pay in total interest and what was his effective annual rate?

Note: Total interest paid = Principal × interest × term in years
$$= \$4,000 \, (.06)(2)$$
$$= \$480$$

$$\text{Effective Interest Rate} = \frac{6(12)(\$480)}{3(\$4,000)(24+1) + \$480(24-1)}$$

$$= \frac{\$34,560}{\$300,000 + \$11,040}$$

$$= 11.11\%$$

.21 Effective Interest Rate—Monthly

Effective Interest Rate = $(1 + \text{monthly interest rate})^{(\text{Number of interest periods})} - 1$

Example: A firm charges its customers a monthly interest carrying charge of 1 3/4%. What is the effective annual rate that reflects the monthly compounding charged to the customers on this accounts receivable balance?

¶635.21

Note: 1 3/4 = 1.75% = .0175

Note: Annual rate is not (12×.0175) = 21% due to monthly compounding

$$\text{Effective interest rate} = (1 + .0175)^{12} - 1$$
$$= (1.0175)^{12} - 1$$
$$= 23.14\%$$

.23 Effective Interest Rate—Constant Ratio Method

The constant ratio method includes repayment of principal plus interest in the same ratio as the original unpaid balance is to interest.

$$\text{Effective Interest Rate} = \frac{2 \text{ (no. of interest payments during a year)(total dollar amount of interest paid)}}{\text{principal (number of interest periods} + 1)}$$

Example: A TV store advertises new TV's for $1,000 cash or for $100 down with the balance in 12 equal monthly installments of $80. Using the constant ratio method, what is the effective interest rate?

Note: Total interest paid:

$$
\begin{array}{rcl}
12 \times \$80 & = & \$960 \\
\$1,000 - \$100 & = & \$900 \\
\hline
& & \$60
\end{array}
$$

$$\text{Effective interest rate} = \frac{2(12)(\$60)}{\$900(12+1)} = \frac{\$1,440}{\$11,700} = 12.31\%$$

.25 Effective Interest Rate—Compounding Period Less Than One Year

Effective Interest Rate =

$$\left[1 + \frac{\text{Nominal Rate}}{\begin{array}{c}\text{Number of times interest}\\\text{is converted in a year}\end{array}} \right]^{\text{No. of times interest is converted in a year}} - 1$$

What is the effective interest rate if the nominal rate of 7% is compounded for the following terms?

Term	No. of periods	Formula	Effective Rate
Annual	1	$\left[1 + \dfrac{.07}{1}\right]^{1} - 1$	$= .07000$
Semi-Annual	2	$\left[1 + \dfrac{.07}{2}\right]^{2} - 1$	$= .07123$
Quarterly	4	$\left[1 + \dfrac{.07}{4}\right]^{4} - 1$	$= .07186$
Monthly	12	$\left[1 + \dfrac{.07}{12}\right]^{12} - 1$	$= .07229$
Weekly	52	$\left[1 + \dfrac{.07}{52}\right]^{52} - 1$	$= .07246$
Daily	365	$\left[1 + \dfrac{.07}{365}\right]^{365} - 1$	$= .07250$

.27 Rate of Interest—Continuous Compounding

$$\text{Effective Rate of Interest} = e^{\text{nominal rate}} - 1$$
$$\text{(continuous compounding)}$$

Note: e is the base of natural logarithms and calculus solves this as e = 2.71828 . . . therefore:

$$\text{Effective Rate of Interest} = 2.71828^{\text{nominal rate}} - 1$$
$$\text{(continuous compounding)}$$

Example: A nominal rate of 8%, converted continuously, corresponds to what effective rate?

$$\text{Effective Rate of Interest} = 2.71828^{(.08)} - 1$$
$$\text{(continuous compounding)}$$
$$= 8.33\%$$

In other words, both rates 8.33% = effective rate, and 8% = nominal rate compounded continually, will yield the same compound sum at the end of one year.

.28 Effective Rate of Interest on Accounts Receivable Financing

Effective Rate of Interest on Accounts Receivable Financing

$$i = \frac{\text{Daily interest rate on face of invoice financed} \times 360}{\text{\% of the face amount of invoice}}$$

Example: Finance company will loan 80% of the face amount of invoice. The charge is 1/30 of 1% per day computed on the face amount. What is the effective interest rate?

$$i = \frac{(.01/30) \times 360}{.80} = 15\%$$

¶ 637 INTEREST—COMPOUND

.01 Basic Concept

Compound Interest—Future Value

Compound interest is interest on interest. The original value has interest applied on it. Then for the next period, the amount is calculated on the original sum, plus the interest earned on the prior period. The process continues. See ¶ 635 on simple interest, ¶ 633 on future value, and ¶ 651 on present value.

Compound Interest—Future Value

FV = Principal × (1 + interest pate per period)^number of periods

Example: How much will $2,000 accumulate to over 10 years at 8% per year compounded annually?

Using the future value formula:

FV = $2,000 (1 + .08)^{10}= $4,317.80

Using the future value factor from table at ¶ 691.09

FV = $2,000 (2.1589) = $4,317.80

Compound Interest—Present Value

Compound Interest—Present Value

$$PV = FV \times (1 + \text{interest rate per period})^{-\text{number of periods}}$$

Example: What is the future value of a 10 year note for $200,000 with 8% interest compounded semi-annually?

If the note is sold immediately for a 7% yield, how much money should be received for the note?

$$\text{Future value} = \$200,000 \left(1 + \frac{.08}{2}\right)^{20}$$

Using the future value factor from table at ¶ 691.09 with 4% per period for 20 periods

$$= \$200,000 \left(2.1911231\right) = \$438,225$$
$$PV = \left(\$438,225\right) \times \left(1 + .07\right)^{-10} = \$222,771.37$$

Using the present value factor from table at ¶691.07 :

$$PV = \$438,225 \times .50834932 = \$222,771.37$$

Example: Present value (non-interest bearing note) What is the PV of a $6,000, 10 year non-interest bearing note if money is worth 6%?

From PV table at ¶ 691.07 for 6% at 10 periods.

= $6,000 (.5583948)

= $3,350.37

.03 Compound Interest—With Fraction of a Year Terms

Example (1): Fractional period method:

FV = Principal × (1 + interest rate)^{term}

Suppose $1,000 is invested for 3 years and 3 months (term = 3 3/12 = 3 1/4 years) at 6% interest. What is the compound future value?

FV		
	=	$1,000 (1.06)$^{13/4}$
	=	$1,000 (1.06)$^{12/4}$ (1.06)$^{1/4}$
	=	$1,000 (1.06)^{3} (1.06)$^{1/4}$
	=	$1,000 (1.1910) (1.0147)
	=	$1,208.51

This value is computed by obtaining whole (annual) periods of compounding times a fractional period of compounding.

Practical method:

$$FV = Principal \left[1 + \left(\frac{\text{Annual interest rate}}{\text{No. of conversions per year}}\right)^{(\text{no. of conversions per year})(\text{no. of years})}\right]$$

$$\times \left[1 + \frac{\text{Annual interest rate}}{\text{No. of conversions per year}}\right]$$

What is the compound future value if $1,000 is invested for 3 years and 3 months at 6% interest?

FV	=	$1,000 (1 + .06 /1)$^{(1)(3)}$ (1 + .06 / 4)
FV	=	$1,000 (1.1910) (1.015)
	=	$1,208.87

Note: That 3 months = 1/4 of a year (or 4 conversions) so interest rate of .06 above is 1/4 ×.06 = .06 / 4

Example (2): Fractional Period Method:

Given:

Principal = $1000

Bank pays 8% annual, compounded quarterly

What does $1000 grow to in two quarters?

Solution:

FV	=	Principal (1 + interest rate)^{term}
	=	$1000 (1.08)$^{1/2}$
	=	$1000 (1.04)
	=	$1040

Example (3): Fractional Period Method:

Given:

$2000

Bank pays 12% annual rate

Interest is compounded monthly

What does $2000 grow to in 1 quarter (3 months)?

Solution:

FV = Principal $(1 + \text{interest rate})^{\text{term}}$

Convert annual interest rate to monthly rate = .12 / 12 = .01 per month

$$\begin{aligned} FV \;&=\; \$2000 \,(1 + .01)^3 \\ &=\; \$2000 \,(1.03) \\ &=\; \$2060 \end{aligned}$$

Example (4): Fractional Period Method:

Given:

Bank lends $20,000 at an annual rate of 16% for one year

The interest is compounded quarterly

What amount is due the bank at the end of one year?

Solution:

Convert annual interest rate to compound quarterly period = .16 / 4 = .04

$$\begin{aligned} FV \;&=\; \text{Principal } (1 + \text{interest rate})^{\text{term}} \\ &=\; \$20,000 \,(1 + .04)^4 \\ &=\; \$20,000 \,(1.16986) \\ &=\; \$23,397.20 \end{aligned}$$

.05 Compound Interest—With Changing Rates

$$(\text{Principal}) \left(\frac{1 + \text{Nominal Rate}}{\text{No. of conversions within a year}} \right)^{(\text{no. of conversions within a year})(\text{no. of years})}$$

How much will $10,000 grow to in a C/D left in the account for 6 years given that:

1st: for 2 years, the bank paid 3%, compounded quarterly;

2nd: for 3 years, the bank paid 4% compounded semi-annually;

3rd: for last year, the bank paid 5%, compounded annually.

Future Value =

$$\begin{aligned} &\$10,000 \,[(1 + .03 \,/\, 4)^{4 \times 2} \,(1 + .04 \,/\, 2)^{2 \times 3} \,(1 + .05 \,/\, 1)^{1 \times 1}] \\ =\; &\$10,000 \,[(1.0075)^8 \,(1.02)^6 \,(1.05)^1] \\ =\; &\$12,553.09 \end{aligned}$$

.09 Compound Interest—Nominal Rate and Effective Rate

What effective rate equals a nominal rate of 10% compounded quarterly on an investment of $1,000 for 1 year?

¶637.05

$$\text{Effective rate} = 1 + \dfrac{\text{(Nominal rate)}}{\left(\begin{array}{c}\text{Number of times interest}\\ \text{is converted in a year}\end{array}\right)}^{\text{No. of times interest is converted in a year}} - 1$$

$$\text{Effective rate} = \left(1 + \dfrac{.10}{4}\right)^{4} - 1$$

$$= (1.025)^4 - 1$$
$$= 1.1038 - 1$$
$$= 10.38\%$$

What nominal rate equals an effective rate of 10% compounded quarterly on an investment of $1,000 for one year?

Nominal rate = No. of times interest (1 + effective rate)$^{1/\text{No. of times interest is converted in a year}} -1$ is converted in a year

Nominal rate $= 4\,[(1 + .10)^{1/4} - 1]$
$\qquad\qquad = 4\,[1.0241 - 1]$
$\qquad\qquad = 4\,[.0241]$
$\qquad\qquad = 9.64\%$

The effective rate is 10% and the nominal rate = 9.64%

.11 Compound Interest—Nominal Rate

When a year is divided into several periods, interest is compounded for each period. If interest is compounded at 2% every 3 months, the nominal interest rate may be stated as 8 percent compounded quarterly. This will be higher than 8% annual, because interest is compounded on interest each quarter.

FV   = $1,000 (1 + .02)^1 = \$1,020$
FV   = $1,020 (1 + .02)^1 = \$1,040$
FV   = $1,040 (1 + .02)^1 = \$1,061$
FV   = $1,061 (1 + .02)^1 = \$1,082$
or
FV   =   Principal (1 + interest rate)^{term}
FV   = $1,000 (1 + .02)^4$
$\qquad$ $1,000 (1.02)^4$
$=$ $1,082$

.13 Compound Interest—Effective Rate

$$\text{Effective rate} \quad = \quad \dfrac{\text{Future value} - \text{principal}}{\text{principal}}$$

If $1,000 is compounded quarterly at 8% (2% per quarter), the effective rate is:

$$\text{Effective rate} \quad = \quad \dfrac{1,082 - 1,000}{1,000} \quad = \quad 8.2\%$$

The nominal rate is the expressed annual rate when interest is compounded more than once a year. (8% above). The effective rate is the rate of interest actually earned with more frequent conversions. (8.2% above).

However, if $1,000 is compounded annually at 8%, the future value is:

$$FV = \$1,000 \ (1 + .08)^1 = \$1,080$$

The effective rate is:

$$\text{Effective rate} \quad = \quad \frac{\$1,080 - \$1,000}{\$1,000} \quad = \quad 8\%$$

¶ 639 INVENTORY

.01 Inventory Analysis

Inventory Management

- Does the inventory system provide information for:
  - Overall composition of inventory
  - Physical stocking location
  - Total inventory levels
  - Stock-out costs
  - Availability
  - Units on hand
  - Cost per unit
- Are there policies concerning obsolescence damage?
- Are there proper safeguards in place to reduce theft?
- Is insurance coverage adequate? Not too high nor too low?
- Have carrying costs of excessive inventory been investigated?
- Is there consignment inventory?
- Is inventory excessive?
- Have clear return policies been established?
- To control "creeping up" inventory levels consider purposefully limiting space for inventory storage.
- Implement time-phased replenishment of inventory for carefully projected needs.
- Fine-tune the inventory forecasting methods.
- Profile the economy and the marketplace. Is it expanding? Contracting? Are more competitors entering the marketplace?
- Understand your customers' purchasing and inventory requirements. What are their short term and immediate plans? Are they changing their product mix? Are they moving into new markets? Seek to obtain more information on what they may buy.
- Miscalculations in projecting sales can cause significant inventories over or under situations.

Proper Inventory Control Advantages

- Provides for advantageous purchasing.
- Provides improved service to customers by:
  — Avoiding stockouts.
  — Providing quick delivery.
- May reduce storage requirement costs.
- Improves product quality.
- Reduces handling costs.
- Reduces losses due to theft or spoilage.
- Provides for more efficient production.
- Provides savings for bulk shipments.

Inventory Costs

- Carrying costs: Storage, obsolescence, taxes, insurance, protection, breakage, opportunity cost of capital
- Interest rates on borrowed funds
- Ordering costs
- Stock out costs
- Market decline
- Production setup costs

Inventory Valuation Methods

- Replacement cost
- Last in, first out
- First in, last out
- Cost
- Lower of cost or market
- Standard cost
- Standard supplier's catalog cost
- Specific identification
- Average cost
- Weighted average cost
- Weighted moving average cost
- Moving average cost
- Retail method
- Gross profit

Inventory Records

- Part number
- Part description
  — Location

— Minimum and maximum on hand quantity

— Reorder point

— Economic order quantity

— Different vendor prices

— Quantity on hand, on order, committed

— Unit cost

— Sales prices

— Historical usage information

.02 Inventory—Total Annual Inventory Cost

The following formula calculates the total annual inventory cost as composed of set-up outlays, plus the value of inventory, plus the annual inventory carrying cost.

$$\text{Total annual inventory cost} =$$

$$\frac{(\text{Annual demand in units per year})(\text{Set - up costs per lot})}{\text{Ecomomic lot size}} +$$

$$\left[\begin{array}{c} (.05)(\text{Unit Cost}) \times (\text{Total company charges as a \% of cost of items carried annually} \\ \text{in inventory}) \times (\text{Economic lot size of units per lot}) \end{array} \right] +$$

$$\left[(\text{Annual demand in units per yr.}) \times (\text{Unit cost}) \right]$$

Example: What is the total annual inventory cost given the following data?

Annual demand in units per year = $500,000

# of lots per year = 5

Set - up cost per lot = $200

Unit cost = $3.00 (Total cost, composed of direct material, labor and overhead for manufactured items.)

Total carrying charge is % of cost of items carried in inventory = 15% (Composed of taxes, insurance, interest, etc.)

Assume economic lot size of 100,000 units (Based on a annual demand / # of lots per year) 100,000=500,000/5

$$\text{Total annual inventory cost (10 lots per year)} =$$

$$\left[\frac{(500,000)(\$200)}{\$50,000} \right] + \left[(.05)(\$3.00)(.15)(10,000) \right] + \left[(500,000)(\$3.00) \right]$$

$$= \$2000 + \$2250 + \$1,500,000$$
$$= \$1,504,250$$

Example: What is the total inventory cost given the data above, except that there are 10 lots per year with an assumed economic lot size of 50,000?

Total annual inventory cost (10 lots per year) =

$$\left[\frac{(500,000)\ (\$200)}{\$50,000}\right] + \left[(.05)(\$3.00)(.15)(50,000)\right] + \left[(500,000)(\$3.00)\right]$$

= \$2000 + \$1125 + \$1,500,000
= \$1,503,125

.03 Inventory—Estimation Methods

Gross Profit Method

Inventory Estimation—Gross Profit Method

Ending Inventory (GPM)

= (Beg. inventory + purchases + freight-in)

– (Sales (1 – Gross profit % of sales))

Example: What is the interim financial ending inventory estimated to be, given the following data?

Gross profit % = 35%

Sales = \$125,000

Purchases = \$ 80,000

Beginning inventory = \$25,000

Freight-in = \$4,000

Ending inventory (GPM)	= (\$25,000 + \$80,000 + \$4,000)
	– (\$125,000 (1 – .35))
	= \$109,000 – \$81,250
	= \$27,750

Retail Inventory Method

Estimating Inventory—Retail Inventory Method

Ending cost inventory (RM)

$$= \text{Ending Retail Inventory}\left(\text{RM}\right)$$

$$\times \left[\frac{\left(\text{Beg. inv. at cost + freight in + purchases at cost}\right)}{\left(\text{Beg. retail inv. + purchases at retail + net markups}\right)}\right]$$

Where Ending Retail Inventory (RM) = [(Beginning retail inventory + Purchases at retail + net markups) – (Sales + worthless inventory + employee discounts + net markdowns)]

Example of estimating the inventory by the retail method, given the following data:

Markups	$2,000	Markdowns	$3,000
Markup cancellations	– 500	Markdown cancellations	– 1,000
Net markups	$1,500	Net markdowns	$2,000

	Retail	Cost
Ending inventory	?	?
Purchases	$75,000	$60,000
Sales	45,000	
Beginning inventory	32,000	25,000
Freight-in		4,000
Worthless inventory	250	
Employee discounts	200	

Answer

Ending Retail Inventory (RM) =

$\quad$ $[(32,000 + 75,000 + 1,500) - (45,000 + 250 + 200 + 2000)]$

$\quad$ = $61,050

$\quad$ $61,050 \times [(25,000 + 4,000 + 60,000)/(32,000 + 75,000 + 1,500)]$

$\quad$ = $[61,050 \times [(89,000)/(108,500)]]$

$\quad$ = $61,050 \times (.8203)$

$\quad$ = $50,079

Ending retail inventory = $61,050

Ending cost inventory = $50,079

.05 Reorder Models

Fixed-Quantity Inventory Reorder Model

This method assumes the following are constant:

- Inventory holding cost is based on average inventory
- Requires no safety stock
- Demand
- Lead time
- Price per unit
- Ordering cost

Fixed-Quantity Inventory Reorder Model

Economic Order Quantity

$$\sqrt{\frac{2DS}{H}}$$

Reorder Point

d × L

Total cost

DC + (D/Q) S + (Q/2)H

Where:
D	= Annual demand
S	= Cost of placing an order
H	= Annual holding cost per unit of average inventory
d	= Average daily demand, D/365
L	= Lead time
C	= Purchase cost per unit
Q	= to be ordered

Fixed Quantity Inventory Reorder With Usage

Production of items and usage take place simultaneously.

Fixed Quantity Inventory Reorder With Usage

Economic Order Quantity

$$\sqrt{\frac{2\,DS}{H} \times \frac{P}{(P-di)}}$$

Reorder Point

di × L

Total cost

DC + (D/Q)S + ((P – di)QH)/2P

Where:
P	= Production rate that produces the item
D	= Demand for item
L	= Lead time
di	= Daily usage rate

Fixed-Period Inventory Reorder Model

A fixed period model is designed to place orders of varying quantity needs on a repetitive *time* basis.

Periodic systems require carrying a larger inventory to prevent stock-outs.

Fixed-Period Inventory Reorder Model with Usage

Optimal Time Period to Order

$$\sqrt{\frac{2S}{DH}}$$

Optimal Order Quantity

D × T

Total cost

$$DC + \frac{DS}{DT} + \frac{DTH}{2}$$

Where:
H	= Annual storage cost per unit of average inventory
T	= Reorder time as fraction of year
S	= Cost of placing an order
D	= Annual demand
C	= Purchase cost per unit
Q	= Quantity to be ordered

.07 Inventory—Fixed Quantity Inventory Reorder Cycle

The following formula calculates how many times a year inventory should be replenished.

$$\text{Number of times inventory should be ordered} = \frac{\text{Annual demand in units}}{\text{Economic order quantity}}$$

Example: If annual demand for a product was 600,000 units and the economic order quantity was 50,000 units, how often should inventory be ordered?

$$\text{No. of times inventory should be ordered} = \frac{600,000}{50,000}$$

$$= 12 \text{ times a year}$$

Inventory should be ordered every 30 days (365 / 12)

.08 Inventory—Economic Order Quantity—Cost of Capital

The annual holding cost per unit is the unit cost times the total carrying charges, expressed as an annual percentage. The carrying charge includes all costs including interest. If the interest factor is separated out and analyzed it will call attention to the interest (cost of capital) in financial inventory decisions. By referring to the following formula, one can note how different interest rates will affect the EOQ.

$$\sqrt{\frac{2 \times (\text{Annual demand}) (\text{Set - up cost})}{(\text{Unit cost}) \times \left[\begin{array}{l}\text{Carrying charges as a \% + Interest rate} \\ \text{of cost of items carried} \\ \text{in inventory}\end{array}\right]}}$$

.09 Inventory—Fixed Quantity Inventory Reorder with Continuously Rising Prices

Use the following formula to compute the EOQ where there is a steady percent price increase. This % rise could be based on historical data, pegged to some index, or just be an anticipated rate of price increase.

Economic order quantity (with continuous price increase) =

$$\sqrt{\frac{2(\text{Annual demand in units}) \times \left[\begin{array}{l}\text{Order cost per order} \\ \text{independent of order size + Fixed cost to maintain inventory for 1 yr}\end{array}\right]}{(\text{Per unit cost})\left[\dfrac{\begin{array}{l}\text{Inventory cost that} \\ \text{varies with quanity and storage}\end{array}}{\text{Per unit cost}} - (2)(\text{Percent price increase}) + \left[1 + \dfrac{\begin{array}{l}\text{Inventory cost that} \\ \text{varies with order size}\end{array}}{\text{Per unit cost}}\right]\right]}}$$

.11 Inventory—Economic Order Size and Volume Discounts

Should a company change its economic order size to take advantage of quantity discounts? Additional costs are the carrying outlays less savings on ordering expenses from fewer ordering cycles. The savings from extra quantity purchases equal the discount per unit, times the usage. The following formula considers the savings from the lower purchase price (the unit discount times the annual demand) less the net increase in costs.

Volume discount net savings =

(Discount savings)-(Additional carrying costs)-(Savings on ordering expenses)

= (Unit discount) (Annual usage)

$$- \left[\frac{(\text{Revised lot size} - \text{original EOQ}) \times \left[\begin{array}{l} \text{Total carrying charges as} \\ \text{a \% of items carried} \\ \text{annually in inventory} \end{array} \right] \times \text{unit cost}}{2} \right]$$

$$- \left[\frac{(\text{Annual usage}) (\text{Ordering cost})}{\text{Original EOQ}} - \frac{(\text{Annual usage}) (\text{Ordering cost})}{\text{Revised lot size}} \right]$$

Example: Given the following data, should the company change its order quantity in order to take advantage of a volume discount offered by its supplier where the supplier offers a per unit discount of $.02, if the company will order 30,000 units each time.

Economic order quantity = 21,000

Annual Demand = 500,000

Unit cost = $3.00

Ordering cost = $100

Revised lot size = 30,000

Total carrying charge as a % of cost of item carried in inventory = 15%

Volume discount savings =

$$(\$.02)(500,000) - \frac{(30,000 - 21,000)(.15)(\$3.00)}{2}$$

$$\left[\frac{(500,000)(\$100)}{21,000} - \frac{(500,000)(\$100)}{30,000} \right]$$

$$= \$10,000 - \$2025 - (\$2381 - \$1667)$$

$$= \$7261$$

This savings favors ordering 30,000 units per order.

.13 Inventory—Sell or Scrap Decision

If obsolete or scrap items have no current value to normal operations, the items should probably be sold and converted to cash. But what should be done with surplus inventory that is slow moving and gathering dust? Should it be sold for salvage or held for possible future sale? The following keep/sell ratio determines the decision as follows:

- If ratio is greater than 1, hold and sell the inventory at a higher price in the future.

- If ratio is less than 1, sell now at salvage value.

Keep / sell ratio =

$$\frac{\text{Probability of sell within a given time period} \times (\text{Normal selling price per item}) \times (\text{Number of items in inventory})}{(\text{Marginal investment rate}) \times (\text{Current salvage value}) \times (\text{Number of items in inventory})}$$

Example: Given the following facts, should the company sell its surplus inventory now for scrap at \$.20, or keep for a possible future sell at the normal price of \$1.00?

Probability of sell whithin 1 year = 25%

Firm's marginal investment rate = 12%

Normal selling price = \$1.00/each

Current salvage value = \$.20/each

Surplus number of items in inventory = 2,000

$$\text{Keep / sell ratio} = \frac{(.25)\,(\$1.00)\,(2,000)}{(.12)\,(\$.20)\,(2,000)} = \frac{500}{48} = 10.41$$

Since the keep/sell ratio is greater than 1, the company should wait and sell in the future, and hope their estimates are reasonable.

Example: If everything in the previous example remains the same, except the probability of a future sell is estimated at 2%, what would be the outcome?

$$\text{Keep / sell ratio} = \frac{(.02)(\$1.00)(2,000)}{(.12)(\$.20)(2,000)}$$

$$= \frac{40}{48}$$

$$= .83$$

Since the ratio is less than 1, the company should sell now for scrap value.

¶639.13

.15 Inventory—Return on Investment—Age Specific

By considering the Age-Specific-Return-on-Invesment of the average inventory per product, one can better analyze the profitability of the business' investment in its inventory. This is the inventory's return on investment (ROI) as it has changed over time on each product.

Such an analysis will help answer inventory questions such as:

- Is money tied up in overstocked inventory?
- Which inventory items are profitable?
- Is the trend of these profits increasing or decreasing?
- Should the older inventory items be discounted, so they can be moved?
- The analysis shows how much you are making on inventory as a function of how much you have on hand.
- The analysis helps to determine which older stock products need to be moved.

Step one: Calculate the Return on Investment of an inventory product.

Step two: Calculate the age-specific ROI of an inventory product.

Example: Product A versus Product B

Data:

Product A = Average Inventory
= (Beginning inventory + Ending inventory)/2
= ($150,000 + $150,000)/2
= $150,000

Product A Gross Profit = $40,000

Step one:

Product A = ROI of Average Inventory
= $40,000/$150,000
= 27%

Product B (in this example) has the same 27% ROI of average inventory.

Product A versus Product B

How does the ROI of product A compare to the ROI of product B? Use step two.

Step two: Age-Specific ROI

Data for Product A

Year	Begin Inventory	+ Purchases	- Sales	= Ending Inventory	Avg Inventory	Gross Profit $	ROI Avg Inventory	
Qtr 1	$150,000	+ $60,000	- $50,000	= $160,000	($150,000 + $160,000) /2 = $155,000	$13,000	$13,000 / $155,000 =	8%
Qtr 2	$160,000	+ $20,000	- $45,000	= $135,000	($160,000 + $135,000) /2 = $148,000	$11,000	$11,000 / $148,000 =	8%
Qtr 3	$135,000	+ $60,000	- $40,000	= $155,000	($135,000 + $155,000) /2 = $145,000	$10,000	$10,000 / $145,000 =	7%
Qtr 4	$155,000	+ $19,000	- $24,000	= $150,000	($155,000 + $150,000) /2 = $153,000	$6,000	$6,000 / $153,000 =	6%
Totals				$600,000		$40,000	$40,000 / $150,000 = 27%	27%

Avg Inventory = ($600,000 / 4) = $150,000

or Avg Inventory = (Beg inventory + Ending inventory) / 2 = ($150,000 + $150,000) / 2 = $150,000

Note that for Product A, the ROI on the avg inventory has declined each year from 8% to 6%.

Data for Product B

Year	Begin Inventory	+ Purchases	- Sales	= Ending Inventory	Avg Inventory	Gross Profit $	ROI Avg Inventory	
Qtr 1	$150,000	+ $60,000	- $70,000	= $140,000	($150,000 + $140,000) /2 = $145,000	$6,000	$6,000 / $145,000 =	4%
Qtr 2	$140,000	+ $20,000	- $10,000	= $150,000	($140,000 + $150,000) /2 = $145,000	$8,000	$8,000 / $145,000 =	6%
Qtr 3	$150,000	+ $40,000	- $30,000	= $160,000	($150,000 + $160,000) /2 = $160,000	$12,000	$12,000 / $160,000 =	8%
Qtr 4	$160,000	+ $20,000	- $30,000	= $150,000	($160,000 + $150,000) /2 = $155,000	$14,000	$14,000 / $155,000 =	9%
Totals				$600,000		$40,000	$40,000 / $150,000 = 27%	27%

Avg Inventory = ($600,000 / 4) = $150,000

or Avg Inventory = (Beg inventory + Ending inventory) / 2 = ($150,000 + $150,000) / 2 = $150,000

Note that for Product B, the ROI on the avg inventory has improved each year from 4% to 9%.

Conclusion:

Although both product A and B show a ROI on average inventory of 27%, the profit on Product A is declining, while the profit on product B is increasing. By preparing an age specific ROI, the owner can better understand the profits and make more appropriate business decisions regarding the inventory.

¶ 641 INVESTMENT

.01 Investment for Capital Asset Pricing—Expected Rate of Returns, Dividend Stream, Future Market Price, Total Asset Value

Solve for the following investment criterion given the following data:

Market price of ABC shares	= $65 /share
Dividend rate	= $3 /share
Dividend expected growth rate	= 10% /year
Interest free rate of return	= 4%
Market rate of return	= 11%
Stock volatility	= 1.2

Investment strategy is to hold security for 4 years
Estimated market price of ABC shares in 4 years = $90/share

$$\text{Expected rate of return} = \begin{bmatrix} \text{interest free} \\ \text{rate of return} \end{bmatrix} + \begin{bmatrix} \text{market rate} & \text{interest free} \\ \text{of return} & - & \text{rate of return} \end{bmatrix} \times$$

$$\begin{bmatrix} \text{stock} \\ \text{volatility} \end{bmatrix} = 4 + (11 - 4) \times 1.2 = 4 + 8.4 = 12.4\%$$

Present value of dividend stream =

$$\text{current dividend} \times \left[\frac{1 - \left[\dfrac{1 + \text{dividend growth rate}}{1 + \text{expected rate of return}} \right]^{\text{No. of periods}}}{\text{expected rate of return} - \text{dividend growth rate}} \right] =$$

$$\$3 \times \left[\frac{1 - \left[\dfrac{1 + .10}{1 + .124} \right]^4}{.124 - .10} \right] = \$3(3.438) = \$10.31$$

Present value of future market price =

$$\text{future market price} \times \left[\frac{1}{(1 + \text{expected rate of return})^{\text{No. of periods}}} \right]$$

$$= \$90 \frac{1}{(1 + .124)^4} = \$90 \frac{1}{1.5961} = \$56.39$$

Total present value of investment = present value of dividend stream + present value of future market price = $10.31 + $56.39 = $66.70

¶ 643 LEASE

.01 Effective Rate of Interest for a Lease

$$\frac{\text{Financial amount}}{\text{Monthly lease payment}}$$

= (Table value factor for present value of annuity of $1 at N lease periods for i interest)

Where: Financial amount is the current cash outlay.

Example: Machinery to be leased costs $8,275, with $640 down, 36 monthly payments of $250/month starting one month hence.

At termination, the machinery can be purchased for one dollar.

What is the annual effective rate of interest?

$$\frac{8,275 - 640}{250} = 30.54$$

30.54 = Table value factor for PV of an annuity for 36 months at i interest

Find *monthly* value in table of 30.54 at ¶ 691.13, then read heading to locate interest of .11 per month.

Formula technique for more effective annual rate

= $(1 + .11/12)^{12} - 1$

= 1.1157–1 = .1157 or 11.57%

Table, "Effective Annual Rate for Different Periods of Compounding," at ¶ 691.05 also provides effective annual rate for monthly compounding at an 11% nominal annual rate.

Effective Annual Rates for Different Periods of Compounding

Nominal Rate	Period of Compounding				
	Daily	Weekly	Monthly	Quarterly	Semi-Annual
10%	10.5155782%	10.5064793%	10.4713067%	10.3812891%	10.2500000%
11%	11.6259572%	11.6148386%	11.5718836%	11.4621259%	11.3025000%
12%	12.7474616%	12.7340987%	12.6825030%	12.5508810%	12.3600000%
13%	13.8802025%	13.8643647%	13.8032482%	13.6475928%	13.4225000%
14%	15.0242923%	15.0057425%	14.9342029%	14.7523001%	14.4900000%
15%	16.1798443%	16.1583394%	16.0754518%	15.8650415%	15.5625000%

.03 Capitalized Value of Lease

Capitalized Lease Value

Monthly lease payments ×

$$\left[\left(\begin{array}{c} \text{Present value of annuity of} \\ \text{\$1 per period} \end{array} \right) + 1 \right] + \left[(\text{Option price}) \times \left(\begin{array}{c} \text{Present value of \$1} \\ \text{at compound interest} \end{array} \right) \right]$$

Example: Company obtains a 3 year lease on machinery with payments of $550/43.03. At the end of the lease, the option purchase price is $3,500. Current interest rates on similar financing are 12% per year. What is the capitalized value of the lease?

Term = 3 years ×12 = 36 months

Interest = .12/12 = .01/month

Capitalized value of lease = $550

$$\times \left[(\text{Factor from present value table of annuity at} \quad \P 691.11 \text{ for 36 months at .01}) + 1 \right]$$
$$+ (\$3,500)(\text{factor from present value table for 36 months at .01})$$
$$= \$550 \left[(44.95504) + 1 \right] + (\$3,500)(.5505)$$
$$= \$550 (45.95055 + 1) + (\$3,500)(.5505)$$
$$= \$550 (46.95055) + (\$3,500)(.5505)$$
$$= \$25,822.80 + \$1,926.75$$
$$= \$27,749.55$$

.05 Lease Versus Purchase—Net Present Value Method

There are several models analyzing the lease-purchase-borrow decision. This technique excludes explicit financing costs from the capital budget decision process. It does not address the financing factor. The following technique incorporates rates that reflect the degree of risk associated with various flows, such as a higher rate that reflects outcomes that are less predictable, such as operating costs on estimated salvage value. The net present value of the flows relating to the leasing option is the present value of the asset's net after-tax cash net income, minus the after-tax present values of the lease payments. The tax savings and lease payments are discounted at a rate reflecting lower risk. The net present value of the flows relating to buying the asset is the sum of the present values of the asset's net after-tax cash operating profits, plus the discounted after-tax residual value, less the initial cost of the asset.

These flows are combined to determine the change in net present value which equals the net present value of the buying option minus the net present value of the leasing option. This complicated formula can be illustrated simply in a tabular format. A positive change in net present value, favors purchasing over leasing. A negative change in net present value, indicates that leasing is preferable to buying.

Example: Given the following data, should the firm lease or purchase the equipment it is considering (Where the decision is based on a numerical answer alone)?

Purchase:

Cost = $50,000

Economic life = 4 years

Depreciation = Straight line

Salvage = $5,000

Tax rate on salvage sale = 15%

Maintenance = $1,000/year

Lease:

Annual fixed lease payment = $15,000

Net income tax rate = 25%

General:

Cost of capital = 12%

Pre-tax rate on recent borrowings = 8%

From data from the table following we conclude:

Change in net present value =

> Present value of purchase − cost + present value of lease
> = $15,565 − $50,000 + $38,984
> = + $4,549

The positive change in net present value favors purchasing over leasing.

.06 Lease Versus Purchase Analysis Illustration Table

	Purchase Analysis					Lease Analysis	
	1	**2**	**3**	**4**	**5**	**6**	**7**
	Tax saved due to Straight Line Depreciation	Maintenance Cost Net of Taxes	Salvage Gain Net of Taxes on Gain Rate	Col. 1 less Col. 2 plus Col. 3	Present Value of Col. 4 at 12%*	Lease Payments Net of Taxes	Present Value of Column 6 at 8% Net of Taxes**
Year							
1	.25 ($12,500)	(1−.25) (1,000)		$3,875	$3,555	(1−.25) ($15,000)	$10,613
2	.25 ($12,500)	(1−.25) (1,000)		$3,875	$3,262	(1−.25) ($15,000)	$10,013
3	.25 ($12,500)	(1−.25) (1,000)		$3,875	$2,992	(1−.25) ($15,000)	$9,447
4	.25 ($12,500)	(1−.25) (1,000)	(1−.15) ($5,000)	$8,125	$5,756	(1−.25) ($15,000)	$8,911
Total					15,565		$38,984

Year	Total × Present value factor at 12% of present value*	Year	Total × Present value factor at 6%** = (1 − .25)(.08) = Present value
1	$3,875 × .9174 = $3.555	1	$11,250 × .9434 = $10,613
2	$3,875 × .8417 = $3,262	2	$11,250 × .8900 = $10,013
3	$3,875 × .7722 = $2,992	3	$11,250 × .8397 = $9,447
4	$8,125 × .7084 = $5,756	4	$11,250 × .7921 = $8,911

.07 Lease Versus Purchase—Basic Interest Rate on Borrowing

The basic interest rate approach (developed by R.F. Vancil) allows 100% financing. The cost of the debt financing is the cash purchase price minus the sum of the present values arising from the annual depreciation changes. The cost of leasing is the equivalent cash price of the asset less the sum of the present cash values arising from the noninterest portion of the lease payments.

> **Example:** Based on the summary of the following data in the analysis charts, the firm should lease the desired equipment.

Purchase:

Cost = $50,000

Economic life = 4 years

Depreciation − straight line = $12,500/year

Loan interest rate = 10%

¶643.06

Lease:

Annual lease payments = $15,000/year

General:

Investment rate = 15%

Tax rate = 25%

Purchase with 100% Debt—Present Value of Cost of Purchase

	1	2	3	4
Year	Annual Depreciation St. Line	Depreciation Expense (tax of .25) Col. 1 × .25	Present Value Factor at 12%	Present Value Cost of Ownership Col. 2 × Col. 3
1	$12,500	$3,125	0.8929	$2,790
2	$12,500	$3,125	0.7972	$2,491
3	$12,500	$3,125	0.7118	$2,246
4	$12,500	$3,125	0.6355	$1,986
			Total	$9,513
			Plus cost	$50,000
			Value cost of purchase	$59,513

.09 Lease versus Purchase—Opportunity Loss

A further analysis (which contemplates early lease termination) regarding the lease versus purchase decision can be made by comparing the present value flows between leasing and purchasing. These are then assigned a probability outcome. Suppose for example, in the lease versus purchase analysis above using the discounted cash flow method, the following flows were instead computed (see column (1) and (2)).

The opportunity loss analysis says that if we leased when we should have bought, then the additional cost of leasing is an "opportunity cost." It represents the incremental loss incurred by not selecting the less expensive alternative of purchasing. Probabilities are assigned that represent the year that the lease might be terminated, i.e., changed or bought-out due to obsolescence; changed by trading to another lease, etc. The following analysis illustrates that the opportunity cost of leasing exceeds buying by $484 ($1,056 – $572), this implies the company should consider purchasing if there is a possibility that the equipment might be "changed" before the lease term ends.

.10 Opportunity Loss Analysis Table

	1 Present value of leasing cost	2 Present value cost of purchase	Probability	Lease Opportunity Loss Col. 1 less Col. 2	Expected Value	Purchase Opportunity Loss Col. 1 less Col. 2	Expected Value
Year							
1	$10,045	$7,584	0.1	$2,461	$246		
2	$8,969	$6,943	0.4	$2,026	$810		
3	$8,008	$9,100	0.4			$1,092	$437
4	$7,149	$8,500	0.1			$1,351	$135
Totals	$34,171	$32,127	1		$1,056		$572

Financial Lease—Present Value of After-Tax Cost

	1 Annual Lease Payment	2 Cost of Lease Payments Net of Tax of 25%	3 Present Value Factor at 12% Investment Rate	4 Present value of Cost of Leasing (Columns 2 × 3)
Year				
1	$15,000	(1-.25) ($15,000) = $11,250	0.8929	$10,045
2	$15,000	(1-.25) ($15,000) = $11,250	0.7972	$8,969
3	$15,000	(1-.25) ($15,000) = $11,250	0.7118	$8,008
4	$15,000	(1-.25) ($15,000) = $11,250	0.6355	$7,149
Total				$34,171

Purchase with Debt—Present Value of After-Tax Cost

	1 Loan Balance	2 Loan Payment (Gross)	3 Loan Payment to Principal	4 Loan Payment to Interest 10%	5 Annual Depreciation-Straight Line
Year					
1	$40,000	$12,619	$8,619	$4,000	$12,500
2	$31,381	$12,619	$9,481	$3,138	$12,500
3	$21,901	$12,619	$10,429	$2,190	$12,500
4	$11,472	$12,619	$11,472	$1,147	$12,500

	6 Deprec. Plus Interest (Columns 4+5)	7 Deprec. Plus Interest Net of Tax Rate of 25% (Columns 6 × .25)	8 Loan Payments Net of Taxes Saved (Columns 2 – 7)	9 Present Value Factor at 12%	10 Present Value of Cost of Purchase
Year					
1	$16,500	$4,125	$8,494	0.8929	$7,584
2	$15,638	$3,910	$8,709	0.7972	$6,943
3	$14,690	$3,673	$8,946	0.7118	$6,368
4	$13,647	$3,412	$9,207	0.6355	$5,851
				Total	$26,746
				plus down payment	$10,000
				Total present value cost of purchase	$36,746

.11 Lease Versus Purchase—Discounted Cash Flow on Borrowing

This method compares discounted cash flows of leasing to borrowing. Leasing should be chosen if the discounted present value cost of lease financing is less than the discounted present value cost of debt financing. Debt financing should be chosen if the discounted present value cost of debt financing is less than the discounted present value cost of lease financing.

> **Example:** Should the firm lease or purchase the desired equipment given the following data?

Purchase:

Economic life = 4 years

Cost = $50,000

Depreciation straight line = $12,500

¶643.11

Down payment = $10,000

Loan = $40,000

Loan financed for 4 years at 10% interest, with amount payable of $12,619 at end of year.

Lease:

Annual lease payments = $15,000/year

General:

Investment rate = 12%

Tax rate = 25%

Note from the following analysis that the present value of a financial lease is $34,171 and the present value cost of purchasing with borrowing is $36,746.

.12 Lease Versus Purchase—Discounted Cash Flow Table

Financial Lease—Present Value of Tax Savings on Non-Interest Portion of Lease Payments

	1	2	3	4	5	
	Imputed interest expenses Lease Cost Balance	Interest exp on leasing at 10 % loan rate	Annual lease payment less imputed interest	Net lease payment times tax rate of 25%	Present value factor at12% interest rate	Present value of cost of leasing on non-interest portion of lease payments
Year	Col. 1-col 3	Col. 1 × .10	=$15,000 - Col. 2	Col. 3 × .25		
1	$50,000	$5,000	$10,000	$2,500	0.8929	$2,232
2	$40,000	$4,000	$11,000	$2,750	0.7972	$2,192
3	$29,000	$2,900	$12,100	$3,025	0.7118	$2,153
4	$16,900	$1,690	$13,310	$3,328	0.6355	$2,115
					Total	$8,692
					Plus cost	$50,000

Total present value cost of non-interest portion of lease payments $58,692

.13 Buy Versus Lease

- Buying outright by paying cash or by using a loan
- Lease

Leasing is "renting" for a specific amount of time. At the end of the lease, the car is turned back in. One is only paying for a portion of the value of the item, not its entire value. Regarding leasing a car, costs for registration, taxes and plates, and maintenance and repairs must still be paid. Most car leases have a surcharge for driving more than a certain number of miles over the term of the lease. Any "excessive" wear and tear on the vehicle must be paid for at the end of the lease.

Leasing Benefits

- Off-balance sheet financing. It does not add to borrowing maximums for other loan qualifications.
- Less up-front money.
- Lower monthly payment, but not lower total costs.

- The higher the cost of the car and the business use percentage, the greater will be the tax advantage.

Buying Benefits

- Car has a residual value and can be resold.
- No restrictions on mileage or use.
- No insurance problems regarding a premature termination.
- The interest charges may be deductible on a tax return if a home equity or investment/business-type loan is used for the financing.
- You can treat the car however you wish.
- No residual valuation concerns.

Questions to analyze:

- How long do I want to drive this make/model car?
- How many miles do I drive per year?
- What kind of monthly payment can I handle?
- What deductible business-use percentage will be available?

Assumptions:

Income Tax Rate 28%	
Payoff Period months 36	
Lease Buyout Price	$ 5,500
Business Use Percent	10%
Interest Deductibility Percent	10%
Pre Tax Investment Rate	10%

Cash:

Cash Price	$18,000

Loan:

Down payment	2,000
Monthly Payment	516
Loan Rate	10%

Lease:

Down payment	3,000
Refundable Deposit	0
Monthly Payment	600
Total Other Expenses for Full Term	1,000

Summary:

	Purchase With Cash	Purchase by Loan	Lease
Initial Payment	$18,000	$2,000	$3,000
Monthly Payment		516	600
Total Payments	18,000	$20,576	$25,600
Foregone Savings	4,325	481	721
Lease Buyout Price			5,500
Tax Savings on Interest		72	

¶643.13

	Purchase With Cash	Purchase by Loan	Lease
Tax Savings on Depreciation		237	237
Expense Write-Off			717
Lease Inclusion Effect			3
Total Cost	22,089	20,748	31,107

.15 Lease Capitalization—Rule of Thumb Estimation

The following formula estimates the total value of lease expenditures which can be used as a guideline to determine the balance sheet lease liability for planning purposes.

Capitalized value of lease indebtedness =

$$(\text{Annual lease payments}) \times \frac{(1 + \text{Interest rate})\, \text{Term in years} - 1}{(1 + \text{Interest rate})\, \text{Term in years}\ (\text{Interest rate})}$$

Example: What is the estimated capitalized value of lease indebtedness given:

Annual lease payments = $15,000

Term = 5 years

The firm can presently borrow at 8%

Capitalized value of lease indebtedness

$$= \$15,000\ \frac{(1 + .08)^8 - 1}{(1 + .08)^8\ (.08)}$$

$$= \$15,000\ \frac{1.8509 - 1}{(1.8509)(.08)}$$

$$= \$15,000\ \frac{.8509}{.1481}$$

$$= \$86,182$$

.17 Lease—Lease Buyout Price

Leasing is the process of "renting" for a specific amount of time. You are only buying a portion of the item, not its entire value. Consider carefully the "lease buyout" price. The higher the lease buyout price at the end, the lower the monthly lease payment.

Assumptions

Pre-Tax Investment Rate of Return	8%
Business Use Percent	100%
Buy out is required on lease completion	
Tax Rate: Federal = 34%	
Retail Purchase price	$20,000

Lease Details

Lease 1

Payoff Period in Months	60
Downpayment	$5,000
Monthly Payment	$350

Lease 2

Payoff Period in Months	40
Downpayment	$5,000
Monthly Payment	$250
Refundable Deposits	$200
Other Expenses for Full Term	$132
Lease Buyout Price	$4,111

Lease 3

Payoff Period in Months	30
Downpayment	$5,000
Monthly Payment	$200

Lease 1

Refundable Deposits	$200
Other Expenses for Full Term	$132
Lease Buyout Price	$4,000

Lease 3

Refundable Deposits	$200
Other Expenses for Full Term	$123
Lease Buyout Price	$4,000

Lease Summary

	Lease #1	Lease #2	Lease #3
Initial Payment	$5,000	$5,000	$5,000
Total Additional Payments	$21,132	$10,132	$6,123
Foregone Savings on Downpayment	$1,567	$998	$732
Lease Inclusion Effect	$233	$101	$101
Lease Buyout Price	$4,000	$4,111	$4,000
Less Business Write-Off Savings	$8,885	$5,145	$3,782
Total Cost	$23,047	$15,197	$12,175

¶ 644 LEVERAGE

.01 Overview

Leverage or trading-on-equity is a method of maximizing the return to a company and raising the total value of the company by borrowing funds at a rate lower than the return rate that can be generated with those borrowed funds. Interest is tax deductible, which reduces the overall cost of the borrowing. Up to a level, borrowing will lower the overall cost of capital. But excessive leverage will increase risk and the possible risk of insolvency. Accumulating too much debt will no longer raise the firm's income, but will reduce the total worth of the business.

As long as earnings before interest and taxes exceed interest costs, net income will be greater in a leveraged firm than in one that is financed entirely with stock. But excessive leverage can reduce the total value of the firm. Businesses with stable incomes, like utility companies, can handle more leverage because of the less variance in their anticipated net income. Businesses with fluctuating incomes will find the marginal cost of capital rising as debt expands.

.03 Leverage—Operating

The concept of operating leverage does not concern itself with debt whatsoever. It seeks to maximize the return to the firm by the best combination of resource employment, such as:

- Determining the least cost of inputs
- Inventory holding costs vs. stockouts
- Different sales levels
- Fixed versus variable costs
- Marketing decisions and customer reactions

An analysis by example of operating leverage data:

Low Operating Leverage (100% Equity)

Probability of Sales	20%	60%	20%
# Units	100,000	150,000	200,000
$ Sales (at $12/unit)	$1,200,000	$1,800,000	$2,400,000
Variable costs (at $8/unit)	$800,000	$1,200,000	$1,600,000
Total fixed costs	$200,000	$200,000	$200,000
Net income before taxes	$200,000	$400,000	$600,000
Taxes (25% rate)	$50,000	$100,000	$150,000
Net Income after taxes	$150,000	$300,000	$450,000
Earnings per share (100,000)	$1.50	$3.00	$4.50

High Operating Leverage (100% Equity)

Probability of Sales	20%	60%	20%
# Units	100,000	150,000	200,000
$ Sales (at $12/unit)	$1,200,000	$1,800,000	$2,400,000
Variable costs (at $6/unit)	$600,000	$900,000	$1,200,000
Total fixed costs	$400,000	$400,000	$400,000
Net income before taxes	$200,000	$500,000	$800,000
Taxes (25% rate)	$50,000	$125,000	$200,000
Net Income after taxes	$150,000	$375,000	$600,000
Earnings per share (100,000)	$1.50	$3.75	$6.00

The low operating leverage firm has a low fixed investment amount and a high variable per unit cost. If it were to shut down operations almost all of its costs would disappear.

The earnings per share vary from $1.50 to $4.50 or by 3 times. The earnings range is relatively small.

However, the high operating leverage firm, with a high fixed investment amount, but lower variable costs, has an earnings per share range from $1.50 to $6.00, or by about 4 times.

The low operating leverage firm could sustain a dip in sales to 50,000 units and achieve Breakeven, but the high operating leverage firm would hit Breakeven at 66,666 units.

$$\text{Breakeven (in units)} = \frac{\text{Fixed expenses}}{\text{Unit sales price - unit variable expenses}}$$

$$\text{Breakeven (low leverage)} = \frac{\$200,000}{12 - 8} = 50,000 \text{ units}$$

$$\text{Breakeven (high leverage)} = \frac{\$400,000}{12 - 6} = 66,666 \text{ units}$$

.05 Leverage—Degree of Operating Leverage—Breakeven Known

Degree of operating leverage (DOL) defines the rate of change in net operating income in relation to a change in sales. If sales rise by some percent, how much will net operating income increase? (Note: This assumes a linear relationship.)

$$\text{DOL (Degree of operating leverage)} = \frac{\text{Given output number of units}}{\text{Given output number of units - breakeven points in units}}$$

Example: What is the degree of operating leverage for the low operating leverage company defined above at 100,000 units.

$$\text{DOL (Low)} = \frac{100,000}{100,000 - 50,000} = 2$$

What is the degree of operating leverage for 100,000 units for the high operating leverage company above?

$$\text{DOL (High)} = \frac{100,000}{100,000 - 66,666} = 3$$

DOL = 2, means that a 10% increase in sales will bring about a 20% rise in net operating income.

DOL = 3, means that a 10% increase in sales will bring about a 30% rise in net operating income.

.07 Leverage—Degree of Operating Leverage—Breakeven Unknown

$$\text{DOL (degree of operating leverage)} = \frac{\text{Given output no. of units (sales price unit - variable cost per unit)}}{\text{Given output no. of units (price per unit - variable cost / unit) - total fixed costs}}$$

Given the low operating leverage company what is the degree of operating leverage at 100,000 units?

$$\text{DOL} = \frac{100,000\,(\$12 - \$8)}{100,000\,(\$12 - \$8) - \$200,000}$$

$$= \frac{400,000}{400,000 - 200,000}$$

$$= 2$$

What is the degree of leverage for the low operating leverage company at 200,000 units?

$$\text{DOL} = \frac{200,000\,(\$12 - \$8)}{200,000\,(\$12 - \$8) - \$200,000}$$

$$= \frac{800,000}{800,000 - 200,000}$$

$$= 1.33$$

The DOL dropped from 2 to 1.33, which means that as the firm has higher outputs, and moves further away from Breakeven, the less will each further increase in sales magnify net income. With higher and higher units sold, the firm will increase its net income by smaller and smaller amounts. The only way to achieve greater returns hinges on debt financing or the use of financial leverage.

.09 Leverage—Financial

The concept of financial leverage relates to some mixture of debt and equity. The purpose is to maximize the return to the company through the use of borrowed funds. A high leverage firm will rely on debt financing as long as the cost of borrowed funds is less than the yield to common shareholders, so that the return on equity rises.

.11 Leverage—Financing with Bonds

The degree of financial leverage (DFL) defines the rate of change in net operating income relative to interest cost (I). The DFL equals earnings before interest and taxes (EBIT) divided by earnings after payment of interest and before payment of taxes.

$$\text{DFLB (Degree of Financial Leverage with Bonds)} = \frac{\text{EBIT}}{\text{EBIT} - \text{I}}$$

> **Example:** Referring to the data at ¶ 644.03 concerning the company relating to operating leverage: Assume the company now finances its growth with 8%, 20 year bonds for 40% debt of its capital structure. For $1,000,000, interest = $80,000. The other 60% of capital structure is raised with 60,000 shares of common stock.

Low Operating Leverage Company (40% Debt)

Probability of Sales	20%	60%	20%
# Units	100,000	150,000	200,000
$ Sales	$1,200,000	$1,800,000	$2,400,000
EBIT	$200,000	$400,000	$600,000
I(interest)	$80,000	$80,000	$80,000
EBT	$120,000	$320,000	$520,000
Taxes (25%)	$30,000	$80,000	$130,000
Earnings after taxes	$90,000	$240,000	$390,000
Earnings per share (60,000)	$1.50	$4.00	$6.50

Note that earnings after taxes is lower than the operating leverage example due to the cost of interest. However, earnings per share increases (on the 60% expected probability) from $3.00 share to $4.00 share since there are only 60,000 shares outstanding. The EPS must be higher than the pure operating example for the common shareholders to assume the additional risk associated with the funding of operations. The debt funding provides shareholders a way to obtain additional funds at a fixed cost.

Referring to the data ¶ 644.03 concerning the company relating to operating leverage:

High Leverage Company (40% Debt)

Probability of Sales	20%	60%	20%
# Units	100,000	150,000	200,000
$ Sales	$1,200,000	$1,800,000	$2,400,000
EBIT	$200,000	$500,000	$800,000
I(interest)	$80,000	$80,000	$80,000
EBT	$120,000	$420,000	$720,000
Taxes (25%)	$30,000	$105,000	$180,000
Earnings after taxes	$90,000	$315,000	$540,000
Earnings per share (60,000)	$1.50	$5.25	$9.00

Financial leverage is concerned with the impact of interest costs on earnings. The return to the shareholders is much higher than the low leverage company.

Using the data from above, the degree of financial leverage is computed as follows with output of 150,000 units.

¶644.11

$$\text{DFL (Low leverage company)} = \frac{\$400,000}{\$400,000 - \$80,000} = 1.25$$

$$\text{DFL (High leverage company)} = \frac{\$500,000}{\$500,000 - \$80,000} = 1.20$$

If interest on the low leverage company were to rise to \$90,000, the financial leverage would increase to 1.29. So, if interest charges rise relative to net operating income, the degree of financial leverage increases.

.13 Leverage—Degree of Financial and Operating Leverage Combined with Breakeven Unknown

The following formula defines the degree of financial and operating leverage combined (DFOL).

DFOL (Degree of financial and operating leverage) =

$$\frac{\text{Given output no. of units (Sales price per unit - variable cost per unit)}}{\text{Given output no. of units (sales price per unit - variable cost per unit) - total fixed costs - interest}}$$

Example: Given data from the low operating leverage company above, what is the degree of financial and operating leverage at output of 100,000 units?

$$\text{DFOL} = \frac{100,000(\$12 - \$8)}{100,000\ (\$12 - \$8) - \$200,000 - \$80,000}$$

$$= \frac{\$400,000}{\$400,000 - \$200,000 - \$80,000}$$

$$= 3.33$$

.15 Leverage—Financing with Preferreds, Common Stock and Bonds

$$\text{DFLBS (Degree of financial leverage with bonds and stock)} = \frac{\text{EBIT}}{\text{EBIT - Interest} + \dfrac{\text{Dividends to preferred owners}}{(1 - \text{tax rate})}}$$

Example: What is the degree of financial leverage if financing is a mixture of preferred and common stock and debt, given the following data?

Interest = \$60,000

Dividends to preferred owners = \$40,000 (Note: dividends are subject to earnings after taxes)

Tax rate (corporate) = 25%

EBIT = Earnings before interest and taxes = \$400,000

(Data relates to low leverage company illustrated previously with 100,000 units sold at a 60% probability)

$$\text{DFLBS} = \frac{\$400,000}{\$400,000 - \$60,000 + \dfrac{\$40,000}{(1 - .25)}}$$

$$= 1.02$$

In summary, for a low leverage company with output of 100,000 units and the facts above.

DOL = 2

DFL = 1.25

DFOL = 3.33

DFLBS = 1.02

Note: That the degree of leverage depends on the combination of factors between debt and equity and fixed interest charges.

.17 Leverage—Indifference Point—Common Stock versus Bonds

The following formula equates the indifference point between 100% equity financing and a mixture of equity and debt financing. In other words, what financing mix equates EBIT and EPS? Note that even though the indifference point is determined, the degree of risk is different.

Let X = EBIT at the indifference point, the amount to be determined

$$\frac{X(1 - \text{tax rate})}{\substack{\text{Number of outstanding common shares} \\ \text{if only common stock is issued}}} = \frac{(X - \text{Interest})(1 - \text{tax rate})}{\substack{\text{Number of outstanding common shares if} \\ \text{both common and bonds are in mix}}}$$

Example: Tax rate = 25%

Interest on debt = $80,000

Number of outstanding shares = 100,000

Number of shares, if debt and common is mix = 60,000

$$\frac{X(1-.25)}{100,000} = \frac{(X - \$80,000)(1-.25)}{60,000}$$

$$\frac{.75X}{100,000} = \frac{.75(X - \$80,000)}{60,000}$$

$$\frac{.75X}{100,000} = \frac{.75X - 60,000}{60,000}$$

$$
\begin{aligned}
60,000\,(.75X) &= 100,000\,(.75X - 60,000) \\
45,000X &= 75,000X - 6,000,000,000 \\
-30,000X &= -6,000,000,000 \\
X &= \$200,000 = \text{EBIT}
\end{aligned}
$$

Low Operating Leverage Firm

	100% Equity	40% Debt
# Units	100,000	100,000
Sales	$1,200,000	$1,200,000
EBIT	$200,000*	$200,000*
Interest	-	$80,000
EBT	$200,000	$120,000

Taxes (25%)	$50,000	$30,000
Net income after taxes	$150,000	$90,000
EPS	$1.50	$1.50
	(100,000 shares)	(60,000 shares)

.19 Leverage—Indifference Point—Common versus Preferred

The following formula determines the indifference point between 100% equity financing and financing with a mixture of debt and equity, with the equity composed on common and preferred shareholders.

X = EBIT at the indifference point, the amount to be determined

X = EBIT at the indifference point, the amount to be determined

$$\frac{X(1 - \text{tax rate})}{\substack{\text{No. of outstanding common shares} \\ \text{if only common stock is issued}}} = \frac{X(1 - \text{tax rate}) - \text{Dividends paid to preferred stockholders}}{\substack{\text{Number of outstanding common shares if} \\ \text{both common and bonds are in mix}}}$$

Example: Tax rate = 25%

Interest on debt = $80,000

Number of outstanding shares = 100,000

Number of shares, if debt and common is mix = 60,000

Dividends paid to preferred stockholders = $40,000

$$\frac{X(1-.25)}{100,000} = \frac{X(1-.25) - \$40,000}{60,000}$$

$$\frac{.75X}{100,000} = \frac{.75X - \$40,000}{60,000}$$

$$60,000(.75X) = 100,000(.75X - 40,000)$$

$$45,000X = 75,000X - 4,000,000,000$$

$$-30,000X = -4,000,000,000$$

$$X = \$133,333 = EBIT$$

.21 Financial Leverage Effect on the Variability of Residual Earnings to Common Stockholders

Symbols are defined as follows:

O = Operating elasticity

f = Financial elasticity

T = Tax elasticity

p = Price per unit of product

Q = Number of units sold

S = Revenue from sales, measured in dollars

v = Variable cost per unit of product

F = Fixed operating expenses

N = pQ −vQ − F (Net operating income)

¶644.19

I = Interest on debt

i = X – i (Taxable income)

t = Average tax rate on net corporate income

m = Marginal tax rate on corporate income

E = i(1– t) (Total earnings to common stockholders)

Operating leverage is the ratio between the percentage change in net operating income and the percentage change in the sales that cause it. Operating leverage varies directly with fixed operating expenses, such that the larger are the fixed operating expenses, the larger is the percentage change in the net operating income in response to a given percentage change in sales. Degree of operating leverage is defined as follows:

$$O = \frac{Q(p - v)}{Q(p - v) - F}$$

Degree of financial leverage is defined as the ratio between change in taxable income and the percentage change in net operating income that causes it. Financial leverage is defined as follows:

$$f = \frac{N}{N - I}$$

The degree of financial leverage varies directly with the debt interest. So, a percentage change in taxable income, resulting from a given change in net income, varies directly with the size of fixed interest expenses.

The degree of tax leverage is the ratio between the percentage change in residual earnings and the percentage change in taxable income that causes it. The degree of tax leverage is defined as follows:

$$T = \frac{1 - \text{marginal tax rate}}{1 - \text{average tax rate}}$$

Total effect on residual earnings = O × f × T

Example of financial leverage effect

By what percentage will the earnings on common stock increase given the following assumptions?

I = Interest on debt = $8

F = Fixed operating expenses = $35

t = Average tax rate = .4

m = Marginal tax rate = .6

Q = Number of units sold in year 1 = 100

P = Selling price = $1

V = Unit variable cost = $.40

A 25% increase in sales is expected in year 2

Net operating income   = net sales – variable costs – fixed expenses
                         = $(100 \times \$1) - (100 \times \$.40) - \$35$
                         = $100 - 40 - 35$
                    N   = $\$25$

Net operating income   = net sales – variable costs – fixed expenses
                         = $(100 \times \$1) - (100 \times \$.40) - \$35$
                         = $100 - 40 - 35$
                    N   = $\$25$

$$O = \frac{Q(P - V)}{Q(P - V) - F}$$

$$O = \frac{100(1 - .40)}{100(1 - .40) - 35} = 2.4$$

$$f = \frac{N}{N - I} = \frac{25}{25 - 8} = 1.47$$

$$T = \frac{1 - .6}{1 - .4} = 67\%$$

Total effect on residual earnings = $O \times f \times T$
                                  = $2.4 \times 1.47 \times .67$
                                  = 2.36

Total effect on residual earnings = $O \times f \times T$
                                  = $2.4 \times 1.47 \times .67$
                                  = 2.36

Therefore earnings on common stock in year 2 will rise by 59% (2.36 × 25% = 59%) if the projected increase in sales of 25% is realized.

O = 2.4 = degree of operating leverage

If sales increase by 25%, then net operating income will increase by 60% (25% × 2.4)

f = 1.47 = degree of financial leverage

A 60% increase in net operating income will result in a 88.2% increase in taxable income (1.47 × 60%)

T = .67 = degree of tax leverage

An 88.2% increase in taxable income will result in an increase of total earnings to common stockholders (residual earnings) of 59% (88.2% × .67).

¶ 645 LINE OF CREDIT VERSUS ACCOUNTS PAYABLE EXTENSION

Use the following formula to estimate the potential interest savings from reduction of line of credit by extending accounts payable by a given number of days.

Potential Interest Savings from Reduction of Line of Credit

Yearly Total of Accounts Payable Balance

(Ending AP balance Q1 total) + (Ending AP balance Q2 total) +

(Ending AP balance Q3 total) + (Ending AP balance Q4 total)

Interest Savings by Extending Accounts Payable

$$\left(\frac{\text{Yearly Total of AP Balance}}{372}\right) \times \text{Number of days to extend payments}$$

372 represents number of days in a year computed on a "quarterly" basis as follows:

Assume 31 days in a month.

Therefore, number of days in 1 quarter = 31×3=93

Therefore, number of days in 1 year on a "quarterly" basis = 93×4=372

Example: Average annual interest rate on line of credit = 8%.

Number of days chosen to extend A/P payments = 15

Quarter Ending	Ending Accounts Payable Balance
3/XI	$60,000
6/XI	$80,000
9/XI	$65,000
12/XI	$75,000

Interest savings by extending accounts payable =

$$[(\text{Yearly total of A/P balance})/372]$$
$$\times \text{Number of days to extend payments}$$
$$\times \text{Average interest rate on line of credit}$$
$$= [(\$60,000 + \$80,000 + \$65,000 + \$75,000)/372] \times 15 \times .08$$
$$= \$752.69 \times 15 \times .08$$
$$= \underline{\$903.23}$$

¶ 646 MARGINAL ANALYSIS

.01 Overview

Suppose a truck line runs truck A everyday between cities B and C. If the truck is fully loaded, profits result. But, if less than full, losses arise. The analysis, here, is to determine if the truck should only run its route if it's fully loaded, i.e., if daily partial load runs should be made?

Data:

Marginal (addition to) revenue	=	$35,000
Fully allocated costs	=	$50,000
Marginal (out-of-pocket) costs	=	$27,000
Fixed costs (whether run or not)	=	$23,000

The analysis should revolve around *marginal* costs. Fixed costs are sunk. They are incurred whether this truck run is made or not. They are costs such as: service crew, mechanics, inspectors, investment in truck, equipment, buildings, etc.

Full cost analysis:

Marginal revenue	$35,000
Total cost	–$50,000
Loss	($15,000)
Marginal analysis:	
Addition to revenue	$35,000
Marginal costs	– $27,000
Addition to profit	+ $8,000

This conclusion would indicate that the route should be run, because it improves profit, even though it doesn't cover fully allocated costs.

.03 Marginal Revenue

Marginal revenue deals with the incremental additions to revenue. Generally, any significant expansion in sales is usually accompanied by lower prices, through discounts, or extra services, or liberal credit policies, etc. The decision regarding marginal revenues is that of revenue versus additions to costs. If revenue increments are greater than cost increments, then net income increases. The average marginal revenue is:

$$\text{Average marginal revenue} = \frac{\text{Change in total revenue}}{\text{Change in sales volume}}$$

The following company data illustrates marginal revenue analysis. The cost data is from the example regarding marginal cost analysis. The general rule that will be illustrated concerning marginal revenue and marginal cost, is so on copy that favorable results will occur at volumes which equate marginal revenue with marginal cost.

Production in Units	Sales Price per Unit*	Total Revenue $	Total Costs $*	Marginal $ Revenue per Unit	Marginal $ Cost per Unit
100,000	$1.65	$165,000	132,000	$.200	$.180
200,000	.925	185,000	150,000	.150	.100
300,000	.667	200,000	160,000	.100	.080
400,000	.525	210,000	168,000	.400	.300
500,000	.500	250,000	198,000	.0120	.120
600,000	.437	262,000	210,000	.130	.200
700,000	.393	275,000	230,000	.070	.300
800,000	.353	282,000	250,000		

* Rounded for illustration purposes.

Average marginal revenue is calculated as follows.

As output increases from 100,000 units to 200,000 units:

$$\text{Average marginal revenue} = \frac{\$185,000 - \$165,000}{\$200,000 - \$100,000} = \frac{\$20,000}{\$100,000} = .200$$

.05 Marginal Cost

Marginal cost analysis deals with the incremental additions to cost. It is the change in total cost associated with some shift in business activity such as variability in output or resource mix, etc. Where costs alone are the pivotal decision making process, then marginal cost is most important. Marginal cost, specifically, is the change in total cost brought about by *one* additional unit change in total production. Marginal analysis focuses on future alternatives, rather than on past historical data. The marginal data is the data that is relevant for decision-making. Average costs reflect total costs and total production. Marginal costs tell how much it will cost to manufacture that last item (or last batch). The average marginal cost is defined as:

$$\text{Average marginal cost} = \frac{\text{Change in total cost}}{\text{Change in total output}}$$

The following company data illustrates marginal cost analysis.

Costs $ Production Units	Variable	Fixed	Total	Average Cost	Marginal Cost Change in total cost/ Change in total output
100,000	$12,000	120,000	$132,000	$1.32	
					$0.18
200,000	30,000	120,000	150,000	0.75	
					$0.10
300,000	40,000	120,000	160,000	0.53	
					$0.08
400,000	48,000	120,000	168,000	0.42	
					$0.30
500,000	68,000	120,000	198,000	0.40	
					$0.12
600,000	90,000	120,000	210,000	0.35	
					$0.20
700,000	110,000	120,000	230,000	0.33	
					$0.30
800,000	140,000	120,000	260,000	0.33	

Example: For the company above, at 300,000 units of production, the average cost is $160,000/300,000 units = $.53 per unit.

At the level of increase from 500,000 units to 600,000 units, the average marginal cost is:

$$\text{Average Marginal Cost} = \frac{\$210,000 - \$198,000}{600,000 - 500,000} = \frac{\$12,000}{\$100,000} = 0.12$$

If one were to analyze the production costs by the average cost alone, it would tend to imply that continued increased output would be proper, since average costs per unit continually decreases from $1.32 per unit at 100,000 units of production to $.33 per unit at 800,000 units of production. However, marginal analysis provides a clearer picture. Note that marginal costs of adding 100,000 more units of production decreases from $.18 to $.12 at an output of 600,000 units. However, to add another increment of 100,000 units to a level of 700,000, would indicate an average marginal cost per unit of $.20. The increase from .12/unit to .20/unit may not be justifiable if considering costs alone.

¶ 647 MARGIN OF SAFETY

.01 Definition of Margin of Safety

Defined as the breakeven sales less net sales at the current operating level. Indicates to what extent sales may decline before a loss is sustained. M/S may be expressed as a % of sales.

Example:

Sales	$1,480,000
Less: breakeven sales	−$1,000,000
= margin of safety	=$ 480,000

$$\text{or, as a \% of sales} = \frac{\$480,000}{\$1,480,000} = .3243 \text{ or } \underline{32.43\%}$$

Sales could decline 32.43% before the firm sustains an operating loss.

¶ 648 OPPORTUNITY COST ANALYSIS

.01 Overview

Opportunity cost analysis is the measurement of sacrifices, or alternatives that could have been implemented, but were not. What a business does not do is as critical as what it does do with certain investments. Opportunity costs are those profits given up when a particular option is chosen.

For example, consider an orange grower who sells oranges for $12.00 per bushel. Could he increase his overall income by adding an incremental processing cost and sell orange juice instead of oranges? This is the essence of opportunity cost analysis. The question does not relate to the growing of oranges. These are costs that do not enter the picture. The relevant figure is the revenue from the alternate use—the selling of orange juice. The selling price of the oranges is income foregone and represents a cost. If additional costs per bushel to process the oranges into juice is $4.00 and the juice can be sold for $20.00, what could be the addition to profit by selling juice instead of oranges?

Market $ for orange juice	$20.00
Less: Market $ for oranges	12.00
Less: Additional processing costs	4.00
Additional profit by selling juice	4.00

.03 Opportunity Cost Analysis—Replacement Cost

In addition to focusing on possible cash inflows and outflows, opportunity replacement cost focuses, not on maximizing profits, but on *minimizing* costs. The following model illustrates keeping an old company vehicle for 5 more years or trading-in for a new vehicle. Concepts such as depreciation are simplified to illustrate the concept of opportunity cost, rather than to track complicated, everchanging tax rules. These costs are analyzed as two mutually exclusive alternatives. The object here is to minimize costs. To further simplify the calculations, the new car will be purchased for cash.

	New Vehicle		Old Vehicle
Cost (new)	$25,000	Book value	$8,000
		Market value (trade-in)	$2,500
		Fix-up cost	$3,000
Cost of capital	9%	Cost of capital	9%
Tax rate	25%	Tax rate	25%
Maintenance	$6,000	Maintenance	$8,500
Useful life	5 years	Useful life	5 years

New vehicle investment base = cost = $25,000
New vehicle depreciation base = cost = $25,000
Annual depreciation (new vehicle) = $25,000 / 5 = $5,000

Old vehicle tax gain forgone:

Tax gain forgone = Tax rate (book value - trade-in value) = .25 ($8,000 – $2,500) = $1,375

Old vehicle investment base:

Investment base = Trade-in value + tax gain forgone + maintenance
= $2,500 + $1,375 + $8,500
= $12,375

Depreciation on old vehicle:

Assume st. line for 5 years

Depreciation base (old vehicle)   = Book value + fix-up cost
= $8,000 + $3,000
= $11,000
Annual depreciation (old vehicle)   = $11,000 / 5 = $2,200

Data Summary

	New	Old
Tax gain forgone	—	$1,375
Investment base	$25,000	12,375
Depreciation - annual	5,000	2,200
Future operating costs:		
Maintenance	6,000	8,500
+ Depreciation - annual	5,000	2,200
	11,000	10,700
× Tax (25%)	2,750	2,675
= Tax		
Maintenance	$6,000	$8,500
– Tax saved	2,750	2,675
= Cash flow	3,250	5,825
× Present value of annuity of 9%, 5 years	× 3.8897	× 3.8897
= Present value of cash flow	$12,641	$22,657
+ Investment base	25,000	12,375
= Total cost	37,641	35,032

Since $37,641 for the new vehicle is practically the same as $35,032, possibly the new vehicle should be considered since the future trade-in value of the new vehicle will be of more value.

¶ 649 MORTGAGE

.01 Adjustable Rate

What is the annual interest rate, principal balance and new monthly payment amount given the following data?

Mr. X financed a new home for $150,000 with a 30 year, 8%, adjustable rate mortgage.

1st monthly payment owed 1/1/X0 for $1,100.65.

Interest would be adjusted by using the one-year treasury index plus a spread of 2.50 points.

The 1/1/X1 index rate = 6.40%

The rate's minimum = 6%

The rate's maximum = 12%

The rate's maximum yearly change allowed = 2%

What is the annual rate of interest?

New interest rate = 6.40% + 2.50% = 8.9%

Subject to:

Minimum rate = 6%

Maximum rate = 12%

Maximum 1/1/X1 annual increase = 8% + 2% = 10%

Note: 8% to 8.9% is a .9% increase, which is within range, less than 2% increase.

What is the principal balance after the 12th payment?

What is the new monthly payment?

Principal (at 360 - 12) = [(total principal payment + interest)]

$$\left[\frac{1-1+\frac{.08}{12}-348}{\frac{.08}{12}}\right]$$

= $1,100.65 (135.1450)

= $148,747

What is the new monthly payment?

$$[\text{current principal balance}]\left[\frac{\frac{1}{1+\left(1+\frac{.08}{12}\right)^{348}}}{\frac{.089}{12}}\right]$$

$$=\left[\$148,747\right]\left[\frac{1}{123.4328}\right]$$

= $1,205.98/month

.03 Loan Amortization Summaries

Use the Loan Amortization Summaries tables at ¶ 691.27 to determine, for a given annual percentage rate by term:

- The annual payment
- The annual amount applied to principal and interest
- The total interest
- The total amount of payments

(Note: Tables are based on $1,000 principal.)

Example: Principal = $20,000

Interest = 10%

Term = 5 years

Conversion factor for table value:

= $20,000/$1,000

= 20

Locate factors for loan by term:

= 5 years.

Information for year two:

	Annual Payment	Total Annual Interest	Interest to Date
Table Factors	$ 255.00	$ 75.70	$ 168.41
Conversion Factor	× 20	× 20	× 20
$20,000 Principal	$5,100.00	$1,514.00	$3,368.20

Total for 5 years:

	Total Payment	Total Interest
Table Factors	$1,274.77	$274.77
Conversion Factor	× 20	× 20
	$25,495.40	$5,495.40

Mortgage Summary Amortization by Interest, Given Term

The Mortgage Summary Amortization by Interest, Given Term tables at ¶ 691.29 provide information on the monthly payment amount, total interest over the term of the loan, and total amount of payments for a $100,000 loan, at various interest rates for various terms.

Example (1): What is the monthly payment, total interest, and total amount of payments for a loan of $100,000 at 10% interest, for 1 year?

- Locate the table header with term of 1 year.
- Read down left column to 10% interest.
- Read across columns for $100,000 at 10%:
  - Monthly payment = $8,791.59
  - Total interest = $5,499.05
  - Total of payments = $105,499.05

Example (2): What are the amounts for a $250,000 loan at 10% interest?

- Convert $100,000 table amount into a conversion ratio for table lookup:

$$\frac{\text{Amount needed}}{\text{Table value}} = \frac{\$250,000}{\$100,000} = 2.5 \text{ times}$$

- Convert table answers for $250,000.
  - Total monthly payment = $8,791.59 × 2.5 = $21,978.98
  - Total interest = $5,499.05 × 2.5 = $13,747.63
  - Total of payments = $105,499.05 × 2.5 = $263,747.63

Mortgage Summary Amortization—By Term

The Mortgage Summary Amortization tables at ¶ 691.25 provide information on the monthly payment amount, total interest over the term of the loan, and total amount of payments for a $100,000 loan, at various interest rates for various terms.

Example (1): What is the monthly payment, total interest, and total amount of payments for a loan of $100,000 at 10% interest, for 5 years?

- Locate the table header with interest of 10%.
- Read down left column to 5 years.
- Read across column for $100,000 at 10%:
  - — Monthly payment = $2,124.70
  - — Total interest = $27,482.00
  - — Total of payments = $127,482.00

Example (2): What are the amounts for a $250,000 loan at 10% interest?

- Convert $100,000 table amount into a conversion ratio for table lookup:

$$\frac{\text{Amount needed}}{\text{Table value}} = \frac{\$250,000}{\$100,000} = 2.5 \text{ times}$$

- Convert table answers for $250,000
  - — Total monthly payment = $2,124.70 × 2.5 = $5,311.75
  - — Total interest = $27,482.00 × 2.5 = $68,705
  - — Total of payments = $127,482.00 × 2.5 = $318,705

Up-Front Mortgage Fees Versus Mortgage Interest Rates

Effective Annual Interest Rate

$$\frac{(\text{mortgage rate} \times \text{expected period of ownership}) + (\text{up-front fee rate})}{\text{expected period of ownership}}$$

Should the purchaser accept a higher interest rate for lower up-front fees? The comparison of points vs. rates depends on the homeowner's expected time frame for owning the home. Generally, for short terms, the points push up the total rate, but become less significant over longer terms. To make the comparison, the total interest and points are converted into an effective annual rate per given time period.

Example: Should a purchaser accept these terms?

Mortgage rate = 8%

Expected period to own home = 5 years

Upfront fees = 5%

$$\text{Effective annual interest rate} = \frac{(.08 \times 5) + .05}{5} = 9\%$$

or from comparision of Up-Front Mortgage Fees Versus Mortgage Interest Rates tables at ¶ 691.31, effective annual rate = 9.00%

Or should a purchaser accept this higher interest rate for lower up-front fees?

Mortgage rate obtainable = 9%

Expected period to own home = 5 years

Upfront fees (reduced from 5%) = 2%

From table ¶ 691.31, effective annual rate = 9.40%

¶ 651 PRESENT VALUE

.01 Present Value of $1 Received n Periods from Now

The present value table is used to compute the discounted present value of a sum at a future date.

The future sum is discounted at a specific interest rate per period for a given number of periods.

> **Example:** What is the present value of $50,000 discounted at 8% APR for 10 years.

Locate table factor for 8% = .4631935

Present Value = $50,000 × .4631935 = $23,159.67

Present Value of $1 Received at End of Period

Period	Interest Rate						
	2%	3%	4%	5%	6%	7%	8%
8	0.8534904	0.7894092	0.7306902	0.6768394	0.6274124	0.5820091	0.5402689
9	0.8203483	0.7664167	0.7025867	0.6446089	0.5918985	0.5439337	0.5002490
10	0.8203483	0.7440939	0.6755642	0.6139133	0.5583948	0.5083493	0.4631935
11	0.8042630	0.7224213	0.6495809	0.5846793	0.5267875	0.4750928	0.4288829
12	0.7884932	0.7013799	0.6245970	0.5568374	0.4969694	0.4440120	0.3971138

See ¶ 691.07 for complete Present Value tables.

.03 Discounting—Continuous

The following formula computes the present value of a sum that has been compounded continuously at a given nominal rate for n periods which yields a future sum at the end of the period. The assumption is that interest is compounded and added to principal an infinite number of intervals each year.

Present value = (future amount) $(2.7183)^{-\text{(rate continuously compounded)(number of years)}}$ (continuous discounting)

> **Example:** What is the present value of a sum that has been compounded continuously at a 7% nominal rate for 10 years to $2,500 at the end of the period?

$$\text{Present value} = \$2,500 \ (2.7183)^{-(.07)(10)}$$
$$= \$2,500 \ (.4966)$$
$$= \$1,241.50$$

.05 Discounting—Continuous—Annuity

The following formula computes the present value of continuous discounted cash flows per period. The formula is for continuous discounting of cash flow rates per period.

$$\text{Present value (Continous discounting of annuity)} = \left[\frac{2.7183^{\text{(nominal rate)(number of years)}} - 1}{\text{(nominal rate)}(2.7183)^{\text{(nominal rate)(number of years)}}} \right]$$

Example: What is the present value of the following cash flow by continuous discounting if the yearly cash flows are $1200 per year for 3 years, using a discount rate of 8%?

$$PV = \$1,200 \left[\frac{2.7183^{\,(.08)(3)} - 1}{(.08)(2.7183)^{\,(.08)(3)}} \right]$$

$$= \$1,200 \left[\frac{.27125}{.10170} \right]$$

$$= \$3,200.59$$

.06 Return on Investment—Present Value of Dividend Growth

The following approximates the present value of perpetual dividend growth at a given discount rate:

$$\text{Present value (of perpetual dividend growth)} = \frac{\text{Dividends beginning of period}}{\dfrac{(1\ +\ \text{discount rate})}{(1\ +\ \text{growth rate of dividends})}\ -\ 1}$$

Note: The discount rate used should appropriately reflect risk.

Example: What is the present value of perpetual dividend growth at a rate of 6% a year, with a discount rate of 12%? The dividends have an average yield of $2.50.

$$\text{Present value (of perpetual dividend growth)} = \frac{\$2.50}{\left[\dfrac{1\ +\ .12}{1\ +\ .06}\right]\ -\ 1} = \$44.17$$

.07 Present Value of Ordinary Annuity

Present Value of Ordinary Annuity

$$\left(\text{Amount per period}\right) \times \frac{1 - \left(1 + \text{interest rate per period}\right)^{(-\text{number of periods})}}{\text{interest rate per period}}$$

Example (1): What is the present value of an annuity of $3,000 per year with payments made at the end of each year for 5 years assuming an interest rate of 5% compounded annually?

$$PV = \$3,000\,\frac{1 - \left(1 + .05\right)^{-5}}{.05}$$

PV factor from table for 5 periods at 5%

$$= \frac{1 - (1 + .05)^{-5}}{.05}$$

$$= 4.3294767$$

Thus, present value of annuity

$$= \$3,000\,(4.3294767) = \underline{\$12,988.43}$$

Present Value of Ordinary Annuity of $1 per Period

Period	Interest Rate					
	2%	3%	4%	5%	6%	7%
3	2.8838833	2.8286114	2.7750910	2.7232480	2.6730119	2.6243160
4	3.8077287	3.7170984	3.6298952	3.5459505	3.4651056	3.3872113
5	4.7134595	4.5797072	4.4518223	4.3294767	4.2123638	4.1001974
6	5.6014309	5.4171914	5.2421369	5.0756921	4.9173243	4.7665397
7	6.4719911	6.2302830	6.0020547	5.7863734	5.5823814	5.3892894

See ¶ 691.11 for complete Present Value of Annuity Tables.

Example (2): A firm is estimated to have annual adjusted Net Income of $20,000 a year for 5 years. What is the present value of these 5 flows of $20,000 discounted at 12%?

- From the table locate discount rate of 12%.
- Read down column to locate a term of 5 years.
- Present value of $20,000 a year = $20,000 × 3.6047762 = $72,095.52

Present Value of Ordinary Annuity of $1 per Period

Period	Interest Rate					
	8%	9%	10%	11%	12%	13%	14%
2	1.7832647	1.7591112	1.7355372	1.7125233	1.6900510	1.6681024	1.6466605
3	2.5770970	2.5312947	2.4868520	2.4437147	2.4018313	2.3611526	2.3216320
4	3.3121268	3.2397199	3.1698654	3.1024457	3.0373493	2.9744713	2.9137123
5	3.9927100	3.8896513	3.7907868	3.6958970	3.6047762	3.5172313	3.4330810
6	4.6228797	4.4859186	4.3552607	4.2305379	4.1114073	3.9975498	3.8886675
7	5.2063701	5.0329528	4.8684188	4.7121963	4.5637565	4.4226104	4.2883048

Example (3): A business is considering incorporating a new training system for its supervisors provided by a consulting firm. The consulting firm claims its supervisory teaching techniques will provide efficiencies to the firm that will save $12,000 a year over the next 7 years. The initial cost to be paid to the consulting firm is $25,000. The additional annual price to be paid to the consulting firm yearly to maintain the training is $5,000. The firm uses 9% for annual interest calculations. Should the firm contract with the consulting firm?

Net annual inflow = Annual savings – annual cost

= $12,000 – $5,000

= $7,000

Present value of annual net inflow $= \$7,000 \times \dfrac{1 - (1 + .09)^{-7}}{.09}$

$\$7,000 \times \dfrac{1 - 5470}{.09}$

= $7,000 (5.033)

= $35,231

Since the present value of the cash inflows of $35,000, exceeds the initial outlay of $25,000, the firm should consider contracting with the consulting firm.

Note: The factor 5.033 may be computed as above, or obtained from the PV table above (See 9% interest and column for Period 7).

.08 Periodic Rent of Annuity

$$\text{Amount Per Period (Total Amount)} = \frac{\text{Interest rate per period}}{1 - (1 + \text{interest rate per period})^{-(\text{number of periods})}}$$

Example: What equal payments should be made at the end of each period for 15 years to pay off a note of $60,000, if money is worth 10% compounded annually.

$$\text{Amount per period} = \$60,000 \left(\frac{.10}{1 - (1 + .10)^{-15}} \right)$$

Take the reciprocal of factor from table (of periodic rent of annuity whose present value is $1) for 15 periods at 10% interest.

$$= \frac{.10}{1\ (1 + .10)^{-15}} = \frac{1}{7.6060795} = .1314$$

Thus, amount per period = $60,000 (.1314) = $7,884

See ¶ 691.11 for complete Present Value of Annuity tables.

.09 Present Value of Ordinary Annuity of $1—Monthly Basis

Example: A firm has a leasehold contract remaining for 39 months. The value of this lease savings compared to having to obtain another lease is a savings of $230 per month. What is the present value of this "lease savings" of $230 a month for the remaining 39 months discounted at 7% for inflation and risk.

- From table, locate discount rate 7%
- Read down column to locate term of 39 months.
- Present value of lease savings of $230 a month for 39 months = $230 × 34.7915872 = $8,002.07

Present Value of Ordinary Annuity of $1 per Month Based on Monthly Compounding of Nominal Annual Rates

Period	Interest Rate					
	2%	3%	4%	5%	6%	7%
35	33.9712460	33.4724313	32.9836690	32.5047250	32.0353713	31.5753855
36	34.9130576	34.3864651	33.8707664	33.3657013	32.8710162	32.3864645
37	35.8533021	35.2982196	34.7549167	34.2231050	33.7025037	33.1928396
38	36.7919821	36.2077003	35.6361296	35.0769511	34.5298544	33.9945381
39	37.7291003	37.1149130	36.5144149	35.9272542	35.3530890	34.7915872
40	38.6646592	38.0198634	37.3897823	36.7740290	36.1722279	35.5840137

See ¶ 691.13 for complete tables.

.11 Present Value of Annuities with Payments Increasing or Decreasing in Constant Amount

Increasing in Constant Amount Using Table

Example: A firm is estimated to have annual Adjusted Net Income of $100,000/year with a constant increase of $10,000/year for 10 years. The discount rate to be applied is 12%. What is the present value of these 10 increasing flows?

Solution: Convert constant dollar amount into ratio for table lookup.

$$\frac{\$10,000}{\$100,000} = \frac{\text{Increase per year}}{\text{Adjusted net income}} = 10\% \text{ Increase}$$

For table usage, % should be rounded to 2%—5%—10%—15% or 20% increase, or use interpolation method to determine nearest rate.

- From the table, locate Header of 10% increase.
- Locate Discount column of 12% for discount rate.
- Read down column to locate Term of 10 years.
- Present value of Adjusted Net Income = $100,000 × 7.6756319 = $767,563.19

See ¶ 691.17 for complete table.

Present Value of Ordinary Annuity of $1 per Period Increasing in Constant Amount of 10 Percent

Period	Interest Rate						
	8%	9%	10%	11%	12%	13%	14%
10	4.6583023	4.4879708	4.3278468	4.1771470	4.0351585	3.9012321	3.7747756
11	4.8078445	4.6230952	4.4500565	4.2877768	4.1353952	3.9921318	3.8572790
12	4.9324630	4.7346657	4.5500462	4.3774767	4.2159426	4.0645298	3.9224132
13	5.0363118	4.8267882	4.6318560	4.4502063	4.2806682	4.1221918	3.9738350
14	5.1228524	4.9028527	4.6987913	4.5091763	4.3326798	4.1681174	4.0144312

Increasing by Constant Amount Using Present Value of Annuity table

Present Value of Increasing Annuity

$$\left[\left[(\text{First payment}) \times \binom{\text{PV of ordinary annuity factor}}{\text{for term of payments}}\right]\right.$$
$$+ \left(\text{dollar amount of increase of each successive payment}\right)$$

$$\left. \times \left[\frac{\binom{\text{PV of ordinary annuity}}{\text{factor for term of payments}} - \binom{\text{Number of payments}}{\times (\text{PV factor})}}{i}\right]\right]$$

Note: The PV Factor is the Present Value of $1 at compound interest due in n periods, i.e., $PV = 1/(1+i)^n$

¶651.11

Example: What is the present value of a series of 5 payments starting at $110, made at the end of year 1, with each subsequent payment increasing by $25.00 with interest at 8% per year?

PV of increasing annuity

$$= \$110 \ (3.9927) + \$25 \quad \frac{3.9927 - (5) \ (.6806)}{.08}$$

$$= \$439.20 + \$184.28$$
$$= \$623.48$$

See ¶ 691.07 for Present Value tables and ¶ 691.13 for Present Value Annuity tables.

Decreasing in Constant Amount

Example (1): A firm is estimated to have annual Adjusted Net Income of $100,000/year with a constant decrease of $10,000/year for 10 years. The discount rate to be applied is 12%. What is the present value of these 10 *decreasing* flows?

Solution

Convert constant dollar amount into *ratio* for table lookup.

$$\frac{\$10,000}{\$100,000} = \frac{\text{Decrease per Year}}{\text{Adjusted Net Income}} = 10\% \text{ Decrease}$$

For table usage, % should be rounded to 2%—5%—10%—15% or 20% decreases, or use interpolation method to determine nearest rate.

- From the table, locate Header of 10% decrease.
- Locate Discount column of 12% for discount rate.
- Read down column to locate Term of 10 years.
- Present value of Adjusted Net Income = $100,000 × 3.6248141 = $362,481.41

Example (2): There are five years remaining on a lease that will save a potential buyer $10,000/year. Inflation will cause the value of this savings to decline by $500/per year. What is the present value of this lease savings discounted at 12%?

Solution

- Convert constant dollar decline into ratio for table lookup.

$$\frac{\$500}{\$10,000} = 5\%$$

- From the table, locate Header of 5% decline.
- Locate Discount column of 12% for discount rate.
- Read down column to locate Term of 5 years.
- Present value of lease savings to potential buyer = $10,000 × 3.2849 = $32,489

¶651.11

See ¶ 691.19 for complete Present Value of Annuity Decreasing in Constant Amount table.

Present Value of Ordinary Annuity of $1 per Period Decreasing in Constant Amount of 10 Percent

Period	Interest Rate						
	8%	9%	10%	11%	12%	13%	14%
6	3.5705523	3.4766801	3.3868436	3.3008171	3.2183902	3.1393662	3.0635616
7	3.8039484	3.6954938	3.5921068	3.4934805	3.3993298	3.3093905	3.2234166
8	3.9660291	3.8460537	3.7320590	3.6236584	3.5204948	3.4888154	3.3900859
9	4.0660789	3.9381393	3.8168786	3.7018434	3.5926168	3.4888154	3.3900859
10	4.1123983	3.9803803	3.8554329	3.7370618	3.6248141	3.5182742	3.4170603

.13 Present Value Annuities with Payments Increasing or Decreasing in Constant Ratio

Present Value of Ordinary Annuity of $1 Increasing in Constant Ratio

Example: A firm is estimated to have annual Adjusted Net Income of $100,000/year with a constant *rate* of increase of 10% per year compounded for 10 years. The discount rate to be applied is 12%. What is the present value of these 10 *increasing* flows?

Solution: For table usage, % rate of increase should be rounded to 5%—10%—15% or 20% increases, or use interpolation method to determine nearest rate.

- From the table, locate Header of 10% increase.
- Locate Discount column of 12% for discount rate.
- Read down column to locate Term of 10 years.
- Present value of Adjusted Net Income.

Starting at $100,000/year and increasing: $100,000 × 8.2442173 = $824,421.73 at 10% per year compounded.

From Table, illustrated by year:

Present Value total at 12% for net income at end of year 1 that is growing at a constant rate of 10% = $100,000 × .8928571 = $89,285.71

Present Value total at 12% for net income at end of year 2 that is growing at a constant rate of 10% = $100,000 × 1.7697704 = $176,977.04

Present Value total at 12% for net income at end of year 3 that is growing at a constant rate of 10% = $100,000 × 2.631045 = $263,104.50

See ¶ 691.21 for complete Present Value Annuity Increasing in Constant Ratio tables.

Present Value of Ordinary Annuity of $1 per Period Increasing in Constant Ratio of 10 Percent

Period	Interest Rate						
	8%	9%	10%	11%	12%	13%	14%
1	0.9259259	0.9174312	0.9090909	0.9009009	0.8928571	0.8849558	0.8771930
2	1.8689986	1.8432792	1.8181818	1.7936856	1.7697704	1.7464171	1.7236073
3	2.8295356	2.7776212	2.7272727	2.6784271	2.6310245	2.5850078	2.5403228
4	3.8078604	3.7205352	3.6363636	3.5551981	3.4768991	3.4013350	3.3283816
5	4.8043022	4.6720997	4.5454545	4.4240702	4.3076687	4.1959898	4.0887893
6	5.8191967	5.6323942	5.4545455	5.2851146	5.1236032	4.9695476	4.8225160
7	6.8528855	6.6014987	6.3636364	6.1384.18	5.9249674	5.7225685	5.5304979
8	7.9057168	7.5794941	7.2727273	6.9840018	6.7120216	6.4555977	6.2136383
9	8.9780448	8.5664620	8.1818182	7.8219838	7.4850212	7.1691659	6.8728089
10	10.0702309	9.5624845	9.0909091	8.6524164	8.2442173	7.8637898	7.5088507

Present Value of an Annuity with Interest Increasing at a Constant Ratio
Present Value of Increasing Interest Annuity

$$\left(\text{First Payment}\right) \times \frac{1 - \left|\dfrac{1 + \text{rate of increase of interest}}{1 + \text{original rate of interest}}\right|^{(\text{number of periods})}}{\text{original rate of interest} - \text{rate of increase of interest}}$$

Example: What is the present value of annuity payments of $1,500 at the end of each year for 10 years at 8% interest where the interest rate (as a hedge against inflation) is to increase by 5% per year?

$$\text{PV of increasing annuity} = 1,500 \times \frac{1 - \left(\dfrac{1 + .05}{1 + .08}\right)^{10}}{.08 - .05}$$

$$= 1,500 \times \frac{1 - \left(\dfrac{1.05}{1.08}\right)^{10}}{.03}$$

$$= 1,500 \times \frac{1 - .97^{10}}{.03}$$

$$= 1,500 \times \frac{1 - .7374}{.03}$$

$$= \$1,500 \times 8.75333$$

$$= \$13,130$$

Present Value of Ordinary Annuity of $1 per Period
Decreasing in Constant Ratio of 10 Percent

Period	Interest Rate						
	8%	9%	10%	11%	12%	13%	14%
10	9.307765	8.854935	8.433701	8.041402	7.675632	7.334213	7.015171
11	10.165530	9.630001	9.134689	8.675969	8.250584	7.855608	7.488406
12	10.999469	10.376624	9.803814	9.276235	8.789602	8.340090	7.924280
13	11.808405	11.094217	10.441075	9.842766	9.293785	8.789252	8.324833
14	12.591465	11.782484	11.046737	10.376354	9.764411	9.204808	8.692166
15	13.348045	12.441375	11.621278	10.877964	10.202882	9.588546	9.028397

¶651.13

Use the following examples to illustrate the concept and the present value of annuity decreasing in constant ratio.

Present Value of Ordinary Annuity of $1 Decreasing in Constant Ratio

Example (1): A firm is estimated to have annual Adjusted Net Income of $100,000/year with a constant rate of decrease of 10% per year compounded for 10 years. The discount rate to be applied is 12%. What is the present value of these 10 *decreasing* flows?

Solution

For table usage, % rate of decrease should be rounded to 5%, 10%, 15%, or 20% decreases, or use interpolation method to determine nearest rate.

- From the table, locate Header of 10% decrease.
- Locate Discount column of 12%.
- Read down column to locate Term of 10 years.
- Present value of adjusted net income.
  - Starting at $100,000 a year = $100,000 × 4.0351585 = $403,515.85 and decreasing at 10% per year.

.15 Finding Interest Rate of Annuity Using Tables

Future Value of Annuity

$$\frac{(1 + \text{interest rate per period})^{(\text{number of periods})} - 1}{\text{interest rate per period}}$$

$$= \frac{\text{Future value of annuity}}{\text{Amount per period}}$$

Example: What interest rate is required if it is desired to accumulate $324,000 at the end of 11 years by setting aside $18,000 per year?

$$\frac{(1 + i)^{11} - 1}{i} = \frac{\$324,000}{\$18,000}$$

$$\frac{(1 + i)^{11} - 1}{i} = 18$$

From factors from table at ¶ 691.15 for Future Value of Annuity of $1 we see that the factors are:

$$\frac{(1 + .09)^{11} - 1}{.09} = 17.5603$$

$$\frac{(1 + .095)^{11} - 1}{.095} = 18.0395$$

Therefore the rate must be between 9% and 9.5%. By interpolation the rate approximates 9.46%.

¶651.15

.17 Capitalized Value

Capitalized Value by Discounted Cash Flow Method

Capitalized Value

	=	Present value factor of year (I) ×cash flow of year (1)
	+	present value factor of year (2) ×cash flow of year (2)
	+	etc.,
	+	Present value factor year final

$$\times \quad \frac{\text{final cash value}}{\text{discount rate}}$$

The discount rate is the appropriate rate that should be applied given the situation.

Example: What purchase price should be paid for a company, given that a discount rate of 15% is a satisfactory measure of the inherent risk of the business, if the next 5 years of cash flows are estimated as follows:

Year 1 =	75,000
Year 2 =	120,000
Year 3 =	125,000
Year 4 =	225,000
Year 5 =	250,000

Capitalized value =

$$(1+.15)^{-1} \times 75,000 + (1 + .15)^{-2} \times 120,000 +$$

$$(1+.15)^{-3} \times 125,000 + (1 + .15)^{-4} \times 225,000 + (1 + .15)^{-5} \times \frac{25,000}{(.15)}$$

$$= (8696)(75,000) + (.7561)(120,000) + (.6575)(125,000)$$

$$+(.5718)(225,000) + (.4972)\frac{(250,000)}{(.15)}$$

$$= \$2,033,461$$

$$= 65,220 + 90,732 + 82,188 + 128,655 + 828,667$$

$$= \$1,195,462$$

Capitalized Value of Endowment Fund

$$\text{Cost} + \frac{\text{Maintenence}}{\text{Interest}} + \left[\frac{\text{Renewal Cost}}{\text{Interest}} \times \frac{1}{\substack{\text{future value of annuity factor} \\ \text{of \$1 for n periods at i interest}}} \right]$$

Example: An endowment is provided to add a wing to a hospital for $2,000,000. The endowment provides $35,000 for annual maintenance. At the end of each 20 year period the building is to be renovated at an estimated allowed cost of $400,000. Interest is assumed to be 9%. How much money is required to fund the endowment?

Capitalized value =

$$2,000,000 + \frac{35,000}{.09} + \left[\frac{400,000}{.09} \times \frac{1}{\text{future value of annuity factor of \$1}} \right]$$
$$\text{for 20 years at 9\%}$$

$$= 2,000,000 + 388,889 + (4,444,444 \times 1/51.1601)$$
$$= \$2,475,762$$

.19 Finance vs. Purchase vs. Straight Lease

Present Value to Finance

= (cost) × (down payment %)

+ present value of periodic payments for number of payments at interest i

− (present value of residual value of assets

− (tax benefits)

Tax Benefits

$$= \Big[\big(\text{Annual depreciation of asset} \big) \Big] \big(\text{tax rate} \big)$$

$$\times \big(\text{present value of annuity for N periods at interest } i \big)$$

Example: Given the following data, what is the best way to finance the purchase?

Data: Vehicle cash cost = $12,000

Lease is $450/month with no buyout option

Financing requires $250/month for 48 months at 8% APR on balance after 10% downpayment

Residual value of vehicle = $2,500

Depreciation is straight line over 5 years

Tax rate is 34%

Company cost of capital = 9%

$$\text{Yearly depreciation} = \frac{\$12,000 - \$2,500}{5} = \$1,900$$

Present value to finance

($12,000) (.10) + present value of annuity of $250 a month for 48 months at 8% APR.

− (present value of $2,500 at 9% for 5 periods)

− (tax benefits)

Tax benefits

= ($1,900 × .34) (present value of annuity factor for 5 periods at 9%)

= ($1,900 × .34) (3.8897) = $2,512.75

Thus, the present value to finance

= ($12,000) (.10) + ($250) (40.9619) – ($2,500) (.64993) – $2,512.75

= $7,302.90

Present value to purchase = cost

– (Present value of residual value of asset) (Tax benefits)

= $12,000 – [($2,500) (present value factor for 5 periods at 9%)]

– [($1,900) (.34) (present value of annuity factor for 5 periods at 9%)]

= $12,000 – [($2,500) (.64993)] – [($1,900) (.34) (3.8897)]

=$12,000 – $1,625 – $2,513 = $7,862

Present value of lease: (lease payments) × (present value of periodic payments of annuity factor at i interest for N months)

– [(periodic payments) × tax rate ×12 × (present value factor of annuity at i interest for N periods)]

Thus, the present value of lease

$$= (\$450)(40.1848) - \left[(\$450 \times .34 \times 12) \times (3.2397)\right]$$

$$= \$12,135.07$$

.21 Internal Rate of Return

The rate of interest which would make the present value of the future cash flows equal to the initial investment.

Example:

- Machine cost = $8,400
- Machine yields a net cash inflow of $3,500 annually.
- Expected useful life = 3 yrs.

Determine the internal rate of return i of this investment.

Multiply the annuity payment A by the annuity factor corresponding to i and n, obtained from a PV of annuity table.

Internal Rate of Return

PV = A × Annuity factor for interest rate i and n periods

Rearrange the equation to solve for the annuity factor. This annuity factor can then be matched to the corresponding interest rate from the table.

Annuity Factor

$$\frac{PV}{A}$$

$$= \frac{\$8,400}{\$3,500}$$

$$= 2.4$$

Present value of Annuity of $1.00 in arrears

Interest Rate	Annuity Factor
i	$1 Annuity, 3 periods
7	2.62
8	2.58
10	2.49
12	2.40
15	2.28

The annuity factor 2.4 corresponds to 12% in the table above: thus the internal rate of return for this investment is 12%.

Compare this rate with the minimum desired rate of return required by management to determine if the investment should be made.

Advantages:

- All of the cash flow over the life of the project is used,

- The time value of money is explicitly recognized, and

- The project's rate of return is estimated.

Disadvantages:

- Cash flows are assumed to be reinvested at the rate earned by the project, and

- It is more complicated than some other techniques.

.23 Interpolation of Table Data

Example: Present value of $1 at compound interest table at ¶ 691.13 shows the following:

	Interest Rate		
	1 1/4	1 3/8	1 1/2
Periods	.0125	.01375	.0150
1	.9877	.9864	.9852
2	.9755	.9731	.9707
3	.9634	.9599	.9563
4	.9515	.9468	.9422
5	.9398	.9340	.9283

Value calculated for 4 periods = .9452 which gives an interest rate between 1.375% and 1.50%. Interpolated interest = 1.42%, as follows:

$$\frac{.9452 - .9468}{.9422 - .9468} = \frac{i - .01375}{.0150 - .01375}$$

$$\frac{.0016}{.0046} = \frac{i - .01375}{.00125}$$

$$i - .01375 = .00043$$
$$i = .01375 + .00043 = .0142 \text{ or } 1.42\%$$

.25 Interest-Period of Compounding—Other Than Annual Compounding

The annual (nominal) interest rate compounded on different time periods provides different factors.

Example: Person borrows $100,000

Nominal interest rate to be charged = 8%

If the interest rate is to be compounded on a daily basis, the effective annual rate = 8.32775%

The daily rate to be applied = 8.32775 / 360 = .0231326

Simple Interest Rate Equivalent to a Compound Interest Rate on a per Year Basis

Effective Rate of Interest

$$\left(1 + \frac{\text{Nominal rate of interest}}{\text{Number of conversion periods per year}}\right)^{(\text{number of conversion periods per year})} - 1$$

Example: What is the effective rate of interest on a note for 1 year that bears interest at a rate of 6% compounded semiannually?

.06/2 = .03, at 2 periods per year

Effective rate = $(1 + .03)^2$ 1 = $(1.03)^2$ 1

From compound interest table at ¶ 691.05 for $(1.03)^2$

= 1.0609, therefore = 1.0609 1 = .0609 or 6.09%

¶ 653 PROBABILITY AND EXPECTED VALUE

.01 Definition of Probability

Probability of Event Happening

$$\frac{\text{Number of elements in event}}{\text{Total number of elements in set}}$$

Example: Employer decides to send one of his 6 employees to a conference. He will draw straws to give each an equal chance of going. He prefers that employee A or B goes. What is the probability of satisfying his preference?

$$\text{Probability} = \frac{\text{Number of employees satisfying performance}}{\text{Total employees}} = \frac{2}{6} \text{ or } 3.33\%$$

.03 Estimating Probability

Estimate of Probability of Event Happening

$$\frac{\left(\begin{array}{c}\text{No. of times}\\\text{event A occurred}\end{array}\right) + \left(\begin{array}{c}\text{No. of times}\\\text{event B occurred}\end{array}\right) + \left(\begin{array}{c}\text{No. of times}\\\text{event C occurred}\end{array}\right) + \left(\text{etc.}\right)}{\text{Total number of events}}$$

Example: An auditor is concerned with two possible errors regarding payroll checks, the dollar amount is incorrect or the payee is incorrect. An analysis of last year's payroll checks showed the following:

Payroll checks written	13,500
Dollar amount incorrect	250
Payroll incorrect	50

Estimate the probability that a payroll check is incorrect:

$$P = \frac{250 + 50}{13,500} = .0222 \text{ or } 2.22\%$$

.05 Expected Value

Expected Value

(Probability of event 1) (net value of event 1) +

(Probability of event 2) (net value of event 2) +

(Probability of event 3) (net value of event 3) +, etc.

Example: Taxpayer A plans to invest $200,000 in a new business venture for which statistics of similar ventures indicate an 85% success probability. If the venture fails, he loses his investment. The expected net present value of the estimated cash flow of the business over the next 7 years is $1,200,000. What is the expected value?

Expected value	= (.85 × $1,200,000) + (.15 × – $200,000)
	= $1,020,000 – $30,000
	= $990,000

.07 Probability Range Expected Value

Characteristic	Projected ×	Estimated Probability=	Weighted Probability
Least Likely-Lowest	_____	.10	_____
Less Likely-Lower	_____	.20	_____
Most Probable	_____	.40	_____
Less Likely-Higher	_____	.20	_____
Least Likely-Highest	_____	.10	_____
Expected Value		=	_____

¶ 654 PRODUCT PRICING

.02 Product Pricing with Nonfinancial Considerations

- Don't be trapped with too small of a clientele that controls your pricing.

- Don't let prices become static. Be sure you don't let prices fall below acceptable market levels.
- Control your pricing by excellent selling. It's often the marketer, not the market, that sets prices.
- On pricing, be aware of features you provide, fast turn around time, free delivery, meeting the customer's specific requirements, etc.
- Don't undervalue your products or services.
- Don't underestimate the public's willingness to pay more for a service or product that stands out from the crowd.
- A high price tag can somtimes make a product more desirable. The concept of "Carriage Trade Pricing," the customer feels its better because it costs more.
- Research your competitor's prices to be sure you are in line.
- Ask the customer what they would pay for the product or service. The customer has a certain value in mind, generally. If a customer, for example, is willing to pay more for a faster turnaround time, the price should reflect that service.

¶ 655 PROFIT

.01 Gross Profit Variations

Gross Profit Variations

Selling price variation due to change in unit selling price =

(period (2) quantity) × (period (2) avg selling price – period (1) avg selling price)

Selling volume variation due to change in units sold =

(period (1) avg selling price) × (period (2) quantity – period (1) quantity)

Cost price variation due to change in unit cost =

(period (2) quantity) × (period (1) avg cost per unit – period (2) avg cost per unit)

Cost volume variation due to change in number of units sold =

(period (1) avg cost per unit) × (period (1) quantity – period (2) quantity)

Example:

Data	Period 1	Period 2
Sales	$225,000	$275,000
COGS	145,000	180,000
G/P	80,000	95,000
Units sold	150,000	165,000

$$\text{Average selling price} = \frac{\$225,000}{150,000} = \$1.50 \qquad \frac{\$275,000}{165,000} = \$1.666$$

$$\text{Average cost} = \frac{\$145,000}{150,000} = \$.966 \qquad \frac{\$180,000}{165,000} = \$1.091$$

What is total gross profit variation and variation by each type?

Total gross profit variation = period (2) – period (1) = $95,000 – $80,000 = $15,000

Selling variation:

Selling price variation due to change in unit selling price = 165,000 × \$(1.666 − 1.50) = \$27,390

Selling volume variation due to change in units sold = 1.50 × (165,000 − 150,000) = \$22,500

Cost variation:

Cost price variation due to change in unit cost = 165,000 × \$(.966 − 1.091) = −\$20,625

Cost volume variation due to change in number of units sold = .966 × (150,000 − 165,000) = −\$14,490

Total variation = \$15,000[1]

Gross Profit Variance Analysis

Variations in gross profit:

- Change in cost of goods sold:
  — Cost price variance
  — Cost volume variance
- Changes in Sales:
  — Sales price variance
  — Sales volume variance

Example:

	Prior Year	Per Unit Data Current Year	Difference
Units Sold	125,000	85,000	(40,000)
Price per Unit	\$10.00	\$14.00	\$4.00
Cost per Unit	\$6.50	\$9.00	\$2.50

	Prior Year	Income Statement Current Year	Difference
Sales	\$1,250,000	\$1,190,000	\$60,000
Cost of Sales	812,500	765,000	47,500
Gross Profit	\$437,500	\$425,000	\$112,500

Sales Volume Variance

Indicates the change in sales dollars due to changes in the number of units sold.

Previous Year Prices:

125,000 × \$10.00 (by *previous* year's units sold)	\$1,250,000
85,000 × \$10.00 (by *current* year's units sold)	−850,000
Unfavorable sales volume variance =	\$400,000

[1] (rounding error)

¶655.01

Sales Price Variance

Indicates the change in sales dollars due to changes in the price.

Current Year Units:

85,000 × $14.00 (at *current* year prices)	$1,190,000
85,000 × $10.00 (at *previous* year prices)	− 850,000
Favorable sales price variance =	$340,000

Cost Volume Variance

Indicates the change in cost of goods sold due to changes in the number of units sold.

Prior Year's Cost:

125,000 × $6.50 (by *previous* year's units sold)	$812,500
85,000 × $6.50 (by *previous* year's units sold)	− 552,500
Favorable cost volume variance =	$260,000

Cost Price Variance

Indicates the change in cost of goods sold due to changes in cost between periods.

Current Year's Units Sold:

85,000 × $9.00 (at *current* year's cost)	$765,000
less 85,000 × $6.50 (at *prior* year's cost)	− 552,500
Unfavorable cost price variance =	$ 212,500

Net Income Summary Variance:

Sales price variance =	$340,000
Sales volume variance =	(400,000)
Cost price variance =	(212,500)
Cost volume variance =	260,000
Net Income Statement change	$(12,500)

.03 Profit Analysis per Product

Analyze profit on a product-by-product basis to indicate the contribution of each product to the total marginal income. This can point out which product's sales should be increased, decreased, or possibly dropped.

Sales – Var = Gross Profit – Fixed Cost Allocation = Net Income

					% of Sales	Total × Fixed	Fixed Allocated	G/P Fixed
Product A	300	−	220	=	80	300/600 = .50	× 100 =	50	30
Product B	100	−	80	=	20	100/600 = .17	× 100 =	17	3
Product C	200	−	150	=	50	200/600 = .33	× 100 =	33	17
Totals	600	−	450	=	150			100	50

¶655.03

Profit Volume Analysis

Analyzes the relationships between the contribution of gross profit margin and sales volume. Answers questions such as:

- What effect on net income will changes of selling price and sales mix volume and expenses have?
- Which products are the most or least profitable?

Profit-volume (P-V) analysis has been developed as an alternative to the breakeven chart.

Marginal Relationships of Cost, Volume, and Revenues

Profit Volume Ratio (P/V) expresses the rate at which marginal income increases with increases in volume. A high ratio may indicate that substantial sales promotion effort per dollar of added sales may be profitable.

Profit Volume Ratio (P/V)   = Change in Profit / Change in Volume
                                            = Δ Profit / Δ Volume

or,

Profit Volume Ratio (P/V) = 1 – [Δ Variable Cost / Δ Sales]

or,

Profit Volume Ratio (P/V) = (Δ Sales – Δ Variable Costs) / Δ Sales

or,

Profit Volume Ratio (P/V) = (Δ Fixed Costs + Δ Profit) / Δ Sales

	Sales	Variable Costs	Gross Profit	Fixed Expenses	Net Income
19x2	$100,000	$65,000	$35,000	$20,000	$15,000
19x1	$80,000	$55,000	$25,000	$20,000	$5,000
Change	$20,000	$10,000	$10,000	$0	$10,000

Profit Volume Ratio (P/V)   = Δ Profit / Δ Volume
                                       = $10,000 / $20,000 = 50%

Profit Volume Ratio (P/V)   = 1 – [Δ Variable Cost / Δ Sales]
                                       = 1 – [$10,000 / $ 20,000] = 50%

or,

Profit Volume Ratio (P/V)   = (Δ Sales – Δ Variable Costs) / Δ Sales
                                       ($20,000 – $10,000) / $20,000 = 50%

or,

Profit Volume Ratio (P/V)   = (Δ Fixed Costs + Δ Profit) / Δ Sales
                                       = ($0 + $10,000) / $20,000 = 50%

Data for following Examples:

	$	%
Sales	100,000	100
Variable expense	65,000	65
Gross profit	35,000	35

	$	%
Fixed expenses	20,000	20
Net income	15,000	15

Net Income or Loss at Various Sales Volume Levels

Net Income (Loss)

= (Gross Profit Margin × Sales) – Fixed Expenses

Example:

Net Income (Loss)	= (.35 × $100,000) – $20,000
	= $35,000 – $20,000
	= $15,000

Variable Expenses at Any Sales Volume

= 100% – gross profit margin

= 100% – 35%

= 65%

.04 Profit Analysis by Contribution Margin

Contribution margin represents the contribution that sales in a defined business unit make toward the fixed costs and profits after all variable costs associated with that business unit have been taken out. Contribution Margin is particularly useful for evaluating different business units or divisions for profitability. The business unit is the portion of the business being analyzed. This could be categorized by product line, geographic location, etc. Contribution Margin is defined as follows:

Sales

– Variable manufacturing or service costs (Direct labor, direct materials, variable overhead)

= Gross Margin

– Variable sales costs (Commissions based on sales volume, etc.)

– Variable admin. costs (rent, depreciation, salaries, - all expenses directly related to that business unit)

= Contribution margin

If postive, then the contribution margin contributes dollars toward covering the fixed expenses of the business unit.

	Divison A	Divison B	Division C
Sales	$250,000	$300,000	$425,000
less: Variable manufacturing			
Direct labor	$115,000	155,000	205,000
direct materials	75,000	85,000	105,000
variable overhead	25,000	30,000	55,000
= Gross Margin	35,000	30,000	60,000

	Divison A	Divison B	Division C
less: Variable sales costs	10,000	15,000	35,000
Commissions	1,000	3,000	5,000
less: Variable admin. costs			
rent	5,000	8,000	9,000
depreciation	200	2,000	2,500
salaries	1,500	5,000	8,000
other,etc.	500	500	300
= Contribution margin	16,800	23,500	200

Ranked by Gross Margin: Divison C, Divison A, Division B
Ranked by Contribution Margin: Divison B, Divison A, Division C

.05 Fixed Expenses Given Any Known Amount of Sales

Fixed Expenses Given Any Known Amount of Sales

$$\text{Fixed Expense} = \frac{\text{Gross Profit Margin} - \text{Net Income}}{\text{Sales}} \times (\text{Sales})$$

Example:

$$\text{Fixed Expenses} = .35 - \frac{\$15,000}{\$100,000} \times \$100,000$$

$$= (.35 - .15) \times \$100,000 = \$20,000$$

.06 Markups

Markup on Cost for Selling Price

The following procedure provides the markup on cost to arrive at a selling price given total deductions from the selling price. Use it to compute the desired markup on cost and requested selling price given a desired net income and other criterion.

Example: What should be the cost markup and resulting selling price on an item purchased for $15.00, if the firm allows a 4% discount off the selling price, pays a commission of 5% of the selling price, covers the overhead at 9% of the selling price, and wishes to attain a net profit of 4% of the selling price?

To determine the selling price.

- Let 100% = total selling price
- Cost = $15.00
- Deduct the total of the "other" costs from 100% (not the cost of the item)
  4% + 5% + 9% + 4% = 22%
  100% – 22% = 78%
- Divide the actual dollar cost by the % determined.
  $15.00 / .78 = $19.23

Proof:

Sale	$19.23	100%
Cost	$15.00	– 78%
G/P	$4.23	= 22%

¶655.05

Less:

Discount	– 4%
Commission	– 5%
Overhead	– 9%
Net Profit	= 4%

Percentage Markup to Cover Deductions

% Markups on Cost For Selling Price to Cover Deductions

% Markup on Cost	Total % Deductions from Selling Price	%Markup on Cost	Total % Deductions from Selling Price
101.01	1	135.14	26
102.04	2	136.99	27
103.09	3	138.89	28
104.17	4	140.85	29
105.26	5	142.86	30
106.38	6	144.93	31
107.53	7	147.06	32
108.7	8	149.25	33
109.89	9	151.52	34
111.11	10	153.85	35
112.36	11	156.25	36
113.64	12	158.73	37
114.94	13	161.29	38
116.28	14	163.93	39
117.65	15	166.67	40
119.05	16	169.49	41
120.48	17	172.41	42
121.95	18	175.44	43
123.46	19	178.57	44
125	20	181.82	45
126.58	21	185.19	46
128.21	22	188.68	47
129.87	23	192.31	48
131.58	24	196.08	49
133.33	25	200	50

Markup on Cost for Gross Profit

Markups on Cost for Gross Profit %

To Make G/P % on Sales $'s	Markup on Cost	To Make G/P % on Sales $'s	Markup on Cost
1	1.01	26	1.351
2	1.02	27	1.37

To Make G/P % on Sales $'s	Markup on Cost	To Make G/P % on Sales $'s	Markup on Cost
3	1.031	28	1.389
4	1.042	29	1.408
5	1.053	30	1.429
6	1.064	31	1.449
7	1.075	32	1.471
8	1.087	33	1.493
9	1.099	34	1.515
10	1.111	35	1.538
11	1.124	36	1.563
12	1.136	37	1.587
13	1.149	38	1.613
14	1.163	39	1.639
16	1.19	40	1.667
17	1.205	41	1.695
18	1.22	42	1.724
19	1.235	43	1.754
20	1.25	44	1.786
21	1.266	45	1.818
22	1.282	46	1.852
23	1.299	47	1.887
24	1.316	48	1.923
25	1.333	49	1.961
		50	2.000

Markup on Cost for Gross Profit

$$\text{Selling price} = \frac{\text{Cost}}{(1 - \text{desired profit rate on sales price})}$$

Example: Compute the selling price so that a profit of 30% will be made on the sales price.

Cost = $10.00

Desired profit on sales price = 30%

Selling price	=	Cost / (1 − .30)
	=	$10.00 / .70
	=	$14.29

Proof:	Sale	$14.29	100%
	Cost	$10.00	70%
	G/P	$ 4.29	30%

This table provides the markup on the cost of an item to achieve a desired gross profit margin.

From table per illustration above, to achieve a gross profit margin of 30% of sales, the markup on cost would be 1.429.

¶655.06

Cost = $10.00

Table value = 1.429

Sale price = $14.29

.07 Mark Downs

Percent Mark Down from Original Price

% Change = (Original Price – New Price) / Original Price

> *Example:* A product is marked down form $125 to $99. By what percent is the product marked down?

% change = ($125 – $99) / $125

= $26 / $125

= 20.8%

Rebate

An auto dealer offers a $1500 discount on a $20,000 auto.

What percent of the original price is the rebate (discount)?

% change = (Rebate) / Original Price

= $1500 / $20,000

= 7.5%

Discounted Price

Given: Product A originally cost $85.00

If product A is marked down by 20 percent, what is the new price?

New Price = Original Price – (Original Price × Discount)

= $85 – (85 × .20)

= $85 – $17

= $68

Or, alternately, compute the one's complement of the discount percent and multiply by the original price.

One's complement = (1 – .20) = .8

New Price = Original Price × One's complement of Discount %

= $85 × .8

= $68

Original Price

Product A is marked down by 25 percent to $50. What was the original price of Product A?

Let x = Original Price

Therefore, x – .25x = $50

.75x = $50

$$x = \$50 \ / \ .75$$

$$x = \$66.67$$

Discount from List Price—Cost of Product

The list price of Product A is $500. The manufacturer sells it to the retailer for 40 percent off list price (discounted). How much did the retailer pay for Product A?

Retailer's Cost = List × (1 – Discount %)

$$= \$500 \times (1 - .40)$$

$$= \$500 \times .60$$

$$= \$300$$

Discount From List Price—List Price of Product

A retailer receives a quantity of 10 of product A at a 20-percent discount and is billed $5,000 total. What is the list price for each product A?

Let x = List Price

Retailer Cost % = 1 – .20 = .8

$$10 \ (\ .8x) = \$5000$$

$$8x = \$5000$$

$$x = \$5000 \ / \ 8$$

$$x = \$625$$

Chain Discount

If a manufacturer provides the following discounts to a retailer, what is the retailer's cost assuming the bill is paid timely for the discount?

Given:

List Price = $100

Trade discount = 25%

Quantity discount = 5%

Terms = 2/10 net 30

Solution:

Retailer's Cost = List × (1 – Trade Discount) × (1 – Quantity Discount) × (100% – 2%)

$$= \$100 \times (1 - .25) \times (1 - .25) \times (1 - .02)$$

$$= \$100 \times .75 \times .95 \times .98$$

$$= \$69.83$$

.08 Profit Change by Price Cut

Percent Change in Profit by Price Cut

$$\% \text{ profit before price cut} = \frac{\text{Total profit before price cut}}{(\text{Sales volume}) \times (\text{selling price before cut})}$$

$$\% \text{ profit after price cut} = \frac{\text{Total profit after price cut}}{(\text{Sales volume}) \times (\text{selling price after cut})}$$

$$\% \text{ cut in profit} = \frac{(\% \text{ profit before price cut}) - (\% \text{ profit after price cut})}{\% \text{ profit before price cut}}$$

Example: Assume no change in variable and fixed expense.

Data:

	19X1 Before Price Cut	19X2 After Price Cut
Units sold: 9,000		
Price per unit	$1.50	$1.35
Total profit	$1,250	$955

$$\% \text{ profit before price cut} = \frac{\$1,250}{9,000(\$1.50)} = 9.26\%$$

$$\% \text{ profit after price cut} = \frac{\$955}{9,000(\$1.35)} = 7.86\%$$

$$\% \text{ cut in profit} = \frac{9.26\% - 7.86\%}{9.26\%} = 15.12\%$$

.09 Sales Volume Required to Recover Lost Profits

Sales Volume Required to Recover Lost Profits

$$\text{Sales volume required} = \frac{\text{Lost Profits}}{\dfrac{\text{Total profit before price cut}}{\text{Sales volume in units}}}$$

Example (given the previous example):

The lost profits are $1,250 – 955 = $295.

Assuming no other variable or fixed changes, how many units of the product must be sold if a new customer will buy the product at the original price of $1.50/per unit?

$$\text{Increase in sales volume required to recover lost profit} = \frac{\$295}{\dfrac{\$1,250}{9,000}} = 2,124 \text{ units}$$

.14 Sales Volume Change Required Given Sales Price Changes

The following illustrates the "sales volume change 'allowed' to not lose money."

Formulas for unit volume % changes:

For price increase:
$$\frac{\text{Gross Profit \%}}{\left(\text{GrossProfit \%}\right)+\left(\text{Price Change \%}\right)}-1$$

For price decrease:
$$\frac{\text{Gross Profit \%}}{\left(\text{GrossProfit \%}\right)-\left(\text{Price Change \%}\right)}-1$$

Example: Given: gross profit = 30%.

If there were a price decrease of 5%, what % increase in sales volume will be needed to maintain the same gross profit dollars?

Use table, "% Change in Unit Sales Volume Allowed to Maintain Gross Profit Margin," at ¶ 691.35.

Locate 30% gross profit on the left hand margin. Read across to heading of 5% price decrease (–5).

The firm would require a 20% increase in sales to maintain the same gross profit dollars.

Example by formula:

$$\frac{.30}{(.30-.05)}-1=\frac{.30}{.25}-1=.20 \text{ or } \underline{20\%}$$

See ¶ 691.35 for related charts.

.15 Sales Volume Required to Cover an Additional Expenditure

Use the following formula to determine the sales volume required to cover an additonal expenditure to the company without changing its net income. Profit margins determine a company's ability to absorb increases in overhead. A company should seek to keep its gross profit margin stable. A company should-never sacrifice its gross profit margin.

Example: Company XZY is thinking of hiring a salesperson at a $40,000 starting salary to increase sales of its products. (This $40,000 covers all expenses associated with hiring this person, such as benefits, travel, etc.) What sales increase is necessary to hire a new salesperson and still keep the same net income?

Annual Sales	= $100,000
Annual COGS	= $70,000
Cost of salesperson	= $40,000
Gross Profit	= Sales – COGS
	= $100,000 – $ 70,000
	= $30,000
Gross Profit / Sales	= Gross Profit Margin %
	$30,000 / $100,000 = 30%
COGS %	= (1 – Gross profit margin %) = (1 – 30%) = 70%

Sales increase needed to keep the
same gross profit margin + net income = (Annual Sales / Annual Gross Profit) × New Expense

= ($100,000 / $30,000) × $40,000

$133,333 of new sales needed to cover cost spent on the new salesperson without reduction in net income.

Proof:

	Before salesperson	After adding salesperson	
Sales	100,000	233,333	
COGS	70,000	163,333	70%
G/P	30,000	70,000	30%
Salesperson	0	40,000	
Net	30,000	30,000	

To calculate by percentages:

Sales increase needed to keep the same
gross profit margin

= (1 / Annual Gross Profit %) × New Expense

= (1 / 30%) × $40,000

= 3.33 × $40,000

= $133,333

Proof:

Sales	$133,333
COGS at 70%	93,333
Less: New Sales person	40,000
Equals additional cost	$0

¶ 656 PRICING

.01 Pricing Strategies

Understand how customers evaluate your product:

- Is it "price"or the "value" of the product?
- Does the customer perceive superiority of a particular brand?

Pricing is an art, not an absolute.

A firm that prices only from internal cost needs might price too low and fail to realize the true profit potential. If the firm prices too high-beyond what buyers will pay, the product will fail to sell, and again profit is lost.

Pricing by product-driven factors = product—price—customer

Pricing by customer-driven focus = customer—price—product

Understanding what features can exist based on the price the customer will pay limits how the product is made.

Pricing should consider the costs, competition, and customer sensitivity to price.

Is pricing done as a tactic? For example, to gain a dominant market share.

To price effectively, you must understand costs and what are the relevant costs to be considered. If your costs continue to rise to replace inventory, and you continue to sell at the same price, your profit is deteriorating with each sell. The company must be sensitive to its costs.

Sunk costs are the costs that a company is irreversibly committed to bear, i.e., rent, past research and development, etc.

Costing analysis:

- Don't average total variable costs to estimate the cost of a single unit. Consider only the actual incremental costs of the particular units affected by the pricing decision.

- Don't treat a single cost as an all-relevant or an all-irrelevant cost.

- Be aware of opportunity costs. Opportunity costs are the foregone profits when a firm uses assets for one purpose rather than another. For example, if instead of paying interest on a note to buy inventory, the firm paid cash for the inventory, and the amount of interest payments was invested instead in an interest bearing investment. The opportunity cost is the earning of interest versus the paying of interest.

.02 Price Sensitivity

Is the product unique?

- How much do buyers value the uniqueness of the product?

- Does the product's uniqueness truly differentiate it from competitors?

Product Carriage Trade

Does the buyer buy the product mostly for the prestigious image it conveys?

Sunk Product

Is the buyer generally more or less locked into those expenditures? For example, computer software use.

Product End-Benefit

What is the end purpose for the use of the product?

Product Expenditures

What is the consumer use of the product?

Product Alternatives

What are the substitute products available to the buyer?

Product Shared Cost Effect

Do buyers share in the overall cost, like insurance, or pay the full cost of the product alone?

Product Comparatives

Are the products easily comparable for the buyers? Or are the products too complex for comparisons?

¶656.02

.03 Competitor Pricing Considerations

Typical Competitor

Charges prices similarly to competitors' changes. Maintains constant market share. Has unit costs similar to competitors.

Normative Adaptive Competitor

Adjusts price changes according to cost changes. Accepts that it can't influence the pricing structure by its actions. Has small market share.

Opportunistic Competitor

Initiates price cuts to increase market share over competitors. Generally has lower unit costs than competitors.

Predatory Competitor

Initiates large price cuts to attack weaker competitors. Constantly seeking to increase market share. Wants to prey on weaker competitors.

.04 Pricing by Segmenting Markets

Segmented pricing examples:

- Theaters offering discounts to "first" showing of the day, discounts before 6:00 PM, or quantity discounts to large groups.
- Barbers charging different prices for a haircut for short hair, long hair, or children's hair.
- Stores, like supermarkets, offering coupons to price-sensitive shoppers.

Price Segmentation by Location

Dentists, doctors, and opticians may have multiple stores in different locations and offer different prices for reasons such as higher prices in the expensive neighborhoods or lower prices in localities where competition is more intense. Other examples include pricing by prestige, pricing by location due to convenience, or theater tickets discounted for location in balcony, etc.

Price Segmentation by Time of Purchase

- Theaters having pricing differences for matinees or weekend afternoons versus weekday prices.
- Periodic sales, offering the same merchandise at discounted prices.

Price Segmentation by Purchase Quantity

- *Volume discounts.* Can be per purchase or over a given time frame.
- *Order discounts.* Where established discounts are published based on quantity bought.
- *Step discounts.* These apply, not to the total quantity purchased, but only to purchases beyond a specific amount. For example, electricity priced at .12 per KWH for the first 100 KWH and .08 per KWH after 100 KWH used.

Price Segmentation by Product Design

Offering different versions of the same product, such as offering an auto with different trim packages—heated seats, sunroof, leather seats, and automatic adjustable seats.

.05 Pricing Product Considerations

- Consider the pricing of complementary products. Should these products by bought and used together, i.e., washer and dryer combinations offered at a discount.
- Does the product have cheaper substitutes?
- Should pricing be done to have loss leaders?
- What is the price perception in the market place of the company's product? High? Low? Cheap?
- Should the company offer price discounts to induce trial use?
- Consider the pricing of the product by how different distribution channels can affect the price. How will reseller's pricing influence the ultimate attractiveness of the product to consumers?

.06 Profit Pricing versus Competitors

- What competitive cost advantages does the company have? For example, a mutual fund family that offers 40 funds versus a family that only offers three selections.
- Does the company have a price advantage by being large scale and having economies of scale on buying or making the product?
- Does the company enjoy economies of experience?
- Does the company enjoy product superiority?

.07 Selling Price (Markup Based on Cost)

Selling Price (Markup Based on Cost)

Selling Price = Cost (1 + % markup on cost)

> **Example:** Established markup on cost= 65%

If an item costs $40, what should be the selling price?

Selling price = $40 (1 + .65) = $66

Selling price (markup based on cost with load factors)

$$\text{Selling price} = \frac{\text{Cost}\left(1 + \% \text{ markup on cost}\right)}{1 - \text{load factor } \% \text{ based on selling price}}$$

> **Example:** Established markup on cost = 65%

Cost of item = $40

Load factor allowed = 10% sales commission to sales representative

Load factor allowed = 2% sales commission to house account

What should be the selling price?

$$\text{Selling price} = \frac{\$40 \ (1 + .65)}{1 - (.10 + .02)} = \$75$$

Selling price (markup based on selling price)

$$\text{Selling price} = \frac{\text{Cost}}{1 - \%\ \text{markup on selling price}}$$

Example: Established markup on selling price = 30%

If an item costs $21, what should be the selling price?

$$\text{Selling price} = \frac{\$21}{1 - .30} = \$30$$

Selling Price (markup based on selling price with load factors)

$$\text{Selling price} =$$

$$\frac{\text{Cost}}{1 - (\%\ \text{markup on selling price} + \text{load factor}\ \%\ \text{based on selling price})}$$

Example: Cost = $21

Desired markup on sales price = 30% (computed after paying loads)

Load factor allowed = 10% sales commission to sales representative.

What should be the selling price?

$$\text{Selling price} = \frac{\$21}{1 - (.30 + .10)} = \$35$$

Proof:	Sale – cost of goods = gross profit
By dollar:	$35 – ($21 + $3.50) = $10.50
By percentage:	100% – 70% = 30%

Note: Load factor = 10% sales commission to sales representative.

$3.50 = $35 × .10 commission

.09 Pricing—Top Down Pricing for Service by Individual

Use this technique for an individual who wishes to provide service (ie. repair glass, garage doors, install ceiling fans, etc.), is just beginning a business, and needs an overall starting point for pricing the service. If, after determing the service hourly rate, it does not compare favorably to local competition, then adjust the target salary, target work hours, benefits or overhead accordingly. The following illustrates an example of top down pricing.

Step 1: Determine target annual hours

Annual hours – 8 hrs × 5 days × 52 weeks	= 2080 hours
Less: Vacation desired – 8 hrs × 5 days × 4 weeks	= 160
Less: Holidays – 8 hrs × 10 days	= 80
Annual adjusted for time off	= 1840
Expected billable percentage	× 70%
Total billable hours	= 1288

Step 2: Determine Target Salary $65,000

Step 3: Determine overhead $

Office Supplies	$2,000
Equipment	$4,300
Small Tools	$800
Advertising	$1,200
Insurance	$3,000
Transportation costs	$1,500
Other, Etc.	$200
(Generally estimate at 15-20% of target Income)	$13,000

Step 4: Determine Benefits

Health benefits (insurance, etc.)	$1,200
Disability	$2,200
Retirement funding	$1,378
Social Security costs	$4,972
(Generally estimate at 15-20% of target Income)	$9,750
Total costs	**$87,750**

Step 5: Determine Hourly billable rate

Divide by Total billable hours	/1288
Hourly billable rate	$68.13
	(Round to $70.00/ hour)

Total cost billed would be $70.00/hour × number of hours, plus direct material costs.

.11 Selling Price—By Job Cost In $'s

Selling Price—By Job Cost in $'s = (Direct Labor + Direct Material + Overhead) + (Marketing + General & Administrative) + (Desired Profit)

.13 Selling Price—Return on Assets Employed Method

A unit selling price can be determined from a target return on assets employed. Management can make decisions regarding detailed definitions of the assets employed. The assets could be historical cost, depreciated cost basis, current replacement cost, etc. The key is that consistency is used. The fixed assets should include assets used in manufacturing and selling the product. The following unit price formula was developed by James Willson, CPA, as published in the *Budget and Profit Planning Manual*.

Unit Selling Price—Return on Assets Employed Method =

$$\frac{\text{Total Cost} + (\text{Before tax desired rate of return on assets employed} \times \text{Fixed Assets})}{\text{Annual Sales Volume in Units}}$$

1 – (Before tax desired rate of return on assets employed) (Variable assets expressed as a % of sales volume)

Where:

Total Assets = Fixed Assets + Variable Assets

Variable Assets = Current assets that are a function of volume, such as accounts receivable and inventory.

¶656.11

Given the following data, what is the Unit Selling Price if management seeks a "Before tax desired rate of return on assets employed" of 20%?

Fixed Assets = $300,000

Planned annual Sales Units = 4,200

Variable Assets (Inventory and Accounts Receivable) = 30 % of Sales

Unit cost = $50.00

Unit Selling Price—Return on Assets Employed Method =

$$\frac{(\$50.00 \times 4,200) + (.20 \times \$300,000)}{\dfrac{4,200}{1 - (.20)(.30)}}$$

= $68.39

Proof:

Shows that Net before tax income = Before tax desired rate of return on assets employed.

Assets Employed

Variable Assets (Inventory and Accounts Receivable) at 30 % of Sales

	4,200 × $68.39 = $287,238
	× .30
	$86,171
Fixed Assets	
	$300,000
	$386,171
Before tax desired rate of return on assets employed of 20%	× .20
	≈$77,238

Income	4,200 × $68.39 =	$287,238
Cost	$50.00 × 4,200 =	$210,000
Net before tax income		= $77,238

.15 Product Pricing Formula

Product Pricing Formula

	Cost Per ____Pieces
Material - Raw	_____
Outside Processing Subcontracted	_____
Purchased Parts for Materials	_____
Subtotal—Materials	_____
Scrap Allowance, Handling, Etc.(____%)	
of Materials Total	_____
Set-Up Costs	_____
Labor Costs	_____

Fixed Overhead (as ____% of Labor) _____

Variable Overhead (as ____% of Labor) _____

Total Manufacturing Cost _____ (A)

General, Administrative, Sales, and Marketing Expense

(____% of Total Manufacturing Cost) _____ (B)

      Subtotal (Lines A + B) _____ (C)

Minimum Selling Price

      (Line C / [1 - desired profit %]) _____ (D)

Sales Commission

([Line D/(1-Commission Rate)]-Line D) _____ (E)

Required Profit or Sales Commission _____

      (Line E × Desired Profit % of ____%) _____ (F)

Target Selling Price (Lines D + E + F) _____

Final Selling Price (Based on Target Price) _____

¶ 657 PROFITABILITY INDEX

Use when several projects vary in size. This can be used for capital budgeting decisions, such as when there is a scarce amount of investment capital and the firm needs to identify its best investment alternatives.

Profitability Index

$$\text{Profitability index} = \frac{\text{Present value of cash in-flows}}{\text{Initial investment}}$$

Data: Machine cost = $12,000

Machine yields cash in-flows of $4,500, $5,000, and $6,000.

Cost of capital is 8%.

Year	Cash Flow	PV Factor at 8%	PV of Cash Flow
1	$4,500	.926	$4,167
2	5,000	.857	4,285
3	6,000	.794	4,764
		Total	$13,216

Net present value = $13,216 $12,000 = $1,216

$$\text{Profitability index} = \frac{\$13,216}{12,000} = 1.101$$

¶ 658 BUSINESS PROFIT TRIANGLE

The business profit triangle visually illustrates the major income statement relationships between sales, gross profit and fixed/overhead expenses.

¶657

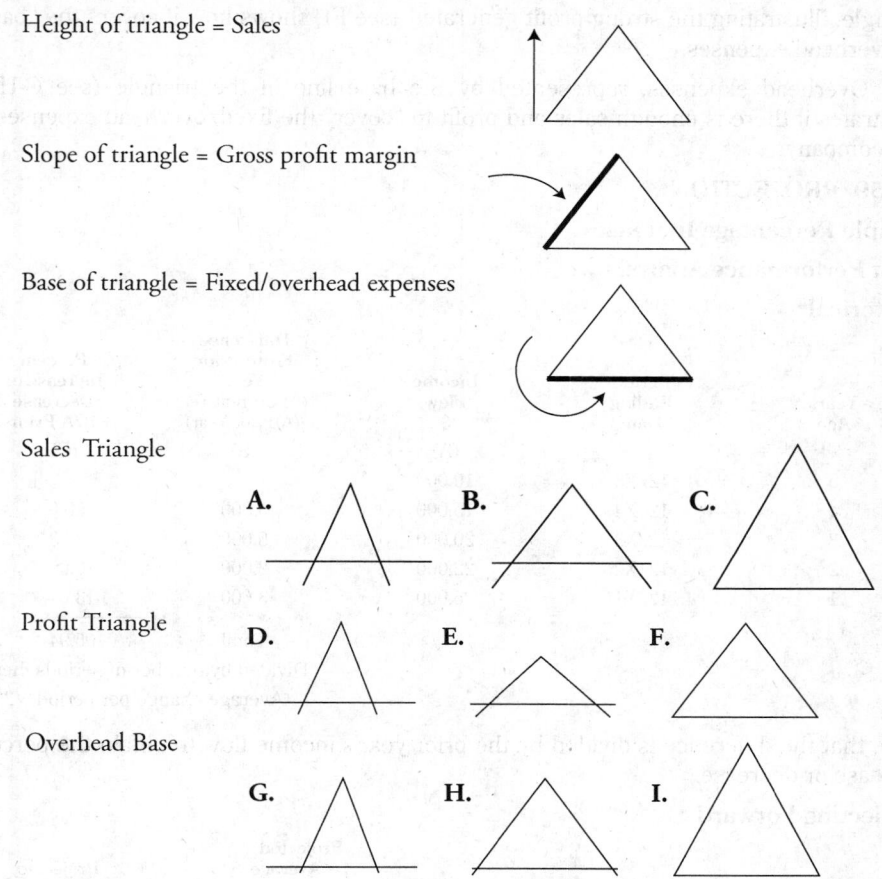

Height of triangle = Sales

Slope of triangle = Gross profit margin

Base of triangle = Fixed/overhead expenses

Sales Triangle

A.   **B.**   **C.**

Profit Triangle

D.   **E.**   **F.**

Overhead Base

G.   **H.**   **I.**

Examples of illustrations regarding a client's company and the Profit Triangle:

Referring to the Sales triangle illustration (see A-B-C), if there is not enough sales, as in triangle A, then there is not enough income to cover the fixed expenses, then the triangle does not form a true triangle, and the company shows a loss by not covering the base line of the triangle.

If there is not enough profit slope, the company must have to have too much required sales (see C) to cover the fixed costs. This not being possible, the company needs to address the Triangles D-E-F.

Referring to the sales triangle illustration (see D), note the difficulty in covering the fixed overhead if there is not a sufficient gross profit. The sales have to be much higher than can be expected to be achieved (see C), given the current assets (i.e., inventory) and employee base. The conclusion might be that increased sales alone (see G) may not be able to achieve a profitable net income for the company.

Referring to the gross profit triangle illustrations (defined by the slope of the triangle sides), the more vertical the slope (see D), the smaller the gross profit. The more horizontal (see F), or wider the slope, the higher the gross profit. Thus the wider triangle, illustrating the strong profit generated (see F), shows how it covers the "base" or overhead expenses.

The Overhead expenses, represented by the base line of the triangle (see G-H-I), illustrates if there is enough sales and profit to "cover" the fixed/overhead expenses of the company.

¶ 659 PROJECTION

Simple Percentage Increase

Past Performance Analysis

Historical

Years Ago	Period Ending Date	Income Flow $ (A)	Difference From Prior Year ((A) Current Year -(A) Prior Year) (B)	Percent Increase or Decrease B/A Prior (C)
5	12/X5	10,000		
4	12/X4	15,000	5,000	50.0
3	12/X3	20,000	5,000	33.3
2	12/X2	22,000	2,000	10.00
1	12/X1	25,000	3,000	13.64
			Total	106.94

Divided by number of periods, here 4

Average change per period = 26.74

Note that the difference is divided by the prior year's income flow to obtain the percent increase or decrease.

Projecting Forward

Projected Years	Period Ending	Income Flow $		Projected 1 + Average Change per Period in %		Projected Income Flow $
1	12/X1	25,000	×	1.2674	=	31,685
2	12/X2	31,685		1.2674		40,158
3	12/X3	40,158		1.2674		50,896
4	12/X4	50,896		1.2674		64,505
5	12/X5	64,505		1.2674		81,753

¶ 661 RANDOM NUMBERS

Use the Random Number tables at ¶ 691.37 when random selections are needed. Often in the auditing process, auditors need to make selections of items based on a daily method. Use the table from 1 to 365 for these daily selections.

¶ 663 RATIOS

.01 Bankruptcy/Solvency Indicator Ratios

The following ratios may be indicators of financial difficulty.

Bankruptcy/Solvency Indicator Ratios

Cash Flow to Debt Ratio

Indicates the firm's earnings ability to cover total debt.

$$\text{Cash flow to debt ratio} = \frac{\text{Net income} + \text{depreciation}}{\text{Total debt}}$$

Working Capital to Total Assets

Indicates liquid assets relative to total capitalization. Consistent firm losses will reduce current assets relative to total assets.

$$\text{Working capital to total assets ratio} = \frac{\text{Net working capital}}{\text{Total assets}}$$

Net Worth to Total Liabilities

Indicates the book value amount the firm's assets can decline before becoming insolvent.

$$\text{Net worth to total liabilities ratio} = \frac{\text{Net worth}}{\text{Total liabilities}}$$

Retained Earnings to Total Assets

Indicates the firm's cumulative profitability as a return on its firm's investment.

$$\text{Retained earnings to total assets ratio} = \frac{\text{Retained earnings}}{\text{Total Assets}}$$

EBIT to Total Assets

Indicates the firm's current earnings as a return on the firm's investment.

$$\text{EBIT to total assets ratio} = \frac{\text{Earnings before interest and taxes}}{\text{Total assets}}$$

Market Equity to Debt

Indicates how much the firm's market value of assets can decline in value before the business becomes insolvent.

$$\text{Market equity to debt ratio} = \frac{\text{Market value of common} + \text{preferred}}{\text{Total current} + \text{long term debt}}$$

Sales to Assets

Indicates number of times sales is earned on assets.

$$\text{Total sales to total assets ratio} = \frac{\text{Total sales}}{\text{Total assets}}$$

Z-Score Analysis

Z-score analysis, developed by Professor Edward Altman of New York University from a study in the mid-1960's, is an analytical tool for measuring a company's financial position in whatever life stage it is in. Tracking a company's Z-score can aid in warning of potential financial problems that may need serious attention and can be used to help

¶663.01

predict the company's future financial strength. If a company's Z-score is low, the company should examine its financial statements to determine the deficiencies and use the Z-score as a guide for corrective or preventative actions. Comparisons of Z-scores readily point out trends in the company.

The Z-Score is based on the following four ratios:

Retained Earnings to Total Assets

This ratio shows the firm's cumulative profitability. A growing positive ratio indicates strong earnings.

$$\frac{\text{Retained Earnings}}{\text{Total Assets}}$$

Working Capital to Total Assets

This ratio indicates liquid assets relative to total capitalization. Consistent losses will shrink current assets relative to total assets.

$$\frac{\text{Net Working Capital}}{\text{Total Assets}}$$

EBIT to Total Assets

This ratio analyzes the productivity of a firm's total assets.

$$\frac{\text{Earnings Before Interest and Taxes}}{\text{Total Assets}}$$

Net Worth to Total Liabilities

This ratio measures how much the firm's assets can decline before the business becomes insolvent.

$$\frac{\text{Net Worth}}{\text{Total Liabilities}}$$

Z-Score = 1.4 (Retained Earnings to Total Assets) + 1.2 (Working Capital to Total Assets)

+ 3.3 (EBIT to Total Assets) + .6 (Net Worth to Total Liabilities)

+ 1 (Sales to Total Assets)

Given a firm's following data, what is the Z-Score?

Sales = $950,000

EBIT = $100,000

Total Assets = $300,000

Working Capital = $200,000

Total Liabilities = $275,000

Net Worth of Equity = $400,000

Retained Earnings = $250,000

Z-Score   = 1.4 (250,000 / 300,000) + 1.2 (200,000 / 300,000)
              + 3.3 (100,000 / 300,000) + .6 (400,000 / 275,000)
              + 1 (950,000 / 300,000)

¶663.01

$$= 1.4 \,(.833) + 1.2 \,(.667) + 3.3 \,(.333) + .6 \,(1.455) + 1 \,(3.167)$$
$$= 7.1056$$

This company is financially sound.

Z-Score Bankruptcy Ratios

If a Company's Z-Score total approaches 1.10 and below, it is an indicator of possible bankruptcy tendencies. If a Company's Z-Score total approaches 2.60, it is an indicator that the company is financially sound.

.03 Coverage Ratios

Indicates the firm's ability to cover items such as interest expenses, debt cash flow, fixed charges, etc.

Coverage Ratios

Total Interest Coverage Ratio

Indicates firm's ability to repay debt and interest.

$$\text{Total interest coverage ratio} = \frac{\text{Earnings before interest and taxes}}{\dfrac{\text{Principal reduction}}{\left(1 - \text{tax rate}\right)} + \text{interest}}$$

Times Interest Earned Ratio

Indicates to what level a company's operating income covers interest costs. The ratio focuses on the firm's cash flow necessary to service debt and indicates to what level earnings can drop with interest still being serviced.

$$\text{Times interest earned ratio} = \frac{\text{Earning before interest and taxes}}{\text{Total interest}}$$

Fixed Charges Coverage Ratio

This ratio indicates the number of times that earnings cover payment of interest and contractual fixed obligations, such as lease payments, rent, etc.

$$\frac{\text{Earnings before interest and taxes}}{\text{Interest payments} + \text{fixed deductible obligations} + \dfrac{\text{sinking fund payments}}{\left(1 - \text{tax rate}\right)}}$$

Debt Cash Flow Coverage

Indicates the number of times interest on debt plus sinking fund payments (net of tax) are covered by cash flow.

Debt cash flow coverage =

$$\frac{\text{Earnings before interest and taxes} + \text{depreciation}}{\text{Interest payments} + \left(\text{sinking fund payments}\right) / \left(1 - \text{tax rate}\right)}$$

Common Stock Cash Flow Coverage

Indicates number of times that cash flow will cover common stock dividends and sinking fund requirements.

Common stock cash flow coverage ratio =

$$\frac{\text{Earnings before interest and taxes + depreciation}}{\begin{array}{l} \text{Interest payments} + \left(\text{Debt sinking fund payments}\right)/\left(1 - \text{tax rate}\right) \\ + \left(\text{Preferred dividend payments}\right)/\left(1 - \text{tax rate}\right) \\ + \left(\text{Sinking fund requirements on preferred}\right)/\left(1 - \text{tax rate}\right) \\ + \left(\text{Dividend payment on common}\right)/\left(1 - \text{tax rate}\right) \end{array}}$$

Preferred Stock Cash Flow Coverage

Indicates number of times that cash flow will cover preferred dividends and sinking fund requirements.

Preferred stock cash flow coverage ratio =

$$\frac{\text{Earnings before interest and taxes + depreciation}}{\begin{array}{l} \text{Interest payments} + \left(\text{Debt sinking fund payments}\right)/\left(1 - \text{tax rate}\right) \\ + \left(\text{Preferred dividend payments}\right)/\left(1 - \text{tax rate}\right) \\ + \left(\text{Sinking fund requirements on preferred}\right)/\left(1 - \text{tax rate}\right) \end{array}}$$

Preferred dividend coverage indicates the probability of preferred owners receiving the agreed upon dividend.

Preferred dividend coverage ratio =

$$\frac{\text{Earnings after taxes}}{\left(\text{Preferred dividend payout}\right) + \left(\text{interest}\right)\left(1 - \text{tax rate}\right)}$$

.04 General Ratios

Accounts Payable Turnover

$$\frac{\text{Purchases on account}}{\dfrac{\text{Accounts payable at beginning of period + accounts payable at end of period}}{2}}$$

Payment Period for Accounts Payable

$$\text{Payment period} = \frac{360}{\text{accounts payable turnover}}$$

.05 Income Ratios

Provide analysis of aspects of income statement items to net sales relating to profits from income. Income ratios should be used to indicate trends over several periods.

Income Ratios

Operating Ratio

Indicates operating income profitability related to ordinary business operations. Operating income excludes extraordinary items, interest on long term obligations, other income, and income taxes.

$$\text{Operating ratio} = \frac{\text{Operating income}}{\text{Net sales}}$$

Gross Margin Ratio

Indicates average markup between cost of goods and selling price. Fluctuations result from interrelations of markups, markdowns, higher sales prices, lower cost of goods, changes in proportionate volumes of higher marginal products.

$$\text{Gross margin ratio} = \frac{\text{Gross margin}}{\text{Net sales}} = \frac{\text{Net sales} - \text{COGS}}{\text{Net sales}}$$

Sales Acceptance Ratio

Indicates the spread of risk of dependency on major accounts related to sales volume. A high sales volume transacted with 3 or 4 major accounts is much riskier than a similar sales volume transacted with 200 accounts. Loss of one account with the former could be losing 1/3 of the firm's business.

$$\text{Sales acceptance ratio} = \frac{\text{Sales opportunity accepted}}{\text{Sales opportunity submitted}}$$

Repairs and Maintenance to Fixed Assets Ratio

Indicates maintenance of property. Use when maintenance does not directly relate to sales.

$$\text{R} + \text{M to fixed assets ratio} = \frac{\text{Maintenance} + \text{repairs expenses}}{\text{Tangible fixed assets} - \text{land}}$$

Depreciation to Fixed Assets Ratio

Indicates age of property, composition of fixed assets. Use when assets are minor and do not directly tie in with sales.

$$\text{Depreciation to fixed assets ratio} = \frac{\text{Depreciation}}{\text{Tangible fixed assets} - \text{land}}$$

Repairs and Maintenance to Net Sales

Indicates maintenance related to sales volume. Use for heavy operating asset companies.

$$\text{Repairs \& maintenance to net sales ratio} = \frac{\text{Maintenance \& repair expenses}}{\text{Net sales}}$$

Operating Expense Ratio

Indicates the amount of sales being absorbed by expenses. Indicates how expenses are adjusted to changing sales.

$$\text{Operating expense ratio} = \frac{\text{Total operating expenses}}{\text{Net sales}}$$

Net Sales to Tangible Net Worth Ratio

Indicates the amount of sales volume transacted on the margin of investment and whether investment is adequately proportionate to sales volume. Tangible net worth is owner's equity less intangible assets.

$$\text{Net sales to tangible net worth ratio} = \frac{\text{Net sales}}{\text{Tangible net worth}}$$

.07 Leverage Ratios

Leverage ratios indicate the proportionate share of business ownership between creditors and equity owners. The stockholder's percentage of ownership represents the margin of safety to creditors. The firm's use of leverage (debt) provides an opportunity to increase the rate of return on owner's equity.

Leverage Ratios

Equity Ratio

Indicates the amount of the firm's financing obtained through ownership rather than debt.

$$\text{Equity ratio} = \frac{\text{Shareholder's equity}}{\text{Total assets}}$$

Debt Ratio

Indicates the amount of the firm's financing obtained through debt rather than equity ownership.

$$\text{Debt ratio} = \frac{\text{Current} + \text{long term debt}}{\text{Total assets}}$$
$$= \frac{\text{Total debt}}{\text{Total assets}}$$

Debt to Equity Ratio

Indicates the proportionate positions between owners and creditors. The greater the proportion from stockholders, the greater the cushion of safety for the firm to meet fixed obligations, but the company will have a higher overall cost of capital.

$$\text{Debt to equity ratio} = \frac{\text{Total debt} + \text{preferred stock}}{\text{Total stockholders equity}}$$

Times Interest Earned Ratio

$$\text{Times Interest Earned} = \frac{\text{Earnings before Interest Expense}}{\text{Interest Expense}}$$

Operating Cash Flows to Fixed Charge Ratio =

$$\frac{\text{Cash flow from operating activities} + \text{interest payments} + \text{income taxes}}{\text{Interest payments} + \text{loan principal payments} + \text{capital lease payments}}$$

.09 Liquidity Ratios

Indicates the relative strength of the firm's ability to meet financial obligations.

Liquidity Ratios

Collection Ratio

Indicates the percentage of accounts paid to total accounts due.

$$\text{Collection ratio} = \frac{\text{Collections during period made}}{\text{Total accounts receivable beginning balance}}$$

Inventory Turnover Ratio

This ratio indicates, on average, the number of times goods are purchased and sold in a year. Since average inventory is used, the ratio indicates how management controls capital committed to inventory. A reduced turnover may indicate increasing inventory resulting from reduced sales and inefficient purchasing. Inventory could be quarterly averaging or any number consistently used.

$$\text{Inventory turnover ratio} = \frac{\text{Cost of goods sold}}{\left(\text{Beginning inventory} + \text{ending inventory}\right)/2}$$

Bad Debt Index

Indicates the portion of sales never collected.

$$\text{Bad debt index} = \frac{\text{Bad debts}}{\text{Credit sales}}$$

Current Ratio

Indicates firm's ability to meet current obligations.

$$\text{Current ratio} = \frac{\text{Current assets}}{\text{Current liabilities}}$$

Quick Ratio

Indicates firm's ability to meet current obligations from assets quickly convertible to cash. Analysts should take note of the current components of the order of liquidity of the ratio—cash, marketable securities, and accounts receivable.

$$\text{Quick ratio} = \frac{\text{Cash} + \text{marketable securities} + \text{accounts receivable}}{\text{Current liabilities}}$$

Liquidity Ratio

Indicates the time period it takes to convert normal current assets into cash. This index should be tracked over a number of periods to analyze the firm's trend.

[(Cash × number of days from cash) + (accounts receivable × number of days from cash) + (inventory × number of days from cash)] / Total cash

Example:

Category	Total	× Days From Cash	= Weighted Total
Cash	$ 25,000	0	0
Accounts Receivable	80,000	25	2,000,000
Inventory	120,000	45	5,400,000
Total	$225,000		7,400,000

Using the formula:

$$\left[(\$25,000 \times 0) + (\$80,000 \times 25) + (\$120,000 \times 45)\right] / \left(\begin{array}{c}\$25,000 + \\ \$80,000 + \$120,000\end{array}\right)$$

$$= (0 + \$2,000,000 + \$5,400,000)/\$225,000$$

$$= \$7,400,000/\$225,000$$

$$= 32.89 \text{ days, i.e., Liquidity Ratio} = 32.89 \text{ days}$$

Absolute Liquidity Ratio

Indicates only "quick cash" items available to cover current obligations. This eliminates any uncertainties regarding accounts receivable.

$$\text{Absolute liquidity ratio} = \frac{\text{Cash + marketable securities}}{\text{Current liabilities}}$$

Quick Accounts Receivable Ratio

Indicates the firm's ability to meet current obligations solely out of accounts receivable net of bad debts allowance.

$$\text{Quick accounts receivable ratio} = \frac{\text{Accounts receivable (net)}}{\text{Current liabilities}}$$

Days Coverage With No Revenue

Indicates the number of days a firm could meet its cash expenses if all revenues ceased without additional financing.

$$\text{Days coverage with no revenue ratio} =$$

$$\frac{365 \left(\text{cash + receivables + marketable securities}\right)}{\text{Operating expenses + interest + income taxes}}$$

Net Sales to Inventory Ratio

Indicates inventory levels as related to sales. A low ratio may indicate slow moving inventory due to overstocking, obsolescence, poor purchasing policy, etc.

$$\text{Net sales to inventory ratio} = \frac{\text{Net sales}}{\text{Inventory}}$$

Operating Cash Flow

$$\frac{\text{Cash flow from operations}}{\text{Current Liabilities}}$$

¶663.09

Past Due Ratio

Indicates proportion of past due receivables relative to total outstanding accounts receivable.

$$\text{Past due ratio} = \frac{\text{Total amount past due}}{\text{Total sum collected}}$$

Collection Ratio

For a given collection period, this ratio indicates the proportion collected to the total amount due. Dividing the net credit due period by this ratio approximates the average collection period.

$$\text{Collection ratio} = \frac{\text{Collections made during period}}{\text{Beginning accounts receivables owing}}$$

Average Collection Period

Indicates the quality of the accounts receivables by expressing them by the length of the collection period.

$$\text{Average collection period} = \frac{365 \,(\text{accounts receivable})}{\text{Annual net credit sales}}$$

Accounts Receivable Turnover Ratio

Indicates the firm's efficiency in employing the funds invested in receivables. The ratio also indicates changes in collections.

$$\text{Accounts receivable turnover ratio} = \frac{\text{Total credit sales}}{\text{Average receivables owing}}$$

Finished Goods Turnover Ratio

$$\text{Finished goods turnover ratio} = \frac{\text{Cost of goods sold}}{\text{Average finished goods inventory}}$$

Work-in-Process Turnover Ratio

$$\text{Work-in-process turnover ratio} = \frac{\text{Cost of goods manufactured}}{\text{Average work-in-process inventory}}$$

Supplies Turnover Ratio

$$\text{Supplies turnover ratio} = \frac{\text{Cost of supplies used}}{\text{Average supply inventory}}$$

Raw Materials Turnover Ratio

$$\text{Raw materials turnover ratio} = \frac{\text{Materials placed into production}}{\text{Average raw materials}}$$

.11 Long-Term Ratios

Indicate the long-term relationships between debt vs. equity funding.

Long-Term Ratios

Total Debt to Net Worth Ratio

Indicates the relative risk creditors assume in relations to stockholders.

$$\text{Total Debt to Net Worth Ratio} = \frac{\text{Total debt}}{\text{Preferred stock} + \text{common stock} + \text{retained earnings} - \text{intangible assets}}$$

$$= \frac{\text{Total debt}}{\text{Tangible net worth}}$$

Current Assets to Total Debt Ratio

Indicates the relative level of risk associated with debt.

$$\text{Current assets to total debt ratio} = \frac{\text{Current assets}}{\text{Current} + \text{non-current liabilities}}$$

$$= \frac{\text{Current assets}}{\text{Total debt}}$$

Stockholder's Equity to Total Assets

Indicates long range liquidity and the firm's financial strength to meet maturing debts and cover fixed interest charges.

$$\text{Stockholder's equity to total assets ratio} = \frac{\text{Stockholder's equity}}{\text{Total assets}}$$

Fixed Assets to Net Worth

Indicates the extent to which owner's equity has been invested in fixed assets.

$$\text{Fixed assets to net worth ratio} = \frac{\text{Fixed assets} - \text{Intangibles}}{\text{Tangible net worth}}$$

Dividend Payout Ratio

Indicates the percent of earnings received by the stockholder each period.

$$\text{Dividend payout ratio} = \frac{\text{Dividends per share}}{\text{Earnings per share}}$$

Dividend Yield Ratio

Indicates cash returns paid currently.

$$\text{Dividend yield ratio} = \frac{\text{Common dividends per share}}{\text{Average market price of common stock}}$$

.13 Profitability Ratios

Indicates management's effectiveness in terms of returns generated.

Profitability Ratios

Gross Profit Ratio

Indicates whether average markup on goods will cover remaining expenses and result in profit.

$$\text{Gross profit ratio} = \frac{\text{Net sales} - \text{cost of goods sold}}{\text{Net sales}}$$

Net Operating Profit Ratio

Indicates return on earnings without considering the financing costs of interest and the tax implications.

$$\text{Net operation profit ratio} = \frac{\text{Earnings before interest and taxes (EBIT)}}{\text{Tangible net worth}}$$

Management Rate of Return Ratio

Indicates use of assets to be compared with a target rate of return.

$$\text{Management rate of return ratio} = \frac{\text{Operating income}}{\text{Tangible fixed assets} + \text{net working capital}}$$

Net Profit to Sales Ratio

Indicates overall profit rate of firm. After breakeven point of operating expenses are covered, profits rise disproportionately greater than sales.

$$\text{Net profit ratio} = \frac{\text{Earnings after taxes}}{\text{Net sales}}$$

Earnings Power Ratio

Indicates sales effect of profits and assets. Earnings power can be increased by increasing sales faster than related costs, lowering the breakeven point, or trading heavier on the assets.

$$\text{Earnings power ratio} = \frac{\text{Net sales}}{\text{Tangible assets}} \times \frac{\text{Earnings after taxes}}{\text{Net sales}}$$

$$= \frac{\text{Earnings after taxes}}{\text{Tangible assets}}$$

Net Profit to Tangible Net Worth

Indicates management's return on the firm's "investment" (tangible net worth)

$$\text{Net profit ratio} = \frac{\text{Earnings after taxes}}{\text{Tangible net worth}}$$

Earnings Per Share Ratio

Indicates company earnings available for distributions to individual shareholders for each share of common stock outstanding.

$$\text{Earnings per share ratio} = \frac{\text{Earnings after taxes} - \text{preferred dividends}}{\text{Average number of outstanding shares}}$$

Rate of Return on Common Stock Equity

Indicates rate of return on book value of owner's equity.

$$\text{Rate of return on common stock equity} =$$
$$\frac{\text{Earnings after taxes} - \text{preferred dividends}}{\text{Tangible net worth} - \text{book value of preferred stock}}$$

Turnover of Total Operating Assets Ratio

Indicates if there is an overinvestment in operating assets. An inadequate sales volume may require a reduced investment in assets. Conversely, sales may rise within a given range without additional asset investment.

Total operating assets equals total assets less intangible assets less long-term investments.

$$\text{Turnover of total operating assets ratio} = \frac{\text{Net sales}}{\text{Total operating assets}}$$

Asset Turnover

$$\text{Asset Turnover} = \frac{\text{Net Sales}}{\dfrac{\text{Total Assets at Beginning of Period} + \text{Total Assets at End of Period}}{2}}$$

Profit Margin

$$\text{Profit Margin} = \frac{\text{Net Income}}{\text{Sales}}$$

Total Asset Turnover

$$\text{Total Asset Turnover} = \frac{\text{Sales}}{\text{Total Assets}}$$

Return on Total Assets

$$\text{Return on Total Assets} = \frac{\text{Net income}}{\text{Total assets}}$$

Return on Equity

$$\text{Return on Equity} = \frac{\text{Net income}}{\text{Total Equity}}$$

Price-Earnings Ratio

Relates market price to earnings per share.

¶663.13

$$\text{Price earnings ratio} = \frac{\text{Market price of common stock}}{\text{Earnings per share}}$$

Return on Assets Employed (ROAE)

The % return on assets employed measures profitability. It is composed of the net income ratio and the utilization of assets in the production of the net income.

$$\text{Return on assets employed ratio} = \frac{\text{Net Income}}{\text{Sales}} \times \frac{\text{Sales}}{\text{Assets Employed}}$$

$$= \text{Net income ratio} \times \text{assets turnover ratio}$$

.15 Return on Equity by Financial Performance

A firm's total Return on Equity (ROE) can be analyzed by two major components:

- Return on "owned" assets (the equity ownership)
- Return on the portion of the business financed with debt. (Both are net of the firm's tax rate.)

The Return on Equity by Financial Performance provides for analysis of a firm's operating performance in relation to its debt structure. It indicates how the level of debt affects the firm's making or losing money and illustrates how the use of leverage can magnify a company's return.

Return on Equity

$$\text{Return on Equity} =$$

$$\text{Return on owned assets} + \text{net return on debt} \times (\text{net of tax effect})$$

$$\text{ROE} = \left(\text{EOA} + \left(\text{Financial Benefit from use of debt}\right)\right) \times \left(1 \text{ tax rate}\right)$$

$$\text{ROE} = \left(\text{EOA} + \left(\text{Debt}/\text{Equity} \times \left(\text{EOA} - \text{Interest rate}\right)\right)\right) \times \left(1 - \text{tax rate}\right)$$

Reduced further by each source or type of debt. Any negative return indicates a negative cost of borrowing, which means the firm's return on assets is less than the firm's borrowing interest rate. In other words, what is earned on every borrowed dollar is less than what is paid on every borrowed dollar.

EBIT = Earnings before interest and taxes.

EOA = Earnings before interest and taxes/total assets.

$$= \frac{\text{EBIT}}{\text{Total Assets}}$$

Debtor's margin = EOA - Interest on borrowed funds

— Use a weighted rate of each note's interest expense to total debt on an annual basis.

Debt/Equity = The total debt divided by total equity.

— Use latest 12 month "average" debt and equity amounts.

Illustration of Firm's Total Return on Equity By the Financial Performance Method

Balance Sheet			Income Statement	
Assets	$150,000		Sales	$125,000
=		–	Expenses	– 95,000
Liabilities	$65,000	=	Net income	= $30,000
+		+	Interest	+ 6,000
Equity	$85,000	+	Taxes	+ 4,000
Corporate tax rate = 15%		=	EBIT	= $40,000

Liabilities by Type:

Accounts payable	= $8,000 at 0% interest
Current debt 1	= 12,000 at 12% interest
Non-Current debt 1	= 20,000 at 8% interest
Non-Current debt 2	= 25,000 at 9% interest
	$65,000

Weighted average interest cost:

	Total Debt	Debt Ratio/ Total Debt	Interest Rate	Weighted Interest %
Accounts Payable	$8,000	8,000/65,000	× .0	= 0
Current debt 1	12,000	12,000/65,000	× .12	= .022
Non-Current debt	20,000	20,000/65,000	× .09	= .025
Non-Current debt	25,000	25,000/65,000	× .09	= .035
	$65,000			
		Weighted Average Interest Cost	= .082 or 8.2%	

Debt/Equity Ratio = $65,000/$85,000 = .76

EOA Ratio = EBIT/Total Assets

= 40,000/150,000

= .27

Financial benefit from use of debt:

Debt/Equity × (EOA – weighted average interest rate)

.76 × (.27 – .0822) = .143 or 14.3%

Financial Benefit by Loan Type

	Debt/Equity × (EOA – interest rate)			
Accounts payable	$8,000/$85,000	×	(.27 – 0)	= .025
Current debt 1	$12,000/$85,000	×	(.27 – .12)	= .021
Non-Current debt 1	$20,000/$85,000	×	(.27 – .08)	= .045
Non-Current debt 2	$25,000/$85,000	×	(.27 – .09)	= .053
				.144 or 14.4%

¶663.15

Firm's total Return on Equity (ROE) by the financial performance formula:

$$\text{ROE} = [\text{EOA} + (\text{Debt/Equity} \times (\text{EOA}\ \text{interest rate}))] \times (1 - \text{tax rate})$$

$$\text{ROE} = [.27 + .76 \times (.27 - .082)] \times (1 - .15)$$

$$\text{ROE} = .3485 \text{ or } 34.85\%$$

.17 Return on Investment

Analyzes the major elements in the interrelationship of income statement items and balance sheet items.

$$\text{ROI} = \text{Capital turnover} \times \text{net income to sales percentage}$$

$$\text{ROI} = \frac{\text{Total sales}}{\text{Capital employed}} \times \frac{\text{Net income}}{\text{Total sales}}$$

"Capital turnover" measures the changes in assets in relation to sales during a period of time. It reflects the general efficiency of management on a given investment in relation to the sales volume generated.

"Net income percentage" is the final return on sales as a % of sales.

- Total sales is usually gross sales or net sales.
- Net income is usually net after taxes.
- Capital employed is current assets less current liabilities plus fixed assets.

Return on Shareholder's Equity

This ratio considers the operating efficiency of the use of the assets, and the financing efficiency of obtaining the assets.

Return on Shareholders Equity

$$= \frac{\text{Assets employed}}{\text{Shareholder's equity}} \times \text{ROAE}$$

$$= \frac{\text{Assets employed}}{\text{Shareholder's equity}} \times \frac{\text{Net income}}{\text{Net sales}} \times \frac{\text{Net sales}}{\text{Assets employed}}$$

Cancel out common assets and sales in formula above

$$\text{Return on shareholder's equity ratio} = \frac{\text{Net income}}{\text{Shareholder's equity}}$$

Return on Investment - Net Worth

$$\text{Return on investment (net worth method)} =$$

$$\frac{\text{net income}}{\text{net worth at beginning of period}\ +\ \text{net worth at end of period}}$$

2

Return on Investment - Total Assets

$$\text{Return on investment (total asset method)} = \frac{\text{net income}}{\dfrac{\text{total assets at beginning of period} + \text{total assets at end of period}}{2}}$$

.19 Residual Income Ratio

Measures the true earnings of the company. It determines if the firm is earning a sufficient amount to cover its minimum return on assets. The higher the ratio, the better is the firm's earning quality. This analysis should be applied over several periods.

Residual Income Ratio

$$\text{Residual income} = \text{Net income} \quad (\text{total assets} \times \text{cost of capital})$$

$$\text{Residual income ratio} = \frac{\text{Residual income}}{\text{Net income}}$$

- Net income is net of taxes.
- Cost of capital is the weighted percentages of different financing instruments. This includes:
  — Stock whose cost is dividends.
  — Loans whose cost is interest.

     Example: Net income = $500,000

Total assets = $2,000,000

Cost of capital = 8% (Average overall weighted cost of capital)

Residual income = Net income – (total assets × cost of capital)

= $500,000 – $(2,000,000 × .08)

= $340,000

$$\text{Residual income ratio} = \frac{340,000}{500,000} = .68$$

Trading on Equity Ratio—Common and Debt

This ratio compares the rate of return on common stock issued with debt to the rate of return on total capitalization.

$$\text{Trading on equity ratio (common)} = \frac{1}{\text{Proportion of equity capital to total capitalization}} \left| \frac{\text{EBIT} - \text{interest}}{\text{EBIT}} \right|$$

     Example: What is the trading on equity ratio for common shareholders given:

Proportion of equity capital to total capitalization = 60%

EBIT	=	$200,000
Interest	=	$80,000

¶663.19

$$\text{Trading on equity (common)} = \frac{1}{.60} \times \frac{\$200,000 - \$80,000}{\$200,000}$$

$$= 1.00$$

Trading on Equity Ratio—Preferred

This ratio compares the rate of return on preferred stock issued with debt to the rate of return on total capitalization. This formula reflects the before-tax burden, the tax rate, and the annual preferred dividend obligation.

$$\text{Trading on equity ratio (preferred)} =$$

$$\frac{1}{\substack{\text{Proportion of equity capital} \\ \text{to total capitalization}}} \left[1 - \frac{1}{\text{EBIT}} \left[\text{Interest} + \frac{\text{Annual preferred dividends paid}}{(1 - \text{tax rate})} \right] \right]$$

Example: What is the trading on equity ratio for preferred given:

Proportion of equity capital to total capitalization = 60%

EBIT = $200,000

Interest = $60,000

Annual preferred dividends = $20,000

Tax rate = 25%

$$\text{Trading on equity (preferred)} = \frac{1}{.60} \left[1 - \frac{1}{\$200,000} \left[\$60,000 + \frac{\$20,000}{(1 - .25)} \right] \right]$$

$$= \frac{1}{.60} \left[1 - .000005 \, (\$60,000 + \$26,667) \right]$$

$$= \frac{1}{.60} \left[1 - .4333 \right]$$

$$= .9445$$

Note that the burden of paying preferred dividends decreases the return to common shareholders.

.21 Working Capital Ratios

Indicates relationships between assets and liabilities.

Working Capital Ratios

Current Asset Turnover Ratio

Indicates the number of times average current assets are used to pay operating costs. It is an indicator of the profitability of the firm's current assets.

$$\text{Current asset turnover ratio} = \frac{\text{Cost of goods sold} + \text{expenses} + \text{interest} + \text{taxes}}{\text{Average current assets}}$$

Working Capital Turnover Ratio

Shows the number of times working capital is covered by sales which indicates if the firm is over or underinvested in assets. The ratio measures how effectively a company's working capital is used to generate sales. When sales rise, then there is also a related rise in inventory, accounts receivable, and accounts payable. This ratio measures the complexity of the relationship between buying and selling. A high ratio may make the company vulnerable to adverse conditions. Too low of a ratio may indicate inefficient use of cash, since a low value indicates availability of cash to sustain operations.

$$\text{Working capital turnover ratio:} \frac{\text{Net sales}}{\text{Working capital}}$$

Inventory to Working Capital

Indicates the amount of risk that may arise from a decline in the firm's inventory.

$$\text{Inventory to working capital ratio} = \frac{\left(\text{Beginning inventory} + \text{ending inventory}\right)/2}{\text{Working capital}}$$

$$= \frac{\text{Average inventory}}{\text{Working capital}}$$

Current Debt to Net Worth

Current debt to net worth ratio Indicates the proportionate relationship of creditors to equity ownership.

Current debt to net ratio =

$$\frac{\text{Current liabilities}}{\text{Preferred stock} + \text{common stock} + \text{retained earnings} - \text{intangible assets}}$$

$$= \frac{\text{Current liabilities}}{\text{Tangible net worth}}$$

Current Liabilities to Inventory

Indicates to what level the firm might rely on inventory to meet current obligations.

$$\text{Current liabilities to inventory ratio} = \frac{\text{Current liabilities}}{\text{Inventory}}$$

Net Earnings to Net Working Capital Ratio

Indicates cushion of earnings to working capital.

$$\text{Net earnings to net working capital ratio} = \frac{\text{Earnings after taxes}}{\text{Net working capital}}$$

Non-current debt to net working capital indicates number of times funded debt over one year exceeds net working capital.

$$\text{Non-current debt to net working capital} = \frac{\text{Non-current debt}}{\text{Net working capital}}$$

¶663.21

¶ 665 REFINANCING

.01 Refinancing Worksheet

Should one refinance a present loan to a lower interest rate loan?

Assumptions:

Present Loan	**New Loan A**	**New Loan B**
Principal = $150,000	Principal = $150,000	Principal = $150,000
Term = 30 years	Term = 30 years	Term = 30 years
Interest = 8%	Interest = 7%	Interest = 7.25%
	Closing costs = 2% of Principal	Closing costs = 1.5% of Principal

	New Loan A	New Loan B
1. Monthly principal and interest payment on current mortgage. (150 × $7.33)	$1100	1100
2. Monthly interest and principal payment on a new mortgage. 7% — 150 × 6.65 = $998 8%—150 × 6.82 = $1023	998	1023
3. Monthly savings. Line 1 less line 2.	$102	77

4.   Refinancing costs (points and any other closing costs).
        7%—$150,000 × .02 = $3,000
        8%—$150,000 × .015 =$2,250
	$3000	2250

5. Number of months needed to recoup refinancing costs. Line 4 divided by line 3.	29	29

Refinance if plans involve remaining in current home longer than line 5.

Do not refinance if plans involve remaining in current home less than line 5.

.03 Choosing from Alternate Mortgages Worksheet

Which new mortgage is a better choice?

Assumptions:

New Loan A	**New Loan B**
Principal = $150,000	Principal = $150,000
Term = 30 years	Term = 30 years
Interest = 7%	Interest = 7.25%
Closing costs = 2% of Principal	Closing costs = 1.5% of Principal

1. Enter the total refinancing costs for the mortgage with the higher up-front closing costs. (Loan A)	3000
2. Enter the total refinancing costs for the mortgage with the lower up-front closing costs. (Loan B)	2250
3. Refinancing costs difference. Line 1 less line 2.	750
4. Monthly savings by switching from current mortgage to the higher up-front closing costs mortgage (from line 3 in part one). (Loan A)	102
5. Monthly savings by switching from current mortgage to the lower up-front closing costs mortgage (from line 3 in part one). (Loan B)	77
6. Monthly savings difference. Line 4 less line 5	25
7. Number of months it will take to come out ahead with the higher-cost mortgage. Line 3 divided by line 6.	30

Higher-cost loan is better if plans involve remaining in current home **longer than** line 7.

Lower-cost loan is better if plans involve moving from current home in **less than** line 7.

.05 Mortgage Monthly Payment Table

To determine monthly payment, divide mortgage by $1,000 and multiply the result by the dollar amount at right for the rate factor given the loan term.

Example: Loan = $150,000 at 8% for 30 years

Monthly payment = $150000 /$1000 = 150 150 x $7.33 = $1099.50 or $1100

Interest rate	30-year fixed rate mortgage	20-year fixed rate mortgage	15-year fixed-rate mortgage
6.50%	$6.32	7.46	$8.71
6.75	6.49	7.75	8.85
7.00	6.65	7.75	8.99
7.25	6.82	7.90	9.13
7.50	6.99	8.06	9.27
7.75	7.16	8.21	9.41
8.00	7.33	8.36	9.56

Note: Payments are per $1,000 / principal.

Also, see ¶ 691.31 Comparison of Up-Front Fees and Mortgage Rates.

Net Savings

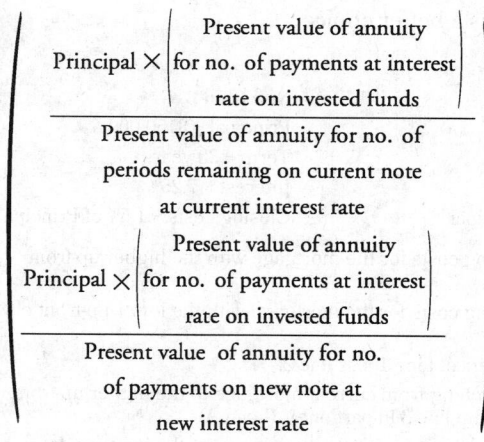

$$\left\{ \frac{\text{Principal} \times \left(\frac{\text{Present value of annuity for no. of payments at interest rate on invested funds}}{\text{Present value of annuity for no. of periods remaining on current note at current interest rate}}\right)}{} - \frac{\text{Principal} \times \left(\frac{\text{Present value of annuity for no. of payments at interest rate on invested funds}}{\text{Present value of annuity for no. of payments on new note at new interest rate}}\right)}{} \right\}$$

— Refinancing costs

Example:

	Present note	New note
Payments remaining	68	120
Interest rate	14%	11%
Principal balance = $125,000		

Refinancing costs = $3,500 which are presently in a savings account earning 6% interest.

Net savings =

$$\left[\frac{\$125,000 \times \left(\begin{array}{c} \text{PV annuity for} \\ \text{68 periods @6\%/12} \end{array} \right)}{\begin{array}{c} \text{PV annuity for} \\ \text{68 periods @14\%/12} \end{array}} \quad \frac{\$125,000 \times \left(\begin{array}{c} \text{PV annuity for} \\ \text{120 periods @6\%/12} \end{array} \right)}{\begin{array}{c} \text{PV annuity for} \\ \text{120 periods @11\%/12} \end{array}} \right]$$

$$- \$3,500$$

$$= \left[\frac{\$125,000 \times 57.5253}{46.7643} - \frac{\$125,000 \times 90.0734}{72.5953} \right] - \$3,500$$

$$= \$2,672.98 \times 57.5253 - \$1,721.87 \times 90.0734 - \$3,500$$

$$= \$153,763.98 - 155,094.69 - \$3,500$$

$$= -\$4,830.71$$

Thus, at a discount rate of only 6%, refinancing is not indicated.

¶ 667 RETURN ON INVESTMENT

.01 Simple Return on Investment

Simple Return on Investment

$$\text{ROI} = \frac{\text{Profit}}{\text{Sales}} \times \frac{\text{Sales}}{\text{Assets}}$$

$$\text{ROI} = \frac{\text{Profit}}{\text{Assets}}$$

Where profit = Net Income

Where profit = Net Income

.03 Payback Method

Payback Method

$$\text{Payback method rate of return} = \frac{\text{Average annual flow of funds}}{\text{Original investment}} = R$$

Reciprocal of R is the number of years to recover the investment.

Example: Investment = $250,000

Cash flow return = $ 80,000 annually

What is the rate of return?

$$R = \frac{\$80,000}{\$250,000} = .32 \text{ or } 32\%$$

What is the number of years to recover the original investment?

$$\text{Number of years} = \frac{1}{R} = \frac{1}{.32} = 3.13 \text{ years}$$

.05 Net Payback Method

Net payback method rate of return adjusts the cash flow by straight line depreciation, which nets out the original investment over the term. The cash flows are not adjusted for timing.

Net Payback Method Rate of Return

$$\frac{\text{Annual cash flow} - \text{depreciation}}{\text{Original investment}}$$

.07 Original Book Method

Original Book Method Rate of Return

$$\frac{\text{Net income} - \text{depreciation}}{\text{Original investment}}$$

.09 Average Book Method

Average Book Method Rate of Return

$$\frac{\text{Net income} - \text{depreciation}}{(\text{Original investment} - \text{salvage value})/2}$$

.11 Earning Power for Company (Return on Investment)

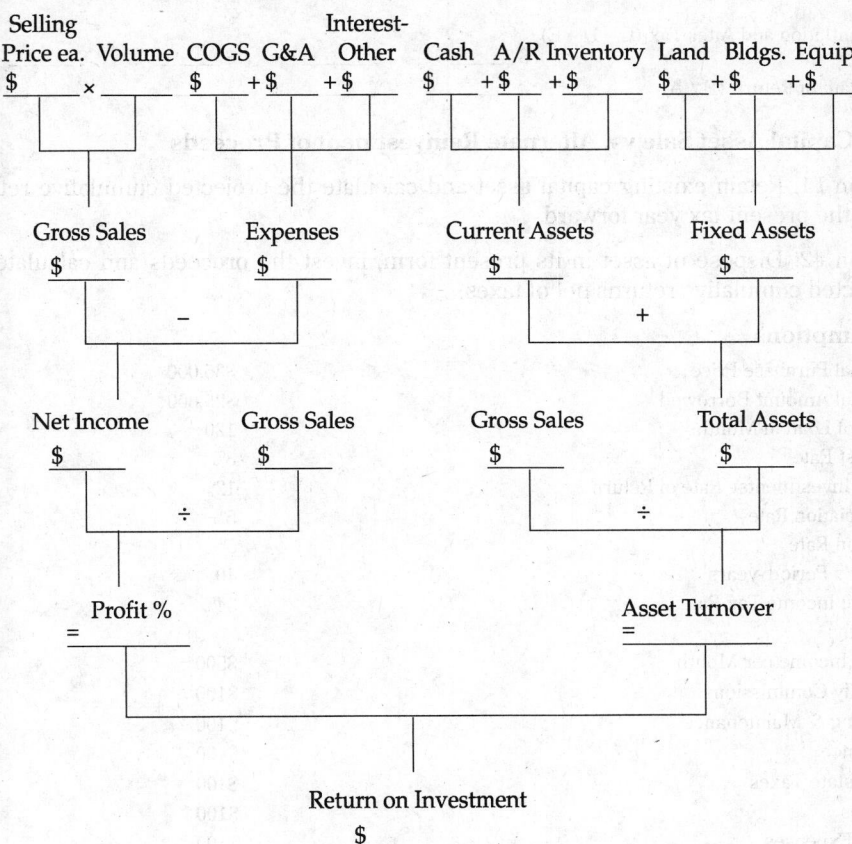

.12 Return On Investment—Dupont Method

Return on Investment =

Sales / Assets x (Sales – Expenses) / Sales = Net Income / Assets x Assets/

Equity = Net Income / Equity

or,

Marketing		Operating				Financial		
Leverage	x	Leverage	=	Return on Assets	x	Leverage	=	Return on Equity

.13 Real Rate of Return on Investment

Investment Project				
A. Original Investment Amount	$ _____	$ _____	$ _____	$ _____
B. Interest Rate	× _____	× _____	× _____	× _____
C. Interest Income (A × B) =	$ _____	$ _____	$ _____	$ _____
D. Inflation (A × 5%) –	$ _____	$ _____	$ _____	$ _____
E. Taxes (C × Tax Bracket) –	$ _____	$ _____	$ _____	$ _____

F. RealReturn:

After Inflation and After Tax (C – D – E)

= $ _____ $ _____ $ _____ $ _____

Real Rate of Return (F / A)   % _____   % _____   % _____   % _____

.14 Capital Asset Sale vs. Alternate Reinvestment of Proceeds

Option #1: Retain existing capital asset and calculate the projected cumulative returns from the present tax year forward.

Option #2: Dispose of asset in its present form, invest the proceeds and calculate the projected cumulative returns net of taxes.

Assumptions

Original Purchase Price	$35,000
Original Amount Borrowed	$25,000
Term of Loan in Months	120
Interest Rate	8%
Other Investments - Rate of Return	12%
Appreciation Rate	5%
Inflation Rate	5%
Analysis Period -years	40
Federal Income Tax Rate	34%
Monthly:	
Rental Income per Month	$500
Monthly Commissions	$100
Cleaning & Maintenance	$100
Insurance	$100
Real Estate Taxes	$100
Utilities	$100
Other Expenses	$100
Annual Depreciation	$2,000
Remaining Years of Depreciation	10
Selling Price / Fair Market Value	$200,000
Tax Due on Sale of Asset	12,222
Payout Amount of Outstanding Loan	25,000
Closing Costs on Sale of Assets	5,000
Required Cash Payouts on Sale	10,000
Net Realized on Sale of Asset	147,778

.15 Rental Property Investment Return

Use the following formulas to analyze whether to invest in rental property solely on a financial basis. Suggested cash on cash return = 10% or better. Suggested Return on investment = 10% or better.

Rental pre-tax cash flow =	(annual rent – vacancy) – (repairs + maintenance + taxes + insurance + manage ment fees + etc.) – (mortgage interest payments)
After-tax cash flow =	[rental pre-tax cash flow] – [(Rental pre-tax cash flow – depreciation) × tax rate]
Cash return % =	after tax cash flow / cash invested

Projected total return =   after tax cash flow + [(purchase price × annual % in crease in value)]

Return on investment =   projected total return / cash invested

Example:

Cost of rental property =$65,000   Down payment = $15,000

Monthly rent = $850   Annual % increase in value = 2%

Tax rate =.45 (combined federal, state, city)

Rental pre-tax cash flow	=	(850 × 12 – 850 × 2
	–	(200 + 300+ 400 + 450 + 200 + 150)
	–	(4000)
	=	$2800

After-tax cash flow =	[2800] – [(2800- 2400) × .45] = 2620
Cash return % =	2620 / 15000 = 17%
Projected total return =	2620 + [(65000 × .02)] = 3920
Return on investment =	3920 / 15000 = 26%

¶ 669 RULE OF 78 FACTORS

"Rule of 78" is a sum-of-the-years weighted declining value factor method.

It can be used for depreciation, a declining balance amortization, or any other systematic amortization of a total over a given number of years. The numbers are accelerated in the early periods and decline in later periods. It approximates interest computations.

The division formula to determine the interest factor is as follows:

Rule of 78

$$\text{Divisor} = \frac{m(m+1)}{2}$$

The "Rule of 78" derives its name from the one-year term, where the sum of the 12 months = 78.

From the table, locate the amortization term desired.

Multiply the value by each month's factor to write off 100% of the item by the end of the term.

    Example: An advertising catalog printed for $25,000 is to be written off over the next 12 months. The annual catalog is seasonal, generating greater sales in the early months with fewer sales in later periods.

Monthly expenses to write off:

	Total	Factor		Monthly Expense
Month 1	$25,000 ×	.154	=	$3,850
Month 2	$25,000 ×	.141	=	$3,525
Month 3	$25,000 ×	.128	=	$3,200
Month 4	$25,000 ×	.115	=	$2,875
etc.				

See Table Section ¶ 691.33 for Interest Factors for Rule of 78 tables.

¶ 671 SALES

.01 Sales Computed from Balance Sheet Items

Sales Computed from Balance Sheet Items

Sales = (A/R collections) + (year end A/R balance) – (beginning of year A/R balance)

    Example: Determine net sales given the following data.

A/R collections = $65,000

Year end A/R balance = $32,000

Beginning of year A/R balance = $42,000

Sales = $65,000 + $32,000 – $42,000 = $55,000

.03 Purchases Computed from Balance Sheet Items

Purchases Computed from Balance Sheet Items

Purchases = (A/P payments) + (year end A/P Balance) – (beginning of year A/P Balance)

    Example: Determine net purchases given the following data.

A/P payments = $75,000

Year end A/P Balance = $65,000

Beginning year A/P Balance = $67,000

Purchases = $75,000 + $65,000 – $67,000 = $73,000

.05 Expenses Computed from Balance Sheet Items

Determination of Expense

Expense = Accrued expenses paid during year + year end accrual of expense – beginning of year accrual of expense

    Example: Determine the wages expensed given the following data:

Accrued wages paid during year = $35,000

Year end accrual of wages = $1,200

Beginning of year accrual of wages = $1,500

Expense of wages for year = $35,000 + $1,200 – $1,500 = $34,700

Expense—With Accruals and Prepaids

The following formula computes the current period expense given prepaids and accruals.

Expense = [prepaid expense at beginning of year - prepaid expense at end of year]

+ [accrual at end of year – accrual at beginning of year]

+ [Expenses paid in cash during year]

    Example: What was the actual expense for the current year's subscriptions service given that:

Unpaid bills at year end for subscriptions = $175

Cancelled checks for subscriptions during the year = $1750

Of the $1750, $250 represents an arrangement for service to be delivered next year

Prior year's subscription supplies = $150

Prior year's accrued subscription = $50

Current year end inventory of subscription supplies = $300

Expense = [$150 − ($300 + $250)] + [$175 − $50] + $1750

= (−$400) + $125 + $1750

= $1475

¶ 673 SALES TAX

Determination of Sales and Sales Tax from Gross Amount

$$\text{Sales} = \frac{\text{Gross amount}}{1 + \text{sales tax rate}}$$

$$\text{Sales tax} = \text{Gross amount} - \text{sales}$$

Example: A small retail store rings up the gross sales for the month on the register which includes the sales tax of 8% in its total. If the gross amount is $35,000, what amount is the sales for the month and the sales tax?

$$\text{Sales} = \frac{\$35,000}{1 + .08} = \$32,407$$

Sales tax = $35,000 − $32,407 = $2,593

¶ 674 STANDARD COSTS

.01 Overhead Rate per Direct Labor Hour

Overhead Rate Data:

	(1)	(2)	(3)	(4)	(5)
Direct Hours	0	125	150	300	400
% Capacity	0	25%	50%	80%	100%
Supervision	2000	2500	2800	3000	3500
Depreciation	2000	2000	2000	2000	2000
Maintenance	300	325	350	400	425
Supplies	50	80	85	90	100
Indirect Labor	500	525	600	650	700
Total	4850	5430	5835	6140	6725

Overhead Rate per Direct Labor Hour at Normal Level of Activity of 300 Hours

(Based on Entire Activity Range)

Fixed Portion of Overhead Rate = col 1 / Hours

= 4850 / 300 = $16.17

Variable Portion of Overhead Rate = (col 4 − col 1) / Hours

= (6140 − 4850) / 300 = $4.30

Total Overhead Rate = col 4 / Hours

= 6140 / 300 = \$20.47

(Also, \$16.17 + \$4.30 = \$20.47)

Overhead Rate per Direct Labor Hour at Normal Level of Activity of 300 Hours

(Based on Relevant Activity Range)

Variable Portion of Overhead Rate = (col 5 – col 3 in \$'s) / (col 5 – col 3 in Hours)

= (6725 – 5835) / (400 – 150) = \$3.56

where (col 6) = \$3.56

Fixed Portion of Overhead Rate = (col 4 – (col 6 x Hours)) / Hours

= (6140 – (3.56 x 300)) / 300

= 16.91

Total Overhead Rate = col 4 / Hours

= 6140 / 300 = \$20.47

(Also, \$3.56 + \$16.19 = \$20.47)

¶ 675 STATISTICS

.01 Standard Deviation of Variables with Ungrouped Data

Standard Deviation

$$\text{Standard Deviation} = \sqrt{\frac{\left[\text{Add all the products from first through last of}\left(F \times X^2\right)\right]}{N}}$$

Where:

F = Frequency or number of times an observation occurs

X = Difference between observation and arithmetic mean

N = Total number of observations

Arithmetic Mean = Total / Number of observations

.02 Sample Arithmetic Mean with Variables

Arithmetic Mean of Sample

Arithmetic Mean of Sample = Sum of all values in sample / Number of items in sample

What is the arithmetic mean of the following sample taken? A CPA's sample of 15 invoices to clients totaled \$3750.

Arithmetic Mean of Sample = \$3750 / 15 = \$250

Sample Arithmetic Mean with Attributes

Sample Arithmetic Mean with Attributes

Proportion of successes in total sample = Number of successes of attribute / Number in total sample

Example: What is the proportion of errors found in a sample of invoices (where any error regarding the invoice represents an error) where 100 invoices were examined and 6 errors were found?

Proportion of successes in total sample = 6 / 100 = 6%

.03 Mean

Mean is a value that results from computing the sum of all observed values, divided by the sum of the total observations defined in that group.

Arithmetic Mean—Grouped Data

$$\text{Arithmetic Mean} = A + \frac{(\Sigma\, B\,(C/D))\, D}{E}$$

Where:

A = Midpoint of centered class

B = Number of observations in a class

C = Difference between midpoint of class and midpoint of centered class

D = Class range

E = Sum of number of observations

Arithmetic Mean = Midpoint of centered class +

[Σ Number of observations in a class x (Difference between midpoint of class and midpoint of centered class / Class range)) x Class range] / Sum of number of observations

What is the average hourly manufacturing wage if the laborers are distributed in wage classes as follows:

Class Description	Hourly Dollar Wage Class	No. of Workers in Class	Deviation Divided by Class Range	Col. 3 x Col.4
Foundry Delivery Carrier	$10.00 – 11.99	6	(11 – 17) / 2 = –3	–18
Foundry Sand Packer	$12.00 – 13.99	9	(13 – 17) / 2 = –2	–18
Foundry Iron Pourer	$14.00 – 15.99	12	(15 – 17) / 2 = –1	–12
Foundry Pattern Operator	$16.00 – 17.99	22	(17 – 17) / 2 = 0	0
Foundry Quality Inspector	$18.00 – 19.99	15	(19 – 17) / 2 = 1	22
Foundry Packer	$20.00 – 21.99	14	(21 – 17) / 2 = 2	28
Foundry Machine Operator	$22.00 – 23.99	8	(23 – 17) / 2 = 3	24
Foundry Shipper	$24.00 – 25.99	4	(25 – 17) / 2 = 16	16
		90		42

$$\text{Arithmetic Mean} = A + \frac{(\Sigma\, B\,(C/D))\, D}{E}$$

Arithmetic Mean = 17 + (42) (2) / 90 = 17.93

Note:

A = Midpoint of centered class = 17

D = Class range = $10.00 – 11.99 = 2

For: Foundry Delivery Carrier   (11–17) / 2 = –3   –18
Deviation divided by class range   Col. 3 x Col. 4

.04 Mode

The mode is the selection of the item that occurs most frequently. The magnitude of the other items does not affect the magnitude of the mode.

Mode—Grouped Data

Mode = Lower limit of modal class +

[[Difference between modal class number of observations less immediately preceding modal class number of observations / (Difference between modal class number of observations less immediately following modal class number of observations + Difference between modal class number of observations less immediately preceding modal class number of observations)] x Range of modal class]

Given the following distribution classes for sales, what is the most frequently occurring amount of sale?

Class of Amount of Sale in $'s	Number of Transactions in Class
0 - $9.99	4
10.00 - 11.99	5
12.00 - 12.99	8
13.00 - 13.99	15
14.00 - 14.99	17
15.00 - 15.99	9
16.00 - 16.99	4
17.00 - 17.99	5
18.00 - 18.99	4
19.00 - 19.99	2
20.00 - Over	1
	74

$14.00 - 14.99 is modal class, since it has the highest frequency

$14.00 is lowest value in modal class

Note: 14.99 - $14.00 is considered $1.00

Mode—Grouped Data   = $14.00 + [(17 – 15) / ((17 – 9) + (17 – 15))] x $1.00
                           = $14.00 + [2 / (8 + 2)] × $1.00
                           = $16.00

¶675.04

¶ 676 STOCK RIGHTS

.01 Stock Right (Theoretical Value)

Stock Right Theoretical Value

$$\frac{\text{Market value of stock} - \text{subscription price of stock}}{\text{No. of rights required to subscribe to 1 share of stock} + 1}$$

Example: Market value of stock = $400.

Taxpayer owns 20 shares of the stock at $100 par value.

Taxpayer has 50 rights.

He is given options to buy one additional share of stock for $150 plus 5 rights.

What is the theoretical value of the rights?

$$\text{Stock rights theoretical value} = \frac{\$400 - \$150}{5 + 1} = \$41.67$$

.03 Stock Right Value—Allocation of Cost

Stock Right Value

$$\frac{\text{Market value of rights on date of issue}}{\text{Market value of rights on date of issue} + \text{market value of stock ex rights}} \times \text{Cost}$$

Example: Taxpayer owns 20 shares of $100 par value common stock at a cost of $150 per share. He received 50 rights. On date rights were received, the stock was quoted ex rights for $200/share with each right quoted at $5/share. What cost should be assigned to each right?

$$\text{Stock right value} = \frac{5}{5 + 200}\ \$150 = \$3.66$$

¶ 677 SUM OF SERIES OF PAYMENTS

.01 Sum of Series of Payments with Constant Dollar Change

Sum of Series of Payments with Constant Dollar Change

Sum of series =

$$\left(\frac{\text{No. of terms in series}}{2}\right)$$

$$\times \left[\left(\begin{array}{c}2 \times \text{first term} \\ \text{of series}\end{array}\right) + \left(\begin{array}{c}\text{first term} \\ \text{of series}\end{array}\right) + \left(\begin{array}{c}\text{number of terms} \\ \text{in series} - 1\end{array}\right)\left(\begin{array}{c}\text{difference between} \\ \text{a term and the} \\ \text{preceeding term}\end{array}\right)\right]$$

Example: What is the sum of a series of 15 payments starting with $100 and decreasing by $5 with each payment?

$$\text{Sum of series} = \left(\frac{15}{2}\right) \times \left[(2 \times 100) + (15-1)(-5)\right]$$

$$= \left(\frac{15}{2}\right) \times (\$200 - 70) = \$975$$

.03 Sum of Series of Payments with Constant Percentage Rate Change

Sum of Series of Payments with Constant Percentage Rate Change

Sum of series =

$$\frac{\text{First term of series} \left(1 - \left(\frac{\text{ratio of a term to}}{\text{the preceding term}}\right)^{\text{(number of terms in series)}}\right)}{1 - \text{ratio of a term to the preceding term}}$$

Example: The production of an oil well has been decreasing at a rate of 15% per year. The well will produce 20,000 barrels of oil this year. How many barrels will be recovered over the next 7 years, at which time the well will be abandoned?

(Rate is decrease, use one's complement 1.00 – .15 = .85), i.e., ratio of a term to its preceding term = (1 – .15) / 1 = .85

$$\text{Sum of series} = \frac{20,000 \left(1 - (.85)^7\right)}{1 - .85}$$

$$= \frac{20,000 \left(1 - .32058\right)}{1 - .85}$$

$$= \frac{13,588.40}{.15} = 90,589.33$$

¶ 678 SUNK COST ANALYSIS

.01 Capital Recovery

Sunk costs are those costs that are historical costs. Nothing that can be done now or later can undo what was done in the past. The proper analysis regarding capital recovery costs on an asset is to base it on present net realizable value. The formula incorporates a sinking fund factor plus an interest rate. To apply sunk cost analysis for a company vehicle, for example, one might consider whether a company should keep a vehicle for two more years, or sell it now. Each year that the company waits, the resale value declines. The capital recovery cost of extending vehicle use for another two years is the decrease in market value plus interest forgone on today's sales price. Sunk cost analysis will consider, "What is it worth if sold today?" The capital recovery cost formula equals the market value of an asset in time period -now, less its market value in time period -future, multiplied by the appropriate capital recovery factor, plus the last resale value, times the appropriate interest rate. Note: In the following example, that the original outlay to purchase the vehicle, the book value, or the depreciation, does not enter into the computation. That is a historical, sunk cost. The analysis focuses on the money difference between selling a vehicle now, or selling it later. The capital recovery cost formula is defined as follows:

$$
\begin{aligned}
\text{Capital recovery cost} \;=\; & \Big[(\text{Market value in time - now} - \text{market value in time - future})\Big] \\
& \times \left[\frac{\text{Interest rate }(1 + \text{Interest rate})^{\text{number of periods}}}{(1 + \text{Interest rate})^{\text{number of periods}} - 1} \right] \\
& + \Big[(\text{Market value in time - future}) \times (\text{Interest rate})\Big]
\end{aligned}
$$

Example: A company purchased a vehicle 3 years ago for $10,000. It is being depreciated by the straight line method over 5 years. The salvage value is $1,200. The current book value is $4,000. The company uses 9% as it's rate of return. Should the company sell the vehicle now or keep it two more years, given the following information?

Market value now = $6,500

Market value 1 year from now = $4,500

Market value 2 years from now = $1,200

Capital Recovery Cost =

$$
(\$6{,}500 - \$1{,}200) \left[\frac{.09\,(1 + .09)^2}{(1 + .09)^2 - 1} \right] \quad (1{,}200)(.09)
$$

$$
= (5{,}300) \left[\frac{(.09)\,(1.1881)}{(1.1881 - 1)} \right] + (108)
$$

$$
= (\$5{,}300)\,(.5685) + (108)
$$

$$
= 3{,}121 \text{ (The cost of retaining the vehicle for an additional two years)}
$$

¶ 679 TAX ANNUALIZED

Annualized Income

$$
\frac{\text{Income}}{\text{number of months}} \times 12
$$

Calculate tax on annualized income

Tax = 15% of taxable income up to $50,000

25% of taxable income on next $25,000

Prorated Annualized Tax

$$
\text{Annualized tax} \times \frac{\text{number of months}}{12}
$$

Example: Company has income through April of $18,500. Given that the tax rates are 15percent on the first $50,000 and 25percent on next $25,000, what is the company's annualized estimated tax?

Annualized income = $18,500 / 4 ×12 = $55,500

Tax on annualized income = .15 ($50,000) + .25 ($5,500) = $8,875

Annualized tax prorated = $8,875 ×4/12 = $2,958

¶ 681 TRENDS

.01 Trend Line-Projection

The trend line equation: $Y = a + b\,x$

Ending Date of Years N	Value for Years X	Years Squared X^2	Flows Y	Flows Weighted by Years XY
↓	↓	↓	↓	↓
Totals:	Totals:	Totals:	Totals:	Totals:
(A)[1]	(B)[2]	(C)	(D)	(E)

[1] This is "number" of years observed. For example if 5 years are chosen, the number of years observed is 5.

[2] This is the total of the years observed. For example, if 5 years are used, the total of years observed is 15, i.e., (5+4+3+2+1=15)

$$\text{Using } a = \frac{\sum y - b\left(\sum x\right)}{N} \quad b = \frac{\left(\sum xy\right) - \left(\sum x\right)\left(\sum y\right)}{N\left(\sum x^2\right) - \left(\sum x\right)^2}$$

Where:

X = Value for the years

N = Number of observations

Y = Income values

$$\text{Trend line: } y = (a) + (b)\ X$$
$$y = \underline{\hspace{1cm}} + \underline{\hspace{1cm}}\ X$$

Where X = the value for the years

Trend Line Method

The trend line formula: $Y = a + b \times$

Ending Date of Years N	Value for Years X	Value for Years Squared X^2	Income Flows $ Y	Income Weighted by Years $ XY
19X1	1	1	10,000	10,000
19X2	2	4	12,000	24,000
19X3	3	9	13,000	39,000
19X4	4	16	14,000	56,000
19X5	5	25	15,000	75,000
Totals: N = 5	15	55	64,000	204,000
(A)[1]	(B)[2]	(C)	(D)	(E)

Complete the formula by using the totals of the columns (A) thru (E).

[1] This is "number" of years observed. For example if all 7 years are chosen, the number of years observed is 7.

[2] This is the total of the years observed. For example, if all 7 years are used, the total of years observed is 28.

$$b = \frac{5(204,000) - (15)(64,000)}{5(55) - (15)^2}$$

$$= 1,200$$

$$a = \frac{64,000 - (1,200)(15)}{5} = 9,200$$

$$y = 9,200 + 1,200\,x$$

Trend Line Shortcut

The methodology of fitting a linear trend line can be simplified if the middle of the time period is designated as zero, where the sum of X = 0.

Trend Line Shortcut Method

Trend line Y = a + bX

Defining a and b in a simplified manner:

$$a \text{ becomes } = \frac{\Sigma Y}{N}$$

$$b \text{ becomes } = \frac{\Sigma XY}{X^2}$$

Years Ago	Year in Transformed Units	Flows $	Flow Times Transformed Years	Transformed Years Squared
	X	Y	XY	X²
5	−2	10,000	(20,000)	4
4	−1	15,000	(15,000)	1
3	0	20,000	0	0
2	+1	22,000	22,000	1
1	+2	25,000	50,000	4
Totals	0	92,000	37,000	10

$$(a) = \frac{\Sigma Y}{N} = \frac{92,000}{5} = 18,400$$

$$(b) = \frac{\Sigma XY}{X^2} = \frac{37,000}{10} = 3,700$$

(c) = the sum of the column X²

Trend Line

Y = a + bX

Where X = year in transformed units

Y = 18,400 + 3,700X

¶681.01

Projected Values:	(a)Value	(b)Value
Current Year (projected)	= $18,400+	($3,700 × 3) = $29,500
1 Year in Future	= $18,400+	($3,700 × 4) = $33,200
2 Years in Future	= $18,400+	($3,700 × 5) = $36,900

.03 Trend Based on Moving Average

Trend Secular—Moving Average Central with Odd Number of Periods

The following formula is used to compute a moving average where the first number in the group is removed from the running total and the next number in the group is included.

Moving Average

$$\frac{\left(\begin{matrix}\text{Value in 1st time}\\\text{period in avg.}\end{matrix}\right) + \left(\begin{matrix}\text{Value in 2nd time}\\\text{period in avg.}\end{matrix}\right) + \left(\begin{matrix}\text{Value in 3rd time}\\\text{period in avg.}\end{matrix}\right) + \left(\begin{matrix}\text{Value in last time}\\\text{period in avg.}\end{matrix}\right)}{\text{Number of time periods in average}}$$

Example: What is the trend of the year end inventory values based on a three year moving average?

Year	Year End Inventory Balance	Period 3	Year Moving Average
1986	$425,000		
1987	475,000	'86-'88	$472,000
1988	515,000	'87-'89	505,000
1989	525,000	'88-'90	521,000
1990	522,000	'89-'91	525,000
1991	528,000		

Moving average above computed as follows:

Moving average on years '86 thru '88 =

$$\frac{\$425,000 + 475,000 + 515,000}{3} = \$471,667$$

Moving average on years '87 thru '89 =

$$\frac{\$475,000 + 515,000 + 525,000}{3} = \$505,000$$

Trend Secular—Moving Average Central with Even Number of Periods

Moving Average with Even Number of Periods

Note that an extra period is used: but *non-end* values are weighted by 2.

¶681.03

$$\left(\begin{array}{c}\text{Value in 1st time}\\ \text{period in avg.}\end{array}\right) + 2\left(\begin{array}{c}\text{Value in 2nd time}\\ \text{period in avg.}\end{array}\right)$$

$$+\, 2\left(\begin{array}{c}\text{Value in 3rd time}\\ \text{period in avg.}\end{array}\right) + 2\left(\begin{array}{c}\text{Value in last time}\\ \text{period in avg.}\end{array}\right)$$

$$\dfrac{+\left(\begin{array}{c}\text{Value after last time}\\ \text{period in avg.}\end{array}\right)}{2\left(\text{Total number of time periods in average} - 1\right)}$$

Example: What is the trend of the year-end accounts receivable balance balanced on a four year moving average?

Year	Year-End A/R Balance	Period	4 Year Moving Average (centered)
1986	$225,000		
1987	255,000		
1988	275,000	'86-'90	= $283,750
1989	315,000	'87-'91	= $313,125
1990	355,000	'88-'92	= $338,750
1991	360,000		
1992	375,000		

Moving average above computed as follows:

four year (centered) moving avg ('86-'90) =

$$= \dfrac{\$225,000 + 2 \times \$255,000 + 2 \times \$275,000 + 2 \times \$315,000 + \$355,000}{2 \times 4}$$

$$= \$283,750$$

4 year (centered) moving avg ('87-'91) =

$$\dfrac{\$255,000 + 2 \times \$275,000 + 2 \times \$315,000 + 2 \times \$355,000 + \$360,000}{2 \times 4}$$

$$= \$313.125$$

.05 Periodic Average

A periodic average is a simple average applied to the same unit of time over several different periods. It points out variations between time units, usually months, or years and indicates trends.

Example of Periodic Average:

Year Ending	12/31/X4	12/31/X3	12/31/X2	Total	Average
January	51,206	50,111	48,102	149,419	49,806
February	55,212	55,200	56,100	166,512	55,504
March	40,717	47,002	43,012	130,731	43,577
April	etc.				

.07 Progressive Average

A progressive or running average is cumulative in nature. The current period result is added to the cumulative prior period total. This amount is divided by the previous divisor plus one. Use to spot trends.

Example of Progressive Average:

		Current Total + Prior Cumulative Total $	Divided by # of Months		Progressive Average $
January		45,000 =			
February	+	47,500 = 92,500	/ 2	=	46,250
March	+	42,750 = 135,250	/ 3	=	45,083
April	+	48,950 = 184,200	/ 4	=	46,050
May	+	etc.= _____	/ 5	=	_____

¶ 682 VEHICLE BUSINESS USE—CASH VS. LOAN VS. LEASE

.01 Recordkeeping Recommendations for Vehicles Are Designed To Be Able to Prove:

- When vehicle was placed in service.
- Adjusted cost basis of vehicle.
- Operating expenses (gas, insurance, etc.).
- Total mileage and business mileage verification.
- Business purpose regarding business miles.

Proof of the actual expenses being claimed is required. Contemporary recordkeeping is recommended, but is not an absolute requirement for IRS purposes.

Assumptions for Cash vs. Loan vs. Lease

Lease Buyout		$8,500
Pre-Tax Investment Rate	12%	
Interest Deductibility Percent		80%
Business Use Percent		80%
Payoff Period - Months	36	
Tax Rates	Federal Income	28%
	Social Security	6.20%
	Medicare	1.45%

Cash:

Cash Price Paid	$25,000	

Loan:

Downpayment		$2,000
Monthly Payment	$764	
Loan Rate		12%

Lease:

Downpayment		$2,000
Monthly Payment	$650	
Deposit-Refundable	$500	
Total other expenses for full term	$2,000	

¶681.07

Cost Analysis

	Purchase With Cash	Purchase w/Loan	Lease
Initial Payment	$25,000	$2,000	$2,000
Monthly Payment	$0	$764	$650
Total Payments	$25,000	$29,504	$27,400
Foregone Savings	$6,615	$529	$661
Lease Buyout Price	$0	$0	$8,500
Lease Inclusion Effect	$0	$0	$128
Total Cost	$31,615	$30,033	$36,689
Less-Tax Savings	$3,101	$4,347	$7,580
Net After-Tax Cost	$8,514	$25,686	$29,110

1997 MACRS and lease inclusion rules used for this analysis.

¶ 683 VENTURE CAPITAL

.01 Investment % of Ownership

% Ownership to Venture Capitalist

$$\frac{\text{Capital Required}}{\left(\begin{array}{c}\text{Est. future value} \\ \text{of company}\end{array}\right) \times \left(\begin{array}{c}1 + \text{rate of return} \\ \text{desired by venture} \\ \text{capitalist}\end{array}\right) - \left(\begin{array}{c}\text{Number of years} \\ \text{to obtain future value}\end{array}\right)}$$

Example: Venture capitalist will invest $250,000 required rate of return is 30 percent. In five years the business is estimated to be valued at $1,500,000. What percent of common stock should be sold to the venture capitalist?

$$\% \text{ ownership} = \frac{\$250,000}{\$1,500,000 \left(1 + .30\right)^{-5}}$$

$$= \frac{\$250,000}{\$1,500,000 \dfrac{1}{1(1+.30)^5}}$$

$$= \frac{\$250,000}{\$1,500,000 \left(.26933\right)}$$

$$= .6188 \text{ or } 61.88\%$$

¶ 685 WAGES

.01 Determining Gross Wages When Net Wages Are Known

Use this formula to estimate what the gross wage is, when all you really have is the net check. Be aware that the FICA rate varies, depending on if the employee has passed the maximum limit for the year.

Gross wages = Net wages

+ Federal % W/H method

+ State % W/H method

+ Gross × (FICA rate)

Gross Wages

= Net wages

$$+ \left[\left[\begin{pmatrix} \text{Federal} \\ \text{W/H} \\ \text{\% rate} \end{pmatrix} \times \text{Gross} - \begin{pmatrix} \text{Dependents} \\ \text{claimed} \end{pmatrix} \frac{\begin{pmatrix} \text{Federal} \\ \text{Exemption} \\ \text{Amount} \end{pmatrix}}{\begin{pmatrix} \text{No. pay} \\ \text{periods} \\ \text{per year} \end{pmatrix}} - \begin{pmatrix} \text{Wage over} \\ \text{limit} \end{pmatrix} \right] + \begin{pmatrix} \text{Tax} \\ \text{base} \end{pmatrix} \right]$$

$$+ \left[\begin{pmatrix} \text{State} \\ \text{W/H} \\ \text{\% rate} \end{pmatrix} \times \left[\text{Gross} - \begin{pmatrix} \text{Dependents} \\ \text{claimed} \end{pmatrix} \frac{\begin{pmatrix} \text{State Exemption} \\ \text{Amount} \end{pmatrix}}{\begin{pmatrix} \text{No. of pay} \\ \text{periods per year} \end{pmatrix}} \right] + \begin{pmatrix} \text{FICA} \\ \text{tax rate} \end{pmatrix} \times \text{Gross} \right]$$

Example: * Employer agrees to allow employee take home pay, regardless of deductions, of $325/week.

FICA = 7.65%

Employee is single and claims 2 exemptions on W-4

Exemption = $2,050, for weekly = $2,050 / 52 = $39.42

Federal optional method for percent withholding for weekly pay is:

Wages	Tax Base +	Tax %	Wage Over Limit
$0 - $250	0	.12	$0
$251-$450	30.12	.15	250
$451- $650, etc	67.65	.18	450

State tax rate = 2% and exemption = $2,000/52 – $38.46

What would the gross wages be, given the above data?

---

* Note: Tax rates, etc., here used for illustration only, check for current rates when applying.

¶685.01

$$G = \$325 + [(.15\,(G - 21\,(\$2,050/52) - \$250)) + 30.121]$$
$$+ (.02\,(G - 2\ (\$2,000/52))) + .0765G$$
$$= \$325 + [1(.15\,(G - \$78.85) - \$250) + 30.121]$$
$$+ [.02\,(G - \$76.92)] + .0765G$$
$$= \$325 + .15G - \$49.33 + \$30.12 + .02G - \$1.54 + .0765G$$
$$G = .2465G + \$304.25$$
$$.7535G = \$304.25$$
$$G = \$403.78$$

Proof :

Gross = \$403.78

SS = \$ 30.89

W/H = \$ 41.35 [.15 (\$403.78 − \$78.85) − \$250)] = 11.24 + 30.12

ST = \$ 6.54 [.02 (\$403.78 − \$76.92)]

Net = \$325.00

*Note: Tax rates, etc., here used for illustration only, check for current rates when applying.

.03 Gross-Up—for Employer's Payment of Employee's Taxes

At certain times, an employer may wish to pay its employee's Federal and FICA taxes without deducting them from the employee's pay. Taxes imposed on the employee but paid by the employer are additional taxable wages to the employee. If an employer pays the employee's FICA taxes, the employee's wages are increased by the amount of the taxes paid, which then increases the amount of wages, etc.

The IRS has addressed the procedure to handle this situation so that the amount of FICA wages can be determined. This is known as "gross-up" (Rev. Proc. 81-48, CB 1981-2, 623; Rev. Rul. 86-14, CB 1986-1, 542). Note: The procedure and formula do not apply when the pay is for domestic service or for agricultural labor.

The formula to determine FICA wages is:

FICA Wages

$$W = \frac{SP \times (\text{amount of original pay})}{1 - R \times (\text{rate of employee FICA taxes})}$$

W = the employee's total FICA wages after the increase
SP = Stated pay (pay before taking into account the increase in wages)
R = Rate of employee FICA tax

Example: Employer agrees to pay an employee \$300 a week and to pay the employee's FICA taxes without deducting them from the \$300.

$$W = \frac{\$300}{1 - 0.0765} = \frac{\$300}{0.9235} = \underline{\$324.85}$$

The employee's weekly wage is $324.85 for FIT, FICA, and FUTA purposes.

Even though $24.85 was not actually withheld, enter it in Boxes 11 and 15, "Social Security tax withheld" and "Medicare Tax withheld."

.05 Wages Benefits Estimate

The following illustrates a calculation technique to determine the percent overhead factor related to benefits provided to an employee as a "real" company cost.

Annual Salary or Hourly Rate =	$11.00 × 2080 Annual hours	=	$22880.00 Base Earnings	100%
FICA (max $65,400)	.062 × 22880 Base Earnings	=	$1419	6.2%
Medicare	.0145 × 22880 Base Earnings	=	$331	1.5%
Federal Unemployment (max $7,000)	.008 × 7000	=	$56	.2%
State Unemployment (max $9,000)	.027 × 9000	=	$243	1%
Paid sick leave	$11.00 Hourly Rate × 42 hours taken	=	$462	2%
Paid breaks	$11.00 Hourly Rate × 121 hours take	=	$1331	5.8%
Paid vacations	$11.00 Hourly Rate × 120 hours taken	=	$1320	5.8%
Paid holidays	$11.00 Hourly Rate × 80 hours taken	=	$880	3.8%
Contribution to pension	.03 Contribution Rate × 22880 Base	=	$686	3%
Medical insurance	.063 Premium Rate × 22880 Base	=	$1441	6.3%
Child care provided		=	$1200	5.2%
Pension adminstrative costs		=	$130	.5%
Training		=	$1800	7.8%
Educational courses/ materials		=	$2200	9.6%
Health/wellness programs		=	$4400	19.2%
Safety, clothing		=	$1800	7.9%
Total Compensation Benefits		=	$19699	86.10%

.07 Percent Wage Increase

Given:

  Salary = $400

  Raise = 10%

What percent was the salary increased?

Solution:

  $ Change / $ Salary = $10 / $400

  = .025 × 100 (for %)

  = 2.5%

.09 Wages—Relationships (Algebra)

Given:

A's salary = $50

A's salary is $10 greater than B's salary

What is B's salary?

Solution:

B + $10 = A

B + $10 = $50

B = $50 – $10

B = $40

Given:

B's salary = $50

B's salary is twice that of A's salary

What is A's salary?

Solution:

2 × A = B

2 × A = $50

A = $50 / 2

A = $25

Given:

C's salary = $280

D's salary is $5 less than 3 times C's salary

What is D's salary?

Solution:

C = $280

D = (3 × C) – 5

D = (3 × $280) – 5

D = $835

Given:

A makes twice as much as B per week. The total salaries combined is $600.

How much does A make?

How much does B make?

Solution:

Let B's salary = x

Therefore, A's salary = 2x

x + 2x = $600

3x = $600

x = $600 / 3

x = $200 B's Salary

Therefore, 2x = $400 A's Salary

Given:

A makes twice as much as B per week.

B makes twice as much as C per week.

Their total salary is $1050.

How much per week does each employee make?

Solution:

Let C's salary = x

Therefore, B's salary = 2x

Therefore, A's salary = 4x

x + 2x + 4x = $1050

7x = $1050

x = $1050 / 7

x = $150

Therefore,

x = $150 C's salary

2x = $300 B's salary

3x = $600 A's salary

Total = $1050

.11 Wages—Commissions

Commission Earned—Single Period

If a salesperson was paid 15-percent commission on $30,000 of sales, what commission was made?

Commission = $30,000 × .15 = $4,500

Commission Earned—Multiple Periods

If a salesperson was paid 15-percent commission on monthly sales, what was the total commission on monthly sales of $35,000, $42,000, and $38,000?

Commission = ($35,000 + $42,000 + $38,000) × .15

= $17,250

Commission Earned—Multiple Rates

Given:

Commission = 12% on new customers

¶685.11

Commission = 10% on existing customers

Sales per period to new customers = $55,000

Sales per period to existing customers = $45,000

What commission was earned?

Commission = ($45,000 × .10) + ($55,000 × .12)

= $4,500 + $6,600

= $11,100

¶ 687 WASTING ASSET

.01 Value of a Wasting Asset

Value of Wasting Asset

$$\text{Net income generated by asset} \bigg/ \left(\text{Rate of return on investment} + \cfrac{1}{\substack{\text{Future value of annuity} \\ \text{for periods at rate of} \\ \text{return on income reinvested}}} \right)$$

Example: A sandpit generates $425,000 cash flow per year. This is estimated to continue for 10 years. A fair rate of return on this type of investment = 12%. A sinking fund is established to recover the cost of the investment which is estimated to earn 7%. Salvage value is to be ignored for the wasting asset. What is the value of the sand pit?

$$\text{Value} = \cfrac{\$425,000}{\left(.12 + \cfrac{1}{\cfrac{(1+.07)^{10}-1}{.07}} \right)}$$

$$= \cfrac{\$425,000}{\left(.12 + \cfrac{1}{\substack{\text{factor from table for future value} \\ \text{of annuity at 7\% for 10 periods} \\ = 13.8164}} \right)}$$

$$= \$2,209.20$$

.02 Wasting Asset—Capitalized Value with Variable Income Stream

Determine the capitalized present value of the following oil field and the proved reserve given the following data:

Remaining life of production = 4 years

Current production = 25,000 barrels of oil/year

Production is decreasing at constant rate of 15% per year

Oil price is expected to escalate at 6% per annum

Current price of oil (net of expense) = $25/barrel

Fair return on investment = 10%

Capitalized present value of oil field:

Year	Annual Production	Selling Price per Barrel (net)	Total Income	PV Factor at 10%	PV of Total Income
0	25,000				
1	21,250	$25.00	$531,250	.9091	$482,959
2	18,063	26.50	478,669	.8264	395,572
3	15,353	28.09	431,266	.7513	324,010
4	13,050	29.78	388,629	.6830	265,43

Proved = 67,716
reserve

Capitalized present value of oil field =1,467,975

Annual production yr 1 = 25,000 * (1 – .15)

Annual production yr 2 = 21,250 * (1 – .15)

Selling price   yr 1 = $25
Selling price   yr 2 = $25 * 1.06

Proved Reserve =

$$\text{1st year production} \times \frac{(1 - (1 - \text{constant decline rate})^{\text{No. of periods}})}{(1 - (1 - \text{constant decline rate}))}$$

$$= 21250 \times \frac{(1 - ((1 - .15)^4))}{(1 - (1 - .15))}$$

$$= 21250 \times \frac{(1 - .522)}{.15}$$

$$= 67,716$$

¶ 688 WORKING CAPITAL

.01 Working Capital Requirement from Projected Growth—Short Cut Method

Over a short range of growth there is a linear relationship between cash, accounts receivable, inventory, and accounts payable. The growth of the firm will require continuing needs for cash, until the growth levels off. The relationship of sales growth rate and profit margin will determine the cash requirement and working capital needs.

Use the following technique to estimate the firm's working capital and cash needs:

(in 000's)	19x1	19x2	19x3	19x4	19x5
Sales	$1500	$2000	$2200	$2500	$3000
COGS	975	1300	1430	1625	1950
Expenses	950	1290	1405	1605	1920
Net Income	25	10	25	20	30

Balance Sheet

	19x1	% of 19x1 Sales	
Cash	$55,000	4	= $55,000 / $1,500,000
Accounts Receivable	125,000	8	
Inventory	225,000	15	
Total Current Assets	405,000	27	
Less: Accounts Payable	250,000	17	
Working Capital	155,000	10	

(in 000's)	19x2	19x3	19x4	19x5
Projected Sales Increase	$500	$200	$300	$500
Working Capital at 10 %	50	20	30	50
= Net Income	10	25	20	30
Less: Net Working Capital 10%	50	20	30	50
= Working Capital Requirement needed From External Funds	40	(5)	10	20
Cumulative WC Requirement From External Funds	40	35	45	65

.02 Working Capital Requirement—Formula Method

External Funds Needed

External Funds Needed =

((Assets that increase spontaneously with sales stated as a % of sales) × (Change in Sales)) – ((Liabilities that increase spontaneously with sales stated as a % of sales) × (Change in Sales)) ((Profit Margin) × (Total projected sales for period × (1 – Dividend payout %)))

From the data in ¶ 688.01

Change in sales = $2,000,000 – $1,500,000 = $500,000

Dividend payout = $0

19x2 External Funds Needed =

(27% × \$500,000) – (17% × \$500,000) – (.005 × (2,000,000 × (1 – 0)))

\$135,000 – \$85,000 – \$10,000

\$40,000

19x3 External Funds Needed =

(27% × \$200,000) – (17% × \$200,000) – (.011 × (2,200,000 × (1 – 0)))

\$54,000 – \$34,000 – \$25,000

(5,000)

Note: No external funds needed.

19x4 External Funds Needed =

(27% × \$300,000) – (17% × \$300,000) – (.008 × (2,500,000 × (1– 0)))

\$81,000 – \$51,000 – \$20,000

10,000

19x5 External Funds Needed =

(27% × \$500,000) – (17% × \$500,000) – (.01 × (3,000,000 × (1– 0)))

\$135,000 – \$85,000 – \$30,000

20,000

.03 Working Capital—Permanent

Permanent Working Capital is only permanent in the sense that it remains relatively constant over numerous operating periods. Permanent Working Capital represents the amount of cash invested in the normal operating assets of A/R and inventory less the cash invested in A/P and other accruals.

The permanent capital working concept to be aware of is that as sales grow or the operating cycle is extended, the need for permanent working capital increases. The permanent working capital formula is:

Permanent Working Capital = (Accounts Receivable + Inventory) – (Accounts Payable + Payroll Accruals)

Working Capital Operation Cycle

Permanent Working Capital Operating Cycle = (Days inventory + Days A/R) – (Days A/P + Days Accruals)

Where:

Days Inventory = (Inventory * 360) / COGS

Days A/R = (A/R * 360) / Sales

Days A/P = (A/P * 360) / Purchases

Days P/Y Accruals = (P/Y Accrual * 360) / (Salaries & P/Y Taxes)

For Accounts Receivable:

$$\text{Days A/R} = \frac{(A/R)\,(360)}{\text{Sales}}$$

¶688.03

or

Sales = $\dfrac{(A/R)\,(360)}{\text{Days A/R}}$

or

A/R = $\dfrac{(\text{Days A/R})\,(\text{Sales})}{360}$

For Inventory:

Days inventory = $\dfrac{(\text{Inventory})\,(360)}{\text{COGS}}$

or

COGS = $\dfrac{(\text{Inventory})\,(360)}{\text{Days inventory}}$

or

Inventory = $\dfrac{(\text{Days inventory})\,(\text{COGS})}{360}$

For P/Y accruals (*i.e.*, salary and P/Y taxes):

Days P/Y accrual = $\dfrac{(\text{P/Y accrual})\,(360)}{\text{salaries and P/Y taxes}}$

or

Salaries + P/Y taxes = $\dfrac{(\text{P/Y accruals})\,(360)}{\text{Days P/Y accruals}}$

or

P/Y accruals = $\dfrac{(\text{Days P/Y accruals})\,(\text{salaries} + \text{P/Y taxes})}{360}$

For Accounts Payable:

Days A/P = $\dfrac{(A/P)\,(360)}{\text{Purchases}}$

or

Purchases = $\dfrac{(A/P)\,(360)}{\text{Days A/P}}$

or

A/P = $\dfrac{(\text{Days A/P})\,(\text{purchases})}{360}$

Use the above formulas to solve for accounts receivable, accounts payable, inventory, and P/Y accruals to determine the increase in permanent working capital that might be required for a given sales volume and calculated operating cycle. These balances are the ending balances of the projection period. Subtract these from the beginning balances to obtain the additional cash requirement for permanent working capital.

Permanent working capital increase:

Given:

A/R	= $6,500	Days A/R	= 28
Inventory	= $6,000	Days Inventory	= 30
A/P	= $1,200	Days payable	= 27
P/Y accruals	= $ 80	Days accrual	= 5

Projections:

Sales	=	$250,000
Cogs	=	75,000
Purchases	=	25,000
Salary + P/Y taxes	=	8,000

Permanent working capital = (A/R + Inventory) – (A/P + P/Y accruals)

$$= \frac{(Days\ A/R)(Sales)}{30} + \frac{(Days\ Inventory)(COGS)}{30} - \frac{(Days\ A/P)(Purchases)}{30} + \frac{(Days\ P/Y\ Accruals)(Salaries + P/Y\ taxes)}{30}$$

$$= \frac{(28)(450,000)}{360} + \frac{(30)(75,000)}{360} - \frac{(27)(25,000)}{360} + \frac{(5)(8,000)}{360}$$

= (19,444 + 6250) – (1875 + 111)

= $23,708

	Ending	–	Beginning	=	Increase
A/R	19,444	–	6,500	=	$12,944
Inventory	6,250	–	6,000	=	250
Less: A/P	1,875	–	1,200	=	675
P/Y Accruals	111	–	80	=	31
Working Capital =	23,708		$11,220		
Permanent capital total increase					$12,488

.04 Working Capital Changes Effect on Cash

Asset Accounts	Change	Description	Cash Effect
Inventory	Increase	Produce or purchase additional Inventory	Decrease
Inventory	Decrease	Liquidate of sale Inventory	Increase
Accounts Receivable	Increase	Customers paying slow or allowance of additional credit	Decrease
Accounts Receivable	Decrease	Collection on accounts or reduction of credit terms	Increase
Prepaid Expenses	Increase	Increased payment for insurance, etc.	Decrease

¶688.04

Asset Accounts	Change	Description	Cash Effect
Prepaid Expenses	Decrease	Decreased payment for insurance, etc.	Increase

Liability Accounts	Change	Description	Cash Effect
Accounts Payable	Increase	Pay vendors slower or purchase more on credit	Increase
Accounts Payable	Decrease	Pay vendors sooner or purchase less on credit	Decrease
Current Notes	Increase	Slower or smaller debt payments	Increase
Current Notes	Decrease	Quicker or larger debt payments	Decrease
Payroll Taxes	Increase	Slower or smaller tax payments	Increase
Payroll Taxes	Decrease	Quicker or larger tax payments	Decrease
Sales Taxes	Increase	Slower or smaller tax payments	Increase
Sales Taxes	Decrease	Quicker or larger tax payments	Decrease

¶ 689 YIELD

.01 Annualized

Annualized Yield

$$\left[1 + \frac{\text{Dividend}}{\text{Market value of investment}} \right]^{(\text{number of periods in year})} - 1$$

Example: A cash management account received a monthly dividend of $100 on its $20,000 investment, which was reinvested in the account. What is the annualized yield?

Annualized yield =

$$\left[1 + \frac{100}{2000} \right]^{12} - 1 = (1 + .005)^{12} - 1 = (1.005)^{12} - 1 = 1.0617 - 1$$

$$= .0617 \text{ or } 6.17\%$$

¶ 691 TABLES

.01 Cost of Debt After Inflation and Taxes

Cost of Debt After Inflation and Taxes Inflation Rate of 0.0 Percent

Interest Rate				Tax Rate			
	0%	15%	25%	28%	33%	34%	35%
2%	2.00%	1.70%	1.50%	1.44%	1.34%	1.32%	1.30%
3%	3.00%	2.55%	2.25%	2.16%	2.01%	1.98%	1.95%
4%	4.00%	3.40%	3.00%	2.88%	2.68%	2.64%	2.60%
5%	5.00%	4.25%	3.75%	3.60%	3.35%	3.30%	3.25%
6%	6.00%	5.10%	4.50%	4.32%	4.02%	3.96%	3.90%
7%	7.00%	5.95%	5.25%	5.04%	4.69%	4.62%	4.55%
8%	8.00%	6.80%	6.00%	5.76%	5.36%	5.28%	5.20%
9%	9.00%	7.65%	6.75%	6.48%	6.03%	5.94%	5.85%
10%	10.00%	8.50%	7.50%	7.20%	6.70%	6.60%	6.50%
11%	11.00%	9.35%	8.25%	7.92%	7.37%	7.26%	7.15%
12%	12.00%	10.20%	9.00%	8.64%	8.04%	7.92%	7.80%
13%	13.00%	11.05%	9.75%	9.36%	8.71%	8.58%	8.45%
14%	14.00%	11.90%	10.50%	10.08%	9.38%	9.24%	9.10%
15%	15.00%	12.75%	11.25%	10.80%	10.05%	9.90%	9.75%
16%	16.00%	13.60%	12.00%	11.52%	10.72%	10.56%	10.40%
17%	17.00%	14.45%	12.75%	12.24%	11.39%	11.22%	11.05%
18%	18.00%	15.30%	13.50%	12.96%	12.06%	11.88%	11.70%
19%	19.00%	16.15%	14.25%	13.68%	12.73%	12.54%	12.35%
20%	20.00%	17.00%	15.00%	14.40%	13.40%	13.20%	13.00%

Cost of Debt After Inflation and Taxes Inflation Rate of 1.0 Percent

Interest Rate				Tax Rate			
	0%	15%	25%	28%	33%	34%	35%
2%	1.00%	0.70%	0.50%	0.44%	0.34%	0.32%	0.30%
3%	2.00%	1.55%	1.25%	1.16%	1.01%	0.98%	0.95%
4%	3.00%	2.40%	2.00%	1.88%	1.68%	1.64%	1.60%
5%	4.00%	3.25%	2.75%	2.60%	2.35%	2.30%	2.25%
6%	5.00%	4.10%	3.50%	3.32%	3.02%	2.96%	2.90%
7%	6.00%	4.95%	4.25%	4.04%	3.69%	3.62%	3.55%
8%	7.00%	5.80%	5.00%	4.76%	4.36%	4.28%	4.20%
9%	8.00%	6.65%	5.75%	5.48%	5.03%	4.94%	4.85%
10%	9.00%	7.50%	6.50%	6.20%	5.70%	5.60%	5.50%
11%	10.00%	8.35%	7.25%	6.92%	6.37%	6.26%	6.15%
12%	11.00%	9.20%	8.00%	7.64%	7.04%	6.92%	6.80%
13%	12.00%	10.05%	8.75%	8.36%	7.71%	7.58%	7.45%
14%	13.00%	10.90%	9.50%	9.08%	8.38%	8.24%	8.10%
15%	14.00%	11.75%	10.25%	9.80%	9.05%	8.90%	8.75%
16%	15.00%	12.60%	11.00%	10.52%	9.72%	9.56%	9.40%
17%	16.00%	13.45%	11.75%	11.24%	10.39%	10.22%	10.05%
18%	17.00%	14.30%	12.50%	11.96%	11.06%	10.88%	10.70%
19%	18.00%	15.15%	13.25%	12.68%	11.73%	11.54%	11.35%
20%	19.00%	16.00%	14.00%	13.40%	12.40%	12.20%	12.00%

Cost of Debt After Inflation and Taxes Inflation Rate of 2.0 Percent

Interest Rate | | | | Tax Rate | | |

	0%	15%	25%	28%	33%	34%	35%
2%	0.00%	-0.30%	-0.50%	-0.56%	-0.66%	-0.68%	-0.70%
3%	1.00%	0.55%	0.25%	0.16%	0.01%	-0.02%	-0.05%
4%	2.00%	1.40%	1.00%	0.88%	0.68%	0.64%	0.60%
5%	3.00%	2.25%	1.75%	1.60%	1.35%	1.30%	1.25%
6%	4.00%	3.10%	2.50%	2.32%	2.02%	1.96%	1.90%
7%	5.00%	3.95%	3.25%	3.04%	2.69%	2.62%	2.55%
8%	6.00%	4.80%	4.00%	3.76%	3.36%	3.28%	3.20%
9%	7.00%	5.65%	4.75%	4.48%	4.03%	3.94%	3.85%
10%	8.00%	6.50%	5.50%	5.20%	4.70%	4.60%	4.50%
11%	9.00%	7.35%	6.25%	5.92%	5.37%	5.26%	5.15%
12%	10.00%	8.20%	7.00%	6.64%	6.04%	5.92%	5.80%
13%	11.00%	9.05%	7.75%	7.36%	6.71%	6.58%	6.45%
14%	12.00%	9.90%	8.50%	8.08%	7.38%	7.24%	7.10%
15%	13.00%	10.75%	9.25%	8.80%	8.05%	7.90%	7.75%
16%	14.00%	11.60%	10.00%	9.52%	8.72%	8.56%	8.40%
17%	15.00%	12.45%	10.75%	10.24%	9.39%	9.22%	9.05%
18%	16.00%	13.30%	11.50%	10.96%	10.06%	9.88%	9.70%
19%	17.00%	14.15%	12.25%	11.68%	10.73%	10.54%	10.35%
20%	18.00%	15.00%	13.00%	12.40%	11.40%	11.20%	11.00%

Cost of Debt After Inflation and Taxes Inflation Rate of 3.0 Percent

Interest Rate | | | | Tax Rate | | |

	0%	15%	25%	28%	33%	34%	35%
2%	-1.00%	-1.30%	-1.50%	-1.56%	-1.66%	-1.68%	-1.70%
3%	0.00%	-0.45%	-0.75%	-0.84%	-0.99%	-1.02%	-1.05%
4%	1.00%	0.40%	0.00%	-0.12%	-0.32%	-0.36%	-0.40%
5%	2.00%	1.25%	0.75%	0.60%	0.35%	0.30%	0.25%
6%	3.00%	2.10%	1.50%	1.32%	1.02%	0.96%	0.90%
7%	4.00%	2.95%	2.25%	2.04%	1.69%	1.62%	1.55%
8%	5.00%	3.80%	3.00%	2.76%	2.36%	2.28%	2.20%
9%	6.00%	4.65%	3.75%	3.48%	3.03%	2.94%	2.85%
10%	7.00%	5.50%	4.50%	4.20%	3.70%	3.60%	3.50%
11%	8.00%	6.35%	5.25%	4.92%	4.37%	4.26%	4.15%
12%	9.00%	7.20%	6.00%	5.64%	5.04%	4.92%	4.80%
13%	10.00%	8.05%	6.75%	6.36%	5.71%	5.58%	5.45%
14%	11.00%	8.90%	7.50%	7.08%	6.38%	6.24%	6.10%
15%	12.00%	9.75%	8.25%	7.80%	7.05%	6.90%	6.75%
16%	13.00%	10.60%	9.00%	8.52%	7.72%	7.56%	7.40%
17%	14.00%	11.45%	9.75%	9.24%	8.39%	8.22%	8.05%
18%	15.00%	12.30%	10.50%	9.96%	9.06%	8.88%	8.70%
19%	16.00%	13.15%	11.25%	10.68%	9.73%	9.54%	9.35%
20%	17.00%	14.00%	12.00%	11.40%	10.40%	10.20%	10.00%

Cost of Debt After Inflation and Taxes Inflation Rate of 4.0 Percent

Interest Rate   Tax Rate

	0%	15%	25%	28%	33%	34%	35%
2%	-2.00%	-2.30%	-2.50%	-2.56%	-2.66%	-2.68%	-2.70%
3%	-1.00%	-1.45%	-1.75%	-1.84%	-1.99%	-2.02%	-2.05%
4%	0.00%	-0.60%	-1.00%	-1.12%	-1.32%	-1.36%	-1.40%
5%	1.00%	0.25%	-0.25%	-0.40%	-0.65%	-0.70%	-0.75%
6%	2.00%	1.10%	0.50%	0.32%	0.02%	-0.04%	-0.10%
7%	3.00%	1.95%	1.25%	1.04%	0.69%	0.62%	0.55%
8%	4.00%	2.80%	2.00%	1.76%	1.36%	1.28%	1.20%
9%	5.00%	3.65%	2.75%	2.48%	2.03%	1.94%	1.85%
10%	6.00%	4.50%	3.50%	3.20%	2.70%	2.60%	2.50%
11%	7.00%	5.35%	4.25%	3.92%	3.37%	3.26%	3.15%
12%	8.00%	6.20%	5.00%	4.64%	4.04%	3.92%	3.80%
13%	9.00%	7.05%	5.75%	5.36%	4.71%	4.58%	4.45%
14%	10.00%	7.90%	6.50%	6.08%	5.38%	5.24%	5.10%
15%	11.00%	8.75%	7.25%	6.80%	6.05%	5.90%	5.75%
16%	12.00%	9.60%	8.00%	7.52%	6.72%	6.56%	6.40%
17%	13.00%	10.45%	8.75%	8.24%	7.39%	7.22%	7.05%
18%	14.00%	11.30%	9.50%	8.96%	8.06%	7.88%	7.70%
19%	15.00%	12.15%	10.25%	9.68%	8.73%	8.54%	8.35%
20%	16.00%	13.00%	11.00%	10.40%	9.40%	9.20%	9.00%

Cost of Debt After Inflation and Taxes Inflation Rate of 5.0 Percent

Interest Rate   Tax Rate

	0%	15%	25%	28%	33%	34%	35%
2%	-3.00%	-3.30%	-3.50%	-3.56%	-3.66%	-3.68%	-3.70%
3%	-2.00%	-2.45%	-2.75%	-2.84%	-2.99%	-3.02%	-3.05%
4%	-1.00%	-1.60%	-2.00%	-2.12%	-2.32%	-2.36%	-2.40%
5%	0.00%	-0.75%	-1.25%	-1.40%	-1.65%	-1.70%	-1.75%
6%	1.00%	0.10%	-0.50%	-0.68%	-0.98%	-1.04%	-1.10%
7%	2.00%	0.95%	0.25%	0.04%	-0.31%	-0.38%	-0.45%
8%	3.00%	1.80%	1.00%	0.76%	0.36%	0.28%	0.20%
9%	4.00%	2.65%	1.75%	1.48%	1.03%	0.94%	0.85%
10%	5.00%	3.50%	2.50%	2.20%	1.70%	1.60%	1.50%
11%	6.00%	4.35%	3.25%	2.92%	2.37%	2.26%	2.15%
12%	7.00%	5.20%	4.00%	3.64%	3.04%	2.92%	2.80%
13%	8.00%	6.05%	4.75%	4.36%	3.71%	3.58%	3.45%
14%	9.00%	6.90%	5.50%	5.08%	4.38%	4.24%	4.10%
15%	10.00%	7.75%	6.25%	5.80%	5.05%	4.90%	4.75%
16%	11.00%	8.60%	7.00%	6.52%	5.72%	5.56%	5.40%
17%	12.00%	9.45%	7.75%	7.24%	6.39%	6.22%	6.05%
18%	13.00%	10.30%	8.50%	7.96%	7.06%	6.88%	6.70%
19%	14.00%	11.15%	9.25%	8.68%	7.73%	7.54%	7.35%
20%	15.00%	12.00%	10.00%	9.40%	8.40%	8.20%	8.00%

¶691.01

Cost of Debt After Inflation and Taxes Inflation Rate of 6.0 Percent

Interest Rate   Tax Rate

	0%	15%	25%	28%	33%	34%	35%
2%	-4.00%	-4.30%	-4.50%	-4.56%	-4.66%	-4.68%	-4.70%
3%	-3.00%	-3.45%	-3.75%	-3.84%	-3.99%	-4.02%	-4.05%
4%	-2.00%	-2.60%	-3.00%	-3.12%	-3.32%	-3.36%	-3.40%
5%	-1.00%	-1.75%	-2.25%	-2.40%	-2.65%	-2.70%	-2.75%
6%	0.00%	-0.90%	-1.50%	-1.68%	-1.98%	-2.04%	-2.10%
7%	1.00%	-0.05%	-0.75%	-0.96%	-1.31%	-1.38%	-1.45%
8%	2.00%	0.80%	0.00%	-0.24%	-0.64%	-0.72%	-0.80%
9%	3.00%	1.65%	0.75%	0.48%	0.03%	-0.06%	-0.15%
10%	4.00%	2.50%	1.50%	1.20%	0.70%	0.60%	0.50%
11%	5.00%	3.35%	2.25%	1.92%	1.37%	1.26%	1.15%
12%	6.00%	4.20%	3.00%	2.64%	2.04%	1.92%	1.80%
13%	7.00%	5.05%	3.75%	3.36%	2.71%	2.58%	2.45%
14%	8.00%	5.90%	4.50%	4.08%	3.38%	3.24%	3.10%
15%	9.00%	6.75%	5.25%	4.80%	4.05%	3.90%	3.75%
16%	10.00%	7.60%	6.00%	5.52%	4.72%	4.56%	4.40%
17%	11.00%	8.45%	6.75%	6.24%	5.39%	5.22%	5.05%
18%	12.00%	9.30%	7.50%	6.96%	6.06%	5.88%	5.70%
19%	13.00%	10.15%	8.25%	7.68%	6.73%	6.54%	6.35%
20%	14.00%	11.00%	9.00%	8.40%	7.40%	7.20%	7.00%

Cost of Debt After Inflation and Taxes Inflation Rate of 7.0 Percent

Interest Rate   Tax Rate

	0%	15%	25%	28%	33%	34%	35%
2%	-5.00%	-5.30%	-5.50%	-5.56%	-5.66%	-5.68%	-5.70%
3%	-4.00%	-4.45%	-4.75%	-4.84%	-4.99%	-5.02%	-5.05%
4%	-3.00%	-3.60%	-4.00%	-4.12%	-4.32%	-4.36%	-4.40%
5%	-2.00%	-2.75%	-3.25%	-3.40%	-3.65%	-3.70%	-3.75%
6%	-1.00%	-1.90%	-2.50%	-2.68%	-2.98%	-3.04%	-3.10%
7%	0.00%	-1.05%	-1.75%	-1.96%	-2.31%	-2.38%	-2.45%
8%	1.00%	-0.20%	-1.00%	-1.24%	-1.64%	-1.72%	-1.80%
9%	2.00%	0.65%	-0.25%	-0.52%	-0.97%	-1.06%	-1.15%
10%	3.00%	1.50%	0.50%	0.20%	-0.30%	-0.40%	-0.50%
11%	4.00%	2.35%	1.25%	0.92%	0.37%	0.26%	0.15%
12%	5.00%	3.20%	2.00%	1.64%	1.04%	0.92%	0.80%
13%	6.00%	4.05%	2.75%	2.36%	1.71%	1.58%	1.45%
14%	7.00%	4.90%	3.50%	3.08%	2.38%	2.24%	2.10%
15%	8.00%	5.75%	4.25%	3.80%	3.05%	2.90%	2.75%
16%	9.00%	6.60%	5.00%	4.52%	3.72%	3.56%	3.40%
17%	10.00%	7.45%	5.75%	5.24%	4.39%	4.22%	4.05%
18%	11.00%	8.30%	6.50%	5.96%	5.06%	4.88%	4.70%
19%	12.00%	9.15%	7.25%	6.68%	5.73%	5.54%	5.35%
20%	13.00%	10.00%	8.00%	7.40%	6.40%	6.20%	6.00%

.03 Simple Interest — Growth of $1.00
Simple Interest — Growth of $1.00

Period	Interest Rate								
	2%	3%	4%	5%	6%	7%	8%	9%	10%
0	1.00	1.00	1.00	1.00	1.00	1.00	1.00	1.00	1.00
1	1.02	1.03	1.04	1.05	1.06	1.07	1.08	1.09	1.10
2	1.04	1.06	1.08	1.10	1.12	1.14	1.16	1.18	1.20
3	1.06	1.09	1.12	1.15	1.18	1.21	1.24	1.27	1.30
4	1.08	1.12	1.16	1.20	1.24	1.28	1.32	1.36	1.40
5	1.10	1.15	1.20	1.25	1.30	1.35	1.40	1.45	1.50
6	1.12	1.18	1.24	1.30	1.36	1.42	1.48	1.54	1.60
7	1.14	1.21	1.28	1.35	1.42	1.49	1.56	1.63	1.70
8	1.16	1.24	1.32	1.40	1.48	1.56	1.64	1.72	1.80
9	1.18	1.27	1.36	1.45	1.54	1.63	1.72	1.81	1.90
10	1.20	1.30	1.40	1.50	1.60	1.70	1.80	1.90	2.00
11	1.22	1.33	1.44	1.55	1.66	1.77	1.88	1.99	2.10
12	1.24	1.36	1.48	1.60	1.72	1.84	1.96	2.08	2.20
13	1.26	1.39	1.52	1.65	1.78	1.91	2.04	2.17	2.30
14	1.28	1.42	1.56	1.70	1.84	1.98	2.12	2.26	2.40
15	1.30	1.45	1.60	1.75	1.90	2.05	2.20	2.35	2.50
16	1.32	1.48	1.64	1.80	1.96	2.12	2.28	2.44	2.60
17	1.34	1.51	1.68	1.85	2.02	2.19	2.36	2.53	2.70
18	1.36	1.54	1.72	1.90	2.08	2.26	2.44	2.62	2.80
19	1.38	1.57	1.76	1.95	2.14	2.33	2.52	2.71	2.90
20	1.40	1.60	1.80	2.00	2.20	2.40	2.60	2.80	3.00
21	1.42	1.63	1.84	2.05	2.26	2.47	2.68	2.89	3.10
22	1.44	1.66	1.88	2.10	2.32	2.54	2.76	2.98	3.20
23	1.46	1.69	1.92	2.15	2.38	2.61	2.84	3.07	3.30
24	1.48	1.72	1.96	2.20	2.44	2.68	2.92	3.16	3.40
25	1.50	1.75	2.00	2.25	2.50	2.75	3.00	3.25	3.50
26	1.52	1.78	2.04	2.30	2.56	2.82	3.08	3.34	3.60
27	1.54	1.81	2.08	2.35	2.62	2.89	3.16	3.43	3.70
28	1.56	1.84	2.12	2.40	2.68	2.96	3.24	3.52	3.80
29	1.58	1.87	2.16	2.45	2.74	3.03	3.32	3.61	3.90
30	1.60	1.90	2.20	2.50	2.80	3.10	3.40	3.70	4.00
31	1.62	1.93	2.24	2.55	2.86	3.17	3.48	3.79	4.10
32	1.64	1.96	2.28	2.60	2.92	3.24	3.56	3.88	4.20
33	1.66	1.99	2.32	2.65	2.98	3.31	3.64	3.97	4.30
34	1.68	2.02	2.36	2.70	3.04	3.38	3.72	4.06	4.40
35	1.70	2.05	2.40	2.75	3.10	3.45	3.80	4.15	4.50
36	1.72	2.08	2.44	2.80	3.16	3.52	3.88	4.24	4.60
37	1.74	2.11	2.48	2.85	3.22	3.59	3.96	4.33	4.70
38	1.76	2.14	2.52	2.90	3.28	3.66	4.04	4.42	4.80
39	1.78	2.17	2.56	2.95	3.34	3.73	4.12	4.51	4.90
40	1.80	2.20	2.60	3.00	3.40	3.80	4.20	4.60	5.00

¶691.03

Simple Interest — Growth of $1.00

Period	Interest Rate									
	11%	**12%**	**13%**	**14%**	**15%**	**16%**	**17%**	**18%**	**19%**	**20%**
0	1.00	1.00	1.00	1.00	1.00	1.00	1.00	1.00	1.00	1.00
1	1.11	1.12	1.13	1.14	1.15	1.16	1.17	1.18	1.19	1.20
2	1.22	1.24	1.26	1.28	1.30	1.32	1.34	1.36	1.38	1.40
3	1.33	1.36	1.39	1.42	1.45	1.48	1.51	1.54	1.57	1.60
4	1.44	1.48	1.52	1.56	1.60	1.64	1.68	1.72	1.76	1.80
5	1.55	1.60	1.65	1.70	1.75	1.80	1.85	1.90	1.95	2.00
6	1.66	1.72	1.78	1.84	1.90	1.96	2.02	2.08	2.14	2.20
7	1.77	1.84	1.91	1.98	2.05	2.12	2.19	2.26	2.33	2.40
8	1.88	1.96	2.04	2.12	2.20	2.28	2.36	2.44	2.52	2.60
9	1.99	2.08	2.17	2.26	2.35	2.44	2.53	2.62	2.71	2.80
10	2.10	2.20	2.30	2.40	2.50	2.60	2.70	2.80	2.90	3.00
11	2.21	2.32	2.43	2.54	2.65	2.76	2.87	2.98	3.09	3.20
12	2.32	2.44	2.56	2.68	2.80	2.92	3.04	3.16	3.28	3.40
13	2.43	2.56	2.69	2.82	2.95	3.08	3.21	3.34	3.47	3.60
14	2.54	2.68	2.82	2.96	3.10	3.24	3.38	3.52	3.66	3.80
15	2.65	2.80	2.95	3.10	3.25	3.40	3.55	3.70	3.85	4.00
16	2.76	2.92	3.08	3.24	3.40	3.56	3.72	3.88	4.04	4.20
17	2.87	3.04	3.21	3.38	3.55	3.72	3.89	4.06	4.23	4.40
18	2.98	3.16	3.34	3.52	3.70	3.88	4.06	4.24	4.42	4.60
19	3.09	3.28	3.47	3.66	3.85	4.04	4.23	4.42	4.61	4.80
20	3.20	3.40	3.60	3.80	4.00	4.20	4.40	4.60	4.80	5.00
21	3.31	3.52	3.73	3.94	4.15	4.36	4.57	4.78	4.99	5.20
22	3.42	3.64	3.86	4.08	4.30	4.52	4.74	4.96	5.18	5.40
23	3.53	3.76	3.99	4.22	4.45	4.68	4.91	5.14	5.37	5.60
24	3.64	3.88	4.12	4.36	4.60	4.84	5.08	5.32	5.56	5.80
25	3.75	4.00	4.25	4.50	4.75	5.00	5.25	5.50	5.75	6.00
26	3.86	4.12	4.38	4.64	4.90	5.16	5.42	5.68	5.94	6.20
27	3.97	4.24	4.51	4.78	5.05	5.32	5.59	5.86	6.13	6.40
28	4.08	4.36	4.64	4.92	5.20	5.48	5.76	6.04	6.32	6.60
29	4.19	4.48	4.77	5.06	5.35	5.64	5.93	6.22	6.51	6.80
30	4.30	4.60	4.90	5.20	5.50	5.80	6.10	6.40	6.70	7.00
31	4.41	4.72	5.03	5.34	5.65	5.96	6.27	6.58	6.89	7.20
32	4.52	4.84	5.16	5.48	5.80	6.12	6.44	6.76	7.08	7.40
33	4.63	4.96	5.29	5.62	5.95	6.28	6.61	6.94	7.27	7.60
34	4.74	5.08	5.42	5.76	6.10	6.44	6.78	7.12	7.46	7.80
35	4.85	5.20	5.55	5.90	6.25	6.60	6.95	7.30	7.65	8.00
36	4.96	5.32	5.68	6.04	6.40	6.76	7.12	7.48	7.84	8.20
37	5.07	5.44	5.81	6.18	6.55	6.92	7.29	7.66	8.03	8.40
38	5.18	5.56	5.94	6.32	6.70	7.08	7.46	7.84	8.22	8.60
39	5.29	5.68	6.07	6.46	6.85	7.24	7.63	8.02	8.41	8.80
40	5.40	5.80	6.20	6.60	7.00	7.40	7.80	8.20	8.60	9.00

.05 Effective Annual Rates for Different Periods of Compounding
Effective Annual Rates for Different Periods of Compounding

Nominal Rate	Period of Compounding				
	Daily	Weekly	Monthly	Quarterly	Semi-Annual
2%	2.0200781%	2.0197417%	2.0184356%	2.0150501%	2.0100000%
3%	3.0453264%	3.0445620%	3.0415957%	3.0339191%	3.0225000%
4%	4.0808493%	4.0794770%	4.0741543%	4.0604010%	4.0400000%
5%	5.1267496%	5.1245842%	5.1161898%	5.0945337%	5.0625000%
6%	6.1831311%	6.1799820%	6.1677812%	6.1363551%	6.0900000%
7%	7.2500983%	7.2457696%	7.2290081%	7.1859031%	7.1225000%
8%	8.3277572%	8.3220474%	8.2999507%	8.2432160%	8.1600000%
9%	9.4162145%	9.4089166%	9.3806898%	9.3083319%	9.2025000%
10%	10.5155782%	10.5064793%	10.4713067%	10.3812891%	10.2500000%
11%	11.6259572%	11.6148386%	11.5718836%	11.4621259%	11.3025000%
12%	12.7474616%	12.7340987%	12.6825030%	12.5508810%	12.3600000%
13%	13.8802025%	13.8643647%	13.8032482%	13.6475928%	13.4225000%
14%	15.0242923%	15.0057425%	14.9342029%	14.7523001%	14.4900000%
15%	16.1798443%	16.1583394%	16.0754518%	15.8650415%	15.5625000%
16%	17.3469730%	17.3222633%	17.2270798%	16.9858560%	16.6400000%
17%	18.5257942%	18.4976235%	18.3891728%	18.1147825%	17.7225000%
18%	19.7164245%	19.6845300%	19.5618171%	19.2518601%	18.8100000%
19%	20.9189820%	20.8830941%	20.7450998%	20.3971278%	19.9025000%
20%	22.1335858%	22.0934279%	21.9391085%	21.5506250%	21.0000000%

.07 Present Value of $1 Received at End of Period

Present Value of $1 Received at End of Period

Period	Interest Rate			
	2%	3%	4%	5%
0	1.0000000	1.0000000	1.0000000	1.0000000
1	0.9803922	0.9708738	0.9615385	0.9523810
2	0.9611688	0.9425959	0.9245562	0.9070295
3	0.9423223	0.9151417	0.8889964	0.8638376
4	0.9238454	0.8884870	0.8548042	0.8227025
5	0.9057308	0.8626088	0.8219271	0.7835262
6	0.8879714	0.8374843	0.7903145	0.7462154
7	0.8705602	0.8130915	0.7599178	0.7106813
8	0.8534904	0.7894092	0.7306902	0.6768394
9	0.8367553	0.7664167	0.7025867	0.6446089
10	0.8203483	0.7440939	0.6755642	0.6139133
11	0.8042630	0.7224213	0.6495809	0.5846793
12	0.7884932	0.7013799	0.6245970	0.5568374
13	0.7730325	0.6809513	0.6005741	0.5303214
14	0.7578750	0.6611178	0.5774751	0.5050680
15	0.7430147	0.6418619	0.5552645	0.4810171
16	0.7284458	0.6231669	0.5339082	0.4581115
17	0.7141626	0.6050164	0.5133732	0.4362967
18	0.7001594	0.5873946	0.4936281	0.4155207
19	0.6864308	0.5702860	0.4746424	0.3957340
20	0.6729713	0.5536758	0.4563869	0.3768895
21	0.6597758	0.5375493	0.4388336	0.3589424
22	0.6468390	0.5218925	0.4219554	0.3418499
23	0.6341559	0.5066917	0.4057263	0.3255713
24	0.6217215	0.4919337	0.3901215	0.3100679
25	0.6095309	0.4776056	0.3751168	0.2953028
26	0.5975793	0.4636947	0.3606892	0.2812407
27	0.5858620	0.4501891	0.3468166	0.2678483
28	0.5743746	0.4370768	0.3334775	0.2550936
29	0.5631123	0.4243464	0.3206514	0.2429463
30	0.5520709	0.4119868	0.3083187	0.2313774
31	0.5412460	0.3999871	0.2964603	0.2203595
32	0.5306333	0.3883370	0.2850579	0.2098662
33	0.5202287	0.3770262	0.2740942	0.1998725
34	0.5100282	0.3660449	0.2635521	0.1903548
35	0.5000276	0.3553834	0.2534155	0.1812903
36	0.4902232	0.3450324	0.2436687	0.1726574
37	0.4806109	0.3349829	0.2342968	0.1644356
38	0.4711872	0.3252262	0.2252854	0.1566054
39	0.4619482	0.3157535	0.2166206	0.1491480
40	0.4528904	0.3065568	0.2082890	0.1420457

Present Value of $1 Received at End of Period

Period			Interest Rate		
	6%	7%	8%	9%	10%
0	1.0000000	1.0000000	1.0000000	1.0000000	1.0000000
1	0.9433962	0.9345794	0.9259259	0.9174312	0.9090909
2	0.8899964	0.8734387	0.8573388	0.8416800	0.8264463
3	0.8396193	0.8162979	0.7938322	0.7721835	0.7513148
4	0.7920937	0.7628952	0.7350299	0.7084252	0.6830135
5	0.7472582	0.7129862	0.6805832	0.6499314	0.6209213
6	0.7049605	0.6663422	0.6301696	0.5962673	0.5644739
7	0.6650571	0.6227497	0.5834904	0.5470342	0.5131581
8	0.6274124	0.5820091	0.5402689	0.5018663	0.4665074
9	0.5918985	0.5439337	0.5002490	0.4604278	0.4240976
10	0.5583948	0.5083493	0.4631935	0.4224108	0.3855433
11	0.5267875	0.4750928	0.4288829	0.3875329	0.3504939
12	0.4969694	0.4440120	0.3971138	0.3555347	0.3186308
13	0.4688390	0.4149644	0.3676979	0.3261786	0.2896644
14	0.4423010	0.3878172	0.3404610	0.2992465	0.2633313
15	0.4172651	0.3624460	0.3152417	0.2745380	0.2393920
16	0.3936463	0.3387346	0.2918905	0.2518698	0.2176291
17	0.3713644	0.3165744	0.2702690	0.2310732	0.1978447
18	0.3503438	0.2958639	0.2502490	0.2119937	0.1798588
19	0.3305130	0.2765083	0.2317121	0.1944897	0.1635080
20	0.3118047	0.2584190	0.2145482	0.1784309	0.1486436
21	0.2941554	0.2415131	0.1986557	0.1636981	0.1351306
22	0.2775051	0.2257132	0.1839405	0.1501817	0.1228460
23	0.2617973	0.2109469	0.1703153	0.1377814	0.1116782
24	0.2469785	0.1971466	0.1576993	0.1264049	0.1015256
25	0.2329986	0.1842492	0.1460179	0.1159678	0.0922960
26	0.2198100	0.1721955	0.1352018	0.1063925	0.0839055
27	0.2073680	0.1609304	0.1251868	0.0976078	0.0762777
28	0.1956301	0.1504022	0.1159137	0.0895484	0.0693433
29	0.1845567	0.1405628	0.1073275	0.0821545	0.0630394
30	0.1741101	0.1313671	0.0993773	0.0753711	0.0573086
31	0.1642548	0.1227730	0.0920160	0.0691478	0.0520987
32	0.1549574	0.1147411	0.0852000	0.0634384	0.0473624
33	0.1461862	0.1072347	0.0788889	0.0582003	0.0430568
34	0.1379115	0.1002193	0.0730453	0.0533948	0.0391425
35	0.1301052	0.0936629	0.0676345	0.0489861	0.0355841
36	0.1227408	0.0875355	0.0626246	0.0449413	0.0323492
37	0.1157932	0.0818088	0.0579857	0.0412306	0.0294083
38	0.1092389	0.0764569	0.0536905	0.0378262	0.0267349
39	0.1030555	0.0714550	0.0497134	0.0347030	0.0243044
40	0.0972222	0.0667804	0.0460309	0.0318376	0.0220949

Present Value of $1 Received at End of Period

Period	Interest Rate				
	11%	**12%**	**13%**	**14%**	**15%**
0	1.0000000	1.0000000	1.0000000	1.0000000	1.0000000
1	0.9009009	0.8928571	0.8849558	0.8771930	0.8695652
2	0.8116224	0.7971939	0.7831467	0.7694675	0.7561437
3	0.7311914	0.7117802	0.6930502	0.6749715	0.6575162
4	0.6587310	0.6355181	0.6133187	0.5920803	0.5717532
5	0.5934513	0.5674269	0.5427599	0.5193687	0.4971767
6	0.5346408	0.5066311	0.4803185	0.4555865	0.4323276
7	0.4816584	0.4523492	0.4250606	0.3996373	0.3759370
8	0.4339265	0.4038832	0.3761599	0.3505591	0.3269018
9	0.3909248	0.3606100	0.3328848	0.3075079	0.2842624
10	0.3521845	0.3219732	0.2945883	0.2697438	0.2471847
11	0.3172833	0.2874761	0.2606977	0.2366174	0.2149432
12	0.2858408	0.2566751	0.2307059	0.2075591	0.1869072
13	0.2575143	0.2291742	0.2041645	0.1820694	0.1625280
14	0.2319948	0.2046198	0.1806766	0.1597100	0.1413287
15	0.2090043	0.1826963	0.1598908	0.1400965	0.1228945
16	0.1882922	0.1631217	0.1414962	0.1228917	0.1068648
17	0.1696326	0.1456443	0.1252179	0.1077997	0.0929259
18	0.1528222	0.1300396	0.1108123	0.0945611	0.0808051
19	0.1376776	0.1161068	0.0980640	0.0829484	0.0702653
20	0.1240339	0.1036668	0.0867823	0.0727617	0.0611003
21	0.1117423	0.0925596	0.0767985	0.0638261	0.0531307
22	0.1006687	0.0826425	0.0679633	0.0559878	0.0462006
23	0.0906925	0.0737880	0.0601445	0.0491121	0.0401744
24	0.0817050	0.0658821	0.0532252	0.0430808	0.0349343
25	0.0736081	0.0588233	0.0471020	0.0377902	0.0303776
26	0.0663136	0.0525208	0.0416831	0.0331493	0.0264153
27	0.0597420	0.0468936	0.0368877	0.0290783	0.0229699
28	0.0538216	0.0418693	0.0326440	0.0255073	0.0199738
29	0.0484879	0.0373833	0.0288885	0.0223748	0.0173685
30	0.0436828	0.0333779	0.0255651	0.0196270	0.0151031
31	0.0393539	0.0298017	0.0226239	0.0172167	0.0131331
32	0.0354540	0.0266087	0.0200212	0.0151024	0.0114201
33	0.0319405	0.0237577	0.0177179	0.0132477	0.0099305
34	0.0287752	0.0212123	0.0156795	0.0116208	0.0086352
35	0.0259236	0.0189395	0.0138757	0.0101937	0.0075089
36	0.0233546	0.0169103	0.0122794	0.0089418	0.0065295
37	0.0210402	0.0150985	0.0108667	0.0078437	0.0056778
38	0.0189551	0.0134808	0.0096165	0.0068804	0.0049372
39	0.0170767	0.0120364	0.0085102	0.0060355	0.0042932
40	0.0153844	0.0107468	0.0075312	0.0052943	0.0037332

Present Value of $1 Received at End of Period

Period	Interest Rate				
	16%	**17%**	**18%**	**19%**	**20%**
0	1.0000000	1.0000000	1.0000000	1.0000000	1.0000000
1	0.8620690	0.8547009	0.8474576	0.8403361	0.8333333
2	0.7431629	0.7305136	0.7181844	0.7061648	0.6944444
3	0.6406577	0.6243706	0.6086309	0.5934158	0.5787037
4	0.5522911	0.5336500	0.5157889	0.4986688	0.4822531
5	0.4761130	0.4561112	0.4371092	0.4190494	0.4018776
6	0.4104423	0.3898386	0.3704315	0.3521423	0.3348980
7	0.3538295	0.3331954	0.3139250	0.2959179	0.2790816
8	0.3050255	0.2847824	0.2660382	0.2486705	0.2325680
9	0.2629530	0.2434037	0.2254561	0.2089668	0.1938067
10	0.2266836	0.2080374	0.1910645	0.1756024	0.1615056
11	0.1954169	0.1778097	0.1619190	0.1475650	0.1345880
12	0.1684628	0.1519741	0.1372195	0.1240042	0.1121567
13	0.1452266	0.1298924	0.1162877	0.1042052	0.0934639
14	0.1251953	0.1110192	0.0985489	0.0875674	0.0778866
15	0.1079270	0.0948882	0.0835160	0.0735861	0.0649055
16	0.0930405	0.0811010	0.0707763	0.0618370	0.0540879
17	0.0802074	0.0693171	0.0599799	0.0519639	0.0450732
18	0.0691443	0.0592454	0.0508304	0.0436671	0.0375610
19	0.0596071	0.0506371	0.0430766	0.0366951	0.0313009
20	0.0513855	0.0432796	0.0365056	0.0308362	0.0260841
21	0.0442978	0.0369911	0.0309370	0.0259128	0.0217367
22	0.0381878	0.0316163	0.0262178	0.0217754	0.0181139
23	0.0329205	0.0270225	0.0222185	0.0182987	0.0150949
24	0.0283797	0.0230961	0.0188292	0.0153770	0.0125791
25	0.0244653	0.0197403	0.0159569	0.0129219	0.0104826
26	0.0210908	0.0168720	0.0135228	0.0108587	0.0087355
27	0.0181817	0.0144205	0.0114600	0.0091250	0.0072796
28	0.0156739	0.0123253	0.0097119	0.0076681	0.0060663
29	0.0135120	0.0105344	0.0082304	0.0064437	0.0050553
30	0.0116482	0.0090038	0.0069749	0.0054149	0.0042127
31	0.0100416	0.0076955	0.0059110	0.0045503	0.0035106
32	0.0086565	0.0065774	0.0050093	0.0038238	0.0029255
33	0.0074625	0.0056217	0.0042452	0.0032133	0.0024379
34	0.0064332	0.0048049	0.0035976	0.0027002	0.0020316
35	0.0055459	0.0041067	0.0030488	0.0022691	0.0016930
36	0.0047809	0.0035100	0.0025837	0.0019068	0.0014108
37	0.0041215	0.0030000	0.0021896	0.0016024	0.0011757
38	0.0035530	0.0025641	0.0018556	0.0013465	0.0009797
39	0.0030629	0.0021916	0.0015725	0.0011315	0.0008165
40	0.0026405	0.0018731	0.0013327	0.0009509	0.0006804

.09 Future Value of $1 at End of Period
Future Value of $1 at End of Period

Period	Interest Rate			
	2%	**3%**	**4%**	**5%**
0	1.0000000	1.0000000	1.0000000	1.0000000
1	1.0200000	1.0300000	1.0400000	1.0500000
2	1.0404000	1.0609000	1.0816000	1.1025000
3	1.0612080	1.0927270	1.1248640	1.1576250
4	1.0824322	1.1255088	1.1698586	1.2155063
5	1.1040808	1.1592741	1.2166529	1.2762816
6	1.1261624	1.1940523	1.2653190	1.3400956
7	1.1486857	1.2298739	1.3159318	1.4071004
8	1.1716594	1.2667701	1.3685691	1.4774554
9	1.1950926	1.3047732	1.4233118	1.5513282
10	1.2189944	1.3439164	1.4802443	1.6288946
11	1.2433743	1.3842339	1.5394541	1.7103394
12	1.2682418	1.4257609	1.6010322	1.7958563
13	1.2936066	1.4685337	1.6650735	1.8856491
14	1.3194788	1.5125897	1.7316764	1.9799316
15	1.3458683	1.5579674	1.8009435	2.0789282
16	1.3727857	1.6047064	1.8729812	2.1828746
17	1.4002414	1.6528476	1.9479005	2.2920183
18	1.4282462	1.7024331	2.0258165	2.4066192
19	1.4568112	1.7535061	2.1068492	2.5269502
20	1.4859474	1.8061112	2.1911231	2.6532977
21	1.5156663	1.8602946	2.2787681	2.7859626
22	1.5459797	1.9161034	2.3699188	2.9252607
23	1.5768993	1.9735865	2.4647155	3.0715238
24	1.6084372	2.0327941	2.5633042	3.2250999
25	1.6406060	2.0937779	2.6658363	3.3863549
26	1.6734181	2.1565913	2.7724698	3.5556727
27	1.7068865	2.2212890	2.8833686	3.7334563
28	1.7410242	2.2879277	2.9987033	3.9201291
29	1.7758447	2.3565655	3.1186515	4.1161356
30	1.8113616	2.4272625	3.2433975	4.3219424
31	1.8475888	2.5000803	3.3731334	4.5380395
32	1.8845406	2.5750828	3.5080587	4.7649415
33	1.9222314	2.6523352	3.6483811	5.0031885
34	1.9606760	2.7319053	3.7943163	5.2533480
35	1.9998896	2.8138625	3.9460890	5.5160154
36	2.0398873	2.8982783	4.1039326	5.7918161
37	2.0806851	2.9852267	4.2680899	6.0814069
38	2.1222988	3.0747835	4.4388135	6.3854773
39	2.1647448	3.1670270	4.6163660	6.7047512
40	2.2080397	3.2620378	4.8010206	7.0399887

Future Value of $1 at End of Period

Period	Interest Rate				
	6%	**7%**	**8%**	**9%**	**10%**
0	1.0000000	1.0000000	1.0000000	1.0000000	1.0000000
1	1.0600000	1.0700000	1.0800000	1.0900000	1.1000000
2	1.1236000	1.1449000	1.1664000	1.1881000	1.2100000
3	1.1910160	1.2250430	1.2597120	1.2950290	1.3310000
4	1.2624770	1.3107960	1.3604890	1.4115816	1.4641000
5	1.3382256	1.4025517	1.4693281	1.5386240	1.6105100
6	1.4185191	1.5007304	1.5868743	1.6771001	1.7715610
7	1.5036303	1.6057815	1.7138243	1.8280391	1.9487171
8	1.5938481	1.7181862	1.8509302	1.9925626	2.1435888
9	1.6894790	1.8384592	1.9990046	2.1718933	2.3579477
10	1.7908477	1.9671514	2.1589250	2.3673637	2.5937425
11	1.8982986	2.1048520	2.3316390	2.5804264	2.8531167
12	2.0121965	2.2521916	2.5181701	2.8126648	3.1384284
13	2.1329283	2.4098450	2.7196237	3.0658046	3.4522712
14	2.2609040	2.5785342	2.9371936	3.3417270	3.7974983
15	2.3965582	2.7590315	3.1721691	3.6424825	4.1772482
16	2.5403517	2.9521637	3.4259426	3.9703059	4.5949730
17	2.6927728	3.1588152	3.7000181	4.3276334	5.0544703
18	2.8543392	3.3799323	3.9960195	4.7171204	5.5599173
19	3.0255995	3.6165275	4.3157011	5.1416613	6.1159090
20	3.2071355	3.8696845	4.6609571	5.6044108	6.7274999
21	3.3995636	4.1405624	5.0338337	6.1088077	7.4002499
22	3.6035374	4.4304017	5.4365404	6.6586004	8.1402749
23	3.8197497	4.7405299	5.8714636	7.2578745	8.9543024
24	4.0489346	5.0723670	6.3411807	7.9110832	9.8497327
25	4.2918707	5.4274326	6.8484752	8.6230807	10.8347059
26	4.5493830	5.8073529	7.3963532	9.3991579	11.9181765
27	4.8223459	6.2138676	7.9880615	10.2450821	13.1099942
28	5.1116867	6.6488384	8.6271064	11.1671395	14.4209936
29	5.4183879	7.1142570	9.3172749	12.1721821	15.8630930
30	5.7434912	7.6122550	10.0626569	13.2676785	17.4494023
31	6.0881006	8.1451129	10.8676694	14.4617695	19.1943425
32	6.4533867	8.7152708	11.7370830	15.7633288	21.1137767
33	6.8405899	9.3253398	12.6760496	17.1820284	23.2251544
34	7.2510253	9.9781135	13.6901336	18.7284109	25.5476699
35	7.6860868	10.6765815	14.7853443	20.4139679	28.1024368
36	8.1472520	11.4239422	15.9681718	22.2512250	30.9126805
37	8.6360871	12.2236181	17.2456256	24.2538353	34.0039486
38	9.1542523	13.0792714	18.6252756	26.4366805	37.4043434
39	9.7035075	13.9948204	20.1152977	28.8159817	41.1447778
40	10.2857179	14.9744578	21.7245215	31.4094201	45.2592556

Future Value of $1 at End of Period

Period			Interest Rate		
	11%	**12%**	**13%**	**14%**	**15%**
0	1.0000000	1.0000000	1.0000000	1.0000000	1.0000000
1	1.1100000	1.1200000	1.1300000	1.1400000	1.1500000
2	1.2321000	1.2544000	1.2769000	1.2996000	1.3225000
3	1.3676310	1.4049280	1.4428970	1.4815440	1.5208750
4	1.5180704	1.5735194	1.6304736	1.6889602	1.7490063
5	1.6850582	1.7623417	1.8424352	1.9254146	2.0113572
6	1.8704146	1.9738227	2.0819518	2.1949726	2.3130608
7	2.0761602	2.2106814	2.3526055	2.5022688	2.6600199
8	2.3045378	2.4759632	2.6584442	2.8525864	3.0590229
9	2.5580369	2.7730788	3.0040419	3.2519485	3.5178763
10	2.8394210	3.1058482	3.3945674	3.7072213	4.0455577
11	3.1517573	3.4785500	3.8358612	4.2262323	4.6523914
12	3.4984506	3.8959760	4.3345231	4.8179048	5.3502501
13	3.8832802	4.3634931	4.8980111	5.4924115	6.1527876
14	4.3104410	4.8871123	5.5347525	6.2613491	7.0757058
15	4.7845895	5.4735658	6.2542704	7.1379380	8.1370616
16	5.3108943	6.1303937	7.0673255	8.1372493	9.3576209
17	5.8950927	6.8660409	7.9860778	9.2764642	10.7612640
18	6.5435529	7.6899658	9.0242680	10.5751692	12.3754536
19	7.2633437	8.6127617	10.1974228	12.0556929	14.2317716
20	8.0623115	9.6462931	11.5230878	13.7434899	16.3665374
21	8.9491658	10.8038483	13.0210892	15.6675785	18.8215180
22	9.9335740	12.1003101	14.7138308	17.8610394	21.6447457
23	11.0262672	13.5523473	16.6266288	20.3615850	24.8914576
24	12.2391566	15.1786289	18.7880905	23.2122069	28.6251762
25	13.5854638	17.0000644	21.2305423	26.4619158	32.9189526
26	15.0798648	19.0400721	23.9905128	30.1665840	37.8567955
27	16.7386500	21.3248808	27.1092794	34.3899058	43.5353148
28	18.5799014	23.8838665	30.6334858	39.2044926	50.0656121
29	20.6236906	26.7499305	34.6158389	44.6931216	57.5754539
30	22.8922966	29.9599221	39.1158980	50.9501586	66.2117720
31	25.4104492	33.5551128	44.2009647	58.0831808	76.1435378
32	28.2055986	37.5817263	49.9470901	66.2148261	87.5650684
33	31.3082145	42.0915335	56.4402118	75.4849017	100.6998287
34	34.7521180	47.1425175	63.7774394	86.0527880	115.8048030
35	38.5748510	52.7996196	72.0685065	98.1001783	133.1755234
36	42.8180846	59.1355739	81.4374123	111.8342033	153.1518519
37	47.5280740	66.2318428	92.0242759	127.4909917	176.1246297
38	52.7561621	74.1796639	103.9874318	145.3397306	202.5433242
39	58.5593399	83.0812236	117.5057979	165.6872929	232.9248228
40	65.0008673	93.0509704	132.7815516	188.8835139	267.8635462

Future Value of $1 at End of Period

Period	Interest Rate				
	16%	**17%**	**18%**	**19%**	**20%**
0	1.0000000	1.0000000	1.0000000	1.0000000	1.0000000
1	1.1600000	1.1700000	1.1800000	1.1900000	1.2000000
2	1.3456000	1.3689000	1.3924000	1.4161000	1.4400000
3	1.5608960	1.6016130	1.6430320	1.6851590	1.7280000
4	1.8106394	1.8738872	1.9387778	2.0053392	2.0736000
5	2.1003417	2.1924480	2.2877578	2.3863537	2.4883200
6	2.4363963	2.5651642	2.6995542	2.8397609	2.9859840
7	2.8262197	3.0012421	3.1854739	3.3793154	3.5831808
8	3.2784149	3.5114533	3.7588592	4.0213853	4.2998170
9	3.8029613	4.1084003	4.4354539	4.7854486	5.1597804
10	4.4114351	4.8068284	5.2338356	5.6946838	6.1917364
11	5.1172647	5.6239892	6.1759260	6.7766737	7.4300837
12	5.9360270	6.5800674	7.2875926	8.0642417	8.9161004
13	6.8857914	7.6986788	8.5993593	9.5964476	10.6993205
14	7.9875180	9.0074542	10.1472440	11.4197727	12.8391846
15	9.2655209	10.5387215	11.9737479	13.5895295	15.4070216
16	10.7480042	12.3303041	14.1290225	16.1715401	18.4884259
17	12.4676849	14.4264558	16.6722466	19.2441327	22.1861111
18	14.4625145	16.8789533	19.6732509	22.9005180	26.6233333
19	16.7765168	19.7483754	23.2144361	27.2516164	31.9479999
20	19.4607595	23.1055992	27.3930346	32.4294235	38.3375999
21	22.5744810	27.0335510	32.3237808	38.5910139	46.0051199
22	26.1863979	31.6292547	38.1420614	45.9233066	55.2061439
23	30.3762216	37.0062280	45.0076324	54.6487348	66.2473727
24	35.2364170	43.2972868	53.1090063	65.0319944	79.4968472
25	40.8742438	50.6578255	62.6686274	77.3880734	95.3962166
26	47.4141228	59.2696558	73.9489803	92.0918073	114.4754600
27	55.0003824	69.3454973	87.2597968	109.5892507	137.3705520
28	63.8004436	81.1342319	102.9665602	130.4112084	164.8446624
29	74.0085146	94.9270513	121.5005410	155.1893379	197.8135948
30	85.8498769	111.0646500	143.3706384	184.6753122	237.3763138
31	99.5858572	129.9456405	169.1773534	219.7636215	284.8515766
32	115.5195944	152.0363994	199.6292770	261.5187095	341.8218919
33	134.0027295	177.8825873	235.5625468	311.2072644	410.1862702
34	155.4431662	208.1226271	277.9638052	370.3366446	492.2235243
35	180.3140728	243.5034738	327.9972902	440.7006071	590.6682292
36	209.1643244	284.8990643	387.0368024	524.4337224	708.8018750
37	242.6306163	333.3319052	456.7034269	624.0761296	850.5622500
38	281.4515149	389.9983291	538.9100437	742.6505943	1,020.6747000
39	326.4837573	456.2980451	635.9138515	883.7542072	1,224.8096400
40	378.7211585	533.8687127	750.3783448	1,051.6675066	1,469.7715680

.11 Present Value of Ordinary Annuity of $1 per Period

Present Value of Ordinary Annuity of $1 per Period

Period		Interest Rate		
	2%	3%	4%	5%
0	0.00000000	0.00000000	0.00000000	0.00000000
1	0.98039216	0.97087379	0.96153846	0.95238095
2	1.94156094	1.91346970	1.88609467	1.85941043
3	2.88388327	2.82861135	2.77509103	2.72324803
4	3.80772870	3.71709840	3.62989522	3.54595050
5	4.71345951	4.57970719	4.45182233	4.32947667
6	5.60143089	5.41719144	5.24213686	5.07569207
7	6.47199107	6.23028296	6.00205467	5.78637340
8	7.32548144	7.01969219	6.73274487	6.46321276
9	8.16223671	7.78610892	7.43533161	7.10782168
10	8.98258501	8.53020284	8.11089578	7.72173493
11	9.78684805	9.25262411	8.76047671	8.30641422
12	10.57534122	9.95400399	9.38507376	8.86325164
13	11.34837375	10.63495533	9.98564785	9.39357299
14	12.10624877	11.29607314	10.56312293	9.89864094
15	12.84926350	11.93793509	11.11838743	10.37965804
16	13.57770931	12.56110203	11.65229561	10.83776956
17	14.29187188	13.16611847	12.16566885	11.27406625
18	14.99203125	13.75351308	12.65929697	11.68958690
19	15.67846201	14.32379911	13.13393940	12.08532086
20	16.35143334	14.87747486	13.59032634	12.46221034
21	17.01120916	15.41502414	14.02915995	12.82115271
22	17.65804820	15.93691664	14.45111533	13.16300258
23	18.29220412	16.44360839	14.85684167	13.48857388
24	18.91392560	16.93554212	15.24696314	13.79864179
25	19.52345647	17.41314769	15.62207994	14.09394457
26	20.12103576	17.87684242	15.98276918	14.37518530
27	20.70689780	18.32703147	16.32958575	14.64303362
28	21.28127236	18.76410823	16.66306322	14.89812726
29	21.84438466	19.18845459	16.98371463	15.14107358
30	22.39645555	19.60044135	17.29203330	15.37245103
31	22.93770152	20.00042849	17.58849356	15.59281050
32	23.46833482	20.38876553	17.87355150	15.80267667
33	23.98856355	20.76579178	18.14764567	16.00254921
34	24.49859172	21.13183668	18.41119776	16.19290401
35	24.99861933	21.48722007	18.66461323	16.37419429
36	25.48884248	21.83225250	18.90828195	16.54685171
37	25.96945341	22.16723544	19.14257880	16.71128734
38	26.44064060	22.49246159	19.36786423	16.86789271
39	26.90258883	22.80821513	19.58448484	17.01704067
40	27.35547924	23.11477197	19.79277388	17.15908635

Present Value of Ordinary Annuity of $1 per Period

Period			Interest Rate		
	6%	7%	8%	9%	10%
0	0.00000000	0.00000000	0.00000000	0.00000000	0.00000000
1	0.94339623	0.93457944	0.92592593	0.91743119	0.90909091
2	1.83339267	1.80801817	1.78326475	1.75911119	1.73553719
3	2.67301195	2.62431604	2.57709699	2.53129467	2.48685199
4	3.46510561	3.38721126	3.31212684	3.23971988	3.16986545
5	4.21236379	4.10019744	3.99271004	3.88965126	3.79078677
6	4.91732433	4.76653966	4.62287966	4.48591859	4.35526070
7	5.58238144	5.38928940	5.20637006	5.03295284	4.86841882
8	6.20979381	5.97129851	5.74663894	5.53481911	5.33492620
9	6.80169227	6.51523225	6.24688791	5.99524689	5.75902382
10	7.36008705	7.02358154	6.71008140	6.41765770	6.14456711
11	7.88687458	7.49867434	7.13896426	6.80519055	6.49506101
12	8.38384394	7.94268630	7.53607802	7.16072528	6.81369182
13	8.85268296	8.35765074	7.90377594	7.48690392	7.10335620
14	9.29498393	8.74546799	8.24423698	7.78615039	7.36668746
15	9.71224899	9.10791401	8.55947869	8.06068843	7.60607951
16	10.10589527	9.44664860	8.85136916	8.31255819	7.82370864
17	10.47725969	9.76322299	9.12163811	8.54363137	8.02155331
18	10.82760348	10.05908691	9.37188714	8.75562511	8.20141210
19	11.15811649	10.33559524	9.60359920	8.95011478	8.36492009
20	11.46992122	10.59401425	9.81814741	9.12854567	8.51356372
21	11.76407662	10.83552733	10.01680316	9.29224373	8.64869429
22	12.04158172	11.06124050	10.20074366	9.44242544	8.77154026
23	12.30337898	11.27218738	10.37105895	9.58020683	8.88321842
24	12.55035753	11.46933400	10.52875828	9.70661177	8.98474402
25	12.78335616	11.65358318	10.67477619	9.82257960	9.07704002
26	13.00316619	11.82577867	10.80997795	9.92897211	9.16094547
27	13.21053414	11.98670904	10.93516477	10.02657992	9.23722316
28	13.40616428	12.13711125	11.05107849	10.11612837	9.30656651
29	13.59072102	12.27767407	11.15840601	10.19828291	9.36960591
30	13.76483115	12.40904118	11.25778334	10.27365404	9.42691447
31	13.92908599	12.53181419	11.34979939	10.34280187	9.47901315
32	14.08404339	12.64655532	11.43499944	10.40624025	9.52637559
33	14.23022961	12.75379002	11.51388837	10.46444060	9.56943236
34	14.36814114	12.85400936	11.58693367	10.51783541	9.60857487
35	14.49824636	12.94767230	11.65456822	10.56682148	9.64415897
36	14.62098713	13.03520776	11.71719279	10.61176282	9.67650816
37	14.73678031	13.11701660	11.77517851	10.65299342	9.70591651
38	14.84601916	13.19347345	11.82886899	10.69081965	9.73265137
39	14.94907468	13.26492846	11.87858240	10.72552261	9.75695579
40	15.04629687	13.33170884	11.92461333	10.75736020	9.77905072

Present Value of Ordinary Annuity of $1 per Period

Period			Interest Rate		
	11%	**12%**	**13%**	**14%**	**15%**
0	0.00000000	0.00000000	0.00000000	0.00000000	0.00000000
1	0.90090090	0.89285714	0.88495575	0.87719298	0.86956522
2	1.71252333	1.69005102	1.66810244	1.64666051	1.62570888
3	2.44371472	2.40183127	2.36115260	2.32163203	2.28322512
4	3.10244569	3.03734935	2.97447133	2.91371230	2.85497836
5	3.69589702	3.60477620	3.51723126	3.43308097	3.35215510
6	4.23053785	4.11140732	3.99754979	3.88866752	3.78448269
7	4.71219626	4.56375654	4.42261043	4.28830484	4.16041973
8	5.14612276	4.96763977	4.79877029	4.63886389	4.48732151
9	5.53704753	5.32824979	5.13165513	4.94637184	4.77158392
10	5.88923201	5.65022303	5.42624348	5.21611565	5.01876863
11	6.20651533	5.93769913	5.68694113	5.45273302	5.23371185
12	6.49235615	6.19437423	5.91764702	5.66029213	5.42061900
13	6.74987040	6.42354842	6.12181152	5.84236151	5.58314696
14	6.98186523	6.62816823	6.30248807	6.00207150	5.72447561
15	7.19086958	6.81086449	6.46237882	6.14216799	5.84737010
16	7.37916178	6.97398615	6.60387506	6.26505964	5.95423487
17	7.54879440	7.11963049	6.72909298	6.37285933	6.04716076
18	7.70161657	7.24967008	6.83990529	6.46742046	6.12796587
19	7.83929421	7.36577686	6.93796928	6.55036883	6.19823119
20	7.96332812	7.46944362	7.02475158	6.62313055	6.25933147
21	8.07507038	7.56200324	7.10155007	6.68695662	6.31246215
22	8.17573908	7.64464575	7.16951334	6.74294441	6.35866274
23	8.26643160	7.71843370	7.22965782	6.79205650	6.39883717
24	8.34813658	7.78431581	7.28288303	6.83513728	6.43377145
25	8.42174466	7.84313911	7.32998498	6.87292744	6.46414909
26	8.48805826	7.89565992	7.37166812	6.90607670	6.49056442
27	8.54780023	7.94255350	7.40855586	6.93515500	6.51353428
28	8.60162183	7.98442277	7.44119988	6.96066228	6.53350807
29	8.65010976	8.02180604	7.47008839	6.98303709	6.55087658
30	8.69379257	8.05518397	7.49565344	7.00266411	6.56597964
31	8.73314646	8.08498569	7.51827738	7.01988080	6.57911273
32	8.76860042	8.11159436	7.53829857	7.03498316	6.59053281
33	8.80054092	8.13535211	7.55601643	7.04823084	6.60046331
34	8.82931614	8.15656438	7.57169596	7.05985161	6.60909853
35	8.85523977	8.17550391	7.58557164	7.07004528	6.61660742
36	8.87859438	8.19241421	7.59785101	7.07898708	6.62313689
37	8.89963458	8.20751269	7.60871771	7.08683078	6.62881468
38	8.91858971	8.22099347	7.61833426	7.09371121	6.63375190
39	8.93566641	8.23302988	7.62684447	7.09974667	6.63804513
40	8.95105082	8.24377668	7.63437564	7.10504094	6.64177837

¶691.11

Present Value of Ordinary Annuity of $1 per Period

Period	Interest Rate				
	16%	17%	18%	19%	20%
0	0.00000000	0.00000000	0.00000000	0.00000000	0.00000000
1	0.86206897	0.85470085	0.84745763	0.84033613	0.83333333
2	1.60523187	1.58521441	1.56564206	1.54650095	1.52777778
3	2.24588954	2.20958496	2.17427293	2.13991677	2.10648148
4	2.79818064	2.74323501	2.69006180	2.63858552	2.58873457
5	3.27429365	3.19934616	3.12717102	3.05763489	2.99061214
6	3.68473591	3.58918475	3.49760256	3.40977722	3.32551012
7	4.03856544	3.92238013	3.81152759	3.70569514	3.60459176
8	4.34359090	4.20716251	4.07756576	3.95436567	3.83715980
9	4.60654388	4.45056624	4.30302183	4.16333249	4.03096650
10	4.83322748	4.65860363	4.49408629	4.33893487	4.19247209
11	5.02864438	4.83641336	4.65600533	4.48649989	4.32706007
12	5.19710722	4.98838748	4.79322486	4.61050411	4.43921673
13	5.34233381	5.11827990	4.90951259	4.71470933	4.53268061
14	5.46752915	5.22929906	5.00806152	4.80227675	4.61056717
15	5.57545616	5.32418723	5.09157756	4.87586282	4.67547264
16	5.66849669	5.40528823	5.16235386	4.93769985	4.72956054
17	5.74870404	5.47460533	5.22233378	4.98966374	4.77463378
18	5.81784831	5.53385071	5.27316422	5.03333087	4.81219482
19	5.87745544	5.58448778	5.31624087	5.07002594	4.84349568
20	5.92884090	5.62776734	5.35274650	5.10086214	4.86957973
21	5.97313871	5.66475841	5.38368347	5.12677490	4.89131644
22	6.01132647	5.69637471	5.40990125	5.14855034	4.90943037
23	6.04424696	5.72339719	5.43211970	5.16684902	4.92452531
24	6.07262669	5.74649332	5.45094890	5.18222607	4.93710442
25	6.09709197	5.76623361	5.46690585	5.19514796	4.94758702
26	6.11818273	5.78310565	5.48042868	5.20600669	4.95632252
27	6.13636443	5.79752619	5.49188872	5.21513167	4.96360210
28	6.15203830	5.80985145	5.50160061	5.22279972	4.96966841
29	6.16555026	5.82038585	5.50983102	5.22924347	4.97472368
30	6.17719850	5.82938962	5.51680595	5.23465837	4.97893640
31	6.18724008	5.83708514	5.52271691	5.23920872	4.98244700
32	6.19589662	5.84366252	5.52772619	5.24303254	4.98537250
33	6.20335916	5.84928420	5.53197135	5.24624583	4.98781042
34	6.20979238	5.85408906	5.53556894	5.24894607	4.98984201
35	6.21533826	5.85819578	5.53861775	5.25121519	4.99153501
36	6.22011919	5.86170579	5.54120148	5.25312201	4.99294584
37	6.22424068	5.86470581	5.54339108	5.25472438	4.99412154
38	6.22779369	5.86726992	5.54524668	5.25607090	4.99510128
39	6.23085663	5.86946147	5.54681922	5.25720244	4.99591773
40	6.23349709	5.87133459	5.54815188	5.25815331	4.99659811

.13 Present Value of Ordinary Annuity of $1 per Month Based on Monthly Compounding of Nominal Annual Rates

Present Value of Ordinary Annuity of $1 per Month Based on Monthly Compounding of Nominal Annual Rates

Period	Nominal Annual Rate			
	2%	3%	4%	5%
0	0.00000000	0.00000000	0.00000000	0.00000000
1	0.99833611	0.99750623	0.99667774	0.99585062
2	1.99501109	1.99252492	1.99004426	1.98756908
3	2.99002771	2.98506227	2.98011056	2.97517253
4	3.98338873	3.97512446	3.96688760	3.95867804
5	4.97509690	4.96271766	4.95038631	4.93810261
6	5.96515497	5.94784804	5.93061759	5.91346318
7	6.95356570	6.93052174	6.90759228	6.88477661
8	7.94033181	7.91074487	7.88132121	7.85205970
9	8.92545605	8.88852357	8.85181516	8.81532916
10	9.90894115	9.86386391	9.81908487	9.77460165
11	10.89078983	10.83677198	10.78314107	10.72989376
12	11.87100483	11.80725384	11.74399442	11.68122200
13	12.84958884	12.77531555	12.70165557	12.62860283
14	13.82654460	13.74096314	13.65613512	13.57205261
15	14.80187481	14.70420264	14.60744364	14.51158766
16	15.77558217	15.66504004	15.55559167	15.44722422
17	16.74766939	16.62348133	16.50058970	16.37897848
18	17.71813916	17.57953250	17.44244821	17.30686654
19	18.68699417	18.53319950	18.38117762	18.23090443
20	19.65423711	19.48448828	19.31678832	19.15110815
21	20.61987066	20.43340477	20.24929069	20.06749359
22	21.58389749	21.37995488	21.17869504	20.98007661
23	22.54632029	22.32414452	22.10501167	21.88887297
24	23.50714172	23.26597957	23.02825083	22.79389839
25	24.46636445	24.20546591	23.94842275	23.69516853
26	25.42399113	25.14260939	24.86553763	24.59269895
27	26.38002442	26.07741585	25.77960561	25.48650517
28	27.33446698	27.00989112	26.69063682	26.37660266
29	28.28732144	27.94004102	27.59864135	27.26300680
30	29.23859046	28.86787134	28.50362925	28.14573291
31	30.18827667	29.79338787	29.40561055	29.02479626
32	31.13638269	30.71659638	30.30459523	29.90021205
33	32.08291118	31.63750262	31.20059325	30.77199540
34	33.02786473	32.55611234	32.09361454	31.64016139
35	33.97124599	33.47243126	32.98366898	32.50472504
36	34.91305756	34.38646510	33.87076642	33.36570128
37	35.85330206	35.29821955	34.75491670	34.22310501
38	36.79198209	36.20770030	35.63612960	35.07695105
39	37.72910025	37.11491302	36.51441488	35.92725416
40	38.66465916	38.01986336	37.38978228	36.77402904
41	39.59866139	38.92255697	38.26224147	37.61729033
42	40.53110954	39.82299947	39.13180213	38.45705261
43	41.46200619	40.72119648	39.99847389	39.29333040
44	42.39135394	41.61715359	40.86226633	40.12613816
45	43.31915535	42.51087640	41.72318903	40.95549028
46	44.24541299	43.40237047	42.58125153	41.78140111
47	45.17012944	44.29164137	43.43646332	42.60388492
48	46.09330726	45.17869463	44.28883387	43.42295594

Present Value of Ordinary Annuity of $1 per Month Based on Monthly Compounding of Nominal Annual Rates

Period	Nominal Annual Rate				
	6%	**7%**	**8%**	**9%**	**10%**
0	0.00000000	0.00000000	0.00000000	0.00000000	0.00000000
1	0.99502488	0.99420050	0.99337748	0.99255583	0.99173554
2	1.98509938	1.98263513	1.98017631	1.97772291	1.97527491
3	2.97024814	2.96533732	2.96044004	2.95555624	2.95068586
4	3.95049566	3.94234034	3.93421196	3.92611041	3.91803557
5	4.92586633	4.91367722	4.90153506	4.88943961	4.87739065
6	5.89638441	5.87938083	5.86245205	5.84559763	5.82881717
7	6.86207404	6.83948384	6.81700535	6.79463785	6.77238066
8	7.82295924	7.79401874	7.76523710	7.73661325	7.70814611
9	8.77906392	8.74301780	8.70718917	8.67157642	8.63617796
10	9.73041186	9.68651314	9.64290315	9.59957958	9.55654013
11	10.67702673	10.62453667	10.57242035	10.52067452	10.46929600
12	11.61893207	11.55712014	11.49578180	11.43491267	11.37450843
13	12.55615131	12.48429509	12.41302828	12.34234508	12.27223976
14	13.48870777	13.40609288	13.32420028	13.24302242	13.16255183
15	14.41662465	14.32254470	14.22933802	14.13699495	14.04550595
16	15.33992502	15.23368156	15.12848148	15.02431261	14.92116292
17	16.25863186	16.13953427	16.02167035	15.90502492	15.78958306
18	17.17276802	17.04013350	16.90894405	16.77918107	16.65082618
19	18.08235624	17.93550969	17.79034177	17.64682984	17.50495158
20	18.98741915	18.82569315	18.66590242	18.50801969	18.35201810
21	19.88797925	19.71071398	19.53566466	19.36279870	19.19208406
22	20.78405896	20.59060213	20.39966688	20.21121459	20.02520734
23	21.67568055	21.46538738	21.25794723	21.05331473	20.85144529
24	22.56286622	22.33509930	22.11054361	21.88914614	21.67085483
25	23.44563803	23.19976732	22.95749365	22.71875547	22.48349240
26	24.32401794	24.05942070	23.79883475	23.54218905	23.28941395
27	25.19802780	24.91408852	24.63460406	24.35949286	24.08867499
28	26.06768936	25.76379968	25.46483847	25.17071251	24.88133057
29	26.93302423	26.60858295	26.28957464	25.97589331	25.66743527
30	27.79405397	27.44846689	27.10884898	26.77508021	26.44704325
31	28.65079997	28.28347993	27.92269766	27.56831783	27.22020818
32	29.50328355	29.11365030	28.73115662	28.35565045	27.98698332
33	30.35152592	29.93900610	29.53426154	29.13712203	28.74742147
34	31.19554818	30.75957524	30.33204789	29.91277621	29.50157501
35	32.03537132	31.57538549	31.12455088	30.68265629	30.24949588
36	32.87101624	32.38646445	31.91180551	31.44680525	30.99123559
37	33.70250372	33.19283955	32.69384653	32.20526576	31.72684521
38	34.52985445	33.99453808	33.47070848	32.95808016	32.45637541
39	35.35308900	34.79158716	34.24242564	33.70529048	33.17987644
40	36.17222786	35.58401374	35.00903209	34.44693844	33.89739813
41	36.98729141	36.37184465	35.77056168	35.18306545	34.60898988
42	37.79829991	37.15510653	36.52704803	35.91371260	35.31470070
43	38.60527354	37.93382588	37.27852453	36.63892070	36.01457921
44	39.40823238	38.70802904	38.02502437	37.35873022	36.70867360
45	40.20719640	39.47774221	38.76658050	38.07318136	37.39703167
46	41.00218547	40.24299143	39.50322566	38.78231401	38.07970083
47	41.79321937	41.00380258	40.23499238	39.48616775	38.75672809
48	42.58031778	41.76020141	40.96191296	40.18478189	39.42816009

¶691.13

Present Value of Ordinary Annuity of $1 per Month Based on Monthly Compounding of Nominal Annual Rates

Period	Nominal Annual Rate				
	11%	**12%**	**13%**	**14%**	**15%**
0	0.00000000	0.00000000	0.00000000	0.00000000	0.00000000
1	0.99091660	0.99009901	0.98928277	0.98846787	0.98765432
2	1.97283230	1.97039506	1.96796317	1.96553661	1.96311538
3	2.94582887	2.94098521	2.93615483	2.93133767	2.92653371
4	3.90998732	3.90196555	3.89397015	3.88600100	3.87805798
5	4.86538793	4.85343124	4.84152034	4.82965502	4.81783504
6	5.81211025	5.79547647	5.77891543	5.76242671	5.74600992
7	6.75023312	6.72819453	6.70626423	6.68444156	6.66272585
8	7.67983463	7.65167775	7.62367443	7.59582362	7.56812429
9	8.60099220	8.56601758	8.53125252	8.49669550	8.46234498
10	9.51378253	9.47130453	9.42910390	9.38717842	9.34552591
11	10.41828162	10.36762825	10.31733279	10.26739218	10.21780337
12	11.31456477	11.25507747	11.19604233	11.13745520	11.07931197
13	12.20270663	12.13374007	12.06533454	11.99748455	11.93018466
14	13.08278113	13.00370304	12.92531035	12.84759593	12.77055275
15	13.95486157	13.86505252	13.77606959	13.68790372	13.60054592
16	14.81902055	14.71787378	14.61771106	14.51852097	14.42029227
17	15.67533002	15.56225127	15.45033246	15.33955945	15.22991829
18	16.52386129	16.39826858	16.27403046	16.15112960	16.02954893
19	17.36468502	17.22600850	17.08890070	16.95334063	16.81930759
20	18.19787120	18.04555297	17.89503779	17.74630046	17.59931613
21	19.02348921	18.85698313	18.69253533	18.53011577	18.36969495
22	19.84160781	19.66037934	19.48148590	19.30489203	19.13056291
23	20.65229510	20.45582113	20.26198110	20.07073347	19.88203744
24	21.45561860	21.24338726	21.03411156	20.82774314	20.62423451
25	22.25164518	22.02315570	21.79796692	21.57602287	21.35726865
26	23.04044114	22.79520366	22.55363586	22.31567335	22.08125299
27	23.82207214	23.55960759	23.30120613	23.04679408	22.79629925
28	24.59660328	24.31644316	24.04076451	23.76948344	23.50251778
29	25.36409904	25.06578530	24.77239688	24.48383866	24.20001756
30	26.12462333	25.80770822	25.49618817	25.18995584	24.88890623
31	26.87823946	26.54228537	26.21222243	25.88792999	25.56929010
32	27.62501020	27.26958947	26.92058278	26.57785502	26.24127418
33	28.36499773	27.98969255	27.62135148	27.25982374	26.90496215
34	29.09826364	28.70266589	28.31460987	27.93392791	27.56045644
35	29.82486901	29.40858009	29.00043845	28.60025823	28.20785822
36	30.54487433	30.10750504	29.67891685	29.25890435	28.84726737
37	31.25833955	30.79950994	30.35012385	29.90995488	29.47878259
38	31.96532408	31.48466330	31.01413736	30.55349741	30.10250133
39	32.66588678	32.16303298	31.67103448	31.18961852	30.71851983
40	33.36008599	32.83468611	32.32089149	31.81840381	31.32693316
41	34.04797952	33.49968922	32.96378383	32.43993787	31.92783522
42	34.72962462	34.15810814	33.59978615	33.05430432	32.52131874
43	35.40507807	34.81000806	34.22897229	33.66158582	33.10747530
44	36.07439611	35.45545352	34.85141529	34.26186407	33.68639536
45	36.73763446	36.09450844	35.46718742	34.85521984	34.25816825
46	37.39484835	36.72723608	36.07636019	35.44173296	34.82288222
47	38.04609250	37.35369909	36.67900431	36.02148233	35.38062442
48	38.69142114	37.97395949	37.27518975	36.59454596	35.93148091

Present Value of Ordinary Annuity of \$1 per Month Based on Monthly Compounding of Nominal Annual Rates

Period			Nominal Annual Rate		
	16%	**17%**	**18%**	**19%**	**20%**
0	0.00000000	0.00000000	0.00000000	0.00000000	0.00000000
1	0.98684211	0.98603122	0.98522167	0.98441345	0.98360656
2	1.96069945	1.95828880	1.95588342	1.95348330	1.95108842
3	2.92174287	2.91696513	2.91220042	2.90744870	2.90270992
4	3.87014099	3.86224992	3.85438465	3.84654507	3.83873107
5	4.80606019	4.79433024	4.78264497	4.77100417	4.75940761
6	5.72966466	5.71339054	5.69718717	5.68105414	5.66499109
7	6.64111644	6.61961270	6.59821396	6.57691958	6.55572894
8	7.54057544	7.51317604	7.48592508	7.45882158	7.43186453
9	8.42819945	8.39425739	8.36051732	8.32697776	8.29363724
10	9.30414419	9.26303111	9.22218455	9.18160239	9.14128253
11	10.16856334	10.11966914	10.07111779	10.02290637	9.97503200
12	11.02160856	10.96434097	10.90750521	10.85109733	10.79511344
13	11.86342950	11.79721378	11.73153222	11.66637965	11.60175093
14	12.69417385	12.61845237	12.54338150	12.46895454	12.39516485
15	13.51398735	13.42821926	13.34323301	13.25902006	13.17557198
16	14.32301384	14.22667470	14.13126405	14.03677118	13.94318556
17	15.12139523	15.01397670	14.90764931	14.80239985	14.69821530
18	15.90927161	15.79028105	15.67256089	15.55609501	15.44086751
19	16.68678120	16.55574138	16.42616837	16.29804267	16.17134509
20	17.45406039	17.31050917	17.16863879	17.02842592	16.88984763
21	18.21124381	18.05473377	17.90013673	17.74742503	17.59657144
22	18.95846428	18.78856247	18.62082437	18.45521742	18.29170961
23	19.69585291	19.51214048	19.33086145	19.15197777	18.97545208
24	20.42353906	20.22561099	20.03040537	19.83787803	19.64798565
25	21.14165039	20.92911519	20.71961120	20.51308748	20.30949408
26	21.85031288	21.62279230	21.39863172	21.17777275	20.96015811
27	22.54965087	22.30677959	22.06761746	21.83209786	21.60015552
28	23.23978704	22.98121242	22.72671671	22.47622431	22.22966117
29	23.92084247	23.64622424	23.37607558	23.11031105	22.84884705
30	24.59293665	24.30194666	24.01583801	23.73451457	23.45788235
31	25.25618749	24.94850944	24.64614582	24.34898892	24.05693345
32	25.91071134	25.58604054	25.26713874	24.95388573	24.64616405
33	26.55662303	26.21466610	25.87895442	25.54935428	25.22573513
34	27.19403588	26.83451050	26.48172849	26.13554154	25.79580505
35	27.82306173	27.44569650	27.07559458	26.71259217	26.35652956
36	28.44381091	28.04834495	27.66068431	27.28064856	26.90806186
37	29.05639235	28.64257513	28.23712740	27.83985092	27.45055265
38	29.66091350	29.22850465	28.80505163	28.39033725	27.98415015
39	30.25748043	29.80624945	29.36458288	28.93224340	28.50900014
40	30.84619779	30.37592386	29.91584520	29.46570310	29.02524604
41	31.42716888	30.93764062	30.45896079	29.99084800	29.53302890
42	32.00049560	31.49151088	30.99405004	30.50780772	30.03248744
43	32.56627855	32.03764426	31.52123157	31.01670981	30.52375814
44	33.12461699	32.57614881	32.04062223	31.51767988	31.00697522
45	33.67560887	33.10713112	32.55233718	32.01084155	31.48227070
46	34.21935086	33.63069626	33.05648983	32.49631654	31.94977446
47	34.75593835	34.14694783	33.55319195	32.97422465	32.40961423
48	35.28546548	34.65598800	34.04255365	33.44468382	32.86191563

¶691.13

.15 Future Value of Ordinary Annuity of $1 per Period

Future Value of Ordinary Annuity of $1 per Period

Period	Interest Rate			
	2%	**3%**	**4%**	**5%**
0	0.0000000	0.0000000	0.0000000	0.0000000
1	1.0000000	1.0000000	1.0000000	1.0000000
2	2.0200000	2.0300000	2.0400000	2.0500000
3	3.0604000	3.0909000	3.1216000	3.1525000
4	4.1216080	4.1836270	4.2464640	4.3101250
5	5.2040402	5.3091358	5.4163226	5.5256313
6	6.3081210	6.4684099	6.6329755	6.8019128
7	7.4342834	7.6624622	7.8982945	8.1420085
8	8.5829691	8.8923360	9.2142263	9.5491089
9	9.7546284	10.1591061	10.5827953	11.0265643
10	10.9497210	11.4638793	12.0061071	12.5778925
11	12.1687154	12.8077957	13.4863514	14.2067872
12	13.4120897	14.1920296	15.0258055	15.9171265
13	14.6803315	15.6177904	16.6268377	17.7129828
14	15.9739382	17.0863242	18.2919112	19.5986320
15	17.2934169	18.5989139	20.0235876	21.5785636
16	18.6392853	20.1568813	21.8245311	23.6574918
17	20.0120710	21.7615877	23.6975124	25.8403664
18	21.4123124	23.4144354	25.6454129	28.1323847
19	22.8405586	25.1168684	27.6712294	30.5390039
20	24.2973698	26.8703745	29.7780786	33.0659541
21	25.7833172	28.6764857	31.9692017	35.7192518
22	27.2989835	30.5367803	34.2479698	38.5052144
23	28.8449632	32.4528837	36.6178886	41.4304751
24	30.4218625	34.4264702	39.0826041	44.5019989
25	32.0302997	36.4592643	41.6459083	47.7270988
26	33.6709057	38.5530423	44.3117446	51.1134538
27	35.3443238	40.7096335	47.0842144	54.6691264
28	37.0512103	42.9309225	49.9675830	58.4025828
29	38.7922345	45.2188502	52.9662863	62.3227119
30	40.5680792	47.5754157	56.0849378	66.4388475
31	42.3794408	50.0026782	59.3283353	70.7607899
32	44.2270296	52.5027585	62.7014687	75.2988294
33	46.1115702	55.0778413	66.2095274	80.0637708
34	48.0338016	57.7301765	69.8579085	85.0669594
35	49.9944776	60.4620818	73.6522249	90.3203074
36	51.9943672	63.2759443	77.5983138	95.8363227
37	54.0342545	66.1742226	81.7022464	101.6281389
38	56.1149396	69.1594493	85.9703363	107.7095458
39	58.2372384	72.2342328	90.4091497	114.0950231
40	60.4019832	75.4012597	95.0255157	120.7997742

Future Value of Ordinary Annuity of $1 per Period

Period	Interest Rate				
	6%	7%	8%	9%	10%
0	0.0000000	0.0000000	0.0000000	0.0000000	0.0000000
1	1.0000000	1.0000000	1.0000000	1.0000000	1.0000000
2	2.0600000	2.0700000	2.0800000	2.0900000	2.1000000
3	3.1836000	3.2149000	3.2464000	3.2781000	3.3100000
4	4.3746160	4.4399430	4.5061120	4.5731290	4.6410000
5	5.6370930	5.7507390	5.8666010	5.9847106	6.1051000
6	6.9753185	7.1532907	7.3359290	7.5233346	7.7156100
7	8.3938376	8.6540211	8.9228034	9.2004347	9.4871710
8	9.8974679	10.2598026	10.6366276	11.0284738	11.4358881
9	11.4913160	11.9779887	12.4875578	13.0210364	13.5794769
10	13.1807949	13.8164480	14.4865625	15.1929297	15.9374246
11	14.9716426	15.7835993	16.6454875	17.5602934	18.5311671
12	16.8699412	17.8884513	18.9771265	20.1407198	21.3842838
13	18.8821377	20.1406429	21.4952966	22.9533846	24.5227121
14	21.0150659	22.5504879	24.2149203	26.0191892	27.9749834
15	23.2759699	25.1290220	27.1521139	29.3609162	31.7724817
16	25.6725281	27.8880536	30.3242830	33.0033987	35.9497299
17	28.2128798	30.8402173	33.7502257	36.9737046	40.5447028
18	30.9056525	33.9990325	37.4502437	41.3013380	45.5991731
19	33.7599917	37.3789648	41.4462632	46.0184584	51.1590904
20	36.7855912	40.9954923	45.7619643	51.1601196	57.2749995
21	39.9927267	44.8651768	50.4229214	56.7645304	64.0024994
22	43.3922903	49.0057392	55.4567552	62.8733381	71.4027494
23	46.9958277	53.4361409	60.8932956	69.5319386	79.5430243
24	50.8155774	58.1766708	66.7647592	76.7898131	88.4973268
25	54.8645120	63.2490377	73.1059400	84.7008962	98.3470594
26	59.1563827	68.6764704	79.9544151	93.3239769	109.1817654
27	63.7057657	74.4838233	87.3507684	102.7231348	121.0999419
28	68.5281116	80.6976909	95.3388298	112.9682169	134.2099361
29	73.6397983	87.3465293	103.9659362	124.1353565	148.6309297
30	79.0581862	94.4607863	113.2832111	136.3075385	164.4940227
31	84.8016774	102.0730414	123.3458680	149.5752170	181.9434250
32	90.8897780	110.2181543	134.2135374	164.0369865	201.1377675
33	97.3431647	118.9334251	145.9506204	179.8003153	222.2515442
34	104.1837546	128.2587648	158.6266701	196.9823437	245.4766986
35	111.4347799	138.2368784	172.3168037	215.7107547	271.0243685
36	119.1208667	148.9134598	187.1021480	236.1247226	299.1268053
37	127.2681187	160.3374020	203.0703198	258.3759476	330.0394859
38	135.9042058	172.5610202	220.3159454	282.6297829	364.0434344
39	145.0584581	185.6402916	238.9412210	309.0664633	401.4477779
40	154.7619656	199.6351120	259.0565187	337.8824450	442.5925557

¶691.15

Future Value of Ordinary Annuity of $1 per Period

Period	Interest Rate				
	11%	**12%**	**13%**	**14%**	**15%**
0	0.0000000	0.0000000	0.0000000	0.0000000	0.0000000
1	1.0000000	1.0000000	1.0000000	1.0000000	1.0000000
2	2.1100000	2.1200000	2.1300000	2.1400000	2.1500000
3	3.3421000	3.3744000	3.4069000	3.4396000	3.4725000
4	4.7097310	4.7793280	4.8497970	4.9211440	4.9933750
5	6.2278014	6.3528474	6.4802706	6.6101042	6.7423813
6	7.9128596	8.1151890	8.3227058	8.5355187	8.7537384
7	9.7832741	10.0890117	10.4046575	10.7304914	11.0667992
8	11.8594343	12.2996931	12.7572630	13.2327602	13.7268191
9	14.1639720	14.7756563	15.4157072	16.0853466	16.7858419
10	16.7220090	17.5487351	18.4197492	19.3372951	20.3037182
11	19.5614300	20.6545833	21.8143165	23.0445164	24.3492760
12	22.7131872	24.1331333	25.6501777	27.2707487	29.0016674
13	26.2116378	28.0291093	29.9847008	32.0886535	34.3519175
14	30.0949180	32.3926024	34.8827119	37.5810650	40.5047051
15	34.4053590	37.2797147	40.4174644	43.8424141	47.5804109
16	39.1899485	42.7532804	46.6717348	50.9803521	55.7174725
17	44.5008428	48.8836741	53.7390603	59.1176014	65.0750934
18	50.3959355	55.7497150	61.7251382	68.3940656	75.8363574
19	56.9394884	63.4396808	70.7494062	78.9692348	88.2118110
20	64.2028321	72.0524424	80.9468290	91.0249277	102.4435826
21	72.2651437	81.6987355	92.4699167	104.7684175	118.8101200
22	81.2143095	92.5025838	105.4910059	120.4359960	137.6316380
23	91.1478835	104.6028939	120.2048367	138.2970354	159.2763837
24	102.1741507	118.1552411	136.8314654	158.6586204	184.1678413
25	114.4133073	133.3338701	155.6195559	181.8708272	212.7930175
26	127.9987711	150.3339345	176.8500982	208.3327430	245.7119701
27	143.0786359	169.3740066	200.8406110	238.4993271	283.5687656
28	159.8172859	190.6988874	227.9498904	272.8892329	327.1040804
29	178.3971873	214.5827539	258.5833762	312.0937255	377.1696925
30	199.0208779	241.3326843	293.1992151	356.7868470	434.7451464
31	221.9131745	271.2926065	332.3151130	407.7370056	500.9569183
32	247.3236237	304.8477192	376.5160777	465.8201864	577.1004561
33	275.5292223	342.4294455	426.4631678	532.0350125	664.6655245
34	306.8374368	384.5209790	482.9033796	607.5199142	765.3653532
35	341.5895548	431.6634965	546.6808190	693.5727022	881.1701561
36	380.1644058	484.4631161	618.7493254	791.6728805	1014.3456796
37	422.9824905	543.5986900	700.1867377	903.5070838	1167.4975315
38	470.5105644	609.8305328	792.2110137	1030.9980755	1343.6221612
39	523.2667265	684.0101967	896.1984454	1176.3378061	1546.1654854
40	581.8260664	767.0914203	1013.7042433	1342.0250990	1779.0903082

¶691.15

Future Value of Ordinary Annuity of $1 per Period

Period	Interest Rate				
	16%	17%	18%	19%	20%
0	0.0000000	0.0000000	0.0000000	0.0000000	0.0000000
1	1.0000000	1.0000000	1.0000000	1.0000000	1.0000000
2	2.1600000	2.1700000	2.1800000	2.1900000	2.2000000
3	3.5056000	3.5389000	3.5724000	3.6061000	3.6400000
4	5.0664960	5.1405130	5.2154320	5.2912590	5.3680000
5	6.8771354	7.0144002	7.1542098	7.2965982	7.4416000
6	8.9774770	9.2068482	9.4419675	9.6829519	9.9299200
7	11.4138733	11.7720124	12.1415217	12.5227127	12.9159040
8	14.2400931	14.7732546	15.3269956	15.9020281	16.4990848
9	17.5185080	18.2847078	19.0858548	19.9234135	20.7989018
10	21.3214692	22.3931082	23.5213086	24.7088621	25.9586821
11	25.7329043	27.1999366	28.7551442	30.4035458	32.1504185
12	30.8501690	32.8239258	34.9310701	37.1802196	39.5805022
13	36.7861961	39.4039932	42.2186628	45.2444613	48.4966027
14	43.6719874	47.1026720	50.8180221	54.8409089	59.1959232
15	51.6595054	56.1101262	60.9652660	66.2606816	72.0351079
16	60.9250263	66.6488477	72.9390139	79.8502111	87.4421294
17	71.6730305	78.9791518	87.0680364	96.0217512	105.9305553
18	84.1407154	93.4056076	103.7402830	115.2658839	128.1166664
19	98.6032298	110.2845609	123.4135339	138.1664019	154.7399997
20	115.3797466	130.0329363	146.6279700	165.4180183	186.6879996
21	134.8405060	153.1385354	174.0210046	197.8474417	225.0255995
22	157.4149870	180.1720864	206.3447855	236.4384557	271.0307195
23	183.6013849	211.8013411	244.4868468	282.3617622	326.2368633
24	213.9776065	248.8075691	289.4944793	337.0104971	392.4842360
25	249.2140235	292.1048559	342.6034855	402.0424915	471.9810832
26	290.0882673	342.7626814	405.2721129	479.4305649	567.3772999
27	337.5023901	402.0323372	479.2210933	571.5223722	681.8527598
28	392.5027725	471.3778345	566.4808901	681.1116229	819.2233118
29	456.3032161	552.5120664	669.4474503	811.5228313	984.0679742
30	530.3117307	647.4391177	790.9479913	966.7121692	1181.8815690
31	616.1616076	758.5037677	934.3186298	1151.3874814	1419.2578828
32	715.7474648	888.4494082	1103.4959831	1371.1511029	1704.1094594
33	831.2670592	1040.4858076	1303.1252601	1632.6698124	2045.9313512
34	965.2697886	1218.3683949	1538.6878069	1943.8770767	2456.1176215
35	1120.7129548	1426.4910221	1816.6516121	2314.2137213	2948.3411458
36	1301.0270276	1669.9944958	2144.6489023	2754.9143284	3539.0093749
37	1510.1913520	1954.8935601	2531.6857047	3279.3480508	4247.8112499
38	1752.8219683	2288.2254653	2988.3891316	3903.4241804	5098.3734999
39	2034.2734833	2678.2237944	3527.2991753	4646.0747747	6119.0481999
40	2360.7572406	3134.5218395	4163.2130268	5529.8289819	7343.8578398

.17 Present Value of Ordinary Annuity Increasing in Constant Amount
$1 per Period, Increasing in Constant Amount of 2 Percent

Period	Interest Rate			
	2%	3%	4%	5%
0	0.0000000	0.0000000	0.0000000	0.0000000
1	0.9803922	0.9708738	0.9615385	0.9523810
2	1.9607843	1.9323216	1.9045858	1.8775510
3	2.9407995	2.8840689	2.8291420	2.7759421
4	3.9200757	3.8258652	3.7352345	3.6480067
5	4.8982650	4.7574827	4.6229157	4.4942150
6	5.8750335	5.6787154	5.4922617	5.3150519
7	6.8500609	6.5893779	6.3433697	6.1110150
8	7.8230399	7.4893044	7.1763565	6.8826119
9	8.7936760	8.3783478	7.9913571	7.6303582
10	9.7616870	9.2563786	8.7885228	8.3547759
11	10.7268027	10.1232842	9.5680199	9.0563910
12	11.6887643	10.9789676	10.3300283	9.7357327
13	12.6473247	11.8233473	11.0747402	10.3933312
14	13.6022472	12.6563557	11.8023588	11.0297168
15	14.5533061	13.4779390	12.5130974	11.6454187
16	15.5002856	14.2880560	13.2071780	12.2409636
17	16.4429802	15.0866777	13.8848307	12.8168753
18	17.3811938	15.8737865	14.5462924	13.3736729
19	18.3147396	16.6493755	15.1918061	13.9118711
20	19.2434400	17.4134480	15.8216201	14.4319786
21	20.1671262	18.1660170	16.4359871	14.9344979
22	21.0856376	18.9071044	17.0351637	15.4199247
23	21.9988221	19.6367405	17.6194097	15.8887474
24	22.9065355	20.3549638	18.1889870	16.3414466
25	23.8086412	21.0618200	18.7441599	16.7784947
26	24.7050101	21.7573621	19.2851937	17.2003558
27	25.5955204	22.4416495	19.8123549	17.6074852
28	26.4800572	23.1147477	20.3259102	18.0003294
29	27.3585124	23.7767280	20.8261264	18.3793257
30	28.2307844	24.4276671	21.3132699	18.7449021
31	29.0967780	25.0676465	21.7876063	19.0974772
32	29.9564039	25.6967525	22.2494002	19.4374604
33	30.8095791	26.3150755	22.6989147	19.7652514
34	31.6562258	26.9227101	23.1364111	20.0812403
35	32.4962722	27.5197542	23.5621491	20.3858080
36	33.3296516	28.1063093	23.9763859	20.6793256
37	34.1563024	28.6824799	24.3793765	20.9621549
38	34.9761681	29.2483735	24.7713732	21.2346482
39	35.7891969	29.8040997	25.1526254	21.4971487
40	36.5953419	30.3497709	25.5233799	21.7499900

Present Value of Ordinary Annuity of $1 per Period, Increasing in Constant Amount of 2 Percent

Period	Interest Rate				
	6%	7%	8%	9%	10%
0	0.0000000	0.0000000	0.0000000	0.0000000	0.0000000
1	0.9433962	0.9345794	0.9259259	0.9174312	0.9090909
2	1.8511926	1.8254869	1.8004115	1.7759448	1.7520661
3	2.7243966	2.6744367	2.6259971	2.5790156	2.5334335
4	3.5640159	3.4831057	3.4051287	3.3299463	3.2574278
5	4.3710548	4.2531307	4.1401586	4.0318722	3.9280228
6	5.1465114	4.9861072	4.8333451	4.6877663	4.5489441
7	5.8913753	5.6835869	5.4868544	5.3004446	5.1236812
8	6.6066254	6.3470773	6.1027609	5.8725722	5.6554996
9	7.2932276	6.9780404	6.6830497	6.4066684	6.1474529
10	7.9521335	7.5778926	7.2296180	6.9051132	6.6023939
11	8.5842785	8.1480039	7.7442775	7.3701526	7.0229866
12	9.1905811	8.6896985	8.2287562	7.8039050	7.4117162
13	9.7719415	9.2042544	8.6847017	8.2083665	7.7709001
14	10.3292407	9.6929042	9.1136826	8.5854170	8.1026974
15	10.8633400	10.1568351	9.5171920	8.9368257	8.4091193
16	11.3750802	10.5971900	9.8966496	9.2642564	8.6920371
17	11.8652812	11.0150682	10.2534046	9.5692730	8.9531921
18	12.3347419	11.4115259	10.5887383	9.8533446	9.1942029
19	12.7842396	11.7875772	10.9038667	10.1178506	9.4165737
20	13.2145301	12.1441954	11.1999432	10.3640852	9.6217020
21	13.6263477	12.4823138	11.4780613	10.5932625	9.8108848
22	14.0204049	12.8028265	11.7392568	10.8065205	9.9853260
23	14.3973930	13.1065900	11.9845108	11.0049257	10.1461426
24	14.7579817	13.3944240	12.2147518	11.1894769	10.2943700
25	15.1028196	13.6671128	12.4308583	11.3611093	10.4309680
26	15.4325347	13.9254061	12.6336610	11.5206981	10.5568262
27	15.7477340	14.1700202	12.8239449	11.6690620	10.6727683
28	16.0490044	14.4016396	13.0024521	11.8069666	10.7795570
29	16.3369129	14.6209176	13.1698830	11.9351276	10.8778985
30	16.6120069	14.8284777	13.3268992	12.0542140	10.9684460
31	16.8748146	15.0249145	13.4741249	12.1648506	11.0518039
32	17.1258456	15.2107951	13.6121489	12.2676207	11.1285311
33	17.3655910	15.3866600	13.7415268	12.3630693	11.1991442
34	17.5945242	15.5530241	13.8627820	12.4517047	11.2641208
35	17.8131009	15.7103779	13.9764080	12.5340013	11.3239020
36	18.0217602	15.8591881	14.0828698	12.6104016	11.3788957
37	18.2209245	15.9998993	14.1826052	12.6813182	11.4294780
38	18.4110001	16.1329343	14.2760267	12.7471358	11.4759967
39	18.5923778	16.2586951	14.3635223	12.8082131	11.5187725
40	18.7654333	16.3775642	14.4454573	12.8648840	11.5581014

Present Value of Ordinary Annuity of $1 per Period, Increasing in Constant Amount of 2 Percent

Period	Interest Rate				
	11%	**12%**	**13%**	**14%**	**15%**
0	0.0000000	0.0000000	0.0000000	0.0000000	0.0000000
1	0.9009009	0.8928571	0.8849558	0.8771930	0.8695652
2	1.7287558	1.7059949	1.6837654	1.6620499	1.6408318
3	2.4891948	2.4462464	2.4045375	2.3640202	2.3246486
4	3.1874497	3.1198955	3.0546554	2.9916253	2.9307071
5	3.8283771	3.7327165	3.6408361	3.5525435	3.4676580
6	4.4164820	4.2900108	4.1691865	4.0536887	3.9432183
7	4.9559394	4.7966419	4.6452544	4.5012825	4.3642678
8	5.4506156	5.2570688	5.0740767	4.9009198	4.7369358
9	5.9040884	5.6753764	5.4602231	5.2576290	5.0666802
10	6.3196661	6.0553048	5.8078373	5.5759267	5.3583582
11	6.7004060	6.4002761	6.1206745	5.8598676	5.6162900
12	7.0491318	6.7134197	6.4021357	6.1130897	5.8443168
13	7.3684495	6.9975957	6.6552997	6.3388557	6.0458514
14	7.6607630	7.2554167	6.8829521	6.5400903	6.2239255
15	7.9282886	7.4892679	7.0876123	6.7194138	6.3812305
16	8.1730684	7.7013261	7.2715574	6.8791730	6.5201547
17	8.3969835	7.8935766	7.4368450	7.0214685	6.6428168
18	8.6017652	8.0678297	7.5853335	7.1481805	6.7510957
19	8.7890068	8.2257349	7.7187006	7.2609902	6.8466565
20	8.9601736	8.3687950	7.8384601	7.3614014	6.9309749
21	9.1166127	8.4983785	7.9459780	7.4507579	7.0053579
22	9.2595623	8.6157308	8.0424859	7.5302606	7.0709627
23	9.3901595	8.7219855	8.1290939	7.6009820	7.1288139
24	9.5094488	8.8181734	8.2068027	7.6638799	7.1798179
25	9.6183888	8.9052319	8.2765136	7.7198094	7.2247768
26	9.7178591	8.9840131	8.3390383	7.7695333	7.2643998
27	9.8086669	9.0552913	8.3951077	7.8137323	7.2993140
28	9.8915522	9.1197700	8.4453795	7.8530135	7.3300737
29	9.9671934	9.1780879	8.4904456	7.8879182	7.3571685
30	10.0362122	9.2308250	8.5308383	7.9189289	7.3810314
31	10.0991784	9.2785078	8.5670366	7.9464756	7.4020443
32	10.1566139	9.3216138	8.5994710	7.9709414	7.4205448
33	10.2089963	9.3605765	8.6285283	7.9926676	7.4368309
34	10.2567631	9.3957889	8.6545563	8.0119581	7.4511653
35	10.3003148	9.4276073	8.6778674	8.0290834	7.4637803
36	10.3400177	9.4563548	8.6987424	8.0442845	7.4748804
37	10.3762068	9.4823242	8.7174331	8.0577757	7.4846462
38	10.4091887	9.5057808	8.7341659	8.0697476	7.4932369
39	10.4392437	9.5269648	8.7491439	8.0803700	7.5007930
40	10.4666280	9.5460941	8.7625493	8.0897938	7.5074382

Present Value of Ordinary Annuity of $1 per Period, Increasing in Constant Amount of 2 Percent

Period	Interest Rate				
	16%	17%	18%	19%	20%
0	0.0000000	0.0000000	0.0000000	0.0000000	0.0000000
1	0.8620690	0.8547009	0.8474576	0.8403361	0.8333333
2	1.6200951	1.5998247	1.5800057	1.5606242	1.5416667
3	2.2863791	2.2491701	2.2129819	2.1777767	2.1435185
4	2.8718077	2.8148391	2.7597181	2.7063656	2.6547068
5	3.3860097	3.3074392	3.2317960	3.1589389	3.0887346
6	3.8374962	3.7362616	3.6392707	3.5462955	3.4571223
7	4.2337853	4.1094404	3.9908667	3.8777235	3.7696938
8	4.5815143	4.4340923	4.2941503	4.1612079	4.0348214
9	4.8865398	4.7164407	4.5556793	4.4036094	4.2596371
10	5.1540264	4.9619248	4.7811354	4.6108202	4.4502137
11	5.3885267	5.1752965	4.9754382	4.7878983	4.6117193
12	5.5940514	5.3607049	5.1428460	4.9391834	4.7485504
13	5.7741323	5.5217715	5.2870428	5.0683979	4.8644456
14	5.9318785	5.6616556	5.4112145	5.1787328	4.9625827
15	6.0700250	5.7831125	5.5181150	5.2729230	5.0456617
16	6.1909777	5.8885438	5.6101242	5.3533111	5.1159760
17	6.2968514	5.9800424	5.6892977	5.4219035	5.1754726
18	6.3895047	6.0594312	5.7574105	5.4804174	5.2258044
19	6.4705704	6.1282976	5.8159947	5.5303227	5.2683736
20	6.5414824	6.1880234	5.8663725	5.5728767	5.3043696
21	6.6034993	6.2398109	5.9096842	5.6091546	5.3348010
22	6.6577259	6.2847060	5.9469135	5.6400757	5.3605228
23	6.7051314	6.3236184	5.9789081	5.6664258	5.3822595
24	6.7465658	6.3573387	6.0063987	5.6888763	5.4006250
25	6.7827745	6.3865544	6.0300150	5.7080007	5.4161392
26	6.8144106	6.4118624	6.0502992	5.7242888	5.4292425
27	6.8420468	6.4337817	6.0677185	5.7381587	5.4403074
28	6.8661845	6.4527625	6.0826748	5.7499675	5.4496496
29	6.8872632	6.4691962	6.0955142	5.7600198	5.4575358
30	6.9056674	6.4834222	6.1065346	5.7685753	5.4641919
31	6.9217339	6.4957350	6.1159922	5.7758559	5.4698088
32	6.9357575	6.5063904	6.1241072	5.7820505	5.4745481
33	6.9479961	6.5156099	6.1310693	5.7873203	5.4785463
34	6.9586752	6.5235860	6.1370413	5.7918027	5.4819188
35	6.9679923	6.5304853	6.1421633	5.7956148	5.4847630
36	6.9761199	6.5364523	6.1465556	5.7988564	5.4871614
37	6.9832089	6.5416123	6.1503217	5.8016125	5.4891836
38	6.9893911	6.5460739	6.1535505	5.8039554	5.4908884
39	6.9947819	6.5499310	6.1563181	5.8059469	5.4923253
40	6.9994819	6.5532652	6.1586903	5.8076395	5.4935364

Present Value of Ordinary Annuity of $1 per Period, Increasing in Constant Amount of 5 Percent

Period	Interest Rate			
	2%	3%	4%	5%
0	0.0000000	0.0000000	0.0000000	0.0000000
1	0.9803922	0.9708738	0.9615385	0.9523810
2	1.9896194	1.9605995	1.9323225	1.9047619
3	3.0261739	2.9672553	2.9102185	2.8549833
4	4.0885962	3.9890154	3.8932433	3.8010911
5	5.1754732	5.0241460	4.8795558	4.7413225
6	6.2854374	6.0710013	5.8674490	5.6740918
7	7.4171656	7.1280202	6.8553421	6.5979775
8	8.5693776	8.1937227	7.8417739	7.5117106
9	9.7408350	9.2667061	8.8253953	8.4141631
10	10.9303400	10.3456423	9.8049634	9.3043373
11	12.1367346	11.4292742	10.7793348	10.1813563
12	13.3588990	12.5164130	11.7474602	11.0444543
13	14.5957510	13.6059352	12.7083788	11.8929684
14	15.8462448	14.6967796	13.6612126	12.7263305
15	17.1093699	15.7879449	14.6051623	13.5440596
16	18.3841501	16.8784870	15.5395016	14.3457548
17	19.6696427	17.9675166	16.4635734	15.1310888
18	20.9649375	19.0541967	17.3767855	15.8998020
19	22.2691560	20.1377401	18.2786061	16.6516965
20	23.5814501	21.2174078	19.1685606	17.3866310
21	24.9010017	22.2925064	20.0462278	18.1045158
22	26.2270217	23.3623860	20.9112364	18.8053080
23	27.5587491	24.4264387	21.7632617	19.4890077
24	28.8954503	25.4840962	22.6020228	20.1556537
25	30.2364182	26.5348285	23.4272798	20.8053198
26	31.5809716	27.5781416	24.2388306	21.4381115
27	32.9284543	28.6135764	25.0365087	22.0541626
28	34.2782345	29.6407068	25.8201807	22.6536327
29	35.6297041	30.6591381	26.5897441	23.2367038
30	36.9822778	31.6685056	27.3451249	23.8035786
31	38.3353927	32.6684735	28.0862755	24.3544773
32	39.6885076	33.6587329	28.8131733	24.8896360
33	41.0411023	34.6390012	29.5258181	25.4093046
34	42.3926769	35.6090201	30.2242312	25.9137448
35	43.7427515	36.5685553	30.9084529	26.4032286
36	45.0908652	37.5173945	31.5785419	26.8780365
37	46.4365758	38.4553467	32.2345731	27.3384563
38	47.7794593	39.3822412	32.8766366	27.7847816
39	49.1191091	40.2979265	33.5048363	28.2173107
40	50.4551358	41.2022692	34.1192890	28.6363454

¶691.17

Present Value of Ordinary Annuity of $1 per Period, Increasing in Constant Amount of 5 Percent

Period			Interest Rate		
	6%	7%	8%	9%	10%
0	0.0000000	0.0000000	0.0000000	0.0000000	0.0000000
1	0.9433962	0.9345794	0.9259259	0.9174312	0.9090909
2	1.8778925	1.8516901	1.8261317	1.8011952	1.7768595
3	2.8014737	2.7496178	2.6993472	2.6505970	2.6033058
4	3.7123814	3.6269473	3.5446315	3.4652860	3.3887713
5	4.6090912	4.4825307	4.3613313	4.2452037	4.1338768
6	5.4902919	5.3154585	5.1490434	4.9905378	4.8394693
7	6.3548661	6.1250331	5.9075809	5.7016823	5.5065748
8	7.2018728	6.9107454	6.6369439	6.3792018	6.1363598
9	8.0305307	7.6722527	7.3372924	7.0238007	6.7300964
10	8.8402031	8.4093591	8.0089230	7.6362964	7.2891342
11	9.6303844	9.1219983	8.6522473	8.2175957	7.8148751
12	10.4006869	9.8102169	9.2677736	8.7686745	8.3087528
13	11.1508294	10.4741600	9.8560903	9.2905603	8.7722158
14	11.8806259	11.1140584	10.4178510	9.7843170	9.2067124
15	12.5899766	11.7302167	10.9537619	10.2510317	9.6136789
16	13.2788575	12.3230022	11.4645702	10.6918037	9.9945299
17	13.9473135	12.8928361	11.9510543	11.1077355	10.3506503
18	14.5954495	13.4401843	12.4140150	11.4999239	10.6833890
19	15.2234242	13.9655502	12.8542679	11.8694543	10.9940542
20	15.8314435	14.4694672	13.2726369	12.2173945	11.2839093
21	16.4197543	14.9524934	13.6699484	12.5447906	11.5541704
22	16.9886397	15.4152054	14.0470265	12.8526631	11.8060047
23	17.5384140	15.8581939	14.4046886	13.1420040	12.0405288
24	18.0694178	16.2820591	14.7437422	13.4137747	12.2588089
25	18.5820148	16.6874073	15.0649815	13.6689039	12.4618601
26	19.0765874	17.0748471	15.3691855	13.9082870	12.6506473
27	19.5535337	17.4449870	15.6571152	14.1327850	12.8260860
28	20.0132645	17.7984322	15.9295124	14.3432238	12.9890429
29	20.4562007	18.1357829	16.1870985	14.5403947	13.1403374
30	20.8827705	18.4576324	16.4305729	14.7250540	13.2807434
31	21.2934076	18.7645649	16.6606131	14.8979236	13.4109901
32	21.6885490	19.0571548	16.8778732	15.0596915	13.5317643
33	22.0686331	19.3359650	17.0829844	15.2110124	13.6437119
34	22.4340987	19.6015462	17.2765545	15.3525086	13.7474396
35	22.7853828	19.8544362	17.4591677	15.4847710	13.8435167
36	23.1229199	20.0951587	17.6313853	15.6083597	13.9324769
37	23.4471408	20.3242234	17.7937453	15.7238054	14.0148203
38	23.7584715	20.5421255	17.9467632	15.8316101	14.0910147
39	24.0573326	20.7493450	18.0909321	15.9322487	14.1614975
40	24.3441380	20.9463471	18.2267233	16.0261696	14.2266775

Present Value of Ordinary Annuity of $1 per Period, Increasing in Constant Amount of 5 Percent

Period	Interest Rate				
	11%	**12%**	**13%**	**14%**	**15%**
0	0.0000000	0.0000000	0.0000000	0.0000000	0.0000000
1	0.9009009	0.8928571	0.8849558	0.8771930	0.8695652
2	1.7531045	1.7299107	1.7072598	1.6851339	1.6635161
3	2.5574150	2.5128690	2.4696149	2.4276026	2.3867839
4	3.3149556	3.2437148	3.1749315	3.1084949	3.0443002
5	4.0270972	3.9246270	3.8262434	3.7317373	3.6409122
6	4.6953982	4.5579159	4.4266416	4.3012205	4.1813217
7	5.3215542	5.1459699	4.9792204	4.8207490	4.6700399
8	5.9073549	5.6912122	5.4870362	5.2940037	5.1113573
9	6.4546496	6.1960663	5.9530750	5.7245148	5.5093247
10	6.9653171	6.6629275	6.3802281	6.1156433	5.8677425
11	7.4412421	7.0941416	6.7712746	6.4705694	6.1901573
12	7.8842954	7.4919880	7.1288687	6.7922860	6.4798634
13	8.2963182	7.8586667	7.4555319	7.0835970	6.7399081
14	8.6791096	8.1962894	7.7536482	7.3471185	6.9731004
15	9.0344170	8.5068731	8.0254625	7.5852825	7.1820210
16	9.3639284	8.7923360	8.2730809	7.8003429	7.3690344
17	9.6692671	9.0544958	8.4984732	7.9943824	7.5363010
18	9.9519881	9.2950690	8.7034759	8.1693205	7.6857905
19	10.2135756	9.5156719	8.8897975	8.3269224	7.8192946
20	10.4554417	9.7178221	9.0590230	8.4688077	7.9384401
21	10.6789263	9.9029413	9.2126200	8.5964599	8.0447015
22	10.8852971	10.0723585	9.3519447	8.7112348	8.1394127
23	11.0757514	10.2273132	9.4782481	8.8143702	8.2237790
24	11.2514171	10.3689597	9.5926823	8.9069939	8.2988877
25	11.4133549	10.4983710	9.6963066	8.9901322	8.3657185
26	11.5625605	10.6165428	9.7900937	9.0647181	8.4251530
27	11.6999670	10.7243980	9.8749354	9.1315982	8.4779837
28	11.8264478	10.8227908	9.9516489	9.1915403	8.5249221
29	11.9428188	10.9125107	10.0209813	9.2452398	8.5666065
30	12.0498417	10.9942866	10.0836157	9.2933260	8.6036090
31	12.1482264	11.0687909	10.1401755	9.3363678	8.6364417
32	12.2386340	11.1366430	10.1912296	9.3748788	8.6655629
33	12.3216793	11.1984131	10.2372960	9.4093227	8.6913822
34	12.3979336	11.2546257	10.2788468	9.4401178	8.7142655
35	12.4679274	11.3057624	10.3163111	9.4676407	8.7345395
36	12.5321526	11.3522657	10.3500794	9.4922307	8.7524956
37	12.5910652	11.3945414	10.3805061	9.5141930	8.7683934
38	12.6450873	11.4329617	10.4079133	9.5338022	8.7824645
39	12.6946097	11.4678673	10.4325929	9.5513051	8.7949148
40	12.7399937	11.4995703	10.4548099	9.5669232	8.8059279

¶691.17

Present Value of Ordinary Annuity of $1 per Period, Increasing in Constant Amount of 5 Percent

Period	Interest Rate				
	16%	**17%**	**18%**	**19%**	**20%**
0	0.0000000	0.0000000	0.0000000	0.0000000	0.0000000
1	0.8620690	0.8547009	0.8474576	0.8403361	0.8333333
2	1.6423900	1.6217401	1.6015513	1.5818092	1.5625000
3	2.3471135	2.3085477	2.2710452	2.2345666	2.1990741
4	2.9822482	2.9222453	2.8642024	2.8080357	2.7536651
5	3.5535838	3.4695786	3.3887335	3.3108949	3.2359182
6	4.0666367	3.9568769	3.8517729	3.7510728	3.6545407
7	4.5266150	4.3900309	4.2598755	4.1357661	4.0173468
8	4.9383994	4.7744871	4.6190270	4.4714713	4.3313137
9	5.3065336	5.1152523	4.9346655	4.7640249	4.6026431
10	5.6352248	5.4169065	5.2117090	5.0186483	4.8368261
11	5.9283502	5.6836211	5.4545875	5.2399958	5.0387081
12	6.1894676	5.9191810	5.6672778	5.4322024	5.2125509
13	6.4218301	6.1270089	5.8533382	5.5989308	5.3620931
14	6.6284024	6.3101905	6.0159439	5.7434170	5.4906060
15	6.8118783	6.4715004	6.1579212	5.8685133	5.6009453
16	6.9746993	6.6134271	6.2817797	5.9767281	5.6955991
17	7.1190725	6.7381979	6.3897435	6.0702631	5.7767309
18	7.2469894	6.8478018	6.4837799	6.1510473	5.8462189
19	7.3602429	6.9440123	6.5656255	6.2207679	5.9056905
20	7.4604446	7.0284074	6.6368115	6.2808985	5.9565544
21	7.5490402	7.1023896	6.6986854	6.3327241	6.0000278
22	7.6273251	7.1672030	6.7524319	6.3773637	6.0371614
23	7.6964581	7.2239502	6.7990906	6.4157909	6.0688607
24	7.7574746	7.2736069	6.8395734	6.4488516	6.0959058
25	7.8112982	7.3170355	6.8746787	6.4772797	6.1189675
26	7.8587524	7.3549976	6.9051051	6.5017119	6.1386224
27	7.9005703	7.3881648	6.9314631	6.5226993	6.1553655
28	7.9374039	7.4171292	6.9542861	6.5407193	6.1696213
29	7.9698326	7.4424118	6.9740391	6.5561842	6.1817539
30	7.9983708	7.4644710	6.9911276	6.5694508	6.1920751
31	8.0234747	7.4837098	7.0059050	6.5808266	6.2008516
32	8.0455489	7.5004821	7.0186787	6.5905774	6.2083116
33	8.0649515	7.5150985	7.0297161	6.5989319	6.2146502
34	8.0819995	7.5278314	7.0392497	6.6060876	6.2200339
35	8.0969734	7.5389195	7.0474815	6.6122142	6.2246050
36	8.1101210	7.5485720	7.0545868	6.6174579	6.2284848
37	8.1216611	7.5569721	7.0607177	6.6219446	6.2317768
38	8.1317872	7.5642798	7.0660061	6.6257822	6.2345690
39	8.1406697	7.5706353	7.0705665	6.6290636	6.2369367
40	8.1484591	7.5761610	7.0744978	6.6318687	6.2389439

¶691.17

Present Value of Ordinary Annuity of $1 per Period, Increasing in Constant Amount of 10 Percent

Period	Interest Rate			
	2%	**3%**	**4%**	**5%**
0	0.0000000	0.0000000	0.0000000	0.0000000
1	0.9803922	0.9708738	0.9615385	0.9523810
2	2.0376778	2.0077293	1.9785503	1.9501134
3	3.1684646	3.1058993	3.0453459	2.9867185
4	4.3694637	4.2609324	4.1565914	4.0562317
5	5.6374868	5.4685847	5.3072893	5.1531683
6	6.9694439	6.7248111	6.4927611	6.2724914
7	8.3623402	8.0257575	7.7086296	7.4095816
8	9.8132738	9.3677532	8.9508030	8.5602085
9	11.3194333	10.7473034	10.2154591	9.7205045
10	12.8780950	12.1610818	11.4990310	10.8869397
11	14.4866211	13.6059243	12.7981929	12.0562983
12	16.1424568	15.0788221	14.1098467	13.2256569
13	17.8431283	16.5769150	15.4311097	14.3923638
14	19.5862409	18.0974860	16.7593024	15.5540201
15	21.3694763	19.6379547	18.0919372	16.7084612
16	23.1905908	21.1958720	19.4267076	17.8537400
17	25.0474135	22.7689148	20.7614780	18.9881114
18	26.9378438	24.3548802	22.0942740	20.1100171
19	28.8598499	25.9516811	23.4232728	21.2180722
20	30.8114668	27.5573408	24.7467949	22.3110517
21	32.7907942	29.1699886	26.0632957	23.3878788
22	34.7959952	30.7878554	27.3713574	24.4476134
23	36.8252942	32.4092690	28.6696817	25.4894416
24	38.8769751	34.0326503	29.9570825	26.5126657
25	40.9493800	35.6565092	31.2324797	27.5166951
26	43.0409075	37.2794408	32.4948920	28.5010377
27	45.1500109	38.9001214	33.7434316	29.4652916
28	47.2751967	40.5173054	34.9772983	30.4091381
29	49.4150235	42.1298215	36.1957736	31.3323341
30	51.5681000	43.7365699	37.3982165	32.2347062
31	53.7330838	45.3365185	38.5840575	33.1161441
32	55.9086804	46.9287003	39.7527950	33.9765953
33	58.0936410	48.5122106	40.9039906	34.8160600
34	60.2867622	50.0862036	42.0372646	35.6345856
35	62.4868837	51.6498906	43.1522926	36.4322629
36	64.6928878	53.2025365	44.2488019	37.2092213
37	66.9036981	54.7434580	45.3265674	37.9656252
38	69.1182779	56.2720209	46.3854089	38.7016704
39	71.3356294	57.7876379	47.4251878	39.4175806
40	73.5547924	59.2897665	48.4458041	40.1136045

¶691.17

Present Value of Ordinary Annuity of $1 per Period, Increasing in Constant Amount of 10 Percent

Period	Interest Rate				
	6%	7%	8%	9%	10%
0	0.0000000	0.0000000	0.0000000	0.0000000	0.0000000
1	0.9433962	0.9345794	0.9259259	0.9174312	0.9090909
2	1.9223923	1.8953620	1.8689986	1.8432792	1.8181818
3	2.9299355	2.8749195	2.8215973	2.7698994	2.7197596
4	3.9596572	3.8666833	3.7771361	3.6908521	3.6076771
5	5.0058187	4.8648639	4.7299526	4.6007561	4.4769669
6	6.0632595	5.8643773	5.6752070	5.4951571	5.3236778
7	7.1273508	6.8607768	6.6087917	6.3704119	6.1447308
8	8.1939519	7.8501923	7.5272488	7.2235845	6.9377934
9	9.2593691	8.8292731	8.4276969	8.0523545	7.7011691
10	10.3203192	9.7951367	9.3077645	8.8549351	8.4337013
11	11.3738942	10.7453223	10.1655303	9.6300008	9.1346891
12	12.4175299	11.6777474	10.9994692	10.3766237	9.8038138
13	13.4489758	12.5906692	11.8084046	11.0942167	10.4410755
14	14.4662680	13.4826489	12.5914650	11.7824836	11.0467374
15	15.4677041	14.3525193	13.3480451	12.4413749	11.6212783
16	16.4518198	15.1993558	14.0777712	13.0710493	12.1653511
17	17.4173673	16.0224492	14.7804705	13.6718396	12.6797473
18	18.3632955	16.8212818	15.4561429	14.2442227	13.1653660
19	19.2887320	17.5955051	16.1049367	14.7887937	13.6231884
20	20.1929657	18.3449202	16.7271265	15.3062433	14.0542549
21	21.0754319	19.0694595	17.3230937	15.7973375	14.4596466
22	21.9356977	19.7691703	17.8933093	16.2629008	14.8404691
23	22.7734489	20.4442003	18.4383182	16.7038012	15.1978392
24	23.5884781	21.0947842	18.9587260	17.1209375	15.5328737
25	24.3806735	21.7212314	19.4551869	17.5152282	15.8466801
26	25.1500086	22.3239156	19.9283931	17.8876020	16.1403492
27	25.8965332	22.9032649	20.3790656	18.2389901	16.4149488
28	26.6203647	23.4597531	20.8079464	18.5703193	16.6715192
29	27.3216803	23.9938918	21.2157910	18.8825066	16.9110690
30	28.0007099	24.5062236	21.6033626	19.1764540	17.1345723
31	28.6577292	24.9973156	21.9714267	19.4530453	17.3429671
32	29.2930545	25.4677542	22.3207469	19.7131427	17.5371531
33	29.9070367	25.9181400	22.6520804	19.9575841	17.7179915
34	30.5000563	26.3490831	22.9661753	20.1871818	17.8863043
35	31.0725192	26.7612001	23.2637672	20.4027205	18.0428743
36	31.6248527	27.1551096	23.5455778	20.6049566	18.1884457
37	32.1575013	27.5314303	23.8123121	20.7946173	18.3237241
38	32.6709239	27.8907775	24.0646574	20.9724006	18.4493779
39	33.1655904	28.2337615	24.3032818	21.1389748	18.5660392
40	33.6419791	28.5609854	24.5288333	21.2949790	18.6743043

Present Value of Ordinary Annuity of $1 per Period, Increasing in Constant Amount of 10 Percent

Period	Interest Rate				
	11%	**12%**	**13%**	**14%**	**15%**
0	0.0000000	0.0000000	0.0000000	0.0000000	0.0000000
1	0.9009009	0.8928571	0.8849558	0.8771930	0.8695652
2	1.7936856	1.7697704	1.7464171	1.7236073	1.7013233
3	2.6711152	2.6239067	2.5780773	2.5335731	2.4903427
4	3.5274655	3.4500802	3.3753916	3.3032774	3.2336219
5	4.3582974	4.2444778	4.1352556	4.0303936	3.9296694
6	5.1602586	5.0044245	4.8557333	4.7137734	4.5781608
7	5.9309121	5.7281832	5.5358304	5.3531931	5.1796600
8	6.6685871	6.4147847	6.1753021	5.9491435	5.7353931
9	7.3722517	7.0638828	6.7744948	6.5026578	6.2470654
10	8.0414022	7.6756319	7.3342127	7.0151710	6.7167163
11	8.6759688	8.2505841	7.8556080	7.4884058	7.1466028
12	9.2762346	8.7896018	8.3400904	7.9242799	7.5391078
13	9.8427659	9.2937850	8.7892523	8.3248326	7.8966693
14	10.3763540	9.7644106	9.2048083	8.6921655	8.2217252
15	10.8779645	10.2028816	9.5885462	9.0283971	8.5166720
16	11.3486950	10.6106858	9.9422868	9.3356262	8.7838339
17	11.7897398	10.9893611	10.2678533	9.6159054	9.0254412
18	12.2023597	11.3404680	10.5670466	9.8712205	9.2436150
19	12.5878570	11.6655669	10.8416258	10.1034759	9.4403579
20	12.9475554	11.9662006	11.0932944	10.3144849	9.6175487
21	13.2827821	12.2438794	11.3236899	10.5059631	9.7769408
22	13.5948551	12.5000712	11.5343760	10.6795253	9.9201626
23	13.8850712	12.7361926	11.7268384	10.8366839	10.0487208
24	14.1546976	12.9536036	11.9024815	10.9788505	10.1640039
25	14.4049651	13.1536028	12.0626282	11.1073371	10.2672879
26	14.6370627	13.3374257	12.2085192	11.2233595	10.3597415
27	14.8521338	13.5062425	12.3413150	11.3280414	10.4424330
28	15.0512737	13.6611588	12.4620979	11.4224183	10.5163360
29	15.2355278	13.8032153	12.5718742	11.5074426	10.5823364
30	15.4058908	13.9333892	12.6715779	11.5839880	10.6412383
31	15.5633064	14.0525960	12.7620737	11.6528547	10.6937707
32	15.7086676	14.1616916	12.8441606	11.7147744	10.7405930
33	15.8428177	14.2614742	12.9185756	11.7704146	10.7823011
34	15.9665511	14.3526869	12.9859976	11.8203840	10.8194326
35	16.0806151	14.4360209	13.0470506	11.8652361	10.8524717
36	16.1857109	14.5121172	13.1023077	11.9054742	10.8818543
37	16.2824958	14.5815702	13.1522945	11.9415552	10.9079721
38	16.3715849	14.6449299	13.1974923	11.9738932	10.9311770
39	16.4535530	14.7027047	13.2383414	12.0028635	10.9517845
40	16.5289366	14.7553640	13.2752441	12.0288054	10.9700774

Present Value of Ordinary Annuity of $1 per Period, Increasing in Constant Amount of 10 Percent

Period			Interest Rate		
	16%	17%	18%	19%	20%
0	0.0000000	0.0000000	0.0000000	0.0000000	0.0000000
1	0.8620690	0.8547009	0.8474576	0.8403361	0.8333333
2	1.6795482	1.6582658	1.6374605	1.6171174	1.5972222
3	2.4483374	2.4075104	2.3678175	2.3292164	2.2916667
4	3.1663158	3.1012555	3.0383431	2.9774858	2.9185957
5	3.8328740	3.7398111	3.6502960	3.5641549	3.4812243
6	4.4485374	4.3245690	4.2059433	4.0923684	3.9835712
7	5.0146646	4.8576816	4.7082233	4.5658371	4.4301019
8	5.5332079	5.3418116	5.1604882	4.9885770	4.8254675
9	6.0065233	5.7799384	5.5663092	5.3647173	5.1743196
10	6.4372221	6.1752094	5.9293316	5.6983618	5.4811802
11	6.8280559	6.5308288	6.2531697	5.9934918	5.7503562
12	7.1818279	6.8499745	6.5413307	6.2539007	5.9858852
13	7.5013264	7.1357378	6.7971637	6.4831522	6.1915057
14	7.7892757	7.3910819	7.0238263	6.6845572	6.3706448
15	8.0483005	7.6188135	7.2242648	6.8611638	6.5264179
16	8.2809018	7.8215660	7.4012055	7.0157564	6.6616377
17	8.4894409	8.0017905	7.5571533	7.1508625	6.7788281
18	8.6761305	8.1617530	7.6943955	7.2687637	6.8802429
19	8.8430304	8.3035368	7.8150101	7.3715099	6.9678853
20	8.9920483	8.4290475	7.9208764	7.4609349	7.0435291
21	9.1249417	8.5400207	8.0136874	7.5386732	7.1087392
22	9.2433238	8.6380312	8.0949625	7.6061771	7.1648924
23	9.3486693	8.7245032	8.1660615	7.6647328	7.2131962
24	9.4423224	8.8007204	8.2281979	7.7154771	7.2547073
25	9.5255044	8.8678374	8.2824515	7.7594115	7.2903481
26	9.5993221	8.9268895	8.3297814	7.7974171	7.3209223
27	9.6647761	8.9788035	8.3710375	7.8302670	7.3471288
28	9.7227695	9.0244069	8.4069715	7.8586388	7.3695742
29	9.7741149	9.0644377	8.4382471	7.8831250	7.3887842
30	9.8195431	9.0995524	8.4654493	7.9042432	7.4052138
31	9.8597094	9.1303345	8.4890932	7.9224445	7.4192562
32	9.8952012	9.1573017	8.5096312	7.9381222	7.4312507
33	9.9265439	9.1809128	8.5274609	7.9516180	7.4414900
34	9.9542067	9.2015737	8.5429305	7.9632291	7.4502259
35	9.9786086	9.2196432	8.5563453	7.9732132	7.4576751
36	10.0001228	9.2354383	8.5679721	7.9817939	7.4640238
37	10.0190816	9.2492384	8.5780443	7.9891648	7.4694320
38	10.0357808	9.2612897	8.5867656	7.9954934	7.4740368
39	10.0504829	9.2718091	8.5943138	8.0009248	7.4779558
40	10.0634211	9.2809874	8.6008438	8.0055841	7.4812896

Present Value of Ordinary Annuity of $1 per Period, Increasing in Constant Amount of 15 Percent

Period	Interest Rate			
	2%	**3%**	**4%**	**5%**
0	0.0000000	0.0000000	0.0000000	0.0000000
1	0.9803922	0.9708738	0.9615385	0.9523810
2	2.0857363	2.0548591	2.0247781	1.9954649
3	3.3107553	3.2445432	3.1804734	3.1184537
4	4.6503312	4.5328495	4.4199394	4.3113723
5	6.0995005	5.9130235	5.7350228	5.5650142
6	7.6534504	7.3786210	7.1180732	6.8708911
7	9.3075147	8.9234948	8.5619171	8.2211857
8	11.0571700	10.5417838	10.0598320	9.6087063
9	12.8980316	12.2279006	11.6055228	11.0268460
10	14.8258501	13.9765213	13.1930986	12.4695421
11	16.8365077	15.7825745	14.8170509	13.9312403
12	18.9260146	17.6412311	16.4722331	15.4068595
13	21.0905056	19.5478949	18.1538406	16.8917593
14	23.3262370	21.4981924	19.8573921	18.3817097
15	25.6295826	23.4879645	21.5787120	19.8728627
16	27.9970315	25.5132570	23.3139136	21.3617252
17	30.4251842	27.5703129	25.0593826	22.8451339
18	32.9107500	29.6555638	26.8117625	24.3202322
19	35.4505438	31.7656221	28.5679394	25.7844479
20	38.0414835	33.8972737	30.3250292	27.2354724
21	40.6805867	36.0474708	32.0803636	28.6712419
22	43.3649687	38.2133247	33.8314784	30.0899188
23	46.0918392	40.3920992	35.5761017	31.4898754
24	48.8584998	42.5812044	37.3121422	32.8696776
25	51.6623418	44.7781900	39.0376795	34.2280704
26	54.5008434	46.9807399	40.7509534	35.5639639
27	57.3715674	49.1866663	42.4503546	36.8764206
28	60.2721589	51.3939039	44.1344158	38.1646435
29	63.2003429	53.6005050	45.8018032	39.4279644
30	66.1539222	55.8046342	47.4513080	40.6658337
31	69.1307750	58.0045635	49.0818394	41.8778108
32	72.1288532	60.1986677	50.6924168	43.0635547
33	75.1461798	62.3854199	52.2821630	44.2228154
34	78.1808474	64.5633871	53.8502979	45.3554265
35	81.2310158	66.7312258	55.3961323	46.4612972
36	84.2949105	68.8876785	56.9190618	47.5404061
37	87.3708205	71.0315693	58.4185617	48.5927941
38	90.4570965	73.1618006	59.8941812	49.6185592
39	93.5521496	75.2773493	61.3455393	50.6178506
40	96.6544490	77.3772637	62.7723192	51.5908635

Present Value of Ordinary Annuity of $1 per Period, Increasing in Constant Amount of 15 Percent

Period	Interest Rate				
	6%	**7%**	**8%**	**9%**	**10%**
0	0.0000000	0.0000000	0.0000000	0.0000000	0.0000000
1	0.9433962	0.9345794	0.9259259	0.9174312	0.9090909
2	1.9668921	1.9390340	1.9118656	1.8853632	1.8595041
3	3.0583972	3.0002212	2.9438475	2.8892017	2.8362134
4	4.2069330	4.1064193	4.0096408	3.9164183	3.8265829
5	5.4025461	5.2471972	5.0985739	4.9563085	4.8200570
6	6.6362270	6.4132961	6.2013707	5.9997763	5.8078864
7	7.8998356	7.5965206	7.3100025	7.0391414	6.7828868
8	9.1860309	8.7896392	8.4175537	8.0679672	7.7392269
9	10.4882075	9.9862935	9.5181014	9.0809084	8.6722417
10	11.8004353	11.1809143	10.6066061	10.0735738	9.5782684
11	13.1174041	12.3686463	11.6788133	11.0424059	10.4545032
12	14.4343729	13.5452780	12.7311647	11.9845729	11.2988748
13	15.7471221	14.7071784	13.7607189	12.8978731	12.1099351
14	17.0519100	15.8512393	14.7650790	13.7806502	12.8867623
15	18.3454317	16.9748220	15.7423283	14.6317181	13.6288777
16	19.6247821	18.0757094	16.6909723	15.4502948	14.3361723
17	20.8874211	19.1520623	17.6098867	16.2359436	15.0088442
18	22.1311416	20.2023792	18.4982708	16.9885214	15.6473429
19	23.3540397	21.2254601	19.3556054	17.7081332	16.2523225
20	24.5544879	22.2203732	20.1816160	18.3950921	16.8246005
21	25.7311095	23.1864256	20.9762390	19.0498844	17.3651227
22	26.8827557	24.1231352	21.7395921	19.6731385	17.8749335
23	28.0084839	25.0302068	22.4719478	20.2655984	18.3551496
24	29.1075384	25.9075093	23.1737099	20.8281004	18.8069385
25	30.1793321	26.7550555	23.8453922	21.3615525	19.2315001
26	31.2234298	27.5729841	24.4876006	21.8669169	19.6300510
27	32.2395327	28.3615429	25.1010160	22.3451951	20.0038117
28	33.2274650	29.1210740	25.6863803	22.7974148	20.3539956
29	34.1871600	29.8520007	26.2444834	23.2246184	20.6818005
30	35.1186492	30.5548148	26.7761522	23.6278540	20.9884013
31	36.0220508	31.2300663	27.2822404	24.0081670	21.2749440
32	36.8975601	31.8783537	27.7636207	24.3665939	21.5425418
33	37.7454402	32.5003149	28.2211765	24.7041559	21.7922711
34	38.5660138	33.0966200	28.6557960	25.0218550	22.0251690
35	39.3596557	33.6679640	29.0683668	25.3206700	22.2422320
36	40.1267855	34.2150606	29.4597704	25.6015534	22.4444144
37	40.8678618	34.7386371	29.8308790	25.8654292	22.6326279
38	41.5833763	35.2394295	30.1825516	26.1131911	22.8077412
39	42.2738483	35.7181781	30.5156314	26.3457009	22.9705808
40	42.9398203	36.1756237	30.8309433	26.5637884	23.1219311

Present Value of Ordinary Annuity of $1 per Period, Increasing in Constant Amount of 15 Percent

Period	Interest Rate				
	11%	**12%**	**13%**	**14%**	**15%**
0	0.0000000	0.0000000	0.0000000	0.0000000	0.0000000
1	0.9009009	0.8928571	0.8849558	0.8771930	0.8695652
2	1.8342667	1.8096301	1.7855744	1.7620806	1.7391304
3	2.7848155	2.7349444	2.6865396	2.6395436	2.5939015
4	3.7399754	3.6564456	3.5758518	3.4980600	3.4229437
5	4.6894975	4.5643286	4.4442677	4.3290499	4.2184265
6	5.6251190	5.4509331	5.2848251	5.1263263	4.9749998
7	6.5402700	6.3103966	6.0924403	5.8856372	5.6892802
8	7.4298193	7.1383572	6.8635681	6.6042833	6.3594288
9	8.2898538	7.9316993	7.5959147	7.2808008	6.9848061
10	9.1174873	8.6883364	8.2881973	7.9146987	7.5656902
11	9.9106956	9.4070266	8.9399414	8.5062422	8.1030482
12	10.6681738	10.0872156	9.5513121	9.0562738	8.5983522
13	11.3892137	10.7289033	10.1229727	9.5660681	9.0534305
14	12.0735984	11.3325318	10.6559685	10.0372126	9.4703500
15	12.7215119	11.8988902	11.1516298	10.4715117	9.8513229
16	13.3334616	12.4290356	11.6114926	10.8709095	10.1986334
17	13.9102125	12.9242264	12.0372335	11.2374285	10.5145814
18	14.4527312	13.3858669	12.4306172	11.5731205	10.8014396
19	14.9621385	13.8154620	12.7934540	11.8800295	11.0614213
20	15.4396690	14.2145790	13.1275658	12.1601621	11.2966574
21	15.8866380	14.5848175	13.4347598	12.4154664	11.5091801
22	16.3044131	14.9277839	13.7168073	12.6478157	11.7009125
23	16.6943910	15.2450721	13.9754286	12.8589977	11.8736626
24	17.0579781	15.5382475	14.2122808	13.0507071	12.0291201
25	17.3965753	15.8088347	14.4289498	13.2245419	12.1688572
26	17.7115649	16.0583085	14.6269447	13.3820009	12.2943301
27	18.0043006	16.2880871	14.8076946	13.5244845	12.4068824
28	18.2760996	16.4995269	14.9725469	13.6532963	12.5077500
29	18.5282369	16.6939199	15.1227672	13.7696453	12.5980663
30	18.7619399	16.8724918	15.2595402	13.8746499	12.6788676
31	18.9783863	17.0364012	15.3839719	13.9693417	12.7510996
32	19.1787012	17.1867403	15.4970916	14.0546700	12.8156231
33	19.3639561	17.3245352	15.5998552	14.1315065	12.8732200
34	19.5351686	17.4507482	15.6931484	14.2006501	12.9245996
35	19.6933028	17.5662794	15.7777900	14.2628315	12.9704038
36	19.8392691	17.6719687	15.8545361	14.3187178	13.0112129
37	19.9739264	17.7685990	15.9240830	14.3689174	13.0475509
38	20.0980825	17.8568981	15.9870713	14.4139842	13.0798896
39	20.2124964	17.9375421	16.0440898	14.4544219	13.1086543
40	20.3178796	18.0111576	16.0956783	14.4906876	13.1342270

Present Value of Ordinary Annuity of \$1 per Period, Increasing in Constant Amount of 15 Percent

Period	Interest Rate				
	16%	**17%**	**18%**	**19%**	**20%**
0	0.0000000	0.0000000	0.0000000	0.0000000	0.0000000
1	0.8620690	0.8547009	0.8474576	0.8403361	0.8333333
2	1.7167063	1.6947914	1.6733697	1.6524257	1.6319444
3	2.5495613	2.5064732	2.4645899	2.4238662	2.3842593
4	3.3503834	3.2802657	3.2124837	3.1469359	3.0835262
5	4.1121642	4.0100436	3.9118585	3.8174149	3.7265303
6	4.8304381	4.6922611	4.5601137	4.4336640	4.3126018
7	5.5027142	5.3253323	5.1565712	4.9959080	4.8428569
8	6.1280164	5.9091362	5.7019495	5.5056826	5.3196214
9	6.7065130	6.4446244	6.1979528	5.9654096	5.7459962
10	7.2392195	6.9335123	6.6469543	6.3780752	6.1255343
11	7.7277617	7.3780366	7.0517519	6.7469878	6.4620042
12	8.1741882	7.7807680	7.4153837	7.0755990	6.7592194
13	8.5808227	8.1444668	7.7409893	7.3673736	7.0209182
14	8.9501489	8.4719733	8.0317086	7.6256975	7.2506836
15	9.2847227	8.7661266	8.2906084	7.8538143	7.4518906
16	9.5871044	9.0297049	8.5206314	8.0547846	7.6276762
17	9.8598094	9.2653830	8.7245631	8.2314618	7.7809253
18	10.1052716	9.4757041	8.9050111	8.3864802	7.9142669
19	10.3258179	9.6630613	9.0643947	8.5222519	8.0300801
20	10.5236519	9.8296876	9.2049414	8.6409713	8.1305037
21	10.7008432	9.9776519	9.3286893	8.7446224	8.2174506
22	10.8593224	10.1088595	9.4374931	8.8349904	8.2926234
23	11.0008805	10.2250562	9.5330324	8.9136748	8.3575316
24	11.1271703	10.3278340	9.6168224	8.9821026	8.4135087
25	11.2397106	10.4186393	9.6902243	9.0415433	8.4617286
26	11.3398917	10.4987815	9.7544578	9.0931223	8.5032222
27	11.4289820	10.5694422	9.8106119	9.1378347	8.5388922
28	11.5081351	10.6316847	9.8596570	9.1765583	8.5695271
29	11.5783972	10.6864636	9.9024552	9.2100658	8.5958144
30	11.6407153	10.7346337	9.9397710	9.2390356	8.6183525
31	11.6959441	10.7769591	9.9722813	9.2640625	8.6376608
32	11.7448535	10.8141213	10.0005837	9.2856670	8.6541899
33	11.7881362	10.8467271	10.0252057	9.3043041	8.6683298
34	11.8264139	10.8753160	10.0466113	9.3203706	8.6804178
35	11.8602437	10.9003670	10.0652090	9.3342122	8.6907451
36	11.8901245	10.9223045	10.0813574	9.3461298	8.6995628
37	11.9165021	10.9415046	10.0953708	9.3563850	8.7070872
38	11.9397743	10.9582996	10.1075250	9.3652047	8.7135045
39	11.9602960	10.9729830	10.1180610	9.3727860	8.7189748
40	11.9783832	10.9858138	10.1271898	9.3792995	8.7236354

.19 Present Value of Ordinary Annuity Decreasing in Constant Amount
$1 per Period, Decreasing in Constant Amount of 2 Percent

Period		Interest Rate		
	2%	3%	4%	5%
0	0.0000000	0.0000000	0.0000000	0.0000000
1	0.9803922	0.9708738	0.9615385	0.9523810
2	1.9223376	1.8946178	1.8676036	1.8412698
3	2.8269670	2.7731538	2.7210401	2.6705539
4	3.6953817	3.6083316	3.5245560	3.4438943
5	4.5286540	4.4019317	4.2807289	4.1647383
6	5.3278283	5.1556675	4.9920120	4.8363322
7	6.0939213	5.8711880	5.6607397	5.4617318
8	6.8279230	6.5500800	6.2891333	6.0438136
9	7.5307974	7.1938700	6.8793061	6.5852851
10	8.2034830	7.8040270	7.4332687	7.0886940
11	8.8468934	8.3819641	7.9529335	7.5564374
12	9.4619181	8.9290404	8.4401192	7.9907706
13	10.0494228	9.4465634	8.8965555	8.3938148
14	10.6102503	9.9357906	9.3238870	8.7675651
15	11.1452209	10.3979312	9.7236775	9.1138974
16	11.6551330	10.8341480	10.0974132	9.4345755
17	12.1407636	11.2455592	10.4465070	9.7312572
18	12.6028687	11.6332397	10.7723016	10.0055009
19	13.0421844	11.9982227	11.0760727	10.2587706
20	13.4594267	12.3415017	11.3590326	10.4924421
21	13.8552922	12.6640312	11.6223328	10.7078075
22	14.2304588	12.9667289	11.8670669	10.9060804
23	14.5855861	13.2504763	12.0942737	11.0884003
24	14.9213157	13.5161205	12.3049393	11.2558370
25	15.2382718	13.7644754	12.5000000	11.4093945
26	15.5370614	13.9963227	12.6803446	11.5500148
27	15.8182752	14.2124135	12.8468166	11.6785820
28	16.0824875	14.4134688	13.0002162	11.7959251
29	16.3302569	14.6001812	13.1413028	11.9028215
30	16.5621267	14.7732156	13.2707967	12.0000000
31	16.7786251	14.9332105	13.3893808	12.0881438
32	16.9802657	15.0807786	13.4977028	12.1678929
33	17.1675481	15.2165080	13.5963767	12.2398470
34	17.3409576	15.3409633	13.6859844	12.3045677
35	17.5009665	15.4546860	13.7670774	12.3625806
36	17.6480334	15.5581957	13.8401780	12.4143778
37	17.7826045	15.6519909	13.9057811	12.4604198
38	17.9051131	15.7365497	13.9643553	12.5011372
39	18.0159807	15.8123306	14.0163442	12.5369327
40	18.1156166	15.8797731	14.0621678	12.5681827

Present Value of Ordinary Annuity of $1 per Period, Decreasing in Constant Amount of 2 Percent

Period	Interest Rate				
	6%	7%	8%	9%	10%
0	0.0000000	0.0000000	0.0000000	0.0000000	0.0000000
1	0.9433962	0.9345794	0.9259259	0.9174312	0.9090909
2	1.8155927	1.7905494	1.7661180	1.7422776	1.7190083
3	2.6216272	2.5741954	2.5281969	2.4835737	2.4402705
4	3.3661953	3.2913169	3.2191250	3.1494934	3.0823031
5	4.0536728	3.9472641	3.8452615	3.7474303	3.6535507
6	4.6881373	4.5469721	4.4124142	4.2840709	4.1615773
7	5.2733876	5.0949919	4.9258857	4.7654610	4.6131564
8	5.8129622	5.5955197	5.3905170	5.1970660	5.0143528
9	6.3101569	6.0524241	5.8107261	5.5838254	5.3705948
10	6.7680406	6.4692705	6.1905448	5.9302022	5.6867403
11	7.1894706	6.8493447	6.5336511	6.2402285	5.9671354
12	7.5771067	7.1956741	6.8433998	6.5175456	6.2156674
13	7.9334244	7.5110471	7.1228502	6.7654414	6.4358123
14	8.2607271	7.7980318	7.3747914	6.9868837	6.6306775
15	8.5611580	8.0589929	7.6017654	7.1845511	6.8030398
16	8.8367104	8.2961072	7.8060887	7.3608600	6.9553801
17	9.0892382	8.5113777	7.9898716	7.5179897	7.0899145
18	9.3204651	8.7066479	8.1550360	7.6579056	7.2086213
19	9.5319934	8.8836133	8.3033317	7.7823790	7.3132664
20	9.7253123	9.0438330	8.4363516	7.8930061	7.4054255
21	9.9018056	9.1887409	8.5555450	7.9912250	7.4865038
22	10.0627585	9.3196545	8.6622305	8.0783304	7.5577545
23	10.2093650	9.4377848	8.7576071	8.1554879	7.6202943
24	10.3427334	9.5442440	8.8427647	8.2237466	7.6751181
25	10.4638927	9.6400535	8.9186940	8.2840499	7.7231120
26	10.5737977	9.7261513	8.9862949	8.3372461	7.7650647
27	10.6733343	9.8033979	9.0463846	8.3840979	7.8016780
28	10.7633242	9.8725829	9.0997049	8.4252902	7.8335760
29	10.8445292	9.9344305	9.1469290	8.4614382	7.8613133
30	10.9176554	9.9896047	9.1886675	8.4930941	7.8853829
31	10.9833573	10.0387139	9.2254739	8.5207532	7.9062224
32	11.0422412	10.0823155	9.2578499	8.5448598	7.9242201
33	11.0948682	10.1209200	9.2862500	8.5658119	7.9397205
34	11.1417581	10.1549946	9.3110854	8.5839661	7.9530290
35	11.1833918	10.1849667	9.3327284	8.5996417	7.9644159
36	11.2202140	10.2112274	9.3515158	8.6131241	7.9741207
37	11.2526361	10.2341339	9.3677518	8.6246686	7.9823550
38	11.2810382	10.2540126	9.3817113	8.6345035	7.9893061
39	11.3057715	10.2711618	9.3936425	8.6428322	7.9951391
40	11.3271604	10.2858535	9.4037693	8.6498364	8.0000000

Present Value of Ordinary Annuity of $1 per Period, Decreasing in Constant Amount of 2 Percent

Period	Interest Rate				
	11%	12%	13%	14%	15%
0	0.0000000	0.0000000	0.0000000	0.0000000	0.0000000
1	0.9009009	0.8928571	0.8849558	0.8771930	0.8695652
2	1.6962909	1.6741071	1.6524395	1.6312712	1.6105860
3	2.3982346	2.3574162	2.3177677	2.2792438	2.2418016
4	3.0174417	2.9548032	2.8942873	2.8357993	2.7792496
5	3.5634169	3.4768359	3.3936264	3.3136184	3.2366522
6	4.0445937	3.9328039	3.8259131	3.7236463	3.6257471
7	4.4684531	4.3308712	4.1999664	4.0753272	3.9565717
8	4.8416299	4.6782108	4.5234639	4.3768080	4.2377072
9	5.1700067	4.9811232	4.8030872	4.6351146	4.4764876
10	5.4587980	5.2451413	5.0446496	4.8563046	4.6791791
11	5.7126246	5.4751221	5.2532078	5.0455985	4.8511337
12	5.9355805	5.6753287	5.4331583	5.2074946	4.9969212
13	6.1312913	5.8495011	5.5883234	5.3458673	5.1204425
14	6.3029675	6.0009198	5.7220240	5.4640527	5.2250257
15	6.4534506	6.1324611	5.8371454	5.5649222	5.3135097
16	6.5852551	6.2466462	5.9361927	5.6509463	5.3883151
17	6.7006053	6.3456844	6.0213409	5.7242501	5.4515047
18	6.8014680	6.4315105	6.0944770	5.7866605	5.5048360
19	6.8895816	6.5058188	6.1572380	5.8397474	5.5498058
20	6.9664827	6.5700922	6.2110430	5.8848597	5.5876880
21	7.0335280	6.6256280	6.2571221	5.9231553	5.6195664
22	7.0919159	6.6735607	6.2965408	5.9556282	5.6463628
23	7.1427037	6.7148819	6.3302217	5.9831310	5.6688604
24	7.1868244	6.7504583	6.3589633	6.0063946	5.6877250
25	7.2251006	6.7810464	6.3834563	6.0260455	5.7035213
26	7.2582574	6.8073068	6.4042979	6.0426201	5.7167290
27	7.2869335	6.8298157	6.4220040	6.0565777	5.7277545
28	7.3116915	6.8490756	6.4370203	6.0683111	5.7369425
29	7.3330261	6.8655242	6.4497312	6.0781560	5.7445846
30	7.3513729	6.8795429	6.4604685	6.0863993	5.7509279
31	7.3671145	6.8914636	6.4695181	6.0932860	5.7561811
32	7.3805870	6.9015749	6.4771262	6.0990249	5.7605208
33	7.3920856	6.9101277	6.4835046	6.1037941	5.7640958
34	7.4018691	6.9173399	6.4888356	6.1077451	5.7670317
35	7.4101647	6.9234005	6.4932759	6.1110071	5.7694346
36	7.4171711	6.9284736	6.4969597	6.1136897	5.7713934
37	7.4230623	6.9327012	6.5000023	6.1158859	5.7729832
38	7.4279907	6.9362062	6.5025026	6.1176748	5.7742669
39	7.4320891	6.9390949	6.5045451	6.1191233	5.7752972
40	7.4354737	6.9414592	6.5062020	6.1202881	5.7761186

Present Value of Ordinary Annuity of $1 per Period, Decreasing in Constant Amount of 2 Percent

Period	Interest Rate				
	16%	17%	18%	19%	20%
0	0.0000000	0.0000000	0.0000000	0.0000000	0.0000000
1	0.8620690	0.8547009	0.8474576	0.8403361	0.8333333
2	1.5903686	1.5706041	1.5512784	1.5323777	1.5138889
3	2.2054000	2.1699999	2.1355640	2.1020568	2.0694444
4	2.7245536	2.6716309	2.6204055	2.5708055	2.5227623
5	3.1625776	3.0912532	3.0225460	2.9563309	2.8924897
6	3.5319756	3.4421079	3.3559344	3.2732590	3.1938979
7	3.8433456	3.7353198	3.6321884	3.5336668	3.4394897
8	4.1056675	3.9802327	3.8609813	3.7475234	3.6394983
9	4.3265480	4.1846918	4.0503644	3.9230555	3.8022959
10	4.5124285	4.3552825	4.2070372	4.0670495	3.9347305
11	4.6687621	4.4975303	4.3365725	4.1851015	4.0424008
12	4.8001631	4.6160701	4.4436037	4.2818248	4.1298830
13	4.9105353	4.7147883	4.5319824	4.3610208	4.2009156
14	5.0031798	4.7969425	4.6049086	4.4258207	4.2585516
15	5.0808873	4.8652620	4.6650401	4.4788026	4.3052836
16	5.1460157	4.9220327	4.7145835	4.5220885	4.3431451
17	5.2005567	4.9691683	4.7553699	4.5574240	4.3737949
18	5.2461919	5.0082703	4.7889180	4.5862443	4.3985852
19	5.2843404	5.0406780	4.8164870	4.6097291	4.4186178
20	5.3161994	5.0675113	4.8391205	4.6288476	4.4347899
21	5.3427781	5.0897059	4.8576827	4.6443952	4.4478319
22	5.3649270	5.1080434	4.8728890	4.6570250	4.4583380
23	5.3833625	5.1231760	4.8853313	4.6672723	4.4667911
24	5.3986875	5.1356479	4.8954991	4.6755759	4.4735839
25	5.4114095	5.1459128	4.9037967	4.6822952	4.4790348
26	5.4219549	5.1543489	4.9105581	4.6877246	4.4834026
27	5.4306821	5.1612707	4.9160590	4.6921046	4.4868968
28	5.4378921	5.1669403	4.9205264	4.6956319	4.4896873
29	5.4438373	5.1715755	4.9241478	4.6984672	4.4919116
30	5.4487296	5.1753571	4.9270773	4.7007414	4.4936809
31	5.4527462	5.1784353	4.9294417	4.7025616	4.4950852
32	5.4560357	5.1809347	4.9313452	4.7040146	4.4961968
33	5.4587222	5.1829585	4.9328734	4.7051714	4.4970745
34	5.4609095	5.1845921	4.9340966	4.7060895	4.4977652
35	5.4626842	5.1859063	4.9350722	4.7068156	4.4983070
36	5.4641185	5.1869593	4.9358474	4.7073876	4.4987303
37	5.4652725	5.1877993	4.9364605	4.7078363	4.4990594
38	5.4661963	5.1884660	4.9369429	4.7081864	4.4993142
39	5.4669314	5.1889919	4.9373203	4.7084580	4.4995101
40	5.4675123	5.1894040	4.9376135	4.7086672	4.4996598

Present Value of Ordinary Annuity of $1 per Period, Decreasing in Constant Amount of 5 Percent

Period	Interest Rate			
	2%	3%	4%	5%
0	0.0000000	0.0000000	0.0000000	0.0000000
1	0.9803922	0.9708738	0.9615385	0.9523810
2	1.8935025	1.8663399	1.8398669	1.8140590
3	2.7415926	2.6899674	2.6399636	2.5915128
4	3.5268612	3.4451814	3.3665471	3.2908099
5	4.2514459	4.1352684	4.0240888	3.9176308
6	4.9174244	4.7633816	4.6168247	4.4772924
7	5.5268165	5.3325457	5.1487672	4.9747693
8	6.0815853	5.8456617	5.6237158	5.4147149
9	6.5836384	6.3055117	6.0452679	5.8014802
10	7.0348300	6.7147634	6.4168282	6.1391325
11	7.4369615	7.0759740	6.7416186	6.4314722
12	7.7917834	7.3915949	7.0226873	6.6820490
13	8.1009964	7.6639755	7.2629169	6.8941776
14	8.3662527	7.8953667	7.4650332	7.0709513
15	8.5891571	8.0879253	7.6316126	7.2152565
16	8.7712686	8.2437170	7.7650896	7.3297844
17	8.9141011	8.3647203	7.8677643	7.4170437
18	9.0191250	8.4528295	7.9418085	7.4793718
19	9.0877681	8.5098581	7.9892727	7.5189452
20	9.1214166	8.5375419	8.0120921	7.5377897
21	9.1214166	8.5375419	8.0120921	7.5377897
22	9.0890747	8.5114473	7.9909943	7.5206972
23	9.0256591	8.4607781	7.9504217	7.4881400
24	8.9324009	8.3869880	7.8919034	7.4416298
25	8.8104947	8.2914669	7.8168801	7.3825693
26	8.6610999	8.1755432	7.7267078	7.3122591
27	8.4853413	8.0404865	7.6226628	7.2319046
28	8.2843102	7.8875097	7.5059457	7.1426218
29	8.0590652	7.7177711	7.3776851	7.0454433
30	7.8106333	7.5323771	7.2389417	6.9413235
31	7.5400104	7.3323835	7.0907116	6.8311437
32	7.2481620	7.1187981	6.9339297	6.7157173
33	6.9360248	6.8925824	6.7694732	6.5957938
34	6.6045065	6.6546532	6.5981644	6.4720632
35	6.2544872	6.4058848	6.4207735	6.3451600
36	5.8868198	6.1471105	6.2380220	6.2156669
37	5.5023311	5.8791242	6.0505845	6.0841184
38	5.1018220	5.6026819	5.8590919	5.9510039
39	4.6860686	5.3185037	5.6641334	5.8167707
40	4.2558227	5.0272747	5.4662588	5.6818273

¶691.19

Present Value of Ordinary Annuity of $1 per Period, Decreasing in Constant Amount of 5 Percent

Period	Interest Rate				
	6%	**7%**	**8%**	**9%**	**10%**
0	0.0000000	0.0000000	0.0000000	0.0000000	0.0000000
1	0.9433962	0.9345794	0.9259259	0.9174312	0.9090909
2	1.7888928	1.7643462	1.7403978	1.7170272	1.6942149
3	2.5445502	2.4990143	2.4548468	2.4119923	2.3703982
4	3.2178298	3.1474753	3.0796222	3.0141537	2.9509596
5	3.8156364	3.7178642	3.6240888	3.5340989	3.4476967
6	4.3443568	4.2176209	4.0967160	3.9812994	3.8710521
7	4.8098967	4.6535457	4.5051593	4.3642233	4.2302628
8	5.2177148	5.0318516	4.8563340	4.6904364	4.5334926
9	5.5728539	5.3582118	5.1564834	4.9666931	4.7879512
10	5.8799710	5.6378040	5.4112398	5.1990190	5.0000000
11	6.1433647	5.8753504	5.6256813	5.3927854	5.1752469
12	6.3670010	6.0751557	5.8043824	5.5527761	5.3186308
13	6.5545366	6.2411415	5.9514616	5.6832475	5.4344966
14	6.7093419	6.3768775	6.0706230	5.7879838	5.5266625
15	6.8345214	6.4856114	6.1651955	5.8703452	5.5984801
16	6.9329330	6.5702950	6.2381681	5.9333126	5.6528874
17	7.0072059	6.6336099	6.2922219	5.9795273	5.6924563
18	7.0597574	6.6779895	6.3297593	6.0113263	5.7194352
19	7.0928087	6.7056403	6.3529305	6.0307753	5.7357860
20	7.1083990	6.7185613	6.3636579	6.0396969	5.7432181
21	7.1083990	6.7185613	6.3636579	6.0396969	5.7432181
22	7.0945237	6.7072756	6.3544608	6.0321878	5.7370758
23	7.0683440	6.6861809	6.3374293	6.0184096	5.7259080
24	7.0312972	6.6566089	6.3137744	5.9994489	5.7106792
25	6.9846975	6.6197591	6.2845708	5.9762553	5.6922200
26	6.9297450	6.5767102	6.2507704	5.9496572	5.6712436
27	6.8675346	6.5284311	6.2132143	5.9203748	5.6483603
28	6.7990641	6.4757903	6.1726445	5.8890329	5.6240901
29	6.7252414	6.4195652	6.1297135	5.8561711	5.5988744
30	6.6468918	6.3604500	6.0849937	5.8222541	5.5730855
31	6.5647644	6.2990635	6.0389857	5.7876802	5.5470362
32	6.4795378	6.2359559	5.9921257	5.7527890	5.5209868
33	6.3918261	6.1716150	5.9447923	5.7178688	5.4951528
34	6.3021836	6.1064725	5.8973129	5.6831622	5.4697102
35	6.2111099	6.0409084	5.8499687	5.6488720	5.4448013
36	6.1190543	5.9752568	5.8030003	5.6151660	5.4205394
37	6.0264198	5.9098098	5.7566117	5.5821815	5.3970127
38	5.9335668	5.8448214	5.7109748	5.5500292	5.3742881
39	5.8408168	5.7805119	5.6662327	5.5187965	5.3524141
40	5.7484557	5.7170706	5.6225033	5.4885508	5.3314239

¶691.19

Present Value of Ordinary Annuity of $1 per Period, Decreasing in Constant Amount of 5 Percent

Period	Interest Rate				
	11%	**12%**	**13%**	**14%**	**15%**
0	0.0000000	0.0000000	0.0000000	0.0000000	0.0000000
1	0.9009009	0.8928571	0.8849558	0.8771930	0.8695652
2	1.6719422	1.6501913	1.6289451	1.6081871	1.5879017
3	2.3300145	2.2907935	2.2526902	2.2156615	2.1796663
4	2.8899358	2.8309839	2.7740112	2.7189297	2.6656566
5	3.3646968	3.2849254	3.2082191	3.1344247	3.0633980
6	3.7656775	3.6648987	3.5684580	3.4761146	3.3876437
7	4.1028384	3.9815432	3.8660005	3.7558607	3.6507996
8	4.3848906	4.2440673	4.1105044	3.9837241	3.8632857
9	4.6194454	4.4604333	4.3102353	4.1682289	4.0338432
10	4.8131469	4.6375186	4.4722589	4.3165879	4.1697948
11	4.9717886	4.7812566	4.6026077	4.4348966	4.2772664
12	5.1004169	4.8967604	4.7064253	4.5282982	4.3613746
13	5.2034226	4.9884301	4.7880911	4.6011260	4.4263858
14	5.2846208	5.0600470	4.8513279	4.6570245	4.4758508
15	5.3473221	5.1148559	4.8992952	4.6990534	4.5127192
16	5.3943952	5.1556363	4.9346692	4.7297763	4.5394354
17	5.4283217	5.1847652	4.9597128	4.7513363	4.5580205
18	5.4512450	5.2042711	4.9763346	4.7655205	4.5701413
19	5.4650128	5.2158818	4.9861410	4.7738153	4.5771678
20	5.4712145	5.2210652	4.9904802	4.7774534	4.5802228
21	5.4712145	5.2210652	4.9904802	4.7774534	4.5802228
22	5.4661811	5.2169330	4.9870820	4.7746540	4.5779128
23	5.4571118	5.2095542	4.9810676	4.7697428	4.5738954
24	5.4448561	5.1996719	4.9730838	4.7632807	4.5686552
25	5.4301344	5.1879073	4.9636634	4.7557226	4.5625797
26	5.4135560	5.1747771	4.9532426	4.7474353	4.5559759
27	5.3956335	5.1607090	4.9421763	4.7387118	4.5490849
28	5.3767959	5.1460547	4.9307509	4.7297843	4.5420941
29	5.3574007	5.1311014	4.9191955	4.7208344	4.5351467
30	5.3377435	5.1160814	4.9076912	4.7120022	4.5283503
31	5.3180665	5.1011805	4.8963792	4.7033938	4.5217838
32	5.2985668	5.0865457	4.8853676	4.6950875	4.5155027
33	5.2794025	5.0722911	4.8747368	4.6871389	4.5095444
34	5.2606986	5.0585031	4.8645452	4.6795854	4.5039315
35	5.2425521	5.0452454	4.8548322	4.6724499	4.4986753
36	5.2250361	5.0325627	4.8456226	4.6657435	4.4937782
37	5.2082040	5.0204839	4.8369293	4.6594686	4.4892360
38	5.1920921	5.0090253	4.8287552	4.6536202	4.4850393
39	5.1767231	4.9981925	4.8210960	4.6481883	4.4811754
40	5.1621079	4.9879830	4.8139414	4.6431587	4.4776288

Present Value of Ordinary Annuity of $1 per Period, Decreasing in Constant Amount of 5 Percent

Period	Interest Rate				
	16%	17%	18%	19%	20%
0	0.0000000	0.0000000	0.0000000	0.0000000	0.0000000
1	0.8620690	0.8547009	0.8474576	0.8403361	0.8333333
2	1.5680737	1.5486887	1.5297328	1.5111927	1.4930556
3	2.1446656	2.1106222	2.0775006	2.0452669	2.0138889
4	2.6141131	2.5642248	2.5159212	2.4691354	2.4238040
5	2.9950035	2.9291137	2.8656085	2.8043749	2.7453061
6	3.3028352	3.2214926	3.1434322	3.0684816	2.9964796
7	3.5505158	3.4547294	3.3631797	3.2756242	3.1918367
8	3.7487824	3.6398379	3.5361045	3.4372600	3.3430059
9	3.9065542	3.7858802	3.6713782	3.5626401	3.4592900
10	4.0312302	3.9003007	3.7764636	3.6592214	3.5481180
11	4.1289386	3.9892056	3.8574231	3.7330039	3.6154120
12	4.2047469	4.0575940	3.9191719	3.7888058	3.6658825
13	4.2628375	4.1095509	3.9656870	3.8304879	3.7032681
14	4.3066559	4.1484076	4.0001791	3.8611365	3.7305284
15	4.3390340	4.1768741	4.0252340	3.8832123	3.7500000
16	4.3622941	4.1971493	4.0429280	3.8986716	3.7635220
17	4.3783356	4.2110128	4.0549240	3.9090644	3.7725366
18	4.3887072	4.2198996	4.0625486	3.9156144	3.7781708
19	4.3946679	4.2249633	4.0668562	3.9192839	3.7813009
20	4.3972372	4.2271273	4.0686815	3.9208258	3.7826051
21	4.3972372	4.2271273	4.0686815	3.9208258	3.7826051
22	4.3953278	4.2255464	4.0673706	3.9197370	3.7816994
23	4.3920358	4.2228442	4.0651488	3.9179071	3.7801899
24	4.3877788	4.2193798	4.0623244	3.9156006	3.7783030
25	4.3828858	4.2154317	4.0591330	3.9130162	3.7762065
26	4.3776131	4.2112137	4.0557523	3.9103015	3.7740226
27	4.3721586	4.2068875	4.0523143	3.9075640	3.7718387
28	4.3666727	4.2025737	4.0489151	3.9048802	3.7697155
29	4.3612679	4.1983599	4.0456230	3.9023027	3.7676934
30	4.3560262	4.1943082	4.0424843	3.8998660	3.7657977
31	4.3510054	4.1904605	4.0395288	3.8975908	3.7640424
32	4.3462443	4.1868429	4.0367737	3.8954877	3.7624334
33	4.3417668	4.1834699	4.0342266	3.8935597	3.7609706
34	4.3375852	4.1803468	4.0318881	3.8918046	3.7596501
35	4.3337031	4.1774721	4.0297540	3.8902162	3.7584650
36	4.3301174	4.1748395	4.0278162	3.8887861	3.7574069
37	4.3268202	4.1724395	4.0260645	3.8875042	3.7564663
38	4.3238002	4.1702600	4.0244872	3.8863596	3.7556335
39	4.3210435	4.1682876	4.0230720	3.8853413	3.7548987
40	4.3185351	4.1665082	4.0218059	3.8844379	3.7542524

Present Value of Ordinary Annuity of $1 per Period, Decreasing in Constant Amount of 10 Percent

Period		Interest Rate		
	2%	**3%**	**4%**	**5%**
0	0.0000000	0.0000000	0.0000000	0.0000000
1	0.9803922	0.9708738	0.9615385	0.9523810
2	1.8454441	1.8192101	1.7936391	1.7687075
3	2.5993019	2.5513234	2.5048361	2.4597776
4	3.2459937	3.1732644	3.1031991	3.0356693
5	3.7894322	3.6908296	3.5963553	3.5057850
6	4.2334179	4.1095718	3.9915126	3.8788927
7	4.5816420	4.4348084	4.2954797	4.1631652
8	4.8376891	4.6716311	4.5146868	4.3662170
9	5.0050401	4.8249145	4.6552041	4.4951388
10	5.0870750	4.8993239	4.7227606	4.5565301
11	5.0870750	4.8993239	4.7227606	4.5565301
12	5.0082257	4.8291859	4.6603008	4.5008464
13	4.8536191	4.6929956	4.5401860	4.3947821
14	4.6262566	4.4946603	4.3669435	4.2432617
15	4.3290507	4.2379155	4.1448377	4.0508549
16	3.9648278	3.9263320	3.8778836	3.8217991
17	3.5363303	3.5633222	3.5698597	3.5600211
18	3.0462187	3.1521459	3.2243200	3.2691567
19	2.4970741	2.6959171	2.8446060	2.9525695
20	1.8913999	2.1976089	2.4338578	2.6133690
21	1.2316241	1.6600597	1.9950242	2.2544266
22	0.5201012	1.0859779	1.5308733	1.8783917
23	-0.2408859	0.4779478	1.0440017	1.4877062
24	-1.0491239	-0.1615660	0.5368437	1.0846179
25	-1.9024671	-0.8302138	0.0116802	0.6711940
26	-2.7988360	-1.5257559	-0.5293536	0.2493329
27	-3.7362153	-2.2460584	-1.0842601	-0.1792244
28	-4.7126520	-2.9890889	-1.6511718	-0.6128836
29	-5.7262542	-3.7529124	-2.2283444	-1.0501870
30	-6.7751889	-4.5356872	-2.8141499	-1.4898041
31	-7.8576808	-5.3356615	-3.4070704	-1.9305231
32	-8.9720107	-6.1511693	-4.0056920	-2.3712420
33	-10.1165139	-6.9806270	-4.6086992	-2.8109616
34	-11.2895787	-7.8225303	-5.2148690	-3.2487776
35	-12.4896450	-8.6754504	-5.8230662	-3.6838743
36	-13.7152029	-9.5380315	-6.4322380	-4.1155179
37	-14.9647913	-10.4089871	-7.0414098	-4.5430505
38	-16.2369967	-11.2870977	-7.6496804	-4.9658850
39	-17.5304517	-12.1712077	-8.2562181	-5.3834993
40	-18.8438339	-13.0602225	-8.8602564	-5.7954318

Present Value of Ordinary Annuity of \$1 per Period, Decreasing in Constant Amount of 10 Percent

Period			Interest Rate		
	6%	7%	8%	9%	10%
0	0.0000000	0.0000000	0.0000000	0.0000000	0.0000000
1	0.9433962	0.9345794	0.9259259	0.9174312	0.9090909
2	1.7443930	1.7206743	1.6975309	1.6749432	1.6528926
3	2.4160884	2.3737126	2.3325967	2.2926900	2.2539444
4	2.9705540	2.9077392	2.8471176	2.7885876	2.7320538
5	3.4189089	3.3355310	3.2554675	3.1785465	3.1046066
6	3.7713892	3.6687021	3.5705523	3.4766801	3.3868436
7	4.0374120	3.9178020	3.8039484	3.6954938	3.5921068
8	4.2256357	4.0924047	3.9660291	3.8460537	3.7320590
9	4.3440154	4.2011914	4.0660789	3.9381393	3.8168786
10	4.3998549	4.2520264	4.1123983	3.9803803	3.8554329
11	4.3998549	4.2520264	4.1123983	3.9803803	3.8554329
12	4.3501580	4.2076252	4.0726869	3.9448269	3.8235698
13	4.2563902	4.1246323	3.9991473	3.8795911	3.7656369
14	4.1236999	4.0082871	3.8970090	3.7898172	3.6866376
15	3.9567939	3.8633087	3.7709123	3.6800020	3.5908807
16	3.7599707	3.6939414	3.6249671	3.5540671	3.4820662
17	3.5371521	3.5039968	3.4628057	3.4154232	3.3633594
18	3.2919114	3.2968920	3.2876314	3.2670276	3.2374582
19	3.0275010	3.0756854	3.1022617	3.1114358	3.1066518
20	2.7468768	2.8431083	2.9091683	2.9508480	2.9728726
21	2.4527213	2.6015952	2.7105126	2.7871500	2.8377420
22	2.1474657	2.3533107	2.5081780	2.6219501	2.7026114
23	1.8333090	2.1001744	2.3037997	2.4566124	2.5685976
24	1.5122369	1.8438838	2.0987905	2.2922860	2.4366144
25	1.1860388	1.5859350	1.8943655	2.1299310	2.3074000
26	0.8563238	1.3276417	1.6915628	1.9703423	2.1815418
27	0.5245351	1.0701532	1.4912639	1.8141698	2.0594975
28	0.1919638	0.8144694	1.2942106	1.6619374	1.9416138
29	-0.1402383	0.5614563	1.1010211	1.5140592	1.8281429
30	-0.4710476	0.3118588	0.9122041	1.3708541	1.7192566
31	-0.7995572	0.0663128	0.7281720	1.2325584	1.6150592
32	-1.1249678	-0.1746436	0.5492519	1.0993378	1.5155981
33	-1.4465775	-0.4105599	0.3756963	0.9712971	1.4208732
34	-1.7637740	-0.6410644	0.2076921	0.8484890	1.3308454
35	-2.0760265	-0.8658555	0.0453692	0.7309224	1.2454436
36	-2.3828784	-1.0846941	-0.1111923	0.6185691	1.1645706
37	-2.6839407	-1.2973971	-0.2619551	0.5113695	1.0881089
38	-2.9788856	-1.5038306	-0.4069194	0.4092387	1.0159248
39	-3.2674411	-1.7039046	-0.5461170	0.3120704	0.9478724
40	-3.5493854	-1.8975677	-0.6796067	0.2197414	0.8837971

Present Value of Ordinary Annuity of $1 per Period, Decreasing in Constant Amount of 10 Percent

Period	Interest Rate				
	11%	12%	13%	14%	15%
0	0.0000000	0.0000000	0.0000000	0.0000000	0.0000000
1	0.9009009	0.8928571	0.8849558	0.8771930	0.8695652
2	1.6313611	1.6103316	1.5897878	1.5697138	1.5500945
3	2.2163142	2.1797558	2.1442279	2.1096910	2.0761075
4	2.6774259	2.6246185	2.5735510	2.5241472	2.4763348
5	3.0334967	2.9650746	2.8992070	2.8357684	2.7746408
6	3.3008171	3.2183902	3.1393662	3.0635616	2.9908046
7	3.4934805	3.3993298	3.3093905	3.2234166	3.1411794
8	3.6236584	3.5204948	3.4222384	3.3285843	3.2392500
9	3.7018434	3.5926168	3.4888154	3.3900859	3.2961024
10	3.7370618	3.6248141	3.5182742	3.4170603	3.3208209
11	3.7370618	3.6248141	3.5182742	3.4170603	3.3208209
12	3.7084777	3.5991466	3.4952037	3.3963043	3.3021302
13	3.6569749	3.5533118	3.4543708	3.3598905	3.2696246
14	3.5873764	3.4919259	3.4001678	3.3119775	3.2272260
15	3.5037747	3.4188473	3.3362115	3.2559389	3.1780682
16	3.4096286	3.3372865	3.2654634	3.1944930	3.1246358
17	3.3078490	3.2498999	3.1903326	3.1298132	3.0688803
18	3.2008735	3.1588722	3.1127640	3.0636204	3.0123167
19	3.0907314	3.0659868	3.0343128	2.9972617	2.9561045
20	2.9791009	2.9726867	2.9562087	2.9317762	2.9011142
21	2.8673586	2.8801271	2.8794103	2.8679501	2.8479835
22	2.7566230	2.7892203	2.8046507	2.8063636	2.7971629
23	2.6477920	2.7006748	2.7324773	2.7474291	2.7489536
24	2.5415755	2.6150280	2.6632845	2.6914240	2.7035390
25	2.4385242	2.5326754	2.5973418	2.6385178	2.6610103
26	2.3390538	2.4538942	2.5348171	2.5887939	2.6213873
27	2.2434667	2.3788645	2.4757967	2.5422686	2.5846355
28	2.1519700	2.3076867	2.4203019	2.4989063	2.5506801
29	2.0646917	2.2403968	2.3683025	2.4586316	2.5194168
30	1.9816943	2.1769788	2.3197289	2.4213403	2.4907210
31	1.9029866	2.1173753	2.2744811	2.3869069	2.4644548
32	1.8285332	2.0614971	2.2324366	2.3551919	2.4404726
33	1.7582642	2.0092301	2.1934573	2.3260470	2.4186255
34	1.6920811	1.9604418	2.1573944	2.2993193	2.3987645
35	1.6298644	1.9149870	2.1240927	2.2748545	2.3807432
36	1.5714779	1.8727112	2.0933943	2.2525000	2.3644195
37	1.5167734	1.8334552	2.0651409	2.2321064	2.3496572
38	1.4655945	1.7970571	2.0391762	2.2135292	2.3363268
39	1.4177798	1.7633551	2.0153476	2.1966299	2.3243057
40	1.3731650	1.7321894	1.9935072	2.1812765	2.3134793

Present Value of Ordinary Annuity of $1 per Period, Decreasing in Constant Amount of 10 Percent

Period	Interest Rate				
	16%	17%	18%	19%	20%
0	0.0000000	0.0000000	0.0000000	0.0000000	0.0000000
1	0.8620690	0.8547009	0.8474576	0.8403361	0.8333333
2	1.5309156	1.5121631	1.4938236	1.4758845	1.4583333
3	2.0434417	2.0116595	1.9807283	1.9506171	1.9212963
4	2.4300455	2.3852145	2.3417805	2.2996852	2.2588735
5	2.7157133	2.6588812	2.6040461	2.5511149	2.5000000
6	2.9209344	2.8538005	2.7892618	2.7271860	2.6674490
7	3.0624662	2.9870787	2.9148318	2.8455532	2.7790816
8	3.1539739	3.0725134	2.9946433	2.9201544	2.8488521
9	3.2065645	3.1211941	3.0397345	2.9619477	2.8876134
10	3.2292328	3.1419979	3.0588409	2.9795080	2.9037640
11	3.2292328	3.1419979	3.0588409	2.9795080	2.9037640
12	3.2123865	3.1268005	3.0451190	2.9671075	2.8925483
13	3.1833412	3.1008220	3.0218614	2.9462665	2.8738555
14	3.1457826	3.0675162	2.9922968	2.9199963	2.8504895
15	3.1026118	3.0295610	2.9588904	2.8905618	2.8245274
16	3.0560916	2.9890105	2.9235022	2.8596433	2.7974834
17	3.0079671	2.9474202	2.8875143	2.8284650	2.7704395
18	2.9595662	2.9059484	2.8519329	2.7978980	2.7441467
19	2.9118804	2.8654388	2.8174716	2.7685419	2.7191060
20	2.8656335	2.8264872	2.7846166	2.7407894	2.6956304
21	2.8213357	2.7894961	2.7536796	2.7148766	2.6738937
22	2.7793292	2.7547182	2.7248400	2.6909236	2.6539684
23	2.7398246	2.7222912	2.6981779	2.6689652	2.6358544
24	2.7029310	2.6922662	2.6736999	2.6489750	2.6195016
25	2.6686796	2.6646298	2.6513602	2.6308844	2.6048260
26	2.6370434	2.6393218	2.6310759	2.6145963	2.5917227
27	2.6079527	2.6162489	2.6127399	2.5999963	2.5800754
28	2.5813071	2.5952960	2.5962297	2.5869606	2.5697626
29	2.5569856	2.5763340	2.5814149	2.5753619	2.5606632
30	2.5348539	2.5592269	2.5681626	2.5650736	2.5526590
31	2.5147708	2.5438358	2.5563407	2.5559729	2.5456378
32	2.4965920	2.5300233	2.5458212	2.5479429	2.5394943
33	2.4801745	2.5176556	2.5364818	2.5408736	2.5341308
34	2.4653781	2.5066045	2.5282074	2.5346631	2.5294582
35	2.4520679	2.4967483	2.5208902	2.5292172	2.5253950
36	2.4401156	2.4879733	2.5144309	2.5244501	2.5218679
37	2.4293997	2.4801733	2.5087379	2.5202840	2.5188111
38	2.4198066	2.4732502	2.5037278	2.5166484	2.5161658
39	2.4112304	2.4671138	2.4993247	2.5134801	2.5138797
40	2.4035730	2.4616818	2.4954600	2.5107225	2.5119066

Present Value of Ordinary Annuity of $1 per Period, Decreasing in Constant Amount of 15 Percent

Period	Interest Rate			
	2%	3%	4%	5%
0	0.0000000	0.0000000	0.0000000	0.0000000
1	0.9803922	0.9708738	0.9615385	0.9523810
2	1.7973856	1.7720803	1.7474112	1.7233560
3	2.4570113	2.4126795	2.3697087	2.3280423
4	2.9651262	2.9013473	2.8398510	2.7805287
5	3.3274186	3.2463909	3.1686218	3.0939392
6	3.5494114	3.4557619	3.3662005	3.2804930
7	3.6364674	3.5370711	3.4421923	3.3515611
8	3.5937929	3.4976006	3.4056577	3.3177192
9	3.4264419	3.3443173	3.2651404	3.1887974
10	3.1393200	3.0838844	3.0286929	2.9739277
11	2.7371884	2.7226738	2.7039025	2.6815881
12	2.2246679	2.2667768	2.2979144	2.3196438
13	1.6062418	1.7220158	1.8174551	1.8953867
14	0.8862606	1.0939538	1.2688538	1.4155721
15	0.0689444	0.3879057	0.6580628	0.8864533
16	-0.8416129	-0.3910530	-0.0093224	0.3138139
17	-1.8414405	-1.2380760	-0.7280449	-0.2970014
18	-2.9266875	-2.1485376	-1.4931685	-0.9410584
19	-4.0936198	-3.1180239	-2.3000606	-1.6138062
20	-5.3386168	-4.1423240	-3.1443765	-2.3110517
21	-6.6581684	-5.2174226	-4.0220437	-3.0289364
22	-8.0488723	-6.3394915	-4.9292478	-3.7639137
23	-9.5074309	-7.5048825	-5.8624183	-4.5127277
24	-11.0306486	-8.7101201	-6.8182159	-5.2723940
25	-12.6154289	-9.9518946	-7.7935196	-6.0401813
26	-14.2587719	-11.2270551	-8.7854150	-6.8135933
27	-15.9577718	-12.5326034	-9.7911831	-7.5903534
28	-17.7096142	-13.8656875	-10.8082894	-8.3683890
29	-19.5115736	-15.2235958	-11.8343739	-9.1458172
30	-21.3610111	-16.6037515	-12.8672414	-9.9209317
31	-23.2553720	-18.0037065	-13.9048523	-10.6921898
32	-25.1921835	-19.4211367	-14.9453138	-11.4582013
33	-27.1690527	-20.8538364	-15.9868717	-12.2177170
34	-29.1836639	-22.2997137	-17.0279024	-12.9696185
35	-31.2337772	-23.7567857	-18.0669059	-13.7129086
36	-33.3172255	-25.2231735	-19.1024979	-14.4467026
37	-35.4319136	-26.6970984	-20.1334041	-15.1702194
38	-37.5758153	-28.1768774	-21.1584528	-15.8827738
39	-39.7469720	-29.6609191	-22.1765696	-16.5837693
40	-41.9434905	-31.1477197	-23.1867715	-17.2726908

Present Value of Ordinary Annuity of $1 per Period, Decreasing in Constant Amount of 15 Percent

Period	Interest Rate				
	6%	7%	8%	9%	10%
0	0.0000000	0.0000000	0.0000000	0.0000000	0.0000000
1	0.9433962	0.9345794	0.9259259	0.9174312	0.9090909
2	1.6998932	1.6770024	1.6546639	1.6328592	1.6115702
3	2.2876267	2.2484109	2.2103465	2.1733876	2.1374906
4	2.7232782	2.6680032	2.6146129	2.5630215	2.5131480
5	3.0221815	2.9531977	2.8868462	2.8229940	2.7615165
6	3.1984216	3.1197833	3.0443886	2.9720609	2.9026350
7	3.2649273	3.1820582	3.1027376	3.0267643	2.9539508
8	3.2335567	3.1529578	3.0757242	3.0016710	2.9306255
9	3.1151770	3.0441710	2.9756744	2.9095854	2.8458059
10	2.9197388	2.8662488	2.8135567	2.7617416	2.7108658
11	2.6563451	2.6287024	2.5991152	2.5679752	2.5356188
12	2.3333150	2.3400946	2.3409913	2.3368777	2.3285088
13	1.9582438	2.0081231	2.0468330	2.0759347	2.0967773
14	1.5380579	1.6396967	1.7233950	1.7916506	1.8466126
15	1.0790663	1.2410061	1.3766291	1.4896587	1.5832814
16	0.5870084	0.8175878	1.0117660	1.1748215	1.3112449
17	0.0670983	0.3743837	0.6333895	0.8513191	1.0342624
18	-0.4759346	-0.0842054	0.2455035	0.5227288	0.7554813
19	-1.0378067	-0.5542696	-0.1484070	0.1920964	0.4775177
20	-1.6146455	-1.0323447	-0.5453212	-0.1380008	0.2025270
21	-2.2029563	-1.5153709	-0.9426327	-0.4653969	-0.0677342
22	-2.7995922	-2.0006542	-1.3381048	-0.7882876	-0.3318530
23	-3.4017259	-2.4858320	-1.7298299	-1.1051848	-0.5887128
24	-4.0068234	-2.9688413	-2.1161933	-1.4148769	-0.8374505
25	-4.6126198	-3.4478891	-2.4958399	-1.7163933	-1.0774201
26	-5.2170974	-3.9214267	-2.8676447	-2.0089727	-1.3081601
27	-5.8184645	-4.3881248	-3.2306865	-2.2920353	-1.5293654
28	-6.4151364	-4.8468515	-3.5842233	-2.5651581	-1.7408626
29	-7.0057180	-5.2966526	-3.9276714	-2.8280526	-1.9425887
30	-7.5889869	-5.7367324	-4.2605855	-3.0805459	-2.1345723
31	-8.1638789	-6.1664379	-4.5826416	-3.3225633	-2.3169177
32	-8.7294733	-6.5852430	-4.8936218	-3.5541134	-2.4897906
33	-9.2849810	-6.9927349	-5.1933997	-3.7752747	-2.6534063
34	-9.8297315	-7.3886013	-5.4819287	-3.9861842	-2.8080193
35	-10.3631629	-7.7726193	-5.7592303	-4.1870271	-2.9539141
36	-10.8848112	-8.1446450	-6.0253848	-4.3780278	-3.0913981
37	-11.3943012	-8.5046039	-6.2805219	-4.5594424	-3.2207949
38	-11.8913380	-8.8524826	-6.5248136	-4.7315518	-3.3424385
39	-12.3756989	-9.1883212	-6.7584666	-4.8946557	-3.4566693
40	-12.8472265	-9.5122060	-6.9817167	-5.0490680	-3.5638297

Present Value of Ordinary Annuity of $1 per Period, Decreasing in Constant Amount of 15 Percent

Period	Interest Rate				
	11%	12%	13%	14%	15%
0	0.0000000	0.0000000	0.0000000	0.0000000	0.0000000
1	0.9009009	0.8928571	0.8849558	0.8771930	0.8695652
2	1.5907800	1.5704719	1.5506304	1.5312404	1.5122873
3	2.1026139	2.0687181	2.0357655	2.0037204	1.9725487
4	2.4649160	2.4182531	2.3730908	2.3293646	2.2870130
5	2.7022965	2.6452238	2.5901948	2.5371121	2.4858837
6	2.8359567	2.7718816	2.7102745	2.6510087	2.5939656
7	2.8841226	2.8171165	2.7527805	2.6909724	2.6315593
8	2.8624262	2.7969223	2.7339725	2.6734445	2.6152142
9	2.7842413	2.7248003	2.6673956	2.6119429	2.5583617
10	2.6609767	2.6121097	2.5642896	2.5175326	2.4718471
11	2.5023350	2.4683716	2.4339408	2.3992239	2.3643754
12	2.3165385	2.3015328	2.2839820	2.2643105	2.2428858
13	2.1105271	2.1181935	2.1206504	2.1186549	2.1128634
14	1.8901320	1.9238047	1.9490077	1.9669305	1.9786012
15	1.6602272	1.7228388	1.7731278	1.8128243	1.8434173
16	1.4248620	1.5189367	1.5962575	1.6592098	1.7098363
17	1.1873763	1.3150346	1.4209524	1.5082902	1.5797401
18	0.9505020	1.1134733	1.2491934	1.3617204	1.4544921
19	0.7164500	0.9160917	1.0824846	1.2207082	1.3350411
20	0.4869872	0.7243082	0.9219373	1.0860990	1.2220056
21	0.2635027	0.5391890	0.7683403	0.9584469	1.1157442
22	0.0470650	0.3615076	0.6222193	0.8380731	1.0164130
23	-0.1615278	0.1917953	0.4838870	0.7251153	0.9240118
24	-0.3617050	0.0303841	0.3534853	0.6195674	0.8384228
25	-0.5530860	-0.1225564	0.2310202	0.5213130	0.7594409
26	-0.7354484	-0.2669887	0.1163915	0.4301525	0.6867988
27	-0.9087001	-0.4029801	0.0094171	0.3458255	0.6201862
28	-1.0728560	-0.5306813	-0.0901472	0.2680283	0.5592661
29	-1.2280174	-0.6503078	-0.1825904	0.1964289	0.5036869
30	-1.3743548	-0.7621238	-0.2682333	0.1306783	0.4530916
31	-1.5120934	-0.8664299	-0.3474171	0.0704199	0.4071258
32	-1.6415003	-0.9635515	-0.4204944	0.0152963	0.3654425
33	-1.7628742	-1.0538310	-0.4878223	-0.0350449	0.3277066
34	-1.8765364	-1.1376194	-0.5497564	-0.0809469	0.2935975
35	-1.9828232	-1.2152715	-0.6066468	-0.1227409	0.2628111
36	-2.0820804	-1.2871403	-0.6588341	-0.1607436	0.2350608
37	-2.1746572	-1.3535736	-0.7066475	-0.1952559	0.2100785
38	-2.2609031	-1.4149111	-0.7504028	-0.2265618	0.1876142
39	-2.3411635	-1.4714823	-0.7904009	-0.2549285	0.1674360
40	-2.4157779	-1.5236043	-0.8269270	-0.2806057	0.1493298

Present Value of Ordinary Annuity of $1 per Period, Decreasing in Constant Amount of 15 Percent

Period	Interest Rate				
	16%	**17%**	**18%**	**19%**	**20%**
0	0.0000000	0.0000000	0.0000000	0.0000000	0.0000000
1	0.8620690	0.8547009	0.8474576	0.8403361	0.8333333
2	1.4937574	1.4756374	1.4579144	1.4405762	1.4236111
3	1.9422178	1.9126968	1.8839560	1.8559673	1.8287037
4	2.2459779	2.2062043	2.1676399	2.1302351	2.0939429
5	2.4364231	2.3886488	2.3424836	2.2978549	2.2546939
6	2.5390337	2.4861084	2.4350915	2.3858904	2.3384184
7	2.5744166	2.5194279	2.4664840	2.4154822	2.3663266
8	2.5591654	2.5051888	2.4531821	2.4030487	2.3546982
9	2.5065748	2.4565081	2.4080908	2.3612553	2.3159368
10	2.4272355	2.3836950	2.3412183	2.2997945	2.2594099
11	2.3295270	2.2947901	2.2602588	2.2260120	2.1921159
12	2.2200262	2.1960069	2.1710661	2.1454093	2.1192141
13	2.1038449	2.0920930	2.0780359	2.0620451	2.0444430
14	1.9849094	1.9866248	1.9844144	1.9788560	1.9704507
15	1.8661896	1.8822478	1.8925468	1.8979114	1.8990547
16	1.7498890	1.7808716	1.8040764	1.8206151	1.8314448
17	1.6375987	1.6838276	1.7201045	1.7478656	1.7683423
18	1.5304251	1.5919973	1.6413173	1.6801816	1.7101227
19	1.4290930	1.5059143	1.5680870	1.6177999	1.6569112
20	1.3340299	1.4258471	1.5005516	1.5607530	1.6086557
21	1.2454342	1.3518649	1.4386776	1.5089275	1.5651823
22	1.1633305	1.2838899	1.3823094	1.4621103	1.5262374
23	1.0876134	1.2217382	1.3312070	1.4200233	1.4915190
24	1.0180831	1.1651527	1.2850754	1.3823495	1.4607002
25	0.9544734	1.1138279	1.2435874	1.3487526	1.4334454
26	0.8964738	1.0674298	1.2063996	1.3188911	1.4094228
27	0.8437468	1.0256102	1.1731655	1.2924287	1.3883120
28	0.7959415	0.9880182	1.1435442	1.2690411	1.3698098
29	0.7527033	0.9543081	1.1172069	1.2484211	1.3536329
30	0.7136817	0.9241455	1.0938409	1.2302812	1.3395203
31	0.6785361	0.8972112	1.0731525	1.2143550	1.3272332
32	0.6469397	0.8732037	1.0548686	1.2003980	1.3165551
33	0.6185821	0.8518413	1.0387370	1.1881875	1.3072910
34	0.5931709	0.8328621	1.0245266	1.1775216	1.2992662
35	0.5704328	0.8160246	1.0120265	1.1682182	1.2923249
36	0.5501138	0.8011070	1.0010456	1.1601142	1.2863289
37	0.5319793	0.7879070	0.9914113	1.1530638	1.2811559
38	0.5158131	0.7762403	0.9829684	1.1469371	1.2766980
39	0.5014173	0.7659400	0.9755774	1.1416189	1.2728607
40	0.4886110	0.7568554	0.9691140	1.1370071	1.2695609

.21 Present Value of Ordinary Annuity Increasing in Constant Ratio
$1 per Period, Increasing in Constant Ratio of 2 Percent

Period	Interest Rate			
	2%	**3%**	**4%**	**5%**
0	0.0000000	0.0000000	0.0000000	0.0000000
1	0.9803922	0.9708738	0.9615385	0.9523810
2	1.9607843	1.9323216	1.9045858	1.8775510
3	2.9411765	2.8844350	2.8294976	2.7762877
4	3.9215686	3.8273046	3.7366227	3.6493461
5	4.9019608	4.7610200	4.6263030	4.4974600
6	5.8823529	5.6856703	5.4988741	5.3213421
7	6.8627451	6.6013434	6.3546650	6.1216847
8	7.8431373	7.5081265	7.1939983	6.8991604
9	8.8235294	8.4061059	8.0171907	7.6544225
10	9.8039216	9.2953670	8.8245524	8.3881057
11	10.7843137	10.1759945	9.6163879	9.1008264
12	11.7647059	11.0480722	10.3929958	9.7931838
13	12.7450980	11.9116832	11.1546690	10.4657595
14	13.7254902	12.7669095	11.9016946	11.1191187
15	14.7058824	13.6138327	12.6343543	11.7538106
16	15.6862745	14.4525334	13.3529244	12.3703684
17	16.6666667	15.2830913	14.0576759	12.9693102
18	17.6470588	16.1055856	14.7488744	13.5511395
19	18.6274510	16.9200945	15.4267807	14.1163450
20	19.6078431	17.7266955	16.0916503	14.6654018
21	20.5882353	18.5254654	16.7437339	15.1987713
22	21.5686275	19.3164803	17.3832775	15.7169016
23	22.5490196	20.0998155	18.0105222	16.2202282
24	23.5294118	20.8755454	18.6257044	16.7091741
25	24.5098039	21.6437440	19.2290563	17.1841501
26	25.4901961	22.4044844	19.8208052	17.6455553
27	26.4705882	23.1578389	20.4011743	18.0937776
28	27.4509804	23.9038793	20.9703825	18.5291934
29	28.4313725	24.6426766	21.5286444	18.9521689
30	29.4117647	25.3743011	22.0761705	19.3630593
31	30.3921569	26.0988224	22.6131672	19.7622100
32	31.3725490	26.8163096	23.1398370	20.1499563
33	32.3529412	27.5268308	23.6563786	20.5266243
34	33.3333333	28.2304538	24.1629867	20.8925302
35	34.3137255	28.9272456	24.6598524	21.2479817
36	35.2941176	29.6172723	25.1471629	21.5932775
37	36.2745098	30.3005997	25.6251021	21.9287077
38	37.2549020	30.9772930	26.0938501	22.2545541
39	38.2352941	31.6474163	26.5535838	22.5710907
40	39.2156863	32.3110336	27.0044764	22.8785833

Present Value of Ordinary Annuity of $1 per Period, Increasing in Constant Ratio of 2 Percent

Period	Interest Rate				
	6%	**7%**	**8%**	**9%**	**10%**
0	0.0000000	0.0000000	0.0000000	0.0000000	0.0000000
1	0.9433962	0.9345794	0.9259259	0.9174312	0.9090909
2	1.8511926	1.8254869	1.8004115	1.7759448	1.7520661
3	2.7247325	2.6747633	2.6263146	2.5793245	2.5337340
4	3.5653086	3.4843538	3.4063341	3.3311110	3.2585534
5	4.3741649	4.2561129	4.1430193	4.0346176	3.9306586
6	5.1524983	4.9918086	4.8387775	4.6929449	4.5538834
7	5.9014606	5.6931259	5.4958824	5.3089943	5.1317828
8	6.6221602	6.3616715	6.1164816	5.8854809	5.6676531
9	7.3156636	6.9989765	6.7026029	6.4249455	6.1645511
10	7.9829971	7.6065010	7.2561620	6.9297655	6.6253110
11	8.6251481	8.1856365	7.7789679	7.4021659	7.0525611
12	9.2430671	8.7377095	8.2727289	7.8442286	7.4487385
13	9.8376683	9.2639848	8.7390588	8.2579020	7.8161030
14	10.4098318	9.7656677	9.1794814	8.6450092	8.1567500
15	10.9604042	10.2439076	9.5954362	9.0072563	8.4726228
16	11.4902002	10.6997997	9.9882823	9.3462399	8.7655229
17	12.0000040	11.1343885	10.3593037	9.6634538	9.0371213
18	12.4905699	11.5486694	10.7097127	9.9602962	9.2889670
19	12.9626238	11.9435914	11.0406546	10.2380754	9.5224967
20	13.4168645	12.3200591	11.3532108	10.4980155	9.7390424
21	13.8539639	12.6789349	11.6484028	10.7412622	9.9398393
22	14.2745690	13.0210407	11.9271953	10.9688876	10.1260328
23	14.6793023	13.3471603	12.1904992	11.1818948	10.2986849
24	15.0687626	13.6580407	12.4391752	11.3812226	10.4587806
25	15.4435263	13.9543939	12.6740358	11.5677496	10.6072329
26	15.8041479	14.2368989	12.8958487	11.7422978	10.7448887
27	16.1511612	14.5062026	13.1053385	11.9056365	10.8725331
28	16.4850796	14.7629221	13.3031901	12.0584855	10.9908944
29	16.8063974	15.0076454	13.4900499	12.2015186	11.1006475
30	17.1155899	15.2409330	13.6665286	12.3353660	11.2024186
31	17.4131148	15.4633193	13.8332030	12.4606177	11.2967882
32	17.6994124	15.6753137	13.9906176	12.5778258	11.3842945
33	17.9749063	15.8774019	14.1392870	12.6875067	11.4654367
34	18.2400041	16.0700467	14.2796970	12.7901439	11.5406777
35	18.4950983	16.2536893	14.4123064	12.8861897	11.6104466
36	18.7405663	16.4287506	14.5375486	12.9760674	11.6751414
37	18.9767714	16.5956314	14.6558330	13.0601732	11.7351311
38	19.2040630	16.7547140	14.7675460	13.1388776	11.7907579
39	19.4227776	16.9063629	14.8730527	13.2125277	11.8423391
40	19.6332388	17.0509254	14.9726979	13.2814479	11.8901690

Present Value of Ordinary Annuity of $1 per Period, Increasing in Constant Ratio of 2 Percent

Period			Interest Rate		
	11%	**12%**	**13%**	**14%**	**15%**
0	0.0000000	0.0000000	0.0000000	0.0000000	0.0000000
1	0.9009009	0.8928571	0.8849558	0.8771930	0.8695652
2	1.7287558	1.7059949	1.6837654	1.6620499	1.6408318
3	2.4894873	2.4465311	2.4048148	2.3642902	2.3249116
4	3.1885379	3.1209479	3.0556735	2.9926106	2.9316608
5	3.8309087	3.7351490	3.6431743	3.5547919	3.4698209
6	4.4211954	4.2945107	4.1734848	4.0577963	3.9471455
7	4.9636210	4.8039294	4.6521721	4.5078528	4.3705116
8	5.4620661	5.2678643	5.0842615	4.9105350	4.7460190
9	5.9200968	5.6903764	5.4742892	5.2708295	5.0790777
10	6.3409898	6.0751642	5.8263495	5.5931983	5.3744863
11	6.7277564	6.4255960	6.1441385	5.8816336	5.6365009
12	7.0831636	6.7447392	6.4309923	6.1397073	5.8688965
13	7.4097539	7.0353875	6.6899222	6.3706153	6.0750212
14	7.7098640	7.3000850	6.9236466	6.5772172	6.2578449
15	7.9856407	7.5411489	7.1346191	6.7620715	6.4200016
16	8.2390573	7.7606891	7.3250544	6.9274675	6.5638275
17	8.4719265	7.9606276	7.4969517	7.0754534	6.6913948
18	8.6859144	8.1427144	7.6521157	7.2078618	6.8045415
19	8.8825520	8.3085435	7.7921753	7.3263325	6.9048977
20	9.0632460	8.4595664	7.9186007	7.4323326	6.9939092
21	9.2292891	8.5971051	8.0327192	7.5271747	7.0728586
22	9.3818693	8.7223636	8.1357288	7.6120335	7.1428833
23	9.5220781	8.8364383	8.2287110	7.6879598	7.2049921
24	9.6509186	8.9403277	8.3126418	7.7558939	7.2600800
25	9.7693126	9.0349413	8.3884023	7.8166770	7.3089405
26	9.8781070	9.1211073	8.4567879	7.8710619	7.3522777
27	9.9780803	9.1995798	8.5185165	7.9197220	7.3907158
28	10.0699477	9.2710459	8.5742362	7.9632601	7.4248088
29	10.1543664	9.3361311	8.6245318	8.0022151	7.4550478
30	10.2319403	9.3954051	8.6699313	8.0370697	7.4818685
31	10.3032244	9.4493868	8.7109115	8.0682553	7.5056573
32	10.3687287	9.4985487	8.7479024	8.0961583	7.5267569
33	10.4289219	9.5433211	8.7812924	8.1211241	7.5454713
34	10.4842345	9.5840960	8.8114321	8.1434619	7.5620702
35	10.5350624	9.6212303	8.8386378	8.1634484	7.5767927
36	10.5817690	9.6550490	8.8631952	8.1813310	7.5898509
37	10.6246886	9.6858482	8.8853620	8.1973312	7.6014330
38	10.6641283	9.7138975	8.9053710	8.2116472	7.6117058
39	10.7003701	9.7394424	8.9234323	8.2244563	7.6208173
40	10.7336735	9.7627064	8.9397353	8.2359170	7.6288988

Present Value of Ordinary Annuity of $1 per Period, Increasing in Constant Ratio of 2 Percent

Period	Interest Rate				
	16%	**17%**	**18%**	**19%**	**20%**
0	0.0000000	0.0000000	0.0000000	0.0000000	0.0000000
1	0.8620690	0.8547009	0.8474576	0.8403361	0.8333333
2	1.6200951	1.5998247	1.5800057	1.5606242	1.5416667
3	2.2866354	2.2494198	2.2132253	2.1780141	2.1437500
4	2.8727311	2.8157335	2.7605846	2.7072053	2.6555208
5	3.3880911	3.3094429	3.2337257	3.1607978	3.0905260
6	3.8412526	3.7398562	3.6427120	3.5495914	3.4602805
7	4.2397221	4.1150883	3.9962426	3.8828431	3.7745717
8	4.5901004	4.4422137	4.3018368	4.1684873	4.0417193
9	4.8981918	4.7274000	4.5659945	4.4133253	4.2687947
10	5.1690997	4.9760239	4.7943343	4.6231864	4.4618089
11	5.4073118	5.1927730	4.9917127	4.8030673	4.6258709
12	5.6167741	5.3817337	5.1623279	4.9572510	4.7653236
13	5.8009566	5.5464687	5.3098089	5.0894084	4.8838584
14	5.9629101	5.6900838	5.4372924	5.2026862	4.9846129
15	6.1053175	5.8152868	5.5474900	5.2997814	5.0702543
16	6.2305378	5.9244380	5.6427456	5.3830059	5.1430495
17	6.3406453	6.0195956	5.7250852	5.4543412	5.2049254
18	6.4374640	6.1025534	5.7962601	5.5154858	5.2575199
19	6.5225976	6.1748756	5.8577841	5.5678954	5.3022253
20	6.5974565	6.2379257	5.9109660	5.6128179	5.3402248
21	6.6632807	6.2928925	5.9569367	5.6513229	5.3725244
22	6.7211607	6.3408123	5.9966741	5.6843272	5.3999791
23	6.7720551	6.3825885	6.0310234	5.7126166	5.4233156
24	6.8168070	6.4190088	6.0607151	5.7368646	5.4431516
25	6.8561579	6.4507598	6.0863809	5.7576487	5.4600122
26	6.8907595	6.4784402	6.1085665	5.7754636	5.4743437
27	6.9211851	6.5025718	6.1277439	5.7907335	5.4865255
28	6.9479386	6.5236096	6.1443210	5.8038220	5.4968800
29	6.9714633	6.5419502	6.1586504	5.8150407	5.5056813
30	6.9921487	6.5579395	6.1710368	5.8246567	5.5131624
31	7.0103377	6.5718789	6.1817436	5.8328990	5.5195214
32	7.0263314	6.5840312	6.1909987	5.8399639	5.5249265
33	7.0403949	6.5946255	6.1989989	5.8460195	5.5295209
34	7.0527610	6.6038615	6.2059143	5.8512100	5.5334261
35	7.0636347	6.6119135	6.2118920	5.8556590	5.5367455
36	7.0731960	6.6189331	6.2170592	5.8594724	5.5395670
37	7.0816034	6.6250528	6.2215258	5.8627410	5.5419653
38	7.0889961	6.6303879	6.2253867	5.8655427	5.5440038
39	7.0954966	6.6350390	6.2287241	5.8679442	5.5457366
40	7.1012125	6.6390938	6.2316089	5.8700026	5.5472094

Present Value of Ordinary Annuity of $1 per Period, Increasing in Constant Ratio of 5 Percent

Period	Interest Rate			
	2%	3%	4%	5%
0	0.0000000	0.0000000	0.0000000	0.0000000
1	0.9803922	0.9708738	0.9615385	0.9523810
2	1.9896194	1.9605995	1.9323225	1.9047619
3	3.0285298	2.9695432	2.9124410	2.8571429
4	4.0979963	3.9980780	3.9019837	3.8095238
5	5.1989178	5.0465844	4.9010412	4.7619048
6	6.3322193	6.1154501	5.9097051	5.7142857
7	7.4988532	7.2050705	6.9280676	6.6666667
8	8.6997998	8.3158485	7.9562221	7.6190476
9	9.9360685	9.4481951	8.9942627	8.5714286
10	11.2086979	10.6025290	10.0422845	9.5238095
11	12.5187577	11.7792771	11.1003834	10.4761905
12	13.8673486	12.9788747	12.1686563	11.4285714
13	15.2556039	14.2017655	13.2472010	12.3809524
14	16.6846903	15.4484017	14.3361164	13.3333333
15	18.1558087	16.7192445	15.4355022	14.2857143
16	19.6701952	18.0147638	16.5454589	15.2380952
17	21.2291225	19.3354388	17.6660883	16.1904762
18	22.8339006	20.6817580	18.7974930	17.1428571
19	24.4858781	22.0542193	19.9397766	18.0952381
20	26.1864431	23.4533304	21.0930437	19.0476190
21	27.9370248	24.8796087	22.2573999	20.0000000
22	29.7390941	26.3335816	23.4329518	20.9523810
23	31.5941655	27.8157871	24.6198071	21.9047619
24	33.5037979	29.3267733	25.8180745	22.8571429
25	35.4695958	30.8670990	27.0278637	23.8095238
26	37.4932114	32.4373339	28.2492854	24.7619048
27	39.5763451	34.0380588	29.4824516	25.7142857
28	41.7207474	35.6698658	30.7274752	26.6666667
29	43.9282203	37.3333583	31.9844702	27.6190476
30	46.2006190	39.0291517	33.2535516	28.5714286
31	48.5398529	40.7578731	34.5348358	29.5238095
32	50.9478878	42.5201619	35.8284400	30.4761905
33	53.4267472	44.3166699	37.1344826	31.4285714
34	55.9785143	46.1480615	38.4530834	32.3809524
35	58.6053333	48.0150142	39.7843631	33.3333333
36	61.3094117	49.9182183	41.1284435	34.2857143
37	64.0930219	51.8583779	42.4854478	35.2380952
38	66.9585029	53.8362105	43.8555002	36.1904762
39	69.9082628	55.8524476	45.2387261	37.1428571
40	72.9447804	57.9078349	46.6352523	38.0952381

Present Value of Ordinary Annuity of $1 per Period, Increasing in Constant Ratio of 5 Percent

Period			Interest Rate		
	6%	**7%**	**8%**	**9%**	**10%**
0	0.0000000	0.0000000	0.0000000	0.0000000	0.0000000
1	0.9433962	0.9345794	0.9259259	0.9174312	0.9090909
2	1.8778925	1.8516901	1.8261317	1.8011952	1.7768595
3	2.8035727	2.7516585	2.7013317	2.6525275	2.6051841
4	3.7205202	3.6348051	3.5522207	3.4726182	3.3958575
5	4.6288172	4.5014442	4.3794738	4.2626139	4.1505913
6	5.5285453	5.3518845	5.1837477	5.0236189	4.8710189
7	6.4197854	6.1864287	5.9656806	5.7566971	5.5586999
8	7.3026176	7.0053740	6.7258932	6.4628733	6.2151226
9	8.1771213	7.8090119	7.4649887	7.1431349	6.8417080
10	9.0433748	8.5976285	8.1835539	7.7984327	7.4398121
11	9.9014562	9.3715046	8.8821589	8.4296828	8.0107298
12	10.7514425	10.1309157	9.5613581	9.0377679	8.5556966
13	11.5934100	10.8761322	10.2216908	9.6235379	9.0758922
14	12.4274344	11.6074195	10.8636809	10.1878117	9.5724426
15	13.2535907	12.3250378	11.4878379	10.7313782	10.0464225
16	14.0719530	13.0292427	12.0946572	11.2549974	10.4988578
17	14.8825950	13.7202849	12.6846204	11.7594012	10.9307279
18	15.6855894	14.3984104	13.2581958	12.2452947	11.3429675
19	16.4810084	15.0638607	13.8158385	12.7133573	11.7364690
20	17.2689234	15.7168726	14.3579911	13.1642432	12.1120841
21	18.0494052	16.3576788	14.8850840	13.5985829	12.4706257
22	18.8225240	16.9865072	15.3975353	14.0169836	12.8128700
23	19.5883493	17.6035818	15.8957519	14.4200300	13.1395577
24	20.3469498	18.2091224	16.3801292	14.8082858	13.4513960
25	21.0983936	18.8033444	16.8510515	15.1822937	13.7490598
26	21.8427484	19.3864594	17.3088927	15.5425765	14.0331935
27	22.5800810	19.9586751	17.7540161	15.8896379	14.3044119
28	23.3104576	20.5201952	18.1867749	16.2239631	14.5633023
29	24.0339438	21.0712196	18.6075126	16.5460195	14.8104249
30	24.7506047	21.6119445	19.0165632	16.8562573	15.0463147
31	25.4605047	22.1425623	19.4142512	17.1551103	15.2714822
32	26.1637075	22.6632621	19.8008924	17.4429961	15.4864148
33	26.8602763	23.1742292	20.1767935	17.7203174	15.6915778
34	27.5502737	23.6756455	20.5422530	17.9874617	15.8874152
35	28.2337616	24.1676895	20.8975608	18.2448025	16.0743508
36	28.9108016	24.6505364	21.2429989	18.4926997	16.2527894
37	29.5814544	25.1243581	21.5788415	18.7314997	16.4231172
38	30.2457803	25.5893234	21.9053552	18.9615364	16.5857028
39	30.9038390	26.0455977	22.2227990	19.1831314	16.7408981
40	31.5556896	26.4933436	22.5314250	19.3965945	16.8890391

Present Value of Ordinary Annuity of $1 per Period, Increasing in Constant Ratio of 5 Percent

Period	Interest Rate				
	11%	12%	13%	14%	15%
0	0.0000000	0.0000000	0.0000000	0.0000000	0.0000000
1	0.9009009	0.8928571	0.8849558	0.8771930	0.8695652
2	1.7531045	1.7299107	1.7072598	1.6851339	1.6635161
3	2.5592430	2.5146484	2.4713476	2.4292900	2.3884277
4	3.3218064	3.2503401	3.1813407	3.1146969	3.0503036
5	4.0431502	3.9400509	3.8410688	3.7459928	3.6546250
6	4.7255024	4.5866549	4.4540904	4.3274495	4.2063967
7	5.3709708	5.1928461	5.0237124	4.8630017	4.7101883
8	5.9815489	5.7611504	5.5530071	5.3562735	5.1701719
9	6.5591229	6.2939356	6.0448296	5.8106028	5.5901570
10	7.1054766	6.7934218	6.5018328	6.2290640	5.9736216
11	7.6222977	7.2616901	6.9264818	6.6144888	6.3237415
12	8.1111825	7.7006916	7.3210671	6.9694853	6.6434161
13	8.5736411	8.1122555	7.6877173	7.2964557	6.9352930
14	9.0111019	8.4980967	8.0284098	7.5976127	7.2017892
15	9.4249162	8.8598228	8.3449826	7.8749942	7.4451119
16	9.8163622	9.1989410	8.6391431	8.1304771	7.6672761
17	10.1866489	9.5168643	8.9124781	8.3657903	7.8701217
18	10.5369202	9.8149174	9.1664620	8.5825262	8.0553285
19	10.8682578	10.0943422	9.4024647	8.7821513	8.2244303
20	11.1816853	10.3563030	9.6217592	8.9660165	8.3788277
21	11.4781708	10.6018912	9.8255285	9.1353661	8.5197992
22	11.7586300	10.8321301	10.0148716	9.2913460	8.6485123
23	12.0239293	11.0479792	10.1908099	9.4350116	8.7660330
24	12.2748881	11.2503376	10.3542924	9.5673353	8.8733345
25	12.5122815	11.4400486	10.5062009	9.6892123	8.9713054
26	12.7368429	11.6179027	10.6473548	9.8014675	9.0607571
27	12.9492658	11.7846410	10.7785155	9.9048604	9.1424304
28	13.1502064	11.9409581	10.9003905	10.0000907	9.2170017
29	13.3402853	12.0875053	11.0136372	10.0878029	9.2850885
30	13.5200897	12.2248934	11.1188664	10.1685904	9.3472547
31	13.6901749	12.3536947	11.2166458	10.2429999	9.4040151
32	13.8510664	12.4744459	11.3075027	10.3115350	9.4558399
33	14.0032610	12.5876502	11.3919273	10.3746594	9.5031582
34	14.1472289	12.6937792	11.4703749	10.4328003	9.5463618
35	14.2834147	12.7932751	11.5432688	10.4863512	9.5858086
36	14.4122391	12.8865526	11.6110019	10.5356743	9.6218253
37	14.5341001	12.9740002	11.6739399	10.5811036	9.6547100
38	14.6493740	13.0559823	11.7324220	10.6229463	9.6847352
39	14.7584168	13.1328406	11.7867638	10.6614856	9.7121496
40	14.8615654	13.2048952	11.8372584	10.6969823	9.7371800

Present Value of Ordinary Annuity of $1 per Period, Increasing in Constant Ratio of 5 Percent

Period	Interest Rate				
	16%	17%	18%	19%	20%
0	0.0000000	0.0000000	0.0000000	0.0000000	0.0000000
1	0.8620690	0.8547009	0.8474576	0.8403361	0.8333333
2	1.6423900	1.6217401	1.6015513	1.5818092	1.5625000
3	2.3487151	2.3101086	2.2725668	2.2360501	2.2005208
4	2.9880611	2.9278753	2.8696569	2.8133215	2.7587891
5	3.5667794	3.4822812	3.4009659	3.3226787	3.2472738
6	4.0906193	3.9798250	3.8737408	3.7721114	3.6746979
7	4.5647847	4.4263387	4.2944304	4.1686698	4.0486940
8	4.9939862	4.8270561	4.6687728	4.5185742	4.3759406
9	5.3824875	5.1866743	5.0018741	4.8273133	4.6622813
10	5.7341481	5.5094085	5.2982778	5.0997302	4.9128295
11	6.0524617	5.7990418	5.5620269	5.3400981	5.1320591
12	6.3405903	6.0589692	5.7967188	5.5521874	5.3238851
13	6.6013964	6.2922373	6.0055549	5.7393250	5.4917328
14	6.8374709	6.5015805	6.1913836	5.9044465	5.6385995
15	7.0511590	6.6894526	6.3567396	6.0501418	5.7671079
16	7.2445836	6.8580557	6.5038785	6.1786966	5.8795528
17	7.4196662	7.0093662	6.6348071	6.2921272	5.9779420
18	7.5781461	7.1451577	6.7513114	6.3922131	6.0640326
19	7.7215978	7.2670219	6.8549805	6.4805242	6.1393618
20	7.8514462	7.3763872	6.9472284	6.5584457	6.2052749
21	7.9689815	7.4745355	7.0293134	6.6272000	6.2629489
22	8.0753712	7.5626173	7.1023552	6.6878655	6.3134136
23	8.1716722	7.6416651	7.1673499	6.7413940	6.3575703
24	8.2588412	7.7126055	7.2251843	6.7886249	6.3962073
25	8.3377442	7.7762699	7.2766470	6.8302993	6.4300147
26	8.4091650	7.8334046	7.3224401	6.8670708	6.4595962
27	8.4738132	7.8846793	7.3631883	6.8995163	6.4854800
28	8.5323309	7.9306951	7.3994472	6.9281446	6.5081284
29	8.5852995	7.9719913	7.4317115	6.9534049	6.5279456
30	8.6332452	8.0090521	7.4604212	6.9756934	6.5452858
31	8.6766444	8.0423117	7.4859680	6.9953597	6.5604584
32	8.7159281	8.0721601	7.5087004	7.0127124	6.5737344
33	8.7514867	8.0989471	7.5289283	7.0280235	6.5853510
34	8.7836733	8.1229867	7.5469277	7.0415333	6.5955154
35	8.8128077	8.1445607	7.5629442	7.0534538	6.6044093
36	8.8391794	8.1639220	7.5771961	7.0639718	6.6121915
37	8.8630503	8.1812975	7.5898779	7.0732525	6.6190009
38	8.8846576	8.1968909	7.6011625	7.0814412	6.6249591
39	8.9042159	8.2108850	7.6112039	7.0886666	6.6301726
40	8.9219196	8.2234438	7.6201391	7.0950420	6.6347343

¶691.21

Present Value of Ordinary Annuity of $1 per Period, Increasing in Constant Ratio of 10 Percent

Period	Interest Rate			
	2%	**3%**	**4%**	**5%**
0	0.0000000	0.0000000	0.0000000	0.0000000
1	0.9803922	0.9708738	0.9615385	0.9523810
2	2.0376778	2.0077293	1.9785503	1.9501134
3	3.1778878	3.1150507	3.0542359	2.9953569
4	4.4075261	4.2976270	4.1919803	4.0903739
5	5.7336066	5.5605725	5.3953637	5.2375345
6	7.1636934	6.9093492	6.6681732	6.4393219
7	8.7059438	8.3497905	8.0144140	7.6983372
8	10.3691551	9.8881257	9.4383225	9.0173057
9	12.1628143	11.5310081	10.9443795	10.3990821
10	14.0971527	13.2855426	12.5373245	11.8466575
11	16.1832039	15.1593173	14.2221701	13.3631649
12	18.4328670	17.1604360	16.0042184	14.9518871
13	20.8589742	19.2975530	17.8890772	16.6162627
14	23.4753643	21.5799110	19.8826778	18.3598942
15	26.2969615	24.0173806	21.9912938	20.1865558
16	29.3398605	26.6205036	24.2215607	22.1002014
17	32.6214181	29.4005378	26.5804969	24.1049729
18	36.1603529	32.3695064	29.0755256	26.2052097
19	39.9768512	35.5402496	31.7144982	28.4054577
20	44.0926826	38.9264801	34.5057193	30.7104795
21	48.5313244	42.5428428	37.4579723	33.1252643
22	53.3180949	46.4049778	40.5805477	35.6550388
23	58.4802985	50.5295879	43.8832716	38.3052787
24	64.0473807	54.9345114	47.3765372	41.0817206
25	70.0510968	59.6387986	51.0713374	43.9903739
26	76.5256926	64.6627946	54.9792992	47.0375346
27	83.5080999	70.0282272	59.1127203	50.2297981
28	91.0381470	75.7583009	63.4846080	53.5740742
29	99.1587859	81.8777971	68.1087200	57.0776016
30	107.9163378	88.4131814	72.9996077	60.7479636
31	117.3607564	95.3927180	78.1726620	64.5931047
32	127.5459138	102.8465920	83.6441618	68.6213478
33	138.5299070	110.8070400	89.4313249	72.8414119
34	150.3753899	119.3084893	95.5523629	77.2624315
35	163.1499303	128.3877071	102.0265377	81.8939759
36	176.9263955	138.0839590	108.8742226	86.7460700
37	191.7833677	148.4391795	116.1169662	91.8292162
38	207.8055926	159.4981529	123.7775604	97.1544170
39	225.0844626	171.3087069	131.8801119	102.7331987
40	243.7185381	183.9219200	140.4501184	108.5776368

Present Value of Ordinary Annuity of $1 per Period, Increasing in Constant Ratio of 10 Percent

Period			Interest Rate		
	6%	7%	8%	9%	10%
0	0.0000000	0.0000000	0.0000000	0.0000000	0.0000000
1	0.9433962	0.9345794	0.9259259	0.9174312	0.9090909
2	1.9223923	1.8953620	1.8689986	1.8432792	1.8181818
3	2.9383316	2.8830825	2.8295356	2.7776212	2.7272727
4	3.9926083	3.8984960	3.8078604	3.7205352	3.6363636
5	5.0866690	4.9423791	4.8043022	4.6720997	4.5454545
6	6.2220150	6.0155299	5.8191967	5.6323942	5.4545455
7	7.4002042	7.1187690	6.8528855	6.6014987	6.3636364
8	8.6228535	8.2529401	7.9057168	7.5794941	7.2727273
9	9.8916404	9.4189104	8.9780448	8.5664620	8.1818182
10	11.2083061	10.6175715	10.0702309	9.5624845	9.0909091
11	12.5746572	11.8498398	11.1826425	10.5676450	10.0000000
12	13.9925688	13.1166577	12.3156544	11.5820270	10.9090909
13	15.4639865	14.4189939	13.4696480	12.6057153	11.8181818
14	16.9909294	15.7578442	14.6450119	13.6387953	12.7272727
15	18.5754928	17.1342324	15.8421417	14.6813531	13.6363636
16	20.2198510	18.5492109	17.0614407	15.7334756	14.5454545
17	21.9262605	20.0038617	18.3033192	16.7952506	15.4545455
18	23.6970627	21.4992970	19.5681955	17.8667666	16.3636364
19	25.5346878	23.0366605	20.8564954	18.9481131	17.2727273
20	27.4416571	24.6171276	22.1686527	20.0393802	18.1818182
21	29.4205876	26.2419069	23.5051093	21.1406589	19.0909091
22	31.4741946	27.9122407	24.8663150	22.2520411	20.0000000
23	33.6052963	29.6294064	26.2527282	23.3736195	20.9090909
24	35.8168169	31.3947168	27.6648158	24.5054875	21.8181818
25	38.1117912	33.2095220	29.1030531	25.6477397	22.7272727
26	40.4933682	35.0752095	30.5679245	26.8004713	23.6363636
27	42.9648160	36.9932060	32.0599231	27.9637783	24.5454545
28	45.5295261	38.9649781	33.5795513	29.1377580	25.4545455
29	48.1910176	40.9920336	35.1273207	30.3225080	26.3636364
30	50.9529428	43.0759224	36.7037526	31.5181274	27.2727273
31	53.8190916	45.2182380	38.3093777	32.7247157	28.1818182
32	56.7933970	47.4206185	39.9447365	33.9423736	29.0909091
33	59.8799402	49.6847480	41.6103798	35.1712028	30.0000000
34	63.0829569	52.0123577	43.3068683	36.4113055	30.9090909
35	66.4068420	54.4052276	45.0347732	37.6627854	31.8181818
36	69.8561568	56.8651872	46.7946765	38.9257467	32.7272727
37	73.4356344	59.3941177	48.5871705	40.2002949	33.6363636
38	77.1501867	61.9939528	50.4128588	41.4865361	34.5454545
39	81.0049107	64.6666804	52.2723562	42.7845777	35.4545455
40	85.0050960	67.4143444	54.1662887	44.0945280	36.3636364

Present Value of Ordinary Annuity of $1 per Period, Increasing in Constant Ratio of 10 Percent

Period	Interest Rate				
	11%	12%	13%	14%	15%
0	0.0000000	0.0000000	0.0000000	0.0000000	0.0000000
1	0.9009009	0.8928571	0.8849558	0.8771930	0.8695652
2	1.7936856	1.7697704	1.7464171	1.7236073	1.7013233
3	2.6784271	2.6310245	2.5850078	2.5403228	2.4969179
4	3.5551981	3.4768991	3.4013350	3.3283816	3.2579215
5	4.4240702	4.3076687	4.1959898	4.0887893	3.9858379
6	5.2851146	5.1236032	4.9695476	4.8225160	4.6821058
7	6.1384018	5.9249674	5.7225685	5.5304979	5.3481012
8	6.9840018	6.7120216	6.4555977	6.2136383	5.9851403
9	7.8219838	7.4850212	7.1691659	6.8728089	6.5944820
10	8.6524164	8.2442173	7.8637898	7.5088507	7.1773306
11	9.4753676	8.9898562	8.5399723	8.1225752	7.7348380
12	10.2909048	9.7221802	9.1982032	8.7147656	8.2681059
13	11.0990948	10.4414270	9.8389588	9.2861773	8.7781883
14	11.9000039	11.1478301	10.4627033	9.8375395	9.2660931
15	12.6936976	11.8416189	11.0698882	10.3695557	9.7327847
16	13.4802408	12.5230185	11.6609531	10.8829046	10.1791854
17	14.2596981	13.1922503	12.2363260	11.3782413	10.6061773
18	15.0321333	13.8495316	12.7964235	11.8561977	11.0146044
19	15.7976095	14.4950757	13.3416512	12.3173838	11.4052738
20	16.5561896	15.1290922	13.8724039	12.7623878	11.7789575
21	17.3079357	15.7517869	14.3890657	13.1917777	12.1363942
22	18.0529092	16.3633622	14.8920109	13.6061013	12.4782901
23	18.7911713	16.9640164	15.3816035	14.0058872	12.8053209
24	19.5227824	17.5539447	15.8581981	14.3916456	13.1181331
25	20.2478024	18.1333385	16.3221397	14.7638686	13.4173447
26	20.9662906	18.7023861	16.7737643	15.1230311	13.7035471
27	21.6783060	19.2612720	17.2133989	15.4695914	13.9773059
28	22.3839069	19.8101779	17.6413618	15.8039917	14.2391622
29	23.0831509	20.3492819	18.0579628	16.1266586	14.4896334
30	23.7760955	20.8787590	18.4635036	16.4380039	14.7292145
31	24.4627974	21.3987811	18.8582778	16.7384249	14.9583791
32	25.1433127	21.9095172	19.2425714	17.0283047	15.1775800
33	25.8176973	22.4111329	19.6166624	17.3080133	15.3872505
34	26.4860063	22.9037913	19.9808218	17.5779076	15.5878048
35	27.1482946	23.3876522	20.3353132	17.8383319	15.7796394
36	27.8046162	23.8628727	20.6803934	18.0896185	15.9631333
37	28.4550251	24.3296071	21.0163122	18.3320880	16.1386492
38	29.0995744	24.7880069	21.3433127	18.5660498	16.3065341
39	29.7383170	25.2382211	21.6616319	18.7918025	16.4671195
40	30.3713051	25.6803957	21.9715001	19.0096339	16.6207230

Present Value of Ordinary Annuity of \$1 per Period, Increasing in Constant Ratio of 10 Percent

Period   Interest Rate

Period	16%	17%	18%	19%	20%
0	0.0000000	0.0000000	0.0000000	0.0000000	0.0000000
1	0.8620690	0.8547009	0.8474576	0.8403361	0.8333333
2	1.6795482	1.6582658	1.6374605	1.6171174	1.5972222
3	2.4547439	2.4137541	2.3739039	2.3351506	2.2974537
4	3.1898434	3.1240423	3.0604188	2.9988787	2.9393326
5	3.8869205	3.7918347	3.7003905	3.6124089	3.5277215
6	4.5479418	4.4196736	4.2969742	4.1795376	4.0670781
7	5.1747724	5.0099496	4.8531115	4.7037743	4.5614882
8	5.7691807	5.5649099	5.3715446	5.1883628	5.0146975
9	6.3328438	6.0866674	5.8548297	5.6363017	5.4301394
10	6.8673519	6.5772087	6.3053497	6.0503629	5.8109611
11	7.3742130	7.0384013	6.7253260	6.4331086	6.1600477
12	7.8548571	7.4720012	7.1168294	6.7869071	6.4800437
13	8.3106404	7.8796593	7.4817901	7.1139477	6.7733734
14	8.7428487	8.2629275	7.8220077	7.4162542	7.0422590
15	9.1527013	8.6232652	8.1391597	7.6956972	7.2887374
16	9.5413547	8.9620442	8.4348099	7.9540058	7.5146759
17	9.9099053	9.2805544	8.7104160	8.1927785	7.7217863
18	10.2593930	9.5800084	8.9673370	8.4134927	7.9116374
19	10.5908037	9.8615463	9.2068395	8.6175143	8.0856676
20	10.9050724	10.1262401	9.4301047	8.8061056	8.2451953
21	11.2030859	10.3750976	9.6382332	8.9804338	8.3914290
22	11.4856849	10.6090661	9.8322512	9.1415774	8.5254766
23	11.7536668	10.8290365	10.0131156	9.2905338	8.6483536
24	12.0077874	11.0358463	10.1817179	9.4282245	8.7609908
25	12.2487640	11.2302828	10.3388896	9.5555016	8.8642415
26	12.4772762	11.4130864	10.4854055	9.6731528	8.9588881
27	12.6939688	11.5849530	10.6219882	9.7819059	9.0456474
28	12.8994531	11.7465371	10.7493110	9.8824340	9.1251768
29	13.0943090	11.8984536	10.8680018	9.9753592	9.1980787
30	13.2790861	12.0412812	10.9786458	10.0612564	9.2649055
31	13.4543058	12.1755635	11.0817884	10.1406572	9.3261634
32	13.6204624	12.3018119	11.1779384	10.2140528	9.3823164
33	13.7780247	12.4205069	11.2675697	10.2818976	9.4337901
34	13.9274372	12.5321005	11.3511243	10.3446112	9.4809742
35	14.0691215	12.6370175	11.4290141	10.4025818	9.5242264
36	14.2034773	12.7356575	11.5016233	10.4561680	9.5638742
37	14.3308836	12.8283960	11.5693099	10.5057016	9.6002180
38	14.4517000	12.9155859	11.6324075	10.5514888	9.6335332
39	14.5662672	12.9975594	11.6912274	10.5938132	9.6640721
40	14.6749086	13.0746285	11.7460594	10.6329366	9.6920661

Present Value of Ordinary Annuity of $1 per Period, Increasing in Constant Ratio of 15 Percent

Period	Interest Rate			
	2%	**3%**	**4%**	**5%**
0	0.0000000	0.0000000	0.0000000	0.0000000
1	0.9803922	0.9708738	0.9615385	0.9523810
2	2.0857363	2.0548591	2.0247781	1.9954649
3	3.3319575	3.2651339	3.2004758	3.1378901
4	4.7370110	4.6164117	4.5005261	4.3891177
5	6.3211398	6.1251198	5.9380818	5.7595099
6	8.1071674	7.8095998	7.5276866	7.2604156
7	10.1208260	9.6903299	9.2854226	8.9042647
8	12.3911274	11.7901741	11.2290731	10.7046708
9	14.9507809	14.1346604	13.3783020	12.6765442
10	17.8366647	16.7522908	15.7548532	14.8362151
11	21.0903573	19.6748878	18.3827703	17.2015689
12	24.7587361	22.9379815	21.2886403	19.7921946
13	28.8946535	26.5812415	24.5018618	22.6295464
14	33.5576975	30.6489589	28.0549434	25.7371223
15	38.8150511	35.1905852	31.9838316	29.1406577
16	44.7424596	40.2613330	36.3282754	32.8683394
17	51.4253221	45.9228475	41.1322276	36.9510384
18	58.9599220	52.2439560	46.4442901	41.4225659
19	67.4548140	59.3015042	52.3182054	46.3199531
20	77.0323884	67.1812911	58.8134002	51.6837581
21	87.8306339	75.9791114	65.9955867	57.5584018
22	100.0051265	85.8019205	73.9374277	63.9925353
23	113.7312701	96.7691346	82.7192710	71.0394434
24	129.2068241	109.0140823	92.4299631	78.7574856
25	146.6547527	122.6856259	103.1677476	87.2105795
26	166.3264368	137.9499706	115.0412594	96.4687299
27	188.5052964	154.9926857	128.1706234	106.6086090
28	213.5108734	174.0209597	142.6886701	117.7141908
29	241.7034357	195.2661201	158.7422794	129.8774470
30	273.4891677	218.9864448	176.4938667	143.1991087
31	309.3260224	245.4703024	196.1230256	157.7895000
32	349.7303194	275.0396580	217.8283457	173.7694523
33	395.2841837	308.0539871	241.8294207	191.2713049
34	446.6439326	344.9146458	268.3690710	210.4400007
35	504.5495318	386.0697502	297.7157996	231.4342864
36	569.8352564	432.0196240	330.1665092	254.4280280
37	643.4417107	483.3228811	366.0495054	279.6116497
38	726.4293797	540.6032168	405.7278184	307.1937116
39	819.9939085	604.5569896	449.6028761	337.4026365
40	925.4833282	675.9616874	498.1185650	370.4886019

¶691.21

Present Value of Ordinary Annuity of \$1 per Period, Increasing in Constant Ratio of 15 Percent

Period	Interest Rate				
	6%	7%	8%	9%	10%
0	0.0000000	0.0000000	0.0000000	0.0000000	0.0000000
1	0.9433962	0.9345794	0.9259259	0.9174312	0.9090909
2	1.9668921	1.9390340	1.9118656	1.8853632	1.8595041
3	3.0772886	3.0185879	2.9617087	2.9065758	2.8531180
4	4.2819641	4.1788562	4.0795972	3.9840020	3.8918960
5	5.5889233	5.4258735	5.2699415	5.1207361	4.9778913
6	7.0068507	6.7661257	6.5374377	6.3200427	6.1132500
7	8.5451683	8.2065837	7.8870864	7.5853661	7.3002159
8	10.2140976	9.7547395	9.3242124	8.9203404	8.5411348
9	12.0247286	11.4186452	10.8544855	10.3287995	9.8384591
10	13.9890923	13.2069551	12.4839428	11.8147885	11.1947527
11	16.1202417	15.1289705	14.2190132	13.3825750	12.6126960
12	18.4323377	17.1946879	16.0665418	15.0366617	14.0950913
13	20.9407437	19.4148515	18.0338177	16.7817990	15.6448682
14	23.6621276	21.8010086	20.1286022	18.6229990	17.2650895
15	26.6145724	24.3655700	22.3591597	20.5655494	18.9589572
16	29.8176965	27.1218743	24.7342905	22.6150291	20.7298189
17	33.2927839	30.0842574	27.2633648	24.7773243	22.5811743
18	37.0629259	33.2681271	29.9563607	27.0586449	24.5166822
19	41.1531743	36.6900432	32.8239026	29.4655428	26.5401678
20	45.5907080	40.3678034	35.8773037	32.0049305	28.6556299
21	50.4050134	44.3205364	39.1286104	34.6841010	30.8672495
22	55.6280806	48.5688008	42.5906500	37.5107487	33.1793972
23	61.2946157	53.1346924	46.2770810	40.4929918	35.5966425
24	67.4422718	58.0419591	50.2024474	43.6393950	38.1237626
25	74.1118986	63.3161243	54.3822356	46.9589947	40.7657518
26	81.3478146	68.9846196	58.8329361	50.4613247	43.5278314
27	89.1981007	75.0769276	63.5721079	54.1564435	46.4154602
28	97.7149206	81.6247353	68.6184482	58.0549633	49.4343447
29	106.9548667	88.6620987	73.9918661	62.1680806	52.5904513
30	116.9793365	96.2256200	79.7135611	66.5076080	55.8900172
31	127.8549405	104.3546384	85.8061068	71.0860084	59.3395635
32	139.6539449	113.0914338	92.2935396	75.9164309	62.9459073
33	152.4547515	122.4814475	99.2014542	81.0127482	66.7161758
34	166.3424191	132.5735183	106.5571040	86.3895967	70.6578201
35	181.4092283	143.4201365	114.3895089	92.0624185	74.7786302
36	197.7552949	155.0777168	122.7295697	98.0475058	79.0867497
37	215.4892350	167.6068919	131.6101900	104.3620474	83.5906929
38	234.7288870	181.0728278	141.0664060	111.0241784	88.2993607
39	255.6020944	195.5455626	151.1355249	118.0530323	93.2220589
40	278.2475552	211.1003710	161.8572719	125.4687955	98.3685162

Present Value of Ordinary Annuity of $1 per Period, Increasing in Constant Ratio of 15 Percent

Period	Interest Rate				
	11%	12%	13%	14%	15%
0	0.0000000	0.0000000	0.0000000	0.0000000	0.0000000
1	0.9009009	0.8928571	0.8849558	0.8771930	0.8695652
2	1.8342667	1.8096301	1.7855744	1.7620806	1.7391304
3	2.8012673	2.7509595	2.7021333	2.6547305	2.6086957
4	3.8031148	3.7175030	3.6349144	3.5552106	3.4782609
5	4.8410649	4.7099362	4.5842049	4.4635896	4.3478261
6	5.9164185	5.7289523	5.5502970	5.3799369	5.2173913
7	7.0305237	6.7752635	6.5334881	6.3043223	6.0869565
8	8.1847768	7.8496009	7.5340808	7.2368163	6.9565217
9	9.3806246	8.9527153	8.5523832	8.1774902	7.8260870
10	10.6195661	10.0853773	9.5887085	9.1264155	8.6956522
11	11.9031540	11.2483784	10.6433759	10.0836648	9.5652174
12	13.2329974	12.4425314	11.7167100	11.0493110	10.4347826
13	14.6107631	13.6686707	12.8090412	12.0234277	11.3043478
14	16.0381780	14.9276529	13.9207056	13.0060894	12.1739130
15	17.5170312	16.2203579	15.0520455	13.9973709	13.0434783
16	19.0491765	17.5476889	16.2034092	14.9973478	13.9130435
17	20.6365342	18.9105735	17.3751509	16.0060965	14.7826087
18	22.2810940	20.3099638	18.5676315	17.0236938	15.6521739
19	23.9849172	21.7468378	19.7812179	18.0502174	16.5217391
20	25.7501395	23.2221996	21.0162837	19.0857457	17.3913043
21	27.5789733	24.7370799	22.2732091	20.1303575	18.2608696
22	29.4737111	26.2925374	23.5523809	21.1841325	19.1304348
23	31.4367277	27.8896590	24.8541930	22.2471512	20.0000000
24	33.4704837	29.5295605	26.1790459	23.3194947	20.8695652
25	35.5775281	31.2133880	27.5273476	24.4012446	21.7391304
26	37.7605021	32.9423181	28.8995131	25.4924836	22.6086957
27	40.0221418	34.7175587	30.2959646	26.5932949	23.4782609
28	42.3652821	36.5403505	31.7171321	27.7037624	24.3478261
29	44.7928598	38.4119670	33.1634531	28.8239708	25.2173913
30	47.3079178	40.3337161	34.6353726	29.9540056	26.0869565
31	49.9136085	42.3069407	36.1333438	31.0939531	26.9565217
32	52.6131980	44.3330195	37.6578277	32.2439000	27.8260870
33	55.4100700	46.4133682	39.2092937	33.4039342	28.6956522
34	58.3077302	48.5494405	40.7882193	34.5741442	29.5652174
35	61.3098106	50.7427291	42.3950904	35.7546191	30.4347826
36	64.4200740	52.9947665	44.0304018	36.9454491	31.3043478
37	67.6424190	55.3071263	45.6946566	38.1467250	32.1739130
38	70.9808846	57.6814244	47.3883674	39.3585384	33.0434783
39	74.4396552	60.1193197	49.1120553	40.5809817	33.9130435
40	78.0230662	62.6225157	50.8662510	41.8141482	34.7826087

Present Value of Ordinary Annuity of $1 per Period, Increasing in Constant Ratio of 15 Percent

Period			Interest Rate		
	16%	17%	18%	19%	20%
0	0.0000000	0.0000000	0.0000000	0.0000000	0.0000000
1	0.8620690	0.8547009	0.8474576	0.8403361	0.8333333
2	1.7167063	1.6947914	1.6733697	1.6524257	1.6319444
3	2.5639761	2.5205215	2.4782841	2.4372181	2.3972801
4	3.4039418	3.3321365	3.2627345	3.1956309	3.1307268
5	4.2366664	4.1298778	4.0272412	3.9285509	3.8336131
6	5.0622124	4.9139824	4.7723113	4.6368349	4.5072126
7	5.8806416	5.6846836	5.4984390	5.3213110	5.1527454
8	6.6920154	6.4422104	6.2061058	5.9827796	5.7713810
9	7.4963946	7.1867880	6.8957811	6.6220139	6.3642401
10	8.2938395	7.9186377	7.5679223	7.2397613	6.9323968
11	9.0844098	8.6379773	8.2229751	7.8367441	7.4768803
12	9.8681649	9.3450204	8.8613740	8.4136603	7.9986769
13	10.6451635	10.0399773	9.4835425	8.9711843	8.4987320
14	11.4154638	10.7230546	10.0898931	9.5099680	8.9779515
15	12.1791236	11.3944554	10.6808280	10.0306414	9.4372036
16	12.9362001	12.0543792	11.2567392	10.5338131	9.8773201
17	13.6867501	12.7030223	11.8180085	11.0200715	10.2990984
18	14.4308298	13.3405775	12.3650083	11.4899850	10.7033026
19	15.1684951	13.9672343	12.8981013	11.9441032	11.0906650
20	15.8998012	14.5831790	13.4176411	12.3829569	11.4618873
21	16.6248029	15.1885947	13.9239723	12.8070592	11.8176420
22	17.3435546	15.7836615	14.4174306	13.2169059	12.1585736
23	18.0561102	16.3685562	14.8983434	13.6129763	12.4852997
24	18.7625230	16.9434527	15.3670296	13.9957334	12.7984122
25	19.4628461	17.5085218	15.8238000	14.3656247	13.0984784
26	20.1571319	18.0639317	16.2689576	14.7230827	13.3860418
27	20.8454325	18.6098474	16.7027977	15.0685253	13.6616234
28	21.5277994	19.1464312	17.1256079	15.4023564	13.9257224
29	22.2042839	19.6738427	17.5376687	15.7249663	14.1788173
30	22.8749366	20.1922385	17.9392534	16.0367321	14.4213666
31	23.5398079	20.7017729	18.3306283	16.3380184	14.6538096
32	24.1989475	21.2025973	18.7120530	16.6291775	14.8765676
33	24.8524048	21.6948606	19.0837805	16.9105496	15.0900439
34	25.5002289	22.1787091	19.4460573	17.1824639	15.2946254
35	26.1424683	22.6542867	19.7991236	17.4452383	15.4906827
36	26.7791712	23.1217348	20.1432137	17.6991798	15.6785709
37	27.4103852	23.5811924	20.4785557	17.9445855	15.8586305
38	28.0361578	24.0327959	20.8053721	18.1817423	16.0311875
39	28.6565357	24.4766797	21.1238796	18.4109275	16.1965547
40	29.2715656	24.9129758	21.4342894	18.6324089	16.3550316

.23 Present Value of Ordinary Annuity Decreasing in Constant Ratio
$1 per Period, Decreasing in Constant Ratio of 2 Percent

Period	Interest Rate			
	2%	3%	4%	5%
0	0.0000000	0.0000000	0.0000000	0.0000000
1	0.9803922	0.9708738	0.9615385	0.9523810
2	1.9223376	1.8946178	1.8676036	1.8412698
3	2.8273439	2.7735198	2.7213957	2.6708995
4	3.6968599	3.6097567	3.5259305	3.4452205
5	4.5322771	4.4053996	4.2840499	4.1679200
6	5.3349329	5.1624190	4.9984316	4.8424397
7	6.1061120	5.8826900	5.6715991	5.4719913
8	6.8470488	6.5679963	6.3059299	6.0595728
9	7.5589292	7.2200353	6.9036647	6.6079823
10	8.2428928	7.8404219	7.4669148	7.1198311
11	8.9000343	8.4306927	7.9976697	7.5975566
12	9.5314055	8.9923096	8.4978042	8.0434338
13	10.1380170	9.5266635	8.9690847	8.4595858
14	10.7208399	10.0350779	9.4131760	8.8479944
15	11.2808069	10.5188119	9.8316466	9.2105091
16	11.8188145	10.9790638	10.2259747	9.5488561
17	12.3357237	11.4169733	10.5975530	9.8646466
18	12.8323620	11.8336251	10.9476942	10.1593845
19	13.3095243	12.2300511	11.2776349	10.4344731
20	13.7679743	12.6072331	11.5885406	10.6912225
21	14.2084459	12.9661052	11.8815094	10.9308553
22	14.6316441	13.3075564	12.1575762	11.1545126
23	15.0382463	13.6324323	12.4177160	11.3632594
24	15.4289033	13.9415376	12.6628478	11.5580897
25	15.8042404	14.2356377	12.8938373	11.7399313
26	16.1648585	14.5154611	13.1115006	11.9096502
27	16.5113346	14.7817009	13.3166063	12.0680545
28	16.8442234	15.0350163	13.5098790	12.2158984
29	17.1640578	15.2760350	13.6920014	12.3538862
30	17.4713497	15.5053537	13.8636167	12.4826747
31	17.7665909	15.7235404	14.0253311	12.6028774
32	18.0502540	15.9311355	14.1777159	12.7150665
33	18.3227930	16.1286532	14.3213092	12.8197763
34	18.5846443	16.3165827	14.4566183	12.9175055
35	18.8362269	16.4953893	14.5841210	13.0087194
36	19.0779434	16.6655161	14.7042679	13.0938524
37	19.3101810	16.8273842	14.8174832	13.1733099
38	19.5333111	16.9813947	14.9241669	13.2474702
39	19.7476911	17.1279289	15.0246957	13.3166865
40	19.9536640	17.2673498	15.1194248	13.3812883

Present Value of Ordinary Annuity of $1 per Period, Decreasing in Constant Ratio of 2 Percent

Period	Interest Rate				
	6%	**7%**	**8%**	**9%**	**10%**
0	0.0000000	0.0000000	0.0000000	0.0000000	0.0000000
1	0.9433962	0.9345794	0.9259259	0.9174312	0.9090909
2	1.8155927	1.7905494	1.7661180	1.7422776	1.7190083
3	2.6219631	2.5745219	2.5285145	2.4838826	2.4405710
4	3.3674753	3.2925527	3.2203187	3.1506467	3.0834178
5	4.0567225	3.9501885	3.8480669	3.7501228	3.6561359
6	4.6939510	4.5525091	4.4176904	4.2891012	4.1663756
7	5.2830867	5.1041672	4.9345709	4.7736873	4.6209528
8	5.8277594	5.6094242	5.4035921	5.2093702	5.0259398
9	6.3313248	6.0721829	5.8291854	5.6010852	5.3867463
10	6.7968852	6.4960180	6.2153720	5.9532692	5.7081922
11	7.2273089	6.8842034	6.5658005	6.2699118	5.9945712
12	7.6252479	7.2397377	6.8837819	6.5545996	6.2497089
13	7.9931537	7.5653672	7.1723206	6.8105574	6.4770134
14	8.3332930	7.8636074	7.4341428	7.0406847	6.6795210
15	8.6477615	8.1367619	7.6717222	7.2475880	6.8599369
16	8.9384965	8.3869408	7.8873034	7.4336113	7.0206711
17	9.2072892	8.6160766	8.0829235	7.6008615	7.1638706
18	9.4557957	8.8259393	8.2604306	7.7512333	7.2914483
19	9.6855469	9.0181500	8.4215018	7.8864299	7.4051085
20	9.8979585	9.1941935	8.5676591	8.0079829	7.5063694
21	10.0943390	9.3554295	8.7002832	8.1172690	7.5965837
22	10.2758983	9.5031037	8.8206274	8.2155263	7.6769563
23	10.4437550	9.6383567	8.9298285	8.3038676	7.7485611
24	10.5989433	9.7622332	9.0289185	8.3832938	7.8123544
25	10.7424193	9.8756902	9.1188334	8.4547046	7.8691885
26	10.8750669	9.9796041	9.2004229	8.5189087	7.9198225
27	10.9977034	10.0747776	9.2744579	8.5766335	7.9649328
28	11.1110842	10.1619459	9.3416377	8.6285329	8.0051219
29	11.2159081	10.2417822	9.4025972	8.6751947	8.0409268
30	11.3128207	10.3149033	9.4579122	8.7171475	8.0728257
31	11.4024191	10.3818741	9.5081055	8.7548666	8.1012447
32	11.4852554	10.4432118	9.5536513	8.7887791	8.1265635
33	11.5618399	10.4993902	9.5949799	8.8192693	8.1491202
34	11.6326444	10.5508434	9.6324818	8.8466825	8.1692162
35	11.6981052	10.5979687	9.6665112	8.8713292	8.1871199
36	11.7586256	10.6411302	9.6973898	8.8934887	8.2030704
37	11.8145784	10.6806613	9.7254093	8.9134118	8.2172809
38	11.8663083	10.7168674	9.7508344	8.9313244	8.2299412
39	11.9141341	10.7500281	9.7739052	8.9474293	8.2412203
40	11.9583504	10.7803995	9.7948399	8.9619089	8.2512690

Present Value of Ordinary Annuity of $1 per Period, Decreasing in Constant Ratio of 2 Percent

Period	Interest Rate				
	11%	**12%**	**13%**	**14%**	**15%**
0	0.0000000	0.0000000	0.0000000	0.0000000	0.0000000
1	0.9009009	0.8928571	0.8849558	0.8771930	0.8695652
2	1.6962909	1.6741071	1.6524395	1.6312712	1.6105860
3	2.3985271	2.3577009	2.3180449	2.2795138	2.2420646
4	3.0185194	2.9558454	2.8952956	2.8367750	2.7801942
5	3.5659000	3.4792219	3.3959200	3.3158241	3.2387742
6	4.0491730	3.9371763	3.8300899	3.7276383	3.6295641
7	4.4758464	4.3378864	4.2066267	4.0816540	3.9625850
8	4.8525491	4.6885077	4.5331807	4.3859832	4.2463768
9	5.1851334	4.9953014	4.8163868	4.6475996	4.4882168
10	5.4787665	5.2637459	5.0619991	4.8724979	4.6943065
11	5.7380100	5.4986348	5.2750081	5.0658316	4.8699307
12	5.9668917	5.7041626	5.4597415	5.2320306	5.0195931
13	6.1689675	5.8839994	5.6199528	5.3749035	5.1471315
14	6.3473767	6.0413566	5.7588972	5.4977241	5.2558164
15	6.5048911	6.1790442	5.8793975	5.6033067	5.3484349
16	6.6439579	6.2995208	5.9839023	5.6940706	5.4273619
17	6.7667376	6.4049378	6.0745347	5.7720958	5.4946214
18	6.8751377	6.4971778	6.1531363	5.8391701	5.5519383
19	6.9708423	6.5778877	6.2213041	5.8968304	5.6007822
20	7.0553383	6.6485089	6.2804230	5.9463981	5.6424057
21	7.1299383	6.7103024	6.3316943	5.9890089	5.6778762
22	7.1958014	6.7643717	6.3761596	6.0256392	5.7081032
23	7.2539508	6.8116824	6.4147225	6.0571284	5.7338618
24	7.3052899	6.8530793	6.4481664	6.0841981	5.7558127
25	7.3506163	6.8893015	6.4771709	6.1074686	5.7745186
26	7.3906342	6.9209960	6.5023252	6.1274730	5.7904594
27	7.4259653	6.9487286	6.5241404	6.1446698	5.8040436
28	7.4571586	6.9729947	6.5430598	6.1594530	5.8156198
29	7.4846986	6.9942275	6.5594678	6.1721613	5.8254847
30	7.5090131	7.0128062	6.5736978	6.1830860	5.8338913
31	7.5304801	7.0290626	6.5860388	6.1924775	5.8410552
32	7.5494329	7.0432869	6.5967416	6.2005508	5.8471601
33	7.5661659	7.0557332	6.6060237	6.2074910	5.8523625
34	7.5809393	7.0666237	6.6140736	6.2134572	5.8567959
35	7.5939824	7.0761528	6.6210550	6.2185860	5.8605739
36	7.6054980	7.0844909	6.6271097	6.2229950	5.8637934
37	7.6156649	7.0917867	6.6323606	6.2267852	5.8665370
38	7.6246411	7.0981705	6.6369145	6.2300434	5.8688750
39	7.6325660	7.1037563	6.6408639	6.2328443	5.8708674
40	7.6395628	7.1086439	6.6442890	6.2352521	5.8725652

Present Value of Ordinary Annuity of $1 per Period, Decreasing in Constant Ratio of 2 Percent

Period	Interest Rate				
	16%	**17%**	**18%**	**19%**	**20%**
0	0.0000000	0.0000000	0.0000000	0.0000000	0.0000000
1	0.8620690	0.8547009	0.8474576	0.8403361	0.8333333
2	1.5903686	1.5706041	1.5512784	1.5323777	1.5138889
3	2.2056562	2.1702496	2.1358075	2.1022942	2.0696759
4	2.7254682	2.6725168	2.6212638	2.5716372	2.5235687
5	3.1646197	3.0932192	3.0244394	2.9581550	2.8942477
6	3.5356270	3.4456024	3.3592802	3.2764638	3.1969690
7	3.8490642	3.7407610	3.6373683	3.5386005	3.4441913
8	4.1138646	3.9879878	3.8683228	3.7544777	3.6460896
9	4.3375752	4.1950667	4.0601325	3.9322589	3.8109732
10	4.5265722	4.3685174	4.2194321	4.0786670	3.9456281
11	4.6862420	4.5138009	4.3517317	4.1992384	4.0555963
12	4.8211355	4.6354914	4.4616077	4.2985325	4.1454036
13	4.9350972	4.7374201	4.5528606	4.3803040	4.2187463
14	5.0313752	4.8227963	4.6286470	4.4476453	4.2786428
15	5.1127136	4.8943080	4.6915882	4.5031029	4.3275583
16	5.1814304	4.9542067	4.7438614	4.5487738	4.3675059
17	5.2394843	5.0043783	4.7872747	4.5863852	4.4001298
18	5.2885299	5.0464023	4.8233298	4.6173592	4.4267727
19	5.3299649	5.0816020	4.8532739	4.6428672	4.4485310
20	5.3649703	5.1110854	4.8781428	4.6638739	4.4663004
21	5.3945439	5.1357809	4.8987965	4.6811734	4.4808120
22	5.4195285	5.1564661	4.9159497	4.6954201	4.4926631
23	5.4406361	5.1737921	4.9301955	4.7071527	4.5023415
24	5.4584684	5.1883045	4.9420268	4.7168148	4.5102456
25	5.4735337	5.2004602	4.9518527	4.7247719	4.5167006
26	5.4862612	5.2106419	4.9600133	4.7313247	4.5219721
27	5.4970138	5.2191701	4.9667907	4.7367212	4.5262772
28	5.5060979	5.2263134	4.9724194	4.7411654	4.5297931
29	5.5137723	5.2322967	4.9770941	4.7448253	4.5326643
30	5.5202559	5.2373084	4.9809764	4.7478393	4.5350092
31	5.5257335	5.2415061	4.9842008	4.7503214	4.5369242
32	5.5303610	5.2450222	4.9868786	4.7523656	4.5384881
33	5.5342705	5.2479673	4.9891026	4.7540489	4.5397653
34	5.5375734	5.2504342	4.9909496	4.7554353	4.5408083
35	5.5403637	5.2525004	4.9924836	4.7565769	4.5416601
36	5.5427211	5.2542311	4.9937575	4.7575171	4.5423558
37	5.5447126	5.2556808	4.9948156	4.7582914	4.5429239
38	5.5463951	5.2568950	4.9956943	4.7589291	4.5433878
39	5.5478166	5.2579121	4.9964241	4.7594542	4.5437667
40	5.5490175	5.2587639	4.9970302	4.7598866	4.5440762

Present Value of Ordinary Annuity of $1 per Period, Decreasing in Constant Ratio of 5 Percent

Period	Interest Rate			
	2%	3%	4%	5%
0	0.0000000	0.0000000	0.0000000	0.0000000
1	0.9803922	0.9708738	0.9615385	0.9523810
2	1.8935025	1.8663399	1.8398669	1.8140590
3	2.7439484	2.6922552	2.6421861	2.5936724
4	3.5360304	3.4540218	3.3750738	3.2990369
5	4.2737538	4.1566221	4.0445386	3.9372239
6	4.9608491	4.8046514	4.6560689	4.5146311
7	5.6007908	5.4023484	5.2146783	5.0370472
8	6.1968150	5.9536223	5.7249465	5.5097094
9	6.7519355	6.4620788	6.1910569	5.9373561
10	7.2689596	6.9310436	6.6168309	6.3242746
11	7.7505016	7.3635839	7.0057590	6.6743437
12	8.1989966	7.7625288	7.3610298	6.9910728
13	8.6167125	8.1304878	7.6855561	7.2776373
14	9.0057616	8.4698673	7.9819983	7.5369100
15	9.3681113	8.7828874	8.2527869	7.7714900
16	9.7055939	9.0715951	8.5001419	7.9837290
17	10.0199159	9.3378790	8.7260912	8.1757548
18	10.3126667	9.5834806	8.9324871	8.3494925
19	10.5853269	9.8100064	9.1210219	8.5066837
20	10.8392750	10.0189380	9.2932412	8.6489043
21	11.0757954	10.2116418	9.4505568	8.7775800
22	11.2960839	10.3893784	9.5942586	8.8940010
23	11.5012546	10.5533101	9.7255247	8.9993342
24	11.6923450	10.7045094	9.8454312	9.0946357
25	11.8703213	10.8439649	9.9549612	9.1808609
26	12.0360836	10.9725890	10.0550127	9.2588741
27	12.1904700	11.0912229	10.1464058	9.3294576
28	12.3342613	11.2006425	10.2298899	9.3933187
29	12.4681845	11.3015634	10.3061494	9.4510979
30	12.5929170	11.3946459	10.3758096	9.5033743
31	12.7090893	11.4804986	10.4394414	9.5506720
32	12.8172891	11.5596832	10.4975667	9.5934651
33	12.9180634	11.6327175	10.5506619	9.6321827
34	13.0119217	11.7000793	10.5991623	9.6672130
35	13.0993389	11.7622090	10.6434656	9.6989070
36	13.1807568	11.8195132	10.6839349	9.7275825
37	13.2565872	11.8723665	10.7209021	9.7535270
38	13.3272136	11.9211148	10.7546702	9.7770006
39	13.3929930	11.9660767	10.7855160	9.7982387
40	13.4542582	12.0075465	10.8136925	9.8174540

Present Value of Ordinary Annuity of $1 per Period, Decreasing in Constant Ratio of 5 Percent

Period			Interest Rate		
	6%	7%	8%	9%	10%
0	0.0000000	0.0000000	0.0000000	0.0000000	0.0000000
1	0.9433962	0.9345794	0.9259259	0.9174312	0.9090909
2	1.7888928	1.7643462	1.7403978	1.7170272	1.6942149
3	2.5466492	2.5010551	2.4568314	2.4139228	2.3722765
4	3.2257706	3.1551423	3.0870276	3.0213088	2.9578751
5	3.8344170	3.7358740	3.6413669	3.5506820	3.4636194
6	4.3799020	4.2514770	4.1289801	4.0120623	3.9003986
7	4.8687801	4.7092552	4.5578992	4.4141827	4.2776170
8	5.3069256	5.1156939	4.9351891	4.7646547	4.6033965
9	5.6996031	5.4765507	5.2670645	5.0701119	4.8847515
10	6.0515311	5.7969375	5.5589919	5.3363360	5.1277399
11	6.3669382	6.0813931	5.8157799	5.5683663	5.3375936
12	6.6496145	6.3339472	6.0416583	5.7705945	5.5188308
13	6.9029564	6.5581774	6.2403475	5.9468484	5.6753539
14	7.1300081	6.7572603	6.4151205	6.1004642	5.8105329
15	7.3334978	6.9340161	6.5688560	6.2343495	5.9272784
16	7.5158707	7.0909489	6.7040863	6.3510386	6.0281041
17	7.6793180	7.2302817	6.8230389	6.4527400	6.1151808
18	7.8258039	7.3539885	6.9276731	6.5413789	6.1903834
19	7.9570884	7.4638215	7.0197124	6.6186330	6.2553311
20	8.0747490	7.5613369	7.1006730	6.6859646	6.3114223
21	8.1801996	7.6479159	7.1718883	6.7446480	6.3598648
22	8.2747072	7.7247852	7.2345314	6.7957941	6.4017014
23	8.3594074	7.7930336	7.2896341	6.8403710	6.4378330
24	8.4353180	7.8536279	7.3381040	6.8792225	6.4690376
25	8.5033510	7.9074267	7.3807397	6.9130838	6.4959870
26	8.5643240	7.9551919	7.4182432	6.9425960	6.5192615
27	8.6189696	7.9976003	7.4512325	6.9683176	6.5393622
28	8.6679445	8.0352526	7.4802508	6.9907355	6.5567219
29	8.7118370	8.0686822	7.5057761	7.0102741	6.5717144
30	8.7511747	8.0983627	7.5282290	7.0273031	6.5846624
31	8.7864302	8.1247145	7.5479792	7.0421449	6.5958448
32	8.8180270	8.1481110	7.5653521	7.0550804	6.6055023
33	8.8463450	8.1688836	7.5806338	7.0663545	6.6138429
34	8.8717243	8.1873266	7.5940760	7.0761805	6.6210462
35	8.8944699	8.2037012	7.6059002	7.0847445	6.6272671
36	8.9148551	8.2182394	7.6163011	7.0922085	6.6326398
37	8.9331248	8.2311471	7.6254500	7.0987138	6.6372798
38	8.9494987	8.2426072	7.6334977	7.1043836	6.6412871
39	8.9641733	8.2527821	7.6405767	7.1093252	6.6447480
40	8.9773252	8.2618159	7.6468036	7.1136320	6.6477369

Present Value of Ordinary Annuity of $1 per Period, Decreasing in Constant Ratio of 5 Percent

Period	Interest Rate				
	11%	12%	13%	14%	15%
0	0.0000000	0.0000000	0.0000000	0.0000000	0.0000000
1	0.9009009	0.8928571	0.8849558	0.8771930	0.8695652
2	1.6719422	1.6501913	1.6289451	1.6081871	1.5879017
3	2.3318424	2.2925730	2.2544229	2.2173489	2.1813101
4	2.8966219	2.8374503	2.7802670	2.7249838	2.6715170
5	3.3799917	3.2996230	3.2223484	3.1480128	3.0764706
6	3.7936866	3.6916445	3.5940097	3.5005370	3.4109975
7	4.1477498	4.0241628	3.9064683	3.7943071	3.6873457
8	4.4507769	4.3062095	4.1691548	4.0391156	3.9156334
9	4.7101243	4.5454456	4.3899974	4.2431226	4.1042189
10	4.9320884	4.7483690	4.5756615	4.4131285	4.2600069
11	5.1220576	4.9204916	4.7317508	4.5548001	4.3887014
12	5.2846439	5.0664884	4.8629764	4.6728597	4.4950142
13	5.4237943	5.1903250	4.9732987	4.7712427	4.5828378
14	5.5428871	5.2953649	5.0660476	4.8532286	4.6553877
15	5.6448132	5.3844613	5.1440223	4.9215501	4.7153203
16	5.7320474	5.4600342	5.2095763	4.9784848	4.7648298
17	5.8067072	5.5241361	5.2646880	5.0259303	4.8057290
18	5.8706053	5.5785083	5.3110209	5.0654682	4.8395152
19	5.9252928	5.6246276	5.3499733	5.0984165	4.8674256
20	5.9720974	5.6637466	5.3827209	5.1258734	4.8904821
21	6.0121555	5.6969279	5.4102521	5.1487542	4.9095287
22	6.0464394	5.7250728	5.4333978	5.1678214	4.9252628
23	6.0757814	5.7489457	5.4528566	5.1837109	4.9382606
24	6.1008940	5.7691950	5.4692157	5.1969520	4.9489979
25	6.1223868	5.7863708	5.4829689	5.2079863	4.9578678
26	6.1407815	5.8009395	5.4945314	5.2171816	4.9651951
27	6.1565247	5.8132969	5.5042521	5.2248443	4.9712482
28	6.1699986	5.8237786	5.5124243	5.2312299	4.9762485
29	6.1815303	5.8326694	5.5192948	5.2365512	4.9803792
30	6.1913998	5.8402106	5.5250708	5.2409857	4.9837915
31	6.1998467	5.8466072	5.5299268	5.2446811	4.9866104
32	6.2070760	5.8520329	5.5340093	5.2477605	4.9889390
33	6.2132633	5.8566351	5.5374414	5.2503268	4.9908627
34	6.2185586	5.8605387	5.5403268	5.2524653	4.9924518
35	6.2230907	5.8638498	5.5427527	5.2542474	4.9937645
36	6.2269695	5.8666583	5.5447921	5.2557325	4.9948489
37	6.2302892	5.8690405	5.5465066	5.2569700	4.9957448
38	6.2331304	5.8710611	5.5479480	5.2580013	4.9964848
39	6.2355621	5.8727751	5.5491598	5.2588608	4.9970961
40	6.2376432	5.8742289	5.5501786	5.2595770	4.9976012

Present Value of Ordinary Annuity of $1 per Period, Decreasing in Constant Ratio of 5 Percent

Period	Interest Rate				
	16%	**17%**	**18%**	**19%**	**20%**
0	0.0000000	0.0000000	0.0000000	0.0000000	0.0000000
1	0.8620690	0.8547009	0.8474576	0.8403361	0.8333333
2	1.5680737	1.5486887	1.5297328	1.5111927	1.4930556
3	2.1462673	2.1121832	2.0790222	2.0467505	2.0153356
4	2.6197879	2.5697214	2.5212467	2.4742966	2.4288074
5	3.0075849	2.9412267	2.8772749	2.8156149	2.7561392
6	3.3251773	3.2428764	3.1639077	3.0880960	3.0152769
7	3.5852745	3.4878056	3.3946715	3.3056228	3.2204275
8	3.7982851	3.6866798	3.5804559	3.4792787	3.3828384
9	3.9727335	3.8481588	3.7300280	3.6179116	3.5114138
10	4.1156007	3.9792742	3.8504463	3.7285849	3.6132026
11	4.2326040	4.0857355	3.9473932	3.8169375	3.6937854
12	4.3284257	4.1721784	4.0254437	3.8874711	3.7575801
13	4.4069004	4.2423671	4.0882809	3.9437795	3.8080842
14	4.4711684	4.2993579	4.1388702	3.9887315	3.8480667
15	4.5238017	4.3456325	4.1795989	4.0246176	3.8797195
16	4.5669066	4.3832058	4.2123890	4.0532661	3.9047779
17	4.6022080	4.4137142	4.2387877	4.0761368	3.9246158
18	4.6311186	4.4384858	4.2600410	4.0943950	3.9403209
19	4.6547954	4.4585996	4.2771516	4.1089708	3.9527540
20	4.6741859	4.4749313	4.2909272	4.1206069	3.9625969
21	4.6900660	4.4881921	4.3020176	4.1298963	3.9703892
22	4.7030713	4.4989594	4.3109464	4.1373122	3.9765581
23	4.7137222	4.5077021	4.3181348	4.1432324	3.9814419
24	4.7224449	4.5148008	4.3239221	4.1479586	3.9853081
25	4.7295885	4.5205648	4.3285813	4.1517317	3.9883689
26	4.7354389	4.5252449	4.3323324	4.1547438	3.9907921
27	4.7402301	4.5290450	4.3353524	4.1571484	3.9927104
28	4.7441540	4.5321306	4.3377837	4.1590680	3.9942291
29	4.7473675	4.5346359	4.3397411	4.1606005	3.9954313
30	4.7499992	4.5366702	4.3413170	4.1618240	3.9963831
31	4.7521545	4.5383220	4.3425857	4.1628006	3.9971367
32	4.7539197	4.5396631	4.3436071	4.1635803	3.9977332
33	4.7553652	4.5407521	4.3444295	4.1642028	3.9982054
34	4.7565491	4.5416363	4.3450915	4.1646997	3.9985793
35	4.7575187	4.5423543	4.3456245	4.1650964	3.9988753
36	4.7583127	4.5429372	4.3460537	4.1654131	3.9991096
37	4.7589630	4.5434106	4.3463991	4.1656659	3.9992951
38	4.7594956	4.5437949	4.3466773	4.1658678	3.9994420
39	4.7599317	4.5441070	4.3469012	4.1660289	3.9995582
40	4.7602889	4.5443604	4.3470815	4.1661575	3.9996503

Present Value of Ordinary Annuity of $1 per Period, Decreasing in Constant Ratio of 10 Percent

Period	Interest Rate			
	2%	**3%**	**4%**	**5%**
0	0.0000000	0.0000000	0.0000000	0.0000000
1	0.9803922	0.9708738	0.9615385	0.9523810
2	1.8454441	1.8192101	1.7936391	1.7687075
3	2.6087252	2.5604748	2.5137261	2.4684159
4	3.2822085	3.2081819	3.1368784	3.0681660
5	3.8764585	3.7741395	3.6761447	3.5822376
6	4.4007967	4.2686656	4.1428176	4.0228703
7	4.8634480	4.7007758	4.5466690	4.4005555
8	5.2716698	5.0783478	4.8961559	4.7242857
9	5.6318655	5.4082650	5.1985965	5.0017687
10	5.9496853	5.6965423	5.4603239	5.2396112
11	6.2301145	5.9484350	5.6868187	5.4434763
12	6.4775520	6.1685354	5.8828239	5.6182178
13	6.6958792	6.3608562	6.0524438	5.7679962
14	6.8885209	6.5289035	6.1992302	5.8963777
15	7.0584988	6.6757409	6.3262569	6.0064190
16	7.2084793	6.8040454	6.4361838	6.1007401
17	7.3408151	6.9161562	6.5313129	6.1815867
18	7.4575819	7.0141171	6.6136362	6.2508839
19	7.5606115	7.0997140	6.6848775	6.3102814
20	7.6515200	7.1745073	6.7465286	6.3611936
21	7.7317333	7.2398608	6.7998805	6.4048326
22	7.8025098	7.2969657	6.8460504	6.4422375
23	7.8649596	7.3468633	6.8860052	6.4742988
24	7.9200624	7.3904630	6.9205814	6.5017799
25	7.9686825	7.4285599	6.9505031	6.5253352
26	8.0115826	7.4618485	6.9763970	6.5455254
27	8.0494356	7.4909356	6.9988051	6.5628313
28	8.0828354	7.5163515	7.0181967	6.5776649
29	8.1123057	7.5385595	7.0349779	6.5903794
30	8.1383090	7.5579646	7.0495001	6.6012776
31	8.1612530	7.5749206	7.0620674	6.6106189
32	8.1814978	7.5897364	7.0729429	6.6186257
33	8.1993608	7.6026823	7.0823545	6.6254887
34	8.2151222	7.6139942	7.0904991	6.6313713
35	8.2290294	7.6238785	7.0975473	6.6364135
36	8.2413005	7.6325152	7.1036467	6.6407354
37	8.2521279	7.6400618	7.1089250	6.6444398
38	8.2616815	7.6466559	7.1134928	6.6476151
39	8.2701111	7.6524178	7.1174457	6.6503368
40	8.2775490	7.6574525	7.1208665	6.6526696

Present Value of Ordinary Annuity of $1 per Period, Decreasing in Constant Ratio of 10 Percent

Period	Interest Rate				
	6%	**7%**	**8%**	**9%**	**10%**
0	0.0000000	0.0000000	0.0000000	0.0000000	0.0000000
1	0.9433962	0.9345794	0.9259259	0.9174312	0.9090909
2	1.7443930	1.7206743	1.6975309	1.6749432	1.6528926
3	2.4244846	2.3818756	2.3405350	2.3004118	2.2614576
4	3.0019209	2.9380262	2.8763717	2.8168538	2.7593744
5	3.4921970	3.4058164	3.3229024	3.2432738	3.1667608
6	3.9084692	3.7992848	3.6950112	3.5953637	3.5000771
7	4.2619078	4.1302396	4.0051020	3.8860801	3.7727903
8	4.5619972	4.4086127	4.2635109	4.1261212	3.9959193
9	4.8167900	4.6427584	4.4788517	4.3243202	4.1784795
10	5.0331236	4.8397033	4.6583023	4.4879708	4.3278468
11	5.2168031	5.0053579	4.8078445	4.6230952	4.4500565
12	5.3727573	5.1446936	4.9324630	4.7346657	4.5500462
13	5.5051713	5.2618918	5.0363118	4.8267882	4.6318560
14	5.6175983	5.3604697	5.1228524	4.9028527	4.6987913
15	5.7130552	5.4433858	5.1949696	4.9656582	4.7535565
16	5.7941034	5.5131282	5.2550673	5.0175159	4.7983644
17	5.8629180	5.5717901	5.3051486	5.0603342	4.8350254
18	5.9213455	5.6211318	5.3468831	5.0956888	4.8650208
19	5.9709537	5.6626343	5.3816619	5.1248807	4.8895625
20	6.0130739	5.6975428	5.4106441	5.1489840	4.9096420
21	6.0488363	5.7269052	5.4347960	5.1688859	4.9260707
22	6.0792007	5.7516025	5.4549226	5.1853186	4.9395124
23	6.1049817	5.7723759	5.4716948	5.1988870	4.9505102
24	6.1268712	5.7898489	5.4856716	5.2100901	4.9595083
25	6.1454567	5.8045458	5.4973189	5.2193405	4.9668704
26	6.1612368	5.8169077	5.5070250	5.2269784	4.9728940
27	6.1746351	5.8273055	5.5151134	5.2332849	4.9778224
28	6.1860109	5.8360514	5.5218538	5.2384921	4.9818547
29	6.1956696	5.8434077	5.5274708	5.2427917	4.9851538
30	6.2038704	5.8495953	5.5321516	5.2463417	4.9878531
31	6.2108334	5.8547998	5.5360522	5.2492730	4.9900616
32	6.2167453	5.8591774	5.5393028	5.2516933	4.9918686
33	6.2217649	5.8628595	5.5420116	5.2536917	4.9933471
34	6.2260268	5.8659566	5.5442689	5.2553418	4.9945567
35	6.2296454	5.8685616	5.5461500	5.2567042	4.9955464
36	6.2327178	5.8707527	5.5477176	5.2578292	4.9963561
37	6.2353264	5.8725958	5.5490239	5.2587580	4.9970186
38	6.2375413	5.8741460	5.5501125	5.2595250	4.9975607
39	6.2394219	5.8754499	5.5510197	5.2601582	4.9980042
40	6.2410186	5.8765466	5.5517757	5.2606811	4.9983671

Present Value of Ordinary Annuity of $1 per Period, Decreasing in Constant Ratio of 10 Percent

Period	Interest Rate				
	11%	**12%**	**13%**	**14%**	**15%**
0	0.0000000	0.0000000	0.0000000	0.0000000	0.0000000
1	0.9009009	0.8928571	0.8849558	0.8771930	0.8695652
2	1.6313611	1.6103316	1.5897878	1.5697138	1.5500945
3	2.2236261	2.1868736	2.1511584	2.1164407	2.0826827
4	2.7038410	2.6501663	2.5982678	2.5480672	2.4994908
5	3.0932044	3.0224551	2.9543725	2.8888250	2.8256884
6	3.4089045	3.3216157	3.2379958	3.1578443	3.0809736
7	3.6648775	3.5620126	3.4638905	3.3702279	3.2807619
8	3.8724232	3.7551887	3.6438066	3.5378993	3.4371180
9	4.0407035	3.9104195	3.7871026	3.6702713	3.5594837
10	4.1771470	4.0351585	3.9012321	3.7747756	3.6552481
11	4.2877768	4.1353952	3.9921318	3.8572790	3.7301942
12	4.3774767	4.2159426	4.0645298	3.9224132	3.7888476
13	4.4502063	4.2806682	4.1221918	3.9738350	3.8347503
14	4.5091763	4.3326798	4.1681174	4.0144312	3.8706741
15	4.5569898	4.3744748	4.2046953	4.0464807	3.8987885
16	4.5957575	4.4080601	4.2338281	4.0717830	3.9207910
17	4.6271908	4.4350483	4.2570312	4.0917585	3.9380103
18	4.6526772	4.4567353	4.2755116	4.1075287	3.9514863
19	4.6733419	4.4741623	4.2902305	4.1199788	3.9620328
20	4.6900970	4.4881661	4.3019535	4.1298078	3.9702865
21	4.7036823	4.4994192	4.3112904	4.1375676	3.9767460
22	4.7146973	4.5084618	4.3187268	4.1436937	3.9818012
23	4.7236285	4.5157283	4.3246497	4.1485301	3.9857575
24	4.7308699	4.5215674	4.3293670	4.1523483	3.9888537
25	4.7367414	4.5262595	4.3331242	4.1553627	3.9912768
26	4.7415020	4.5300299	4.3361166	4.1577425	3.9931731
27	4.7453620	4.5330598	4.3384999	4.1596213	3.9946572
28	4.7484917	4.5354945	4.3403982	4.1611045	3.9958187
29	4.7510293	4.5374509	4.3419101	4.1622755	3.9967277
30	4.7530868	4.5390231	4.3431142	4.1631999	3.9974391
31	4.7547551	4.5402864	4.3440733	4.1639298	3.9979958
32	4.7561077	4.5413016	4.3448371	4.1645060	3.9984315
33	4.7572045	4.5421173	4.3454455	4.1649609	3.9987725
34	4.7580937	4.5427728	4.3459300	4.1653200	3.9990393
35	4.7588147	4.5432996	4.3463160	4.1656035	3.9992482
36	4.7593993	4.5437229	4.3466233	4.1658273	3.9994116
37	4.7598733	4.5440630	4.3468681	4.1660040	3.9995395
38	4.7602577	4.5443364	4.3470631	4.1661435	3.9996396
39	4.7605693	4.5445560	4.3472184	4.1662537	3.9997180
40	4.7608219	4.5447325	4.3473421	4.1663406	3.9997793

¶691.23

Present Value of Ordinary Annuity of $1 per Period, Decreasing in Constant Ratio of 10 Percent

Period	Interest Rate				
	16%	17%	18%	19%	20%
0	0.0000000	0.0000000	0.0000000	0.0000000	0.0000000
1	0.8620690	0.8547009	0.8474576	0.8403361	0.8333333
2	1.5309156	1.5121631	1.4938236	1.4758845	1.4583333
3	2.0498483	2.0179032	1.9868146	1.9565513	1.9270833
4	2.4524685	2.4069341	2.3628247	2.3200808	2.2786458
5	2.7648463	2.7061886	2.6496121	2.5950191	2.5423177
6	3.0072083	2.9363844	2.8683482	2.8029556	2.7400716
7	3.1952478	3.1134581	3.0351808	2.9602185	2.8883870
8	3.3411405	3.2496686	3.1624260	3.0791569	2.9996236
9	3.4543332	3.3544459	3.2594775	3.1691102	3.0830510
10	3.5421551	3.4350439	3.3334998	3.2371422	3.1456216
11	3.6102927	3.4970423	3.3899575	3.2885949	3.1925495
12	3.6631581	3.5447334	3.4330184	3.3275088	3.2277455
13	3.7041744	3.5814189	3.4658615	3.3569394	3.2541425
14	3.7359974	3.6096384	3.4909113	3.3791979	3.2739402
15	3.7606876	3.6313458	3.5100171	3.3960320	3.2887885
16	3.7798439	3.6480438	3.5245893	3.4087637	3.2999247
17	3.7947064	3.6608884	3.5357037	3.4183927	3.3082768
18	3.8062378	3.6707688	3.5441808	3.4256752	3.3145410
19	3.8151845	3.6783692	3.5506464	3.4311829	3.3192391
20	3.8221259	3.6842156	3.5555777	3.4353484	3.3227626
21	3.8275115	3.6887129	3.5593390	3.4384988	3.3254053
22	3.8316899	3.6921723	3.5622077	3.4408814	3.3273873
23	3.8349318	3.6948334	3.5643957	3.4426834	3.3288738
24	3.8374471	3.6968804	3.5660645	3.4440463	3.3299887
25	3.8393986	3.6984550	3.5673373	3.4450770	3.3308249
26	3.8409127	3.6996662	3.5683081	3.4458566	3.3314520
27	3.8420875	3.7005980	3.5690486	3.4464462	3.3319223
28	3.8429989	3.7013147	3.5696133	3.4468920	3.3322751
29	3.8437060	3.7018660	3.5700441	3.4472293	3.3325396
30	3.8442547	3.7022901	3.5703726	3.4474843	3.3327381
31	3.8446804	3.7026163	3.5706232	3.4476772	3.3328869
32	3.8450106	3.7028672	3.5708143	3.4478231	3.3329985
33	3.8452669	3.7030603	3.5709600	3.4479334	3.3330822
34	3.8454657	3.7032088	3.5710712	3.4480169	3.3331450
35	3.8456199	3.7033230	3.5711560	3.4480800	3.3331921
36	3.8457396	3.7034108	3.5712207	3.4481277	3.3332274
37	3.8458324	3.7034784	3.5712700	3.4481638	3.3332539
38	3.8459045	3.7035304	3.5713076	3.4481911	3.3332737
39	3.8459604	3.7035704	3.5713363	3.4482118	3.3332886
40	3.8460037	3.7036012	3.5713582	3.4482274	3.3332998

Present Value of Ordinary Annuity of $1 per Period, Decreasing in Constant Ratio of 15 Percent

Period	Interest Rate			
	2%	3%	4%	5%
0	0.0000000	0.0000000	0.0000000	0.0000000
1	0.9803922	0.9708738	0.9615385	0.9523810
2	1.7973856	1.7720803	1.7474112	1.7233560
3	2.4782135	2.4332702	2.3897111	2.3474787
4	3.0455701	2.9789123	2.9146677	2.8527208
5	3.5183672	3.4291994	3.3437188	3.2617264
6	3.9123648	3.8007957	3.6943856	3.5928261
7	4.2406962	4.1074527	3.9809882	3.8608592
8	4.5143057	4.3605192	4.2152307	4.0778384
9	4.7423135	4.5693605	4.4066790	4.2534883
10	4.9323201	4.7417053	4.5631511	4.3956810
11	5.0906589	4.8839316	4.6910369	4.5107894
12	5.2226079	5.0013027	4.7955590	4.6039723
13	5.3325654	5.0981625	4.8809858	4.6794062
14	5.4241967	5.1780952	4.9508057	4.7404717
15	5.5005560	5.2440592	5.0078700	4.7899056
16	5.5641889	5.2984954	5.0545091	4.8299236
17	5.6172162	5.3434186	5.0926277	4.8623191
18	5.6614057	5.3804910	5.1237822	4.8885440
19	5.6982302	5.4110848	5.1492451	4.9097737
20	5.7289173	5.4363322	5.1700561	4.9269597
21	5.7544899	5.4571673	5.1870651	4.9408721
22	5.7758004	5.4743614	5.2009666	4.9521346
23	5.7935592	5.4885506	5.2123285	4.9612518
24	5.8083581	5.5002602	5.2216146	4.9686324
25	5.8206906	5.5099235	5.2292043	4.9746072
26	5.8309677	5.5178980	5.2354073	4.9794439
27	5.8395319	5.5244790	5.2404772	4.9833594
28	5.8466687	5.5299098	5.2446208	4.9865290
29	5.8526161	5.5343916	5.2480073	4.9890949
30	5.8575722	5.5380902	5.2507752	4.9911721
31	5.8617024	5.5411424	5.2530375	4.9928536
32	5.8651441	5.5436612	5.2548864	4.9942148
33	5.8680123	5.5457398	5.2563975	4.9953167
34	5.8704024	5.5474552	5.2576326	4.9962088
35	5.8723941	5.5488708	5.2586420	4.9969309
36	5.8740539	5.5500390	5.2594670	4.9975155
37	5.8754371	5.5510031	5.2601413	4.9979887
38	5.8765897	5.5517986	5.2606924	4.9983718
39	5.8775503	5.5524552	5.2611429	4.9986820
40	5.8783507	5.5529970	5.2615110	4.9989330

Present Value of Ordinary Annuity of $1 per Period, Decreasing in Constant Ratio of 15 Percent

Period			Interest Rate		
	6%	**7%**	**8%**	**9%**	**10%**
0	0.0000000	0.0000000	0.0000000	0.0000000	0.0000000
1	0.9433962	0.9345794	0.9259259	0.9174312	0.9090909
2	1.6998932	1.6770024	1.6546639	1.6328592	1.6115702
3	2.3065181	2.2667776	2.2282077	2.1907618	2.1543952
4	2.7929627	2.7352906	2.6796079	2.6258234	2.5738508
5	3.1830361	3.1074738	3.0348766	2.9650916	2.8979756
6	3.4958308	3.4031334	3.3144862	3.2296586	3.1484357
7	3.7466568	3.6380032	3.5345493	3.4359723	3.3419731
8	3.9477908	3.8245820	3.7077472	3.5968591	3.4915246
9	4.1090775	3.9727988	3.8440603	3.7223213	3.6070872
10	4.2384112	4.0905411	3.9513437	3.8201589	3.6963856
11	4.3421222	4.1840747	4.0357798	3.8964541	3.7653889
12	4.4252867	4.2583771	4.1022341	3.9559505	3.8187096
13	4.4919752	4.3174024	4.1545361	4.0023467	3.8599119
14	4.5454518	4.3642916	4.1956997	4.0385272	3.8917501
15	4.5883340	4.4015400	4.2280970	4.0667414	3.9163524
16	4.6227206	4.4311299	4.2535949	4.0887433	3.9353632
17	4.6502949	4.4546359	4.2736626	4.1059008	3.9500534
18	4.6724063	4.4733089	4.2894567	4.1192804	3.9614049
19	4.6901371	4.4881426	4.3018872	4.1297141	3.9701765
20	4.7043552	4.4999264	4.3116705	4.1378504	3.9769546
21	4.7157565	4.5092873	4.3193703	4.1441953	3.9821922
22	4.7248991	4.5167236	4.3254303	4.1491431	3.9862394
23	4.7322304	4.5226309	4.3301998	4.1530015	3.9893668
24	4.7381093	4.5273236	4.3339535	4.1560104	3.9917834
25	4.7428235	4.5310514	4.3369079	4.1583567	3.9936508
26	4.7466037	4.5340128	4.3392331	4.1601864	3.9950938
27	4.7496351	4.5363653	4.3410631	4.1616133	3.9962089
28	4.7520659	4.5382341	4.3425033	4.1627259	3.9970705
29	4.7540151	4.5397187	4.3436369	4.1635936	3.9977363
30	4.7555781	4.5408980	4.3445290	4.1642703	3.9982508
31	4.7568315	4.5418349	4.3452312	4.1647979	3.9986483
32	4.7578366	4.5425791	4.3457838	4.1652094	3.9989555
33	4.7586426	4.5431703	4.3462187	4.1655302	3.9991929
34	4.7592888	4.5436400	4.3465610	4.1657805	3.9993763
35	4.7598071	4.5440131	4.3468304	4.1659756	3.9995181
36	4.7602227	4.5443094	4.3470425	4.1661278	3.9996276
37	4.7605559	4.5445449	4.3472094	4.1662464	3.9997122
38	4.7608231	4.5447319	4.3473407	4.1663389	3.9997776
39	4.7610374	4.5448805	4.3474441	4.1664111	3.9998282
40	4.7612093	4.5449985	4.3475254	4.1664674	3.9998672

Present Value of Ordinary Annuity of $1 per Period, Decreasing in Constant Ratio of 15 Percent

Period	Interest Rate				
	11%	12%	13%	14%	15%
0	0.0000000	0.0000000	0.0000000	0.0000000	0.0000000
1	0.9009009	0.8928571	0.8849558	0.8771930	0.8695652
2	1.5907800	1.5704719	1.5506304	1.5312404	1.5122873
3	2.1190657	2.0847332	2.0513592	2.0189073	1.9873428
4	2.5236089	2.4750207	2.4280135	2.3825186	2.3384708
5	2.8333942	2.7712211	2.7113376	2.6536323	2.5980001
6	3.0706172	2.9960160	2.9244575	2.8557785	2.7898262
7	3.2522744	3.1666193	3.0847689	3.0065015	2.9316107
8	3.3913813	3.2960950	3.2053571	3.1188827	3.0364079
9	3.4979046	3.3943578	3.2960651	3.2026757	3.1138667
10	3.5794765	3.4689323	3.3642968	3.2651529	3.1711189
11	3.6419415	3.5255289	3.4156215	3.3117368	3.2134357
12	3.6897750	3.5684818	3.4542285	3.3464704	3.2447133
13	3.7264043	3.6010799	3.4832693	3.3723683	3.2678316
14	3.7544537	3.6258196	3.5051140	3.3916781	3.2849190
15	3.7759330	3.6445952	3.5215460	3.4060758	3.2975488
16	3.7923812	3.6588446	3.5339063	3.4168109	3.3068839
17	3.8049766	3.6696588	3.5432038	3.4248151	3.3137838
18	3.8146217	3.6778661	3.5501976	3.4307832	3.3188837
19	3.8220076	3.6840948	3.5554583	3.4352331	3.3226531
20	3.8276635	3.6888219	3.5594156	3.4385510	3.3254393
21	3.8319946	3.6924095	3.5623922	3.4410249	3.3274986
22	3.8353111	3.6951322	3.5646313	3.4428694	3.3290207
23	3.8378509	3.6971986	3.5663156	3.4442447	3.3301457
24	3.8397957	3.6987668	3.5675825	3.4452702	3.3309773
25	3.8412850	3.6999569	3.5685355	3.4460348	3.3315919
26	3.8424255	3.7008602	3.5692524	3.4466049	3.3320462
27	3.8432988	3.7015457	3.5697916	3.4470300	3.3323820
28	3.8439675	3.7020659	3.5701972	3.4473469	3.3326301
29	3.8444796	3.7024607	3.5705023	3.4475832	3.3328136
30	3.8448718	3.7027604	3.5707319	3.4477594	3.3329492
31	3.8451721	3.7029878	3.5709045	3.4478908	3.3330494
32	3.8454021	3.7031604	3.5710344	3.4479887	3.3331235
33	3.8455782	3.7032914	3.5711320	3.4480618	3.3331782
34	3.8457130	3.7033908	3.5712055	3.4481162	3.3332187
35	3.8458163	3.7034662	3.5712608	3.4481568	3.3332486
36	3.8458953	3.7035235	3.5713024	3.4481871	3.3332707
37	3.8459559	3.7035669	3.5713336	3.4482097	3.3332870
38	3.8460023	3.7035999	3.5713572	3.4482265	3.3332991
39	3.8460378	3.7036249	3.5713749	3.4482391	3.3333080
40	3.8460650	3.7036439	3.5713882	3.4482484	3.3333146

Present Value of Ordinary Annuity of \$1 per Period, Decreasing in Constant Ratio of 15 Percent

Period	Interest Rate				
	16%	17%	18%	19%	20%
0	0.0000000	0.0000000	0.0000000	0.0000000	0.0000000
1	0.8620690	0.8547009	0.8474576	0.8403361	0.8333333
2	1.4937574	1.4756374	1.4579144	1.4405762	1.4236111
3	1.9566326	1.9267451	1.8976502	1.8693192	1.8417245
4	2.2958084	2.2544729	2.2144090	2.1755641	2.1378882
5	2.5443423	2.4925658	2.4425828	2.3943105	2.3476708
6	2.7264577	2.6655393	2.6069452	2.5505579	2.4962668
7	2.8599044	2.7912037	2.7253419	2.6621632	2.6015223
8	2.9576886	2.8824984	2.8106276	2.7418813	2.6760783
9	3.0293408	2.9488237	2.8720623	2.7988228	2.7288888
10	3.0818445	2.9970086	2.9163161	2.8394953	2.7662962
11	3.1203171	3.0320148	2.9481938	2.8685470	2.7927932
12	3.1485082	3.0574467	2.9711565	2.8892983	2.8115618
13	3.1691655	3.0759228	2.9876975	2.9041206	2.8248563
14	3.1843023	3.0893456	2.9996126	2.9147080	2.8342732
15	3.1953939	3.0990972	3.0081955	2.9222704	2.8409435
16	3.2035214	3.1061818	3.0143781	2.9276722	2.8456683
17	3.2094769	3.1113286	3.0188317	2.9315305	2.8490151
18	3.2138408	3.1150678	3.0220398	2.9342865	2.8513857
19	3.2170385	3.1177843	3.0243507	2.9362551	2.8530649
20	3.2193817	3.1197578	3.0260153	2.9376612	2.8542543
21	3.2210987	3.1211916	3.0272144	2.9386656	2.8550968
22	3.2223568	3.1222332	3.0280782	2.9393830	2.8556935
23	3.2232787	3.1229899	3.0287004	2.9398954	2.8561163
24	3.2239542	3.1235397	3.0291486	2.9402614	2.8564157
25	3.2244492	3.1239391	3.0294714	2.9405229	2.8566278
26	3.2248119	3.1242293	3.0297040	2.9407096	2.8567780
27	3.2250777	3.1244401	3.0298715	2.9408430	2.8568844
28	3.2252724	3.1245932	3.0299922	2.9409383	2.8569598
29	3.2254152	3.1247045	3.0300791	2.9410063	2.8570132
30	3.2255197	3.1247853	3.0301417	2.9410549	2.8570510
31	3.2255964	3.1248440	3.0301869	2.9410897	2.8570778
32	3.2256525	3.1248867	3.0302193	2.9411145	2.8570968
33	3.2256936	3.1249177	3.0302427	2.9411322	2.8571102
34	3.2257238	3.1249402	3.0302596	2.9411448	2.8571197
35	3.2257459	3.1249565	3.0302717	2.9411539	2.8571265
36	3.2257621	3.1249684	3.0302805	2.9411603	2.8571313
37	3.2257739	3.1249771	3.0302868	2.9411649	2.8571346
38	3.2257826	3.1249833	3.0302913	2.9411682	2.8571370
39	3.2257890	3.1249879	3.0302946	2.9411706	2.8571387
40	3.2257937	3.1249912	3.0302970	2.9411723	2.8571399

.25 Mortgage Summary Amortization — Various Rates

Mortgage Summary Amortization of $100,000

Interest Rate = 6%   **Interest Rate = 7%**

Term Years	Monthly Payment	Total Interest	Total Payments	Monthly Payment	Total Interest	Total Payments
1	$8,606.64	$3,279.68	$103,279.68	$8,652.67	$3,832.04	$103,832.04
2	$4,432.06	$6,369.44	$106,369.44	$4,477.26	$7,454.24	$107,454.24
3	$3,042.19	$9,518.84	$109,518.84	$3,087.71	$11,157.56	$111,157.56
4	$2,348.50	$12,728.00	$112,728.00	$2,394.62	$14,941.76	$114,941.76
5	$1,933.28	$15,996.80	$115,996.80	$1,980.12	$18,807.20	$118,807.20
6	$1,657.29	$19,324.88	$119,324.88	$1,704.90	$22,752.80	$122,752.80
7	$1,460.86	$22,712.24	$122,712.24	$1,509.27	$26,778.68	$126,778.68
8	$1,314.14	$26,157.44	$126,157.44	$1,363.37	$30,883.52	$130,883.52
9	$1,200.57	$29,661.56	$129,661.56	$1,250.63	$35,068.04	$135,068.04
10	$1,110.21	$33,225.20	$133,225.20	$1,161.08	$39,329.60	$139,329.60
11	$1,036.70	$36,844.40	$136,844.40	$1,088.41	$43,670.12	$143,670.12
12	$975.85	$40,522.40	$140,522.40	$1,028.38	$48,086.72	$148,086.72
13	$924.72	$44,256.32	$144,256.32	$978.07	$52,578.92	$152,578.92
14	$881.24	$48,048.32	$148,048.32	$935.40	$57,147.20	$157,147.20
15	$843.86	$51,894.80	$151,894.80	$898.83	$61,789.40	$161,789.40
16	$811.44	$55,796.48	$155,796.48	$867.21	$66,504.32	$166,504.32
17	$783.10	$59,752.40	$159,752.40	$839.66	$71,290.64	$171,290.64
18	$758.16	$63,762.56	$163,762.56	$815.50	$76,148.00	$176,148.00
19	$736.08	$67,826.24	$167,826.24	$794.19	$81,075.32	$181,075.32
20	$716.43	$71,943.20	$171,943.20	$775.30	$86,072.00	$186,072.00
21	$698.86	$76,112.72	$176,112.72	$758.47	$91,134.44	$191,134.44
22	$683.07	$80,330.48	$180,330.48	$743.42	$96,262.88	$196,262.88
23	$668.85	$84,602.60	$184,602.60	$729.92	$101,457.92	$201,457.92
24	$655.98	$88,922.24	$188,922.24	$717.76	$106,714.88	$206,714.88
25	$644.30	$93,290.00	$193,290.00	$706.78	$112,034.00	$212,034.00
26	$633.68	$97,708.16	$197,708.16	$696.84	$117,414.08	$217,414.08
27	$623.99	$102,172.76	$202,172.76	$687.81	$122,850.44	$222,850.44
28	$615.12	$106,680.32	$206,680.32	$679.61	$128,348.96	$228,348.96
29	$607.00	$111,236.00	$211,236.00	$672.13	$133,901.24	$233,901.24
30	$599.55	$115,838.00	$215,838.00	$665.30	$139,508.00	$239,508.00
31	$592.69	$120,480.68	$220,480.68	$659.06	$145,170.32	$245,170.32
32	$586.38	$125,169.92	$225,169.92	$653.34	$150,882.56	$250,882.56
33	$580.55	$129,897.80	$229,897.80	$648.10	$156,647.60	$256,647.60
34	$575.17	$134,669.36	$234,669.36	$643.28	$162,458.24	$262,458.24
35	$570.19	$139,479.80	$239,479.80	$638.86	$168,321.20	$268,321.20
36	$565.58	$144,330.56	$244,330.56	$634.78	$174,224.96	$274,224.96
37	$561.30	$149,217.20	$249,217.20	$631.03	$180,177.32	$280,177.32
38	$557.33	$154,142.48	$254,142.48	$627.57	$186,171.92	$286,171.92
39	$553.64	$159,103.52	$259,103.52	$624.38	$192,209.84	$292,209.84
40	$550.21	$164,100.80	$264,100.80	$621.43	$198,286.40	$298,286.40
41	$547.02	$169,133.84	$269,133.84	$618.71	$204,405.32	$304,405.32
42	$544.05	$174,201.20	$274,201.20	$616.19	$210,559.76	$310,559.76
43	$541.28	$179,300.48	$279,300.48	$613.86	$216,751.76	$316,751.76
44	$538.70	$184,433.60	$284,433.60	$611.70	$222,977.60	$322,977.60
45	$536.28	$189,591.20	$289,591.20	$609.70	$229,238.00	$329,238.00
46	$534.03	$194,784.56	$294,784.56	$607.85	$235,533.20	$335,533.20
47	$531.93	$200,008.52	$300,008.52	$606.13	$241,857.32	$341,857.32
48	$529.96	$205,256.96	$305,256.96	$604.54	$248,215.04	$348,215.04
49	$528.12	$210,534.56	$310,534.56	$603.06	$254,599.28	$354,599.28
50	$526.40	$215,840.00	$315,840.00	$601.69	$261,014.00	$361,014.00

¶691.25

Mortgage Summary Amortization of $100,000

Interest Rate = 8%   **Interest Rate = 9%**

Term Years	Monthly Payment	Total Interest	Total Payments	Monthly Payment	Total Interest	Total Payments
1	$8,698.84	$4,386.08	$104,386.08	$8,745.15	$4,941.80	$104,941.80
2	$4,522.73	$8,545.52	$108,545.52	$4,568.47	$9,643.28	$109,643.28
3	$3,133.64	$12,811.04	$112,811.04	$3,179.97	$14,478.92	$114,478.92
4	$2,441.29	$17,181.92	$117,181.92	$2,488.50	$19,448.00	$119,448.00
5	$2,027.64	$21,658.40	$121,658.40	$2,075.84	$24,550.40	$124,550.40
6	$1,753.32	$26,239.04	$126,239.04	$1,802.55	$29,783.60	$129,783.60
7	$1,558.62	$30,924.08	$130,924.08	$1,608.91	$35,148.44	$135,148.44
8	$1,413.67	$35,712.32	$135,712.32	$1,465.02	$40,641.92	$140,641.92
9	$1,301.87	$40,601.96	$140,601.96	$1,354.29	$46,263.32	$146,263.32
10	$1,213.28	$45,593.60	$145,593.60	$1,266.76	$52,011.20	$152,011.20
11	$1,141.54	$50,683.28	$150,683.28	$1,196.08	$57,882.56	$157,882.56
12	$1,082.45	$55,872.80	$155,872.80	$1,138.03	$63,876.32	$163,876.32
13	$1,033.07	$61,158.92	$161,158.92	$1,089.68	$69,990.08	$169,990.08
14	$991.32	$66,541.76	$166,541.76	$1,048.94	$76,221.92	$176,221.92
15	$955.65	$72,017.00	$172,017.00	$1,014.27	$82,568.60	$182,568.60
16	$924.93	$77,586.56	$177,586.56	$984.52	$89,027.84	$189,027.84
17	$898.26	$83,245.04	$183,245.04	$958.80	$95,595.20	$195,595.20
18	$874.96	$88,991.36	$188,991.36	$936.44	$102,271.04	$202,271.04
19	$854.50	$94,826.00	$194,826.00	$916.90	$109,053.20	$209,053.20
20	$836.44	$100,745.60	$200,745.60	$899.73	$115,935.20	$215,935.20
21	$820.43	$106,748.36	$206,748.36	$884.58	$122,914.16	$222,914.16
22	$806.18	$112,831.52	$212,831.52	$871.17	$129,988.88	$229,988.88
23	$793.45	$118,992.20	$218,992.20	$859.27	$137,158.52	$237,158.52
24	$782.05	$125,230.40	$225,230.40	$848.66	$144,414.08	$244,414.08
25	$771.82	$131,546.00	$231,546.00	$839.20	$151,760.00	$251,760.00
26	$762.60	$137,931.20	$237,931.20	$830.72	$159,184.64	$259,184.64
27	$754.28	$144,386.72	$244,386.72	$823.13	$166,694.12	$266,694.12
28	$746.76	$150,911.36	$250,911.36	$816.30	$174,276.80	$274,276.80
29	$739.95	$157,502.60	$257,502.60	$810.16	$181,935.68	$281,935.68
30	$733.76	$164,153.60	$264,153.60	$804.62	$189,663.20	$289,663.20
31	$728.15	$170,871.80	$270,871.80	$799.63	$197,462.36	$297,462.36
32	$723.04	$177,647.36	$277,647.36	$795.12	$205,326.08	$305,326.08
33	$718.38	$184,478.48	$284,478.48	$791.03	$213,247.88	$313,247.88
34	$714.14	$191,369.12	$291,369.12	$787.34	$221,234.72	$321,234.72
35	$710.26	$198,309.20	$298,309.20	$783.99	$229,275.80	$329,275.80
36	$706.72	$205,303.04	$305,303.04	$780.96	$237,374.72	$337,374.72
37	$703.48	$212,345.12	$312,345.12	$778.20	$245,520.80	$345,520.80
38	$700.52	$219,437.12	$319,437.12	$775.70	$253,719.20	$353,719.20
39	$697.80	$226,570.40	$326,570.40	$773.43	$261,965.24	$361,965.24
40	$695.31	$233,748.80	$333,748.80	$771.36	$270,252.80	$370,252.80
41	$693.03	$240,970.76	$340,970.76	$769.48	$278,584.16	$378,584.16
42	$690.94	$248,233.76	$348,233.76	$767.77	$286,956.08	$386,956.08
43	$689.01	$255,529.16	$355,529.16	$766.21	$295,364.36	$395,364.36
44	$687.25	$262,868.00	$362,868.00	$764.80	$303,814.40	$403,814.40
45	$685.63	$270,240.20	$370,240.20	$763.50	$312,290.00	$412,290.00
46	$684.13	$277,639.76	$377,639.76	$762.33	$320,806.16	$420,806.16
47	$682.76	$285,076.64	$385,076.64	$761.25	$329,345.00	$429,345.00
48	$681.50	$292,544.00	$392,544.00	$760.28	$337,921.28	$437,921.28
49	$680.34	$300,039.92	$400,039.92	$759.38	$346,515.44	$446,515.44
50	$679.27	$307,562.00	$407,562.00	$758.57	$355,142.00	$455,142.00

Mortgage Summary Amortization of $100,000

Interest Rate = 10%   **Interest Rate = 11%**

Term Years	Monthly Payment	Total Interest	Total Payments	Monthly Payment	Total Interest	Total Payments
1	$8,791.59	$5,499.08	$105,499.08	$8,838.17	$6,058.04	$106,058.04
2	$4,614.49	$10,747.76	$110,747.76	$4,660.78	$11,858.72	$111,858.72
3	$3,226.72	$16,161.92	$116,161.92	$3,273.87	$17,859.32	$117,859.32
4	$2,536.26	$21,740.48	$121,740.48	$2,584.55	$24,058.40	$124,058.40
5	$2,124.70	$27,482.00	$127,482.00	$2,174.24	$30,454.40	$130,454.40
6	$1,852.58	$33,385.76	$133,385.76	$1,903.41	$37,045.52	$137,045.52
7	$1,660.12	$39,450.08	$139,450.08	$1,712.24	$43,828.16	$143,828.16
8	$1,517.42	$45,672.32	$145,672.32	$1,570.84	$50,800.64	$150,800.64
9	$1,407.87	$52,049.96	$152,049.96	$1,462.59	$57,959.72	$157,959.72
10	$1,321.51	$58,581.20	$158,581.20	$1,377.50	$65,300.00	$165,300.00
11	$1,251.99	$65,262.68	$165,262.68	$1,309.23	$72,818.36	$172,818.36
12	$1,195.08	$72,091.52	$172,091.52	$1,253.56	$80,512.64	$180,512.64
13	$1,147.85	$79,064.60	$179,064.60	$1,207.53	$88,374.68	$188,374.68
14	$1,108.20	$86,177.60	$186,177.60	$1,169.05	$96,400.40	$196,400.40
15	$1,074.61	$93,429.80	$193,429.80	$1,136.60	$104,588.00	$204,588.00
16	$1,045.90	$100,812.80	$200,812.80	$1,109.00	$112,928.00	$212,928.00
17	$1,021.21	$108,326.84	$208,326.84	$1,085.38	$121,417.52	$221,417.52
18	$999.84	$115,965.44	$215,965.44	$1,065.05	$130,050.80	$230,050.80
19	$981.26	$123,727.28	$223,727.28	$1,047.46	$138,820.88	$238,820.88
20	$965.02	$131,604.80	$231,604.80	$1,032.19	$147,725.60	$247,725.60
21	$950.78	$139,596.56	$239,596.56	$1,018.87	$156,755.24	$256,755.24
22	$938.25	$147,698.00	$247,698.00	$1,007.22	$165,906.08	$265,906.08
23	$927.18	$155,901.68	$255,901.68	$997.01	$175,174.76	$275,174.76
24	$917.39	$164,208.32	$264,208.32	$988.03	$184,552.64	$284,552.64
25	$908.70	$172,610.00	$272,610.00	$980.11	$194,033.00	$294,033.00
26	$900.98	$181,105.76	$281,105.76	$973.13	$203,616.56	$303,616.56
27	$894.10	$189,688.40	$289,688.40	$966.95	$213,291.80	$313,291.80
28	$887.96	$198,354.56	$298,354.56	$961.48	$223,057.28	$323,057.28
29	$882.48	$207,103.04	$307,103.04	$956.63	$232,907.24	$332,907.24
30	$877.57	$215,925.20	$315,925.20	$952.32	$242,835.20	$342,835.20
31	$873.18	$224,822.96	$324,822.96	$948.50	$252,842.00	$352,842.00
32	$869.24	$233,788.16	$333,788.16	$945.09	$262,914.56	$362,914.56
33	$865.70	$242,817.20	$342,817.20	$942.06	$273,055.76	$373,055.76
34	$862.53	$251,912.24	$351,912.24	$939.36	$283,258.88	$383,258.88
35	$859.67	$261,061.40	$361,061.40	$936.96	$293,523.20	$393,523.20
36	$857.10	$270,267.20	$370,267.20	$934.81	$303,837.92	$403,837.92
37	$854.79	$279,526.76	$379,526.76	$932.90	$314,207.60	$414,207.60
38	$852.71	$288,835.76	$388,835.76	$931.19	$324,622.64	$424,622.64
39	$850.84	$298,193.12	$398,193.12	$929.66	$335,080.88	$435,080.88
40	$849.15	$307,592.00	$407,592.00	$928.29	$345,579.20	$445,579.20
41	$847.62	$317,029.04	$417,029.04	$927.07	$356,118.44	$456,118.44
42	$846.25	$326,510.00	$426,510.00	$925.98	$366,693.92	$466,693.92
43	$845.00	$336,020.00	$436,020.00	$925.01	$377,305.16	$477,305.16
44	$843.88	$345,568.64	$445,568.64	$924.14	$387,945.92	$487,945.92
45	$842.87	$355,149.80	$455,149.80	$923.36	$398,614.40	$498,614.40
46	$841.96	$364,761.92	$464,761.92	$922.66	$409,308.32	$509,308.32
47	$841.13	$374,397.32	$474,397.32	$922.03	$420,024.92	$520,024.92
48	$840.39	$384,064.64	$484,064.64	$921.47	$430,766.72	$530,766.72
49	$839.71	$393,749.48	$493,749.48	$920.97	$441,530.36	$541,530.36
50	$839.11	$403,466.00	$503,466.00	$920.52	$452,312.00	$552,312.00

¶691.25

Mortgage Summary Amortization of $100,000

Interest Rate = 12%   Interest Rate = 13%

Term Years	Monthly Payment	Total Interest	Total Payments	Monthly Payment	Total Interest	Total Payments
1	$8,884.88	$6,618.56	$106,618.56	$8,931.73	$7,180.76	$107,180.76
2	$4,707.35	$12,976.40	$112,976.40	$4,754.18	$14,100.32	$114,100.32
3	$3,321.43	$19,571.48	$119,571.48	$3,369.40	$21,298.40	$121,298.40
4	$2,633.38	$26,402.24	$126,402.24	$2,682.75	$28,772.00	$128,772.00
5	$2,224.44	$33,466.40	$133,466.40	$2,275.31	$36,518.60	$136,518.60
6	$1,955.02	$40,761.44	$140,761.44	$2,007.41	$44,533.52	$144,533.52
7	$1,765.27	$48,282.68	$148,282.68	$1,819.20	$52,812.80	$152,812.80
8	$1,625.28	$56,026.88	$156,026.88	$1,680.73	$61,350.08	$161,350.08
9	$1,518.42	$63,989.36	$163,989.36	$1,575.36	$70,138.88	$170,138.88
10	$1,434.71	$72,165.20	$172,165.20	$1,493.11	$79,173.20	$179,173.20
11	$1,367.79	$80,548.28	$180,548.28	$1,427.61	$88,444.52	$188,444.52
12	$1,313.42	$89,132.48	$189,132.48	$1,374.63	$97,946.72	$197,946.72
13	$1,268.67	$97,912.52	$197,912.52	$1,331.21	$107,668.76	$207,668.76
14	$1,231.43	$106,880.24	$206,880.24	$1,295.26	$117,603.68	$217,603.68
15	$1,200.17	$116,030.60	$216,030.60	$1,265.24	$127,743.20	$227,743.20
16	$1,173.73	$125,356.16	$225,356.16	$1,239.99	$138,078.08	$238,078.08
17	$1,151.22	$134,848.88	$234,848.88	$1,218.61	$148,596.44	$248,596.44
18	$1,131.95	$144,501.20	$244,501.20	$1,200.43	$159,292.88	$259,292.88
19	$1,115.39	$154,308.92	$254,308.92	$1,184.90	$170,157.20	$270,157.20
20	$1,101.09	$164,261.60	$264,261.60	$1,171.58	$181,179.20	$281,179.20
21	$1,088.70	$174,352.40	$274,352.40	$1,160.11	$192,347.72	$292,347.72
22	$1,077.94	$184,576.16	$284,576.16	$1,150.23	$203,660.72	$303,660.72
23	$1,068.56	$194,922.56	$294,922.56	$1,141.68	$215,103.68	$315,103.68
24	$1,060.38	$205,389.44	$305,389.44	$1,134.27	$226,669.76	$326,669.76
25	$1,053.22	$215,966.00	$315,966.00	$1,127.84	$238,352.00	$338,352.00
26	$1,046.95	$226,648.40	$326,648.40	$1,122.24	$250,138.88	$350,138.88
27	$1,041.45	$237,429.80	$337,429.80	$1,117.38	$262,031.12	$362,031.12
28	$1,036.61	$248,300.96	$348,300.96	$1,113.13	$274,011.68	$374,011.68
29	$1,032.36	$259,261.28	$359,261.28	$1,109.43	$286,081.64	$386,081.64
30	$1,028.61	$270,299.60	$370,299.60	$1,106.20	$298,232.00	$398,232.00
31	$1,025.31	$281,415.32	$381,415.32	$1,103.37	$310,453.64	$410,453.64
32	$1,022.40	$292,601.60	$392,601.60	$1,100.90	$322,745.60	$422,745.60
33	$1,019.83	$303,852.68	$403,852.68	$1,098.74	$335,101.04	$435,101.04
34	$1,017.56	$315,164.48	$415,164.48	$1,096.85	$347,514.80	$447,514.80
35	$1,015.55	$326,531.00	$426,531.00	$1,095.19	$359,979.80	$459,979.80
36	$1,013.78	$337,952.96	$437,952.96	$1,093.74	$372,495.68	$472,495.68
37	$1,012.21	$349,421.24	$449,421.24	$1,092.47	$385,056.68	$485,056.68
38	$1,010.82	$360,933.92	$460,933.92	$1,091.35	$397,655.60	$497,655.60
39	$1,009.59	$372,488.12	$472,488.12	$1,090.37	$410,293.16	$510,293.16
40	$1,008.50	$384,080.00	$484,080.00	$1,089.51	$422,964.80	$522,964.80
41	$1,007.54	$395,709.68	$495,709.68	$1,088.76	$435,669.92	$535,669.92
42	$1,006.68	$407,366.72	$507,366.72	$1,088.10	$448,402.40	$548,402.40
43	$1,005.93	$419,059.88	$519,059.88	$1,087.52	$461,160.32	$561,160.32
44	$1,005.26	$430,777.28	$530,777.28	$1,087.01	$473,941.28	$573,941.28
45	$1,004.66	$442,516.40	$542,516.40	$1,086.56	$486,742.40	$586,742.40
46	$1,004.13	$454,279.76	$554,279.76	$1,086.17	$499,565.84	$599,565.84
47	$1,003.67	$466,069.88	$566,069.88	$1,085.83	$512,408.12	$612,408.12
48	$1,003.25	$477,872.00	$577,872.00	$1,085.52	$525,259.52	$625,259.52
49	$1,002.89	$489,699.32	$589,699.32	$1,085.26	$538,132.88	$638,132.88
50	$1,002.56	$501,536.00	$601,536.00	$1,085.02	$551,012.00	$651,012.00

¶691.25

.27 Loan Amortization Summaries

Loan Amortization Summaries

Term 3.0 Years

Principal $1,000.00   Interest 8.00%

Yearly Term	Yearly Payments	For Interest	For Principal	Remaining Balance	Interest Accuml.
1	376.08	68.90	307.18	692.82	68.90
2	376.08	43.40	332.68	360.14	112.30
3	375.92	15.78	360.14	0.00	128.08
Total	1,128.08	128.08	1,000.00		

Term 5.0 Years

Yearly Term	Yearly Payments	For Interest	For Principal	Remaining Balance	Interest Accuml.
1	243.36	73.87	169.49	830.51	73.87
2	243.36	59.81	183.55	646.96	133.68
3	243.36	44.56	198.80	448.16	178.24
4	243.36	28.06	215.30	232.86	206.30
5	243.07	10.21	232.86	0.00	216.51
Total	1,216.51	216.51	1,000.00		

Term 10.0 Years

Yearly Term	Yearly Payments	For Interest	For Principal	Remaining Balance	Interest Accuml.
1	145.56	77.54	68.02	931.98	77.54
2	145.56	71.87	73.69	858.29	149.41
3	145.56	65.79	79.77	778.52	215.20
4	145.56	59.15	86.41	692.11	274.35
5	145.56	51.97	93.59	598.52	326.32
6	145.56	44.23	101.33	497.19	370.55
7	145.56	35.83	109.73	387.46	406.38
8	145.56	26.70	118.86	268.60	433.08
9	145.56	16.83	128.73	139.87	449.91
10	146.01	6.14	139.87	0.00	456.05
Total	1,456.05	456.05	1,000.00		

Loan Amortization Summaries

Term 15.0 Years

Principal $1,000.00   Interest 8.00%

Yearly Term	Yearly Payments	For Interest	For Principal	Remaining Balance	Interest Accuml.
1	114.72	78.72	36.00	964.00	78.72
2	114.72	75.71	39.01	924.99	154.43
3	114.72	72.48	42.24	882.75	226.91
4	114.72	68.98	45.74	837.01	295.89
5	114.72	65.17	49.55	787.46	361.06
6	114.72	61.02	53.70	733.76	422.08
7	114.72	56.60	58.12	675.64	478.68
8	114.72	51.77	62.95	612.69	530.45
9	114.72	46.55	68.17	544.52	577.00
10	114.72	40.89	73.83	470.69	617.89
11	114.72	34.78	79.94	390.75	652.67
12	114.72	28.15	86.57	304.18	680.82
13	114.72	20.96	93.76	210.42	701.78
14	114.72	13.15	101.57	108.85	714.93
15	113.61	4.76	108.85	0.00	719.69
Total	1,719.69	719.69	1,000.00		

Term 20.0 Years

Yearly Term	Yearly Payments	For Interest	For Principal	Remaining Balance	Interest Accuml.
1	100.32	79.24	21.08	978.92	79.24
2	100.32	77.49	22.83	956.09	156.73
3	100.32	75.59	24.73	931.36	232.32
4	100.32	73.55	26.77	904.59	305.87
5	100.32	71.32	29.00	875.59	377.19
6	100.32	68.91	31.41	844.18	446.10
7	100.32	66.31	34.01	810.17	512.41
8	100.32	63.48	36.84	773.33	575.89
9	100.32	60.43	39.89	733.44	636.32
10	100.32	57.12	43.20	690.24	693.44
11	100.32	53.53	46.79	643.45	746.97
12	100.32	49.65	50.67	592.78	796.62
13	100.32	45.42	54.90	537.88	842.04
14	100.32	40.88	59.44	478.44	882.92
15	100.32	35.96	64.36	414.08	918.88
20	504.26	90.18	414.08	0.00	1,009.06
Total	2,009.06	1,009.06	1,000.00		

Loan Amortization Summaries

Term 3.0 Years

Principal $1,000.00   Interest 9.00%

Yearly Term	Yearly Payments	For Interest	For Principal	Remaining Balance	Interest Accuml.
1	381.60	77.66	303.94	696.06	77.66
2	381.60	4,914.00	332.46	363.60	126.80
3	381.58	17.98	363.60	0.00	144.78
Total	1,144.78	144.78	1,000.00		

Term 5.0 Years

Yearly Term	Yearly Payments	For Interest	For Principal	Remaining Balance	Interest Accuml.
1	249.12	83.27	165.85	834.15	83.27
2	249.12	67.72	181.40	652.75	150.99
3	249.12	50.70	198.42	454.33	201.69
4	249.12	32.09	217.03	237.30	233.78
5	249.02	11.72	237.30	0.00	245.50
Total	1,245.50	245.50	1,000.00		

Term 10.0 Years

Yearly Term	Yearly Payments	For Interest	For Principal	Remaining Balance	Interest Accuml.
1	152.04	87.36	64.68	935.32	87.36
2	152.04	81.31	70.73	864.59	168.67
3	152.04	74.65	77.39	787.20	243.32
4	152.04	67.40	84.64	702.56	310.72
5	152.04	59.46	92.58	609.98	370.18
6	152.04	50.78	101.26	508.72	420.96
7	152.04	41.30	110.74	397.98	462.26
8	152.04	30.90	121.14	276.84	493.16
9	152.04	19.55	132.49	144.35	512.71
10	151.46	7.11	144.35	0.00	519.82
Total	1,519.82	519.82	1,000.00		

¶691.27

Loan Amortization Summaries

Term 15.0 Years
Principal $1,000.00   Interest 9.00%

Yearly Term	Yearly Payments	For Interest	For Principal	Remaining Balance	Interest Accuml.
1	121.68	88.67	33.01	966.99	88.67
2	121.68	85.56	36.12	930.87	174.23
3	121.68	82.18	39.50	891.37	256.41
4	121.68	78.47	43.21	848.16	334.88
5	121.68	74.43	47.25	800.91	409.31
6	121.68	69.98	51.70	749.21	479.29
7	121.68	65.14	56.54	692.67	544.43
8	121.68	59.84	61.84	630.83	604.27
9	121.68	54.04	67.64	563.19	658.31
10	121.68	47.67	74.01	489.18	705.98
11	121.68	40.73	80.95	408.23	746.71
12	121.68	33.16	88.52	319.71	779.87
13	121.68	24.83	96.85	222.86	804.70
14	121.68	15.75	105.93	116.93	820.45
15	122.76	5.83	116.93	0.00	826.28
Total	1,826.28	826.28	1,000.00		

Term 20.0 Years

Yearly Term	Yearly Payments	For Interest	For Principal	Remaining Balance	Interest Accuml.
1	108.00	89.24	18.76	981.24	89.24
2	108.00	87.48	20.52	960.72	176.72
3	108.00	85.55	22.45	938.27	262.27
4	108.00	83.45	24.55	913.72	345.72
5	108.00	81.14	26.86	886.86	426.86
6	108.00	78.63	29.37	857.49	505.49
7	108.00	75.84	32.16	825.33	581.33
8	108.00	72.85	35.15	790.18	654.18
9	108.00	69.56	38.44	751.74	723.74
10	108.00	65.95	42.05	709.69	789.69
11	108.00	62.02	45.98	663.71	851.71
12	108.00	57.70	50.30	613.41	909.41
13	108.00	52.96	55.04	558.37	962.37
14	108.00	47.81	60.19	498.18	1,010.58
15	108.00	42.19	65.81	432.37	1,052.37
20	538.11	105.74	432.37	0.00	1,158.11
Total	2,158.11	1,158.11	1,000.00		

Loan Amortization Summaries

Term 3.0 Years

Principal $1,000.00   Interest 10.00%

Yearly Term	Yearly Payments	For Interest	For Principal	Remaining Balance	Interest Accuml.
1	387.24	86.46	300.78	699.22	86.46
2	387.24	54.98	332.26	366.96	141.44
3	387.18	20.17	366.96	0.00	161.61
Total	1,161.61	161.61	1,000.00		

Term 5.0 Years

Yearly Term	Yearly Payments	For Interest	For Principal	Remaining Balance	Interest Accuml.
1	255.00	92.71	162.29	837.71	92.71
2	255.00	75.70	179.30	658.41	168.41
3	255.00	56.91	198.09	460.32	225.32
4	255.00	36.19	218.81	241.51	261.61
5	254.77	13.26	241.51	0.00	274.77
Total	1,274.77	274.77	1,000.00		

Term 10.0 Years

Yearly Term	Yearly Payments	For Interest	For Principal	Remaining Balance	Interest Accuml.
1	158.64	97.23	61.41	938.59	97.23
2	158.64	90.81	67.83	870.76	188.04
3	158.64	83.72	74.92	795.84	271.76
4	158.64	75.86	82.78	713.06	347.62
5	158.64	67.19	91.45	621.61	414.81
6	158.64	57.62	101.02	520.59	472.43
7	158.64	47.03	111.61	408.98	519.46
8	158.64	35.35	123.29	285.69	554.81
9	158.64	22.43	136.21	149.48	577.24
10	157.66	8.18	149.48	0.00	585.42
Total	1,585.42	585.42	1,000.00		

Loan Amortization Summaries

Term 15.0 Years

Principal $1,000.00   Interest 10.00%

Yearly Term	Yearly Payments	For Interest	For Principal	Remaining Balance	Interest Accuml.
1	129.00	98.62	30.38	969.62	98.62
2	129.00	95.46	33.54	936.08	194.08
3	129.00	91.95	37.05	899.03	286.03
4	129.00	88.06	40.94	858.09	374.09
5	129.00	83.78	45.22	812.87	457.87
6	129.00	79.04	49.96	762.91	536.91
7	129.00	73.81	55.19	707.72	610.72
8	129.00	68.03	60.97	646.75	678.75
9	129.00	61.64	67.36	579.39	740.39
10	129.00	54.60	74.40	504.99	794.99
11	129.00	46.79	82.21	422.78	841.78
12	129.00	38.18	90.82	331.96	879.96
13	129.00	28.70	100.30	231.66	908.66
14	129.00	18.19	110.81	120.85	926.85
15	127.42	6.57	120.85	0.00	933.42
Total	1,933.42	933.42	1,000.00		

Term 20.0 Years

Yearly Term	Yearly Payments	For Interest	For Principal	Remaining Balance	Interest Accuml.
1	115.80	99.25	16.55	983.45	99.25
2	115.80	97.53	18.27	965.18	196.78
3	115.80	95.61	20.19	944.99	292.39
4	115.80	93.50	22.30	922.69	385.89
5	115.80	91.16	24.64	898.05	477.05
6	115.80	88.59	27.21	870.84	565.64
7	115.80	85.75	30.05	840.79	651.39
8	115.80	82.58	33.22	807.57	733.97
9	115.80	79.12	36.68	770.89	813.09
10	115.80	75.26	40.54	730.35	888.35
11	115.80	71.04	44.76	685.59	959.39
12	115.80	66.33	49.47	636.12	1,025.72
13	115.80	61.14	54.66	581.46	1,086.86
14	115.80	55.44	60.36	521.10	1,142.30
15	115.80	49.11	66.69	484.41	1,191.41
20	579.36	124.95	454.41	0.00	1,316.36
Total	2,316.36	1,316.36	1,000.00		

Loan Amortization Summaries

Term 3.0 Years

Principal $1,000.00   Interest 12.00%

Yearly Term	Yearly Payments	For Interest	For Principal	Remaining Balance	Interest Accuml.
1	398.52	104.18	294.34	705.66	104.18
2	398.52	66.83	331.69	373.97	171.01
3	398.75	24.78	373.97	0.00	195.79
Total	1,195.79	195.79	1,000.00		

Term 5.0 Years

Yearly Term	Yearly Payments	For Interest	For Principal	Remaining Balance	Interest Accuml.
1	266.88	111.65	155.23	844.77	111.65
2	266.88	91.95	174.93	669.84	203.60
3	266.88	69.78	197.10	472.74	273.38
4	266.88	44.79	222.09	250.65	318.17
5	267.26	16.61	250.65	0.00	334.78
Total	1,334.78	334.78	1,000.00		

Term 10.0 Years

Yearly Term	Yearly Payments	For Interest	For Principal	Remaining Balance	Interest Accuml.
1	172.20	117.03	55.17	944.83	117.03
2	172.20	110.04	62.16	882.67	227.07
3	172.20	102.17	70.03	812.64	329.24
4	172.20	93.27	78.93	733.71	422.51
5	172.20	83.27	88.93	644.78	505.78
6	172.20	71.98	100.22	544.56	577.76
7	172.20	59.28	112.92	431.64	637.04
8	172.20	44.96	127.24	304.40	682.00
9	172.20	28.81	143.39	161.01	710.81
10	171.63	10.62	161.01	0.00	721.43
Total	1,721.43	721.43	1,000.00		

Loan Amortization Summaries

Term 15.0 Years

Principal $1,000.00   Interest 12.00%

Yearly Term	Yearly Payments	For Interest	For Principal	Remaining Balance	Interest Accuml.
1	144.00	118.64	25.36	974.64	118.64
2	144.00	115.42	28.58	946.06	234.06
3	144.00	111.79	32.21	913.85	345.85
4	144.00	107.70	36.30	877.55	453.55
5	144.00	103.10	40.90	836.65	556.55
6	144.00	97.93	46.07	790.58	654.58
7	144.00	92.07	51.93	738.65	746.65
8	144.00	85.47	58.53	680.12	832.12
9	144.00	78.07	65.93	614.19	910.19
10	144.00	69.68	74.32	539.87	979.87
11	144.00	60.28	83.72	456.15	1,040.15
12	144.00	49.65	94.35	361.80	1,089.80
13	144.00	37.68	106.32	255.48	1,127.48
14	144.00	24.19	119.81	135.67	1,151.67
15	144.67	9.00	135.67	0.00	1,160.67
Total	2,160.67	1,160.67	1,000.00		

Term 20.0 Years

Yearly Term	Yearly Payments	For Interest	For Principal	Remaining Balance	Interest Accuml.
1	132.12	119.32	12.80	987.20	119.32
2	132.12	117.69	14.43	972.77	237.01
3	132.12	115.86	16.26	956.51	352.87
4	132.12	113.81	18.31	938.20	466.68
5	132.12	111.47	20.65	917.55	578.15
6	132.12	108.84	23.28	894.27	686.99
7	132.12	105.90	26.22	868.05	792.89
8	132.12	102.58	29.54	838.51	895.47
9	132.12	98.84	33.28	805.23	994.31
10	132.12	94.60	37.52	767.71	1,088.91
11	132.12	89.85	42.27	725.44	1,178.76
12	132.12	84.47	47.65	677.79	1,263.23
13	132.12	78.45	53.66	624.13	1,341.69
14	132.12	71.65	60.47	563.66	1,413.34
15	132.12	63.97	68.15	495.51	1,477.31
20	661.63	166.12	495.51	0.00	1,643.43
Total	2,643.43	1,643.43	1,000.00		

¶691.27

Loan Amortization Summaries

Term 3.0 Years

Principal $1,000.00   Interest 14.00%

Yearly Term	Yearly Payments	For Interest	For Principal	Remaining Balance	Interest Accuml.
1	410.16	121.97	288.19	711.81	121.97
2	410.16	78.94	331.22	380.59	200.91
3	410.06	29.46	380.59	0.00	230.37
Total	1,230.37	230.37	1,000.00		

Term 5.0 Years

Yearly Term	Yearly Payments	For Interest	For Principal	Remaining Balance	Interest Accuml.
1	279.24	130.72	148.52	851.48	130.72
2	279.24	108.53	170.71	680.77	239.25
3	279.24	83.04	196.20	484.57	322.29
4	279.24	53.73	225.51	259.06	376.02
5	279.11	20.05	259.06	0.00	396.07
Total	1,396.07	396.07	1,000.00		

Term 10.0 Years

Yearly Term	Yearly Payments	For Interest	For Principal	Remaining Balance	Interest Accuml.
1	186.36	136.91	49.45	950.55	136.91
2	186.36	129.52	56.84	893.71	266.43
3	186.36	121.05	65.31	828.40	387.48
4	186.36	111.28	75.08	753.32	498.76
5	186.36	100.07	86.29	667.03	598.83
6	186.36	87.18	99.18	567.85	686.01
7	186.36	72.35	114.01	453.84	758.36
8	186.36	55.34	131.02	322.82	813.70
9	186.36	35.78	150.58	172.24	849.48
10	185.52	13.28	172.24	0.00	862.76
Total	1,862.76	862.76	1,000.00		

Loan Amortization Summaries
Term 15.0 Years
Principal $1,000.00   Interest 14.00%

Yearly Term	Yearly Payments	For Interest	For Principal	Remaining Balance	Interest Accuml.
1	159.84	138.70	21.14	978.86	138.70
2	159.84	135.53	24.31	954.55	274.33
3	159.84	131.90	27.94	926.61	406.13
4	159.84	127.71	32.13	894.48	533.84
5	159.84	122.92	36.92	857.56	656.76
6	159.84	117.41	42.43	815.13	774.17
7	159.84	111.07	48.77	766.36	885.24
8	159.84	103.80	56.04	710.32	989.04
9	159.84	95.42	64.42	645.90	1,084.46
10	159.84	85.80	74.04	571.86	1,170.26
11	159.84	74.74	85.10	486.76	1,245.00
12	159.84	62.04	97.80	388.96	1,307.04
13	159.84	47.42	112.42	276.54	1,354.46
14	159.84	30.63	129.21	147.33	1,385.09
15	158.67	11.34	147.33	0.00	1,396.43
Total	2,396.43	1,396.43	1,000.00		

Term 20.0 Years

Yearly Term	Yearly Payments	For Interest	For Principal	Remaining Balance	Interest Accuml.
1	149.28	139.38	9.90	990.10	139.38
2	149.28	137.90	11.38	978.72	277.28
3	149.28	136.20	13.08	965.64	413.48
4	149.28	134.26	15.02	950.62	547.74
5	149.28	132.00	17.28	933.34	679.74
6	149.28	129.44	19.84	913.50	809.18
7	149.28	126.46	22.82	890.68	935.64
8	149.28	123.05	26.23	864.45	1,058.69
9	149.28	119.16	30.12	834.33	1,177.85
10	149.28	114.64	34.64	799.69	1,292.49
11	149.28	109.48	39.80	759.89	1,401.97
12	149.28	103.53	45.75	714.14	1,505.50
13	149.28	96.70	52.58	661.56	1,602.20
14	149.28	88.85	60.43	601.13	1,691.05
15	149.28	79.82	69.46	531.67	1,770.87
20	740.49	208.82	531.67	0.00	1,979.69
Total	2,979.69	1,979.69	1,000.00		

.29 Mortgage Summary Amortization — Given Term

Mortgage Summary Amortization by Interest, Given Term

	Term 1 Year				Term 2 Years	
		Principal $100,000.00				
Interest Rate	Monthly Payment	Total Interest	Total Payment	Monthly Payment	Total Interest	Total Payment
1.5	8,401.20	814.36	100,814.36	4,232.08	1,569.98	101,569.98
2.0	8,423.89	1,086.65	101,086.65	4,254.03	2,096.62	102,096.62
2.5	8,446.61	1,359.33	101,359.33	4,276.04	2,624.93	102,624.93
3.0	8,469.37	1,632.44	101,632.44	4,298.12	3,154.89	103,154.89
3.5	8,492.16	1,905.97	101,905.97	4,320.27	3,686.52	103,686.52
4.0	8,514.99	2,179.88	102,179.88	4,342.49	4,219.84	104,219.84
4.5	8,537.85	2,454.24	102,454.24	4,364.78	4,754.75	104,754.75
5.0	8,560.75	2,728.98	102,728.98	4,387.14	5,291.34	105,291.34
5.5	8,583.68	3,004.13	103,004.13	4,409.57	5,829.53	105,829.53
6.0	8,606.64	3,279.73	103,279.73	4,432.06	6,369.48	106,369.48
6.5	8,629.64	3,555.70	103,555.70	4,454.63	6,911.00	106,911.00
7.0	8,652.67	3,832.09	103,832.09	4,477.26	7,454.18	107,454.18
7.5	8,675.74	4,108.91	104,108.91	4,499.96	7,999.01	107,999.01
8.0	8,698.84	4,386.11	104,386.11	4,522.73	8,545.52	108,545.52
8.5	8,721.98	4,663.74	104,663.74	4,545.57	9,093.60	109,093.60
9.0	8,745.15	4,941.77	104,941.77	4,568.47	9,643.37	109,643.37
9.5	8,768.35	5,220.23	105,220.23	4,591.45	10,194.79	110,194.79
10.0	8,791.59	5,499.05	105,499.05	4,614.49	10,747.84	110,747.84
10.5	8,814.86	5,778.33	105,778.33	4,637.60	11,302.53	111,302.53
11.0	8,838.17	6,057.98	106,057.98	4,660.78	11,858.86	111,858.86
11.5	8,861.51	6,338.05	106,338.05	4,684.03	12,416.74	112,416.74
12.0	8,884.88	6,618.53	106,618.53	4,707.35	12,976.34	112,976.34
12.5	8,908.29	6,899.44	106,899.44	4,730.73	13,537.55	113,537.55
13.0	8,931.73	7,180.72	107,180.72	4,754.18	14,100.39	114,100.39
13.5	8,955.20	7,462.44	107,462.44	4,777.70	14,664.84	114,664.84
14.0	8,978.71	7,744.54	107,744.54	4,801.29	15,230.91	115,230.91
14.5	9,002.25	8,027.05	108,027.05	4,824.94	15,798.63	115,798.63
15.0	9,025.83	8,309.97	108,309.97	4,848.66	16,367.97	116,367.97
15.5	9,049.44	8,593.30	108,593.30	4,872.45	16,938.91	116,938.91
16.0	9,073.09	8,877.03	108,877.03	4,896.31	17,511.48	117,511.48
16.5	9,096.76	9,161.16	109,161.16	4,920.24	18,085.62	118,085.62
17.0	9,120.48	9,445.70	109,445.70	4,944.23	18,661.41	118,661.41
17.5	9,144.22	9,730.66	109,730.66	4,968.28	19,238.83	119,238.83
18.0	9,168.00	10,015.99	110,015.99	4,992.41	19,817.83	119,817.83
18.5	9,191.81	10,301.75	110,301.75	5,016.60	20,398.47	120,398.47
19.0	9,215.66	10,587.90	110,587.90	5,040.86	20,980.73	120,980.73
19.5	9,239.54	10,874.45	110,874.45	5,065.19	21,564.51	121,564.51
20.0	9,263.45	11,161.39	111,161.39	5,089.58	22,149.95	122,149.95
20.5	9,287.40	11,448.76	111,448.76	5,114.04	22,736.95	122,736.95
21.0	9,311.38	11,736.54	111,736.54	5,138.57	23,325.51	123,325.51
21.5	9,335.39	12,024.70	112,024.70	5,163.16	23,915.75	123,915.75
22.0	9,359.44	12,313.26	112,313.26	5,187.82	24,507.55	124,507.55
22.5	9,383.52	12,602.22	112,602.22	5,212.54	25,100.96	125,100.96
23.0	9,407.63	12,891.60	112,891.60	5,237.33	25,695.94	125,695.94
23.5	9,431.78	13,181.35	113,181.35	5,262.19	26,292.49	126,292.49
24.0	9,455.96	13,471.53	113,471.53	5,287.11	26,890.63	126,890.63
24.5	9,480.17	13,762.09	113,762.09	5,312.10	27,490.35	127,490.35
25.0	9,504.42	14,053.05	114,053.05	5,337.15	28,091.66	128,091.66
25.5	9,528.70	14,344.40	114,344.40	5,362.27	28,694.55	128,694.55
26.0	9,553.01	14,636.17	114,636.17	5,387.46	29,298.99	129,298.99

Mortgage Summary Amortization by Interest, Given Term

Term 3 Years   Term 4 Years

Principal $100,000.00

Interest Rate	Monthly Payment	Total Interest	Total Payment	Monthly Payment	Total Interest	Total Payment
1.5	2,842.48	2,329.38	102,329.38	2,147.76	3,092.47	103,092.47
2.0	2,864.26	3,113.30	103,113.30	2,169.51	4,136.57	104,136.57
2.5	2,886.14	3,900.95	103,900.95	2,191.40	5,187.35	105,187.35
3.0	2,908.12	4,692.33	104,692.33	2,213.43	6,244.78	106,244.78
3.5	2,930.21	5,487.45	105,487.45	2,235.60	7,308.84	107,308.84
4.0	2,952.40	6,286.34	106,286.34	2,257.91	8,379.47	108,379.47
4.5	2,974.69	7,088.93	107,088.93	2,280.35	9,456.72	109,456.72
5.0	2,997.09	7,895.26	107,895.26	2,302.93	10,540.64	110,540.64
5.5	3,019.59	8,705.22	108,705.22	2,325.65	11,631.03	111,631.03
6.0	3,042.19	9,519.01	109,519.01	2,348.50	12,728.15	112,728.15
6.5	3,064.90	10,336.43	110,336.43	2,371.50	13,831.72	113,831.72
7.0	3,087.71	11,157.53	111,157.53	2,394.62	14,942.04	114,942.04
7.5	3,110.62	11,982.41	111,982.41	2,417.89	16,058.70	116,058.70
8.0	3,133.64	12,810.92	112,810.92	2,441.29	17,182.07	117,182.07
8.5	3,156.75	13,643.15	113,643.15	2,464.83	18,311.81	118,311.81
9.0	3,179.97	14,479.06	114,479.06	2,488.50	19,448.27	119,448.27
9.5	3,203.29	15,318.66	115,318.66	2,512.31	20,591.10	120,591.10
10.0	3,226.72	16,161.84	116,161.84	2,536.26	21,740.37	121,740.37
10.5	3,250.24	17,008.80	117,008.80	2,560.34	22,896.16	122,896.16
11.0	3,273.87	17,859.40	117,859.40	2,584.55	24,058.55	124,058.55
11.5	3,297.60	18,713.62	118,713.62	2,608.90	25,227.27	125,227.27
12.0	3,321.43	19,571.51	119,571.51	2,633.38	26,402.50	126,402.50
12.5	3,345.36	20,433.07	120,433.07	2,658.00	27,584.01	127,584.01
13.0	3,369.40	21,298.18	121,298.18	2,682.75	28,771.97	128,771.97
13.5	3,393.53	22,166.98	122,166.98	2,707.63	29,966.39	129,966.39
14.0	3,417.76	23,039.48	123,039.48	2,732.65	31,167.06	131,167.06
14.5	3,442.10	23,915.52	123,915.52	2,757.80	32,374.09	132,374.09
15.0	3,466.53	24,795.25	124,795.25	2,783.07	33,587.73	133,587.73
15.5	3,491.07	25,678.42	125,678.42	2,808.49	34,807.25	134,807.25
16.0	3,515.70	26,565.33	126,565.33	2,834.03	36,033.27	136,033.27
16.5	3,540.44	27,455.80	127,455.80	2,859.70	37,265.69	137,265.69
17.0	3,565.27	28,349.86	128,349.86	2,885.50	38,504.30	138,504.30
17.5	3,590.21	29,247.36	129,247.36	2,911.44	39,748.92	139,748.92
18.0	3,615.24	30,148.66	130,148.66	2,937.50	41,000.02	141,000.02
18.5	3,640.37	31,053.39	131,053.39	2,963.69	42,257.24	142,257.24
19.0	3,665.60	31,961.69	131,961.69	2,990.01	43,520.66	143,520.66
19.5	3,690.93	32,873.53	132,873.53	3,016.46	44,790.12	144,790.12
20.0	3,716.36	33,788.91	133,788.91	3,043.04	46,065.69	146,065.69
20.5	3,741.88	34,707.84	134,707.84	3,069.74	47,347.47	147,347.47
21.0	3,767.51	35,630.17	135,630.17	3,096.57	48,635.35	148,635.35
21.5	3,793.23	36,556.12	136,556.12	3,123.53	49,929.10	149,929.10
22.0	3,819.05	37,485.56	137,485.56	3,150.61	51,229.11	151,229.11
22.5	3,844.96	38,418.59	138,418.59	3,177.82	52,535.00	152,535.00
23.0	3,870.97	39,355.04	139,355.04	3,205.15	53,847.01	153,847.01
23.5	3,897.08	40,294.95	140,294.95	3,232.60	55,165.05	155,165.05
24.0	3,923.29	41,238.14	141,238.14	3,260.18	56,488.94	156,488.94
24.5	3,949.59	42,185.04	142,185.04	3,287.89	57,818.44	157,818.44
25.0	3,975.98	43,135.45	143,135.45	3,315.71	59,154.33	159,154.33
25.5	4,002.47	44,089.18	144,089.18	3,343.66	60,495.77	160,495.77
26.0	4,026.06	45,046.28	145,046.28	3,371.73	61,843.03	161,843.03

Mortgage Summary Amortization by Interest, Given Term

	Term 5 Years			Term 6 Years		
		Principal $100,000.00				
Interest Rate	Monthly Payment	Total Interest	Total Payment	Monthly Payment	Total Interest	Total Payment
1.5	1,730.99	3,859.29	103,859.29	1,453.19	4,629.96	104,629.96
2.0	1,752.78	5,166.53	105,166.53	1,475.04	6,203.20	106,203.20
2.5	1,774.74	6,484.13	106,484.13	1,497.10	7,791.37	107,791.37
3.0	1,796.87	7,812.15	107,812.15	1,519.37	9,394.44	109,394.44
3.5	1,819.17	9,150.53	109,150.53	1,541.84	11,012.46	111,012.46
4.0	1,841.65	10,499.17	110,499.17	1,564.52	12,645.27	112,645.27
4.5	1,864.30	11,858.13	111,858.13	1,587.40	14,293.03	114,293.03
5.0	1,887.12	13,227.51	113,227.51	1,610.49	15,955.60	115,955.60
5.5	1,910.12	14,606.90	114,606.90	1,633.79	17,632.82	117,632.82
6.0	1,933.28	15,996.84	115,996.84	1,657.29	19,324.77	119,324.77
6.5	1,956.61	17,396.95	117,396.95	1,680.99	21,031.54	121,031.54
7.0	1,980.12	18,807.22	118,807.22	1,704.90	22,752.86	122,752.86
7.5	2,003.79	20,227.72	120,227.72	1,729.01	24,488.84	124,488.84
8.0	2,027.64	21,658.40	121,658.40	1,753.32	26,239.45	126,239.45
8.5	2,051.65	23,099.28	123,099.28	1,777.84	28,004.31	128,004.31
9.0	2,075.84	24,550.08	124,550.08	1,802.55	29,783.89	129,783.89
9.5	2,100.19	26,011.11	126,011.11	1,827.47	31,577.66	131,577.66
10.0	2,124.70	27,482.30	127,482.30	1,852.58	33,386.13	133,386.13
10.5	2,149.39	28,963.42	128,963.42	1,877.90	35,208.51	135,208.51
11.0	2,174.24	30,454.64	130,454.64	1,903.41	37,045.32	137,045.32
11.5	2,199.26	31,955.65	131,955.65	1,929.12	38,896.18	138,896.18
12.0	2,224.44	33,466.83	133,466.83	1,955.02	40,761.29	140,761.29
12.5	2,249.79	34,987.73	134,987.73	1,981.12	42,640.41	142,640.41
13.0	2,275.31	36,518.40	136,518.40	2,007.41	44,533.52	144,533.52
13.5	2,300.98	38,059.21	138,059.21	2,033.90	46,440.36	146,440.36
14.0	2,326.83	39,069.35	139,609.35	2,060.57	48,361.51	148,361.51
14.5	2,352.83	41,169.61	141,169.61	2,087.44	50,295.98	150,295.98
15.0	2,378.99	42,739.66	142,739.66	2,114.50	52,244.17	152,244.17
15.5	2,405.32	44,319.05	144,319.05	2,141.75	54,205.84	154,205.84
16.0	2,431.81	45,908.25	145,908.25	2,169.18	56,181.40	156,181.40
16.5	2,458.45	47,507.16	147,507.16	2,196.81	58,169.84	158,169.84
17.0	2,485.26	49,115.40	149,115.40	2,224.61	60,172.24	160,172.24
17.5	2,512.22	50,733.35	150,733.35	2,252.60	62,187.83	162,187.83
18.0	2,539.34	52,360.66	152,360.66	2,280.78	64,215.99	164,215.99
18.5	2,566.62	53,997.30	153,997.30	2,309.14	66,257.34	166,257.34
19.0	2,594.06	55,643.09	155,643.09	2,337.67	68,312.51	168,312.51
19.5	2,621.64	57,298.85	157,298.85	2,366.39	70,379.89	170,379.89
20.0	2,649.39	58,963.28	158,963.28	2,395.28	72,460.55	172,460.55
20.5	2,677.29	60,636.93	160,636.93	2,424.35	74,553.67	174,553.67
21.0	2,705.34	62,319.97	162,319.97	2,453.60	76,659.17	176,659.17
21.5	2,733.54	64,012.21	164,012.21	2,483.02	78,777.43	178,777.43
22.0	2,761.89	65,713.49	165,713.49	2,512.61	80,908.28	180,908.28
22.5	2,790.39	67,423.89	167,423.89	2,542.38	83,050.88	183,050.88
23.0	2,819.05	69,142.66	169,142.66	2,572.31	85,206.47	185,206.47
23.5	2,847.85	70,870.72	170,870.72	2,602.41	87,374.07	187,374.07
24.0	2,876.80	72,607.61	172,607.61	2,632.68	89,553.51	189,553.51
24.5	2,905.89	74,353.60	174,353.60	2,663.12	91,744.35	191,744.35
25.0	2,935.13	76,108.01	176,108.01	2,693.72	93,947.53	193,947.53
25.5	2,964.52	77,870.88	177,870.88	2,724.48	96,162.60	196,162.60
26.0	2,994.05	79,642.59	179,642.59	2,755.40	98,389.33	198,389.33

¶691.29

Mortgage Summary Amortization by Interest, Given Term

	Term 7 Years			Term 8 Years		
		Principal $100,000.00				
Interest Rate	Monthly Payment	Total Interest	Total Payment	Monthly Payment	Total Interest	Total Payment
1.5	1,254.81	5,404.29	105,404.29	1,106.07	6,182.37	106,182.37
2.0	1,276.74	7,246.49	107,246.49	1,128.09	8,296.35	108,296.35
2.5	1,298.92	9,108.91	109,108.91	1,150.38	10,436.96	110,436.96
3.0	1,321.33	10,991.64	110,991.65	1,172.96	12,603.83	112,603.83
3.5	1,343.99	12,894.75	112,894.75	1,195.81	14,797.20	114,797.20
4.0	1,366.88	14,817.97	114,817.97	1,218.93	17,017.02	117,017.02
4.5	1,390.02	16,761.29	116,761.29	1,242.32	19,263.13	119,263.13
5.0	1,413.39	18,724.81	118,724.81	1,265.99	21,535.25	121,535.25
5.5	1,437.00	20,708.43	120,708.43	1,289.93	23,833.55	123,833.55
6.0	1,460.86	22,711.78	122,711.78	1,314.14	26,157.83	126,157.83
6.5	1,484.94	24,735.40	124,735.40	1,338.62	28,507.96	128,507.96
7.0	1,509.27	26,778.48	126,778.48	1,363.37	30,883.77	130,883.77
7.5	1,533.83	28,841.45	128,841.45	1,388.39	33,285.05	133,285.05
8.0	1,558.62	30,924.29	130,924.29	1,413.67	35,712.05	135,712.05
8.5	1,583.65	33,026.43	133,026.43	1,439.21	38,164.57	138,164.57
9.0	1,608.91	35,148.14	135,148.14	1,465.02	40,641.99	140,641.99
9.5	1,634.40	37,289.44	137,289.44	1,491.09	43,144.43	143,144.43
10.0	1,660.12	39,449.90	139,449.90	1,517.42	45,671.73	145,671.73
10.5	1,686.07	41,629.62	141,629.62	1,544.00	48,224.18	148,224.18
11.0	1,712.24	43,828.65	143,828.65	1,570.84	50,801.04	150,801.04
11.5	1,738.65	46,046.03	146,046.03	1,597.94	53,401.75	153,401.75
12.0	1,765.27	48,283.15	148,283.15	1,625.28	56,027.48	156,027.48
12.5	1,792.12	50,538.62	150,538.62	1,652.88	58,676.65	158,676.65
13.0	1,819.20	52,812.31	152,812.31	1,680.73	61,349.39	161,349.39
13.5	1,846.49	55,105.11	155,105.11	1,708.82	64,045.98	164,045.98
14.0	1,874.00	57,416.21	157,416.21	1,737.15	66,766.40	166,766.40
14.5	1,901.73	59,745.29	159,745.29	1,765.73	69,509.26	169,509.26
15.0	1,929.68	62,092.39	162,092.39	1,794.54	72,275.91	172,275.91
15.5	1,957.83	64,458.48	164,458.48	1,823.59	75,065.13	175,065.13
16.0	1,986.21	66,841.17	166,841.17	1,852.88	77,876.19	177,876.19
16.5	2,014.79	69,242.15	169,242.15	1,882.40	80,709.78	180,709.78
17.0	2,043.58	71,660.78	171,660.78	1,912.15	83,565.57	183,565.57
17.5	2,072.58	74,096.66	174,096.66	1,942.12	86,443.78	186,443.78
18.0	2,101.78	76,550.19	176,550.19	1,972.32	89,343.20	189,343.20
18.5	2,131.19	79,020.30	179,020.30	2,002.74	92,263.94	192,263.94
19.0	2,160.80	81,507.57	181,507.57	2,033.39	95,204.73	195,204.73
19.5	2,190.61	84,011.60	184,011.60	2,064.25	98,167.10	198,167.10
20.0	2,220.62	86,532.01	186,532.01	2,095.32	101,150.77	201,150.77
20.5	2,250.82	89,069.70	189,069.70	2,126.61	104,153.55	204,153.55
21.0	2,281.22	91,623.06	191,623.06	2,158.10	107,177.88.	207,177.88
21.5	2,311.81	94,192.71	194,192.71	2,189.80	110,221.41	210,221.41
22.0	2,342.59	96,778.41	196,778.41	2,221.71	113,283.57	213,283.57
22.5	2,373.56	99,379.74	199,379.74	2,253.81	116,367.27	216,367.27
23.0	2,404.72	101,996.28	201,996.28	2,286.12	119,467.35	219,467.35
23.5	2,436.06	104,628.86	204,628.86	2,318.62	122,587.35	222,587.35
24.0	2,467.58	107,277.00	207,277.00	2,351.31	125,726.49	225,726.49
24.5	2,499.28	109,940.27	209,940.27	2,384.20	128,882.05	228,882.05
25.0	2,531.16	112,618.34	212,618.34	2,417.27	132,056.93	232,056.93
25.5	2,563.22	115,310.54	215,310.54	2,450.52	135,250.46	235,250.46
26.0	2,595.45	118,017.79	218,017.79	2,483.96	138,459.62	238,459.62

Mortgage Summary Amortization by Interest, Given Term

Term 9 Years   Term 10 Years
Principal $100,000.00

Interest Rate	Monthly Payment	Total Interest	Total Payment	Monthly Payment	Total Interest	Total Payment
1.5	990.41	6,964.23	106,964.23	897.91	7,749.87	107,749.87
2.0	1,012.53	9,352.90	109,352.90	920.13	10,416.22	110,416.22
2.5	1,034.96	11,775.15	111,775.15	942.7	13,123.83	113,123.83
3.0	1,057.69	14,231.03	114,231.03	965.61	15,872.91	115,872.91
3.5	1,080.74	16,720.09	116,720.09	988.86	18,662.99	118,662.99
4.0	1,104.10	19,242.38	119,242.38	1,012.45	21,494.25	121,494.25
4.5	1,127.76	21,797.97	121,797.97	1,036.38	24,366.21	124,366.21
5.0	1,151.73	24,386.56	124,386.56	1,060.66	27,278.47	127,278.47
5.5	1,176.00	27,007.95	127,007.95	1,085.26	30,231.56	130,231.56
6.0	1,200.57	29,662.25	129,662.25	1,110.21	33,224.33	133,224.33
6.5	1,225.45	32,348.85	132,348.85	1,135.48	36,257.61	136,257.61
7.0	1,250.63	35,067.59	135,067.59	1,161.08	39,330.35	139,330.35
7.5	1,276.10	37,819.07	137,819.07	1,187.02	42,442.01	142,442.01
8.0	1,301.87	40,602.25	140,602.25	1,213.28	45,592.79	145,592.79
8.5	1,327.94	43,416.75	143,416.75	1,239.86	48,782.60	148,782.60
9.0	1,354.29	46,263.47	146,263.47	1,266.76	52,010.76	152,010.76
9.5	1,380.94	49,140.89	149,140.89	1,293.98	55,276.70	155,276.70
10.0	1,407.87	52,049.70	152,049.70	1,321.51	58,580.56	158,580.56
10.5	1,435.09	54,989.09	154,989.09	1,349.35	61,922.09	161,922.09
11.0	1,462.59	57,959.00	157,959.00	1,377.50	65,300.02	165,300.02
11.5	1,490.37	60,959.21	160,959.21	1,405.95	68,715.02	168,715.02
12.0	1,518.42	63,989.97	163,989.97	1,434.71	72,165.06	172,165.06
12.5	1,546.76	67,049.19	167,049.19	1,463.76	75,651.58	175,651.58
13.0	1,575.36	70,138.69	170,138.69	1,493.11	79,172.62	179,172.62
13.5	1,604.23	73,257.09	173,257.09	1,522.74	82,729.55	182,729.55
14.0	1,633.37	76,403.90	176,403.90	1,552.66	86,320.38	186,320.38
14.5	1,662.77	79,579.60	179,579.60	1,582.87	89,943.89	189,943.89
15.0	1,692.43	82,783.28	182,783.28	1,613.35	93,601.96	193,601.96
15.5	1,722.35	86,014.26	186,014.26	1,644.11	97,291.86	197,291.86
16.0	1,752.53	89,272.10	189,272.10	1,675.13	101,016.12	201,016.12
16.5	1,782.95	92,558.17	192,558.17	1,706.42	104,771.26	204,771.26
17.0	1,813.62	95,870.71	195,870.71	1,737.98	108,556.58	208,556.58
17.5	1,844.53	99,210.12	199,210.12	1,769.79	112,374.10	212,374.10
18.0	1,875.69	102,574.24	202,574.24	1,801.85	116,222.59	216,222.59
18.5	1,907.08	105,965.03	205,965.03	1,834.17	120,098.85	220,098.85
19.0	1,938.71	109,380.15	209,380.15	1,866.72	124,007.54	224,007.54
19.5	1,970.57	112,820.44	212,820.44	1,899.52	127,943.31	227,943.31
20.0	2,002.65	116,286.39	216,286.39	1,932.56	131,906.01	231,906.01
20.5	2,034.96	119,775.05	219,775.05	1,965.82	135,899.68	235,899.68
21.0	2,067.49	123,287.94	223,287.94	1,999.32	139,917.12	239,917.12
21.5	2,100.23	126,825.28	226,825.28	2,033.03	143,965.10	243,965.10
22.0	2,133.19	130,384.69	230,384.69	2,066.97	148,036.15	248,036.15
22.5	2,166.36	133,966.23	233,966.23	2,101.12	152,133.87	252,133.87
23.0	2,199.73	137,571.62	237,571.62	2,135.48	156,256.69	256,256.69
23.5	2,233.31	141,196.96	241,196.96	2,170.04	160,406.59	260,406.59
24.0	2,267.08	144,846.40	244,846.40	2,204.81	164,577.07	264,577.07
24.5	2,301.06	148,512.96	248,512.96	2,239.77	168,773.57	268,773.57
25.0	2,335.22	152,203.74	252,203.74	2,274.93	172,991.55	272,991.55
25.5	2,369.57	155,914.46	255,914.46	2,310.27	177,234.61	277,234.61
26.0	2,404.11	159,643.38	259,643.38	2,345.80	181,497.89	281,497.89

¶691.29

Mortgage Summary Amortization by Interest, Given Term

Term 11 Years Term 12 Years

Principal $100,000.00

Interest Rate	Monthly Payment	Total Interest	Total Payment	Monthly Payment	Total Interest	Total Payment
1.5	822.27	8,539.09	108,539.09	759.25	9,332.16	109,332.16
2.0	844.59	11,486.00	111,486.00	781.68	12,562.50	112,562.50
2.5	867.29	14,482.98	114,482.98	804.53	15,852.22	115,852.22
3.0	890.38	17,529.64	117,529.64	827.79	19,201.27	119,201.27
3.5	913.83	20,626.25	120,626.25	851.45	22,609.53	122,609.53
4.0	937.67	23,772.06	123,772.06	875.53	26,076.08	126,076.08
4.5	961.87	26,967.33	126,967.33	900.01	29,601.09	129,601.09
5.0	986.45	30,211.24	130,211.24	924.89	33,184.23	133,184.23
5.5	1,011.39	33,504.08	133,504.08	950.17	36,824.91	136,824.91
6.0	1,036.70	36,845.08	136,845.08	975.85	40,522.32	140,522.32
6.5	1,062.38	40,233.49	140,233.49	1,001.92	44,276.72	144,276.72
7.0	1,088.41	43,670.11	143,670.11	1,028.38	48,087.00	148,087.00
7.5	1,114.80	47,153.75	147,153.75	1,055.23	51,952.24	151,952.24
8.0	1,141.54	50,684.35	150,684.35	1,082.45	55,873.42	155,873.42
8.5	1,168.64	54,260.25	154,260.25	1,110.06	59,847.57	159,847.57
9.0	1,196.08	57,882.62	157,882.62	1,138.03	63,876.55	163,876.55
9.5	1,223.86	61,550.65	161,550.65	1,166.37	67,958.11	167,958.11
10.0	1,251.99	65,262.18	165,262.18	1,195.08	72,091.08	172,061.08
10.5	1,280.45	69,018.34	169,018.34	1,224.14	76,276.37	176,276.37
11.0	1,309.23	72,819.63	172,819.63	1,253.56	80,511.24	180,511.24
11.5	1,338.35	76,662.25	176,662.25	1,283.32	84,796.99	184,796.99
12.0	1,367.79	80,547.74	180,547.74	1,313.42	89,132.32	189,132.32
12.5	1,397.54	84,476.05	184,476.05	1,343.86	93,515.04	193,515.04
13.0	1,427.61	88,444.66	188,444.66	1,374.63	97,945.05	197,945.05
13.5	1,457.99	92,453.65	192,453.65	1,405.72	102,422.66	202,422.66
14.0	1,488.67	96,503.16	196,503.16	1,437.13	106,945.58	206,945.58
14.5	1,519.64	100,593.58	200,593.58	1,468.85	111,514.08	211,514.08
15.0	1,550.91	104,721.60	204,721.60	1,500.88	116,125.50	216,125.50
15.5	1,582.47	108,887.45	208,887.45	1,533.20	120,782.72	220,782.72
16.0	1,614.32	113,089.18	213,089.18	1,565.83	125,477.36	225,477.36
16.5	1,646.44	117,329.24	217,329.24	1,598.73	130,218.69	230,218.69
17.0	1,678.83	121,606.38	221,606.38	1,631.92	134,997.82	234,997.82
17.5	1,711.49	125,918.20	225,918.20	1,665.39	139,814.55	239,814.55
18.0	1,744.42	130,262.54	230,262.54	1,699.12	144,673.03	244,673.03
18.5	1,777.60	134,642.98	234,642.98	1,733.11	149,570.35	249,570.35
19.0	1,811.03	139,057.06	239,057.06	1,767.36	154,502.37	254,502.37
19.5	1,844.71	143,502.97	243,502.97	1,801.86	159,470.68	259,470.68
20.0	1,878.63	147,981.21	247,981.21	1,836.61	164,471.14	264,471.14
20.5	1,912.79	152,489.08	252,489.08	1,871.59	169,508.47	269,508.47
21.0	1,947.18	157,027.66	257,027.66	1,906.80	174,579.77	274,579.77
21.5	1,981.79	161,598.48	261,598.48	1,942.24	179,681.21	279,681.21
22.0	2,016.63	166,194.42	266,194.42	1,977.89	184,818.79	284,818.79
22.5	2,051.68	170,820.69	270,820.69	2,013.76	189,983.04	289,983.04
23.0	2,086.94	175,475.12	275,475.12	2,049.84	195,175.22	295,175.22
23.5	2,122.40	180,158.73	280,158.73	2,086.11	200,403.09	300,403.09
24.0	2,158.07	184,863.75	284,863.75	2,122.59	205,649.60	305,649.60
24.5	2,193.93	189,597.23	289,597.23	2,159.25	210,929.78	310,929.78
25.0	2,229.98	194,354.93	294,354.93	2,196.09	216,239.73	316,239.73
25.5	2,266.21	199,140.07	299,140.07	2,233.12	221,566.49	321,566.49
26.0	2,302.62	203,950.14	303,950.14	2,270.31	226,928.16	326,928.16

Mortgage Summary Amortization by Interest, Given Term

Principal $100,000.00

Interest Rate	Term 13 Years			Term 14 Years		
	Monthly Payment	Total Interest	Total Payment	Monthly Payment	Total Interest	Total Payment
1.5	705.95	10,129.09	110,129.09	660.29	10,929.59	110,929.59
2.0	728.50	13,645.46	113,645.46	682.95	14,735.21	114,735.21
2.5	751.49	17,231.74	117,231.74	706.08	18,622.03	118,622.03
3.0	774.92	20,887.69	120,887.69	729.70	22,588.61	122,588.61
3.5	798.80	24,612.56	124,612.56	753.78	26,635.94	126,635.94
4.0	823.12	28,405.92	128,405.92	778.35	30,761.73	130,761.73
4.5	847.87	32,267.96	132,267.96	803.38	34,966.84	134,966.84
5.0	873.06	36,197.29	136,197.29	828.87	39,250.30	139,250.30
5.5	898.68	40,193.73	140,193.73	854.83	43,610.46	143,610.46
6.0	924.72	44,257.08	144,257.08	881.24	48,047.22	148,047.22
6.5	951.19	48,385.66	148,385.66	908.10	52,599.76	152,559.76
7.0	978.07	52,579.95	152,579.95	935.40	57,147.33	157,147.33
7.5	1,005.37	56,837.85	156,837.85	963.14	61,808.49	161,808.49
8.0	1,033.07	61,160.00	161,160.00	991.32	66,541.18	166,541.18
8.5	1,061.18	65,543.84	165,543.84	1,019.92	71,346.09	171,346.09
9.0	1,089.68	69,990.22	169,990.22	1,048.94	76,221.20	176,221.20
9.5	1,118.57	74,497.57	174,497.57	1,078.37	81,165.41	181,165.41
10.0	1,147.85	79,063.89	179,063.89	1,108.20	86,178.58	186,178.58
10.5	1,177.50	83,690.48	183,690.48	1,138.43	91,257.68	191,257.68
11.0	1,207.53	88,373.75	188,373.75	1,169.05	96,401.98	196,401.98
11.5	1,237.92	93,114.62	193,114.62	1,200.06	101,608.09	201,608.09
12.0	1,268.67	97,911.13	197,911.13	1,231.43	106,880.30	206,880.30
12.5	1,299.77	102,762.88	202,762.88	1,263.17	112,211.78	212,211.78
13.0	1,331.21	107,668.70	207,668.70	1,295.26	117,605.45	217,605.45
13.5	1,362.99	112,627.41	212,627.41	1,327.71	123,053.65	223,053.65
14.0	1,395.10	117,637.01	217,637.01	1,360.49	128,561.98	228,561.98
14.5	1,427.54	122,695.07	222,695.07	1,393.60	134,126.86	234,126.86
15.0	1,460.29	127,804.11	227,804.11	1,427.04	139,742.74	239,742.74
15.5	1,493.35	132,960.32	232,960.32	1,460.79	145,412.85	245,412.85
16.0	1,526.70	138,167.51	238,167.51	1,494.85	151,131.69	251,131.69
16.5	1,560.36	143,414.66	243,414.66	1,529.20	156,903.94	256,903.94
17.0	1,594.30	148,708.21	248,708.21	1,563.84	162,723.90	262,723.90
17.5	1,628.51	154,048.84	254,048.84	1,598.76	168,590.96	268,590.96
18.0	1,663.00	159,428.39	259,428.39	1,633.95	174,503.82	274,503.82
18.5	1,697.75	164,851.29	264,851.29	1,669.41	180,456.99	280,456.99
19.0	1,732.76	170,311.82	270,311.82	1,705.11	186,462.35	286,462.35
19.5	1,768.02	175,811.79	275,811.79	1,741.07	192,500.37	292,500.37
20.0	1,803.52	181,351.03	281,351.03	1,777.27	198,577.28	298,577.28
20.5	1,839.26	186,923.22	286,923.22	1,813.69	204,699.92	304,699.92
21.0	1,875.22	192,536.55	292,536.55	1,850.34	210,855.99	310,855.99
21.5	1,911.41	198,178.89	298,178.89	1,887.20	217,051.87	317,051.87
22.0	1,947.81	203,857.45	303,857.45	1,924.27	223,280.96	323,280.96
22.5	1,984.42	209,567.01	309,567.01	1,961.54	229,543.19	329,543.19
23.0	2,021.23	215,307.61	315,307.61	1,999.01	235,831.93	335,831.93
23.5	2,058.23	221,084.06	321,084.06	2,036.66	242,156.84	342,156.84
24.0	2,095.42	226,886.35	326,886.35	2,074.49	248,510.76	348,510.76
24.5	2,132.79	232,721.36	332,721.36	2,112.49	254,896.34	354,896.34
25.0	2,170.34	238,577.99	338,577.99	2,150.66	261,304.24	361,304.24
25.5	2,208.06	244,461.35	344,461.35	2,188.98	267,750.93	367,750.93
26.0	2,245.95	250,363.37	350,363.37	2,227.46	274,213.88	374,213.88

¶691.29

Mortgage Summary Amortization by Interest, Given Term

Term 15 Years   Term 16 Years

Principal $100,000.00

Interest Rate	Monthly Payment	Total Interest	Total Payment	Monthly Payment	Total Interest	Total Payment
1.5	620.74	11,733.83	111,733.83	586.15	12,514.80	112,541.80
2.0	643.51	15,831.58	115,831.58	609.03	16,934.67	116,934.67
2.5	666.79	20,021.98	120,021.98	632.46	21,432.55	121,432.55
3.0	690.58	24,304.76	123,304.76	656.43	26,035.40	126,035.40
3.5	714.88	28,678.95	128,678.95	680.95	30,714.60	130,741.60
4.0	739.69	33,143.79	133,143.79	706.00	35,550.96	135,550.96
4.5	764.99	37,699.06	137,699.06	731.58	40,462.25	140,462.25
5.0	790.79	42,343.24	142,343.24	757.68	45,474.00	145,474.86
5.5	817.08	47,075.43	147,075.43	784.30	50,586.78	150,586.78
6.0	843.86	51,893.80	151,893.80	811.44	55,795.71	155,795.71
6.5	871.11	56,798.89	156,798.89	839.08	61,101.68	161,101.68
7.0	898.83	61,788.73	161,788.73	867.21	66,503.53	166,503.53
7.5	927.01	66,862.61	166,862.61	895.83	71,998.53	171,998.53
8.0	955.65	72,017.71	172,017.71	924.93	77,584.62	177,584.62
8.5	984.74	77,253.05	177,253.05	954.49	83,262.37	183,262.37
9.0	1,014.27	82,567.37	182,567.37	984.52	89,026.15	189,026.15
9.5	1,044.22	87,961.54	187,961.54	1,014.99	94,878.00	194,878.00
10.0	1,074.61	93,427.99	193,427.99	1,045.90	100,813.74	200,813.74
10.5	1,105.40	98,971.63	198,971.63	1,077.24	106,831.39	206,831.39
11.0	1,136.60	104,586.46	204,586.46	1,109.00	112,928.09	212,928.09
11.5	1,168.19	110,274.02	210,274.02	1,141.16	119,105.33	219,105.33
12.0	1,200.17	116,029.68	216,029.68	1,173.73	125,353.58	225,353.58
12.5	1,232.52	121,854.86	221,854.86	1,206.67	131,680.50	231,680.50
13.0	1,265.24	127,744.33	227,744.33	1,239.99	138,076.90	238,076.90
13.5	1,298.32	133,696.75	233,696.75	1,273.67	144,543.23	244,543.23
14.0	1,331.74	139,714.18	239,714.18	1,307.70	151,077.75	251,077.75
14.5	1,365.50	145,790.72	245,790.72	1,342.07	157,677.53	257,677.53
15.0	1,399.59	151,924.45	251,924.45	1,376.77	164,339.30	264,339.30
15.5	1,433.99	158,118.70	258,118.70	1,411.79	171,061.22	271,061.22
16.0	1,468.70	164,366.68	264,366.68	1,447.11	177,845.25	277,845.25
16.5	1,503.71	170,666.63	270,666.63	1,482.73	184,684.07	284,684.07
17.0	1,539.00	177,023.72	277,023.72	1,518.63	191,580.71	291,580.71
17.5	1,574.58	183,422.35	283,422.35	1,554.81	198,526.92	298,526.92
18.0	1,610.42	189,876.52	289,876.52	1,591.26	205,517.09	305,517.09
18.5	1,646.52	196,376.68	296,376.68	1,627.95	212,569.41	312,569.41
19.0	1,682.88	202,914.59	302,914.59	1,664.89	219,662.32	319,662.32
19.5	1,719.47	209,504.48	309,504.48	1,702.07	226,793.61	326,793.61
20.0	1,756.30	516,129.97	316,129.97	1,739.47	233,973.04	333,973.04
20.5	1,793.35	222,799.01	322,799.01	1,777.08	241,199.35	341,199.35
21.0	1,830.61	229,512.51	329,512.51	1,814.90	248,461.10	348,461.10
21.5	1,868.08	236,260.80	336,260.80	1,852.92	255,756.25	355,756.25
22.0	1,905.76	243,031.78	343,031.78	1,891.12	263,099.27	363,099.27
22.5	1,943.62	249,849.00	349,849.00	1,929.51	270,463.05	370,463.05
23.0	1,981.66	256,704.64	356,704.64	1,968.07	277,862.40	377,862.40
23.5	2,019.88	263,585.28	363,585.28	2,006.79	285,299.68	385,299.68
24.0	2,058.27	270,495.15	370,495.15	2,045.67	292,763.51	392,763.51
24.5	2,096.82	277,435.28	377,435.28	2,084.69	300,273.14	400,273.14
25.0	2,135.53	284,393.44	384,393.44	2,123.87	307,771.85	407,771.85
25.5	2,174.38	291,391.90	391,391.90	2,163.17	315,331.37	415,331.37
26.0	2,213.38	298,397.95	398,397.95	2,202.61	322,888.22	422,888.22

Mortgage Summary Amortization by Interest, Given Term

Term 17 Years   Term 18 Years
Principal $100,000.00

Interest Rate	Monthly Payment	Total Interest	Total Payment	Monthly Payment	Total Interest	Total Payment
1.5	555.65	13,353.61	113,353.61	528.56	14,168.86	114,168.86
2.0	578.65	18,043.85	118,043.85	551.67	19,159.96	119,159.96
2.5	602.22	22,853.25	122,853.25	575.39	24,284.18	124,284.18
3.0	626.37	27,780.68	127,780.68	599.72	29,540.45	129,540.45
3.5	651.10	32,824.45	132,824.45	624.66	34,926.98	134,926.98
4.0	676.39	37,984.56	137,984.56	650.20	40,442.38	140,442.38
4.5	702.25	43,258.13	1,432,581.13	676.32	46,086.57	146,086.57
5.0	728.66	48,645.16	148,645.16	703.03	51,855.71	151,855.71
5.5	755.61	54,144.19	154,144.19	730.32	57,747.73	157,747.73
6.0	783.10	59,752.60	159,752.60	758.16	63,763.44	163,763.44
6.5	811.12	65,468.92	165,468.92	786.56	69,897.54	169,897.54
7.0	839.66	71,290.84	171,290.84	815.50	76,149.02	176,149.02
7.5	868.71	77,216.63	177,216.63	844.97	82,514.98	182,514.98
8.0	898.26	83,243.63	183,243.63	874.96	88,992.66	188,992.66
8.5	928.29	89,372.18	189,372.18	905.46	95,578.25	195,578.25
9.0	958.80	95,597.12	195,597.12	936.44	102,273.67	202,273.67
9.5	989.78	101,915.53	201,915.53	967.91	109,069.49	209,069.49
10.0	1,021.21	108,327.22	208,327.22	999.84	115,967.73	215,967.73
10.5	1,053.08	114,828.82	214,828.82	1,032.23	122,960.49	222,960.49
11.0	1,085.38	121,418.04	221,418.04	1,065.05	130,050.78	230,050.78
11.5	1,118.10	128,090.00	228,090.00	1,098.30	137,229.76	237,229.76
12.0	1,151.22	134,846.00	234,846.00	1,131.95	144,501.71	244,501.71
12.5	1,184.73	141,682.23	241,682.23	1,166.00	151,856.58	251,856.58
13.0	1,218.61	148,599.67	248,599.67	1,200.43	159,294.90	259,294.90
13.5	1,252.87	155,584.93	255,584.93	1,235.23	166,810.97	266,810.97
14.0	1,287.48	162,643.09	262,643.09	1,270.38	174,405.16	274,405.16
14.5	1,322.42	169,777.51	269,777.51	1,305.87	182,071.96	282,071.96
15.0	1,357.70	176,971.40	276,971.40	1,341.69	189,805.54	289,805.54
15.5	1,393.29	184,233.35	284,233.35	1,377.82	197,608.76	297,608.76
16.0	1,429.19	191,553.29	291,553.29	1,414.25	205,473.95	305,473.95
16.5	1,465.38	198,932.84	298,932.84	1,450.96	213,408.20	313,408.20
17.0	1,501.84	206,379.44	306,379.44	1,487.95	221,394.04	321,394.04
17.5	1,538.58	213,869.25	313,869.25	1,525.19	229,449.21	329,449.21
18.0	1,575.57	221,420.00	321,420.00	1,562.69	237,542.86	337,542.86
18.5	1,612.81	229,016.85	329,016.85	1,600.42	245,699.51	345,699.51
19.0	1,650.29	236,655.52	336,655.52	1,638.38	253,897.17	353,897.17
19.5	1,687.99	244,346.55	344,346.55	1,676.56	262,133.90	362,133.90
20.0	1,725.90	252,088.92	352,088.92	1,714.94	270,419.24	370,419.24
20.5	1,764.02	259,863.62	359,863.62	1,753.51	278,753.66	378,753.66
21.0	1,802.34	267,672.80	367,672.80	1,792.26	287,135.60	387,135.60
21.5	1,840.84	275,530.63	375,530.63	1,831.19	295,546.58	395,546.58
22.0	1,879.52	283,416.73	383,416.73	1,870.29	303,979.45	403,979.45
22.5	1,918.36	291,356.45	391,356.45	1,909.54	312,460.32	412,460.32
23.0	1,957.37	299,308.02	399,308.02	1,948.94	320,968.12	420,968.12
23.5	1,996.53	307,296.07	407,296.07	1,988.48	329,502.57	429,502.57
24.0	2,035.84	315,297.51	415,297.51	2,028.15	338,077.02	438,077.02
24.5	2,075.28	323,345.57	423,345.57	2,067.94	346,692.14	446,692.14
25.0	2,114.85	331,419.60	431,419.60	2,107.86	355,288.25	455,288.25
25.5	2,154.54	339,529.39	439,529.39	2,147.88	363,949.03	463,949.03
26.0	2,194.35	347,650.45	447,650.45	2,188.01	372,610.79	472,610.79

Mortgage Summary Amortization by Interest, Given Term

Term 19 Years   Term 20 Years

Principal $100,000.00

Interest Rate	Monthly Payment	Total Interest	Total Payment	Monthly Payment	Total Interest	Total Payment
1.5	504.33	14,988.18	114,988.18	482.55	15,810.76	115,810.76
2.0	527.56	20,282.56	120,282.56	505.88	21,412.23	121,412.23
2.5	551.43	25,725.22	125,725.22	529.90	27,177.01	127,177.01
3.0	575.94	31,314.68	131,314.68	554.60	33,103.24	133,103.24
3.5	601.09	37,049.03	137,049.03	579.96	39,190.29	139,190.29
4.0	626.87	42,926.40	142,926.40	605.98	45,435.21	145,435.21
4.5	653.27	48,945.26	148,945.26	632.65	51,835.75	151,835.75
5.0	680.28	55,102.99	155,102.99	659.96	58,388.59	158,388.59
5.5	707.89	51,397.51	161,397.51	687.89	65,092.46	165,092.46
6.0	736.08	67,827.55	167,827.55	716.43	71,943.81	171,943.81
6.5	764.86	74,386.25	174,386.25	745.57	78,938.28	178,938.28
7.0	794.19	81,076.45	181,076.45	775.30	86,071.47	186,071.47
7.5	824.08	87,889.66	187,889.66	805.59	93,343.39	193,343.39
8.0	854.50	94,826.80	194,826.80	836.44	100,745.53	200,745.53
8.5	885.45	101,880.12	201,880.12	867.82	408,279.05	208,279.05
9.0	916.90	109,051.26	209,051.26	899.73	115,932.83	215,932.83
9.5	948.84	116,335.32	216,335.32	932.13	123,712.12	223,712.12
10.0	981.26	123,726.58	223,726.58	965.02	131,606.05	231,606.05
10.5	1,014.14	131,222.92	231,222.92	998.38	139,611.02	239,611.02
11.0	1,047.46	138,823.56	238,823.56	1,032.19	147,724.22	247,724.22
11.5	1,081.22	146,516.37	246,516.37	1,066.43	155,942.92	255,942.92
12.0	1,115.39	154,305.30	254,305.30	1,101.09	164,257.65	26,457.65
12.5	1,149.95	162,189.34	262,189.34	1,136.14	172,674.25	272,674.25
13.0	1,184.90	170,155.05	270,155.05	1,171.58	181,174.64	281,174.64
13.5	1,220.21	178,209.52	278,209.52	1,207.37	189,774.34	289,774.34
14.0	1,255.88	189,335.95	286,335.95	1,243.52	198,446.68	298,446.68
14.5	1,291.88	194,544.16	294,544.16	1,280.00	207,196.66	307,196.66
15.0	1,328.20	202,826.99	302,826.99	1,316.79	216,029.11	316,029.11
15.5	1,364.83	211,175.93	311,175.93	1,353.88	224,932.25	324,932.25
16.0	1,401.75	219,593.66	319,593.66	1,391.26	233,895.32	333,895.32
16.5	1,439.94	228,086.00	328,086.00	1,428.90	242,937.02	342,937.02
17.0	1,476.41	236,618.77	336,618.77	1,466.80	252,033.55	352,033.55
17.5	1,514.12	245,226.12	345,226.12	1,504.94	261,189.59	361,189.59
18.0	1,552.08	253,870.74	353,870.74	1,543.31	270,398.02	370,398.02
18.5	1,590.26	262,576.90	362,576.90	1,581.90	279,647.85	379,647.85
19.0	1,628.66	271,323.58	371,323.58	1,620.68	288,975.47	388,975.47
19.5	1,667.25	280,143.71	380,143.71	1,659.66	298,331.31	398,331.31
20.0	1,706.05	288,969.77	388,969.77	1,698.82	307,730.79	407,730.79
20.5	1,745.02	297,864.87	397,864.87	1,738.15	317,169.89	417,169.89
21.0	1,784.17	306,777.46	406,777.46	1,777.64	326,645.14	426,645.14
21.5	1,823.47	315,761.12	415,761.12	1,817.28	336,153.43	436,153.43
22.0	1,862.93	324,758.06	424,758.06	1,857.06	345,695.45	445,695.45
22.5	1,902.54	333,769.66	433,769.66	1,896.97	355,273.92	455,273.92
23.0	1,942.28	342,828.39	442,828.39	1,937.00	364,897.13	464,897.13
23.5	1,982.14	351,942.09	451,942.09	1,977.15	374,526.86	474,526.86
24.0	2,022.13	361,043.77	461,043.77	2,017.41	384,166.61	484,166.61
24.5	2,062.23	370,180.29	470,180.29	2,057.77	393,832.06	493,832.06
25.0	2,102.43	379,368.48	479,368.48	2,098.22	403,544.17	503,544.17
25.5	2,142.74	388,521.95	488,521.95	2,138.76	413,264.83	513,264.83
26.0	2,183.13	397,765.87	497,765.87	2,179.38	423,023.08	523,023.08

.31 Comparison of Up-Front Fees and Mortgage Interest Rates

Comparison of Up-Front Fees and Mortgage Interest Rates

Mortgage Interest Rate	Years to Own Home	Total Interest Rate	Up-Front Mortgage Points	Total Interest and Points	Effective Annual % Rate
8	5	40.00	2.00	42.00	8.40
8	5	40.00	3.00	43.00	8.60
8	5	40.00	4.00	44.00	8.80
8	5	40.00	5.00	45.00	9.00
8	5	40.00	6.00	46.00	9.20
8	10	80.00	2.00	82.00	8.20
8	10	80.00	3.00	83.00	8.30
8	10	80.00	4.00	84.00	8.40
8	10	80.00	5.00	85.00	8.50
8	10	80.00	6.00	86.00	8.60
8	15	120.00	2.00	122.00	8.13
8	15	120.00	3.00	123.00	8.20
8	15	120.00	4.00	124.00	8.27
8	15	120.00	5.00	125.00	8.33
8	15	120.00	6.00	126.00	8.40
8	20	160.00	2.00	162.00	8.10
8	20	160.00	3.00	163.00	8.15
8	20	160.00	4.00	164.00	8.20
8	20	160.00	5.00	165.00	8.25
8	20	160.00	6.00	166.00	8.30
8	25	200.00	2.00	202.00	8.08
8	25	200.00	3.00	203.00	8.12
8	25	200.00	4.00	204.00	8.16
8	25	200.00	5.00	205.00	8.20
8	25	200.00	6.00	206.00	8.24
8	30	240.00	2.00	242.00	8.07
8	30	240.00	3.00	243.00	8.10
8	30	240.00	4.00	244.00	8.13
8	30	240.00	5.00	245.00	8.17
8	30	240.00	6.00	246.00	8.20

Comparison of Up-Front Fees and Mortgage Interest Rates

Mortgage Interest Rate	Years to Own Home	Total Interest Rate	Up-Front Mortgage Points	Total Interest and Points	Effective Annual % Rate
9	5	45.00	2.00	47.00	9.40
9	5	45.00	3.00	48.00	9.60
9	5	45.00	4.00	49.00	9.80
9	5	45.00	5.00	50.00	10.00
9	5	45.00	6.00	51.00	10.20
9	10	90.00	2.00	92.00	9.20
9	10	90.00	3.00	93.00	9.30
9	10	90.00	4.00	94.00	9.40
9	10	90.00	5.00	95.00	9.50
9	10	90.00	6.00	96.00	9.60
9	15	135.00	2.00	137.00	9.13
9	15	135.00	3.00	138.00	9.20
9	15	135.00	4.00	139.00	9.27
9	15	135.00	5.00	140.00	9.33
9	15	135.00	6.00	141.00	9.40
9	20	180.00	2.00	182.00	9.10
9	20	180.00	3.00	183.00	9.15
9	20	180.00	4.00	184.00	9.20
9	20	180.00	5.00	185.00	9.25
9	20	180.00	6.00	186.00	9.30
9	25	225.00	2.00	227.00	9.08
9	25	225.00	3.00	228.00	9.12
9	25	225.00	4.00	229.00	9.16
9	25	225.00	5.00	230.00	9.20
9	25	225.00	6.00	231.00	9.24
9	30	270.00	2.00	272.00	9.07
9	30	270.00	3.00	273.00	9.10
9	30	270.00	4.00	274.00	9.13
9	30	270.00	5.00	275.00	9.17
9	30	270.00	6.00	276.00	9.20

.33 Interest Factors for the Rule of 78

Interest Factors for the Rule of 78

Month	Weight	Interest Factor	Weight	Interest Factor	Weight	Interest Factor	Weight	Interest Factor
1	12	0.15385	24	0.08000	36	0.05405	48	0.04082
2	11	0.14103	23	0.07667	35	0.05255	47	0.03997
3	10	0.12821	22	0.07333	34	0.05105	46	0.03912
4	9	0.11538	21	0.07000	33	0.04955	45	0.03827
5	8	0.10256	20	0.06667	32	0.04805	44	0.03741
6	7	0.08974	19	0.06333	31	0.04655	43	0.03656
7	6	0.07692	18	0.06000	30	0.04505	42	0.03571
8	5	0.06410	17	0.05667	29	0.04354	41	0.03486
9	4	0.05128	16	0.05333	28	0.04204	40	0.03401
10	3	0.03846	15	0.05000	27	0.04054	39	0.03316
11	2	0.02564	14	0.04667	26	0.03904	38	0.03231
12	1	0.01282	13	0.04333	25	0.03754	37	0.03146
13			12	0.04000	24	0.03604	36	0.03061
14			11	0.03667	23	0.03453	35	0.02976
15			10	0.03333	22	0.03303	34	0.02891
16			9	0.03000	21	0.03153	33	0.02806
17			8	0.02667	20	0.03003	32	0.02721
18			7	0.02333	19	0.02853	31	0.02636
19			6	0.02000	18	0.02703	30	0.02551
20			5	0.01667	17	0.02553	29	0.02466
21			4	0.01333	16	0.02402	28	0.02381
22			3	0.01000	15	0.02252	27	0.02296
23			2	0.00667	14	0.02102	26	0.02211
24			1	0.00333	13	0.01952	25	0.02126
25					12	0.01802	24	0.02041
26					11	0.01652	23	0.01956
27					10	0.01502	22	0.01871
28					9	0.01351	21	0.01786
29					8	0.01201	20	0.01701
30					7	0.01051	19	0.01616
31					6	0.00901	18	0.01531
32					5	0.00751	17	0.01446
33					4	0.00601	16	0.01361
34					3	0.00450	15	0.01276
35					2	0.00300	14	0.01190
36					1	0.00150	13	0.01105
37							12	0.01020
38							11	0.00935
39							10	0.00850
40							9	0.00765
41							8	0.00680
42							7	0.00595
43							6	0.00510
44							5	0.00425
45							4	0.00340
46							3	0.00255
47							2	0.00170
48							1	0.00085
	78	1.00000	300	1.00000	666	1.00000	1176	1.00000

.35 Percent Change in Units Allowed to Maintain Gross Profit Margin

% Change in Unit Sales Volume Allowed to Maintain Gross Profit Margin When Prices Are Increased

% Change in Price

Gross Profit%	1	2	3	4	5	6	7
5	-16.67	-28.57	-37.50	-44.44	-50.00	-54.55	-58.33
6	-14.29	-25.00	-33.33	-40.00	-45.45	-50.00	-53.85
7	-12.50	-22.22	-30.00	-36.36	-41.67	-46.15	-50.00
8	-11.11	-20.00	-27.27	-33.33	-38.46	-42.86	-46.67
9	-10.00	-18.18	-25.00	-30.77	-35.71	-40.00	-43.75
10	-9.09	-16.67	-23.08	-28.57	-33.33	-37.50	-41.18
11	-8.33	-15.38	-21.43	-26.67	-31.25	-35.29	-38.89
12	-7.69	-14.29	-20.00	-25.00	-29.41	-33.33	-36.84
13	-7.14	-13.33	-18.75	-23.53	-27.78	-31.58	-35.00
14	-6.67	-12.50	-17.65	-22.22	-26.32	-30.00	-33.33
15	-6.25	-11.76	-16.67	-21.05	-25.00	-28.57	-31.82
16	-5.88	-11.11	-15.79	-20.00	-23.81	-27.27	-30.43
17	-5.56	-10.53	-15.00	-19.05	-22.73	-26.09	-29.17
18	-5.26	-10.00	-14.29	-18.18	-21.74	-25.00	-28.00
19	-5.00	-9.52	-13.64	-17.39	-20.83	-24.00	-26.92
20	-4.76	-9.09	-13.04	-16.67	-20.00	-23.08	-25.93
21	-4.55	-8.70	-12.50	-16.00	-19.23	-22.22	-25.00
22	-4.35	-8.33	-12.00	-15.38	-18.52	-21.43	-24.14
23	-4.17	-8.00	-11.54	-14.81	-17.86	-20.69	-23.33
24	-4.00	-7.69	-11.11	-14.29	-17.24	-20.00	-22.58
25	-3.85	-7.41	-10.71	-13.79	-16.67	-19.35	-21.88
26	-3.70	-7.14	-10.34	-13.33	-16.13	-18.75	-21.21
27	-3.57	-6.90	-10.00	-12.90	-15.63	-18.18	-20.59
28	-3.45	-6.67	-9.68	-12.50	-15.15	-17.65	-20.00
29	-3.33	-6.45	-9.38	-12.12	-14.71	-17.14	-19.44
30	-3.23	-6.25	-9.09	-11.76	-14.29	-16.67	-18.92
31	-3.13	-6.06	-8.82	-11.43	-13.89	-16.22	-18.42
32	-3.03	-5.88	-8.57	-11.11	-13.51	-15.79	-17.95
33	-2.94	-5.71	-8.33	-10.81	-13.16	-15.38	-17.50
34	-2.86	-5.56	-8.11	-10.53	-12.82	-15.00	-17.07
35	-2.78	-5.41	-7.89	-10.26	-12.50	-14.63	-16.67
36	-2.70	-5.26	-7.69	-10.00	-12.20	-14.29	-16.28
37	-2.63	-5.13	-7.50	-9.76	-11.90	-13.95	-15.91
38	-2.56	-5.00	-7.32	-9.52	-11.63	-13.64	-15.56
39	-2.50	-4.88	-7.14	-9.30	-11.36	-13.33	-15.22
40	-2.44	-4.76	-6.98	-9.09	-11.11	-13.04	-14.89

% Change in Unit Sales Volume Allowed to Maintain Gross Profit Margin When Prices Are Increased

% Change in Price

Gross Profit%	1	2	3	4	5	6	7
41	-2.38	-4.65	-6.82	-8.89	-10.87	-12.77	-14.58
42	-2.33	-4.55	-6.67	-8.70	-10.64	-12.50	-14.29
43	-2.27	-4.44	-6.52	-8.51	-10.42	-12.24	-14.00
44	-2.22	-4.35	-6.38	-8.33	-10.20	-12.00	-13.73
45	-2.17	-4.26	-6.25	-8.16	-10.00	-11.76	-13.46
46	-2.13	-4.17	-6.12	-8.00	-9.80	-11.54	-13.21
47	-2.08	-4.08	-6.00	-7.84	-9.62	-11.32	-12.96
48	-2.04	-4.00	-5.88	-7.69	-9.43	-11.11	-12.73
49	-2.00	-3.92	-5.77	-7.55	-9.26	-10.91	-12.50
50	-1.96	-3.85	-5.66	-7.41	-9.09	-10.71	-12.28
51	-1.92	-3.77	-5.56	-7.27	-8.93	-10.53	-12.07
52	-1.89	-3.70	-5.45	-7.14	-8.77	-10.34	-11.86
53	-1.85	-3.64	-5.36	-7.02	-8.62	-10.17	-11.67
54	-1.82	-3.57	-5.26	-6.90	-8.47	-10.00	-11.48
55	-1.79	-3.51	-5.17	-6.78	-8.33	-9.84	-11.29
56	-1.75	-3.45	-5.08	-6.67	-8.20	-9.68	-11.11
57	-1.72	-3.39	-5.00	-6.56	-8.06	-9.52	-10.94
58	-1.69	-3.33	-4.92	-6.45	-7.94	-9.38	-10.77
59	-1.67	-3.28	-4.84	-6.35	-7.81	-9.23	-10.61
60	-1.64	-3.23	-4.76	-6.25	-7.69	-9.09	-10.45
61	-1.61	-3.17	-4.69	-6.15	-7.58	-8.96	-10.29
62	-1.59	-3.13	-4.62	-6.06	-7.46	-8.82	-10.14
63	-1.56	-3.08	-4.55	-5.97	-7.35	-8.70	-10.00
64	-1.54	-3.03	-4.48	-5.88	-7.25	-8.57	-9.86
65	-1.52	-2.99	-4.41	-5.80	-7.14	-8.45	-9.72
66	-1.49	-2.94	-4.35	-5.71	-7.04	-8.33	-9.59
67	-1.47	-2.90	-4.29	-5.63	-6.94	-8.22	-9.46
68	-1.45	-2.86	-4.23	-5.56	-6.85	-8.11	-9.33
69	-1.43	-2.82	-4.17	-5.48	-6.76	-8.00	-9.21
70	-1.41	-2.78	-4.11	-5.41	-6.67	-7.89	-9.09
71	-1.39	-2.74	-4.05	-5.33	-6.58	-7.79	-8.97
72	-1.37	-2.70	-4.00	-5.26	-6.49	-7.69	-8.86
73	-1.35	-2.67	-3.95	-5.19	-6.41	-7.59	-8.75
74	-1.33	-2.63	-3.90	-5.13	-6.33	-7.50	-8.64
75	-1.32	-2.60	-3.85	-5.06	-6.25	-7.41	-8.54

% Change in Unit Sales Volume Allowed to Maintain Gross Profit Margin When Prices Are Increased

% Change in Price

Gross Profit%	8	9	10	11	12	13	14
5	-61.54	-64.29	-66.67	-68.75	-70.59	-72.22	-73.68
6	-57.14	-60.00	-62.50	-64.71	-66.67	-68.42	-70.00
7	-53.33	-56.25	-58.82	-61.11	-63.16	-65.00	-66.67
8	-50.00	-52.94	-55.56	-57.89	-60.00	-61.90	-63.64
9	-47.06	-50.00	-52.63	-55.00	-57.14	-59.09	-60.87
10	-44.44	-47.37	-50.00	-52.38	-54.55	-56.52	-58.33
11	-42.11	-45.00	-47.62	-50.00	-52.17	-54.17	-56.00
12	-40.00	-42.86	-45.45	-47.83	-50.00	-52.00	-53.85
13	-38.10	-40.91	-43.48	-45.83	-48.00	-50.00	-51.85
14	-36.36	-39.13	-41.67	-44.00	-46.15	-48.15	-50.00
15	-34.78	-37.50	-40.00	-42.31	-44.44	-46.43	-48.28
16	-33.33	-36.00	-38.46	-40.74	-42.86	-44.83	-46.67
17	-32.00	-34.62	-37.04	-39.29	-41.38	-43.33	-45.16
18	-30.77	-33.33	-35.71	-37.93	-40.00	-41.94	-43.75
19	-29.63	-32.14	-34.48	-36.67	-38.71	-40.63	-42.42
20	-28.57	-31.03	-33.33	-35.48	-37.50	-39.39	-41.18
21	-27.59	-30.00	-32.26	-34.38	-36.36	-38.24	-40.00
22	-26.67	-29.03	-31.25	-33.33	-35.29	-37.14	-38.89
23	-25.81	-28.13	-30.30	-32.35	-34.29	-36.11	-37.84
24	-25.00	-27.27	-29.41	-31.43	-33.33	-35.14	-36.84
25	-24.24	-26.47	-28.57	-30.56	-32.43	-34.21	-35.90
26	-23.53	-25.71	-27.78	-29.73	-31.58	-33.33	-35.00
27	-22.86	-25.00	-27.03	-28.95	-30.77	-32.50	-34.15
28	-22.22	-24.32	-26.32	-28.21	-30.00	-31.71	-33.33
29	-21.62	-23.68	-25.64	-27.50	-29.27	-30.95	-32.56
30	-21.05	-23.08	-25.00	-26.83	-28.57	-30.23	-31.82
31	-20.51	-22.50	-24.39	-26.19	-27.91	-29.55	-31.11
32	-20.00	-21.95	-23.81	-25.58	-27.27	-28.89	-30.43
33	-19.51	-21.43	-23.26	-25.00	-26.67	-28.26	-29.79
34	-19.05	-20.93	-22.73	-24.44	-26.09	-27.66	-29.17
35	-18.60	-20.45	-22.22	-23.91	-25.53	-27.08	-28.57
36	-18.18	-20.00	-21.74	-23.40	-25.00	-26.53	-28.00
37	-17.78	-19.57	-21.28	-22.92	-24.49	-26.00	-27.45
38	-17.39	-19.15	-20.83	-22.45	-24.00	-25.49	-26.92
39	-17.02	-18.75	-20.41	-22.00	-23.53	-25.00	-26.42
40	-16.67	-18.37	-20.00	-21.57	-23.08	-24.53	-25.93

% Change in Unit Sales Volume Allowed to Maintain Gross Profit Margin When Prices Are Increased

% Change in Price

Gross Profit%	8	9	10	11	12	13	14
41	-16.33	-18.00	-19.61	-21.15	-22.64	-24.07	-25.45
42	-16.00	-17.65	-19.23	-20.75	-22.22	-23.64	-25.00
43	-15.69	-17.31	-18.87	-20.37	-21.82	-23.21	-24.56
44	-15.38	-16.98	-18.52	-20.00	-21.43	-22.81	-24.14
45	-15.09	-16.67	-18.18	-19.64	-21.05	-22.41	-23.73
46	-14.81	-16.36	-17.86	-19.30	-20.69	-22.03	-23.33
47	-14.55	-16.07	-17.54	-18.97	-20.34	-21.67	-22.95
48	-14.29	-15.79	-17.24	-18.64	-20.00	-21.31	-22.58
49	-14.04	-15.52	-16.95	-18.33	-19.67	-20.97	-22.22
50	-13.79	-15.25	-16.67	-18.03	-19.35	-20.63	-21.88
51	-13.56	-15.00	-16.39	-17.74	-19.05	-20.31	-21.54
52	-13.33	-14.75	-16.13	-17.46	-18.75	-20.00	-21.21
53	-13.11	-14.52	-15.87	-17.19	-18.46	-19.70	-20.90
54	-12.90	-14.29	-15.63	-16.92	-18.18	-19.40	-20.59
55	-12.70	-14.06	-15.38	-16.67	-17.91	-19.12	-20.29
56	-12.50	-13.85	-15.15	-16.42	-17.65	-18.84	-20.00
57	-12.31	-13.64	-14.93	-16.18	-17.39	-18.57	-19.72
58	-12.12	-13.43	-14.71	-15.94	-17.14	-18.31	-19.44
59	-11.94	-13.24	-14.49	-15.71	-16.90	-18.06	-19.18
60	-11.76	-13.04	-14.29	-15.49	-16.67	-17.81	-18.92
61	-11.59	-12.86	-14.08	-15.28	-16.44	-17.57	-18.67
62	-11.43	-12.68	-13.89	-15.07	-16.22	-17.33	-18.42
63	-11.27	-12.50	-13.70	-14.86	-16.00	-17.11	-18.18
64	-11.11	-12.33	-13.51	-14.67	-15.79	-16.88	-17.95
65	-10.96	-12.16	-13.33	-14.47	-15.58	-16.67	-17.72
66	-10.81	-12.00	-13.16	-14.29	-15.38	-16.46	-17.50
67	-10.67	-11.84	-12.99	-14.10	-15.19	-16.25	-17.28
68	-10.53	-11.69	-12.82	-13.92	-15.00	-16.05	-17.07
69	-10.39	-11.54	-12.66	-13.75	-14.81	-15.85	-16.87
70	-10.26	-11.39	-12.50	-13.58	-14.63	-15.66	-16.67
71	-10.13	-11.25	-12.35	-13.41	-14.46	-15.48	-16.47
72	-10.00	-11.11	-12.20	-13.25	-14.29	-15.29	-16.28
73	-9.88	-10.98	-12.05	-13.10	-14.12	-15.12	-16.09
74	-9.76	-10.84	-11.90	-12.94	-13.95	-14.94	-15.91
75	-9.64	-10.71	-11.76	-12.79	-13.79	-14.77	-15.73

¶691.35

% Change in Unit Sales Volume Allowed to Maintain Gross Profit Margin When Prices Are Decreased

% Change in Price

Gross Profit%	-1	-2	-3	-4	-5	-6	-7
8	14.29	33.33	60.00	100.00	166.67	300.00	700.00
9	12.50	28.57	50.00	80.00	125.00	200.00	350.00
10	11.11	25.00	42.86	66.67	100.00	150.00	233.33
11	10.00	22.22	37.50	57.14	83.33	120.00	175.00
12	9.09	20.00	33.33	50.00	71.43	100.00	140.00
13	8.33	18.18	30.00	44.44	62.50	85.71	116.67
14	7.69	16.67	27.27	40.00	55.56	75.00	100.00
15	7.14	15.38	25.00	36.36	50.00	66.67	87.50
16	6.67	14.29	23.08	33.33	45.45	60.00	77.78
17	6.25	13.33	21.43	30.77	41.67	54.55	70.00
18	5.88	12.50	20.00	28.57	38.46	50.00	63.64
19	5.56	11.76	18.75	26.67	35.71	46.15	58.33
20	5.26	11.11	17.65	25.00	33.33	42.86	53.85
21	5.00	10.53	16.67	23.53	31.25	40.00	50.00
22	4.76	10.00	15.79	22.22	29.41	37.50	46.67
23	4.55	9.52	15.00	21.05	27.78	35.29	43.75
24	4.35	9.09	14.29	20.00	26.32	33.33	41.18
25	4.17	8.70	13.64	19.05	25.00	31.58	38.89
26	4.00	8.33	13.04	18.18	23.81	30.00	36.84
27	3.85	8.00	12.50	17.39	22.73	28.57	35.00
28	3.70	7.69	12.00	16.67	21.74	27.27	33.33
29	3.57	7.41	11.54	16.00	20.83	26.09	31.82
30	3.45	7.14	11.11	15.38	20.00	25.00	30.43
31	3.33	6.90	10.71	14.81	19.23	24.00	29.17
32	3.23	6.67	10.34	14.29	18.52	23.08	28.00
33	3.13	6.45	10.00	13.79	17.86	22.22	26.92
34	3.03	6.25	9.68	13.33	17.24	21.43	25.93
35	2.94	6.06	9.38	12.90	16.67	20.69	25.00
36	2.86	5.88	9.09	12.50	16.13	20.00	24.14
37	2.78	5.71	8.82	12.12	15.63	19.35	23.33
38	2.70	5.56	8.57	11.76	15.15	18.75	22.58
39	2.63	5.41	8.33	11.43	14.71	18.18	21.88
40	2.56	5.26	8.11	11.11	14.29	17.65	21.21

% Change in Unit Sales Volume Allowed to Maintain Gross Profit Margin When Prices Are Decreased

% Change in Price

Gross Profit%	-1	-2	-3	-4	-5	-6	-7
40	2.56	5.26	8.11	11.11	14.29	17.65	21.21
41	2.50	5.13	7.89	10.81	13.89	17.14	20.59
42	2.44	5.00	7.69	10.53	13.51	16.67	20.00
43	2.38	4.88	7.50	10.26	13.16	16.22	19.44
44	2.33	4.76	7.32	10.00	12.82	15.79	18.92
45	2.27	4.65	7.14	9.76	12.50	15.38	18.42
46	2.22	4.55	6.98	9.52	12.20	15.00	17.95
47	2.17	4.44	6.82	9.30	11.90	14.63	17.50
48	2.13	4.35	6.67	9.09	11.63	14.29	17.07
49	2.08	4.26	6.52	8.89	11.36	13.95	16.67
50	2.04	4.17	6.38	8.70	11.11	13.64	16.28
51	2.00	4.08	6.25	8.51	10.87	13.33	15.91
52	1.96	4.00	6.12	8.33	10.64	13.04	15.56
53	1.92	3.92	6.00	8.16	10.42	12.77	15.22
54	1.89	3.85	5.88	8.00	10.20	12.50	14.89
55	1.85	3.77	5.77	7.84	10.00	12.24	14.58
56	1.82	3.70	5.66	7.69	9.80	12.00	14.29
57	1.79	3.64	5.56	7.55	9.62	11.76	14.00
58	1.75	3.57	5.45	7.41	9.43	11.54	13.73
59	1.72	3.51	5.36	7.27	9.26	11.32	13.46
60	1.69	3.45	5.26	7.14	9.09	11.11	13.21
61	1.67	3.39	5.17	7.02	8.93	10.91	12.96
62	1.64	3.33	5.08	6.90	8.77	10.71	12.73
63	1.61	3.28	5.00	6.78	8.62	10.53	12.50
64	1.59	3.23	4.92	6.67	8.47	10.34	12.28
65	1.56	3.17	4.84	6.56	8.33	10.17	12.07
66	1.54	3.13	4.76	6.45	8.20	10.00	11.86
67	1.52	3.08	4.69	6.35	8.06	9.84	11.67
68	1.49	3.03	4.62	6.25	7.94	9.68	11.48
69	1.47	2.99	4.55	6.15	7.81	9.52	11.29
70	1.45	2.94	4.48	6.06	7.69	9.38	11.11
71	1.43	2.90	4.41	5.97	7.58	9.23	10.94
72	1.41	2.86	4.35	5.88	7.46	9.09	10.77
73	1.39	2.82	4.29	5.80	7.35	8.96	10.61
74	1.37	2.78	4.23	5.71	7.25	8.82	10.45
75	1.35	2.74	4.17	5.63	7.14	8.70	10.29

¶691.35

% Change in Unit Sales Volume Allowed to Maintain Gross Profit Margin When Prices Are Decreased

% Change in Price

Gross Profit%	-8	-9	-10	-11	-12	-13	-14
15	114.29	150.00	200.00	275.00	400.00	650.00	1400.00
16	100.00	128.57	166.67	220.00	300.00	433.33	700.00
17	88.89	112.50	142.86	183.33	240.00	325.00	466.67
18	80.00	100.00	125.00	157.14	200.00	260.00	350.00
19	72.73	90.00	111.11	137.50	171.43	216.67	280.00
20	66.67	81.82	100.00	122.22	150.00	185.71	233.33
21	61.54	75.00	90.91	110.00	133.33	162.50	200.00
22	57.14	69.23	83.33	100.00	120.00	144.44	175.00
23	53.33	64.29	76.92	91.67	109.09	130.00	155.56
24	50.00	60.00	71.43	84.62	100.00	118.18	140.00
25	47.06	56.25	66.67	78.57	92.31	108.33	127.27
26	44.44	52.94	62.50	73.33	85.71	100.00	116.67
27	42.11	50.00	58.82	68.75	80.00	92.86	107.69
28	40.00	47.37	55.56	64.71	75.00	86.67	100.00
29	38.10	45.00	52.63	61.11	70.59	81.25	93.33
30	36.36	42.86	50.00	57.89	66.67	76.47	87.50
31	34.78	40.91	47.62	55.00	63.16	72.22	82.35
32	33.33	39.13	45.45	52.38	60.00	68.42	77.78
33	32.00	37.50	43.48	50.00	57.14	65.00	73.68
34	30.77	36.00	41.67	47.83	54.55	61.90	70.00
35	29.63	34.62	40.00	45.83	52.17	59.09	66.67
36	28.57	33.33	38.46	44.00	50.00	56.52	63.64
37	27.59	32.14	37.04	42.31	48.00	54.17	60.87
38	26.67	31.03	35.71	40.74	46.15	52.00	58.33
39	25.81	30.00	34.48	39.29	44.44	50.00	56.00
40	25.00	29.03	33.33	37.93	42.86	48.15	53.85
41	24.24	28.13	32.26	36.67	41.38	46.43	51.85
42	23.53	27.27	31.25	35.48	40.00	44.83	50.00
43	22.86	26.47	30.30	34.38	38.71	43.33	48.28
44	22.22	25.71	29.41	33.33	37.50	41.94	46.67
45	21.62	25.00	28.57	32.35	36.36	40.63	45.16

¶691.35

% Change in Unit Sales Volume Allowed to Maintain Gross Profit Margin When Prices Are Decreased

% Change in Price

Gross Profit%	-8	-9	-10	-11	-12	-13	-14
46	21.05	24.32	27.78	31.43	35.29	39.39	43.75
47	20.51	23.68	27.03	30.56	34.29	38.24	42.42
48	20.00	23.08	26.32	29.73	33.33	37.14	41.18
49	19.51	22.50	25.64	28.95	32.43	36.11	40.00
50	19.05	21.95	25.00	28.21	31.58	35.14	38.89
51	18.60	21.43	24.39	27.50	30.77	34.21	37.84
52	18.18	20.93	23.81	26.83	30.00	33.33	36.84
53	17.78	20.45	23.26	26.19	29.27	32.50	35.90
54	17.39	20.00	22.73	25.58	28.57	31.71	35.00
55	17.02	19.57	22.22	25.00	27.91	30.95	34.15
56	16.67	19.15	21.74	24.44	27.27	30.23	33.33
57	16.33	18.75	21.28	23.91	26.67	29.55	32.56
58	16.00	18.37	20.83	23.40	26.09	28.89	31.82
59	15.69	18.00	20.41	22.92	25.53	28.26	31.11
60	15.38	17.65	20.00	22.45	25.00	27.66	30.43
61	15.09	17.31	19.61	22.00	24.49	27.08	29.79
62	14.81	16.98	19.23	21.57	24.00	26.53	29.17
63	14.55	16.67	18.87	21.15	23.53	26.00	28.57
64	14.29	16.36	18.52	20.75	23.08	25.49	28.00
65	14.04	16.07	18.18	20.37	22.64	25.00	27.45
66	13.79	15.79	17.86	20.00	22.22	24.53	26.92
67	13.56	15.52	17.54	19.64	21.82	24.07	26.42
68	13.33	15.25	17.24	19.30	21.43	23.64	25.93
69	13.11	15.00	16.95	18.97	21.05	23.21	25.45
70	12.90	14.75	16.67	18.64	20.69	22.81	25.00
71	12.70	14.52	16.39	18.33	20.34	22.41	24.56
72	12.50	14.29	16.13	18.03	20.00	22.03	24.14
73	12.31	14.06	15.87	17.74	19.67	21.67	23.73
74	12.12	13.85	15.63	17.46	19.35	21.31	23.33
75	11.94	13.64	15.38	17.19	19.05	20.97	22.95
76	11.76	13.43	15.15	16.92	18.75	20.63	22.58
77	11.59	13.24	14.93	16.67	18.46	20.31	22.22
78	11.43	13.04	14.71	16.42	18.18	20.00	21.88
79	11.27	12.86	14.49	16.18	17.91	19.70	21.54
80	11.11	12.68	14.29	15.94	17.65	19.40	21.21

¶691.35

.37 Random Number Tables
Random Numbers

Greater than 0 Less than 365

00000000	00000001	00000002	00000011
00000013	00000017	00000017	00000018
00000019	00000021	00000022	00000025
00000026	00000028	00000028	00000029
00000030	00000032	00000033	00000035
00000035	00000038	00000038	00000039
00000043	00000046	00000047	00000049
00000050	00000055	00000057	00000063
00000063	00000064	00000066	00000067
00000068	00000068	00000069	00000069
00000072	00000074	00000076	00000079
00000084	00000084	00000084	00000084
00000086	00000088	00000089	00000091
00000092	00000092	00000095	00000096
00000096	00000097	00000098	00000099
00000099	00000100	00000102	00000102
00000104	00000105	00000107	00000108
00000110	00000110	00000112	00000116
00000117	00000117	00000123	00000126
00000130	00000134	00000136	00000138
00000142	00000143	00000145	00000145
00000148	00000149	00000150	00000152
00000153	00000158	00000159	00000162
00000162	00000162	00000164	00000166
00000168	00000169	00000169	00000169
00000169	00000173	00000175	00000175
00000176	00000180	00000181	00000183
00000183	00000184	00000190	00000195
00000197	00000198	00000200	00000201
00000203	00000204	00000205	00000206
00000211	00000213	00000213	00000213
00000215	00000215	00000219	00000226
00000228	00000231	00000235	00000237
00000240	00000240	00000240	00000241
00000242	00000242	00000243	00000245
00000246	00000246	00000247	00000251
00000252	00000252	00000255	00000257
00000263	00000264	00000267	00000267
00000268	00000270	00000273	00000280
00000283	00000286	00000287	00000288
00000289	00000290	00000292	00000294
00000296	00000297	00000298	00000298
00000299	00000300	00000300	00000301
00000304	00000306	00000309	00000314
00000316	00000320	00000321	00000323
00000326	00000332	00000334	00000335
00000337	00000338	00000338	00000341
00000346	00000348	00000354	00000355
00000356	00000358	00000358	00000360
00000360	00000362	00000363	00000363

Random Numbers

Greater than 0 and Less than 50000

00000142	00000190	00000266	00000438	00000323	00000525	00000768	00001041
00000516	00000770	00001176	00001256	00001200	00001455	00001502	00001759
00001365	00001552	00002179	00002665	00001874	00002049	00002784	00002839
00003037	00003208	00003856	00004080	00003482	00003547	00003549	00004277
00004290	00004447	00004759	00004841	00004329	00004436	00004638	00004647
00005117	00005198	00005580	00005605	00004917	00004967	00005119	00005732
00005968	00006068	00006131	00006187	00005887	00005905	00006034	00006102
00006198	00006312	00006465	00006545	00006243	00006520	00006789	00006830
00006939	00007112	00007335	00007789	00006977	00007040	00007494	00007547
00007859	00008415	00008549	00091136	00007677	00007967	00007976	00007995
00009182	00009403	00009715	00009897	00008132	00008305	00008361	00008473
00009924	00010209	00010235	00010931	00008670	00008792	00008798	00008922
00011023	00011436	00011593	00012457	00008941	00008944	00008986	00009003
00012739	00013261	00013657	00013729	00009084	00009577	00009591	00009880
00014137	00014691	00015150	00015284	00010171	00010332	00010458	00010752
00015451	00015586	00015942	00015971	00010853	00010984	00011142	00011196
00016308	00016389	00016403	00016643	00011415	00011461	00011517	00011680
00016655	00016830	00016903	00017187	00012650	00013516	00013597	00014063
00017822	00018243	00018669	00018883	00015869	00015877	00016070	00016260
00019017	00019058	00019407	00019645	00016323	00017085	00017158	00017730
00019645	00019703	00020079	00020189	00017909	00018267	00018565	00018808
00020380	00020680	00024164	00022104	00019046	00019302	00019516	00019634
00022590	00022603	00022646	00022744	00019889	00020351	00020540	00020610
00022828	00023380	00023410	00023709	00020745	00020791	00021178	00021415
00024396	00024566	00024687	00024708	00021901	00022188	00022569	00023207
00025637	00025807	00025818	00026176	00023527	00023596	00024108	00024245
00026358	00026691	00026925	00027100	00024848	00025999	00026060	00026188
00027256	00027423	00027484	00027671	00026533	00026693	00026767	00026824
00027785	00027789	00027850	00028708	00027312	00027338	00027640	00027710
00029091	00029413	00029928	00030159	00028532	00029102	00029157	00029426
00030393	00030586	00030674	00031170	00030224	00030264	00030365	00030380
00031324	00031902	00031919	00031977	00030768	00030802	00031082	00031226
00032744	00033663	00034397	00035222	00031477	00031809	00031929	00032141
00035238	00035267	00035361	00036073	00032588	00032759	00033140	00033460
00036242	00036690	00037402	00037472	00034130	00034197	00034727	00034956
00037652	00038005	00038376	00038471	00035109	00035424	00035562	00036006
00038472	00038604	00038630	00038712	00036228	00036314	00037123	00038147
00038900	00039056	00039203	00039530	00038707	00038783	00038878	00039243
00039990	00040205	00402334	00040393	00039544	00039548	00039576	00039770
00040455	00040466	00040783	00040978	00039902	00039956	00040132	00040493
00041310	00041385	00041466	00041555	00041150	00041751	00041881	00041940
00041617	00042067	00042200	00042724	00042108	00042114	00042156	00042499
00042732	00042997	00043350	00043696	00042798	00012805	00043195	00043213
00043809	00044304	00044547	00044686	00043290	00044143	00044464	00044509
00044787	00046302	00046358	00046410	00044548	00044781	00044969	00045868
00046421	00046488	00046581	00046686	00046076	00046090	00046147	00046357
00046875	00047598	00047780	00047991	00046485	00046771	00046886	00047209
00048121	00048230	00048329	00048525	00047964	00048193	00048206	00048319
00048621	00049009	00049270	00049309	00048549	00048599	00048925	00049173
00049579	00049659	00049892	00049925	00049216	00049337	00049753	00049821

¶ 693　LOANS

.01　Debt vs. Equity Financing

Equity

- Equity buy-back is not deductible.
- The cost of reacquiring future ownership from equity owners can be substantial.
- Equity funds do not have to be repaid.

Debt

- Debt principal repayment is not deductible.
- Debt owners have no direct claim on future earnings of the company.
- Debt interest repayments are tax deductible.
- Debt must be repaid.
- Debt repayment amounts are more clearly defined and planned for.
- Debt does not dilute the company's ownership.
- Debt instruments may contain restrictive covenants that limit the company's future actions.

Types of Money Available

- Equity financing requires no payback, dilutes ownership.
- Funds increase firm's net worth.
- Long-term loans are longer than one year.
- Used for capital asset purchases and longer term situations.
- Loans are paid back out of accumulated profits.
- Short-term loans of 1 to 6 months in length.
  - Usually provided by banks.
  - Loans are paid back from sales dollars profits.
  - Usually secured by accounts receivables, or inventory.
- Trade credit. Open account purchases provided by suppliers.

Financing Sources

- Banks—Commercial
- Brokerage Houses
- Charge Accounts
- Commissions—Advances
- Credit Cards
- Credit Unions
- Economic Development Agency
- Finance Companies
- Friends
- Insurance Companies
- Investment Groups

¶693.01

- Leasing Companies
- Minority Enterprise—Small Business Investment Companies
- Mortgage Companies
- Pawnbrokers
- Small Business Investment Companies
- Suppliers—Trade Credit

.03 Financing Sources

Banks—Commercial

- Often the first source approached.
- Borrowing costs are comparably low with rates ranging from 10% to 18%.
- Successful borrowing and repayment makes future loans from the bank easier to obtain and less expensive.
- Advantages
  - Relatively inexpensive
  - Loan processing simplicity
- Disadvantages:
  - Often credit rating requirements are too rigid
  - There may be strict penalties if the creditor does not meet monthly installments

Brokerage House

- If the firm has stock certificates in street name with a broker-dealer and has a margin account, it has a ready source of credit depending on the current market value of the stocks.

Interest and Maturity

- Interest—The interest rate is generally about 1% above the broker's loan rate.
- Maturity
  - Generally no maximum maturity on the borrowings as long as the stocks do not decline below the credit line allowed by the regulation.
  - If the margin account drops below the established minimum, a margin call will be issued requiring the borrower to restore the account's equity to the proper level.
- Advantages
  - Reasonable interest rate
  - Quick and easy to obtain
  - No debt amortization required
- Disadvantages
  - A sudden drop in the security's portfolio may produce margin calls forcing one to pay back part of the loan on an extremely short notice.
  - Interest rates can fluctuate widely such that one is not aware of the true cost of borrowing.
  - The debtor may continue to postpone payments.

¶693.03

Charge Accounts

An open account is one in which the store accepts the promise to repay within a certain period from the purchase, typically 30 days.

A revolving account is one in which the store specifies a maximum which may be owed at any one time. Interest is paid on the outstanding balance.

A flexible account is one in which monthly installment payments are based on the size of the account balance and interest is charged on the unpaid balance.

Commissions—Advances Interest and Maturities

- Interest—generally interest is not charged on salary advances.
- Maturities are typically short term—6 months to a year.
- Advantage
  - Repayment periods may be available and terms may often be very easy to handle.
- Disadvantage
  - Reduced pay periods in the future may cause cash flow problems. Personal information may have to be revealed.

Credit Cards

- Interest rates usually range from 12% to 18%.
- Maximum Credit Limit—usually from $500-$5,000.

Credit Unions

- Generally associated with groups whose members share a common interest, such as employees, or trade union members.
- Deal exclusively with individuals.
- Can be more lenient to borrowers with repayment problems.
- Generally provide low rates and excellent service to their members.

Economic Development Agency

- EDA loans usually range $1-5 million dollars.
- Are usually long-term loans ranging from 20 to 30 years.
- Interest rates are usually well below the prime rate.
- The firm should be considered a growth industry firm.
- It will not loan to a firm that can obtain commercial bank loans.
- It can loan up to 85% of the required capital.
- The firm must be located in a high unemployment area and must be labor intensive.

Finance Companies

- Small, independent, private companies designed for the very small borrower of small amounts.
  - One of the most expensive ways to obtain money.

¶693.03

- Their source of capital is from banks.
- Interest rates generally range from 10% to 24% or higher.
- Maximum rates are regulated by the individual states.
- Advantages
  - Small amounts can be borrowed.
  - Funds can be obtained quickly.
  - Funds may be available when one would normally not qualify with a commercial bank.
  - They will take greater risks because they charge higher rates.
- Disadvantages
  - The amount of funds obtained may not be adequate.
  - The interest is in the highest range.
  - Many times the borrower will need a cosigner.

Friends

- Advantages
  - Quick source of cash.
  - Minimum of paperwork involved.
  - A friend may be willing to lend for purposes that general lenders would not consider.
  - Loan may be obtained at little or no interest.
- Disadvantages
  - Friends will resent it if you don't repay the loan.
  - Puts stress on your relationship with friends.
  - Often causes uneasiness when you are around friends with whom you owe money.

Insurance Companies

- Easy to obtain.
- Usually no maximum maturity on the loan.
- Will lend up to about 95% of the cash surrender value in the policy.
- Interest rates are low, usually about 6% to 8%.
- No reasons required to secure the loan.
- Interest is usually charged at a flat rate on the unpaid balance of the loan.

Investment Groups

- Many cash rich individuals such as doctors, lawyers, and executives often join together and form investment groups.
- These groups are sometimes hard to work with, or sometimes easy to work with. It just depends on the individuals that are involved.
- Often they take the attitude that they want to control the whole situation, since they have "put up" the money.
- Sometimes they are not involved.

Leasing Companies

- Uses:
    - When flexibility is needed.
    - When the risk of obsolescence is great.
    - When off balance sheet financing is desired.
    - When convenience is an important consideration.
    - When interest costs are not important.
    - When equipment is not available for direct purchase.

Minority Enterprise Small Business Investment Companies (MESBIC)

- SBA licensed specialized type of SBIC helps small businesses owned and managed by socially or economically disadvantaged firms.
- Assists members of minority groups who want to start their own small businesses or expand existing ones.
- SBA has combined its own programs with those of private industry, banks, local communities and other Federal agencies.

For information contact:

American Association of Minority Enterprise

Small Business Investment Companies

1413 K Street, N.W.

Washington, D.C. 20005

Mortgage Companies

- Mortgage companies will lend funds against a house on a second mortgage.
- Advantages:
    - One can generally borrow up to about 85% of the equity in the house.
    - Generally a quick way to raise funds.
    - Repayment can be spread over a number of years such as 2 to 10.
- Disadvantages:
    - Cost can easily run 2 or 3 times as much as from a more conventional source.
    - Mismatching of purpose with life of loan results in an expensive financing choice.
    - Leads to unsound borrowing methods.
    - Can be complex agreement.
    - Funds generally will be limited in amount.

Pawnbrokers

The pawnbroker will generally loan only 50% to 60% of the auction value of the asset. Redemptions are usually expected within 30 to 60 days or the property will be offered for sale.

¶693.03

- Advantages:
  - — Quick and easy transactions.
  - — No signed note or complex paperwork.
  - — Money obtained immediately.
- Disadvantages:
  - — Interest rates are usually the highest possible.
  - — One does not have the use of the asset during the term of the loan.
  - — One can borrow only a fraction of the auction value of the asset placed as collateral.

Small Business Investment Companies (SBIC)

- Provide growth capital to established businesses.
- SBIC's are privately capitalized and obtain financial assistance from the SBA.
- Write Office of SBIC Operations, Small Business Administration, 1441 Street, N.W., Washington, D.C. 20416.
- Write The National Association of Small Business Investment Companies, 618 Washington Building, Washington, D.C. 20005. Ask for membership directory.

Suppliers—Trade Credit

- Trade credit is the credit extended by suppliers' invoice terms. These may be generally thought of initially as free funds.
- Trade credit grows natually as the business grows.

.04 Automation of the Loan Process

The loan process at regional and national banks is becoming more automated. Banks are using autodecisioning in two primary ways—credit scoring and automatic loan decisions. Loan applicants should seek to know and understand this process.

Credit Scoring—The process in which the computer calculates an applicant's credit worthiness.

Auto Decisions—Where a bank bases loan approvals or rejections "solely" on the applicants credit score.

Generally, the smaller the loan, the more automated will be the loan decision.

Advantages

- The automated process can allow lenders to quickly offer loan decisions.
- The automated process means lending decisions become objective, eliminating possible subjective bias such as race or sexism.

.05 Loan Application Information

Checklist

- Date
- Business name
- Company history
- Contact

- Phone
- Purpose of loan
- Long-term or short-term need
- Type of loan
- Potential sources of lenders
- Loan amount
- Desired take down (amounts and dates the money is to be provided)
- Desired term of loan
- Desired interest rate
- Loan cost considerations
- Collateral
- Guarantor
- Contingent guarantor
- Repayment schedule
- Source of repayment
- Contingency repayment plan
- Potential lender restrictions
- Owner/management team resumes
- Owner/management team personal financials
- Insurance summary on key personnel
- Provide business financials for latest 3 to 5 periods on:
  — Balance sheet
  — Income statement
  — Cash flow statement
  — Working capital analysis
  — Details on debt structure
- Forcasts and projections
- Major customers
- Major suppliers
- Fixed asset details, conditions and descriptions
- Inventory details
- Production and labor information
- Industry and competition data
- Company strengths and weaknesses
- Future plans and goals
- Detail credit history of major financing

Details Regarding Request for Funds for Growth

- The opportunity that exists
- Loan amount needed
- Amounts to be provided by equity
- Best, expected and worst case scenarios
- What risks are associated with the opportunity

.07 Small Business Administration

Business of SBA—Overview (see ¶ 501 for detailed information)

To help people get into business and to stay in business. The Agency provides the small business community with financial assistance, management counseling and training. The Agency makes special efforts to assist women, minorities, the handicapped and veterans in business. The agency has about 3,700 permanent employees and more than 100 offices across the nation. SBA has delegated decision-making authority to its field offices in most of the program areas.

Small Business Defined

- SBA generally defines a small business as one which is independently owned and operated and is not dominant in its field.

Eligibility

- Most small, independent businesses are eligible for SBA assistance.

Regular Business Loans

- Most SBA loans are made by private lenders and then guaranteed by the Agency.
- Maturity may be up to 25 years.
- The average size of a guaranteed business loan is $175,000 and the average maturity is about eight years.

How to Apply for a Loan to SBA

- For new businesses:
  - Prepare current personal financial statements.
  - Prepare a detailed projection of earnings for the first year of operations.
  - Estimate how much the owners can invest in the business and how much will need to be borrowed.
  - List collateral offered as security for the loan, indicating the present market values of each item.
  - Apply at bank for loan and ask for a direct bank loan.
  - If the loan is declined, ask the bank to make the loan under SBA's Loan Guarantee Plan or Immediate Participation Plan.
  - If the bank is interested in an SBA guaranteed or participation loan, ask the banker to contact the SBA for discussion of the application.
  - In most cases of guaranteed or participation loans, SBA will deal directly with the bank.

- For existing businesses:
  - Describe the type of business to be established.
  - Describe experience and management capabilities.
  - State the amount of the loan requested and exact purposes for which it can be used.
  - Provide a current balance sheet listing all assets and liabilities of the business.
  - Provide a profit and loss statement for the current period.
  - List collateral offered as security for the loan, with estimates of the present market value.
  - Provide a current personal financial statement of the owner, or each partner or stockholder owning 20 percent or more of the corporate stock in the business.
  - Apply for a direct bank loan.
  - If the loan is declined, ask the bank to make the loan under SBA's Loan Guarantee Plan or Immediate Participation Plan.
  - If the bank is interested in an SBA guaranteed or participation loan, ask the banker to contact the SBA for discussion of the application.
  - In most cases of guaranteed or participation loans, SBA will deal directly with the bank.

Renegotiating Loan

- Cooperate with the lender.
- Prepare a formal business plan of where the firm intends to head and how it will get there.
- Be open and honest.
- Describe the present situation fully.
- Define the problem and what caused the problem.
- Provide detailed steps for a solution.
- Prepare a written repayment plan.
- Negotiate payments with other creditors.
- Provide cash flow projections that show how repayment can be made.
- Restructure any of the present loan terms—principal, interest amount, repayment term.
- Consider asking for forgiveness of part of the debt.
- Consider asking for payment of principal only for a certain time.
- Seek ways to accelerate cash collections.
- Review assets that may be sold.

Chapter 7
Investments

Concepts . . . . *¶ 701-715*

Investment Instruments . . . . *¶ 717-727*

CONCEPTS

¶ 701 BASICS AND RISK

.01 Basic Considerations of Saving and Investing

Cash Management Objectives

- Evaluate debt level
- Save for retirement
- Eliminate cash flow problems
- Clearly understand flow of expenditures
- Increase income flow
- Establish control over expenditures
- Decrease expenditures
- Expand standard of living
- Purchase wisely
- Have control over interest costs
- Schedule properly for major cash commitments

Education Planning

- To fund all or a portion of children's college education.
- The best time to start funding for college is when the child is in diapers.
- Start early and invest regularly.
- Stocks are the best hedge against rising college costs.
- To provide for grandchildren's education.
- To provide for elementary or secondary private school.
- To properly utilize funds, given time frame.

Financial Concerns

- Growth
- Income
- Safety
- Liquidity
- Tax considerations
- Level of investment risk
- Term

Goals—Investment Goals

One of the most important things an investor should do is to set personal investment goals. To be successful, decide what you are willing to do to achieve your goals. Make goals realistic and tangible. Investment goals must be:

- Specific—Goals must be concrete, not vague.
- Relevant—Be sure the goal leads to where you want to go.
- Measurable—One must be able to measure the goal.
- Attainable—The goal must be realistic both in content and time involved.
- Time Bound—The goal must have a definite time period.
- Short-Medium-Long Range—Medium may be college expenses. Long range may be the retirement lake house.
- Reasonable goals increase odds for long-term success.
- Goals should balance acceptable risk against potential return.
- A goal that avoids all risk will not earn a fair return. It will provide for chronic under-performance.
- In goal planning, temporary price fluctuations don't mean much. What matters is the average growth rate the stock returns over longer periods of time.
- Goals must line up against inflation. If your returns are so risk-free that they only earn four percent and inflation is four percent, you haven't accomplished anything.
- Proper goal planning requires a portfolio that is properly diversified. This can boost your long-term returns. An ideal portfolio reacts to economic changes in opposite ways. It's usually composed of stocks and bonds.
- Long-term goal planning avoids market timing on making big portfolio changes.
- Long-term goal planning strives for value investing.
- Goal planning is not a one time act. It should be adjusted as conditions change.
- Goal planning is an art not a science.
- Potential profits—In goal planning, don't overestimate the size of potential profits.
- Avoid the herd mentality, where everyone is chasing the same "hot" stocks. The investor usually overpays for these stocks.
- P/Es above 50 will rarely keep outperforming the market for long.
- Consider the P/E in relation to the company's growth rate. A company that has a 12-percent growth rate might have a P/E of 24, or be trading at twice its growth rate. A company's stock that is trading at P/Es more than twice their growth rate will rarely sustain that price for long.
- The average range of P/Es for publicly traded companies is 15-20.
- Consistency is the key to long-term profits.

Be More Specific. One way to be sure the goal is specific enough is to *begin* the plan for its achievement. Writing down investment goals is important, as it forces you to clearly define the goals.

¶701.01

- Begin with the end in mind. Define exactly what you wish the investment outcome to be.
- Define where you currently stand in relation to your goal.
- Order the steps to bridge the gap in a logical manner.
- Take action. Without stepping forward with your plan, there is no successful plan.
- Make each step along the way a distinct, clear, and measurable action step.
- Post the written, step-by-step plan in an area where you will be able to see it often as an ongoing reminder.

Goals—Measuring Progress

The key to measuring process is to have clear, distinct, benchmark steps to the action plan and to use measurements that relate to the outcome.

The best way to ensure that the measurement method is related to your outcome is to have a clearly defined outcome.

Measurement is important not only as a yardstick but also as a motivator.

Attainable goals. One way to be sure the goals are attainable is to develop an action plan. The clear, specific action plan is the roadmap to accomplishing the objective.

Relevant goals. Your beliefs and values simply will not allow you to achieve a goal that is not consistent with them. A way to be sure your goal matches your beliefs and values is to be clear as to what those beliefs and values are.

Time constraints. Realistic time constraints come from setting up an acceptable schedule based on the steps in the plan.

Investment Goals—Long Term

- Long-term thinking is best for portfolio development.
- Adopting a long-term strategy requires patience.
- Expect more reasonable returns 9 to 12 percent, not 18 percent.
- Have trust in the basic strength and resilience of the markets.
- Hang on during periods of great turbulence, with the long-term view in mind.
- Short-term thinking for portfolio building is not very reliable.
- Old truths will endure precisely.
- Don't abandon investment practices that have succeeded over long times. There is no reason to abandon discipline. Remain confident with your long-term strategy in the face of short-term challenges.
- Rely on practices that have proven successful over long periods of time.
- Focus on elements that you can control, accept things that are beyond your control.
- Recognize that periodic losses are an inevitable, natural part of investing.
- Stocks have historically delivered the highest returns over any other asset over long periods of time.
- A long-term portfolio should include stocks and bonds.

¶701.01

- Trying to time the market is a mistake. Don't constantly be moving money back and forth from money market and stocks.
- Be rational about risk.
- Buying low and selling high happens more consistently when an investor takes advantage of dollar cost averaging through systematic investing into a mutual fund. When prices are down, your investment is buying more shares. The name of the game with dollar cost averaging is to accumulate shares (this is a good form of avoiding any market timing strategies).
- Consider at least annual rebalancing of your portfolio consistent with your investment goals.
- Diversification is important. Consider index investing as a key part of your portfolio design.
- Realize there is no such thing as risk-free investing.
- Don't try to get rich quick; try to get rich slowly.
- Long-term investing in stock is a process—a learning process where over time we develop a feel for what works best for us personally, until it grows and becomes an art.

Inflation and Investing

Many people are afraid to invest in, say, stocks because of the "risk" involved. But there are many ways to view risk. One risk is the risk of inflation on your money. If you don't put your principal "at risk," it has no way to outgrow inflation. Historically, stocks have been an excellent hedge against inflation. Should you be a "saver" or an "investor?" You are a "saver" if your principal cannot grow. You are an "investor" if the principal is subject to market fluctuations.

Inflation Rates of Consumer Price Index for All Items

1997	2.3
1996	3.0
1995	2.8
1994	2.6
1993	3.0
1992	3.0
1991	4.2
1990	5.4

Source: Statistical Abstract of U.S. 1998

Consider the following in terms of time. How long would it take your money to "double" given the historical returns on the following with inflation at 3.5 percent?

	Historical Rate of Return	# of Years to Double Money	
	1950 - 1997	**Without Inflation**	**With Inflation**
Stocks	13.14	5 years	8 years
Bond	6.05 (10 year)	12 years	28 years
CD's	4.5 (6 month)	16 years	70 years
Money Market	3.8	19 years	231 years

How do you view your "risk" now?

¶701.01

Investment and the Importance of Time—Illustration for Client

Consider there is a target location that you would like to drive to that is 60 miles away and you need to get there in an hour. If you leave immediately and drive at 60 miles per hour, you will reach your location. However, if you wait 10 minutes, you will have to drive at 72 miles an hour to hit the same arrival time. If you wait 30 minutes before you leave, you'll have to drive at 120 miles per hour to hit your target arrival. The same time constraint holds true for investing. The longer you wait, the more precarious your situation and the more difficult the journey. Having a longer timeframe for investing allows you to invest smaller amounts, at reduced risk and achieve more in the long run. In summary, start investing today.

Investment Characteristics

The Patient Investor:

- Uses and depends on logic to dictate important decisions.
- Respects the advantages financial consultants can provide.
- Understands the benefits of regular, disciplined investing.
- Develops long-term financial goals and stays with them.
- Ignores short-term market fluctuations.
- Considers a loss an opportunity to buy.
- Trusts expertise and experience of proven management.

The Restless Trader:

- Succombs to the emotion of the moment.
- Refuses to listen to the wisdom of a financial consultant.
- Fails to explore the benefits of consistent investing by using dollar-cost averaging.
- Waffles between daily and weekly periods of price changes.
- Frets over daily price changes.
- Panics by selling shares at the first indication of a loss.
- Solicits hot tips from friends and neighbors.

Investment Concepts

- There is no such thing as one perfect investment.
- There is no such thing as no risk in investing.
- The greater the risk, the greater the return.
- The greater your rate of return and time horizon, the greater your ability to accumulate wealth and achieve your financial goals.
- Combinations of various investments can decrease risk and yet maintain return.
- The compounding impact of time can make a significant difference in the amount of accumulation.
- The longer the time span you have to reach a goal, the less risk of losing your money.
- "Time" provides a greater opportunity to earn higher rates of return.

¶701.01

- Best time to start investing is now.
- How much an investor wants to be involved in investment process determines type of investment preferred.
- Long-term investing reduces the risk of loss.

Investment Risk

- Risk is fear of losing money
- Risk cannot be completely eliminated
- Interest rate risk
- Financial risk
- Timing or marketability—relates to liquidity
- Political risk—Congress's power to change existing laws
- Purchasing power risk—risk due to inflation

Mistakes in Investing

- All investors make mistakes.
- Thinking you will not make a mistake is a mistake.
- Skipping research. Usually doing adequate homework pays off.
- Regarding the market, thinking, "it's different this time."
- If you fail to understand the market's past, you'll not understand its future.
- Thinking that what happened to the market in the past will not happen again.
- Buying stock just by your feelings.
- Misjudging risk. Sometimes erring too much on the side of caution is a risk.
- Do not exceed 10 percent of the total portfolio in one company's stock.
- Buying too fast.
- Investing too much money in start-up companies.
- We're not as smart in investing as we think we are.
- Being overly confident.
- Losing sight of the big picture and long-term goals.
- To help minimize mistakes ask:
  — Why am I buying or selling now?
  — Have I done due diligence?
  — What are the tax ramifications?
  — Does the trade suit my overall financial strategy?
- Investing in complicated deals, especially that lock you in for a set amount of time.
- Trading too excessively. Trading too often and taking more chances increases the chances for more mistakes.
- To help minimize mistakes regarding an advisor ask:
  — Is the person qualified? Degrees? Accreditations?
  — What is the basic philosophy of the person providing financial advice?

    — Does the advisor have something to gain?

    — Does the advisor know the company and the stock?

    — Does the advisor know my risk tolerance and goals?

- Acting on hot tips—relying on E-message boards.
- Following the crowd.
- Being paralyzed by indecision.

Personal Expenditure Review

- Contributions
- Food
- Entertainment
- Household goods
- Mortgage
- Clothing
- Auto
- Entertainment
- Debt amortization
- Medical
- Insurance

(Source: Finances—Personal Overview, Managing Your Personal Finances, United States Department of Agriculture, Home and Garden Bulletin No. HG-245-2)

Retirement Planning

- Put target goals in writing—plan ahead and use discipline.
- Set a target time to retire.
- Increase saving amount—eliminating a $3 a day habit will provide almost $1100 a year in investment money for something such as IRA.
- Reduce interest on credit cards by eliminating or reducing their use.
- Keep investments growing by leaving them alone.

Savings—A Comparison of Savings and Investing

- Both accumulate wealth
- Differences are determined by
  - The degree of risk
  - The availability of funds for use
  - The rate and stability of return
  - The amount of protection against inflation

¶701.01

Savings and Investment Types

Instrument	Maturity	Risk	Usual minimum balance	Taxable	Characteristics
Passbook accounts	Immediate	None	$5	Yes	Safe and convenient
Certificates of deposit	90 days and up	None	$1,000	Yes	Safe—but locked in form term
I Bonds	10-30 years	None	$50-$10,000	Yes	Safe
EE Series	10 years	None	$25 for $50 bond	Yes, Federal; no State and local	Safe and convenient Long maturity
HH Series	10 years	None	$500		
Corporate	5-30 years	Some	$1,000	Yes	Usually for large investors
Municipal	1-20 Years	Some	1,000	No Federal; some states	Usually for long-term returns
Stocks	Immediate	Low to high	Varies	Yes	Risky
Bills	1 year or less	None	$10,000	Yes	Partial protection against inflation
Notes	1-10 years	None	$1,000	Yes	
Bonds	10-30 years	None	$1,000	Yes	
Mutual Funds	Varies	Low to moderately high	$1,000 sometimes less	Yes, except for tax- exempt bond found	Provides investors opportunity to have expert invest money

Savings—Adjusting for Inflation When Setting Long-Term Goals

Using the table below, multiply the current cost of your goals by the multiplier that matches the time required to reach the target goal. Inflation has averaged about 4 percent over the past 25 years. Example: Your Target goal is $500,000. Your term is 20 years. At an inflation rate of 4 percent, you need $1,095,000 in 20 years to equal today's dollars of $500,000.

Inflation % Rate	Years to Goal						
	5	10	15	20	25	30	35
3%	1.15	1.34	1.56	1.81	2.09	2.43	2.81
4%	1.22	1.48	1.80	2.19	2.67	3.24	3.95
5%	1.28	1.63	2.08	2.65	3.39	4.32	5.52
6%	1.34	1.79	2.40	3.21	4.29	5.74	7.69

Savings—Savings Analysis

- How safe is money in this particular institution and savings plan?
- How convenient is it to make deposits and withdrawals?
- Are there minimum-balance requirements?
- Are there penalties and fees for transactions?
- What special features or services are offered?
- At what rate and how often is interest compounded?
- Are there any tax advantages or disadvantages associated with this saving instrument or institution?

¶701.01

Savings—Increase Savings by Writing Down Long-Term Financial Goals

The simple failure of not writing down financial goals keeps people from attaining their financial goals. A written plan allows one to formulate concrete goals. If you aim at nothing, you will hit it every time. One must develop a plan to reach one's goal. The act of planning itself leads to achieving financial goals.

When setting goals, consider the following:

Be sure the goals are realistic.

Avoid setting goals that are so unrealistic that they can never be realized.

Avoid setting goals that are too vague.

Use input from financial planners or a spouse, but remember, it is your plan. Be sure you are determining what *you* want.

Savings—What Savings Will Grow To

Using the table below, multiply the current savings by the multiplier that matches the time required to reach the target goal. Example: Your savings is $10,000 once a year. Your term is 20 years. At an investment return of 10 percent, your savings will grow to $73,281.

Estimated Annual % Rate	Years to Goal						
	5	10	15	20	25	30	35
6%	1.34	1.79	2.40	3.21	4.29	5.74	7.69
8%	1.47	2.16	3.17	4.66	6.85	10.06	14.79
10%	1.61	2.59	4.18	6.73	10.84	17.45	28.10
12%	1.76	3.11	5.47	9.64	17.00	29.96	52.80

Savings—Reserve Cash for a Crisis

How much money should be set aside for emergencies?

Consider the following guideline:

Two earners in a household where each separately brings home enough money to pay the monthly bills—provide for an emergency fund equal to three months of fixed expenses.

One earner or two incomes needed to make ends meet—provide for an emergency fund equal to six months of fixed expenses.

Keep the emergency fund in a stable, highly liquid form—money-market or short-term bond funds.

Reserve Cash Emergency Fund Worksheet

Expenses	Monthly Cost
1. Transportation (auto-loan payments, insurance, gas, repairs, parking and other commuting costs)	_____
2. Taxes (annual total divided by 12)	_____
3. Housing (rent or mortgage payments, utilities, property taxes and insurance)	_____
4. Food (eating out, eating in)	_____
5. Medical Costs (insurance premiums, expenses, unreimbursed prescription drugs)	_____
6. Loan/Credit Payments	_____
7. Other Fixed Expenses	_____
Total Monthly Expenses (Add lines 1 through 7)	_____
Multiply by 3 or 6 (Multiply by 3 (for two earners) or 6 (for one earner))	X 3 or 6
Total Needed for Emergency Fund =	_____

.02 Investment Funding

To free-up money for potential investments, consider the following cut-the-fat strategies to trim expenses.

Auto

Purchase two year-old cars, instead of brand new. A car loses 40-60 percent of its value in first two years.

Auto Insurance

- Vehicle model and make has significant impact on premium rate.
- Raise deductible.
- Personal injury protection should be dropped, if your health policy already covers.

Auto Maintenance

- Find a reputable mechanic and use regularly.
- Use premium gasoline only occasionally if your car feels sluggish and needs a cleaning.

Clothing

- Use hand-me-downs for toddlers.
- Buy quality.
- Don't buy quantity.
- Don't impulse buy.
- Shop sales.
- Shop manufacture-owned outlets.
- Use a clothing budget.

Credit Cards

- Do not use them.

¶701.02

- If you must use them, pay off the entire balance each month.
- Shop for the lowest interest rate.
- Credit card debt—The average consumer has $5,000 in credit card debt at all times. The average rate is 18 percent interest. If you add no more charges, but only pay the minimum required payment of $75.00 per month (cards differ), you will be debt free in 20 years. Your total interest paid will be $13,511.

Debt

Reduce all debts to free up money. The amount you save on interest will astound you. While you're cleaning up the debt, order a copy of your credit report from one of the three major credit bureaus: Equifax (800-997-2493), Trans Union (800-888-4213), and Experian (800-888-3742). Reports cost around $8. Check for inaccuracies. If you find any, report them. The bureaus are required to investigate and correct them.

Education

- Seek scholarships/grants.
- Work part-time during school.
- Have child continue to live at home one to four years while attending college.
- Non-resident status usually doubles tuition expense.
- Obtain college loans.
- Consider public, rather than private schools.

Entertainment

- Attend community sponsored events.
- Go to matinees.
- Wait 1-2 months and go to "dollar theater."
- Wait 4-6 months and rent videos.

Food

- Make a grocery list before shopping that bases purchases on a weekly food plan.
- Join a discount club.
- Grow a garden.

Gifts

- Purchase gift in off-season.
- Use a gift budget.
- Don't impulse buy.
- Can you give of yourself? Consider non-financial gifts—like babysitting or tennis/golf lessons.

Homeowner Insurance

- Seek all discounts—dead bolt locks, smoke detectors, house/auto policies, etc., may reduce premiums.
- Raise overall deductible.
- Insure for replacement cost not market value.
- Purchase an umbrella policy.

Home Maintenance

- Implement own bug control service at home.
- Cancel maid service.
- Cancel lawn service.

Medical

- Quit smoking—a pack-a-day savings = $1,000 per year.
- Enroll in a health maintenance organization.
- Eat smart.
- Exercise.
- Schedule preventive medical check-ups.
- Purchase generic drugs.

Mortgage

Refinance when lower interest rates are available.

Mortgage Insurance

Seek ways to reduce. Obtain quotes from several carriers. Be sure all the details are correct.

Mortgage Property Taxes

Pay these yourself. Save each month in a savings/investment account that earns interest for you, rather than in a non-interest bearing escrow account at the mortgage company.

Property Taxes

Challenge your property tax assessment. Usually you can have it reduced by doing so. A typical reduction is 10 percent.

Rent

Consider three or six month advance payments. Many landlords will allow discounts on prepaying. Consider this if it will beat other rates of returns you could make on investments.

Restaurants

- Be frugal when you dine out.
- Eat-in more regularly.
- Brown bag your daily lunches.
- Leave credit cards at home. Paying cash will have you reviewing the menu more closely.

Telephone

- Decline all bells and whistles.
- Select the correct long-distance carrier.
- Set up a budget.

¶701.02

Utilities

Install an electric L or D controller. Turn off lights when not in room. Monitor thermostat setting.

Vacations

- Don't take every year.
- Never borrow to go on vacation.
- Travel locally.
- When appropriate, stay with family rather than in a hotel.
- Use vacation packages.
- Drive rather than fly.
- Consider bed and breakfasts.

.03 Savings Institutions

Banks vs. Savings

Money in banks is safe. FDIC insures each deposit of up to $100,000 for each account. But money in banks is not "investing."

Convenience and safety comes at a cost:

- Savings accounts pay about 1.5 percent.
- Interest bearing accounts pay about 1.2 percent.

Inflation is higher than what you will earn at a bank. Depending on what period you are viewing, general inflation is typically three to four percent.

Interest rates. Banks use different methods to calculate interest. Don't look at the "interest rate," look at the APR (Annual Percentage Rate).

Bank fees will eat up any interest you may earn.

Commercial Banks

Commercial banks are convenient, flexible financial institutions that offer a wide variety of services such as savings and checking accounts and loans. Most commercial banks are members of the Federal Deposit Insurance Corporation (FDIC), insuring each account up to $100,000.

Savings and Loan Associations

Savings and loan associations offer a more limited range of financial services. Their main purpose has been to offer savings accounts and to make housing loans. The Federal Deposit Insurance Corporation (FDIC) insures the safety of deposits up to $100,000 at participating savings and loan associations.

Mutual Savings Banks

Mutual savings banks are found in some areas. Their main activities involve savings accounts and mortgage loans. Most are also insured by FDIC.

Credit Unions

One must be a member of an organization in order to use its credit union. The National Credit Union Association (NCUA) insures accounts up to $100,000.

.04 Savings Instruments

Passbook Savings

Passbook savings accounts require a low minimum balance and are convenient to use, but pay low interest rates. The amount of interest income earned depends on not only the stated interest rate, but also on the method by which the interest is compounded and credited to the account. If stated rates are the same at several places, consider using saving institutions that use the day-of-deposit-to-day-of-withdrawal method of computing interest to earn the most on the savings account.

NOW Account

NOW and Super NOW (negotiable order of withdrawal) accounts are checking accounts that earn interest. Super NOW accounts require larger minimum balances and pay higher interest rates than regular NOW accounts. Some NOW accounts charge fees.

Certificates of Deposit

Certificates of deposit, savings certificates, and other time accounts generally pay higher interest rates than passbook accounts. There are many types of certificates requiring different minimum deposits and terms. There is a penalty for early withdrawal of funds.

U.S. Government Savings Bonds

U.S. Government savings bonds are currently issued in Series EE (replacing the old Series E) and Series HH (replacing the old Series H). Both series must be held at least six months before redeeming. Series EE bonds are available in denominations ranging from $50 to $10,000 and are purchased for one-half the amount of their face value. Series EE bonds held five years or more accrue interest calculated semiannually at 85 percent of the average yield on outstanding five-year U.S. Treasury marketable securities. Bonds held less than five years accrue interest on a graduated scale. EE bonds reach full maturity at 10 years. Series HH bonds are no longer purchased with cash; they are sold in exchange for Series E or EE bonds in denominations of $500 or more. These are purchased for the full face amount and pay interest semiannually by check at a flat rate. Accrued interest is exempt from state and local taxes, and federal tax on EE bonds may be deferred until the HH bonds are cashed or reach maturity. Payroll deduction for bonds is available through many employers, making them a convenient way to save. Bonds can also be replaced if lost, stolen, or destroyed.

.05 Investment Instrument Survey

Bonds

A bond represents an agreement between investors and an issuing corporation or municipality. The issuing organization agrees to pay investors a fixed interest rate for a certain period of time. At maturity, the issuer redeems the bond at its face value.

Corporate Bonds

Corporate bonds are sold by private companies for the purpose of borrowing money from a large number of investors. The company must pay the interest and redeem the bonds whether or not it has made a profit. Corporate bonds are traded in the open market and are generally for investors with at least $5,000 to invest. A degree of risk is involved. How prompt a corporation is in making its interest payments will depend on its financial condition. There is also the risk that over time the interest rate paid on the bond will not be as high as the interest rate available on alternative investments.

DRIPs (Dividend Reinvestment Plans)

DRIPs and direct-purchase programs are stock offerings of companies where investors can trade without a broker. See *www.buyandhold.com, www.sharebuilder.com,* and *www.netstockdirect.com* for online centers for DRIP investing. These sites will let you buy stocks through automatic withdrawals from your bank account.

Municipal Bonds

Municipal bonds are issued by cities, states, and other local authorities. Interest paid on municipal bonds comes either from taxes paid to the issuing organization or from revenue received from some special project. The earned interest is exempt from federal income tax. Some risk is involved with the purchase of municipal bonds, as interest payments depend on the financial condition of the issuing municipality. The pre-tax rate of return on these bonds is often less than that for corporate bonds, but the tax advantages make them a good investment for persons in high tax brackets.

Stocks

Stock investments should be expected to make solid long-term returns and with careful selection provide a good rate of return on the investment dollar. Owning stock in a corporation means that you are a part owner of the company and are entitled to a share of the profits.

Earnings may be realized in two ways:

- Profits may be divided among shareholders in the form of dividends. Most corporations pay dividends to shareholders quarterly.
- Profits can be made through an increase in the value of the stock on the open market.

If the market value of the stock goes down, the loss could be considerable. Selecting and managing stock requires study and often the assistance of a good brokerage firm.

U.S. Treasury Bills, Bonds, and Notes

The U.S. Treasury issues bills, bonds, and notes to help finance its debt and raise money. They are sold at a discount and cashed in for the face value at maturity. Bills, bonds, and notes can be bought and sold on the open market. Interest rates fluctuate with market conditions. Since they are backed by the U.S. government, safety is their primary advantage. Those with short maturities also can provide protection against inflation, but on average reflect overall market conditions rather than very high returns. Treasury bills mature in 1 year or less. The minimum denomination available is $10,000. Bonds are available in denominations of $1,000 with maturities from 10 to 30 years. Notes can be purchased in denominations of $1,000 with maturities from 1 to 10 years. Both bonds and notes pay interest at a fixed rate twice a year until maturity.

Mutual Funds

Mutual funds are professionally managed investment portfolios in which individuals can buy shares. The fund uses the money from the sale of these shares to purchase stocks, bonds, and other investments. Profits are returned to shareholders monthly, quarterly, or semiannually in the form of dividends. Investors also earn money through the appreciation of the shares. Mutual funds allow small investors to enjoy the advantages of professional account management and diversification normally reserved for the large investor. Investment objectives vary. When selecting a fund, choose one whose investment goals are compatible with your own. For example, a fund with a growth objective might invest in stocks, sacrificing current income for long-term growth; a money-market fund would purchase bank certificates or government bonds to provide safe short-term income.

Life Insurance

Life insurance has several important purposes:

- To protect survivors against loss of income
- To provide money to pay burial expenses and outstanding debts
- To serve as a form of savings

Insurance is usually purchased on the lives of the persons who provide the household income and household services. Insurance can also build a savings fund for education, retirement, and other purposes.

The amount of the premium for an insurance policy is determined by several factors:

- The size of the benefit that will be paid at death—the larger the face value of the policy, the more it will cost.
- The risk or likelihood of death—for one young and healthy, premiums are lower than for someone older or ill.
- The administrative and sales fees charged by the insurance company.
- The type of policy desired—"pure" insurance costs less than insurance policies with a savings component.

Insurance Types

The three basic types of insurance are term, whole life, and endowment. These types can be combined and modified to provide hybrids to meet the needs of all kinds of households.

Term Insurance

Term insurance pays benefits only at the death of the insured. This is the least expensive type of insurance available. It is most useful when a large amount of coverage is needed or income is low. Term insurance provides coverage for a certain period of time—5 years, 10 years, 20 years—or to a certain age. Most term policies are for 5-year periods, after which they can be renewed for another 5-year period at a higher premium. Term insurance has many variations. A convertible term policy can be converted to a whole life policy without a medical examination. Level term insurance premiums stay the same over the life of the policy, but these premiums are higher than those of straight term in early years and lower in later years. With decreasing term, the amount of coverage decreases each year while the premium stays the same.

Whole Life Insurance

Whole life insurance provides protection over one's life-span without an increase in premiums in later years. Policies that provide protection throughout the life-span are called permanent life insurance. This is in contrast to term insurance, which is temporary, providing coverage for a limited number of years. Whole life insurance has the lowest premium and the smallest cash value accumulation of the permanent type life insurance policies. There are two basic kinds of whole life insurance. Straight life requires one to pay premiums continuing throughout life and limited payment insurance will have premiums scheduled so that the policy is paid up after a certain number of years. Whole life policies build a reserve, which can be cashed in for a lump-sum payment or money can be borrowed against it.

Endowment Insurance

Endowment insurance is an insured savings plan paying the face value of the policy at the end of a specified period, at which time insurance protection ends. The insured receives the face value in a lump sum or by monthly payments. Endowment policies are expensive, but if purchased at a young age, the cash value may exceed the total amount paid. This type of policy is sometimes used for an educational fund or retirement fund.

Universal Life Insurance

Universal life insurance combines a term insurance policy with an interest-earning savings account that is geared to current market rates. The premiums go into a cash-value fund. The cost of the term insurance and fees to the company are deducted from this fund. The remainder of the premium earns interest at a variable rate that is often higher than the fixed rate paid by whole life insurance policies. Universal life policyholders receive yearly statements listing the interest rate they have earned, the amount that has accumulated in their policy, and fees they have been charged. Annual premiums for universal life are not fixed. When needed, premium payments can be taken out of the accumulated cash value. Withdrawals, as well as loans, can be made from the cash-value fund. Interest earned is tax-exempt until the money is withdrawn.

Variable Life Insurance

A variable life insurance policy invests most of the premium payments into investment funds that one selected. The death benefit and the cash value vary with the investment. Joint life and survivorship joint life insurance policies cover two or more persons. These policies can be term or whole life. Joint life pays on the death of the first insured person; survivorship joint life pays on the death of the second. Various family income policies provide monthly payments to the survivors of the insured.

Insurance Savings

For the main purpose of providing income protection for survivors in case of death of the wage earner, term insurance is considered the best buy. It gives the greatest amount of protection at the lowest cost. For persons who would not meet their savings goals without a carefully administered system, whole life, endowment or hybrid insurance may serve a purpose. One should select his insurance plan with care. Often it is cheaper and more profitable in the long run to buy the separate components of the plans and invest elsewhere.

Reasons for Life Insurance

If one's death would cause financial stress for the spouse, children, parents, or anyone else an individual wants to protect, then one should consider purchasing life insurance. A person's stage in the life cycle and the type of household will influence this decision. Single persons living alone or with their parents may have little or no need for life insurance. A two-earner couple may have a moderate need for life insurance, especially if they have a mortgage or other large debts. Households with small children most often have the greatest need for life insurance. Families may also want small amounts of insurance to cover burial expenses for children and other household members or may decide to self-insure for this.

How Much Life Insurance Is Needed

To estimate the amount of life insurance needed, decide what the family's financial needs would be if death were to occur today. Consider how much would have to be spent to pay off medical expenses and debts and to support the family until graduation, marriage, retirement, death, or until family members could become self-sufficient. Consider all necessary expenses, such as:

- Burial expenses.
- Medical expenses not covered by health insurance.
- Probate and estate taxes, if on how long each will need support.

Balance these expenses with the family's current assets and income:

- Savings and investments.
- Social Security.
- Life insurance.
- Pensions.
- Spouse's and dependents' incomes.
- Other assets or income.

The difference between the total expenses and total assets represents an approximate amount of life insurance that one needs. A decision may be made to purchase additional insurance or to increase the investment to make up the difference. Inflation and interest rates will affect the value of the long-term investments.

Insurance Types Overview

Type policy: Term: Level

Period covered: For a stated no. of years such as 1, 5, 20

Cash value: None

Insurance protection: High

Premium: Same until renewal

Coverage: Stays same

Comments: Pure insurance coverage

Type policy: Term: Decreasing

Period covered: For a stated no. of years such as 1, 5, 20

Cash value: None

Insurance protection: High

Premium: Stays same until renewal

¶701.05

Coverage: Decreases

Comments: Least expensive type of insurance

Type policy: Whole Life: Straight

Period covered: Whole life

Cash value: Low

Insurance protection: Moderate

Premium: Stays same

Coverage: Stays same

Type policy: Whole Life: Limited payment

Period covered: Whole life

Cash value: Low

Insurance protection: Moderate

Premium: Stays same

Coverage: Stays same until paid up

Comments: Paid up after certain number of years.

Type policy: Whole Life: Endowment

Period covered: For a stated period of time

Cash value: High

Insurance protection: Low

Premium: Stays same

Coverage: Same until paid up

Comments: Savings accumulation; no insurance protection after policy is paid up.

Type policy: Whole Life: Universal life

Period covered: Varies

Cash value: Low to high

Insurance protection: Low to high

Premium: Varies

Coverage: Varies

Comments: Combines renewable term insurance with a market-rate-interest savings account.

Limited Partnerships—Direct Participation Programs

Advantages

- Limited liability
- Direct participation—cash distributions
- Growth—equity buildup
- Tax benefits—deductions
- Deferral vs. conversion

Disadvantages

- Business risks, loss of principal
- Tax risks, tax law changes, IRS challenges
- Liquidity risks—not a ready market for trading partnership interest

General Partners

- Provide management knowledge and expertise
- Have fiduciary responsibility
- Have unlimited liability

Limited Partners

- Provide capital, not active role in management
- Passive investor
- Limited liability—to contribution guarantee

Abusive Tax Shelters

- Have no real business purpose
- Usually disallowed

Tax Deduction

Tax Reduction

= Tax deduction × Marginal tax rate

Return Analysis

- Cash flow
- Tax deduction
- Capital appreciation
- Safety of investment

Phantom Income to

- Secured creditors
- General creditors
- Limited partners
- General partners

Write-offs

- Usually depreciation (depletion), interest, credits

¶701.05

Limited Partnership Types

Existing Commercial Property

Advantages

- Installment purchase may be arranged with seller
- Lower risk than new property

Disadvantages

- Requires maintenance and upkeep

New Commercial Property

Advantages

- Good appreciation potential

Disadvantages

- Possible phantom income

New Residential Property

Advantages

- Tax deductions for depreciation

Disadvantages

- Accelerated depreciation creates tax preference item
- Possible phantom income

Government-Assisted Housing

Advantages

- No investment interest problem
- Risk of loss of principal is low
- Property vacancy rate low
- High tax write-off

Disadvantages

- Highly leveraged
- Phantom income will occur
- Cash flow minimal
- Appreciation of property is unlikely

Raw Land

Advantages

- Capital gain rates apply
- Potential for appreciation
- No phantom income
- Little management is required

Disadvantages

- Highly speculative

- Investment interest problem
- Minimal tax benefits

Oil and Gas Developmental

Advantages

- Moderate tax write-off
- Sheltered cash flow due to depletion
- Higher probability of being successful than exploratory
- No investment interest

Disadvantages

- Tax preference items
- Large economic gain is not available

Oil and Gas Exploratory

Advantages

- No investment interest
- Opportunity for large economic gain
- Sheltered cash flow due to depletion
- High tax write-off

Disadvantages

- Phantom income possible
- Tax preference items
- High risk of total loss of investment
- No cash flow in early periods

Equipment Leasing

Advantages

- No investment interest problem
- Stable, long-term cash flow

Disadvantages

- Tax preference items result
- Recapture of depreciation
- Phantom income
- If leased equipment becomes obsolete before cash investment is recovered, a loss may occur

Real Estate Investment Trusts (REIT)

Advantages

- An REIT is a company that buys, develops, manages, and sells real estate.
- An REIT trades like a stock on a stock exchange with no minimum purchase requirement; therefore, it's easy to purchase or liquidate.

¶701.05

- An REIT allows investors to invest in a professionally managed portfolio of real estate properties.

- An REIT is a pass-through entity for tax purposes that passes 90 percent of its profits to the investors.

- There are over 300 publicly traded REITs totaling over $300 billion in assets.

  — Equity REITs—invest and own properties

  — Mortgage REITs—invest and own mortgages

  — Hybrid REITs—own properties and mortgages

- REITs can provide the investor with current income dividends and long-term appreciation.

- REITs possess low relative historical volatility.

- An REIT acts similar to a small-cap stock with higher than bond returns of dividends.

- REITs vs. Limited Partnerships

  — Partnerships provide the investor complicated year-end K-1 schedules for tax purposes.

  — REITs provide a single 1099-DIV.

- Mutual funds also specialize in REIT investment and ownership.

- For investors who lack real estate experience but wish to invest in the real estate market.

- Investments are made into hotels and shopping malls, etc.

- Annual returns are typically 10 to 12 percent.

- REITs tend to have a negative correlation to the stock market.

- Some Returns:

REIT 1972-2001	12.5%
S&P Index 1972-2001	12.2%
Bonds 1972-2001	8.9%

- At least 75 percent of the corporation's assets (by IRC provisions) must be invested in real estate, and at least 75 percent of its income must come from rents on mortgage interest.

- Investors should consider real estate when developing a diversified portfolio. Real estate is a great diversifier.

- Real estate stocks (REITS) are an asset class that march to a different drummer. They move out of step with other stocks, even performing well in a down market. This is because real estate firms get most of their income from long-term leases. Also, land and buildings are hard assets that on average grow in value over time.

- Adding REIT reduces a portfolio's volatility.

- No minimum investment requirement.

- REITS are reasonably liquid since their shares trade on major exchanges— which is much more liquid than to buy/sell real estate properties in private markets.

What are Commercial Mortgage Obligations (CMOs)?

Commercial Mortgage Obligations (CMOs) and commercial mortgage backed securities (CMBSs) are debt products, while REITs are equity products. In general, debt instruments have a fixed expiration debt, rate of return, and priority on the income stream. Equity investments have an infinite life and the rate of return varies over time based on the operation's success or failure. There are also no guarantees that the investment will be returned; rather the return of investment is obtained by selling the equity interest in the market place.

What is "Funds From Operations (FFO)"?

Funds From Operations (FFO) is a supplemental measure of a REIT's operating performance. FFO is different from corporate "earnings" as typically reported in the financial press. The National Association of Real Estate Investment Trusts (NAREIT) defines FFO as net income (computed in accordance with generally accepted accounting principles) excluding gains or losses from sales of property or debt restructuring, and adding back depreciation of real estate.

Historically, commercial real estate maintains residual value to a much greater extent than machinery, computers, or other personal property. Therefore, current depreciation used in normal earnings measures overstates the real depreciation of REIT corporate assets. Thus, the company does not require as much cash flow to maintain and replace its physical assets, which may in fact be appreciating. FFO recaptures that cash flow and presents it as part of a REIT's annual performance.

Real Estate Mutual Funds

- Provides strong diversification in your portfolio.
- Mutual fund REITs can specialize in investment and diversification.

Examples:

Columbia Real Estate

Cohen & Steens

Third Avenue Real Estate

Public Storage

Franklin—FRTCX

Phoenix—REITX

Fidelity—FSAVX

Scudder—KTCAX

Wells Fargo—WFHAX

Morgan Stanley—MSITX

Disadvantages

- Liquidity
- Difficulty in selling current shares
- Highly speculative

¶701.05

To learn more about REITs visit internet sites *www.reitnet.com* or *www.advisorinsight.com*.

.07 Investment Earnings Demonstrating Small Gain Difference

$10,000 Investment Growth Earning 10% Compared with 1% Extra Gain

Table illustrates potential return on $10,000 investment at 10% return versus a 1% higher rate of return for given time periods.

Example:

Investment = $10,000
Interest earned = 10%
vs. interest earned = 11% (10% + 1% extra)
Period of growth = 7 years
$10,000 grows to $19,487 at 10% interest
$10,000 grows to $20,762 at 11% interest

Extra gain over 7 years	= $20,762
by obtaining 1% extra	– $19,487
	$1,275

$10,000 Investment Earning 10% Extra Gain per Extra 1% of Interest per Year for Given Periods

Term Years	$10,00 Grows to	$10% Return*	Cumulative Gain	$10,000 at 11%	Extra 1% Gain*	Cumulative Extra 1%
1	$11,000.00	$1,000.00	$1,000.00	$11,100.00	$100.00	$100.00
2	$12,100.00	$1,100.00	$2,100.00	$12,321.00	$121.00	$221.00
3	$13,310.00	$1,210.00	$3,310.00	$13,676.31	$145.31	$366.00
4	$14,641.00	$1,331.00	$4,641.00	$15,180.70	$173.39	$540.00
5	$16,105.10	$1,464.10	$6,105.10	$16,850.58	$205.78	$746.00
6	$17,715.61	$1,610.51	$7,715.61	$18,704.15	$243.05	$988.00
7	$19,487.17	$1,771.56	$9,487.17	$20,761.60	$285.90	$1,275.00
8	$21,435.89	$1,948.72	$11,435.89	$23,045.38	$335.06	$1,609.00
9	$23,579.48	$2,143.59	$13,579.48	$25,580.37	$391.40	$2,001.00
10	$25,937.42	$2,357.95	$15,937.42	$28,394.21	$455.89	$2,457.00
11	$28,531.17	$2,593.74	$18,531.17	$31,517.57	$529.62	$2,987.00
12	$31,384.28	$2,853.12	$21,384.28	$34,984.51	$613.82	$3,601.00
13	$34,522.71	$3,138.43	$24,522.71	$38,832.80	$709.87	$4,310.00
14	$37,974.98	$3,452.27	$27,974.98	$43,104.41	$819.34	$5,129.00
15	$41,772.48	$3,797.50	$31,772.48	$47,845.89	$943.99	$6,074.00
16	$45,949.73	$4,177.25	$35,949.73	$53,108.94	$1,085.80	$7,159.00
17	$50,544.70	$4,594.97	$40,544.70	$58,950.93	$1,247.01	$8,406.00
18	$55,599.17	$5,054.47	$45,499.17	$65,435.53	$1,430.13	$9,837.00
19	$61,159.09	$5,559.92	$51,159.09	$72,633.44	$1,637.99	$11,474.00
20	$67,275.00	$6,115.91	$57,275.00	$80,623.12	$1,873.77	$13,348.00
21	$74,002.50	$6,727.50	$64,002.50	$89,491.66	$2,141.04	$15,490.00
22	$81,402.75	$7,400.25	$71,402.75	$99,335.74	$2,443.83	$17,933.00
23	$89,543.02	$8,140.27	$79,543.02	$110,262.67	$2,786.66	$20,720.00
24	$98,497.33	$8,954.30	$88,497.33	$122,391.57	$3,174.59	$23,895.00
25	$108,347.06	$9,849.73	$98,347.06	$135,854.64	$3,613.34	$27,508.00
26	$119,181.77	$10,834.71	$109,181.77	$150,798.65	$4,109.30	$31,617.00
27	$131,099.94	$11,918.18	$121,099.94	$167,386.50	$4,669.67	$36,286.00
28	$144,209.94	$13,109.99	$134,209.94	$185,799.01	$5,302.52	$41,589.00
29	$158,630.93	$14,420.99	$148,630.93	$206,236.91	$6,016.90	$47,606.00
30	$174,494.02	$15,863.09	$164,494.02	$228,922.97	$6,822.97	$54,429.00
31	$191,943.42	$17,449.40	$181,943.42	$254,104.49	$7,732.12	$62,161.00
32	$211,137.77	$19,194.34	$201,137.77	$282,055.99	$8,757.15	$70,918.00
33	$232,251.54	$21,113.78	$222,251.54	$313,082.14	$9,912.38	$80,830.00
34	$255,476.70	$23,225.15	$245,476.70	$347,521.18	$11,213.88	$92,044.00
35	$281,024.37	$25,547.67	$271,024.37	$385,748.51	$12,679.66	$104,725.00
36	$309,126.81	$28,102.44	$299,126.81	$428,180.85	$14,329.90	$119,054.00
37	$340,039.49	$30,912.68	$330,039.49	$475,280.74	$16,187.21	$135,242.00
38	$374,043.43	$34,003.95	$364,043.43	$527,561.62	$18,276.93	$153,519.00
39	$411,447.78	$37,404.34	$401,447.78	$585,593.40	$20,627.43	$174,145.00
40	$452,592.56	$41,144.78	$442,592.56	$650,008.67	$23,270.50	$197,416.00

* For final year of term

.09 Investment and Growth of Various Instruments

No investment returns are guaranteed, but the following chart provides a reasonable guideline of possible returns given different investment vehicles and risk levels.

The chart illustrates the tremendous potential of higher percent returns and of lengthening time frames.

> ***Example:*** If series "EE" bonds or a similar investment were purchased for $10,000 and earned 7-percent interest, the $10,000 investment would grow to:

For Periods	Value of Investment
22 years	$44,304
24 years	$50,724
26 years	$58,074
28 years	$66,488

Possible Value of $10,000 Investment in Various Instruments

Typical Investment	Possible Return	Value per Given Periods			
		5	7	9	11
Passbook Savings	5%	$12,762.82	$14,071.00	$15,513.28	$17,103.39
Cash Value Life Instr.	6%	$13,382.26	$15,036.30	$16,894.79	$18,982.99
Series E Bonds	7%	$14,025.52	$16,057.81	$18,384.59	$21,048.52
Money Market Instr.	8%	$14,693.28	$17,138.24	$19,990.05	$23,316.39
Govt. Bonds	9%	$15,386.24	$18,280.39	$21,718.03	$25,804.26
Bond Funds	10%	$16,105.10	$19,487.17	$23,579.48	$28,531.17
Treasury Notes	12%	$17,623.42	$22,106.81	$27,730.79	$34,785.50
Fixed Annuities	14%	$19,254.15	$25,022.69	$32,519.49	$42,262.32
Variable Annuities	16%	$21,003.42	$28,262.20	$38,029.61	$51,172.65
Bonds	18%	$22,877.58	$31,854.74	$44,354.54	$61,759.26
Mutual Funds	20%	$24,883.20	$35,831.81	$51,597.80	$74,300.84
Growth Mutual Fund	22%	$27,027.08	$40,227.11	$59,874.03	$89,116.50
Individual Stocks	24%	$29,316.25	$45,076.67	$69,309.88	$106,570.88
Speculatives	26%	$31,757.97	$50,418.95	$80,045.13	$127,079.65
Speculatives	28%	$34,359.74	$56,295.00	$92,233.72	$151,115.73

		14	16	18	20
Passbook Savings	5%	$19,799.32	$21,828.75	$24,066.19	$26,532.98
Cash Value Life Instr.	6%	$22,609.04	$25,403.52	$28,543.39	$32,071.35
Series E Bonds	7%	$25,785.34	$29,521.65	$33,799.32	$38,696.84
Money Market Instr.	8%	$29,371.94	$34,259.43	$39,960.19	$46,609.57
Govt. Bonds	9%	$33,417.27	$39,703.06	$47,171.20	$56,044.11
Bond Funds	10%	$37,974.98	$45,949.73	$55,599.17	$67,275.00
Treasury Notes	12%	$48,871.12	$61,303.94	$76,899.66	$96,462.93
Fixed Annuities	14%	$62,613.49	$81,372.49	$105,751.69	$137,433.40
Variable Annuities	16%	$79,875.18	$107,408.04	$144,625.14	$194,607.59
Bonds	18%	$101,472.44	$141,290.23	$196,732.51	$273,930.35
Mutual Funds	20%	$128,391.85	$184,884.26	$266,233.33	$383,376.00
Growth Mutual Fund	22%	$161,822.02	$240,855.90	$358,489.92	$533,576.40
Individual Stocks	24%	$203,190.59	$312,425.85	$480,385.99	$738,641.50
Speculatives	26%	$254,207.07	$403,579.15	$640,722.26	$1,017,210.66
Speculatives	28%	$316,912.65	$519,229.69	$850,705.92	$1,393,796.57

		22	24	26	28
Passbook Savings	5%	$29,252.61	$32,251.00	$35,556.73	$39,201.29
Cash Value Life Instr.	6%	$36,035.37	$40,489.35	$45,493.83	$51,116.87
Series E Bonds	7%	$44,304.02	$50,723.67	$58,073.53	$66,488.38
Money Market Instr.	8%	$54,365.40	$63,411.81	$73,963.53	$86,271.06
Govt. Bonds	9%	$66,586.00	$79,110.83	$93,991.58	$111,671.40
Bond Funds	10%	$81,402.75	$98,497.33	$119,181.77	$144,209.94
Treasury Notes	12%	$121,003.10	$151,786.29	$190,400.72	$238,838.66
Fixed Annuities	14%	$178,610.39	$232,122.07	$301,665.84	$392,044.93
Variable Annuities	16%	$261,863.98	$352,364.17	$474,141.23	$638,004.44
Bonds	18%	$381,420.61	$531,090.06	$739,489.80	$1,029,665.60
Mutual Funds	20%	$552,061.44	$794,968.47	$1,144,754.60	$1,648,446.62
Growth Mutual Funds	22%	$794,175.12	$1,182,050.24	$1,759,363.58	$2,618,636.75
Individual Stocks	24%	$1,135,735.17	$1,746,306.39	$2,685,120.71	$4,128,641.60
Speculatives	26%	$1,614,923.64	$2,563,852.77	$4,070,372.66	$6,462,123.64
Speculatives	28%	$2,283,596.31	$3,741,444.19	$6,129,982.16	$10,043,362.78

.11 Yields at Various Interest Rates After Taxes and Inflation

Actual Yield on $1,000 Investment after Federal and State Taxes and After Inflation per Given Interest Rate

Example: Investment = $1,000

Interest rate earned = 9%

Federal tax rate = 15%

State tax rate = 3%

Inflation = 4%

Table shows net remaining as follows:

$	1,000.00	
+	90.00	interest
$	1,090.00	
$	– 13.50	15% federal tax ($90 × .15)
$	– 2.70	3% state tax
$	– 40.00	4% inflation
$	1,033.80	net

Effective yield is as follows

$1,033.80 – $1,000 = $33.80 or a yield of 3.38%

Actual Yield on $1,000 Investment After Federal Taxes of 15% After State Taxes of 3% and After 3% to 6% Inflation

Interest Rate	Return	Federal Tax	Federal Tax	State Tax	Inflation	Net	Yield
6%	$60.00	15.00%	$9.00	$1.80	$30.00	$1,019.20	1.92%
6%	$60.00	15.00%	$9.00	$1.80	$40.00	$1,019.20	0.92%
6%	$60.00	15.00%	$9.00	$1.80	$50.00	$999.20	−0.08%
6%	$60.00	15.00%	$9.00	$1.80	$60.00	$989.20	−1.08%
7%	$70.00	15.00%	$10.50	$2.10	$30.00	$1,027.40	2.74%
7%	$70.00	15.00%	$10.50	$2.10	$40.00	$1,017.40	1.74%
7%	$70.00	15.00%	$10.50	$2.10	$50.00	$1,007.40	0.74%
7%	$70.00	15.00%	$10.50	$2.10	$60.00	$997.40	−0.26%
8%	$80.00	15.00%	$12.00	$2.40	$30.00	$1,035.60	3.56%
8%	$80.00	15.00%	$12.00	$2.40	$40.00	$1,025.60	2.56%
8%	$80.00	15.00%	$12.00	$2.40	$50.00	$1,015.60	1.56%
8%	$80.00	15.00%	$12.00	$2.40	$60.00	$1,005.60	0.56%
9%	$90.00	15.00%	$13.50	$2.70	$30.00	$1,043.80	4.38%
9%	$90.00	15.00%	$13.50	$2.70	$40.00	$1,033.80	3.38%
9%	$90.00	15.00%	$13.50	$2.70	$50.00	$1,023.80	2.38%
9%	$90.00	15.00%	$13.50	$2.70	$60.00	$1,013.80	1.38%
10%	$100.00	15.00%	$15.00	$3.00	$30.00	$1,052.00	5.20%
10%	$100.00	15.00%	$15.00	$3.00	$40.00	$1,042.00	4.20%
10%	$100.00	15.00%	$15.00	$3.00	$50.00	$1,032.00	3.20%
10%	$100.00	15.00%	$15.00	$3.00	$60.00	$1,022.00	2.20%
11%	$110.00	15.00%	$16.50	$3.30	$30.00	$1,060.20	6.02%
11%	$110.00	15.00%	$16.50	$3.30	$40.00	$1,050.20	5.02%
11%	$110.00	15.00%	$16.50	$3.30	$50.00	$1,040.20	4.02%
11%	$110.00	15.00%	$16.50	$3.30	$60.00	$1,030.20	3.02%
12%	$120.00	15.00%	$18.00	$3.60	$30.00	$1,068.40	6.84%
12%	$120.00	15.00%	$18.00	$3.60	$40.00	$1,058.40	5.84%
12%	$120.00	15.00%	$18.00	$3.60	$50.00	$1,048.40	4.84%
12%	$120.00	15.00%	$18.00	$3.60	$60.00	$1,038.40	3.84%

Actual Yield on $1,000 Investment After Federal Taxes of 28% After State Taxes of 3% and After 3% to 6% Inflation

Interest Rate	Return	Federal Tax	Federal Tax	State Tax	Inflation	Net	Yield
6%	$60.00	28.00%	$16.80	$1.80	$30.00	$1,011.40	1.14%
6%	$60.00	28.00%	$16.80	$1.80	$40.00	$1,001.40	0.14%
6%	$60.00	28.00%	$16.80	$1.80	$50.00	$991.40	−0.86%
6%	$60.00	28.00%	$16.80	$1.80	$60.00	$981.40	−1.86%
7%	$70.00	28.00%	$19.60	$2.10	$30.00	$1,018.30	1.86%
7%	$70.00	28.00%	$19.60	$2.10	$40.00	$1,008.30	0.83%
7%	$70.00	28.00%	$19.60	$2.10	$50.00	$998.30	−0.17%
7%	$70.00	28.00%	$19.60	$2.10	$60.00	$988.30	−1.17%
8%	$80.00	28.00%	$22.40	$2.40	$30.00	$1,025.20	2.52%
8%	$80.00	28.00%	$22.40	$2.40	$40.00	$1,015.20	1.52%
8%	$80.00	28.00%	$22.40	$2.40	$50.00	$1,005.20	0.52%
8%	$80.00	28.00%	$22.40	$2.40	$60.00	$995.20	−0.48%
9%	$90.00	28.00%	$25.20	$2.70	$30.00	$1,032.10	3.21%
9%	$90.00	28.00%	$25.20	$2.70	$40.00	$1,022.10	2.21%
9%	$90.00	28.00%	$25.20	$2.70	$50.00	$1,012.10	1.21%
9%	$90.00	28.00%	$25.20	$2.70	$60.00	$1,002.10	0.21%
10%	$100.00	28.00%	$28.00	$3.00	$30.00	$1,039.00	3.90%
10%	$100.00	28.00%	$28.00	$3.00	$40.00	$1,029.00	2.90%
10%	$100.00	28.00%	$28.00	$3.00	$50.00	$1,019.00	1.90%
10%	$100.00	28.00%	$28.00	$3.00	$60.00	$1,009.00	0.90%
11%	$110.00	28.00%	$30.80	$3.30	$30.00	$1,045.90	4.59%
11%	$110.00	28.00%	$30.80	$3.30	$40.00	$1,035.90	3.59%
11%	$110.00	28.00%	$30.80	$3.30	$50.00	$1,025.90	2.59%
11%	$110.00	28.00%	$30.80	$3.30	$60.00	$1,015.90	1.59%
12%	$120.00	28.00%	$33.60	$3.60	$30.00	$1,052.80	5.28%
12%	$120.00	28.00%	$33.60	$3.60	$40.00	$1,042.80	4.28%
12%	$120.00	28.00%	$33.60	$3.60	$50.00	$1,032.80	3.28%
12%	$120.00	28.00%	$33.60	$3.60	$60.00	$1,022.80	2.28%

Actual Yield on $1,000 Investment After Federal Taxes of 33% After State Taxes of 3% and After 3% to 6% Inflation

Interest Rate	Return	Federal Tax	Federal Tax	State Tax	Inflation	Net	Yield
6%	$60.00	33.00%	$19.80	$1.80	$30.00	$1,008.40	0.84%
6%	$60.00	33.00%	$19.80	$1.80	$40.00	$998.40	−0.16%
6%	$60.00	33.00%	$19.80	$1.80	$50.00	$988.40	−1.16%
6%	$60.00	33.00%	$19.80	$1.80	$60.00	$978.40	−2.16%
7%	$70.00	33.00%	$23.10	$2.10	$30.00	$1,014.80	1.48%
7%	$70.00	33.00%	$23.10	$2.10	$40.00	$1,004.80	0.48%
7%	$70.00	33.00%	$23.10	$2.10	$50.00	$994.80	−0.52%
7%	$70.00	33.00%	$23.10	$2.10	$60.00	$984.80	−1.52%
8%	$80.00	33.00%	$26.40	$2.40	$30.00	$1,021.20	2.12%
8%	$80.00	33.00%	$26.40	$2.40	$40.00	$1,011.20	1.12%
8%	$80.00	33.00%	$26.40	$2.40	$50.00	$1,001.20	0.12%
8%	$80.00	33.00%	$26.40	$2.40	$60.00	$991.20	−0.88%
9%	$90.00	33.00%	$29.70	$2.70	$30.00	$1,027.60	2.76%
9%	$90.00	33.00%	$29.70	$2.70	$40.00	$1,017.60	1.76%
9%	$90.00	33.00%	$29.70	$2.70	$50.00	$1,007.60	0.76%
9%	$90.00	33.00%	$29.70	$2.70	$60.00	$997.60	−0.24%
10%	$100.00	33.00%	$33.00	$3.00	$30.00	$1,034.00	3.40%
10%	$100.00	33.00%	$33.00	$3.00	$40.00	$1,024.00	2.40%
10%	$100.00	33.00%	$33.00	$3.00	$50.00	$1,014.00	1.40%
10%	$100.00	33.00%	$33.00	$3.00	$60.00	$1,004.00	0.40%
11%	$110.00	33.00%	$36.30	$3.30	$30.00	$1,040.40	4.04%
11%	$110.00	33.00%	$36.30	$3.30	$40.00	$1,030.40	3.04%
11%	$110.00	33.00%	$36.30	$3.30	$50.00	$1,020.40	2.04%
11%	$110.00	33.00%	$36.30	$3.30	$60.00	$1,010.40	1.04%
12%	$120.00	33.00%	$39.60	$3.60	$30.00	$1,045.80	4.68%
12%	$120.00	33.00%	$39.60	$3.60	$40.00	$1,036.80	3.68%
12%	$120.00	33.00%	$39.60	$3.60	$50.00	$1,026.80	2.68%
12%	$120.00	33.00%	$39.60	$3.60	$60.00	$1,016.80	1.68%

.13 Goals and the Investment Required to Reach Them

Investing Annual Amount to Achieve Long-Term Goals

Annual Investment Required at Given Interest Rate to Grow to $100,000 per Specified Period

The sinking fund requirements show how much must be invested at the end of each period to grow to $100,000, given different interest rates.

Example (1): If interest was 7 percent and the term was 10 years, then $7,238 must be deposited at the end of each year to grow to $100,000.

Example (2): To obtain a fund of $250,000, develop a conversion factor for the table values.

If interest were 7 percent and the term were 10 years, then

$7,238 × 2.5 = $18,095 must be deposited at the end of each year to grow to $250,000.

Annual Investment Required at Given Interest Rate to Grow to $100,000 per Specified Period

Term (Yrs.)	Interest Rate			
	2%	3%	4%	5%
1	$100,000.00	$100,000.00	$100,000.00	$100,000.00
2	$49,504.95	$49,261.08	$49,019.61	$48,780.49
3	$32,675.47	$32,353.04	$32,034.85	$31,720.86
4	$24,262.38	$23,902.70	$23,549.00	$23,201.18
5	$19,215.84	$18,835.46	$18,462.71	$18,097.48
6	$15,852.58	$15,459.75	$15,076.19	$14,701.75
7	$13,451.20	$13,050.64	$12,660.96	$12,281.98
8	$11,650.98	$11,245.64	$10,852.78	$10,472.18
9	$10,251.54	$9,843.39	$9,449.30	$9,069.01
10	$9,132.65	$8,723.05	$8,329.09	$7,950.46
11	$8,217.79	$7,807.74	$7,414.90	$7,038.89
12	$7,455.96	$7,046.21	$6,655.22	$6,282.54
13	$6,811.84	$6,402.95	$6,014.37	$5,645.58
14	$6,260.20	$5,852.63	$5,466.90	$5,102.40
15	$5,782.55	$5,376.66	$4,994.11	$4,634.23
16	$5,365.01	$4,961.08	$4,582.00	$4,226.99
17	$4,996.98	$4,595.25	$4,219.85	$3,869.91
18	$4,670.21	$4,270.87	$3,899.33	$3,554.62
19	$4,378.18	$3,981.39	$3,613.86	$3,274.50
20	$4,115.67	$3,721.57	$3,358.18	$3,024.26
21	$3,878.48	$3,487.18	$3,128.01	$2,799.61
22	$3,663.14	$3,274.74	$2,919.88	$2,597.05
23	$3,466.81	$3,081.39	$2,730.91	$2,413.68
24	$3,287.11	$2,904.74	$2,558.68	$2,247.09
25	$3,122.04	$2,742.79	$2,401.20	$2,095.25
26	$2,969.92	$2,593.83	$2,256.74	$1,956.43
27	$2,829.31	$2,456.42	$2,123.85	$1,829.19
28	$2,698.97	$2,329.32	$2,001.30	$1,712.25
29	$2,577.84	$2,211.47	$1,887.99	$1,604.55
30	$2,464.99	$2,101.93	$1,783.01	$1,505.14
31	$2,359.63	$1,999.89	$1,685.54	$1,413.21
32	$2,261.06	$1,904.66	$1,594.86	$1,328.04
33	$2,168.65	$1,815.61	$1,510.36	$1,249.00
34	$2,081.87	$1,732.20	$1,431.48	$1,175.54
35	$2,000.22	$1,653.93	$1,357.73	$1,107.17
36	$1,923.29	$1,580.38	$1,288.69	$1,043.45
37	$1,850.68	$1,511.16	$1,223.96	$983.98
38	$1,782.06	$1,445.93	$1,163.19	$928.42
39	$1,717.11	$1,384.39	$1,106.08	$876.46
40	$1,655.57	$1,326.24	$1,052.35	$827.82

¶701.13

Annual Investment Required at Given Interest Rate to Grow to $100,000 per Specified Period

Term (Yrs.)	Interest Rate				
	6%	7%	8%	9%	10%
1	$100,000.00	$100,000.00	$100,000.00	$100,000.00	$100,000.00
2	$48,543.69	$48,309.18	$48,076.92	$47,846.89	$47,619.05
3	$31,410.98	$31,105.17	$30,803.35	$30,505.48	$30,211.48
4	$22,859.15	$22,522.81	$22,192.08	$21,866.87	$21,547.08
5	$17,739.64	$17,389.07	$17,045.65	$16,709.25	$16,379.75
6	$14,336.26	$13,979.58	$13,631.54	$13,291.98	$12,960.74
7	$11,913.50	$11,555.32	$11,207.24	$10,869.05	$10,540.55
8	$10,103.59	$9,746.78	$9,401.48	$9,067.44	$8,744.40
9	$8,702.22	$8,348.65	$8,007.97	$7,679.88	$7,364.05
10	$7,586.80	$7,237.75	$6,902.95	$6,582.01	$6,274.54
11	$6,679.29	$6,335.69	$6,007.63	$5,694.67	$5,396.31
12	$5,927.70	$5,590.20	$5,269.50	$4,965.07	$4,676.33
13	$5,296.01	$4,965.08	$4,652.18	$4,356.66	$4,077.85
14	$4,758.49	$4,434.49	$4,129.69	$3,843.32	$3,574.62
15	$4,296.28	$3,979.46	$3,682.95	$3,405.89	$3,147.38
16	$3,895.21	$3,585.76	$3,297.69	$3,029.99	$2,781.66
17	$3,544.48	$3,242.52	$2,962.94	$2,704.62	$2,466.41
18	$3,235.65	$2,941.26	$2,670.21	$2,421.23	$2,193.02
19	$2,962.09	$2,675.30	$2,412.76	$2,173.04	$1,954.69
20	$2,718.46	$2,439.29	$2,185.22	$1,954.65	$1,745.96
21	$2,500.45	$2,228.90	$1,983.23	$1,761.66	$1,562.44
22	$2,304.56	$2,040.58	$1,803.21	$1,590.50	$1,400.51
23	$2,127.85	$1,871.39	$1,642.22	$1,438.19	$1,257.18
24	$1,967.90	$1,718.90	$1,497.80	$1,302.26	$1,129.98
25	$1,822.67	$1,581.05	$1,367.88	$1,180.63	$1,016.81
26	$1,690.43	$1,456.10	$1,250.71	$1,071.54	$915.90
27	$1,569.72	$1,342.57	$1,144.81	$973.49	$825.76
28	$1,459.26	$1,239.19	$1,048.89	$885.20	$745.10
29	$1,357.96	$1,144.87	$961.85	$805.57	$672.81
30	$1,264.89	$1,058.64	$882.74	$733.64	$607.92
31	$1,179.22	$979.69	$810.73	$668.56	$549.62
32	$1,100.23	$907.29	$745.08	$609.62	$497.17
33	$1,027.29	$840.81	$685.16	$556.17	$449.94
34	$959.84	$779.67	$630.41	$507.66	$407.37
35	$897.39	$723.40	$580.33	$463.58	$368.97
36	$839.48	$671.53	$534.47	$423.50	$334.31
37	$785.74	$623.68	$492.44	$387.03	$302.99
38	$735.81	$579.51	$453.89	$353.82	$274.69
39	$689.38	$538.68	$418.51	$323.56	$249.10
40	$646.15	$500.91	$386.02	$295.96	$225.94

Annual Investment Required at Given Interest Rate to Grow to $100,000 per Specified Period

Term (Yrs.)	Interest Rate				
	11%	12%	13%	14%	15%
1	$100,000.00	$100,000.00	$100,000.00	$100,000.00	$100,000.00
2	$47,393.36	$47,169.81	$46,948.36	$46,728.97	$46,511.63
3	$29,921.31	$29,634.90	$29,352.20	$29,073.15	$28,797.70
4	$21,232.64	$20,923.44	$20,619.42	$20,320.48	$20,026.54
5	$16,057.03	$15,740.97	$15,431.45	$15,128.35	$14,831.56
6	$12,637.66	$12,322.57	$12,015.32	$11,715.75	$11,423.69
7	$10,221.53	$9,911.77	$9,611.08	$9,319.24	$9,036.04
8	$8,432.11	$8,130.28	$7,838.67	$7,557.00	$7,285.01
9	$7,060.17	$6,767.89	$6,486.89	$6,216.84	$5,957.40
10	$5,980.14	$5,698.42	$5,428.96	$5,171.35	$4,925.21
11	$5,112.10	$4,841.54	$4,584.15	$4,339.43	$4,106.90
12	$4,402.73	$4,143.68	$3,898.61	$3,666.93	$3,448.08
13	$3,815.10	$3,567.72	$3,335.03	$3,116.37	$2,911.05
14	$3,322.82	$3,087.12	$2,866.75	$2,660.91	$2,468.85
15	$2,906.52	$2,682.42	$2,474.18	$2,280.90	$2,101.71
16	$2,551.67	$2,339.00	$2,142.62	$1,961.54	$1,794.77
17	$2,247.15	$2,045.67	$1,860.84	$1,691.54	$1,536.69
18	$1,984.29	$1,793.73	$1,620.09	$1,462.12	$1,318.63
19	$1,756.25	$1,576.30	$1,413.44	$1,266.32	$1,133.64
20	$1,557.56	$1,387.88	$1,235.38	$1,098.60	$976.15
21	$1,383.79	$1,224.01	$1,081.43	$954.49	$841.68
22	$1,231.31	$1,081.05	$947.95	$830.32	$726.58
23	$1,097.12	$956.00	$831.91	$723.08	$627.84
24	$978.72	$846.34	$730.83	$630.28	$542.98
25	$874.02	$750.00	$642.59	$549.84	$469.94
26	$781.26	$665.19	$565.45	$480.00	$406.98
27	$698.92	$590.41	$497.91	$419.29	$352.65
28	$625.71	$524.39	$438.69	$366.45	$305.71
29	$560.55	$466.02	$386.72	$320.42	$265.13
30	$502.46	$414.37	$341.07	$280.28	$230.02
31	$450.63	$368.61	$300.92	$245.26	$199.62
32	$404.33	$328.03	$265.59	$214.68	$173.28
33	$362.94	$292.03	$234.49	$187.96	$150.45
34	$325.91	$260.06	$207.08	$164.60	$130.66
35	$292.75	$231.66	$182.92	$144.18	$113.49
36	$263.04	$206.41	$161.62	$126.31	$98.59
37	$236.42	$183.96	$142.82	$110.68	$85.65
38	$212.54	$163.98	$126.23	$96.99	$74.43
39	$191.11	$146.20	$111.58	$85.01	$64.68
40	$171.87	$130.36	$98.65	$74.51	$56.21

¶701.13

Annual Investment Required at Given Interest Rate to Grow to $100,000 per Specified Period

Term (Yrs.)	Interest Rate				
	16%	17%	18%	19%	20%
1	$100,000.00	$100,000.00	$100,000.00	$100,000.00	$100,000.00
2	$46,296.30	$46,082.95	$45,871.56	$45,662.10	$45,454.55
3	$28,525.79	$28,257.37	$27,992.39	$27,730.79	$27,472.53
4	$19,737.51	$19,453.31	$19,173.87	$18,899.09	$18,628.91
5	$14,540.94	$14,256.39	$13,977.78	$13,705.02	$13,437.97
6	$11,138.99	$10,861.48	$10,591.01	$10,327.43	$10,070.57
7	$8,761.27	$8,494.72	$8,236.20	$7,985.49	$7,742.39
8	$7,022.43	$6,768.99	$6,524.44	$6,288.51	$6,060.94
9	$5,708.25	$5,469.05	$5,239.48	$5,019.22	$4,807.95
10	$4,690.11	$4,465.66	$4,251.46	$4,047.13	$3,852.28
11	$3,886.08	$3,676.48	$3,477.64	$3,289.09	$3,110.38
12	$3,241.47	$3,046.56	$2,862.78	$2,689.60	$2,526.50
13	$2,718.41	$2,537.81	$2,368.62	$2,210.22	$2,062.00
14	$2,289.80	$2,123.02	$1,967.81	$1,823.46	$1,689.31
15	$1,935.75	$1,782.21	$1,640.28	$1,509.19	$1,388.21
16	$1,641.36	$1,500.40	$1,371.01	$1,252.34	$1,143.61
17	$1,395.22	$1,266.16	$1,148.53	$1,041.43	$944.01
18	$1,188.49	$1,070.60	$963.95	$867.56	$780.54
19	$1,014.17	$906.75	$810.28	$723.76	$646.25
20	$866.70	$769.04	$682.00	$604.53	$535.65
21	$741.62	$653.00	$574.64	$505.44	$444.39
22	$635.26	$555.02	$484.63	$422.94	$368.96
23	$544.66	$472.14	$409.02	$354.16	$306.53
24	$467.34	$401.92	$345.43	$296.73	$254.79
25	$401.26	$342.34	$291.88	$248.73	$211.87
26	$344.72	$291.75	$246.75	$208.58	$176.25
27	$296.29	$248.74	$208.67	$174.97	$146.66
28	$254.78	$212.14	$176.53	$146.82	$122.07
29	$219.15	$180.99	$149.38	$123.23	$101.62
30	$188.57	$154.45	$126.43	$103.44	$84.61
31	$162.30	$131.84	$107.03	$86.85	$70.46
32	$139.71	$112.56	$90.62	$72.93	$58.68
33	$120.30	$96.11	$76.74	$61.25	$48.88
34	$103.60	$82.08	$64.99	$51.44	$40.71
35	$89.23	$70.10	$55.05	$43.21	$33.92
36	$76.86	$59.88	$46.63	$36.30	$28.26
37	$66.22	$51.15	$39.50	$30.49	$23.54
38	$57.05	$43.70	$33.46	$25.62	$19.61
39	$49.16	$37.34	$28.35	$21.52	$16.34
40	$42.36	$31.90	$24.02	$18.08	$13.62

Sinking Fund—Reflecting Taxes and Inflation—Monthly

Monthly Investment Required at Given Interest Rate to Grow to $100,000 per Specified Period After Annual Taxes of 15% and Inflation of 5%

The table determines how much to set aside at the end of each month to grow to $100,000 at various interest rates and time periods, given the effects of taxes and inflation.

> *Example:* Interest rate earned = 7%

Term to invest = 10 years

From table, $795/month will grow to $100,000 given the annual deflation effects of 15% taxes and 5% inflation.

Monthly Investment Required at Given Interest Rate to Grow to $100,000 per Specified Period After Annual Taxes of 15% and After Inflation of 5%

Term (Yrs.)	Annual Interest Rate				
	5%	6%	7%	8%	9%
1	$8,362.02	$8,329.51	$8,297.11	$8,264.81	$8,232.60
2	$4,196.69	$4,162.67	$4,128.86	$4,095.24	$4,061.82
3	$2,808.28	$2,773.73	$2,739.48	$2,705.54	$2,671.89
4	$2,114.09	$2,079.26	$2,044.83	$2,010.79	$1,977.16
5	$1,697.59	$1,662.57	$1,628.06	$1,594.04	$1,560.52
6	$1,419.94	$1,384.78	$1,350.23	$1,316.28	$1,282.93
7	$1,221.63	$1,186.36	$1,151.80	$1,117.94	$1,084.78
8	$1,072.90	$1,037.55	$1,003.00	$969.25	$936.29
9	$957.24	$921.80	$887.27	$853.64	$820.91
10	$864.71	$829.21	$794.71	$761.21	$728.70
11	$789.02	$753.45	$718.98	$685.62	$653.35
12	$725.95	$690.32	$655.89	$622.66	$590.63
13	$672.58	$636.89	$602.51	$569.43	$537.64
14	$626.85	$591.11	$556.77	$523.83	$492.28
15	$587.22	$551.42	$517.13	$484.34	$453.04
16	$552.55	$516.70	$482.46	$449.82	$418.76
17	$521.96	$486.06	$451.87	$419.38	$388.57
18	$494.77	$458.83	$424.69	$392.35	$361.79
19	$470.45	$434.46	$400.38	$368.19	$337.88
20	$448.57	$412.53	$378.50	$346.47	$316.41
21	$428.77	$392.69	$358.71	$326.83	$297.02
22	$410.78	$374.65	$340.73	$309.01	$279.45
23	$394.35	$358.18	$324.32	$292.75	$263.44
24	$379.30	$343.09	$309.28	$277.86	$248.80
25	$365.46	$329.20	$295.45	$264.19	$235.38
26	$352.68	$316.38	$282.68	$251.58	$223.02
27	$340.85	$304.51	$270.87	$239.92	$211.61
28	$329.87	$293.48	$259.91	$229.11	$201.05
29	$319.65	$283.22	$249.70	$219.06	$191.25
30	$310.11	$273.64	$240.18	$209.70	$182.13
31	$301.19	$264.68	$231.28	$200.95	$173.63
32	$292.83	$256.28	$222.94	$192.77	$165.69
33	$284.98	$248.39	$215.11	$185.09	$158.26
34	$277.60	$240.97	$207.74	$177.88	$151.30
35	$270.64	$233.96	$200.79	$171.09	$144.75
36	$264.06	$227.35	$194.24	$164.69	$138.60
37	$257.85	$221.09	$188.04	$158.65	$132.80
38	$251.96	$215.17	$182.18	$152.94	$127.33
39	$246.38	$209.54	$176.61	$147.53	$122.16
40	$241.08	$204.20	$171.33	$142.41	$117.28

Monthly Investment Required at Given Interest Rate to Grow to $100,000 per Specified Period After Taxes of 15% and After Inflation of 5%

Term (Yrs.)	Annual Interest Rate					
	10%	11%	12%	13%	14%	15%
1	$8,200.50	$8,168.49	$8,136.58	$8,104.77	$8,073.07	$8,041.45
2	$4,028.61	$3,995.59	$3,962.77	$3,930.15	$3,897.73	$3,865.50
3	$2,638.54	$2,605.49	$2,572.74	$2,540.29	$2,508.14	$2,476.28
4	$1,943.93	$1,911.10	$1,878.67	$1,846.63	$1,814.99	$1,783.74
5	$1,527.51	$1,494.99	$1,462.97	$1,431.44	$1,400.41	$1,369.86
6	$1,250.17	$1,218.02	$1,186.45	$1,155.48	$1,125.10	$1,095.31
7	$1,052.32	$1,020.55	$989.47	$959.09	$929.38	$900.36
8	$904.14	$872.78	$842.20	$812.41	$738.40	$755.16
9	$789.07	$758.13	$728.07	$698.88	$670.57	$643.12
10	$697.19	$666.67	$637.12	$608.55	$580.94	$554.27
11	$622.17	$592.07	$563.05	$535.09	$508.17	$482.30
12	$559.79	$530.12	$501.62	$474.27	$448.06	$422.96
13	$507.13	$477.90	$449.92	$423.18	$397.66	$373.34
14	$462.12	$433.32	$405.86	$379.74	$354.90	$331.34
15	$423.22	$394.85	$367.92	$342.39	$318.25	$295.44
16	$389.28	$361.35	$334.94	$310.01	$286.54	$264.48
17	$359.43	$331.93	$306.04	$281.71	$258.91	$237.59
18	$332.99	$305.92	$280.55	$256.81	$234.67	$214.07
19	$309.42	$282.78	$257.92	$234.77	$213.28	$193.39
20	$288.29	$262.08	$237.72	$215.15	$194.31	$175.12
21	$269.25	$243.47	$219.61	$197.61	$177.40	$158.89
22	$252.01	$226.65	$203.29	$181.87	$162.28	$144.44
23	$236.34	$211.40	$188.54	$167.67	$148.70	$131.51
24	$222.05	$197.53	$175.16	$154.84	$136.47	$119.92
25	$208.96	$184.85	$162.97	$143.19	$125.41	$109.50
26	$196.93	$173.24	$151.84	$132.60	$115.40	$100.09
27	$185.86	$162.58	$141.65	$122.94	$106.31	$91.60
28	$175.63	$152.76	$132.30	$114.11	$98.04	$83.90
29	$166.16	$143.70	$123.70	$106.03	$90.49	$76.92
30	$157.38	$135.31	$115.78	$98.60	$83.60	$70.58
31	$149.21	$127.54	$108.46	$91.78	$77.29	$64.81
32	$141.60	$120.32	$101.69	$85.49	$71.52	$59.54
33	$134.49	$113.61	$95.41	$79.69	$66.21	$54.74
34	$127.85	$107.35	$89.59	$74.34	$61.34	$50.35
35	$121.62	$101.51	$84.18	$69.38	$56.86	$46.34
36	$115.79	$96.05	$79.15	$64.80	$52.73	$42.67
37	$110.31	$90.95	$74.46	$60.55	$48.93	$39.30
38	$105.15	$86.17	$70.08	$56.60	$45.42	$36.22
39	$100.30	$81.68	$66.00	$52.94	$42.18	$33.39
40	$95.72	$77.47	$62.18	$49.54	$39.18	$30.79

Monthly Investment Required at Given Interest Rate to Grow to $100,000 per Specified Period After Annual Taxes of 15% and After Inflation of 5%

Term (Yrs.)	Annual Interest Rate				
	16%	17%	18%	19%	20%
1	$8,009.94	$7,978.53	$7,947.21	$7,916.00	$7,884.88
2	$3,833.48	$3,801.65	$3,770.02	$3,738.58	$3,707.35
3	$2,444.72	$2,413.46	$2,382.49	$2,351.81	$2,321.43
4	$1,752.89	$1,722.43	$1,692.36	$1,662.68	$1,633.38
5	$1,339.81	$1,310.24	$1,281.16	$1,252.56	$1,224.44
6	$1,066.10	$1,037.47	$1,009.41	$981.93	$955.02
7	$872.02	$844.34	$817.33	$790.97	$765.27
8	$727.69	$700.97	$675.00	$649.78	$625.28
9	$616.52	$590.76	$565.83	$541.72	$518.42
10	$528.54	$503.74	$479.84	$456.84	$434.71
11	$457.43	$433.57	$410.69	$388.77	$367.79
12	$398.95	$376.02	$354.14	$333.28	$313.42
13	$350.18	$328.17	$307.26	$287.44	$268.67
14	$309.02	$287.91	$267.96	$249.15	$231.43
15	$273.94	$253.71	$234.70	$216.87	$200.17
16	$243.79	$224.42	$206.32	$189.44	$173.73
17	$217.69	$199.16	$181.95	$165.99	$151.22
18	$194.95	$177.24	$160.89	$145.81	$131.95
19	$175.03	$158.12	$142.60	$128.38	$115.39
20	$157.50	$141.37	$126.65	$113.25	$101.09
21	$142.00	$126.63	$112.68	$100.07	$88.70
22	$128.25	$113.61	$100.41	$88.56	$77.94
23	$116.01	$102.08	$89.60	$78.47	$68.56
24	$105.09	$91.84	$80.05	$69.61	$60.38
25	$95.31	$82.72	$71.60	$61.81	$53.22
26	$86.54	$74.59	$64.10	$54.93	$46.95
27	$78.65	$67.31	$57.43	$48.86	$41.45
28	$71.55	$60.80	$51.50	$43.49	$36.61
29	$65.14	$54.96	$46.21	$38.73	$32.36
30	$59.35	$49.71	$41.49	$34.51	$28.61
31	$54.10	$44.99	$37.27	$30.76	$25.31
32	$49.35	$40.74	$33.49	$27.44	$22.40
33	$45.05	$36.91	$30.11	$24.48	$19.83
34	$41.13	$33.45	$27.09	$21.85	$17.56
35	$37.58	$30.33	$24.37	$19.50	$15.55
36	$34.35	$27.51	$21.93	$17.42	$13.78
37	$31.40	$24.96	$19.75	$15.56	$12.21
38	$28.72	$22.65	$17.78	$13.90	$10.82
39	$26.27	$20.56	$16.02	$12.42	$9.59
40	$21.04	$18.67	$14.43	$11.10	$8.50

Monthly Investment Required at Given Interest Rate to Grow to $100,000 per Specified Period After Annual Taxes of 28% and After Inflation of 5%

Term (Yrs.)	Annual Interest Rate				
	5%	6%	7%	8%	9%
1	$8,386.94	$8,359.34	$8,331.81	$8,304.35	$8,276.96
2	$4,222.84	$4,193.88	$4,165.07	$4,136.40	$4,107.87
3	$2,834.90	$2,805.42	$2,776.16	$2,747.11	$2,718.28
4	$2,141.00	$2,111.20	$2,081.70	$2,052.49	$2,023.56
5	$1,724.71	$1,694.69	$1,665.03	$1,635.73	$1,606.79
6	$1,447.23	$1,417.02	$1,387.25	$1,357.90	$1,328.99
7	$1,249.07	$1,218.70	$1,188.83	$1,159.47	$1,130.61
8	$1,100.48	$1,069.96	$1,040.02	$1,010.65	$981.86
9	$984.94	$954.29	$924.28	$894.91	$866.20
10	$892.54	$861.75	$831.68	$802.33	$773.70
11	$816.96	$786.05	$755.92	$726.59	$698.05
12	$754.01	$722.97	$692.79	$663.48	$635.03
13	$700.75	$669.59	$639.37	$610.08	$581.73
14	$655.13	$623.85	$593.58	$564.32	$536.07
15	$615.61	$584.21	$553.90	$524.67	$496.51
16	$581.04	$549.53	$519.18	$489.97	$461.92
17	$550.56	$518.94	$488.54	$459.37	$431.41
18	$523.48	$491.74	$461.31	$432.16	$404.31
19	$499.26	$467.42	$436.94	$407.83	$380.08
20	$477.48	$445.52	$415.01	$385.93	$358.29
21	$457.78	$425.72	$395.17	$366.13	$338.59
22	$439.89	$407.72	$377.13	$348.12	$320.69
23	$423.57	$391.29	$360.66	$331.69	$304.37
24	$408.62	$376.23	$345.56	$316.63	$289.41
25	$394.87	$362.37	$331.67	$302.77	$275.66
26	$382.19	$349.59	$318.85	$289.99	$262.99
27	$370.46	$337.75	$306.98	$278.15	$251.26
28	$359.58	$326.77	$295.96	$267.17	$240.38
29	$349.46	$316.54	$285.70	$256.94	$230.26
30	$340.02	$307.00	$276.12	$247.40	$220.83
31	$331.20	$298.07	$267.16	$238.48	$212.01
32	$322.94	$289.70	$258.76	$230.11	$203.76
33	$315.19	$281.85	$250.87	$222.26	$196.01
34	$307.90	$274.45	$243.44	$214.87	$188.73
35	$301.04	$267.48	$236.44	$207.91	$181.87
36	$294.56	$260.90	$229.82	$201.33	$175.40
37	$288.44	$254.68	$223.57	$195.11	$169.29
38	$282.65	$248.79	$217.64	$189.22	$163.51
39	$277.17	$243.20	$212.02	$183.64	$158.04
40	$271.96	$237.89	$206.67	$178.33	$152.84

¶701.13

Monthly Investment Required at Given Interest Rate to Grow to $100,000 per Specified Period After Taxes of 28% and After Inflation of 5%

Term (Yrs.)	Annual Interest Rate					
	10%	**11%**	**12%**	**13%**	**14%**	**15%**
1	$8,249.64	$8,222.39	$8,195.22	$8,168.11	$8,141.08	$8,114.12
2	$4,079.49	$4,051.25	$4,023.15	$3,995.20	$3,967.39	$3,939.72
3	$2,689.66	$2,661.26	$2,633.08	$2,605.11	$2,577.35	$2,549.81
4	$1,994.92	$1,966.57	$1,938.50	$1,910.72	$1,883.22	$1,856.01
5	$1,578.21	$1,549.98	$1,522.12	$1,494.61	$1,467.46	$1,440.66
6	$1,300.51	$1,272.46	$1,244.84	$1,217.64	$1,190.87	$1,164.53
7	$1,102.25	$1,074.39	$1,047.04	$1,020.18	$993.82	$967.95
8	$953.64	$925.99	$898.92	$872.41	$846.47	$821.09
9	$838.13	$810.70	$783.92	$757.77	$732.26	$707.38
10	$745.79	$718.59	$692.10	$666.32	$641.24	$616.85
11	$670.29	$643.32	$617.14	$591.72	$567.08	$543.20
12	$607.44	$580.70	$554.82	$529.78	$505.58	$482.20
13	$554.31	$527.81	$502.23	$477.56	$453.80	$430.92
14	$508.81	$482.55	$457.28	$432.99	$409.66	$387.28
15	$469.43	$443.41	$418.44	$394.52	$371.63	$349.76
16	$435.01	$409.23	$384.57	$361.03	$338.57	$317.19
17	$404.67	$379.14	$354.79	$331.62	$309.60	$288.71
18	$377.75	$352.46	$328.42	$305.62	$284.03	$263.62
19	$353.69	$328.64	$304.91	$282.48	$261.32	$241.40
20	$332.08	$307.27	$283.85	$261.78	$241.05	$221.61
21	$312.55	$287.98	$264.87	$243.17	$222.86	$203.89
22	$294.83	$270.50	$247.70	$226.37	$206.47	$187.97
23	$278.67	$254.59	$232.09	$211.12	$191.65	$173.61
24	$263.90	$240.06	$217.86	$197.25	$178.19	$160.61
25	$250.33	$226.73	$207.83	$184.58	$165.93	$148.80
26	$237.82	$214.47	$192.87	$172.98	$154.73	$138.04
27	$226.27	$203.16	$181.86	$162.32	$144.47	$128.22
28	$215.57	$192.69	$171.69	$152.51	$135.05	$119.24
29	$205.63	$182.99	$162.29	$143.45	$126.38	$110.99
30	$196.37	$173.97	$153.56	$135.07	$118.39	$103.42
31	$187.73	$165.57	$145.45	$127.30	$111.00	$96.45
32	$179.65	$157.72	$137.90	$120.09	$104.17	$90.01
33	$172.08	$150.39	$130.86	$113.38	$97.83	$84.07
34	$164.97	$143.51	$124.27	$107.12	$91.94	$78.58
35	$158.29	$137.07	$118.11	$101.29	$86.47	$73.49
36	$151.99	$131.01	$112.33	$95.84	$81.37	$68.77
37	$146.05	$125.30	$106.91	$90.74	$76.62	$64.39
38	$140.45	$119.92	$101.81	$85.96	$72.19	$60.32
39	$135.14	$114.85	$97.02	$81.48	$68.05	$56.53
40	$130.12	$110.06	$92.50	$77.27	$64.17	$53.00

Monthly Investment Required at Given Interest Rate to Grow to $100,000 per Specified Period After Annual Taxes of 28% and After Inflation of 5%

Term (Yrs.)	Annual Interest Rate				
	16%	17%	18%	19%	20%
1	$8,087.23	$8,060.41	$8,033.66	$8,006.98	$7,980.37
2	$3,912.20	$3,884.81	$3,857.57	$3,830.47	$3,803.52
3	$2,522.48	$2,495.36	$2,468.46	$2,441.77	$2,415.29
4	$1,829.08	$1,802.44	$1,776.08	$1,750.00	$1,724.21
5	$1,414.22	$1,388.13	$1,362.39	$1,337.01	$1,311.97
6	$1,138.61	$1,113.12	$1,988.04	$1,063.38	$1,039.14
7	$942.58	$917.69	$893.30	$869.38	$845.95
8	$796.27	$772.01	$748.30	$725.14	$702.52
9	$683.12	$659.48	$636.47	$614.06	$592.25
10	$593.16	$570.16	$547.83	$526.17	$505.17
11	$520.08	$497.70	$476.06	$455.14	$434.95
12	$459.64	$437.89	$416.93	$396.75	$377.34
13	$408.92	$387.79	$367.51	$348.06	$329.43
14	$365.85	$345.33	$325.72	$306.98	$289.12
15	$328.87	$308.97	$290.01	$271.99	$254.87
16	$296.86	$277.55	$259.25	$241.91	$225.53
17	$268.92	$250.21	$232.54	$215.89	$200.22
18	$244.38	$226.25	$209.21	$193.22	$178.25
19	$222.69	$205.14	$188.71	$173.38	$159.08
20	$203.42	$186.44	$170.62	$155.92	$142.28
21	$186.22	$169.80	$154.57	$140.49	$127.49
22	$170.81	$154.94	$140.29	$126.81	$114.43
23	$156.95	$141.62	$127.53	$114.64	$102.86
24	$144.45	$129.64	$116.10	$103.78	$92.58
25	$133.12	$118.83	$105.83	$94.06	$83.42
26	$123.85	$109.06	$96.59	$85.35	$75.25
27	$113.50	$100.20	$88.24	$77.52	$67.94
28	$104.97	$92.16	$80.69	$70.47	$61.39
29	$97.18	$84.84	$73.85	$64.11	$55.51
30	$90.05	$78.16	$67.64	$58.37	$50.23
31	$83.51	$72.07	$62.00	$53.18	$45.48
32	$77.50	$66.50	$56.87	$48.48	$41.20
33	$71.98	$61.40	$52.19	$44.22	$37.35
34	$66.89	$56.72	$47.92	$40.35	$33.86
35	$62.20	$52.43	$44.02	$36.84	$30.72
36	$57.86	$48.48	$40.46	$33.64	$27.87
37	$53.86	$44.85	$37.20	$30.74	$25.30
38	$50.16	$41.52	$34.22	$28.09	$22.97
39	$46.73	$38.44	$31.48	$25.68	$20.87
40	$43.55	$35.61	$28.98	$23.48	$18.96

Sinking Fund

Monthly Multiplier Required at Given Interest Rate to Reach a Sum After Taxes of Given Percent and Inflation of Given Percent per Given Periods

This table determines how much to set aside to reach a given sum.

> **Example:** Investor wants to purchase a new boat in five years for $30,000. He will invest an amount at the end of each month earning 8%. (This rate is reduced by 15% taxes and 5% inflation.) Locate from table, 8% interest and five-year term, for factor of 62.73. The monthly amount to invest is: $30,000 / 62.73 = $478.24

Monthly Multiplier Required at Given Interest Rate After Taxes of 15% and After Inflation of 5%

Term (Yrs.)	Annual Interest Rate				
	5%	6%	7%	8%	9%
1	11.9588	12.0055	12.0524	12.0995	12.1468
2	23.8283	24.0230	24.2198	24.4186	24.6195
3	35.6090	36.0525	36.5033	36.9613	37.4267
4	47.3017	48.0941	48.9039	49.7316	50.5775
5	58.9070	60.1477	61.4229	62.7337	64.0810
6	70.4255	72.2134	74.0614	75.9717	77.9468
7	81.8580	84.2912	86.8204	89.4501	92.1845
8	93.2050	96.3810	99.7012	103.1730	106.8041
9	104.4672	108.4829	112.7049	117.1450	121.8158
10	115.6452	120.5970	125.8327	131.3706	137.2303
11	126.7397	132.7231	139.0857	145.8544	153.0582
12	137.7512	144.8614	152.4652	160.6010	169.3107
13	148.6805	157.0118	165.9723	175.6153	185.9992
14	159.5280	169.1744	179.6083	190.9021	203.1353
15	170.2945	181.3492	193.3744	206.4663	220.7311
16	180.9805	193.5361	207.2719	222.3130	238.7988
17	191.5867	205.7352	221.3019	238.4473	257.3513
18	202.1135	217.9466	235.4659	254.8745	276.4013
19	212.5617	230.1701	249.7650	271.5997	295.9624
20	222.9318	242.4059	264.2005	288.6286	316.0482
21	233.2244	254.6539	278.7737	305.9665	336.6728
22	243.4401	266.9142	293.4860	323.6190	357.8506
23	253.5794	279.1867	308.3387	341.5920	379.5965
24	263.6429	291.4715	323.3331	359.8911	401.9258
25	273.6312	303.7686	338.4706	378.5223	424.8539
26	283.5448	316.0780	353.7524	397.4917	448.3971
27	293.3843	328.3998	369.1802	416.8054	472.5719
28	303.1504	340.7338	384.7551	436.4696	497.3951
29	312.8434	353.0802	400.4786	456.4907	522.8842
30	322.4639	365.4390	416.3521	476.8751	549.0570
31	332.0126	377.8101	432.3771	497.6296	575.9319
32	341.4899	390.1935	448.5550	518.7607	603.5276
33	350.8963	402.5894	464.8873	540.2753	631.8636
34	360.2324	414.9977	481.3754	562.1804	660.9597
35	369.4988	427.4184	498.0208	584.4830	690.8363
36	378.6959	439.8515	514.8251	607.1904	721.5143
37	387.8243	452.2971	531.7896	630.3100	753.0152
38	396.8844	464.7551	548.9161	653.8491	785.3611
39	405.8768	477.2255	566.2059	677.8155	818.5746
40	414.8020	489.7085	583.6608	702.2168	852.6791

¶701.13

Monthly Multiplier Required at Given Interest Rate After Annual Taxes of 15% and After Inflation of 5%

Term (Yrs.)	Annual Interest Rate					
	10%	11%	12%	13%	14%	15%
1	12.1944	12.2422	12.2902	12.3384	12.3869	12.4356
2	24.8225	25.0276	25.2349	25.4449	25.6560	25.8699
3	37.8997	38.3804	38.8690	39.3655	39.8702	40.3831
4	51.4421	52.3259	53.2292	54.1527	55.0968	56.0620
5	65.4661	66.8901	68.3543	69.8598	71.4079	73.0000
6	79.9889	82.1007	84.2848	86.5439	88.8808	91.2984
7	95.0283	97.9863	101.0638	104.2658	107.5981	111.0664
8	110.6025	114.5769	118.7363	123.0902	127.6486	132.4221
9	126.7307	131.9038	137.3501	143.0856	149.1272	155.4929
10	143.4325	149.9995	156.9552	164.3248	172.1356	180.4165
11	160.7284	168.8984	177.6044	186.8852	196.7827	207.3419
12	178.6394	188.6359	199.3533	210.8490	223.1853	236.4297
13	197.1874	209.2493	222.2605	236.3035	251.4684	267.8536
14	216.3951	230.7775	246.3877	263.3415	281.7660	301.8013
15	236.2860	253.2611	271.7998	292.0613	314.2215	338.4754
16	256.8844	276.7424	298.5654	322.5677	348.9887	378.0950
17	278.2154	301.2658	326.7564	354.9718	386.2321	420.8965
18	300.3050	326.8775	356.4487	389.3917	426.1281	467.1355
19	323.1803	353.6258	387.7224	425.9526	468.8658	517.0881
20	346.8693	381.5611	420.6617	464.7879	514.6474	571.0526
21	371.4007	410.7361	455.3552	506.0389	563.6897	629.3511
22	396.8047	441.2059	491.8964	549.8561	616.2251	692.3317
23	423.1122	473.0278	530.3837	596.3989	672.5023	760.3705
24	450.3554	506.2619	570.9208	645.8370	732.7878	833.8737
25	478.5676	540.9709	613.6167	698.3504	797.3671	913.2801
26	507.7832	577.2202	658.5865	754.1305	866.5461	999.0640
27	538.0378	615.0782	705.9513	813.3804	940.6523	1,091.737
28	569.3686	654.6162	755.8386	876.3161	1,020.036	1,191.853
29	601.8137	695.9088	808.3828	943.1667	1,105.075	1,300.010
30	635.4127	739.0339	863.7253	1,014.175	1,196.170	1,416.853
31	670.2068	784.0728	922.0153	1,089.602	1,293.753	1,543.081
32	706.2384	831.1104	983.4096	1,169.720	1,398.287	1,679.446
33	743.5516	880.2355	1,048.073	1,254.822	1,510.266	1,826.763
34	782.1918	931.5406	1,116.181	1,345.218	1,630.221	1,985.911
35	822.2064	985.1225	1,187.916	1,441.238	1,758.720	2,157.841
36	863.6441	1,041.082	1,263.472	1,543.230	1,896.371	2,343.579
37	906.5557	1,099.525	1,343.051	1,651.567	2,043.826	2,544.235
38	950.9935	1,160.562	1,426.869	1,766.643	2,201.783	2,761.006
39	997.0118	1,224.307	1,515.150	1,888.877	2,370.991	2,995.186
40	1,044.666	1,290.881	1,608.133	2,018.715	2,552.250	3,248.174

¶701.13

Monthly Multiplier Required at Given Interest Rate After Annual Taxes of 15% and After Inflation of 5%

Term (Yrs.)	Annual Interest Rate				
	16%	17%	18%	19%	20%
1	12.4845	12.5336	12.5830	12.6326	12.6825
2	26.0860	26.3044	26.5251	26.7481	26.9735
3	40.9044	41.4343	41.9729	42.5204	43.0769
4	57.0487	58.0576	59.0892	60.1440	61.2226
5	74.6375	76.3217	78.0541	79.8383	81.6697
6	93.7999	96.3885	99.0673	101.8400	104.7099
7	114.6769	118.4359	122.3500	126.4264	130.6723
8	137.4218	142.6594	148.1474	153.8988	159.9273
9	162.2017	169.2739	176.7310	184.5958	192.8926
10	189.1987	198.5153	208.4017	218.8960	230.0387
11	218.6112	230.6428	243.4930	257.2223	271.8959
12	250.6553	265.9415	282.3743	300.0473	319.0616
13	285.5664	304.7242	325.4550	347.8990	372.2091
14	323.6011	347.3348	373.1886	401.3674	432.0970
15	365.0389	394.1512	426.0776	461.1119	499.5802
16	410.1842	445.5885	484.6788	527.8691	575.6220
17	459.3687	502.1028	549.6092	602.4621	661.3078
18	512.9539	564.1952	621.5524	685.8108	757.8606
19	571.3335	632.4163	701.2658	778.9428	866.6588
20	634.9364	707.3709	789.5885	883.0064	989.2554
21	704.2300	789.7238	887.4505	999.2849	1,127.4002
22	779.7234	880.2051	995.8820	1,129.2120	1,283.0653
23	861.9715	979.6171	1,116.0246	1,274.3897	1,458.4726
24	951.5784	1,088.8413	1,249.1431	1,436.6080	1,656.1259
25	1,049.2026	1,208.8461	1,396.6389	1,617.8674	1,878.8466
26	1,155.5615	1,340.6958	1,560.0650	1,820.4026	2,129.8139
27	1,271.4365	1,485.5593	1,741.1417	2,046.7111	2,412.6101
28	1,397.6791	1,644.7212	1,941.7755	2,299.5833	2,731.2720
29	1,535.2169	1,819.5928	2,164.0787	2,582.1372	3,090.3481
30	1,685.0606	2,011.7246	2,410.3915	2,897.8568	3,494.9641
31	1,848.3110	2,222.8203	2,683.3072	3,250.6351	3,950.8956
32	2,026.1678	2,454.7517	2,985.6989	3,644.8219	4,464.6505
33	2,219.9379	2,709.5752	3,320.7503	4,085.2777	5,043.5625
34	2,431.0449	2,989.5504	3,691.9886	4,577.4335	5,695.8949
35	2,661.0402	3,297.1598	4,103.3223	5,127.3577	6,430.9595
36	2,911.6136	3,635.1311	4,559.0818	5,741.8311	7,259.2486
37	3,184.6064	4,006.4609	5,064.0653	6,428.4304	8,192.5855
38	3,482.0244	4,414.4418	5,623.5891	7,195.6216	9,244.2929
39	3,806.0530	4,862.6915	6,243.5440	8,052.8643	10,429.3832
40	4,159.0732	5,355.1844	6,930.4566	9,010.7289	11,764.7725

¶701.13

Monthly Multiplier Required at Given Interest Rate After Annual Taxes of 28% and After Inflation of 5%

Term (Yrs.)	Annual Interest Rate				
	5%	6%	7%	8%	9%
1	11.9233	11.9627	12.0022	12.0419	12.0817
2	23.6807	23.8442	24.0092	24.1756	24.3435
3	35.2746	35.6453	36.0210	36.4019	36.7880
4	46.7072	47.3663	48.0376	48.7214	49.4179
5	57.9808	59.0079	60.0590	61.1349	62.2360
6	69.0976	70.5706	72.0853	73.6430	75.2451
7	80.0597	82.0548	84.1163	86.2465	88.4480
8	90.8693	93.4613	96.1522	98.9462	101.8477
9	101.5286	104.7904	108.1928	111.7427	115.4471
10	112.0396	116.0427	120.2383	124.6368	129.2491
11	122.4043	127.2187	132.2886	137.6292	143.2567
12	132.6249	138.3190	144.3437	150.7207	157.4731
13	142.7033	149.3440	156.4037	163.9121	171.9013
14	152.6416	160.2943	168.4685	177.2041	186.5445
15	162.4415	171.1704	180.5381	190.5974	201.4059
16	172.1052	181.9727	192.6125	204.0929	216.4887
17	181.6344	192.7018	204.6918	217.6913	231.7963
18	191.0311	203.3582	216.7758	231.3934	247.3320
19	200.2970	213.9423	228.8648	245.2000	263.0992
20	209.4341	244.4547	240.9585	259.1119	279.1013
21	218.4441	234.8959	253.0571	273.1299	295.3419
22	227.3287	245.2662	265.1606	287.2549	311.8245
23	236.0897	255.5663	277.2689	301.4875	328.5526
24	244.7289	265.7965	289.3820	315.8287	345.5301
25	253.2479	275.9574	301.5000	330.2793	362.7605
26	261.6484	286.0494	313.6228	344.8400	380.2476
27	269.9320	296.0729	325.7505	359.5119	397.9954
28	278.1004	306.0286	337.8830	374.2956	416.0076
29	286.1552	315.9167	350.0204	389.1920	434.2881
30	294.0979	325.7378	362.1626	404.2021	452.8411
31	301.9302	335.4924	374.3097	419.3267	471.6706
32	309.6535	345.1808	386.4616	434.5666	490.7806
33	317.2693	354.8036	398.6185	449.9227	510.1753
34	324.7793	364.3611	410.7801	465.3959	529.8591
35	332.1847	373.8538	422.9467	480.9872	549.8362
36	339.4871	383.2822	435.1181	496.6973	570.1109
37	346.6880	392.6466	447.2944	512.5273	590.6877
38	353.7887	401.9476	459.4755	528.4780	611.5712
39	360.7906	411.1855	471.6615	544.5503	632.7658
40	367.6951	420.3608	483.8524	560.7452	654.2763

Monthly Multiplier Required at Given Interest Rate After Annual Taxes of 28% and After Inflation of 5%

Term (Yrs.)	Annual Interest Rate					
	10%	11%	12%	13%	14%	15%
1	12.1217	12.1619	12.2022	12.2427	12.2834	12.3242
2	24.5129	24.6837	24.8561	25.0300	25.2055	25.3825
3	37.1794	37.5761	37.9784	38.3861	38.7995	39.2187
4	50.1274	50.8501	51.5863	52.3364	53.1005	53.8790
5	63.3631	64.5168	65.6979	66.9071	68.1451	69.4126
6	76.8930	78.5881	80.3319	82.1260	83.9720	85.8715
7	90.7235	93.0757	95.5075	98.0218	100.6219	103.3108
8	104.8614	107.9921	114.2448	114.6248	118.1376	121.7889
9	119.3135	123.3499	127.5646	131.9662	136.5640	141.3677
10	134.0868	139.1622	144.4884	150.0791	155.9487	162.1127
11	149.1884	155.4425	162.0387	168.9976	176.3414	184.0935
12	164.6255	172.2046	180.2385	188.7577	197.7944	207.3835
13	180.4058	189.4627	199.1120	209.3967	220.3631	232.0610
14	196.5367	207.2316	218.6841	230.9538	244.1052	258.2083
15	213.0261	225.5263	238.9806	253.4698	269.0820	285.9132
16	229.8820	244.3624	260.0283	276.9873	295.3576	315.2684
17	247.1125	263.7560	281.8551	301.5510	322.9994	346.3721
18	264.7258	283.7235	304.4898	327.2073	352.0787	379.3286
19	282.7306	304.2819	327.9622	354.0048	382.6700	414.2483
20	301.1356	325.4487	352.3035	381.9944	414.8521	451.2480
21	319.9495	347.2420	377.5457	411.2289	448.7076	490.4517
22	339.1815	369.6802	403.7222	441.7639	484.3236	531.9906
23	358.8410	392.7824	430.8676	473.6571	521.7917	576.0038
24	378.9373	416.5683	459.0177	506.9690	561.2080	622.6388
25	399.4802	441.0581	488.2098	541.7627	602.6740	672.0517
26	420.4797	466.2727	518.4824	578.1041	646.2963	724.4079
27	441.9459	492.2335	549.8754	616.0620	692.1868	779.8829
28	463.8891	518.9625	582.4304	655.7083	740.4637	838.6623
29	486.3199	546.4826	616.1905	697.1182	791.2509	900.9431
30	509.2492	574.8171	651.2000	740.3701	844.6790	966.9337
31	532.6881	603.9901	687.5054	785.5459	900.8854	1,036.855
32	556.6479	634.0265	725.1546	832.7312	960.0145	1,110.941
33	581.1401	664.9518	764.1973	882.0154	1,022.218	1,189.441
34	606.1766	696.7923	804.6852	933.4919	1,087.656	1,272.616
35	631.7696	729.5750	846.6716	987.2581	1,156.497	1,360.747
36	657.9313	763.3280	890.2121	1,043.416	1,228.918	1,454.126
37	684.6743	798.0798	935.3641	1,102.071	1,305.105	1,553.068
38	712.0117	833.8601	982.1874	1,163.336	1,385.253	1,657.904
39	739.9566	870.6992	1,030.743	1,227.327	1,469.569	1,768.985
40	768.5226	908.6286	1,081.097	1,294.163	1,558.270	1,886.682

¶701.13

Monthly Multiplier Required at Given Interest Rate After Annual Taxes of 28% and After Inflation of 5%

Term (Yrs.)	Annual Interest Rate				
	16%	17%	18%	19%	20%
1	12.3652	12.4063	12.4476	12.4891	12.5307
2	25.5611	25.7413	25.9230	26.1064	26.2915
3	39.6436	40.0744	40.5111	40.9539	41.4029
4	54.6722	55.4803	56.3037	57.1427	57.9977
5	70.7104	72.0394	73.4003	74.7940	76.2213
6	87.8262	89.8380	91.9085	94.0398	96.2337
7	106.0919	108.9688	111.9450	115.0243	118.2105
8	125.5848	129.5316	133.6358	137.9044	142.3445
9	146.3873	151.6335	157.1177	162.8515	168.8474
10	168.5874	175.3898	182.5384	190.0522	197.9518
11	192.2789	200.9243	210.0580	219.7102	229.9130
12	217.5622	228.3701	239.8500	252.0475	265.0114
13	244.5441	257.8703	272.1019	287.3060	303.5550
14	273.3387	289.5786	307.0167	325.7497	345.8819
15	304.0679	323.6603	344.8145	367.6663	392.3636
16	336.8616	360.2930	385.7332	413.3696	443.4077
17	371.8586	399.6678	430.0306	463.2016	499.4622
18	409.2067	441.9898	477.9855	517.5353	567.0189
19	449.0641	487.4797	592.9000	576.7774	628.6179
20	491.5992	536.3746	586.1011	641.3714	702.8521
21	536.9921	588.9293	646.9426	711.8006	784.3731
22	585.4346	645.4179	712.8078	788.5922	873.8959
23	637.1317	706.1347	784.1115	872.3210	972.2060
24	692.3020	771.3962	861.3026	963.6136	1,080.1661
25	751.1788	841.5426	944.8673	1,063.1535	1,198.7232
26	814.0113	916.9396	1,035.3320	1,171.6856	1,328.9175
27	881.0651	997.9802	1,133.2662	1,290.0222	1,471.8914
28	952.6239	1,085.0868	1,239.2868	1,419.0491	1,628.8993
29	1,028.9902	1,178.7134	1,354.0614	1,559.7320	1,801.3187
30	1,110.4872	1,279.3482	1,478.3128	1,713.1239	1,990.6623
31	1,197.4595	1,387.5156	1,612.8236	1,880.3729	2,198.5941
32	1,290.2749	1,503.7794	1,758.4409	2,062.7308	2,426.9303
33	1,389.3261	1,628.7458	1,916.0817	2,261.5625	2,677.6824
34	1,495.0319	1,763.0661	2,086.7388	2,478.3563	2,953.0477
35	1,607.8395	1,907.4405	2,271.4868	2,714.7347	3,255.4421
36	1,728.2259	2,062.6215	2,471.4894	2,972.4670	3,587.5188
37	1,856.7004	2,229.4180	2,688.0061	3,253.4823	3,952.1912
38	1,993.8064	2,408.6995	2,922.4004	3,559.8839	4,352.6591
39	2,140.1237	2,601.4005	3,176.1484	3,893.9652	4,792.4358
40	2,296.2711	2,808.5254	3,450.8483	4,258.2266	5,275.3799

¶701.13

.14 Investing After Age 50

Step one—Realize the investing time span for a 50-year-old isn't 5-10 years; it's 30-40 years. A 65-year-old has a 50 percent chance of living to age 85.

- Investments into very liquid money markets or short-term bonds won't exceed inflation by much.
- Stocks will beat inflation by a good margin over the long haul.
- The "over 50" investor is looking for higher returns with low risk.
- Stick with fundamental investment strategies for the 50-year-old.

3 Basic Strategies:

- Diversification: Different types of stocks and bonds.
- Dollar cost averaging.
- Asset allocation—stocks, bonds, and money market funds behave differently under different conditions. Allocation determines what mix provides the optimal blend of risk and reward.

Diversification

Larger stocks versus small caps performance usually runs in cycles, each taking turns somewhat. If you own both, your portfolio benefits. Small stocks represent about 10 percent of U.S. stocks; so a portfolio should, maybe, be composed of only 10-20 percent small caps.

- Stocks generate the best returns over the long haul. So recent retirees should keep a larger percentage of their investments in stocks.
- Consider international stocks into the portfolio. Stock markets around the world move in different directions at different times.
- Some portion of bonds (say 25 percent) in the portfolio will add stability in a stock market turndown. Short-term bonds will hold better than long-term bonds if interest rates rise.
- Buy bonds at different times with different maturities. This spreads risk.

Consider the low risk of buying treasuries. You can buy directly from the government at "treasury direct" at www.treasurydirect.gov.

.15 Risk

Risk Under Uncertainty—Psychology

The greatest investment risk is the risk of doing nothing, and then missing out on superior returns and the concept of your money making you money. Remember, the greatest risk in investing is not taking one. Sometimes the biggest risk you can take is trying to play it too safe.

Risk and Psychology

- To invest more successfully, an investor needs to separate how risky a situation feels from how risky it really is.
- Psychologists say that people chronically mislead themselves about risk by overestimating how often bad things occur and underestimating our powers of recuperation.

¶701.14

- Psychologists say we underestimate risk when we think we are in control.
- To invest more successfully, an investor needs to recognize he is driven partly by feelings and integrate those feelings into his analytical decisions.
- Successful investing is about managing one's reaction to risk.
- How risky something is has nothing to do with how risky we think it is.
- Investing seems riskier to us when we realize we cannot control the market.
- Long-term investment returns have little to do with how the investor feels right now.

Risk Strategy—Volatility

- Volatility is the measure of risk. Stocks have inherent volatility.
- The only way one can reduce risk is by diversification.
- An investor increases risk when he panics and sells during a short-term market meltdown.
- Realize that the stock's long-term gains are a reality.
- The risk of investing in stocks goes down over time.
- Risk is composed of volatility and uncertainty.
- Risk—we do not know the future with 100 percent certainty.
- Standard deviation is the measure of volatility—It's how much a stock's (or portfolio's) short-term return varies around its long-term average.
- Short-term volatility has huge effects on returns that accumulate over the long-term.
- Avoid extreme positions and diversify among several asset classes.
- The larger the stocks' standard deviation, the wider the range of possible future returns. The longer you hold the stock, the closer the extreme highs and lows draw to the median, narrowing the range of possible annualized returns. So the range of possible annualized returns decreases over time, as does the odds of losing money. It's in this sense that stocks become less risky over time.
- An investor typically takes more risks when stock prices are high. They buy on margin and make other borrowings.

Risk Measures

Beta:

- A Beta of 1 is in perfect correlation with the market index that it's related to.
  - If market index increases 10 percent, then the stock portfolio will increase 10 percent.
  - If Beta is 1.10 and market increases 10 percent, then the stock fund will increase 10% × 1.10 = 11%.
- Beta works well for a portfolio of stocks such as a mutual fund. The Beta will explain 90 to 95 percent of the movement of a portfolio of stocks or a mutual fund. But a Beta will only explain 30 to 35 percent of the volatility of an individual stock. This is because Beta is just capturing movement in the market. It does not consider non-market factors such as management, industry, etc. These non-market factors tend to cancel each other out in a portfolio of stocks.

¶701.15

Standard deviation:

- Standard deviation is a measure of volatility purely as a mathematical concept, i.e., without regard to interest rates, the market's perception, etc.

- Standard deviation shows how much the short-term returns of a security (or portfolio) fluctuate around its long-term average, and thus predicts its future behavior.

- The larger the standard deviation, the larger the fluctuation and the more volatile it is.

- If the investor concentrates on too low of a standard deviation, he might be sacrificing stronger returns just to have less fluctuation.

- An investment that's been volatile in the past, will generally be volatile in the near future.

Risk vs. Return vs. Time

Value of investment of $1,000 per given time periods and extra percent of return per increasing risk levels.

Bond Grades	Relative Risk Level	Actual % Return 1988	Percent Increase Per Risk Level	Total Value		Extra $ Return By Increasing Risk Level	
				10 yrs.	20 yrs.	10 yrs.	20 yrs.
State & local Aaa	Lowest	7.35%	—	2,032	4,130	—	—
State & local Baa	Low	7.84%	.49%	2,127	4,525	95	395
Corporate Aaa	High	9.71%	1.87%	2,526	6,382	399	1,857
Corporate Baa	Highest	10.89%	1.18%	2,811	7,904	285	1,522

Risk By Vehicle

Increased Risk of Loss of Capital; Increased Potential for High Return

Highest Risk	Commodities
	Tax shelters
	Precious stones, gold, silver, coins, stamps
	Exploratory drilling
High Risk	Real estate development
	Stock options
	Development drilling, raw land speculation
Medium Risk	Individual stock trading, gas and oil income funds, option
	income programs, managed funds, variable annuities
Low Risk	Convertible bonds, discount bonds
	High quality income securities
	Municipal bonds, long-term government bonds
	Municipal bond funds, fixed annuities
	Treasury bills, treasury notes
	Money market accounts, savings and loan accounts
	Cash value of life insurance
	Passbook savings, insured municipals
	Series EE & HH bonds
Lowest Risk	Checking accounts

¶701.15

Increased Safety of Principal; Increased Risk of Loss of Purchasing Power

Risk by Portfolio Size

Number of Stocks	Risk Ratio
1	6.56
2	3.77
4	2.38
10	1.55
50	1.10
100	1.04
500	1.00

Example: It is 6.56 times risky (risk being the probability of gain versus loss) to invest in one stock as opposed to investing in a portfolio of say, a mutual fund, that has 500 stocks in the portfolio. This is based purely on statistics and is a function of the number of stocks in a portfolio.

.17 Return—Total Portfolio Estimated Return

Use this worksheet to determine an estimate of a portfolio's total return.

Steps				Example
1.	Enter the value of total portfolio at beginning of year			$75,000
2.	Determine net additions or withdrawals to the portfolio during the year.			
Stocks: Additions = Purchases & reinvested dividends			$5500	
Withdrawals = Sales proceeds & cash withdrawals			−1500	
Bonds: Additions = Purchases			2000	
Withdrawals = Interest & Bond sales			−3000	
Mutual Funds: Additions = Purchases & reinvested dividends			2000	
Withdrawals = Sale proceeds & dividends and Capital gain withdrawals taken in cash			−3000	2,000

3. Multiply the result of step 2 by timing factor.

Most transactions Jan – June = .6

Most transactions June – Aug = .5

Most transactions Aug – Dec = .4

Most transactions evenly throughout year = .5 $\qquad$ × .5

$\qquad$ = 1,000

4.	Enter the total value of portfolio at year-end		88,500	
	For CDs, add accrued interest		+ 500	= 89,000
5.	Combining Values:	Step 4	$89,000	
		Plus step 3	+ 1,000	
		Less step 2	− 2,000	= 88,000
6.	Combining Values:	Step 1	75,000	
		Plus step 3	1,000	= 76,000
7.	Step 5 divided by step 6		88,000 / 76,000	= 1.16
8.	**Estimated total return for the year**		(1.16 – 1) × 100	= 16%

(From the result of step 7, subtract 1. Then multiply by 100.)

.19 Risk: Market Decline vs. Time Needed to Recover

What is the time period needed to recover from a market decline? The chart below illustrates the cumulative returns necessary to break even when an investment is down a certain percentage.

If a stock is down 80 percent, it will take a return of 400 percent to get the investment back to even.

The following chart provides the time in years required given the following return rates: 2% return (Money Market), 8% return (junk bond fund), 10% return (conservative equities), 12% return (aggressive equities), 15% return (very aggressive equities), and 20%.

| Initial Investment: $100,000 | | | | Years needed to break-even given returns of— | | | | | |
If investment is down . . .	Current value is equal to:	Amt needed to break even	% Return for break even	2.00%	8.00%	10.00%	12.00%	15.00%	20.00%
10%	$90,000	$10,000	11.1%	5.32	1.36	1.11	0.93	0.75	0.58
20%	$80,000	$20,000	25.0%	11.27	2.90	2.34	1.97	1.60	1.22
30%	$70,000	$30,000	42.9%	18.01	4.63	3.74	3.1	2.55	1.96
40%	$60,000	$40,000	66.7%	25.80	6.64	5.36	4.51	3.65	2.80
50%	$50,000	$50,000	100.0%	35.00	9.01	7.27	6.12	4.96	3.80
60%	$40,000	$60,000	150.0%	46.27	11.91	9.61	8.09	6.56	5.03
70%	$30,000	$70,000	233.3%	60.80	15.64	12.63	10.62	8.61	6.60
80%	$20,000	$80,000	400.0%	81.27	20.91	16.89	14.20	11.52	8.83
90%	$10,000	$90,000	900.0%	116.28	29.92	24.16	20.32	16.48	12.63

¶ 703 COLLEGE FUNDING—MONTHLY INVESTMENT REQUIRED

Monthly Investment Required to Fund College Expense of $100,000 After Annual Taxes of 15% and Inflation of 5%, Given Child's Age

Example (1): If child is 10 years old, monthly investments can be made for 8 years before entering college. If the investment fund is to receive 8% interest, then $969/month should be set aside for a college fund to grow up to $100,000 assuming an annual loss of 15% to taxes and 5% to inflation.

Example (2): Assume same facts as above, except child is 2 years old. At 8% growth, $450/month should be set aside to grow to $100,000 by time child reaches 18 years old.

Example (3): How much should be set aside each month to have a college fund of $50,000 available?

Develop conversion factor for table values:

To have a fund of $50,000 available, where child is 2 years old, and fund is to grow at 8% interest, then $450 × .50 = $225/month should be set aside.

Monthly Investment Required to Fund College Expense After Annual Taxes of 15% and After Inflation of 5% to Grow to $100,000

Child's Age	Term (Yrs.)	Interest Rate				
		5%	6%	7%	8%	9%
17	1	$8,362	$8,330	$8,297	$8,265	$8,233
16	2	$4,197	$4,163	$4,129	$4,095	$4,062
15	3	$2,808	$2,774	$2,739	$2,706	$2,672
14	4	$2,114	$2,079	$2,045	$2,011	$1,977
13	5	$1,698	$1,663	$1,628	$1,594	$1,561
12	6	$1,420	$1,385	$1,350	$1,316	$1,283
11	7	$1,222	$1,186	$1,152	$1,118	$1,085
10	8	$1,073	$1,038	$1,003	$969	$936
9	9	$957	$922	$887	$854	$821
8	10	$865	$829	$795	$761	$729
7	11	$789	$753	$719	$686	$653
6	12	$726	$690	$656	$623	$591
5	13	$673	$637	$603	$569	$538
4	14	$627	$591	$557	$524	$492
3	15	$587	$551	$517	$484	$453
2	16	$553	$517	$482	$450	$419
1	17	$522	$486	$452	$419	$389
0	18	$495	$459	$425	$392	$362

Child's Age	Term (Yrs.)	Interest Rate				
		10%	11%	12%	13%	14%
17	1	$8,200	$8,168	$8,137	$8,105	$8,073
16	2	$4,029	$3,996	$3,963	$3,930	$3,898
15	3	$2,639	$,2,605	$2,573	$2,540	$2,508
14	4	$1,944	$1,911	$1,879	$1,847	$1,815
13	5	$1,528	$1,495	$1,463	$1,431	$1,400
12	6	$1,250	$1,218	$1,186	$1,155	$1,125
11	7	$1,052	$1,021	$989	$959	$929
10	8	$904	$873	$842	$812	$783
9	9	$789	$758	$728	$699	$671
8	10	$697	$667	$637	$609	$581
7	11	$622	$592	$563	$535	$508
6	12	$560	$530	$502	$474	$448
5	13	$507	$478	$450	$423	$398
4	14	$462	$433	$406	$380	$355
3	15	$423	$395	$368	$342	$318
2	16	$389	$361	$335	$310	$287
1	17	$359	$332	$306	$282	$259
0	18	$333	$306	$281	$257	$235

Monthly Investment Required to Fund College Expense After Annual Taxes of 28% and After Inflation of 5% to Grow to $100,000

Child's Age	Term (Yrs.)	Interest Rate				
		5%	6%	7%	8%	9%
17	1	$8,387	$8,359	$8,332	$8,304	$8,277
16	2	$4,223	$4,194	$4,165	$4,136	$4,108
15	3	$2,835	$2,805	$2,776	$2,747	$2,718
14	4	$2,141	$2,111	$2,082	$2,052	$2,024
13	5	$1,725	$1,695	$1,665	$1,636	$1,607
12	6	$1,447	$1,417	$1,387	$1,358	$1,329
11	7	$1,249	$1,219	$1,189	$1,159	$1,131
10	8	$1,100	$1,070	$1,040	$1,011	$982
9	9	$985	$954	$924	$895	$866
8	10	$893	$862	$832	$802	$774
7	11	$817	$786	$756	$727	$698
6	12	$754	$723	$693	$663	$635
5	13	$701	$670	$639	$610	$582
4	14	$655	$624	$594	$564	$536
3	15	$616	$584	$554	$525	$497
2	16	$581	$550	$519	$490	$462
1	17	$551	$519	$489	$459	$431
0	18	$523	$492	$461	$432	$404

Child's Age	Term (Yrs.)	Interest Rate				
		10%	11%	12%	13%	14%
17	1	$8,250	$8,222	$8,195	$8,168	$8,141
16	2	$4,079	$4,051	$4,023	$3,995	$3,967
15	3	$2,690	$2,661	$2,633	$2,605	$2,577
14	4	$1,995	$1,967	$1,938	$1,911	$1,883
13	5	$1,578	$1,550	$1,522	$1,495	$1,467
12	6	$1,301	$1,272	$1,245	$1,218	$1,191
11	7	$1,102	$1,074	$1,047	$1,020	$994
10	8	$954	$926	$899	$872	$846
9	9	$838	$811	$784	$758	$732
8	10	$746	$719	$692	$666	$641
7	11	$670	$643	$617	$592	$567
6	12	$607	$581	$555	$530	$506
5	13	$554	$528	$502	$478	$454
4	14	$509	$483	$457	$433	$410
3	15	$469	$443	$418	$395	$372
2	16	$435	$409	$385	$361	$339
1	17	$405	$379	$355	$332	$310
0	18	$378	$352	$328	$306	$284

¶ 705 DOLLAR COST AVERAGING

.01 Definition

Dollar cost averaging is the technique of making equal investments at fixed intervals for a given period. The average cost per share will always be less than the average price per share, unless the trend continues downward continually.

- When price is down, payments buy more shares.
- The objective is to accumulate shares.
- If the investment is discontinued when market value of accumulated shares is less than cost, a loss will be incurred.

.02 Dollar-Cost Averaging and Timing the Market

The biggest selling points of dollar cost averaging:

- It eliminates the temptation to try to "time" the market purchases and sells.
- It eliminates the need to "time" the market.
- It is an investment strategy that does not consider the "timing" situation.
- Market timing, in the long run, would require consistence and recurring perfection on both the purchase and the sell. You must "get in" and "get out" at the right time.

.03 Illustration

Example: Illustration of systematic purchasing of mutual fund A, whose value continues to grow, and mutual fund B, whose value declines and then increases, but not above the original starting value.

$100/month is invested for 7 months = $700 total cost. Total value is computed at end of 7 months.

Month Recorded	Mutual Fund A		Mutual Fund B	
	Market Price	Number of Shares Purchased	Market Price	Number of Shares Purchased
1	12	8.3	12	8.3
2	12.5	8	10	10
3	14	7.1	8	12.5
4	15	6.6	6	16.7
5	16	6.3	2	50
6	16.5	6.1	8	12.5
7	18	5.6	9	11.1
Totals	104	48	55	121.1

Mutual Fund A Value		Mutual Fund B Value
18 × 48 Shares = $864		9 × 121.1 Shares = $1,090
104/7 = $14.86	Average price per share	55/7 = $7.86
700/48 = $14.58	Average cost per share	700/121.1 = $5.78

If the cost of the shares being purchased were to decrease, a larger number of shares could be purchased, given the "set" investment each month.

The investment goal using dollar cost averaging is to accumulate shares.

The following table provides illustrations of market value fluctuations and shows a fund whose share price drops from $18.00 down to $2.00 in month nine, and then increases to $17.00 over the two-year period.

The amount invested is $2,400 at $100/month. The current value of the portfolio is $5,701.80, for a gain of $3,301.80. This gain is the result of using dollar cost averaging, even though the current value of $17.00/share is less than the initial starting value of $18.00/share.

Dollar Cost Averaging

Month	Market Price Per Share	Number of Shares Purchased	Accumulated Number of Shares	Total Value of Portfolio	Total Amount Invested
\$100 per Month Invested in a Volatile Market					
1	\$18.00	5.56	5.56	\$100.08	\$100.00
2	\$16.00	6.25	11.81	\$188.96	\$200.00
3	\$14.00	7.14	18.95	\$265.30	\$300.00
4	\$12.00	8.33	27.38	\$327.36	\$400.00
5	\$10.00	10.00	37.28	\$372.80	\$500.00
6	\$8.00	12.50	49.78	\$398.24	\$600.00
7	\$6.00	16.67	66.45	\$398.70	\$700.00
8	\$4.00	25.00	91.45	\$365.80	\$800.00
9	\$2.00	50.00	141.45	\$282.90	\$900.00
10	\$3.00	33.33	174.78	\$524.34	\$1,000.00
11	\$4.00	25.00	199.78	\$799.12	\$1,100.00
12	\$5.00	20.00	219.78	\$1,098.90	\$1,200.00
13	\$6.00	16.67	236.45	\$1,418.70	\$1,300.00
14	\$7.00	14.29	250.74	\$1,755.18	\$1,400.00
15	\$8.00	12.50	263.24	\$2,105.92	\$1,500.00
16	\$9.00	11.11	274.35	\$2,469.15	\$1,600.00
17	\$10.00	10.00	284.35	\$2,843.50	\$1,700.00
18	\$11.00	9.09	293.44	\$3,227.84	\$1,800.00
19	\$12.00	8.33	301.77	\$3,621.24	\$1,900.00
20	\$13.00	7.69	309.46	\$4,022.98	\$2,000.00
21	\$14.00	7.14	316.60	\$4,432.40	\$2,100.00
22	\$15.00	6.67	323.27	\$4,849.05	\$2,200.00
23	\$16.00	6.25	329.52	\$5,272.32	\$2,300.00
24	\$17.00	5.88	335.40	\$5,701.80	\$2,400.00

Dollar Cost Averaging

Month	Market Price Per Share	Number of Shares Purchased	Accumulated Number of Shares	Total Value of Portfolio	Total Amount Invested
		\$100 per Month Invested in a Volatile Market			
1	\$25.00	4.00	4.00	\$100.00	\$100.00
2	\$23.60	4.24	8.24	\$194.46	\$200.00
3	\$23.43	4.27	12.51	\$293.11	\$300.00
4	\$22.92	4.36	16.87	\$386.66	\$400.00
5	\$21.90	4.57	21.44	\$469.54	\$500.00
6	\$21.77	4.59	26.03	\$566.67	\$600.00
7	\$20.65	4.84	30.87	\$637.47	\$700.00
8	\$19.03	5.25	36.12	\$687.36	\$800.00
9	\$17.63	5.67	41.79	\$736.76	\$900.00
10	\$19.52	5.12	46.91	\$915.68	\$1,000.00
11	\$20.90	4.78	51.69	\$1,080.32	\$1,100.00
12	\$21.27	4.70	56.39	\$1,199.42	\$1,200.00
13	\$22.40	4.46	60.85	\$1,363.04	\$1,300.00
14	\$23.15	4.32	65.17	\$1,508.69	\$1,400.00
15	\$24.39	4.10	69.27	\$1,689.50	\$1,500.00
16	\$24.39	4.10	73.37	\$1,789.49	\$1,600.00
17	\$26.12	3.83	77.20	\$2,016.46	\$1,700.00
18	\$26.37	3.79	80.99	\$2,135.71	\$1,800.00
19	\$26.95	3.71	84.70	\$2,282.67	\$1,900.00
20	\$28.08	3.56	88.26	\$2,478.34	\$2,000.00
21	\$28.40	3.52	91.78	\$2,606.55	\$2,100.00
22	\$29.18	3.43	95.21	\$2,778.23	\$2,200.00
23	\$31.05	3.22	98.43	\$3,065.25	\$2,300.00
24	\$31.61	3.16	101.59	\$3,211.26	\$2,400.00

¶ 707 ESTATE PLANNING

.01 Basic Estate Concepts

Estate planning is a master plan for the disposition of one's assets at death and for lifetime transfers.

- Minimize taxes at death
- Help avoid probate costs and delays
- Provide for timely payment of estate obligations
- Provide for estate liquidity as needed
- Assure that accumulated wealth passes according to owner's wishes
- Limit administration costs
- Execute dispositive documents

Attention to estate planning depends on:

- Amount of liabilities

- Heirs
- Number of family members
- Nature and size of estate

Expenses of Dying

- Death taxes—federal and state
- Funeral expenses, such as burial plot, funeral director fees
- Administrative costs—executor fees, attorney fees, court costs, appraisal costs, insurance, repairs and maintenance of property
- Satisfying creditors and debtors
- Expenses of final illness
- Income taxes

Property Disposition Techniques

- Trust agreement
- Real estate deeds
- Last will and testament
- Lifetime gifts

Estate Shrinkage

- Funeral expense
- Federal estate taxes
- Federal and state income taxes
- Burial plots
- Attorney's fees
- Executor's fees
- Appraisal fees
- Property insurance
- Liquidation costs
- Debts
- Final illness expenses
- Property taxes

.03 Estate Information Worksheet

Name:_____   Date:_____

Employer:_____   Phone:_____

Birthdate:_____   Age:_____

                            Bus. phone:_____

Spouse: _____   Phone: _____

Employer: _____   Bus. phone: _____

Birthdate: _____   Age: _____

Location of will: _____

Attorney: _____

Accountant: _____

Financial Agent: _____

Trust Officer: _____

Life Insurance:

Amount ($)	Insured	Insurance Company
_____	_____	_____
_____	_____	_____
_____	_____	_____

Prior Taxable Gifts:

Date: _____   Amount($): _____

Donee: _____   Taxes Paid: _____

Date: _____   Amount ($): _____

Donee: _____   Taxes Paid: _____

Date: _____   Amount($): _____

Donee: _____   Taxes Paid: _____

Liquidity Need

Income:

Target amount desired   _____

    Less Social Security   _____

    Less: _____

    Less: _____

= Income Needed   _____ (A)

Capital Required to Produce Income (Divide (A) by
rate of return)   _____ (B)

Pay off Mortgage   _____ (C)

Final Expenses (taxes, probate, etc.   _____ (D)

    Other: _____ (E)

    Other: _____ (F)

Total Capital Needed   _____ (G)

(B+C+D+E+F)

Less current liquid assets   _____

Less current life insurance   _____

Liquidity need   _____

.05 Property Ownership

Fee simple—property owned full and outright.

Joint Ownership

- Joint tenancy with rights of survivorship.
  - All joint tenants hold an equal share in the property.
  - When one joint owner dies, the surviving co-owner, by law, succeeds to his interest in the property.
  - A will has no effect on the passage of property at the decedent's death.
  - A joint tenant may convey his interest in the property during life without consent of the other joint tenant.
- Tenancy in common.
  - No right of survivorship exists.
  - Each co-owner may freely dispose of his interest at death or during life.
  - Tenant in common may hold unequal shares.
  - At death, the surviving co-owner takes no automatic additional rights in the property.
  - There can be any number of tenants in common, each owning a fractional share of the whole.
- Tenancy by the entirety.
  - Can only exist between husband and wife.
  - Can only be two owners—each owns 50%.
  - When one spouse dies, the surviving spouse succeeds to full ownership.
  - Property interest cannot be conveyed without the consent of the other.

Community Property States

Arizona, California, Idaho, Louisiana, Nevada, New Mexico, Texas, Washington, Wisconsin

Community Property Issues

- Community property generally will retain its character if the owner moves to a noncommunity state.
- Community property is property acquired during marriage in which each spouse owns a 50-percent interest. It is assumed that property acquired during marriage is the product of effort and consideration of both spouses equally.
- Income earned in community property states is community income.
  - Property acquired prior to marriage remains seperate property.
  - A gift or inheritance to one's spouse after marriage remains seperate property.

How Property Passes at Death

- By law—Example: Jointly owned property with right of survivorship will suceed to joint owner at death

- Dower (in some states)—Wife has right to a certain percent, no matter what the will states
- Dying Intestate (to die without a will)—Property will pass by state law statute
- By Contract—Example: Owner of policy names beneficiary to receive death benefits when insured dies
- By Will—Document details how property is to pass by the owner
- By Gift—Gift taxes have to be paid on credits used

Estate (or Probate) Administration

- Estate administration is the process by which the decedent's affairs are put in order—taxes paid, debts paid, property inventoried, bequests satisfied, etc.
- Objective of Estate Administrators
  - Conserve assets
  - Satisfy creditor claims
  - Pay any taxes owed
  - Distribute net assets to beneficiaries

Estate Concepts

- Probate—the personal representative proves the validity of the will and carries out its designs.
- Spouse election against the will—one cannot disinherit a spouse. If too small a share of the estate is given in the will, the spouse can elect against the will and take the share of the estate guaranteed by the state intestacy laws.
- Per capita—property divided equally among a group of named beneficiaries.
- Per stirpes—a distribution by line of descent.
- Adopted child—generally stands in position of natural child with respect to his mother or mother's blood relatives.
- Posthumous child—child born after a parent's death. Takes full child's share of the estate of the parent.
- Half-brother or half-sister—generally takes share like a natural child.
- Escheat—if no heirs, then property passes to the state.
- After-born children—children born after will is signed to the testator parent usually entitled to a child's intestate share if overlooked by the will.
- Will—has no effect until owner dies.

.07 Wills

States wishes of owner regarding disposition of assets after death (Example: specific assets for specific individuals). The will applies only to the situation at death. Property that is mentioned in the will, but no longer owned, is not affected by the will.

Validity of Will

- Must meet strict legal requirements.
- Person must have reached minimum legal age to make a will (generally, age 18).

- Must be of sound mind at the time the will is signed.
- Will made under fraud or duress will generally be invalidated by the court.
- Generally must be in writing.
- Most states require the will to be signed in the presence of witnesses.
- Holographic will is one written entirely in the testator's own handwriting.
- Noncupative will (oral will)—generally,
  - Must be made during final illness.
  - Witnesses must hear the testator's wishes and convert those wishes to writing within specified number of days.
  - The will must be probated within a specified number of days.

Revocation of Will

- By physical destruction
- By operation of law
- By execution of a later will

Contesting the will—if ruled invalid by the court, state intestacy laws will apply.

Reason to Revise Will

- When survivor's income needs change
- When major changes occur in the testator's property values
- When divorce or marriage occurs
- When one moves to another state
- When a beneficiary predeceases the testator
- If executor, guardian or trustee must be changed

.08 Power of Attorney

Having a will is not of much use to a client who is in a coma, or mentally incompetent. To provide for protection in these situations, a client should have a power of attorney. A statutory durable power of attorney is the most powerful type. It is important to consult an attorney for a drafting specific to the client's needs. The following is an example to illustrate what should be addressed.

Statutory Durable Power of Attorney

Notice: The powers granted by this document are broad and sweeping. They are explained in the durable Power of Attorney Act, Chapter XII, Texas Probate Code. If you have any questions about these powers, obtain competent legal advice. This document does not authorize anyone to make medical and other health-care decisions for you. You may revoke this power of attorney if you later wish to do so.

I, John Charles Wisdom (my social security number being (xxx-xx-xxxx) appoint Tracy Leigh Wisdom (her social security number being (xxx-xx-xxx) residing at xxxx xxxx , as my agent and attorney-in-fact to act for me in any lawful way with respect to the following initialed subjects:

- To grant all of the following powers, initial the line in front of power designated by the letter "N" and ignore the lines in front of the other powers.

- To grant one or more, but fewer than all, of the following powers, initial the line in front of each power you are granting.
- To withhold a power, do not initial the line in front of it. You may, but need not, cross out each power withheld.

Initial

_____(A) real property transactions;

_____(B) tangible personal property transactions;

_____(C) stock and bond transactions;

_____(D) commodity and option transactions;

_____(E) banking and other financial institutions transactions:

_____(F) business operating transactions;

_____(G) insurance and annuity transactions;

_____(H) estate, trust, and other beneficiary transactions;

_____(I) claims and litigation;

_____(J) personal and family maintenance;

_____(K) benefits from social security, Medicare, Medicaid, or other gov't programs

_____(L) retirement plan transactions;

_____(M) tax matters;

_____(N) All of the powers listed (A) through (M).

You need not initial any other lines if you initial line (N).

Unless you direct otherwise above, this Power of Attorney is effective immediately and will continue until it is revoked.

Choose one of the following alternatives by crossing out the alternative not chosen:

You should choose alternative (A) if this power of attorney is to become effective on the date it is executed. If neither (A) nor (B) is crossed out, it will be assumed that you chose alternative (A).

    (A) This power of attorney is not affected by my subsequent disability or incapacity.

    (B) This power of attorney becomes effective upon my disability or incapacity.

I agree that any third party who receives a copy of this document may act under it. Revocation of the durable power of attorney is not effective as to a third party until the third party receives actual notice of the revocation. I agree to indemnify the third party for any claims that arise against the third party because of reliance on this power of attorney.

If any agent named by me dies, becomes legally disabled, resigns or refuses to act, I name the following (each to act alone and successively, in the order named) as successor(s) to that agent: none.

Signed this_____day of July, 20XX

John Charles Wisdom

State of Texas

County of xxxx

This document was acknowledged before me on the _____ day of July, 20XX, by John Charles Wisdom.

Notary Public in and for the State of Texas

My Commission expires: _____

The attorney in fact or agent, by accepting or acting under the appointment, assumes the fiduciary and other legal responsibilities of an agent.

.20 Estate Planning for Business Owners

Two-Man Partnership

- Decision to be made by surviving partner:
  - — Buy interests of heirs
  - — Take heirs in as partners
  - — A buyer of the heirs' interests could become a partner
  - — Sell interest to heirs

Corporation—Closely Held

- Decision to be made at major stockholder's death.
  - — Sell out to heirs
  - — Buy out heirs
  - — Accept the heirs into the business
  - — Accept the purchaser of the heirs' shares into the business
- Estate and heirs are generally interested in income.
- Problems of lack of ready market for shares.
- Shareholders may not themselves be able to afford the purchase price to redeem the shares.
- Logical plan is to have cash available to buy a stockholder's interest when he dies.

.21 Buy-Sell Agreements

The general objective is for surviving owners to buy deceased's interest and continue operating the business.

Cross-Purchase Agreement for Buy-Sell

- A contract entered among the business owners.
- In the event of death, the shareholder agrees to sell the shares to the other owners, and they agree to buy the shares.

- The buy-out price is specifically agreed to as a fixed price or defined by a formula.
- The value must approximate the market value of the business interest.
- The prospective purchaser usually buys life insurance of the prospective seller to have the funds available to make the purchase.
- Number of policies required for a cross-agreement:
- $P = N \times (N - 1)$
- where P = number of policies needed and N = number of shareholders

    Example: If there are 3 shareholders, then 6 policies are required.

$P = 3 \times (3 - 1) = 3 \times 2 = 6$

- Flow of cross-purchase agreement.
    — All principals agree that each will pay for, own, and be the beneficiary of insurance on the life of the other principals.
    — They individually pay premiums.
    — Upon death, the insurance company pays death benefits to the surviving principal.
    — The surviving principal buys out the deceased's business interest.
- Cash values of the policies a stockholder owns on other stockholders are included in his estate.
- A cross-purchase plan can allow any ratio desired to be achieved through the purchase of specific percentages of a deceased's interest.
- Policy proceeds received individually by each stockholder are not subject to a corporation's creditors—they are not assets of the corporation.
- In a cash-purchase agreement, the insurance has no effect on the value of the business.

Entity Purchase—Stock Redemption for Buy-Sell

- A contract between the business owner and the business itself.
- A stock redemption may convert a present minority situation into a majority or controlling interest.
- Flow of stock redemption agreement.
    — All business principals agree that the business will pay for, own, and be the beneficiary of insurance on the life of each principal in an amount equal to each principal's proportionate share of the business.
    — The business will pay the premiums.
    — Upon death of the insured, the insurance company will pay death benefits to the corporation.
    — The business will then purchase the deceased's business interest.
    — The surviving principals' percentage ownership will be adjusted to reflect the proportionate increase in each survivor's share of the business.
- The insurance proceeds are a corporate asset, which increase the value of the deceased's stock.

- If the corporation is insolvent at the death of the shareholder, the proceeds will be subject to the claims of the creditors.
- Since the stockholders possess no incidents of ownership in the policies owned on their lives, the values of the policies are not included in their estates.

¶ 709 INVESTMENT MIX

.01 Asset Allocation

One of the single most important things an investor can do is practice asset allocation. Studies have shown that asset allocation is the single greatest determinant of investment performance. Obtain professional advice to help develop an effective asset allocation plan. Practicing asset allocation is the engineering of the overall investment plan. Typically the allocation is among stocks, bonds, and money market accounts.

- If you have a longer time frame, put more stock into the portfolio.
- If you have a higher risk tolerance, put more stock into the portfolio.

Diversification and Correlation

- Diversification is also called asset allocation.
- The best way to balance risk and return.
- A diversified portfolio will not give you a grand slam, but it helps avoid a shut out.

The relations among movements of different stocks, their ups and downs in relation to one another, are measured statistically by the coefficient of correlation. If two investments move precisely in tandem, they have a correlation of +10. If they move precisely in opposite directions, their correlation is –1. If their movements are unrelated, the correlation is 0. Research has shown that adding volatile assets with low correlation to one's current portfolio can actually lower the volatility of the overall holdings. Blending assets with low correlation can provide the biggest with the less pain. This technique, known as optimization, can help provide the highest return with the amount of volatility one is willing to accept. But remember, stocks do not behave statistically based on their past performance. In general, a portfolio simply composed of large-caps, small-caps, bonds, and some foreign stocks should provide a nice diversified portfolio.

Diversification and Portfolio Size

- To diversify your portfolio properly, one only needs between eight to 15 stocks.
- Consider focusing on a small select group of stocks—between eight to 15 stocks for your portfolio.
- When you reduce the number of stocks in a portfolio, you increase the probability of returns that are higher than the market's. But this also increases your chances of underperforming, and this is why stock selection is so critical.
- The most you can lose on a stock is 100 percent, but the most you can win is unlimited.
- Maximize your portfolio by getting the highest projected earnings growth at the lowest price. Look for companies that dominate their industry in an industry that is growing faster than the overall economy, and avoid stocks that are trading at P/Es that are more than double their projected earnings growth rates. A good

value would be a stock that has a P/E no more than 60 percent above its growth rate. So the PEG (price/earnings to growth) ratio would be 1.6 or less.

- Minimize risk with the growth stocks above by adding the financially strongest stocks to the portfolio. Add a group of stocks that consistently and regularly turn in 16 percent or more earnings growth. After these star performers, add the solid companies with 12- to 15-percent returns. Then balance your portfolio with the overlooked companies with earnings growth rates of eight to 12 percent. These may be ready to turn it on and outpace other companies. Now you have minimized your overall portfolio risk by being more balanced across the board.

Sound asset allocation strategies capitalize on the opportunity created by the differences among asset classes to build combinations of investments that help reduce risk. Sound asset allocation strategies seek competitive investment returns. Asset allocation is the process of combining investments into a portfolio designed to meet an individual investor's needs. Asset allocation involves knowing how to combine these investments so that they work together to help reduce investment risk. Asset allocation involves knowing how to combine investments to seek competitive investment returns. Asset allocation involves understanding the distinct characteristics of a number of types of investments. By investing in different asset classes, one's chances for success may be enhanced—simply by the fact that more investments are owned. Should one investment perform poorly, others may offset those losses.

An example of a diversified portfolio in theory would provide for the following concepts:

	100% Stock Portfolio	vs.	Portfolio of
			30% International Stocks
			30% Corporate Bonds
			30% US Stocks
			10% Government Bonds
Annualized Return	17%		15%
Annualized Risk	14%		10%
Percentage of Periods with Positive Returns	90%		95%

.02 The Asset Allocation Process

The asset allocation process should create an optimal combination of investments that will address specific investment goals and reduce risk. Investment goals are best reached through a diversified portfolio with different investment objectives. One should consider: size and maturity, style and type, asset class, and geographic area.

Determining Investor Profile

Step one in developing an asset allocation model is to gather information about your financial objectives, risk tolerance, time horizon and available resources.

Step Two. Determine which investment categories have characteristics that match your investor goals.

Step Three. Select specific investments to create and build a portfolio that meets your investment needs.

Step Four. Monitor the portfolio. A portfolio "checkup" should be conducted periodically to review and rebalance the investment portfolio because:

¶709.02

The investment time frame will change as one moves closer to the goal.

The portfolio mix, over time, will shift as some assets outperform others.

Life circumstances such as career or family needs may change.

.03 Asset Allocation Diversification Worksheet Example

Stocks	70%		
Domestic		40%	
Large Company			25%
Growth			15%
Value			10%
Small Company			15%
Growth			10%
Value			5%
International		30%	
Regional			18%
Emerging			10%
Diversified Broadly			2%
Bonds	30%		
International		20%	
Long Term			10%
Intermediate			10%
Domestic		10%	
Long Term			5%
Intermediate			2%
Short Term			3%
	100%	100%	100%

.04 Investor Assessment Questionnaire for Asset Allocation Strategy

Circle the answer that best describes your current investment situation (Circle all that apply). Total the points and use the chart at the end of the questionnaire to obtain an indication of your investor profile.

My investment experience is:

10 I have a great deal of experience investing in stocks and other types of investments.

5 I have some experience investing in stocks or stock funds.

2 I have invested in stocks basically through my company retirement plan.

0 I have rarely invested in stocks.

Investment Resources Currently Available

Approximately what percentage of your current investment portfolio is in the following categories?

Individual stocks	_____	%
Individual bonds	_____	%
Mutual funds—Stocks	_____	%
Mutual funds—Bonds	_____	%
International stocks	_____	%
International mutual funds	_____	%
Cash (CDs, savings accounts, etc.)	_____	%
Other:_____	_____	%
Other:_____	_____	%

What is your current age?

10	Under 25
8	26 to 40
5	41 to 50
3	51 to 60
1	Over 60

Which order (choose one) of investment objectives is most important to you:

0	Safety of principal—Current income—Growth of capital
0	Safety of principal—Growth of capital—Current income
5	Current income—Safety of principal—Growth of capital
5	Current income—Growth of capital—Safety of principal
10	Growth of capital—Safety of principal—Current income
10	Growth of capital—Current income—Safety of principal

Investment Objectives

What are your primary investment goals?

5	Retirement
5	Wealth accumulation
2	College funding
0	Wealth preservation
0	Seeking current income

Attitude and Risk Tolerance

Which statement best describes your Risk Tolerance?

0	I would rather accept a lower rate of return than put my investment at risk.
5	I am willing to accept day-to-day fluctuations in the value of my investment in exchange for a higher potential return over the long-run.
10	I am willing to accept more risk in order to seek the highest return. I am a long-term investor seeking a maximum return on my investments.

Which of the following best describes your reaction if your portfolio value suddenly declined 20%?

¶709.04

10	I understand that there are temporary changes due to market fluctuations. I invest for long-term growth.
7	A temporary decline would concern me, even though I invest for long-term growth
2	It would not bother me, if the amount of income I received was unaffected.
0	I would be very concerned. Fluctuations of my portfolio bother me greatly.

How long before you need to start receiving income from your investment?

0	In less than 3 years
5	3 to 7 years
10	8 to 20 years
20	More than 20 years

When will you need to draw down the principal?

0	In less than 3 years
5	3 to 10 years
10	11 to 15 years
20	More than 15 years

Investor Profile Summary

Add up the points from each question to determine your final score. Then, use the scale below to get an idea of your investor profile.

Total Score = _____

Conservative Investor (0-25) = A portfolio that emphasizes income. It seeks to preserve and protect principal.

Balanced Investor (26-50) = A portfolio that balances growth and income. It seeks to protect accumulated income while seeking growth.

Growth Investor (51-75) = A portfolio that moderately emphasizes growth over income.

Aggressive Investor (76-100) = A portfolio that greatly emphasizes growth over income.

.05 Model Portfolios

Each of the following model portfolios represents a distinct asset allocation strategy.

Aggressive portfolio—Emphasizes growth through equities over income.

For a long-term investment of 20 years or greater.

80% equities

35% International stocks

20% Large capitalization stocks

25% Small capitalization stocks

20% income

10% Corporate bonds

10% Government bonds

Balanced portfolio—Balances equities and income to protect accumulated income. It seeks to maintain growth. For an investment term of 10 years.

60% equities

30% Large capitalization stocks

30% Small capitalization stocks

40% income

15% Government bonds

25% Corporate bonds

Growth portfolio—Emphasizes growth over income, but to a lesser degree than an aggressive portfolio. For an investment term of 15 years.

75% equities

30% International stocks

20% Small capitalization stocks

20% Large capitalization stocks

25% income

20% Corporate bonds

5% Government bonds

Conservative portfolio—Emphasizes income and protection. For an investment of about five years.

40% equities

15% International stocks

25% Large capitalization stocks

60% income

30% Government bonds

30% Corporate bonds

.06 Diversification by Investment

Diversification of Investment

Recommended Investment Diversification of Portfolio

Risk Tolerance	Years to Retirement			
	1 Year	**5 Years**	**10 Years**	**20 Years**
Conservative	Growth	Growth	Growth	Growth
	0%	10%	20%	30%
	Income	Income	Income	Income
	20%	30%	30%	30%
	Risk Free	Risk Free	Risk Free	Risk Free
	80%	60%	50%	40%
	100%	100%	100%	100%
Aggressive	Growth	Growth	Growth	Growth
	20%	40%	60%	80%
	Income	Income	Income	Income
	20%	40%	20%	20%

Risk Tolerance	Years to Retirement			
	1 Year	**5 Years**	**10 Years**	**20 Years**
	Risk Free	Risk Free	Risk Free	Risk Free
	60%	20%	20%	0%
	100%	100%	100%	100%
Moderate	Growth	Growth	Growth	Growth
	5%	35%	55%	65%
	Income	Income	Income	Income
	15%	25%	25%	25%
	Risk Free	Risk Free	Risk Free	Risk Free
	80%	40%	20%	10%
	100%	100%	100%	100%

.07 Equity-Bond Formula

The following is a guideline for estimating the amount of stocks and bonds for an individual's investment portfolio.

Equity-Bond Formula for Individuals

100 – age = % in equities

> **Example (1):** 34 year old

100 – 34 = 66

EQUITY = 66% BONDS = 34%

> **Example (2):** 44 year old

100 – 44 = 56

EQUITY = 56% BONDS = 44%

.09 Investment Mix by Fund Type

Fund Type	Stocks	Bonds	Bond Yield	Investment Risk
Aggressive Growth	100%	0%	Lower	Higher
Growth Mostly	90%	10%	Lower	Higher
Growth and Income	70-80%	30-20%	Medium	Medium
Income and Growth	60-70%	30-40%	Medium	Medium
Income	25%	75%	Medium	Lower
Bond Mostly	10-15%	85-100%	Higher	Lower

.11 Mix by Life Stage

Age: Over 60 or retired

Goal: Income with inflation protection

10% - 25% Growth

15% - 35% Growth and income

50% - 70% Income or 50% - 70% tax-free

Age: Late 40s to late 50s

Goal: Income with some growth

20% - 40% Growth

30% - 40% Growth and income

25% - 50% Income or 25% - 50% tax-free

Age: Late 30s to early 40s

Goal: Growth with some income

25% - 50% Growth

25% - 50% Growth and income

25% - 40% Income or 25% - 40% tax-free

Age: 20s to early 30s

Goal: Maximum growth

40% - 60% Growth

25% - 35% Growth and income

15% - 25% Income or 15% - 25% tax-free

¶ 713 PRICE/EARNINGS RATIO—PROJECTED FOR GIVEN PERIODS FOR GIVEN PROJECTED ANNUAL GROWTH RATES

This table projects what the price/earnings ratio (P/E) will be for a stock's given growth rate at 3, 5, 7, and 9 year intervals.

Example: Stock is currently selling at a price/earnings ratio of 9.00. If the compounded annual rate of growth is 6%, what will be the projected P/E ratio:

in 3 years?	7.56
5 years?	6.73
7 years?	5.99
9 years?	5.33

Projected Price/Earnings Ratios for Given Periods for Given Projected Annual Growth Rates

Current P/E Ratio	No.Years Projected	Growth Rates							
		5%	6%	7%	8%	9%	10%	11%	12%
5.00	3	4.32	4.20	4.08	3.97	3.86	3.76	3.66	3.56
5.00	5	3.92	3.74	3.56	3.40	3.25	3.10	2.97	2.84
5.00	7	3.55	3.33	3.11	2.92	2.74	2.57	2.41	2.26
5.00	9	3.22	2.96	2.72	2.50	2.30	2.12	1.95	1.80
6.00	3	5.18	5.04	4.90	4.76	4.63	4.51	4.39	4.27
6.00	5	4.70	4.48	4.28	4.08	3.90	3.73	3.56	3.40
6.00	7	4.26	3.99	3.74	3.50	3.,28	3.08	2.89	2.71
6.00	9	3.87	3.55	3.26	3.00	2.76	2.54	2.35	2.16
7.00	3	6.05	5.88	5.71	5.56	5.41	5.26	5.12	4.98
7.00	5	5.48	5.23	4.99	4.76	4.55	4.35	4.15	3.97
7.00	7	4.97	4.66	4.36	4.08	3.83	3.59	3.37	3.17
7.00	9	4.51	4.14	3.81	3.50	3.22	2.97	2.74	2.52
8.00	3	6.91	6.72	6.53	6.35	6.18	6.01	5.85	5.69
8.00	5	6.27	5.98	5.70	5.44	5.20	4.97	4.75	4.54
8.00	7	5.69	5.32	4.98	4.67	4.38	4.11	3.85	3.62
8.00	9	5.16	4.74	4.35	4.00	3.68	3.39	3.13	2.88
9.00	3	7.77	7.56	7.35	7.14	6.95	6.76	6.58	6.41
9.00	5	7.05	6.73	6.42	6.13	5.85	5.59	5.34	5.11
9.00	7	6.40	5.99	5.60	5.25	4.92	4.62	4.33	4.07
9.00	9	5.80	5.33	4.90	4.50	4.14	3.82	3.52	3.25
10.00	3	8.64	8.40	8.16	7.94	7.72	7.51	7.31	7.12
10.00	5	7.84	7.47	7.13	6.81	6.50	6.21	5.93	5.67
10.00	7	7.11	6.65	6.23	5.83	5.47	5.13	4.82	4.52
10.00	9	6.45	5.92	5.44	5.00	4.60	4.24	3.91	3.61
15.00	3	12.96	12.59	12.24	11.91	11.58	11.27	10.97	10.68
15.00	5	11.75	11.21	10.69	10.21	9.75	9.31	8.90	8.51
15.00	7	10.66	9.98	9.34	8.75	8.21	7.70	7.22	6.79
15.00	9	9.67	8.88	8.16	7.50	6.91	6.36	5.86	5.41
20.00	3	17.28	16.79	16.33	15.88	15.44	15.03	14.62	14.24
20.00	5	15.67	14.95	14.26	13.61	13.00	12.42	11.87	11.35
20.00	7	14.21	13.30	12.45	11.67	10.94	10.26	9.63	9.05
20.00	9	12.89	11.84	10.88	10.00	9.21	8.48	7.82	7.21
25.00	3	21.60	20.99	20.41	19.85	19.30	18.78	18.28	17.79
25.00	5	19.59	18.68	17.82	17.01	16.25	15.52	14.84	14.19
25.00	7	17.77	16.63	15.57	14.59	13.68	12.83	12.04	11.31
25.00	9	16.12	14.80	13.60	12.51	11.51	10.60	9.77	9.02
30.00	3	25.92	25.19	24.49	23.81	23.17	22.54	21.94	21.35
30.00	5	23.51	22.42	21.39	20.42	19.50	18.63	17.80	17.02
30.00	7	21.32	19.95	18.68	17.50	16.41	15.39	14.45	13.57
30.00	9	19.34	17.76	16.32	15.01	13.81	12.72	11.73	10.82
35.00	3	30.23	29.39	28.57	27.78	27.03	26.30	25.59	24.91
35.00	5	27.42	26.15	24.95	23.82	22.75	21.73	20.77	19.86
35.00	7	24.87	23.28	21.80	20.42	19.15	17.96	16.86	15.83
35.00	9	22.56	20.72	19.04	17.51	16.11	14.84	13.68	12.62

Current P/E Ratio	No. Years Projected	Growth Rates							
		5%	6%	7%	8%	9%	10%	11%	12%
40.00	3	34.55	33.58	32.65	31.75	30.89	30.05	29.25	28.47
40.00	5	31.34	29.89	28.52	27.22	26.00	24.84	23.74	22.70
40.00	7	28.43	26.60	24.91	23.34	21.88	20.53	19.27	18.09
40.00	9	25.78	23.68	21.76	20.01	18.42	16.96	15.64	14.42

¶ 715 RETIREMENT

.01 Retirement in General

- Retirement is not a race if you start early enough.
- If you start planning early, there are many routes to retirement funding.
- Set the right goal in your financial planning.
- Use asset allocation to spread your money among several different types of investments to increase returns and reduce risk.
- Only stocks (not bonds) can provide the growth to stay ahead of inflation and taxes.
- At age 65, plan on your retirement money needing to last for another 20 years.
- At retirement, withdraw your funds wisely.
  - Draw from taxable investments first.
  - Let the tax free investments continue to grow tax free.
  - Minimize your mandatory distributions from your IRAs, 401(k)s, and other retirement accounts. This allows the funds to grow tax-free for as long as possible.
  - Does it make sense for you to convert your regular IRA to a Roth IRA? You will have to pay income tax on the money you convert to a Roth, but you don't have to take mandatory withdrawals from the Roth. It can continue to grow tax-free and can be left tax-free to heirs. When they withdraw it, possibly at a higher tax rate, there will be no income tax.

.02 IRA Investment Comparisons

IRA Investment of $2,000/Year Given Percent Return and Various Terms

No investment returns are guaranteed, but the following chart provides a reasonable guideline of possible returns given different investment vehicles and risk levels.

The chart illustrates the tremendous potential of higher percent returns and of lengthening time frames.

> **Example:** If series "EE" bonds or a similar investment were purchased at $2,000/year for a period of 22 years earning 7% interest, the $44,000 investment would grow to $98,011.

Possible Value of $2,000 Per Year Put into IRA Investments

Typical Investment	Possible Return	Value per Given Periods			
		6	8	10	12
Passbook Savings	5%	$13,603.83	$19,098.22	$25,155.79	$31,834.25
Cash Value Life Ins.	6%	$13,950.64	$19,794.94	$26,361.59	$33,739.88
Series E Bonds	7%	$14,306.58	$20,519.61	$27,632.90	$35,776.90
Money Market Instr.	8%	$14,671.86	$21,273.26	$28,973.12	$37,954.25
Govt. Bonds	9%	$15,046.67	$22,056.95	$30,385.86	$40,281.44
Bond Funds	10%	$15,431.22	$22,871.78	$31,874.85	$42,768.57
Treasury Notes	12%	$16,230.38	$24,599.39	$35,097.47	$42,266.27
Fixed Annuities	14%	$17,071.04	$26,465.52	$38,674.59	$54,541.50
Variable Annuities	16%	$17,954.95	$28,480.19	$42,642.94	$61,700.34
Bonds	18%	$18,883.94	$30,653.99	$47,042.62	$69,862.14
Mutual Funds	20%	$19,859.84	$32,998.17	$51,917.36	$79,161.00
Growth Mutual Funds	22%	$20,884.58	$35,524.61	$57,314.83	$89,747.39
Individual Stocks	24%	$21,960.13	$38,245.89	$63,286.88	$101,789.91
		14	16	18	20
Passbook Savings	5%	$39,197.26	$47,314.98	$56,264.77	$66,131.91
Cash Value Life Ins.	6%	$42,030.13	$51,345.06	$61,811.31	$73,571.18
Series E Bonds	7%	$45,100.98	$55,776.11	$67,998.07	$81,990.98
Money Market Instr.	8%	$48,429.84	$60,648.57	$74,900.49	$91,523.93
Govt. Bonds	9%	$52,038.38	$66,006.80	$82,602.68	$102,320.24
Bond Funds	10%	$55,949.94	$71,899.46	$91,198.35	$114,550.00
Treasury notes	12%	$64,785.90	$85,506.56	$111,499.43	$144,104.88
Fixed Annuities	14%	$75,162.13	$101,960.70	$136,788.13	$182,049.86
Variable Annuities	16%	$87,343.97	$121,850.05	$168,281.43	$230,759.49
Bonds	18%	$101,636.04	$145,878.03	$207,480.57	$293,255.94
Mutual Funds	20%	$118,391.85	$174,884.26	$256,233.33	$373,376.00
Growth Mutual Funds	22%	$138,020.02	$209,869.00	$316,809.02	$475,978.55
Individual Stocks	24%	$160,992.16	$252,021.54	$391,988.32	$607201.25
		22	24	26	28
Passbook Savings	5%	$77,010.43	$89,004.00	$102,226.91	116,805.17
Cash Value Life Ins.	6%	$86,784.58	$101,631.15	$118,312.77	$137,056.22
Series E Bonds	7%	$98,011.48	$116,353.34	$137,352.94	$161,395.38
Money Market Instr.	8%	$110,913.51	$133,529.52	$159,908.83	$190,677.66
Govt. Bonds	9%	$125,746.68	$153,579.63	$186,647.95	$225,936.43
Bond Funds	10%	$142,805.50	$176,994.65	$218,363.53	$268,190870
Treasury notes	12%	$185,005.17	$236,310.48	$300,667.87	$381,397.77
Fixed Annuities	14%	$240,871.99	$317,317.24	$416,665.49	$545,778.47
Variable Annuities	16%	$314,829.97	$427,955.21	$580,176.53	$785,005.55
Bonds	18%	$412,689.57	$578,988.96	$810,544.23	$1,132,961.78
Mutual Funds	20%	$542,061.44	$784,968.47	$1,134,754.60	$1,638,446.62
Growth Mutual Funds	22%	$712,886.47	$1,065,500.22	$1,590,990.53	$2,371,487.96
Individual Stocks	24%	$938,112.64	$1,446,921.99	$2,229,267.26	$3,432,201.34

.03 Retirement Planning

Retirement planning is the business of making trade-offs. The decision is to put money aside today instead of spending it on something to save for tomorrow.

Assumptions:

Current Tax Rate-Federal	34.00%
Assumed Inflation Rate	5.00%

Tax Deferred Accounts (401(k), IRA, Keogh, etc.)

Current Value of Tax Deferred Accounts	$100,000
Annual Amount invested in Tax Deferred Accounts	$10,000
Investment Rate on Tax Deferred Accounts	8.00%

Other Savings

Current Value of Other Savings Accounts	$20,000
Annual Amount Saved in Other Savings Accounts	$5,000
Investment Rate on Other Savings Accounts	6%

Married? Y   Current Age of Taxpayer: 38, Spouse 33
Retirement Age of Taxpayer 65
Younger Spouse will continue to work

Current Annual Wages	Taxpayer: $50,000	Spouse: $25,000
Annual Wages After Retirement	Taxpayer $8,000	Spouse=$0
Annual $ Needed today for Retirement Expenses	$100,000	

Projected Social Security	Taxpayer: $8,000	Spouse $5,000
Projected Annual Pension	Taxpayer: $50,000	Spouse $0

Other taxable income at Retirement $35,000-Non-Tax $500
Allowable Item. Deductions- Exempt at Retirement $20,000
Annual Surplus/(Shortfall) at Retirement

Pension Taxpayer	$50,000	
Pension Spouse	$0	
Social Security Taxpayer	$8,000	
Social Security Spouse	$0	
Income From Savings & Investments	$151,252	
Other Taxable Income at Retirement	$43,000	
Other Non-Taxable Income at Retirement	$500	
Taxable Earnings from Working Spouse	$25,000	
Total Annual Retirement Income		$277,752
Annual Retirement Expense	$373,346	
Estimated Federal Income Taxes	$77,102	
Total Annual Retirement Expenses	$450,447	
Shortfall		($172,696)

Options—In order to allow for this shortfall, consider the following options:

Earn Extra After-Tax Retirement Income of	$172,696
Reduce Yearly Retirement Spending by	$172,696
Increase Yearly Taxable Savings to	$27,700
Increase Average Rate-of-Return on Taxable Earnings by	
Additional 14%, or on Tax-Deferred Investments by Additional 1%	

.04 Withdrawal of Savings by Periods

The following chart provides amounts by totals of how long an investment portfolio of $100,000 will last given different withdrawal periods and earned interest rates.

Example (1): Table headers:

Principal $100,000

Interest earned = 10% APR

Choose the liquidation period only by reading down the left-handed column.

From the chart, to liquidate the principal of $100,000 over 20 years with the principal earning 10% interest, the monthly amount to withdraw is $965, the yearly amount to withdraw = $11,580.

Over the 20-year liquidation period, $131,607 will be withdrawn from earned interest, plus the $100,000 return of principal, for a total received of $231,607.

Example (2): For a principal of $225,000:

Compute conversion factor for table lookup.

Multiply 2.25 times table rates. In the example above, if $225,000 were the principal, then:

Monthly withdrawal = $965 × 2.25 = $2,171.25

Yearly withdrawal = $11,580 × 2.25 = $26,055

Total interest withdrawn = $131,607 × 2.25 = $296,115.75

Totals of Savings Withdrawal for Given Terms

| | Principal $100,000 | | Interest Earned 6.00% | | |
Year	Monthly Withdrawal	Yearly Withdrawal	Rec'd from Interest	Rec'd from Principal	Total Received
20	716	8,592	71,955	100,000	171,955
19	736	8,832	67,830	100,000	167,830
18	758	9,096	63,760	100,000	163,760
17	783	9,396	59,758	100,000	159,758
16	810	9,731	55,801	100,000	155,801
15	843	10,127	51,893	100,000	151,893
14	880	10,571	48,049	100,000	148,049
13	925	11,100	44,257	100,000	144,257
12	975	11,711	40,517	100,000	140,517
11	1,037	12,444	36,853	100,000	136,853
10	1,109	13,319	33,220	100,000	133,220
9	1,201	14,412	29,663	100,000	129,663
8	1,314	15,768	26,160	100,000	126,160
7	1,460	17,531	22,712	100,000	122,712
6	1,657	19,884	19,325	100,000	119,325
5	1,933	23,196	15,999	100,000	115,999

Totals of Savings Withdrawal for Given Terms

| | Principal $100,000 | | Interest Earned 7.00% | | |
Year	Monthly Withdrawal	Yearly Withdrawal	Rec'd from Interest	Rec'd from Principal	Total Received
20	774	9,299	86,072	100,000	186,072
19	794	9,528	81,068	100,000	181,068
18	816	9,792	76,150	100,000	176,150
17	839	10,079	71,293	100,000	171,293
16	866	10,403	66,500	100,000	166,500
15	898	10,787	61,793	100,000	161,793
14	935	11,220	57,147	100,000	157,147
13	978	11,736	52,578	100,000	152,578
12	1,028	12,336	48,092	100,000	148,092
11	1,088	13,056	43,670	100,000	143,670
10	1,161	13,932	39,330	100,000	139,330
9	1,250	15,011	35,069	100,000	135,069
8	1,363	16,356	30,887	100,000	130,887
7	1,509	18,108	26,779	100,000	126,779
6	1,704	20,459	22,753	100,000	122,753
5	1,980	23,760	18,806	100,000	118,806

Totals of Savings Withdrawal for Given Terms

Principal $100,000   Interest Earned 8.00%

Year	Monthly Withdrawal	Yearly Withdrawal	Rec'd from Interest	Rec'd from Principal	Total Received
20	836	10,032	100,748	100,000	200,748
19	855	10,260	94,824	100,000	194,824
18	875	10,500	88,999	100,000	188,999
17	897	10,775	83,245	100,000	183,245
16	924	11,099	77,583	100,000	177,583
15	956	11,472	72,015	100,000	172,015
14	990	11,891	66,543	100,000	166,543
13	1,033	12,396	61,163	100,000	161,163
12	1,082	12,984	55,873	100,000	155,873
11	1,142	13,704	50,861	100,000	150,861
10	1,212	14,555	45,591	100,000	145,591
9	1,302	15,624	40,607	100,000	140,607
8	1,413	16,967	35,711	100,000	135,711
7	1,558	18,707	30,926	100,000	130,926
6	1,753	21,036	26,238	100,000	126,238
5	2,027	24,335	21,655	100,000	121,655

Totals of Savings Withdrawal for Given Terms

Principal $100,000   Interest Earned 9.00%

Year	Monthly Withdrawal	Yearly Withdrawal	Rec'd from Interest	Rec'd from Principal	Total Received
20	899	10,799	115,929	100,000	215,929
19	916	11,003	109,054	100,000	209,054
18	936	11,232	102,278	100,000	202,278
17	959	11,508	95,595	100,000	195,595
16	984	11,819	89,029	100,000	189,029
15	1,013	12,167	82,577	100,000	182,577
14	1,048	12,587	76,225	100,000	176,225
13	1,089	13,079	69,986	100,000	169,986
12	1,138	13,656	63,880	100,000	163,880
11	1,196	14,352	57,882	100,000	157,882
10	1,266	15,203	52,011	100,000	152,011
9	1,354	16,248	46,261	100,000	146,261
8	1,465	17,580	40,645	100,000	140,645
7	1,608	19,307	35,149	100,000	135,149
6	1,802	21,635	29,782	100,000	129,782
5	2,075	24,911	24,551	100,000	124,551

Total of Savings Withdrawal for Given Terms

Principal $100,000   Interest Earned 10.00%

Year	Monthly Withdrawal	Yearly Withdrawal	Rec'd from Interest	Rec'd from Principal	Total Received
20	965	11,580	131,607	100,000	231,607
19	980	11,771	123,730	100,000	223,730
18	1,000	12,000	115,971	100,000	215,971
17	1,021	12,252	108,323	100,000	208,323
16	1,046	12,552	100,816	100,000	200,816
15	1,074	12,899	93,426	100,000	193,426
14	1,108	13,296	86,176	100,000	186,176
13	1,147	13,775	79,066	100,000	179,066
12	1,194	14,339	72,091	100,000	172,091
11	1,251	15,023	65,268	100,000	165,268
10	1,321	15,863	58,578	100,000	158,578
9	1,407	16,895	52,049	100,000	152,049
8	1,516	18,203	45,675	100,000	145,675
7	1,659	19,919	39,447	100,000	139,447
6	1,852	22,235	33,382	100,000	133,382
5	2,125	25,500	27,483	100,000	127,483

Total of Savings Withdrawal for Given Terms

Principal $100,000   Interest Earned 11.00%

Year	Monthly Withdrawal	Yearly Withdrawal	Rec'd from Interest	Rec'd from Principal	Total Received
20	1,031	12,383	147,719	100,000	247,719
19	1,047	12,564	138,824	100,000	238,824
18	1,065	12,780	130,053	100,000	230,053
17	1,085	13,020	121,423	100,000	221,423
16	1,109	13,308	12,926	100,000	212,926
15	1,136	13,643	104,592	100,000	204,592
14	1,169	14,028	96,405	100,000	196,405
13	1,207	14,495	88,373	100,000	188,373
12	1,253	15,047	80,515	100,000	180,515
11	1,309	15,708	72,822	100,000	172,822
10	1,377	16,535	65,301	100,000	165,301
9	1,462	17,555	57,956	100,000	157,956
8	1,571	18,852	50,802	100,000	150,802
7	1,712	20,544	43,833	100,000	143,833
6	1,903	22,836	37,042	100,000	137,042
5	2,174	26,088	30,457	100,000	130,457

Total of Savings Withdrawal for Given Terms

	Principal $100,000			**Interest Earned 12.00%**	
Year	**Monthly Withdrawal**	**Yearly Withdrawal**	**Rec'd from Interest**	**Rec'd from Principal**	**Total Received**
20	1,100	13,211	164,256	100,000	264,256
19	1,114	13,379	154,308	100,000	254,308
18	1,132	13,584	144,502	100,000	244,502
17	1,150	13,811	134,847	100,000	234,847
16	1,173	14,087	125,356	100,000	225,356
15	1,199	14,399	116,033	100,000	216,033
14	1,231	14,772	106,882	100,000	206,882
13	1,268	15,227	97,917	100,000	197,917
12	1,313	15,756	89,132	100,000	189,132
11	1,367	16,415	80,552	100,000	180,552
10	1,434	17,219	72,170	100,000	172,170
9	1,518	18,216	63,994	100,000	163,994
8	1,625	19,500	56,027	100,000	156,027
7	1,765	21,180	48,284	100,000	148,284
6	1,954	23,459	40,763	100,000	140,763
5	2,224	26,688	33,466	100,000	133,466

Total of Savings Withdrawal for Given Terms

	Principal $100,000			**Interest Earned 13.00%**	
Year	**Monthly Withdrawal**	**Yearly Withdrawal**	**Rec'd from Interest**	**Rec'd from Principal**	**Total Received**
20	1,171	14,063	181,175	100,000	281,175
19	1,184	14,219	170,160	100,000	270,160
18	1,200	14,400	159,292	100,000	259,292
17	1,219	14,628	148,606	100,000	248,606
16	1,239	14,879	138,081	100,000	238,081
15	1,265	15,180	127,743	100,000	227,743
14	1,295	15,540	117,604	100,000	217,604
13	1,331	15,972	107,664	100,000	207,664
12	1,374	16,499	97,946	100,000	197,946
11	1,427	17,135	88,444	100,000	188,444
10	1,492	17,915	79,173	100,000	179,173
9	1,575	18,900	70,135	100,000	170,135
8	1,680	20,171	61,350	100,000	161,350
7	1,818	21,827	52,811	100,000	152,811
6	2,007	24,084	44,535	100,000	144,535
5	2,275	27,300	36,515	100,000	136,515

Total of Savings Withdrawal for Given Terms

	Principal $100,000			Interest Earned 14.00%	
Year	Monthly Withdrawal	Yearly Withdrawal	Rec'd from Interest	Rec'd from Principal	Total Received
20	1,244	14,928	198,443	100,000	298,443
19	1,255	15,071	186,341	100,000	286,341
18	1,270	15,240	174,406	100,000	274,406
17	1,286	15,443	162,639	100,000	262,639
16	1,307	15,695	151,083	100,000	251,083
15	1,332	15,984	139,717	100,000	239,717
14	1,360	16,320	128,559	100,000	228,559
13	1,395	16,740	117,643	100,000	217,643
12	1,436	17,243	106,947	100,000	206,947
11	1,488	17,867	96,498	100,000	196,498
10	1,553	18,636	86,324	100,000	186,324
9	1,633	19,596	76,400	100,000	176,400
8	1,737	20,844	66,766	100,000	166,766
7	1,874	22,488	57,418	100,000	157,418
6	2,061	24,732	48,363	100,000	148,363
5	2,326	27,923	39,609	100,000	139,609

Total of Savings Withdrawal for Given Terms

	Principal $100,000			Interest Earned 15.00%	
Year	Monthly Withdrawal	Yearly Withdrawal	Rec'd from Interest	Rec'd from Principal	Total Received
20	1,316	15,803	216,025	100,000	316,025
19	1,327	15,935	316,025	100,000	416,025
18	1,342	16,104	89,805	100,000	289,805
17	1,358	16,296	176,969	100,000	276,969
16	1,376	16,523	164,340	100,000	264,340
15	1,399	16,799	151,920	100,000	251,920
14	1,427	17,124	139,752	100,000	239,752
13	1,459	17,519	127,807	100,000	227,807
12	1,500	18,011	116,131	100,000	216,131
11	1,551	18,612	104,724	100,000	204,724
10	1,613	19,356	93,607	100,000	193,607
9	1,692	20,304	82,781	100,000	182,781
8	1,794	21,159	72,276	100,000	172,276
7	1,929	23,159	62,093	100,000	162,093
6	2,114	25,379	52,246	100,000	152,246
5	2,379	28,548	42,740	100,000	142,740

Total of Savings Withdrawal for Given Terms

	Principal $100,000			Interest Earned 16.00%	
Year	Monthly Withdrawal	Yearly Withdrawal	Rec'd from Interest	Rec'd from Principal	Total Received
20	1,390	16,691	233,902	100,000	333,902
19	1,401	16,823	219,594	100,000	319,594
18	1,413	16,967	205,474	100,000	305,474
17	1,428	17,147	191,557	100,000	291,557
16	1,447	17,364	177,849	100,000	277,849
15	1,469	17,628	164,372	100,000	264,372
14	1,494	17,939	151,133	100,000	251,133
13	1,527	18,324	138,171	100,000	238,171
12	1,565	18,791	125,476	100,000	225,476
11	1,613	19,367	113,090	100,000	213,090
10	1,675	20,100	101,014	100,000	210,014
9	1,752	21,035	89,275	100,000	189,275
8	1,852	22,235	77,879	100,000	177,879
7	1,985	23,831	66,836	100,000	166,836
6	2,169	26,028	56,182	100,000	156,182
5	2,431	29,183	45,910	100,000	145,910

Total of Savings Withdrawal for Given Terms

	Principal $100,000			Interest Earned 17.00%	
Year	Monthly Withdrawal	Yearly Withdrawal	Rec'd from Interest	Rec'd from Principal	Total Received
20	1,467	17,604	252,032	100,000	352,032
19	1,475	17,711	236,618	100,000	336,618
18	1,487	17,855	221,394	100,000	321,394
17	1,502	18,024	206,373	100,000	306,373
16	1,519	18,228	191,582	100,000	291,582
15	1,239	18,468	177,025	100,000	277,025
14	1,563	18,767	162,725	100,000	262,725
13	1,593	19,127	148,705	100,000	248,705
12	1,632	19,584	135,002	100,000	235,002
11	1,679	20,148	121,606	100,000	221,606
10	1,737	20,855	108,559	100,000	208,559
9	1,813	21,767	95,871	100,000	195,871
8	1,911	22,943	83,572	100,000	183,572
7	2,043	24,527	71,663	100,000	171,663
6	2,224	26,699	60,175	100,000	160,175
5	2,485	29,820	49,117	100,000	149,117

Projected Price/Earnings Ratios for Given Periods for Given Projected Annual Growth Rates

Current P/E Ratio	No.Years Projected	Growth Rates							
		5%	6%	7%	8%	9%	10%	11%	12%
5.00	3	4.32	4.20	4.08	3.97	3.86	3.76	3.66	3.56
5.00	5	3.92	3.74	3.56	3.40	3.25	3.10	2.97	2.84
5.00	7	3.55	3.33	3.11	2.92	2.74	2.57	2.41	2.26
5.00	9	3.22	2.96	2.72	2.50	2.30	2.12	1.95	1.80
6.00	3	5.18	5.04	4.90	4.76	4.63	4.51	4.39	4.27
6.00	5	4.70	4.48	4.28	4.08	3.90	3.73	3.56	3.40
6.00	7	4.26	3.99	3.74	3.50	3.,28	3.08	2.89	2.71
6.00	9	3.87	3.55	3.26	3.00	2.76	2.54	2.35	2.16
7.00	3	6.05	5.88	5.71	5.56	5.41	5.26	5.12	4.98
7.00	5	5.48	5.23	4.99	4.76	4.55	4.35	4.15	3.97
7.00	7	4.97	4.66	4.36	4.08	3.83	3.59	3.37	3.17
7.00	9	4.51	4.14	3.81	3.50	3.22	2.97	2.74	2.52
8.00	3	6.91	6.72	6.53	6.35	6.18	6.01	5.85	5.69
8.00	5	6.27	5.98	5.70	5.44	5.20	4.97	4.75	4.54
8.00	7	5.69	5.32	4.98	4.67	4.38	4.11	3.85	3.62
8.00	9	5.16	4.74	4.35	4.00	3.68	3.39	3.13	2.88
9.00	3	7.77	7.56	7.35	7.14	6.95	6.76	6.58	6.41
9.00	5	7.05	6.73	6.42	6.13	5.85	5.59	5.34	5.11
9.00	7	6.40	5.99	5.60	5.25	4.92	4.62	4.33	4.07
9.00	9	5.80	5.33	4.90	4.50	4.14	3.82	3.52	3.25
10.00	3	8.64	8.40	8.16	7.94	7.72	7.51	7.31	7.12
10.00	5	7.84	7.47	7.13	6.81	6.50	6.21	5.93	5.67
10.00	7	7.11	6.65	6.23	5.83	5.47	5.13	4.82	4.52
10.00	9	6.45	5.92	5.44	5.00	4.60	4.24	3.91	3.61
15.00	3	12.96	12.59	12.24	11.91	11.58	11.27	10.97	10.68
15.00	5	11.75	11.21	10.69	10.21	9.75	9.31	8.90	8.51
15.00	7	10.66	9.98	9.34	8.75	8.21	7.70	7.22	6.79
15.00	9	9.67	8.88	8.16	7.50	6.91	6.36	5.86	5.41
20.00	3	17.28	16.79	16.33	15.88	15.44	15.03	14.62	14.24
20.00	5	15.67	14.95	14.26	13.61	13.00	12.42	11.87	11.35
20.00	7	14.21	13.30	12.45	11.67	10.94	10.26	9.63	9.05
20.00	9	12.89	11.84	10.88	10.00	9.21	8.48	7.82	7.21
25.00	3	21.60	20.99	20.41	19.85	19.30	18.78	18.28	17.79
25.00	5	19.59	18.68	17.82	17.01	16.25	15.52	14.84	14.19
25.00	7	17.77	16.63	15.57	14.59	13.68	12.83	12.04	11.31
25.00	9	16.12	14.80	13.60	12.51	11.51	10.60	9.77	9.02
30.00	3	25.92	25.19	24.49	23.81	23.17	22.54	21.94	21.35
30.00	5	23.51	22.42	21.39	20.42	19.50	18.63	17.80	17.02
30.00	7	21.32	19.95	18.68	17.50	16.41	15.39	14.45	13.57
30.00	9	19.34	17.76	16.32	15.01	13.81	12.72	11.73	10.82
35.00	3	30.23	29.39	28.57	27.78	27.03	26.30	25.59	24.91
35.00	5	27.42	26.15	24.95	23.82	22.75	21.73	20.77	19.86
35.00	7	24.87	23.28	21.80	20.42	19.15	17.96	16.86	15.83
35.00	9	22.56	20.72	19.04	17.51	16.11	14.84	13.68	12.62

Current P/E Ratio	No. Years Projected	Growth Rates							
		5%	6%	7%	8%	9%	10%	11%	12%
40.00	3	34.55	33.58	32.65	31.75	30.89	30.05	29.25	28.47
40.00	5	31.34	29.89	28.52	27.22	26.00	24.84	23.74	22.70
40.00	7	28.43	26.60	24.91	23.34	21.88	20.53	19.27	18.09
40.00	9	25.78	23.68	21.76	20.01	18.42	16.96	15.64	14.42

.05 Monthly Income Based on Various Principals

This table illustrates the amount of monthly income that can be provided from various principal amounts given different interest rates with no reduction to the principal.

    Example: Principal = 300,000

Interest Earned = 12%

Monthly Income = $3,000

Monthly Income from Various Principals

Principal	Interest Rate				
	5%	6%	7%	8%	9%
$10,000.00	$41.67	$50.00	$58.33	$66.67	$75.00
$20,000.00	$83.33	$100.00	$116.67	$133.33	$150.00
$30,000.00	$125.00	$150.00	$175.00	$200.00	$225.00
$40,000.00	$166.67	$200.00	$233.33	$266.67	$300.00
$50,000.00	$208.33	$250.00	$291.67	$333.33	$375.00
$60,000.00	$250.00	$300.00	$350.00	$400.00	$450.00
$70,000.00	$291.67	$350.00	$408.33	$466.67	$525.00
$80,000.00	$333.33	$400.00	$466.67	$533.33	$600.00
$90,000.00	$375.00	$450.00	$525.00	$600.00	$675.00
$100,000.00	$416.67	$500.00	$583.33	$666.67	$750.00
$110,000.00	$458.33	$550.00	$641.67	$733.33	$825.00
$120,000.00	$500.00	$600.00	$700.00	$800.00	$900.00
$130,000.00	$541.67	$650.00	$758.33	$866.67	$975.00
$140,000.00	$583.33	$700.00	$816.67	$933.33	$1,050.00
$150,000.00	$625.00	$750.00	$875.00	$1,000.00	$1,125.00
$160,000.00	$666.67	$800.00	$933.33	$1,066.67	$1,200.00
$170,000.00	$708.33	$850.00	991.67	$1,133.33	$1,275.00
$180,000.00	$750.00	$900.00	$1,050.00	$1,200.00	$1,350.00
$190,000.00	$791.67	$950.00	$1,108.33	$1,266.67	$1,425.00
$200,000.00	$833.33	$1,000.00	$1,166.67	$1,333.33	$1,500.00
$210,000.00	$875.00	$1,050.00	$1,225.00	$1,400.00	$1,575.00
$220,000.00	$916.67	$1,100.00	$1,283.33	$1,466.67	$1,650.00
$230,000.00	$958.33	$1,150.00	$1,341.67	$1,533.33	$1,725.00
$240,000.00	$1,000.00	$1,200.00	$1,400.00	$1,600.00	$1,800.00
$250,000.00	$1,041.67	$1,250.00	$1,458.33	$1,666.67	$1,875.00
$260,000.00	$1,083.33	$1,300.00	$1,516.67	$1,733.33	$1,950.00
$270,000.00	$1,125.00	$1,350.00	$1,575.00	$1,800.00	$2,025.00
$280,000.00	$1,166.67	$1,400.00	$1,633.33	$1,866.67	$2,100.00
$290,000.00	$1,208.33	$1,450.00	$1,691.67	$1,933.33	$2,175.00
$300,000.00	$1,250.00	$1,500.00	$1,750.00	$2,000.00	$2,250.00
$310,000.00	$1,291.67	$1,550.00	$1,808.33	$2,066.67	$2,325.00
$320,000.00	$1,333.33	$1,600.00	$1,866.67	$2,133.33	$2,400.00
$330,000.00	$1,375.00	$1,650.00	$1,925.00	$2,200.00	$2,475.00
$340,000.00	$1,416.67	$1,700.00	$1,983.33	$2,266.67	$2,550.00

Principal	Interest Rate				
	5%	6%	7%	8%	9%
$350,000.00	$1,458.33	$1,750.00	$2,041.67	$2,333.33	$2,625.00
$360,000.00	$1,500.00	$1,800.00	$2,100.00	$2,400.00	$2,700.00
$370,000.00	$1,541.67	$1,850.00	$2,158.33	$2,466.67	$2,775.00
$380,000.00	$1,583.33	$1,900.00	$2,216.67	$2,533.33	$2,850.00
$390,000.00	$1,625.00	$1,950.00	$2,275.00	$2,600.00	$2,925.00
$400,000.00	$1,666.67	$2,000.00	$2,333.33	$2,666.67	$3,000.00
$410,000.00	$1,708.33	$2,050.00	$2,391.67	$2,733.33	$3,075.00
$420,000.00	$1,750.00	$2,100.00	$2,450.00	$2,800.00	$3,150.00
$430,000.00	$1,791.67	$2,150.00	$2,508.33	$2,866.67	$3,225.00
$440,000.00	$1,833.33	$2,200.00	$2,566.67	$2,933.33	$3,300.00
$450,000.00	$1,875.00	$2,250.00	$2,625.00	$3,000.00	$3,375.00
$460,000.00	$1,916.67	$2,300.00	$2,683.33	$3,066.67	$3,450.00
$470,000.00	$1,958.33	$2,350.00	$2,741.67	$3,133.33	$3,525.00
$480,000.00	$2,000.00	$2,400.00	$2,800.00	$3,200.00	$3,600.00
$490,000.00	$2,041.67	$2,450.00	$2,858.33	$3,266.67	$3,675.00
$500,000.00	$2,083.33	$2,500.00	$2,916.67	$3,333.33	$3,750.00

Monthly Income from Various Principals

Principal	Interest Rate					
	10%	11%	12%	13%	14%	15%
$10,000.00	$83.33	$91.67	$100.00	$108.33	$116.67	$125.00
$20,000.00	$166.67	$183.33	$200.00	$216.67	$233.33	$250.00
$30,000.00	$250.00	$275.00	$300.00	$325.00	$350.00	$375.00
$40,000.00	$333.33	$366.67	$400.00	$433.33	$466.67	$500.00
$50,000.00	$416.67	$458.33	$500.00	$541.67	$583.33	$625.00
$60,000.00	$500.00	$550.00	$600.00	$650.00	$700.00	$750.00
$70,000.00	$583.33	$641.67	$700.00	$758.33	$816.67	$875.00
$80,000.00	$666.67	$733.33	$800.00	$866.67	$933.33	$1,000.00
$90,000.00	$750.00	$825.00	$900.00	$975.00	$1,050.00	$1,125.00
$100,000.00	$833.33	$916.67	$1,000.00	$1,083.33	$1,166.67	$1,250.00
$110,000.00	$916.67	$1,008.33	$1,100.00	$1,191.67	$1,283.33	$1,375.00
$120,000.00	$1,000.00	$1100.00	$1,200.00	$1,300.00	$1,400.00	1,500.00
$130,000.00	$1,083.33	$1,191.67	$1,300.00	$1,408.33	$1,516.67	1,625.00
$140,000.00	$1,166.67	$1,283.33	$1,400.00	$1,516.67	$1,633.33	$1,750.00
$150,000.00	$1,250.00	$1,375.00	$1,500.00	$1,625.00	$1,750.00	$1,875.00
$160,000.00	$1,333.33	$1,466.67	$1,600.00	$1,733.33	$1,866.67	$2,000.00
$170,000.00	$1,416.67	$1,558.33	$1,700.00	$1,841.67	$1,983.33	$2,125.00
$180,000.00	$1,500.00	$1,650.00	$1,800.00	$1,950.00	$2,100.00	$2,250.00
$190,000.00	$1,583.33	$1,741.67	$1,900.00	$2,058.33	$2,216.67	$2,375.00
$200,000.00	$1,666.67	$1,833.33	$2,000.00	$2,166.67	$2,333.33	$2,500.00
$210,000.00	$1,750.00	$1,925.00	$2,100.00	$2,275.00	$2,450.00	$2,625.00
$220,000.00	$1,833.33	$2,016.67	$2,200.00	$2,383.33	$2,566.67	$2,750.00
$230,000.00	$1,916.67	$2,108.33	$2,300.00	$2,491.67	$2,683.33	$2,875.00
$240,000.00	$2,000.00	$2,200.00	$2,400.00	$2,600.00	$2,800.00	$3,000.00
$250,000.00	$2,083.33	$2,291.67	$2,500.00	$2,708.33	$2,916.67	$3,125.00
$260,000.00	$2,166.67	$2,383.33	$2,600.00	$2,816.67	$3,033.33	$3,250.00
$270,000.00	$2,250.00	$2,475.00	$2,700.00	$2,925.00	$3,150.00	$3,375.00
$280,000.00	$2,333.33	$2,566.67	$2,800.00	$3,033.33	$3,266.67	$3,500.00
$290,000.00	$2,416.67	$2,658.33	$2,900.00	$3,141.67	$3,383.33	$3,625.00
$300,000.00	$2,500.00	$2,750.00	$3,000.00	$3,250.00	$3,500.00	$3,750.00
$310,000.00	$2,583.33	$2,841.67	$3,100.00	$3,358.33	$3,616.67	$3,875.00
$320,000.00	$2,666.67	$2,933.33	$3,200.00	$3,466.67	$3,733.33	$4,000.00
$330,000.00	$2,750.00	$3,025.00	$3,300.00	$3,575.00	$3,850.00	$4,125.00
$340,000.00	$2,833.33	$3,116.67	$3,400.00	$3,683.33	$3,966.67	$4,250.00
$350,000.00	$2,916.67	$3,208.33	$3,500.00	$3,791.67	$4,083.33	$4,375.00
$360,000.00	$3,000.00	$3,300.00	$3,600.00	$3,900.00	$4,200.00	$4,500.00
$370,000.00	$3,083.33	$3,391.67	$3,700.00	$4,008.33	$4,316.67	$4,625.00
$380,000.00	$3,166.67	$3,483.33	$3,800.00	$4,116.67	$4,433.33	$4,750.00
$390,000.00	$3,250.00	$3,875.00	$3,900.00	$4,225.00	$4,550.00	$4,875.00
$400,000.00	$3,333.33	$3,666.67	$4,000.00	$4,333.33	$4,666.67	$5,000.00
$410,000.00	$3,416.67	$3,758.33	$4,100.00	$4,441.67	$4,783.33	$5,125.00

Principal	Interest Rate					
	10%	11%	12%	13%	14%	15%
$420,000.00	$3,500.00	$3,850.00	$4,200.00	$4,550.00	$4,900.00	$5,250.00
$430,000.00	$3,583.33	$3,941.67	$4,300.00	$4,658.33	$5,106.67	$5,375.00
$440,000.00	$3,666.67	$4,033.33	$4,400.00	$4,766.67	$5,133.33	$5,500.00
$450,000.00	$3,750.00	$4,125.00	$4,500.00	$4,875.00	$5,250.00	$5,625.00
$460,000.00	$3,833.33	$4,216.67	$4,600.00	$4,983.33	$5,366.67	$5,750.00
$470,000.00	$3,916.67	$4,308.33	$4,700.00	$5,091.67	$5,483.33	$5,875.00
$480,000.00	$4,000.00	$4,400.00	$4,800.00	$5,200.00	$5,600.00	$6,000.00
$490,000.00	$4,083.33	$4,491.67	$4,900.00	$5,308.33	$5,716.67	$6,125.00
$500,000.00	$4,166.67	$4,583.33	$5,000.00	$5,416.67	$5,833.33	$6,250.00

¶715.05

Monthly Income from Various Principals

Principal	Interest Rate				
	16%	17%	18%	19%	20%
$10,000.00	$133.33	$141.67	$150.00	$158.33	$166.67
$20,000.00	$266.67	$283.33	$300.00	$316.67	$333.33
$30,000.00	$400.00	$425.00	$450.00	$475.00	$500.00
$40,000.00	$533.33	$566.67	$600.00	$633.33	$666.67
$50,000.00	$666.67	$708.33	$750.00	$791.67	$833.33
$60,000.00	$800.00	$850.00	$900.00	$950.00	$1,000.00
$70,000.00	$933.33	$991.67	$1,050.00	$1,108.33	$1,166.67
$80,000.00	$1,066.67	$1,133.33	$1,200.00	$1,266.67	$1,333.33
$90,000.00	$1,200.00	$1,275.00	$1,350.00	$1,425.00	$1,500.00
$100,000.00	$1,333.33	$1,416.67	$1,500.00	$1,583.33	$1,666.67
$110,000.00	$1,466.67	$1,558.33	$1,650.00	$1,741.67	$1,833.33
$120,000.00	$1,600.00	$1,700.00	$1,800.00	$1,900.00	$2,000.00
$130,000.00	$1,733.33	$1,841.67	$1,950.00	$2,058.33	$2,166.67
$140,000.00	$1,866.67	$1,983.33	$2,100.00	$2,216.67	$2,333.33
$150,000.00	$2,000.00	$2,125.00	$2,250.00	$2,375.00	$2,500.00
$160,000.00	$2,133.33	$2,266.67	$2,400.00	$2,533.33	$2,666.67
$170,000.00	$2,266.67	$2,408.33	$2,550.00	$2,691.67	$2,833.33
$180,000.00	$2,400.00	$2,550.00	$2,700.00	$2,850.00	$3,000.00
$190,000.00	$2,533.33	$2,691.67	$2,850.00	$3,008.33	$3,166.67
$200,000.00	$2,666.67	$2,833.33	$3,000.00	$3,166.67	$3,333.33
$210,000.00	$2,800.00	$2,975.00	$3,150.00	$3,325.00	$3,500.00
$220,000.00	$2,933.33	$3,116.67	$3,300.00	$3,483.33	$3,666.67
$230,000.00	$3,066.67	$3,258.33	$3,450.00	$3,641.67	$3,833.33
$240,000.00	$3,200.00	$3,400.00	$3,600.00	$3,800.00	$4,000.00
$250,000.00	$3,333.33	$3,541.67	$3,750.00	$3,958.33	$4,266.67
$260,000.00	$3,466.67	$3,683.33	$3,900.00	$4,116.67	$4,333.33
$270,000.00	$3,600.00	$3,825.00	$4,050.00	$4,275.00	$4,500.00
$280,000.00	$3,733.33	$3,966.67	$4,200.00	$4,433.33	$4,666.67
$290,000.00	$3,866.67	$4,108.33	$4,350.00	$4,591.67	$4,833.33
$300,000.00	$4,000.00	$4,250.00	$4,500.00	$4,750.00	$5,000.00
$310,000.00	$4,133.33	$4,391.67	$4,650.00	$4,908.33	$5,166.67
$320,000.00	$4,266.67	$4,533.33	$4,800.00	$5,066.67	$5,333.33
$330,000.00	$4,400.00	$4,675.00	$4,950.00	$5,225.00	$5,500.00
$340,000.00	$4,533.33	$4,816.67	$5,100.00	$5,383.33	$5,666.67
$350,000.00	$4,666.67	$4,958.33	$5,250.00	$5,541.67	$5,833.33
$360,000.00	$4,800.00	$5,100.00	$5,400.00	$5,700.00	$6,000.00
$370,000.00	$4,933.33	$5,241.67	$5,550.00	$5,858.33	$6,166.67
$380,000.00	$5,066.67	$5,383.33	$5,700.00	$6,016.67	$6,333.33
$390,000.00	$5,200.00	$5,525.00	$5,850.00	$6,175.00	$6,500.00
$400,000.00	$5,333.33	$5,666.67	$6,000.00	$6,333.33	$6,666.67
$410,000.00	$5,466.67	$5,808.33	$6,150.00	$6,491.67	$6,833.33

Principal	Interest Rate				
	16%	17%	18%	19%	20%
$420,000.00	$5,600.00	$5,950.00	$6,300.00	$6,650.00	$7,000.00
$430,000.00	$5,733.33	$6,091.67	$6,450.00	$6,808.33	$7,166.67
$440,000.00	$5,866.67	$6,233.33	$6,600.00	$6,966.67	$7,333.33
$450,000.00	$6,000.00	$6,375.00	$6,750.00	$7,125.00	$7,500.00
$460,000.00	$6,133.33	$6,516.67	$6,900.00	$7,283.33	$7,666.67
$470,000.00	$6,266.67	$6,658.33	$7,050.00	$7,441.67	$7,833.33
$480,000.00	$6,400.00	$6,800.00	$7,200.00	$7,600.00	$8,000.00
$490,000.00	$6,533.33	$6,941.67	$7,350.00	$7,758.33	$8,166.67
$500,000.00	$6,666.67	$7,083.33	$7,500.00	$7,916.67	$8,333.33

Monthly Income from Various Principals

Principal	Interest Rate				
	5%	6%	7%	8%	9%
$510,000.00	$2,125.00	$2,550.00	$2,975.00	$3,400.00	$3,825.00
$520,000.00	$2,166.67	$2,600.00	$3,033.33	$3,466.67	$3,900.00
$530,000.00	$2,208.33	$2,650.00	$3,091.67	$3,533.33	$3,975.00
$540,000.00	$2,250.00	$2,700.00	$3,150.00	$3,600.00	$4,050.00
$550,000.00	$2,291.67	$2,750.00	$3,208.33	$3,666.67	$4,125.00
$560,000.00	$2,333.33	$2,800.00	$3,266.67	$3,733.33	$4,200.00
$570,000.00	$2,375.00	$2,850.00	$3,325.00	$3,800.00	$4,275.00
$580,000.00	$2,416.67	$2,900.00	$3,383.33	$3,866.67	$4,350.00
$590,000.00	$2,458.33	$2,950.00	$3,441.67	$3,933.33	$4,425.00
$600,000.00	$2,500.00	$3,000.00	$3,500.00	$4,000.00	$4,500.00
$610,000.00	$2,541.67	$3,050.00	$3,558.33	$4,066.67	$4,575.00
$620,000.00	$2,583.33	$3,100.00	$3,616.67	$4,133.33	$4,650.00
$630,000.00	$2,625.00	$3,150.00	$3,675.00	$4,200.00	$4,725.00
$640,000.00	$2,666.67	$3,200.00	$3,733.33	$4,266.67	$4,800.00
$650,000.00	$2,708.33	$3,250.00	$3,791.67	$4,333.33	$4,875.00
$660,000.00	$2,750.00	$3,300.00	$3,850.00	$4,400.00	$4,950.00
$670,000.00	$2,791.67	$3,350.00	$3,908.33	$4,466.67	$5,025.00
$680,000.00	$2,833.33	$3,400.00	$3,966.67	$4,533.33	$5,100.00
$690,000.00	$2,875.00	$3,450.00	$4,025.00	$4,600.00	$5,175.00
$700,000.00	$2,916.67	$3,500.00	$4,083.33	$4,666.67	$5,250.00
$710,000.00	$2,958.33	$3,550.00	$4,141.67	$4,733.33	$5,325.00
$720,000.00	$3,000.00	$3,600.00	$4,200.00	$4,800.00	$5,400.00
$730,000.00	$3,041.67	$3,650.00	$4,258.33	$4,866.67	$5,475.00
$740,000.00	$3,083.33	$3,700.00	$4,316.67	$4,933.33	$5,550.00
$750,000.00	$3,125.00	$3,750.00	$4,375.00	$5,000.00	$5,625.00
$760,000.00	$3,166.67	$3,800.00	$4,433.33	$5,066.67	$5,700.00
$770,000.00	$3,208.33	$3,850.00	$4,491.67	$5133.33	$5,775.00
$780,000.00	$3,250.00	$3,900.00	$4,550.00	$5,200.00	$5,850.00
$790,000.00	$3,291.67	$3,950.00	$4,608.33	$5,266.67	$5,925.00
$800,000.00	$3,333.33	$4,000.00	$4,666.67	$5,333.33	$6,000.00
$810,000.00	$3,375.00	$4,050.00	$4,725.00	$5,400.00	$6,075.00
$820,000.00	$3,416.67	$4,100.00	$4,783.33	$5,466.67	$6,150.00
$830,000.00	$3,458.33	$4,150.00	$4,841.67	$5,533.33	$6,225.00
$840,000.00	$3,500.00	$4,200.00	$4,900.00	$5,600.00	$6,300.00
$850,000.00	$3,541.67	$4,250.00	$4,958.33	$5,666.67	$6,375.00
$860,000.00	$3,583.33	$4,300.00	$5,016.67	$5,733.33	$6,450.00
$870,000.00	$3,625.00	$4,350.00	$5,075.00	$5,800.00	$6,525.00
$880,000.00	$3,666.67	$4,400.00	$5,133.33	$5,866.67	$6,600.00
$890,000.00	$3,708.33	$4,450.00	$5,191.67	$5,933.33	$6,675.00
$900,000.00	$3,750.00	$4,500.00	$5,250.00	$6,000.00	$6,750.00
$910,000.00	$3,791.67	$4,550.00	$5,308.33	$6,066.67	$6,825.00

Principal	Interest Rate				
	5%	6%	7%	8%	9%
$920,000.00	$3,833.33	$4,600.00	$5,366.67	$6,133.33	$6,900.00
$930,000.00	$3,875.00	$4,650.00	$5,425.00	$6,200.00	$6,975.00
$940,000.00	$3,916.67	$4,700.00	$5,483.33	$6,266.67	$7,050.00
$950,000.00	$3,958.33	$4,750.00	$5,541.67	$6,333.33	$7,125.00
$960,000.00	$4,000.00	$4,800.00	$5,600.00	$6,400.00	$7,200.00
$970,000.00	$4,041.67	$4,850.00	$5,658.33	$6,466.67	$7,275.00
$980,000.00	$4,083.33	$4,900.00	$5,716.67	$6,533.33	$7,350.00
$990,000.00	$4,125.00	$4,950.00	$5,775.00	$6,600.00	$7,425.00
$1,000,000.00	$4,166.67	$5,000.00	$5,833.33	$6,666.67	$7,500.00

Monthly Income from Various Principals

Principal	Interest Rate					
	10%	11%	12%	13%	14%	15%
$510,000.00	$4,250.00	$4,675.00	$5,100.00	$5,525.00	$5,950.00	$6,375.00
$520,000.00	$4,333.33	$4,766.67	$5,200.00	$5,633.33	$6,066.67	$6,500.00
$530,000.00	$4,416.67	$4,858.33	$5,300.00	$5,741.67	$6,183.33	$6,625.00
$540,000.00	$4,500.00	$4,950.00	$5,400.00	$5,850.00	$6,300.00	$6,750.00
$550,000.00	$4,583.33	$5,041.67	$5,500.00	$5,958.33	$6,416.67	$6,875.00
$560,000.00	$4,666.67	$5,133.33	$5,600.00	$6,066.67	$6,533.33	$7,000.00
$570,000.00	$4,750.00	$5,225.00	$5,700.00	$6,175.00	$6,650.00	$7,125.00
$580,000.00	$4,833.33	$5,316.67	$5,800.00	$6,283.33	$6,766.67	$7,250.00
$590,000.00	$4,916.67	$5,408.33	$5,900.00	$6,391.67	$6,883.33	$7,375.00
$600,000.00	$5,000.00	$5,500.00	$6,000.00	$6,500.00	$7,000.00	$7,500.00
$610,000.00	$5,083.33	$5,591.67	$6,100.00	$6,608.33	$7,116.67	$7,625.00
$620,000.00	$5,166.67	$5,683.33	$6,200.00	$6,716.67	$7,233.33	$7,750.00
$630,000.00	$5,250.00	$5,775.00	$6,300.00	$6,825.00	$7,350.00	$7,875.00
$640,000.00	$5,333.33	$5,866.67	$6,400.00	$6,933.33	$7,466.67	$8,000.00
$650,000.00	$5,416.67	$5,958.33	$6,500.00	$7,041.67	$7,583.33	$8,125.00
$660,000.00	$5,500.00	$6,050.00	$6,600.00	$7,150.00	$7,700.00	$8,250.00
$670,000.00	$5,583.33	$6,141.67	$6,700.00	$7,258.33	$7,816.67	$8,375.00
$680,000.00	$5,666.67	$6,233.33	$6,800.00	$7,366.67	$7,933.33	$8,500.00
$690,000.00	$5,750.00	$6,325.00	$6,900.00	$7,475.00	$8,050.00	$8,625.00
$700,000.00	$5,833.33	$6,416.67	$7,000.00	$7,583.33	$8,166.67	$8,750.00
$710,000.00	$5,916.67	$6,508.33	$7,100.00	$7,691.67	$8,283.33	$8,875.00
$720,000.00	$6,000.00	$6,600.00	$7,200.00	$7,800.00	$8,400.00	$9,000.00
$730,000.00	$6,083.33	$6,691.67	$7,300.00	$7,908.33	$8,516.67	$9,125.00
$740,000.00	$6,166.67	$6,783.33	$7,400.00	$8,016.67	$8,633.33	$9,250.00
$750,000.00	$6,250.00	$6,875.00	$7,500.00	$8,125.00	$8,750.00	$9,375.00
$760,000.00	$6,333.33	$6,966.67	$7,600.00	$8,233.33	$8,866.67	$9,500.00
$770,000.00	$6,416.67	$7,058.33	$7,700.00	$8,341.67	$8,983.33	$9,625.00
$780,000.00	$6,500.00	$7,150.00	$7,800.00	$8,450.00	$9,100.00	$9,750.00
$790,000.00	$6,583.33	$7,241.67	$7,900.00	$8,558.33	$9,216.67	$9,875.00
$800,000.00	$6,666.67	$7,333.33	$8,000.00	$8,666.67	$9,333.33	$10,000.00
$810,000.00	$6,750.00	$7,425.00	$8,100.00	$8,775.00	$9,450.00	$10,125.00
$820,000.00	$6,833.33	$7,516.67	$8,200.00	$8,883.33	$9,566.67	$10,250.00
$830,000.00	$6,916.67	$7,608.33	$8,300.00	$8,991.67	$9,683.33	$10,375.00
$840,000.00	$7,000.00	$7,700.00	$8,400.00	$9,100.00	$9,800.00	$10,500.00
$850,000.00	$7,083.33	$7,791.67	$8,500.00	$9,208.33	$9,916.67	$10,625.00
$860,000.00	$7,166.67	$7,883.33	$8,600.00	$9,316.67	$10,033.33	$10,750.00
$870,000.00	$7,250.00	$7,975.00	$8,700.00	$9,425.00	$10,150.00	$10,875.00
$880,000.00	$7,333.33	$8,066.67	$8,800.00	$9,533.33	$10,266.67	$11,000.00
$890,000.00	$7,416.67	$8,158.33	$8,900.00	$9,641.67	$10,383.33	$11,125.00
$900,000.00	$7,500.00	$8,250.00	$9,000.00	$9,750.00	$10,500.00	$11,250.00
$910,000.00	$7,583.33	$8,341.67	$9,100.00	$9,858.33	$10,616.67	$11,375.00
$920,000.00	$7,666.67	$8,433.33	$9,200.00	$9,966.67	$10,733.33	$11,500.00
$930,000.00	$7,750.00	$8,525.00	$9,300.00	$10,075.00	$10,850.00	$11,625.00
$940,000.00	$7,833.33	$8,616.67	$9,400.00	$10,183.33	$10,966.67	$11,750.00
$950,000.00	$7,916.67	$8,708.33	$9,500.00	$10,291.67	$11,083.33	$11,875.00

¶715.05

Principal	Interest Rate					
	10%	11%	12%	13%	14%	15%
$960,000.00	$8,000.00	$8,800.00	$9,600.00	$10,400.00	$11,200.00	$12,000.00
$970,000.00	$8,083.33	$8,891.67	$9,700.00	$10,508.33	$11,316.67	$12,125.00
$980,000.00	$8,166.67	$8,983.33	$9,800.00	$10,616.67	$11,433.33	$12,250.00
$990,000.00	$8,250.00	$9,075.00	9,900.00	$10,725.00	$11,550.00	$12,375.00
$1,000,000.00	$8,333.33	$9,166.67	$10,000.00	$10,833.33	$11,666.67	$12,500.00

Monthly Income from Various Principals

Principal	Interest Rate				
	16%	17%	18%	19%	20%
$510,000.00	$6,800.00	$7,225.00	$7,650.00	$8,075.00	$8,500.00
$520,000.00	$6,933.33	$7,366.67	$7,800.00	$8,233.33	$8,666.67
$530,000.00	$7,066.67	$7,508.33	$7,950.00	$8,391.67	$8,833.33
$540,000.00	$7,200.00	$7,650.00	$8,100.00	$8,550.00	$9,000.00
$550,000.00	$7,333.33	$7,791.67	$8,250.00	$8,708.33	$9,166.67
$560,000.00	$7,466.67	$7,933.33	$8,400.00	$8,866.67	$9,333.33
$570,000.00	$7,600.00	$8,075.00	$8,550.00	$9,025.00	$9,500.00
$580,000.00	$7,733.33	$8,216.67	$8,700.00	$9,183.33	$9,666.67
$590,000.00	$7,866.67	$8,358.33	$8,850.00	$9,341.67	$9,833.33
$600,000.00	$8,000.00	$8,500.00	$9,000.00	$9,500.00	$10,000.00
$610,000.00	$8,133.33	$8,641.67	$9,150.00	$9,658.33	$10,166.67
$620,000.00	$8,266.67	$8,783.33	$9,300.00	$9,816.67	$10,333.33
$630,000.00	$8,400.00	$8,925.00	$9,450.00	$9,975.00	$10,500.00
$640,000.00	$8,533.33	$9,066.67	$9,600.00	$10,133.33	$10,666.67
$650,000.00	$8,666.67	$9,208.33	$9,750.00	$10,291.67	$10,833.33
$660,000.00	$8,800.00	$9,350.00	$9,900.00	$10,450.00	$11,000.00
$670,000.00	$8,933.33	$9,491.67	$10,050.00	$10,608.33	$11,166.67
$680,000.00	$9,066.67	$9,633.33	$10,200.00	$10,766.67	$11,333.33
$690,000.00	$9,200.00	$9,775.00	$10,350.00	$10,925.00	$11,500.00
$700,000.00	$9,333.33	$9,916.67	$10,500.00	$11,083.33	$11,666.67
$710,000.00	$9,466.67	$10,058.33	$10,650.00	$11,241.67	$11,833.33
$720,000.00	$9,600.00	$10,200.00	$10,800.00	$11,400.00	$12,000.00
$730,000.00	$9,733.33	$10,341.67	$10,950.00	$11,558.33	$12,166.67
$740,000.00	$9,866.67	$10,483.33	$11,100.00	$11,716.67	$12,333.33
$750,000.00	$10,000.00	$10,625.00	$11,250.00	$11,875.00	$12,500.00
$760,000.00	$10,133.33	$10,766.67	$11,400.00	$12,033.33	$12,666.67
$770,000.00	$10,266.67	$10,908.33	$11,550.00	$12,191.67	$12,833.33
$780,000.00	$10,400.00	$11,050.00	$11,700.00	$12,350.00	$13,000.00
$790,000.00	$10,533.33	$11,191.67	$11,850.00	$12,508.33	$13,166.67
$800,000.00	$10,666.67	$11,333.33	$12,000.00	$12,666.67	$13,333.33
$810,000.00	$10,800.00	$11,475.00	$12,150.00	$12,825.00	$13,500.00
$820,000.00	$10,933.33	$11,616.67	$12,300.00	$12,983.33	$13,666.67
$830,000.00	$11,066.67	$11,758.33	$12,450.00	$13,141.67	$13,833.33
$840,000.00	$11,200.00	$11,900.00	$12,600.00	$13,300.00	$14,000.00
$850,000.00	$11,333.33	$12,041.67	$12,750.00	$13,458.33	$14,166.67
$860,000.00	$11,466.67	$12,183.33	$12,900.00	$13,616.67	$14,333.33
$870,000.00	$11,600.00	$12,325.00	$13,050.00	$13,775.00	$14,500.00
$880,000.00	$11,733.33	$12,466.67	$13,200.00	$13,933.33	$14,666.67
$890,000.00	$11,866.67	$12,608.33	$13,350.00	$14,091.67	$14,833.33
$900,000.00	$12,000.00	$12,750.00	$13,500.00	$14,250.00	$15,000.00
$910,000.00	$12,133.33	$12,891.67	$13,650.00	$14,408.33	$15,166.67

Principal	Interest Rate				
	16%	17%	18%	19%	20%
$920,000.00	$12,266.67	$13,033.33	$13,800.00	$14,566.67	$15,333.33
$930,000.00	$12,400.00	$13,175.00	$13,950.00	$14,725.00	$15,500.00
$940,000.00	$12,533.33	$13,316.67	14,100.00	$14,883.33	$15,666.67
$950,000.00	$12,666.67	$13,458.33	$14,250.00	$15,041.67	$15,833.33
$960,000.00	$12,800.00	$13,600.00	$14,400.00	$15,200.00	$16,000.00
$970,000.00	$12,933.33	$13,741.67	$14,550.00	$15,358.33	$16,166.67
$980,000.00	$13,066.67	$13,883.33	$14,700.00	$15,516.67	$16,333.33
$990,000.00	$13,200.00	$14,025.00	$14,850.00	$15,675.00	$16,500.00
$1,000,000.00	$13,333.33	$14,166.67	$15,000.00	$15,833.33	$16,666.67

.06 Savings Withdrawal Term (Static Reserve and Exponential Reserve Formulas)

To make one realize how short of a time a given sum of money will last if it's not put in an "earnings" position (i.e., it's kept in a non-interest bearing checking account or under your mattress), use the model depletion or non-renewable source formulas.

Static Reserve. The static reserve is how long the supply S will last at a particular constant rate of use U, namely

S/U units of time.

Static Reserve Formula Example. If you have retirement savings of $500,000 and you wish to live draw out $50,000/year, and there is no inflation, how long will the retirement savings last?

Use static reserve formula:

Static reserve = S/U

$500,000 / $50,000 = 10 years

Exponential Reserve. The exponential reserve is how long the supply S will last at an initial rate of use U that is increasing by a proportion "r" each year—

$$\frac{Ln\,[1 + (S/U)\,r\,]}{Ln\,(1 + r)} \quad \text{units of time.}$$

(Where, Ln is natural logarithm)

Exponential Reserve Formula Example. You have retirement savings of $500,000 and wish to maintain a standard of living in today's dollars of $50,000 year. But inflation is at 4% per year, and it will cost increasingly more to live each year. How long will the nest egg last?

Use exponential reserve formula:

S/U = $500,000 / $50,000 = 10 years

$$\text{Term} = \frac{Ln\,[1 + (10)\,(.04)\,]}{Ln\,1.04}$$

$$= \frac{\text{Ln } 1.40}{\text{Ln } 1.04}$$

= 8.58 years

By contrast, if the investor had the $500,000 in a mutual fund, he could have withdrawn $50,000 a year for 30 years, or $1,500,000, earned a 12.32-percent return, and still have a fund remaining worth $3,671,323. (Computed from actual returns from American Funds AMCAP Fund from 12/31/70 through12/31/00.)

Example of Static and Exponential Reserve Formula of $1,000,000. If facts are the same, but the nest egg is $1,000,000, how long will it last?

Static Reserve: (No inflation)

S/U = $1,000,000 / $50,000 = 20 years

Exponential reserve (inflation of 4%)

$$\text{Term} = \text{Ln} \quad [1 + (20)\,(.04)]$$

$$= \frac{\text{Ln } (1.04)}{\text{Ln } 1.80}$$

$$\frac{}{\text{Ln } 1.04}$$

$$= \quad \frac{14.99}{\text{years}}$$

.07 Savings Accumulation from Five-Year IRA Investment

Impact of Time on IRA Investment of $2,000 per Year Invested for Five Years—Investment Fund Grows to Retirement Age per Given Interest Rate

This table illustrates "the cost of waiting" to invest in a retirement vehicle.

A five year period can result in a significant loss of potential growth.

Note that a younger investor who waits five years to invest is losing tremendous potential growth (due to his longer time frame of growth to age 65) than is an older investor who waits five years.

Example (1): A person is 40 years old, invests $2,000/year for 5 years and receives 8% interest. At age 65, the value of the funds will be $54,688. Assume the same person waits until he is 45 and then invests $2,000/year for 5 years and receives 8% interest. At age 65, the value of the fund will be $37,220. This investor has lost a potential growth of $54,688 – $37,220 = $17,468 by waiting 5 years to start his retirement account.

Example (2):
Loss to Younger Investor

Investor	At 8% Interest Value of Fund at Age 65
Age 20	$254,898
Age 25	$173,479
Loss of potential	$ 81,419

Loss to Older Investor

Investor	At 8% Interest Value of Fund at age 65
Age 40	$54,688
Age 45	$37,220
Loss of Potential	$17,468

Waiting five years cost the 20-year-old investor $81,419, while waiting five years cost the 40-year-old $17,468 in potential growth.

The Impact of Time on IRA Investment of $2,000 per Year Invested for Five Years (Investment Fund Grows to Retirement Age per Specified Interest Rates)

Investor's Age	Years to Age 65	Interest Rate			
		5%	6%	7%	8%
20	45	$77,800.76	$115,963.10	$172,228.40	$254,898.20
21	44	$74,095.97	$109,399.15	$160,961.12	$236,016.85
22	43	$70,567.59	$103,206.74	$150,430.95	$218,534.12
23	42	$67,207.22	$97,364.85	$140,589.68	$202,346.41
24	41	$64,006.88	$91,853.63	$131,392.22	$187,357.78
25	40	$60,958.93	$86,654.37	$122,796.47	$173,479.43
26	39	$58,056.13	$81,749.41	$114,763.05	$160,629.10
27	38	$55,291.55	$77,122.08	$107,255.19	$148,730.65
28	37	$52,658.62	$72,756.68	$100,238.50	$137,713.56
29	36	$50,151.07	$68,638.38	$93,680.84	$127,512.56
30	35	$47,762.92	$64,753.19	$87,552.18	$118,067.19
31	34	$45,488.49	$61,087.91	$81,824.47	$109,321.47
32	33	$43,322.38	$57,630.11	$76,471.47	$101,223.58
33	32	$41,259.41	$54,368.02	$71,468.66	$93,725.54
34	31	$39,296.47	$51,290.59	$66,793.14	$86,782.91
35	30	$37,423.50	$48,387.35	$62,423.50	$80,354.54
36	29	$35,641.43	$45,648.44	$58,339.72	$74,402.35
37	28	$33,944.22	$43,064.57	$54,523.10	$68,891.07
38	27	$32,327.82	$40,626.95	$50,956.17	$63,788.03
39	26	$30,788.40	$38,327.31	$47,622.59	$59,062.99
40	25	$29,322.29	$36,157.84	$44,507.09	$54,687.95
41	24	$27,925.99	$34,111.17	$41,595.41	$50,636.99
42	23	$26,596.18	$32,180.35	$38,874.22	$46,886.10
43	22	$25,329.70	$30,358.82	$36,331.04	$43,413.06
44	21	$24,123.52	$28,640.40	$33,954.25	$40,197.28
45	20	$22,974.78	$27,019.24	$31,732.94	$37,219.70
46	19	$21,880.74	$25,489.85	$29,656.95	$34,462.69
47	18	$20,838.80	$24,047.03	$27,716.78	$31,909.89
48	17	$19,846.48	$22,685.88	$25,903.53	$29,546.20
49	16	$18,901.41	$21,401.77	$24,208.91	$27,357.59
50	15	$18,001.34	$20,190.35	$22,625.15	$25,331.10
51	14	$17,144.14	$19,047.50	$21,145.00	$23,454.72
52	13	$16,327.75	$17,969.34	$19,761.68	$21,717.34
53	12	$15,550.24	$16,952.21	$18,468.86	$20,108.65
54	11	$14,809.75	$15,992.65	$17,260.62	$18,619.12
55	10	$14,104.52	$15,087.40	$16,131.42	$17,239.92
56	9	$13,432.88	$14,233.40	$15,076.09	$15,962.89
57	8	$12,793.22	$13,427.74	$14,089.81	$14,780.46
58	7	$12,184.02	$12,667.68	$13,168.04	$13,685.61
59	6	$11,603.83	$11,950.64	$12,306.58	$12,671.86
60	5	$11,051.26	$11,274.19	$11,501.48	$11,733.20

The Impact of Time on IRA Investment of $2,000 per Year Invested for Five Years (Investment Fund Grows to Retirement Age per Specified Interest Rates)

Investor's Age	Years to Age 65	Interest Rate			
		9%	10%	11%	12%
20	45	$375,952.58	$552,624.56	$809,624.99	$1,182,277.22
21	44	$344,910.62	$502,385.97	$729,391.88	$1,055,604.66
22	43	$316,431.76	$456,714.51	$657,109.80	$942,504.16
23	42	$290,304.37	$415,195.01	$591,990.81	$841,521.58
24	41	$266,334.29	$377,450.01	$53,3325.06	$751,358.55
25	40	$244,343.38	$343,136.37	$480,473.02	$670,855.85
26	39	$224,168.24	$311,942.16	$432,858.58	$598,978.44
27	38	$205,658.94	$238,583.78	$389,962.68	$534,802.17
28	37	$188,677.92	$257,803.44	$351,317.73	$477,501.94
29	36	$173,099.01	$234,366.76	$316,502.46	$426,341.02
30	35	$158,806.43	$213,060.69	$285,137.35	$380,661.62
31	34	$145,693.97	$193,691.54	$256,880.50	$339,876.45
32	33	$133,664.20	$176,083.22	$231,423.87	$303,461.12
33	32	$122,627.70	$160,075.65	$208,489.98	$270,947.43
34	31	$112,502.48	$145,523.32	$187,828.81	$241,917.34
35	30	$103,213.28	$132,293.93	$169,215.14	$215,997.63
36	29	$94,691.09	$120,267.21	$152,446.07	$192,855.03
37	28	$86,872.56	$109,333.82	$137,338.80	$172,191.99
38	27	$79,699.59	$99,394.39	$123,728.65	$153,742.85
39	26	$73,118.89	$90,358.53	$111,467.25	$137,270.40
40	25	$67,081.55	$82,144.12	$100,420.95	$122,562.86
41	24	$61,542.71	$74,676.47	$90,469.32	$109,431.12
42	23	$56,461.20	$67,887.70	$81,503.90	$97,706.36
43	22	$51,799.27	$61,716.09	$73,426.93	$87,237.82
44	21	$47,522.26	$56,105.54	$66,105.39	$77,890.91
45	20	$43,598.41	$51,005.04	$59,594.95	$69,545.46
46	19	$39,998.54	$46,368.21	$53,689.14	$62,094.16
47	18	$36,695.91	$42,152.92	$48,368.60	$55,441.21
48	17	$33,665.97	$38,320.84	$43,573.51	$49,501.08
49	16	$30,886.21	$34,837.13	$39,257.04	$44,197.39
50	15	$28,335.97	$31,670.11	$35,366.70	$39,461.96
51	14	$25,996.31	$28,791.01	$31,861.89	$35,233.89
52	13	$23,849.82	$26,173.65	$28,704.41	$31,458.83
53	12	$21,880.57	$23,794.23	$25,859.83	$28,088.24
54	11	$20,073.92	$21,631.11	$23,297.14	$25,078.79
55	10	$18,416.44	$19,664.65	$20,988.42	$22,391.78
56	9	$16,895.81	$17,876.95	$18,908.48	$19,992.66
57	8	$15,500.75	$16,251.78	$17,034.67	$17,850.59
58	7	$14,220.87	$14,774.34	$15,346.55	$15,938.02
59	6	$13,046.67	$13,431.22	$13,825.72	$14,230.38
60	5	$11,969.42	$12,210.20	$12,455.60	$12,705.69

¶715.07

The Impact of Time on IRA Investment of $2,000 per Year Invested for Five Years (Investment Fund Grows to Retirement Age per Specified Interest Rates)

Investor's Age	Years to Age 65	Interest Rate			
		13%	14%	15%	16%
20	45	$3,170,684	$4,807,913	$7,265,175	$10,940,749
21	44	$2,805,915	$4,217,467	$6,317,544	$9,431,680
22	43	$2,483,111	$3,699,533	$5,493,516	$8,130,759
23	42	$2,197,443	$3,245,204	$4,776,970	$7,009,275
24	41	$1,944,640	$2,846,670	$4,153,887	$6,042,478
25	40	$1,720,920	$2,497,079	$3,612,076	$5,209,033
26	39	$1,522,938	$2,190,420	$3,140,935	$4,490,545
27	38	$1,347,733	$1,921,421	$2,731,248	$3,871,160
28	37	$1,192,984	$1,685,457	$2,374,998	$3,337,207
29	36	$1,055,472	$1,478,471	$2,065,216	$2,876,902
30	35	$934,046	$1,296,904	$1,795,840	$2,480,088
31	34	$826,590	$1,137,635	$1,561,600	$2,138,007
32	33	$731,495	$997,926	$1,357,913	$1,843,109
33	32	$647,341	$875,373	$1,180,794	$1,588,887
34	31	$572,868	$767,871	$1,026,777	$1,369,730
35	30	$506,963	$673,571	$892,850	$1,180,802
36	29	$448,640	$590,852	$776,391	$1,017,933
37	28	$397,026	$518,291	$675,122	$877,528
38	27	$351,350	$454,641	$587,063	$756,490
39	26	$310,930	$398,808	$510,489	$652,146
40	25	$275,159	$349,832	$443,904	$562,195
41	24	$243,503	$306,870	$386,003	$484,651
42	23	$215,490	$269,184	$335,655	$417,802
43	22	$190,699	$236,126	$291,874	$360,174
44	21	$168,760	$207,128	$253,803	$310,495
45	20	$149,345	$181,691	$220,698	$267,668
46	19	$132,164	$159,378	$191,912	$230,748
47	18	$116,959	$139,805	$166,880	$198,921
48	17	$103,503	$122,636	$145,113	$171,483
49	16	$91,596	$107,576	$126,185	$147,830
50	15	$81,058	$94,365	$109,726	$127,440
51	14	$71,733	$82,776	$95,414	$109,862
52	13	$63,480	$72,610	$82,968	$94,709
53	12	$56,177	$63,693	$72,146	$81,645
54	11	$49,714	$55,871	$62,736	$70,384
55	10	$43,995	$49,010	$54,553	$60,676
56	9	$38,934	$42,991	$47,437	$52,306
57	8	$34,454	$37,711	$41,250	$45,092
58	7	$30,491	$33,080	$35,869	$38,872
59	6	$26,983	$29,017	$31,191	$33,510
60	5	$23,878	$25,454	$27,122	$28,888

¶715.07

The Impact of Time on IRA Investment of $2,000 per Year Invested for Five Years (Investment Fund Grows to Retirement Age per Specified Interest Rates)

Investor's Age	Years to Age 65	Interest Rate			
		17%	18%	19%	20%
20	45	$16,420,422	$24,563,033	$36,623,824	$54,431,761
21	44	$14,034,548	$20,816,129	$30,776,322	$45,359,801
22	43	$11,995,340	$17,640,787	$25,862,456	$37,799,834
23	42	$10,252,428	$14,949,820	$21,733,156	$31,499,862
24	41	$8,762,759	$12,669,339	$18,263,156	$26,249,885
25	40	$7,489,537	$10,736,728	$15,347,190	$21,874,904
26	39	$6,401,314	$9,098,922	$12,896,798	$18,229,086
27	38	$5,471,208	$7,710,950	$10,837,645	$15,190,905
28	37	$4,676,246	$6,534,704	$9,107,265	$12,659,088
29	36	$3,996,792	$5,537,884	$7,653,164	$10,549,240
30	35	$3,416,061	$4,693,122	$6,431,230	$8,791,033
31	34	$2,919,710	$3,977,222	$5,404,395	$7,325,861
32	33	$2,495,479	$3,370,527	$4,541,508	$6,104,884
33	32	$2,132,888	$2,856,379	$3,816,393	$5,087,403
34	31	$1,822,981	$2,420,660	$3,207,053	$4,239,502
35	30	$1,558,103	$2,051,407	$2,695,003	$3,532,919
36	29	$1,331,712	$1,738,480	$2,264,708	$2,944,099
37	28	$1,138,215	$1,473,288	$1,903,116	$2,453,416
38	27	$972,834	$1,248,549	$1,599,257	$2,044,513
39	26	$831,482	$1,058,093	$1,343,913	$1,703,761
40	25	$710,668	$896,689	$1,129,339	$1,419,800
41	24	$607,408	$759,905	$949,024	$1,183,167
42	23	$519,152	$643,988	$797,499	$985,972
43	22	$443,720	$545,752	$670,167	$821,644
44	21	$379,248	$462,502	$563,166	$684,703
45	20	$324,143	$391,951	$473,248	$570,586
46	19	$277,046	$332,161	$397,688	$475,488
47	18	$236,791	$281,493	$334,191	$396,240
48	17	$202,385	$238,553	$280,833	$330,200
49	16	$172,979	$202,163	$235,994	$275,166
50	15	$147,845	$171,325	$198,314	$229,305
51	14	$126,363	$145,191	$166,650	$191,088
52	13	$108,003	$123,043	$140,042	$159,240
53	12	$92,310	$104,273	$117,683	$132,700
54	11	$78,897	$88,367	$98,893	$110,583
55	10	$67,434	$74,887	$83,103	$92,152
56	9	$57,635	$63,464	$69,834	$76,794
57	8	$49,261	$53,783	$58,684	$63,995
58	7	$42,103	$45,579	$49,315	$53,329
59	6	$35,986	38,626	$41,441	$44,440
60	5	$30,757	$32,734	$34,824	$37,034

.09 Value of Retirement Income After Inflation

This chart provides the value of a retirement fund in today's dollars given inflation rate assumption and years in retirement.

> *Example:*
>
> - Fund available for retirement = $200,000
> - Current age of worker = 55
> - If retirement is planned 10 years from now at age 65; then years to retirement = 10
> - If inflation is assumed as 3%

Answer: Value of retirement fund in today's dollars = $200,000 × .7441 = $148,820

> - If inflation is assumed as 5%

Answer: Value of retirement fund in today's dollars = $200,000 × .6139 = $122,780

Value of Retirement Income

Years to Retirement	Rate of Inflation					
	2%	3%	4%	5%	6%	7%
0	1.0000	1.0000	1.0000	1.0000	1.0000	1.0000
1	0.9804	0.9709	0.9615	0.9524	0.9434	0.9346
2	0.9612	0.9426	0.9246	0.9070	0.8900	0.8734
3	0.9423	0.9151	0.8890	0.8638	0.8396	0.8163
4	0.9238	0.8885	0.8548	0.8227	0.7921	0.7629
5	0.9057	0.8626	0.8219	0.7835	0.7473	0.7130
6	0.8880	0.8375	0.7903	0.7462	0.7050	0.6663
7	0.8706	0.8131	0.7599	0.7107	0.6651	0.6227
8	0.8535	0.7894	0.7307	0.6768	0.6274	0.5820
9	0.8368	0.7664	0.7026	0.6446	0.5919	0.5439
10	0.8203	0.7441	0.6756	0.6139	0.5584	0.5083
11	0.8043	0.7224	0.6496	0.5847	0.5268	0.4751
12	0.7885	0.7014	0.6246	0.5568	0.4970	0.4440
13	0.7730	0.6810	0.6006	0.5303	0.4688	0.4150
14	0.7579	0.6611	0.5775	0.5051	0.4423	0.3878
15	0.7430	0.6419	0.5533	0.4810	0.4173	0.3624
16	0.7284	0.6232	0.5339	0.4581	0.3936	0.3387
17	0.7142	0.6050	0.5134	0.4363	0.3714	0.3166
18	0.7002	0.5874	0.4936	0.4155	0.3503	0.2959
19	0.6864	0.5703	.4746	0.3957	0.3305	0.2765
20	0.6730	0.5537	0.4564	0.3769	0.3118	0.2584
21	0.6598	0.5375	0.4388	0.3589	0.2942	0.2415
22	0.6468	0.5219	0.4220	0.3418	0.2775	0.2257
23	0.6342	0.5067	0.4057	0.3256	0.2618	0.2109
24	0.6217	0.4919	0.3901	0.3101	0.2470	0.1971
25	0.6095	0.4776	0.3751	0.2953	0.2330	0.1842
26	0.5976	0.4637	0.3607	0.2812	0.2198	0.1722
27	0.5859	0.4502	0.3468	0.2678	0.2074	0.1609
28	0.5744	0.4371	0.3335	0.2551	0.1956	0.1504
29	0.5631	0.4243	0.3207	0.2429	0.1846	0.1406
30	0.5521	0.4120	0.3083	0.2314	0.1741	0.1314
31	0.5412	0.4000	0.2965	0.2204	0.1643	0.1228
32	0.5306	0.3883	0.2851	0.2099	0.1550	0.1147
33	0.5202	0.3770	0.2741	0.1999	0.1462	0.1072
34	0.5100	0.3660	0.2636	0.1904	0.1379	0.1002
35	0.5000	0.3554	0.2534	0.1813	0.1301	0.0937
36	0.4902	0.3450	0.2437	0.1727	0.1227	0.0875
37	0.4806	0.3350	0.2343	0.1644	0.1158	0.0818
38	0.4712	0.3252	0.2253	0.1566	0.1092	0.0765
39	0.4619	0.3158	0.2166	0.1491	0.1031	0.0715
40	0.4529	0.3066	0.2083	0.1420	0.0972	0.0668
41	0.4440	0.2976	0.2003	0.1353	0.0917	0.0624
42	0.4353	0.2890	0.1926	0.1288	0.0865	0.0583
43	0.4268	0.2805	0.1852	0.1227	0.0816	0.0545
44	0.4184	0.2724	0.1780	0.1169	0.0770	0.0509

INVESTMENT INSTRUMENTS

¶ 717 ANNUITIES

Comparison of Fixed and Variable Annuities

Fixed	Variable
Inflation risk	Less inflation risk
Fixed payments guaranteed	Payments variable
Minimum interest rate guaranteed	Rate of return variable
Premiums: Single or installment	Premiums: Single or installment
Portfolio: Fixed income securities	Portfolio: Equity or other securities
Subject to insurance regulations	Regulated by SEC, NASD, and Insurance regulations
Insurance company takes risk	Annuitant takes risk

.01 Definition and Overview

An annuity is a contract between the insurance company and the annuitant (the person who purchases the annuity). The annuitant agrees to invest a certain amount of money and the insurance company agrees to pay back to the annuitant under established conditions.

Annuity Types

- Fixed
  - Fixed income—guaranteed for annuity period
  - Guaranteed interest rate
  - Expense guarantee
- Variable Annuities
  - Expressed in units
  - Varies according to market value of securities in the portfolio
  - Variable income
  - Guaranteed payments of variable amount
  - Interest rate variable
  - Excess expenses charged to separate account
  - Funds invested in separate insurance account to support guaranteed payments

Annuity Risk

Variable annuities carry risk. They must be kept in a separate account. The separate account for a variable annuity is invested primarily in common stocks. The separate account can maintain a diversified portfolio much like that of the diversified common stock mutual fund. The SEC treats a separate account as either a unit investment trust or as an open-end investment company.

Annuity Purchase Plans

- Single premium deferred
- Single premium immediate
- Period payment plan-installments
- Sales charge-level load, front-end, downscaling (breakpoint discounts)

Taxation of Variable Annuities

Non-Tax Qualified Annuity

Accumulation period income and gross income accrue tax deferred. If payments stop, contract becomes a reduced paid-up contract. If owner surrenders contract before annuitization, then cost basis is recovered tax free, excess over tax is ordinary income, and there is a 10-percent penalty tax if taken before age 59 1/2.

Annuity Distribution

- Excess over cost is taxed as ordinary income when received.
- After contract annuitization use exclusion ratio to determine percentage of payments that represents return of capital.

Tax Qualified Annuities

- During accumulation period, income and gains accrue in separate account tax deferred.

If Owner Surrenders Contract Before Annuitization

- Non-deductible contributions recovered tax free.
- Excess is ordinary income.
- Deductible contributions—entire value is taxable in year received as ordinary income, 10-percent penalty if taken before age 59 1/2.
- After contract annuitization—recover cost tax free, remainder is taxed as ordinary income.

Payment Settlement Options

- Installments for designated amount.
- Installments for designated period.
- Life annuity period certain—annuitant receives payment for life.
  - If death occurs before end of designated period, the payments go to beneficiary for remainder of period.
- Joint and last survivor.
- Payments until death—then to surviving annuitant.
  - Payments continue to survivor in group.
- Life annuity payments end at death of annuitant.
- Unit refund life annuity.
  - Number of units guaranteed.

.03 Annuity Units

Accumulation Units

- Shares in separate accounts during pay-in period—pay-in is after sales charge and fees

Variable Annuity Value

= units × unit value

500 units × $5.00 = $2,500

Accumulation Units

$$= \frac{\text{annuity value}}{\text{unit value}}$$

1,000 units = $10,000 divided by $10.00 per unit

Value of Accumulation Unit

$$= \frac{\text{value of annuity}}{\text{number of accumulation units}}$$

$6.00 = $15,000 divided by 2,500

Annuity Units

- Annuity units - measures of value during payout period
- Accumulation units—convert to annuity using actuarial tables
- Variables
  — Age and sex of the annuitant
  — Accumulated value in the separate account
  — Payout method
  — Assumed investment rate

Number of Annuity Units

$$\frac{\text{Initial annuity payment}}{\text{Value of one annuity unity}}$$

Example: Accumulated units 5,000

Value per Acc unit $6.00

Payout value (from annuity tables) of $8 per 1,000 = $125 value

Annuity unit value $10.00

1st annuity payment = (5,000 × $6.00) / 125 = $240

$$\text{Annuity Units} = \frac{\$240}{\$10} = 24 \text{ units}$$

If annuity unit increases next month to $11, annuitant receives 24 units:

24 units × $11.00 per unit = $264.00

.05 Payout Provisions

Gross Income on Annuities: Certain Proceeds of Endowment and Life Insurance Contracts

Generally, gross income includes any amount received as an annuity (whether for a period certain or during one or more lives) under an annuity, endowment, or life insurance contract. (Code Sec. 72(a))

¶717.05

Exclusion Ratio

Gross income does not include that part of any amount received as an annuity under an annuity, endowment, or life insurance contract which bears the same ratio to such amount as the investment in the contract (as of the annuity starting date) bears to the expected return under the contract (as of such date). (Code Sec. 72(b)(1))

Exclusion Limited to Investment

The portion of any amount received as an annuity which is excluded from gross income shall not exceed the unrecovered investment in the contract immediately before the receipt of such amount. (Code Sec. 72(b)(2))

Deduction Where Annuity Payments Cease Before Entire Investment Recovered

- If after the annuity starting date, payments as an annuity under the contract cease by reason of the death of an annuitant,
- And as of the date such cessation, there is unrecovered investment in the contract,
- Then the amount of such unrecovered investment shall be allowed as a deduction to the annuitant for his last taxable year. (Code Sec. 72 (b)(3))

Payments to Other Persons

The deduction shall be allowed to the person entitled to such payments for the taxable year in which such payments are received.

Unrecovered Investment in the Contract as of Any Date

- The investment in the contract as of the annuity starting date, reduced by
- The aggregate amount received under the contract on or after such annuity starting date and before the date as of which the determination is being made, to the extent such amount was excludable from gross income. (Code Sec. 72(b)(4))

Definitions

Initial investment in the contract: The investment in the contract as of the annuity starting date is the aggregate amount of premiums or other consideration paid for the contract, minus the aggregate amount received under the contract before such date, to the extent that such amount was excludable from gross income under income tax laws.

Adjustment in investment where there is refund feature: If the expected return under the contract depends in whole or in part of the life expectancy of one or more individuals, the contract provides for payments to be made to a beneficiary on or after the death of the annuitant or annuitants, and such payments are in the nature of a refund of the consideration paid, then the value of such payments on the annuity starting date shall be subtracted from the amount determined above under "Investment in the Contract."

Such value shall be computed in accordance with actuarial tables prescribed by the Secretary. The term "refund of the consideration paid" includes amounts payable after the death of an annuitant by reason of a provision in the contract for a life annuity with minimum period of payments certain, but does not include that part of any payment to a beneficiary which is not attributable to the consideration paid by the employee for the contract as the aggregate amount of premiums or other consideration paid for the contract. (Code Sec. 72(c)(2))

Expected Return Shall Be Determined as Follows

- Life expectancy: If the expected return depends on the life expectancy, the expected return shall be computed with reference to actuarial tables prescribed by the Secretary.

- Installment payments: If the above does not apply, the expected return is the aggregate of the amounts receivable under the contract as an annuity. (Code Sec. 72(c)(3))

Amounts Not Received as Annuities

Dividends: Any amount received which is in the nature of a dividend or similar distribution shall be treated as an amount not received as an annuity. (Code Sec. 72 (e)(1))

General Rule: Any amount

- If received on or after the annuity starting date, shall be included in gross income, or

- If received before the annuity starting date, shall be included in gross income to the extent allocable to income on the contract, and shall not be included in gross income to extent allocable to the investment in the contract. (Code Sec 72 (e)(2))

Allocation of Amounts to Income and Investment

- Any amount to which these rules apply shall be treated as allocable to income from the contract to the extent that such amount does not exceed the excess (if any) of:

  — The cash value of the contract (determined without regard to any surrender charge) immediately before the amount is received, over

  — The investment in the contract at such time. (Code Sec. 72 (e)(3))

Loans Treated as Distributions

If, during any taxable year, an individual receives any amount as a loan or assigns or pledges any portion of the value of any such contract, such amount or portion shall be treated as received under the contract as an amount not received as an annuity. (Code Sec. 72 (a)(4)(A))

Treatment of Policyholder Dividends

Any dividend amount treated as not received as an annuity shall not be included in gross income to the extent such amount is retained by the issuer as a premium or other consideration paid for the contract. (Code Sec. 72 (e)(4)(B))

Treatment of Transfers Without Adequate Consideration

- If an individual who holds an annuity contract transfers it without full and adequate consideration, such individual shall be treated as receiving an amount equal to the excess of:

  — The cash surrender value of such contract at the time of transfer, over

— The investment in such contract at such time, under the contract as an amount not received as an annuity.

- The above clause shall not apply to any transfer (relating to transfers of property between spouses or incident to divorce). (Code Sec. 72 (e)(4)(c))

If an amount is included in the gross income of the transferor of an annuity contract, the investment in the contract of the transferee in such contract shall be increased by the amount so included. (Code Sec. 72 (e)(4)(c))

Option to Receive Annuity in Lieu of Lump Sum

- If a contract provides for payment of a lump sum in full discharge of an obligation under the contract, subject to an option to receive an annuity in lieu of such lump sum,

- The option is exercised within 60 days after the day on which such lump sum first became payable, and

- Part or all of such lump sum would be includible in gross income by the rules under "Amounts Not Received as Annuities," no part of such lump sum shall be considered as includible in gross income at the time such lump sum first became payable. (Code Sec. 72(h))

Interest

If any amount is held under an agreement to pay interest thereon, the interest payments shall be included in gross income. (Code Sec. 72 (j))

Loans Treated as Distributions

Treatment as Distributions

Loans: If during any taxable year a participant or beneficiary receives any amount as a loan from a qualified employer plan, such amount shall be treated as having been received by such individual as a distribution under such plan. (Code Sec. 72 (p)(1))

Assignments or pledges: If during any taxable year a participant or beneficiary assigns any portion of his interest in a qualified employer plan, such portion shall be treated as having been received by such individual as a loan from such plan. (Code Sec. 72 (p)(1))

Exception for Certain Loans

The rules regarding "treatment as distributions" shall not apply to any loan to the extent that such loan when added to the outstanding balance of all other loans from such plan does not exceed the lesser of:

- $50,000, reduced by the excess (if any) of

- The highest outstanding balance of loans from the plan during the 1 year period ending on the day before the date on which such loan was made, over

- The outstanding balance of loans from the plan on the date on which such loan was made, or

- The greater of: one-half of the present value of the nonforfeitable accrued benefit of the employee under the plan, or $10,000. (Code Sec. 72(p)(2))

Denial of Interest Deduction in Certain Cases

No deduction shall be allowed for any interest paid or accrued on any loan that is not treated as a distribution due to the exceptions for certain loans regarding the $50,000 limit, e.g., loans with a term in excess of five years. (Code Sec. 72(p)(3))

.07 10-Percent Penalty for Premature Distributions from Annuity Contracts

Imposition of penalty: If any taxpayer receives any amount under an annuity contract, the taxpayer's tax for the taxable year in which such amount is received shall be increased by an amount equal to 10 percent of the portion of such amount which is includible in gross income. (Code Sec. 72 (q)(1))

Exceptions to 10-Percent Penalty

This shall not apply to any distribution:

- Made on or after the date on which the taxpayer attains age 59 ½,
- Made on or after the death of the holder (or, where the holder is not an individual, the death of the primary annuitant),
- Attributable to the taxpayer's becoming disabled,
- Which is a part of a series of substantially equal periodic payments (not less frequently than annually) made for the life (or life expectancy) of the taxpayer or the joint lives (or joint life expectancies) of such taxpayer and his designated beneficiary,
- From a plan, contract, account, trust, or annuity described in subsection (e)(5)(D), allocable to investment in the contract before August 14, 1982,
- Under a qualified funding asset,
- Under an immediate annuity contract (within the meaning of section 72(u)(4)), or
- Which is purchased by an employer upon the termination of a plan described in section 401(a) or 403(a) and which is held by the employer until such time as the employee separates from service. (Code Sec. 72 (q)(2))

Required Distributions Where Holder Dies Before Entire Interest Is Distributed

A contract shall not be treated as an annuity contract unless it provides that:

- If any holder of such contract dies on or after the annuity starting date and before the entire interest in such contract has been distributed, the remaining portion of such interest will be distributed at least as rapidly as under the method of distributions being used as of the date of his death, and
- If any holder of such contract dies before the annuity starting date, the entire interest in such contract will be distributed within five years after the death of such holder. (Code Sec. 72 (s)(1))

Exception for certain amounts payable over the life of beneficiary. If:

- Any portion of the holder's interest is payable to a designated beneficiary,
- Such portion will be distributed over the life of such designated beneficiary, and
- Such distributions begin not later than one year after the date of the holder's death or such later date as the Secretary may by regulations prescribe, then the portion remaining, that has not been distributed when a holder dies after the

annuity starting date and before the entire interest in the contract has been distributed, shall be treated as distributed on the day on which such distributions begin. (Code Sec. 72 (s)(2))

Special rule where holder is corporation or other non-individual:

- If the holder of the contract is not an individual, the primary annuitant shall be treated as the holder of the contract. (Code Sec. 72 (s)(6))

Treatment of Changes in Primary Annuitant Where Holder of Contract Is Not an Individual

In the case of a holder of an annuity contract which is not an individual, if there is a change in a primary annuitant such change shall be treated as the death of the holder. (Code Sec 72 (s)(7))

10-Percent Additional Tax on Early Distributions from Qualified Retirement Plans

Imposition of additional tax: If any taxpayer receives any amount from a qualified retirement plan, the taxpayer's tax under this chapter for the taxable year in which such amount is received shall be increased by an amount equal to 10 percent of the portion of such amount which is includible in gross income. (Code Sec. 72 (t)(1))

Treatment of Annuity Contracts Not Held by Natural Persons

- Such contract shall not be treated as an annuity contract for purposes of this subtitle (other than subchapter L)
- The income on the contract for any taxable year of the policyholder shall be treated as ordinary income received or accrued by the owner during such taxable year. (Code Sec. 72 (u)(1))

Income on the contract means, the excess of:

- The sum of the net surrender value of the contract as of the close of the taxable year plus all distributions under the contract received during the taxable year or any prior taxable year, reduced by
- The sum of the amount of net premiums under the contract for the taxable year and prior taxable years and amounts includible in gross income for prior taxable years within respect to such contract under this subsection (Code Sec. 72 (u)(2))

Exceptions: This subsection shall not apply to any annuity contract which is:

- Acquired by the estate of a decedent by reason of the death of the decedent.
- Held under a plan described in section 401(a) or 403(a), under a program described in section 403(b), or under an individual retirement plan.
- A qualified funding asset.
- Purchased by an employer upon the termination of a plan described in section 401(a) or 403(a) and which is held by their employer until all amounts under such contract are distributed to the employee for whom such contract was purchased or the employee's beneficiary, or which is an immediate annuity. (Code Sec. 72 (u)(3))

Immediate annuity:

- The annuity starting date commences no later than one year from the date of the purchase of the annuity, and
- Provides for a series of substantially equal periodic payments (to be made not less frequently than annually) during the annuity period. (Code Sec. 72 (u) (4))

Amounts to be considered as a return of premiums: In general "amounts received as annuities" are amounts which are payable at regular intervals over a period of more than one full year from the date on which they are deemed to begin, provided the total of the amounts so payable or the period for which they are to be paid can be determined as of that date. (Reg. § 1.72-1(b))

"Amounts received as annuities": A proportionate part of each amount so received is considered to represent a return of premiums or other consideration paid. The proportionate part of each annuity payment which is thus excludable from gross income is determined by the ratio which the investment in the contract as of the date on which the annuity is deemed to begin bears to the expected return under the contract as of that date. (Reg. § 1.72-1(c))

.09 Annuity Exclusion Ratio

To determine the proportionate part of the total amount received each year as an annuity which is excludable from the gross income of a recipient in the taxable year of receipt, an exclusion ratio is to be determined for each contract. In general, this ratio is determined by dividing the investment in the contract as found under Reg. § 1.72-6 by the expected return under such a contract. (Reg. § 1.72-4(a)) The exclusion ratio for the particular contract is then applied to the total amount received as an annuity during the taxable year by each recipient. (Reg. § 1.72-4(a))

> **Example:** Taxpayer "A" purchased an annuity contract providing for payments of $100 per month for a consideration of $12,650. Assuming that the expected return under this contract is $16,000 the exclusion ratio to be used by "A" is $12,650 / $16,000; or 79.1 percent (79.06 rounded to the nearest tenth). If 12 such monthly payments are received by 'A' during his taxable year, the total amount he may exclude from his gross income in such year is $949.20 ($1,200 × 79.1 percent). The balance of $250.80 ($1,200 less $949.20) is the amount to be included in gross income. If "A" instead received only five such payments during the year, he should exclude $395.50 (500 × 79.1%) of the total amounts received. (Reg. § 1.72-4(a))

After an exclusion ratio has been determined for a particular contract, it shall be applied to any amounts received as an annuity thereunder unless or until:

- The contract is assigned or transferred for a valuable consideration;
- The contract matures or is surrendered, redeemed or discharged;
- The contract is exchanged in a manner regarding amounts not received as annuity payments. (See paragraph (e) of Reg. § 1.72-11). (Reg. § 1.72-4(a))

Exceptions to the General Rule

Where the provisions of section 72 would otherwise require an exclusion ratio to be determined, but the investment in the contract (determined under Reg. § 1.72-6) is an amount of zero or less, no exclusion ratio shall be determined and all amounts received under such a contract shall be includible in the gross income of the recipient for the purposes of section 72. (Reg. § 1.72-4(d)(1))

Where the investment in the contract is equal to or greater than the total expected return, the exclusion ratio shall be considered to be 100 percent and all amounts received as an annuity under such contract shall be excludable from the recipient's gross income. (Reg. § 1.72-4(d)(2))

Exclusion Ratio in the Case of Two or More Annuity Elements Acquired for a Single Consideration

Where two or more annuity elements are provided under a contract, an exclusion ratio shall be determined for the contract as a whole and applied to all amounts received as an annuity under any of the annuity elements. To obtain this ratio, the investment in the contract shall be divided by the aggregate of the expected returns found with respect to each of the annuity elements. It is immaterial that payments under one or more of the annuity elements involved have not commenced at the time when an amount is first received as an annuity under one or more of the other annuity elements. (Reg. § 1.72-4(e))

¶ 719 BONDS

Bonds are long-term obligations to pay a fixed number of dollars at the end of a specified number of years at a fixed interest rate.

.01 Bond Overview

- Bonds vs. Stocks
  - Bonds offer more certainty. Consider a non-callable bond held to maturity. You know when you will receive the money and how much you will receive. Normally, the longer the term, the higher the yield.
  - Bonds can provide the investor a more "safe" steady stream of income. Bonds are more predictable than stocks. You loan money to a government agency or a corporation, and they agree to pay it back at a fixed interest rate over a fixed period of time. Bonds can provide a steady and reasonably secure income flow, if kept to maturity to avoid market fluctuations.
  - The longer the period, the higher the interest rate. This is because the higher the risk, the higher the return. The investor is at greater risk on a longer term, because interest rates can rise and he is left with a low rate.
- Bond savers—People who buy and hold bonds to maturity to earn a guaranteed rate of return.
- Bond investors—Bond buyers who hope to make money on bonds when interest rates decline which sends the bond price higher.
- Bond prices move in the opposite direction of interest rates. When interest rates decline, bond prices rise. When interest rates increase, bond prices fall. But bonds held to maturity will pay the principal back along with the interest returns.
- When buying bonds, purchase new issues. Older bonds trade in the secondary market, and their prices include a dealer's markup.
- If you are in a higher tax bracket, consider tax-free bonds.

- For bond capital gains, go long. When interest rates fall, longer term bonds gain more in price than shorter-term bonds.
- For steady income, purchase short or intermediate bonds.
- **Bond return.** When purchasing bonds, don't just consider the interest or coupon rate. You must be aware of your "total return"—all the money you earn off the bond. If you sell the bond, consider your capital gain or loss, plus the interest earned.
- **Security**. U.S. Treasuries are safe, liquid investments. Treasuries can be bought directly from the government with no fees or expenses (*www.publicdebt.treas.gov* or call 800-943-6864).

.02 Bond Types

Corporate Bonds

- Bonds with a fixed obligation to pay a certain sum at a certain time (usually 10 to 30 years after issuance).

Convertible Bonds

- Can be changed into stock or another security at a certain conversion price.
- Convertible bonds pay income the way regular bonds do.
- Growth potential is available by redeeming for stock shares of the issuing company.

Debentures

- Backed only by the general credit of a corporation without the specific property as collateral.

Zero-Coupon Bonds

- Priced at a discount from face value, and increases to it by the maturity date.
- The bonds don't pay interest before maturity.
- The interest accumulates at the original rate and becomes part of the final value.

U.S. Savings Bonds

- Series EE issued at half price and build up to face value.
- Series HH bonds are current income bonds.

Municipal Bonds

- Issued by municipalities
- Exempt from federal income tax

Investment Pitfalls

- Each municipal bond issue is a stand-alone investment with specific contract terms spelled out in a detailed, lengthy prospectus.
- General Obligation Bonds
  — Backed by the full taxing power of the political unit issuing them
  — Generally have the highest rating
- Revenue Bonds

— Obligations that are secured by the revenues of a particular project, such as a toll highway or a bridge

- Special Assessment Bonds
  - Secured by special assessments levied against property owners for improvements benefiting them directly
- Moral Obligation Bonds
  - Bonds that aren't debts of the state or federal government
  - Guaranteed by the "moral obligation" of the state in the event the issuing authority defaults.

Investment Pitfalls of Tax-Exempts

- Price fluctuation and unmarketability.
- Defaults in tax-exempts are extremely rare.
- Price fluctuates with changes in the prevailing interest rates, although this doesn't matter if you intend to hold the bond until its maturity.
- Unmarketability is a common problem for bonds issued by small taxing districts.

.03 Bond Ratings—Municipal

Description of Ratings

	S&P	Moody's
Extremely strong capacity to pay interest and repay principal	AAA	Aaa
Very strong capacity to pay interest and repay principal—differs from highest-rated issue only by a small degree	AA	Aa
Strong capacity to pay interest and repay principal somewhat more susceptible to adverse effects of changes in circumstances and economic conditions	A	A
Adequate capacity to pay interest and repay principal—adverse economic conditions or changing circumstances are more likely to weaken capacity to pay interest and repay principal	BBB	Baa
Speculative ability to pay interest and repay principal	BB	Ba
Low grade, speculative in nature	B	B
More speculative than higher-rated bonds	CC	Caa
Highest speculative grade	CC	Ca
Lowest-rated class of bonds—may pay no interest	C	C

.05 Bond Types Defined

Bonds—Types

- Fully registered for principal and interest.
- Registered bond with coupons for interest.
- Coupon bearer bond—not registered.

Corporate Bonds

Purchaser is a creditor of the corporation.

Secured Bonds

- Mortgage bond—secured by a lien on real estate.

- Collateral trust bond—secured by financial assets of corporation (other stocks and bonds).
- Guaranteed bonds—secured by another corporation (parent - subsidiary).

Unsecured Bonds

- Debentures—unsecured promise by issuer to pay.
  - Issued by corporations with high credit rating.
- Subordinated debentures—unsecured and ranks be other corporate debt (but ahead of common and preferred stock).
- Income bonds
  - Issued by corporations as an alternative to bankruptcy as an adjustment to their capital structure.
  - Pay interest only if issuer has sufficient income to pay.

Flat Bonds

- Bonds that trade without interest.

Convertible Bonds

- Corporate debt securities that can be converted into stock.

Municipal Securities

- Issued by states, counties, cities, or school districts for capital expenditures.

General Obligation Bonds

- Issued by states and municipalities.
- Repayment from general revenues.

Revenue Bonds

- Not issued by states or municipalities, but by authorities of states or municipalities, e.g., airports, or transit authorities.
- Repayment is from general revenues.

U.S. Treasury Obligations

Treasuries are the safest bonds of all because the interest and principal payments are guaranteed by the "full faith and credit of the U.S. Government" (that is, the taxing power). Interest is exempt from state and local taxes but not from federal tax. Because of their almost total lack of default risk, Treasuries carry some of the lowest yields around. Treasuries are among the most liquid of debt instruments.

- Treasury bills
  - Have the shortest maturities: 13 weeks, 26 weeks, and one year.
  - Buy them at a discount to their $10,000 face value and receive the full $10,000 at maturity. The difference reflects the interest you earn.
  - Very liquid
  - No gain or loss if held to maturity
- Treasury Notes
  - Mature in two to 10 years.

- Interest is paid semiannually at a fixed rate.
- Minimum investment: $1,000 or $5,000, depending on maturity.

- Treasury Bonds
  - Term: 10 to 30 years
  - Coupon or book-entry registered bonds
  - Series HH or EE bonds are non-marketable debt.
  - Pay interest semiannually
  - Sold in denominations of $1,000.
- Zero-coupon bonds, ("strips" or "zeros"), are Treasury-based securities that are sold by brokers at a deep discount and redeemed at full face value when they mature in six months to 30 years.
  - The investor doesn't actually receive interest until the bond matures, but must pay taxes each year on the "phantom interest" earned. This is based on the bond's market value, which usually rises steadily during the holding period. For that reason, they are best held in tax-deferred accounts.
  - Because they pay no coupon interest, zeros can be highly volatile in price.
- Inflation-indexed Treasuries.
  - Issued in 10- and 30-year maturities.
  - Inflation-indexed Treasuries pay a real rate of interest on a principal amount that rises or falls with the consumer price index.
  - You don't collect the inflation adjustment to your principal until the bond matures or you sell it.
  - The owner owes federal income tax on the phantom income amount each year.
  - The owner owes federal income tax on the interest received currently.
  - Inflation bonds are best held in tax-deferred accounts.

.07 Bond Terms

Refunding—issuing more bonds to retire existing bonds.

Bond Values

- Discounted bonds—bond prices go down if interest rates go up.
- Premium bonds—bond prices go up if interest rates go down.

Bond Rating

- Higher rating—AAA means safer bond, but lower yield.
- Lower rating—BBB means higher risk bond, but higher yield.

Bond Quotes and Trading

- Bond par value = $1,000 (unless stated otherwise)
- Bond price quoted at 96 means a bond price of $960
- Point = 1% of 1,000
  - 1 point on bond = $10

— 1/4 point on bond = $2.50

— 1/8 point on bond = $1.25

— One Basis point = 1 of 1,000 or = .1%, or =.001 or, in money = 100 cents or $1.00

.08 Bond Risks

Inflation risk. The longer the bond term, the higher the inflation risk.

Interest rate risk

- Bond prices move in the opposite direction of interest rates.
- When interest rates rise, bond prices fall because new bonds are issued paying higher coupon rates.
- The longer the term of the bond, the greater the price fluctuation.
- This only matters if the bond is not held to maturity and needs to be sold before maturity.

Risk of call. Many bond issuers have the right to redeem the bond before its maturity. They are required to pay bond holders only the par value. This happens when interest rates fall, and the issuer can lower his cost by selling new bonds at lower yields. The investor may receive less than the market value and may have to reinvest in new bonds paying lower rates of interest. Non-callable bonds can be purchased if a target maturity (college funding) is desired.

Credit risk

- This is where the issuer does not make it's interest payments on time, or at all.
- Insured bonds will guarantee the investor the return of interest and principal, but not against interest rate or market risk.
- U.S. Treasuries are considered to have no credit risk.
- Junk bonds have the highest credit risk.
- Bonds with the highest credit worthiness are rated AAA.

Liquidity risk

- Bonds are not as liquid, because most investors are buying and holding to maturity to receive the coupon yield.
- Treasuries have a more ready market for trading.
- Munis and junk bonds can be highly illiquid.

Market risk

- Changes in interest rates cause changes in bond prices.
- Bond prices move in the opposite direction of interest rates.
- Bond prices follow the law of supply and demand.
- A popular bond commands a higher price.
- A less plentiful bond commands a higher price.

.09 Bond Yields

Bond Bought at Face

Nominal yield = interest rate on face of bond

A $1,000 6% bond = $60.00/year

Bond Bought at Discount

$$\text{Current yield} = \frac{\text{Nominal Yield}}{\text{Cost of Security}}$$

$$\text{Current yield} \frac{\$60}{\$950} \quad .063 \text{ or } 63\%$$

Where bond was bought for $950

Yield to Maturity

$$= \frac{\text{Adjusted interest}}{\text{Average price}}$$

Yield to Maturity for Bond Bought at Discount

$$= \frac{\text{Annual Nominal Interest} + \text{Prorated Discount}}{(\text{Purchase Price} + \text{Maurity Price})/2}$$

Yield to Maturity for Bond Bought at Premium

$$= \frac{\text{Annual Nominal Interest Prorated Discount}}{(\text{Purchase Price} + \text{Maurity Price})/2}$$

Bond Bought at Discount

Face	$1,000
Cost	−$910

$$\$90 \quad \frac{\$90}{2} = \$45$$

Average price = $910 + $45 = $955

$$\frac{\$90}{6} \text{ years to maturity} = \$15/\text{yr}$$

Nominal yield = $1,000 at 6% equals; $60/yr

$$\text{Yield to maturity} \quad \frac{\$60 + \$15}{\$910 + \$45} = .0785 \text{ ir } 7.8\%$$

Bond Bought at Premium

$$\text{Average price} = \frac{\$1,090 + \$1,000}{2} = \$1,045$$

$$\frac{\$90}{6} \text{ years} = \$15/\text{year}$$

$$\text{Yield to maturity} = \frac{\$60 - \$15}{\$1,045} = .043 \text{ or } 4.3\%$$

Tax Exempt Bond "Called At" for Capital Gain

Bond bought at . . . . 96.00 = $960
Called at . . . . 104.00 = $1,040.00
Capital Gain of . . . . $80.00 per bond

Tax Exempt Bond Sold for Capital Gain

Bond bought at par . . . . 100.00 = $1,000
Then sold at . . . . 104.00 = $1,040.00
Capital Gain of . . . . $40.00 per bond

Tax Exempt Bond Bought Back and Sold Later for Capital Gain

Bond bought at . . . . 99.00 = $990
Sold at . . . . 95.00 = $950.00
Capital loss of . . . . $40.00 per bond

Bond Yield Comparisons

Bond Price	Lowest Yield	Medium Yield		Highest Yield
Discount	NY	CY	YTM	YTC
Premium	YTC	YTM	CY	NY

NY	=	Nominal Yield
CY	=	Current Yield
YTM	=	Yield o Maturity
YTC	=	Yield to the call

Bond Trust Indenture

Agreement on borrowing terms between the debtor and its creditors

- Trust Indenture Act of 1939 requires that a corporation appoint a trustee for its bonds.

Protective Covenants

The debtor corporation agrees to:

- Specify the places for payment.
- Pay the interest and principal of every bond.
- Defend the legal title.
- Pay all taxes.
- Not do anything to diminish the claims of the bonds.
- Establish a sinking fund, if provided by covenant.

Bondholder Remedies

- The right of entry.
- The right to foreclose.
- The right to declare the principal due before the maturity date.
- The right to bring suit.
- The right to sell property to the highest bidder.
- Protection for bondholders in consolidations and mergers.
- Acceleration of maturity in cases of default.

Bonds—Corporate Pricing

(1)	(2)	(3)	(4)	(5)	(6)	(7)	(8)
Agency	Bond Description	Current Yield	Volume	High	Low	Close	Net Change
AMR	952000	8.5	25	96 1/2	96	96	+ 3/8

1. Corporation issuing bond
2. Description states that bond pays 9% interest
3. Current annual yield = 8.5% which indicates bond is selling at a premium
4. Number of bonds sold the previous day
5. Highest trading price—on trading day
6. Lowest trading price—on trading day
7. Closing trading price—on trading day
8. Net change in closing trading price from previous day to trade day

Bonds—Government Pricing

Government bonds transfer at par, at a premium over par, or at a discount from par. The par value of a bond is normally $1,000. Government notes are quoted with variations at 1/32 of 1% of par, or 1/32 of a point. Treasury bills are quoted with variations of 1/100 of a point.

A bid of:	Means:	Or:
98.1	98 + 1/32% of $1,000	$980.3125
98.9	98 + 9/32% of $1,000	$982.8125
98.12	98 + 12/32% of $1,000	$983.7500

Bonds—Tax-Exempt Price

(1) Agency	(2) Coupon	(3) Mat Date	(4) Bid	(5) Ask	(6) Change	(7) Yield
Jacksonville Electric	10 1/2	Jan. 21	62	65	+ 2	3.11

1. Agency issuing bond
2. Coupon rate
3. Maturity date of bond
4. Bid price—sell price
5. Ask price—buy price
6. Change from ending value on prior day
7. Current percentage yield on current price

Yield to Call

Call—where the issuer redeems the bonds before maturity by paying off the principal

Yield to Call for Bond Bought at Discount

$$= \frac{(\text{annual interest} + \text{prorated premium})/2}{(\text{purchase price} + \text{call price})/2}$$

Yield to Call for Bond Bought at Premium

$$= \frac{(\text{annual interest} - \text{prorated premium})/2}{(\text{purchase price} + \text{call price})/2}$$

Tax Equivalent Yield

Tax Equivalent Yield

$$= \frac{\text{Tax free yield}}{(1 - \text{tax rate}}$$

Example: A taxpayer in the 28% tax bracket receives a 5% yield from a tax exempt municipal bond.

$$\text{Tax equivalent yield} = \frac{.05}{(1 - .28)} = .0694 \text{ or } 6.94\%$$

Comparison of Tax Exempt vs. Taxable Investment

Compare net after-tax return:

Comparison of Tax-Exempt vs. Taxable Investment

$$\text{Taxpayer's marginal tax rate} - \left[1 - \frac{\text{Tax exempt investment interest rate}}{\text{Taxable investment interest rate}} \right]$$

= positive or negative value

If positive, then choose tax free

If negative, then choose taxable

Example (1): Tax-exempt rate of investment alternative 1 = 8.5%

Taxable rate of investment alternative 2 = 11.0%

Marginal tax rate of taxpayer = 34%

$$(.34) - [1 - \frac{8.5}{11.0}]$$

.34 – .23 = .11 = positive, then choose tax-free

Proof : Convert tax-free rate to tax equivalent rate = $\frac{.085}{1.00 - .34}$ – .1288, which is greater than .11

¶719.09

Example (2): Same data as above, except taxpayer marginal rate = 15%

$$(.15) - [1 \ \frac{8.5}{11.0} \ ]$$

.15 – .23 = –.08 = negative, then choose taxable

Proof: Convert tax-free rate to taxable rate equivalent = $\dfrac{.085}{1.00 - .15}$ = .10, which is less than .11

.10 BOND YIELD CHARTS

Bond Yields

	Lowest Yield			Highest Yield	
Premium bond	Yield to call	Yield to maturity	Current yield	Nominal yield	Bond price
Discount bond	Bond price	Nominal yield	Current yield	Yield to maturity	Yield to call
Par Bond	All yields for par bond are equal				

Bond Yields: 1985 to 1999 (Percent per year. Annual averages of daily figures.)

Type	1985	1989	1990	1991	1992	1993	1994	1995	1996	1997	1999
U.S. Treasury, constant maturities:											
1 year	8.42	8.53	7.89	5.86	3.89	3.43	5.32	5.94	5.52	5.63	5.08
2 year	9.27	8.57	8.16	6.49	4.77	4.05	5.94	6.15	5.84	5.99	5.43
3 year	9.64	8.55	8.26	6.82	5.30	4.44	6.27	6.25	5.99	6.10	5.49
5 year	10.12	8.50	8.37	7.37	6.19	5.14	6.69	6.38	6.18	6.22	5.55
7 year	10.50	8.52	8.52	7.68	6.63	5.54	6.91	6.50	6.34	6.33	5.79
10 year	10.62	8.49	8.55	7.86	7.01	5.87	7.69	6.57	6.44	6.35	5.65
10 year	(NA)	(NA)	(NA)	(NA)	(NA)	6.29	7.47	6.95	6.83	6.69	6.20
30 year	10.79	8.45	8.61	8.14	7.67	6.59	7.37	6.88	6.71	6.61	5.87
U.S. Govt. long-term bonds	10.75	8.58	8.74	8.16	7.52	6.45	7.41	6.93	6.80	6.67	6.14
State/local govt. bonds, Aaa	8.60	7.00	6.97	6.56	6.09	5.38	5.77	5.80	5.52	5.32	5.29
State/local govt. bonds, Baa	9.58	7.40	7.30	6.99	6.48	5.83	6.17	6.10	5.79	5.50	5.70
Municipal (Bond Buyer, 20 bonds.	9.10	7.23	7.27	6.92	6.44	5.60	6.18	5.95	5.76	5.52	5.43
Corporate Aaa Seasoned	11.37	9.26	9.32	8.77	8.14	7.22	7.97	7.59	7.37	7.27	7.05
Corporate Baa seasoned	12.72	10.18	10.36	9.80	8.98	7.93	8.63	8.20	8.05	7.87	7.88
Corp. (Moody's)	12.05	9.66	9.77	9.23	8.55	7.54	8.26	7.83	7.66	7.54	7.44

Type	1985	1989	1990	1991	1992	1993	1994	1995	1996	1997	1999
Industrials (49 bonds)	11.80	9.66	9.77	9.25	8.52	7.51	8.21	7.76	7.58	7.47	7.33
Public Utilities (51 bonds)	12.29	9.66	9.76	9.21	8.57	7.56	8.30	7.90	7.74	7.63	7.54

Source: Except as noted, Board of Governors of the Federal Reserve System, Federal Reserve Bulletin, monthly.

Bond Yields

Average Yields of Long-Term Treasury, Corporate, and Municipal Bonds

Type	1990	1995	1996	1997	1999
Federal funds, effective rate	8.10	5.83	5.30	5.46	4.97
Commercial paper, 3-month	8.06	5.93	5.41	5.58	N/A
Commercial paper, 6-month	7.95	5.93	5.42	5.62	N/A
Prime rate charged by banks	10.01	8.83	8.27	8.44	8.00
Eurodollar deposits, 3-month	8.16	5.93	5.38	5.61	5.31
Finance paper, 3-month	7.87	5.78	5.29	5.48	N/A
Finance paper, 6-month	7.53	5.68	5.21	5.48	N/A
Bankers acceptances, 3-month	7.93	5.81	5.31	5.54	5.24
Bankers acceptances, 6-month	7.80	5.80	5.31	5.57	5.30
Large negotiable CD's:					
3-month, secondary market 13.07	5.92	5.39	5.62	N/A	5.19
6-month, secondary market 12.94	5.98	5.47	5.73	N/A	5.33
Taxable money market funds	7.82	5.48	4.95	5.10	4.64
Tax-exempt money market funds	5.45	3.39	2.99	3.14	2.72
Certificates of deposit (CD's):					
6-month	7.35	4.92	4.68	4.86	4.27
1-year	7.42	5.39	4.95	5.16	4.56
2 1/2-year	7.52	5.69	5.14	5.40	4.74
5-year	7.71	6.00	5.46	5.67	4.93
U.S. Government securities:					
Secondary market:					
3-month Treasury bill	7.50	5.49	5.01	5.06	4.64
6-month Treasury bill	7.46	5.56	5.08	5.18	4.75
1-month Treasury bill	7.35	5.60	5.22	5.36	4.81
Auction average:					
3-month Treasury bill	7.51	5.51	5.02	5.07	4.66
6-month Treasury bill	7.47	5.59	5.09	5.18	4.76
1-month Treasury bill	7.36	5.69	5.23	5.36	4.78
Home mortgages:					
HUD series:					
FHA insured, secondary market	10.17	8.18	8.18	7.89	7.74
Conventional, new-home	10.08	8.05	8.03	7.76	7.45
Conventional, existing-home	10.08	8.05	8.03	7.76	7.47
Conventional, 15 year fixed	9.67	7.39	7.28	7.16	7.09
Conventional, 30 year fixed	10.01	7.86	7.76	7.57	7.46

.11 Zero-Coupon Bonds

A zero-coupon bond is a bond which is issued at a discount and pays no interest. At maturity, the bond is redeemed at its face value.

A zero-coupon bond is an original issue discount bond. Code Sec. 1272 provodes that there shall be included in the gross income of the holder an amount equal to the sum of the daily portion of the original discount.

The annual accrued interest is not taxable to the holder under Code Sec. 103(a), if a state or municipal obligation is issued at a discount. (Rev. Rul. 72-587.)

> **Example:** Bond cost = $422.41

Term = 10 year

Bond effectively earns 9% per year

Year	Bond Price Plus Accrued Interest	Interest	Value at End of Year
1	$422.41	$38.02	$460.43
2	460.43	41.44	501.87
3	501.87	45.17	547.04
4	547.04	49.23	596.27
5	596.27	53.66	649.93
6	649.93	58.49	708.42
7	708.42	63.76	772.18
8	772.18	69.50	841.68
9	841.68	75.75	917.43
10	917.43	82.57	1,000.13

Market price is effected by the bond's remaining term to maturity and market interest rates. The following table shows the market price of a zero-coupon bond with a $1,000 face maturity value.

> **Example:** A zero bond priced to yield 7%, with 16 years to maturity sells for $333. If interest rates drop to 6% two years later, the bond will sell for $437.

Years to Maturity	Yield to Maturity					
	5%	6%	7%	8%	9%	10%
25	$290	$228	$179	$141	$111	$ 87
20	372	307	253	208	172	142
16	454	388	333	285	244	210
14	501	437	382	333	292	255
12	553	492	438	390	348	310
8	674	623	577	534	494	458
6	744	701	662	625	590	557

.13 Government Bond Types

Government Securities

Marketable Government Securities

Type	Maturity	Denomination	Pricing	Form
Treasury Bills (T-Bills)	90 days to one year (short term)	$10,000 to $1million	Issued and quoted at discount	Book-entry
Treasury	One to 10 years	$1,000 to	Issued close to par;	Book-entry

Type	Maturity	Denomination	Pricing	Form
Notes	(intermediate)	$1 million	priced at a percentage of par	or registered
Treasury Bonds	10 to 30 years (long-term)	$1,000 to $1 million	Priced at a percentage of par (variations in 32nds)	Book-entry or registered

Nonmarketable Government Securities

Series EE Bonds	10 years	$50 to $10,000	Issued at 50% discount	Registered
Series HH Bonds	10 years	$500 to $10,000	Issued at par and interest-bearing	Registered
Series I Bonds	10 to 30 years	$50 to $10,000	Issued at par with inflation indexed farthest	Registered

.15 I-Savings Bonds

The Treasury Department now sells an inflation-indexed version savings bond. The I-bond is designed to guarantee that the return will out-pace inflation. The new savings bond is called the U.S. Series I savings bond. The I-bond is a new type of federal savings bond whose return will rise and fall with the inflation rate.

The interest rate on the bond is composed of two parts. The government will guarantee a fixed minimum interest rate for the life of the bond—up to 30 years. That rate will be based on a fraction of the interest rate paid for auctioned five-year Treasury notes.

The rate could be different for the new I-bonds because the government will adjust the rate for new issues every six months. In addition to the fixed rate, the government will add on an additional interest rate based on the official inflation rate. The flexible rate will be readjusted every six months, depending on increases in the Consumer Price Index.

It is similar to the 10- to 30-year inflation-indexed Treasuries already on the market. I-bond interest is exempt from state and local taxes. I-bonds are similar to traditional Series EE savings bonds that are sold by most banks and credit unions. An I-bond should be an excellent investment for conservative long-term savers.

The I-savings bonds are offered in eight denominations: $50, $75, $100, $200, $500, $1,000, $5,000 and $10,000. Interest payments are deferred until the bonds are cashed in. Earnings are exempt from state and local taxes, and federal taxes are deferred until you cash in the bonds or they reach their 30-year earning limit. Earnings, for certain level income individuals, if they are used to paying for qualified college expenses, can escape federal tax. A $100 EE bond sells for $50, then gradually matures to $100. The I-bonds will be sold at their face value, unlike EE bonds, which sell at half their face value. A $50 I-bond will sell for $50 and interest will be earned on it in addition to that.

When inflation is low, the I-bond's payout is unlikely to beat that of a regular savings bond. However, when inflation picks up, so will the I-bond's appeal. A guarantee that you will beat inflation for the next 30 years is something bank savings accounts, certificates of deposit and other savings bonds cannot match. Interest on the I-bond will equal the inflation rate plus a fixed rate of return (typically about 3.0% to 3.5%).

When interest rates rise, the value of bonds fall, and stocks typically slow as well. I-bonds, on the other hand, would provide a minimal return above inflation regardless of how high it climbs. If the fixed I-bond rate remains too far below the real return of EE bonds, EE bonds usually will remain more attractive even in an inflationary period. However, there have been times when interest rates could not keep up with the inflation rate, at which point I-bonds would be very attractive. Another risk for I-bonds is if the economy suffers deflation. In this case, I-bonds would eliminate their inflation add-on rate and actually lower their fixed interest rate.

Once you buy an I-bond, the fixed rate stays the same until the bond matures and stops earning interest after 30 years. Interest rate changes every May and November are based on open-market interest rates. Since an I-bond's rate is reset every six months, there is a lot of upside potential. For I-bonds, see *www.savingsbonds.gov*.

¶ 721 INSURANCE

.01 Insurance Overview

Insurance Planning

Purposes of insurance:

- To provide for family income in event of death
- To provide needed liquidity for emergency
- To provide income flow in case of disability
- To provide for liquidation of long-term debts, like mortgage
- To provide resources for major purchases
- To provide coverage for property loss—fire, etc.
- Buy-sell agreements for business interests

Insurance Features

- Tax shelter
  - Tax-free accumulations
  - Tax-free death benefits
- Forced savings program
- Pure protection—guaranteeing income continuation in case of death or disability
- Business planning—keeping control of business by designated group
- Compensation planning
  - Funding deferred compensation
  - Funding retirement arrangements
- Estate planning—assuring needed liquidity to pay taxes
- Spreads the result of financial loss among many persons so that cost to any one person is minimal
- Unilateral contract—only insurance company is legally bound to agreement
- Improves credit position

— Credit more readily available to a person with a sound insurance program than one having an inadequate program

- Convenience of purchasing units, convenience of paying for the units purchased, physical maintenance or upkeep, safety of principal, return on investment

Universal Life Insurance

- Insurance elements and savings components separate
- Insurance cost—cost similar to renewable term policy

Investment

- Interest earned above guaranteed rate is paid directly into cash value fund
- Pays interest at close to market rates

Premiums and Death Benefit

- Permits policyholder to change the amount and taxing of premiums and size of death benefit as policyholder's needs change

Flexible Premium and variable benefit—qualifies as insurance if policy meets:

- Cash value accumulation test or
- Guideline premium and cash value corridor test

Disabilty Insurance

Statistical studies show that the possibility of permanent disability is far greater than the possibility of death during a person's normal working lifetime. Total and permanent disability is not only more common than death but can also have a much greater financial impact on the family. Both death and premature disability can remove a source of family income. However, in the case of disability, family expenditures might actually increase. The disabled person must be fed, clothed and sheltered. The family is faced with the possibilty of large medical costs.

Disability Need—Funds for Income Replacement Methods

- Non-contributing plan where employer pays premiums and owns policy, then pays taxable income to the employee
- Employer gives pay raise and employee pays premiums—employee owns policy and receives tax-free benefits

Trade or Business Expense—Insurance

- There shall be allowed as a deduction all the ordinary and necessary expenses paid or incurred during the taxable year in carrying on any trade or business. (Code Sec. 162 (a))

General Rule for Disallowance of Deductions

- In computing taxable income, no deduction shall in any case be allowed in respect of the items specified in this part. (Code Sec. 261)

Personal, Living, and Family Expenses

- Except as otherwise expressly provided, no deduction shall be allowed for personal, living, or family expenses. (Code Sec. 262)

¶721.01

Life Insurance Contract Defined (Code Sec. 7702)

- The term "life insurance contract" means any contract which is a life insurance contract under the applicable law, but only if such contract:
    - — Meets the following cash value accumulation test, or
    - — Meets the following guideline premium requirements, and
    - — Falls within the following cash value corridor.

Cash Value Accumulation Test

A contract meets the cash value accumulation test if, by the terms of the contract, the cash surrender value of such contract may not at any time exceed the net single premium which would have to be paid at such time to fund future benefits under the contract. These rules shall be made:

- On the basis of interest at the greater of an annual effective rate of four percent or the rate or rates guaranteed on issuance of the contract,
- By taking into account only current and future and death benefits and qualified additional benefits.

Guideline Premium Requirements

A contract meets the guideline premium requirements if the sum of the premiums paid under such contract does not at any time exceed the guideline premium limitation as of such time.

The term "guideline level premium" means the level annual amount, payable over a period not ending before the insured attains age 95, computed on the same basis as the guideline single premium.

.02 Life Insurance Techniques

Insurance-Related Employee Benefit Evaluation Techniques

Evaluate benefits considering tax rates of the business entity and of the employee.

Poor

Benefit that is nondeductible to the employer and taxable to the employee.

Examples:

- A benefit that results in unreasonable compensation and is disallowed and is reclassified as a dividend.
- A loan to stockholder/employee disallowed and reclassified as a dividend. The opportunity to be deductible as wages would have saved on at least the corporation's tax.

Better

A benefit is that is deductible to the employer but still taxable to the employee.

Examples:

- Salary allotment plans
- Executive equity plans
- Survivor income plans
- Deferred compensation arrangements
- Bonused split-dollar insurance techniques

Best

A benefit that is both deductible to the employer and nontaxable to the employee.

Examples:

- Cafeteria plans
- Qualified retirement plans
- Group term insurance
- Medical expense reimbursement

Survivor Income

This assures that continuing income will be available to the family. Should be a written agreement between the employer and the employee. Benefits usually provide for ongoing and periodic payments for a specified number of years following the employee's death. These payments are usually stated as a certain percentage of the employee's salary at time of death.

During Life—Employer purchases a life insurance contract insuring the employee. The employer is both owner and beneficiary of the contract. The premium payments are not tax deductible to the employer. The premiums are not taxable income to the employee. The employee has no rights whatsoever in the policy. This technique is similar to key person insurance, the difference being the purpose for which the death benefit will be used.

Upon Death—At the employee's death, the insurance company pays a death benefit directly to the employer, as beneficiary of the contract. The employer then provides a survivor income benefit to the family, according to the pre-existing agreement. These payments are tax deductible by the employer, and are received as taxable income by the family. This provides tax leverage to the employer, in that receipt of the death benefit by the employer is tax free, yet the payments to the surviving family are tax deductible.

Tax Consequences—The premiums paid by the corporation are not taxable to the insured employee if the corporation is the owner and beneficiary of the policy. Any proceeds paid to a widow are taxable income as compensation for past services. Death benefits payable under contract are taxable income.

Key Person Insurance

The existence of business debt may require the future possible need for insurance. Key person insurance can function as a form of commercial loan protection. It can provide needed funds when a business is sold, liquidated, or is to be continued.

During Life—The business obtains insurance on the life of the key employee. The business pays the premium directly to the insurance company. The business is owner and beneficiary of the contract. The business is beneficiary of the contract. The contract's cash value is carried as a business asset. The cash value is available as collateral for securing commercial loans. The cash value is available for borrowing from the insurance company at favorable interest rates.

Upon Death of the Key Employee—The funds received are treated as an addition to capital and are received free of income taxes. The insurance company pays this death benefit directly to the business, not the key employee. The proceeds can be used as the business sees fit: for liquidation of the business, the cash can benefit the surviving family by providing funds for lost business value. If the business is to be sold, money is available to fund a full stock redemption. The proceeds can be used to: provide a financial cushion, fund a partial stock redemption, make survivor income payments. obtain a qualified replacement, replace lost profits, and protect the business' credit position.

Cross Purchase Agreement

Provides for the disposition of a business interest by having the owners agree, among themselves, to buy and sell their respective interests. Such an agreement helps to establish a market value for estate tax purposes.

During Lifetime—The owners enter into a binding agreement providing for the purchase and sale of their respective interests. This obligates both parties to either buy or sell upon the death, disability, or retirement of either. Each obtains a life insurance contract insuring the other. The insurance is used to fully fund their mutual obligations to each other. Each pays the premiums, and each is both owner and beneficiary of the contract that insures the other party.

Upon Death—The business interest passes to the family or estate. The insurance company pays a tax-free death benefit to the survivor, as beneficiary of the contract insuring the decedent's life. This is paid, pursuant to the agreement, to the decedent's family or estate, who transfers to the survivor the entire interest in the business. The fully funded agreement assures that the decedent's surviving family receives a fair price for the interest in the business.

Tax Consequences of Premium Payments—Premiums that are paid by a key employee for insurance on life of sole proprietor are not deductible. The life insurance proceeds are not included in the insured's estate.

Premiums paid by a partner for insurance on his own life are not deductible if the proceeds are payable to a copartner. Premiums paid by a partner for insurance on life of copartner are not deductible. Stockholder cannot deduct premiums paid on policy purchased on life of another stockholder. Premiums paid by corporation on insurance policies owned by stockholders is taxable income to the stockholders.

Split-Dollar Insurance

Split-dollar is a technique of a sharing of premiums, cash values, and death benefits between two parties, such as an employer and an employee. Split-dollar is easy to implement, can be made available to selected employees, and has few restrictions that apply to group insurance and other qualified plans.

During Life—The employer and the employee enter into an agreement under which a permanent life insurance contract on the employee's life is purchased. Premiums are to be split between the employer and the employee. Almost any splitting arrangement can be implemented. Typically the employee pays the part of the premium which is equal to the "economic benefit" of the coverage received by the employee for each year. The employer pays the remaining balance of the premium. One particular variation of split-dollar is the "single bonus" split-dollar. Here the employer provides a bonus to the employee, in an amount equal to the employee's share of the premium. This enables the employer to pay the entire premium and deduct the part which is considered an employee bonus for tax purposes. The employee pays taxes on only the bonuses received. The employer will generally own the cash values accruing in the policy.

Upon Death—The insurance company pays an amount that equals the employer's cumulative contributions to the plan as a death benefit to the employer. The balance of the death benefit goes to the employee's beneficiary.

Split-Dollar Funding Cross Purchase Agreement

Split-dollar insurance could fund the insurance needs of an employee, spouse, child, another stockholder whose stock interest he was obligated to purchase, etc.

During Life—Assume a corporation is owned equally by two individuals, Employee A and Employee B, who enter into a cross-purchase agreement providing for the purchase and sale of their respective business interests. To fund the purchase obligations, A and B each obtain a life insurance contract on the life of the other. They each enter into a split-dollar agreement with the corporation providing for a sharing of premiums and death benefits. The agreements are intended to provide employee benefits, not stockholder benefits. However, this is one and the same individual. Each employee pays the premium which is equal to the "economic benefit" of the coverage received in that year. But, the life used to measuure the "economic benefit" is based on the insured co-stockholder, not the employee-stockholder who enters the split-dollar agreement with the corporation. The corporation provides a bonus so the employee can pay the premiums. The employee pays taxes only on the bonuses received.

Upon Death—The employee's stock interest passes to his family or estate. The insurance company pays a part of the death benefit to the corporation to reimburse it under the terms of the split-dollar agreement. The balance of the death benefit is paid to the surviving employee. This is then used by the survivor to purchase the deceased's entire stock interest from the family or estate.

Split-Dollar Funding Life Insurance Trust

This trust uses employer provided dollars to pay premiums for life insurance required for estate taxes and other estate settlement costs.

During Life—Employee establishes a trust. The trustee of the trust obtains insurance on the employee's life. The trust owns the insurance policy. The employer and trustee enter into a split-dollar agreement providing for the sharing of premiums and death benefits, and cash values. The trust agrees to pay the part of the premium equal to the "economic benefit" of the coverage received each year. The remaining portion of the premium is paid by the employer. The employee is given a bonus by his employer, equal in amount to the trust's share of the premium. The employee's cost is limited to the taxes paid on the bonus received. The employee makes cash gifts to the trust to provide the trust with funds to pay its portion of the premiums. If the trust beneficiaries are given the opportunity to withdraw the funds, the gifts will qualify for the annual $10,000 gift tax exclusion.

Upon Death—The policy proceeds are split between the employer and the trust. The employer receives a return equal to its cumulative contributions to the plan. The balance of the proceeds are paid directly to the trust. Funds are then available to be disbursed by the trustee pursuant to the trust provisions, which will end with the eventual distribution of trust corpus to beneficiaries.

¶721.02

Consequences—The death proceeds are received by the trust free of income taxes. Revenue Ruling 64-328 determines the basic tax consequences of split dollar arrangements. The employee is taxed on the value of the economic benefit he receives from the employer's participation in the split-dollar arrangement. Revenue Ruling 64-328 provides that the employer cannot take a business deduction on its share of the premiums when the employer is the beneficiary.

Gross Income (Rev. Rul. 64-328, 1964-2 CB 11)—Where an insurance policy is purchased on the life of an employee under a so-called "split-dollar" arrangement in which the employer provides the funds to pay the portions of the premiums equal to the increases in the cash surrender value of the policy and the employee is to pay the balance, if any, of the premiums, and in which, from the proceeds of the policy payable at the employee's death, the employer will receive an amount generally equal to the cash surrender value of the policy and the employee's beneficiary will receive the balance, the employee must include in his income the value of the insurance protection in excess of the portions, if any, of premiums provided by him. *Held also:* no deduction shall be allowed to the employer for premium payments made. *Held also:* the proceeds of the policy payable upon the death of the employee are subject to section 101(a) of the Internal Revenue Code.

Reverse Split-Dollar

This insurance technique provides a method where a business can obtain key person insurance to protect itself from financial losses which may occur when a key employee dies. With Reverse split-dollar, most of the death benefit will be received by the business. The employee generally owns all the policy cash values.

During Lifetime—The employee purchases a life insurance contract on his life. Then a formal agreement is adopted by the company specifying the exact death benefit to be received by the employer. Terms such as the length of the agreement are specified. Any sharing arrangement may be possible. For example, a portion of the death benefit equal to the cash value could be retained by the employee and made payable to his beneficiary. The agreement provides that the business will pay a share of the premium. Typically, this is an amount equal to the "P.S. 58 table" cost of the coverage received each year. The employee pays the balance of the premium. After the first few years, this amount is usually very low because of the high "P.S. 58" costs attributed to the business. The employee's share of premiums could be paid with bonuses from the business. The employee's total compensation must be reasonable. If the employee is still alive when the agreement terminates, the business will then relinquish all of its interests in the death benefits. The employee, as owner, can withdraw the cash value in a lump sum, retain the policy as paid-up insurance, or purchase a retirement annuity, etc.

Upon Death—If the employee dies prior to the end of the agreement, the insurance company pays to the business most of the death benefit.

.03 Miscellaneous Insurance Techniques

Deferred Compensation Insurance Funding

A plan that provides for selected management to defer income until after retirement.

- This is a non-qualified plan that can be unique and specific with each employer.
- The plan postpones payment for current services until some future date.

- This postpones taxation until receipt by the employee.
- Generally the employee gives up some current payment for future payments.

Deduction for Contributions of an Employer to an Employee's Trust or Annuity Plan and Compensation under a Deferred-Payment Plan (Code Sec. 404)

If contributions are paid by an employer to or under a stock bonus, pension, profit-sharing, or annuity plan, or if compensation is paid or accrued on account of any employee under a plan deferring the receipt of such compensation, such contributions or compensation shall not be deductible until includible in the employee's income.

Technique:

A typical deferred compensation plan might provide for retirement payments (tax-deductible to the corporation when made), at age 65, of a specified or variable sum per year for a specified number of years. This saves current fund expenses. If funding is required in the contract, it will allow for smaller amounts due to the potential future growth of any funding. These payments are taxable to the retired employee. The concept is that the retiree would pay less tax, due to a reduced retirement income and a resulting lower marginal tax bracket.

Generally, deferred compensation plans provide for survivor payments if the employee dies prior to retirement. Life insurance on the employee can provide the employer with funds to meet its obligation. These payments would be taxable income to the family.

Deferred compensation plans may also provide disability benefits to the employee, usually provided by a disability income contract.

Life Insurance Funding

By using life insurance with an increasing death benefit, the benefit received will likely produce a gain to corporate capital when the employee dies. This amount can then be used to make the survivor payments. This gain is the amount by which the death benefit exceeds the cumulative outlay by the corporation. This outlay is the sum of the premium payments prior to retirement and the after-tax cost of the retirement payments. If the agreement is formally funded, the IRS argues that a present economic value accrues and should be included in the employee's income. However, Letter Ruling 8509023 states that a plan that sets aside assets in escrow is not considered formally funded if its assets are subject to the claims of generally creditors.

Executive Equity Insurance Technique

Executive equity is a benefit plan where the employer provides life insurance for a selected employee. The employer has total discretion to select the amount of insurance coverage and who is to be covered by the agreement. This is available to both the stockholder-employee and the non-stockholder-employee. Ease of installation, and premium payments with a business check are advantages.

During Lifetime

The employee purchases and owns a permanent life insurance contract on his own life. The employer pays premiums to the insurance company. These premiums are tax-deductible by the employer as compensation to the employee. The compensation is taxable income to the employee. The employee owns the life insurance contract, including all policy cash values. The annual increase in these values usually more than offsets any taxes paid by the employee.

Upon Death

The insurance company pays the total death benefit (which is tax-free) directly to the employee's beneficiary. Executive plans are attractive to corporations that have marginal tax brackets, which are higher than the marginal tax brackets of their employee-stockholders. This costs the employee-stockholder less to use executive equity to take profits out of his corporation, than to leave the money in his corporation.

Salary Allotment Insurance Technique

Under a salary allotment plan, employees are given the opportunity to supplement their existing group with life or disability income insurance. Each employee takes advantage of the plan through an individual pay allotment to the insurance company.

- Compensation consists of both salary and benefits.
- Benefits can range from 10-30% of direct payroll costs.
- A salary allotment plan can help contain benefit expenses.

By purchasing a base of permanent life insurance during working years, the employee can avoid the prohibitive costs associated with converting group life insurance upon retirement. This guarantees that some life insurance will be available. Employees view such plans as an extension of existing benefits packages. Employees can pay modest premiums, which will provide substantial life, disability, and annuity benefits for themselves and their families.

The employer should:

- Arrange for payroll deductions.
- Provide notice of enrollment opportunity.
- Provide for enrollment at work during business hours.

Advantages

- No physical examinations required.
- Convenient payroll deduction of premiums.
- Discounted premiums from group billing.
- Level insurance premiums, which do not increase.
- No lapse of policy upon retirement.

Entity Purchase Agreement Insurance Technique

This arrangement provides for a contract with the business, rather than with each owner to provide for the complete disposition of a business interest.

During Life

Assume a business which is owned equally by X and Y. Each enters into an agreement with the business for the purchase and sale of their respective interests. This agreement is binding. It obligates both X and Y, and their estates, to sell their business interest, upon the death, disability or retirement of either. It further obligates the business to buy the interest. The business obtains separate life insurance contracts insuring X and Y in order to provide for funds to meet its obligations to purchase these interests. The business is thus amortizing the cost of the buyout purchase over the lifetime of the insured. The business pays the premiums and is owner and beneficiary of the contracts.

Upon Death

Upon the first to die, the business interest passes to the family or estate. The insurance company pays a tax-free death benefit to the business as beneficiary of the contract. In return for cash, X's family, or estate, will then transfer X's entire interest to the business. This fully funded agreement guarantees that the surviving family will receive a fair price for X's interest.

Certain Death Benefits

Generally, gross income does not include amounts received (whether in a single sum or otherwise) under a life insurance contract, if such amounts are paid by reason of the death of the insured. (Code Sec. 101)

Transfer for Valuable Consideration

In the case of a transfer for a valuable consideration, by assignment or otherwise, of a life insurance contract or any interest therein, the amount excluded from gross income shall not exceed an amount equal to the sum of the actual value of such consideration and the premiums and other amounts subsequently paid by the transferee.

The preceding sentence shall not apply in the case of such a transfer—

- If such contract or interest therein has a basis for determining gain or loss in the hands of a transferee determined in whole or in part by reference to such basis of such contract or interest therein in the hands of the transferor, or

- If such transfer is to the insured, to a partner of the insured, to a partnership in which the insured is a partner, or to a corporation in which the insured is a shareholder or officer.

Proceeds and Premiums

- Life insurance proceeds are not directly included in the insured's estate when partnership or corporation is owner and beneficiary.

- Premiums paid by partnership are not deductible.

- Premiums paid on key person life insurance, where the employer is both owner and beneficiary of the policy, are not taxable to the insured employee. (Rev. Rul. 59-184.)

Group Medical Insurance Technique

Group insurance provides a tax-favored benefit, which the employer can provide for his employees. Plans offered with life insurance can provide employees up to $50,000 of life coverage, free of income taxes on the premium payments. Insurance premiums on a plan that discriminates in favor of "key employees" are not excluded from income.

The group term life insurance plan must meet four basic requirements to be excluded:

- It must be provided under a policy carried directly or indirectly by the employer.

- It must be provided to a group of employees as compensation for personal services.

¶721.03

- The amount of insurance must be computed under a formula (such as age, years of service, compensation or position) that precludes individual selection of such amounts.
- It must provide a general death benefit that is excludable from income.

During Lifetime

The employer pays the premiums to the insurance company. These premiums are tax-deductible to the employer and not taxable to the covered employee.

Upon Death

The insurance company pays the death benefit directly to the employee's family or estate, as beneficiary of the insurance. This payment is income tax free.

Medical Expense Reimbursement Plan

- Pays for the medical expenses of an employee and the employee's dependents.
- Reimbursement is tax exempt.
- Self-insured plans will cause highly compensated individuals to be taxed on part or all of any reimbursements, unless the plan is nondiscriminatory as to benefits.

Amounts Received Under Accident and Health Plans (Code Sec. 105)

AMOUNT PAID TO HIGHLY COMPENSATED INDIVIDUALS UNDER A DISCRIMINATORY SELF-INSURED MEDICAL EXPENSE REIMBURSEMENT PLAN. (Code Sec. 105(h))

In the case of amounts paid to a highly compensated individual under a self-insured medical reimbursement plan which does not satisfy the requirements following for a plan year, the tax exemption shall not apply to such amounts to the extent they constitute an excess reimbursement of such highly compensated individual. (Code Sec. 105(h)(1))

PROHIBITION OF DISCRIMINATION—A self-insured medical reimbursement plan satisfies the requirements of only if—the plan does not discriminate in favor of highly compensated individuals as to eligibility to participate; and the benefits provided under the plan do not discriminate in favor of participants who are highly compensated individuals. (Code Sec. 105(h)(2))

NONDISCRIMINATORY ELIGIBILITY CLASSIFICATIONS—(Code Sec. 105(h)(3))

A self-insured medical reimbursement plan does not satisfy the requirements unless such plan benefits—

- Percent or more of all employees, or 80 percent or more of all the employees who are eligible to benefit under the plan if 70 percent or more of all employees are eligible to benefit under the plan; or
- Such employees as qualify under a classification set up by the employer and found by the Secretary not to be discriminatory in favor of highly compensated individuals. (Code Sec. 105(h)(3)(A))

EXCLUSION OF CERTAIN EMPLOYEES

There may be excluded from consideration—

- Employees who have not completed 3 years of service;

- Employees who have not attained age 25;
- Part-time or seasonal employees;
- Employees not included in the plan who are included in a unit of employees covered by an agreement between employee representatives and one or more employers which the Secretary finds to be a collective bargaining agreement, if accident and health benefits were the subject of good faith bargaining between such employee representatives and such employer or employers; and
- Employees who are nonresident aliens and who receive no earned income from the employer which constitutes income from sources within the United States. (105(h)(3)(B))

NONDISCRIMINATORY BENEFITS

A self-insured medical reimbursement plan does not meet the requirement unless all benefits provided for participants who are highly compensated individuals are provided for all other participants. (105(h)(4))

HIGHLY COMPENSATED INDIVIDUAL DEFINED

The term "highly compensated individual" means an individual who is—

- One of the 5 highest paid officers,
- A shareholder who owns (with the application of section 318) more than 10 percent in value of the stock of the employer, or
- Among the highest paid 25 percent of all employees. (105(h)(5))

SELF-INSURED MEDICAL REIMBURSEMENT PLAN

The term "self-insured medical reimbursement plan" means a plan of an employer to reimburse employees for expenses for which reimbursement is not provided under a policy of accident and health insurance. (105(h)(6))

EXCESS REIMBURSEMENT OF HIGHLY COMPENSATED INDIVIDUAL.

The excess reimbursement of a highly compensated individual which is attributable to a self-insured medical reimbursement plan is—(105(h)(7))

- In the case of a benefit available to highly compensated individuals but not to all other participants, amount reimbursed under the plan to the employee with respect to such benefit, and (105(h)(7)(A))
- In the case of benefits (other than benefits paid to a highly compensated individual by a plan which fails to satisfy the requirements, the total amount reimbursed to the highly compensated individual for the plan year multiplied by a fraction—105(h)(7)(B)
- The numerator of which is the total amount reimbursed to all participants who are highly compensated individuals under the plan for the plan year, and the denominator of which is the total amount reimbursed to all employees under the plan for such plan year.

In determining the fraction, there shall not be taken into account any reimbursement which is attributable to a benefit described above.

TIME OF INCLUSION

Any amount paid for a plan year that is included in income by reason of this subsection shall be treated as received or accrued in the taxable year of the participant in which the plan year ends. (105(h)(10))

Disability Income Plan Insurance Technique

Many corporations will informally continue a disabled employee's salary for an extended period of time. If the employee is an employee-stockholder, the resulting tax effect could be very unwanted.

No Plan

If this employee-stockholder becomes disabled without a pre-existing plan, continued salary payments might be treated by the IRS as nondeductible dividends. Thus the corporation would lose the benefit of the salary deduction.

Disability Income Plan

A pre-existing disability income plan would enable the corporation to preserve the tax-deductibility of continued salary payments to the disabled employee-stockholder.

To establish a plan:

- A corporate resolution must be adopted;
- A plan document must be prepared;
- Notification of the plan's existence must be given to the covered employee.

Stockholders must be covered in their capacity as employees.

The plan may be selective in its coverage. A class may consist of just one employee. The class defined must be a "reasonable" classification.

Reduced Risk Plan

Part of the corporation's liability is covered by an insurance company. The premium is deductible by the corporation, yet not taxable to the employee. With an individual disability income contract, a portion of the benefit could be paid directly to the disabled employee-stockholder by the insurance company. The corporation would deduct a continued salary payment.

Compensation for Injuries or Sickness (Sec. 104)

Except in the case of amounts attributable to (and not in excess of) deductions allowed under section 213 (relating to medical, etc., expenses) for any prior taxable year, gross income does not include—

- Amounts received under workmen's compensation acts as compensation for personal injuries or sickness; (104(a)(1))
- The amount of any damages (other than punitive damages) received (whether by suit or agreement and whether as lump sums or as periodic payments) on account of personal physical injuries or physical sickness; (104(a)(2))
- Amounts received through accident or health insurance (or through an arrangement having the effect of accident or health insurance) for personal injuries or sickness (other than amounts received by an employee, to the extent such amounts are attributable to contributions by the employer which were not

¶721.03

includible in the gross income of the employee, or are paid by the employer). (104(a)(3))

Contributions by Employer to Accident and Health Plans

Except as otherwise provided, gross income of an employee does not include employer-provided coverage under an accident or health plan. (Code Sec. 106.)

Amounts Received under Accident and Health Plans (Code Sec. 105)

AMOUNTS ATTRIBUTABLE TO EMPLOYER CONTRIBUTIONS

Except as otherwise provided, amounts received by an employee through accident or health insurance for personal injuries or sickness shall be included in gross income to the extent such amounts are attributable to contributions by the employer which were not includible in the gross income of the employee, or are paid by the employer.

AMOUNTS EXPENDED FOR MEDICAL CARE

Except in the case of amounts attributable to (and not in excess of) deductions allowed under section 213 (relating to medical, etc., expenses) for any prior taxable year, gross income does not include reimbursable medical amounts if such amounts are paid, directly or indirectly, to the taxpayer to reimburse the taxpayer for expenses incurred by him for the medical care of the taxpayer, his spouse, and his dependents.

Certain Employee Benefits (Reg. § 1.162-10)

Amounts paid or accrued by a taxpayer on account of injuries received by employees and lump-sum amounts paid or accrued as compensation for injuries are proper deductions as ordinary and necessary expenses. Such deductions are limited to the amount not compensated for by insurance or otherwise. Amounts paid or accrued within the taxable year for dismissal wages, unemployment benefits, guaranteed annual wages, vacations, or a sickness, accident, hospitalization, medical expense, recreational, welfare, or similar benefit plan, are deductible if they are ordinary and necessary expenses of the trade or business. However, such amounts shall not be deductible, under any circumstances, they may be used to provide benefits under a stock bonus, pension, annuity, profit-sharing, or other deferred compensation plan of the type referred to in section 404(a). In such an event, the extent to which these amounts are deductible from gross income shall be governed by the provisions of section 404 and the regulations issued thereunder.

.04 Cash Value Corridor

A contract falls within the cash value corridor if the death benefit under the contract at any time is not less than the applicable percentage of the cash surrender value.

Applicable Percentage

In the case of an insured with an attained age as of the beginning of the contract year of: The applicable percentage shall decrease by a rationable portion for each full year:

More than:	But not more than:	From:	To:
0	40	250	250
40	45	250	215
45	50	215	185
55	60	150	130
60	65	130	120

More than:	But not more than:	From:	To:
65	70	120	115
70	75	115	105
75	90	105	105
90	95	105	100

Treatment of Certain Contracts Which Do Not Meet Certain Tests

Income Inclusion

If at any time any contract which is a life insurance contract under the applicable law does not meet the definition of life insurance contract as above, the income on the contract for any taxable year of the policyholder shall be treated as ordinary income received or accrued by the policyholder during such year.

Income on the contract—the term "income on the contract" means with respect to any taxable year of the policyholder, the excess of the sum of the increase in the net surrender value of the contract during the taxable year and the cost of the life insurance protection provided under the contract during the taxable year over the premiums paid under the contract during the taxable year.

.05 Insurance and Taxation

Premiums on Life Insurance Taken Out in a Trade or Business

When Premiums Are Not Deductible

Premiums paid by a taxpayer on a life insurance policy are not deductible from the taxapayer's gross income, even though they would otherwise be deductible as trade or business expenses, if they are paid on a life insurance policy covering the life of any officer or employee of the taxpayer or any person (including the taxpayer) who is financially interested in any trade or business carried on by the taxpayer, when the taxpayer is directly or indirectly a beneficiary of the policy. (Reg. § 1.264-1 (a))

When Taxpayer Is a Beneficiary

If a taxpayer takes out a policy for the purpose of protecting himself from loss in the event of the death of the insured, the taxpayer is considered a beneficiary directly or indirectly under the policy. However, if the taxpayer is not a beneficiary under the policy, the premiums so paid will not be disallowed as deductions merely because the taxpayer may derive a benefit from the increased efficiency of the officer of the employee insured. A taxpayer is considered a beneficiary under a policy where, for example, he, as a principal member of a partnership, takes out an insurance policy on his own life irrevocably designating his partner as the sole beneficiary in order to induce his partner to retain his investment in the partnership. Whether or not the taxpayer is a beneficiary under a policy, the proceeds of the policy paid by reason of the death of the insured may be excluded from gross income whether the beneficiary is an individual or a corporation, except in the case of:

- Certain transferees (as provided in section 101(a)(2)),

- Portions of amount of life insurance proceeds received at a date later than death under the provisions of section 101(d), and

- Life insurance policy proceeds which are includable in the gross income of a husband or wife under section 71 (relating to alimony) or section 682 (relating to income of an estate or trust in case of divorce, etc.). (Reg. § 1.264-1 (b))

Interest Relating to Tax-Exempt Income

No amount shall be allowed as a deduction for interest on any indebtedness incurred or continued to purchase or carry obligations, the interest on which is wholly exempt. (Reg. § 1.265-2(a))

Property Transferred in Connection with the Performance of Services

Life Insurance

The cost of life insurance protection under a life insurance contract, retirement income contract, endowment contract, or other contract providing life insurance protection is taxable during the period such contract remains substantially nonvested (as defined in Reg. § 1.83-3(b)). The cost of such life insurance protection is the reasonable net premium cost of the current life insurance protection (as defined in Reg. § 1.72-16 (b) (3)) provided by such contract.

Compensation for Services, Including Fees, Commissions, and Similar Items

Compensation Paid Other Than in Cash

Property transferred to employee or independent contractor: If property is transferred by an employer to an employee or if property is transferred to an independent contractor, as compensation for services, for an amount less than its fair market value, then regardless of whether the transfer is in the form of a sale or exchange, the difference between the amount paid for the property and the amount of its fair market value at the time of the transfer is compensation and shall be included in the gross income of the employee or independent contractor. In computing the gain or loss from the subsequent sale of such property, its basis shall be the amount paid for the property increased by the amount of such difference included in grosss income. (Reg. § 1.61-2(d) (2))

Cost of life insurance on the life of the employee: Generally, life insurance premiums paid by an employer on the life of an employee, where the proceeds of such insurance are payable to the beneficiary of such employee, are part of the gross income of the employee. However, whether the amount is includable in the employee's gross income is determined with regard to the provisions of section 403 in the case of an individual contract issued after December 31, 1962, or a group contract, which provides incidental life insurance insurance protection. (Reg. § 1.61-2(d) (ii) (a))

Cost of group-term life insurance on the life of an individual other than an employee: the cost of group-term life insurance of the life of an individual other than an employee (such as the spouse or dependent of the employee) provided in connection with the performance of services by the employee is includable in the gross income of the employee. (Reg. § 1.61-2(d) (2) (ii) (b))

Compensation for Personal Services

There may be included among the ordinary and necessary expenses paid or incurred in carrying on any trade or business a reasonable allowance for salaries or other compensation for personal services actually rendered. The test of deductibility in the case of compensation payments is whether they are reasonable and are in fact payments purely for services. (Reg. § 1.162-7(a))

¶721.05

An ostensible salary may be in part payment for property. (Reg. § 1.162-7(b)(1))

The compensation paid may not exceed what is reasonable under all the circumstances. It is, in general, just to assume that reasonable and true compensation is only such amount as would ordinarily be paid for like services by like enterprises under like circumstances. The circumstances to be taken into consideration are those existing at the date when the contract for services was made, not those existing at the date when the contract is questioned. (Reg. § 1.162-7(b)(3))

Premiums paid for life insurance by the insured are not deductible. (Reg. § 1.262-1(b)(1))

Certain Death Benefits

Gross Income

Proceeds of life insurance contracts payable by reason of death: generally, gross income does not include amounts received under a life insurance contract, if such amount are paid by reason of death of the insured. (Code Sec. 101 (a)(1))

Transfer for Valuable Consideration

In the case of a transfer for a valuable consideration, by assignment or otherwise, or a life insurance contract or any interest therein, the amount excluded from gross income above shall not exceed an amount equal to the sum of the actual value of such consideration and the premiums and other amounts subsequently paid by the transferee. The preceding sentence shall not apply in the case of such a transfer if such contract or interest therein has a basis of determining gain or loss in the hands of such a transferee determined in whole or in part by reference to such basis of such contract or interest therein in the hands of the transferor, or if such transfer is to the insured, to a partner of the insured, to a partnerhsip in which the insured is a partner, or to a corporation in which the insured is a shareholder or officer. (Code Sec. 101(a)(2))

Treatment of Self-Employed Individuals

The term "employee" does not include a self-employed individual. (Code Sec. 101(b)(3)(A))

Exclusion from Gross Income of Proceeds of Life Insurance Contracts Payable by Reason of Death

Transfers of life insurance policies: In the case of a series of transfers, if the last transfer of a life insurance policy or an interest therein is for valuable consideration.

- The general rule is that the final transferee shall exclude from the gross income, with repect to the proceeds of such policy or interest therein, only the sum of :
  — The actual value of the consideration paid by him, and
  — The premiums and other amounts subsequently paid by him.

If the final transfer is to the insured, to a partner of the insured, to a partnership in which the insured is a partner, or to a corporation in which the insured is a shareholder or officer, the final transferee shall exclude the entire amount of the proceeds from gross income.

Except for the above, if the basis of the policy of interest transferred, for the purpose of determining gain or loss with respect to the final transferee, is determinable, in whole or in part, by reference to the basis of such policy or interest therein in the hands of the transferor, the amount of the proceeds which is excludable by the final transferee is limited to the sum of:

- The amount which would have been excludable by his transferor if no such transfer had taken place, and any premiums and other amounts subsequently paid by the final transferee himself. (Reg. § 1.101-1(b)(3))

Accelerated Death Benefits

In situations where an insured person is chronically or terminally ill, amounts received after 1996 under a life insurance contract or from the sale or assignment of any portion of the death benefit under a life insurance contract to a viatical settlement provider may be excluded from income. The excludable amount for a chronically ill individual is capped at $175 per day, adjusted for inflation.

Exclusion From Employer-Provided Death Benefits

The $5,000 exclusion from income for employer-provided death benefits is repealed for employees dying after the date of enactment of the Small Business Act (8/20/96).

Distribution of Property

A distribution of property made by a corporation to a shareholder with respect to its stock shall be treated in the manner following. (Code Sec. 301(a))

Amount Taxable

Amount constituting dividend: That portion of the distribution which is a dividend shall be included in gross income. (Code Sec. 301(c)(1))

Exchange of Stock for Property

Nonrecognition of gain or loss: No gain or loss shall be recognized to a corporation on the receipt of money or other property in exchange for stock (including treasury stock) of such corporation. No gain or loss shall be recognized by a corporation with respect to any lapse or acquisition of an option to buy or sell its stock (including treasury stock). (Code Sec. 1032(a))

Certain Exchanges of Insurance Policies

No gain or loss shall be recognized on the exchange of:

- A contract of life insurance for another contract of life insurance or for an endowment or annuity contract; or
- A contract of endowment insurance (A) for another contract of endowment insurance which provides for regular payments beginning at a date not later than the date payments would have begun under the contract exchanged, or (B) for an annuity contract; or
- An annuity contract for an annuity contract. (Code Sec. 1035(a))

Health Insurance Costs

30% Deduction Amount

Self-Employed Health Insurance Deduction

The deduction increase for health insurance expenses of self-employed individuals and their spouses and dependents is phased in as follows:

¶721.05

Tax Year Beginning In:	Applicable Percentage
2001	60%
2002	70%
2003	100%

Example: Barbara Wright is a self-employed accountant and earned $40,000 during 2001. She spent $2,400 on medical insurance for herself and her family. Barbara may deduct $1,440 ($2,400 × 60%) from her gross income.

Dollar Amount Limitations

No deduction shall be allowed to the extent that the amount of such deduction exceeds the taxpayer's earned income derived by the taxpayer from the trade or business with respect to which the plan providing the medical care coverage is established. (Code Sec. 162(1)(2)(A))

Coordination with Medical Deduction

Medical Deduction

Any amount paid by a taxpayer for insurance to which the above applies shall not be taken into account in computing the amount allowable to the taxpayer as a deduction under section 213(a). (Code Sec. 162(1)(3)(A))

Deduction Not Allowed for Self-Employment Tax Purposes

The deduction allowable by reason of this subsection shall not be taken into account in determining an individual's net earnings from self-employement. (Code Sec. 162(1)(4))

Treatment of Certain S Corporation Shareholders

These rules shall apply in the case of any individual treated as a partner, except that

- Such individual's wages from the S corporation shall be treated as such individual's earned income. (Code Sec. 162(1)(5)(A))

.07 Co-Insurance

Co-Insurance provides that if the insured fails to carry an adequate amount of insurance equal to a stated percentage of the value of the property to be insured, then the insured becomes a co-insurer and must proportionately bear the loss. Recovery for partial loss is computed by the following formula:

Recovery for Co-Insurance Loss

$$\text{Recovery} = \frac{\text{Face value of insurance}}{\text{Co-insurance\%} \times \text{FMV of property}} \times \text{Loss}$$

Example (1): A company with property worth $150,000 and an 80% insurance clause must carry at least $120,000 of insurance to fully cover a loss.

If the company carried only $100,000, the deficit would be $20,000 ($120,000 − $100,000).

Example (2): Face value of policy = $150,000 (note: maximum that can be recovered)

Co-insurance % = 80%

¶721.07

Fair market value of property before fire disaster = $250,000

Fire damage= $ 42,500

$$42,500 \times \frac{\$150,000}{(.80) \times (\$250,000)} = \$31,875$$

Business Interruption Insurance

Co-Insurance: Should a client be underinsured the co-insurance formula will be in effect and the client will collect only a portion of the loss.

Business Interruption Insurance—Co-Insurance

$$\frac{\text{Insurance Carried}}{\text{Insurance Required}}$$

Business Interruption Insurance

% of loss paid x

= [(Gross sales – COGS – labor) × policy co-insurance requirements] × estimated sales for the year

.09 Insurance Checklists

Life Insurance Annual Review Checklist

- Review each policy presently owned.
  — Suitability.
  — Death benefits to be detailed.
  — Is the "savings" element satisfactory?
  — Should different types of insurance be considered? Term? Whole life? Universal life?
  — What policy riders are desired?
  — Is there an accidental death benefit?
  — Are policies lapse-proof?
- Review current beneficiaries—add, change, delete.
  — Have contingent beneficiaries been assigned properly?
  — Has income increased or decreased significantly?
  — Has the family situation changed dramatically since the last review? Marriage? Divorce? Additional children or aging parent responsibilities?
  — Are cash value build-ups adequate?
- Insurance coverage.
  — Will there be adequate income replacement at retirement?
  — Are death benefits appropriate?
  — Are disability benefits adequate?
- Insurance settlement options.
  — Are they appropriate for the beneficiaries' situation?
  — Does the insurance plan provide for adequate retirement?

¶721.09

- Premiums.
  - What is the amount?
  - Would a change from monthly to annual payment provide a reduction in cost?
  - Would a different carrier provide comparable coverage at reduced cost?
- Policy loans.
  - Are additional loans a valid consideration for the businessman's current needs?
  - What loans are outstanding?
  - Should they be paid back or refinanced?

Life Insurance Considerations for Married Couples

- Do you think your existing insurance is adequate to take care of your goals?
- How much insurance do each of you have—through work and outside of work?
- What do each of you make?
- Would you be willing to sell any noncommitted assets in the event of either death?
- Do you want to consider Social Security as income in the event of death?
- How much income would each of you need in the event of either death?
- Would you pay off the mortgage?
- Would you still want to send the kids to college?
- Are there any debts you would like to pay off?

Reducing Unemployment Insurance Costs

Classification: Be sure the company is classified properly.

Stabilize the labor force: Constant turnover of new employees does not allow the wages to exceed the wage base limit.

Excludable wages: Be sure that no exempt wages (such as those exceeding the wage base) are reported as taxable wages to the taxing authority.

When acquiring an ongoing business, the successor should seek to obtain the predecessor's previous rate, if lower.

Check account charges. Verify:

- The chargeback is of the correct amount.
- The chargeback period ends correctly.
- The employee was employed by the employer.
- Wages are correct.
- The period of employment is correct.

Control Claims

- Keep written records concerning employment history.
- The employee's job performance.

— Document carefully all warnings concerning job performance.

— Doument any infractions of company rules, unexplained absences, misconduct.

— Document carefully what was said at the termination meeting.

— Document the reasons and conditions surrounding the termination.

Common Disqualifying Conditions

- A statute of federal, state, or municipality requiring that the employer separate the individual from service.
- Unemployment because of strike or labor dispute.
- Discharge for misconduct.
- Voluntary leave.
- Failure to apply for or accept suitable work without good cause.

Insurance Coverage Review

- Have various premium rates been analyzed from different carriers?
- Is the policy adequate in how it is supposed to perform?
- Ask different agents to review the firm's insurance needs and make recommendations.
- Seek comprehensive policies.
- Is insurance lacking in some areas?
- Do insurance gaps exist?
- Is there overinsurance or underinsurance in certain areas?

Insurance Total Coverage Summary Analysis

- Workman's compensation
- Personal liability
- Pension—P/S plans
- General liability
- Product liability
- Fire
- Business Interruption
- Credit
- Auto
- Disability
- Life
- Major medical
- Destruction of records
- Contractual liability
- Criminal acts

¶721.09

.11 Health Insurance

Health insurance is used to pay medical expenses. Preventative care, medical examinations and tests, optical and dental work, inoculations and treatments for physical and mental illnesses are some of the things that health insurance policies may cover. Almost every household will eventually need health insurance. Policies can include any or all of the following coverages:

- Hospitalization—covers hospital room and board, medications, tests and services.
- Major medical—covers expenses that exceed the dollar limit of the basic coverage.
- Surgical—covers operations.
- Medical—covers visits to the doctor's office and diagnostic laboratory tests.
- Comprehensive—includes all of the above.
- Dental—covers most dental expenses.
- Prescriptions—pays for prescribed medication.

Skyrocketing medical costs have made it necessary for many households to economize when planning for medical expenses. Consider purchasing health insurance through a group plan, or self-insuring for routine medical costs and buying insurance.

When selecting a health insurance policy and company, ask:

- Is there a limit to the amount the insurance will pay or to what is considered a "reasonable and customary" fee?
- Is there a waiting period before coverage begins?
- Is there a deductible (an amount that you pay before coverage begins)? How much is it, and how many persons in the family would have to pay the deductible per year?
- What is the percentage or allowance of medical fees that are paid?
- How many days of hospitalization are covered?

.13 Disability Insurance

For young workers chances of becoming disabled are greater than the chances of dying. Disability insurance protects from loss of income if the wage earner is unable to work due to illness or accident. It pays an income until one is able to return to work or until benefits run out. If one becomes unable to work in his current job, but would be able to work in another field, some policies provide benefits while one retrains.

Regarding disability insurance, consider how long and how much the employer will pay if the employees could not work. Check to see if one qualifies to receive disability payments from other sources, such as a health insurance policy, Social Security, worker's compensation, veteran's benefits, and mortgages. If one can cover 60 to 70 percent of present income from other sources, one is probably safe. If not, one may want to consider purchasing additional disability coverage. Disability insurance can be purchased as an option on a life insurance policy or as a separate policy. Either way one might want to be sure of the following:

The policy is renewable.

The company cannot cancel the policy, increase the premium, or lower benefits for a certain period.

The waiting period ends about the time the personal emergency fund runs out.

The premiums can be waived while one is disabled.

Disability-Client Questions

What concerns do you have about disability?

If you became disabled today:

    — How much income would you need to cover your expenses?

    — How much income would you need to cover your expenses?

    — What would you want to happen to your family?

Do you have a disability policy?

Is it group or individual?

Who is paying the premium?

Is it short-term or long-term?

How long will the benefits last?

What percent of your income is covered?

Is that percent adequate for your monthly needs?

How would you feel about your ability to pay your mortgage and maintain your home?

Do you know if what you have in place today is adequate to meet your needs?

Did you know that more homes are lost due to disability than to death?

.15 Saving on Insurance Costs

Insurance premiums can account for a substantial portion of the household budget. There are several ways to reduce the amount spent on insurance. Insurance premiums for similar coverage vary widely from one company to the next. Rates should be checked before making a decision.

Deductibles

A deductible is the money that must be paid toward a loss before the insurance will pay—the larger the deductible, the lower the premium. A large deductible can result in large savings in the premium.

Fewer Payments

Savings can often be obtained by paying insurance premiums once or twice a year instead of breaking them down into monthly payments.

Group Insuring

Group plans usually result in a substantial premium savings over individual plans-especially with health insurance.

Preventative Measures

Being a good insurance risk can also result in lower premiums. For example, non-smokers often qualify for lower life or health insurance premiums. Alarms in a house or apartment may qualify for a reduction in homeowners' insurance rates, and safe driver rates are available from most auto insurers.

Self-Insuring

It may make sense to self-insure against a loss. For example, suppose a personal car has a low value of about $1000. Savings on automobile insurance premiums can be obtained by dropping the collision insurance and putting $1000 in a savings account where it can earn interest. Later, if damage occurs to the car, money for repairs would come from savings instead of from the insurance company. When cutting premium costs, beware of underinsuring. Find out if the insurance will rebuild the house and replace the belongings at current prices. Underinsuring can cause considerable financial stress if after a loss one does not receive enough money to return to prior financial position.

.16 Life Insurance—How Much a Person Needs

This analysis worksheet is based on estimates of current net worth, and the future needs of your survivors. Our primary calculations are based on the assumption that survivors will only use the income that the life insurance proceeds will generate and not the principal.

Assumptions

Tax Rate-Federal	28%
Pre Tax Investment Rate-of-Return	12%

Assets Available:

Life Insurance	$200,000
Company Death Benefits	10,000
Investment Assets	100,000
Other Assets	100,000
	410,000

Expenses:

Estate Taxes, Probate	1,000
Funeral Expenses	5,000
Reserve for College	20,000
Number of Children	2
	46,000

Current Proceeds Available	**364,000**
Annual Cash Inflow:	
Survivor's Annual Income	50,000
Other Annual Proceeds	10,000
Annual Return-on-Investments	31,450
	91,450

Annual Cash Outflow:	
Annual Living Expenses	100,000
Annual Shortfall	(8850)

¶721.16

Shortfall

Annual Shortfall to be covered   8,550

Additional Insurance Required to Cover shortfall $ 98,963

($98,963 × .12 = $11,876 Less Tax ($11,876 × .28 = $ 3,325) = $8,551)

Insurance Needs Worksheet #2

Assumptions:

The surviving spouse will be self-supporting through retirement after children are independent.

This does not consider investment rate of return and growth.

This does not consider inflation factor.

		Estimate
Estimated Funds Need:		
A. Higher education expenses (for all children to complete college and/or graduate school).		$120,000
B. Survivors' living expenses (70% to 85% of current expenses until youngest child is independent)		$400,000
C. Projected expenses (add lines A and B)		$520,000
Estimated Funds Total:		
1. Total assets that can be readily converted to cash (existing life insurance, savings, CDs, home equity)		$50,000
2. Investment fund (with short term liquidity)		$100,000
3. Survivors' future income (until youngest child is independent)	$440,000	
Less: Emergency fund of three to six months of living expenses	10,000	
		$430,000
4. Total liquid assets (add lines 1 through 3)		$580,000
5. Liabilities expected (medical bills, outstanding debt, funeral costs, etc.)		$150,000
6. Net liquid assets (line 4 less line 5)		$430,000
Projected insurance need (line C less line 6)		$90,000

.17 Life Insurance as an Investment

Life insurance is the primary method of creating an estate. It guarentees that a certain target amount will be reached.

The following table illustrates the percentage gain return if death occurs at a given period for the cost of $1,000 of insurance at different annual premium rates.

> **Example:** Cost of insurance = $20 per $1000 of coverage

Death occurs after 10 years.

% return on cost = 400%

Percentage Gain Given Various Premium Rates (Per $1000 of Insurance)

Year of Death	Premium Rate				
	$10	$20	$30	$40	$50
1	9900%	4900%	3233%	2400%	1900%
2	4900%	2400%	1567%	1150%	900%
3	3233%	1567%	1011%	733%	567%
4	2400%	1150%	733%	525%	400%
5	1900%	900%	567%	400%	300%
6	1567%	733%	456%	317%	233%
7	1329%	614%	376%	257%	186%
8	1150%	525%	317%	213%	150%
9	1011%	456%	270%	178%	122%
10	900%	400%	233%	150%	100%
11	809%	355%	203%	127%	82%
12	733%	317%	178%	108%	67%
13	669%	285%	156%	92%	54%
14	614%	257%	138%	79%	43%
15	567%	233%	122%	67%	33%
16	525%	213%	108%	56%	25%
17	488%	194%	96%	47%	18%
18	456%	178%	85%	39%	11%
19	426%	163%	75%	32%	5%
20	400%	150%	67%	25%	0%
21	376%	138%	59%	19%	−5%
22	355%	127%	52%	14%	−9%
23	335%	117%	45%	9%	−13%
24	317%	108%	39%	4%	−17%
25	300%	100%	33%	0%	−20%
26	285%	92%	28%	−4%	−23%
27	270%	85%	23%	−7%	−26%
28	257%	79%	19%	−11%	−29%
29	245%	72%	15%	−14%	−31%
30	233%	67%	11%	−17%	−33%

.19 Lost Earnings Due to Death

Amount of Earnings Lost Before Age 65 Due to Death

These tables provide guidelines of sums that should be made available from life insurance given each person's age at death, increase in annual income, and annual income to cover lifetime loss of earnings.

> *Example:* Given: A person's annual income is $40,000 a year, and this income increases at 4% each year. If the person were age 60 and death ocurred, then $40,000 (plus 4% growth each year) for 5 years would be a sum of $225,320 that the family would lose in earnings.

Using Amount-of-Earnings-Lost Table:

Locate amount for 60 year old, with $10,000 income, at 4% growth = $56,330.

Use conversion factor for 4 (4 × $10,000 = $40,000).

4 × 56,330 = $225,320

If the person were age 50, and the facts were as above, then the family would lose $832,980 in total earnings.

Amount of Earnings Lost Before Age 65 Due to Death (Per $10,000 of Annual Income)

Age at Death	Annual Growth Rate of Income				
	2%	4%	6%	8%	10%
20	$733,306	$1,258,706	$2,255,081	$4,174,261	$7,907,953
21	$708,927	$1,200,294	$2,117,435	$3,855,056	$7,179,048
22	$685,027	$1,144,129	$1,987,580	$3,559,496	$6,516,408
23	$661,595	$1,090,124	$1,865,076	$3,285,830	$5,914,007
24	$638,622	$1,038,196	$1,749,505	$3,032,435	$5,366,370
25	$616,100	$988,265	$1,640,477	$2,797,810	$4,868,518
26	$594,020	$940,255	$1,537,620	$2,580,565	$4,415,926
27	$572,372	$894,091	$1,440,585	$2,379,412	$4,004,478
28	$551,149	$849,703	$1,349,042	$2,193,159	$3,630,434
29	$530,343	$807,022	$1,262,681	$2,020,703	$3,290,395
30	$509,944	$765,983	$1,181,209	$1,861,021	$2,981,268
31	$489,945	$726,522	$1,104,348	$1,713,168	$2,700,244
32	$470,338	$688,579	$1,031,838	$1,576,267	$2,444,767
33	$451,116	$652,095	$963,432	$1,449,506	$2,212,515
34	$432,270	$617,015	$898,898	$1,332,135	$2,001,378
35	$413,794	$583,283	$838,017	$1,223,459	$1,809,434
36	$395,681	$550,849	$780,582	$1,122,832	$1,634,940
37	$377,922	$519,663	$726,398	$1,029,659	$1,476,309
38	$360,512	$489,676	$675,281	$943,388	$1,332,099
39	$343,443	$460,842	$627,058	$863,508	$1,200,999
40	$326,709	$433,117	$581,564	$789,544	$1,081,818
41	$310,303	$406,459	$538,645	$721,059	$973,471
42	$294,219	$380,826	$498,156	$657,648	$874,973
43	$278,450	$356,179	$459,958	$598,933	$785,430
44	$262,990	$332,480	$423,923	$544,568	$704,027
45	$247,833	$309,692	$389,927	$494,229	$630,025
46	$232,974	$287,781	$357,856	$447,620	$562,750
47	$218,406	$266,712	$327,600	$404,463	$501,591
48	$204,123	$246,454	$299,057	$364,502	$445,992
49	$190,121	$226,975	$272,129	$327,502	$395,447
50	$176,393	$208,245	$246,725	$293,243	$349,497
51	$162,935	$190,236	$222,760	$261,521	$307,725
52	$149,739	$172,919	$200,151	$232,149	$269,750
53	$136,803	$156,268	$178,821	$204,953	$235,227
54	$124,121	$140,258	$158,699	$179,771	$203,843
55	$111,687	$124,864	$139,716	$156,455	$175,312
56	$99,497	$110,061	$121,808	$134,866	$149,374
57	$87,546	$95,828	$104,913	$114,876	$125,795
58	$75,830	$82,142	$88,975	$96,366	$104,359
59	$64,343	$68,983	$73,938	$79,228	$84,872
60	$53,081	$56,330	$59,753	$63,359	$67,156

.21 Life Expectancy Table

Selected Life Table Values: 1990 to 1996

Age and Sex

Average Expectation of Life in Years		1990	1991	1996
At Birth:	Male	71.8	72.0	73.0
	Female	78.8	78.9	79.0
Age 20:	Male	53.3	53.4	54.2
	Female	59.8	59.9	59.9
Age 40:	Male	35.1	35.3	35.9
	Female	40.6	40.7	40.7
Age 50:	Male	26.4	26.6	27.1
	Female	31.3	31.5	31.5
Age 65:	Male	15.1	15.3	15.7
	Female	18.9	19.1	18.9

Source: U.S. National Center for Health Statistics, U.S. Life Tables and Actuarial Tables; Vital Statistics of the United States, annual; and unpublished data.

Published data: Statistical Abstract of the United States, 1994 and 1998

.23 Insurance—Long Term Care (LTC)

Long-term care (LTC) insurance should be a cornerstone in retirement planning.

Facts and Figures Regarding Aging

- Life expectancy has doubled in the last 200 years.
- In the 1800's, only 1 out of 10 people could expect to see age 65.
- Life expectancy in 1990 of a male was 71.8, and 78.8 for a female.
- Life expectancy in 1996 of a male was 73, and 79 for a female.

Per Capital health care costs:

	1980	1990	1995
Hospital care	$434	$986	$1270
Physician Services	$192	$563	$720
Home heath care	$10	$50	$199
Nursing home care	$75	$196	$276

- Elder care will replace childcare as the number one dependent care need in the next century.
- There's a one in four chance of someone over 65 needing long term-care for one year or more. The actual risk of needing long-term care (nursing home or home care) is greater than 50 percent.
- One out of three workers will be caring for an aging parent.
- In 1990, there were 54,000 people age 100.
- In year 2000, there are 108,000 people age 100.
- In year 2000, 80 percent of Americans will live past 65.
- In year 2000, there are 34 million people over 65; 12 percent of the population.
- By 2030, 68 million will be over 65.

- In year 2000, life expectancy for men is 80 years, for women 84 years.
- In year 2040, life expectancy for men will be 86 years, for women 94 years.
- In year 2000, the average annual cost nationally for nursing home care is about $38,000 or $105 per day for total cost including room and board, drugs and medical supplies.
- The fastest-growing segment of the elderly population consists of women over age 85.
- Because women outlive men by several years, they face a 50 percent greater likelihood of entering a nursing home after age 65 than a man.

Purpose of LTC Insurance

- To protect against the high cost of nursing homes.
- To protect against the professional home care.
- To protect investment assets.
- Without LTC insurance, funding must come from family, friends, personal assets, or government programs.

Evaluating a LTC Insurance Policy

Long-Term Care Questions

- Do you know how much the average nursing home stay costs?
- Do you want to rely on Medicaid to cover any LTC expenses?
- Do you want to consider the cost of LTC in your investment plan?
- Are you a smoker?
- Do you have any health concerns?
- What is the benefit period of your policy?
- Does it include home health care coverage?
- What is the elimination period?
- Is there a rider that allows the benefits to increase with inflation?
- Financially or emotionally?
- What concerns you most about LTC?
- Do you know anyone who has been placed in a nursing home? How did it impact them?
- What is the daily benefit of your policy?

Plan Questions

- The plan premiums must be affordable.
- The plan must be flexible.
- The plan should allow a high level of customization.

Benefit Periods

- Usually a stated number of years, or
- Lifetime benefits.
- Benefit maximums are structured as a lifetime dollar limit.

Elimination Period

- The number of days 30-60-90 etc. before the policy starts to pay.
- Usually, the elimination period has to be met only once in a lifetime.

Type of Care

- Nursing home
- Assisted living
- Home care

Inflation Protection

- The policy should have an automatic built-in increase for inflation to increase daily and lifetime benefit maximums.

Future Purchase Options

- This feature guarantees the opportunity to buy additional coverage, generally every two or three years.

Guaranteed Renewability

- The policy is automatically renewed, but premiums rise.

Non-forfeiture—If policy lapses, insurance company will offer reduced benefits or return of premiums.

Pre-existing Conditions

- Generally, the policy will not pay for care for first six months regarding a pre-existing condition.

Reinstatement

- If policy lapses, it can be reinstated if payments are caught up within 90 days.

Waiver of Premium

- If person is confined to a hospital, the premium is temporarily waived.

Prior to Hospitalization

- The policy may require a hospital stay before benefits will be paid.

Prior Hospitalization

- The policy may require a hospital stay before benefits will be paid.

Coverage Types of Care

LTC coverage types by LTC insurance:

- Intensive 24 hour/day by highly trained medical personnel.
- Generally provided in a hospital requiring constant supervision and monitoring.

Acute Care

- Partial day care requiring assistance of medical personnel.

Skilled Care

- Usually provided by a licensed medical professional in a nursing home and based on physician's orders.

¶721.23

Intermediate Care

- Such as a patient recovering from surgery. Requires supervision by a licensed medical professional.

Custodial Care

- For activities of daily living—eating, personal hygiene, press, walking, etc.
- Typically provided in patient's home or in assisted living facility.

¶ 723 MUTUAL FUNDS

.01 Overview

"Investment Companies" Defined

Subchapter "M" of Internal Revenue Code:

- Net investment income taxed only to shareholder.
- An investment company that provides for many people to pool their money in order to obtain greater diversification of their investments.
- Professional advisors.
- Investment Company Act of 1940—highly regulated to insure professionalism and protection of the investor.
- Open end companies
  - One class of common stock only.
  - Can leverage borrowed money subject to 300%.
  - Asset coverage.
  - Continuing public offering redeemed at net asset value.
  - Company continually issues and redeems.
  - Always new issue, no margin.
- Redemption—net asset value, normally no redemption charge.
- Purchase price—Public Offering Price = net asset value plus sales charge.
- Closed end.
  - Common stock.
  - Preferred stock and bonds.
  - No leverage.
  - Fixed number of shares.
  - Trade by supply and demand, etc. Company does not redeem.

Mutual Fund Income Distributions

- Investment income and realized short-term capital gains are distributed monthly.
- Long-term capital gains are distributed yearly.
- Capital gains are determined from holding period of company—not shareholder's holding period.

Mutual Fund Issuance of Shares

No-load Companies

- Do not charge the commission against the client's account.
- Shares issued by company directly to investor.
- Issued at net asset value.
- Usually have higher management fees.
- Usually have redemption fees.

Mutual Fund Loaded Companies

- Issued at NAV plus sales charge.
- NASD member firm is underwriter.
- 90% of companies.

12(b)(1) Funds—Back End Loads

- Deferred Sales charge—pay a load to redeem shares plus redemption fee.
- Could be no load if held long enough.

Mutual Fund Types

- Growth—long term growth of invested capital with little current income return.
- Aggressive growth funds—very aggressive, greater risk.
- Growth and income funds—reasonable income return of dividends with good growth. Generally are more stable in a declining market.
- Specialty Funds—concentrate on investments in special types of securities.
- Income Funds—pay highest current dividends commensurate with related risks desired.
- Balanced Funds—maintain a balance between common stocks and senior securities (preferred stocks, bonds, U.S. government obligations).
- Common Stock Funds—invest almost 100% in stocks.
- Municipal Bond Funds—bonds issued by states, cities, legal governments—interest earned is tax free.
- Money-Market Funds—short term, high yield securities—interest varies on a daily basis. Considered safe investments. No cost to deposit or withdraw funds.
- Ginnie Mae Funds—mortgage backed securities guaranteed by the government National Mortage Assoc. Pay a fixed return higher than long term bonds. Ginnie Mae Funds' advantages: Government guarantee, minimized risk, certain rate of return is assured. Investor receives monthly checks—part return of capital and part interest.

Mutual Fund Selection Concepts

- Growth and Aggressive Growth Funds—seek capital appreciation—negligible cash flow
- Blue Chip Stock Fund—high yield—good for dividend exclusion for corporations
- High Yield Funds—high default risk

- High Quality Bond Funds—safe, very low default risk
- Option Income Funds—write covered call options against their positions, higher yield than bonds but usually little capital gain
- Money-Market Funds—good place to keep funds while waiting for next investment opportunity
- U.S. Government Securities—safest of funds
- Municipal Securities—tax free income—ideal for "older" client who wishes steady flow of income and safety
- Convertible Funds—average yields

Mutual Fund Advantages

- Diversification
- Versatility
- Simplicity
- Convenience
  - Purchasing ease
  - Single certificate
  - Withdrawal plans
  - Exchange privileges
  - Accumulation plans
  - Redemption privileges
  - Immediate liquidity. Company has up to 7 days to send check
  - Provides for lower brokerage costs by taking advantage of volume discounts and net trading markets
  - Reinvestment
  - Immediate valuation of assets at close of each business day
- Quality purchase discounts
  - Letter of intent—investor intends to purchase a required dollar amount over an extended period of time (usually 3 months)
  - Cumulative quality discount—if total cumulative shares owned have a dollar value equal to or in excess of a breakpoint
- Professional management
- Selection of portfolio mix
- Changes to portfolio
- Supervision of portfolio
- Timing of purchases and sales
- Retention of cash—keeping pace with changing conditions of industries and markets

Chasing Winners

Mutual funds may rank high over one period, but rarely will in the next. Look for long-term consistent results.

¶723.01

Index funds

These funds are composed of the same stocks as certain market indexes, such as the S&P 500. They are not actively managed, so they tend to charge lower expenses. The cost of research administration, manager salaries, etc. are lower. They usually are more tax efficient. There is no risk that the fund manager will make large sudden changes to the fund portfolio. The fund's return will equal the index "market" return.

Fund Selling

Don't be in a hurry to sell a fund that had down year. Compare its returns to the benchmark of comparable sector funds. If earnings have been consistently below par for several years, then consider selling.

- Sell if the investment strategy of the fund has changed and that changes your portfolio mix.
- Maybe sell if the fund manager changes. Give him one year to prove himself.
- Sell if you can use the tax loss to offset other capital gains.
- Don't make bad investment decisions just for tax purposes.

Value Funds

These funds are composed of stocks that are "cheap" or under valued on the basis of the earnings power of the company.

.03 Pricing and Commissions

Sales Commissions (maximum 8.50%) are included in the public offering price.

- Sales charge is a percentage of POP (Public Offering Price).
- Forward pricing on next computed NAV (Net Asset Value) at day's end.
- Newspaper mutual fund quotes example:

Net Asset Value or Bid Price

$11.00

$11.75 – $11.00 = .75

Public Offering Price or Asked Price

$11.75

Sales charge is .75 / 11.75 = .0638 or 6.38%

Net asset value that fund will pay to buy back the stock is $11.00. It costs $11.75 for an investor to buy the stock.

Net Asset Value Per Share (NAV)

$$= \frac{\text{(Cash \& Market Value of Securities – Liabilities)}}{\text{Number of shares outstanding}}$$

Sales Charges

Maximum = 8.50%

Public Offering Price (POP)

= Net asset value + sales charge

$$\frac{\text{NAV}}{\text{(100\% – sales charge percentage)}}$$

Where sales charge % = $\dfrac{\text{Sales Charge}}{\text{POP}}$

Example: Given: NAV = $9.15

sales charge percentage = 7%

How many shares can be bought for $10,000?

$$\text{POP} = \frac{\text{NAV}}{(100\% - \text{sales charge percentage})} = \frac{\$9.15}{1.00 - .07} = \$9.84$$

$$\text{Number of shares} - \frac{\$10,000}{\$9.84 \ / \ \text{share}} = 1,016.26 \text{ shares}$$

.04 Ex-Distribution Date of Purchasing Mutual Funds

The following is an example of the benefit of purchasing mutual funds on or soon after the ex-distribution date.

If purchased immediately before ex-distribution date:

On December 12, Taxpayer A pays $5,000 for 500 shares of Amazing Growth Mutual Fund.

All capital gains and dividends are to be reinvested in additional shares.

On December 14, the ex-distribution date, the fund declares a taxable distribution equal to 10 percent of its net asset value.

Taxpayer A receives a taxable distribution of $500.

$5,000 × .10

The net asset value declines to $9.00 as a result of the distribution.

$9 = $10 – ($10 × 10%)

$9 = $10 – $1

With the $500 distribution, Taxpayer A purchases 55.55 additional shares at $9 per share.

$500 \ $9 per share = 55.55 shares

The basis increases to $5,500.

= (500 shares × $10 per share) + (55.55 shares × $9 per share)

Taxpayer A reports $500 of taxable income.

Taxpayer A's basis has increased by $500 to compensate for the $500 taxable distribution.

Taxpayer A's equity in the fund remains the same, $5,000.

$9 × 555.55 shares

If, before another distribution, Taxpayer A redeems his shares when the net asset value is $15 for a total redemption value of $8,333 ($15 × 555.55 shares), he recognizes a $2833 capital gain ($8,333 – $5,500).

If purchased on ex-distribution date:

Assume instead that Taxpayer A acquired 555.55 shares of Growth Mutual Fund on December 14, the ex-distribution date, for $5,000 ($9 per share × 555.55 shares).

There is no taxable income since the purchase occurred on the distribution date.

If Taxpayer A redeems his shares for $8,333 when the net asset value is $15 per share, he would recognize a capital gain of $3,333 ($8,333 – $5,000).

This is $500 more than in the previous example, which compensates for not recognizing $500 from the December 14 distribution.

$500 = $3,333 – $2,833

Taxpayer A has shifted income recognition to a later period for a current tax advantage.

.05 Investing Wisely in Mutual Funds

Mutual Fund Investment Checklist

- Choosing.
  - Look for low fund expenses.
  - Seek funds with consistent returns with itself and with its sector peers.
  - Seek low taxes.
- Don't choose funds by yields alone.
  - High yield might be achieved at the expense of the fund's net asset value.
- Seek professional advice.
- Be aware for shareholder privileges.
  - Telephone exchanges
  - Redemption requirements
  - Exchange privileges
  - Wire redemptions
  - Purchase plans
  - Withdrawal plans
- Choose a fund that has the same objectives as the investor.
  - Long-term objectives for long-term goals
  - Income fund for income needs
  - Tax-free fund if objective is for tax-free income, etc.
- Understand fund's expenses, fees and charges.
  - Don't purchase only by comparing sales charges.
  - Managment fees and general expenses vary.
- Consider a fund that is a member of a larger family of funds.
- Consider record and history of management company.
- Don't choose fund entirely by magazine or newspaper rankings.
  - These rankings may be based only on yield.
  - Seek to analyze by fund's total return.

¶723.05

- Risk
  - Standard deviation indicates how much a fund fluctuates from its own average returns.
  - Beta measures the volatility to a certain index, typically the S&P 500. A beta with 1.0 moves in perfect correlation to the index. A beta of 1.10 means the fund is 10 percent more volatile than the index and will move 10 percent more in either direction than the index. A beta of .80 means the fund will only move 80 percent as much as the index.

Mutual Fund Open End vs. Closed-End Fund Comparison

	Open-End	Closed-End
Capitalization	Unlimited	Fixed number issued
Shares	Full or fractional shares	Full units only
Pricing	Mathematical formula from NAV	Supply and demand or market
Issues	One class of equity (common) No debt	Several classes Equity and debt
Trading	Sold only by fund Redeemed by fund Always primary offering	Primary offering and secondary trading OTC or exchange
Shareholder rights	Dividend (when declared) Voting	Dividends (when declared) Voting Preemptive rights

.07 Performance

The following technique is designed to estimate the total return on an annualized basis over short periods (1 to 2 years) of an individual's mutual fund where uneven investments and redemptions are taking place.

Total Return on Annualized Basis Over Short Periods

$$\left[\frac{\left(\binom{\text{Current value}}{\text{of investment}} + \binom{\text{Dividend \& capital gain}}{\text{distributions paid in cash}}\right) - \frac{\binom{\text{Total investments}}{\text{- Total redemptions}}}{2}}{(\text{Beg. value of investment}) + \frac{\binom{\text{Total investment}}{\text{- Total redemptions}}}{2}}\right]$$

$$\times \left(\frac{12}{\text{no. of mos. in perf. period}}\right) \times 100$$

Note: Total investments do not include reinvested dividends. Dividend and capital gain distributions do not include those reinvested in the fund. The reinvested dividends and capital gain are included in the current value of the investment amount.

Example: Current value of investment = $9,000 (Total shares owned at current share price)

Beginning value of investment = $5,500

Data in performance period:

Number of months in performance period = 18

Dividend + capital gain distributions paid in cash = $150

Total investments = $2,500

Total redemptions = $700

$$\text{Estimated fund total} = \left[\frac{(9,000+150)-\dfrac{(2,500-700)}{2}}{5,500+\dfrac{(2,500-700)}{2}} - 1 \right] \times \frac{(12 \cdot 100)}{18}$$

$$= \left[\frac{(9,150 - 900)}{5,550 + 900} - 1 \right] \times (.667 \times 100)$$

$$= \left[\frac{(8,250)}{6,450} - 1 \right] \times 66.7$$

$$= [(1.289) - 1] \times 66.7$$

$$= .289 \times 66.7$$

$$= 19.28\%$$

.08 Total Return on Annualized Basis Worksheet

1	18	Number of months in performance period
2	$5500	Beginning value of investment
3	9000	Current value of investment
4	150	Dividends and capital-gain distributions received in cash
5	2500	Total investments throughout period
6	700	Total redemptions throughout period
7	6400	Beginning Net Averaged Gain

(Line 5 less line 6) × .5 + Line 2

[(2500 – 700) × .5] + 5500

8	8250	Ending Net Averaged Gain

(Line 3 + line 4) less ((line 5 less line 6) × .5)

(9000 + 150) – ((2500 – 700) × .5)

9	1.2891	Gain Return Ratio

Line 8 / line 7

8250 / 6400

10	28.91%	Overall Gain Return Percentage

(Line 9 less 1) × 100

(1.2891 – 1) × 100

11	.667	Annualization Factor

12 / Line 1

12 / 18

12	19.28	Total Annualized Return

Line 11 × Line 10

.667 × 28.914

.09 Mutual Fund Portfolio Strategy

Build your mutual fund portfolio based on your risk tolerance and goals.

Aggressive	Moderate	Conservative
30% Large growth	40% Large growth	60% Large blend
30% Large value	30% Large value	30% Small blend

¶723.08

Aggressive	Moderate	Conservative
10% Foreign	10% Foreign	10% Foreign
10% Small growth	10% Small growth	
10% Small value	10% Small value	
10% Emerging markets		
100%	100%	100%

.10 Mutual Fund Closings

What happens if a mutual fund closes down?

- Sometimes a fund is merged into a similar fund offered by the same fund family.
- Sometimes a fund hires another fund management company.
- Killing off funds allows fund managers to bury their mistakes. It eliminates the records of their weaker performing funds.

Mutual Fund Bankruptcy

Under the Investment Company Act of 1940, each fund is a subchapter M-Corporation owned by the shareholders and separate from the fund sponsor. The fund hires the fund company to manage the assets of the fund. The fund manager may go bankrupt, but the fund manager's creditors are not able to touch the money in the fund, which is a separate entity.

Small Funds

Often funds close because they are too small. To cover the cost of operation, the expense ratio often exceeds two percent of the assets annually. This cost lowers performance and hurts the funds ability to attract new customers. Generally, these small funds are merged into other funds.

Liquidation of Funds

- The fund closes its doors to new investors.
- The fund sells off its securities to liquidate to cash.
- The shareholder receives a check for its shares of the proceeds.

¶ 724 PROPERTY

.01 Section 1031 Exchanges

Like-Kind Exchanges-IRC 1031

IRC 1031 exchanges of property are not taxable. The gain or loss will not be recognized until disposition of the property received. A 1031 exchange is a powerful tool that can help accomplish a variety of investment goals, especially in structuring real estate transactions.

Benefit of IRC section 1031 exchange:

- The tax bill is put on hold and deferred to a future time.
- The full amount of equity in the property continues to compound.

Delayed Exchanges

- The sale of existing property and the acquisition of new take place at different times.

- This requires the services of a qualified intermediary.
- The exchanger has 45 days after the sale to identify a list of potential replacement properties.
- The exchanger has 180 days after the sale to acquire one of those replacement properties.

Advantages of Exchanging

- Investment property can be transferred from one location to another.
- An exchange may be a way to obtain replacement property in a site ideal for future retirement.
- An investment property that requires time-consuming attention may be exchanged for one requiring less hands-on management.
- An investor may want a property that produces a higher monthly cash flow income instead of the property that has equity increase over time.
- An investor may want a property that has equity increase over time instead of a higher monthly cash flow income.
- Investors who move can exchange for properties closer to home.
- Investment properties can be consolidated or diversified.

Like-Kind Exchanges Basic Rules

The exchange of property for the same kind of property is the most common type of nontaxable exchange. To be a like-kind exchange, the property traded and the property received must be qualifying property, and like property. Additional requirements apply to exchanges in which the property received is not received immediately upon the transfer of the property given up. If the like-kind exchange involves the receipt of money or unlike property or the assumption of liabilities, there may have been a taxable gain.

Multiple-Party Transactions

The like-kind exchange rules also apply to property exchanges that involve three- and four-party transactions. Any part of these multiple-party transactions can qualify as a like-kind exchange if it meets all of the requirements.

Receipt of Title from Third Party

If one receives property in a like-kind exchange and the other party who transfers the property does not transfer the title, but a third party does, the receiving party may still treat this transaction as a like-kind exchange if it meets all the requirements.

Basis of Property Received in a Like-Kind Exchange

The basis of that property is the same as the basis of the property transferred.

> *Example:* Investor A exchanged real estate held for investment with an adjusted basis of $25,000 for other real estate held for investment. The FMV of both properties is $50,000. The basis of investor A's new property is the same as the basis of the old ($25,000).

¶724.01

Money Paid

If, in addition to giving up like property, money is paid in a like-kind exchange, the investor still has no taxable gain or deductible loss. The basis of the property received is the basis of the property given up, increased by the money paid.

> *Example:* Investor A trades an old cab for a new one. The new cab costs $10,800. He is allowed $2,000 for the old cab and pays $8,800 cash. He has no taxable gain or deductible loss on the transaction regardless of the adjusted basis of his old cab. If investor A sold the old cab to a third party for $2,000 and bought a new one, he would have a recognized gain or loss on the sale of his old cab equal to the difference between the amount realized and the adjusted basis of the old cab.

Sale and Purchase

If the investor sells property and buys similar property in two mutually dependent transactions, the investor may have to treat the sale and purchase as a single nontaxable exchange.

> *Example:* Investor A used his car for business for 2 years. Its adjusted basis is $3,500 and its trade-in value is $4,500. A new car that costs $10,500 is desired. Ordinarily, the investor would trade his old car for the new one and pay the dealer $6,000. The basis for depreciation of the new car would then be $9,500 ($6,000 plus $3,500 adjusted basis of the old car). Because the investor wants the new car to have a larger basis for depreciation, he arranges to sell the old car to the dealer for $4,500. He then buys the new one for $10,500 from the same dealer. However, he is treated as having exchanged his old car for the new one because the sale and purchase are reciprocal and mutually dependent. The basis for depreciation for the new car is $9,500, the same as if he traded the old car.

Exchange Expenses

Exchange expenses are generally the closing costs that are paid. They include such items as brokerage commissions, attorney fees, and deed preparation fees. Subtract these expenses from the consideration received to figure the amount realized on the exchange. Also add them to the basis of the like-kind property received. If the investor receives cash or unlike property in addition to the like-kind property and realizes a gain on the exchange, subtract the expenses from the cash or fair market value of the unlike property. Then use the net amount to figure the recognized gain.

Qualifying Property

In a like-kind exchange, both the property given up and the property received must be held by for investment or for productive use in a trade or business. Machinery, buildings, land, trucks, and rental houses are examples of property that may qualify.

The rules for like-kind exchanges do not apply to exchanges of the following property.

- Property you use for personal purposes, such as your home and your family car.
- Stock in trade or other property held primarily for sale, such as inventories, raw materials, and real estate held by dealers.
- Stocks, bonds, notes, or other securities or evidences of indebtedness, such as accounts receivable.
- Partnership interests.

¶724.01

- Certificates of trust or beneficial interest.

- Choses in action.

- An exchange of the assets of a business for the assets of a similar business cannot be treated as an exchange of one property for another property.

Like Property

There must be an exchange of like property. The exchange of real estate for real estate and the exchange of personal property for similar personal property are exchanges of like property. For example, the trade of land improved with an apartment house for land improved with a store building, or a panel truck for a pickup truck, is a like-kind exchange. An exchange of personal property for real property does not qualify as a like-kind exchange. For example, an exchange of a piece of machinery for a store building does not qualify. Nor does the exchange of livestock of different sexes qualify. An exchange of city property for farm property, or improved property for unimproved property is a like-kind exchange. The exchange of real estate for a real estate lease that runs 30 years or longer is a like-kind exchange. However, not all exchanges of interests in real property qualify. The exchange of a life estate expected to last less than 30 years for a remainder interest is not a like-kind exchange. An exchange of a remainder interest in real estate for a remainder interest in other real estate is a like-kind exchange if the nature and character of the two property interests are the same.

Foreign Real Property Exchanges

Real property located in the United States and real property located outside the United States are not considered like-kind property under the like-kind exchange rules. Gain or loss on this exchange is recognized.

Deferred Exchanges

A deferred exchange is one in which the investor transfers property used in business or held for investment and, at a later time, receives like-kind property to be used in business or held for investment. The transaction must be an exchange (that is, property for property) rather than a transfer of property for money that is used to buy replacement property. If, before the investor receives the replacement property, he actually or constructively receives money or unlike property in full payment for the property transferred, the transaction will be treated as a sale rather than a deferred exchange. The investor constructively receives money or unlike property when the money or property is credited to his account or made available to him. He also constructively receives money or unlike property when any limits or restrictions on it expire or are waived.

Identification Requirement

The investor must identify the property to be received within 45 days after the date of transfer of the property given up in the exchange. Any property received during that time is considered to have been identified. If the investor transferred more than one property (as part of the same transaction) and the properties are transferred on different dates, the identification period and the receipt period begin on the date of the earliest transfer.

¶724.01

Identifying Replacement Property

The investor must identify the replacement property in a signed written document and deliver it to the other person involved in the exchange. He must clearly describe the replacement property in the written document. For example, he could use the legal description or street address for real property and the make, model, and year for a car. In the same manner, the investor can cancel an identification of replacement property at any time before the end of the identification period.

Identifying Alternative and Multiple Properties

The maximum number of replacement properties that can be identified is the larger of the following.

- Three.
- Any number of properties whose total fair market value (FMV) at the end of the identification period is not more than double the total FMV, on the date of transfer, of all properties given up.

If, as of the end of the identification period, the investor has identified more properties than permitted, the only property that will be considered identified is:

- Any replacement property received before the end of the identification period, and
- Any replacement property identified before the end of the identification period and received before the end of the receipt period, but only if the FMV of the property is at least 95 percent of the total FMV of all identified replacement properties. FMV is determined on the earlier of the date the investor received the property or the last day of the receipt period.

Replacement Property to Be Produced or Constructed

Gain or loss from a deferred exchange can qualify for nonrecognition even if the replacement property is not in existence or is being produced at the time the investor identifies it as replacement property. If the investor needs to know the FMV of the replacement property to identify it, he should estimate its FMV as of the date he expects to receive it. To determine whether the replacement property received qualifies as like-kind by being substantially the same as the property identified, do not take into account any variations due to usual production changes. Substantial changes in the property to be produced, however, will disqualify it as like-kind property. If the identified replacement property is personal property to be produced, it must be completed by the date the property is received it to qualify as like-kind property.

If the investor's identified replacement property is real property to be constructed and it is not completed by the date he receives the property, it may still qualify as like-kind property. It will qualify as like-kind property only if, had it been completed on time, the property received would have been considered to be substantially the same as the property identified. It is considered to be substantially the same only to the extent the property received is considered real property under local law. However, any additional production on the replacement property after the investor receives it does not qualify as like-kind property.

Receipt Requirement

The property must be received by the earlier of the following dates.

- The 180th day after the date on which you transfer the property given up in the exchange.
- The due date, including extensions, for your tax return for the tax year in which the transfer of the property given up occurs.

Like-Kind Exchanges Using Qualified Intermediaries

If an investor transfers property through a qualified intermediary, the transfer of the property given up and receipt of like-kind replacement property is treated as an exchange. This rule applies even if the investor receives money or other property directly from a party to the transaction other than the qualified intermediary.

A qualified intermediary is a person who enters into a written exchange agreement with the investor to acquire and transfer the property given up and to acquire the replacement property and transfer it to the investor. This agreement must expressly limit the investor's rights to receive, pledge, borrow, or otherwise obtain the benefits of money or other property held by the qualified intermediary.

A qualified intermediary cannot be either of the following.

- The investor's agent at the time of the transaction. This includes a person who has been an employee, attorney, accountant, investment banker or broker, or real estate agent or broker within the 2-year period before the transfer of property given up.
- A person who is related to the investor or his agent.

An intermediary is treated as acquiring and transferring property if all the following requirements are met.

- The intermediary acquires and transfers legal title to the property.
- The intermediary enters into an agreement with a person other than the investor for the transfer to that person of the property given up and that property is transferred to that person.
- The intermediary enters into an agreement with the owner of the replacement property for the transfer of that property and the replacement property is transferred to the investor.

An intermediary is treated as entering into an agreement if the rights of a party to the agreement are assigned to the intermediary and all parties to that agreement are notified in writing of the assignment by the date of the relevant transfer of property.

Reverse Exchange of Property Technique

The investor may find the desired replacement property before the relinquished property is even on the market. Using the reverse exchange method, a third party, unrelated to the exchanger, purchases and holds the replacement property. When the investor sells his relinquished property, he purchases the "held" property from the unrelated third party as his replacement property, which completes the exchange.

Reverse Exchange Summary

- The replacement property must be purchased before the relinquished property can be sold.
- A third party entity purchases the replacement property and holds it until the exchanger sells the relinquished property.

¶724.01

- The exchanger net leases or manages the replacement property.
- When the relinquished property is sold, a qualified intermediary holds the net proceeds.
- The exchanger purchases the replacement property from the third party.

Construction Exchange

An investor might consider purchasing a lot and building the replacement property instead of buying exchanger property outright. The land cost must equal or exceed the relinquished property price, or only part of the taxes may be deferred. But the unimproved lot typically is much less than the value of the relinquished property. By using a construction exchange, a third party purchases the lot on which the improvements will be built and holds title to the property during the construction period. Once the cost of the lot and improvements equals or exceeds the value of the relinquished property, the third party transfers the new property to the investor. During the acquisition and construction period, cash draws requested from a third-party lender never must be controlled by the exchanger; they must flow through the qualified intermediary directly to the contractor. This concludes the tax-free exchange.

Construction Exchange Summary

- The exchanger wants to build the replacement property.
- When the relinquished property is sold, a qualified intermediary holds the proceeds.
- The qualified intermediary purchases the replacement property and holds it during the construction period.
- The exchanger supervises the construction using a written agreement.
- All funds for acquisition and construction are handled by the qualified intermediary and are never controlled by the exchanger.
- When the construction is complete, the qualified intermediary transfers the replacement property to the exchanger.

Reverse Construction Exchange

With a reverse construction exchange the lot is purchased and improved before selling the relinquished property, or when construction is expected to take more than 180 days.

Reverse Construction Exchange Summary

- The exchanger wants to build the replacement property and the lot must be purchased before the relinquished property can be sold.
- The exchanger follows various steps from the reverse and construction methods.

Finding a Qualified Intermediary

Contact the Federation of Exchange Accommodators (FEA) at 916-388-1031or website: *www.1031.org.*

Partially Nontaxable Exchanges

If, in addition to like property, the investor receives money or unlike property in an exchange in which he realizes a gain, he has a partially nontaxable exchange. He is taxed on the gain realized, but only to the extent of the money and the fair market value of the unlike property received. A loss is never deductible in a nontaxable exchange in which the investor receives unlike property or cash.

To figure the amount of taxable gain, first determine the fair market value of any unlike property received and add it to the amount of any money received. The total is the maximum amount of gain that can be taxed. Next, determine the amount of gain on the whole exchange. The recognized (taxable) gain is the lesser of these two amounts.

> *Example:* The investor exchanges real estate held for investment with an adjusted basis of $8,000 for other real estate that he wants to hold for investment. The fair market value of the real estate the investor received is $10,000. He also receives $1,000 in cash. The investor paid $500 in exchange expenses. Although the total gain realized on the transaction is $2,500, only $500 ($1,000 cash received minus the $500 exchange expenses) is recognized.

Assumption of Liabilities

If the other party to a nontaxable exchange assumes any liabilities, the investor will be treated as if he received cash in the amount of the liability.

> *Example:* The facts are the same as in the previous example, except the property given up is subject to a $3,000 mortgage for which the investor was personally liable. The other party in the trade has agreed to pay off the mortgage. Compute the gain realized as follows.

FMV of like property received	$ 10,000
Cash	1,000
Mortgage treated as assumed by other party	3,000
Total received	$ 14,000
Minus: Exchange expenses	(500)
Amount realized	$ 13,500
Minus: Adjusted basis of property you transferred	(8,000)
Realized gain	$ 5,500

The realized gain is taxed only up to $3,500, the sum of the cash received ($1,000 - $500 exchange expenses) and the mortgage ($3,000).

Unlike Property Given Up

If, in addition to like property, the investor gives up unlike property, he must recognize gain or loss on the unlike property given up. The gain or loss is equal to the difference between the fair market value of the unlike property and its adjusted basis.

> *Example:* The investor exchanges stock and real estate that he held for investment for real estate that he also intended to hold for investment. The stock transferred has a fair market value of $1,000 and an adjusted basis of $4,000. The real estate exchanged has a fair market value of $19,000 and an adjusted basis of $15,000. The real estate the investor received has a fair market value of $20,000. The investor does not have a taxable gain on the exchange of the real estate because it qualifies as a nontaxable exchange. However, the investor must recognize a $3,000 loss on the stock because it is unlike property.

¶724.01

Basis of Property Received

The total basis for all properties (other than money) received in a partially nontaxable exchange is the total adjusted basis of the properties given up, with the following adjustments.

Add—

- Any additional costs you incur, and
- Any gain you recognize on the exchange.

Subtract—

- Any money you receive, and
- Any loss you recognize on the exchange.

Allocate this basis first to the unlike property, other than money, up to its fair market value on the date of the exchange. The rest is the basis of the like property.

Multiple Property Exchanges

Under the like-kind exchange rules, the investor must generally make a property-by-property comparison to determine the recognized gain and the basis of the property received in the exchange. However, for exchanges of multiple properties, the investor does not make a property-by-property comparison if he does either of the following.

- Transfer and receive properties in two or more exchange groups.
- Transfer or receive more than one property within a single exchange group.

Compute the recognized gain and the basis of the property received by comparing the properties within each exchange group.

Exchange Groups

Each exchange group consists of properties transferred and received in the exchange that are of like kind or like classes. If property could be included in more than one exchange group, the investor can include it in any one of those groups. The following may not be included in an exchange group.

- Money.
- Stock in trade or other property held primarily for sale.
- Stocks, bonds, notes, or other securities or evidences of debt or interest.
- Interests in a partnership.
- Certificates of trust or beneficial interests.
- Choses in action.

Treatment of Liabilities

Offset all liabilities assumed as part of the exchange against all liabilities of which the investor is relieved. Offset these liabilities whether they are recourse or nonrecourse and regardless of whether they are secured by or otherwise relate to specific property transferred or received as part of the exchange.

If the investor assumes more liabilities than he is relieved of, allocate the difference among the exchange groups in proportion to the total fair market value of the properties you received in the exchange groups. The difference allocated to each exchange group may not be more than the total fair market value of the properties you received in the exchange group.

The amount allocated to an exchange group reduces the total fair market value of the properties received in that exchange group. This reduction is made in determining whether the exchange group has a surplus or a deficiency. This reduction is also made in determining whether a residual group is created.

If the investor is relieved of more liabilities than assumed, treat the difference as cash, demand deposits and like accounts, and similar items when making allocations to the residual group.

The treatment of liabilities and any differences between amounts the investor assumes and amounts he is relieved of will be the same even if the like-kind exchange treatment applies to only a portion of a larger transaction. If so, determine the difference in liabilities based on all liabilities assumed or are relieved of as part of the larger transaction.

> **Example:** The fair market value of and liabilities secured by each property are as follows.

	Fair Market Value	Liability
Investor Transfers:		
Computer A	$1,500	$ -0-
Automobile A	2,500	500
Truck A	2,000	-0-
Investor Receives:		
Computer R	$1,600	$ -0-
Automobile R	3,100	750
Truck R	1,400	250
Cash	400	

All liabilities assumed by the investor ($1,000) are offset by all liabilities of which he is relieved ($500), resulting in a difference of $500. The difference is allocated among the investor's exchange groups in proportion to the fair market value of the properties received in the exchange groups as follows.

- $131 ($500 × $1,600 ÷ $6,100) is allocated to the first exchange group (computers A and R). The fair market value of computer R is reduced to $1,469 ($1,600 – $131).

- $254 ($500 × $3,100 ÷ $6,100) is allocated to the second exchange group (automobiles A and R). The fair market value of automobile R is reduced to $2,846 ($3,100 – $254).

- $115 ($500 × $1,400 ÷ $6,100) is allocated to the third exchange group (trucks A and R). The fair market value of truck R is reduced to $1,285 ($1,400 – $115).

In each exchange group, the investor uses the reduced fair market value of the properties received to figure the exchange group's surplus or deficiency and to determine whether a residual group has been created.

¶724.01

Like-Kind Exchanges Between Related Persons

Special rules apply to like-kind exchanges made between related persons. These rules affect both direct and indirect exchanges. Under these rules, if either person disposes of the property within two years after the exchange, the exchange is disqualified from nonrecognition treatment. The gain or loss on the original exchange must be recognized as of the date of that later disposition.

Related Persons Defined

Related persons include, for example, the investor and a member of his family (spouse, brother, sister, parent, child, etc.), the investor and a corporation in which he has more than 50 percent ownership, the investor and a partnership in which he directly or indirectly owns more than a 50 percent interest of the capital or profits, and two partnerships in which the investor directly or indirectly owns more than 50 percent of the capital interests or profits.

> ***Example:*** The investor used a panel truck in his house painting business. His sister used a station wagon in her landscaping business. In December 20X2, the investor exchanged his truck, plus $200, for his sister's station wagon. At that time, the fair market value (FMV) of the investor's truck was $7,000 and its adjusted basis was $6,000. The FMV of his sister's station wagon was $7,200 and its adjusted basis was $1,000. The investor realized a gain of $1,000 (the $7,200 FMV of the station wagon minus the $200 paid minus the $6,000 adjusted basis of the truck). The sister realized a gain of $6,200 (the $7,000 FMV of the investor's truck plus the $200 paid minus the $1,000 adjusted basis of the station wagon).
>
> However, because this was a like-kind exchange, the investor recognized no gain. His basis in the station wagon was $6,200 (the $6,000 adjusted basis of the truck plus the $200 paid). The investor's sister recognized gain only to the extent of the money she received, $200. Her basis in the truck was $1,000 (the $1,000 adjusted basis of the station wagon minus the $200 received, plus the $200 gain recognized).
>
> In year 20X3, the investor sold the station wagon to a third party for $7,000. Because he sold it within two years after the exchange, the exchange is disqualified from nonrecognition treatment. On his tax return, he must report $1,000 gain on the exchange. He must also report a loss on the sale of $200 (the adjusted basis of the station wagon, $7,200 (its $6,200 basis plus the $1,000 gain recognized) minus the $7,000 amount realized from the sale).
>
> In addition, the investor's sister must report on her tax return the $6,000 balance of her gain on the 20X2 exchange. Her adjusted basis in the truck is increased to $7,000 (its $1,000 basis plus the $6,000 gain recognized).

Two-Year Holding Period

The two-year holding period begins on the date of the last transfer of property that was part of the like-kind exchange. If the holder's risk of loss on the property is substantially diminished during any period, however, that period is not counted toward the two-year holding period. The holder's risk of loss on the property is substantially diminished by any of the following events.

- The holding of a put on the property.
- The holding by another person of a right to acquire the property.
- A short sale or other transaction.

A put is an option that entitles the holder to sell property at a specified price at any time before a specified future date.

A short sale involves property one generally does not own. One borrows the property to deliver to a buyer and, at a later date, buys substantially identical property and delivers it to the lender.

Exceptions to the Rules for Related Persons

The following kinds of property dispositions are excluded from these rules.

- Dispositions due to the death of either related person.
- Involuntary conversions.
- Dispositions if it is established to the satisfaction of the IRS that neither the exchange nor the disposition had as a main purpose the avoidance of federal income tax.

.02 Rental Property

A rental property is a "tax-favored" investment. It has the potential to provide "tax sheltering" of income as well as to take advantage of the tax rate spread between capital gains rates and ordinary income tax rates. An active owner will report the rental income received and deduct all the ordinary and necessary expenses. Generally the owner is allowed to write-off up to $25,000 in rental property losses per year against other forms of income if it is an actively managed property. A rental property can provide tax-rate savings if it is sold for a profit by taking advantage of the long term capital gain treatment.

Category 1: Cash In/Out

This category reports the total after-tax change in cash position as a result of buying a rental property. The cash out includes principal payments. Points are taken as a cash expense in the first year, but the tax benefit from the points is amortized over the life of the loan. The formula is:

Rental Income + tax benefit – total mortgage payments – rental expenses

Category 2: Investing Downpayment

This is an opportunity-cost comparison. This category reports the total after-tax return on investing the downpayment, rather than in the rental property. The is calculated as a straight compounding of the initial deposit at the after-tax investment rate.

Category 3: Investment Analysis

This category reports the total after-tax benefit/cost of investing in a rental property. The principal portion of mortgage payments is not included since the principal will be returned at the time of sale. The formula is:

Rental Income + tax benefit + appreciation – interest expense – rental expenses

Category 4: Difference Between Category 2 & Category 3

Indicates the financial returns associated with the risks of being a landlord.

Assumptions:

Purchase Price = $125,000 Down Payment = $10,000

¶724.02

Term of Loan = 240 months, Interest Rate = 8%,

Points Paid on Loan = 1%

Rate of Return on other investments = 12%

Property Appreciation Rate = 5%, Inflation Rate = 3%

Tax Rate = Federal = 28%

Per Month Assumptions:

Rental Income per Month	$900
Monthly Commissions	$50
Utilities	$50
Other Expenses	$50
Cleaning & Maintenance	$50
Insurance	$50
Real Estate Taxes	$50
Depreciation Basis	$100,000

Cumulative After Tax Profit From Rental Property

	Cash Flow Analysis	Return on Investing Downpayment	Rental Property Value	Landlord's Return Value
Year 1	($3,923)	$899	$4,758	$3,858
Year 2	($6,597)	$1,879	$11,278	$9,399
Year 3	($9,172)	$2,947	$18,445	$15,498
Year 4	($11,649)	$4,111	$26,291	$22,180
Year 5	($14,027)	$5,380	$34,854	$29,474
Year 6	($16,308)	$6,762	$44,171	$37,409
Year 7	($18,493)	$8,269	$54,284	$46,014
Year 8	($20,583)	$9,912	$65,235	$55,324
Year 9	($22,581)	$11,702	$77,072	$65,370
Year 10	($24,488)	$13,653	$89,842	$76,189
Year 11	($26,309)	$15,780	$103,597	$87,818
Year 12	($28,045)	$18,097	$118,393	$100,296
Year 13	($29,703)	$20,623	$134,288	$113,665
Year 14	($31,285)	$23,376	$151,344	$127,968
Year 15	($32,799)	$26,377	$169,627	$143,250
Year 16	($34,261)	$29,648	$189,237	$159,590
Year 17	($35,673)	$33,212	$210,232	$177,020
Year 18	($37,038)	$37,097	$232,682	$195,585
Year 19	($38,367)	$41,331	$256,673	$215,342
Year 20	($39,671)	$45,946	$282,295	$236,348

¶ 725 SECURITIES

.01 Overview

Investing in Stocks

Stock—Owning a share of stock is a share of ownership in a company. Each share owned by the shareholder represents a claim on the assets and earnings of the corporation.

Stock Prices

- A stock's value depends generally on its earnings.
  - Over the short-term, the market price is based on demographics, rumors, tax laws, savings patterns, fear, news, enthusiasm, the day of the week, etc.
  - Over the long-term, the company's *earnings* are the primary factor that determines the stock price.
- Investment in stocks can provide a return above the pace of inflation.
- An individual stock is not the market. It may, and often does, move opposite of the market indexes.
- A stock's past record does not predict its future price.
- Stock prices are usually based on projections of future earnings.
- Stock prices are relative. A $100 share price may be cheap, and a $5 share price may be expensive.
- For steady long-term returns on a stock investment, look to stocks of sound companies with steady long-term profits.

Stock Investment Goal Planning

- Narrow your objectives.
- Prioritize goals by importance to you. What are your top five financial goals?
- Resolve conflicting goals.
- Time is your most important ally on preparing a long-term goal. The longer you wait, the harder it is to reach the goal.
- Keep your daily spending in light of your long-term goal.
- Be willing to change and re-examine your priorities. Review every two years.
- Develop a disciplined savings and investment approach.
- Resolve conflicts regarding current spending vs. current investing. Keep your goals realistic.

Stock Performance

- Over the long-term, stocks have historically outperformed all other investments. Depending on the time frame chosen (25 year period, etc.), stocks have generally returned 10-12 percent annually.
- Over the short-term, stocks can be hazardous. It's a roller coaster ride.
- The longer the time frame, the more important are earnings trends.

Equity participation is regarded as one of the best inflation fighters available.

Growth Stocks—stocks that have good long-term prospects.

- A solid growth strategy is to buy quality growth stocks when they are temporarily depressed.
- Stock prices follow earnings in the long run.
- Seek companies that have "above-average" growth rates.
- Identify growth stocks
  - Does the company have a unique service or product?

— Does the company have recurring revenues?

— Sustainable earnings growth comes from steadily rising revenues.

— Is the company early in its growth curve? It will eventually start to level off. If everyone seems to know of the company, is familiar with its successes, and assumes it will grow forever, it probably won't.

— Is the company at the forefront of its industry?

— A company with a strong sustainable growth rate will have a high return on equity.

— A Return on Equity (ROE) of 12-15 percent will provide for sustainable growth for the company.

— Solid growth companies have little or reasonable debt.

Advantages of growth stock ownership:

- Offers opportunity for captial gain.
- Offers opportunity for meeting retirement needs because the hoped-for appreciation may be realized at retirement when it's needed and because taxes will be less because of reduced income.

Disadvantages of growth stock ownership:

- Poor rate of income return in terms of dividends.
- A long period of time may be needed to realize any appreciable gain.

Blue Chips Stocks—tried and true companies with long histories of earnings.

Price/Earnings (P/E) Ratio—represents the relationship of a stock's market price per share to its earnings per share.

$$\text{Price to Earnings} = \frac{\text{Stock Market Price}}{\text{Net Profit After Taxes per Share}}$$

It is a company's earnings that drive the market prices. As earnings go, so do company stock prices go. Investors buy stocks for their earning power; they are buying shares of a company's future profit stream. Although at times the relationship seems out of whack, in the long run it's corporate profits that drive share prices.

When a growth and price variance diverges, it's because the money investors will shell out for a company's earning power varies tremendously. The relationship is the P/E ratio. The average P/E ratio for the last 50 years has been about 14, i.e., the investor will pay $14 for $1 of a company's annual earnings.

Investors spend more for firms that grow earnings quickly. When the market is running high P/E ratios, say at 20 to 30 or more, the market is overvalued and prices will one day fall and come back more in line with the company's earnings.

- The P/E indicates how much investors are willing to pay for a dollar of earnings.
- A "trailing" P/E calculates its value based on past earnings, i.e., the P/E is calculated by dividing the company's current stock price by the past year's earnings.
- A "forward" P/E reflects predictions of future earnings potential.

- For investment decisions, one should look to a company's stock P/E on a relative basis. How does its P/E compare to prior levels, current levels, and projected levels. How does it compare to the overall market itself?
- The P/E ratio for the Standard & Poor's 500 composite index from 1950 to 2000 was 15.7. So use 15-16 as the benchmark P/E ratio. Is a P/E of 30 for a stock overpriced? Is P/E of 10 a good value?

Yield—the yield on a stock is the relationship of the dividend to the market price.

- Most yields are quoted at a current market price.

Investment Principles and Analysis

- Invest only surplus.
- Diversify.
- Practice continuous planning—know when changed circumstances warrant a new investment approach.
- Check with reputable sources before making investments.
- Consider liquidity.
- Consider the benefits, current cash flow needs, appreciation and safety.

Capitalization

Total Capitalization

= Long term debt + preferred stock + common stock + paid in capital + retained earnings

Security Features

- Equity
  - Preferred stock
  - Non-cumulative
  - Cumulative
  - Callable
  - Convertible
  - Participating
- Types
  - Bond
  - Registered by name
  - Bearer
  - Not registered where interest is paid by coupons
- Stock
  - Growth
  - Income
  - Defensive
- Common Stock
  - Generally only one class
  - Has voting rights for board of directors and major changes

¶725.01

- — Shares in profits through dividends
- — Last claim on earnings and assets
- Preferred Stock
  - — Pays ahead of common in dividends and assets
  - — Pays behind bonds and general creditors
  - — Dividends are a stated amount or a percentage of par

Dates of Stock

- Declaration Date—date directors declare a dividend.
- Record date—on this date stockholders of record will receive a dividend.
- Trade date—date of purchase or sale of security.
- Settlement date—date of delivery or payment.
- Ex-dividend date—date on or after which seller will receive a declared dividend.

Selling Dividends

- Encouraging purchase of shares just prior to upcoming ex-date for declared but not paid dividends.
- Violates rules of fair practice.
- Purchaser receiving dividends must pay income tax.
- The price paid includes the dividend.
- The market price will drop by the amount of the dividend on ex-dividend date.
- The purchaser is essentially paying tax on returned capital.

Stock Rights

- Are securities.
- Trade separate from stock.
- Short periods of time to subscribe.
- On ex-date market price drops by value of right.

Value of Right

Stock trading with right	Stock trading ex-right
$$\frac{M - S}{N + 1}$$	$$\frac{M - S}{N}$$

M = Market price per share
S = Subscrption price of new share
N = Number of rights to get one new share

Stock Definitions

Par value—an arbitrary value printed on the face of a stock certificate assigned at the time of issuance.

Premium—stocks sold above par value.

Paid-in Capital—amount of money paid for stock in excess of par value.

Market value—value of stock determined by supply and demand.

¶725.01

Book Value—measure of how much a common shareholder could expect to receive for each share if the corporation were to liquidate.

Book Value =

$$\frac{\text{Stockholder's equity} - (\text{par value of preferred} + \text{intangible assets})}{\text{Number of shares of common outstanding}}$$

or

Book Value =

$$\frac{\text{Total assets} - (\text{liabilities} + \text{intangible assets} + \text{par value of preferred stock})}{\text{Number of shares of common outstanding}}$$

Stock point—1 point represents $1 per share.

Portions of stock are quoted in fractions of $\dfrac{1}{16}$

Example:

Stock quoted for $26 \dfrac{3}{8} = \$ 26.375$ per share

.02 Stock Market Declines

It's time in the market that counts, not timing the market.

Considerations of Market Declines

- Stock market corrections are an inevitable part of investing.
- An intelligent investor understands how to live with market declines.
- Market declines are a natural part of the investment process.
- We can never know when a decline will occur.
- How one reacts to stock market declines will play a crucial role in long-term investment success.
- When the asset portfolio has significantly dropped, that is the time to reassess one's risk tolerance. Then determine how assets should be allocated.
- Long-term planning is always paramount to short-term performance.
- Are investor expectations realistic over time?
- Educated investors will endure Bear markets.
- Remember the "ride" on the stock market is a "roller-coaster" ride.
- Don't become emotional and sell stocks at market bottoms. One will then miss the bulk of the rebound.
- When the market is at a downturn is the time to buy.
- The stock market is like a roller coaster ride. The only time people get hurt is when they get off in the middle of the ride.
- Tough market cycles occur on average every three to five years. Just plan on it happening. It will.

- Remain focused on long-term goals.
- Do not let the short-term market conditions cause you to abandon the commitment you made to achieve long-term success.
- Regarding the market decline lows. If you are looking for the right time to invest, consider this as the right time to invest.

How Investors Should Cope with Market Declines

Invest for income.

- Investments that tend to fare well in market declines include stocks that pay high dividends, as well as bonds.

Talk with your financial adviser.

- Examine your investment goals, time horizon, risk tolerance and financial circumstances.
- Market declines may prompt you to re-examine your strategy. Keep a long-term perspective.
- Don't quit.
- History shows that the market will recover. So the investor should have patience.

Maintain a diversified investment portfolio.

- Spread your risks by investing in a carefully selected mix of mutual funds that invest in stocks and bonds.

Invest regularly.

- Invest regularly in both bear and bull markets.
- Investing regularly, using dollar cost averaging, can take the emotion out of investing.
- By investing regularly, you don't have to guess which way the market is going.
- It takes the timing problem out of the investment decision. You won't be waiting for the perfect time to buy.
- When there is a down market, you can view it as an opportunity to buy good companies at lower prices through your mutual funds.

Lessons from Market Declines

- No one can predict consistently when market declines will happen.
- Generally, market declines have been brief and, for the long-term investor, relatively painless.
- A common mistake investors make is to lose patience and sell at or near the bottom of a downturn.
- A long look at history shows that long-term investors have come out ahead.

Forget market timing.

- Successful market timing during a decline is extremely difficult because it requires two near-perfect actions—getting out at the right time and getting back in at the right time.
- Stocks can be very volatile, especially in the short run.

¶725.02

- Average investors can protect themselves against this inherent riskiness by staying in for the long haul.
- History shows that while stocks may bounce around wildly for periods of a year or two, their prices rise over the long-term (periods of five years or more).
- Stocks have provided annual average returns of 11 to 14 percent over the years, surpassing bonds and Treasury bills.
- Being in the market during an abrupt downturn is a risk that comes with investing.
- Endurance in and of the market is key to long term gains.
- Risk—A greater risk on your investments, is not being in the market at all.
- Diversification reduces risk.
- In the investment world of stocks, the smart investor will learn to ignore day-to-day bumps and grinds.
- When the market declines, sit tight through these corrections. Market ups and downs are a normal, healthy part of every bull market.
- Don't try to time the market to avoid fluctuations.
- A company's future earnings and dividends won't be affected by short-term corrections.
- Try to spot trends in the market.

.03 Stock Market Information

U/D	(1) High	(2) 52 Weeks Low	(3) Stock	(4) Dividend	(5) Yield %	(6) P.E. Ratio	(7) Sales 100s	(8) High	(9) Low	(10) Close	(11) Net Change	SV
U	44 1/8	30	AAMR	1.20	2.9	16	10	42 3/8	42	42	–5/8	S

U/D: U = Stock traded at highest (or D = lowest) value over the last 52 weeks.

1. The highest value the stock has sold for in the last 52 weeks.

2. The lowest value the stock has sold for in the last 52 weeks.

3. The abbreviation of the stock company name.

4. The current annual dividend per share the stock is now paying—based on the latest quarterly or semi-annual declaration.

5. The annual yield of % return represented by the annual dividend at the current stock price.

6. The price to earnings ratio per share.

7. Number of shares sold on preceding day in hundreds.

8. The highest trading price in dollars on the preceding day.

9. The lowest trading price in dollars on the preceding day.

10. The closing trading price in dollars on the preceding day.

11. The net change in the day's closing price from the prior day.

S/V: S indicates a stock split, V indicates trading was halted.

.05 Types of Security Orders

Order Type	Order Description
Market	Buy or sell at the best available market price
Limit	Client specifies a minimum selling price or a maximum buying price
Buy Stop	Protects profits—client issues a buy order at price above the current market price
Sell Stop	Protects profits—client issues a sell order at a price below the current market price
Stop Limit	A stop order that becomes a limit order once the stop price has been attained

¶725.03

.06 Stock—Returns

	Stock Total Return	Treasury Bills Total Return	Bonds (10-year) Total Return
1950 to 1959	19.25	2.02	0.69
1960 to 1969	7.78	4.06	2.35
1970 to 1979	5.88	6.48	5.94
1980 to 1989	17.55	9.13	13.01
1990 to 1999	18.21	4.95	8.02
2000 to 2004	-2.30	2.66	8.41
2001	-11.89	3.32	5.51
2002	-22.10	1.61	15.15
2003	28.68	1.03	0.54
2004	10.88	1.43	4.59
2005	4.91	3.30	3.16

Source: Statistical Abstract of the United States: 2007

.07 Stock Market—Indexes

Purpose of Indexes

- Used to measure market performance.

- Provides standards of investment performance to compare against actual performance.

- Used to measure historical market returns.

Capitalization Weights Indexes

- Reflect the total common stock investing experience.

- Market value of stock in the index is determined by multiplying the number of common shares outstanding by the current price per share. The total market value of all the stocks is then the total values of the individual stocks in the index. Each stock is, thus, weighted.

- Stock splits or dividends have no effect on the weighted index because the number of shares increases, but the price is reduced by the proportionate amount, keeping the total market value constant.

- A capitalization weighted index uses an arbitrary number like 50 or 100 to represent the initial market value of the stocks at the base date.

- The current market value is then expressed relative to the base period market value.

Standard and Poor's Stock Price Indexes

- Composed of 500 common stocks, divided as:

  — 400 industrial stocks

  — 40 utility stocks

— 40 financial stocks

— 20 transportation stocks

- Composed of large, highly capitalized companies.
- The 500 stocks are now divided into 95 industry groups.

Standard and Poor's 500 Index

Date	Close
12/31/94	470.42
06/30/95	544.75
12/29/95	615.93
06/28/96	670.64
12/31/96	740.74
06/30/97	885.20
12/31/97	970.43
06/30/98	1133.86
12/31/98	1229.40
06/30/99	1372.86
12/31/99	1469.25
08/24/00	1508.31
12/29/00	1320.50
06/29/01	1224.54
12/31/01	1148.08
07/15/02	917.93
01/17/03	901.78
02/18/05	1201.59
06/12/06	1236.40
01/09/07	1412.11

New York Stock Exchange Indexes

- In 1966, NY Stock Exchange began publishing indexes on every common stock listed on the exchange.
- Intitial indexes were set to a 1965 base of 50.
- A composite index is composed of all indexes plus four sub-indexes:

— Finance index

— Transportation index

— Industrial index

— Utility index

American Stock Exchange Indexes

- Indexes on every common stock, warrant, and American depository receipt listed on the exchange.
- Indexes were set to base values of 100 on 8-31-73.
- A composite index is composed of all indexes plus eight sub-indexes:

— Manufactured capital goods

— Manufactured consumer goods

¶725.07

— Housing/construction/local development

— Retailing

— Finance

— High technology

— Natural resources

— Services

Dow Jones Composite Average

- 65 stock composite average, including:

  — Industrial Index of 30 stocks

  — Transportation Index of 20 stocks

  — Utility Index of 15 stocks

- Dow Industrial Average

  — Represents companies that are among largest in the U.S.

  — Sum of its composite stocks divided by 30 comprises average.

  — Average is adjusted for stock splits, stock dividends and changes in list of component stocks.

  — Stock splits are adjusted by reducing the divisor.

Dow Jones Industrial Average

1985	Jan. 4	1184.96
1986	Jan. 22	1502.29
1987	Oct. 19	1738.74
1988	Jan. 20	1879.14
1989	Jan. 3	2144.64
1990	Oct. 11	2365.10
1991	Jan. 9	2470.30
1992	Oct. 9	3136.58
1993	Jan. 20	3241.95
1994	Oct. 10	3821.32
1995	Jan. 20	3869.43
1996	Oct. 14	6010.00
1997	Jan. 20	6843.87
1998	Apr. 1	8868.32
1999	Jan. 4	9184.27
2000	Jan. 31	10940.53
2001	Apr. 30	10734.90
2002	Jan. 31	9920
2002	July 15	8639
2003	Jan. 17	8586.74
2005	Feb. 18	10785.22
2006	June 12	10792.58
2007	Jan. 9	12416.60

Components of Dow Jones Industrial Average

Alcoa	DuPont	Johnson & Johnson
Altria Group	Exxon Mobil	McDonald's
American Express	General Electric	Merck
American Intl. Group	General Motors	Microsoft
AT&T Inc.	Hewlett-Packard	Pfizer
Boeing	Home Depot	Proctor & Gamble
Caterpillar	Honeywell	3M Corp.
Citigroup	IBM	United Technologies
Coca-Cola	Intel	Verizon Communications
Disney (Walt)	J.P. Morgan Chase & Co.	Wal-Mart Stores

Components of Dow Jones Transportation Average

Alexander & Baldwin	Expeditors Intl. of Wash.	Overseas Shipholding Group
AMR Corp.	Federal Express	Ryder System
Burlington Northern SF	GATX Corp.	Southwest Airlines
C.H. Robinson Worldwide	J.B. Hunt	Union Pacific
Continental Airlines	JetBlue Airways	UPS
Con-way	Landstar System	YRC Worldwide
CSX Corp.	Norfolk Southern	

Dow Jones Utility Average Components

American Electric Power	Duke Energy	Pacific Gas & Electric
AES Corp.	Edison Int.	Public Service Enterprises
Centerpoint Energy	Exelon	Southern Co.
Consolidated Edison	First Energy Corp.	Texas Utilities
Dominion Resources	NiSource Inc.	Williams Cos.

Here are some of the more popular indexes available.

Symbol	Index Name	Symbol	Index Name
XAX.X	AMEX Composite	IXCO.X	NASDAQ Computer
DFI.X	AMEX Defense	COMP.X	NASDAQ Composite Index
XMI.X	AMEX Major Market Index	OFIN.X	NASDAQ Financial 100
COMP	DOW Jones 65 Composite	NYA.X	NYSE Composite
INDU.X	DOW Jones 30 Industrials	NF.X	NYSE Financial
TRAN.X	DOW Jones 20 Transport	RUT.X	Russell 2000
UTIL.X	DOW Jones 15 Utilities	OEX.X	S&P 100 Index
DJAT	DOW Jones Asian Titans 50	SML.X	S&P 600 Small Cap Index
DJGT	DOW Jones Global Titans 50	SPX.X	S&P 500 Index
WLX	DOW Jones Wilshire 5000	MID.X	S&P Midcap 400 Index
NDX.X	NASDAQ 100 Index	VLFVD	Value Line

.09 Stocks—Convertible

Convertible Securities

Convertible bonds and convertible preferred stock can be converted into shares of common stock.

Conversion price—amount of par value exchangeable for one share of common stock.

¶725.09

Stock Conversion Price

$$= \frac{\text{Principal}}{\text{Equivalent common share}}$$

$$= \frac{\$1,000}{\$40} = \$25$$

Conversion ratio—number of shares of common stock that can be received when a bond is converted.

Equivalent Common Shares

$$= \frac{\text{Principal}}{\text{Conversion price}}$$

$$= \frac{\$1,000}{\$25} = \$40$$

Parity—calculating parity between convertible securities and the underlying common stock.

Conversion ratio

$$= \frac{\text{Par Value convertible}}{\text{Conversion price}}$$

Parity of Common

$$= \frac{\text{Market Value of Bond}}{\text{Conversion price}}$$

Parity of Convertible

$$\text{Market value of common} \times \text{Conversion ratio}$$

In rising market, market value of convertible rises with increase in market.

In declining market, market value of convertible tends to level off when yield becomes competitive and may not decline as far as the stock drops.

> ***Example:*** Bonds sells at $900 and stock trades at $15/share

Conversion price = $25

Conversion ratio = 40 or 40 to 1

Parity of convertible = $15 × 40 = $600, which is below $900 of bond price

.11 Stock Exemptions from the Securities Act of 1933

Securities of certain issuers are automatically granted exemptions:

- The U.S. Government
- Banks
- State and political sub-divisions
- Charitable organizations

Exemptions of certain types of securities:

- Insurance policies and fixed annuity contracts
- Commercial paper
- Banker's acceptances

Regulation A allows up to $5,000,000 in capital to be raised in a twelve-month period (including no more than $1,500,000 in non-issuer resales) without full registration. The issuer must file an "offering statement" with the SEC. Purchases are provided with an "offering circular."

Intra-State Offering (Within One State); Rule 147 Safe Harbor

The SEC does not have jurisdiction over the issue.

- All purchasers must be residents of that state.
- The broker-dealer must be resident and have office in the state.
- The issuer must have its principal office and at least 80% of its assets in that state.
- At least 80% of the proceeds from the securities transaction in question must stay within that state.
- Purchasers may not resell the stock purchased in an intrastate offering to a person outside the state of issue for at least nine months after the underwriting is completed.

Private Placement

There is no public offering of securities.

There is no limit to the amount of capital that can be raised.

Regulation D

- No general advertising can be made for the underwriting.
- Must be sold to no more than 35 nonaccredited investors.
- An unlimited number of sales may be made to "accredited investors."
- An accredited investor must have $1,000,000 in net worth or an annual income of $200,000, which may not be more than 20% of the investor's total net worth.
- The purchaser must intend to hold the stock for investment purposes only.
- The certificate may indicate that it cannot be transferred without registration or exemption.

Rule 144

Rule 144 places requirements for resale on restricted stock purchased in a private placement.

- If the securities are to be sold, the current owner must have owned the securities, fully paid, for two years.
- There is no volume limitation if the securities were owned for at least three years.
- Current financial information must be available to the buyer.

¶725.11

- Offering cannot be advertised.
- A notice is filed with the SEC on Form 144 if the amount to be sold exceeds 500 shares or $10,000.
- If the sale is less than 500 shares and less than $10,000, no filing is necessary.
- Filing is effective for 90 days.
- Resales of securities owned between two and three years are limited to the greater of 1% of the outstanding shares of the company, or the average weekly trading volume for the four weeks preceding the sale.

.13 Stock Options

Option Definitions

Contract giving right to buy or sell stock and requiring the writer to buy or sell if the buyer chooses to excerise the contract.

Holders of option contracts have three choices:

- Exercise the option and buy the stock.
- Let the option expire worthless.
- Trade the option contract before the expiration date.

Call—the right to buy stock for a limited time at a specified price.

Put—the right to sell stock for a limited time at a specified price.

Strike Price—the price at which the underlying stock will be sold if the buyer exercises the rights in the contract.

Option Buyer—the person who pays the premium and becomes the owner of the contract.

Option Writer—the person who recieves the premium and becomes the seller of the contract.

Premium—the cash price paid to the writer by the option buyer.

Premium = Intangible Value + Time Value

Where,

Time Value = arises from its distance of its expiration date. (A buyer is willing to pay more for a contract that has a long time to run, rather than a contract that is about to expire.)

Where,

Intrinsic Value = market value of underlying instrument minus the exercise price of the option.

The intrinsic value of an option changes as the underlying stock price changes.

If stock is trading at $87/share, the owner of a call with an exercise price of $80 is "in the money" or has an intrinsic value of $7. A call is "in the money" whenever the stock price exceeds the strike price. A call is "out-of-the-money" whenever the strike price exceeds the stock price.

Long options—The holder of an option (or owner or buyer) is said to have a long position. This person has paid a premium in exchange for rights in the contract.

Long call—The right to purchase the underlying security at a specific target price at any time through the expiration date.

Long put—The right to sell the underlying security at the strike price until the expiration date.

Short options—The writer or seller of the option receives the premium and is said to have a short position.

Short call—The person agrees to sell the underlying security at the specified target price to the holder of the long call if the option is exercised by the expiration date.

Short put—The person agrees to buy the underlying security at the strike price at any time through the expiration date if a put owner exercises the option.

Stock Option Positions

Buy calls:	Write calls:
Bull view	Bear view
Right to buy stock	Right to sell stock
Gain is unlimited	Gain is limited to premium
Loss is limited to premium	Loss is unlimited
Break-even = strike price + premium	Break-even = strike price + premium
Position is long call	Position is short call

Buy puts:	Write puts:
Bear view	Bull view
Right to buy stock	Right to sell stock
Break-even = strike price – premium	Break-even = strike price – premium
Gain = strike price – premium	Profit is limited to premium
Loss is limited to premium	Loss = strike price – premium

Stock Option Spreads

Spreads are always of same type (both call or both puts), are of the same class of security (like stock), but of a different series (like price or expiration date).

Call spread = long call and short call

Put spread = long put and short put

Straddles

Straddles differ in type (calls and puts) and are of the same class and same series.

Long straddle = long call and long put (buy call and buy put)

Short straddle = short call and short put (sell call and sell put)

Stock Option Tax Consequences of Options

Investment Strategy	Option Expires	Option Exercised	Position Closed at Intrinsic Value
Buy a Put (Right to Sell)	Capital Loss	Proceeds = Strike price + premium	Capital Gain or Loss
Sell a Put (Obligation to Buy)	Capital Gain	Cost basis = Strike price + premium	Capital Gain or Loss
Buy a Call (Right to Buy)	Capital Gain	Cost basis = Strike price + premium	Capital Gain or Loss
Sell a Call (Obligation to Sell)	Capital Gain	Proceeds = Strike price + premium	Capital Gain or Loss

Stock Option Basic Options Strategies

Position	Strategy	Long	Short
Call	**Strategy**	**Bullish**	**Bearish**
	Maximum Gain =	Unlimited	Premium
	Maximum Loss =	Premium	Unlimited
	Breakeven point =	Strike price + premium	Strike price + premium
Call Spread	**Strategy**	**Dr—Bullish**	**Cr—Bearish**
Net DR = Bought spread	Maximum gain =	Difference between strike price minus net premium	Net premium
Net CR = sold spread	Maximum loss =	Net premium	Difference between strike price minus net premium
(Net premium is net debit or net credit)	Break-even point =	Lower strike price + net premium	Lower strike price + net premium
Put	**Strategy**	**Bearish**	**Bullish**
	Maximum gain =	Strike price – premium	Premium
	Maximum loss =	Premium	Strike price – premium
	Breakeven point =	Strike price – premium	Strike price – premium
Put Spread	**Strategy**	**Dr—Bearish**	**Cr—Bullish**
Net DR bought spread	Maximum gain =	Difference between strike price minus net premium	Net premium
Net CR = sold spread	Maximum loss =	Net premium	Difference between strike price minus net premium
	Break-even point =	Higher strike price - net premium	Higher strike price - net premium
Straddle	**Strategy**	Wants volatile market	Wants steady market
	Maximum gain =	Unlimited, on call side	Premiums received
	Maximum loss =	Premiums paid	Unlimited, on call side
	Break-even points	Strike price +/– combined premiums	Strike price +/– combined premiums

.14 Stock Options—Employee Stock Options

An employee stock option plan gives the employee the right to:

- Buy ("exercise") a certain number of shares of the employer's stock at a

- Stated price ("strike" "exercise" or "grant") over a certain period of

- Time (the "exercise" period)

Qualified—Incentive Stock Option (ISO) Plan

ISOs usually qualify for special tax treatment, such as gains being taxed at capital gain rates instead of ordinary income rates. No income tax is due at the exercise.The tax is deferred until the stock is later sold. At the time of the sell, the initial spread at exercise, plus subsequent appreciation, is taxed at long-term capital gain rates—if the stock is sold at least two years after the option is granted and one year after exercised.

Non-Qualified Plans

A Non-Qualified plan can be granted at a discount to the stock's market price.

No tax is incurred when options are granted. However, when the employee purchases or "exercises" the stock, the employee will pay ordinary income tax on the difference between the purchase price and the stock's current market value. The company deducts this difference as compensation expense, with appropriate W/H, FICA, and Medicare deducted from the employee. The stock is often sold at the same time to obtain funds to cover the purchase of the stock and taxes due from the employee. In reality, the employee is borrowing enough money from the broker needed to exercise the purchase, and then simultaneously selling at least enough shares to cover the cash flow costs.

If the stock has steady, consistent growth, hold the stock options until they are about to expire, so that exercise of them will provide for maximum gain through stock appreciation. If the stock is held and later sold at a profit over its adjusted basis (cost plus compensation), capital gains rates will apply.

.15 Stock Trading

Investor taking a long position buys security now and sells after the security price has risen. Investor taking a short position borrows the stock from a dealer and sells at the high price, then when ask price drops, buys at the lower price and pays off the loan. Short positioning represents about 25 percent of trading in the stock market.

Insider Trading

Insider trading is the trading by executives, directors, and managers who run the business. Many investors feel that paying attention to their trading habits of their own companies might provide buy and sell guidance. Many investors pay attention to the people who are running the company, as they know most about where it's heading. Consider smaller companies when you analyze insider trading. Here the executives have a better sense of the underlying value of the company. Insiders often purchase early, before the returns are generated. They might buy as early as six months before the stock starts rising.

Selling. Ask—Is the insider selling for estate tax planning purposes? Diversification? Quick cash he needs? Etc. If the insider is selling because the stock price is falling, that may be a signal they are worried.

Buying—The insider has one main reason for buying—he thinks it's a good investment. Studies have shown that heavy insider trading of the company's stock that had low price/earnings ratios averaged superior returns in the following periods, than stocks with the higher P/E ratios. The more insiders that are buying, the stronger is the growth increase signal of the stock.

Stock options of executives—Be aware if there is a lot of buying activity just because the executive is exercising stock options that were granted at rock bottom prices. This is not an insider trading buying signal.

New Security Issues of Corporations, By Type of Offering and Industry Group: 1990 to1996

(In billions of dollars. Represents gross proceeds of issues maturing in more than one year. Figures are the principal amounts or numbers of units multiplied by the offering price. Excludes secondary offerings, employee stock plans, investment companies other than closed-end, intracorporate transactions, equities sold abroad, and Yankee bonds. Stock data include ownership securities issued by limited partnerships.)

Type of Offering and Industry Group	1990	1993	1994	1995	1996[1]
Total	339.1	769.1	583.2	673.6	665.2
Bonds, total	298.9	646.6	498.0	573.0	548.9
Public, domestic	188.8	487.0	365.2	408.7	465.5
Private placement, domestic	87.0	121.2	76.1	87.5	(NA)
Sold abroad	23.1	38.4	56.8	76.8	83.4
Manufacturing	51.8	88.2	43.4	60.8	49.5
Commercial and miscellaneous	40.7	58.6	40.7	50.7	40.5
Transportation	12.8	10.8	6.9	8.5	5.7
Public utility	17.6	56.3	13.3	13.8	9.5
Communication	6.7	31.9	13.3	23.0	14.5
Real estate and financial	169.3	400.8	380.4	416.2	429.2

Type of Offering and Industry Group	1990	1993	1994	1995	1996[1]
Stocks, total	40.2	122.5	85.2	100.9	116.6
Preferred	4.0	18.9	12.5	11.0	33.2
Common	19.4	82.7	47.8	57.8	83.4
Private placement	16.7	20.9	24.8	32.1	(NA)
Manufacturing	5.6	22.3	17.8	21.8	21.3
Commercial and miscellaneous	10.2	25.8	15.7	27.8	44.5
Transportation	0.4	2.2	2.2	0.8	1.7
Public utility	0.4	7.1	2.2	1.9	3.7
Communication	3.8	3.4	0.5	1.1	4.8
Real estate and financial	19.7	61.0	46.7	47.4	40.5

N/A = Not available

[1] Excludes private placements.

Source: Board of Governors of the Federal Reserve System, Federal Reserve Bulletin, monthly and Annual Statistical Digest.

.16 ETFs (Exchange-Traded Funds)—Index Tracking Stocks

Exchange traded funds are "tracking stocks" that mirror the price of major market indexes. Each ETF share represents a stake in a unit investment trust that holds shares of companies that compose a particular index. The trust is designed to track closely the price and yield of that index. For example, shares in the (QQQ) NASDAQ 100 trust are created in blocks of 50,000 by large investors or institutions and are priced at 1/20 the value of the NASDAQ 100 index. Individual investors buy and sell the QQQ shares in the secondary market, where prices are subject to supply and demand.

ETFs are similar to regular index mutual funds except that they trade like stocks on a stock exchange, rather than directly from the fund company. A commission is paid on each purchase.

Investing in an ETF may be more tax efficient than an index tracking mutual fund, since it is not actively managed.

ETFs:

- ETFs can be bought or sold, just like normal stocks, any time the market is open. Mutual funds do not trade intraday. They are priced and sold at the end of the day.
- ETFs provide for diversification, since they make up the stocks that mirror an index.
- ETFs, compared to mutual funds, can help shield investors from the cost and tax impact of portfolio turnover—costs such as commissions, bid/ask spreads, transaction taxes, etc.
- Investing in ETFs lets you know exactly what you are investing in.
- ETFs offer a broad range of indexes to choose from.
- An ETF is an automatic implementation of asset allocation.

With ETFs the investor could invest by:

- Market capitalization
- Industry sector
- Country
- By value
- By growth, etc.

ETFs reduce the guess work in developing an investment strategy.

- With ETFs, more of your investment is at work versus a managed index fund.
- ETFs can provide faster action than indexed mutual funds.

Some examples of ETFs:

- DSV = Street tracks Dow Jones vs. small cap value
- XLI = SPDR of industrial index
- FFF = Fortune 500 tracking stocks
- FEF = Fortune e-50 index tracking stock
- MDY = SPDR that tracks mid cap

Some Internet sites to analyze index stocks:

- See *www.IShares.com*
- See symbol "FFF" that tracks the Fortune 500 stocks at *www.streetracks.com*
- See QQQ that tracks the NASDAQ 100 index

¶725.16

- See SPDR's (AMEX symbol: SPY) that tracks the S&P 500
- See Diamonds (AMEX symbol: DIA) that tracks the Dow Jones industrial average
- See *www.stockmarkettimer.com*
- See *www.NASDAQ.com*

.17 Initial Public Offerings (IPOs)

An IPO is the first issue of stocks sold by a company to the public.

Assessing the value of an IPO of stock to purchase is very difficult. There is no trading record. There is no market perception.

To purchase IPOs successfully, one must size up the company, its market, and investor's attitudes before and immediately after it goes public.

Typically, successful IPOs dip after several months, when the "hotness" wears off.

Research the company carefully:

- Look for good past earnings record.
- Look for good growth record.
- Look for an experienced management team.
- Does the firm have a market niche?
- Who are the firm's customers?

.18 Stock—Growth vs. Value

Growth Stock Indicators

Successful strategies on picking winning stocks revolve around two concepts—growth stocks and value stocks. Value stocks are selling at what investors believe are discounted prices to what they feel they are currently worth. Value investors must show patience and hold on to the stock with their purchases until the market recognizes the stocks' value. They try to uncover undervalued assets and are not concerned with growth and future potential of a company. They look for a deal now.

Growth investors look for stocks that they feel have strong earnings growth and feel that the company's record will propel the stock upward. They are more optimistic for quick growth and must be aware of higher risk potentials. A successful stock portfolio strategy will contain both growth and value stocks depending on the investor's risk tolerance and investing style. Generally, the two types of stock work in opposite directions. If value stocks are performing successfully, then growth stocks are usually on the decline, and vice versa.

Growth Stock Indicators

Criteria	Current Stock Under Analysis
Return on Equity— Annual average ROE over the past three years (Net Income/Shareholder's Equity) Large-cap target: 15% or better Small-cap target: 10% or better (Be sure that the company has not leveraged its profits by taking on too much debt.)	_____
Price/Earnings Ratio (on estimated next 12 months' earnings) divided by Growth rate (on annual next 5 years) Acceptable Range: 0.80 to 1.25 (The relationship of P/E less than the growth rate would indicate an excellent fast growing company.)	_____
Annual Earnings Growth Rate—past three years Large-cap target: 12% or better Small-cap target: 15% or better (Past record indicates that the earnings are no fluke.)	_____
Projected Annual Earnings Growth Rate—next 3 years Large-cap target: 12% or better Small-cap target: 15% or better (Look at the potential 3-year growth.)	_____
Annual Sales Growth—past three years Large-cap target: 10% or better Small-cap target: 15% or better (Profits must come from sales growth and not just cost cutting procedures, or profits will stop)	_____

Value Stock Indicators

Criteria	Current Stock Under Analysis
Price to Book Value Ratio (Assets-Liabilities) Target: less than 3 (A stock trading for less than its book value allows one to buy the company for less than the value of the things it owns.)	_____
Price/Earnings Ratio Target: less than 20 (A ratio lower than its peers might indicate a bargain.)	_____
Long-Term Debt-to-Equity Ratio Large-cap target: less than 40% Small-cap target: less than 20% (The lower the ratio, the less risk.)	_____
Annual Earnings Growth Rate—recent 3 years Target: 8% or more (Indicates expanding or steady profits.)	_____

¶725.18

Value Stock Indicators
Criteria

	Current Stock Under Analysis
Gross Profit Ratio ((Net Sales – cost of goods sold)/Net Sales) Target: 30% or higher (If there really is no profit at the top, the value cannot continue to exist.)	_____

.19 Stock—Sell vs. Keeping Analysis

Comparing Selling a Winning Stock with Replacement Stock versus Keeping

Is an investor better off holding on to a stock on which there is a large profit or replacing it with another? In other words, will a person have more money by hanging on to or selling the stock after consideration of the tax consequences?

Assumptions:

Original cost of stock = $10,000

Capital gain tax rate on stock = 20%

Income dividends with related tax consequences and commissions are immaterial.

Current stock rate of return = 12%

Projected stock rate of return = 14%

Analysis holding period = 4 years

Retention of Stock

1. Current stock's value.

Number of shares owned	200	
Multiplied by the current share price	$100	
		$20,000

2. Number of years projected to retain stock	4	
3. Projected annualized rate of return.	12%	
4. Investment multiplier from table below for holding period and stock's projected annualized return.		1.57
5. Estimated future value of stock. Line 1 multiplied by line 4.		$31,400
6. Original cost of stock.		$10,000
7. Capital gain. Line 5 less line 6.		$21,400
8. Capital gain tax. Line 7 multiplied by 20%.		$4,280
9. Net Cash after-tax position. Line 5 less line 8.		$27,120

Replacement of Stock with Another

10. Capital gain on present stock. Line 1 less line 6.		$10,000
11. Capital gain tax. Line 10 multiplied by 20%.		$2,000
12. Net assets available after taxes for investing. Line 1 less line 11.		$18,000
13. Projected annualized rate of return on new stock.	14%	
14. Investment multiplier. Enter the number from the multiplier table below that reflects the estimate of the stock's return and the holding period on line 2.		1.69
15. Future value of new stock. Line 12 multiplied by line 14.		$30,420

16. Capital gain on new stock. Line 15 less line 12. $12,420

17. Capital gain tax on sale of new stock. Line 16 multiplied by 20%. $2,484

18. Net Cash after-tax position. Line 15 less line 17. $27,936

If line 18 is greater than line 9, consider selling and replacing.

If line 18 is less than line 9, consider keeping.

Investment Multiplier Factors

Return %	1 year	2 years	3 years	4 years	5 years	8 years
6	1.06	1.12	1.19	1.26	1.34	1.59
8	1.08	1.17	1.26	1.36	1.47	1.85
10	1.10	1.21	1.33	1.46	1.61	2.14
12	1.12	1.25	1.40	1.57	1.76	2.48
14	1.14	1.30	1.48	1.69	1.93	2.85

.20 When To Sell Stock—Nonfinancial Decisions

Generally, unless the investor is a day trader, he or she should buy a stock with the intention of keeping it for a long time. Every time one looks at returns on the stock market for 10-, 15-, 20-, and 25-year intervals, he or she will usually see annualized returns of about 12 percent. Sometimes these are 10 percent. Sometimes these are 14 percent. So keeping a stock will generally provide the investor with a 12-percent return on the investment. (This refers to normal returns, not a bad stock or a super stock.)

If one doesn't sell the stock (turning stocks too often), he or she won't have to pay the capital gain tax. If one holds the stock, he or she won't have the problem of what to do with the proceeds—Buy another stock? Will it be as good?

One should not necessarily sell just because the stock's value has declined. The stock could simply be on "sale." Maybe the investor should buy more of the stock at the discounted price. Maybe it's just flowing a little with the ups and downs of the market.

Company reasons for selling stock:

- One should consider selling if something is going wrong with the company. The company itself is key to the underlying value of the stock price. One should expect the price to flow with the economy or the market. The market and the economy will rebound. So, one should check the company's fundamentals: Is management stable? How are sales? How are profits? How is the company's industry?

- One should consider selling if there has been a deterioration of management. If there is any doubt about the integrity or competence of management, one should consider selling.

- One should consider selling if the company no longer has the prospect of increasing its profits in the markets in the way it formerly did. One should consider selling if the business isn't generating profit as much as he or she feels that it should be.

- One should consider selling if the P/E (Profit/Earnings) ratio has significantly increased, but the company's earnings are not keeping pace with its rising stock price.

¶725.20

Noncompany reasons for selling stock:

- One should consider selling a stock if it has risen so much in value that it represents too much of his or her portfolio of investments. Generally, one should not keep a stock if it represents over 20 percent of the portfolio. Rebalancing might be needed.

- One should consider selling stock if he or she truly needs the money. This might be a medical need or the time to buy that retirement cabin on the lake.

.21 Stock vs. Bond—Taxable/Nontaxable

Stock Deferred and Bond Taxable vs. Stock Taxable and Bond Deferred

If all of one's investments could be in tax-deferred accounts, one could maximize his or her portfolio return during its growth period. This, of course, is not possible, unless one's total investments are only in retirement accounts. If that is so, he or she is way under-invested. It makes sense to put bonds in tax-deferred accounts and keep stocks or stock funds in taxable portfolios. Why? Interest on bonds is at ordinary income tax rates—up to 39.6 percent. Long-term capital-gains taxes on stock sales are capped at 20 percent.

Generally speaking, one may maximize the return on his or her portfolio by keeping stocks in tax-deferred accounts and placing bonds in a taxable account. To the extent that gains from those sales outpace losses in the fund's portfolio, the gains are taxable. He or she will be paying a lower tax rate than on bond interest, but he or she will likely be taxed on a far bigger gain over time. That is because stocks historically have returned more than twice as much as 30-year Treasury bonds.

Be sure to understand the tax consequences of where investments are placed. Assuming that one has both taxable and nontaxable accounts, the most critical decision is what to do with stocks, since they are likely to produce the larger return. Then turn to bonds. Keep tax-exempt municipal bonds in a taxable account. If they are in a tax-deferred plan, when finally withdrawn, they will be taxed as ordinary income.

Assumptions:

$100,000 invested. 50% into stocks and 50% into bonds. Total stock return of 12%, with 100% coming from capital gain. 6% bond return, all as ordinary income. Federal income tax rate is 28%. The analysis will not work at a 20% rate for mutual funds, since so much of the portfolio is turned within a 12-month period. This analysis will not work where there is excessive short-term trading, and the benefit of a 20% tax rate is not available.

Example:

Invest $100,000
(50% in stocks and 50% in bonds)

After 20 years

Stock deferred	=	$482,315
Bond taxable	=	116,498
Total Value:	=	598,813
Taxes paid	=	49,859
Net Cash Position	=	548,954

Invest $100,000
(50% in stocks and 50% in bonds)

After 20 years

¶725.21

	Stock taxable	=	$312,738
	Bond deferred	=	160,357
	Total Value:	=	473,095
	Taxes paid	=	169577
	Net Cash Position	=	303,518
Gain of Stock deferred and Bond taxable over		$	548,954
Stock taxable and Bond deferred			303,518
	Net Cash Gain	=	245,436

.23 Stock vs. Interest Rates vs. Bonds

When interest rates are raised, bond prices initially drop. With this drop, investors shift money into stocks. After three to six months, when the prices have stabilized, investors begin investing in the higher interest returns of the bonds. This draws away funds from the higher, more uncertain risk of stocks, and drives the stock prices down.

Estimate of Potential Relationship of Stock Prices Given Bond Rates

If Treasury rates are	Then stocks could decline this much
5.75%	3-5%
6%	5-7%
6.25%	8-10%
6.5%	11-12%
6.75%	13-16%
7.0%	17-20%

.25 Stocks—Bear Market

Bear Market Defined

Stock ownership is a roller coaster ride: the market goes up, the market goes down. One just hopes the lows are not too deep and too long. Market declines are natural. The investor should stick to his long-term financial strategies through good times and bad.

What is a bear market? Most define a bear market as a decline of 20 percent or more in a major stock index that stays down three months or more. A decline of 10 to 20 percent is generally considered a correction, especially if the market rebounds rather quickly. What usually causes a bear market is rising interest rates, typically driven by inflation. But, this isn't always the case.

Bear Market Investment Facts

Facts regarding the Dow-Jones Industrial Average:

Decline %	# of Times	Type
10% - 14%	102	Market Correction
15% - 19%	51	Market Correction
20% more %	28	Bear Market

Source: Dow Jones Average Index 1900 through 6/2001 (computer research)

Bull Market Returns

After market declines, come market rises. Long-term investors are rewarded for their patience.

¶725.23

	Average Annual Compound Return	
Date of Bear Market	10 years after Market High	10 years after Market Low
10/90	16.5	18.8
10/8	14.7	19.9
8/82	16.0	20.4
2/78	11.5	16.3
12/74	5.8	13.3

Source: Dow Jones Industrial Average Index (1950-2000) (computer research)

How to Deal with a Bear Market

- Realize it will one day become a Bull Market.
- Have your portfolio (given your risk/reward acceptance level) positioned so you don't have to do a lot of re-jiggering when the Bear hits. That is, hold a diversified portfolio of stocks and bonds that is comfortable to you.
- Continue buying stocks with new money that you have to invest. When the Bull market returns, the purchased stocks of the depressed prices will provide nice returns.

¶ 727 UNIT INVESTMENT TRUSTS

Unit Investment Trust Features

- Fixed portfolio of municipal bonds, government securities, corporate bonds, preferred stock.
- Portfolio—closed-end fund—known when fund is started. No new bonds can be added.
- Safety of principal is goal.
- Redemption
  - No redemption charge.
  - Company redeems at net asset value at any time.
  - Determined by independent evaluator.
  - Proceeds from any sale or redemption of bonds may not be reinvested in the fund.
  - They are redistributed to unit holders, which may result in a gain or loss.
- Investment
  - Represents a fractional undivided share of all securitites in the portfolio.
- Sales charge on purchase
  - Public offering price equals value per unit of bond in portfolio plus sales charge, usually 3.5 to 5 percent of public offering price.
- No management fee.
- Tax free if distributions are from municipal investment.
- Rate of return
  - Steady, known interest.
  - Determined by dividing the net interest earned by the public offering price paid for the units.

Unit Investment Trust Advantages

- Organized by experienced investment firms.
- Diversification—fund hold 12 to 50 securities of different issues diversified by type, by location, and by purpose. Spreads the risk to conserve capital.
- Professional selection—most are top rated AAA to BBB.
- Convenience—the trust handles all details of collecting and disbursing income, and safekeeping of securities.
- Ready Resale—one may redeem all or a portion of trust units at any time per prospectus terms at market value (by independent evaluation) with no redemption charge.
- Fixed Maturity Value—one knows when purchasing the trust units what the bonds will be worth at maturity.

Bond Vehicles

- Revenue bonds
  - Issued by "Authorities" of states or municipalities to finance public projects.
  - Repayment from fees charged to public using the facility.
- Municipal securities issued by states, cities, counties, school districts etc.
  - Security promise of issuer to pay interest and repay principal.
- General Obligation Bonds (GO)—issued by states and munipalities to finance public projects.
  - Supported by general revenues
  - Tax collections

Chapter 8
Taxation

2006 Change Highlights and Other Significant Issues	¶ 801
Business Tax Issues	¶ 802
Estate and Other Taxes	¶ 805
Gains and Losses—Business, Capital, and Depreciation	¶ 807
Gains and Losses—Passive Activity	¶ 809
Individual Returns—Tables	¶ 811
Penalties Tables	¶ 813
Record Retention Requirements	¶ 815
Internal Revenue Service	¶ 817
Tax Audits—Substantiation of Expenses	¶ 821

¶ 801 2006 CHANGE HIGHLIGHTS AND OTHER SIGNIFICANT ISSUES

.01 Six Acts Passed in 2006 Affecting Practitioners

The Tax Increase Prevention and Reconciliation Act of 2005 was signed by President Bush on May 17, 2006. The Act provides for $70 billion in net tax cuts and $20 billion in revenue raisers. Many of the items were extensions of tax provisions expiring in the future.

The Heroes Earned Retirement Opportunities Act allows members of the armed forces to include their combat zone compensation (otherwise excludable from gross income) in their calculation of earned income for purposes of determining their allowable income tax deduction on contributions to retirement savings plans.

State Taxation of Retirement Income Act states that retired partners cannot be taxed by the state where the deferred pay was earned after they have moved out of state. This applies to amounts received after December 31, 1995.

The Pension Protection Act of 2006 makes permanent many provisions passed in 2001. In addition the Act tightens several charitable contribution provisions.

The Financial Services Regulatory Relief Act of 2006 includes a provision exempting certified public accountants from the requirement in the Gramm-Leach-Bliley Act that CPAs send their clients an annual privacy notice. CPAs are certified or licensed by state boards of accountancy and are already subject to state laws and regulations that prohibit disclosure of nonpublic personal information without the expressed consent of the client.

The Tax Relief and Health Care Act of 2006 extended provisions that expired at the end of 2005 and made some changes to the Health Savings Accounts. In addition, some new provisions were added.

.02 AMT Exemption

The AMT exemptions for individuals were increased for 2006 only and the use of certain nonrefundable personal credits were extended for 2006. The exemption amounts are:

- $62,550 for married filing jointly
- $42,500 for singles
- $31,275 for married filing separately

.03 Roth IRAs

The $100,000 adjusted gross income ceiling for converting a traditional individual retirement account (IRA) to a Roth IRA is eliminated for tax years after 2009. The conversion is treated as a taxable distribution, but is not subject to the 10-percent early withdrawal penalty. Taxpayers who convert in 2010 can elect to recognize the conversion income in 2010 or average it over the next two years.

.04 Offers-in-Compromise

Taxpayers are required to make partial payments of their liability in addition to any user fee now imposed by the IRS; however, the user fee will be applied to the outstanding tax liability. For a lump sum offer, taxpayers will pay 20-percent of the amount offered. A lump-sum offer means any offer of payments made in five or fewer installments. For an installment payment offer, taxpayers will make their proposed scheduled payments while the IRS considers the offer. If the IRS fails to process the offer within two years, the offer will be deemed to be accepted.

.05 Kiddie Tax

The Tax Reconciliation Act raises the age limit to under 18, from under 14. This provision is effective immediately for the entire 2006 tax year. The kiddie tax does not apply to a child who is married and files a joint return.

.06 Wage Limitation in Code Sec. 199

Partners and shareholders in S corporations will be allocated their share of the passthrough entity's W-2 wages, but will include in their wage limit only wages paid to determine qualified production activities income (QPAI).

.07 Code Sec. 911 Housing Exclusion

The new base housing amount is set at 16 percent (computed on a daily basis) of the foreign earned income exclusion limitation, multiplied by the number of days of foreign residence or presence in that year. Reasonable foreign housing expenses over the base amount may be excluded from gross income. The exclusion amount is limited to 30 percent of the maximum amount of a taxpayer's foreign earned income exclusion. Any income over the exclusion will be subject to the tax rate applicable had the taxpayer not elected the exclusion. The maximum foreign income exclusion for 2006 is $82,400.

.08 Tax-Exempt Bond Interest

Interest paid on tax-exempt bonds will be reported to the IRS starting in 2006—a factor in computing the alternative minimum tax and the taxation of Social Security benefits.

.09 Loans to Continuing-Care Facilities

Lenders are not taxed on the imputed interest on loans to continuing-care facilities for five years, 2006 through 2010. The rule that lenders need not require immediate care when moving in also is waived. Facilities can assess residents who need extra care without triggering imputed income.

.10 Charitable Contribution Provisions

No deduction is allowed for any contribution of a cash, check, or other monetary gift unless the donor maintains as a record of such contribution a bank record or written communication from the charity showing, among other things, the amount of the contribution. Self-created records, such as a log book of donations, no longer suffice.

No deduction is allowed for donations of clothing and household goods unless they are in "good" condition.

Tax-free distributions from an IRA are allowed for charitable purposes. Taxpayers age 70 1/2 and older may distribute up to $100,000 in 2006 and again in 2007 from their IRAs tax-free to charitable organizations. The distribution is not reported as income to the taxpayer. The distribution does count for purposes of satisfying any required minimum distribution (RMD) amount.

Basis adjustment to stock of S corporations contributing property for 2006 and 2007. The amount of a shareholder's basis reduction in the stock of an S corporation by reason of a charitable contribution equals only the shareholder's *pro rata* share of the adjusted basis of the contributed property.

Contributions of fractional interests. The provision provides for recapture of the income tax charitable deduction and gift tax charitable deduction. If a donor makes an initial fractional contribution, then fails to contribute all of the donor's remaining interest in such property to the same donee before the earlier of 10 years from the initial fractional contribution or the donor's death, then the donee's charitable and gift tax deduction for all previous contributions of interests in the item shall be recaptured (plus interest). If the donee of a fractional interest in an item of tangible personal property fails to take substantial physical possession of the item during the 10 years or fails to use the property for an exempt use during the 10 years, then the donee's charitable and gift tax deductions for all previous contributions of interests in the item shall be recaptured (plus interest). There is also an additional tax in an amount equal to 10 percent of the amount recaptured.

Taxpayer penalties. The new law lowers the thresholds for imposing accuracy-related penalties on a taxpayer. A substantial valuation misstatement exists when the claimed value of any property is 150 percent or more of the amount determined to be the correct value. A gross valuation misstatement occurs when the claimed value of any property is 200 percent or more of the amount determined to be the correct value. The new law tightens the thresholds for imposing accuracy-related penalties with respect to the estate or gift tax. A substantial estate or gift tax valuation misstatement exists when the claimed value of any property is 65 percent or less of the amount determined to be the correct value. A gross estate or gift tax valuation exists when the claimed value of any property is 40 percent or less of the amount determined to be the correct value. The reasonable cause exception to the accuracy-related penalty does not apply in the case of gross valuation misstatements.

.11 Damage Awards

A terminated worker won a suit over the size of a lump-sum payout he received from the retirement plan maintained by his former employer. The IRS says that attorney fees paid can be netted against the taxable recovery. Although this relief is normally associated with awards for employment discrimination, a claim for pension benefits under federal law also qualified for this favorable income tax treatment. (IRS Letter Ruling 200550004, Sept. 9, 2005)

The entire amount of an individual's settlement of his claims against the District of Columbia was included in income. The taxpayer suffered physical symptoms related to emotional trauma; therefore, the settlement did not qualify for exclusion under Code Sec. 104. (*J. Goode,* 91 TCM 901, Dec. 56,454(M), TC Memo. 2006-48)

The Court of Appeals for the District of Columbia held that a whistleblower who suffered emotional distress and loss of reputation because of mistreatment by her employer did not have to pay income tax on amounts awarded to her as damages. (*M. Murphy,* CA-DC, 2006-2 USTC ¶ 50,476, 460 F3d 79 (8-22-06)) The appellate panel found that it was unconstitutional to limit the exclusion to physical injuries.

.12 Home-Makeovers

The value of home improvements is taxable to the winners of home-makeover TV shows. Even if the arrangement is structured as a rental of a house for fewer than 15 days, the income tax exclusion for such short-term rentals does not apply to the home improvements. (INFO 2006-0012) Producers of the television program Extreme Makeover: Home Edition pay applicants $50,000 to rent their homes for 10 days. The producers advise the applicants that the home improvements are nontaxable under Code Sec. 280A(g). Under Reg. § 1.740-1, prizes and awards includible in gross income include, but are not limited to, amounts received from radio and television giveaway shows. To the extent that the value of the improvement constitutes a prize or an award, it cannot also be considered rent, and therefore could not qualify for the exclusion from gross income under Code Sec. 280A(g).

.13 Gambling Winnings

After receiving three installments of a jackpot, a lottery winner sold her rights to the remaining annual payments for $7.1 million. The company that bought her out gave her Form 1099-B listing sales proceeds of $7.1 million, so she reported the payment on her Form 1040 as capital gain. The sales proceeds are ordinary income, the Tax Court says, not capital gain. The amount she received is a substitute for payouts that would have been taxed as ordinary income. (*S.B. Prebola,* 90 TCM 485, Dec. 56,190(M), TC Memo. 2005-261)

.14 Employer Fuel Reimbursements

When an employer pays an employee both a mileage reimbursement and the amount of fuel purchased on a company credit card, the amount of fuel purchased by each employee is additional wages to the employee, as is the excess of any mileage reimbursement over the standard mileage rate. In addition, the payments for fuel by the employer are subject to payroll taxes. (INFO 2005-0218)

.15 Hybrid Vehicle Cash Incentives

Employers that offer rebates or cash incentives to encourage employees to purchase hybrid cars must include the amounts on the employee's year-end Form W-2. The incentives are taxable compensation just like other forms of compensation. (IRS News Release, IR-2006-112, July 13, 2006) They are also subject to income tax withholding and employment taxes.

¶801.12

.16 Unmarried Cohabitants

For unmarried cohabitants in community property states, each partner must report his or her share of earned income. The IRS does not allow the partners to report one-half of the combined income on their separate returns. (CCA 200608038, Feb. 24, 2006)

.17 Refunds of State Income Taxes

Refunds of 2004 income taxes are tax free for filers who deducted state sales taxes. A state income tax refund is taxed only if the recipient deducted income taxes on Schedule A. A state income tax refund is taxable only to the extent the deduction for state income taxes is more than the available sales tax write-off. Assume that a taxpayer could have deducted $5,000 in sales taxes but instead elected to deduct $6,000 in state income taxes. A refund of state income taxes of $2,500 would only be taxable to the extent of $1,000.

.18 Personal Use Employer-Provided Vehicles

For 2006, the cents-per-mile method can be used for passenger automobiles with a fair market value of $15,000 or less on the day they were first made available to employees. The cents-per-mile method can only be used for trucks and vans with a fair market value (FMV) of $16,400 or less. (Rev. Proc. 2006-15, IRB 2006-5, 387) For vehicles that are more expensive, the IRS's annual lease value tables must be used. Trucks and vans are defined as passenger automobiles built on a truck chassis, including minivans and SUVs that are built on a truck chassis.

.19 Options

A software designer received income when he exercised his options through a margin account. The Tax Court rejected the taxpayer's argument that under Code Sec. 83 principles, the exercise of an option through a margin account should be treated as the grant of another option to buy the share, and, therefore, the income should be taxed only when the shares are sold to pay off the margin account. (*J. Facq,* 91 TCM 1201, Dec. 56,529(M), TC Memo. 2006-111)

.20 Payment for Wife's Infidelity

A police officer discovered his wife was having an affair with her doctor. He told the doctor he knew of the affair and was going to sue him. The doctor apologized and paid him $25,000. The doctor's accountant sent the cop a Form 1099 showing the payment as income. The Tax Court ruled that the payment was not a tax-free gift but taxable income. (*M.D. Peebles,* TC Summ. Op. 2006-61, 2006 Tax Ct. Summary LEXIS 157 (Apr. 19, 2006))

.21 Adoption Assistance

Adoption assistance provided by a charity is tax free. The aid is treated as a nontaxable gift and is exempt from Form 1099 reporting if given directly to the individual. (INFO 2006-0027)

.22 Selling Depreciable Assets to a Related Firm

Gain on the sale is taxed as ordinary income. For this purpose, actual or constructive ownership of 50 percent or more of the buyer is sufficient to trigger ordinary-income treatment of the profit made by the seller. It does not matter if the buyer is a partnership, C corporation, or an S corporation. The IRS ruled that sales of oil and gas reserves are not affected by this rule, because depletion is claimed on those assets, not depreciation. The same rule also applied to other mineral deposits. (IRS Letter Ruling 200602018, Oct. 5, 2005)

.23 Mark-to-Market Election

Taxpayers have until April 15 to elect special tax status for the preceding year using Form 3115. Called a section 475(f) election, it allows traders to recognize their gains or losses for tax purposes as if they had sold all their holdings on the last day of the tax year. The election cannot be revoked unless the IRS agrees. (Rev. Proc. 99-17, 1999-1 CB 503)

A taxpayer reported a Schedule C net profit of $18,520,775 in 1999 and $16,966,055 in 2000 from settling a class action lawsuit. He decided to wind down his law practice and began securities trading on 1/28/00 using margin borrowing. Unfortunately his account was liquidated on 4/14/00 for failing to cover a margin call after a sharp decline in technology stocks. On that date his net trading losses totaled $15,196,152. After his 1999 return preparer failed to make the section 475(f) mark-to-market election, a law firm filed a late election for him on 7/21/00. In allowing the taxpayer to make the election under Reg. § 301.9100-3, the Tax Court notes that the government was not prejudiced because the taxpayer did not trade any securities between 4/17/00 and 7/21/00, so his losses were the same on both dates. (*L.S. Vines,* 126 TC 279, Dec. 56,512 (2006))

.24 Relocating Workers

The IRS is limiting employer deductions of home-sale losses in cases where an outside relocation firm is issued to assist with the sale. If title to the home passes to the employer or to the relocation company, the company must treat any loss on the sale as a capital loss. If the worker keeps title, the employer can write off the reimbursement to a relocation firm for the home's decline in value. (Rev. Rul. 2005-74, 2005-2 CB 1153) Any amounts paid by the employer constitute taxable compensation to the employee.

.25 Deferred Exchange Escrow Earnings

Earnings on escrows in deferred swaps are taxed to the seller, even when part of the money goes to the intermediary as a fee, the IRS says in proposed regulations. If the contract says the intermediary is entitled to all the earnings, the seller is treated as lending the proceeds in the escrow account to the intermediary. For tax purposes, the intermediary is deemed to transfer the earnings on the funds to the seller, who then must pay tax on the phantom interest. (Prop. Reg. § 113365-04)

.26 Sale of Residence

The IRS allowed a partial exclusion for taxpayers in a senior-only community who had to sell their home after circumstances forced their child and grandchild to live with them. (IRS Letter Ruling 200601023, Sept. 30, 2005) A couple from out of state was allowed a partial exclusion when they did not realize their new home was in a high-crime area. They sold after their neighbors assaulted them. (IRS Letter Ruling 200601009, Sept. 30, 2005)

The IRS determined that an adoption qualified as an unforeseen circumstance allowing the taxpayers to claim a partial home sale exclusion. The taxpayer had sold their home, which they had occupied for less than two years, to rent a larger home so they would have room for an adopted child. (IRS Letter Ruling 200613009, Dec. 19, 2005)

¶801.23

A taxpayer who had to vacate his home because of fear for his personal safety and the safety of his family is eligible for a reduced home sale exclusion. The sale was by reason of unforseen circumstances. The taxpayer, a police officer, arrested an alleged drug dealer in a highly publicized anti-drug sting. Soon after, the police department learned that the drug dealer's associates had discovered the taxpayer's address and planned to kill him. The taxpayer subsequently sold the house. (IRS Letter Ruling 200615011, Dec. 8, 2005)

.27 Health Savings Accounts

Distributions are allowed from Flexible Spending Accounts (FSAs) and Health Reimbursement Accounts and may be rolled into Health Savings Accounts (HSAs). The amount allowed as a rollover is the smaller of the balance in the account on September 21, 2006, or the balance at the time of the rollover. The rollover must be made before 2012.

The Flexible Spending Account is disregarded for Health Savings eligibility if the FSA balance is zero at the beginning of the year.

The annual plan deductible for 2007 is repealed for 2007. A deduction is allowed for the full year if the taxpayer is eligible at any time during the year. A one-time rollover from an IRA to an HSA is allowed after 2006 and before 2012.

.28 Failed Rollover Requests

Requests for waivers of the 60-day rollover period will now cost from $500 to $3,000, depending on the amount of the rollover. (Rev. Proc. 2006-8, IRB 2006-1, 245)

- $3,000 for a rollover of $100,000 or more.
- $1,500 for a rollover of $50,000 or more but less than $100,000.
- $500 for smaller rollovers.

It was $95 under Rev. Proc. 2005-8.

.29 Manufacturing Deduction

The manufacturing deduction is capped at 50 percent of W-2 wages attributable to production activities. It affects tax years beginning after May 17, 2006.

Land clearing, grading, and demolition qualify as construction. The deduction is retroactive to 2005.

.30 Self-Employed Health Insurance

The IRS has made its position crystal clear that a self-employed individual cannot deduct health insurance costs from his or her self-employment income reported on Schedule C of Form 1040. (CCA 200623001, March 3, 2006) Instead, the insurance costs must be deducted on Form 1040 as an adjustment to the individual's gross income.

Premiums on policies purchased by sole owners of one-person S corporations are not eligible for the 100-percent deduction. The above-the-line deduction for medical premiums applies only to policies purchased in the name of the S corporation. (*Headliner,* Volume 163, May 15, 2006)

.31 Payment of Alimony

Assigning a third party's debt is not a payment of alimony, the Tax Court said. To satisfy an obligation of alimony to his ex-wife, the taxpayer transferred the right to receive future payments on a debt that their son owed him. Only the payment of cash or a cash equivalent such as a check or money order payable on demand qualifies as alimony. (*D.E. Lofstrom,* 125 TC 271, Dec. 56,204 (2005))

An alimony payment made before the due date for the first payment in the decree does not qualify for a deduction. To be deductible, the obligation to pay must be imposed by the decree. Any payments made after that date are deductible alimony, even if paid ahead of schedule. (*J.R. Ray,* TC Summ. Op. 2006-110, 2006 Tax Ct. Summary LEXIS 11 (Jul. 17, 2006))

.32 Costs to Avoid Fines

Environmental remediation project costs to avoid a fine or penalty cannot be depreciated. (TAM 200629030, Mar. 31, 2006) The taxpayer and the EPA came to a project agreement that required the taxpayer to make capital improvements to its facility. The agreement was made after talk of imposing a fine for certain violations had begun. The IRS maintained that if the costs incurred by the taxpayer were related to a fine or penalty, it must be denied under the same public policy underlying Code Sec. 162(f).

.33 Mileage Rates (Rev. Proc. 2005-78, 2005-2 CB 1177)

The optional mileage rate for business use of an automobile (including vans, pickups, and panel trucks) in 2006 is set at 44.5 cents a mile. This is a change from 40.5 cents for the first eight months of 2005 and to 48.5 cents for September through December. The standard mileage rate for using an automobile for medical reasons or moving for 2006 is 18 cents. This is a change from 15 cents for the first eight months and 22 cents for the last four months of 2005. For 2007 the mileage rate for business use of an automobile is set at 48.5 cents a mile. The standard mileage rate for using an automobile for medical reasons or moving is 20 cents.

.34 Luxury Automobiles (Rev. Proc. 2006-18, IRB 2006-12, 645)

The dollar limit on depreciation of business cars placed in service in 2006 is $100 higher for the second and fourth years than the 2005 limits. Electric cars were increased by $100 to $200 for each year from 2005.

Year	Nonelectric	Electric
First year	$2,960	$8,980
Second year	4,800	14,400
Third year	2,850	8,650
Succeeding years	1,775	5,225

The method of calculating the price inflation amount for trucks and vans placed in service in or after 2003 uses a "new trucks" component, resulting in somewhat higher depreciation deductions for trucks and vans. The term "trucks and vans" refers to passenger automobiles that are built on a truck chassis, including minivans and sport utility vehicles (SUVs) that are build on a truck chassis.

Year	Nonelectric
First year	$3,260
Second year	5,200
Third year	3,150
Succeeding years	1,875

¶801.32

.35 Section 179

The section 179 deduction is increased to $108,000 for 2006 with the phaseout beginning at $430,000. To determine any reduction in the dollar limit for costs over $430,000, the partner does not include any of the cost of section 179 property placed in service by the partnership. (IRS Pub. 946, at 21)

To figure the net income (or loss) from a trade or business actively conducted by an S corporation, take into account the items from that trade or business that are passed through to the shareholders and used in determining each shareholder's tax liability. However, do not take into account any credits, tax-exempt income, the section 179 deduction, and deductions for compensation paid to shareholder-employees.

.36 In the Business of Gambling

A regular gambler is engaged in a business. He puts in 40 hours a week studying races and spends most days at the track. His losing wagers are deducted on Schedule C, instead of as a miscellaneous itemized deduction. Gambling losses can be deducted only to the extent that they offset gambling winnings. (*J. Castagnetta,* TC Summ. Op. 2006-24, 2006 Tax Ct. Summary LEXIS 112 (Feb. 13, 2006))

.37 Cost of Removing Mold

The cost of cleaning up mold is a deductible business expense. Most of the drywall, ceilings, doors, sinks, and electrical fixtures were removed during the cleanup of a nursing home after the owner discovered mold. Except for sums reimbursed by insurance, the cost of returning the building to its original shape is deductible. (IRS Letter Ruling 200607003, Nov. 10, 2005) The taxpayer used the building as a nursing home both before and after the remediation project. The existing floor plan was not altered. The mold problem did not appear until after the taxpayer owned the building. The project did not cause a material appreciation or prolong the life of the building.

.38 Takeover Expenses

Exploratory expenses can be deducted by the takeover targets, the IRS says. This includes all expenses incurred before the decision is made to proceed with the acquisition and a mate is chosen. However, merger-related expenses after that date must be capitalized and cannot be deducted. Such costs do not qualify for the amortization of start-up expenses. (IRS Letter Ruling 200548022, Aug. 23, 2005)

.39 Amortizing Customer List

Amounts paid to acquire customer accounts can be amortized ratably over 15 years. (IRS Letter Ruling 200616015, Jan. 10, 2006) The taxpayer is also allowed to amortize contingent payments that the contract requires the buyer to make to the seller in future years if the buyer turns a profit on the new customers. Those additional payments made can be amortized over the remainder of the 15-year period.

.40 Truck Lease

A taxpayer was responsible for all aspects of on-site job management and supervision. The employer did not have a formal written expense reimbursement policy. The employer's verbal reimbursement policy was to pay $25 per day for the use of a personal vehicle while driving on corporate business. For two years the taxpayer filed a Schedule C listing his principal business or profession: "Truck Lease" and reported business income and deducted business expenses resulting in business losses. The Tax Court agreed that the taxpayer's vehicle expenses were unreimbursed employee business expenses that should be deducted on Schedule A, subject to the two-percent floor as miscellaneous itemized deductions. The taxpayer was not in the business of leasing. (*W.M. Alley,* TC Summ. Op. 2006-4, 2006 Tax Ct. Summary LEXIS 93 (Jan. 19, 2006))

.41 Trips Near Family

The IRS disallowed $2,710 of an attorney's driving deductions for his 70-plus-mile trips to a distant law library to conduct research for clients. It said that several other law libraries were available much closer to his home, but the attorney's family lived near the distant library and he was making the trips to visit them. He answered that the distant library was superior to the nearby ones. The Tax Court allowed the deductions. The attorney documented the trips and the fact that he performed work for clients on them, so they had a primary business purpose. Visiting his family on these trips did not make them nondeductible. (*R.O. Berge,* TC Summ. Op. 2006-29, 2006 Tax Ct. Summary LEXIS 102 (Feb. 21, 2006))

.42 Away from Home

The Tax Court recently held that a demanding 17-hour work day that included a mid-trip four-hour snooze was enough to qualify meals and incidentals at the away-from-home location for a deduction. The Tax Court also found that the day was long enough that the standard per diem rate need not be prorated. (*M.G. Bissonnette,* 127 TC No. 10, Dec. 56,648 (2006)) The Court stated: "If the nature of the taxpayer's employment is such that when away from home, during released time, it is reasonable for him or her to need and obtain sleep or rest in order to meet the exigencies of his employment or the business demands of his or her employment, his or her expenditures... for the purpose of obtaining sleep or rest are deductible traveling expenses." Ninety minutes of sleep or rest is not enough to qualify expenses. A four-hour nap between work assignments during a six-hour layover was sufficient.

.43 Guarantee Paid on Loan

Taxpayer paid on a loan that he had guaranteed for a friend's business. He took a deduction on his tax return as a theft loss claiming that he had been fraudulently induced into guaranteeing the loan. The court ruled the friend only took the third party's money. Never did he take control of the taxpayer's funds directly or gained any kind of encumbrance on/control over the taxpayer's property. His loss, if any, had to be treated as a bad debt subject to the capital loss limitations. (*M.B. Stoltz,* DC Ind., 2006-1 USTC ¶ 50,210, 410 FSupp2d 734)

.44 Medical Expense

An IRS legal memo concludes that the cost of male-to-female gender reassignment surgery (GRS), along with related medications, treatments, and transportation, were not deductible as medical expenses under Code Sec. 213. After noting that there is no case law, regulation, or ruling addressing the deductions, the IRS stated that: "In light of the Congressional emphasis on denying a deduction for procedures relating to appearance in all but a few circumstances and the controversy surrounding whether GRS is a treatment for an illness or disease, the materials submitted do not support a deduction. Only an unequivocal expression of Congressional intent that expenses of this type qualify under Sec. 213 would justify the allowance of the deduction in this case." (IRS Letter Ruling 200603025, Oct. 14, 2005)

The cost of special education for a dyslexic child can be treated as a deductible medical expense. (IRS Letter Ruling 200552003, Sept. 27, 2005) The IRS has set up three conditions for deducting special education to overcome a learning disability as a medical expense:

- A doctor must diagnose the condition.

- The school must have a professional staff competent to design and supervise a program to help a child overcome a learning disability.

- Overcoming the learning disability must be the primary motivation for attending the school. Ordinary education must be considered incidental to the treatment provided at the school.

.45 Charitable Contributions

A couple sent their children to a school offering religious education along with traditional instruction. The school gave the parents a letter estimating that 55 percent of the tuition payments were for religious education. The Tax Court denied the deduction, stating that the parents received value from the education for their children from the tuition. (*M. Sklar,* 125 TC 281, Dec. 56,225 (2005))

Some charities have sold donated vehicles at auction and have secured documentation from the auction that the vehicle will be transferred to a needy individual. If a vehicle is sold at auction, the IRS has ruled that the vehicle is not sold or otherwise transferred to a needy individual. The donor's deduction is limited to the charity's gross proceeds from the sale. (IRS News Release, IR-2004-145, Dec. 6, 2004; IRS News Release IR-2005-149, Dec. 22, 2005)

.46 Premiums on Mortgage Insurance

For 2007, premiums on mortgage insurance are treated as home mortgage interest and are deductible. The deduction is phased out for incomes exceeding $100,000. The insurance must be on acquisition indebtedness on policies issued in 2007.

.47 Casualty Losses

An income tax deduction cannot be taken for a blown-down tree on residential property in most cases. No basis allocation is made to individual trees when a home is purchased. The casualty loss deduction is limited to the decline in value of the home without the tree, not the total cost of replacing it.

.48 Miscellaneous Itemized Deductions

Kenneth Graves lent his solely owned corporation $86,000 when it had financial difficulties. The business then failed without repaying him. Being the owner of a corporation is not a "trade or business" that enables one to take a business deduction for related losses. However, being an employee is a trade or business. Graves was an employee of his corporation, and his loan to it had the business purpose of protecting his employment with it. The loss is deductible as an employee business expense. (*K.W. Graves,* 87 TCM 1409, Dec. 55,663(M), TC Memo. 2004-140) Employee business expenses are deductible as a miscellaneous itemized deduction subject to the two-percent limitation. This deduction is added back in computing the AMT.

.49 Energy Credits

The manufacturer of a building envelope component can establish that the component is eligible for the 10-percent qualified energy efficiency improvements credit by providing the consumer with a certification statement that satisfies the IRS guidelines outlined in Notice 2006-26. The statement can be included with the product's packaging, it can be made available in printable form on the manufacturer's website, or it can be furnished in any other manner that permits the consumer to retain the statement for recordkeeping purposes. Consumers are not required to attach these statements to their returns.

An exterior window or skylight that bears the Energy Star label and is installed in the appropriate region(s) identified on the label is automatically treated as being eligible for the 10-percent credit. No manufacturer's certification statement is required for these products.

The manufacturer of a qualified residential energy product can establish that the product is eligible for the 100-percent credit by providing the consumer with a certification statement that satisfies the IRS guidelines outlined in Notice 2006-26.

The IRS has issued rules for owners of energy efficient commercial building property to certify that the property satisfies the requirements of Code Sec. 179D(c)(1) and (d). The IRS also provides a procedure allowing developers of computer software to certify to the Energy Department that the software is acceptable for calculating energy and power consumption for Code Sec. 179D purposes. (Notice 2006-52, IRB 2006-26, 1175)

.50 Education Credits

Prepaid tuition is normally creditable in the year paid. Neither the Hope credit nor the lifetime learning credit can be claimed in the year for which the tuition applies. (*J.B. Patel,* TC Summ. Op. 2006-40, 2006 Tax Ct. Summary LEXIS 154 (Mar. 16, 2006)) The same rules apply for the $3,000 and $4,000 tuition deduction claimed for AGI.

.51 Dependent Care Credit

The IRS has issued proposed regulations under Code Sec. 21 on the credit for household and dependent care services necessary for gainful employment. While the proposed regulations will not be in force until they are finalized, the taxpayer may elect to apply them to tax years that remain open for refund or credit as of May 24, 2006. (NPRM REG-139059-02) The regulations clarify that the dollar limit of $6,000 for taxpayers taking into account employment-related expenses for more than one qualifying individual may be applied in unequal proportions. A credit may be taken in the tax year in which the services are provided or in the tax year in which the expenses are paid, whichever is later, regardless of accounting methods. Expenses for pre-school or other pre-kindergarten programs are allowed as employment-related expenses if they otherwise qualify, even though education may be a big part of these programs.

Programs starting at the kindergarten level and higher are excluded because they are principally for education and not child care that is an employment-related expense. In the past, IRS rules were silent on kindergarten tuition.

Specialty day camps qualify for employment-related expenses. Specialty day camps refer to camps that focus on one activity, like soccer or computer. Overnight camps are still not included, with no pro-ration of expense for day and night supervision.

¶801.49

Transportation provided by a dependent care provider may be an employment-related expense if all other requirements are met. This includes transportation to a day camp or after-school activity. Transportation costs incurred by a qualified individual in getting from the taxpayer's household to a care provider are not allowed as employment-related expenses.

.52 Employee Tip Credit

The federal minimum wage must be used to calculate the Employee Tip Credit, even if the employer's state minimum wage is higher. The credit is equal to FICA and Medicare taxes paid on tips to servers that exceed the portion of tips treated as part of the minimum wage. Employers that claimed smaller credits using the state minimum wage figures can file amended returns to obtain refunds.

.53 Employment Taxes

Retired insurance agents owe SECA tax on renewal commissions, the Tax Court stated. Although a 1997 law exempted a variety of payments for retired agents from self-employment tax, that relief does not apply to any post-retirement renewal commissions based on policies they sold while working. (*G.R. Gilbert,* TC Summ. Op. 2005-176, 2005 Tax Ct. Summary LEXIS 64 (Dec. 1, 2005))

.54 Notary Public

Income for notary services is exempt from self-employment taxes. For federal tax purposes, the performance of functions of a public office, including work as a notary public, is not a trade or business. (INFO 2006-0022; Reg. § 1.1402(c)-2) Notary income is reported on Schedule C, but Schedule SE need not be filed. Retirement plan contributions cannot be based on notary income.

.55 Back Pay

Back pay generally is treated as wages subject to income tax withholding, FICA, and FUTA in the year paid, rather than in the year(s) in which it should have been paid. (INFO 2006-0023)

.56 Alternative Minimum Tax

Alternative minimum tax (AMT) income is not reduced by capital losses in a succeeding year. An individual was granted stock options by his employer in 1999. The options qualified as incentive stock options. On December 21, 2000, the individual exercised an option to purchase 46,125 shares at $.20 a share. The total exercise price was $9,225. On that date, the stock was worth $23.21 a share. The Tax Court concluded that the taxpayer's shares were not subject to a substantial risk of forfeiture and that he had AMTI of $1,066,064, based on the December 21, 2000, value. The stock became worthless in 2001 and the taxpayer had a capital loss of $1,075,289 for AMT. The Tax Court concluded that the loss limitation rules of Code Sec. 1212(a) also apply when computing AMTI. Therefore the taxpayer could not carry back the losses realized in 2001 to offset the individual's AMTI that he realized in 2000. The Tax Court also stated that the capital losses are excluded from the NOL computation. (*R.J. Merlo,* 126 TC 205 (2006))

In 1998, the taxpayer entered into an ISO agreement with his employer. The agreement permitted him to purchase shares of his employer's common stock at a set price, which he did on March 15, 2000. At that time the shares had a fair market value of $2.1 million.

The taxpayer's ISO price was $100,000. The taxpayer realized no income or loss on the exercise of the ISOs for the purpose of computing his 2000 taxable income. However, he realized $2 million in income for the purpose of computing his 2000 AMTI. The taxpayer sold the shares in 2001 for $250,000. The transaction generated a regular tax capital gain of $150,000 and a $1.9 million AMT capital loss. For 2001, the taxpayer reported $561,000 in taxable income. His regular tax liability was $191,000. He reported his AMTI as negative $1.34 million ($561,000 taxable income minus the $1.9 million adjustment). His 2001 tentative minimum tax and 2001 AMT were both $0. (*J.N. Palahnuk,* 127 TC No. 9, Dec. 56,644 (2006)) The IRS disallowed the $1.9 million adjustment. The $1.9 million is a capital loss and not a net operating loss. It cannot be carried back and is carried forward and limited to $3,000 per year.

.57 Federal Telephone Excise Tax

The three-percent federal telephone excise tax will no longer apply to long-distance calls. The tax is eliminated on all long-distance calls. The IRS could have chosen to continue to apply the tax to long-distance charges that vary by distance. The telephone tax still applies to local calls. Credit or refunds of taxes paid after February 28, 2003, and before August 1, 2006, will be issued, along with interest. Individuals seeking a credit or refund will make their requests on their 2006 Form 1040. Entities will make the request on their tax returns.

Individuals who do not have records to show how much tax they paid may seek a credit or refund under a special safe harbor rule.

.58 Overseas Tax Preparers

The IRS will make it harder for U.S. preparers to use overseas help. Preparers will have to get written permission from their client before Form 1040s can be sent abroad to be prepared. The IRS is making the change because it cannot hold overseas preparers accountable for errors. Proposed regulations become effective after the final regulations are published. (Prop. Reg. § 137243-02)

.59 Single Member LLC Tax Deposits

Deposits will soon not be allowed to be made in the owner's name, the IRS says in proposed regulations. The rule change requiring tax deposits to be made using the entity's name and ID number will take effect on Jan. 1, 2007, so firms will have time to gear up. (REG-114371-05)

.60 Tax Software Glitch

The IRS has ruled in favor of two different taxpayers who had a common problem: their tax preparation software program misled them on the proper calculations needed to determine the extent to which they should make the election to treat qualified dividend income as investment income. The software program included all qualified income as investment income. They had missed the part in the software instructions that advised them to make manual computations to determine the optimal amount of qualified dividend income that should be treated as investment income. Both taxpayers were given 60 days from the date of the rulings to amend their elections. (IRS Letter Ruling 200620018, Feb. 8, 2006, and IRS Letter Ruling 200620019, Feb. 8, 2006)

.61 Online Payment Agreement Application

The IRS is implementing the new Online Payment Agreement (OPA) application through national partnerships with the tax professional community. Members of tax professional organizations are using the OPA to apply for payment agreements for clients who owe taxes. This application will eliminate the need to write or call the IRS toll-free number for assistance. When fully implemented, the OPA will provide an easier way for taxpayers on their own or with the help of tax professionals to voluntarily resolve tax liabilities. (IRS News Release, IR-2006-159, Oct. 16, 2006) The IRS estimates that 90 percent of taxpayers who qualify for a payment agreement will be able to obtain one through the OPA once the application is available to the general public later in 2006.

.62 Frivolous Tax Submissions

The penalty for frivolous tax submissions is increased form $500 to $5,000.

.63 Partnerships

A limited liability company (taxed as a partnership) converted into a corporation by filing a certificate of conversion with the appropriate state office. The incorporation was carried out in anticipation of an initial public offering (IPO) of the corporation's stock. However, due to a "precipitous and unexpected deterioration in market conditions," the IPO was canceled and there are no plans to attempt another public offering "in the near future." The IRS concluded that the reconversion from a corporation to an LLC taxable as a partnership will not be treated as a liquidation of the corporation. Furthermore, the entity will be treated as a partnership at all times during the year, and the owners will be treated as partners during the year. (IRS Letter Ruling 200613027, Dec. 16, 2005)

.64 S Corporations

A taxpayer personally guaranteed a $4 million loan to his S corporation from a commercial lender, pledging his assets as collateral. He used this to report increased basis and claim corresponding deductions. The Tax Court ruled that neither the guarantee of a loan nor a pledge of collateral is an "economic outlay." The taxpayer had not increased his basis in the firm, and his deductions were disallowed. (*W.H. Maloof,* 89 TCM 1022, Dec. 55,985(M), TC Memo. 2005-75) The taxpayer gave his fully recourse $1 million promissory note to the bank to replace the S corporation's $1 million promissory note on which the taxpayer had formerly served as guarantor. The Tax Court concluded that the taxpayer had actually "made an economic outlay, which left him poorer in the material sense, by becoming the fully recourse obligor on an enforceable debt had by an independent third-party lender." The taxpayer, who then re-lent the proceeds of the indebtedness to the S corporation, created direct indebtedness of his S corporation to him. He was considered to have sufficient basis to cover the losses claimed. (*T.J. Miller,* 91 TCM 1267, Dec. 56,544(M), TC Memo. 2006-125)

.65 Gift and Estate Taxes

Prepayments of tuition qualify for a special gift tax unlimited exclusion for tuition paid directly to a school. A grandmother arranged with the private school her six grandchildren attended to prepay tuition through grade 12 for each one. The payments she made were nonrefundable if the grandchildren switched to another school. (IRS Letter Ruling 200602002, Sept. 6, 2005) Code Sec. 2503(e)(1) excludes from the gift tax certain qualified transfers that ordinarily would be deemed gifts and be subject to the gift tax. These include amounts paid on behalf of individuals as tuition if paid to an education institution. Code Sec. 2601 imposes an additional generation-skipping tax (GST) on any transfer made to a skip person. Under Code Sec. 2611(b)(1), *inter vivos* transfers which would not be treated as gifts under Code Sec. 2503(e) are not treated as generation-skipping transfers.

Lavish funeral luncheon. A 12-year-old decedent's estate could not deduct as a funeral expense the $3,636 cost of a funeral luncheon because the Tax Court was not satisfied that sufficient proof of its reasonable relationship to the funeral was presented. (*S.M. Davenport Est.*, 92 TCM 324, Dec. 56,642(M), TC Memo. 2006-215) The court questioned whether recognizing and thanking third parties for their support during the decedent's life was consistent with traditional activities typically associated with funeral services that focus on eulogizing and laying to rest the deceased.

.66 Trust Reporting

The Second Circuit Court of Appeals has held that a trust's deduction for investment advice was subject to the two-percent floor for miscellaneous itemized deductions. (*W.L. Rudkin Testamentary Trust*, CA-2, 2006-2 USTC ¶ 50,569, 467 F3d 149) The court analyzed Code Sec. 67(e)(1), which requires that the adjusted gross income of a trust be computed in the same manner as an individual. Code Sec. 67(e)(1) provides an exception to the two-percent floor for an expense (1) that is paid to administer the trust and (2) that would not have been incurred if the property were not held in trust. The court sided with the Tax Court, the Court of Federal Claims, and several appeals courts. Only the Sixth Circuit in *W.J. O'Neill* (CA-6, 93-1 USTC ¶ 50,332, 994 F2d 302) has concluded that a trust could deduct investment advisor fees in full.

.67 Social Security Benefits

The Supreme Court ruled that the government can take part of Social Security benefits to pay off student loans no matter how old the debt is. The ruling settles a conflict among the lower courts, some of which had ruled that the government had only 10 years to collect. (*J. Lockhart,* SCt, 546 US 142 (2005))

.68 Medicare Part B Premiums

Medicare Part B premiums will increase in 2007 for up to 2 million people. The more income a beneficiary has, the higher the premium due.

For Singles

If your 2005 modified AGI is		Your month 2007
More than	*But not over*	*premium surcharge will be*
$80,000	$100,000	13.3%
100,000	150,000	33.3%
300,000	400,000	53.3%
400,000		73.3%

Modified adjusted gross income is 2005 adjusted gross income plus tax-exempt interest, EE bond interest used for educational expenses, and any excluded foreign earned income. The premium increase is owed even if you did not sign up for prescription drug coverage. The add-on percentages for 2008 will be double those of 2007 and be based on 2006 income. In 2009, the percentages will triple.

.69 Extenders

The following tax provisions that had expired at the end of 2005 were extended for 2006 and 2007:

- Deduction for higher education expenses
- Deduction for state and local sales taxes
- Research credit
- Work opportunity credit and welfare-to-work credit
- Using combat pay in the earned income credit computation
- $250 above-the-line teachers' deduction
- Five-year recovery for leasehold improvements and restaurants
- Archer medical savings accounts

¶ 802 BUSINESS TAX ISSUES

.01 Amount of Corporate Tax

The amount of the corporate income tax is the sum of:

- 15% of first $50,000 of taxable income.
- 25% of next $25,000 of taxable income.
- 34% of next $25,000 of taxable income.
- 39% of next $235,000 of taxable income.
- 34% of next $9,665,000 of taxable income.
- 35% of next $5,000,000 of taxable income.
- 38% of next $3,333,333 of taxable income.
- 35% of any additional amount of taxable income.

The purpose of the 39-percent bracket is to impose an additional tax of $11,750 to bring the first two brackets up to the 34-percent bracket. Thus, at $335,000 of taxable income, the result is the equivalent of a "flat tax" of 34 percent. The 38 percent bracket is to bring the previous brackets taxed at 34 percent up to the 35-percent bracket. When corporations reach $18,333,333 of taxable income they will be at a "flat tax" of 35 percent. (Code Sec. 11(b)(1))

.03 Alternative Minimum Tax for Corporations

Simplified Calculation

Taxable income

+ Net Operating loss deduction

+/– Adjustments

+ Tax preference items

+/ – Adjusted current earnings adjustment

– AMT net operating loss deduction

– Allowable AMT exemption

= Alternate Minimum Taxable income

× .20

– AMT foreign tax credit

= Tentative minimum tax

– AMT general business credit

– Regular income tax

= Alternative minimum tax

Alternative minimum tax (AMT) rules have been devised to ensure that no taxpayer with substantial economic income can avoid significant tax liability by using exclusions, deductions, and credits. The starting point for computing the AMT is the corporation's taxable income. Taxable income is modified for adjustments, tax preferences, and an adjustment for current earnings and profits. The modifications result primarily from differences in computing taxable income and deductions allowed for AMT purposes.

Small Corporations

The tentative minimum tax of a corporation is zero for any taxable year if the corporation's average annual gross receipts for all three taxable periods ending before such taxable year do not exceed $7,500,000. If a corporation ceases to be a small corporation, the AMT will only apply prospectively.

First taxable year corporation in existence. The tentative minimum tax of a corporation for its first year will be zero.

.05 Accumulated Earnings Tax

Reasonable Needs of Business

An accumulation of earnings and profits is considered in excess of the reasonable needs of the business if it exceeds the amount that a prudent businessman would consider appropriate for present business purposes and for the reasonable anticipated future needs of the business. (Reg. § 1.537-1(a))

Reasonable Anticipated Needs

In order for a corporation to justify an accumulation of earnings and profits for reasonable anticipated future needs, there must be an indication that the future needs of the business require such accumulation, and the corporation must have specific, definite, and feasible plans for the use of such accumulation. Such an accumulation need not be used immediately, nor must the plans for its use be consummated within a short period after the close of the taxable year, provided that such accumulation will be used within a reasonable time depending upon all the facts and circumstances relating to the future needs of the business. (Reg. § 1.536-7(B)(i))

Reasonable Accumulation of Earnings and Profits

Although the following grounds are not exclusive, one or more of such grounds, if supported by sufficient facts, may indicate that the earnings and profits of a corporation are being accumulated for the reasonable needs of the business:

- To provide necessary working capital for the business, such as for the procurement of inventories;
- To provide for bona fide expansion of business or replacement of plant;

- To provide for the retirement of bona fide indebtedness created in connection with the trade or business, such as the establishment of a sinking fund for the purpose of retiring bonds issued by the corporation in accordance with contract obligations incurred on issue;
- To acquire a business enterprise through purchasing stock or assets;
- To provide for investments or loans to suppliers or customers if necessary in order to maintain the business of the corporation; or
- To provide for the payment of reasonably anticipated product liability losses. (Reg. § 1.537-2(b))

Contingencies as Reasonable

Accumulations have been justified as a result of various forms of contingencies, including the following:

- Accumulations to guard against competition has been justified in some cases.
- A possible liability arising out of some contractual obligation.
- An actual or potential lawsuit.
- A possible business reversal resulting from the loss of a customer.
- An accumulation to provide funds to finance a self-insurance plan; this includes key person, as well as the more common types of risk insurance.
- Accumulations to provide a retirement plan for employees. (MT 4233-16 Internal Revenue Manual, p. 4233-151, 154, Sec. 637.4)

Unreasonable Accumulations of Earnings and Profits

Although the following purposes are not exclusive, accumulations of earnings and profits to meet any one of such objectives may indicate that the earnings and profits of a corporation are being accumulated beyond the reasonable needs of the business:

- Loans having no reasonable relation to the conduct of the business made to relatives or friends of shareholders, or to other persons;
- Loans to shareholders, or the expenditure of funds of the corporation for the personal benefit of the shareholders;
- Loans to another corporation, the business of which is not that of the taxpayer corporation, if the capital stock of such other corporation is owned, directly or indirectly, by the shareholder or shareholders of the taxpayer corporation and such shareholder or shareholders are in control of both corporations;
- Investments in properties, or securities which are unrelated to the activities of the business of the taxpayer corporation; or
- Retention of earnings and profits to provide against unrealistic hazards. (Reg. § 1.537-2(c))

The rate of tax on improper accumulations is 15 percent after 2002 of accumulated taxable income.

.06 Manufacturing Deduction

Under Code Sec. 199(c)(1), qualified production activities income (QPAI) is the excess of domestic production gross receipts (DPGR) over the sum of:

a. The costs of goods sold allocable to such receipts;

b. Other deductions, expenses, or losses directly allocable to such receipts; and

c. A ratable portion of deductions, expenses, and losses not directly allocable to such receipts or another class of income.

The deduction is equal to 3 percent of the lesser of:

a. Qualified production activity income (QPAI), or

b. Taxable income.

Code Sec. 199(c)(4)(A) defines DPGR to mean the taxpayer's gross receipts that are derived from:

a. Any lease, rental, license, sale, exchange, or other disposition of (1) qualifying production property (QPP) that was manufactured, produced, grown, or extracted (MPGE) by the taxpayer in whole or in significant part with the United States; (2) any qualified film produced by the taxpayer; or (3) electricity, natural gas, or potable water (collectively, utilities) produced by the taxpayer in the United States.

b. Construction performed in the United States; or

c. Engineering or architectural services performed in the United States for construction projects in the United States.

Code Sec. 199(c)(4)(B) excepts from DPGR gross receipts of the taxpayer that are derived from:

a. The sale of food and beverages prepared by the taxpayer at a retail establishment;

b. The transmission or distribution of electricity, natural gas, or potable water; and

c. Gross receipts from ticket sales for viewing qualified films.

Distribution and delivery of QPP are not DPGR because distribution and delivery are properly regarded as services regardless of whether the taxpayer retains the benefits and burden of ownership of the property at the time it is delivered. As a matter of administrative convenience, the taxpayer can treat embedded distribution and delivery services similar to the qualified warranty exception.

Services and nonqualifying property are not considered embedded if they are either separately offered or separately bargained for, or a charge for the service or nonqualifying property is separately stated. Separately stated for bargained for amounts will not be respected unless they reflect the fair market value of the service or nonqualifying property.

The installation activity will be considered MPGE activity only if the contractor retains the benefits and burdens of ownership with respect to the parts while the parts are being installed. If the benefits and burdens of ownership pass to the customer prior to the installation of the QPP, the taxpayer is performing a service by installing the customer's property. It is appropriate to treat embedded installation similar to an embedded qualified warranty, qualified delivery, and a qualified operating manual.

Code Sec. 199(c)(7) provides that DPGR does not include any gross receipts of the taxpayer derived from property leased, licensed, or rented by the taxpayer for use by any related person. This rule does not apply to sales to related persons.

¶802.06

Taxpayers do not construct land and thus any gain attributable to the disposition of land (including zoning, planning, entitlement costs, and other cost capitalized to the land such as the demolition of structures under Code Sec. 280B) is not eligible for the Code Sec. 199 deduction. Income from land improvements such as adding roads, sidewalks, or utilities will receive the write-off.

A taxpayer must determine the portion of its gross receipts that is DPGR and the portion of its gross receipts that is non-DPGR. All of a taxpayer's gross receipts may be treated as DPGR if less than 5 percent of the taxpayer's total gross receipts are non-DPGR. If the amount of a taxpayer's gross receipts that do not qualify as DPGR equals or exceeds 5 percent of the taxpayer's total gross receipts, the taxpayer is required to allocate all gross receipts between DPGR and non-DPGR.

Gross receipts and costs are taken into account for purposes of computing QPAI in the taxable year they are recognized for federal income tax purposes under the taxpayer's methods of accounting, even if the related gross receipts or costs, as applicable, are taken into account in different taxable years.

Any reasonable method may be used to identify direct materials, direct labor, factory overhead, and general/administrative cost properly allocated to cost of goods sold (COGS). The method must be consistent with the approach used to determine DPGR. The principles under Code Secs. 263A and 861 (Income from Sources within the U.S.) should be utilized to determine if the allocation method is reasonable.

If the three-year prior gross receipts average $5 million or less, costs are allocated on the basis of the ratio of DPGR to total GR derived from all sources. If the three-year prior GR average is $25 million or less, the simplified method may be utilized to allocate all other costs associated with DPGR. Otherwise, the Code Sec. 861 method must be utilized.

Sec. 4.04(11)(a) of Notice 2005-14 defines the term "construction" to mean the construction or erection of real property by a taxpayer that is in a trade or business that is considered construction for purposes of the North American Industry Classification System (NAICS). In order for a taxpayer to be considered in a construction NAICS code, it must be engaged in a construction trade or business (but not necessarily its primary trade or business) on a regular and ongoing basis.

The amount of the deduction allowable to a taxpayer for any taxable year shall not exceed 50 percent of the W-2 wages of the taxpayer. Payments to independent contractors and self-employment income, including guaranteed payments made to partners, are not included in determining W-2 wages. In determining W-2 wages, a taxpayer may take into account any wages paid by another entity and reported by the other entity on Forms W-2 with the other entity as the employer listed in Box c of the Forms W-2, provided that the wages were paid to employees of the taxpayer for employment by the taxpayer (Prop. Reg. 1.199-2(a)(1)).

For employees leased from a third-party, common law employee definitions will determine who can apply the W-2 wages of the leased employees for Code Sec. 199. For employees leased through noncorporate related parties, there are issues as to whom may utilize the W-2 wages for Code Sec. 199.

Code Sec. 199(d)(1) provides that, in the case of an S corporation, partnership, estate, or trust, or other pass-through entity, Code Sec. 199 generally is applied at the shareholder, partner, or similar level, except as otherwise provided in rules applicable to patrons of cooperatives. DPGR, COGS, W-2 wages, and related expenses must be allocated to each owner. Code Sec. 199 does not apply to taxable years of pass-through entities beginning before January 1, 2005.

Code Sec. 199(d)(1)(B) provides that such person is treated as having been allocated W-2 wages from such entity in an amount equal to the lesser of:

  a. Such person's allocable share of such wages from such entity; or

  b. 2 times 3 percent of the QPAI of that entity allocated to such person for the taxable year.

The computation of a company's Code Sec. 199 deduction in computing alternative minimum taxable income (AMTI) is the same as in computing the regular tax, except that, in the case of a corporation, the taxable income limitation is the corporation's AMTI.

.07 Limited Liability Companies

In most cases, a multi-member limited liability company will be, or will elect to be, treated as a partnership. All 50 states and the District of Columbia permit the creation of limited liability companies in their jurisdictions. A limited liability company offers more advantages and greater flexibility than other passthrough entities, such as limited partnerships and S corporations. A typical limited liability company will limit the liability of its members for the debts of the company. A typical limited liability company will also provide for centralized management. Generally, all partnership attributes, such as basis, capital interests, flow through items, etc., carry over to the limited liability company.

Note: See Chapter 3, Business Entitites, for further discussion of limited liability companies and the "check-the-box" regulations on business entity classification for federal tax purposes.

The Treasury Department has issued regulations allowing unincorporated entities to elect to be treated as corporations or partnerships for tax purposes. The entities merely check a box on the tax return indicating their preference to be treated as a partnership, corporation, or a disregarded entity.

.09 Educational Assistance Plans

The term "educational assistance" means:

- The payment, by an employer, of expenses incurred by or on behalf of an employee for education of the employee (including, but not limited to, tuition, fees, and similar payments, books, supplies, and equipment);

- The provision, by an employer, of courses of instruction for such employee (including books, supplies, and equipment), but does not include payment for, or the provision of, tools or supplies which may be retained by the employee after completion of a course of instruction, or meals, lodging or transportation. (Code Sec. 127(c))

After the term "educational assistance" also includes any payment for, or the provision of any benefits with respect to, any graduate level course. $5,250 is the maximum exclusion of an educational assistance program. (Code Sec. 127(a)(2))

¶802.07

.11 Dependent Care Assistance Plans

Dependent Care Exclusion

Gross income of an employee does not include amounts paid or incurred by the employer for dependent care assistance provided to such employees if the assistance is furnished pursuant to a program. (Code Sec. 129(a)(1))

A dependent care assistance program is a separate written plan of an employer for the exclusive benefit of his employees to provide such employees with dependent care assistance. (Code Sec. 129(d)(1))

Limitation of Dependent Care Exclusion

The amount shall not exceed $5,000 ($2,500 in the case of a separate return by a married individual). (Code Sec. 129(a)(2))

No amount paid is excludable if paid to an individual:

- With respect to whom a deduction is allowable (for personal exemptions for dependents);
- Who is a child of such employee under the age of 19 at the close of such taxable year. (Code Sec. 129(c)(2)

Dependent Care Plan Specifics

Not more than 25 percent of the amounts paid or incurred by the employer for dependent care assistance during the year may be provided for the class of individuals who are shareholders or owners (or their spouses or dependents), each of whom (on any day of the year) owns more than five percent of the stock or of the capital or profits interest in the employer. (Code Sec. 129(d)(4))

Reasonable notification of the availability of the program must be provided to eligible employees. (Code Sec. 129(d)(6))

No funding is required regarding a dependent care program. (Code Sec. 129(d)(5))

The plan is required to furnish to an employee, on or before January 31, a written statement showing the amounts paid.

Certain employees may be excluded from the plan:

- Employees who have not attained the age of 21 and completed one year of service.
- Employees not included in a dependent care assistance program who are included in a unit of employees covered by a collective bargaining agreement. (Code Sec. 129(d)(9))

.12 Health Reimbursement Arrangements

The IRS has ruled that money provided by employers to employees to cover out-of-pocket medical expenses through a health reimbursement arrangement (HRA) is not subject to tax. And, unspent funds may be rolled over from one year to the next. If the employee retires or otherwise terminates employment, any unused reimbursement amount remaining in the HRA is unavailable. (Rev. Rul. 2002-41, 2002-28 IRB 75, IRS Notice 2002-45, 2002-28 IRB 93)

HRAs are not subject to the highly complicated rules that apply to flexible spending accounts (FSAs), which are often available under cafeteria plans. The IRS requires

HRAs to be funded solely by employer contributions. HRAs cannot be funded through a salary reduction agreement signed by an employee. HRAs can be used to reimburse for health insurance premiums. If the HRA provides for payments or other benefits irrespective of medical expenses, all amounts provided under the HRA become taxable, including previous medical reimbursements.

Medical expense reimbursement plans cannot apply retroactively. In December, a firm set up a plan to reimburse employees for medical expenses incurred during the year, even for costs arising before the plan was adopted. Payments for medical expenses incurred before the plan was set up are taxable, the IRS says. Only subsequent costs are reimbursable. (Rev. Rul. 2002-58)

.13 Fringe Benefits

Gross income shall not include any fringe benefit which qualifies as a:

- No-additional-cost service,
- Qualified employee discount,
- Working condition fringe,
- De minimis fringe,
- Qualified transportation fringe, and
- Qualified moving expense reimbursement. (Code Sec. 132(a))

No-additional-cost service means any service provided by an employer to an employee for use by such employee if:

- Such service is offered for sale to customers in the ordinary course of the line of business of the employer in which the employee is performing services, and
- The employer incurs no substantial additional cost in providing such service to the employee without regard to any amount. (Code Sec. 132(b))

Qualified employee discount means any employee discount with respect to qualified property or services to the extent such discount does not exceed:

- In the case of property, the gross profit percentage of the price at which the property is being offered by the employer to customers, or
- In the case of services, 20 percent of the price which the services are being offered by the employer to customers. (Code Sec. 132(c)(1))

The term "*de minimis* fringe" means any property or service the value of which is so small as to make accounting for it unreasonable or administratively impracticable. (Code Sec. 132(e)(1))

Limitation on Exclusion Regarding Vehicles

The amount of the fringe benefits which are provided by an employer to any employee and which may be excluded from gross income cannot exceed $110 per month for 2007 ($105 for 2006) in the case of the aggregate of auto travel benefits, and $215 per month for 2007 ($205 for 2006) in the case of qualified parking. (Code Sec. 132(f)(2))

No constructive receipt. No amount is included in the gross income of an employee solely because the employee may choose between any qualified transportation fringe and compensation which would otherwise be includible in gross income of such employee. (Code Sec. 132(f)(4))

Inflation adjustment. The dollar amounts allowed are increased by an inflation factor.

Fringe Benefits and Occasional Meal Money or Local Transportation Fare

Meals, meal money, or local transportation fare provided to an employee is a *de minimis* fringe benefit if the benefit provided is reasonable and is provided:

- On an occasional basis;
- With overtime. The meals, meal money, or local transportation fare is provided to an employee because overtime work necessitates an extension of the employee's normal work schedule. This condition does not fail to be satisfied merely because the circumstances giving rise to the need for overtime work are reasonably foreseeable; and
- As meal money. In the case of a meal or meal money, the meal or meal money is provided to enable the employee to work overtime. (Reg. § 1.132-6(d) (2))

Fringe Benefits Not Excludable as *De Minimis* Fringes

Examples of fringe benefits that are not excludable from gross income as *de minimis* fringes are: season tickets to sporting or theatrical events; the commuting use of an employer-provided automobile or other vehicle more than one day a month; membership in a private country club or athletic facility, regardless of the frequency with which the employee uses the facility; employer-provided group-term life insurance on the life of the spouse or child of an employee; and use of employer-owned or leased facilities (such as an apartment, hunting lodge, boat, etc.) for a weekend. (Reg. § 1.132-6(e) (2))

Fringe Benefit Nondiscrimination Rules

A highly compensated employee who receives a fringe is not permitted to exclude such benefit from income unless the benefit is available on substantially the same terms to:

- All employees of the employer; or
- A group of employees of the employer which is defined under a reasonable classification set up by the employer that does not discriminate in favor of highly compensated employees. (Reg. § 1.132-8(a) (1))

Fringe Benefits and Meals for Employer's Convenience

In determining whether meals are furnished for the convenience of the employer, the fact that a charge is made for such meals, and the fact that the employee may accept or decline such meals, shall not be taken into account. (Code Sec. 119(b) (2))

Meals Furnished to Employees on Business Premises Where Meals of Most Employees Are Otherwise Excludable

All meals furnished on the business premises of an employer to such employer's employees are treated as furnished for the convenience of the employer if, without regard to this paragraph, more than half of the employees to whom such meals are furnished on such premises are furnished such meals for the convenience of the employer. (Code Sec. 119(b) (4))

Employee Available for Emergency

Meals will be regarded as furnished for a substantial noncompensatory business reason of the employer when the meals are furnished to the employee during working hours to have the employee available for emergency call during the meals period. (Reg. § 1.119-1(a)(2)(i))

Restriction to Short Business Meal

Meals will be regarded as furnished for a substantial noncompensatory business reason of the employer when the meals are furnished to the employee during working hours because the employer's business is such that the employee must be restricted to a short meal period, such as 30 or 45 minutes, and because the employee could not be expected to eat elsewhere in such a short meal period.

Non-Availability of Proper Meal Source

Meals will be regarded as furnished for a substantial noncompensatory business reason of the employer when the meals are furnished to the employee during working hours because the employee could not otherwise secure proper meals within a reasonable meal period. For example, meals may qualify when there are insufficient eating facilities in the vicinity of the employer's premises. (Reg. § 1.119-1(a)(2)(ii)(c))

Meals Furnished to Restaurant Employees

A meal furnished to a restaurant employee or other food service employee for each meal period in which the employee works will be regarded as furnished for a substantial noncompensatory business reason of the employer, irrespective of whether the meal is furnished during, immediately before, or immediately after the working hours of the employee. (Reg. § 1.119v-1(a)(2)(ii)(d))

Lodging Specifics and Fringe Benefits

The value of lodging furnished to an employee by the employer is excluded from the employee's gross income if three tests are met:

— The lodging is furnished on the business premises of the employer,

— The lodging is furnished for the convenience of the employer, and

— The employee is required to accept such lodging as a condition of his employment.

This means that the employee be required to accept the lodging in order to enable the employee properly to perform the duties of employment. (Reg. § 1.119-1(b))

Valuation of Fringe Benefits

An employee must include in gross income the amount by which the fair market value of the fringe benefit exceeds the sum of:

• The amount, if any, paid for the benefit by or on behalf of the recipient, and

• The amount, if any, specifically excluded from gross income by some other section. (Reg. § .61-21(b)(1))

> *Example:* The employer allows an employee to use the company automobile for personal purposes during the year. The personal use is valued at $1,500. The employee reimburses the employer $800 for the personal use of the automobile. The employee must include $700 in income, the excess of the personal use value over the employee's reimbursement to the employer.

.15 Cafeteria Plan

An employee may receive certain employer-sponsored benefits that represent a form of compensation. However, these employer-sponsored benefits are tax free to the employee if certain conditions are met and are deductible by the employer. Other than educational assistance and dependent care assistance discussed above, examples of employer-sponsored benefits include group-term life insurance, health and hospitalization insurance, meals and lodging, scholarships and fellowships, and vanpooling.

Certain of these employer-sponsored benefits may be placed in a cafertia plan offered by the employer. The employee is able to select the benefits they need and desire. Certain employer-sponsored benefits specifically excluded from cafeteria plans include qualified scholarships, educational assistance, and fringe benefits discussed above.

The term "cafeteria plan" means a written plan under which:

- All participants are employees, and
- The participants may choose among two or more benefits consisting of cash and qualified benefits. (Code Sec. 125(d)(1))

No amount is included in the gross income of a participant in a cafeteria plan solely because, under the plan, the participant may choose among the benefits of the plan. (Code Sec. 125(a))

Discrimination

This exclusion from gross income does not apply to any benefit attributable to a plan year for which the plan discriminates in favor of:

- Highly compensated individuals as to eligibility to participate, or
- Highly compensated participants as to contributions and benefits. (Code Sec. 125(b)(1))

Highly Compensated Participant

The term "highly compensated participant" means a participant who is:

- An officer,
- A shareholder owning more than five percent of the voting power or value of all classes of stock of the employer,
- Highly compensated, or
- A spouse or dependent of an individual described above. (Code Sec. 125(e)(1))

Health Benefits

A cafeteria plan which provides health benefits is not treated as discriminatory if:

- Contributions under the plan on behalf of each participant include an amount which:
- Equals 100 percent of the cost of the health benefit coverage under the plan of the majority of the highly compensated participants similarly situated; or
- Equals or exceeds 75 percent of the cost of the health benefit coverage of the participant having the highest cost health benefit coverage under the plan; and

- Contributions or benefits under the plan in excess of those described in the previous sentence bear in uniform relationship to compensation. (Code Sec. 125(g)(2))

   Example: Assume a typical employee pays the following nondeductible expenses on a monthly basis:

$400	Dependent Medical Insurance
250	Medical Cost Not Covered by Insurance
150	Disability Insurance
$800	

Without a cafeteria plan the employee receives wages of $4,000 per month and pays the $800 in nondeductible expenses. The employee net spendable income computed below is $2,592. If the employer were to reduce each employee's pay by $800 per month and install an $800 per month maximum benefit cafeteria plan, the employee's net spendable income increases to $2,773. The $181 savings per month creates a $2,172 yearly savings that results from the 15 percent income tax savings plus the 7.65 percent social security savings.

	Without Plan	With Plan
Monthly Income	$4,000	$4,000
Cafe Plan Expense	0	(800)
Taxable Income	$4,000	$3,200
Less Taxes		
W/H	(302)	(182)
F.I.C.A.	(306)	(245)
Adjusted Net Pay	$3,392	$2,773

	Without Plan	With Plan
Personal Expenses:		
Health Ins.	400	
Medical Exp.	250	
Disability Insurance	150	
	800	
Net Spendable Income w/o Plan		$2,592
Net Spendable Income with Plan		$2,773
Net Savings Per Month		$181
Net Savings Per Year ($181 × 12)		$2,172

The employer also realizes payroll tax savings on all compensation dollars redirected into the Cafeteria Plan. The payroll savings are 7.65 percent on wages below the FICA wage base of $92,400 for 2006 and 1.45 percent on wages above $92,400 ($97,500 for 2007).

.17 Reimbursements or Allowances

Reimbursements and Other Expense Allowance Arrangements

An arrangement will not be treated as a reimbursement or other expense allowance arrangement if:

- Such arrangement does not require the employee to substantiate the expenses covered by the arrangement to the payor.

- Such arrangement provides the employee the right to retain any amount in excess of the substantiated expenses covered under the arrangement. (Regs. § 1.62-2(b))

- The plan does not require the employee to return to the payor within a reasonable period of time any amount paid under the arrangement in excess of the expenses substantiated. (Regs. § 1.62-2(f)(1))

A payor may have more than one arrangement with respect to a particular employee. (Regs. § 1.62-2(c))

.19 Treatment of Payments

Treatment of Payments Under Accountable Plans

Amounts treated as paid under an accountable plan are excluded from the employee's gross income, are not required to be reported on the employee's Form W-2, and are exempt from the withholding and payment of employment taxes (FICA and FUTA). (Regs. § 1.62-2(c)(4))

Treatment of Payments Under Non-Accountable Plans

Amounts treated as paid under a non-accountable plan are included in the employee's gross income, must be reported to the employee on Form W-2, and are subject to withholding and payment of employment taxes (FICA and FUTA and income tax). (Regs. § 1.62-2(d))

.21 Returning Excess Within Reasonable Period

Fixed Date Method—as Reasonable Period

An advance made within 30 days of when an expense is paid or incurred, an expense substantiated to the payor within 60 days after it is paid or incurred, or an amount returned to the payor within 120 days after an expense is paid or incurred is treated as having occurred within a reasonable period of time. (Regs. § 1.62-2(g)(2)(i))

Periodic Statement Method—as Reasonable Period

If a payor provides employees with periodic statements (no less frequently than quarterly) stating the amount, if any, paid under the arrangement in excess of the expenses the employee has substantiated, and requesting the employee to substantiate any additional business expenses that have not yet been substantiated (whether or not such expenses relate to the expenses with respect to which the original advance was paid) and/or to return any amounts remaining unsubstantiated within 120 days of the statement, an expense substantiated or an amount returned within that period is treated as being substantiated or returned within a reasonable period of time. (Regs. § 1.62-2(g)(ii))

¶802.21

Withholding

If the expenses covered under an arrangement are not substantiated to the payor within a reasonable period of time, or if any amounts in excess of the substantiated expenses are not returned to the payor within a reasonable period of time; the amount which is treated as paid under a non-accountable plan is subject to withholding and payment of employment taxes no later than the first payroll period following the end of the reasonable period. (Regs. § 1.62-2(h))

.23 Depreciation

Over the years various depreciation methods have been placed into law. First we had system called Guideline Life where the government provided expected lives of various depreciable assets. This was followed by a system called Asset Depreciation Range (ADR) where the lives from Guideline Life were converted into a range of years for each asset. In 1981, Congress passed the Accelerated Cost Recovery System (ACRS) which was an adaption of of the ADR system that placed all assets into 3, 5, 10, or 15 year lives. The lives under ACRS were significantly shorter than under the previous ADR system. The Tax Reform Act of 1986 made some modification to ACRS. The present depreciation system is referred to as MACRS (Modified Accelerated Cost Recovery System). Technically we are no longer under a depreciation system but under cost recovery. When a taxpayer acquires and begins depreciating an asset, the taxpayer stays under that depreciation system even though a new depreciation system becomes law.

Modified Accelerated Cost Recovery System

Depreciation shall be determined by using:

- The applicable recovery period,
- The applicable depreciation method, and
- The applicable convention. (Code Sec. 168(a))

Applicable Depreciation Method

The applicable depreciation method is:

- The 200 percent declining balance method (150 percent for 15 and 20 year property),
- Switching to the straight-line method for the first taxable year for which using the straight-line method with respect to the adjusted basis as of the beginning of such year will yield a larger allowance. (Code Sec. 168(b)(1))

The applicable depreciation method shall be the straight-line method in the case of the following property:

- Nonresidential real property.
- Residential rental property. (Code Sec. 168(b)(3))

An election may be made to use straight-line depreciation with respect to one or more classes of property for any taxable year and once made with respect to any class shall apply to all property in such class placed in service during such taxable year. Such an election, once made, shall be irrevocable. (Code Sec. 168(b)(5))

The basis of depreciation is not required to be reduced by the salvage value. (Code Sec. 168(b)(4))

¶802.23

Year to Switch to Straight-Line Method

Class Year	Declining Balance Rate	Year
3	66.67%	3rd
5	40%	4th
7	28.57%	5th
10	20%	7th
15	10%	7th
20	7.5%	9th

(IRS Pub. 534)

Half-Year Convention

The half-year convention is a convention which treats all property placed in service during any taxable year as placed in service on the mid-point of such taxable year. (Code Sec. 168(d)(4)(A))

Mid-Quarter Convention

The mid-quarter convention is a convention which treats all property placed in service during any quarter of a taxable year as placed in service on the mid-point of such quarter. (Code Sec. 168(d)(4)(C))

If During Any Taxable Year

- The aggregate bases of tangible personal property placed in service during the last three months of the taxable year exceed 40 percent of the aggregate bases of tangible personal property placed in service during such taxable year, the applicable convention shall be the mid-quarter convention. (Code Sec. 168(d)(3))

Classification of Certain Property

3-Year Property

1. Property with an ADR class life of four years or less except autos and light-duty trucks.
2. Race horses that are more than two years old when placed in service and any other horses that are more than 12-years old when placed in service.

5-Year Property

1. Property with an ADR class life of more than four years and less than 10 years.
2. Automobiles and light duty trucks.
3. Research and experimentation equipment.

7-Year Property

1. Property with an ADR class life of 10 or more years but less than 16 years.
2. Property which does not have a class life.

10-Year Property

1. Property with an ADR class life of 16 or more years but less than 20 years.
2. Single purpose agricultural or horticultural structure.
3. Any tree or vine bearing fruit.

¶802.23

15-Year Property

1. Property with an ADR class life of 20 or more years but less than 25 years.
2. Any municipal wastewater treatment plant.

20-Year Property

1. Property with an ADR class life of 25 or more years.
2. Any municipal sewers.

27.5-Year Property

1. Residential real property.

39-Year Property

1. Nonresidential real property.

.25 Section 1245 Depreciable Personal Property Used in a Trade or Business

The purpose of section 1245 is to prevent taxpayers from taking ordinary depreciation deductions and then receiving long-term capital gain treatment through section 1231 at the time of sale of the property.

Ordinary Income—Gain from Disposition of Certain Depreciable Property

On the disposition of section 1245 property, ordinary income is recognized to the extent of the total depreciation taken (including immediate expensing under section 179), but not to exceed the realized gain from the disposition.

> *Example:* Alex purchased a machine for use in his business for $10,000. After taking $3,600 in depreciation, he sold the asset for $8,000. He will recognize the entire $1,600 ($8,000 - ($10,000 - $3,600)) gain from the sale as ordinary income. Had he sold the asset for $11,000, only the $3,600 in depreciation taken would be recaptured as ordinary income. The remaining $1,000 of gain is section 1231 gain.

Losses. Section 1245 does not apply to losses. Thus if Alex sold the asset for $6,000, the $400 loss would be section 1231 loss and no depreciation recapture would apply.

.27 Section 1250 Depreciable Real Property of a Business or Trade

If section 1250 property is disposed, the basic depreciation recapture rule states that only the excess of accelerated depreciation over straight-line depreciation is recaptured as ordinary income.

Thus, section 1250 property depreciated under MACRS will have no depreciation recapture since both residential real estate and nonresidential require straight-line depreciation.

Section 1250 property depreciated under ACRS has some special rules. Residential real estate depreciated using accelerated methods requires only the depreciation recapture of the excess of the accelerated depreciation over straight-line depreciation. Nonresidential real estate depreciated using accelerated methods requires full depreciation recapture under the section 1245 rules. Nonresidential real estate using the straight-line method required no depreciation recapture.

Real estate acquired prior to the implementation of ACRS requires the recapture of the excess of accelerated depreciation over straight-line depreciation. However, the amount of depreciation recapture may be reduced for assets acquired before 1977 based on the amount of time the asset is held.

Section 291 subjects corporations to an additional depreciation rule. A corporation must report 20 percent of the excess of any amount that would be treated as ordinary income under Sec. 1245 over the amount treated as ordinary income under Sec. 1250 as ordinary income.

When a Section 1250 asset is sold there is a special computation for what is referred to as "unrecaptured Section 1250 gain." Unrecaptured Section 1250 gain is the amount of long-term gain that would be treated as ordinary income if the asset had been a Section 1245 asset. The unrecaptured Section 1250 gain is subject to a maximum 25 percent tax rate.

> **Example:** Alpha Corporation purchased a building for $390,000. After taking $50,000 in depreciation, the building was sold for $450,000. The gain on the sale is $110,000 ($450,000 - ($390,000 - $50,000)). Assuming no Section 1231 losses for the year, $50,000 of the gain will be unrecaptured Section 1250 gain taxed at 25%; the remaining $60,000 of the gain will be taxed at 20%.

When an asset is sold on the installment method of accounting, any depreciation recapture must be reported as ordinary income in the year of sale. The depreciation recapture amount is added to basis for determining the remaining gross profit, contract price, and gross profit percentage.

.29 Example of Installment Sale With Depreciation Recapture

Facts:

Cost of building acquired in 1977	$190,000
Accelerated depreciation to date	35,000
If straight line depreciation used	12,000
Capital improvements	25,000
Building sold 1/1/06 for	225,000
Cash down	50,000
Expenses of sale	10,000
Note received	175,000
Payments received in 2006	15,000
Payments received in 2007	30,000

Installment Sale Computation

Part I: Gross Profit

1.	Cash down payment	$50,000	
2.	Mortgage assumed by purchaser	0	
3.	Mortgage carried by seller	175,000	
4.	Fair Market Value of other property received	————	
5.	Total sales price (Combine lines 1 - 4)		225,000
6.	Expense of sale		(10,000)
7.	Adjusted sales price		205,000
8.	Original cost or other basis	190,000	
9.	Capital improvements	25,000	
10.	Less: Depreciation	(35,000)	

11.	Adjusted basis		180,000
12.	Realized gain (line 7 less line 11)		25,000
13.	Depreciation recapture (if applicable)		
	Excess of accelerated depreciation	35,000	
	Over straight line depreciation	- 12,000	(23,000)
14.	Gross profit (subtract line 13 from line 12)		$2,000

Part II: Contract Price

15.	Mortgage assumed by purchaser (line 2 above)	0
16.	Recomputed basis (combine line 11 and line 13)	203,000
17.	Excess of mortgage assumed over basis (subtract line 16 from line 15)	0
18.	Contract price (subtract line 17 from line 5)	225,000
19.	Gross profit ratio (divide line 14 by line 18)	.8889%

Part III: Summary of Reportable Gain

Tax Year	Payment Received	Gross Profit %	Gain Reported
Recapture	-0-	100%	$23,000
1	50,000 + 15,000	.8889%	578
2	30,000	.8889%	267
etc.			

Proof: $225,000
           × .8889%
           _____
           2,000

.31 Section 179 Depreciation and Additional First-Year Depreciation

The amount of tangible business property that may be current expenses under Code Sec. 179, rather than depreciated over time, has been increased to $100,000. The increase was phased in over a seven-year period beginning in 1997. After 2003, the amount is indexed for inflation.

Year	Maximum Deduction
1997	$18,000
1998	$18,500
1999	$19,000
2000	$20,000
2001	$24,000
2003	$100,000
2004	$102,000
2005	$105,000
2006	$108,000
2007	$112,000

Taxpayers were allowed to claim an additional first-year depreciation allowance on new MACRS property for which the recovery period is 20 year or less, MACRS water utility property, computer software which is depreciable under Sec. 167, and qualified leasehold improvement property. The additional allowance is equal to 30 percent of the adjusted basis of the property after reduction by the Sec. 179 expense allowance. The allowance applies to property acquired after September 10, 2001, and before September 11, 2004, and placed in service before January 1, 2005. The additonal bonus depreciation is 50 percent for assets acquired after May 5, 2003.

IRS has issued an automatic consent procedure for correcting underdepreciation on property still owned by the taxpayer. No user fee required for making the change. Form 3115 must be filed with the IRS national office by the end-of-the year of change. The difference between the total amount of depreciation that should have been claimed and what was actually claimed is a Section 481 adjustment taken into account in the year of change. The taxpayer is required to own the asset on the first day of the tax year for which Form 3115 is filed.

.33 Depreciation for Business Use of Car Table

Depreciation for Business Use of Car

Maximum Limits[1]—Cars Placed in Service After 1986

Placed in Service	Depreciation First Year[2]	Depreciation Later Years
1987-1988	$2,560	$4,100 2nd yr.
		2,450 3rd yr.
		1,475[3]
1989-1990	$2,660	$4,200 2nd yr.
		2,550 3rd yr.
		1,475[3]
1991	$2,660	$4,300 2nd yr.
		2,550 3rd yr.
		1,575[3]
1992	$2,760	$4,400 2nd yr.
		2,650 3rd yr.
		1,575[3]
1993	$2,860	$4,600 2nd yr.
		2,750 3rd yr.
		1,675[3]
1994	$2,960	$4,700 2nd yr.
		2,850 3rd yr.
		1,675[3]
1995-1996	$3,060	$4,900 2nd yr.
		2,950 3rd yr.
		1,775[3]
1997	$3,160	5,000 2nd yr.
		3,050 3rd yr.
		1,775[3]
1998	$3,160	$5,000 2nd yr.
		2,950 3rd yr.
		1,775[3]
1999	$3,060	$5,000 2nd yr.
		2,950 3rd yr.
		1,775[3]

Maximum Limits[1]—Cars Placed in Service After 1986

Placed in Service	Depreciation First Year[2]	Depreciation Later Years
2000-2003	$3,060	4,900 2nd yr.
		2,950 3rd yr.
		1,775[3]
2004	$2,960	4,800 2nd yr.
		2,850 3rd yr.
		1,675[3]
2005	$2,960	4,700 2nd yr.
		2,850 3rd yr.
		1,675[3]
2006	$2,960	4,800 2nd yr.
		2,850 3rd yr.
		1,775[3]

[1] These amounts must be reduced if the car is used less than 100% for business purposes.

[2] This is the maximum amount of your section 179 deduction and depreciation allowed for the tax year the car is placed in service.

[3] This amount is also the limit on deductions taken in years after the recovery period.

Source: IRS Pub. 534

.35 Basis Summary Chart

Basis for Computing Gain or Loss, and Holding Period on Property Acquired in Common Transactions

Type of Acquisition	Basis for Gains or Losses	Holding Period Begins
Purchase	Purchase price PLUS acquisition and installation charges	On date of acquisition
Inherited Property decedent's death	FMV on date of decedent's death	Considered Held Long Term
Acquired by nontaxable exchange	Basis of old property traded-in PLUS any boot paid	Begins on date old property trade-in was acquired
Repossessed real property by seller	Adjusted basis of the debt due, PLUS gain from the repossession, PLUS any repossession expenses	Includes both the holding period before the sale and after the repossession
Residence after sale of old residence without recognition of gain under § 1034	Cost of new residence LESS gain NOT recognized	Begins on date original home was acquired and on which gain has been deferred
Gift Property: Sold at a GAIN	Donor's basis	On date donor's holding period began
Gift Property: Sold at a LOSS	Lesser of: — Donor's basis, or — FMV of property at time of gift	— On date donor's holding period began — Begins on date of gift

.37 Automobile Expenses

Reporting Car Expenses and Reimbursements

Type of Reimbursement expense (or other account arrangement) Accountable	Employer Reports on Form W-2	Employee Shows on Form 2106
Actual expense reimbursement Adequate accounting and excess returned	Not reported	Not shown if expenses do not exceed reimbursement
Actual expense reimbursement Adequate accounting and return of excess required but excess not returned	Excess reported as wages in Box 1. Amount adequately accounted for is reported only in Box 12 it is not reported in Box 1.*	All expenses and reimbursements reported on Form W-2, Box 1, only if some or all of the unreturned expenses are claimed. Otherwise, form is not filed.
Mileage allowance (up to standard mileage rate). Adequate accounting and excess returned	Not reported.	All expenses and reimbursements only if excess expenses are claimed.* Otherwise, form is not filed.
Mileage allowance (exceeds standard mileage rate). Adequate accounting up to the standard mileage rate only and excess not returned.	Excess reported as wages in Box 1. Amount up to the standard mileage rate is reported only in Box 12 it is not reported in Box 1.	All expenses and reimbursements equal to the standard mileage rate only if expenses in excess of the standard mileage rate are claimed.* Otherwise, form is not filed.
Non-accountable		
Either adequate accounting or return of excess, or both, not required by plan.	Entire amount is reported as wages in Box 1.	All expenses.*
No reimbursement.	Normal reporting of wages, etc.	All expenses.*

* Any allowable business expense is carried to Schedule A and deducted as a miscellaneous itemized deduction. Subject to the 2% disallowance.

.39 Automobile Fixed and Variable Rate Allowance Revenue Procedure 2003-76 Summary

Fixed and Variable Rate (FAVR)

- Must be based on data:

    — Derived from the base locality

    — Reflect retail prices paid by consumers

    — Be reasonably and statistically defensible in approximating actual expenses

- FAVR includes periodic fixed and periodic variable payments.

- Mileage allowance is a payment or reimbursement paid at a flat rate, a standard mileage rate, or a stated schedule.

- The rate must be applied uniformly and objectively to all employees that participate.
- Business mileage percentage use:
  - Business percentage is annual business mileage divided by total mileage.
  - The business use may not exceed 75 percent.

The following percentage may be used in lieu of actual mileage:

Mileage	Business Use %
6,250 - 9,999	45%
10,000 - 14,999	55%
15,000 - 19,999	65%
20,000 or more	75%

- A FAVR allowance may be paid only to an employee who substantiates to the employer at least 5,000 miles per year.
  - For use less than calendar year, prorate on a monthly basis.
- Depreciation
  - A FAVR allowance may not be paid with respect to an automobile for which the employee has claimed:
    - Depreciation other than straight-line
    - Additional first year depreciation
    - Depreciation using MACRS
- A majority of the employees covered by a FAVR allowance cannot be management employees.
- A FAVR may not be paid to a control employee.
- At least 10 employees must be covered by one or more FAVR allowances at all times.
- The employee must provide to the payor within 30 days:
  - Purchase price of auto
  - Depreciation method claimed
  - Make, model, and year of auto
  - Proof of insurance coverage
  - Odometer reading
- The payor must maintain written records setting forth:
  - Statistical data on which FAVR payments are based.
  - Information provided by employees.

.41 Auto Lease Valuation

If an employer provides an employee with an automobile that is available to the employee for an entire calendar year, the value of the benefit provided is the Annual Lease Value of that automobile. For an automobile that is available to an employer for less than an entire calendar year, the value of the benefit provided is either a pro-rated Annual Lease Value, or the Daily Lease Value, whichever is applicable. (Regs. § 1.61-21(d)(i))

¶802.41

Annual Lease Value Table

Automobile Fair Market Value (1)	Annual Lease Value (2)
$0 to 999	$600
1,000 to 1,999	850
2,000 to 2,999	1,100
3,000 to 3,999	1,350
4,000 to 4,999	1,600
5,000 to 5,999	1,850
6,000 to 6,999	2,100
7,000 to 7,999	2,350
8,000 to 8,999	2,600
9,000 to 9,999	2,850
10,000 to 10,999	3,100
11,000 to 11,999	3,350
12,000 to 12,999	3,600
13,000 to 13,999	3,850
14,000 to 14,999	4,100
15,000 to 15,999	4,350
16,000 to 16,999	4,600
17,000 to 17,999	4,850
18,000 to 18,999	5,100
19,000 to 19,999	5,350
20,000 to 20,999	5,600
21,000 to 21,999	5,850
22,000 to 22,999	6,100
23,000 to 23,999	6,350
24,000 to 24,999	6,600
25,000 to 25,999	6,850
26,000 to 27,999	7,250
28,000 to 29,999	7,750
30,000 to 31,999	8,250
32,000 to 33,999	8,750
34,000 to 35,999	9,250
36,000 to 37,999	9,750
38,000 to 39,999	10,250
40,000 to 41,999	10,750
42,000 to 43,999	11,250
44,000 to 45,999	11,750
46,000 to 47,999	12,250

Automobile Fair Market Value	Annual Lease Value
48,000 to 49,999	12,750
50,000 to 51,999	13,250
52,000 to 53,999	13,750
54,000 to 55,999	14,250
56,000 to 57,999	14,750
58,000 to 59,999	15,250

For vehicles having a fair market value in excess of $59,999, the annual lease value is equal to: (.25 × the fair market value of the automobile) + $500. (Regs. § 1.61-21(d)(2)(iii))

Standard Auto Mileage Rate (2000-2007)

Year	2000	2001	2002	2003	2004	2005	2006	2007
All business mileage	.325	.345	.365	.36	.375	.485	.445	.485
Charity work	.14	.14	.14	.14	.14	.22	.18	.20
Moving or medical	.10	.12	.13	.12	.14	.22	.18	.20

Standard Mileage Rate with Taxes and Interest for Self-Employed

Taxpayers can claim any related parking fees and tolls, in addition to claiming the standard mileage rate. Taxpayers are also allowed to deduct interest expense related to purchasing the vehicle and state or local taxes (other than those included in the cost of gasoline) that relate to the business (or charitable, medical, or moving) use of the vehicle to the extent such expenses are otherwise allowable under Code Sec. 163 or 164 (Rev. Proc. 2003-76).

Example (1): Taxpayer is self-employed and uses his automobile in his business. He did keep a record of mileage showing that 8,000 of the 14,000 miles he put on the car in 2006 were business related.

He also paid $1,000 of interest on the loan used to buy the car and $900 of property taxes related to the car.

By using the standard mileage rate, the taxpayer can claim the following expenses related to using her car for business purposes in 2006:

8,000 miles at 44.5 cents/mile	$3,560
Allocable interest expense (8,000 / 14,000 × $1,000)	571
Allocable property taxes (8,000 / 14,000 × $900)	514
	$4,645

Example (2): Assume the same facts above except that the taxpayer is an employee rather than self-employed, and the $900 was for sales taxes paid on the purchase of the car in 2006. The employer did not reimburse the taxpayer for any of the costs of using the car.

Because the taxpayer is an employee rather than self employed, the unreimbursed business expenses have to be reported on Form 2106 and claimed on Form 1040,

¶802.41

Schedule A, as miscellaneous itemized deductions subject to the two percent of adjusted gross income floor. None of the $900 in sales taxes is deductible but instead adds to the basis of the car (Code Sec. 164(a)). The taxpayer does not get any deduction for the interest expense on the car note because interest on debt allocable to the trade or business of performing services as an employee is treated as personal interest. ((Code Sec. 163(h)(2)(A))

.42 Expensing of Roof Repairs

The Tax Court's Small Tax Case Division allowed a deduction for the $8,000 cost of removing and replacing the roof-covering material on the roof of a rental house. There was no replacement or substitution of the roof. The only purpose in having the work done to the roof was to prevent the leakage and keep the rental house in operating condition and not to prolong the life of the property, increase its value, or make it adaptable to another use. (*Nevia Campbell*, TC Summary Opinion 2002-117)

The Tax Court had previously come to the same conclusion when it observed that the taxpayer's only purpose was to prevent leakage and keep the leased property in operating condition over its probable useful life and not to prolong the life of the property, increase its value, or make it adaptable to another use. (*Oberman Manufacturing Co.*, 47 TC 471 (1967))

.43 Bad Debts

Deductible bad debts are:

- *Wholly worthless debts.* A deduction is allowed for any debt which becomes worthless within the taxable year.

- *Partially worthless debts.* When satisfied that a debt is recoverable only in part, an amount not in excess of the part charged off within the taxable year is allowed as a deduction. Partial worthlessness only applies to business bad debts. Nonbusiness bad debts can only be deducted when they become worthless. Code Sec. 166(a))

A bona fide debt is a debt which arises from a debtor-creditor relationship based upon a valid and enforceable obligation to pay a fixed or determinable sum of money. A gift or contribution to capital is not considered a debt. (Regs. § 1.166-1(c))

The following amounts are deductible as bad debts:

- Notes or accounts receivable.

- *Bankruptcy claim.* Only the difference between the amount received in distribution of the assets of a bankrupt and the amount of the claim may be deducted as a bad debt. (Regs. § 1.166-1(d))

Deduction Amount

The basis for determining the amount of the deduction for any bad debt is the adjusted basis for determining the loss from the sale or other disposition of property. (Code Sec. 166(b))

Prior Inclusion in Income Required for Deductibility

Worthless debts are not allowed as a deduction unless the income such items represent has been included in the return of income for the year for which the deduction as a bad debt is claimed or for a prior taxable year. (Regs. § 1.166-1(e)) Thus, cash basis taxpayers are not allowed a bad debt deduction for an uncollected receivable.

Recovery of Bad Debts

Any amount attributable to the recovery during the taxable year of a bad debt, or of a part of a bad debt, which was allowed as a deduction from gross income in a prior taxable year is included in gross income for the taxable year of recovery. (Regs. § 1.166-1(f))

Non-Business Debt Defined

A non-business debt is defined as a debt other than:

- A debt created or acquired (as the case may be) in connection with a trade or business of the taxpayer; or
- A debt the loss from the worthlessness of which is incurred in the taxpayer's trade or business. (Code Sec. 166.(d)(2))

Allowance of Deduction as Capital Loss

In the case of a taxpayer other than a corporation:

- The allowance in total as an ordinary deduction will not apply to any non-business debt.
- Where any non-business debt becomes worthless within the taxable year, the loss resulting is considered a loss from the sale or exchange, during the taxable year, of a capital asset held for not more than one year. (Code Sec. 166(d)(1))

The loss resulting from any non-business debt's becoming partially or wholly worthless within the taxable year is not allowed as a deduction in determining the taxable income of a taxpayer other than a corporation. (Regs. § 1.166-5(a))

.45 Sole Proprietor Employing Child Under Age 18

Significant tax savings can be achieved when a sole proprietor parent employs a child under18. The parent is allowed a deduction for reasonable wages and wages paid to a child under 18 are not subject to employment taxes.

Example:

Assumptions:

Parent's tax rate	= 28%
Social Security rate	= 7.65%
Standard deduction	= $5,000
Child's tax rate	= 10%
Child's wages	= $8,000

1.	Parent's tax savings:	$8,000	
	Tax rate	× .28	
			$2,240
2.	Parent's SE saved:	$8,000	
	SE tax rate (2 × 7.65) =	× .153	
			$1,224
	Gross parent tax savings		$3,464

Less: Child's Tax:	
Gross income	$8,000
- No exemption allowed	0
- Standard deduction	5,000
	$3,000
Child's tax rate	×.10
	300
Net tax savings	3,164

.47 Entertainment Expenses

"Entertainment" means any activity which is of a type generally considered to constitute entertainment, amusement, or recreation, such as entertaining at night clubs, cocktail lounges, theaters, country clubs, golf and athletic clubs, and sporting events. It also includes hunting, fishing, vacation, and similar trips, including such activity relating solely to the taxpayer or the taxpayer's family. (Regs. § 1.274-2(b)(1)(i))

An objective test is used to determine whether an activity is of a type generally considered to constitute entertainment (Regs. § 1.274-2(b)(1)(ii)) unless the taxpayer substantiates by adequate records or by sufficient evidence corroborating the taxpayer's own statement:

- The amount of such expenses or other item,
- The time and place of the travel, entertainment, amusement, recreation, or use of the facility or property, or the description of the gift,
- The business purpose, and
- The business relationship to the taxpayer of persons entertained. (Code Sec. 274(d))

No deduction is allowed for any expenditure with respect to entertainment unless the taxpayer establishes:

- That the expenditure was directly related to the active conduct of the taxpayer's trade or business; and
- In the case of an expenditure directly preceding or following a substantial and bona fide business discussion (including business meetings at a convention or otherwise), that the expenditure was associated with the active conduct of the taxpayer's trade or business. (Regs. § 1.274-2(a)(1))

Such deduction may not exceed the portion of the expenditure directly related to the active conduct of the taxpayer's trade or business. (Regs. § 1.274-2(a)(1))

Expenditures Generally Considered Not Directly Related Regarding Entertainment

Expenditures for entertainment, even if connected with the taxpayer's trade or business, will generally be considered not directly related to the active conduct of the taxpayer's trade or business if the entertainment occurred under circumstances where there was little or no possibility of engaging in the active conduct of trade or business. The following circumstances will generally be considered circumstances where there was little or no possibility of engaging in the active conduct of a trade or business:

- The taxpayer was not present;

- The distractions were substantial, such as: a meeting or discussion at night clubs, theaters, and sporting events, or during essentially social gatherings such as cocktail parties; or
- A meeting or discussion, if the taxpayer meets with a group which includes persons other than business associates, at places such as cocktail lounges, country clubs, golf and athletic clubs, or at vacation resorts. An expenditure for entertainment in any such case is considered not to be directly related to the active conduct of the taxpayer's trade or business unless the taxpayer clearly establishes to the contrary. (Regs. § 1.274-2(c)(7))

Specific Exceptions to Disallowance of Certain Entertainment Expenses

The disallowance rules do not apply to:

- Expenses for food and beverages furnished on the business premises of the taxpayer primarily for his or her employees; (Code Sec. 274(e)(1))
- Expenses treated as compensation; (Code Sec. 274(e)(2))
- Reimbursed expenses; (Code Sec. 274(e)(3))
- Expenses for recreational, social, or similar activities including facilities primarily for the benefit of employees other than employees who are highly compensated employees; (Code Sec. 274(e)(4))
- Expenses incurred by a taxpayer which are directly related to business meetings of the taxpayer's employees, stockholders, agents, or directors; (Code Sec. 274(e)(5))
- Meetings of business leagues, etc; (Code Sec. 274(e)(6))
- Expenses for goods, services, and facilities made available by the taxpayer to the general public; (Code Sec. 274(7))
- Expenses for goods or services (including the use of facilities) which are sold by the taxpayer in a bona fide transaction for an adequate and full consideration in money or money's worth; and (Code Sec. 274(e)(8))
- Expenses paid or incurred by the taxpayer for goods, services, and facilities to the extent that the expenses are includable in the gross income of a recipient of the entertainment, amusement, or recreation who is not an employee of the taxpayer as compensation for services rendered. (Code Sec. 274(e)(9))

Only 50 Percent of Meal and Entertainment Expenses Allowed as Deduction

The amount allowable as a deduction for:

- Any expense for food or beverages, and
- Any item with respect to an activity which is of a type generally considered to constitute entertainment, amusement, or recreation, or with respect to a facility used in connection with such activity, can not exceed 50 percent of the amount of such expense or item. (Code Sec. 274(n)(1))

Exceptions to 50-Percent Rule

- Such expenses are:
  - Treated as compensation;
  - Reimbursed expenses;

— Recreational expenses for employees;

— Items available to the public;

— Entertainment sold to customers; and

— Expenses includable in income of persons who are not employees.

- In the case of an expense for food or beverages, if such expense is excludable from the gross income, such expenses are considered *de minimis* fringes.

- In the case of an employer who pays or reimburses moving expenses of an employee, such expenses that may be includable in the income of the employee under Code Sec. 82. (Code Sec. 274(n)(2))

Application of the 50-Percent Limitation on Meal Expenses for Entertainment

When a per diem for meal and incidental expenses is computed using the optional method, an amount equal to the lesser of the per diem allowance or the federal M&IE rate for the locality of travel for the period away from home is treated as an expense for food and beverages. When a per diem allowance is paid for lodging, meal, and incidental expenses, the payor must treat an amount equal to the federal M&IE rate for the locality of travel for the period the employee is away from home as an expense for food and beverages. An employee may deduct an amount computed under the optional method only as an itemized deduction subject to the 50-percent limitation on meal and entertainment expenses and the two-percent floor on miscellaneous itemized deductions. (Rev. Proc. 90-15)

Self-Employed Deduction and Entertainment

A self-employed individual may deduct an amount computed under the optional method in determining adjusted gross income. This deduction is subject to the 50-percent limitation on meal and entertainment expenses. (Rev. Proc. 90-15)

Self-employed individuals are not entitled to use the federal per diem rates to substantiate lodging expenses. (Stan, TC CCH Dec. 56,064(M)).

.49 Entertainment Expenses Chart

When Deductible

General Rule

— You can deduct ordinary and necessary expenses to entertain a client, customer, or employee if the expenses meet the directly related test or the associated test.

Definitions

— Entertainment includes any activity generally considered to provide entertainment, amusement, or recreation, and includes meals provided to a customer or client.

— An ordinary expense is one that is common and accepted in your field of business, trade, or profession.

— A necessary expense is one that is helpful and appropriate, although not necessarily indispensable, for your business.

Tests To Be Met

Directly Related Test

— Entertainment took place in a clear business setting, or

— Main purpose of entertainment was the active conduct of business, and

— You did engage in business with the customer or client during the entertainment period, and

— You had more than a general expectation of realizing income or some other specific business benefit.

Associated Test

— Entertainment is associated with your trade or business, and

— Entertainment directly precedes or follows a substantial business discussion.

Other Rules

— You cannot deduct the cost of your meal as an entertainment expense if you are claiming the meal as a travel expense.

— You can deduct expenses only to the extent they are not lavish or extravagant under the circumstances.

— You generally can deduct only 50 percent of your unreimbursed entertainment expenses (see 50% Limit).

(Source: IRS Pub. 463)

.51 Health Insurance Deduction for Self-Employed Individuals

Health insurance deduction is 100 percent after 2002. The deduction is also allowed for S corporations shareholders owning two percent or more of the stock. The deduction for health insurance cost of self-employed individuals and their spouses and dependents was increased to 100 percent, phased in as follows:

Year	Percent Deductible
1999 through 2001	60%
2002	70%
2003 and thereafter	100%

.53 Hobby Losses Versus Business Losses

Business losses qualify under Code Section 162, or Code Section 212 regarding trade or business and/or the production of income. But be aware of the hobby loss rules. IRS will consider the following in possibly disallowing the losses:

- Amounts of profits earned must show a profit in three of five years.

- Reasons for, or history of losses. Were losses due to circumstances beyond control, such as weather, casualty, market condition, etc.

- The degree of personal pleasure in the activity.

- Degree of benefit of losses. Does this offset a lot of other taxable income?

- Experience, or expertise of the taxpayer. If taxpayer knows little about the field, IRS will be more suspect that it's not entered into for profit.

- Time spent on the activity.

- The "business-like" nature of the activity. Is the activity run professionally with accounting and marketing activities?

.55 Home Expenses

Disallowance of Deduction

No deduction is allowed with respect to the use of a dwelling unit which is used by the taxpayer during the taxable year as a residence, except as provided by the following. (Code Sec.280A(a))

Deductions for interest, taxes, casualty losses, etc., are allowed to the taxpayer without regard to their connection with the trade or business. (Code Sec. 280A(b))

Home—Exceptions for Certain Business or Rental Use

The deduction is allowed if the dwelling unit portion is exclusively used on a regular basis:

- As the principal place-of-business for any trade or business of the taxpayer;
- As a place of business which is used by patients, clients, or customers in meeting or dealing with the taxpayer in the normal course of the trade or business; or
- In the case of a separate structure which is not attached to the dwelling unit, in connection with the taxpayer's trade or business. (Code Sec. 280A(c) (l))

Home and Storage Use

The disallowance rule shall not apply to any dwelling unit which is used on a regular basis as a storage unit for the inventory of the taxpayer that is held for use in the taxpayer's trade or business of selling products at retail or wholesale, but only if the dwelling unit is the sole fixed location of such trade or business. The 1996 Small Business Act expanded this provision to include product samples as well as inventory. (Code Sec. 280A(c)2))

.57 Home Office Deduction

In the Taxpayer Relief Act of 1997, Congress effectively overturned the U.S. Supreme Court's decision in *N.E. Soliman* which restricted an individual's principal place of business to where the primary income-generating functions of the trade or business were performed. Starting in 1999, the definition of "principal place of business" has been expanded so that a home office qualifies as a taxpayer's principal place of business if:

(1) The office is used by the taxpayer to conduct administrative or management activities of the taxpayer's trade or business; and

(2) There is no other fixed location of the trade or business where the taxpayer conducts substantial administrative or management activities of the trade or business (Code Sec. 280A(c) (1), as amended by P.L. 105-34).

If a taxpayer does not meet the new definition, the taxpayer may be entitled to a home office deduction under the current principal place of business definition set forth in *Soliman* or one of the other tests of Code Sec. 280A.

Taxpayers who perform administrative or management activities for their trade or business at places other than the home office are not automatically prohibited from taking the deduction based on failure to meet the principal place of business requirement. According to the House Committee Report to P.L. 105-34, the following taxpayers are not prevented from taking a home office deduction under the new definition:

(1) Taxpayers who do not conduct substantial administrative or management activities at a fixed location other than the home office, even if administrative or management activities (e.g., billing activities) are performed by other people at other locations;

(2) Taxpayers who carry out administrative and management activities at sites that are not fixed locations of the business (e.g., cars or hotel rooms) in addition to performing the activities at the home office;

(3) Taxpayers who conduct an insubstantial amount of administrative and management activities at a fixed location other than the home office (e.g., occasionally doing minimal paperwork at another fixed location); and

(4) Taxpayers who conduct substantial *nonadministrative* and *nonmanagement* business activities at a fixed location other than the home office (e.g., meeting with, or providing services to customers, clients or patients at a fixed location other than the home office).

There is no other fixed location where the taxpayer conducts substantial administrative or management activities if the taxpayer does not *actually* perform such functions at a fixed location other than the home office. In other words, the second prong of the new definition of "principal place of business" can be met if the taxpayer chose to perform administrative and management functions at home even though another fixed location was available. However, employees do not have this flexibility. The fact that other space for administrative activities at a fixed location was available to an employee is relevant to determining whether the home office use was for the convenience of the employer.

Under the *Soliman* definition, many taxpayers who managed their business activities from their homes but performed significant business functions outside their home were considered to have no principal place of business. Thus, not only were they denied any deduction for their home office expenses, they were often denied related travel expenses on the ground that the costs were nondeductible commuting expenses. The expanded definition of a principal place of business will enable many taxpayers to establish a home office and deduct the cost of traveling to and from their homes to other locations at which they conduct business. (Rev. Rul. 94-47).

Sale of Residence Rules Can Raise Problems

Although the exclusion of gain on the sale of a residence ($500,000 for joint filers, $250,000 for others) was intended to simplify tax compliance for most taxpayers, it may raise questions for others. What impact a home office deduction has on the exclusion is a significant one.

Taxpayers using part of their home for business must adjust the basis of their home for any depreciation that was allowable for its business use - even if not claimed. The amount of the depreciation taken after May 6, 1997, must be taken into income and taxed at 25 percent.

> **Example:** A taxpayer purchased a residence on February 19, 1996, for $234,000. Twenty percent of the home was for business use for a home office. The taxpayer ceased using the home office on December 31, 2002. The residence was sold for $300,000 on June 3, 2003. The taxpayer would have a realized gain on the

¶802.57

sale of $73,850 ($300,000 selling price minus a $226,150 basis ($234,000 – $7,850 depreciation taken)). The taxpayer would have to report a gain of $6,781 because of the depreciation taken after May 6, 1997 ($81 depreciation for May 1997 + 67 months @ $100 per month). This gain would be reported at the 25 percent rate. Under the regulations, no allocation of gain is required if both the residential and non-residential portions of the property are within the same dwelling unit.

.59 Home Office Deduction Tax Savings

Assumptions

Federal Income Tax Rate:	25%
State Income Tax Rate:	2%
Social Security Tax Rate:	6.20%
Medicare Tax Rate:	1.45%
Business Use of Home:	
Business Use (sq. ft.):	200
Total Area (sq. ft.):	2000
Business Use = 200/2000 =	10%

Annual Expenses

Utilities:	5,000
Maintenance/Repairs:	4,000
Insurance:	1,000
Interest Expense:	10,000
Real Estate Taxes:	2,500
Other:	1,000
Depreciation:	4,000
Total Home Expenses	$27,500
Multiplied by business use 10%	= 2,750
Tax savings—including interest & taxes	953
Tax savings—excluding interest & taxes	520

.61 Loan Comparisons

Comparison of the after-tax costs associated with various loan options.

The following analysis considers the amount of the loan, length of the loan, the interest rate one will be paying, the costs of obtaining the loan (bank fees, legal fees, etc.), and any "points" or "loan origination fees" that will be paid to obtain the loan. The expected tax bracket is 34 percent.

Loan	Loan Amount	Loan Term	Interest	Closing	Points
Loan 1	$100000	240	8%	$2000	2%
Loan 2	$100000	240	10%	1000	1%
Loan 3	$100000	240	11%	1000	1%

Conclusion

Loan	Loan 1	Loan 2	Loan 3
Monthly Payment:	$836.44	$965.02	$1,032.19

Over term of Loan = 240 months

Total payments made:	$204,746	$233,605	$249,725
Total tax savings:	34,934	45,086	50,567

Total after-tax cost	169,812	188,519	199,159
Over the Analysis Period = 240 months			
Total payments made:	$204,746	$233,605	$249,725
Tax savings over period:	34,934	45,086	50,567
Total after-tax cost:	169,812	188,519	199,159

Total after-tax cost includes after-tax interest and points, plus closing costs and payoff of total principal on the loan.

Should Debt Be Paid Off Early?

Analysis of total after-tax costs of paying off the debt vs. alternatively investing the money one would use to pay off this debt. This is an opportunity cost comparison.

The analysis considers the savings on the remaining interest one would have had to continue paying (adjusted for any tax deductibility) versus giving up the potential income this money being used to pay off the debt could earn if invested instead. Can one make more on the money in after-tax dollars by investing it than can be saved in interest expense paid out in after tax dollars? Is this a consumer debt in which the interest expense is not deductible? Reducing an interest-paying debt is the same as increasing one's assets since net worth increases.

Assumptions:

The rate of return that can be made by investing

Appropriate tax bracket

What will happen to the open-market interest rates over the life of analysis?

How much of the interest being paid on the debt is tax deductible?

What are current and future liquidity needs?

Compounding calculations are based on a monthly, mid-point methodology.

All assumed rates (interest rates, inflation rates, appreciation rates, business use percentages, federal and/or state tax brackets, and federal/state tax rates) are constant over the life of the analysis.

The current Income, Estate, and Gift tax laws in effect will remain in effect over the life of the analysis period in question.

Any tax savings calculations using a fixed, overall, or marginal tax bracket are based on that bracket remaining the same even after the changes resulting from the tax savings are considered in regard to taxable income.

Marginal tax bracket: The uppermost tax bracket in which ones tax liability occurs.

Federal and state tax rates and brackets used will stay constant over the life of the analysis period.

Opportunity cost: The foregone savings/investment income one is losing on a particular amount of money because one chose to use this money for something else.

Tax savings: Income taxes saved as a result of some type of allowable deduction on your tax returns.

Pre-tax interest rate paid: The stated rate of interest paid on a loan before it is adjusted for any effects of tax deductibility.

¶802.61

Assumption details:

Loan Interest Rate	8%
Pre-Tax Investment Rate	12%
Amount of Loan	$100,000
Term of Loan in Months	240
Income Tax Rate = 34%	Interest is Tax Deductible

Result:

After-tax total of payments remaining to be paid on loan	$166,492
To pay off the loan now	$100,000
Considering the lost interest earnings on the cash used to pay off the loan, the actual total cost of loan payoff	484,911

The after-tax cost of paying out the loan is higher than continuing the loan. One should invest the payoff amount and continue to pay the loan in installments.

.63 Archer Medical Savings Account

A restricted number of participants will be able to take advantage of a new type of savings vehicle called the Archer Medical Savings Account (MSA) for tax years beginning after 1996. The MSA expired at the end of 2005. Assuming the MSA is renewed, individual minimum deductible coverage for 2006 is $1,800 and maximum is $2,700; maximum out-of-pocket limitation is $3,650. Family minimum deductible coverage is $3,650 and maximum is $5,450; maximum out-of-pocket limitation is $6,650. For 2007, individual minimum deductible coverage is $1,900 and maximum is $2,850; maximum out-of-pocket limitation is $3,750. Family minimum deductible coverage is $3,750 and maximum is $5,650; maximum out-of-pocket limitation is $6,900. Within limits, contributions to an MSA will be deductible if made by an eligible individual and excludable from income if made by an employer on behalf of an eligible individual. Individuals may contribute and deduct up to 65 percent of the deductible amount; the family coverage amount is 75 percent of the deductible. Distributions from an MSA that are not used for payment of medical expenses are includible in income and subject to an additional 15-percent tax unless made after the participant reaches age 65, dies, or becomes disabled. Generally, an eligible individual is a self-employed person or an employee who is covered by a high-deductible plan sponsored by a small employer and by no other health plan. A small employer is one who employs, on average, 50 or fewer workers.

.64 Health Savings Accounts (HSAs)

Health Savings Accounts (HSAs) were created by the Medicare Prescription Drug, Improvement and Modernization Act of 2003, passed in December 2003, the law provides tax benefits for individuals with high-deductible health plans (HDHP). An HDHP is one in which the deductible for individuals is $1,050 or $2,100 for a family (for 2006). The annual out-of-pocket, including deductibles and co-pays, cannot exceed $5,250 for self-only coverage and $10,500 for family coverage. For 2007, the minimum deductible for individuals is $1,100 or $2,200 for a family. The annual out-of-pocket, including deductibles and co-pays, cannot exceed $5,650 for self-only coverage and $11,000 for family coverage.

Contributions to an HSA are tax deductible for eligible individuals, regardless of who makes the contribution or whether the individual itemizes deductions. Employers may also contribute to HSAs under stand-alone plans or as part of a cafeteria plan. In either case, the contributions are excluded from the employee's gross income and are not subject to FICA, FUTA, or the Railroad Retirement Tax Act. For 2007, the maximum aggregate annual contribution that can be made to an HSA is $2,850 in the case of self-only coverage and $5,650 in the case of family coverage. For those 55 and older, the contribution limit is raised by $500 in 2004 and will increase $100 annually thereafter to $1,000 in 2009. Contributions for the year may be made up to April 15 of the following year.

The HSA account is tax-exempt. Earnings and growth on amounts held in the HSA grow tax-free. Money not spent in one year can roll over to the next year.

Distributions made exclusively for the purpose of paying qualified medical expenses are excluded from gross income, including expenses paid where the individual ceases to be qualified to make contributions. Payments made that are not qualified are included in gross income and are subject to a 10-percent penalty excise tax. Distributions made as a result of death, disability, or upon reaching age 65 are not subject to the penalty.

There is no substantiation requirement. Neither an employer-sponsor nor an HSA trustee needs to take steps to verify that the expense is qualified. The individual must keep records demonstrating that the expense is qualified.

Individuals may rollover contributions from Archer Medical Savings Accounts (MSAs) or other HSAs into an HSA. Such rollovers need not be in the form of cash, as is required of all other contributions, and are not subject to the annual contribution limits. Rollovers from IRAs, Health Reimbursement Arrangements (HRAs), and Flexible Spending Accounts (FSAs) are not permitted.

The HSA stays with the individual if the individual changes employers or leaves the workforce.

Upon death, any balance remaining in the decedent's health account is includible in his or her gross estate. Upon death, any balance remaining in the account beneficiary's HSA becomes the property of the individual named in the HSA instrument as the beneficiary of the account. If the surviving spouse is named the beneficiary, the account becomes the HSA of the surviving spouse. The amount is eligible for the estate marital deduction. It is not included in the spouse's gross income. The HSA can be used to pay qualified medical expenses of the decedent. If someone other than the spouse is named the beneficiary, the beneficiary includes the fair market value of the account in gross income. The includible amount is reduced by any decedent qualified medical expenses paid within one year after death. The income in respect of a decedent is eligible for the federal estate tax deduction. When there is no named beneficiary, the fair market value is included in the decedent's gross income in the year of death. This rule applies even if the surviving spouse is the sole beneficiary of the decedent's estate.

.65 Flexible Spending Accounts

The IRS has relaxed the "use-it-or-lose-it" rule for flexible spending accounts (FSAs). Employers can give employees an additional 2½-month "grace period" into the next year to use the funds in their FSAs. (Notice 2005-42)

The rule applies to a participant who has unused contributions for a particular benefit, such as health expenses, at the end of the 12-month plan year and who incurs expenses for the same benefit during the grace period. The employee may be reimbursed for those expenses from the unused contributions as if the expenses had been incurred in the immediately preceding 12-month period.

During the grace period, a cafeteria plan may not permit unused benefits or contributions to be cashed out or converted to another benefit. Unused contributions relating to a particular benefit may only be used to pay or reimburse expenses incurred for that particular benefit. Employers can adopt a grace period for the current cafeteria plan year, or for future years, by amending their plan documents before the end of the plan year.

If, due to the additional 2½-month grace period, the employer does not know at the time the Form W-2 must be sent the tax year amount actually reimbursed to the employee from the account, the employer may continue to make a reasonable estimate by determining the amount the employee elected to use in the account plus any matching funds the employer may furnish. (Notice 2005-61)

.66 Roth 401(k) Plans

In 2006, firms can amend their 401(k) plans to add a special Roth IRA account that can be funded by payroll deduction. The IRS will require that the nondeductible Roth contributions be segregated from deductible 401(k) pay-ins and accounted for separately.

The Roth 401(k) contribution cap will be higher than for a regular Roth. The standard 401(k) limits apply, a $15,000 maximum for 2006, plus an additional $5,000 for anyone 50 or older. Any Roth 401(k) contributions will count toward the regular 401(k) limit. There is no income limit on contributions to Roth 401(k)s, unlike the $160,000 income limit on regular Roths.

Employer matches of employee Roth 401(k) contributions are not tax-favored. The matches go into a regular 401(k) and are taxed as income when paid out.

The Roth 401(k) accounts are subject to the minimum pay-out rules after the taxpayer reaches age 70½.

.67 Appreciated Employer Stock and 401(k)s

Taxpayers can have the retirement plan distribute appreciated employer stock. The taxpayer pays tax only on the cost to the company when it contributed to the plan. The amount taxed becomes the basis of the stock. Any appreciation over basis is long-term capital gain and will be taxed when the stock is sold. (Notice 98-24) If stock is held more than one year any further gain will be long-term capital gain.

To qualify for the tax break, the taxpayer must take a lump-sum distribution of the entire retirement account within a single tax year. The shares must be held in a taxable investment account. Other parts of the distribution can be rolled into an IRA.

A taxpayer made a mistake in filling out the paperwork for the withdrawal and the distribution was not completed within the same calendar year. The IRS denied the tax break. (IRS Letter Ruling 200434002)

A taxpayer took proceeds from his properly completed lump-sum distribution and rolled them over to an IRA. Following the mistaken advice of his financial adviser, he included the distributed stock shares in the rollover. The IRS stated that the requirements can not be waived. (IRS Letter Ruling 200442032) Any distributions will be taxed at ordinary income rates.

.68 NOL Carryovers

The net operating loss of a taxpayer, which is generally the excess of the taxpayer's business deductions over its gross income, may be carried back and applied against taxable income for prior years and then carried forward and applied against taxable income for years after the NOL year. Under the 1997 Act, the NOL carryback period is shortened from three years to two years, but the NOL carryforward period is extended from 15 years to 20 years. The three-year carryback period is retained for the portion of the NOL that relates to casualty and theft losses of individual taxpayers and to NOLs that are attributable to a Presidentially declared disaster and are incurred by taxpayers engaged in farming or by a small business. The new carryover rules are effective for NOLs for tax years beginning after August 5, 1997; NOLs carried forward from prior tax years are not eligible to use the 20-year carryover period. Farmers are allowed a special five-year carryback for farming losses (Code Sec. 172(b)(1)(G)).

For net operating losses arising in tax ending in 2001 and 2002, the 2002 Tax Act extended the two- and three-year carryback period to five years.

.69 Travel Expenses

Traveling expenses include travel fares, meals and lodging, and expenses incident to travel such as expenses for sample rooms, telephone and telegraph, public stenographers, etc. Only such traveling expenses as are reasonable and necessary in the conduct of the taxpayer's business and directly attributable to it may be deducted. If the trip is solely on business, the reasonable and necessary traveling expenses, including travel fares, meals and lodging, and expenses incident to travel, are business expenses. If the trip is undertaken for other than business purposes, the travel fares and expenses incident to travel are personal expenses and the meals and lodging are living expenses. (Reg. § 1.162-2(a))

Personal and Business Travel

If the trip is primarily personal in nature, the traveling expenses to and from the destination are not deductible even though the taxpayer engages in business activities while at such destination. (Temp. Reg. § 1.162-2(b)(l)) If a taxpayer travels to a destination and while at such destination engages in both business and personal activities, traveling expenses to and from such destination are deductible only if the trip is related primarily to the taxpayer's trade or business. (Code Sec. 274(m)(3))

Spouse Accompaniment

Where a spouse accompanies the taxpayer on a business trip, expenses attributable to the spouse's travel are not deductible unless it can be adequately shown that the spouse's presence on the trip has a bona fide business purpose and the spouse is an employee of the taxpayer. The same rules apply to any other members of the taxpayer's family who accompany the taxpayer on such a trip. (Code Sec. 274(m)(3))

Convention Attendance

Expenses paid or incurred by a taxpayer in attending a convention or other meeting may constitute an ordinary and necessary business expense under Section 162 depending upon the facts and circumstances of each case. No distinction will be made between self-employed persons and employees. The fact that an employee uses vacation or leave time or that his attendance at the convention is voluntary will not necessarily prohibit

¶802.68

the allowance of the deduction. The allowance of deduction for such expenses will depend upon whether there is a sufficient relationship between the taxpayer's trade or business and his or her attendance at the convention or other meeting so that he is benefiting or advancing the interests of his trade or business by such attendance. If the convention is for political, social, or other purposes unrelated to the taxpayer's trade or business, the expenses are not deductible. (Reg. § 1.162-2(d))

Federal Per Diem Rate

The Federal per diem rate is equal to the sum of the Federal lodging expense rate and the Federal meal and incidental expense (M&IE) rate for the locality of travel. Each of these rates is for a particular locality in the continental United States (CONUS). (Rev. Proc. 2005-67)

Specific High-Low Rates

Beginning November 1, 2005, the per diem rate is $226 for travel to any "high-cost locality," or $141 for travel to any other locality within CONUS. Whichever per diem rate applies, it is applied as if it were the Federal per diem rate for the locality of travel. For purposes of applying the high-low substantiation method, the Federal M&IE rate shall be treated as $58 for a high-cost locality and $45 for any other locality within CONUS. (Rev. Proc. 2005-67)

Beginning November 1, 2006, the per diem is $246 for travel to any "high-cost locality" or $148 for travel to any other locality within CONUS. For purposes of applying the high-low substantiation method, the federal M&IE rate is the same as 2005. (Rev. Proc. 2006-41)

Deductible Travel Expenses

Expense	Description
Transportation	The cost of travel by airplane, train, or bus between your home and your business destination.
Taxi, commuter bus and limousine	Fares of these and other types of transportation between the airport or station and your hotel, or between the hotel and your work site away from home.
Baggage and shipping	The cost of sending baggage and sample or display material between your regular and temporary work sites.
Car	The costs of operating and maintaining your car when traveling away from home on business. You may deduct actual expenses or the standard mileage rate, including business-related tolls and parking. If you lease a car while away from home or business, you can deduct business-related expenses only.
Lodging	The cost of lodging if your business trip is overnight or long enough to require you to get substantial sleep or rest to properly perform your duties.
Meals	The cost of meals only if your business trip is overnight or long enough to require you to get substantial sleep or rest. Includes amounts spent for food, beverages, taxes and related tips.

Expense	Description
Cleaning	Cleaning and laundry expenses while away from home overnight.
Telephone	The cost of business calls while on your business trip, including business communication by fax machine or other communication devices.
Tips	Tips you pay for any expenses in this chart.
Other	Other similar ordinary and necessary expenses related to your business travel such as public stenographer's fees and computer rental fees.

Source: IRS Pub. 463

.70 Work Opportunity Credit

A work opportunity credit replaced the old targeted jobs credit for those hired after September 30, 1996, and before January 1, 2006. The credit is 40 percent of qualified first-year wages for those performing 400 or more hours of service and 25 percent for those performing at least 120 hours but less than 400 hours of service. It is expected that the work opportunity credit will be renewed by Congress.

.71 Welfare-to-Work Credit

The welfare-to-work credit is available for employers for wages paid to long-term family assistance recipients who begin work after 1997 and before 2006. The amount of the credit for a tax year is 35 percent of the qualified first-year wages for such year plus 50 percent of the qualified second-year wages for such year. The credit applies only to the first $10,000 of wages in each year with respect to any individual. Thus, the maximum total credit per qualified employee is $8,500 for the two years. It is expected that the welfare to work credit will be renewed by Congress.

¶ 805 ESTATE AND OTHER TAXES

.01 Gift Tax

Imposition of Tax

A tax is imposed for each calendar year on the transfer of property by gift during such calendar year by any individual, resident or nonresident. (Code Sec. 2501(a))

Rate of Tax

The tax imposed by section 2501 for each calendar year shall be an amount equal to the excess of:

- A tentative tax, computed under section 2001(c), on the aggregate sum of the taxable gifts for such calendar year and for each of the preceding calendar periods, over

- A tentative tax, computed under such section, on the aggregate sum of the taxable gifts for each of the preceding calendar periods. (Code Sec. 2502(a))

Tax to Be Paid by Donor

The tax shall be paid by the donor. (Code Sec. 2502(c))

Taxable Gifts

The term "taxable gifts" means the total amount of gifts less the deductions provided in subchapter C (section 2522 and following). (Code Sec. 2503(a))

Exclusion from Gifts

In the case of gifts (other than gifts of future interests in property) made to any person by the donor during the calendar year, the first $12,000 of such gifts to such a person are not included in the total amount of gifts made during such year. Where there has been a transfer to any person of a present interest in property, the possibility that such interest may be diminished by the exercise of a power is disregarded in applying this subsection if no part of such interest will at any time pass to any other person. (Code Sec. 2503(b))

Taxable Gifts for Preceding Calendar Periods

In computing taxable gifts for preceding calendar periods for purposes of computing the tax for any calendar year:

- There will be treated as gifts such transfers as were considered to be gifts under the gift tax laws applicable to the calendar period in which the transfers were made. (Code Sec. 2504(a)(1))

Unified Credit Against Gift Tax

In the case of a citizen or resident of the United States, a credit is allowed against the tax imposed by section 2501 for each calendar year an amount equal to:

- $345,800 after 2001, reduced by
- The sum of the amounts allowable as credits to the individual for all preceding calendar periods. (Code Sec. 2505(a))

Gift Splitting

A gift by a husband or wife to a third party may elect to be treated as made one-half by each, but only if at the time of the gift each spouse is a citizen or resident of the United States. (Code Sec. 2513(a)(1))

Consent of both spouses is required. (Code Sec. 2513(a)(2))

.03 Definition of Gross Estate

The value of the gross estate of the decedent is determined by including the value at the time of death of all property, real or personal, tangible or intangible, wherever situated. (Code Sec. 2031)

Alternate Valuation

The value of the gross estate may be determined, if the executor so elects, by valuing all the property included in the gross estate as follows:

- In the case of property not distributed, sold, exchanged, or otherwise disposed of, within six months after the decedent's death such property is valued as of the date six months after the decedent's death.
- In the case of property distributed, sold, exchanged, or otherwise disposed of within six months after the decedent's death such property is valued as of the date of distribution, sale, exchange, or other disposition.

- Any interest or estate which is affected by mere lapse of time is included at its value as of the time of death (instead of the later date), with adjustment for any difference in its value as of the later date not due to mere lapse of time. (Code Sec. 2032)

To use the alternative valuation both the gross estate and the estate tax liability must be reduced.

Adjustments for Gift Made Within Three Years of Decedent's Death

Certain gifts made within three years of death are included in the decedent's gross estate. The proceeds of any life insurance policy transferred within three years of death must be included in the gross estate (Code Sec. 2042). Where a decedent retained a life estate in a trust, the trust would be included in the gross estate. However, if the decedent had given up the retained life interest, a taxable gift was created. If the gift took place within three years of death, the trust is still included in the gross estate (Code Sec. 2036). If the decedent had a reversionary interest in property that exceeded five percent of the value of the trust immediately prior to death, the property is included in the gross estate. (Code Sec. 2037)

The gift tax on any taxable gift made within three years of death are pulled back into the estate. (Code Sec. 2035) This is to prevent taxpayers from making deathbed gifts and then reducing the gross estate by the liability for the gift tax.

.05 Estate Tax Rates Chart

Estate Tax Rates for 2006

If the Amount with Respect to Which the Tentative Tax to Be Computed Is:		The Tentative Tax Is:	
Over	Tax	Plus %	of Excess
Not over $10,000	$ 0	18	$ 0
Over $10,000 but not over $20,000	1,800	20	10,000
Over $20,000 but not over $40,000	3,800	22	20,000
Over $40,000 but not over $60,000	8,200	24	40,000
Over $60,000 but not over $80,000	23,000	26	60,000
Over $80,000 but not over $100,000	18,200	28	80,000
Over $100,000 but not over $150,000	23,800	30	100,000
Over $150,000 but not over $250,000	38,800	32	150,000
Over $250,000 but not over $500,000	70,800	34	250,000
Over $500,000 but not over $750,000	155,800	37	500,000
Over $750,000 but not over $1,000,000	248,300	39	750,000
Over $1,000,000 but not over $1,250,000	345,800	41	1,000,000
Over $1,250,000 but not over $1,500,000	448,300	43	1,250,000
Over $1,500,000 but not over $2,000,000	555,800	45	1,500,000
Over $2,000,000	780,800	46	2,000,000

After 2006, the marginal tax rate is 45 percent on taxable estates over $1,500,000.

Any of the unified credit ($780,800 and 2006) that has not been used for gift tax purposes can be applied against the estate tax liability. The effect of the unified credit is to shield $2,000,000 of taxable gifts and estate from the gift and estate taxes.

After 1997 the unified credit amount is replaced by an "applicable credit amount." The applicable credit amount is the amount of the tentative tax that would be determined under the rate schedule if the amount with respect to which such tentative tax is to be computed were the "applicable exclusion amount."

After 2003 the unified credit increases for estate purposes but remains at $345,800 for gift tax purposes.

.07 State Death Taxes

After 2004, the state death tax credit was replaced by a deduction.

.09 State Sales and Use Taxes

State Sales and Use Taxes as of Feb. 2006

State	Rate	Food Exempt	Local Sales Tax
Alabama	4%		X
Alaska	None		X
Arizona	5.6%	X	X
Arkansas	6%		X
California	6.25%	X	X
Colorado	2.9%	X	X
Connecticut	6%	X	
Delaware	None		
District of Colombia	5.75%	X	
Florida	6%	X	X
Georgia	4%	X	X
Hawaii	4%		
Idaho	6%		X
Illinois	6.25%		X
Indiana	6%	X	
Iowa	5%	X	X
Kansas	5.3%		X
Kentucky	6%		X
Louisiana	4%		X
Maine	5%		
Maryland	5%		
Massachusetts	5%	X	
Michigan	6%	X	
Minnesota	6.5%	X	X
Mississippi	7%		
Missouri	4.225%		X
Montana	None		
Nebraska	5.5%	X	X
Nevada	6.5%	X	X
New Hampshire	None		
New Jersey	6%	X	
New Mexico	5%		X
New York	4.25%	X	X
North Carolina	4.5%		X

State	Rate	Food Exempt	Local Sales Tax
North Dakota	5%	X	X
Ohio	6%	X	X
Oklahoma	4.5%		X
Oregon	None		
Pennsylvania	6%	X	X
Rhode Island	7%	X	
South Carolina	5%		X
South Dakota	4%		X
Tennessee	7%		X
Texas	6.25%	X	X
Utah	4.75%		X
Vermont	6%	X	
Virginia	4%		X
Washington	6.5%	X	X
West Virginia	6%		
Wisconsin	5%	X	X
Wyoming	4%		X

¶ 807 GAINS AND LOSSES—BUSINESS, CAPITAL, AND DEPRECIATION

.01 Business Expense Definitions

Economic Performance Rule

Business expenses are generally not deductible until economic performance occurs. If the expense is for property or services provided the taxpayer, or for use of property by the taxpayer, economic performance occurs as the property or services are provided, or as the property is used. If the expense is for property or services that the taxpayer provides to others, economic performance occurs as property or services are provided. An exception allows certain recurring expenses to be treated as incurred during a tax year even though economic performance has not occurred. (Source: IRS Pub. 583)

Capital Asset

"Capital asset" means property held by the taxpayer (whether or not connected with the taxpayer's trade or business), but it does not include:

- Stock in trade of the taxpayer or other property of a kind that would properly be included in the inventory of the taxpayer if on hand at the close of the taxable year, or property held by the taxpayer primarily for sale to customers in the ordinary course of the trade or business.

- Property, used in the trade or business, of a character that is subject to the allowance for depreciation or real property used in the trade or business.

- Accounts or notes receivable acquired in the ordinary course of trade or business for services rendered or from the sale of property. (Code Sec. 1221)

Property Used in Trade or Business

Section 1231 Gain

The term "section 1231 gain" means:

¶807.01

- Any recognized gain on the sale or exchange of property used in the trade or business and

- Any recognized gain from the compulsory or involuntary conversion into other property or money:

- The property must be held more than a year and be property held in connection with a trade or business or a transaction entered into for profit.

Section 1231 Loss

The term "section 1231 loss" means any recognized loss from the sale or exchange.

In determining whether gains exceed losses:

- The section 1231 gains shall be included only if and to the extent taken into account in computing gross income, and

- The section 1231 losses shall be included only if and to the extent taken into account in computing taxable income, except that section 1211 shall not apply. (Code Sec. 1231(a)(3)(B))

Losses on the destruction (in whole or in part), theft or seizure, or requisition or condemnation of:

- Property used in the trade or business or

- Capital assets which are held for more than one year and are held in connection with a trade or business or a transaction entered into for profit, shall be treated as losses from a compulsory or involuntary conversion. (Code Sec. 1231(a)(4)(B))

Gains Exceed Losses

If the section 1231 gains for any taxable year exceed the section 1231 losses for such taxable year, such gains and losses shall be treated as long-term capital gains or long-term capital losses, as the case may be.

Gains Do Not Exceed Losses

If the section 1231 gains for any taxable year do not exceed the section 1231 losses for such taxable year, such gains and losses shall not be treated as gains and losses from sales or exchanges of capital assets. (Code Sec. 1231(a))

Recapture of Net Ordinary Losses

The net section 1231 gain for any taxable year is treated as ordinary income to the extent of any unrecaptured losses within the previous five years.

Example: Cowen Corporation incurred a net section 1231 loss of $5,000 in 2003. This loss will be classified as ordinary. In 2006, Cowen has a net section 1231 gain of $12,000. Because of the $5,000 unrecaptured loss from 2003, Cowen will classify the $12,000 net section gain as $5,000 ordinary income and $7,000 long-term capital gain.

¶807.01

.03 Capital Gains Tax Rates

Capital Gains Tax Rates

Years	Maximum Rate	Years	Maximum Rate
1913 - 1921	7.0 %	1971	32.5 %
1922 - 1933	12.5	1972 - 1978	35.0
1934 - 1937	18.9	1979 - 1981	28.0
1938 - 1941	15.0	1982 - 1986	20.0
1942 - 1967	25.0	1987	28.0
1968	26.9	1988 - 1990	33.0
1969	27.5	1991	28.0
1970	30.2	1992 - 1996	28.0
		1997 - 2002	20.0
		2003	15.0

Maximum Capital Gains Rate

If a taxpayer has a net capital gain for any taxable year, the tax for such taxable year will not exceed the sum of a tax computed at the rates and in the same manner as if this subsection had not been enacted on the greater of taxable income reduced by the net capital gain, or the lesser of:

- The amount of taxable income taxed at a rate below 25 percent, or
- Taxable income reduced by the adjusted net capital gain, plus

  25 percent of the excess (if any) of:

  — The unrecaptured *section 1250* gain (or, if less, the net capital gain), over the excess (if any) of—the sum of the amount on which tax is determined plus the net capital gain, over taxable income, plus

  — 28 percent of the amount of taxable income in excess of the sum of:

  - The adjusted net capital gain, plus

  - The sum of the amounts on which tax is determined, plus

  - 10 percent of so much of the taxpayer's adjusted net capital gain (or, if less, taxable income) as does not exceed the excess (if any) of:

  - The amount of taxable income which would (without regard to this paragraph) be taxed at a rate below 25 percent, over

  - The taxable income reduced by the adjusted net capital gain, plus

  - 15 percent of the taxpayer's adjusted net capital gain (or, if less, taxable income) in excess of the amount on which a tax is determined. (Code Sec. 1(h)(1))

In some of the years the maximum rate on capital gains was computed by taking the allowed capital gain deduction and multiplying the includable income by the maximum tax rate for individuals. For example, during the period 1982-1986, taxpayers were allowed to deduct 60 percent of the net long-term capital gain, subject to a maximum tax rate of 50 percent.

¶807.03

The maximum tax rate on long-term capital gains was 28 percent on gains received prior to May 7, 1997. The rate dropped to 20 percent for most gains after May 6, 1997. The rate dropped to 15 percent for most gains after May 5, 2003.

All net long-term capital gains of corporations are taxed as ordinary income. However, capital losses of corporations are only deductible against capital gains. The carryover period for corporation capital losses is back three years and forward five. Individuals are allowed to deduct up to $3,000 of excess capital losses over capital gains each year, with an unlimited carryforward of any unused losses.

.05 Allocation Rules for Applicable Asset Acquisitions

When a taxpayer sells an unincorporated business, referred to as an applicable asset acquisition, the transferor and the transferee must agree in writing as to the allocation of the selling price of any of the assets.

An applicable asset acquisition is any transfer of a group of assets if:

- The assets transferred constitute a trade or business in the hands of either the seller or the purchaser and

- Except for the exclusion on like-kind exchanges, the purchaser's basis in the transferred assets is determined wholly by reference to the purchaser's consideration. (Temp. Reg. § 1.1060-1T(b)(1))

Consideration Defined

The purchaser's consideration is the cost of the assets acquired in the applicable asset acquisition. The seller's consideration is the amount realized from the applicable asset acquisition regarding the determination of and recognition of gain or loss. (Temp. Reg. § 1.1060-1T(c)(1))

Consideration is first reduced by the amount of Class I assets (if any) transferred by the seller.

Consideration is allocated among Class II assets transferred by the seller in proportion to the fair market values of such Class II assets on the purchase date, then among Class III assets transferred by the seller in proportion to the fair market values of such Class III assets on that date, and finally to Class IV assets. (Temp. Reg. § 1.1060-1T(d)(2))

Class I Assets

Class I assets are cash, demand deposits, and like accounts in banks, savings and loan associations, and other similar items. The amount of the consideration remaining after the reduction is to be allocated to the other assets transferred. (Temp. Reg. § 1.1060-1T(d)(1))

Class II Assets

Class II assets are certificates of deposit, U.S. government securities, readily marketable stock or securities, and other items designated. (Temp. Reg. § 1.1060-1T(d)(2)(i))

Class III Assets

Class III assets are all assets (other than Class I, II, and IV assets), both tangible and intangible, including furniture and fixtures, land, buildings, equipment, accounts receivable, and covenants not to compete. (Temp. Reg. § 1.1060-1T(d)(2)(ii))

Class IV Assets

Class IV assets are intangible assets in the nature of goodwill and going concern value. (Temp. Reg. § 1.1060-1T(d)(2)(iii))

The amount of consideration allocated to an asset (other than Class IV assets) shall not exceed the fair market value of that asset on the purchase date. (Temp. Reg. § 1.1060-1T(e)(1))

Internal Revenue Service Authority

The Internal Revenue Service may challenge the taxpayer's determination of the fair market value of any asset by any appropriate method and take into account all factors, including any lack of adverse tax interests between the parties. For example, in certain cases the Internal Revenue Service may make an independent showing of the value of goodwill and going concern value as a means of calling into question the validity of the taxpayer's valuation of other assets. (Temp. Reg. § 1.1060-1T(e)(4))

> *Example:* S, a sole proprietor, sells to P, a corporation, a group of assets which constitute a trade or business. P pays S $2,000 in cash and assumes $1,000 in liabilities. Thus, the total consideration is $3,000. (Temp. Reg. § 1.1060-1T(g)(i))

Assume that P acquires no Class I assets and that on the purchase date, the fair market values of the Class II and III assets S sold to P are as follows:

Asset Class	Asset	Fair Market Value
II	Portfolio of marketable securities	$ 400
	Total Class II	400
III	Furniture and fixtures	800
	Building	800
	Land	200
	Equipment	400
	Accounts receivable	100
	Covenant not to compete	100
	Total Class III	$2,400

(Temp. Reg. § 1.1060-1T(g))

The amount of consideration allocable to the Class I, II, III, and IV assets is the total consideration reduced by the amount of any Class I assets. Since P acquired no Class I assets, the total consideration of $3,000 is next allocated first to Class II and then to Class III assets. Since the fair market value of the Class II assets is $400, $400 of consideration is allocated to the Class II assets. Since the remaining amount of consideration is $2,600 (i.e., $3,000 - $400), an amount which exceeds the sum of the fair market values of the total amount of Class III assets, the amount allocated to each Class III asset is its fair market value. Thus, the total amount allocated to Class III assets is $2,400. (Temp. Reg. § 1.1060-1T(g))

The amount allocated to the Class IV assets (assets in the nature of goodwill and going concern value) is $200 (i.e., $2,600 - $2,400). (Temp. Reg. § 1.1060-1T(g))

¶807.05

.06 Example of Asset Purchase Using the Residual Method

Acquisition of Assets Constituting a Business. Taxpayer A forms a proprietorship and purchases 100% of the assets of ABC Bookkeeping for $225,000. Purchase date was 6/15/06.

The purchase price is as follows:

Note Payable	$150,000
Cash Paid	75,000
	$225,000

FMV on the acquisition date for the assets acquired were as follows:

Asset Class	Asset	FMV
3	Furniture and Fixtures	$ 25,000
3	Equipment	30,000
3	Noncompete Agreement-Seller (5 years-start 6/15/05)	10,000
3	Office Supplies	5,000
3	Lease on Office Space (2 years-start 6/15/05)	10,000
3	Franchise Agreement	15,000
3	Tax Return and write up clients	105,000
	Total	$200,000

1.	Purchase or sale price (consideration)		$225,000
2.	Class I		
	Cash	$_____	
	Checking Accounts	_____	
	Savings Accounts	_____	
	Demand Deposits	_____	
	_____	_____	
	Total Class I		-0-
3.	Remaining balance (line 1 - line 2)		225,000
4.	Class II		
	Time Deposits	$_____	
	U.S. Securities	_____	
	Readily Marketable Securities & Stocks	_____	
	Foreign Currency	_____	
	_____	_____	
	Total Class II		-0-
5.	Remaining balance (line 3 - line 4)		225,000
6.	Class III		
	Furniture & Fixtures	25,000	
	Equipment	30,000	
	Non-Compete	10,000	
	Office Supplies	5,000	
	Office Space	10,000	
	Franchise Agreement	15,000	
	Tax Return Clients	105,000	
	Customer List	_____	

Accounts Receivable	_____
Inventory	_____
Machinery	_____
Buildings	_____
Land	_____
Total Class III	200,000

7.   Class IV Goodwill (line 5 - line 6) $ 25,000

Asset Acquisition Statement Under Section 1060

Date of sale   Total sales price
6/15/05   225,000
Assets Transferred

1. Assets	Aggregate Fair Market Value (Actual Amount for Class I)	Allocation of Sales Price
Class I	$	$
Class II	$	$
Class III	$200,000	$200,000
Class IV		$ 25,000
Total		$225,000

3.   In connection with the purchase of the group of assets, did you also purchase a license or a covenant not to compete, or enter into a lease agreement, employment contract, management contract, or similar arrangement with the seller (or managers, directors, owners, or employees of the seller)?   Yes _X_ No___

NONCOMPETE $10,000

Class III, Intangible Amortizable Assets Only

Assets	Fair Market Value	Useful Life	Allocation of Sales Price
Noncompete Agreement	$ 10,000	15	$ 10,000
Tax Returns Clients	105,000	15	105,000
Franchise Agreement	15,000	15	15,000
Lease—Office	10,000	15	10,000
Furniture & Fixtures	25,000		
Equipment	30,000		
Noncompete Agreement—seller	10,000		
Office Supplies	5,000		
Office Space	10,000		
Franchise Agreement	15,000		
Tax Return Clients	105,000		
Goodwill	25,000		
Capital		75,000	
Note Payable		150,000	

.07 Amortization of Goodwill and Certain Other Intangibles (Code Sec. 197)

A taxpayer is entitled to an amortization deduction with respect to any amortizable section 197 intangible. The amount of such deduction shall be determined by amortizing the adjusted basis (for purposes of determining gain) of such intangible ratably over the 15-year period beginning with the month in which such intangible was acquired. (Code Sec. 197(a))

A taxpayer is allowed to deduct up to $5,000 of start-up and $5,000 of organizational expenditures in the tax year in which the trade or business begins. Each $5,000 amount is reduced, but not below zero, by the amount by which the cumulative cost of start-up or organizational expenditures exceeds $50,000, respectively. Start-up and organizational expenditures that are not deductible in the year in which the trade or business begins would be amortized over a 15-year period consistent with the amortization period for Code Sec. 197 intangibles. The law is effective for start-up and organizational expenditures incurred after October 22, 2004.

Amortizable Section 197 Intangible

The term "amortizable section 197 intangible" means any section 197 intangible which is acquired by the taxpayer after 8/6/93 and which is held in connection with the conduct of a trade or business or an activity for the production of income. (Code Sec. 197(c)(1))

The term "section 197 intangible" means:

- Goodwill,
- Going concern value,
- Any of the following intangible items:
  — Any patent, copyright, formula, process, design, pattern, know-how, format, or other similar item,
  — Any customer-based intangible,
  — Any supplier-based intangible,
  — A work force in place, including its composition and terms and conditions (contractual or otherwise) of its employment,
  — Business books and records, operating systems, or any other information base (including lists or other information with respect to current or prospective customers), or
  — Any other similar item,
- Any license, permit, or other right granted by a governmental unit or an agency or instrumentality thereof,
- Any covenant not to compete (or other arrangement to the extent such arrangement has substantially the same effect as a covenant not to compete) entered into in connection with an acquisition (directly or indirectly) of an interest in a trade or business or substantial portion thereof, and
- Any franchise, trademark, or trade name. (Code Sec. 197(d)(1))

Exclusion of Self-Created Intangibles

The term "amortizable section 197 intangible" does not include any section 197 intangible that is not described here in section 197 and that is created by the taxpayer. Intangibles created in connection with a transaction (or series of related transactions) involving the acquisition of assets constituting a trade or business or substantial portion thereof are subject to section 197 amortization. (Code Sec. 197(c)(2))

¶807.07

Covenants Not to Compete

In the case of any section 197 intangible that is a covenant not to compete (or other arrangement), described in subsection (d)(1)(E), in no event will such covenant or other arrangement be treated as disposed of (or becoming worthless) before the disposition of the entire interest described in such subsection in connection with which such covenant (or other arrangement) was entered into. (Code Sec. 197(f)(1)(B))

.09 Exchanges—Like-Kind

Property Held for Productive Use in Trade or Business or for Investment

Section 1031(a) provides an exception to the general rule requiring the recognition of gain or loss upon the sale or exchange of property. Under section 1031(a), no gain or loss is recognized if property held for productive use in trade or business or for investment is exchanged solely for property of a like kind to be held either for productive use in trade or business or for investment. Property held for productive use in trade or business may be exchanged for property held for investment. Similarly, property held for investment may be exchanged for property held for investment. Similarly, property held for investment may be exchanged for property held for productive use in trade or business. Property held for productive use in trade or business or for investment does not include stock in trade or other property held primarily for sale, nor stocks, bonds, notes, choses in action, certificates of trust or beneficial interest, or other securities or evidences of indebtedness or interest. (Reg. § 1.1031(a)-1(a))

Like-Kind Refers to Character

The words "like kind" refer to the nature or character of the property and not to its grade or quality. One kind or class of property may not be exchanged for property of a different kind or class. (Reg. § 1.1031(a)-1(b))

Provisions for Gain or Loss Recognized

No gain or loss is recognized if:

- A taxpayer exchanges property held for productive use in his or her trade or business, together with cash, for other property of like kind for the same use, such as a truck for a new truck or a passenger automobile for a new passenger automobile to be used for a like purpose.
- A taxpayer who is not a dealer in real estate exchanges city real estate for a ranch or a farm or improved real estate for unimproved real estate.
- A taxpayer exchanges investment property and cash for investment property of a like kind. (Reg. § 1.1031(a)-1(c))

Receipt of Other Property or Money in Tax-Free Exchange

If the taxpayer receives other property (in addition to property permitted to be received without recognition of gain) or money:

- In an exchange of insurance policies or annuity contracts,
- In an exchange of property held for investment or productive use in trade or business for property of like kind to be held either for productive use or for investment, or
- In an exchange of common stock for common stock, or preferred stock for preferred stock, in the same corporation and not in connection with a corporate

reorganization, the gain, if any, to the taxpayer will be recognized under section 1031(b) in an amount not in excess of the sum of the money and the fair market value of the other property, but the loss, if any, to the taxpayer from such an exchange will not be recognized under section 1031(c) to any extent. (Reg. § 1.1031(b)-1(a))

.10 Tax Basis and Holding Period of Like-Kind Property and Boot Received

Under Code Sec. 1031(d), the tax basis of the like-kind property received is adjusted for any unrecognized gain or loss from the like-kind property given up. The tax basis of the like-kind property received equals:

	The tax basis of the like-kind property given up
Plus	FMV of boot given (if any)
Plus	Gain recognized on like-kind property given (if any)
Less	FMV of boot received (if any).

Since any noncash boot received is taxable, its tax basis will be equal to its FMV, and a new holding period begins on the transaction date.

The holding period for the like-kind property received includes the holding period of the like-kind property given up. (Code Sec. 1223(1))

Facts:

Taxpayer A owns land with a FMV of $36,000 and a tax basis of $16,000.

Taxpayer B owns land with a FMV of $31,000 and a tax basis of $9,000.

In the exchange she gives Taxpayer A $5,000 of cash.

Taxpayer B's realized gain is $22,000 = $36,000 – $9,000 – $5,000. She has no recognized gain.

Taxpayer A's realized gain is $20,000 = $31,000 + $5,000 – $16,000. Taxpayer A recognizes only $5,000, lesser of realized gain or boot received.

Taxpayer A's basis in the like-kind property received is $16,000 ($16,000 + zero + $5,000 – $5,000), computed as follows:

$16,000		The tax basis of the like-kind property given up
0	Plus	FMV of boot given (if any)
5,000	Plus	Gain recognized on like-kind property given (if any)
5,000	Less	FMV of boot received (if any).
$16,000		

The property Taxpayer A now holds has a FMV of $31,000. In effect, the $15,000 unrecognized gain from the old property has become a $15,000 "built-in" gain in the new property.

Taxpayer B's basis in the like-kind property received is $14,000 ($9,000 + $5,000 + zero – zero).

$9,000		The tax basis of the like-kind property given up
5,000	Plus	FMV of boot given (if any)
0	Plus	Gain recognized on like-kind property given (if any)
0	Less	FMV of boot received (if any).
$14,000		

The property Taxpayer B now holds has a FMV of $36,000. Taxpayer B's $21,000 unrecognized gain from the old property has become a "built-in" gain in the new property.

Assume the same facts above, except that Taxpayer B's basis in her original parcel was $50,000. Her basis in the like-kind property received now equals $55,000 ($50,000 + $5,000 + zero – zero). The $19,000 unrecognized loss from the original parcel has become a $19,000 "built-in" loss in the parcel she now holds ($36,000 FMV and $55,000 basis).

Realized Gain with Liabilities Involved

When liabilities are involved, computing the transferor's realized gain equals:

	Gross amount of debt shifted to the transferee
Plus	FMV of boot received in form of cash and/or dissimilar property (if any)
Plus	FMV of like-kind property received
Less	Tax basis of like-kind property given plus any boot given
Less	Gross amount of liabilities taken on by transferor

Recognized Gain

The transferor's recognized gain equals the lesser of the realized gain or the boot received.

When the transferee assumes a liability or takes property subject to a liability, this counts as boot received by the transferor for gain recognition. The amounts are netted for gain recognition purposes, when both parties to the exchange assume liabilities or take property subject to liabilities. If the swap results in the transferor taking on more liabilities than is shifted to the transferee, the transferor is deemed to give the net amount as boot and the transferee is deemed to receive the net amount as boot.

For gain recognition purposes, deemed net boot given from liabilities cannot be used to offset actual boot received in the form of cash and/or dissimilar property. The transferor will still recognize gain equal to the lesser of the realized gain or the actual boot received even when the transferor has deemed net boot given from liabilities.

Taxpayer A owns Taxpayer A Land (FMV of $2,500,000, mortgage of $1,725,000, and tax basis of $1,700,000). The equity in Taxpayer A Land is $600,000.

He swaps the property with Taxpayer B.

Taxpayer B owns Taxpayer B Land (FMV of $2,350,000, mortgage of $1,850,000, and tax basis of $1,300,000). The equity in Taxpayer B Land is $500,000.

Taxpayer B pays $275,000 of cash to balance the land swap.

Taxpayer A's realized gain is computed as follows:

$1,725,000	Taxpayer A Land debt shifted to Taxpayer B
+ 275,000	FMV of boot received
+ 2,350,000	FMV of like-kind property received
– (1,700,000)	Tax basis of property given
– (1,850,000)	Taxpayer B Land debt assumed by Taxpayer A
800,000	

¶807.10

Taxpayer A's recognized gain is limited to the actual boot received of $275,000. Taxpayer A gets no "credit" for the fact that he gave $125,000 of deemed net boot from liabilities (excess of $1,850,000 assumed by Taxpayer A over $1,725,000 shifted to Taxpayer B).

Taxpayer A's basis in Taxpayer B Land is computed (using the formula presented earlier) as follows:

$1,700,000 Tax basis of Taxpayer A Land
+ 125,000 Boot given (from liabilities)
+ 275,000 Gain recognized on Taxpayer A Land disposition
– (275,000) Boot received
$1,825,000

The deemed net boot given adds to Taxpayer A's basis in the like-kind property received.

Thus, Taxpayer A has an unrecognized "built-in" gain of $525,000 in Taxpayer B Land (FMV of $2,350,000 less his basis of $1,825,000).

Taxpayer B's realized gain is computed as follows:

$1,850,000 Taxpayer B Land debt shifted to Taxpayer A
+ 0 FMV of boot received
+ 2,500,000 FMV of like-kind property received
– (1,575,000) Tax basis of property and boot given
– (1,725,000) Taxpayer A Land debt assumed by Taxpayer B
$ 1,050,000

Taxpayer B's recognized gain is zero because he is able to offset the $125,000 of deemed net boot received from liabilities with the $275,000 of actual boot given.

Taxpayer B's basis in Taxpayer A Land is computed as follows:

$1,300,000 Tax basis of Taxpayer B Land
+ 275,000 Boot given
+ 0 Gain recognized on Taxpayer B Land disposition
– (125,000) Boot received (from liabilities)
$ 1,450,000

Thus, Taxpayer B has an unrecognized "built-in" gain of $1,050,000 in Taxpayer A Land (FMV of $2,500,000 less his basis of $1,450,000).

.11 Treatment of Assumption of Liabilities

The amount of any liabilities of the taxpayer assumed by the other party to the exchange (or of any liabilities to which the property exchanged by the taxpayer is subject) is to be treated as money received by the taxpayer upon the exchange, whether or not the assumption resulted in a recognition of gain or loss to the taxpayer under the law applicable to the year in which the exchange was made.

> ***Example (1):*** B, an individual, owns an apartment house which has an adjusted basis in his hands of $500,000, but which is subject to a mortgage of $150,000. He transfers the apartment house to C, receiving in exchange therefor $50,000 in cash and another apartment house with a fair market value on that date

of $600,000. The transfer to C is made subject to the $150,000 mortgage. B realizes a gain of $300,000 on the exchange, computed as follows:

Value of property received	$600,000
Cash	50,000
Liabilities subject to which old property was transferred	150,000
Total consideration received	800,000
Less: Adjusted basis of property transferred	500,000
Gain realized	300,000

Under section 1031(b), $200,000 of the $300,000 gain is recognized.

The basis of the apartment house acquired by B upon the exchange is $500,000, computed as follows:

Adjusted basis of property transferred	$500,000
Less: Amount of money received:	
Cash	$ 50,000
Amount of liabilities subject to which property was transferred	150,000
	200,000
Difference	300,000
Plus: Amount of gain recognized upon the exchange	200,000
Basis of property acquired upon the exchange	$500,000

Example (2): D, an individual, owns an apartment house. On December 1, 20X5, the apartment house owned by D has an adjusted basis in his hands of $100,000, a fair market value of $220,000, but is subject to a mortgage of $80,000. E, an individual, also owns an apartment house. On December 1, 20X5, the apartment house owned by E has an adjusted basis of $175,000, a fair market value of $250,000, but is subject to a mortgage of $150,000. On December 1, 20X5, D transfers his apartment house to E, receiving in exchange therefor $40,000 in cash and the apartment house owned by E. Each apartment house is transferred subject to the mortgage on it.

D realizes a gain of $120,000 on the exchange, computed as follows:

Value of property received		$250,000
Cash		40,000
Liabilities subject to which old property was transferred		80,000
Total consideration received		370,000
Less: Adjusted basis of property transferred	$100,000	
Liabilities to which new property is subject	150,000	
		$250,000
Gain realized		$120,000

The amount of "other property or money" received by D is $40,000. (Consideration received by D in the form of a transfer subject to a liability of $80,000 is offset by consideration given in the form of a receipt of property subject to a $150,000 liability. Thus, only the consideration received in the form of cash, $40,000, is treated as "other property or money." $40,000 of the $120,000 gain is recognized.

The basis of the apartment house acquired by D is $170,000, computed as follows:

Adjusted basis of property transferred	$100,000
Liabilities to which new property is subject	150,000
Total	$250,000
Less: Amount of money received:	
Cash	$40,000
Amount of liabilities subject to which property was transferred	80,000
	$120,000
Difference	$130,000
Plus: Amount of gain recognized upon the exchange	40,000
Basis of property acquired upon the exchange	$170,000

E realizes a gain of $75,000 on the exchange, computed as follows:

Value of property received	$220,000
Liabilities subject to which old property was transferred	$150,000
Total consideration received	370,000
Less: Adjusted basis of property transferred	$175,000
Cash	40,000
Liabilities to which new property is subject	80,000
	$295,000
Gain realized	$ 75,000

The amount of "other property or money" received by E is $30,000. (Consideration received by E in the form of a transfer subject to a liability of $150,000 is offset by consideration given in the form of a receipt of property subject to an $80,000 liability and by the $40,000 cash paid by E. Although consideration received in the form of cash or other property is not offset by consideration given in the form of an assumption of liabilities or a receipt of property subject to a liability, consideration given in the form of cash or other property is offset against consideration received in the form of an assumption of liabilities or a transfer of property subject to a liability.) $30,000 of the $75,000 gain is recognized.

The basis of the apartment house acquired by E is $175,000, computed as follows:

Adjusted basis of property transferred	$175,000
Cash	40,000
Liabilities to which new property is subject	80,000
Total	295,000

```
Less: Amount of money received:
      Amount of liabilities subject to which property
      was transferred  . . . . . . . . . . . . . . . . . . . . . .$150,000
                                                            150,000
                                                         ──────────
Difference  . . . . . . . . . . . . . . . . . . . . . . . . . . . .$145,000
Plus: Amount of gain recognized upon the exchange   . . . 30,000
                                                         ──────────
Basis of property acquired upon the exchange  . . . . . .$175,000
```

[Reg. § 1.1031(d)-2.]

.12 Conversions

Involuntary Conversions

An "involuntary conversion" may be the result of the destruction of property, in whole or in part, the theft of property, the seizure of property, the requisition or condemnation of property, or the threat or imminence of requisition or condemnation of property. The proceeds arising from the disposition of the converted property must (within the time limits specified) be reinvested in similar property in order to avoid recognition of any gain realized. (Reg. §1.1033(a)-1(a)) The property must generally be replaced no later than two years after the end of the year in which any gain from the conversion is realized. (Code Sec. 1033(a)(2)(B))

Conversion into Similar Property

If property (as a result of its destruction, in whole or in part, theft, seizure, or requisition or condemnation, or threat or imminence thereof) is compulsorily or involuntarily converted only into property similar or related in service or use to the property so converted, no gain is recognized. Such nonrecognition of gain is mandatory. (Reg. § 1.1033(a)-2(b))

Conversion into Money or into Dissimilar Property

If property is compulsorily or involuntarily converted into money or into property not similar or related in service or use to the converted property, the gain, if any, is recognized, at the election of the taxpayer, only to the extent that the amount realized upon such conversion exceeds the cost of other property purchased by the taxpayer which is similar or related in service or use to the property so converted, or the cost of stock of a corporation owning such other property that is purchased by the taxpayer in the acquisition of control of such corporation, if the taxpayer purchased such other property, or such stock, for the purpose of replacing the property so converted and during the period required. (Reg. § 1.1033(a)-2(c)(1))

Basis of Property Acquired as a Result of an Involuntary Conversion

The basis of the acquired property is the same as the property so converted, decreased in the amount of any money received by the taxpayer that was not expended in accordance with the provisions of law determining the taxable status of the gain or loss upon such conversion, and increased in the amount of gain or decreased in the amount of loss to the taxpayer recognized upon such conversion under the law applicable to the year in which such conversion was made. In the case of property purchased by the taxpayer in a transaction, which resulted in the nonrecognition of any part of the gain realized as the result of a compulsory or involuntary conversion, the basis is the cost of such property decreased in the amount of the gain not so recognized; and if the property purchased consists of more than one piece of property, the basis is allocated to the purchased properties in proportion to their respective costs. (Code Sec. 1033(b))

Involuntary Conversion Rules for Property Damaged in Disaster

For purposes of the nonrecognition-of-gain rule regarding involuntarily converted property that is replaced with similar property, any tangible property that is acquired and held for productive use in a business is treated as similar or related to business or investment property that was involuntarily converted as a result of a Presidential-declared disaster.

Basis of Real Property Acquired in Involuntary Conversions

Real Property Only

If only depreciable real property is acquired to replace depreciable real property in an involuntary conversion in which gain is realized, and tax on the gain is postponed under the rules for involuntary conversions, the basis of the replacement property is its cost less the gain on which tax is postponed. If the replacement property consists of more than one piece of depreciable real property, the cost of each piece is reduced by an allocable part of the gain. (Code Sec. 1033(b))

Real and Other Property in Exchange

The basis must be figured as follows:

1. Subtract from cost the ordinary income because of additional depreciation that is not required to be reported,
2. Add the tentative basis figured in (1) to the cost of the other property acquired,
3. Subtract from the total in (2) the excess of gain on which tax is postponed over the ordinary income because of additional depreciation not required to be reported, and finally
4. Allocate the amount obtained in (3) to each asset in proportion to its cost, as listed in (2).

   Example: Property was condemned by the state. The property had an adjusted basis of $26,000, and the state paid the taxpayer $31,000 for it. The taxpayer realized a gain of $5,000 ($31,000 – $26,000). New property that is similar in use to the old property was bought for $29,000, and the taxpayer recognizes a gain of $2,000 ($31,000 – $29,000), the unspent part of the payment from the state. The basis of the new property is as follows:

Cost of new property	$29,000
Minus: Gain not recognized	3,000
Basis of the new property	$26,000

   (IRS Publication 544)

Example of Basis for Property Converted to Business or Rental Use From Personal Use

Depreciable basis (if real estate, do not include fair market value of land)

1. Original cost or other basis of property	$75,000
2. Plus improvements since acquisition	25,000
3. Minus deductible casualty loss	(4,000)
4. Minus other decreases to basis	( )
5. Adjusted basis of property on date of conversion	96,000
6. Fair market value of property on date of conversion	85,000
7. Depreciation basis (lesser of line 5 or line 6)	85,000

Example of Basis for Subsequent Sale or Property Converted to Business Use

	(A) Adjusted Basis	(B) FMV Basis
1. Original cost	$75,000	
2. Fair market value on date of conversion		$115,000
3. Add:		
(a) Improvements prior to conversion to business	20,000	
(b) Improvements after conversion to business	15,000	15,000
4. Less:		
(a) Deductible casualty loss prior to conversion	(4,000)	
(b) Deductible casualty loss after conversion	( )	( )
(c) Amount received for easement prior to conversion	( )	
(d) Amount received for easement after conversion	( )	( )
(e) Depreciation total taken	(14,000)	(14,000)
5. Basis	$92,000	$86,000
6. Adjusted basis for gain (Column A)	92,000	
7. Adjusted basis for loss (lesser of Column A or B)	86,000	

1. If the fair market value basis exceeds the adjusted basis, then the adjusted basis is used in the calculation of gain or loss.

2. If the fair market value basis is below the adjusted basis and the sales price is between both, neither gain or loss is recognized on the sale.

.13 Foreclosure, Repossession, or Abandonment

Loss

No deduction is allowed for a loss on:

- A personal residence or other property held for personal use, unless the loss is from a personal casualty or theft (and the $100 and 10%-of-AGI rules are met), or
- The transfer of any property between related parties.
- The owner will have a deductible loss if the adjusted basis of business or investment property transferred through foreclosure or repossession exceeds the amount realized. Depending on whether the property is a capital asset, the loss may be an ordinary loss or a capital loss.

Gain

If the amount realized by the owner of property transferred through foreclosure or repossession is greater than its adjusted basis, the excess is a gain, taxed in the same way as a gain from sales or exchanges generally. A gain from property held for personal use is taxed as a capital gain. Property used in a trade or business and held for more than one year is section 1231 property. A gain on a sale or exchange of section 1231 property, whether by foreclosure or repossession, may qualify as a long-term capital gain.

Cancellation of Debt

Income from cancellation of debt is in addition to the gain or loss from the sale or exchange (transfer of property). This ordinary income from the cancellation of debt may arise if:

¶807.13

- The owner is personally liable for repayment of the debt secured by the property transferred to satisfy the debt and

- The fair market value (FMV) of the property transferred is less than the amount of canceled debt.

The amount realized by the owner does not include the amount of cancelled debt that is more than the FMV of the property transferred. However, the owner may have ordinary income from cancellation of debt for that part of the cancelled debt not included in the amount realized. (IRS Publication 544)

Example of Gain Recognition on Repossession

Real property with an adjusted basis of $40,000 is sold for $100,000. Buyer made a down payment of $20,000 and defaulted after making total payments of $30,000 (plus interest). The seller used installment reporting and incurred $4,000 in repossessions expenses. Upon reacquisition the property was worth $120,000 and the mortgage was canceled. The realized gain on repossession equals:

Fair market value received	$120,000
Less adjusted basis in installment obligation (40% of $70,000)	(28,000)
and less repossession expenses	(4,000)
Realized gain	$88,000

Because of Section 1038 the gain recognition is limited to the lesser of

Amount collected	30,000
Amount collected less gain recognized (60% of $30,000)	(18,000)
	$ 12,000

or	
Gain realized originally	$60,000
less gain recognized	(18,000)
and less repossession cost	(4,000)
	$38,000

Thus, of the actual realized gain of $88,000, only $12,000 is recognized upon repossession and the fair market value is disregarded. Because of the nonrecognition the seller's new basis equals:

Basis in canceled installment obligation	$28,000
plus gain recognized	12,000
plus repossession cost	4,000
Basis after repossession	$44,000

Example of Benefiting from the Rollover of Gain Provision after its Repeal

Rita sold her residence with an adjusted basis of $40,000 for $100,000 in 1996, taking back a mortgage. She purchases a replacement residence for $200,000. After making total payments of $50,000 (plus interest) the buyer defaulted and Rita reacquired the property in exchange for canceling the purchase money mortgage. If she resells the house within a year of acquisition for $170,000, she is deemed to have sold it for $220,000 in 1996 for the purpose of applying Section 1034 with the following tax consequences:

1. She has realized a gain of $180,000 on the original sale. ($50,000 + $170,000 - $40,000).
2. Only $20,000 of gain must be recognized, eligible for the 20% maxitax in section 1(h) on capital gains from assets held over 12 months. This is because she reinvested all but $20,000 of the recomputed selling price. ($200,000 out of $220,000).
3. The rollover provision applies despite its repeal for sales after May 6, 1997, as long as the original sale took place prior to May 7, 1997. There is no time limit on the period elapsing between the sale and the resale.
4. Rita's adjusted basis in her residence acquired years earlier is reduced from $140,000 ($200,000 less gain of $60,000 originally deferred), to $40,000 ($140,000 less $100,000, the latter representing the portion of the extra $120,000 gain deferred). The adjustment takes place in the year of resale, e.g., in year 2003.

Example of Increasing Gain on Original Rollover

Same as the previous example, except Rita purchased a replacement residence for $85,000, recognizing a $15,000 gain on the original sale. If she resold the house within a year of acquisition for $170,000, resulting in a recomputed selling price of $220,000, the following tax consequences occur:

1. Her realized gain of $60,000 of which $15,000 was recognized (or is being recognized under the installment method) and $45,000 of which reduced the adjusted basis of her replacement residence to $40,000, must all be revisited. Any recomputations are made as if the resale took place in 1994 (the year of original sale), but the necessary adjustments are effective in the year of resale, e.g., year 2008.
2. Her realized gain is now $180,000 ($220,000 less $40,000) which adds $120,000 of gain in the year of resale, since the replacement residence did not exceed the original selling price ($45,000 of gain is still deferred, leaving $135,000 of total gain to be recognized, $15,000 of which was recognized in 1994).
3. Her basis in the replacement residence stays the same because the deferred gain is unchanged.
4. By not reselling the house within a year of repossession, the nonrecognition provision in Section 1038 applies and it no longer matters that a greater portion of the new recomputed selling price was not invested in the replacement residence.
5. Under Section 1038 the gain recognized on repossession equals the lesser of:

(a) Amount collected prior to repossession	$50,000
less gain reported so far, for example $10,000 (of a maximum $15,000)	(10,000)
	$40,000

(b) Amount realized less adjusted basis at the time of original sales	$60,000
less gain reported so far	(10,000)
and less repossession expense, for example	(3,000)
	(13,000)
	$47,000

Thus, by retaining the property for over a year, Rita's recognized gain is reduced from $120,000 to $40,000.

Example of Avoiding Gain on Original Rollover by Making "Old" Exclusion Election

Same as the previous example, except that Rita was over age 55 when the original sale took place. (It is irrelevant that she has turned 55 subsequently.) She was therefore eligible to make the "old" Section 121 election, but she saved it, since the recognized gain was only $15,000 with the rollover and could be reported over many years on the installment method. By making the "old" $125,000 exclusion election by April 15 the fourth year after the year of original sale, even if prior to the resale (within the one year limitation) and even if prior to repossession (for example because of any sign of possible default and because the statute was running out on making the election) the following tax consequences result:

1. $125,000 of the $180,000 of realized gain is excluded from gross income.

2. The Section 1034 rollover provision still applies and has to be revisited.

3. The adjusted selling price is recomputed and is $95,000 ($220,000 less $125,000).

4. Since $85,000 was reinvested in a replacement residence, the recognized gain in 1996 should have been $10,000 instead of $15,000.

5. Since all adjustments are made in the year of resale, taxpayer should receive a deduction of $5,000 in the year of sale (presumably a long-term capital loss, since the original gain was a long-term capital gain, by virtue of the Arrowsmith doctrine).

6. Since $45,000 of the $55,000 realized gain is deferred, the basis in the replacement residence remains at $40,000 (plus/minus unrelated post-acquisition adjustments, such as improvements, cost recovery deductions, and casualty losses).

Example of Increased Use of New Exclusion

Rita sold her condo on June 15, 2001, for $200,000 with a $50,000 adjusted basis. She provided seller financing and the buyer defaulted. Rita reacquired the condo on October 31, 2005, canceling the purchase money mortgage in the process. If Rita resells the condo by October 31, year 2006, she can exclude up to $100,000 under the original $250,000 exclusion, $150,000 of which was used up in the original sale, for a total of $250,000. It is sufficient to resell the condo by October 31, 2006 (within one year of the repossession). She does not have to sell within three years of the original sale to continue to meet the "two years of last five years" ownership and use requirement. Since the resale is deemed to take place on the date of the original sale (as part of it), it is only necessary to have met the ownership and use requirements at the time of original sale, regardless of time elapsed.

Sale of Residence—Exclusion of Gain From Sale of Principal Residence

(Effective for sales and exchanges after May 6, 1997.)

Exclusion. Gross income shall not include gain from the sale or exchange of property if, during the five year period ending on the date of the sale or exchange, such property has been owned and used by the taxpayer as the taxpayer's principal residence for periods aggregating two years or more. (Code Sec. 121(a))

Limitation. The amount of gain excluded from gross income shall not exceed $250,000. This shall be applied by substituting "$500,000" for "$250,000" if either spouse meets the ownership requirements with respect to such property, both spouses meet the use requirements with respect to such property, and neither spouse is ineligible for the benefits with respect to such property.

Other joint returns. If such spouses do not meet the above requirements, the limitation shall be the sum of the limitations above to which each spouse would be entitled if such spouses had not been married. Each spouse shall be treated as owning the property during the period that either spouse owned the property. (Code Sec. 121(b)(2))

Application to only one sale or exchange every two years. These rules do not apply to any sale or exchange by the taxpayer if, during the two-year period ending on the date of such sale or exchange, there was any other sale or exchange by the taxpayer to which these rules are applied.

Exclusion for taxpayers failing to meet certain requirements. In the case of a sale or exchange to which these rules apply, the ownership and use requirements do not apply; and the dollar limitation is equal to the amount which bears the same ratio to such limitation (determined without regard to this paragraph) as the shorter of:

- The aggregate periods, during the five-year period ending on the date of such sale or exchange, such property has been owned and used by the taxpayer as the taxpayer's principal residence, or

- The period after the date of the most recent prior sale or exchange by the taxpayer and before the date of such sale or exchange, bears to two years. (Code Sec. 121(c)(1))

Joint returns. If a husband and wife make a joint return for the taxable year of the sale or exchange of the property, the exemption applies if either spouse meets the ownership and use requirements regarding the property.

Property of deceased spouse. In the case of an unmarried individual whose spouse is deceased on the date of the sale or exchange of property, the period such unmarried individual owned and used such property includes the period such deceased spouse owned and used such property before death.

Property Owned by Spouse or Former Spouse

Property transferred to individual from spouse or former spouse. In the case of an individual holding property transferred to such individual, the period such individual owns such property includes the period the transferor owned the property.

¶807.13

Property used by former spouse pursuant to divorce decree. An individual is treated as using property as such individual's principal residence during any period of ownership while such individual's spouse or former spouse is granted use of the property under a divorce or separation instrument.

Involuntary conversions. The destruction, theft, seizure, requisition, or condemnation of property is treated as the sale of such property. In applying section 1033, the amount realized from the sale or exchange of property is treated as being the amount determined without regard to this section, reduced by the amount of gain not included in gross income.

Property acquired after involuntary conversion. The holding and use by the taxpayer of the converted property is treated as holding and use by the taxpayer of the property sold or exchanged.

Recognition of gain attributable to depreciation. The sale-of-residence exclusion does not apply to so much of the gain from the sale of any property as does not exceed the portion of the depreciation adjustments (as defined in section 1250(b)(3)) attributable to periods after May 6, 1997, in respect of such property.

Determination of use during periods of out-of-residence care. In the case of a taxpayer who becomes physically or mentally incapable of self-care, and owns property and uses such property as the taxpayer's principal residence during the 5-year period for periods aggregating at least 1 year, then the taxpayer is treated as using such property as the taxpayer's principal residence during any time during such 5-year period in which the taxpayer owns the property and resides in any facility (including a nursing home) licensed by a State or political subdivision to care for an individual in the taxpayer's condition.

Sales of remainder interests. At the election of the taxpayer, these rules apply to the sale or exchange of an interest in a principal residence by reason of such interest being a remainder interest in such residence, but the exclusion does not apply to any other interest in such residence which is sold or exchanged separately.

Exception for sales to related parties. The exemption does not apply to any sale to, or exchange with, any person who bears a relationship to the taxpayer which is described in section 267(b) or 707(b). (Code Sec. 121(d))

Election to have section not apply. These rules do not apply to any sale or exchange with respect to which the taxpayer elects not to have these rules apply. (Code Sec. 121(f))

¶ 809 GAINS AND LOSSES—PASSIVE ACTIVITY

The Tax Reform Act of 1986 significantly impacted investment decisions with the passage of the passive activity rules. Essentially all limited partnerships, rental properties, and businesses in which an owner does not materially participate have been affected. The general rule is that losses arising from a passive activity are not deductible, except against income from a passive activity. The unused portion of the loss is suspended until offset by passive income in a future tax year or until the entire activity is disposed of in a fully taxable transaction.

.01 Passive Activity—Form 8582 Comprehensive Example (IRS Pub. 925)

Reporting Passive Activity Losses

In this example, in addition to Form 1040, the taxpayers (Charles and Lily) use Form 8582 (to figure allowed passive activity deductions), Schedule E (to report rental activities and partnership activities), Form 4797 (to figure the gain and allowable loss from assets sold that were used in the activities), and Schedule D (to report the sale of partnership interests). No matter how many activities, report each activity on the form as if the activity were not passive. Fill out Form 8582 to determine if the passive loss rules disallow any of the losses. Fill out Schedule E for the rental activities. Use Form 4797 to show gains and losses from the sale of business assets.

Charles and Lily are married, file a joint return, and have combined wages of $132,000 in the current year. They own interests in the following activities. They are at risk for all of their investments in the activities. They did not materially participate in any of the business activities. They actively participated in the rental real estate activities in the current year and all prior years.

Activity A is a rental real estate activity. Its income and expenses are reported on Schedule E. Charles and Lily's records show a loss from operations of $15,000 in the current year. Their records also show a gain of $2,776 in the current year from the sale of section 1231 assets used in the activity. That section 1231 gain is reported in Part I of Form 4797. In the previous year, they completed the Worksheets in the Instructions for Form 8582 and calculated that $6,667 of Activity A's Schedule E loss for the previous year was disallowed by the passive loss rules. That loss is carried over to the current year as a prior year unallowed Schedule E loss.

Activity B is a rental real estate activity. Its income and expenses are reported on Schedule E. Charles and Lily's records show a loss from operations of $11,600 in the current year. In the previous year, they completed the Worksheets in the Instructions for Form 8582 and calculated that $8,225 of Activity B's Schedule E loss for the previous year was disallowed by the passive loss rules. That loss is carried over to the current year as a prior year unallowed Schedule E loss.

Partnership #1 holds a trade or business activity and is not a publicly traded partnership (PTP). Partnership #1 reports a $4,000 distributive share of its current year profits to Charles and Lily on line 1 of Schedule K-1, Form 1065. They report that profit on Schedule E. In the previous year, they completed the Worksheets in the Instructions for Form 8582 and calculated that $2,600 of their distributive share of Partnership #1's previous year loss was disallowed by the passive loss rules. That loss is carried over to the current year as a prior year unallowed Schedule E loss.

Partnership #2 is a PTP that holds a trade or business activity. In the current year, Charles and Lily disposed of their entire interest in Partnership #2. They do not report that gain on Form 8582 because Partnership #2 is a PTP. They recognize a long-term capital gain of $15,300 ($25,300 selling price less $10,000 adjusted basis), which they report on Schedule D. The partnership reports a $1,200 distributive share of its current year losses to them on line 1 of Schedule K-1, Form 1065. They report that loss on Schedule E. In the previous year, they completed the PTP Worksheet in the Instructions for Form 8582 and calculated that $2,445 of their distributive share of Partnership #2's the previous year loss was disallowed by the passive loss rules. That loss is carried over and added to the $1,200 Schedule E loss.

¶809.01

Partnership #3 holds a single trade or business activity and is not a publicly traded partnership. Charles and Lily sold their entire interest in partnership #3 in November of the current year. The sale represents a disposition of their entire interest in this activity. They recognize a $4,000 ($15,000 selling price less $11,000 adjusted basis) long-term capital gain, which they report on Schedule D.

In the previous year, they completed the Worksheets in the Instructions for Form 8582 and calculated that $3,000 of their distributive share of the partnership's loss for the previous year was disallowed by the passive loss rules. That loss is carried over to the current year as a prior year unallowed Schedule E loss. Charles and Lily's distributive share of partnership losses for the current year reported on line 1 of Schedule K-1, Form 1065, is $6,000.

Partnership #4 is a limited partnership that holds a trade or business activity. Charles and Lily are limited partners who did not meet any of the material participation tests. Their distributive share of the current year partnership loss, reported on line 1 of Schedule K-1, Form 1065, is $2,400. In the previous year, they completed the Worksheets in the Instructions for Form 8582 and calculated that $1,500 of their distributive share of loss for the previous year was disallowed by the passive loss rules. That loss is carried over to the current year as a prior year unallowed Schedule E loss.

.03 Worksheets

Step One: Completing the Tax Forms Before Determining the Passive Activity Loss Limits

Charles and Lily enter their combined wages, $132,000, on Form 1040. They complete line 8 of Schedule D showing long-term capital gains of $15,300 from Partnership #2 and $4,000 from Partnership #3 in column (g). Because Partnership #2 is a PTP, it is not entered on Form 8582. Since the disposition of Partnership #3 represents a disposition of an entire interest in an activity with an overall loss of $5,000, that partnership is also not entered on Form 8582. They combine the PTP $1,200 current year loss with its $2,445 prior year loss, and also combine the Partnership #3's $6,000 current year loss with its $3,000 prior year loss and enter the two combined amounts in column (g) of Schedule E, Part II. They complete Schedule E, Part I, through line 22. Since their rental activities are passive, they must complete Form 8582 to figure the deductible losses to enter on line 23. They enter the gain from the sale of the section 1231 assets of Activity A on Form 4797. They enter the $4,000 profit from Partnership #1 on Schedule E, Part II.

Step Two: Completing Worksheets 1 and 2

Charles and Lily now complete Form 8582 and the worksheets that apply to their passive activities. Because they are at risk for all amounts invested in their activities, they do not complete Form 6198 before Form 8582.

Worksheet 1

Charles and Lily compute the gains and losses on Worksheet 1 for Activity A (a rental real estate activity). They enter all amounts from the activity, even though they already reported the gain of $2,776 on Form 4797, since all income or loss from an activity must be taken into account to figure the loss allowed. They write Activity A under Name of Activity. Then they enter: $2,776 gain in column (a) from Form 4797, line 2(h); ($15,000) loss in column (b) from Schedule E, line 22, column A; and ($6,667) prior year unallowed loss in column (c) from their worksheets used in the previous year. They combine the three amounts. Since the result ($18,891) is an overall loss, they enter it in column (e).

Activity B is a rental activity with a current year loss and a prior year unallowed loss. Charles and Lily write Activity B under Name of Activity. Then they enter: ($11,600) loss in column (b) from Schedule E, line 22, column B; ($8,225) prior year unallowed loss in column (c) from their previous year worksheets; Then they combine these two figures and enter the total loss ($19,825) in column (e).

They separately add columns (a), (b), and (c). They enter $2,776 in column (a) on the Total line and also on Form 8582, Part I, line 1a. They enter ($26,600) in column (b) on the Total line and also on Form 8582, Part I, line 1b. They enter ($14,892) in column (c) on the Total line and also on Form 8582, Part I, line 1c. They combine lines 1a, 1b, and 1c on Form 8582 and put the net loss ($38,716) on line 1d.

Worksheet 2

Because Partnership #1 and Partnership #4 are nonrental passive activities, Charles and Lily enter the appropriate information on Worksheet 2, similar to the way they reported their rental activities on Worksheet 1. Then they enter the totals on Form 8582, Part I, lines 2a through 2d.

Reporting Income from Column (d), Worksheets 1 and 2. Activities that have an overall gain in column (d) are not used any further in the calculations for Form 8582. At this point, overall gain activities should be entered on the forms or schedules that would normally be used. They have one activity with an overall gain ($4,000 - $2,600 = $1,400). This is Partnership #1, which is shown in Worksheet 2. They enter this partnership directly on Part II, Schedule E. They write: Partnership #1 on line c in column (a); "P" in column (b) since this entity is a partnership; no entry in (c) since it is not a foreign partnership; the employer identification number in (d); a check mark in (e) since all of their investment is at-risk; ($2,600) in column (g) which is the prior year unallowed Schedule E loss; and $4,000 in column (h), their distributive share of the current year profit.

Step Three: Completing Form 8582

Charles and Lily must now fill out Part II, Form 8582, since they will need the figure on line 9 to complete Worksheet 3. They enter all amounts without brackets as though they were positive. They can then complete Part III of Form 8582. They enter $38,716 on line 4, since this is the smaller of line 1d or line 3. They enter $150,000 on line 5, since they are married and filing a joint return. They enter $138,655, their modified adjusted gross income, on line 6. The $138,655 is made up of their wages, $132,000, plus their overall gain, $11,655, from the entire disposition of Partnership #2, a PTP, plus a $5,000 overall loss from the entire disposition of Partnership #3.

Charles and Lily reported on Schedule D their long-term gains of $15,300 from the PTP disposition and $4,000 from the partnership #3 disposition. Also, on Schedule E they combined the PTP current year loss of $1,200 with its prior loss of $2,445, and combined the Partnership #3 current year loss of $6,000 with its prior year loss of $3,000. Netting these amounts gives them the PTP overall gain of $11,655 and the Partnership #3 overall loss of $5,000 that were used in figuring modified adjusted gross income. They subtract line 6 from line 5 and enter the result, $11,345, on line 7. They multiply line 7 by 50 percent and enter the result, $5,673, on line 8. No matter what the result, they cannot enter more than $25,000 on line 8. They enter the smaller of line 4 or line 8 on line 9, or $5,673. They add the income on lines 1a and 2a and enter the result, $6,776, on line 10. They add lines 9 and 10 and enter the result, $12,449, on line 11.

Step Four: Completing Worksheet 3

Charles and Lily must complete Worksheet 3 since they have an overall loss in column (e) of Worksheet 1 and an amount on line 9 of Form 8582. In the two left-hand columns, they write the names of the activities, A and B, and the schedules the activities are reported on, Schedule E. They fill in column (a) with the losses from Worksheet 1, column (e). They add up the amounts, and enter the result, $38,716, in the Total line without brackets. They figure the ratios for column (b) by dividing each amount in column (a) by the Total line and entering the result in column (b). These ratios, when added, should equal 1.00.

Now, they are ready to prorate their special allowance for active participation in rental real estate activities (from Form 8582, Part II, line 9). They multiply the amount from line 9, Form 8582, $5,673, by each of the ratios in Worksheet 3, column (b) and enter the results on the appropriate line in column (c). The total should equal $5,673. They subtract column (c) from column (a) and enter each result in column (d).

Step Five: Completing Worksheet 4

One must complete Worksheet 4 if one has an overall loss in column (e) of Worksheet 2 or losses in column (d) of Worksheet 3 (or column (e) of Worksheet 1 if one did not have to complete Worksheet 3). Charles and Lily fill out Worksheet 4 with the activities from Worksheet 3. They have one activity showing a loss in Worksheet 2, column (e). They fill in the names of the activities and the schedules or forms each will be reported on in the two left-hand columns of Worksheet 4. In column (a), they enter the losses from Worksheet 2, column (e) and Worksheet 3, column (d). These losses are entered as positive numbers, not in brackets. They add the numbers and enter the total, $36,943, on the Total line. They divide each of the losses in column (a) by the amount on the column (a) Total line, and enter each result in column (b). These numbers should also add up to 1.00.

Now, they use the computation worksheet for column (c) under Worksheet 4 of the Instructions for Form 8582 to figure the unallowed loss to allocate in column (c). On line A of the computation worksheet, they enter the amount from line 3 of Form 8582, $41,216, as a positive number. On line B, they enter the amount from line 9 of Form 8582, $5,673. They subtract line B from line A and enter the result, $35,543, on line C. They multiply line C, $35,543, by each of the ratios in column (b) and enter the results in column (c). This is their total unallowed loss for the current year.

Step Six: Using Worksheets 5 and 6

Charles and Lily now decide whether they must use Worksheet 5, Worksheet 6, or both, to figure their allowed losses. If the losses from each activity entered on Worksheet 4 are reported on only one form or schedule, then Worksheet 5 is used. If any activity has a loss that is reported on two or more schedules or forms (for example, a loss that must be reported partly on Schedule C and partly on Form 4797), Worksheet 6 is used. They must only use Worksheet 5 to figure their allowed losses.

Worksheet 5. Charles and Lily determine that three of the activities they entered on Worksheet 4 should go on Worksheet 5, since the losses are only reported on Schedule E. The activities are A, B, and Partnership #4. They enter the names of the activities and the schedules to be used in the two left-hand columns of Worksheet 5. In column (a), they enter the total loss for each activity. These losses include the current year loss plus the prior year unallowed loss. They find these amounts by adding columns (b) and (c) on Worksheets 1 and 2. In column (b), they enter the unallowed loss for each activity already figured in Worksheet 4, column (c). They must save this information to use next year in figuring their passive losses.

In column (c), they figure their allowed losses for the current year by subtracting their unallowed losses, column (b), from their total losses, column (a). These allowed losses are entered on the appropriate schedules. They enter their allowed losses from Activities A and B on Schedule E, Part I, line 23, because these are rental properties. They report their allowed loss from Partnership #4 on Schedule E, Part II, by writing: The name of the activity on line 27D, column (a); "P" in column (b); the employer identification number in column (d); a check mark in column (e) since all their investment is at-risk; and ($148) in column (g).

Step Seven: Finishing the Reporting of the Passive Activities

Charles and Lily summarize the entries on Schedule E, Schedule D, and Form 4797, and enter the amounts on the appropriate lines of their Form 1040. They enter: the total Schedule D gain, $22,076, on line 13; Schedule E loss ($21,094) on line 17. Charles and Lily are now able to complete their return, having limited their losses from their passive activities as required.

.05 Filling in the Forms

Schedule E Form 1040

Part II Income or Loss from Partnerships and S Corporations

Name	(b) Enter P for Partnership; S for S Corporation	(d)Employer Identification Number
A Partnership #2	P	10-1672810
B Partnership #3	P	10-9876243
C Partnership #1	P	10-5566650
D Partnership #4	P	10-7435837

Passive Income and Loss

	(g) Passive Loss Allowed (attach Form 8582 if required)	(h) Passive Income from Schedule K-1
APTP (3,645)		
B	(9,000)	
C	(2,600)	4,000
D	(198)	
28a	Totals	4,000
b	Totals	15,393
29	Add columns (h) and (k) of line 28a	4,000
30	Add columns (g), (i), and (j) of line 28b	(15,393)
31	Total partnership and S corporation income or loss. Combine lines 29 and 30.	(11,393)

Part V: Summary

40 Total income or loss. Combine lines 26, 31, 36, 38 and 39. Enter the result here and on Form 1040 line 17. (21,094)

Worksheet 1—Form 8582. Lines 1a, 1b, and 1c

Name of Activity	Current Year (a) Net Income (line 1a)	(b) Net Loss (line 1b)	Prior Year (c) Unallowed Loss (line 1c)	Overall Gain or Loss (d) Gain	(e) Loss
Activity A	2,776	(15,000)	(6,667)		(18,891)
Activity B		(11,600)	(8,225)		(19,825)
Total, Enter on Form 8582, lines 1a, 1b, 1c.	2,776	(26,000)	(14,892)		

Worksheet 2—For Form 8582, Lines 2a, 2b, and 2c

Name of Activity	Current Year (a) Net Income (line 2a)	(b) Net Loss (line 2b)	Prior Year (c) Unallowed Loss (line 2c)	Overall Gain or Loss (d) Gain	(e) Loss
Partnership #1	4,000		(2,600)	1,400	
Partnership #4		(2,400)	(1,500)		(3,900)
Total, Enter on Form 8582, lines 2a, 2b, 2c	4,000	(2,400)	(4,100)		

Worksheet 3—Use This Worksheet if an Amount Is Shown on Form 8582, line 9

Name of Activity	Form or Schedule to Be Reported on	(a) Loss	(b) Ratio	(c) Special Allowance	(d) Subtract Column (c) from Column (a)
Activity A	Sch E	18,891	.487938	2,768	16,123
Activity B	Sch E	19,825	.512062	2,905	16,920
Total		38,716	1.000000	5,673	33,043

Worksheet 4—Allocation of Unallowed Losses

Name of Activity	Form or Schedule to Be Reported on	(a) Loss	(b) Ratio	(c) Unallowed Loss
Activity A	Sch. E	16,123	.436429	15,512
Activity B	Sch. E	16,920	.458003	16,279
Partnership #4	Sch. E	3,900	.105568	3,752
Total		36,943	1.000000	35,543

Worksheet 5—Allowed Losses

Name of Activity	Form or Schedule to Be Reported on	(a) Loss	(b)Unallowed Loss	(c)Allowed Loss
Activity A	Sch. E	21,667	15,512	6,155
Activity B	Sch. E	19,825	16,279	3,546
Partnership #4	Sch. E	3,900	3,752	148
Total		45,392	35,543	9,849

Source: IRS Pub. 925

Form 8582 Passive Activity Loss Limitations the Current Year

Name	Identifying Number
Charles Eric and Lily Woods	123-00-4567

Part I The Current Year Passive Activity Loss
Rental Real Estate Activities with Active Participation

1	a	Activities with net income (from Worksheet 1, column (a))	1a	2,776
1	a	Activities with net income (from Worksheet1, column (a))	1a	2,776
	b	Activities with net loss (from Worksheet 1, column (b))	1b	(26,600)
	c	Prior year unallowed losses (from Worksheet 1, column (c))	1c	(14,892)
	d	Combine lines 1a, 1b, and 1c	1d	(38,716)

All Other Passive Activities

2	a	Activities with net income (from Worksheet 1, column (a))	2a	4,000
	b	Activities with net loss (from Worksheet 2, column (b))	2b	(2,400)
	c	Prior year unallowed losses (from Worksheet 2, column (c))	2c	(4,100)
	d	Combine lines 2a, 2b, and 2c	2d	(2,500)
3		Combine lines 1d and 2d	3	(41,216)

Part II Special Allowance for Rental Real Estate with Active Participation

4	Enter the smaller of the loss on line 1d or the loss on line 3	4	38,716
5	Enter $150,000. If married and filing separately, see instructions	5	150,000
6	Enter modified adjusted gross income, but not less than zero	6	138,655
7	Subtract line 6 from line 5	7	11,345
8	Multiply line 7 by 50%	8	5,673
9	Enter the smaller of line 4 or line 8	9	5,673

Part III Total Losses Allowed

10	Add the income, if any, on lines 1a and 2a and enter the total	10	6,776
11	Total losses allowed from all passive activities for the current year. Add lines 9 and 10.	11	12,449

Source: IRS Pub. 925

¶ 811 INDIVIDUAL RETURNS—TABLES

.01 Tax Rate Schedules (2006-2007)

Tax Return Schedules 2006

Married individuals filing joint returns and surviving spouses:

If taxable income is:	The tax is:
Not over $15,100	10% of the taxable income
Over $15,100 but not over $61,300	$1,510.00 + 15% of the excess over $15,100
Over $61,300 but not over $123,700	$8,440.00 + 25% of the excess over $61,300
Over $123,700 but not over $188,450	$24,040.00 + 28% of the excess over $123,700
Over $188,450 but not over $336,550	$42,170.00 + 33% of the excess over $188,450
Over $336,550	$91,043.00 + 35% of the excess over $336,550

Heads of households:

If taxable income is:	The tax is:
Not over $10,750	10% of the taxable income
Over $10,750 but not over $41,050	$1,075.00 + 15% of the excess over $10,750
Over $41,050 but not over $106,000	$5,620.00 + 25% of the excess over $41,050
Over $106,000 but not over $171,650	$21,857.50 + 28% of the excess over $106,000
Over $171,650 but not over $336,550	$40,239.50 + 33% of the excess over $171,650
Over $336,550	$94,656.50 + 35% of the excess over $336,550

Unmarried individuals (other than surviving spouses and heads of households):

If taxable income is:	The tax is:
Not over $7,550	10% of the taxable income
Over $7,550 but not over $30,650	$755.00 + 15% of the excess over $7,550
Over $30,650 but not over $74,200	$4,220.00 + 25% of the excess over $30,650
Over $74,200 but not over $154,800	$15,107.50 + 28% of the excess over $74,200
Over $154,800 but not over $336,550	$37,675.50 + 33% of the excess over $154,800
Over $336,550	$97,653.00 + 35% of the excess over $336,550

Married individuals filing separate returns:

If taxable income is:	The tax is:
Not over $7,550	10% of the taxable income
Over $7,550 but not over $30,650	$755.00 + 15% of the excess over $7,550
Over $30,650 but not over $61,850	$4,220.00 + 25% of the excess over $30,650
Over $61,850 but not over $94,225	$12,020.00 + 28% of the excess over $61,850
Over $94,225 but not over $168,275	$21,085.00 + 33% of the excess over $94,225
Over $168,275	$45,521.50 + 35% of the excess over $168,275

Estates and Trusts:

If taxable income is:	The tax is:
Not over $2,050	15% of the taxable income
Over $2,050 but not over $4,850	$307.50 + 25% of the excess over $2,050
Over $4,850 but not over $7,400	$1,007.50 + 28% of the excess over $4,850
Over $7,400 but not over $10,050	$1,721.50 + 33% of the excess over $7,400
Over $10,050	$2,596.00 + 35% of excess over $10,050

Tax Return Schedules 2007

Married individuals filing joint returns and surviving spouses:

If taxable income is:	The tax is:
Not over $15,650	10% of the taxable income
Over $15,650 but not over $63,700	$1,565.00 + 15% of the excess over $15,650
Over $63,700 but not over $128,500	$8,772.50 + 25% of the excess over $63,700
Over $128,500 but not over $195,850	$24,972.50 + 28% of the excess over $128,500
Over $195,850 but not over $349,700	$43,830.50 + 33% of the excess over $195,850
Over $349,700	$94,601.00 + 35% of the excess over $349,700

Heads of households:

If taxable income is:	The tax is:
Not over $11,200	10% of the taxable income
Over $11,200 but not over $42,650	$1,120.00 + 15% of the excess over $11,200
Over $42,650 but not over $110,100	$5,837.50 + 25% of the excess over $42,650
Over $110,100 but not over $178,350	$22,700.00 + 28% of the excess over $110,100
Over $178,350 but not over $349,700	$41,810.00 + 33% of the excess over $178,350
Over $349,700	$98,355.50 + 35% of the excess over $349,700

Unmarried individuals (other than surviving spouses and heads of households):

If taxable income is:	The tax is:
Not over $7,825	10% of the taxable income
Over $7,825 but not over $31,850	$782.50 + 15% of the excess over $7,825
Over $31,850 but not over $77,100	$4,386.25 + 25% of the excess over $31,850
Over $77,100 but not over $160,850	$15,698.75 + 28% of the excess over $77,100
Over $160,850 but not over $349,700	$39,148.75 + 33% of the excess over $160,850
Over $349,700	$101,469.75 + 35% of the excess over $349,700

Married individuals filing separate returns:

If taxable income is:	The tax is:
Not over $7,825	10% of the taxable income
Over $7,825 but not over $31,850	$782.50 + 15% of the excess over $7,825
Over $31,850 but not over $64,250	$4,386.25 + 25% of the excess over $31,850
Over $64,250 but not over $97,925	$12,486.25 + 28% of the excess over $64,250
Over $97,925 but not over $174,850	$21,915.25 + 33% of the excess over $97,925
Over $174,850	$47,300.50 + 35% of the excess over $174,850

Estates and Trusts:

If taxable income is:	The tax is:
Not over $2,150	15% of the taxable income
Over $2,150 but not over $5,000	$322.50 + 25% of the excess over $2,150
Over $5,000 but not over $7,650	$1,035.00 + 28% of the excess over $5,000
Over $7,650 but not over $10,450	$1,777.00 + 33% of the excess over $7,650
Over $10,450	$2,701.00 + 35% of excess over $10,450

.03 Personal Exemptions, Standard Deductions and Taxable Income Brackets

Following is a table of personal exemptions, standard deductions and taxable income brackets.

¶811.03

	1999	2000	2001	2002	2003	2004	2005	2006	2007
Personal exemptions	$2,750	$2,800	$2,900	3,000	3,050	3,100	3,200	3,300	$3,400
Standard deductions:									
Joint	7,200	7,350	7,600	7,850	9,500	9,700	10,000	10,300	10,700
Single	4,300	4,400	4,550	4,700	4,750	4,850	5,000	5,150	5,350
Head of household	6,350	6,450	6,650	6,900	7,000	7,150	7,300	7,550	7,850
Additional standard deductions for elderly/blind:									
Joint (ea. ind.)	850	850	900	900	950	950	1,000	1,000	1,050
Single/hd of household	1,050	1,100	1,100	1,150	1,150	1,200	1,250	1,250	1,300

Taxable Income Brackets:

Joint returns:

	1999	2000	2001	2002	2003	2004	2005	2006	2007
10% rate ends at				12,000	14,000	14,300	14,600	15,100	15,650
15% rate ends at	43,050	43,850	45,200	46,700	56,800	58,100	59,400	61,300	63,700
27% rate ends at	104,050	105,950	109,250	112,850	114,650	117,250	119,950	123,700	128,500
30% rate ends at	158,550	161,450	166,500	171,950	174,700	178,650	182,800	188,450	195,850
35% rate ends at	283,150	288,350	297,350	307,050	311,950	319,100	326,450	336,550	349,700

Single returns:

	1999	2000	2001	2002	2003	2004	2005	2006	2007
10% rate ends at				6,000	7,000	7,150	7,300	7,550	7,825
15% rate ends at	25,750	26,250	27,050	27,950	28,400	29,050	29,900	30,650	31,850
27% rate ends at	62,450	63,550	65,550	67,700	68,800	70,350	71,950	74,200	77,100
30% rate ends at	130,250	132,600	136,750	141,250	143,500	146,750	150,250	154,800	160,850
35% rate ends at	283,150	288,350	297,350	307,050	311,950	319,100	326,450	336,550	349,700

Heads of households:

	1999	2000	2001	2002	2003	2004	2005	2006	2007
10% rate ends at				10,000	10,000	10,200	10,450	10,750	11,200
15% rate ends at	34,550	35,150	36,250	37,950	38,050	38,900	39,800	41,050	42,650
27% rate ends at	89,150	90,800	93,650	96,700	98,250	100,500	102,800	106,000	110,100
30% rate ends at	144,400	147,050	151,650	156,600	159,100	162,700	166,850	171,650	178,350
35% rate ends at	283,150	288,350	297,350	307,050	311,950	319,100	326,450	336,550	349,700

.05 Filing Requirements

Filing Requirements—For Most People 2004-2007

To use this chart, first find your marital status at the end of the current year. Then, read across to find your filing status and age at the end of the current year. You must file a return if your gross income was at least the amount shown in the last column. Gross income means all income you received in the form of money, goods, property, and services that is not exempt from tax, including any excluded gain from the sale of your home from the Section 121 exclusion.

Filing Requirements For Most People 2004-2007

Marital Status	Filing Status	Age*	2003 Gross Income	2004 Gross Income	2005 Gross Income	2006 Gross Income	2007 Gross Income
Single (including divorced)	Single	under 65	$7,800	$7,950	$8,200	$8,450	$8,750
		65 or older	8,950	9,150	9,450	9,700	10,050
Head of household	Head of household	under 65	10,050	10,250	10,500	10,850	11,250
		65 or older	11,200	11,450	11,750	12,100	12,550
Married with a child and living apart from your spouse during the last 6 months of the current year	Head of household	under 65	10,050	10,250	10,500	10,850	11,250
		65 or older	11,200	11,450	11,750	12,100	12,550
Married and living with your spouse at end of the current year (or on the date your spouse died)	Married, joint return	under 65 (both spouses)	15,600	15,900	16,400	16,900	17,500
		65 or older (one spouse)	16,550	16,850	17,400	17,900	18,550
		65 or older (both spouses)	17,500	17,800	18,400	18,900	19,600
	Married, separate return	any age	3,050	3,100	3,200	3,300	3,400
Married, not living with your spouse at end of the current year (or on the date your spouse died)	Married, joint or separate return	any age	3,050	3,100			
Widowed before the current year and not remarried in the current year.	Single	under 65	7,800	7,950	8,200	8,450	8,750
		65 or older	8,950	9,150	9,450	9,700	10,050
	Head of household	under 65	10,050	10,250	10,500	10,850	11,250
		65 or older	11,200	11,450	11,750	12,100	12,550
	Qualifying widow(er) with dependent child	under 65	12,550	12,800	13,200	13,600	14,100
		65 or older	15,500	13,750	14,200	14,600	15,150

* If you turned age 65 on January 1 of the next year, you are considered to be age 65 at the end of the current year.

¶811.05

.07 Self-Employment Income Tax Chart
Self-Employment Income Tax

Maximum Self-Employment Income and Tax Rates

Years	Wage Base	Tax Rate	Maximum Tax
1973	$10,800	8.000 %	$ 864.00
1974	13,200	7.900	1,042.80
1975	14,100	7.900	1,113.90
1976	15,300	7.900	1,208.70
1977	16,500	7.900	1,303.50
1978	17,700	8.100	1,433.70
1979	22,900	8.100	1,854.90
1980	25,900	8.100	2,097.90
1981	29,700	9.300	2,762.10
1982	32,400	9.350	3,029.40
1983	35,700	9.350	3,337.95
1984	37,800	14.000	4,271.40
1985	39,600	14.000	4,672.80
1986	42,000	14.300	5,166.00
1987	43,800	14.300	5,387.40
1988	45,000	15.020	5,859.00
1989	48,000	15.020	7,209.60
1990	51,300	15.300	7,848.90

Maximum Self-Employment Income and Tax Rates For Years after 1990

Years	Wage Base (old age, survivors disability)	Tax Rate	Wage Base Medicare	Rate
1991	$53,400	12.40%	$125,000	2.9%
1992	$55,500	12.40%	$130,200	2.9%
1993	$57,600	12.40%	$135,000	2.9%
1994	$60,600	12.40%	All Wages	2.9%
1995	$61,200	12.40%	All Wages	2.9%
1996	$62,700	12.40%	All Wages	2.9%
1997	$65.400	12.40%	All Wages	2.9%
1998	$68,400	12.40%	All Wages	2.9%
1999	$72,600	12.40%	All Wages	2.9%
2000	$76,200	12.40%	All Wages	2.9%
2001	$80,400	12.40%	All Wages	2.9%
2002	$84,900	12.40%	All Wages	2.9%
2003	$87,000	12.40%	All Wages	2.9%
2004	$87,900	12.40%	All Wages	2.9%
2005	$90,000	12.40%	All Wages	2.9%
2006	$94,200	12.40%	All Wages	2.9%
2007	$97,500	12.40%	All Wages	2.9%

Source: Reg. § 1.1402(b)-1(b) and Circular E

.09 Estimated Tax Payment Chart

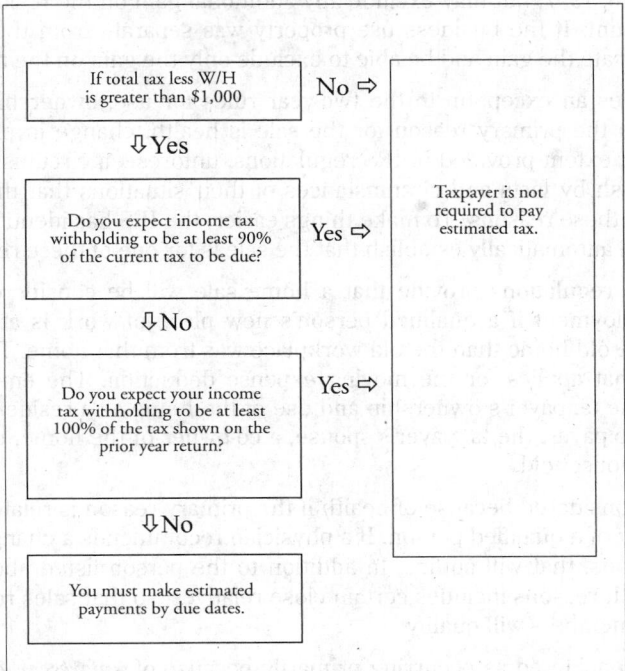

If total tax less W/H is greater than $1,000 — No ⇨

⇩ Yes

Do you expect income tax withholding to be at least 90% of the current tax to be due? — Yes ⇨

⇩ No

Do you expect your income tax withholding to be at least 100% of the tax shown on the prior year return? — Yes ⇨

⇩ No

You must make estimated payments by due dates.

Taxpayer is not required to pay estimated tax.

The de minimis threshold for an underpayment of estimated tax for individuals has been increased from $500 to $1,000 after 1997. The safe harbor provision for individual taxpayers with adjusted gross income of more than $150,000 was 110 percent of the prior year's taxes. For 1998 the law provides that such individuals can avoid an estimated tax penalty if they paid in at least the lesser of 90 percent of the 1998 tax or 100 percent of their 1997 tax liability. For 1999 the 110-percent safe harbor rule was changed to 105 percent of the 1998 tax liability. The percent increased to 108.6 percent for 2000, 110 percent for 2001, 112 percent for 2002, and 110 percent after 2002.

.11 Sale of Residence Regulations

In late December 2002, the IRS issued guidance in the form of both final and temporary regulations related to excluding gain on the sale of a principal residence.

For taxpayers with multiple homes, the regulations list several factors relevant to determining which home is the principal residence. Among these are amount of time used; place of employment; where other family members live; the address used for tax returns, driver's license, car and voter registration, bills, and correspondence; and the location of the taxpayer's banks, religious organizations, or recreational clubs.

The home sale exclusion may include gain from the sale of vacant land that has been used as part of the residence, if the land sale occurs within two years before or after the sale of the residence.

Taxpayers need not allocate gain between business and residential use if the business use and residential use if the business use occurred within the same dwelling unit as

¶811.11

the residential use. They must pay tax on the gain equal to the total depreciation they took after May 6, 1997, but may exclude any additional gain on the residence, up to the maximum amount. If the business use property was separate from the dwelling unit, they would allocate the gain and be able to exclude only the gain on the residential unit.

The law provides an exception to the two-year rules for use, ownership, and claimed exclusion when the primary reason for the sale is health, change in place of employment, or, to the extent provided in IRS regulations, unforeseen circumstances. Taxpayers may establish by facts and circumstances of their situations that their home sales were for one of these reasons. To make things easier, the IRS has identified various *safe harbors* that will automatically establish that the sale is for one of these reasons.

The temporary regulations provide that a home sale will be considered related to a change in employment if a qualified person's new place of work is at least 50 miles farther from the old home than the old workplace was from that home. This is the same distance rule that applies for the moving expense deduction. The employment must occur during the taxpayer's ownership and use of the home as a residence. A qualified person is the taxpayer, the taxpayer's spouse, a co-owner of the home, or a member of the taxpayer's household.

A sale will be considered because of health if the primary reason is related to a disease, illness, or injury of a qualified person. If a physician recommends a change in residence for health reasons, that will suffice. In addition to the person listed above, a qualified person for health reasons includes certain close relatives, so that sales related to caring for sick family members will qualify.

A sale will be considered as occurring primarily because of *unforeseen circumstances* if any of these events occur during the taxpayer's period of use and ownership of the residence:

- Death,
- Divorce or legal separation,
- Becoming eligible for unemployment compensation,
- A change in employment that leaves the taxpayer unable to pay the mortgage or reasonable basic living expenses,
- Multiple births resulting from the same pregnancy,
- Damage to the residence resulting from a natural or man-made disaster or an act of war or terrorism, and
- Condemnation, seizure, or other involuntary conversion of the property.

Any of the first five situations listed must involve the taxpayer, spouse, co-owner, or a member of the taxpayer's household to qualify. The regulations also give the IRS commissioner the discretion to determine other circumstances as unforeseen.

.12 Moving Expenses

Moving Expense Deduction Allowed

There shall be allowed as a deduction moving expenses paid or incurred during the taxable year in connection with the commencement of work by the taxpayer as an employee or as a self-employed individual at a new principal place of work. (Code Sec. 217(a))

Moving Expenses Defined

The term "moving expenses" means only the reasonable expenses:

- Of moving household goods and personal effects from the former residence to the new residence.
- Of traveling (including lodging) from the former residence to the new place of residence. (Code Sec. 217(b)(1))

Commencement of Work

A deduction is not allowable unless employment or self-employment actually does occur. Moving expenses incurred within one year of the date of the commencement of work are considered to be reasonably proximate in time to such commencement. The taxpayer need not remain employed by the same employer or remain self-employed in the same trade or business for the required number of weeks. However, he must be employed in the same general location of the new principal place of work during such period. (Regs. § 1.217-2(c)(3))

Rules for Self-Employed Individuals

"Self-employed individual" means an individual who performs personal services:

- As the owner of the entire interest in an unincorporated trade or business.
- As a partner in a partnership carrying on a trade or business. (Code Sec. 217(f))

When Self-Employed Work Commences

An individual who commences work at a new principal place of work as a self-employed individual shall be treated as having obtained employment when he has made substantial arrangements to commence such work. (Code Sec. 217(f)(2))

Expenses of Traveling from the Former Residence to the New Place of Residence

These expenses include the cost of transportation and lodging enroute from the taxpayer's former residence to his new place of residence. (Regs. § 1.217-2(b)(4)) Meals are not allowed as a moving expense deduction.

Minimum Distance Condition

No deduction shall be allowed unless:

- The taxpayer's new principal place of work:
  - Is at least 50 miles farther from his residence than his former principal place of work.
  - If he had no former principal place of work and is at least 50 miles from his former residence.
- The taxpayer must meet either of the following work requirements:
  - During the 12-month period immediately following his arrival to the general location of his new principal place of work, the taxpayer is a full-time employee, in such general location, during at least 39 weeks.
  - During the 24-month period immediately following his arrival in the general location of his new principal place of work, the taxpayer is a full-time employee or performs services as a self-employed individual on a full-time

basis, in such general location, during at least 78 weeks, of which not less than 39 weeks are during the 12-month period referred to.

- The distance between two points shall be the shortest of the more commonly traveled routes between such two points. (Code Sec. 217(c))

.13 Student Loan Interest Deduction

Individuals are allowed to deduct interest paid during the tax year on any qualified education loan. The maximum deductible amount of interest increased from $1,000 in 1998 to $2,500 after 2002. A qualified education loan is any debt incurred to pay the qualified higher education expenses of the taxpayer, the taxpayer's spouse, or an individual who was the taxpayer's dependent at the time the debt was incurred. The expenses must be attributable to a period during which the student was attending an eligible educational institution at least half-time. Qualified higher education expenses generally include the costs of tuition, fees, room and board, and related expenses such as books and supplies. However, such expenses must be reduced by amounts excludable from income such as (1) employer-provided educational assistance; (2) amounts received from U.S. savings bonds where the bonds are used to pay higher education costs; (3) amounts distributed from education individual retirement accounts; and (4) qualified scholarships, educational assistance allowances, and other excludable payments for education expenses that do not constitute a gift or inheritance. Before 2002, the deduction for interest on a qualified education loan is allowed only with respect to interest paid on the loan during the first 60 months in which interest payments are required. The amount of interest deduction is phased out for taxpayers at moderate income levels. The interest deduction phases out for single taxpayers between $50,000 and $65,000 of modified adjusted gross income and between $100,000 and $130,000 for joint filers. Taxpayers considered married for tax purposes must file a joint return to qualify for the interest deduction. The deduction is not allowed for any year which the taxpayer is a dependent. There is no requirement as to when the loan was incurred, but only interest paid after 1997 is eligible for the above-the-line deduction.

.15 Personal Exemptions

The federal income tax code allows a taxpayer to claim a personal exemption for taxpayer and taxpayer's spouse and a dependency exemption for each dependent. To qualify as a dependent, the person must be either a qualifying child or a qualifying relative.

An individual meeting the definition of a qualifying child qualifies the taxpayer for the dependency exemption, the child tax credit, earned income tax credit, dependent care credit, and head of household filing status. A child is a qualifying child of a taxpayer if the child satisfies each of three tests:

a. The child has the same principal place of abode as the taxpayer for more than one half the tax year.

b. The child has a specified relationship to the taxpayer. The child must be the taxpayer's son, daughter, stepson, stepdaughter, brother, sister, stepbrother, stepsister, or a descendant of any such individual.

c. The child has not yet attained a specified age. In general, a child must be under age 19 (or 24 in the case of a full-time student) in order to be a qualifying child. In general, no age limit applies with respect to individuals who are totally and permanently disabled at any time during the calendar year. The present-law requirements are retained that a child must be under age 13 for purposes of the dependent care credit, and under age 17 for purposes of the child tax credit.

The present-law support and gross income tests for determining dependency do not apply to a child who meets the requirements of the uniform definition of qualifying child. A child who provides over half of his or her own support generally is not considered a qualifying child of another taxpayer.

Taxpayers generally may claim an individual who does not meet the uniform definition of qualifying child with respect to any taxpayer as a dependent if the present-law dependency requirements (including the gross income and support tests) are satisfied.

The law retains the present rule that allows a custodial parent to release the claim to a dependency exemption (and, therefore, the child credit) to a noncustodial parent.

Five tests must be met for a qualifying relative: (1) the person must live with the taxpayer for the entire year as a member of the taxpayer's household or be related to the taxpayer; (2) the dependent's gross income must be less than the exemption amount, unless the dependent is under age 19 or a full-time student under age 24; (3) over half of the dependent's support must be furnished by the taxpayer (without certain exceptions for children of divorced parents); (4) the dependent must not have filed a joint return; and (5) the dependent must be a citizen, national, or resident of the United States, a resident of Canada or Mexico, or a child who, although not a U.S citizen, has been legally adopted by a U.S. citizen living abroad. An individual who can be claimed as a dependent by another taxpayer cannot claim an exemption for himself.

The IRS is authorized to deny claimed dependency exemptions, child tax credits, and dependent care credits if a taxpayer failed to provide a correct taxpayer identification number for the dependent. Denial of the exemption may impact the taxpayer's ability to claim head-of-household filing status, dependent-care credit, earned income credit, and the child-tax credit.

.17 Medical and Dental Expenses Chart

Qualified medical expenses include:

- Prescription medicines (those requiring a prescription by a doctor for their use by an individual) and insulin.
- Medical services fees (from doctors, dentists, surgeons, specialists, and other medical practitioners).
- Special items (artificial limbs, false teeth, eye-glasses, contact lenses, hearing aids, crutches, wheelchair, etc.).
- Meals and lodging provided by a hospital during medical treatment.
- Psychiatric care at a specially equipped medical center (includes meals and lodging).
- Special school or home for mentally or physically handicapped persons (see Pub. 502).
- Legal abortion.
- Expenses of an organ donor.
- Hospital services fees (lab work, therapy, nursing services, surgery, etc.).

- Treatment at a drug or alcohol center (includes meals and lodging provided by the center).

- Birth control pills prescribed by your doctor.

- Oxygen equipment and oxygen.

- Transportation for needed medical care.

- Cost and care of guide dogs or other animals aiding the blind, deaf, and disabled.

- Legal operation to prevent having children.

- Stop smoking program. (Rev. Rul. 99-28)

- Part of life-care fee paid to retirement home designated for medical care.

- Cost of lead-based paint removal. (see Pub. 502)

- Social Security tax for worker providing medical care. (see Pub. 926)

- Medical and hospital insurance premiums.

- Wages for nursing services. (see Pub. 502)

- Capital expenses for equipment or improvements to your home needed for medical care. (see Pub. 502)

- Long-term care insurance.

You cannot include:

- Medicine you buy without a prescription.

- Medical insurance included in a car insurance policy covering all persons injured in or by your car.

- Expenses for your general health (even if following your doctor's advice) such as:

  — Trip for general health improvement

  — Household help (even if you are physically unable to do housework)

  — Weight loss program

  — Social activities, such as dancing or swimming lessons

  — Health club dues

- Toothpaste, toiletries, cosmetics, etc.

- Life insurance or income protection policies, or policies providing payment for loss of life, limb, sight, etc.

- Nursing care for a healthy baby.

- Maternity clothes.

- Diaper service.

- Surgery for purely cosmetic reasons.

- Funeral, burial, or cremation expenses.

- Illegal operation or treatment.

(Source: IRS Pub. 17)

¶811.17

.19 Medical Expense Deduction

Long-term care insurance premiums are treated like other medical insurance. The deductible premiums are limited to a dollar amount based on age as follows:

	Maximum Deduction	
Age	2006	2007
40 years or less	$280	$290
More than 40, but not more than 50	530	550
More than 50, but not more than 60	1,060	1,100
More than 60, but not more than 70	2,830	2,950
More than 70	3,530	3,680

.21 Property Tax Expenses

Disallowance of Certain Taxes

No deduction shall be allowed for the following taxes:

- Federal income taxes, estate, inheritance, legacy, succession, and gift taxes.

- Taxes on real property, to the extent that section 164(d) requires such taxes to be treated as imposed on another taxpayer. (Code Sec. 275)

State or Local Taxes

A state or local tax includes only a tax imposed by a state, a possession of the United States, or a political subdivision of any of the foregoing, or by the District of Columbia. (Regs. § 1.164-3(a))

Real Property

The term "real property taxes" means taxes imposed on interests in real property and levied for the general public welfare, but it does not include taxes assessed against local benefits. (Reg. § 1.164-4, 1.64-3(b))

Personal Property Taxes

The term "personal property tax" means an ad valorem tax which is imposed on an annual basis in respect of personal property. To qualify as a personal property tax, a tax must meet the following three tests:

- The tax must be ad valorem, that is, substantially in proportion to the value of personal property; a tax which is based on criteria other than value does not qualify as ad valorem.

- The tax must be imposed on an annual basis, even if collected more frequently or less frequently.

- The tax must be imposed in respect of personal property. A tax may be considered to be imposed in respect of personal property even if it is imposed on the exercise of a privilege. Thus, state and local taxes on the registration or licensing of highway motor vehicles are not deductible as personal property taxes unless and to the extent that the tests prescribed in this subparagraph are met. For example, an annual ad valorem tax qualifies as a personal property tax although it is denominated a registration fee imposed for the privilege of registering motor vehicles or of using them on the highways. (Regs. § 1.164-3(c)(3))

Schedule A: Taxes—Deductible vs. Non-Deductible

	You Can Deduct	You Cannot Deduct
Income Taxes	Higher of state and local income taxes or state and local sales taxes. Foreign income taxes. Employee contributions to state disability fund, or state unemployment fund.	Federal income taxes. Employee contributions to private or voluntary disability plan.
Real Estate Taxes	State and local real estate taxes. Foreign real estate taxes. Tenant's share of real estate taxes paid by cooperative housing corporation.	Taxes for local benefits. Trash and garbage pickup fees. Rent increase due to higher real estate taxes.
Personal Property Taxes	State and local personal property taxes.	
Other Taxes	Taxes that are expenses of producing income.	Many taxes, such as federal excise taxes, generally are not deductible.
Fees and Charges		Fees and charges, such as for driver's licenses or water bills generally are not deductible.

Source: IRS Pub. 17

.23 Casualty Losses Chart

Deduction Limit Rules
(These rules apply to a casualty or theft loss to non-business property)

	$100 Rule	10% Rule
Definition of Rule	You must reduce each casualty or theft loss by $100 when figuring your deduction. Apply this rule AFTER you reduce your loss by any reimbursement.	You must reduce your total casualty or theft loss by 10% of your adjusted gross income. Apply this rule AFTER you reduce each loss by any reimbursement and by $100 (the $100 rule).
Single Event	Apply this rule only once, even if many pieces of property are affected.	Apply this rule only once, even if many pieces of property are affected.
More Than One Loss	Apply this rule to EACH loss.	Apply this rule to the TOTAL of your losses.
More Than One Person With Loss From the Same Event (Other Than Married Taxpayers)	Apply the rule SEPARATELY to each person.	Apply this rule SEPARATELY to each person.
Married Taxpayers With Loss From the Same Event		
Filing Jointly	Apply this rule as if you were one person.	Apply this rule as if you were one person.

	$100 Rule	10% Rule
Filing Separately	Apply this rule SEPARATELY to each spouse.	Apply this rule SEPARATELY to each spouse.
More Than One Owner (Other Than Married Taxpayers)	Apply this rule SEPARATELY to each owner of jointly owned property.	Apply this rule SEPARATELY to each owner of jointly owned property.

Source: IRS Pub. 547

.25 Education Expense Deduction

Education expenses incurred and not covered by employer educational assistance plans may still qualify for a deduction on the tax return. However, the education expenses must meet certain requirements discussed below.

Minimum Education Requirements

Expenditures made by an individual for education (including research undertaken as part of an educational program) which are not expenditures to meet minimum educational requirements or to qualify one for a new trade or business, are deductible as ordinary and necessary business expenses (even though the education may lead to a degree) if the education:

- Maintains or improves skills required by the individual in his or her employment or other trade or business;

- Meets the express requirements of the individual's employer, or the requirements of applicable law or regulations, imposed as a condition to the retention by the individual of an established employment relationship, status or rate of compensation. (Reg. § 1.162-5(a))

Deductible Educational Expenditures for Maintaining or Improving Skills

Deductible education costs to improve skills required by the individual in his or her employment includes refresher courses or courses dealing with current developments as well as academic or vocational courses. (Reg. § 1.162-5(c)(1))

Meeting Requirements of Employer and Educational Assistance

An individual is considered to have undertaken education in order to meet the express requirements of the employer, or the requirements of applicable law or regulations, imposed as a condition to the retention by the taxpayer of his or her established employment relationship, status, or rate of compensation only if such requirements are imposed for a bona fide business purpose of the individual's employer. Only the minimum education necessary for the retention by the individual of the established employment relationship, status, or rate of compensation may be considered as undertaken to meet the express requirements of the taxpayer's employer. (Reg. § 1.162-5(c)(2))

.27 Deductibility Summary for Schedule A

Non-Deductible Expenses

One cannot deduct the following expenses:

- Adoption expenses; however, the expenses may qualify for a credit.

- Burial or funeral expenses, including the cost of a cemetery lot.
- Campaign expenses.
- Capital expenses.
- Check-writing fees.
- Commuting expenses.
- Expenses to influence general public on legislation or elections.
- Fees and licenses, such as car licenses, marriage licenses, and dog tags.
- Fines and penalties, such as parking tickets.
- Health spa expenses.
- Hobby losses.
- Home repairs, insurance, and rent.
- Illegal bribes and kickbacks. (see Bribes and Kickbacks in Chapter 13 of Publication 535)
- Investment-related seminars. (Code Sec. 274 (h) (7))
- Life insurance premiums.
- Losses from the sale of your home, furniture, personal car, etc.
- Lost or misplaced cash or property.
- Lunches with co-workers.
- Meals while working late.
- Personal disability insurance premiums.
- Personal legal expenses.
- Personal, living, or family expenses.
- Political contributions.
- Professional accreditation fees.
- Professional reputation, expenses to improve.
- Relief fund contributions.
- Residential telephone line.
- Stockholders' meeting, expenses of attending.
- Tax-exempt income expenses.
- Voluntary unemployment benefit fund contributions.
- Wristwatches.

.35 Child and Dependent Care Tax Credit

The child and dependent care tax credit is a limited credit against the costs of care for a qualifying individual. A qualifying individual is a person who is (1) under the age of 13 and for whom the taxpayer may claim a dependency exemption or is (2) a physically or mentally incapacitated dependent or spouse who is incapable of caring for himself or herself. The costs of care must be incurred to enable a taxpayer (or a taxpayer's spouse, if married) to work or look for work. Qualified expenses include the costs of household services. Payments for services outside the home qualify if they involve the care of a child under age 13 or a disabled spouse or dependent who regularly spends at least 8 hours a day in the taxpayer's home. Payments made to a relative also qualify unless the payments are made to a relative that the taxpayer may claim as a dependent or to a taxpayer's child who is under age 19.

The dependent care tax credit is equal to a percentage of a taxpayer's qualified expenses. The amount of qualified expenses that can be taken into account in calculating the credit cannot exceed certain limits. The maximum amount of qualified expenses is limited to $3,000 for one qualifying individual and $6,000 for two or more qualifying individuals. In addition, the amount of qualified expenses cannot exceed the lesser of the earned income of the taxpayer or, if married, the taxpayer's spouse. A nonworking spouse who is a full-time student is assumed to have $250 of earned income per month (while a student) if there is one qualifying individual, and $500 per month if there are two or more qualifying individuals. The amount of work-related expenses that can be taken into account in calculating the credit is reduced by the amount of dependent care expenses excluded from a taxpayer's gross income under a qualified dependent care assistance program (Code Sec.129). Generally, a married couple must file a joint return in order to claim the credit.

The percentage used to calculate the credit depends on a taxpayer's adjusted gross income (AGI). A taxpayer whose AGI is $15,000 or less is allowed a credit equal to 30 percent of qualified work-related expenses. The credit percentage is reduced by one percentage point for each additional $2,000 in AGI, or portion of, above $15,000. For taxpayers whose AGI is greater than $43,000, the credit is equal to 20 percent of qualified expenses. The maximum amount of the credit is $1,050 for one qualifying individual and $2,100 for two or more qualifying individuals. Because the credit is not refundable, it cannot exceed a taxpayer's tax liability.

.37 Adoption Credit and Exclusion

For adoptive parents the tax credit is up to $10,960 (for 2006) for qualifying expenses paid to adopt an eligible child. Credit is subtracted from the tax liability. Also $10,960 paid or reimbursed by one's employer for qualifying adoption expenses under an adoption assistance program is excludable from gross income. The excluded amounts are subject to FICA and FUTA employment taxes. Taxpayers can use both provisions, but not to cover the same expenses. For 2007 the amount is $11,390.

Qualifying Expenses

Qualifying adoption expenses are reasonable and necessary adoption fees, court costs, attorney fees, traveling expenses (including amounts spent for meals and lodging) while away from home, and other expenses directly related to, and whose principal purpose is for, the legal adoption of an eligible child.

Nonqualifying Expenses

- Those that violate state or federal law.
- For carrying out any surrogate parenting arrangement.
- For the adoption of your spouse's child.
- Paid using funds received from any federal, state, or local program.
- Allowed as a credit or deduction under any other federal income tax rule.

¶811.37

- Paid or reimbursed by employer or otherwise (except that amounts paid or reimbursed under an adoption assistance program may be qualifying expenses for the exclusion).

Eligible Child

An eligible child must be under 18 years old, or physically or mentally incapable of caring for himself or herself.

Maximum Credit Allowed from Prior Expenses

You are adopting an eligible child, your qualifying adoption expenses for the credit, before you apply the dollar limit, are $1,000 for 2005 and $12,000 for 2006. The maximum amount of expenses you can take into account for the total adoption effort is $10,960. If you take the $1,000 into account for 2005, the maximum amount of expenses you can take into account for 2006 must be reduced by the expenses you took into account for 2005. Therefore your maximum credit for 2006 is $9,960 ($10,960 – $1,000).

Maximum Credit Amount Two Children

You adopt two brothers, Bobby and Sam, neither of whom is a child with special needs. Your qualifying adoption expenses for the credit, before you apply the dollar limit, are $12,500 for Bobby and $12,500 for Sam. Under the dollar limit, the maximum amount of expenses you can take into account for both adoptions is $21,920 ($10,960 for each child).

Your pay $6,000 of qualifying adoption expenses in an effort to adopt an eligible child. However, the adoption is not successful. You then pay an additional $8,000 of qualifying adoption expenses for the successful adoption of a different eligible child. For the dollar limit on the credit, you must treat the $14,000 of expenses as paid in one adoption effort. The maximum amount of expenses you can take into account is $10,960. (Publication No. 968)

Income Limit

The income limit on the adoption credit or exclusion is based on modified adjusted gross income (modified AGI). Use the following table to see if the income limit will affect your credit or exclusion.

If your modified AGI is . . .	Then the income limit is . . .
$164,410 or less	Will not affect your income credit or exclusion
$164,410 to $204,410	Will reduce your credit or exclusion
$204,410 or more	Will eliminate your credit or exclusion

Example: You are adopting an eligible child. You take into account, after applying the dollar limit, $1,000 of qualifying expenses for 2005 and $9,960 for 2006. Your modified AGI for 2005 is $169,450, and your modified AGI for 2006 is $184,410. Under the income limit, your credit for both years is reduced ratably. Your 2005 credit is reduced by 25%, to $750. Your 2006 credit is reduced by 50%, to $4,980. You cannot take any further credit for this adoption effort.

For 2007 the credit or exclusion phases out between $170,820 and $210,820.

Modified AGI

To figure your modified AGI for the purpose of the credit and exclusion, add back the following items to adjusted gross income:

- The foreign earned income exclusion,

- The foreign housing exclusion or deduction, and

- The exclusion for income from Guam, American Samoa, Northern Mariana Islands and Puerto Rico.

Modified AGI for purposes of the exclusion also includes the payments from your employer's adoption assistance program. (Publication No. 968)

Tax Liability Limit

The amount of the allowable adoption credit for a year cannot be more than the regular tax liability for that year, minus the following:

- Any credit for child and dependent care expenses,

- Any credit for the elderly or the disabled, and

- Any mortgage interest credit.

If the credit is more than this limit, you can carry forward the unused credit to your next five tax years, or unit used, whichever comes first. (Code Sec. 23(c))

Child Who is a U.S. Citizen or Resident

If the eligible child is a U.S. citizen or resident you can take the adoption credit or exclusion even if the adoption never become final.

If you pay qualifying expenses in . . .	Then take the credit in . . .
Any year before the year the adoption becomes final	The year after the year of the payment
The year the adoption becomes final	The year the adoption becomes final
Any year after the year the adoption becomes final	The year of the payment

If your employer pays for qualifying expenses under an adoption assistance program in any year, then take the exclusion in the year of the payment.

Foreign Child

If the eligible child is not a U.S. citizen or resident, a taxpayer cannot take the adoption credit or exclusion unless the adoption becomes final. Take the credit or exclusion as shown in the following table.

If you pay qualifying expenses in . . .	Then take the credit in . . .
Any year before the year the adoption becomes final	The year the adoption becomes final
The year the adoption becomes final	The year the adoption becomes final
Any year after the year the adoption becomes final	The year of the payment

If your employer pays for qualifying expenses under an adoption assistance program in . . .	Then take the exclusion in . . .
Any year before the year the adoption becomes final	The year the adoption becomes final
The year the adoption becomes final	The year the adoption becomes final
Any year after the year the adoption becomes final	The year of the payment

How to Take the Credit or Exclusion

File form 8839 with either Form 1040 or 1040A to take the credit or exclusion. The taxpayer should maintain records to support any adoption credit or exclusion claimed.

Joint Return Required

If married, a taxpayer must file a joint return to take the adoption credit or exclusion. However, one can take the credit or exclusion on a separate return if legally separated under a decree of divorce or separate maintenance, or if one lived apart from the spouse for the last six months or the tax year and the home is the eligible child's home for more than half the year, and one pays more than half the cost of keeping up your home for the year.

.39 Child Tax Credit

A Child Tax Credit of $1,000 can be claimed for children under age 17. An additional credit is available to families with three or more qualifying children or for taxpayers with earned income above certain levels. Eligibility for the credit phases out based on income levels.

.41 Education Credits

After 1997 two tax credits may be elected by low- and middle-income individuals for tuition expenses incurred by students pursuing college or graduate degrees or vocational training. HOPE Scholarship Credit provides a maximum nonrefundable tax credit of $1,650 per student for each of the first two years of post-secondary education. The Lifetime Learning Credit allows a credit of 20 percent of qualified tuition expenses paid by the taxpayer for any year the HOPE credit is not claimed.

The Hope Scholarship Credit

After 1997, taxpayers may be eligible to claim a nonrefundable Hope Scholarship Credit against their federal income taxes. The Hope Scholarship Credit may be claimed for the qualified tuition and related expenses of *each* student in the taxpayer's family (i.e., the taxpayer, the taxpayer's spouse, or an eligible dependent) who is enrolled at least half-time in one of the first two years of postsecondary education and who is enrolled in a program leading to a degree, certificate, or other recognized educational credential. For 2006 and 2007, the amount that may be claimed as a credit is generally equal to: (1) 100 percent of the first $1,100 of the taxpayer's out-of-pocket expenses for each student's qualified tuition and related expenses, plus (2) 50 percent of the next $1,100 of the taxpayer's out-of-pocket expenses for each student's qualified tuition and related expenses. Thus, the maximum credit a taxpayer may claim for a taxable year is $1,650 multiplied by the number of students in the family who meet the enrollment criteria described above. (Notice 97-60, October 27, 1997. 1997-46 I.R.B.)

¶811.39

The amount a taxpayer may claim as a Hope Scholarship Credit for 2006 is gradually reduced for taxpayers who have modified adjusted gross income between $45,000 ($90,000 for married taxpayers filing jointly) and $55,000 ($110,000 for married taxpayers filing jointly). Taxpayers with modified adjusted gross income over $55,000 ($110,000 for married taxpayers filing jointly) may not claim the Hope Scholarship Credit. Both the dollar limitation on the expenses for which the credit may be claimed and the modified adjusted gross income limitation is indexed for inflation after 2001.

For 2007 the Hope Scholarship Credit phases out between $47,000 and $57,000 ($104,000 and $114,000 for married taxpayers filing jointly).

Lifetime Learning Credit

As of July 1, 1998, taxpayers may be eligible to claim a nonrefundable Lifetime Learning Credit against their federal income taxes. The Lifetime Learning Credit may be claimed for the qualified tuition and related expenses of the students in the taxpayer's family (i.e., the taxpayer, the taxpayer's spouse, or an eligible dependent) who are enrolled in eligible educational institutions. Through 2002, the amount that may be claimed as a credit was equal to 20 percent of the taxpayer's first $5,000 of out-of-pocket qualified tuition and related expenses for all the students in the family. After 2002, the credit amount is equal to 20 percent of the taxpayer's first $10,000 of out-of-pocket qualified tuition and related expenses. Thus, the maximum credit a taxpayer may claim for a taxable year is $1,000 through 2002 and $2,000 thereafter. These amounts are not indexed for inflation. (Notice 97-60, October 27, 1997. 1997-46 I.R.B.)

If the taxpayer is claiming a Hope Scholarship Credit for a particular student, none of that student's expenses for that year may be applied toward the Lifetime Learning Credit. The amount a taxpayer may claim as a Lifetime Learning Credit is gradually reduced for taxpayers who have modified adjusted gross income between $45,000 ($90,000 for married taxpayers filing jointly) and $55,000 ($110,000 for married taxpayers filing jointly). Taxpayers with modified adjusted gross income over $55,000 ($110,000 for married taxpayers filing jointly) may not claim a Lifetime Learning Credit. The modified adjusted gross income limitation is indexed for inflation after 2001. The definition of modified adjusted gross income is the same as it is for purposes of the Hope Scholarship Credit.

For 2007 the Lifetime Learning Credit phases out between $47,000 and $57,000 ($104,000 and $114,000 for married taxpayers filing jointly).

Who may claim the Lifetime Learning Credit? An individual paying qualified tuition and related expenses at a postsecondary educational institution may claim the credit, provided the institution is an eligible educational institution. Unlike the Hope Scholarship Credit, students are not required to be enrolled at least half-time in one of the first two years of postsecondary education. Nonresident aliens generally are not eligible to claim the Lifetime Learning Credit.

May an individual claim a Lifetime Learning Credit for paying qualified tuition and related expenses for other family members? Yes. An individual may claim the credit for his/her own qualified tuition and related expenses and the qualified tuition and related expenses of his/her spouse and other eligible dependents (including children) for whom the dependency exemption is allowed. Generally, a parent may claim the dependency exemption for his/her unmarried child if: the parent supplies more than half the

¶811.41

child's support for the taxable year, and the child is under age 19 or is a full-time student under age 24. (Notice 97-60, October 27, 1997. 1997-46 I.R.B.)

.43 Earned Income Credit

The earned income credit (EIC) offers cash aid to working parents who have relatively low earnings and a dependent child. The EIC is a "refundable" tax credit. The Internal Revenue Service (IRS) makes a direct payment of the credit to those whose income is too low to owe income taxes or whose tax liability is smaller than the credit.

To receive the credit, a person must apply for the credit, either by filing an income tax return at the end of the tax year or by filing an earned income eligibility certificate with his/her employer for advance payments of the credit. To be eligible for the EIC, married couples must file a joint return. The earned income credit is denied to individuals not authorized to be employed in the United States.

Earned income credit for 2007 is:

- $2,853 with one qualifying child,
- $4,716 with more than one qualifying child, or
- $428 without a qualifying child.

Earned income credit for 2006 is:

- $2,447 with one qualifying child,
- $4,536 with more than one qualifying child, or
- $412 without a qualifying child.

Earned income amount for 2007. The amount a taxpayer can earn must be less than:

- $32,241 with one qualifying child,
- $37,783 with more than one qualifying child, or
- $12,590 without a qualifying child.

Earned income amount for 2006. The amount a taxpayer can earn must be less than:

- $32,001 with one qualifying child,
- $36,348 with more than one qualifying child, or
- $12,120 without a qualifying child.

The phaseouts for taxpayers filing jointly are $2,000 higher.

Social security numbers must be provided for the taxpayer, spouse, and any qualifying children. If an SSN is missing or incorrect, the taxpayer may not receive the credit.

The maximum amount of investment income a taxpayer can have and still get the credit is $2,800 for 2006, and the amount for 2007 is $2,900. For most people, investment income is taxable interest and dividends, tax-exempt interest, and capital gain net income.

Earned Income Credit Denied

The earned income credit will be denied for a period of years if improperly claimed because of reckless or intentional disregard of IRS rules or regulations, or fraud. Also, taxpayers denied the earned income credit as a result of deficiency procedures, must recertify their eligibility before they can claim the credit again. (Publication No. 17)

Modified AGI (Adjusted Gross Income)

Prior to 2002, modified AGI is used to limit a taxpayer's credit and is an individual's adjusted gross income without regard to amounts for: (1) capital losses, subject to certain limitations, (2) losses from trusts and estates, (3) lossses from nonbusiness rents and royalties and (4) 75% of the net losses from a trade or business. Modified AGI includes tax-exempt interest, and nontaxable distributions from a pension, annuity, or individual retirement arrangement (IRA), unless rolled over into a similar type of plan during the period allowed for rollovers.

After 2001, the earned income credit limitations are calculated based on the individual's adjusted gross income.

Disqualified Income

Disqualified income includes an individual's capital gain net income and net passive income in addition to interest, dividends, tax-exempt interest, and non-business rents or royalties. Credit percentages and phaseout percentages are provided for low-income individuals who have no qualifying children, one qualifying child, and more than one qualifying child.

Earned Income

The credit is based on earned income, which includes all wages, salaries, tips, and other employee compensation plus the amount of the taxpayer's net earnings from self-employment (determined with regard to the deduction for one-half of self-employment taxes). Earned income is determined without regard to community property laws.

Credit Has No Effect on Certain Welfare Benefits

The earned income credit and the advance earned income credit payments received will not be used to determine eligibility for the following benefit programs or how much can be received from the programs:

- Temporary assistance to needy families,
- Medicaid,
- Supplemental Security Income (SSI),
- Food stamps, and
- Low-income housing. (Publication No. 17)

For Those Who Have a Qualifying Child

Four tests must be met for a qualifying child. The four tests are: relationship, residency, age, and social security number. If a taxpayer's child does not meet all four tests of a qualifying child, then the taxpayer cannot claim the credit for persons with a qualifying child.

Relationship Test

To meet the relationship test, the child must be the taxpayer's:

- Son, daughter, or adopted child (or a descendant of the taxpayer's son, daughter, or adopted child—for example, grandchild),
- Stepson or stepdaughter, or
- Eligible foster child.

¶811.43

An adopted child includes a child placed with a taxpayer for adoption by an authorized placement agency, even if the adoption is not final.

An eligible foster child is any child you cared for as your own, who lived with you for more than half of the year, and who is:

(1) Your brother, sister, stepbrother, stepsister, or

(2) A descendant (such as a child) of your brother, sister, stepbrother, stepsister, or

(3) A child placed with you by an authorized placement agency.

Qualifying Child Who is Married

To meet the relationship test, the taxpayer generally must claim an exemption for the taxpayer's married qualifying child. However, the taxpayer does not have to claim an exemption, if the taxpayer meets either of the following exceptions:

(1) The taxpayer cannot claim his or her child's exemption only because he or she gave that right to the child's other parent by filling out Form 8332 or a similar written statement.

(2) The taxpayer cannot claim his or her child's exemption only because he or she gave that right to the child's other parent in a pre-1985 agreement (such as a separation agreement or divorce decree). (Publication No. 17)

Residency Test

To meet the residency test, the child: Must have lived with the taxpayer for more than half the year, and the home must be in the United States (one of the 50 states or the District of Columbia). To meet the residency test, the taxpayer does not need a traditional home. For example, if the taxpayer's child lived with him or her for more than half the year in a homeless shelter, the residency test is met.

U.S. military personnel stationed outside the United States on extended active duty are considered to live in the United States during that duty period for the earned income credit.

Birth or Death of a Child

The child is considered to have lived with the taxpayer for all of the year if both of the following apply: (1) the child was born or died during the year; or (2) your home was the child's home for the entire time he or she was alive during the year.

Temporary Absences

Count time that you or the qualifying child are away from home on a temporary absence due to a special circumstance as time lived at home. Examples of a special circumstance include: Illness, Attending school, Business, Vacation, and Military service. (Publication No. 17)

Age Test

To meet the age test, a child must be: Under age 19 at the end of the year; a full-time student under age 24 at the end of the year; or permanently and totally disabled at any time during the tax year, regardless of age.

¶811.43

.51 Rent vs. Own

Home ownership vs. renting—Comparison of the after-tax costs of owning vs. renting a residence.

Deductible interest you pay on your mortgage (up to certain limits) and property taxes. The amount of income taxes saved depends on tax bracket.

Investment—A house can be a benefit, or a disadvantage. It can appreciate or depreciate over the time owned.

If the house has any qualifying equity in it—(if it is worth more than the mortgage on it)—one may be eligible to take out a home equity loan. This creates favorable tax treatment since the loan interest is deductible. The use of the money is of no concern.

Assumptions

Income Tax Bracket- Federal	34 %
Analysis Period -Years	5
Pre-Tax Investment Rate-of-Return	10.00 %
Rental Cost Inflation Rate	8 %
Inflation Rate	5 %
House Property Inflation Rate	5 %

	House Purchase	Rental
Utilities per month	$200	$200
Property Insurance per month	$600	$600
Repairs/Maintenance per month	$232	$200
Rent per month		$1,500
Rent Security Deposit		$500
Property Tax per month	$122	
Interest Rate	10.0%	
Mortgage Payment per month	$834	
Life of Mortgage in months	360	
House Cost	$100,000	
House Down Payment	$5,000	
Points Paid for Mortgage ($)	$2	

Year	Cumulative Purchase Cost	Cumulative Rent Cost	Purchase Cost Difference
1	$14,936	$30,033	($15,097)
2	$30,298	$62,108	($31,810)
3	$46,108	$96,371	($50,263)
4	$62,386	$132,977	($70,591)
5	$79,153	$172,095	($92,942)

.53 Purchase of Residence

A home provides for an investment and tax shelter.

Many ordinary income tax savings will be because of the allowable tax write-offs associated with having a qualified, deductible mortgage on a home. A home provides important tax write-offs. One may be able to deduct interest and property taxes. For the purchase of a home, most of the "points" paid are deductible.

The federal tax laws favor home ownership in two important areas. From an estate planning basis, the current tax laws allow one to pass the residence to an heir at its appreciated basis. This is called a "stepped up basis," and can result in excellent income tax savings. The heirs can then sell the house, and avoid any tax on the appreciated value since their tax basis is the appreciated (or stepped up) basis.

Assumptions/Results	
Filing Status = Married filing jointly	
Personal Exemptions = 4	
Taxpayer's Adjusted Gross Income	$85,000
Itemized Deductions—other than house	$12,800
Amount Financed on House	$135,000
Mortgage Term in months	240
Interest Rate	10.00%
Real Estate Taxes per month	$250
Total Points Paid on Mortgage	1.00%

The additional tax savings resulting from the purchase of home:

Additional Tax Savings	
Year one tax savings	$1,915
Year two tax savings	$4,576
Year three tax savings	$4,435
Year four tax savings	$4,262
Year five tax savings	$4,052

.55 Real Property Cost Treatment Chart

Treatment of Settlement Costs on Sale or Purchase of Real Property

	Personal Residence		Investment Property	
	Buyer	**Seller**	**Buyer**	**Seller**
Closing costs incident to procuring a mortgage	Not Deductible	Reduce amount realized	Amortize over Mortgage	Reduce amount realized
Loan origination fee — for the use of money	Deductible	Reduce amount realized	Amortize over Mortgage	Reduce amount realized
Loan origination fee — for services only	Not Deductible	Reduce amount realized	Amortize over Mortgage	Reduce amount realized
VA origination fees — sometimes called "points"	Not Deductible	Reduce amount realized	Amortize over Mortgage	Reduce amount realized
FHA origination fees — "points"	Not Deductible	Reduce amount realized	Amortize over Mortgage	Reduce amount realized
Real estate taxes	Deductible	Deductible	Deductible	Deductible
Interest	Partial Deduction	Partial Deduction	Partial Deduction	Partial Deduction
Rent income	N/A	N/A	Partial income	Partial income
Escrow for bills, insurance, etc.	Not Deductible	Not Deductible	Partial Deductible	Partial Deductible

	Personal Residence		Investment Property	
	Buyer	**Seller**	**Buyer**	**Seller**
Misc.—abstracts of title, surveys, recording of deed, etc.	Increase basis	Reduce amount realized	Increase basis	Reduce amount realized
Insurance premium—fire	Not Deductible	Not Deductible	Partial Deductible	Partial Deductible
Transfer taxes	Increase basis	Reduce amount realized	Deductible	Deductible
Title policy fees	Increase basis	Reduce amount realized	Increase basis	Reduce amount realized
Attorney's fees for obtaining property	Increase basis	Reduce amount realized	Increase basis	Reduce amount realized
Attorney's fees for obtaining mortgage	Not Deductible	Reduce amount realized	Amortize over Mortgage	Reduce amount realized
Commissions	Increase basis	Reduce amount realized	Increase basis	Reduce amount realized

Home Items That Could Add to the Cost Basis of Home

Inside Additions and Improvements

- Windows, window seats, and storms
- Inside wall alterations and plastering
- Closets and shelves
- Cabinets and cupboards
- Wood paneling
- Room dividers
- Carpeting
- Bookcases and other built-in cabinets
- Conversion of attics or basement into bedrooms
- Installed furniture—booths, bars, and counters
- Wood flooring, tile, or linoleum
- Radiator covers and ventilators
- Fireplace
- Ceilings and lighting

Equipment Installed: Bathroom

- Tub, towel racks, and hangers
- Shower cabinet
- Sliding doors and heater
- Faucet controls
- Medicine cabinet and mirrors

¶811.55

Hardware, Fixtures, and Locks

- Lighting fixtures
- For curtain and drapes
- For doors and windows
- For cabinets and closets

Plumbing and Sanitation

- Pumps, septic system
- Pipes, tubing, drains, and traps
- Caulking and waterproofing
- Fixtures and controls

Communication

- Intercommunication system
- Chimes
- Fire or burglar alarms

Electricity and Lighting

- Wiring system and circuit breakers
- Conduit, fuse, and junction boxes
- Lightning rods and TV antenna
- Fixtures and switches

Kitchen and Laundry

- Chutes, table, and racks
- Cabinets, tops, and built-ins
- Washer, dryer
- Dishwasher
- Refrigerator
- Counters, sinks, and drainboards
- Range, oven, hood, and ventilators
- Disposal and freezer

Mechanical Equipment

- Humidifier and dehumidifier
- Radiators, valves
- Fans, duct work, and louvers
- Furnace
- Space heaters
- Air conditioning and cooling
- Soft water system
- Hot water system

¶811.55

Insulation

- Pipes, ducts, and weather stripping
- Roof, attic, and basement
- Ceilings, floors, and walls

Lawn, Garden, and Grounds

- Fences and gates
- Kennel
- Bird bath, patio, etc.
- Water well, pump, and sprinkler system
- Cement or asphalt
- Terraces, patios, and retaining wall

Special Assessments

- Water
- Sewer and storm sewer
- Streets, sidewalks, and alleys

Outside Improvements

- Gutters, leaders, and drains
- Windows, screens, and screen doors
- Garage and storage
- Flashing and siding
- Additions to buildings
- Roof repair and replacement
- Porch and wings
- Additional acreage
- Sod, fertilizers, seed, and plants
- Trees and shrubs
- Waste collecting
- Grading, fill, and topsoil
- Mail box
- Clothes dryers and lines

COMPLIANCE

¶ 813 PENALTIES TABLES

.01 Taxpayer Penalties Chart

Following is a listing of violations and the corresponding penalties.

Taxpayer Penalties

Violation	IRC Sec.	Penalty	Exceptions to Penalty
Late filing of tax return. (Failure to file.) (Can be combined with late penalty)	6651(a)(1)	5% of tax per month not to exceed 25% of tax. If return is over 60 days late, the minimum penalty is the lesser of $100 of the tax due.	Reasonable cause excuses: • Death or serious illness • Fire destroyed records • Wrong info from IRS • Return filed at wrong IRS office • Unavoidable absence of taxpayer • Insufficient postage • First return of taxpayer ignorant of law • Timely request for tax forms not answered by IRS Note: IRS is not required to accept any of these excuses.
Unpaid tax or deficiency — or paying late	6651	0.5% per month penalty (maximum 25%) and interest from the due date of tax or deficiency.	Reasonable cause.
Failure to file tax return—fraudulently	6651(f)	15% of tax per month not to exceed 75% of tax.	
Failure to report tips to employer.	6652(b)	50% of Social Security tax on unreported tips.	
Individuals' underpayment of estimated tax.	6654	Annual interest rate charged on underpaid amount, until paid. (See 6621)	• 90% tax liability was paid each quarter • Underpayment is less than $1,000 for the year • Previous year's tax liability was paid each quarter • Annualized computation of tax liability for a specific quarter

¶813.01

Violation	IRC Sec.	Penalty	Exceptions to Penalty
Underpayment of estimated tax by corporation.	6655	Annual interest rate charged on underpaid amount until paid. (See 6621)	• 90% of tax liability was paid each quarter • Previous year's tax liability was paid each quarter • Annualized method is used • Tax liability is $500 or less
Failure to make tax deposits with federal depository—insufficient amount or late.	6656	• 2% of undeposited tax if less than 6 days late. • 5% of undeposited tax if more than 5 days late but less than 16 days late. • 10% of undeposited tax if more than 15 days late. • 15% of undeposited tax if tax is not paid within 10 days of delinquency notice or the day demand for immediate payment is given, whichever is earlier.	Reasonable cause
Paying tax with bad check.	6657	2% of amount of check.	Reasonable cause
Imposition of Accuracy-Related Penalty.	6662	20% of underpayment which is attributable to one or more of the following: • Negligence or disregard of rules or regulations • Substantial understatement of income tax • Substantial estate or gift tax valuation understatement • Substantial valuation overstatement of property • Substantial valuation overstatement of pension liabilities	Reasonable cause
Fraud.	6663	75% of underpayment attributable to fraud.	
Failure to collect and pay over tax, or attempt to evade or defeat tax.	6672	100% of tax evaded, or not collected.	

¶813.01

Violation	IRC Sec.	Penalty	Exceptions to Penalty
Frivolous tax court actions.	6673	Up to $25,000 if taxpayer position is groundless.	
False withholding information on W-4.	6682	Civil penalty up to $500.	Civil penalty waived if credits or estimated tax payments cover such taxes.
	7205	If fraudulent, criminal penalty up to $1,000, one year in prison, or both.	
Failure to file partnership return.	6698	$50 times the number of partners for each month (or fraction of a month) not to exceed five months.	Reasonable cause.
Frivolous or incomplete return.	6702	$500	Reasonable cause.
Failure to register a tax shelter.	6707 (a)	1% of the amount invested in the tax shelter. Minimum penalty: $500.	Reasonable cause.
Failure to furnish Tax Shelter I.D. number to investor.	6707 (b) (1)	$100 for each failure.	
Failure to include Tax Shelter I.D. number on income tax return.	6707 (b) (2)	$250 for each tax shelter.	Reasonable cause.
Failure to file certain information returns.	6721 (a)	$50 for each failure, not to exceed a total of $250,000. But, higher penalty and no limit if failures are intentional.	Reasonable cause.
Failure to comply with other information reporting requirements.	6723	$50 for each failure, not to exceed a total of $100,000.	Reasonable cause.
Willful attempt to evade or defeat tax.	7201	Felony — up to $100,000 fine or five years in prison, or both.	
Willful failure to collect or pay over tax.	7202	Felony — up to $10,000 fine or five years in prison, or both.	

Violation	IRC Sec.	Penalty	Exceptions to Penalty
Willful failure to pay tax or file return.	7203	Misdemeanor — up to $25,000 fine or one year in prison, or both.	
Willful making and subscribing to false return.	7206 (1)	Felony — up to $100,000 fine or three years in prison, or both.	
Negligent or intentional disregard of rules resulting in understatement of taxpayer's tax liability.	6694 (a)	$250 per return.	
Preparer's understatement of tax liability.	6694 (b)	$1,000 per return.	
Failure to furnish copy of return to taxpayer.	6695 (a)	$50 per return.*	
Preparer's failure to sign return.	6695 (b)	$50 per return.*	
Failure to furnish preparer's I.D. number.	6695 (c)	$50 per return.*	
Failure to maintain copies of returns prepared or maintain a listing of clients.	6695 (d)	$50 per return.*	
Failure (under Sec. 6060) for maintaining information on all preparers employed during a return period.	6695 (e)	$50 per preparer or per item missing from required information.*	
Endorsing or negotiating a tax refund check.	6695 (f)	$500 per check.	
Improper disclosure or use of return information.	6713	Civil — $250 for each disclosure or use up to $10,000 per year.	
	7216	Misdemeanor — $1,000 or one year in prison or both.	

Violation	IRC Sec.	Penalty	Exceptions to Penalty
Misrepresentation of eligibility to practice before the IRS, or experience or education, as an income tax preparer.	7407(b)(1)(B)	Court action to stop preparer from such conduct.	

* Note: Maximum penalty shall not exceed $25,000 in any return period.

Return Preparer Penalties

Code Sec.	Violation	Employer Return Preparer	Employee Return Preparer	Amount
6695(a)	Failure to furnish copy of return to taxpayer.	Yes	No	$50 per failure
6695(b)	Failure of preparer to sign return.	No	Yes	$50 per failure
6695(c)	Failure to furnish identifying numbers.	Yes	No	$50 per failure
6695(d)	Failure to maintain copies of returns prepared or maintain a listing.	Yes	No	$50 per failure
6695(e)(1)	Failure to retain and make available a record of the preparers employed (or engaged) during a return period as required by Code Sec. 6060.	Yes	No	$50 per failure
6695(e)(2)	Failure to provide all information on return required by Code Sec. 6060.	Yes	No	$50 per item
6695(f)	Endorsing or negotiating a tax refund check.	Yes	Yes	$500 per item

¶ 815 RECORD RETENTION REQUIREMENTS

.01 Business Tax Records Retention

The time a business should keep records and the types of records required varies according to the statutory requirements of the particular government or agency involved.

- Wage and Hour Division, Immigration and Naturalization
- Social Security Administration
- Equal Employment Opportunity Commission
- Internal Revenue Service
- US Department of Labor
- State agencies

The following is a suggested guideline.

Holding Period

Item	Suggested Holding Period From Filing Date
Bank Deposit Slips	6 years
Bank Statements	6 years
Inventory Records	6 years
Tax Returns	3 years
Cancelled Checks	3 years
Journals, Ledgers	3 years
Minutes of Meetings	Life of organization
Depreciation Schedules	Life of organization
Sales, Purchase Invoices	6 years
Travel & Entertainment Reports	3 years
W-2's, 1099's, 1098's	6 years
Proof of Tax Return Deductions	6 years
Credit Card Slips, Statements	3 years
Corporate Stock Records	Permanent

Item	Suggested Holding Period From Filing Date
Financial Statements	6 years
Retirement Information	Permanent
Security Sales/Purchase Slips	3 years beyond the year the asset was sold
Closing Papers on Properties	3 years beyond the year the property is sold
Employee Payroll Records	3 Years beyond the year of termination of employee
Financial/Insurance Contracts	6 years beyond final year of contract
Capital Expenditures/Improvements	3 years beyond final year property is disposed of

.03 Return Preparers

Income Tax Return Preparers—Employers

An employer is required to retain a record of the name, taxpayer identification number, and principal place of work during the return period for each income tax return preparer employed (or engaged) at any time during the return period and to make the record available for inspection upon request. The employer may choose any form of documentation to be used as a record of the preparers employed (or engaged) during the return period. Sole proprietors and partnerships are also required to retain a record.

Retention period: three-year period following the close of the return period to which the record relates. (26 CFR 1.6060-1)

Income Tax Return Preparers—Returns

To retain a completed copy of the return or claim for refund, or record, by list, card file, or otherwise, of the name, the taxpayer identification number, and taxable year of the taxpayer (or nontaxable entity) for whom the refund or claim for refund was prepared, and the type of return or claim for refund prepared, and the name of the individual preparer required to sign the return or claim for refund. To retain the copy of a return or claim for refund manually signed by the preparer that is photocopied together with a record of arithmetical errors corrected after signature; the information submitted with respect to a computer-prepared return together with a record of arithmetical and clerical errors corrected; and a manually signed copy of the letter submitted to the Internal Revenue Service with respect to facsimile signatures on a return or claim for a nonresident alien individual together with a record of arithmetical errors corrected after the signature is affixed. Retention period: three years following the close of the return period during which the return or claim for refund was presented for signature to the taxpayer, or three years following the close of a later return period in which the return became due. (26 CFR 1.6107-1)

¶ 817 INTERNAL REVENUE SERVICE

.01 Internal Revenue Service Overview

The function of the Internal Revenue Service is to administer the Internal Revenue Code. Tax policy for raising revenue is determined by Congress. The purpose of the Internal Revenue Service is to collect the proper amount of tax revenues at the least cost to the public, and in a manner that warrants the highest degree of public confidence in the IRS's integrity, efficiency, and fairness. To achieve that purpose, the IRS will:

- Encourage and achieve the highest possible degree of voluntary compliance in accordance with the tax law and regulations;

- Advise the public of their rights and responsibilities;

- Determine the extent of compliance and the causes of non-compliance;

- Do all things needed for the proper administration and enforcement of the tax laws; and

- Continually search for and implement new, more efficient and effective ways of accomplishing the mission.

Arrangement of the Internal Revenue Code

Code Format:

Title	26 Internal Revenue Code
Subtitle	A. Income Taxes
Chapter	1. Normal Taxes and Surtaxes
Subchapter	A. Determination of Tax Liability
Part	IV. Credits Against Tax
Subpart	A. Credits Available
Section	31. Tax Withheld on Wages
Subsection	(a) Wage Withholding for Income Tax Purposes
Paragraph	(2) Year of Credit
Subparagraph	(A) —
Clause	(i) —

The key to the Code is usually the section number involved. To designate section 31(a)(2) of the Code, for example, it would be unnecessary to include Title 26, Subtitle A, Chapter 1, Subchapter A, Part IV. Mentioning section 31(a)(2) will suffice because section numbers run consecutively and do not begin again with each new Subtitle, Chapter, Subchapter, or Part.

Citing the Code Sections

Code sections are broken down into subparts. Example: § 441(f)(1)(A)

- § = Abbreviation for "Section"

- 441 = Section Number. Period for computation of taxable income

- (f) = Subsection. Election of year consisting of 52-53 weeks

- (1) = Paragraph designation. General rule. A taxpayer who, in keeping his books . . .

- (A) = Subparagraph designation. On whatever date such same day . . .

Treasury Department Regulations/Procedures

Regulations are issued by the U.S. Treasury Department under the authority granted by Congress. Regulations carry considerable weight and are an important factor to consider in complying with the tax law, although they are not issued by Congress.

¶817.01

Regulation Format

Regulations interpret the Code and are arranged in a similar sequence.

- The prefix 1 designates the regulations under the income tax law.
- Regulations under Code Sec. 2 would be cited as Reg. § 1.2.
- Subparts are added for further identification. Subparts, however, often have no correlation in their numbering with the Code subsections.

Temporary Regulations

Temporary regulations are issued by the Treasury Department relating to elections and other matters where speed is critical. Temporary regulations usually are necessitated by legislation recently enacted by Congress that takes effect immediately.

Regulation Changes

New regulations and changes are usually issued in proposed form before they are finalized. The time interval between proposal and finalization permits for comments on the propriety of the proposal. Example: Prop. Reg. § 1.3.

Rulings and Procedures

These are official pronouncements of the National Office of the IRS designed to provide interpretation of the tax law. They do not carry the same legal force and effect of regulations and usually deal with more restricted problems. Revenue procedures are issued in the same manner as are revenue rulings, but they deal with the internal management practices and procedures of the IRS.

Internal Revenue Bulletin

Both revenue rulings and revenue procedures are published weekly by the U.S. government in the Internal Revenue Bulletin (I.R.B.). Semiannually, the Bulletins for a six-month period are gathered together, reorganized by Code section classification, and published in a bound volume designated Cumulative Bulletin (C.B.).

Individual Letter Rulings

Individual rulings are issued at a taxpayer's specific request and describe how the IRS will treat proposed transactions for tax purposes. They apply only to the taxpayer who asks for the ruling. (Source: Internal Revenue Bulletin)

Treasury Decisions

Treasury decisions (T.D.) are issued by the Treasury Department to promulgate new regulations, to amend or change existing regulations, or to announce the position of the government on selected court decisions.

Definition of Terms for Rulings and Procedures

"Obsoleted" describes a previously published ruling that is not considered determinative with respect to future transactions.

"Modified" is used where the substance of a previously published position is being changed.

"Clarified" is used in those instances where the language in a prior ruling is being made clear because the language has caused or may cause some confusion.

¶817.01

"Amplified" describes a situation where no change is being made in a prior published position, but the prior position is being extended to apply to a variation of the fact situation set forth therein.

"Distinguished" describes a situation where a ruling mentions a previously published ruling and points out an essential difference between them.

"Revoked" describes situations where the position in the previously published ruling is not correct and the correct position is being stated in the new ruling.

"Suspended" is used in rare situations to show that the previous published rulings will not be applied pending some future action, such as the issuance of new or unended requisitions, the outcome of cases in litigation, or the outcome of an I.R.S. study. (Source: Internal Revenue Bulletin)

"Superseded" describes a situation where the new ruling does nothing more than restate the substance and situation of a previously published ruling.

"Supplemented" is used in situations in which a list is published in a ruling and that list is expanded by adding more names in subsequent ruling.

IRS Bulletin Abbreviations

Acq. — Acquiescence

B.T.A. — Board of Tax Appeals

C.B. — Cumulative Bulletin

CFR — Code of Federal Regulations

Ct.D. — Court Decision

Del. Order — Delegation Order

DISC — Domestic International Sales Corporation

DR — Donor

EE — Employee

E.O. — Executive Order

ER — Employer

FICA — Federal Insurance Contributions Act

FISC — Foreign International Sales Company

FPH — Foreign Personal Holding Company

F.R. — Federal Register

FUTA — Federal Unemployment Tax Act

FC — Foreign Corporation

G.C.M. — General Counsel's Memorandum

GP — General Partner

GR — Grantor

I.R.B — Internal Revenue Bulletin

Ltr. Rul. — Letter Ruling

Nonacq. — Nonacquiescence

P — Parent Corporation

PHC — Personal Holding Company

PO — Possession of the U.S.

PTE — Prohibited Transaction Exemption

Pub. L. — Public Law

REIT — Real Estate Investment Trust

Rev. Proc. — Revenue Procedure

Rev. Rul. — Revenue Ruling

S.P.R. — Statements of Procedural Rules

Stat. — Statutes at Large

T — Target Corporation

T.C. — Tax Court

T.D. — Treasury Decision

TFE — Transferee

TFR — Transferor

T.I.R. — Technical Information Release

TP — Taxpayer

TR — Trust

TT — Trustee

¶ 821 TAX AUDITS—SUBSTANTIATION OF EXPENSES

.01 Vehicle Substantiation

Not Personal

Vehicles are not used for personal purposes. Employer-employee substantiation requirements are satisfied if:

- Under written policy, the employee is allowed no personal use of the vehicle.
- The employer reasonably believes there has been no personal use of the vehicle.
- The vehicle is owned by the employer and provided to the employee in connection with business purposes.
- No employee using the vehicle lives at the business premises.
- There must be evidence to substantiate the above.

Commuting With No Other Personal Use

Vehicles not used for personal purposes other than commuting. Employer-employee substantiation requirements are satisfied if:

- The employer reasonably believes there has been no personal (other than commuting) use of the vehicle.
- The employee using the vehicle is not a control employee.

- The employer includes in the employee's income the commuting value.
- The vehicle is owned by the employer and provided to the employee in connection with business purposes.
- Under written policy, the employee is allowed no personal use of the auto, other than commuting.
- There is evidence to substantiate the above.

Entirely Personal

- Vehicles are treated as used entirely for personal purposes.
  - Employers may satisfy the substantiation requirements by including the value of the use of the automobile in the employee's gross income.
  - Any employee business use is taken as an itemized deduction in the two-percent miscellaneous category.
- No deduction is allowed for commuting expenses.

Substantiation by Independent Contractors

An independent contractor is substantiate, with respect to required reimbursements, each element of an expenditure, and to the extent not so substantiated the independent contractor is required to include such reimbursements in income. An independent contractor is required to substantiate a reimbursement for entertainment regardless of whether he or she accounts for such entertainment. (Temp. Reg. § 1.274-5T(h)(2))

Substantiation with Respect to Certain Types of Listed Property

Written Policy Statements as to Vehicles

Two types of written policy statements, if initiated and kept by an employer to implement a policy of no personal use, or no personal use except for commuting, of a vehicle provided by the employer, qualify as sufficient evidence corroborating the taxpayer's own statement and, therefore, will satisfy the employer's substantiation requirements under Code Sec. 274(d). Therefore, the employee need not keep a separate set of records for purposes of the employer's substantiation requirements under Code Sec. 274(d) with respect to use of a vehicle satisfying these written policy federal government rules. (Temp. Reg. § 1.274-6T(a)(1))

Vehicles Not Used for Personal Purposes—Employers

A policy statement that prohibits personal use by an employee satisfies an employer's substantiation requirements if all the following conditions are met:

- No employee using the vehicle lives at the employer's business premises,
- When the vehicle is not used in the employer's trade or business, it is kept on the employer's business premises, unless it is temporarily located elsewhere—for example, for maintenance or because of a mechanical failure,
- The vehicle is owned or leased by the employer and is provided to one or more employees for use in connection with the employer's trade or business,
- Under a written policy of the employer, neither an employee, nor any individual whose use would be taxable to the employee, may use the vehicle for personal purposes, except for *de minimis* personal use (such as a stop for lunch between two business deliveries), and

- The employer reasonably believes that, except for *de minimis* use, neither the employee, nor any individual whose use would be taxable to the employee, uses the vehicle for any personal purpose.
- There must be evidence that would enable the Commissioner to determine whether the use of the vehicle meets the preceding five conditions. (Temp. Reg. § 1.274-6T(a)(2)(i))

Vehicles Not Used for Personal Purposes—Employees

An employee, in lieu of substantiating the business/investment use of an employer-provided vehicle, may treat all use of the vehicle as business/investment use if the following conditions are met:

- No employee using the vehicle lives at the employer's business premises,
- When the vehicle is not used in the employer's trade or business, it is kept on the employer's business premises, unless it is temporarily located elsewhere—for example, for maintenance or because of a mechanical failure,
- The vehicle is owned or leased by the employer and is provided to one or more employees for use in connection with the employer's trade or business,
- Under a written policy of the employer, neither the employee, nor any individual whose use would be taxable to the employee, may use the vehicle for personal purposes, except for *de minimis* personal use (such as a stop for lunch between two business deliveries), and
- Except for *de minimis* personal use, neither the employee, nor any individual whose use would be taxable to the employee, uses the vehicle for any personal purpose.
- There must also be evidence that would enable the Commissioner to determine whether the use of the vehicle meets the preceding five conditions. (Temp. Reg. § 1.274 6T(a)(2)(ii))

Vehicles Not Used for Personal Purposes Other Than Commuting—Employers

A policy statement that prohibits personal use by an employee, other than commuting, satisfies an employer's substantiation requirements if all of the following conditions are met:

- The employer has established a written policy under which neither the employee nor any individual whose use would be taxable to the employee may use the vehicle for personal purposes, other than for commuting or *de minimis* personal use (such as a stop for a personal errand on the way between a business delivery and the employee's home),
- For bona fide noncompensatory business reasons, the employer requires the employee to commute to and/or from work in the vehicle,
- The vehicle is owned or leased by the employer and is provided to one or more employees for use in connection with the employer's trade or business and is used in the employer's trade or business,
- The employer reasonably believes that, except for *de minimis* personal use, neither the employee nor any individual whose use would be taxable to the employee uses the vehicle for any personal purpose other than commuting,

- The employer accounts for the commuting use by including in the employee's gross income the commuting value provided in Temp. Reg. § 1.61-2T(f)(3) (to the extent not reimbursed by the employee),

- The employee required to use the vehicle for commuting is not a control employee required to use an automobile, and

- There must be evidence that would enable the Commissioner to determine whether the use of the vehicle met the preceding six conditions. (Temp. Reg. § 1.274-6T(a)(3)(i))

Vehicles Not Used for Personal Purposes Other Than Commuting—Employees

An employee, in lieu of substantiating the business/investment use of an employer-provided vehicle, may substantiate a working condition fringe benefit by including in income the commuting value of the vehicle if all the following conditions are met:

- Under a written policy of the employer, neither the employee nor any individual whose use would be taxable to the employee may use the vehicle for personal purposes, other than for commuting or *de minimis* personal use (such as a stop for a personal errand on the way between a business delivery and the employee's home),

- For bona fide noncompensatory business reasons, the employer requires the employee to commute to and/or from work in the vehicle,

- The vehicle is owned or leased by the employer, is provided to one or more employees for use in connection with the employer's trade or business and is used in the employer's trade or business,

- Except for *de minimis* personal use, neither the employee nor any individual whose use would be taxable to the employee uses the vehicle for any personal purpose other than commuting,

- The employee required to use the vehicle for commuting is not a control employee and is required to use an automobile,

- The employee includes in gross income the commuting value determined by the employer (to the extent that the employee does not reimburse the employer for the commuting use), and

- There must be evidence that would enable the Commissioner to determine whether the use of the vehicle met the preceding six conditions. (Temp. Reg. § 1.274-6T(a)(3)(ii))

.02 Substantiation of Expenses Summary

- This regulation supersedes the doctrine founded in *Cohan v. Commissioner* where approximations of expenses were allowed. This regulation contemplates that no deduction shall be allowed a taxpayer on the basis of approximations or unsupported testimony of the taxpayer.

- No deduction, in general, is allowed for the following unless each element of expenditure is substantiated:
  - Travel away from home
  - Entertainment
  - Gifts
  - Listed property deductions

- Travel substantiation required.
  — Business purpose. Reason for travel or nature of business derived or expected to be derived.
  — Amount of each separate expenditure, except that expenses may be aggregated in reasonable categories.
  — Time. Dates of departure and return and number of days on each trip.
  — Place. Destinations described by name.
- Entertainment substantiation in general.
  — Business purpose. Business reason, business benefit expected to be derived from the entertainment, nature of business discussion or activity.
  — Business relationship. Occupation or other information regarding the person(s) entertained, including name, title or other designation sufficient to establish the business relationship to the taxpayer.
  — Amount of each separate expenditure, except that incidentals may be aggregated on a daily basis.
  — Time. Date of entertainment.
  — Place. Name, address or location and designation of type of entertainment.
- Entertainment directly preceding or following a substantial and bona fide business discussion. In addition to the above, the following elements must be provided:
  — Time. Date and duration of business discussion.
  — Place. Place of business discussion.
  — Business purpose. Business reason and nature of business discussion.
  — Business relationship. Identification of those persons entertained who participated in the business discussion.
- Listed property substantiation.
  — Expenditures. The amount of each separate expenditure.
  — Use. The amount of business use and amount of total use.
  — Time. Date of expenditure or use.
  — Business purpose and explanation.
- Gift substantiation.
  — Amount. Cost of gift to taxpayer.
  — Time. Date of gift.
  — Description of gift.
  — Business purpose. Business reason for gift or business benefit expected to be derived.
  — Business relationship. Occupation of recipient of gift, name, title, to establish business relationship to the taxpayer.
- Written evidence has more probative value than oral.

¶821.02

— Substantiation requirements are designed to encourage taxpayers to maintain records, together with needed documentary evidence.

— A taxpayer should maintain an account or expense book, but this is not necessary if it just duplicates information reflected on a receipt as long as the account book and receipt complement each other in an orderly manner.

— Written evidence is greater the closer in time it relates to the expenditure. A loss maintained on a weekly basis is considered timely.

- Reimbursements with adequate accounting to employer.
  — Reimbursement equals expenses.
    - Employee reports nothing, no income or deductions.
  — Reimbursement in excess of expenses.
    - Employee reports excess as income.
  — Expenses in excess of reimbursements.
    - Employee deducts excess if substantiated.
- Expenses where no adequate accounting is made to employer.
  — Employee must maintain records and supporting evidence to substantiate each expenditure.
  — Employee must use Form 2106 to claim deduction.
- Documentary evidence, such as receipts, paid bills, etc. is required for:
  — Any expenditure for lodging while traveling.
  — Any expenditure of $75 or more (except for transportation).
- Substantiation by other sufficient evidence.
  — By taxpayer's own statement, written or oral, containing specific information in detail to each element.
  — By other corroborative evidence sufficient to establish such element.
- Additional information may be necessary by personal interview.
  — To clarify information in the records.
  — To establish reliability of accuracy of such records. (Temp. Reg. § 1.274-5T)

Substantiation Requirements

For taxable years beginning on or after January 1, 1986, no deduction or credit shall be allowed with respect to each of the following items unless the taxpayer substantiates each element of the expenditure or use in the manner provided in the substantiation rules of this section. (Temp. Reg. § 1.274-5T(a))

- Traveling away from home (including meals and lodging),
- Any activity which is of a type generally considered to constitute entertainment, amusement, or recreation, or with respect to a facility used in connection with such an activity,
- Gifts,
- Any listed property.

.03 Travel Away from Home

The elements to be proved for expenditures for travel away from home are:

- *Time.* Dates of departure and return for each trip away from home, and number of days away from home spent on business.
- *Place.* Destinations or locality of travel, described by name of city or town or other similar designation.
- *Amount.* Amount of each separate expenditure for traveling away from home, such as cost of transportation or lodging, except that the daily cost of the traveler's own breakfast, lunch, and dinner and of expenditures incidental to such travel may be aggregated if set forth in reasonable categories, such as for meals, for gasoline and oil, and for taxi fares.
- *Business purpose.* Business reason for travel or nature of the business benefit derived or expected to be derived as a result of travel. (Temp. Reg. § 1.274-5T(b)(2))

.05 Entertainment in General

The elements to be proved for expenditures for entertainment are:

- *Time.* Date of entertainment.
- *Place.* Name, if any, address or location, and designation of type of entertainment, such as dinner or theater, if such information is not apparent from the designation of the place.
- *Amount.* Amount of each separate expenditure for entertainment, except that such incidental items as taxi fares or telephone calls may be aggregated on a daily basis.
- *Business purpose.* Business reason for the entertainment or nature of business benefit derived or expected to be derived as a result of the entertainment and, except in the case of business meals described in section 274(e)(1), the nature of any business discussion or activity.
- *Business relationship.* Occupation or other information relating to the person or persons entertained, including name, title, or other designation, sufficient to establish business relationship to the taxpayer. (Temp. Reg. § 1.274-5T(b)(3))

Entertainment Directly Preceding or Following a Substantial and Bona Fide Business Discussion

If a taxpayer claims a deduction for entertainment directly preceding or following a substantial and bona fide business discussion on the ground that such entertainment was associated with the active conduct of the taxpayer's trade or business, the elements to be proved for such expenditures must include:

- *Time.* Date and duration of business discussion.
- *Place.* Place of business discussion.
- *Business purpose.* Nature of business discussion and business reason for the entertainment or nature of business benefit derived or expected to be derived as the result of the entertainment.
- *Business relationship.* Identification of those persons entertained who participated in the business discussion. (Temp. Reg. § 1.274-5T(b)(4))

.07 Gifts

The elements to be proved with respect to expenditures for gifts are:

- *Description.* Description of the gift.

- *Amount.* Cost of the gift to the taxpayer.

- *Time.* Date of the gift.

- *Business purpose.* Business reason for the gift or nature of business benefit derived or expected to be derived as a result of the gift.

- *Business relationship.* Occupation or other information relating to the recipient of the gift, including name, title, or other designation, sufficient to establish business relationship to the taxpayer. (Temp. Reg. § 1.274-5T(b)(5))

.09 Listed Property

The term "listed property" means:

- Any passenger automobile;

- Any other property used as a means of transportation;

- Any property of a type generally used for purposes of entertainment, recreation, or amusement;

- Any computer or peripheral equipment;

- Any cellular telephone (or similar telecommunications equipment); and

- Any other property of a type specified by the Secretary by regulations.

The elements to be proved for listed property are:

- *Uses.* The amount of each business/investment use, based on the appropriate measure (i.e., mileage for automobiles and other means of transportation and time for other listed property, unless the Commissioner approves an alternative method), and the total use of the listed property for the taxable period.

- *Expenditures.* The amount of each separate expenditure with respect to an item of listed property, such as the cost of acquisition, the cost of capital improvements, lease payments, the cost of maintenance and repairs, or other expenditures.

- *Time.* Date of the expenditure or use with respect to listed property.

- *Business or investment purpose.* The business purpose for an expenditure or use with respect to any listed property. (Temp. Reg. § 1.274-5T(b)(6))

.11 Proving Business Expenses — Summary Chart

Elements to Prove Certain Business Expenses — Summary

Element to Be Proved (1)	Expense — Travel (2)	Expense — Entertainment (3)	Expense — Gift (4)	Expense — Transportation (car) (5)
Amount	Amount of each separate expense for travel, lodging, and meals. Incidental expenses may be totaled in reasonable categories, such as taxis, daily meals for traveler, etc.	Amount of each separate expense. Incidental expenses such as taxis, telephones, etc., may be totaled on a daily basis.	Cost of gift.	1) Amount of each separate expense, including cost of the car, 2) Mileage for business use of the car, and 3) Total miles for the tax year.
Time	Date you left and returned for each trip, and number of days for business.	Date of entertainment or use of a facility for entertainment. For meals or entertainment directly before or after a business discussion, the date and duration of the business discussion.	Date of gift.	Date of the expense or use.
Place	Name of city or other designation.	Name and address or location of place of entertainment, or place of use of a facility for entertainment. Type of entertainment if not otherwise apparent. Place where business discussion was held if entertainment is directly before or after a business discussion.	Not applicable.	Name of city or other designation if applicable.
Business Purpose	Business reason for travel or the business benefit gained or expected to be gained.	Business reason or the business benefit gained or expected to be gained. Nature of business discussion or activity.	Business reason for giving the gift or the business benefit gained or expected to be gained.	Business reason for the expense or use of the car.

Element to Be Proved (1)	Expense — Travel (2)	Expense — Entertainment (3)	Expense — Gift (4)	Expense — Transportation (car) (5)
Business Relationship	Not applicable.	Occupation or other information — such as names or other designations — about persons entertained that shows their business relationship to you. If all people entertained did not take part in business discussion, identify those who did. You must also prove that you or your employee was present if entertainment was a business meal.	Occupation or other information — such as a name or other designation — about recipient that shows his or her business relationship to you.	Not applicable.

.13 Substantiation of Evidence Rules

A taxpayer must substantiate each element of an expenditure or use by adequate records or by sufficient evidence corroborating his own statement. A taxpayer should maintain and produce such substantiation as will constitute proof of each expenditure or use. Written evidence has considerably more probative value than oral evidence alone. A contemporaneous log is not required, but a record of the elements of an expenditure or of a business use of listed property made at or near the time of the expenditure or use, supported by sufficient documentary evidence, has a high degree of credibility not present with respect to a statement prepared subsequent thereto when generally there is a lack of accurate recall. Substantiation requirements are designed to encourage taxpayers to maintain records, together with needed documentary evidence. (Temp. Regs. § 1.274-5T(c)(1))

Documentary Evidence

Documentary evidence, such as receipts, paid bills, or similar evidence sufficient to support an expenditure, shall be required for:

- Any expenditure for lodging while traveling away from home.
- Any other expenditure of $75 or more.

Documentary evidence will be considered adequate to support an expenditure if it includes sufficient information to establish the amount, date, place and the essential character of the expenditure. For example, a hotel receipt is sufficient to support expenditures for business travel if it contains the name, location, date and separate amounts for charges, such as for lodging, meals, and telephone. Similarly, a restaurant receipt is sufficient to support an expenditure for a business meal if it contains the name and location of the restaurant, the date and amount of the expenditure, the number of people served and an indication if a charge is made for an item other than meals and beverages. (Temp. Regs. § 1.274-5T(c)(2)(iii))

Loss of Records Due to Circumstances Beyond Control of the Taxpayer

Where the taxpayer establishes that the failure to produce adequate records is due to the loss of such records through circumstances beyond the taxpayer's control, such as destruction by fire, flood, earthquake or other casualty, the taxpayer has the right to substantiate a deduction by reasonable reconstruction of his expenditures or use. (Temp. Regs. § 1.274-5T(c)(5))

Business Use of Passenger Automobiles and Other Vehicles

Taxpayers that claim a deduction or credit with respect to any vehicle are required to answer certain questions providing information about the use of the vehicle. Any employer that provides the use of a vehicle to an employee must obtain information from the employee sufficient to complete the employer's tax return. Any employer that provides more than five vehicles to its employees need not include any information on its return. The employer must instead obtain the information from its employees, indicate on its return that it has obtained the information, and return the information received. Any employer:

- That can satisfy the requirements of Temp. § 1.274-6T(a)(3), relating to vehicles not used for personal purposes other than commuting.

- That can satisfy the requirements of Temp. § 1.274-6T(a)(2), relating to vehicles not used for personal purposes.

- That treats all use of vehicles by employees as personal use need not obtain information with respect to those vehicles, but instead must indicate on its return that it has vehicles exempt from the mileage reporting requirements. (Temp. Regs. § 1.274-5T(d)(2)(ii))

Business Disclosure of Other Listed Property

Taxpayers that claim a deduction or credit with respect to any listed property other than a vehicle (for example, a yacht, airplane, or certain computers) are required to provide the following information:

- The percentage of business use.

- The date that the property was placed in service.

- Whether evidence is available to support the percentage of business use claimed on the return.

- Whether the evidence is written. (Temp. Regs. § 1.274-5T(d)(3))

Reporting of Expenses for Which the Employee Is Required to Make an Adequate Accounting to His Employer Reimbursements Equal to Expenses

For purposes of computing tax liability, an employee need not report on his or her tax return business expenses for travel, transportation, entertainment, gifts, or with respect to listed property, paid or incurred by the employee solely for the benefit of the employer for which the employee is required to, and does, make an adequate accounting to the employer and which are charged directly or indirectly to the employer (for example, through credit cards) or for which the employee is paid through advances, reimbursements, or otherwise, provided that the total amount of such advances, reimbursements, and charges is equal to such expenses. (Temp. Regs. § 1.274-5T(f)(2)(i))

Reimbursements in Excess of Expenses

In a case where the total of the amounts charged directly or indirectly to the employer or received from the employer as advances, reimbursements, or otherwise, exceeds the business expenses paid or incurred by the employee, and the employee is required to,

¶821.13

and does, make an adequate accounting to the employer for such expenses, the employee must include such excess (including amounts received for expenditures not deductible by the employee) in income. (Temp. Regs. § 1.274-5T(f)(2)(ii))

Expenses in Excess of Reimbursements

If an employee incurs deductible business expenses on behalf of the employer which exceed the total of the amounts charged directly or indirectly to the employer and received from the employer as advances, reimbursements or otherwise, and the employee makes an adequate accounting to the employer, the employee must be able to substantiate any deduction for such excess with such records and supporting evidence as will substantiate each element of an expenditure. (Temp. Regs. § 1.274-5T(f)(2)(iii))

Reporting of Expenses for Which the Employee Is Not Required to Make an Adequate Accounting to His Employer

If the employee is not required to make an adequate accounting to the employer for business expenses or, though required, fails to make an adequate accounting for such expenses, the employee must submit—as a part of his or her tax return—the appropriate form issued by the Internal Revenue Service for claiming deductions for employee business expenses (e.g., Form 2106, Employee Business Expenses) and provide the information requested on that form, including the information regarding dates and percentages of business use if the employee's business expenses are with respect to the use of listed property. In addition, the employee must maintain such records and supporting evidence as will substantiate each element of an expenditure or use. (Temp. Regs. § 1.274-5T(f)(3))

.15 Relief from Joint and Several Liability on Joint Return

An individual who has made a joint return may elect to seek relief from joint liability. The individual may elect to limit the individual's liability for any deficiency with respect to such joint return as being made without regard to community property laws. (Code Sec. 6015(a))

Procedures for Relief from Liability Applicable to All Joint Filers

If a joint return has been made for a taxable year, on such return there is an understatement of tax attributable to erroneous items of one individual filing the joint return, the other individual filing the joint return establishes that in signing the return he or she did not know, and had no reason to know, that there was such understatement, taking into account all the facts and circumstances, it is inequitable to hold the other individual liable for the deficiency in tax for such taxable year attributable to such understatement, and the other individual elects (in such form as the Secretary may prescribe) the benefits of this subsection not later than the date which is two years after the date the Secretary has begun collection activities with respect to the individual making the election, then the other individual shall be relieved of liability for tax (including interest, penalties, and other amounts) for such taxable year to the extent such liability is attributable to such understatement. (Code Sec. 6015(b)(1))

Apportionment of Relief

If an individual establishes that in signing the return such individual did not know, and had no reason to know, the extent of such understatement, then such individual is relieved of liability for tax (including interest, penalties, and other amounts) for such taxable year to the extent that such liability is attributable to the portion of such understatement of which such individual did not know and had no reason to know. (Code Sec. 6015(b)(2))

Fair Tax Collection Practices

Communication with the Taxpayer

Without the prior consent of the taxpayer given directly to the Secretary or the express permission of a court of competent jurisdiction, the Secretary may not communicate with a taxpayer in connection with the collection of any unpaid tax—at any unusual time or place or a time or place known or which should be known to be inconvenient to the taxpayer; if the Secretary knows the taxpayer is represented by any person authorized to practice before the Internal Revenue Service with respect to such unpaid tax and has knowledge of, or can readily ascertain, such person's name and address, unless such person fails to respond within a reasonable period of time to a communication from the Secretary or unless such person consents to direct communication with the taxpayer; or at the taxpayer's place of employment if the Secretary knows or has reason to know that the taxpayer's employer prohibits the taxpayer from receiving such communication. In the absence of knowledge of circumstances to the contrary, the Secretary shall assume that the convenient time for communicating with a taxpayer is after 8 a.m. and before 9 p.m., local time at the taxpayer's location. (Code Sec. 6304(a))

Prohibition of Harassment and Abuse

The Secretary may not engage in any conduct the natural consequence of which is to harass, oppress, or abuse any person in connection with the collection of any unpaid tax. Without limiting the general application of the foregoing, the following conduct is a violation of this subsection: The use or threat of use of violence or other criminal means to harm the physical person, reputation, or property of any person. The use of obscene or profane language or language the natural consequence of which is to abuse the hearer or reader. Causing a telephone to ring or engaging any person in telephone conversation repeatedly or continuously with intent to annoy, abuse, or harass any person at the called number. (Code Sec. 6304(b))

Burden of Proof

Burden Shifts Where Taxpayer Produces Credible Evidence

If, in any court proceeding, a taxpayer introduces credible evidence with respect to any factual issue relevant to ascertaining the liability of the taxpayer, the Secretary shall have the burden of proof with respect to such issue. (Code Sec. 7491(a))

Limitations

The burden of proof shift applies with respect to an issue only if the taxpayer has complied with the requirements to substantiate any item, the taxpayer has maintained all records required and has cooperated with reasonable requests by the Secretary for witnesses, information, documents, meetings, and interviews. (Code Sec. 7491(a))

Use of Statistical Information on Unrelated Taxpayers

In the case of an individual taxpayer, the Secretary has the burden of proof in any court proceeding with respect to any item of income which was reconstructed by the Secretary solely through the use of statistical information on unrelated taxpayers.

Penalties

The Secretary has the burden of production in any court proceeding with respect to the liability of any individual for any penalty, addition to tax, or additional amount imposed. (Code Sec. 7491(a))

Confidentiality Privileges Relating To Taxpayer Communications

Uniform Application to Taxpayer Communications with Federally Authorized Practitioners

With respect to tax advice, the same common law protections of confidentiality which apply to a communication between a taxpayer and an attorney also applies to a communication between a taxpayer and any federally authorized tax practitioner to the extent the communication would be considered a privileged communication if it were between a taxpayer and an attorney. This may only be asserted in any noncriminal tax matter before the Internal Revenue Service, and any noncriminal tax proceeding in Federal court brought by or against the United States. The term "federally authorized tax practitioner" means any individual who is authorized under Federal law to practice before the Internal Revenue Service if such practice is subject to Federal regulation under section 330 of title 31, United States Code. The term "tax advice" means advice given by an individual with respect to a matter which is within the scope of the individual's authority to practice described in subparagraph (A). (Code Sec. 7525(a))

Rules Not to Apply to Communications Regarding Corporate Tax Shelters

The privilege does not apply to any written communication between a federally authorized tax practitioner and a director, shareholder, officer, or employee, agent, or representative of a corporation in connection with the promotion of the direct or indirect participation of such corporation in any tax shelter. (Code Sec. 7525(b))

Penalties

The Secretary has the burden of production in any court proceeding with respect to the liability of any individual for any penalty, addition to tax, or additional amount imposed. (Code Sec. 7491(c))

Confidentiality Privilege Extended To Taxpayer Communications

Uniform Application to Taxpayer Communications with Federally Authorized Practitioners

With respect to tax advice, the same common law protections of confidentiality which apply to a communication between a taxpayer and an attorney also apply to a communication between a taxpayer and any federally authorized tax practitioner to the extent the communication would be considered a privileged communication if it were between a taxpayer and an attorney. This may only be asserted in any noncriminal tax matter before the Internal Revenue Service and any noncriminal tax proceeding in federal court brought by or against the United States. The term "federally authorized tax practitioner" means any individual who is authorized under federal law to practice before the Internal Revenue Service (such as attorneys, certified public accountants, enrolled agents, and enrolled actuaries). Practitioner privilege under Code Sec. 7525. The term "tax advice" means advice given by an individual with respect to a matter which is within the scope of the individual's authority to practice described in subparagraph (A). (Code Sec. 7525(a))

Rules Relating to Communications Regarding Corporate Shelters

The privilege does not apply to any written communication between a federally authorized tax practitioner and a director, shareholder, officer, or employee, agent, or representative of a corporation in connection with the promotion of the direct or indirect participation of such corporation in any tax shelter. (Code Sec. 7525(b))

Chapter 9
Human Resources

Employment .... ¶ *903-908*
Legal Compliance .... ¶ *909-920*
Retirement .... ¶ *922-924*

EMPLOYMENT

¶ 903 EMPLOYEE BENEFITS

.01 Pre-Tax Savings Plan

Employee benefits represent a significant portion of an employee's compensation. (See ¶ 907.02) The employer should pay careful attention to employee benefits for several reasons. Employee benefits that are competitive with the area or industry are a significant factor in helping the employer to attract and retain qualified workers. The selection and design of various benefits plans also affects employment costs and has an impact on tax consideration as well.

The U.S. Department of Labor, Bureau of Labor statistics periodically surveys employers and reports on competitive practices relating to the proportion of employees receiving certain kinds of benefits. Shown below is the percent of workers in private industry with access to and participating in certain health care and retirement benefits.

Benefit type	Percent of employees with Access to Plans	Percent of employees Participating
Retirement Benefits		
All Plans	60	51
Defined Benefit Plan	21	20
Defined Contribution Plan	54	43
Health Care Benefits		
Medical Care	71	52
Dental Care	46	36
Vision Care	29	22
Prescription Drugs	67	49
Life Insurance	52	50
Short Term Disability	39	37
Long Term Disability	30	29
Paid Holidays	76	
Paid Sick Leave	57	
Paid Vacations	77	
Paid Personal Leave	37	
Paid Funeral Leave	68	
Paid Jury Duty Leave	70	
Paid Military Leave	48	
Paid Family Leave	8	
Unpaid Family Leave	82	

Source: Employee Benefits in Private Industry, 2006
http://www.bls.gov

For most, a pre-tax savings plan is an excellent long-term program to accumulate wealth. The following illustrates the growth in "pre" versus "post" tax gain.

Assumptions:

Amount to be contributed each year	$3,000
Amount matched by Company each year	$3,000
Contribution investment Rate of Return	12%
Age at initial contribution year	42
Age required to avoid penalty	60
Withdrawal age	60
Penalty for early withdrawal	10%
Pre tax rate-of-return if invested outside	12%
Income tax rate	Federal 27% / State 5%
Estimated tax bracket at withdrawal	15%

Pre-Tax Savings Plan

Assumptions:
1. Employer and employee each contribute $3,000 each year
2. The tax rate during the accumulation period is 32% (27% federal and 5% state)
3. Tax savings equal 32% of the sum of the $6,000 deposited each year and the earnings thereon each year
4. The deposits are assumed to be made at the end of the year and earn 12% compounded annually
5. The tax due if withdrawn early is 42% of the total amount (27% federal, 10% federal penalty, and 5% state)
6. At age 60, the tax due if withdrawn is 19% of the total amount (15% federal and 4% state)

	Pre-Tax Investing					Post-Tax Investing				Advantage or (Disadvantage) of Pre-Tax Over Post-Tax
Age	Amount Deposited	Earnings at 12%	Total	Tax Due if Withdrawn	Total Net of Tax	Amount Deposited	Earnings at 12%	Less Tax at 32% (19% at age 60)	Total	
42	$6,000	$0	$6,000	$2,520	$3,480	$6,000	$0	$1,920	$4,080	($600)
43	$6,000	$720	$12,720	$5,342	$7,378	$6,000	$490	$2,077	$8,493	($1,115)
44	$6,000	$1,526	$20,246	$8,503	$11,743	$6,000	$1,019	$2,246	$13,266	($1,523)
45	$6,000	$2,430	$28,676	$12,044	$16,632	$6,000	$1,592	$2,429	$18,428	($1,796)
46	$6,000	$3,441	$38,117	$16,009	$22,108	$6,000	$2,211	$2,628	$24,012	($1,904)
47	$6,000	$4,574	$48,691	$20,450	$28,241	$6,000	$2,881	$2,842	$30,052	($1,811)
48	$6,000	$5,843	$60,534	$25,424	$35,110	$6,000	$3,606	$3,074	$36,584	($1,474)
49	$6,000	$7,264	$73,798	$30,995	$42,803	$6,000	$4,390	$3,325	$43,649	($846)
50	$6,000	$8,856	$88,654	$37,235	$51,419	$6,000	$5,238	$3,596	$51,291	$128
51	$6,000	$10,638	$105,292	$44,223	$61,070	$6,000	$6,155	$3,890	$59,556	$1,513
52	$6,000	$12,635	$123,927	$52,050	$71,878	$6,000	$7,147	$4,207	$68,496	$3,382
53	$6,000	$14,871	$144,799	$60,815	$83,983	$6,000	$8,220	$4,550	$78,165	$5,818
54	$6,000	$17,376	$168,175	$70,633	$97,541	$6,000	$9,380	$4,922	$88,623	$8,918
55	$6,000	$20,181	$194,356	$81,629	$112,726	$6,000	$10,635	$5,323	$99,935	$12,791
56	$6,000	$23,323	$223,678	$93,945	$129,733	$6,000	$11,992	$5,758	$112,170	$17,564
57	$6,000	$26,841	$256,520	$107,738	$148,781	$6,000	$13,460	$6,227	$125,403	$23,378
58	$6,000	$30,782	$293,302	$123,187	$170,115	$6,000	$15,048	$6,735	$139,716	$30,399
59	$6,000	$35,196	$334,498	$140,489	$194,009	$6,000	$16,766	$7,285	$155,197	$38,812
60	$6,000	$40,140	$380,638	$72,321	$308,317	$6,000	$18,624	$4,678	$175,142	$133,175

.03 Fringe Benefits—Tax Savings

Fringe benefit plans offer an attractive way to maximize a company's investment when compensating employees for their labor. Good plans can attract and maintain good workers. Employers' costs for such plans can be reduced when deductible fringe benefit plans like Cafeteria Plans under Code Sec. 125 are offered. For the employer, a $1000 expenditure in a cafeteria plan may cost much less than the face amount of this "investment" assuming the money would have gone unspent and therefore taxed to the business as profit.

Business Net Cost:

Gross Fringe Benefit Expenditure	$1,000	
Business Tax Assumptions:		
Federal Social Security Rate:		6.2%
Federal Medicare Tax Rate:		1.45%
Federal Income Tax Rate:*		25%
Total Percentage Deductions:		32.65%
Less Total Fringe Benefit Tax Savings:	$326.50	
Net Cost to Business	$673.50	

---

* Assuming 25% rate paid by sole proprietorship or pass through entity.

Employee Savings

Salary Reduction Amount	$1,000	
Individual Tax Assumptions:		
Federal Social Security Rate:		6.2%
Federal Medicare Tax Rate:		1.45%
Federal Income Tax Rate:		25%
Total Percentage Deductions:		32.65%
Plus Total Fringe Benefit Tax Savings:	$326.50	
Net Benefit to Employee	$1,326.50	

Thus, the business contributes $1,000 to a Cafeteria Benefit Plan at a net cost of $673.50 and a participating employee receives $1,000 in plan benefits and saves $326.50 in taxes.

.05 Welfare Benefit Trust

A welfare benefit trust (WBT) is a fund into which an employer makes deposits to provide specific future benefits for employees, such as severance pay and pre-retirement death benefits. Contributions can be deductible when made, with special limitations. A WBT Plan cannot provide medical and life insurance benefits exclusively for retirees. Those limitations do not apply to contributions made to a "10 or more employer plan" that does not maintain experience ratings with respect to individual employers. A "10 or more employer plan" is a plan: to which more than one employer contributes; and to which no individual employer normally contributes more than 10 percent of the total contributions. The WBT is not a plan of deferred compensation. The WBT is not a qualified plan. To avoid classification as deferred compensation, plans must be designed to: cover businesses with more than one employee, include a broad group of employees; base funding on actuarial determinations; and avoid any reversion of assets to employers.

.07 VEBAs—A Special Form of WBT

A voluntary employees' beneficiary association (VEBA) is a special form of a WBT. A VEBA is exempt from regular federal income tax and subject to prescribed guidelines.

Voluntary employees' beneficiary associations (VEBAs), are a type of employee welfare benefit plan, that can be used as a low-cost method of offering employees not only the standard type of insurance-related benefits, but also a variety of fringes. VEBAs reserves can be accumulated tax free. Employer contributions to VEBAs are tax deductible to employers and excludable from employees' gross income until benefits are actually received. VEBAs are not qualified plans, but VEBAs do have tax-exempt status. In order to be exempt, there must be an entity, such as a corporation or trust established under applicable local law, having an existence independent of the member-employees or their employer. (Reg § 1.501(c)(9)-2(c)(1))

A trust does not qualify as a voluntary employees' beneficiary association if it is not controlled by an independent trustee. (*Lima Surgical Associates, Inc. Voluntary Employees' Beneficiary Ass'n Plan Trust v. U.S.*, 20 Cl Ct 674, 90-1 USTC ¶ 50,329)

An organization which includes employers or individuals other than employees among its membership is not a VEBA. (Rev Rul 82-148, 1982-2 CB 401, with respect to future transactions of Code Sec. 501(c)(9) organizations)

Membership in a Voluntary Employees' Beneficiary Association

The membership must consist of individuals who become entitled to participate by reason of their being employees and whose eligibility for membership is defined by reference to objective standards that constitute an employment-related common bond among such individuals. Typically, those eligible for membership in an organization described in Code Sec. 501(c)(9) are defined by reference to a common employer (or affiliated employers), to coverage under one or more collective bargaining agreements (with respect to benefits provided by reason of such agreement(s)), to membership in a labor union, or to membership in one or more locals of a national or international labor union.

For example, membership in an association might be open to all employees of a particular employer, or to employees in specified job classifications working for certain employers at specified locations and who are entitled to benefits by reason of one or more collective bargaining agreements. In addition, employees of one or more employers engaged in the same line of business in the same geographic locale will be considered to share an employment-related bond for purposes of an organization through which their employers provide benefits.

Employees of a labor union also will be considered to share an employment-related common bond with members of the union, and employees of an association will be considered to share an employment-related common bond with members of the association. Whether a group of individuals is defined by reference to a permissible standard or standards is a question to be determined with regard to all the facts and circumstances, taking into account the guidelines set forth in this paragraph. Exemption will not be denied merely because the membership of an association includes some individuals who are not employees, provided that such individuals share an employment-related bond with the employee-members. Such individuals may include, for example, the proprietor of a business whose employees are members of the association. An association will be considered to be composed of employees if 90 percent of the total membership of the association on one day of each quarter of the association's taxable year consists of employees.

Restrictions

Eligibility for membership may be restricted by geographic proximity, or by objective conditions or limitations reasonably related to employment, such as a limitation to a reasonable classification of workers, a limitation based on a reasonable minimum period of service, a limitation based on maximum compensation, or a requirement that a member be employed on a full-time basis. Similarly, eligibility for benefits may be restricted by objective conditions relating to the type or amount of benefits offered. Any objective criteria used to restrict eligibility for membership or benefits may not, however, be selected or administered in a manner that limits membership or benefits to officers, shareholders, or highly compensated employees of an employer contributing to or otherwise funding the employees' association. Similarly, eligibility for benefits may not be subject to conditions or limitations that have the effect of entitling officers, shareholders, or highly compensated employees of an employer contributing to or otherwise funding the employees' association to benefits that are disproportionate in relation to benefits to which other members of the association are entitled. Whether the selection or administration of objective conditions has the effect of providing disproportionate benefits to officers, shareholders, or highly compensated employees generally is to be determined on the basis of all the facts and circumstances.

Meaning of "Employee"

Whether an individual is an "employee" is determined by reference to the legal and bona fide relationship of employer and employee. The term "employee" includes the following:

An individual who is considered an employee for employment tax purposes, or for purposes of a collective bargaining agreement, whether or not the individual could qualify as an employee under applicable common law rules. This would include any person who is considered an employee for purposes of the Labor Management Relations Act of 1947, 61 Stat. 136, *as amended,* 29 USC 141 (1979).

Note: Different labor, employment, and tax laws have different definitions for the meaning of employee. Be sure to check the definitions of applicable laws. (See ¶ 912 - ¶ 919.03)

Description of Voluntary Association of Employees

There must be an entity, such as a corporation or trust established under applicable local law, having an existence independent of the member-employees or their employer.

Voluntary—Generally, membership in an association is voluntary if an affirmative act is required on the part of an employee to become a member rather than the designation as a member due to employee status. However, an association shall be considered voluntary although membership is required of all employees, provided that the employees do not incur a detriment (for example, in the form of deductions from pay) as the result of membership in the association. An employer is not deemed to have imposed involuntary membership on the employee if membership is required as the result of a collective bargaining agreement or as an incident of membership in a labor organization.

Of employees, an organization must be controlled—by its membership, by independent trustee(s) (such as a bank), or by trustees or other fiduciaries at least some of whom are designated by, or on behalf of, the membership. Whether control by or on behalf of the membership exists is a question to be determined with regard to all of the facts and circumstances, but generally such control will be deemed to be present when the membership (either directly or through its representative) elects, appoints or otherwise designates a person or persons to serve as chief operating officer(s), administrator(s), or trustee(s) of the organization.

Benefits

The life, sick, accident or other benefits provided by a VEBA must be payable to its members, their dependents or their designated beneficiaries. (Reg § 1.501(c)(9)-3(a)).

A trust that provides deferred compensation in the form of retirement benefits that is similar to a nonqualifying pension benefit and does not provide for the payment of life, sickness, accident or other benefits cannot qualify as a voluntary employees' beneficiary association. (*Lima Surgical Associates, Inc. Voluntary Employees' Beneficiary Ass'n Plan Trust v. U.S.* 20 Cl Ct 674 90-1 USTC, ¶ 50,329 (Cl Ct 1990). (See Reg § 1.501(c)(9)-1(c).)

Voluntary Employees' Beneficiary Associations: Life, Sick, Accident, etc. (Reg. § 1.501(c)(9)-3)

The life, sick, accident, or other benefits provided by a voluntary employee's beneficiary association must be payable to its members, their dependents, or their designated beneficiaries. A"dependent" means the member's spouse; any child of the member or the member's spouse who is a minor or a student (within the meaning of Code Sec. 151(c)(4)); any other minor child residing with the member; and any other individual who an association, relying on information furnished to it by a member, in good faith believes is a person described in Code Sec. 152(a). Life, sick, accident, or other benefits may take the form of cash or noncash benefits. A voluntary employees' beneficiary association is not operated for the purpose of providing life, sick, accident, or other benefits unless substantially all of its operations are in furtherance of the provision of such benefits. Further, an organization is not described in this section if it systematically and knowingly provides benefits (of more than a *de minimis* amount) that are not permitted by these rules.

Life Benefits

The term "life benefit" means a benefit (including a burial benefit or a wreath) payable by reason of the death of a member or dependent. A "life benefit" may be provided directly or through insurance. It generally must consist of current protection, but also may include a right to convert to individual coverage on termination of eligibility for coverage through the association, or a permanent benefit as defined in, and subject to the conditions in, the regulations under section 79. A "life benefit" also includes the benefit provided under any life insurance contract purchased directly from an employee-funded association by a member or provided by such an association to a member. The term "life benefit" does not include a pension, annuity or similar benefit, except that a benefit payable by reason of the death of an insured may be settled in the form of an annuity to the beneficiary in lieu of a lump-sum death benefit (whether or not the contract provides for settlement in a lump sum).

Sick and Accident Benefits

The term "sick and accident benefits" means amounts furnished to or on behalf of a member or a member's dependents in the event of illness or personal injury to a member or dependent. Such benefits may be provided through reimbursement to a member or a member's dependents for amounts expended because of illness or personal injury, or through the payment of premiums to a medical benefit or health insurance program. Similarly, a sick and accident benefit includes an amount paid to a member in lieu of income during a period in which the member is unable to work due to sickness or injury. Sick benefits also include benefits designed to safeguard or improve the health of members and their dependents. Sick and accident benefits may be provided directly by an association to or on behalf of members and their dependents, or may be provided indirectly by an association through the payment of premiums or fees to an insurance company, medical clinic, or other program under which members and their dependents are entitled to medical services or to other sick and accident benefits. Sick and accident benefits may also be furnished in noncash form, such as, for example, benefits in the nature of clinical care services by visiting nurses, and transportation furnished for medical care.

Other Benefits

The term "other benefits" includes only benefits that are similar to life, sick, or accident benefits. A benefit is similar to a life, sick, or accident benefit if it is intended to safeguard or improve the health of a member or a member's dependents, or it protects against a contingency that interrupts or impairs a member's earning power.

Examples of "Other Benefits"

Paying vacation benefits, providing vacation facilities, reimbursing vacation expenses, and subsidizing recreational activities such as athletic leagues are considered "other benefits." The provision of child-care facilities for preschool and school-age dependents is also considered "other benefits." The provision of job readjustment allowances, income maintenance payments in the event of economic dislocation, temporary living expense loans and grants at times of disaster (such as fire or flood), supplemental unemployment compensation benefits, severance benefits and education or training benefits or courses (such as apprentice training programs) for members, are considered "other benefits" because they protect against a contingency that interrupts earning power. Personal legal service benefits which consist of payments or credits to one or more organizations or trusts described in Code Sec. 501(c)(20) are considered "other benefits." Generally, "other benefits" also include any benefit provided in the manner permitted by paragraphs (5) et seq. of section 302(c) of the Labor Management Relations Act of 1947, 61 Stat. 136, as amended, 29 USC 186(c) (1979).

Examples of Nonqualifying Benefits

"Other benefits" do not include the payment of commuting expenses, such as bridge tolls or train fares, the provision of accident or homeowner's insurance benefits for damage to property, the provision of malpractice insurance, or the provision of loans to members except in times of distress. "Other benefits" also do not include the provision of savings facilities for members. The term "other benefits" does not include any benefit that is similar to a pension or annuity payable at the time of mandatory or voluntary retirement, or a benefit that is similar to the benefit provided under a stock bonus or profit-sharing plan. A benefit will be considered similar to that provided under a pension, annuity, stock bonus or profit-sharing plan if it provides for deferred compensation that becomes payable by reason of the passage of time, rather than as the result of an unanticipated event. Thus, for example, supplemental unemployment benefits, which generally become payable by reason of unanticipated layoff, are not, for purposes of these regulations, considered similar to the benefit provided under a pension, annuity, stock bonus or profit-sharing plan.

Nondiscrimination Requirements

Voluntary employees' benefit associations (VEBAs) are not tax-exempt unless they meet certain nondiscrimination requirements as follows: A plan meets the requirements only if—each class of benefits under the plan is provided under a classification of employees which is set forth in the plan and which is found by the Secretary not to be discriminatory in favor of employees who are highly compensated individuals, and in the case of each class of benefits, such benefits do not discriminate in favor of employees who are highly compensated individuals. A life insurance, disability, severance pay, or supplemental unemployment compensation benefit shall not be considered to fail to meet the requirements merely because the benefits available bear a uniform relationship to the total compensation, or the basic or regular rate of compensation, of employees covered by the plan.

Exclusion of Certain Employees

There may be excluded from consideration—employees who have not completed three years of service, employees who have not attained age 21, seasonal employees or less than half-time employees, employees not included in this plan who are included in a unit of employees covered by an agreement between employee representatives and one or more employers which the Secretary finds to be a collective bargaining agreement if the class of benefits involved was the subject of good faith bargaining between such employee representatives and such employer or employers, and employees who are nonresident aliens and who receive no earned income from the employer which constitutes income from sources within the United States.

Notification Requirements

In order to be exempt from tax, a voluntary employees' beneficiary society must notify the Service that it is applying for recognition of such status. The notification deadline is the day 15 months from the end of the month in which the entity was organized. Exemption applies for any period before the giving of such notice, if the notice is given within the time prescribed by the Service. Notice is given by filing Form 1024 with the trust instrument. A notice will not be considered complete unless, in addition to a properly completed and executed Form 1024, the organization or trust submits a full description of the benefits available to participants under Code Sec. 501(c)(9) or (17). Moreover, both the terms and conditions of eligibility for membership and the terms and conditions of eligibility for benefits must be set forth. This information may be contained in a separate document, such as a "plan document," or it may be contained in the creating document of the entity). For benefits provided through a policy or policies of insurance, all such policies must be included with the notice. Where individual policies of insurance are provided to the participants, single exemplar copies, typical of policies generally issued to participants, are acceptable, provided they adequately describe all forms of insurance available to participants. In providing a full description of the benefits available, the benefits provided must be sufficiently described so that each benefit is definitely determinable. A benefit is definitely determinable if the amount of the benefit, its duration, and the persons eligible to receive it are ascertainable from the plan document or other instrument. Thus, a benefit is not definitely determinable if the rules governing either its amount, its duration, or its recipients are not ascertainable from the plan document or other instrument but are instead subject to the discretion of a person or committee. Likewise, a benefit is not definitely determinable if the amount for any individual is based upon a percentage share of any item that is within the discretion of the employer. However, a disability benefit will not fail to be considered definitely determinable merely because the determination of whether an individual is disabled is made under established guidelines by an authorized person or committee.

.08 Paid Time Off Benefits

Paid time off benefits, often referred to as PTO, represent an emerging trend in the design and administration of benefits providing time away from work with pay for eligible employees. PTO is a new approach which combines the vacation benefit with various other paid absence programs into a consolidated Paid Time Off benefit. This section examines the growth of this new benefit trend, examines pros and cons of this form of benefit for employees, and identifies policy administration issues to consider when implementing a PTO plan.

The PTO benefit or paid time off goes beyond the traditional vacation benefit or sick leave benefit plans. PTO creates a combined paid absence benefit that may include two or more of the following benefits:

- Vacation
- Paid holidays
- Paid sick leave
- Funeral leave
- Personal days
- Other paid absence plans

Recent Growth of PTO Plans

Over the past few years, CCH, a Wolters Kluwer business, has conducted an Unscheduled Absence Survey. The Unscheduled Absence Survey queries CCH subscribers about frequency of absences and actions taken by survey respondents to control unscheduled absences. In the Unscheduled Absence Survey conducted by CCH in 2005, data reveals that the use of paid leave banks is one of the tools used by employers for absence control, and that use of PTO plans is increasing over the past several years, as shown below:

Year	Respondents Offering PTO
2003	59%
2004	63%
2005	67%

¶ 903.08

Other absence control plans currently used by employers were rated by respondents for their effectiveness and frequency of use of such practices as shown below:

Absence Control Program	Effectiveness Rating*	Percentage of Respondents Using Program
Disciplinary action	3.4	90%
Yearly (performance) reviews	3.0	79%
Verification of illness	3.2	76%
Paid leave bank	3.5	67%
Personal recognition	2.6	66%
No fault attendance procedure	3.0	63%
Buy back plan	3.5	58%
Bonus	3.3	57%

*Rating:
  1 = Not very effective
  5 = Very effective

Pros and Cons of PTO Plans

When considering whether on not to implement a PTO plan, the following pros and cons have been identified:

Pros

Throughout the various studies and anecdotal data, the following arguments have been identified in support of the PTO type of paid absence benefit:

- Employees have greater flexibility.
- Supervisors do not worry about legitimate use of sick days.
- PTO plan removes the need for an employee to lie about an absence.
- Fewer absence categories mean greater ease in tracking and administration.
- PTO helps to control unscheduled absences.
- PTO provides an incentive to the employee not to call in sick excessively, because excessive absences reduce potential vacation time.

Cons

Throughout the various studies and anecdotal data, the following arguments have been identified as potential concerns in implementing a PTO type of paid absence benefit:

- Employees with high illness rates will not like the PTO plan.
- Careful communication is needed to introduce the plan to assure employee understanding.
- Careful communication is needed because many PTO plans reduce the total number of potential paid absences and such change is seen as a "take-away."
- State law in some areas requires payment of earned vacation and PTO at separation, but not for sick leave.
- Employee resistance to PTO is likely to occur in a culture of entitlement on absence benefits.

¶903.08

Policy Administration Issues to Consider

Consideration of the following issues is recommended when developing and implementing a paid absence or PTO plan.

- What is the current usage level of the various paid time off benefits currently in place?
- Are there any abuses occurring related to the paid time off benefits currently in place?
- What will be the eligibility requirements for PTO benefit?
- Will the PTO benefit be limited to full-time employees or will part-time workers be permitted to participate?
- Will benefits be earned in lump sum on an action date or be accrued incrementally or monthly?
- Will the benefit accrual or eligibility be keyed to length of service?
- How will the policy address the disposition of any unused benefits, i.e., forfeit at year-end, carryover to next year, cash payout, or conversion to some other form or benefit?
- Will there be a maximum benefit accumulation permitted, and if so, how much?
- Will there be a limit or reserved number of days be defined for a specific purpose, such as illness or sickness?
- Will there be any policy features related to attendance control?
- What notice or request forms or timeliness of requests will be imposed?
- How will the benefit correlate to FMLA leave?
- Will the PTO benefit be required to be used during FMLA?
- Will there be any payout at separation, as may be required by law in some states?
- Will there be any maximum or minimum increments defined for usage of the PTO benefit?
- Will the PTO plan include features for buying added days, selling days, or donating to others?
- Are there any collective bargaining or civil service limitations to defining or implementing such benefit plan?

.09 Health Savings Accounts and Other Tax-Favored Health Plans

Recent legislation relating to Medicare reform and the Health Insurance Portability and Accountability Act have created new tax favorable health plans, which may be offered by employers, or may be set up by employed or self employed individuals. Among the new plans are the following:

- Health Savings Accounts referred to as HSAs
- Medical Savings Accounts referred to as MSAs
- Flexible Spending Arrangements referred to as FSAs
- Health Reimbursement Arrangements referred to as HRAs

Health Savings Accounts (HSAs)

A health savings account is a tax exempt trust or custodial account that an eligible individual sets up with a qualified HSA trustee to pay or reimburse certain medical expenses. A qualified trustee can be a bank, an insurance company, or anyone already approved by the IRS to be a trustee of individual retirement arrangements (IRAs).

The HSA provides these benefits:

- The individual may claim a tax deduction for HSA contributions if deductions are not itemized on Form 1040.
- Any employer contributions may be excluded from the individual's gross income.
- Contributions remain in the account from year to year until used.
- Interest or other earnings on account assets are tax free.
- Distributions may be tax free if applied to qualified medical expenses.
- The HSA is "portable," meaning the employee keeps the account even if changing employers or leaving the work force.

To qualify for an HSA, an individual must have a high deductible health plan (HDHP) on the first day of the month, must have no other health coverage except as permitted under the plan, must not be enrolled in Medicare, and cannot be claimed as a dependent on another's tax return.

A high deductible health plan has a higher annual deductible than typical health plans and a maximum limit on the sum of the annual deducible and out of pocket medical expenses that the individual pays for covered expenses. Maximum deductibles and expenses for 2007 are shown in the chart below:

Type of Coverage	Minimum Annual Deductible	Maximum Annual Deductible and Other Out of Pocket Expenses
Self only	$1,100	$5,500
Family	$2,200	$11,000

Contributions to an HSA: HSA contributions must be made in cash. Stock or property contributions are not permitted. Contributions to the HSA may be made by the individual, by the individual's employer, and by family members on behalf of the individual. Generally, for 2007, contributions for an individual are limited to not more than $2,850, and up to $5,650 for a family plan. Contributions to the HSA must be reported on Form 8889 and filed with Form 1040.

Medical payments: The individual generally makes payments for medical expenses during the year without being reimbursed by the HDHP until reaching the annual deducible limit of the plan. The individual may receive tax free distributions from the HSA for qualified medical expenses. Qualified medical expenses are those expenses that would generally qualify for the medical and dental expenses deduction. Distributions must be reported on Form 8889 and filed with Form 1040.

The individual must keep records sufficient to show that:

- The distributions were exclusively to pay or reimburse qualified medical expenses,

¶903.09

- The qualified medical expenses had not been previously paid or reimbursed from another source, and

- The medical expenses had not been taken as an itemized deduction in any year.

Effect of Other Health Plans

An employee covered by an HDHP and a health FSA or an HRA that pays or reimburses qualified medical expenses generally cannot make contributions to an HSA.

Medical Savings Accounts (MSAs)

A medical savings account may be established by a self-employed individual or by certain small employers to meet the medical care costs of the account holder, the account holder's spouse, or dependents. Referred to as an Archer MSA, this plan is a tax exempt trust or custodial account that is set up with a U.S. financial institution such as a bank or insurance company. The MSA is used to save money for future medical expenses. The MSA provides these benefits:

- The individual may claim a tax deduction for MSA contributions if deductions are not itemized on Form 1040.

- Contributions remain in the account from year to year until used.

- Interest or other earnings on account assets are tax free.

- Distributions may be tax free if applied to qualified medical expenses.

- The MSA is "portable," meaning the employee keeps the account even if changing employers or leaving the work force.

To qualify for an MSA, the individual must be an employee or spouse of an employee who works for a small employer who maintains an individual or family HDHP, or is a self employed person or spouse of a self employed person that maintains an individual or family HDHP. A small employer is one who has 50 or fewer employees. Growing employers with less than 200 employees may also qualify.

A high deductible health plan has a higher annual deductible than typical health plans and a maximum limit on the sum of the annual deducible and out of pocket medical expenses that the individual pays for covered expenses. Maximum deductibles and expenses for 2007 are shown in the chart below:

Type of Coverage	Minimum Annual Deductible	Maximum Annual Deductible	Maximum Annual Out of Pocket Expenses
Self only	$1,900	$2,850	$3,750
Family	$3,750	$5,650	$6,900

Contributions to an MSA: MSA contributions must be made in cash. Stock or property contributions are not permitted. Contributions to the MSA may be made by the individual, or by the individual's employer, but not by both in the same year. There are contribution limits including an annual deductible limit and an income limit. Contributions to the MSA must be reported on Form 8853 and filed with Form 1040.

Medical payments: The individual generally makes payments for medical expenses during the year without being reimbursed by the HDHP until reaching the annual deducible limit of the plan. The individual may receive tax free distributions from the MSA for qualified medical expenses. Qualified medical expenses are those expenses that would generally qualify for the medical and dental expenses deduction. Distributions must be reported on Form 8853 and filed with Form 1040.

The individual must keep records sufficient to show that:

- The distributions were exclusively to pay or reimburse qualified medical expenses,
- The qualified medical expenses had not been previously paid or reimbursed from another source, and
- The medical expenses had not been taken as an itemized deduction in any year.

Flexible Spending Arrangements (FSAs)

A flexible spending arrangement is set up by an employer to allow the employee to be reimbursed for medical expenses. FSAs are usually funded through voluntary salary reduction agreements with the employer. This means that the employee agrees to deduct a portion of income from the employer for contribution to the plan. No employment or federal income taxes are deducted from the employee's contribution. Contributions to this plan are used to pay certain medical expenses.

An FSA provides the following benefits:

- Contributions made by the employer for the individual can be excluded from gross income,
- No employment or federal income taxes are deducted from the contributions,
- Withdrawals may be tax free if you pay qualified medical expenses,
- An individual may withdraw funds from the account to pay qualified medical expenses even if funds have not yet been placed into the account.

FSAs are employer established benefit plans. These may be offered in conjunction with other employer provided benefits as part of a cafeteria plan. Employers have complete flexibility to offer various combinations of benefits in designing their plan. The employee does not have to be covered under any other health care plan to participate. Self-employed persons are not eligible for an FSA.

An individual contributes to the FSA by electing an amount to voluntarily be withheld by the employer from salary. The employer may also contribute to the FSA if specified in the plan. The individual does not pay federal income tax or employment taxes on the amount of salary contributed to the plan and any employer contributions are not taxable. However, contributions made by the employer to provide coverage for long-term care insurance must be included in income.

There is no limit in the regulations on the amount of money that the individual or employer can contribute to the FSA; however, the plan must prescribe a maximum limit. Unspent contributions to an FSA are forfeited at year end. For this reason, it is important that the individual base his or her contribution on a reasonable estimate of qualifying expenses to be incurred during the year.

Distributions from the health FSA must be paid only to reimburse the individual for qualified medical expenses. The individual must provide to the health FSA a written statement from an independent third party stating that the medical expense was incurred, cite the amount of the expense, and state that the expense was not paid or reimbursed under any other health plan coverage.

Health Reimbursement Arrangements (HRAs)

A health reimbursement arrangement must be funded solely by the employer. Employees are reimbursed tax free for qualified medical expenses up to a maximum dollar amount for the coverage period. A health reimbursement arrangement may be offered with other health plans, including FSAs. An HRA provides the following benefits:

- Contributions made by the employer for an individual can be excluded from the individual's gross income,
- Reimbursements may be tax free if used for qualified medical expenses,
- Any unused amounts in the HRA can be carried forward for reimbursements in later years.

HRAs are employer established benefit plans. These may be offered in conjunction with other employer provided health benefits. The employer has the flexibility to offer various combinations of benefits, and the employee does not have to be covered by any other plan to participate. Self-employed persons are not eligible for an HRA.

There is no limit on the amount of money that the employer can contribute to an HRA account. Distributions from an HRA are paid to the individual for reimbursement of qualified medical expenses incurred on or after the date of enrollment into the HRA. Reimbursements can be made to current and former employees, spouses and dependents of those employees, and spouses and dependents of deceased employees. Unused amounts at year-end remain in the plan and generally can be carried forward to the next year. If any reimbursements are made for other than qualified medical expenses, then all reimbursements are subject to inclusion in the individual's gross income for tax purposes.

The foregoing summaries were drawn from Pub. 969 (2007).

¶ 904 HIRING

.01 Family Members

Tax savings and net cost to business for putting a family member (child under 18) on payroll.

Assumptions		Employee Costs
Gross Wages		$35,000
FICA/Medicare		2,678
State Unemployment, etc		160
Fringes Benefits Coverage		400
Worker's Compensation		400
Other		75
Employer Assumptions:		
Federal Income Tax Rate:	25%	
State Income Tax Rate:	3%	
Social Security Tax Rate:	6.2%	
Medicare Tax Rate:	1.45%	
Total Cost of Employing Family Member		$38,713
(Less) Tax Savings		13,801
Net Cost to Business		24,912

Thus, the business contributes $38,713 to pay a son or daughter wages, but the net cost to the business is only $24,912. For this $24,912 expenditure, the child receives $35,000 in wages less the child's tax liability and the business gets $35,000 worth of labor.

Family members should perform services for the business to justify the tax deductions. If a child were to earn $4,900 for the year, and the marginal federal/state tax bracket (including self-employment tax) were 45 percent, this would translate into a tax savings of $2,205 per year.

Sole Proprietor's Concepts

A sole proprietor is allowed to hire children even if the children are not of "legal" working age. It is possible to hire your 12 year old. The Code states that the sole proprietor does not have to pay social security taxes on children's wages, if the children are under 18 years old.

Assume taxpayer business owner is currently paying income taxes at the 28-percent rate. A sole proprietor must pay self-employment taxes on the profits. The rate is 15.3 percent before adjustments—and approximately 12 percent in round numbers after adjustments. The overall marginal federal tax bracket would be 40 percent. (40 cents of taxes are being paid for every additional dollar being earned). This means that 40 cents of taxes would be saved for every additional dollar of deductions.

If taxpayer business owner were to hire his child for the year, and pay a reasonable wage, the savings could be as high as 40 cents on every dollar paid out. If the child was paid $4,000 for the year, the savings would be $1,600/year.

Will the child be taxed on this money? It depends on how much the child is paid, and how much other income the child has for the year. Current tax law allows the dependent child to earn up to at least $8,750 (in 2007) without paying tax. Generally, the child's tax bracket would probably still be significantly lower than the sole proprietor's.

Consequences of paying sole proprietor's spouse. The exception regarding not paying self employment taxes does not apply for a spouse. Also, the spouse's marginal tax bracket is normally the same as that of the sole proprietor since a joint tax return is usually filed, so there would be no tax savings.

.03 Identification Numbers

Employee—Requirement of Application for Employee Identification Number

Every employee who does not have a social security number and who is in employment for wages which are subject to the taxes imposed by the Federal Insurance Contributions Act (FICA) or who is subject to the withholding of income tax from wages must obtain a number by filing a Form SS-5, Application for a Social Security Card. (Reg. § 31.6011(b)-2(a)(ii))

Time for Filing Form SS-5

The application shall be filed on or before the seventh day after the occurrence of the first day of employment to which reference is made. (Reg. § 31.6011(b)-2(a)(2))

Employer—Requirement of Application

Every employer who on any day has in his employ one or more individuals in employment for wages which are subject to the taxes imposed by the Federal Insurance Contributions Act (FICA) or which are subject to the withholding of income tax from wages, but who prior to such day neither has been assigned an identification number nor has applied therefore, must apply for one by filing Form SS-4, Application for Employer Identification Card. (Reg. § 31.6011(b)-1(a)(ii))

Use of Identification Number

The identification number assigned to an employer must be included in the employer's records and in all returns to the extent required by the applicable forms, regulations, and instructions. (Reg. § 31.6011(b)-1(d))

Time for Filing Form SS-4

The application for an identification number shall be filed on or before the seventh day after the first payment of wages. (Reg. § 31.6011(b)-1(a)(2))

Correcting Errors in Social Security Numbers

The Social Security Administration (SSA) stepped up its verification of names and social security numbers (SSNs) on file compared to employer wage and tax statements (Form W-2). Employers are now more likely to be notified by letter when discrepancies are found. The SSA letter asks the employer to help provide accurate and corrected information and notes that the IRS could penalize the employer or the employee for providing incorrect information.

Filing Tips to Ensure Accuracy

Before you file your next annual wage report, please make sure your employment records and the Forms W-2 you report have your employees' correct name and SSNs. Use the tips below to ensure accuracy.

- We encourage you to use SSA's Employee Verification Service (EVS) prior to submitting Forms W-2 to SSA for processing. EVS is a free, convenient and secure method for employers to verify that employee names and SSNs match SSA's records. EVS is not to be used to screen job applicants. A negative EVS response makes no statement about your employee's immigration status. Visit our website at *www.ssa.gov/employer* and select SSN Verification or call toll free 1-800-772-6270 for further details.

- Ask your employees to check their latest Form W-2 against their Social Security cards and to inform you of any name or SSN differences on the two. If the Form W-2 is incorrect, correct your records and prepare a Form W-2c. If the card is incorrect, advise the employee to request a corrected card from the nearest Social Security office.

- Remind your employees near the end of the year to report to Social Security name changes due to marriage, divorce, or other reasons.

- Ask each new employee to check his or her Social Security card and inform you of the name and SSN exactly as shown on the card. (While the employee must furnish the SSN to you, the employee is not required to show the Social Security card. But seeing the card will help ensure that all records are correct.)

- Direct those who do not have SSNs or have lost their cards to contact their nearest Social Security office to apply for a number or replacement card.

- Ensure that the SSNs you report are valid. A valid SSN must have a total of nine digits. The first three digits are referred to as the area, the next two as the group, and the last four as the serial. No SSNs with a 000 area number, or an area number in the 800 or 900 series, have been issued.

- If you file electronically, be sure that all of your employees' names are correctly entered in the appropriate fields of the Code RW "Employee Wage Record." For more information see SSA Publication "Magnetic Media Reporting and Electronic Filing (MMREF-1)."

- If you file on paper, be sure to enter your employees' names on the Forms W-2 as follows: first name, middle name or initial, and last name exactly as shown on their Social Security cards.

See IRS Publication 393, "Federal Employment Tax Forms." SSA Publication 31-011, "Software Specifications and Edits for Annual Wage Reporting" can be obtained through SSA's website or by contacting the SSA Employer 800 Number.

For IRS forms or publications, call 1-800-TAX-FORM (829-3676) or visit the IRS' website at *www.irs.gov*. For SSA forms or publications, call SSA's Employer 800 Number, 1-800-772-6270 or visit SSA's website at *www.ssa.gov/employer*.

Social Security Number Verification

The Social Security Administration has added new resources for employers providing a range of free services designed to help employers file timely and accurate W-2 wage reports.

Employer Reporting Service Center

The Social Security Administration has established a help desk referred to as the Employer Reporting Service Center. At the help center, wage reporting specialists in cities around the country are experts in paper, magnetic media and electronic wage reporting. They can help solve even the toughest problems. For the phone number of the specialist servicing your area, call the toll free number at 1-800-772-6270.

Verify Employee Names and Social Security Numbers

There are three convenient ways to verify payroll records for W-2 reporting purposes.

- *Phone verification.* To verify employee names and numbers, call the Employer Reporting Service Center. (see toll free number above)

- *Local Social Security Office.* Contact your nearest Social Security Office to verify up to 50 employee names and numbers.

- *Large volume request.* Files larger than 50 names and numbers may be submitted on paper listing, magnetic tape, or diskettes. You must register for this service. For details, call the toll free number above.

Online Electronic Filing

Transmit W-2 data from a personal computer. All you need is a modem, and software compatible with the Online Wage Reporting Bulletin Board. Filing is fast and easy, and you'll get transmission acknowledgment and processing status. You must register for this service. Modem dial in number is 1-410-966-8450. For more details, call the toll free number above. Requirements and software specifications are the same as for diskette reporting. Check SSA Pub. 42-007 for further details.

Additional resources for employers are displayed at http://www.ssa.gov/employer.

¶904.03

How To Correct SSNs

Complete Forms W-2c (Correct Wage and Tax Statement) for each of the SSNs listed that you are able to correct. You don't need to prepare Form W-2c for all the SSNs that you reported. If an employee does not provide corrected information or no longer works for you and you are unable to contact him/her, document your records with the information you relied on in completing the W-2 or the efforts you made to contact your former employee. Retain this information in your files; do not send it to SSA. You should provide all corrections as soon as possible. Please follow the guidelines below before preparing Forms W-2c.

- Compare your employment records to the Forms W-2 you reported for the SSNs included on the attached list.

- If your employment records and Forms W-2 do not match, prepare Forms W-2c with the corrected information from your employment records. (Do not send copies of proofs of identity or other documents in addition to, or in place of, the Form W-2c.)

- If your employment records and Forms W-2 match, ask your employee to check his/her Social Security card and to inform you of any name or SSN difference between your records and his/her card. If your employment records are incorrect, correct your records.

- If your records match the information on the employee's Social Security card, have the employee contact any Social Security office to resolve the issue. Tell the employee that once he/she has visited the Social Security office he/she should inform you of any changes you make to your employment records.

- SSA may also send the employee a notice regarding this issue. You should discuss with the employee any changes you make to your employment records.

- If you wish to file your Form W-2c corrections electronically, call SSA at 1-800-772-6270 to request a copy of the "Magnetic Medial Reporting and Electronic Filing of W-2c Information (MMREf-2)."

- We suggest using AccuW2C to identify possible "Magnetic Media Reporting and Electronic Filing of W-2c Information (MMREF-2)" formatting errors. You can download AccuW2C from the Internet at *www.ssa.gov/employer/accuwage*.

.04 Understanding Employment at Will

Employment at will is a concept that defines the employment relationship. The employment-at-will concept comes from common law. Common law is the historical development of law, often referred to as judge made law. Common law develops as various issues are presented in a claim or lawsuit by one person against another. The matter is adjudicated in court based upon legislated laws with consideration given to precedent previously set by judicial decisions on similar matters.

Employment at will refers to the employer-employee relationship. A basic definition of employment at will is that an employer can hire/fire at any time, and, likewise, an employee can seek/quit work at any time.

There are certain limits to employment at will. The limits can be defined by law and may vary from state to state. Various employment laws include a provision that states it is a violation of the law to discriminate against or discharge an individual for exercise of rights under the law. For example, the equal employment opportunity law prohibits an employer from discriminating against an employee or discharging an employee because the employee filed a claim of discrimination against the employer. Other laws, such many state workers compensation laws and the federal Occupational Safety and Health Act (OSHA), have similar protections for employees who exercise rights under these laws.

Another example of a limitation to the prerogative of employment at will is referred to as a Public Policy Limitation. An example of a Public Policy Limitation to employment at will is the limitation that an employer should not discriminate against an employee or discharge an employee because the employee participated in jury duty as summoned or cooperated with law enforcement in the conduct of an investigation.

A third example of a limitation to employment at will is referred to as breach of implied contract. Leading cases applying this concept to limit the employment-at-will prerogative have resulted from an employer discharging an employee in a manner that was contrary to a policy or procedure stated in the employer's personnel policy manual or employee handbook.

Employment-at-will matters are normally decided in state courts resulting from an individual's lawsuit against a former employer for wrongful discharge. The employee's lawsuit will typically assert that the individual was wrongfully discharged in a manner that is contrary to one or more of the recognized limitations to employment at will. The matter may be presented in a jury trial.

In the event that the individual's case is found by the court to have merit, the courts may award to the individual one or more of the following: job reinstatement, back pay, attorney fees, and punitive damages. Often, such awards can be in the hundreds of thousands of dollars.

Employer Protections

There are various actions for an employer to consider to protect the employment-at-will prerogative and to avoid wrongful discharge claims. Among these are:

- Be sure that your employee handbook contains a prominent disclaimer asserting that the handbook is not a contract and that it does not guarantee employment, tenure, or specific benefits.
- Avoid oral or written promises of job tenure.
- Include an employment-at-will statement in the applicant certification section of your firm's employment application.
- Follow policies defined in a personnel policy manual or employee handbook.
- Avoid complex predischarge procedures, such as defining in a handbook that all discharges will occur only after a specified number of warnings or following a probationary period.
- Be sure to review and follow procedures defined in an employee handbook before taking termination of employment action against an employee.
- Take care to document employee performance problems to show how you attempted to work with an employee to improve performance, and that, in spite of continued efforts, the employee still failed to perform properly.
- Instruct supervisors to confer with Human Resources or superiors prior to separating an individual from employment.

¶904.04

.05 Recruiting and Hiring Checklist

Steps to consider that will help to avoid discrimination or limit liability in implementing recruitment and hiring initiatives include:

Recruiting

- Establish a policy for recruitment and hiring, including criteria, procedures, responsible individuals.
- Identify the applicable barriers to equal employment opportunity.
- Prepare a list of job tasks or duties.
- Define hiring criteria based on job duties.
- Identify and develop a recruiting network notifying interested persons of opportunities, including advertising within the organization and, where applicable, not only with the general media, but with minority, persons with disabilities, older persons, and women-focused media.
- Communicate the competencies, skills, and abilities required for available positions.
- Communicate about family-friendly and work-friendly programs.
- Participate in career and job fairs and open houses.
- Work with professional associations, civic associations, and educational institutions with attractive numbers of minorities, women, persons with disabilities and/or older persons to recruit.
- Use employment services recruiter, referral, and search firms with instructions to present diverse candidate pools to expand search networks.
- Partner with organizations that have missions to serve targeted groups.
- Use internships, work/study, co-op, and scholarship programs to attract interested persons and to develop interested and qualified candidates.
- Develop and support educational programs and become more involved with educational institutions that can refer a more diverse talent pool.
- Ensure that personnel involved in the recruitment and hiring process are well trained in their equal employment opportunity responsibilities.
- Explore community involvement options so the company's higher profile may attract more interested persons.
- Eliminate practices which exclude or present barriers to minorities, women, persons with disabilities, older persons, or any individual.
- Include progress in equal employment opportunity recruitment and hiring as factors in management evaluation.

Internet Recruiting

- Consider the Internet as a recruiting resource.
- Post job opening announcements on your organization's website.
- Check employment or recruiting websites as a source for posting job opening announcements.
- Establish an e-mail address to recevie resumes.

- Invite candidates to apply by e-mail.
- Target Internet recruiting efforts for technical or computer oriented jobs or job opportunities for new graduates through Internet recruiting resources.
- Recognize that Internet recruiting broadens your recruiting base resulting in out-of-area or out-of-country applications. Specify whether you will or will not pay for relocation.

Hiring

- Use a job description to develop interview questions.
- Ask questions to elicit candidates' knowledge, skills, and abilities.
- Ask candidate to describe tasks performed on prior jobs.
- Evaluate candidates based on job-related criteria.
- Avoid inquiries relating to age, race, sex, religion, national origin, disability, or other non-job-related factors.
- Evaluate all candidates for a job based on the same criteria.
- Avoid creating arbitrary or unreasonable hiring standards.

Background Checks

Employer use of background checks to screen candidates has grown significantly in recent years. In addition to security concerns raised by the events of September 11, 2001, employers also are concerned about verifying education and credentials, work experience, driving records, credit records and criminal convictions.

Reference Checking

Verification of employment and personal references has traditionally been an activity handled by employers and their human resources specialists.

Contacts may be made by telephone, by fax or by e-mail to former employers to verify information stated by the candidate on an employment application. It is recommended that the screening employer obtain a signed release from the candidate which can be forwarded to the organization where references and employment are verified.

Social Security Number Verification

This practice has increased in the past several years, due in part to IRS and Social Security Administration cross matching of employer W-2 records with employee tax reports and notice provided to employers where mismatches occur. Social security number verification is described at ¶ 904.03 in this chapter.

Education and Professional Credentials

Candidates for certain positions must possess specified educational or professional credentials. Employers involved in hiring candidates for such jobs generally verify credentials by contacting educational institutions, state licensing agencies or similar certifying organizations to verify that the candidate posseses proper credentials for the job.

Driving Records

Candidates hired for positions operating certain vehicles or equipment must posses an appropriate license for the job. Loss of the driver's license may disqualify the individual for the job. Employers involved in hiring candidates for such jobs generally verify driver's license credentials by contacting state licensing agencies or similar certifying organizations to verify that the candidate posseses proper credentials for the job.

Criminal and Civil Court Records

Employers hiring candidates for certain jobs may be concerned about the individual's civil or criminal history. For example, an employer's failure to conduct a background check on an individual who had a violent past and then became violent causing harm to a customer while on the job lead to a negligent hiring claim against the employer. As a result, an employer may check an individual for criminal or civil history and screen out candidates who pose a threat on the job.

Credit Checks

Employers hiring candidates for certain jobs may be concerned about the individual's credit-worthiness. For example, an employer hiring individuals who are responsible for handling large amounts of money may conduct a credit check on job candidates for the position. The use of a credit check in employment is subject to the Fair Credit Reporting Act which requires notice to the individual, a written consent for conducting the check, and specified content of notice to the.individual if an adverse employment decision is made as a result of the credit check.

In 2005, the Fair and Accurate Credit Transactions Act requires employers who hold consumer information to properly dispose of such information by taking reasonable measures to protect against unauthorized access to or use of the information in connection with its disposal. When such records are no longer needed for a business purpose, the employer holding such records should destroy or shred such records to avoid unauthorized disclosures of personal financial data.

Various organizations now offer background checking services. For a fee, the service will conduct a background check on a candidate or employee, conducting those record searches specified by the employer and providing a report of results Background check specialists recommend that the employer notify candidates or employees that background checks are used in the screening and employment process, that the candidate or employee be instructed to sign a consent for the check, and that any legally required notices be provided.

Employment Eligibility

Employers hiring employees must verify the identity and employment eligibility of each new employee in the manner prescribed by the Immigration Reform and Control Act of 1986. See further details at ¶ 917.

.07 Hiring and Relocation

The cost of relocating new hire employees continues to climb. According to the Employee Relocation Council, between 1999 and 2000, the cost to relocate a new hire homeowner rose 10 percent from $41,780 to $45,948. During the same period, costs to relocate a new hire renter rose 22 percent from $11,072 in 1999 to $13,456 in 2000. (Source: Employee Relocation Council, "2001 Transfer Volume and Cost Survey," *Mobility* (July 2001).)

There are certain tax deductions available to the employer for reimbursement of qualified moving expenses. (Code Sec. 217) A qualified move must meet time and distance tests. To qualify, the employee must remain at the new job site at least 39 weeks, and the move must be at least 50 miles further from the residence than the old workplace was.

Checklist to Evaluate Your Employment Application

The employment application is an important tool that many employers use for employee screening and selection. While some firms prepare a custom imprinted employment application, many others purchase preprinted applications available from the office supply store. The choice between a standardized "off the shelf" type form versus a customized form is typically weighed by cost and suitability of available application forms. An important consideration is that the application must be designed to collect sufficient information about the candidate to evaluate his or her suitability for employment. Further, the application must be designed to comply with various state and federal labor laws. Here is a checklist of items to aid in evaluating an employment application form. Does the application contain or elicit the following items?

- Equal employment opportunity statement.
- Personal information, including name, address, and telephone number.
- Position sought and desired salary.
- Education and degrees.
- Listing of special job skills, occupational license, and certifications.
- Employment history, including prior employers, dates, job responsibilities, and pay.
- Reason for leaving prior jobs.
- Reference contact at each prior job.
- Military service including dates and responsibilities.
- Personal references.
- Applicant certification including employment-at-will statement, authorization for reference checking, and acknowledgement that falsification of information is grounds to deny employment.

Items to Avoid on Your Application

Your firm's employment application should not seek certain information in violation of various state and federal labor laws. Make sure that your application does not include inquiries that may identify any of the following: race, color, age, sex, religion, national origin, and physical or mental disability.

In addition, certain state or local laws prohibit inquiries related to one or more of the following issues: ancestry, marital status, sexual preference or orientation, nature of discharge from military service, prior workers compensation claims, or arrest record. There may be other prohibited inquiries identified in state or local law.

Recently, some states have passed laws designed to protect unnecessary disclosures of an individual's social security number. While the social security number is needed at time of employment for payroll, income tax, background or credit checks, and employment identification purposes, it may not be necessary to require the candidate to enter the number on the employment application prior to hire.

¶904.07

Retaining Job Applications and Resumes

Employers that are subject to federal anti-discrimination laws are responsible for retaining hiring records for a period of one year from the date of the employment decision such as the hiring or rejection of a candidate. The federal employment laws include Title VII of the Civil Rights Act of 1964, the Americans with Disabilities Act, and the Age Discrimination in Employment Act. Employers with 15 or more employees (20 or more employees under the age law) are subject to these federal laws. There may be different requirements imposed by state law in various areas.

Examples of covered employment records may include applications, resumes, selection testing results, and background investigations.

In the event the employer is subject to legal claim or discrimination charge, all relevant employment records must be retained until the claim is resolved. In the event that the candidate is employed, then the employer should retain the information through the duration of the individual's employment.

¶ 907 WAGES AND WITHHOLDING

.01 Wages Defined

- Wages include all remuneration for services by cash or other than cash, except:
    — Qualified fringe benefits.
    — Qualified plan contributions.
    — Group term life insurance (up to $50,000).
    — Services not in course of employer's business.
    — Educational assistance (up to $5,250).
    — Moving expense reimbursements, if a deduction is allowed and not taken in previous year.
    — Dependent care assistance up to $5,000 excludible amount; $2,500 for married individual filing separately.
- Basis on which work is paid is immaterial.
- Payment medium is immaterial.
    — For other than cash, use fair market value.
- Payments of unsubstantiated reimbursements and unreturned excess payments are treated as paid under a non-accountable plan and are included in wages.
- Dismissal, severances and termination payments are wages.
- Vacation allowances are wages.
- Advances or reimbursements for travel or other necessary expenses are not wages, if paid under an accountable plan.
    — Make a separate payment, or
    — Specifically identify the payment.
- The name by which wages are called is immaterial.
- Payment for services rendered after termination is still wages.
- Supplemental unemployment compensation benefits required to be included in gross income of individuals are wages.
- Payments of taxes for employees are wages.

Included and Excluded Wages

Wages or Not

If a portion of the remuneration paid by an employer to his employee for services performed during a payroll period of not more than 31 consecutive days constitutes wages, and the remainder does not constitute wages, all the remuneration paid the employee for services performed during such period shall, for purposes of withholding, be treated alike, that is, either all included as wages or all excluded. (Reg. § 31.3402(e)-1(a))

Wages If More Than Half

If one-half or more of the employee's time in the employ of a particular employer in a payroll period is spent in performing services the remuneration for which constitutes wages, then all the remuneration paid the employee for services performed in that payroll period shall be deemed to be wages. (Reg. § 31.3402(e)-1(b))

Not Wages If Less Than Half

If less than one-half of the employee's time in the employ of a particular employer in a payroll period is spent in performing services the remuneration for which constitutes wages, then none of the remuneration paid the employee for services performed in that payroll period shall be deemed to be wages. (Reg. § 31.3402(e)-1(c))

Requirement of Withholding

The employer is required to collect the tax by deducting and withholding the amount from the employee's wages when paid, either actually or constructively. Wages are constructively paid when they are credited to the account of or set apart for an employee so that they may be drawn upon by him at any time, although not actually in his possession.

To constitute payment, the wages:

- Must be credited to or set apart for the employee without any substantial limitation or restriction as to the time or manner of payment or condition upon which payment is to be made.
- Must be made available to him so that they may be drawn upon at any time.
- Their payment brought within his own control and disposition. (Reg. § 31.3402(a)-1(b))

Wages Paid in Property

An employer is required to deduct and withhold the tax even though the wages are paid in something other than money (for example, wages paid in stock or bonds) and to pay over the tax in money. If wages are paid in property other than money, the employer should make necessary arrangements to insure that the amount of the tax required to be withheld is available for payment in money. (Reg. § 31.3402(a)-1(c))

Employer Liability for Correct Amount of Tax Whether Deducted or Not

Every employer required to deduct and withhold tax from the wages of an employee is liable for the payment of such tax whether or not it is collected from the employee by the employer. If, for example, the employer deducts less than the correct amount of tax, or if he fails to deduct any part of the tax, he is nevertheless liable for the correct amount of the tax. The employer is relieved of liability to any other person for the amount of any such tax withheld and paid to the district director or deposited with a duly designated depositary of the United States. (Reg. § 31.3403-1)

.02 Tax Treatment of Military Pay

If an employer continues to pay an employee full salary or the difference between his salary and the amounts received from the military, the employee should be aware that the employment relationship between the employee and the company was terminated when the worker was called for active military service with the U.S. government or for active service with the state National Guard. Under the circumstances, the payments made by the company to the former employees while they are in military service with the U.S. government or active service with the state National Guard are not "wages" for services performed in employment for the companies. These payments, therefore, are not "wages" subject to the taxes imposed by the Federal Insurance Contributions Act and the Federal Unemployment Tax Act or to the Collection of Income Tax at Source of Wages. Note: However, these payments are includable to the taxpayer as income. Businesses are required to issue Form 1099 Miscellaneous for any amounts paid.

(Source: SSA/IRA Reporter, Fall 2004)

.03 Employer Compensation Costs

In September 2006, private sector employers paid an average of $27.31 per hour in total compensation costs for employees. This breaks down to an average of $19.12 per hour (70 percent) for wages and salaries, and $8.18 (30 percent) for benefits. This compares to data from 2005 with total compensation averaging $24.24 per hour, wages and salaries at $17.21 per hour, and benefits at $7.03 per hour.

.04 Employment Taxes Defined

Under Reg. § 31.6302-1(e)(1), the term "employment taxes" means:

- The employee portion of the tax withheld under Code Sec. 3102.
- The employer tax under Code Sec. 3111.
- The employer tax under Code Sec. 3301.
- The income tax withheld under Code Secs. 3402 and 3405.
- The income tax withheld under Code Sec. 3406 relating to backup withholding with respect to reportable payments.

The term "employment taxes" does not include taxes with respect to wages for domestic service in a private home of the employer, unless the employer is otherwise required to file a Form 941 under Reg. § 31.6011(a)(4) or (5). In the case of employers paying advance earned income credit amounts, the amount of taxes required to be deposited shall be reduced by advance amounts paid to employees. (Reg. § 31.6302-1(e)(2))

.05 Deposit Requirements for Employers

An employer must generally deposit employment taxes under one of two rules: the Monthly rule or the Semiweekly rule. Various exceptions and safe harbors are provided. Certain safe harbors are provided for employers who inadvertently fail to deposit the full amount of taxes. There is an overriding exception to the Monthly and Semiweekly rules where an employer has accumulated \$100,000 or more of employment taxes. (Reg. § 31.6302-1(a))

Determination of Status

The determination of whether an employer is a monthly or semiweekly depositor for a calendar year is based on an annual determination and generally depends upon the aggregate amount of employment taxes reported by the employer for a lookback period. (Reg. § 31.6302-1(b)(1))

Monthly Depositor

An employer is a monthly depositor for the entire calendar year if the aggregate amount of employment taxes reported for the lookback period is \$50,000 or less. An employer ceases to be a monthly depositor on the first day after the employer is subject to the One-Day (\$100,000) rule. See discussion of One-Day rule at ¶ 907.07. At that time, the employer immediately becomes a semiweekly depositor for the remainder of the calendar year and for the following calendar year. (Reg. § 31.6302-1(b)(2))

Semiweekly Depositor

An employer is a semiweekly depositor for the entire calendar year if the aggregate amount of employment taxes reported for the lookback period exceeds \$50,000. (Reg. § 31.6302-1(b)(3))

Lookback Period

The lookback period for each calendar year is the twelve-month period ending the preceding June 30. For example, the lookback period for calendar year 2007 is the period July 1, 2005, to June 30, 2006. In determining status as either a monthly or semiweekly depositor, an employer should determine the aggregate amount of employment tax liabilities reported on its quarterly returns (Form 941) for the four quarters constituting this period. New employers shall be treated as having employment tax liabilities of zero for any calendar quarter during which the employer did not exist. (Reg. § 31.6302-1(b)(4))

Electronic Deposit Requirement

If an employer's total deposit of all depository taxes including: social security, Medicare, railroad retirement, and withheld income taxes were more than \$200,000 in 2005, or the employer was required to use EFTPS in 2006, the employer must make electronic deposits for all depository tax liabilities that occur in 2007. If required to deposit by electronic funds transfer in prior years, an employer must continue to do so.

Adjustments

The tax liability shown on an original return for the return period shall be the amount taken into account in determining whether more than \$50,000 has been reported during the lookback period. In determining the aggregate employment taxes for each quarter in a lookback period, an employer does not take into account any adjustments for the quarter made on a supplemental return filed after the due date of the return. However, adjustments made on a Form 941c, Statement to Correct Information, attached to a Form 941 filed for a subsequent quarter, are taken into account in determining the employment tax liability for the subsequent quarter. (Reg. § 31.6302-1(b)(5))

¶907.05

.07 Deposit Rules

Monthly Rule

An employer that is a monthly depositor must deposit employment taxes accumulated with respect to payments made during a calendar month in an authorized financial institution on or before the 15th day of the following month. If the 15th day of the following month is not a banking day, taxes will be treated as timely deposited if deposited on the first banking day thereafter. (Reg. § 31.6302-1(c)(1))

Semiweekly Rule

An employer that is a semiweekly depositor for a calendar year must deposit its employment taxes in an authorized financial institution on or before the dates set forth below:

Payment dates/semiweekly periods	Deposit date
Wednesday, Thursday and/or Friday	On or before the following Wednesday.
Saturday, Sunday, Monday and/or Tuesday	On or before the following Friday.

(Reg. § 31.6302-1(c)(2)(i))

Semiweekly Period Spanning Two Return Periods

A special rule is provided in the case of a return period (quarterly or annual) that ends during a semiweekly period. In this case, an employer must complete the Federal Tax Deposit (FTD) coupon in a manner which designates the proper return period for which the deposit relates (the return period in which the payment is made). In addition, if the return period ends during a semiweekly period in which an employer has two or more payment dates, two deposit obligations may exist. For example, if one quarterly return period ends on Thursday and a new quarterly return period begins on Friday, employment taxes from payments on Wednesday and Thursday are subject to one deposit obligation, and taxes from payments on Friday are subject to a separate obligation. Two separate Federal Tax Deposit coupons are required. (Reg. § 31.6302-1(c)(2)(ii))

Special Rule for Non-Banking Days

Semiweekly depositors shall have at least three banking days following the close of the semiweekly period by which to deposit employment taxes accumulated during the semiweekly period. Thus, if any of the three weekdays following the close of a semiweekly period is a holiday on which banks are closed, the employer shall have an additional banking day by which to make the required deposit. For example, if the Monday following the close of a Wednesday to Friday semiweekly period is a holiday on which banks are closed, the required deposit for the semiweekly period may be made by the following Thursday rather than the following Wednesday. (Reg. § 31.6302-1(c)(2)(iii))

Exception: One-Day Rule

If, on any day within a deposit period (monthly or semiweekly), an employer has accumulated $100,000 or more of employment taxes, those taxes must be deposited in an authorized financial institution by the close of the next banking day. For purposes of determining whether the $100,000 threshold is met:

- A monthly depositor takes into account only those employment taxes accumulated in the calendar month in which the day occurs; and
- A semiweekly depositor takes into account only those employment taxes accumulated in the Wednesday-Friday or Saturday-Tuesday semiweekly period in which the day occurs. (Reg. § 31.6302-1(c)(3))

Deposits Required Only on Banking Days

If taxes are required to be deposited on any day that is not a banking day, the taxes will be treated as timely deposited if deposited on the first banking day thereafter. (Reg. § 31.6302-1(c)(4))

Example 1. Monthly Depositor

Determination of Status

For the calendar year 2007, Employer A determines its depositor status using the lookback period July 1, 2005, to June 30, 2006. For the four calendar quarters within this period, A reported aggregate employment tax liabilities of $42,000 on its quarterly Forms 941. Because the aggregate amount did not exceed $50,000, A is a monthly depositor for the entire calendar year 2007. (Reg. § 31.6302-1(d))

Monthly Rule

During June 2007, Employer A (a monthly depositor) accumulates $3,500 in employment taxes. A has a $3,500 deposit obligation that must be satisfied by the 15th day of the following month. Since July 15, 2007, is a Sunday and not a banking day, A's deposit obligation will be satisfied if the deposit is made by the next banking day after July 15. (Reg. § 31.6302-1(d))

Example 2. Semiweekly Depositor

Determination of Status

For the four calendar quarters spanning July 2005 to June 2006, Employer B reported $88,000 in aggregate employment tax liabilities on its Forms 941. Because that amount exceeds $50,000, B is a semiweekly depositor for the entire calendar year 2007. (Reg. § 31.6302-1(d))

Semiweekly Rule

On Friday, January 5, 2007, B (semiweekly depositor) has a payday on which it accumulates $4,000 in employment taxes. B has a $4,000 deposit obligation that must be filed on or before the following Wednesday (January 10, 2007). (Reg. § 31.6302-1(d))

Deposit Made within Three Banking Days after Payroll

The premise is the same as above, except that B deposits its accumulated employment taxes within three banking days after payroll. B deposits its $4,000 in employment taxes on Wednesday, January 10, three banking days after its Friday payroll. Because B deposited its employment taxes on or before the following Wednesday, B has satisfied its semiweekly deposit obligation. An employer that deposits within three banking days after payroll will always meet the Semiweekly Rule. (Reg. § 31.6302-1(d))

Example 3. One-Day Rule

On Monday, January 8, 2007, Employer C accumulates $110,000 in employment taxes with respect to wages paid on that date. C has a deposit obligation of $110,000 that must be satisfied by the next banking day. If C was not subject to the semiweekly rule on January 8, C becomes subject to that rule as of January 9. (Reg. § 31.6302-1(d))

Example 4. One-Day Rule in Combination with Subsequent Deposit Obligation

Employer D is subject to the semiweekly rule for calendar year 2007. On Monday, January 8, 2007, D accumulates $110,000 in employment taxes. D has a $110,000 deposit obligation that must be satisfied by the next banking day. On Tuesday, January 9, D accumulates an additional $30,000 in employment taxes. Although D has a previous $110,000 deposit obligation incurred earlier in the semiweekly period, D has an additional and separate deposit obligation of $30,000 on Tuesday that must be satisfied by the following Friday. (Reg. § 31.6302-1(d))

Example 5. Special Non-Banking Day Rule for Semiweekly Depositors

Employer E, a semiweekly depositor, accumulates $8,000 in employment taxes on Friday, February 16, 2007, a payment date. Under the general rule, E would be required to deposit the employment taxes on or before the following Wednesday, February 21. However, because Monday, February 19, is President's Day (a holiday on which banks are closed), E will have an additional day by which to satisfy its $8,000 deposit obligation. E's deposit obligation is due on or before Thursday, February 22, 2007. (Reg. § 31.6302-1(d))

.09 Safe Harbor/*De Minimis* Rules

Single Deposit Safe Harbor

An employer will be considered to have satisfied its deposit obligation if:

- The amount of any shortfall does not exceed the greater of $100 or two percent of the amount of employment taxes required to be deposited; and
- The employer deposits the shortfall on or before the shortfall makeup date. (Reg. § 31.6302-1(f)(1))

Shortfall Defined

The term "shortfall" means the excess of the amount of employment taxes required to be deposited for the period over the amount deposited for the period. For this purpose, a period is either monthly, semiweekly or daily. (Reg. § 31.6302-1(f)(2))

Shortfall Makeup Date-Monthly Rule

A shortfall with respect to a deposit required under the Monthly Rule must be deposited or remitted no later than the due date for the quarterly return, in accordance with the applicable form and instructions. (Reg. § 31.6302-1(f)(3)(i))

Semiweekly Rule and One-Day Rule

A shortfall with respect to a deposit required under the Semiweekly Rule or the One-Day Rule must be deposited on or before the first Wednesday or Friday (whichever is earlier), falling on or after the 15th day of the month following the month in which the deposit was required to be made. (Reg § 31.6302-1(f)(3)(ii))

De Minimis Rule

If the total amount of accumulated employment taxes for the quarter is less than $2,500, and the amount is fully deposited or remitted with a timely filed return for the quarter, the amount deposited or remitted will be deemed to have been timely deposited. (Reg. § 31.6302-1(f)(4))

Example 1. Safe-Harbor Rule Satisfied

On Tuesday, January 2, 2007, J (a semiweekly depositor), pays wages and accumulates employment taxes. As required under this Sec., J makes a deposit on or before the following Friday, January 5, 2007, in the amount of $4,000. Subsequently, J determines that it was actually required to deposit $4,090 by Friday. J has a shortfall of $90. The $90 shortfall does not exceed the greater of $100 or 2% of the amount required to be deposited (2% of $4,090 = $81.80). Therefore, J satisfies the safe harbor as long as the $90 shortfall is deposited by the first deposit date (Wednesday or Friday) on or after the 15th day of the next month. (Reg. § 31.6302-1(f)(5))

Example 2. Safe-Harbor Rule Not Satisfied

The facts are the same as in Example 1, except that on Friday, January 5, 2007, J makes a deposit of $25,000, and later determines that it was actually required to deposit $26,000. Since the $1,000 shortfall ($26,000 less $25,000) exceeds $520 (the greater of $100 or 2% of the amount required to be deposited (2% of $26,000 = $520)), the safe harbor is not satisfied, and absent reasonable cause, J will be subject to a failure-to-deposit penalty under Code Sec. 6656. (Reg. § 31.6302-1(h)(5))

.11 Federal Tax Deposit (FTD) Coupon/Timing of Deposits

Each deposit required to be made must be accompanied by an FTD coupon (Form 8109). The FTD coupon shall be prepared in accordance with the instructions applicable thereto. The deposit, together with the FTD coupon, shall be forwarded to a financial institution authorized as a depository for federal taxes. (Reg. § 31.6302-1(i)(3))

Procurement of FTD Coupons

A new employer should receive its initial supply of FTD coupon books after receiving its employer identification number. In the event that a deposit is required to be made before receipt of the FTD coupon books, the employer should contact the local IRS office and furnish the following information: the business name as it appears on IRS records, the employer identification number, address where the coupon books are to be sent and the number of coupon books being requested. Employers who do not automatically receive a resupply should call 1-800-829-4933.

Filers of Form 1120, 990-C, 990PF (with net investment income), 990-T or 2438 must also provide the month that the employer's tax year ends. If an employer has applied for an employer identification number but has not received it, and a deposit is required to be made, the employer should send a check or money order for the deposit amount to its Internal Revenue Service center. Included on the payment should be the name and address of the entity as shown on Form SS-4, Application for Employer Identification Number, the kind of tax, the period covered and the date on which the employer applied for the employer identification number. (Reg. § 31.6302-1(i)(4))

Time Deemed Deposited

The timeliness of a deposit will be determined by the date stamped on the FTD coupon by the authorized financial institution or, if Code Sec. 7502(e) applies, by the date the deposit is treated as received under Code Sec. 7502(e). (Reg. § 31.6302-1(i)(5))

Time Deemed Paid

In general, amounts deposited will be considered as paid at the time deemed deposited above, or on the last day prescribed for filing the return (determined without regard to any extension of time for filing the return), whichever is later. For purposes of Code Sec. 6511 (relating to the period of limitation on credit or refund), if an amount is deposited prior to April 15th of the calendar year immediately succeeding the calendar year that contains the period for which the amount was deposited, the amount will be considered paid on April 15th. (Reg. § 31.6302-1(i)(6))

Deposit System (EFTPS)

Employers must make electronic deposits of *all* depository tax liabilities that occur if:

- The threshold that determines whether an employer must use the Electronic Federal Tax Payment System (EFTPS) has been increased from $50,000 to $200,000.

- *All* Federal tax deposits (such as deposits for employment tax, excise tax, and corporate income tax) made during a calendar year are combined to determine whether the employer exceeded the $200,000 threshold. If the total of Federal tax deposits made in 2005 exceeded $200,000, the employer must use EFTPS beginning January 1, 2007.

- Participation in EFTPS is voluntary if deposits do not exceed the new $200,000 threshold, even if the employer was required to electronically deposit under the previous $50,000 threshold. However, businesses that exceed the new $200,000 threshold must continue to use EFTPS in all later years.

- Those required to make electronic deposits by electronic funds transfer and fail to do so, may be subject to a 10-percent penalty.

Taxpayers who are not required to make electronic deposits may voluntarily participate in EFTPS. To enroll in EFTPS, employers can call 1-800-555-4477.

When to Deposit Employment Taxes

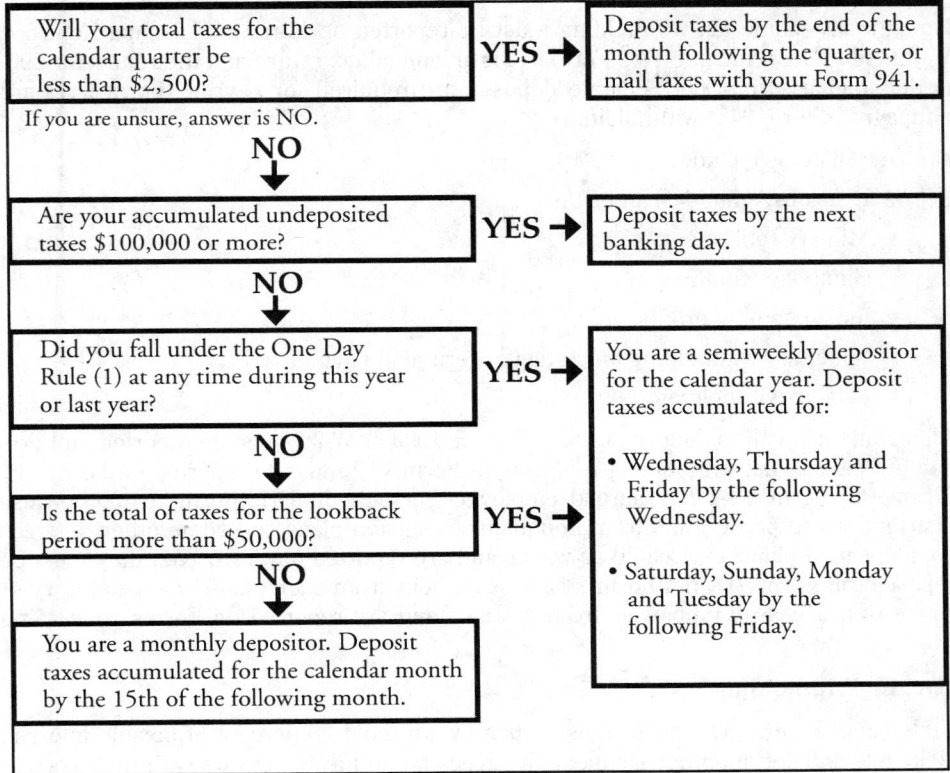

Will your total taxes for the calendar quarter be less than $2,500?	**YES →**	Deposit taxes by the end of the month following the quarter, or mail taxes with your Form 941.

If you are unsure, answer is NO.

NO ↓

Are your accumulated undeposited taxes $100,000 or more?	**YES →**	Deposit taxes by the next banking day.

NO ↓

Did you fall under the One Day Rule (1) at any time during this year or last year?	**YES →**	You are a semiweekly depositor for the calendar year. Deposit taxes accumulated for:

NO ↓

Is the total of taxes for the lookback period more than $50,000?	**YES →**	• Wednesday, Thursday and Friday by the following Wednesday. • Saturday, Sunday, Monday and Tuesday by the following Friday.

NO ↓

You are a monthly depositor. Deposit taxes accumulated for the calendar month by the 15th of the following month.

(1) You fall under the One-Day Rule if your accumulated undeposited taxes are $100,000 or more on any day during a semiweekly or monthly deposit period.

Federal Unemployment Tax

Deposit Due Dates

If at the end of any calendar quarter, the business owes, but has not yet deposited, more than $100 in federal unemployment (FUTA) tax for the year, it must make a deposit by the end of the next month. If a due date falls on a Saturday, Sunday or legal holiday, it is postponed until the next date that is not a Saturday, Sunday or legal holiday.

If undeposited FUTA tax is more than $100 on:	**Deposit the full amount by:**
March 31	April 30
June 30	July 31
September 30	October 31
December 31	January 31

¶907.11

.13 Nonpayroll Tax Withholding Deposits

Nonpayroll Income Tax Withholding

Nonpayroll income tax withholding must be reported on Form 945, Annual Return of Withheld Federal Income Tax. Form 945 is an annual tax return and the return for 2007 is due January 31, 2008. Separate deposits are required for payroll (Form 941) and nonpayroll (Form 945) withholding.

Nonpayroll items include:

- Pensions, annuities, and IRAs.
- Military retirement.
- Gambling winnings.
- Indian gaming profits.
- Voluntary withholding on certain government payments.
- Backup withholding.

All income tax withholding reported on Forms 1099 or W-2G must be reported on Form 945. All income tax withholding reported on Form W-2 must be reported on Form 941, Form 943, Form CT-1 for railroad employees, or Schedule H (Form 1040). Because distributions to participants from nonqualified pension plans and some other deferred compensation plans are treated as wages and are reported on Form W-2, they must be reported on Form 941, not Form 945. Distributions from such plans to a beneficiary or estate of a deceased employee are not wages and are reported on Forms 1099-R and 945.

Backup Withholding

Under Sec. 3406(a)(1), payers must generally withhold 28 percent of taxable interest, dividends and certain other payments if payees fail to furnish payers with their correct taxpayer identification numbers. There are other circumstances when the payer is also required to withhold. This withholding is referred to as backup withholding. Backup withholding does not apply to wages, pensions, or annuities. (Circular E)

Income Tax Withholding from Pensions and Annuities

Generally, payers or plan administrators must withhold federal income tax at specified rates on certain periodic, nonperiodic, and eligible rollover distributions (that are not direct rollovers) from pensions, annuity, deferred income, and IRA payments. (IRS Publication 15-A)

Withholding on Periodic Payments

Generally, periodic payments are those payable for more than one year that are not eligible rollover distributions. Periodic payments include substantially equal payments made at least once a year over the life of the employee and/or beneficiaries or for 10 years or more. These payments are treated as if they are wages. Recipients of periodic payments can submit to you a Form W-4P to specify the number of withholding allowances and any additional amount they want withheld. They may also claim an exemption from withholding on Form W-4P or revoke a previously claimed exemption. If they do not submit a Form W-4P, you must figure withholding by treating a recipient as married with three withholding allowances. (IRS Publication 15-A)

Withholding on Nonperiodic Payments

Withhold 10 percent of a nonperiodic payment that is not an eligible rollover distribution. The recipient may request additional withholding on Form W-4P or claim exemption from withholding. (IRS Publication 15-A)

Withholding on an Eligible Rollover Distribution

Withhold 20 percent of an eligible rollover distribution unless the recipient elected to have the distribution paid in a direct rollover to an eligible retirement plan, including an IRA. An eligible rollover distribution is the taxable part of any distribution from a qualified plan or tax-sheltered annuity (but not an IRA), except one of a series of substantially equal periodic payments (at least annually) made for the life or life expectancy of the employee and the employee's beneficiary or for a specified period of 10 years or more, any part of a distribution that is a minimum distribution required by Code Sec. 401(a)(9) a hardship distribution, and certain other exceptions. A recipient of an eligible rollover distribution cannot claim exemption from the 20 percent withholding. It is not necessary to claim exemption from withholding on a direct transfer to an IRA or other pension plan since withholding is not required in this situation. Therefore, do not provide the recipient Form W-4P for eligible rollover distributions. You are not required to withhold 20 percent of an eligible rollover distribution that, when aggregated with other eligible rollover distributions made to one person during the year, is less than $200. (Reg. § 31.3405(c)-2)

.15 Withholding: Allowances

Items That May Be Taken into Account for Withholding Allowances

According to Reg. § 31.3402(m)-1(b):

- The estimated trade and business deductions of employees.
- The estimated deduction for payments to pension, profit-sharing.
- The estimated net losses from schedules C, D, E, and F of Form 1040 and from the last line of Part II of Form 4797.
- The estimated deduction for alimony, etc., payments.
- The estimated tax credit.
  - For the credit for tax withheld on wages relating to wage withholding.
  - That the employee may claim the credit for earned income only to the extent the employee has not filed for advance payments of the credit on Form W-5.
- Estimated itemized deductions.
- The estimated deduction for net operating loss carryovers.
- The estimated deductions for certain retirement savings but only to the extent that the amount of such deduction is not excluded from the definition of wages.
- The estimated deduction for moving expenses but only to the extent that the amount of such deduction is not excluded from the definition of wages.
- The estimated deduction for penalties forfeited because of premature withdrawal of funds from time saving accounts or deposits.

¶907.15

Employees Incurring No Income Tax Liability

An employer shall not deduct and withhold any tax if there is in effect, with respect to the payment, a withholding exemption certificate furnished to the employer by the employee which contains statements that:

- The employee incurred no liability for income tax for his preceding taxable year; and
- The employee anticipated that he will incur no liability for income tax for his current taxable year. (Reg. § 31.3402(n)-1)

Only One Certificate to Be in Effect

An employee who is entitled to one or more withholding allowances and who has, at the same time, two or more employers, may claim such withholding allowances or allowances with only one of his employers. (Regs. § 31.3402(m)-1(f)(2))

.17 Withholding Benefits

Fringe Benefits Included in Gross Income

Unless the law specifically states otherwise, fringe benefits must be included in an employee's gross income. The benefits are subject to income and employment taxes. Fringe benefits include cars provided, flights on aircraft provided, free or discounted commercial flights, vacations, discounts on property or services, memberships in country clubs or other social clubs, and tickets to entertainment or sporting events. In general, the amount that must be included is the amount by which the fair market value of the benefits is more than the sum of what the employee paid for it plus any amount the law excludes. (Circular E)

When Are Fringe Benefits Treated as Paid

Certain noncash fringe benefits may be treated as paid by the pay period, or by the quarter, or on any other basis as long as the benefits are treated as paid at least as often as once a year. The business does not have to make a formal choice of payment dates or notify the IRS of the dates chosen. The business does not have to make this choice for all employees. It may change methods as often as it likes, as long as the business treats all benefits provided in a calendar year as paid by December 31 of the calendar year. The business may treat a single fringe benefit as paid on one or more dates in the same calendar year, even if the employee gets the entire benefit at one time. However one may choose the payment dates, the business must report the taxes on the employee's return in the same tax period in which the employer treated them as paid. This election does not apply to a fringe benefit where real property or investment personal property is transferred. (Circular E)

Withholding on Fringe Benefits at a Flat 25-Percent Rate

If the business withholds less than the required amount of taxes from an employee in a calendar year but reports the proper amount, it should ask the employee for the social security or railroad retirement and income taxes it paid on his or her behalf. The business must recover income taxes before April 1of the next year. The business may add the value of fringe benefits to regular wages for a payroll period and figure wages for a payroll period and figure withholding taxes on the total, or it may withhold federal income tax on the value of the fringe benefits at the flat 25-percent supplemental wage rate. (Circular E)

¶907.17

Election Not to Withhold Income Tax on Personal Use of a Vehicle

The business may choose not to withhold income tax on the value of an employee's personal use of a vehicle provided. It must, however, withhold social security on the use of the vehicle. The business does not have to make the choice for all employees. If it makes the choice, it must do it in such a way that all of the affected employees will be aware of it. For example, the business can do this by including the notice with the employee's paycheck, or by displaying the notice. The business may change methods at any time by notifying affected employees in a similar way. It must give notice by the later of January 31 of the year to which the business wants a different method to apply, or within 30 days after first providing a vehicle to the employee. (IRS Publication 15-A)

Depositing Taxes on Fringe Benefits

Once the business chooses payment dates for fringe benefits, it must deposit taxes in the same tax period in which it determined to treat the fringe benefit as paid. To avoid a penalty, deposit the taxes following the general deposit rules for that tax period. The business may reasonably estimate the value of the fringe benefits provided on the date(s) chosen, for purposes of making deposits on time.

When to Report Fringe Benefits

In general, the business must figure the value of fringe benefits no later than January 31 of the next year. If the business provides a vehicle, it may either figure the actual value of the benefit for the whole calendar year or consider the employee's use of the vehicle during the year to be entirely personal and include 100 percent in the employee's income.

Special Accounting Rule for Fringe Benefits Provided During November and December

The business may choose to treat the value of noncash fringe benefits provided during November and December, or any shorter period, as paid in the next year. However, this applies only to those benefits actually provided during November and December, not to those merely treated as paid during those months. If the business does this, it must notify each affected employee between the time of the employee's last paycheck of the calendar year and at or near the time it provides a Form W-2. If the business uses the special accounting rule, the employee must also use it for all purposes (e.g., for deductions related to the fringe benefit) and for the same period. The business cannot use this rule for a fringe benefit where it transfers real property or investment personal property to the employee. (IRS Publication 535)

.19 Withholding—Allowances

Allowances Claimed

The number of exemptions to which an employee is entitled on any day depends upon his status:

- As married or single.
- As to old age.
- As to blindness.
- Upon the number of his dependents.
- Upon the number of allowances claimed by his spouse (if he is married).
- Upon the number of withholding allowances to which he is entitled under Code Sec. 3402(m). (Reg.§ 31.3402(f)(1)-1(a))

Withholding Allowances to Which an Employee Is Entitled in Respect of Himself

- One withholding allowance for himself.
- An additional withholding allowance for himself if he will have attained the age of 65 before the close of his taxable year.
- If the employee is blind, he may claim an additional withholding allowance for blindness.
  - Individual shall be considered blind only if his central visual acuity does not exceed 20/200 in the better eye with correcting lenses.

Withholding Allowances to Which an Employee Is Entitled in Respect of His Spouse

A married employee, whose spouse is an employee receiving wages, is entitled to claim any withholding allowance to which his spouse is entitled, unless the spouse has in effect a withholding allowance certificate claiming such withholding allowance. A married employee, whose spouse is not an employee receiving wages, is entitled to claim any withholding allowance to which his spouse would be entitled. (Reg. § 31.3402(f)(1)-1(c))

Withholding Allowances to Which an Employee Is Entitled in Respect of Dependents

An employee shall be entitled on any day to a withholding allowance for each individual who may reasonably be expected to be his dependent for his taxable year beginning in, or with, the calendar year in which such day falls. (Reg. § 31.3402(f)(1)-1(d))

For withholding allowance for an individual as a dependent, such individual must:

- Have less than $3,400 of gross income for the year 2007.
  - Gross income test does not apply if dependent is child of taxpayer under 19.
  - Gross income test does not apply if dependent is child of taxpayer, full time student and under 24.
- Receive over half support from taxpayer.
  - Some exceptions relate to multiple support agreements and children of divorced parents.
- Must be one of the following to taxpayer.
  - Son/daughter, grandchild, stepchild, adopted child.
  - Brother/sister or brother/sister by half blood.
  - Stepbrother/stepsister.
  - Mother/father or ancestor of either.
  - Stepmother/stepfather.
  - Son/daughter of taxpayer's brother or sister.
  - Brother/sister of taxpayer's mother or father.
  - Son-in-law, daughter-in-law, father-in-law, mother-in-law, brother-in-law, sister-in-law (but not widow of taxpayer's deceased wife's brother).
  - Non-spouse who lived with taxpayer as member of household entire year as long as relationship is not in violation of local law.
- Must not have filed joint return with dependent's spouse.

¶907.19

- Must be US citizen, national, US resident, Canadian resident or Mexican resident.

  — Dependent can also be alien child living with US citizen or national as member of household for entire year.

If Dependent Dies

A withholding allowance for a dependent who dies continues for the portion of the calendar year which occurs after the dependent's death. (Reg. § 31.3402(f)(1)-1(d)(1))

Child Alive Only Momentarily

Parents may claim a dependency exemption for a child born alive during the taxable year, even though the child lived only momentarily, providing applicable state and local law recognizes the child's life and there is official documentation of its life. (Reg. § 1.152-1.) (Code Sec. 152, '86 Code) (Rev. Rul. 73-156, 1973-1 C.B. 58.)

Additional Withholding Allowance to Which an Employee Is Entitled in Respect of the Standard Deduction

An employee is entitled to one additional withholding allowance unless:

- The employee is married and the employee's spouse is an employee receiving wages subject to withholding, or

- The employee has withholding allowance certificates in effect with respect to more than one employer. These restrictions do not apply if the combined wages of the employee and the spouse (if any) from other than one employer is less than the amount specified in the instructions to Form W-4 (Employee's Withholding Allowance Certificate). (Reg. § 31.3402 (f)(1)-1(e))

Determination of Marital Status by Employer

An employer, in computing the tax to be deducted and withheld from an employee's wages, shall apply the method for the pertinent payroll period which relates to employees who are single persons, unless there is in effect with respect to such payment of wages a withholding allowance certificate furnished to the employer by the employee indicating that the employee is married, in which case the employer shall apply the applicable table relating to employees who are married persons. (Reg. § 31.3402(f)(2)-1)

Disclosure of Marital Status by Employee

An employee shall be entitled to furnish the employer with a withholding allowance certificate indicating he is married only if, on the day of such furnishing, he is married. Thus, an employee who is contemplating marriage may not, prior to the actual marriage, furnish the employer with a withholding allowance certificate indicating that he is a married person.

Death of Spouse

If an employee who has in effect a withholding allowance certificate indicating that he is a married person and his spouse died during the taxable year which precedes by two years the current taxable year, the employee must, on or before December 1 of the current taxable year, furnish the employer with a new withholding allowance certificate indicating that he is a single person.

Married to Single

The employee must within 10 days after the change occurs furnish the employer with a new withholding allowance certificate indicating that the employee is a single person.

Single to Married

The employee must furnish the employer with a new withholding allowance certificate indicating that the employee is a married person.

Determination of Marital Status

An employee shall on any day be considered as a married person if:

- His spouse died within the portion of his taxable year which precedes such day, or
- His spouse died during one of the two taxable years immediately preceding the current taxable year and, on the basis of facts existing at the beginning of such day, he reasonably expects, at the close of the current taxable year, to be a surviving spouse.

An employee shall on any day be considered as a single person if:

- He is legally separated from his spouse under a decree of divorce or separate maintenance, or
- Either he or his spouse is, of on any preceding day within the same calendar year was, a nonresident alien.

.21 Withholding Penalties

There are penalties for payroll tax amounts not properly or timely deposited.

The penalty rates are:

2% — Deposits made 1 to 5 days late.

5% — Deposits made 6 to 15 days late.

10% — Deposits made 16 or more days late. Also applies to amounts paid to the IRS within 10 days of the date of the first notice the IRS sent you asking for the tax due.

10% — Deposits made at unauthorized financial institutions or directly to the IRS.

10% — Amounts subject to electronic deposit requirements but not deposited using the Electronic Federal Tax Payment System (EFTPS).

15% — Amounts still unpaid more than 10 days after the date of the first notice the IRS sent you asking for the tax due or the day on which you receive notice and demand for immediate payment, whichever is earlier.

Order in Which Deposits Are Applied

Deposits generally are applied to the most recent tax liabilities within the quarter (Rev. Proc. 2001-58, 2001-50 IRB 579). Before 2002, deposits were applied first to the oldest tax liability. The IRS may grant relief from any penalties imposed because multiple failure to deposit penalties have been caused by a single payment. (Rev. Proc 99-10, 1999-2 IRB 11(1/15/99))

> **Example:** Employer A is required to make a deposit of $1,000 on June 15 and $1,500 on July 15. A does not make the deposit on June 15. On July 15, A deposits $2,000. Under the new rule, which applies deposits to the most recent tax liabilities,

$1,500 of the deposit is applied to the July 15 deposit and the remaining $500 is applied to the June deposit. Accordingly, $500 of the June 15 liability remains undeposited and is subject to penalties.

.23 Record Keeping

An employer must kept all records on employment taxes (income tax withholding, social security taxes, federal unemployment tax and advance earned income credit (EIC) payments) for a minimum of four years after the due date of the return or after the tax is paid, whichever is later. (Circular E)

Records for Income Tax Withholding

Records that must be kept for income tax withholding are:

- Employee's name, address and social security number.
- The amount subject to withholding for each wage payment.
- The amount of withholding tax collected on each payment and the date it was collected.
- The total amount and date of each wage payment and the period of time the payment covers.
- Copies of any statements furnished by employees relating to nonresident alien status, residence in Puerto Rico or the Virgin Islands or residence or physical presence in a foreign country.
- The reason why the taxable amount is less than the total payment, if they differ.
- Information about the amount of each payment for wage continuation plans.
- The fair market value and date of each payment of noncash compensation made to a retail commission salesperson, if no income tax was withheld.
- Requests by employees to have the tax withheld figured on the basis of their individual cumulative wages.
- The dates in each calendar quarter on which the employee worked.
- Any agreement between the employer and the employee on Form W-4 for the voluntary withholding of additional amounts of tax.
- Copies of statements furnished by employees reporting tips received in their work.
- The withholding allowance certificates (Form W-4) filed by each employee. (Circular E)

Employer Rules for Record keeping of SS, FUTA, EIC

Records for Social Security Taxes

- The amount of each wage payment subject to social security tax.
- The amount of social security tax collected for each payment and the date collected.
- The reason why the total wage payment is more than the taxable amount, if it differs.

Federal Unemployment Tax

- The total amount paid to employees during the calendar year.

- The amount of compensation subject to the unemployment tax.
- Why it differs from the total compensation, if it differs.
- The amount paid into the state unemployment fund.
- Any other information required to be shown on the unemployment tax return, including the amount of the tax.

Records for Earned Income Credit (EIC)

- Copies of employees' W-5 Forms.
- Amounts and dates of all wage payments and advance EIC payments. (Circular E)

Personnel Records

As described in the preceding sections, wage and employment laws specify that certain employment records must be maintained. Many organizations maintain employment information in a central location often referred to as a personnel record.

- Keep personnel records confidential.
- Keep personnel records locked when unattended.
- Designate a specific individual(s) with responsibility to maintain personnel records.
- Maintain one file on employment information and a separate file on health or medical information.
- Limit personnel records to job-related information such as pay, contact information, employment actions, job assignments, attendance, performance ratings, or disciplinary documents.
- Limit access to personnel information to supervisors or managers with a job-related need to know.
- Some states require the employer to permit an employee to view the contents of his/her personnel file upon proper request.

Protecting Personnel Records

When an organization hires one or more employees, there typically is a need to create and maintain some records related to the individual's pay, hours, benefits, or other terms of employment. In fact, certain income tax regulations and employment laws require that the employer maintain specified employment records.

Some of the records that must be maintained under federal law include income tax exemptions, wages, hours worked, workplace accidents, employment eligibility, as well as employee name and address. In addition, state or local law may define other requirements for maintaining certain employment records.

An employer that maintains accurate personnel records is better able to demonstrate compliance with the law. Employment records also serve to document employment decisions. As an organization grows larger, there is a greater need for accurate personnel records to document the various personnel decisions made by managers or supervisors.

¶907.23

Information That Should Be Kept in a Personnel File

The employer should be sure to create and maintain the minimum files required by law. To protect the confidentiality of personnel records, a management policy guideline is recommended to clarify what records should be maintained.

Human resources specialists recommend that the employer limit the collection of personnel records to strictly job related information that is used for specific business purposes. The employer should avoid collecting miscellaneous or non-job related information on an employee and tossing it into the personnel file. In particular, do not collect or maintain information about an employee that may be viewed as discriminatory in nature. See ¶ 909 Discrimination Law.

In order to comply with the Americans with Disabilities Act and similar state anti-bias laws relating to handicap discrimination, the employer should take care to separate medical information about an employee. Medical records should be maintained in separate medical files that are not a part of the employee's personnel file.

.24 State Laws on Wage Payments

Wage payments are subject to various state laws. Specific laws and their applicability varies from state to state. State laws on wage payments may deal with one or more of the following topics:

- Minimum wage.
- Overtime compensation.
- Equal pay.
- Timeliness of way payment.
- Wage payments at separation of employment.
- Record keeping requirements.

.25 Determining How Much to Pay Employees

Setting a fair and competitive wage for employees is important. Low wages may reduce the salary expense, but such a practice may contribute to unnecessary turnover, difficulty in hiring, or hiring of poorly qualified workers. On the other hand, excessively high wages may create cost pressures that affect competitive pricing of the organization's products or services.

Salary surveys are one source of information about competitive pay levels for various jobs. Salary surveys are available for a specified cost through selected local employer associations, industry and trade associations, and from firms that specialize in employee compensation.

A source on salary information without charge is the U.S. Department of Labor Bureau of labor Statistics (*www.BLS.gov*).

Listed below are some tips for working with salary survey data:

- Recognize that there typically are pay differentials based on geographic area and industry.
- Select a salary survey(s) that best represent the geographical area and/or industry of your organization.

- Avoid making pay comparisons solely on job titles. Review any job description data contained in the survey in order to obtain the best comparison to comparable jobs in your organization.
- Salary data may be reported as a mean (average of rates) or as a median (a middle value of all the rates reported).
- Consider salary survey data as a general guide in the wage determination process.
- Determine your organization's pay philosophy. Identify whether you want to set pay levels that lead the area, trail the area, or generally match pay levels in the area.

Formulating a Job Offer

The formal communication made by an employer to a job candidate in which the employer offers a job to the individual is referred to as a job offer. A job offer can be a verbal offer, such as an offer of employment made in person or over the telephone. A job offer can also be a written offer, communicated in a letter or by electronic means such as e-mail.

A job offer normally includes elements that specify the job, the pay, and a starting date and time. The offer may also specify job location and work schedule. The job offer may also include other details or information that was discussed or agreed to in the course of the employment interview. A job offer normally includes elements that specify the job, the pay, and a starting date and time. The offer may also specify job location and work schedule. Human resources experts recommend that the job offer identify compensation on an hourly, weekly, or monthly basis rather than an annual basis.

An example of a job offer would be, "I would like to offer you the job of sales representative, at a salary of $750.00 per week, to begin employment on March 1, 2007, working at our Andersonville office. You will be working from 8:30 AM until 5:00 PM Monday through Friday."

.26 Performance Appraisal

Use of a performance appraisal system has traditionally been recognized as an effective management tool for promoting communication between employees and management. In addition, many organizations believe in a philosophy of paying for performance. A performance appraisal system provides an objective basis to achieve this goal.

A performance appraisal system is useful for evaluating employee performance, correcting performance problems, coaching for improved performance, justifying pay adjustments, and documenting personnel actions.

Performance appraisals are typically prepared by the supervisor or manager and then discussed with the employee. Some organizations also use peer ratings where fellow employees or other managers provide performance feedback to the individual. Another variation is to have the employee prepare a self-evaluation, and then the results of this evaluation are discussed with the manager providing his/her assessment of the employee's performance.

The appraisal may be conducted at specified time intervals such as quarterly, semi-annually, or annually. Some organizations schedule pay and performance discussions together, while others choose to conduct these discussions separately.

Here are some tips for effective performance appraisals:

- Develop a written policy and procedure to guide the appraisal process.

- Conduct appraisals on time.

- Take time to prepare for the appraisal discussion; record objective and documented facts or work results.

- Allow adequate time for the discussion and conduct it at a time and place that allows for a private discussion without interruptions.

- Praise the individual for results achieved and note any deficiencies that should be improved.

- Permit the employee to make a comment about performance ratings on the appraisal form.

- It is recommended that the employee be asked to sign the appraisal form to acknowledge participating in the appraisal process.

.27 Setting Performance Objectives

In order to have a fair measure of an employee's performance, there must be a standard or basis for comparison. This is accomplished by defining a performance standard or goal for the job. The definition of a performance standard creates an objective measure for identifying good performance that meets or exceeds the standard and for noting performance that fails to meet the defined standard. Performance objectives can be defined for any significant activity related to the job department or organization.

The performance appraisal process, because it is administered by people, is affected by a degree of subjectivity. However, this subjectivity can be minimized by creating job related performance objectives, thus providing the following benefits:

- Improved objectivity of performance ratings,

- Greater consistence of performance ratings,

- Defined performance "targets" which help to improve productivity, accuracy, attendance, etc.

- A clearly defined basis for comparing and rating the employee's performance,

- Clearer employee understanding of job accountabilities, and

- Accurate documentation of performance results.

Performance objectives should be definable, measurable, and achievable. It is recommended that the supervisor obtain employee input and a consensus on performance objectives. To be measurable, the performance goal must be quantified in some way. In addition, the goal must specify a measurement period or timeline for achievement of the objective. Job activity or performance records must be used or created to track work results for comparison against the objective.

WITHHOLDING TAX RULES

15. Special Rules for Various Types of Services and Payments
(Section references are to the Internal Revenue Code unless otherwise noted.)

Special Classes of Employment and Special Types of Payments	Treatment Under Employment Taxes		
	Income Tax Withholding	Social Security and Medicare	Federal Unemployment
Aliens, nonresident.	See pages 14 and 16 and Publication 515, Withholding of Tax on Nonresident Aliens and Foreign Entities, and Publication 519, U.S. Tax Guide for Aliens.		
Aliens, resident: 1. Service performed in the U.S.	Same as U.S. citizen.	Same as U.S. citizen. (Exempt if any part of service as crew member of foreign vessel or aircraft is performed outside U.S.)	Same as U.S. citizen.
2. Service performed outside U.S.	Withhold	Taxable if (1) working for an American employer or (2) an American employer by agreement covers U.S. citizens and residents employed by its foreign affiliates.	Exempt unless on or in connection with an American vessel or aircraft and either performed under contract made in U.S., or alien is employed on such vessel or aircraft when it touches U.S. port.
Cafeteria plan benefits under section 125.	If employee chooses cash, subject to all employment taxes. If employee chooses another benefit, the treatment is the same as if the benefit was provided outside the plan. See Publication 15-B for more information.		
Deceased worker: 1. Wages paid to beneficiary or estate in same calendar year as worker's death. See Instructions for Forms W-2 and W-3 for details.	Exempt	Taxable	Taxable
2. Wages paid to beneficiary or estate after calendar year of worker's death.	Exempt	Exempt	Exempt
Dependent care assistance programs (limited to $5,000; $2,500 if married filing separately).	Exempt to the extent that it is reasonable to believe that amounts are excludable from gross income under section 129.		
Disabled worker's wages paid after year in which worker became entitled to disability insurance benefits under the Social Security Act.	Withhold	Exempt, if worker did not perform any service for employer during period for which payment is made.	Taxable
Employee business expense reimbursement: 1. Accountable plan. a. Amounts not exceeding specified government rate for per diem or standard mileage.	Exempt	Exempt	Exempt
b. Amounts in excess of specified government rate for per diem or standard mileage.	Withhold	Taxable	Taxable
2. Nonaccountable plan. See page 10 for details.	Withhold	Taxable	Taxable
Family employees: 1. Child employed by parent (or partnership in which each partner is a parent of the child).	Withhold	Exempt until age 18; age 21 for domestic service.	Exempt until age 21
2. Parent employed by child.	Withhold	Taxable if in course of the son's or daughter's business. For domestic services, see section 3.	Exempt
3. Spouse employed by spouse. See section 3 for more information.	Withhold	Taxable if in course of spouse's business.	Exempt
Fishing and related activities.	See Publication 334, Tax Guide for Small Business.		
Foreign governments and international organizations.	Exempt	Exempt	Exempt

¶907.27

Special Classes of Employment and Special Types of Payments	Treatment Under Employment Taxes		
	Income Tax Withholding	Social Security and Medicare	Federal Unemployment
Foreign service by U.S. citizens: 1. As U.S. government employee.	Withhold	Same as within U.S.	Exempt
2. For foreign affiliates of American employers and other private employers.	Exempt if at time of payment (1) it is reasonable to believe employee is entitled to exclusion from income under section 911 or (2) the employer is required by law of the foreign country to withhold income tax on such payment.	Exempt unless (1) an American employer by agreement covers U.S. citizens employed by its foreign affiliates or (2) U.S. citizen works for American employer.	Exempt unless (1) on American vessel or aircraft and work is performed under contract made in U.S. or worker is employed on vessel when it touches U.S. port or (2) U.S. citizen works for American employer (except in a contiguous country with which the U.S. has an agreement for unemployment compensation) or in the U.S. Virgin Islands.
Fringe benefits	Taxable on excess of fair market value of the benefit over the sum of an amount paid for it by the employee and any amount excludable by law. However, special valuation rules may apply. Benefits provided under cafeteria plans may qualify for exclusion from wages for social security, Medicare, and FUTA taxes. See Publication 15-B for details.		
Government employment: State/local governments and political subdivisions, employees of: 1. Salaries and wages (Includes payments to most elected and appointed officials. See Chapter 3 of Publication 963, Federal-State Reference Guide.)	Withhold	Generally, taxable for (1) services performed by employees who are either (a) covered under a section 218 agreement or (b) not covered under a section 218 agreement and not a member of a public retirement system (mandatory social security and Medicare coverage), and (2) (for Medicare tax only) for services performed by employees hired or rehired after 3/31/86 who are not covered under a section 218 agreement or the mandatory social security provisions, unless specifically excluded by law. See Publication 963.	Exempt
2. Election workers. Election individuals are workers who are employed to perform services for state or local governments at election booths in connection with national, state, or local elections. **Note:** File Form W-2 for payments of $600 or more even if no social security or Medicare taxes were withheld.	Exempt	Taxable if paid $1,300 or more in 2007 (lesser amount if specified by a section 218 social security agreement). See Rev. Proc. 2000-6.	Exempt
3. Emergency workers. Emergency workers who were hired on a temporary basis in response to a specific unforeseen emergency and are not intended to become permanent employees.	Withhold	Exempt if serving on a temporary basis in case of fire, storm, snow, earthquake, flood, or similar emergency.	Exempt
U.S. federal government employees	Withhold	Taxable for Medicare. Taxable for social security unless hired before 1984. See IRC 3121(b)(5).	Exempt

¶907.27

Special Classes of Employment and Special Types of Payments	Treatment Under Employment Taxes		
	Income Tax Withholding	Social Security and Medicare	Federal Unemployment
Homeworkers (industrial, cottage industry):			
1. Common law employees.	Withhold	Taxable	Taxable
2. Statutory employees. See page 7 for details.	Exempt	Taxable if paid $100 or more in cash in a year.	Exempt
Hospital employees:			
1. Interns	Withhold	Taxable	Exempt
2. Patients	Withhold	Taxable (Exempt for state or local government hospitals.)	Exempt
Household employees:			
1. Domestic service in private homes. Farmers, see Publication 51 (Circular A).	Exempt (withhold if both employer and employee agree).	Taxable if paid $1,500 or more in cash in 2007. Exempt if performed by an individual under age 18 during any portion of the calendar year and is not the principal occupation of the employee.	Taxable if employer paid total cash wages of $1,000 or more in any quarter in the current or preceding calendar year.
2. Domestic service in college clubs, fraternities, and sororities.	Exempt (withhold if both employer and employee agree).	Exempt if paid to regular student; also exempt if employee is paid less than $100 in a year by an income-tax-exempt employer.	Taxable if employer paid total cash wages of $1,000 or more in any quarter in the current or preceding calendar year.
Insurance for employees:			
1. Accident and health insurance premiums under a plan or system for employees and their dependents generally or for a class or classes of employees and their dependents.	Exempt (except 2% shareholder-employees of S corporations).	Exempt	Exempt
2. Group-term life insurance costs. See Publication 15-B for details.	Exempt	Exempt, except for the cost of group-term life insurance that is includible in the employee's gross income. (Special rules apply for former employees.)	Exempt
Insurance agents or solicitors:			
1. Full-time life insurance salesperson.	Withhold only if employee under common law. See page 7.	Taxable	Taxable if (1) employee under common law and (2) not paid solely by commissions.
2. Other salesperson of life, casualty, etc., insurance.	Withhold only if employee under common law.	Taxable only if employee under common law.	Taxable if (1) employee under common law and (2) not paid solely by commissions.
Interest on loans with below-market interest rates (foregone interest and deemed original issue discount).	See Publication 15-A.		
Leave-sharing plans: Amounts paid to an employee under a leave-sharing plan.	Withhold	Taxable	Taxable
Newspaper carriers and vendors: Newspaper carriers under age 18; newspaper and magazine vendors buying at fixed prices and retaining receipts from sales to customers. See Publication 15-A for information on statutory nonemployee status.	Exempt (withhold if both employer and employee voluntarily agree).	Exempt	Exempt
Noncash payments:			
1. For household work, agricultural labor, and service not in the course of the employer's trade or business.	Exempt (withhold if both employer and employee voluntarily agree).	Exempt	Exempt
2. To certain retail commission salespersons ordinarily paid solely on a cash commission basis.	Optional with employer.	Taxable	Taxable
Nonprofit organizations.	See Publication 15-A.		
Officers or shareholders of an S Corporation. Distributions and other payments by an S corporation to a corporate officer or shareholder must be treated as wages to the extent the amounts are reasonable compensation for services to the corporation by an employee. (See the Instructions for Form 1120S.)	Withhold	Taxable	Taxable

¶907.27

Special Classes of Employment and Special Types of Payments	Treatment Under Employment Taxes		
	Income Tax Withholding	Social Security and Medicare	Federal Unemployment
Partners: Payments to general or limited partners of a partnership. (See Publication 541, Partnerships, for partner reporting rules.)	Exempt	Exempt	Exempt
Railroads: Payments subject to the Railroad Retirement Act.	Withhold	Exempt	Exempt
Religious exemptions.	See Publication 15-A and Pub. 517, Social Security and Other Information for Members of the Clergy and Religious Workers.		
Retirement and pension plans: 1. Employer contributions to a qualified plan.	Exempt	Exempt	Exempt
2. Elective employee contributions and deferrals to a plan containing a qualified cash or deferred compensation arrangement (for example, 401(k)).	Generally exempt, but see section 402(g) for limitation.	Taxable	Taxable
3. Employer contributions to individual retirement accounts under simplified employee pension plan (SEP).	Generally exempt, but see section 402(g) for salary reduction SEP limitation.	Exempt, except for amounts contributed under a salary reduction SEP agreement.	
4. Employer contributions to section 403(b) annuities.	Generally exempt, but see section 402(g) for limitation.	Taxable if paid through a salary reduction agreement (written or otherwise).	
5. Employee salary reduction contributions to a SIMPLE retirement account.	Exempt	Taxable	Taxable
6. Distributions from qualified retirement and pension plans and section 403(b) annuities. See Publication 15-A for information on pensions, annuities, and employer contributions to nonqualified deferred compensation arrangements.	Withhold, but recipient may elect exemption on Form W-4P in certain cases; mandatory 20% withholding applies to an eligible rollover distribution that is not a direct rollover; exempt for direct rollover. See Publication 15-A.	Exempt	Exempt
Salespersons: 1. Common law employees.	Withhold	Taxable	Taxable
2. Statutory employees.	Exempt	Taxable	Taxable, except for full-time life insurance sales agents.
3. Statutory nonemployees (qualified real estate agents, direct sellers, and certain companion sitters). See Pub. 15-A for details.	Exempt	Exempt	Exempt
Scholarships and fellowship grants: (includible in income under section 117(c)).	Withhold	Taxability depends on the nature of the employment and the status of the organization. See Students on next page.	
Severance or dismissal pay.	Withhold	Taxable	Taxable
Service not in the course of the employer's trade or business, other than on a farm operated for profit or for household employment in private homes.	Withhold only if employee earns $50 or more in cash in a quarter and works on 24 or more different days in that quarter or in the preceding quarter.	Taxable if employee receives $100 or more in cash in a calendar year.	Taxable only if employee earns $50 or more in cash in a quarter and works on 24 or more different days in that quarter or in the preceding quarter.
Sick pay. (See Publication 15-A for more information.)	Withhold	Exempt after end of 6 calendar months after the calendar month employee last worked for employer.	

¶907.27

Special Classes of Employment and Special Types of Payments	Treatment Under Employment Taxes		
	Income Tax Withholding	Social Security and Medicare	Federal Unemployment
Students, scholars, trainees, teachers, etc.: 1. Student enrolled and regularly attending classes, performing services for:			
a. Private school, college, or university.	Withhold	Exempt	Exempt
b. Auxillary nonprofit organization operated for and controlled by school, college, or university.	Withhold	Exempt unless services are covered by a section 218 (Social Security Act) agreement	Exempt
c. Public school, college, or university.	Withhold	Exempt unless services are covered by a section 218 (Social Security Act) agreement	Exempt
2. Full-time student performing service for academic credit, combining instruction with work experience as an integral part of the program.	Withhold	Taxable	Exempt unless program was established for or on behalf of an employer or group of employers.
3. Student nurse performing part-time services for nominal earnings at hospital as incidental part of training.	Withhold	Exempt	Exempt
4. Student employed by organized camps.	Withhold	Taxable	Exempt
5. Student, scholar, trainee, teacher, etc., as nonimmigrant alien under section 101(a)(15)(F), (J), (M), or (Q) of Immigration and Nationality Act (that is, aliens holding F-1, J-1, M-1, or Q-1 visas).	Withhold unless excepted by regulations.	Exempt if service is performed for purpose specified in section 101(a)(15)(F), (J), (M), or (Q) of Immigration and Nationality Act. However, these taxes may apply if the employee becomes a resident alien. See the special residency tests for exempt individuals in chapter 1 of Publication 519.	
Supplemental unemployment compensation plan benefits.	Withhold	Exempt under certain conditions. See Publication 15-A.	
Tips: 1. If $20 or more in a month.	Withhold	Taxable	Taxable for all tips reported in writing to employer.
2. If less than $20 in a month. See section 6 for more information.	Exempt	Exempt	Exempt
Worker's compensation.	Exempt	Exempt	Exempt

(Published source: IRS Publication 15, Circular E, Employer's Tax Guide)

¶907.27

¶ 908 LABOR AND EMPLOYMENT LAWS

.01 Family and Medical Leave Act of 1993 (FMLA) (29 USC § 2601 et seq.; 29 CFR 825)

Who is Covered

The Family and Medical Leave Act (FMLA) provides a means for employees to balance their work and family responsibilities by taking unpaid leave for certain reasons. The Act is intended to promote the stability and economic security of families as well as the nation's interest in preserving the integrity of families.

The FMLA applies to any employer in the private sector who engages in commerce, or in any industry or activity affecting commerce, and who has 50 or more employees each working day during at least 20 calendar weeks in the current or preceding calendar year.

The law covers all public agencies (state and local governments) and local education agencies (schools, whether public or private). These employers do not need to meet the "50 employee" test. Title II of FMLA covers most federal employees, who are subject to regulations issued by the Office of Personnel Management.

To be eligible for FMLA leave, an individual must (1) be employed by a covered employer and work at a worksite within 75 miles of which that employer employs at least 50 people; (2) have worked at least 12 months (which do not have to be consecutive) for the employer; and (3) have worked at least 1,250 hours during the 12 months immediately before the date FMLA leave begins.

Basic Provisions/Requirments

The FMLA provides an entitlement of up to 12 weeks of job-protected, unpaid leave during any 12-month period for the following reasons:

- Birth and care of the employee's child, or placement for adoption or foster care of a child with the employee;
- Care of an immediate family member (spouse, child, parent) who has a serious health condition; or
- Care of the employee's own serious health condition.

If an employee was receiving group health benefits when leave began, an employer must maintain them at the same level and in the same manner during periods of FMLA leave as if the employee had continued to work. Usually, an employee may elect (or the employer may require) the use of any accrued paid leave (vacation, sick, personal, etc.) for periods of unpaid FMLA leave.

Employees may take FMLA leave in blocks of time less than the full 12 weeks on an intermittent or reduced leave basis when medically necessary. Taking intermittent leave for the placement, adoption, or foster care of a child is subject to the employer's approval. Intermittent leave taken for the birth and care of a child is also subject to the employer's approval except for pregnancy-related leave that would be leave for a serious health condition.

When the need for leave is foreseeable, an employee must give the employer at least 30 days notice, or as much notice as is practicable. When the leave is not foreseeable, the employee must provide such notice as soon as possible.

An employer may require medical certification of a serious health condition from the employee's health care provider. An employer may also require periodic reports during the period of leave of the employee's status and intent to return to work, as well as "fitness-for-duty" certification upon return to work in appropriate situations.

An employee who returns from FMLA leave is entitled to be restored to the same or an equivalent job (defined as one with equivalent pay, benefits, responsibilities, etc.) The employee is not entitled to accrue benefits during periods of unpaid FMLA leave, but the employer must return him or her to employment with the same benefits at the same levels as existed when leave began.

Employers are required to post a notice for employees outlining the basic provisions of FMLA and are subject to a $100 civil money penalty per offense for willfully failing to post such notice. Employers are prohibited from discriminating against or interfering with employees who take FMLA leave.

Employee Rights

The FMLA provides that eligible employees of covered employers have a right to take up to 12 weeks of job-protected leave in any 12-month period for qualifying events without interference or restraint from their employers. The FMLA also gives employees the right to file a complaint with the Wage and Hour Division, file a private lawsuit under the Act (or cause a complaint or lawsuit to be filed), and testify or cooperate in other ways with an investigation or lawsuit without being fired or discriminated against in any other manner.

Compliance Assistance Available

The Wage and Hour Division of the Employment Standards Administration administers FMLA. More detailed information, including copies of explanatory brochures, may be obtained by contacting the local Wage and Hour offices.

Penalties/Sanctions

Employees and other persons may file complaints with the Employment Standards Administration (usually through the nearest office of the Wage and Hour Division). The Department of Labor may file suit to ensure compliance and recover damages if a complaint cannot be resolved administratively. Employees also have private rights of action, without involvement of the Department of Labor, to correct violations and recover damages through the courts.

Relation to State, Local, and Other Federal Laws

A number of states have family leave statutes. Nothing in the FMLA supersedes a provision of state law that is more beneficial to the employee, and employers must comply with the more beneficial provision. Under some circumstances, an employee with a disability may have rights under the Americans with Disabilities Act.

(Source: Employment Law Guide, *www.dol.gov*)

.02 Worker Adjustment and Retraining Notification Act (WARN) (29 USC §2101 et seq.; 20 CFR 639)

Who is Covered

The Worker Adjustment and Retraining Notification Act (WARN) generally covers employers with 100 or more employees, not counting those who have worked less than six months in the last 12 months and those who work an average of less than 20 hours a week. Regular federal, state, and local government entities that provide public services are not covered. Employees entitled to notice under WARN include managers and supervisors as well as hourly and salaried workers.

Basic Provisions/Requirements

WARN protects workers, their families, and communities by requiring employers to provide notification 60 calendar days in advance of plant closings and mass layoffs. Advance notice gives workers and their families some transition time to adjust to the prospective loss of employment, to seek and obtain other jobs, and, if necessary, to enter skill training or retraining that will allow these workers to compete successfully in the job market. WARN also provides for notice to state dislocated worker units so that they can promptly offer dislocated worker assistance.

A covered plant closing occurs when a facility or operating unit is shut down for more than six months, or when 50 or more employees lose their jobs during any 30-day period at a single site of employment. A covered mass layoff occurs when a layoff of six months or longer affects either 500 or more workers or at least 33 percent of the employer's workforce when the layoff affects between 50 and 499 workers. The number of affected workers is the total number laid off during a 30-day (or in some cases 90-day) period.

WARN does not apply to closure of temporary facilities, or the completion of an activity when the workers were hired only for the duration of that activity. WARN also provides for less than 60 days notice when the layoffs resulted from closure of a faltering company, unforeseeable business circumstances, or a natural disaster.

Employee Rights

Workers, or their representatives, and units of local government may bring individual or class action suits. U.S. district courts enforce WARN requirements. The court may allow reasonable attorney's fees as part of any final judgment.

Penalties/Sanctions

An employer who violates the WARN provisions is liable to each employee for an amount equal to back pay and benefits for the period of the violation, up to 60 days. This may be reduced by the period of any notice that was given, and any voluntary payments that the employer made to the employee.

An employer who fails to provide the required notice to the unit of local government is subject to a civil penalty not to exceed $500 for each day of violation. The employer may avoid this penalty by satisfying the liability to each employee within three weeks after the closing or layoff.

Relation to State, Local, and Other Federal Laws

WARN does not preempt any other federal, state, or local law, or any employer/ employee agreement that requires other notification or benefit. Rather, the rights provided by WARN supplement those provided by other federal, state, or local laws.

(Source: www.dol.gov, The Employment Law Guide)

¶908.02

.03 Uniformed Services Employment and Reemployment Rights Act (USERRA) (38 USC §§ 4301 through 4333)

Who is Covered

The Uniformed Services Employment and Reemployment Rights Act (USERRA) was signed on October 13, 1994. The Act applies to persons who perform duty, voluntarily or involuntarily, in the "uniformed services," which include the Army, Navy, Marine Corps, Air Force, Coast Guard, and Public Health Service commissioned corps, as well as the reserve components of each of these services. Federal training or service in the Army National Guard and Air National Guard also gives rise to rights under USERRA. In addition, under the Public Health Security and Bioterrorism Response Act of 2002, certain disaster response work (and authorized training for such work) is considered "service in the uniformed services" as well.

Uniformed service includes active duty, active duty for training, inactive duty training (such as drills), initial active duty training, and funeral honors duty performed by National Guard and reserve members, as well as the period for which a person is absent from a position of employment for the purpose of an examination to determine fitness to perform any such duty.

USERRA covers nearly all employees, including part-time and probationary employees. USERRA applies to virtually all U.S. employers, regardless of size.

Basic Provisions/Requirements

The pre-service employer must reemploy service members returning from a period of service in the uniformed services if those service members meet five criteria:

1. The person must have held a civilian job;
2. The person must have given notice to the employer that he or she was leaving the job for service in the uniformed services, unless giving notice was precluded by military necessity or otherwise impossible or unreasonable;
3. The cumulative period of service must not have exceeded five years;
4. The person must not have been released from service under dishonorable or other punitive conditions; and
5. The person must have reported back to the civilian job in a timely manner or have submitted a timely application for reemployment.

USERRA establishes a five-year cumulative total on military service with a single employer, with certain exceptions allowed for situations such as call-ups during emergencies, reserve drills and annually scheduled active duty for training.

USERRA also allows an employee to complete an initial period of active duty that exceeds five years (e.g., enlistees in the Navy's nuclear power program are required to serve six years).

Employee Rights

Under USERRA, restoration rights are based on the duration of military service rather than the type of military duty performed (e.g., active duty for training or inactive duty), except for fitness-for-service examinations. The time limits for returning to work are as follows:

¶908.03

- Less than 31 days of service: By the beginning of the first regularly scheduled work period after the end of the calendar day of duty, plus time required to return home safely, and an eight hour rest period. If this is impossible or unreasonable, then as soon as possible.

- 31 to 180 days: The employee must apply for reemployment no later than 14 days after completion of military service. If this is impossible or unreasonable through no fault of the employee, then as soon as possible.

- 181 days or more: The employee must apply for reemployment no later than 90 days after completion of military service.

Service-connected injury or illness: Reporting or application deadlines are extended for up to two years for persons who are hospitalized or convalescing.

USERRA guarantees pension plan benefits that accrued during military service, regardless of whether the plan is a defined benefit plan or a defined contribution plan. Also, USERRA provides health benefits continuation for service members and their families during military service for up to 18 months. In addition, USERRA prohibits employment discrimination against a person on the basis of past military service, current military obligations, or an intent to serve.

Enforcement

The Veterans' Employment and Training Service (VETS) enforces USERRA. However, the law also allows an employee to enforce his or her rights by filing a court action directly, without filing a complaint with VETS.

Penalties/Sanctions

A court may order an employer to compensate a prevailing claimant for lost wages or benefits. USERRA allows for liquidated damages for "willful" violations.

Relation to State, Local, and Other Federal Laws

USERRA does not preempt state laws providing greater or additional rights, but it does preempt state laws providing lesser rights or imposing additional eligibility criteria.

(Source: www.dol.gov, The Employment Law Guide)

Posting Requirements

During 2005, the U.S. Department of Labor published a particular form of notice that must be posted regarding employee rights under USERRA. A sample of the poster is available on the Labor Department's Web site at http://www.dol.gov.

.04 Whistleblower Protections

The Occupational Safety and Health Administration (OSHA) administers the employee protection (or "whistleblower") provisions of fourteen statutes.

- Occupational Safety & Health Act (OSH Act), 29 USC § 660(c)
- Surface Transportation Assistance Act (STAA), 49 USC § 31105
- Asbestos Hazard Emergency Response Act (AHERA), 15 USC § 2651
- International Safety Container Act (ISCA), 46 USC App. § 1506
- Energy Reorganization Act of 1974 (ERA), 42 USC § 5851
- Clean Air Act (CAA), 42 USC § 7622

- Safe Drinking Water Act (SDWA), 42 USC § 300j-9(i)
- Federal Water Pollution Control Act (FWPCA), 33 USC § 1367
- Toxic Substances Control Act (TSCA), 15 USC § 2622
- Solid Waste Disposal Act (SWDA), 42 USC § 6971
- Comprehensive Environmental Response, Compensation and Liability Act (CER-CLA), 42 USC § 9610
- Wendell H. Ford Aviation Investment and Reform Act (AIR21), 49 USC § 42121
- Sarbanes-Oxley Act (SOA), 18 USC § 1514A
- Pipeline Safety Improvement Act (PSIA), 49 USC § 60129

Who is Covered

Under the OSH Act, employees who believe that their employer has discriminated or retaliated against them for raising or reporting safety or health concerns may file a complaint with OSHA. Under the STAA, employees in the trucking industry may file complaints with OSHA if they believe that their employer has discriminated against them for reporting safety concerns or for refusing to drive under dangerous circumstances or in violation of safety rules.

Similarly, under the other statutes, employees also may file complaints with OSHA if they believe that their employer has discriminated against them for reporting protected safety concerns involving the airline or pipeline industries, for reporting protected environmental concerns including asbestos in schools, or for reporting potential securities fraud.

The Department of Labor also enforces the anti-retaliation provisions of several other statutes that are not administered by OSHA. Information concerning many of these additional anti-retaliation statutes is available in other sections of the Guide describing the statutes enforced by different Department agencies, such as the Wage and Hour Division, the Employee Benefits Security Administration, and the Mine Safety and Health Administration.

Basic Provisions/Requirements

Generally, the employee protection provisions listed above prohibit an "employer" or any "person" (the definition of which may vary from statute to statute) from discharging or otherwise discriminating against any employee with respect to the employee's compensation, terms, conditions, or privileges of employment because the employee engaged in specified "protected" activities.

The protected activities typically include: (1) initiating a proceeding under, or for the enforcement of, any of these statutes, or causing such a proceeding to be initiated; (2) testifying in any such proceeding; (3) assisting or participating in any such proceeding or in any other action to carry out the purposes of these statutes; or (4) complaining about a violation.

The ERA, the AIR21, the SOA, and the PSIA specifically cover an employee's internal complaints to his or her employer, and it is the Secretary's position, as set forth in regulations, that employees who express safety or quality assurance concerns internally to their employers are protected under the other whistleblower statutes. With the exception of the Fifth Circuit, the courts of appeals that have considered whether internal complaints are protected have agreed with the Secretary.

Employee Rights

An employee who believes that he or she has been discriminated against in violation of any of the statutes listed above may file a complaint with OSHA. Complaints must be filed within 30 days after the occurrence of the alleged violation under the OSH Act, the CAA, the CERCLA, the SWDA, the FWPCA, the SDWA, and the TSCA; within 60 days under the ISCA; within 90 days under the AIR21, the SOA, and the AHERA; and within 180 days under the STAA, the ERA, and the PSIA. Under the SOA, if the Secretary has not issued a final decision within 180 days of the filing of the complaint, and there is no showing that there has been delay due to the bad faith of the employee, the employee may bring an action at law or equity in district court.

Investigations/Penalties/Sanctions

Upon receipt of a timely complaint, OSHA notifies the employer and, if conciliation fails, conducts an investigation. Where OSHA finds that complaints filed under the OSH Act, the AHERA, and the ISCA have merit, they are referred to the Solicitor's Office for legal action. Complaints under these three statutes found not to have merit will be dismissed.

Where OSHA finds a violation after investigating complaints under the other statutes listed above, it will issue a determination letter requiring the employer to pay back wages, reinstate the employee, reimburse the employee for attorney's and expert witness fees, and take other steps to provide necessary relief. Complaints found not to have merit will be dismissed.

Parties who object to OSHA's determinations under the statutes listed above (except for the OSH Act, the AHERA, and the ISCA) may request a hearing before the Department of Labor's Office of Administrative Law Judges (OALJ). Judges' decisions are reviewed by the Department of Labor's Administrative Review Board, which the Secretary has designated to issue final agency decisions.

Under the STAA, if OSHA finds in favor of the employee, litigation usually is conducted by the Solicitor's Office, but sometimes by the employee. Under the other statutes, litigation generally is conducted by the private parties themselves. Employers and employees may seek judicial review of an adverse ARB decision.

Under the AIR21, the SOA, and the PSIA, employees who file complaints frivolously or in bad faith may be liable for attorney's fees up to $1,000.

Relation to State, Local, and Other Federal Laws

The Supreme Court has held that the employee protection provisions of the Energy Reorganization Act do not preempt existing state statutes and common law claims. The other statutes listed above should be consulted separately to determine whether or not their employee protection provisions are supplementary to protection provided by state laws.

(Source: www.dol.gov, The Employment Law Guide)

.05 Wage Garnishment Protections

Title III, Consumer Credit Protection Act (CCPA) (15 USC § 1671 et seq.; 29 CFR 870)

Who is Covered

Title III of the Consumer Credit Protection Act (CCPA) protects employees from discharge by their employers because their wages have been garnished for any one debt, and it limits the amount of an employee's earnings that may be garnished in any one week. Title III applies to all employers and individuals who receive earnings for personal services (including wages, salaries, commissions, bonuses, and income from a pension or retirement program, but ordinarily not including tips).

Basic Provisions/Requirements

Wage garnishment occurs when an employer withholds the earnings of an individual for the payment of a debt as the result of a court order or other equitable procedure. Title III prohibits an employer from discharging an employee because his or her earnings have been subject to garnishment for any one debt, regardless of the number of levies made or proceedings brought to collect it. Title III does not, however, protect an employee from discharge if the employee's earnings have been subject to garnishment for a second or subsequent debt.

Title III also protects employees by limiting the amount of earnings that may be garnished in any workweek or pay period to the lesser of 25 percent of disposable earnings or the amount by which disposable earnings are greater than 30 times the federal minimum hourly wage prescribed by Section 6(a)(1) of the Fair Labor Standards Act of 1938. This limit applies regardless of how many garnishment orders an employer receives. As of September 1, 1997, the federal minimum wage is $5.15 per hour.

In court orders for child support or alimony, Title III allows up to 50 percent of an employee's disposable earnings to be garnished if the employee is supporting a current spouse or child, and up to 60 percent if the employee is not doing so. An additional five percent may be garnished for support payments over 12 weeks in arrears. The restrictions noted in the preceding paragraph do not apply to such garnishments.

"Disposable earnings" is the amount of earnings left after legally required deductions (e.g., federal, state and local taxes, Social Security, unemployment insurance, and state employee retirement systems) have been made. Deductions not required by law (e.g., union dues, health and life insurance, and charitable contributions) are not subtracted from gross earnings when the amount of disposable earnings for garnishment purposes is calculated.

Title III specifies that garnishment restrictions do not apply to bankruptcy court orders and debts due for federal and state taxes. Nor do they affect voluntary wage assignments, i.e., situations where workers voluntarily agree that their employers may turn over a specified amount of their earnings to a creditor or creditors.

Employee Rights

In most cases, Title III gives wage earners the right to receive at least partial compensation for the personal services they provide despite wage garnishment. This law also prohibits an employer from discharging an employee because of garnishment of wages for any one indebtedness. The Wage and Hour Division of the Employment Standards Administration accepts complaints of alleged Title III violations.

¶908.05

Enforcement

The Wage and Hour Division administers and enforces Title III.

Penalties/Sanctions

Violations of Title III may result in reinstatement of a discharged employee, payment of back wages, and restoration of improperly garnished amounts. Where violations cannot be resolved through informal means, the Department of Labor may initiate court action to restrain violators and remedy violations. Employers who willfully violate the discharge provisions of the law may be prosecuted criminally and fined up to $1,000, or imprisoned for not more than one year, or both.

Relation to State, Local, and Other Federal Laws

If a state wage garnishment law differs from Title III, the employer must observe the law resulting in the smaller garnishment, or prohibiting the discharge of an employee because his or her earnings have been subject to garnishment for more than one debt.

(Source: www.dol.gov, The Employment Law Guide)

.06 Lie Detector Tests

Employee Polygraph Protection Act of 1988 (EPPA) (29 USC § 2001 et seq.; 29 CFR 801)

Who is Covered

The Employee Polygraph Protection Act (EPPA) applies to most private employers. The law does not cover federal, state, and local governments.

Basic Provisions/Requirements

The EPPA prohibits most private employers from using lie detector tests, either for pre-employment screening or during the course of employment.

Employers generally may not require or request any employee or job applicant to take a lie detector test or discharge, discipline, or discriminate against an employee or job applicant for refusing to take a test or for exercising other rights under the Act.

Employers may not use or inquire about the results of a lie detector test or discharge or discriminate against an employee or job applicant on the basis of the results of a test, for filing a complaint, or for participating in a proceeding under the Act.

Subject to restrictions, the Act permits polygraph (a type of lie detector) tests to be administered to certain job applicants of security service firms (armored car, alarm, and guard) and of pharmaceutical manufacturers, distributors, and dispensers.

Subject to restrictions, the Act also permits polygraph testing of certain employees of private firms who are reasonably suspected of involvement in a workplace incident (theft, embezzlement, etc.) that resulted in specific economic loss or injury to the employer.

Where polygraph examinations are allowed, they are subject to strict standards for the conduct of the test, including the pretest, testing, and post-testing phases. An examiner must be licensed and bonded or have professional liability coverage. The Act strictly limits the disclosure of information obtained during a polygraph test.

Employee Rights

The EPPA provides that employees have a right to employment opportunities without being subjected to lie detector tests, unless a specific exemption applies. The Act also provides employees the right to file a lawsuit for violations of the Act. In addition, the Wage and Hour Division accepts complaints of alleged EPPA violations.

Enforcement

The Wage and Hour Division of the Employment Standards Administration administers and enforces the EPPA.

Penalties/Sanctions

The Secretary of Labor can bring court action to restrain violators and assess civil money penalties up to $10,000 per violation. An employer who violates the law may be liable to the employee or prospective employee for legal and equitable relief, including employment, reinstatement, promotion, and payment of lost wages and benefits.

Any person against whom a civil money penalty is assessed may, within 30 days of the notice of assessment, request a hearing before an administrative law judge. If dissatisfied with the administrative law judge's decision, such person may request a review of the decision by the Secretary of Labor. Final determinations on violations are enforceable through the courts.

Relation to State, Local, and Other Federal Laws

The law does not preempt any provision of any state or local law or any collective bargaining agreement that is more restrictive with respect to lie detector tests.

(Source: www.dol.gov, The Employment Law Guide)

.07 The National Labor Relations Act (29 USC § 151 et seq.)

Introduction

The National Labor Relations Act is one of several federal laws that define the relationship between employers, their employees, and unions. Employers who operate in areas in which there is a strong union presence may encounter employment issues relating to the role of unions in the workplace. An understanding of the National Labor Relations Act can help to guide proper and lawful employment decisions. To help in understanding the provisions of the Act, the National Labor Relations Board (NLRB) provides an easy to understand guide. A portion of this guide is reproduced below.

Summary of the Act

Purpose of the Act. It is in the national interest of the United States to maintain full production in its economy. Industrial strife among employees, employers, and labor organizations interferes with full production and is contrary to our national interest. Experience has shown that labor disputes can be lessened if the parties involved recognize the legitimate rights of each in their relations with one another. To establish these rights under law, Congress enacted the National Labor Relations Act. Its purpose is to define and protect the rights of employees and employers, to encourage collective bargaining, and to eliminate certain practices on the part of labor and management that are harmful to the general welfare.

What the Act provides. The National Labor Relations Act states and defines the rights of employees to organize and to bargain collectively with their employers through representatives of their own choosing or not to do so. To ensure that employees can freely choose their own representatives for the purpose of collective bargaining, or choose not to be represented, the Act establishes a procedure by which they can exercise their choice at a secret-ballot election conducted by the National Labor Relations Board. Further, to protect the rights of employees and employers, and to prevent labor disputes that would adversely affect the rights of the public, Congress has defined certain practices of employers and unions as unfair labor practices.

How the Act is enforced. The law is administered and enforced principally by the National Labor Relations Board and the General Counsel acting through 52 regional and other field offices located in major cities in various sections of the country. The General Counsel and the staff of the Regional Offices investigate and prosecute unfair labor practice cases and conduct elections to determine employee representatives. The five-member Board decides cases involving charges of unfair labor practices and determines representation election questions that come to it from the Regional Offices.

How this material is organized. The rights of employees, including the rights to self-organization and collective bargaining that are protected by Section 7 of the Act, are presented first in this guide. The Act's provisions concerning the requirements for union-security agreements are covered in the same section, which also includes a discussion of the right to strike and the right to picket. The obligations of collective bargaining and the Act's provisions for the selection of employee representatives are treated in the next section. Unfair labor practices of employers and of labor organizations are then presented in separate sections. The final section, entitled "How the Act Is Enforced," sets forth the organization of the NLRB; its authority and limitations; its procedures and powers in representation matters, in unfair labor practice cases, and in certain special proceedings under the Act; and the Act's provisions concerning enforcement of the Board's orders.

The Rights of Employees

The Section 7 Rights. The rights of employees are set forth principally in Section 7 of the Act, which provides as follows:

Sec. 7. Employees shall have the right to self-organization, to form, join, or assist labor organizations, to bargain collectively through representatives of their own choosing, and to engage in other concerted activities for the purpose of collective bargaining or other mutual aid or protection, and shall also have the right to refrain from any or all of such activities except to the extent that such right may be affected by an agreement requiring membership in a labor organization as a condition of employment as authorized in section 8(a)(3).

Examples of Section 7 rights. Examples of the rights protected by this section are the following:

- Forming or attempting to form a union among the employees of a company.

- Joining a union whether the union is recognized by the employer or not.

- Assisting a union to organize the employees of an employer. Going out on strike to secure better working conditions.

- Refraining from activity on behalf of a union.

Union Security. The Act permits, under certain conditions, a union and an employer to make an agreement, called a union-security agreement, that requires employees to make certain payments to the union in order to retain their jobs. A union-security agreement cannot require that applicants for employment be members of the union in order to be hired, and such an agreement cannot require employees to join or maintain membership in the union in order to retain their jobs. Under a union-security agreement, individuals choosing to be dues-paying nonmembers may be required, as may employees who actually join the union, to pay full initiation fees and dues within a certain period of time (a "grace period") after the collective-bargaining contract takes effect or after a new employee is hired. However, the most that can be required of nonmembers who inform the union that they object to the use of their payments for nonrepresentational purposes is that they pay their share of the union's costs relating to representational activities (such as collective bargaining, contract administration, and grievance adjustment).

Union-security agreements. The grace period, after which the union-security agreement becomes effective, cannot be less than 30 days except in the building and construction industry. The Act allows a shorter grace period of 7 full days in the building and construction industry (Section 8(f). A union-security agreement that provides a shorter grace period than the law allows is invalid, and any employee discharged because he or she has not complied with such an agreement is entitled to reinstatement.

Requirements for union-security agreements. Under a union-security agreement, employees who have religious objections to becoming members of a union or to supporting a union financially may be exempt from paying union dues and initiation fees. These employees may, however, be required to make contributions to a nonreligious, nonlabor tax exempt organization instead of making payments to a union. Unions representing such employees may also charge them the reasonable cost of any grievances processed at the employees' request.

Prehire agreements in the construction industry. For a union-security agreement to be valid, it must meet all the following requirements:

1. The union must not have been assisted or controlled by the employer (see Section 8(a)(2) under "Unfair Labor Practices of Employers" [. . .]).

2. The union must be the majority representative of the employees in the appropriate collective-bargaining unit covered by such agreement when made.

3. The union's authority to make such an agreement must not have been revoked within the previous 12 months by the employees in a Board election.

4. The agreement must provide for the appropriate grace period.

Section 8(f) of the Act allows an employer engaged primarily in the building and construction industry to sign a union-security agreement with a union without the union's having been designated as the representative of its employees as otherwise required by the Act. The agreement can be made before the employer has hired any employees for a project and will apply to them when they are hired. As noted above, however, the union-security provisions of a collective-bargaining contract in the building and construction industry may become effective with respect to new employees after 7 full days. If the agreement is made while employees are on the job, it must allow existing employees the same 7-day grace period to comply. As with any other union-security agreement, the union involved must be free from employer assistance or control.

Collective-bargaining contracts in the building and construction industry can include, as stated in Section 8(f), the following additional provisions:

1. A requirement that the employer notify the union concerning job openings.

2. A provision that gives the union an opportunity to refer qualified applicants for such jobs.

3. Job qualification standards based on training or experience.

4. A provision for priority in hiring based on length of service with the employer, in the industry, or in the particular geographic area.

These four hiring provisions may lawfully be included in collective-bargaining contracts which cover employees in other industries as well.

Finally, pursuant to Section 14(b) of the Act, individual States may prohibit, and some States have prohibited, certain forms of union-security agreements.

The Right to Strike. Section 7 of the Act states in part, "Employees shall have the right. . . to engage in other concerted activities for the purpose of collective bargaining or other mutual aid or protection." Strikes are included among the concerted activities protected for employees by this section. Section 13 also concerns the right to strike. It reads as follows:

Nothing in this Act, except as specifically provided for herein, shall be construed so as either to interfere with or impede or diminish in any way the right to strike, or to affect the limitations or qualifications on that right.

It is clear from a reading of these two provisions that: the law not only guarantees the right of employees to strike, but also places limitations and qualifications on the exercise of that right. [One example is] restrictions on strikes in health care institutions [. . .].

Lawful and unlawful strikes. The lawfulness of a strike may depend on the object, or purpose, of the strike, on its timing, or on the conduct of the strikers. The object, or objects, of a strike and whether the objects are lawful are matters that are not always easy to determine. Such issues often have to be decided by the National Labor Relations Board. The consequences can be severe to striking employees and struck employers, involving as they do questions of reinstatement and backpay.

It must be emphasized that the following is only a brief outline. A detailed analysis of the law concerning strikes, and application of the law to all the factual situations that can arise in connection with strikes, is beyond the scope of this material. Employees and employers who anticipate being involved in strike action should proceed cautiously and on the basis of competent advice.

Strikes for a lawful object. Employees who strike for a lawful object fall into two classes "economic strikers" and "unfair labor practice strikers." Both classes continue as employees, but unfair labor practice strikers have greater rights of reinstatement to their jobs.

Economic strikers defined. If the object of a strike is to obtain from the employer some economic concession such as higher wages, shorter hours, or better working conditions, the striking employees are called economic strikers. They retain their status as employees and cannot be discharged, but they can be replaced by their employer. If the employer has hired bona fide permanent replacements who are filling the jobs of the economic strikers when the strikers apply unconditionally to go back to work, the strikers are not entitled to reinstatement at that time. However, if the strikers do not obtain regular and substantially equivalent employment, they are entitled to be recalled to jobs for which they are qualified when openings in such jobs occur if they, or their bargaining representative, have made an unconditional request for their reinstatement.

Unfair labor practice strikers defined. Employees who strike to protest an unfair labor practice committed by their employer are called unfair labor practice strikers. Such strikers can be neither discharged nor permanently replaced. When the strike ends, unfair labor practice strikers, absent serious misconduct on their part, are entitled to have their jobs back even if employees hired to do their work have to be discharged.

If the Board finds that economic strikers or unfair labor practice strikers who have made an unconditional request for reinstatement have been unlawfully denied reinstatement by their employer, the Board may award such strikers backpay starting at the time they should have been reinstated.

(Source: Office of the General Counsel National Labor Relations Board, "Basic Guide to the National Labor Relations Act," U.S. Government Printing Office (Washington: 1997), www.nlrb.gov)

.08 The Labor-Management Reporting and Disclosure Act of 1959, as amended (LMRDA) (29 USC § 401 et seq.; 29 CFR Parts 401 to 453)

Who is Covered

The Labor-Management Reporting and Disclosure Act of 1959, as amended (LMRDA) directly affects millions of people throughout the United States. The LMRDA covers unions, officers and employees of unions, union members, employees who work under collective bargaining agreements (even if they are not union members), employers, labor relations consultants, surety companies, trusts in which a union is interested, and other "persons" as defined in the LMRDA who may be covered by particular provisions of the Act.

LMRDA also covers unions representing U.S. Postal Service employees by virtue of the Postal Reorganization Act of 1970. Act Sec. 7120 of the Civil Service Reform Act, and its implementing regulations, apply many LMRDA standards to unions representing employees in most agencies of the executive branch of the federal government. LMRDA does not cover unions composed solely of state and local government employees.

Basic Provisions/Requirements

The LMRDA consists of seven titles:

1. Title I, the "Bill of Rights," sets forth certain basic rights that Congress believed federal law should guarantee to union members. Members may enforce these rights through private suit in federal district court. Act Sec. 104 of the LMRDA, which establishes the right to receive or examine collective bargaining agreements, applies not only to union members but also to all nonunion employees whose rights are directly affected by a collective bargaining agreement.

   The Secretary of Labor also has enforcement responsibilities with regard to Act Sec. 104. The Office of Labor-Management Standards (OLMS) of the Department's Employment Standards Administration handles these responsibilities.

2. Title II requires unions to file an information report (Form LM-1), copies of their constitution and bylaws, and annual financial reports (Form LM-2, LM-3, or LM-4) with OLMS. The reports and documents filed with OLMS are public information, and any person may examine them or obtain copies at OLMS offices.

   Officers and employees of unions must file a Form LM-30 with OLMS if they have any loans or benefits from, or certain financial interests in, employers whose employees their union represents and businesses that deal with their union.

   Labor relations consultants who enter into an agreement with an employer to persuade employees about their union activities, or to supply certain information to the employer, must file a Form LM-20, *Agreement and Activities Report,* and a Form LM-21, *Receipts and Disbursements Report.*

   Employers who enter into such an agreement or engage in certain specified financial dealings with their employees, unions, union officers, or labor relations consultants must file a Form LM-10.

   Finally, surety companies that issue bonds required by the LMRDA or the Employee Retirement Income Security Act of 1974 (ERISA) must file a Form S-1 to report data such as premiums received, total claims paid, and amounts recovered. The Secretary of Labor has authority to enforce the reporting requirements of the Act.

¶908.08

3. Title III concerns the imposition of trusteeships over subordinate unions. A parent union may impose a trusteeship only for a purpose specified in the LMRDA, and it must establish and administer the trusteeship in accordance with its own constitution and bylaws. A parent union that places a subordinate union in trusteeship must file initial, semiannual, and terminal trusteeship reports (Forms LM-15, LM-15A, and LM-16).

Under the LMRDA, the parent union may not engage in certain specified acts involving the funds and delegate votes from a union under trusteeship. The Secretary of Labor has the authority to investigate and enforce alleged violations of Title III, and a union member or subordinate union may also enforce the provisions of this title, except for the reporting requirements, through private suit in federal district court.

4. Title IV establishes standards for elections of union officers. Local unions must elect their officers by secret ballot; national and international unions and intermediate bodies must elect their officers either by secret ballot of the members or by delegates chosen by secret ballot. Title IV requires elections to be held by national and international unions at least every five years, intermediate bodies at least every four years, and local unions at least every three years.

Unions and employers may not use their funds to promote the candidacy of any candidate, although union funds may be used to conduct an election. A union member in good standing has the right to nominate candidates, be a candidate subject to reasonable qualifications uniformly imposed, hold office, and support and vote for the candidates of the member's choice. Unions must mail a notice of election to every member at the member's last-known home address at least 15 days before the election.

A union member who has exhausted internal election remedies, or invoked such remedies without obtaining a final decision within three calendar months, may file a complaint with the Secretary within one calendar month thereafter, alleging a violation of Title IV of the LMRDA. The Secretary of Labor has authority to file suit in a federal district court to set aside an invalid union election and to request a new election under the supervision of the Secretary.

5. Title V provides a number of safeguards for unions. Union officers have a duty to manage the funds and property of the union solely for the benefit of the union in accordance with its constitution and bylaws. A union may not have outstanding loans to any one officer or employee that exceed $2,000. Union officials who handle union funds or property must be bonded to provide protection against losses.

A union officer or employee who embezzles or otherwise misappropriates union funds or other assets commits a federal crime punishable by a fine and/or imprisonment. Persons convicted of certain crimes, including a violation of Title II or III of the LMRDA, may not hold union office or employment for up to 13 years after conviction or the end of imprisonment.

6. Title VI includes the authority to investigate (see "Penalties/Sanctions" below); a prohibition on a union fining, suspending, expelling, or otherwise disciplining members for exercising their rights under the LMRDA; and a

prohibition on the use or threat of force or violence to interfere with a union member in the exercise of LMRDA rights.

7. Title VII amends the Labor Management Relations Act (LMRA), otherwise known as the Taft-Hartley Act, concerning strikes, boycotts, and picketing. The National Labor Relations Board (NLRB), an independent federal agency, administers the LMRA.

Employee Rights

Title I of the LMRDA guarantees certain rights to all union members. These include the right to nominate candidates, to vote in elections or referendums, to attend membership meetings, and to participate in the deliberations and vote upon the business of such meetings, subject to reasonable rules and regulations in the organization's constitution and bylaws.

They also include the right to meet and assemble freely with other members, to express any views, arguments, or opinions, and to express views at meetings about candidates in an election of the labor organization or about any business properly before the meeting, subject to the organization's established and reasonable rules pertaining to the conduct of meetings. Additional rights outlined in Title I address dues, initiation fees and assessments, protection of the right to sue, and safeguards against improper disciplinary action.

Compliance Assistance Available

Additional compliance assistance materials appear on the OLMS home page. OLMS field office staff members are available to answer questions about the LMRDA and to help individuals and organizations affected by the law.

The OLMS National Office Public Disclosure Room has copies of all reports and documents filed with OLMS, and OLMS field offices have copies of reports filed by organizations and individuals located within their jurisdictions. Copies of Form LM-1, LM-2, LM-3, and LM-4 reports filed by unions may be ordered on the OLMS website.

In addition, all OLMS field offices as well as the OLMS National Office have blank reporting forms and instructions as well as explanatory pamphlets about the law. For additional compliance assistance, contact the department's toll-free help line at 1-866-4-USA-DOL.

Penalties/Sanctions

The LMRDA authorizes the Secretary of Labor to investigate "in order to determine whether any person has violated or is about to violate" any provisions of the Act (except the Bill of Rights of Union Members and amendments made by the LMRDA to other laws) and to "enter such places and inspect such records and accounts and question such persons" as may be necessary to determine whether a violation has occurred. The Secretary may issue subpoenas to compel testimony or to obtain records and other materials needed to complete an investigation.

The Secretary may file civil actions in federal district court to restrain or correct violations and to bring about compliance with the LMRDA. The embezzlement of union funds is subject to a fine of up to $250,000 and/or imprisonment up to five years. Criminal penalties also apply to other Title V provisions as well as to certain reporting violations under Titles II and III.

¶908.08

Relation to State, Local, and Other Federal Laws

Federal laws related to the LMRDA include the National Labor Relations Act of 1935, the Taft-Hartley Act of 1947, the Racketeer-Influenced and Corrupt Organizations (RICO) Act, the Service Contract Act, and the Civil Service Reform Act of 1978.

(Source: www.dol.gov, Employment Law Guide)

.09 Jury Service Protections (28 USC § 1875)

Federal law at 28 USC defines federal government policy relating to the right to a jury trial and defines certain procedures relating to the selection of jurors. This law is relevant to employers because it is likely that employees will be summoned for jury duty and the employer must properly handle leave for jury service in a manner that does not violate the law. Among the protections defined include a provision for the protection of a juror's employment. While federal law requirements are summarized here, the employer also will be subject to similar state laws dealing with jury service at the state level. Highlights of selected portions of the law are summarized here.

- *Declaration of policy.* It is the policy of the federal government that all litigants in federal courts entitled to trial by jury shall have the right to grand and petit juries selected at random from a fair section of the community.

- *Discrimination prohibited.* The law further states that no citizen shall be excluded from service as a grand or petit juror in district courts of the United States because of race, color, religion, sex, national origin, or economic status.

- *Plan for random jury selection.* The law defines procedures for the random selection of jurors and provides for penalties for individuals failing to comply with summons to serve as a juror.

- *Qualifications for jury service.* The law defines certain qualifications to serve as a juror. A person shall be deemed qualified to serve as a juror unless he:

  — Is not a citizen of the United States 18 years or older who has resided for a period of one year in the judicial district,

  — Is unable to read, write, and understand English with a degree of proficiency needed,

  — Is unable to speak the English language,

  — Is incapable by reason of mental or physical infirmity to render satisfactory jury service, or

  — Has a criminal charge against him or her punishable by one year or more incarceration.

- *Protection of juror's employment.* The law provides that no employer shall discharge, threaten to discharge, intimidate, or coerce any permanent employee by reason of such employee's jury service or the attendance or scheduled attendance in connection with such service in any court in the United States. This section further provides for the following corrective action,

  (b) Any employer who violates the provisions of this section—

    (1) shall be liable for damages for any loss of wages or other benefits suffered by an employee by reason of such violation;

(2) may be enjoined from further violations of this section and ordered to provide other appropriate relief, including but not limited to the reinstatement of any employee discharged by reason of his jury service; and

(3) shall be subject to a civil penalty of not more than $1,000 for each violation as to each employee.

Only brief highlights of the law are summarized here. Employers are advised to:

- Define a jury service leave policy,
- Allow an employee time off from work when summoned for jury service,
- Avoid any form of retaliation for such service,
- Reemploy the individual upon return to work from jury service,
- Provide compensation for jury service if required by law or applicable union or employment agreement,
- Consider competitive practices related to jury service pay.

LEGAL COMPLIANCE

¶ 909 DISCRIMINATION LAW

.01 Civil Rights Act of 1964, Title VII, as Amended (42 USC § 2000e)

Definitions

The term "employer" means a person engaged in an industry affecting commerce who has fifteen or more employees for each working day in each of twenty or more calendar weeks in the current or preceding calendar year, and any agent of such a person. (42 USC § 2000e(b))

The term "employee" means an individual employed by an employer. (42 USC § 2000(f))

The term "commerce" means trade, traffic, commerce, transportation, transmission, or communication among the several states; or between a state and any place outside thereof or within the District of Columbia, or a U.S. possession, or between points in the same state but through a point outside the state. (42 USC § 2000(g))

Civil Rights Act Exemption

This act shall not apply to any employer with respect to the employment of aliens outside any state, or to a religious corporation, association, education institution, or society with respect to the employment of individuals of a particular religion to perform work connected with the carrying on by such corporation, association, educational institution, or society of its activities. (42 USC § 2000e-(1))

Discrimination Because of Race, Color, Religion, Sex, or National Origin

It shall be an unlawful employment practice for an employer: to fail or refuse to hire or to discharge any individual, or otherwise to discriminate against any individual with respect to his compensation, terms, conditions, or privileges of employment, because of such individual's race, color, religion, sex, or national origin; (42 USC § 2000e-(a)(1)) or to limit, segregate, or classify his employees or applicants for employment in any way which would deprive or tend to deprive any individual of employment opportunities or otherwise adversely affect his status as an employee, because of such individual's race, color, religion, sex, or national origin. (42 USC § 2000e-(a)(2))

Notwithstanding any other provision of this act, it shall not be an unlawful employment practice for an employer to hire an employee, where religion, sex, or national origin is a bona fide occupational qualification reasonably necessary to the normal operation of that particular business or enterprise. (42 USC § 2000(e)-2(e))

.03 Race or Color Discrimination

Under Title VII and the Civil Rights Act of 1866

- Employers may not base privileges of employment or compensation, or limit, segregate or classify employees (or applicants for employment) on race or color.
- Employers have a responsibility to maintain a bias-free work atmosphere, and to investigate and correct discriminatory situations.
- Racial and ethnic epithets, slurs or jokes directed at, or made in the presence of, minority employees are deemed to be unlawful racial harassment.
- Failure of a nonminority employee to adequately train a minority coworker could be a form of racial harassment.
- Employers may discharge or discipline an employee for unsatisfactory job performance, insubordination, unauthorized absences or for any valid reason, as long as similarly situated employees of a different race or color are discharged or disciplined under the same or similar circumstances.
- Almost any factor might be used to determine if minorities have been treated differently from nonminorities, including a comparison of the two groups' performance ratings, average salaries, records of terminations and reasons for termination, or even such things as records of employee training. For this reason, it is important for managers and supervisors to maintain accurate and complete records of their employment decisions.

.05 Religious Discrimination

Title VII of the 1964 Civil Rights Act prohibits employment discrimination on the basis of religion and defines "religion" as including all aspects of religious observance and practice, as well as belief.

- Religious discrimination occurs when an individual is required by an employment rule or policy to choose between abandoning a fundamental precept of religion or giving up an employment opportunity.
- Not only are religious believers protected from discrimination, but so are agnostics and atheists. For example, an atheist cannot be compelled to attend staff meetings that begin with a prayer.
- The employer is required to consider what reasonable accommodation may be made if there is a conflict between an employment policy or practice and the individual's religious beliefs.
- Examples of reasonable accommodation include the use of voluntary substitutes and swaps, flexible scheduling, lateral transfer and change of job assignment.
- Unlawful religious bias may occur when a policy on overtime pay results in a disadvantage to employees observing a Sabbath day other than Sunday (i.e., denying Sunday overtime to a Seventh Day Adventist who refused to work Saturdays while offering Saturday overtime to employees whose religion prevented Sunday work).

- An employer is under an obligation to maintain a work environment free of religious bias. Permitting a supervisor to espouse his religious beliefs to employees while at work may amount to religious discrimination.

- An employer must make alternative arrangements if it is notified that an employee cannot be present at a scheduled test or other selection procedure because the time conflicts with the tenets of the employee's religion, unless the employer can demonstrate undue hardship.

- An employer may refuse to accommodate the dress or grooming requirements of an employee that are based on his or her religion only when the employer can demonstrate undue hardship on the conduct of its business (i.e., safety factors, etc.).

.07 Sex Discrimination

Discrimination in employment against any individual, male or female, on the basis of sex is barred by Title VII of the Civil Rights Act of 1964.

- When the sex of an individual is one of the factors upon which a decision is based, the resulting employment decision is probably unlawful.

- There are two general exceptions to the use of sex as a factor in employment decisions: bona fide occupational qualification (BFOQ) and business necessity.

  — The BFOQ exception recognizes that in some extremely rare instances a person's sex, religion, or national origin may be reasonably necessary to carrying out a particular job function in the normal operation of an employer's business or enterprise.

  — Business necessity is a defense to a charge of discrimination. It is primarily used if it is reasonably necessary to such factors as the safety or efficiency of the operation. Reasons such as "Women are less stable and have poorer attendance records" and "A male image is desired" are not sufficient to justify a business necessity for discrimination.

- The use of height and weight standards as part of the requirements of a job may be challenged and discriminatory if those standards eliminate a significantly greater number of females than males.

- To avoid a charge of sex discrimination, any rule against husband-wife employment should provide the two individuals with a choice as to which one will stay.

- The assumption that parenthood may result in a female employee being absent is not a lawful basis for refusing employment to a mother.

.09 Sexual Harassment Discrimination

Sexual harassment is an unlawful employment practice in violation of Title VII of the Civil Rights Act of 1964.

- Sexual harassment is unwelcome verbal or physical sexual conduct that is a term or condition of employment. There are two types of sexual harassment, "quid pro quo" and "environmental."

  — The quid pro quo type of harassment occurs when submission to verbal or physical conduct of a sexual nature, unwelcome sexual advances, or requests for sexual favors is made either explicitly or implicitly a term or condition of an individual's employment.

¶909.09

- — The environmental type of harassment occurs when the unwelcome conduct unreasonably interferes with an individual's job performance or creates an intimidating, hostile or offensive working environment, even if it does not lead to any tangible or economic job consequences.
- Employers must not only correct, but prevent a working environment that is hostile to an employee on the basis of their membership in a protected class.
- Employers must ensure that supervisory personnel and other workers do not engage in unlawful harassment.
- Liability can arise for a hostile work environment created by conduct based on an employee's sex, race, color, national origin, religion, age or disability, as well as gender-based conduct that is nonsexual in nature.
- An employer will be liable for the actions of coworkers that create a hostile work environment in either of the following circumstances:
  - — The employer knew or should have known that the harassment was taking place and failed to take immediate, corrective action.
  - — The employer did not establish and disseminate an explicit policy against harassment and did not provide a reasonable avenue for victims to complain to someone with authority to investigate and remedy the problem.
- In the 1998 *Faragher* and *Ellerth* cases, the US Supreme Court held that an employer will be vicariously liable for the misconduct of a supervisor with authority over an employee when the misconduct results in a tangible job action or hostile environment sexual harassment.
  - — Although the Supreme Court's holding pertained only to sexual harassment, the EEOC takes the position that the vicarious liability standard applies to harassment claims based on any protected class.
  - — Under this vicarious liability standard, if the harassment develops into tangible adverse employment action suffered by the employee, the employer will be automatically liable for the harassment. If no tangible action is taken against the employee, the employer is still vicariously liable, but may raise an affirmative defense by showing that the employer exercised reasonable care to prevent and correct harassment and that the employee unreasonably failed to take advantage of these measures provided, or to otherwise avoid the harm.
- Unlike supervisory sexual harassment, employers are not strictly liable for coworker sexual harassment. Employer liability for harassing conduct by co-workers attaches when:
  - — The employer knew or should have known of the conduct, and
  - — Fails to take immediate and appropriate corrective action.
- Employers may be liable for the sexual harassment of an employee by a non-employee under certain circumstances:
  - — The employer knew or should have known of the conduct,
  - — The employer has some control over the situation or is otherwise legally responsible for the non-employee's conduct, and
  - — The employer fails to take immediate and appropriate corrective action

- Voluntary submission to the sexual conduct will not necessarily defeat a claim of sexual harassment. Neither will occasional use of sexually explicit language nor provocative dress by the harassed necessarily negate a claim.

- The employer should take all necessary steps to prevent sexual harassment, including: developing a written policy prohibiting sexual harassment; informing managers and employees of the policy and how to raise and pursue their rights if harassed; promptly investigating any complaints; and taking appropriate action when needed, including disciplining the offender.

.11 Pregnancy Discrimination

Under the Pregnancy Discrimination Act of 1978, a female applicant and employee may not be treated differently from a male applicant and employee because of the female's pregnancy or capacity to become pregnant.

- A woman is protected against such practices as being fired, or refused a job or promotion, merely because she is pregnant or has had an abortion.

- In terms of employment decisions, leave policies, and receipt of benefits, an employer should treat pregnancy and related medical conditions the same as other disability conditions are treated.

- As long as they can still work, expectant employees cannot be forced to go on leave.

- If other employees who take disability leave are entitled to get their jobs back when they are able to work again, so are women who have been unable to work because of pregnancy.

- If an employer cannot make reasonable accommodations to a female employee's need to take maternity leave and cannot guarantee her return to work, the worker should be given preference in recall where such preference is possible.

- An employer would have to show a business necessity in order to refuse to hire a pregnant applicant.

- An employer may not condition the availability of maternity leave on an employee's having been employed for a specified period of time that is different from other disabilities (e.g., one year).

- Special problems arise when a company deals with materials or processes that may have a harmful effect on female reproductivity of unborn offspring. A policy that expressly excludes women only from the workplace because of reproductive or fetal hazards will violate Title VII. As long as pregnant or potentially pregnant women are as capable of doing their jobs as their male counterparts, they cannot be forced away from jobs on the basis of pregnancy or reproductive capacity.

.13 National Origin Discrimination

Title VII bans employment practices that foster national origin discrimination. National origin discrimination is defined broadly as including the denial of equal employment opportunity because of an individual's (or his or her ancestor's) place of origin or because an individual has the physical, cultural or linguistic characteristics of a national origin group.

- Ethnic slurs, jokes, and other verbal or physical conduct relating to an individual's national origin constitute harassment when this conduct: creates an intimidating, hostile or offensive working environment; unreasonably interferes with an individual's work performance; or otherwise adversely affects an individual's employment opportunities.

- An employer is responsible for the conduct of its agents and supervisory employees where ethnic slurs and other actions amount to harassment on the basis of national origin, regardless of whether the employer knew or should have known of their occurrence.

- Where the acts of harassment on the basis of national origin were committed by coworkers, an employer is responsible only if it knew or should have known of the conduct but failed to take immediate and appropriate corrective action.

- Employers may not require the use of the English language only for all working hours, but it may be lawful to have a more limited rule requiring that employees speak only in English at certain times. Still, the rule must be justified by business necessity.

- The EEOC's Guidelines on National Origin Discrimination require that all employees be notified of the general circumstances when speaking only in English is required and the consequences of violating the rule.

  — A foreign accent that interferes with an employee's ability to perform a task may constitute a legitimate nondiscriminatory reason for an adverse employment decision.

- Height and weight requirements, without basis on true business necessity, may be deemed unlawful national origin bias.

- Employers can use aptitude or other employment tests if they are applied equally to all applicants, or are related to successful job performance and do not disproportionately disqualify applicants of a particular national origin.

.15 Affirmative Action Requirements

Presidential Executive Order 11246 mandates non-discriminative and affirmative action by federal contractors and subcontractors. Affirmative action is a government policy intended for the promotion and insuring of equal employment opportunity for all persons.

Generally, federal government agencies contracting for goods or services must include an equal opportunity clause in government contracts of $10,000 or more. The equal opportunity clause requires the contractor to agree not to discriminate against applicants or employees because of race, color, religion, sex, or national origin. The contractor must take affirmative action to insure that employment decisions are not made based on the protected class categories.

Any contractor or subcontractor with a contract of $25,000 or more with the federal government must take affirmative action to hire and promote qualified targeted veterans which includes, special disabled veterans, veterans of the Vietnam-era, recently separated veterans, and any other veterans who served on active duty during a war or in a campaign or expedition for which a campaign badge has been authorized.

Contractors and subcontractors with openings for jobs, other than executive or top management positions, positions which are to be filled from within the contractor's organization, and positions lasting three days or less, must list them with the nearest State Job Service (also known as State Employment Service) office. The requirement applies to vacancies at all locations of a business not otherwise exempt under the company's federal contract. Qualified targeted veterans receive priority for referral to Federal contractor job openings listed at those offices. The priority for referral does not guarantee that referred veterans will be hired.

Federal contractors are not required to hire those referred but must have affirmative action plans. Contractors with at least 50 employees and a contract of $50,000 or more must have a written affirmative action plan. They must be able to show they have followed the plans and that they have not discriminated against veterans or other covered groups. They must also show that they have actively recruited targeted veterans and disseminated all promotion information internally regarding promotion activities.

The written affirmative action plan must show the following:

- A workforce analysis showing representation of minorities and females in various job categories.
- An analysis of availability of individuals by race and sex in the workforce.
- An analysis of hiring and employment practices to determine whether equal opportunity is afforded.
- Definition of goals and other plans to achieve equal opportunity.

(Source: 41 CFR Part 60)

Companies must file an annual VETS-100 report, which shows the number of targeted veterans in their work force by job category, hiring location, and number of new hires, including targeted veterans hired during the reporting period, and the maximum number of minimum provided at VETS-100 Internet site at http://vets100.cudenver.edu, or employers may contact the VETS-100 Processing Center at (703) 461-2460 or e-mail at mailto:helpdesk@vets100.com.

For information about how to list a job opening, contact the nearest State Job Service office listed in the telephone book.

According to the Supreme Court and the EEOC, affirmative action, even without proof of past discrimination by an employer, is sometimes permitted by Title VII of the Civil Rights Act of 1964, even though Title VII generally disallows the consideration of race, sex, and national origin in making employment decisions. Presidential Executive Order No. 11246 mandates nondiscrimination and affirmative action by federal contractors and subcontractors.

- The existence of an affirmative action plan only applies as a justification if the employer's action actually involved consideration of race, sex, or national origin.
- If an employer's affirmative action plan is voluntary (i.e., not the result of a court order or Executive Order No. 11246), the EEOC cannot compel the employer to implement it.
- An affirmative action plan must be reviewed and revised annually.
- The discharge of an incumbent white or male employee to make room for a minority or female candidate would not be an appropriate implementation of an affirmative action plan.

¶909.15

- Plans that create an absolute bar to the employment or advancement of persons not covered by the affirmative action plan (e.g., a training program that admits women and minorities only) are not permitted under Title VII.
- Plans that are designed to *maintain* racial, sexual or ethnic balance rather than to correct an imbalance are not permitted by Title VII.
- Recruitment directed towards minority group members and women can be an allowable part of an affirmative action plan.
- The Supreme Court has ruled that whites may not be selected for layoff ahead of minorities in order to protect the gains in minority employment.

.17 Age Discrimination

The Age Discrimination in Employment Act of 1967 (ADEA) addresses age discrimination; it was not part of the original 1964 Title VII law. Like the other forms of discrimination, age harassment has been made the subject of guidelines. The employer's obligations are similar to the ones for sexual harassment.

- Individuals 40 years of age and older are protected from employment discrimination on the basis of age by the Age Discrimination in Employment Act of 1967.
- It is against federal policy for contractors and subcontractors, in the performance of federal government contracts, to discriminate against employees or job applicants on account of age.
- Under the ADEA, most workers age 40 and over are protected from mandatory retirement.
- An employer, generally, cannot refuse to hire or promote an individual because he or she is age 70 or older and cannot force an employee to retire after turning 70.
- An employer has an affirmative duty under the law to maintain a work environment free from age harassment.
- Cost-cutting is not a legitimate, nondiscriminatory reason for firing an older worker and replacing that employee with an equally proficient younger employee merely because the older employee happens to be earning more money.
- An employer must show a bona fide occupational qualification if challenged on a practice of eliminating applicants or employees from certain positions because of age. Usually, this requires the showing of some legitimate safety factor which would impact the company.

.19 Disability

Employment discrimination against qualified individuals with disabilities is prohibited by the Rehabilitation Act of 1973 and by the Americans with Disabilities Act of 1990 (ADA). Conceptually, ADA can be thought of as adding to the Civil Rights Act of 1964 the additional category, *persons with disabilities*, as protected from discrimination in various aspects of life. For a more extensive coverage of ADA see the Legal Basics Chapter.

The Rehabilitation Act operates in three areas:

- Section 501 applies to federal government agencies prohibiting discrimination against qualified individuals with disabilities and requiring the agencies to take affirmative action to promote employment opportunities for the disabled.

- Section 503 applies to private sector employers holding federal government contracts or subcontracts of $10,000 or more. These employers are required to take affirmative action to promote employment opportunities for the disabled.

- Section 504 applies to private sector organizations receiving federal assistance, prohibiting such organizations from discriminating against individuals with disabilities.

While the two laws have different, although sometimes overlapping, coverage requirements, their bans on employment discrimination on the basis of disability are substantively the same.

- A person with a disability is defined as someone who has a physical or mental impairment that substantially one or more major life activities, a record of such impairment, or is regarded as having such an impairment.

- To be protected under the law, the must be a person with a disability and must be able to perform the essential functions of the job with or without reasonable accommodation.

- Employers must undertake reasonable accommodation for qualified individuals with a disability if such accommodation would allow that person to perform the essential functions of the job.

- The ADA provides protection not only for those who have physical or mental conditions that actually limit their major life activities, but also for those who are perceived to have handicaps.

- Alcoholics or drug abusers whose use of alcohol or drugs prevents them from carrying out their duties or threatens the property or safety of others are not protected under the law.

In October 2004, the Equal Employment Opportunity Commission issued new guidance for dealing with individuals with intellectual disabilities, a new term for mental retardation. Under the new guideline, an individual with an intellectual disability is one: (1) with an IQ below 70-75, (2) with significant limits on basic adaptive skills needed for everyday life and (3) where such disability originated before the age of 18.

If an individual has two or more impairments that individually may not be substantial, but when taken together substantially limit a major life activity of the individual, such individual should be afforded protection under the law. When encountering such an individual, the employer is obligated to consider and make a reasonable accommodation for qualified disabled individuals.

.21 Vietnam Veterans Discrimination

The Vietnam Era Veterans' Readjustment Assistance Act of 1974 requires federal contractors and subcontractors with contracts of $25,000 or more (including construction contracts) to not discriminate against and to take affirmative action to employ and promote qualified disabled veterans and veterans of the Vietnam era.

- If an employer's voluntary veterans' preference has an adverse impact on female employees or applicants for employment, the preference violates Title VII as sex discrimination unless the employer can show that the preference serves, in a significant way, the legitimate employment goals of the employer.

- A qualified disabled veteran is one who is capable of performing a particular job with reasonable accommodation to his or her disability.

- The Readjustment Act requires that the results of a preemployment physical or mental examination be kept confidential. However, they may be revealed to supervisors and managers to the extent that restrictions are imposed on the duties of the disabled veteran and to the extent that accommodations must be made.

- Veterans must be invited to identify themselves as entitled to protection under the Readjustment Act; the contractor can include this invitation in its application form or as an attachment to the application and may also distribute the invitation to employees.

- Reemployment protection in the form of leave-of-absence rights is afforded under federal law to veterans, reservists and National Guardsmen who perform active/inactive duty training, and to persons who are required to report for a preinduction examination for their physical fitness to enter the armed forces and are rejected. They must still be qualified to do the job when they apply for reemployment.

- Where accommodations to the physical and mental limitations of disabled veterans can be made without imposing an undue hardship on the business in terms of safety and efficiency or financial costs and expenses, the contractor is required to make such arrangements.

.22 State Anti-bias Laws

In addition to the federal laws described in the preceding paragraphs, employers may be subject to various state or local anti-bias laws. Depending upon the area or jurisdiction, such laws may prohibit discrimination on one or more protected class categories such as:

- Sex
- Marital status
- Age
- Sexual orientation or preference
- Race
- Military status
- Religion
- Source of income
- National origin
- Disability
- Or other factors

¶909.22

¶ 911 ENFORCEMENT PROCEDURES

.01 The EEOC and Equal Employment

If an employee believes that he has been discriminated against by an employer when applying for a job or on the job in the terms or conditions of employment because of race, color, sex, religion, national origin or age, he may file a charge of discrimination against the employer, labor union or employment agency with the Equal Employment Opportunity Commission (EEOC). The EEOC enforces Title VII of the Civil Rights Act of 1964, as amended, the Age Discrimination in Employment Act (ADEA) of 1967, as amended, the Equal Pay Act (EPA) of 1963 and Sections 501 and 505 of the Rehabilitation Act of 1973, as amended. Charges/complaints of employment discrimination may be filed at any field office of the U.S. Equal Employment Opportunity Commission (EEOC). Field offices are located throughout the United States. To be connected with the nearest EEOC field office call toll free (800) 669-4000.

The EEOC shall have power:

- To cooperate with and, with their consent, to utilize regional, state, local, and other agencies, both public and private, and individuals;

- To pay to witnesses whose depositions are taken or who are summoned before the Commission or any of its agents the same witness and mileage fees as are paid to witnesses in the courts of the United States;

- To furnish to persons subject to this title such technical assistance as they may request to further their compliance with this title or an order issued thereunder;

- Upon the request of any employer whose employees, or some of them, or any labor organization whose members, or some of them, refuse or threaten to refuse to cooperate in effectuating the provisions of this title, to assist in such effectuation by conciliation or such other remedial action as is provided by this title; to make such technical studies as are appropriate to effectuate the purposes and policies of this title; and to make the results of such studies available to the public;

- To intervene in a civil action brought under Sec. 2000e-5 of the Civil Rights Act by an aggrieved party against a respondent other than a government, governmental agency, or political subdivision. (42 USC § 2000e-g). Also, the EEOC has the power to enforce Titles I and V of the Americans with Disabilities Act of 1990 and the Civil Rights Act of 1991.

.03 Records/Notice Requirements

Every employer, employment agency, and labor organization subject to this title shall:

- Make and keep such records relevant to the determinations of whether unlawful employment practices have been or are being committed,

- Preserve such records for such periods, and

- Make such reports therefrom, as the Commission shall prescribe by regulation or order, after public hearing, as reasonable, necessary, or appropriate for the enforcement of this title or the regulations or orders thereunder.

The Commission shall require each employer that controls a training program to maintain such records as are reasonably necessary to carry out the purpose of this title including, but not limited to, a list of applicants who wish to participate in such program, including the chronological order in which applications were received, and to furnish to the Commission, upon request, a detailed description of the manner in which persons are selected to participate in the apprenticeship or other training program. (42 USC § 2000e-8(c))

Notices to Be Posted

Every employer, employment agency, and labor organization, as the case may be, shall post and keep posted in conspicuous places upon its premises where notices to employees, applicants for employment, and members are customarily posted a notice to be prepared or approved by the Commission setting forth excerpts from, or summaries of, the pertinent provisions of this title and information pertinent to the filing of a complaint. A willful violation shall be punishable by a fine of not more than $100 for each separate offense. (42 USC § 2000e-10)

.04 Equal Opportunity Interviewing Checklist

- *Do* ask questions which are job related or necessary for determining an applicant's qualifications for employment.
- *Do* question candidates in a consistent and uniform manner, regardless of race, sex, national origin, age, or handicap.
- *Do* evaluate applicants on job related criteria, in accord with the actual requirements for successful performance of the job.
- *Do* select the best-qualified individual for the job. Equal opportunity laws do not require that you select unqualified workers.
- *Do* accord reasonable accommodations for qualified disabled applicants. Consider whatever minor adjustments or accommodations may be made to enable the handicapped to perform the job successfully.
- *Do* make reasonable accommodations to the religious observance obligations of associates.
- State attendance requirements and ask whether the applicant can meet them.
- Information about previous work attendance records may be obtained in the interview, on the applicant form, or in reference checks, but the question should not refer to illness or disability.
- Ask whether the person knows of any reason that he or she cannot perform the essential functions of the job (since the person may not be able to perform essential job functions for reasons unrelated to a disability).
- Ask questions about an applicant's ability to perform job-related functions.
- Questions may be asked regarding ability to perform all job functions, not just those that are essential to the job. However, an applicant cannot be screened out because of his or her inability to perform marginal or non-essential job functions.
- Describe or demonstrate a job function and ask all applicants whether they can perform the functions with or without reasonable accommodations.
- *Do not* ask any questions of a female applicant that would not be asked of a male candidate (i.e., inquiries pertaining to child care, marital status, birth control methods, or hindrances to travel or working weekends).

¶911.04

- *Do not* ask questions of one race that would not be asked of another (i.e., questioning one's ability to work in a location with members of another racial group).

- *Do not* establish a negative tone to the interview in an effort to discourage any applicant from seeking the position.

- *Do not* give undue emphasis to the hazardous or tedious aspects of a job, especially if such occurs on an infrequent basis.

- *Do not* inform an applicant that the position is "reserved" or must be filled by a female or minority group applicant due to equal opportunity or affirmative action obligations or regulations. A possible exception to this suggestion may occur when a court or regulatory agency has made a finding of discrimination and directs remedial action in the form of specific hiring goals.

- *Do not* impose additional "desirable" qualifications in excess of actual requirements of your job opening.

- *Do not* devise additional testing requirements as part of a pre-employment screening procedure, unless such testing is job related and properly validated.

- *Do not* ask the birthplace of an applicant. Since birthplace may indicate a person of foreign origin, it is better to avoid this question than to risk a discrimination charge on this basis.

- *Do not* ask questions that tend to identify the age of the applicant, where age is not a valid or necessary factor to successful job performance.

- *Do not* ask a person's religious affiliation.

- *Do not* ask the citizenship of an applicant. Ask whether the person is a citizen or is legally authorized for full time permanent employment.

- *Do not* ask about an applicant's type of military discharge or general military service. You may ask about job related experience in the Armed Forces of the United States of America.

- *Do not* ask if the applicant has ever been arrested. You may ask if the person has ever been convicted.

- *Do not* ask questions on the general physical or mental condition of an applicant.

- *Do not* ask about any physical characteristics such as scars, burns, or missing limbs.

- *Do not* ask if the applicant has ever received counseling or seen a psychiatrist.

- *Do not* ask if the person has had a drug or alcohol problem.

- *Do not* ask about an applicant's worker's compensation history.

- *Do not* ask how a disability occurred or if the disability is indicative of an underlying impairment.

- *Do not* ask whether the applicant will need leave for treatment.

- If the applicant volunteers information about a medical condition such as cancer, *do not* ask about the progress of the illness or whether it is in remission.

- *Do not* ask if family members have had a history of illness.

- *Do not* ask if the person has any disability or medical condition that will prevent the person from performing the job.

¶911.04

.05 Firing Fairly

There are times when it is necessary to face up to firing a subordinate. Terminations, like hiring and a host of other people-related actions, are basic supervisory responsibilities. Terminations are generally the ultimate result of a disciplinary or performance problem.

Firings come under the province of state and federal equal employment opportunity laws. As such, discharge of a white male employee should be given just as much consideration as termination of a minority to assure uniformity of treatment for all your workers. Consistent and fair treatment of all workers is the key to good employee relations and your best defense in the event of employment discrimination allegation or other legal claim. To accomplish good employee relations, the following steps are recommended:

- Investigate all facts.
- Ensure uniform enforcement of rules.
- Consider all alternatives.
- Consult with your superior or the personnel department.
- Check to insure that the firing is consistent with any applicable published employment policies.
- Document your decision.
- Handle the firing in a private meeting.
- Check and comply with state or local law regarding the handling of final pay and other matters relating to the separation.

.06 Investigating a Complaint of Discrimination

A complaint about discrimination may come to an employer's attention in one of several ways. A complaint may be made by an employee, an applicant for employment, or by a former employee. The complaint may be presented directly by the individual or through a third party such as an attorney, union, or a government agency. Regardless of who presented the complaint or the manner in which it is presented, the employer should take the complaint seriously and seek to resolve the matter.

A workplace investigation is recommended to clarify the facts of the situation and then to determine an appropriate course of action. A designated manager or human resources specialist may coordinate or conduct the investigation. The investigation may begin with a detailed discussion with the complainant to identify circumstances occurring that prompt the complaint. As necessary, the investigation should include a discussion with the individual(s) alleged to have acted improperly as well as obtaining statements of any witnesses. Any applicable workplace records, documents, or policies should also be examined. Information uncovered in an investigation conducted by an attorney is considered to be attorney work product, and as such it has an added degree of protection from discovery in subsequent proceedings.

If a complaint is filed by the U.S. Equal Employment Opportunity Commission (EEOC) or similar state agency, a formal notification and investigative process will occur. Listed below are investigative guidelines offered by the EEOC.

EEOC Investigations—What An Employer Should Know

What is EEOC?

1. The Equal Employment Opportunity Commission is an independent federal agency created by Congress in 1964 to eradicate discrimination in employment. The various statutes enforced by the Commission prohibit employment discrimination on the basis of race, color, sex, national origin, religion, retaliation, age, and disability.

2. The EEOC has authority to receive, initiate, and investigate charges of discrimination filed against employers who have a *statutory minimum* number of employees.

3. The EEOC's role in an investigation is to fairly and accurately evaluate the charge allegations in light of all the evidence obtained.

What happens when a charge has been filed against me?

1. You will always be notified that a charge of discrimination has been filed, and you will be provided with the name and contact information for the investigator assigned to your case. A charge does not constitute a finding that your company engaged in discrimination. The EEOC has a responsibility to investigate and determine whether there is a reasonable cause to believe discrimination occurred.

2. In many cases, you may opt to resolve a charge early in the process through mediation or settlement. At the start of an investigation, the EEOC will advise you if your charge is eligible for mediation, but feel free to ask the investigator about the settlement option. Mediation and settlement are voluntary resolutions.

3. During the investigation, you and the Charging Party will be asked to provide information. Your investigator will evaluate the information submitted to determine whether unlawful discrimination has taken place. You may be asked to:

   - Submit a statement of position. This is your opportunity to tell your side of the story and you should take advantage of it.

   - Respond to a Request for Information (RFI). The RFI may ask you to submit copies of personnel policies, Charging Party's personnel files, the personnel files of other individuals, and other relevant information.

   - Permit an on-site visit. While you may view such a visit as being disruptive to your operations, our experience has been that such visits greatly expedite the fact-finding process and may help achieve quicker resolutions. In some cases, an on-site visit may be an alternative to an RFI if requested documents are made available for viewing or photocopying.

   - Provide contact information for or have employees available for witness interviews. You may be present during interviews with management personnel, but an investigator is allowed to conduct interviews of non-management level employees without your presence or permission.

4. If the charge was not dismissed by the EEOC when it was received, that means there was some basis for proceeding with further investigation. There are many cases where it is unclear whether discrimination may have occurred and

an investigation is necessary. You are encouraged to present any facts that you believe show the allegations are incorrect or do not amount to a violation of the law. An employer's input and cooperation will assist the EEOC in promptly and thoroughly investigating a charge.

- Work with the investigator to identify the most efficient and least burdensome way to gather relevant evidence.
- You should submit a prompt response to the EEOC and provide the information requested, even if you believe the charge is frivolous.
  - If there are extenuating circumstances preventing a timely response from you, contact your investigator to work out a new due date for the information.
- Provide complete and accurate information in response to requests from your investigator.
- The average time it takes to process an EEOC investigation is about 182 days.
  - Our experience shows that undue delay in responding to requests for information extends the time it takes to complete an investigation.
- If you have concerns regarding the scope of the information being sought, advise the investigator. Although the EEOC is entitled to all information relevant to the allegations contained in the charge and has the authority to subpoena such information, in some instances, the information request may be modified.
- Keep relevant documents. If you are unsure whether a document is needed, ask your investigator. By law, you are required to keep certain documents for a set period of time.

5. Your investigator will:
- Be available to answer most questions you have about the process.
- Keep you informed about the charge process, including the rights and responsibilities of the parties at the conclusion of the investigation.
- Conduct an appropriate, thorough, and timely investigation.
- Allow you to respond to the allegations.
- Inform you of the outcome of the investigation.

6. Once the investigator has completed the investigation, the EEOC will make a determination on the merits of the charge.
- If the EEOC determines that there is no reasonable cause to believe that discrimination occurred, the charging party will be issued a letter called a Dismissal and Notice of Rights that tells the charging party he/she has the right to file a lawsuit in federal court within 90 days from the date of receipt of the letter. The employer will also receive a copy of this document.
- If the EEOC determines there is reasonable cause to believe discrimination has occurred, both parties will be issued a Letter of Determination stating that there is reason to believe that discrimination occurred and inviting the parties to join the agency in seeking to resolve the charge, through an informal process known as conciliation.

¶911.06

- Where conciliation fails, the EEOC has the authority to enforce violations of its statutes by filing a lawsuit in federal court. If the EEOC decides not to litigate, the charging party will receive a Notice of Right to Sue and may file a lawsuit in federal court within 90 days.

How does a charge get resolved?

The EEOC offers employers many opportunities to resolve charges of discrimination. Successfully resolving the case through one of these voluntary processes may save you time, effort, and money. Methods of resolution include: mediation, settlement, and conciliation.

Mediation

The EEOC has greatly expanded its mediation program. The program is free, quick, voluntary, and confidential. If mediation is successful, there is no investigation.

If the charge filed against your company is eligible for mediation, you will be invited to take part in the mediation process. If mediation is unsuccessful, the charge is referred for investigation.

Settlement

Charges of discrimination may be settled at any time during the investigation. The EEOC investigators are experienced in working with the parties to reach satisfactory settlements. You should contact the investigator if you are interested in resolving your charge through settlement.

Conciliation

The EEOC is statutorily required to attempt to resolve findings of discrimination through "informal methods of conference, conciliation, and persuasion." (See 42 USC 2000e-5.) After the parties have been informed by letter that the evidence gathered during the investigation establishes that there is "reasonable cause" to believe that discrimination has occurred, the parties will be invited to participate in conciliation discussions. During conciliation, your investigator will work with you and the Charging Party to develop an appropriate remedy for the discrimination. We encourage you to take advantage of this final opportunity to resolve the charge prior to the EEOC considering the matter for litigation.

Statutory Minimums

- Title VII of the Civil Rights Act of 1964 applies to employers with fifteen (15) or more employees.

- The Age Discrimination in Employment Act of 1967 (ADEA) applies to employers with twenty (20) or more employees.

- Title I of the Americans with Disabilities Act of 1990 (ADA) applies to employers with fifteen (15) or more employees.

- The Equal Pay Act of 1963 (EPA) applies to most employers with one or more employees.

(Source: www.eeoc.gov)

¶911.06

¶ 912 FAIR LABOR STANDARDS ACT

.01 Definitions

"Act" or "FLSA" means the Fair Labor Standards Act of 1938, as amended (29 USC § 201 et seq.).

Employer and Employee

An employee includes any person acting directly or indirectly in the interest of an employer in relation to an employee and includes a public agency, but does not include any labor organization (other than when acting as an employer) or anyone acting in the capacity of officer or agent of such labor organization.

An employee means any individual employed by an employer, except for those types of individuals excluded by Section 3(e), paragraphs (2), (3), and (4), of the FLSA.

Workweek

A workweek is a period of 168 hours during seven consecutive 24-hour periods. It may begin on any day of the week and any hour of the day established by the employer. Generally, for purposes of minimum wage and overtime payment, each workweek stands alone; there can be no averaging of two or more workweeks. Employee coverage, compliance with wage payment requirements, and the application of most exemptions are determined on a workweek basis.

Hours Worked

Covered employees must be paid for all hours worked in a workweek. In general, "hours worked" includes all time an employee must be on duty or on the employer's premises or at any other prescribed place of work. Also included is any additional time the employee is required or permitted to work.

Overtime Pay/Overtime Rate

Overtime must be paid at a rate of at least one and one-half times the employee's regular rate of pay for each hour worked in a workweek in excess of the maximum allowable in a given type of employment. Generally, the regular rate includes all payments made by the employer to or on behalf of the employee (excluding certain statutory exceptions). The following examples are based on a maximum 40-hour workweek. (See ¶ 912.14 for examples of overtime pay computations.)

Hourly Rate

If more than 40 hours are worked, at least one and one-half times the regular rate for each hour over 40 is due.

Piece Rate

The regular rate of pay for an employee paid on a piecework basis is obtained by dividing the total weekly earnings by the total number of hours worked in the same week. The employee is entitled to an additional one-half times this regular rate for each hour over 40, plus the full piecework earnings.

.03 Enterprises Covered by FLSA

- Engaged in the business of construction or reconstruction; or
- Engaged in the operating of (regardless of dollar volume):

¶912.01

— A hospital,

— An institution primarily engaged in the care of the sick, the aged, or the mentally ill or defective who reside on the premises,

— A school for mentally or physically handicapped or gifted children,

— A preschool,

— An elementary or secondary school, or

— An institution of higher education (whether public or private or operated for profit or not-for-profit); or

- Comprised exclusively of one or more retail or service establishments (as defined in FLSA) whose annual gross volume of sales made or business done is not less than $500,000; or

- Engaged in laundering or cleaning or repairing of clothing or fabrics (whose sales volume is not less than $500,000);

- An activity of a public agency; or

- Any other type of enterprise having an annual gross volume of sales made or business done of not less than $500,000.

The dollar volume above excludes excise taxes at the retail level which are separately stated.

.05 Employees Covered

Employees Covered Regarding Interstate Commerce

Employees of firms which are not covered enterprises under FLSA may still be subject to its minimum wage, overtime pay, and child labor provisions if they are individually engaged in interstate commerce or in the production of goods for interstate commerce. (See exemptions defined at ¶ 912.09.)

Domestic Service Workers

Domestic service workers, such as day workers, housekeepers, chauffeurs, cooks, or full-time baby sitters, are covered if they:

- Receive at least $50 in cash wages in a calendar quarter from their employers, or

- Work a total of more than eight hours a week for one or more employers.

.06 Exemptions to the Fair Labor Standards Act

Act Sec. 13(a)(1) of the FLSA, defined in the Code of Federal Regulations at 29 CFR part 541, provides details relating to Defining and Delimiting the Exemptions for Executive, Administrative, Professional, Outside Sales and Computer Employees. The U.S. Department of Labor recently announced revisions to the federal regulations implementing this section of the Fair Labor Standards Act (FLSA). The revisions took effect on August 23, 2004. Employers are urged to re-examine and revise certain employment policies to comply with these changes to the federal wage-hour law rules.

Under the FLSA, certain jobs are exempt from the minimum wage and overtime pay requirements. The exempted jobs affect employees in executive, administrative, professional, outside sales, and certain computer related jobs. One effect of this law is that many jobs are paid on an hourly basis while the exempt jobs are paid on a salaried basis. The revised regulations updated definitions of the exempted jobs that were originally defined in 1938. Another significant change to the regulation is referred to as the Salary Basis Test.

Salary Basis Requirement

To qualify for exemption, employees generally must be paid at not less than $455 per week on a salary basis. These salary requirements do not apply to outside sales employees, teachers, and employees practicing law or medicine. Exempt computer employees may be paid at least $455 on a salary basis or on an hourly basis at a rate not less than $27.63 an hour.

Being paid on a "salary basis" means an employee regularly receives a predetermined amount of compensation each pay period on a weekly, or less frequent, basis. The predetermined amount cannot be reduced because of variations in the quality or quantity of the employee's work. Subject to exceptions listed below, an exempt employee must receive the full salary for any week in which the employee performs any work, regardless of the number of days or hours worked. Exempt employees do not need to be paid for any workweek in which they perform no work. If the employer makes deductions from an employee's predetermined salary, i.e., because of the operating requirements of the business, that employee is not paid on a "salary basis." If the employee is ready, willing, and able to work, deductions may not be made for time when work is not available.

Circumstances in Which the Employer May Make Deductions from Pay

Deductions from pay are permissible when an exempt employee: is absent from work for one or more full days for personal reasons other than sickness or disability; for absences of one or more full days due to sickness or disability if the deduction is made in accordance with a bona fide plan, policy, or practice of providing compensation for salary lost due to illness; to offset amounts employees receive as jury or witness fees, or for military pay; for penalties imposed in good faith for infractions of safety rules of major significance; or for unpaid disciplinary suspensions of one or more full days imposed in good faith for workplace conduct rule infractions. Also, an employer is not required to pay the full salary in the initial or terminal week of employment, or for weeks in which an exempt employee takes unpaid leave under the Family and Medical Leave Act.

Effect of Improper Deductions from Salary

The employer will lose the exemption if it has an "actual practice" of making improper deductions from salary. Factors to consider when determining whether an employer has an actual practice of making improper deductions include, but are not limited to: the number of improper deductions, particularly as compared to the number of employee infractions warranting deductions; the time period during which the employer made improper deductions; the number and geographic location of both the employees whose salary was improperly reduced and the managers responsible; and whether the employer has a clearly communicated policy permitting or prohibiting improper deductions. If an "actual practice" is found, the exemption is lost during the time period of the deductions for employees in the same job classification working for the same managers responsible for the improper deductions.

Isolated or inadvertent improper deductions will not result in loss of the exemption if the employer reimburses the employee for the improper deductions.

¶912.06

Safe Harbor

If an employer (1) has a clearly communicated policy prohibiting improper deductions and including a complaint mechanism, (2) reimburses employees for any improper deductions, and (3) makes a good faith commitment to comply in the future, the employer will not lose the exemption for any employees unless the employer willfully violates the policy by continuing the improper deductions after receiving employee complaints.

Fee Basis

Administrative, professional, and computer employees may be paid on a "fee basis" rather than on a salary basis. If the employee is paid an agreed sum for a single job, regardless of the time required for its completion, the employee will be considered to be paid on a "fee basis." A fee payment is generally paid for a unique job, rather than for a series of jobs repeated a number of times and for which identical payments repeatedly are made. To determine whether the fee payment meets the minimum salary level requirement, the test is to consider the time worked on the job and determine whether the payment is at a rate that would amount to at least $455 per week if the employee worked 40 hours. For example, an artist paid $250 for a picture that took 20 hours to complete meets the minimum salary requirement since the rate would yield $500 if 40 hours were worked.

(Source: Fact Sheet #17G: Salary Basis Requirement and the Part 541 Exemptions Under the Fair Labor Standards Act (FLSA))

Exemption for Executive Employees

To qualify for the executive employee exemption, all of the following tests must be met:

- The employee must be compensated on a salary basis (as defined in the regulations) at a rate not less than $455 per week;
- The employee's primary duty must be managing the enterprise, or managing a customarily recognized department or subdivision of the enterprise;
- The employee must customarily and regularly direct the work of at least two or more other full-time employees or their equivalent; and
- The employee must have the authority to hire or fire other employees, or the employee's suggestions and recommendations as to the hiring, firing, advancement, promotion, or any other change of status of other employees must be given particular weight.

Primary Duty

"Primary duty" means the principal, main, major, or most important duty that the employee performs. Determination of an employee's primary duty must be based on all the facts in a particular case, with the major emphasis on the character of the employee's job as a whole.

Management

Generally, "management" includes, but is not limited to, activities such as interviewing, selecting, and training of employees; setting and adjusting their rates of pay and hours of work; directing the work of employees; maintaining production or sales records for use in supervision or control; appraising employees' productivity and efficiency for the purpose of recommending promotions or other changes in status; handling employee complaints and grievances; disciplining employees; planning the work; determining the techniques to be used; apportioning the work among the employees; determining the type of materials, supplies, machinery, equipment or tools to be used or merchandise to be bought, stocked, and sold; controlling the flow and distribution of materials or merchandise and supplies; providing for the safety and security of the employees or the property; planning and controlling the budget; and monitoring or implementing legal compliance measures.

Department or Subdivision

The phrase "a customarily recognized department or subdivision" is intended to distinguish between a mere collection of employees assigned from time to time to a specific job or series of jobs and a unit with permanent status and function.

Customarily and Regularly

The phrase "customarily and regularly" means greater than occasional but less than constant; it includes work normally done every workweek, but does not include isolated or one-time tasks.

Two or More

The phrase "two or more other employees" means two full-time employees or their equivalent. For example, one full-time and two half-time employees are equivalent to two full-time employees. The supervision can be distributed among two, three, or more employees, but each such employee must customarily and regularly direct the work of two or more other full-time employees or the equivalent. For example, a department with five full-time nonexempt workers may have up to two exempt supervisors if each supervisor directs the work of two of those workers.

Particular Weight

Factors to be considered in determining whether an employee's recommendations as to hiring, firing, advancement, promotion, or any other change of status are given "particular weight" include, but are not limited to, whether it is part of the employee's job duties to make such recommendations, and the frequency with which such recommendations are made, requested, and relied upon. Generally, an executive's recommendations must pertain to employees whom the executive customarily and regularly directs. It does not include occasional suggestions. An employee's recommendations may still be deemed to have "particular weight" even if a higher level manager's recommendation has more importance and even if the employee does not have authority to make the ultimate decision as to the employee's change in status.

Exemption of Business Owners

Under a special rule for business owners, an employee who owns at least a bona fide 20-percent equity interest in the enterprise in which employed, regardless of the type of business organization (e.g., corporation, partnership, or other), and who is actively engaged in its management, is considered a bona fide exempt executive.

Highly Compensated Employees

Highly compensated employees performing office or non-manual work and paid total annual compensation of $100,000 or more (which must include at least $455 per week paid on a salary or fee basis) are exempt from the FLSA if they customarily and

¶912.06

regularly perform at least one of the duties of an exempt executive, administrative, or professional employee identified in the standard tests for exemption.

(Source: Fact Sheet #17B: Exemption for Executive Employees Under the Fair Labor Standards Act (FLSA))

Exemption for Administrative Employees

To qualify for the administrative employee exemption, all of the following tests must be met:

- The employee must be compensated on a salary or fee basis (as defined in the regulations) at a rate not less than $455 per week;
- The employee's primary duty must be the performance of office or non-manual work directly related to the management or general business operations of the employer or the employer's customers; and
- The employee's primary duty includes the exercise of discretion and independent judgment with respect to matters of significance.

Primary Duty

"Primary duty" means the principal, main, major, or most important duty that the employee performs. Determination of an employee's primary duty must be based on all the facts in a particular case, with the major emphasis on the character of the employee's job as a whole.

Directly Related to Management or General Business Operations

To meet the "directly related to management or general business operations" requirement, an employee must perform work directly related to assisting with the running or servicing of the business, as distinguished, for example from working on a manufacturing production line or selling a product in a retail or service establishment. Work "directly related to management or general business operations" includes, but is not limited to, work in functional areas such as tax; finance; accounting; budgeting; auditing; insurance; quality control; purchasing; procurement; advertising; marketing; research; safety and health; personnel management; human resources; employee benefits; labor relations; public relations; government relations; computer network, Internet, and database administration; legal and regulatory compliance; and similar activities.

Employer's Customers

An employee may qualify for the administrative exemption if the employee's primary duty is the performance of work directly related to the management or general business operations of the employer's customers. Thus, employees acting as advisors or consultants to their employer's clients or customers—as tax experts or financial consultants, for example—may be exempt.

Discretion and Independent Judgment

In general, the exercise of discretion and independent judgment involves the comparison and the evaluation of possible courses of conduct and acting or making a decision after the various possibilities have been considered. The term must be applied in the light of all the facts involved in the employee's particular employment situation, and implies that the employee has authority to make an independent choice, free from immediate direction or supervision. Factors to consider include, but are not limited to:

whether the employee has authority to formulate, affect, interpret, or implement management policies or operating practices; whether the employee carries out major assignments in conducting the operations of the business; whether the employee performs work that affects business operations to a substantial degree; whether the employee has authority to commit the employer in matters that have significant financial impact; whether the employee has authority to waive or deviate from established policies and procedures without prior approval, and other factors set forth in the regulation. The fact that an employee's decisions are revised or reversed after review does not mean that the employee is not exercising discretion and independent judgment. The exercise of discretion and independent judgment must be more than the use of skill in applying well-established techniques, procedures, or specific standards described in manuals or other sources.

Matters of Significance

The term "matters of significance" refers to the level of importance or consequence of the work performed. An employee does not exercise discretion and independent judgment with respect to matters of significance merely because the employer will experience financial losses if the employee fails to perform the job properly. Similarly, an employee who operates very expensive equipment does not exercise discretion and independent judgment with respect to matters of significance merely because improper performance of the employee's duties may cause serious financial loss to the employer.

Educational Establishments and Administrative Functions

The administrative exemption is also available to employees compensated on a salary or fee basis at a rate not less than $455 a week and whose primary duty is performing administrative functions directly related to academic instruction or training in an educational establishment. Academic administrative functions include operations directly in the field of education, and do not include jobs relating to areas outside the educational field. Employees engaged in academic administrative functions include: the superintendent or other head of an elementary or secondary school system, and any assistants responsible for administration of such matters as curriculum, quality and methods of instructing, measuring and testing the learning potential and achievement of students, establishing and maintaining academic and grading standards, and other aspects of the teaching program; the principal and any vice-principals responsible for the operation of an elementary or secondary school; department heads in institutions of higher education responsible for the various subject matter departments; academic counselors and other employees with similar responsibilities. Having a primary duty of performing administrative functions directly related to academic instruction or training in an educational establishment includes, by its very nature, exercising discretion and independent judgment with respect to matters of significance.

Highly Compensated Employees

Highly compensated employees performing office or non-manual work and paid total annual compensation of $100,000 or more (which must include at least $455 per week paid on a salary or fee basis) are exempt from the FLSA if they customarily and regularly perform at least one of the duties of an exempt executive, administrative, or professional employee identified in the standard tests for exemption.

(Source: Fact Sheet #17C: Exemption for Administrative Employees Under the Fair Labor Standards Act (FLSA))

Exemption for Professional Employees

The specific requirements for exemption as a bona fide professional employee are summarized below. There are two general types of exempt professional employees: learned professionals and creative professionals.

Learned Professional Exemption

To qualify for the learned professional employee exemption, all of the following tests must be met:

- The employee must be compensated on a salary or fee basis (as defined in the regulations) at a rate not less than $455 per week;
- The employee's primary duty must be the performance of work requiring advanced knowledge, defined as work which is predominantly intellectual in character and which includes work requiring the consistent exercise of discretion and judgment;
- The advanced knowledge must be in a field of science or learning; and
- The advanced knowledge must be customarily acquired by a prolonged course of specialized intellectual instruction.

Primary Duty

"Primary duty" means the principal, main, major, or most important duty that the employee performs. Determination of an employee's primary duty must be based on all the facts in a particular case, with the major emphasis on the character of the employee's job as a whole.

Work Requiring Advanced Knowledge

"Work requiring advanced knowledge" means work which is predominantly intellectual in character, and which includes work requiring the consistent exercise of discretion and judgment. Professional work is therefore distinguished from work involving routine mental, manual, mechanical, or physical work. A professional employee generally uses the advanced knowledge to analyze, interpret, or make deductions from varying facts or circumstances. Advanced knowledge cannot be attained at the high school level.

Field of Science or Learning

Fields of science or learning include law, medicine, theology, accounting, actuarial computation, engineering, architecture, teaching, various types of physical, chemical and biological sciences, pharmacy and other occupations that have a recognized professional status and are distinguishable from the mechanical arts or skilled trades where the knowledge could be of a fairly advanced type, but is not in a field of science or learning.

Customarily Acquired by a Prolonged Course of Specialized Intellectual Instruction

The learned professional exemption is restricted to professions where specialized academic training is a standard prerequisite for entrance into the profession. The best evidence of meeting this requirement is having the appropriate academic degree. However, the word "customarily" means the exemption may be available to employees in such professions who have substantially the same knowledge level and perform substantially the same work as the degreed employees, but who attained the advanced knowledge through a combination of work experience and intellectual instruction. This exemption does not apply to occupations in which most employees acquire their skill by experience rather than by advanced specialized intellectual instruction.

Creative Professional Exemption

To qualify for the creative professional employee exemption, all of the following tests must be met:

- The employee must be compensated on a salary or fee basis (as defined in the regulations) at a rate not less than $455 per week;
- The employee's primary duty must be the performance of work requiring invention, imagination, originality, or talent in a recognized field of artistic or creative endeavor.

Invention, Imagination, Originality, or Talent

This requirement distinguishes the creative professions from work that primarily depends on intelligence, diligence, and accuracy. Exemption as a creative professional depends on the extent of the invention, imagination, originality, or talent exercised by the employee. Whether the exemption applies, therefore, must be determined on a case-by-case basis. The requirements are generally met by actors, musicians, composers, soloists, certain painters, writers, cartoonists, essayists, novelists, and others as set forth in the regulations. Journalists may satisfy the duties requirements for the creative professional exemption if their primary duty is work requiring invention, imagination, originality, or talent. Journalists are not exempt creative professionals if they only collect, organize and record information that is routine or already public, or if they do not contribute a unique interpretation or analysis to a news product.

Recognized Field of Artistic or Creative Endeavor

This includes such fields as, for example, music, writing, acting, and the graphic arts.

Teachers

Teachers are exempt if their primary duty is teaching, tutoring, instructing, or lecturing in the activity of imparting knowledge, and if they are employed and engaged in this activity as a teacher in an educational establishment. Exempt teachers include, but are not limited to, regular academic teachers, kindergarten or nursery school teachers, teachers of gifted or disabled children, teachers of skilled and semi-skilled trades and occupations, teachers engaged in automobile driving instruction, aircraft flight instructors, home economics teachers, and vocal or instrument music teachers. The salary and salary basis requirements do not apply to bona fide teachers. Having a primary duty of teaching, tutoring, instructing, or lecturing in the activity of imparting knowledge includes, by its very nature, exercising discretion and judgment.

Practice of Law or Medicine

An employee holding a valid license or certificate permitting the practice of law or medicine is exempt if the employee is actually engaged in such a practice. An employee who holds the requisite academic degree for the general practice of medicine is also exempt if he or she is engaged in an internship or resident program for the profession. The salary and salary basis requirements do not apply to bona fide practitioners of law or medicine.

Highly Compensated Employees

Highly compensated employees performing office or non-manual work and paid total annual compensation of $100,000 or more (which must include at least $455 per week paid on a salary or fee basis) are exempt from the FLSA if they customarily and regularly perform at least one of the duties of an exempt executive, administrative, or professional employee identified in the standard tests for exemption.

(Source: Fact Sheet #17D: Exemption for Professional Employees Under the Fair Labor Standards Act (FLSA))

Exemption for Employees in Computer-Related Occupations

Job titles do not determine exempt status. In order for this exemption to apply, an employee's specific job duties and compensation must meet all the requirements of the Department's regulations. The specific requirements for the computer employee exemption are summarized below.

Computer Employee Exemption

To qualify for the computer employee exemption, the following tests must be met:

- The employee must be compensated either on a salary or fee basis at a rate not less than $455 per week or, if compensated on an hourly basis, at a rate not less than $27.63 an hour;
- The employee must be employed as a computer systems analyst, computer programmer, software engineer, or other similarly skilled worker in the computer field performing the duties described below;
- The employee's primary duty must consist of:
  1) The application of systems analysis techniques and procedures, including consulting with users, to determine hardware, software, or system functional specifications;
  2) The design, development, documentation, analysis, creation, testing, or modification of computer systems or programs, including prototypes, based on and related to user or system design specifications;
  3) The design, documentation, testing, creation, or modification of computer programs related to machine operating systems; or
  4) A combination of the aforementioned duties, the performance of which requires the same level of skills.

The computer employee exemption does not include employees engaged in the manufacture or repair of computer hardware and related equipment. Employees whose work is highly dependent upon, or facilitated by, the use of computers and computer software programs (e.g., engineers, drafters, and others skilled in computer-aided design software), but who are not primarily engaged in computer systems analysis and programming or other similarly skilled computer-related occupations identified in the primary duties test described above, are also not exempt under the computer employee exemption.

Primary Duty

"Primary duty" means the principal, main, major, or most important duty that the employee performs. Determination of an employee's primary duty must be based on all the facts in a particular case, with the major emphasis on the character of the employee's job as a whole.

(Source: Fact Sheet #17E: Exemption for Employees in Computer-Related Occupations Under the Fair Labor Standards Act (FLSA))

Exemption for Outside Sales Employees

To qualify for the outside sales employee exemption, all of the following tests must be met:

- The employee's primary duty must be making sales (as defined in the FLSA), or obtaining orders or contracts for services or for the use of facilities for which a consideration will be paid by the client or customer; and

- The employee must be customarily and regularly engaged away from the employer's place or places of business.

- The salary requirements of the regulation do not apply to the outside sales exemption. An employee who does not satisfy the requirements of the outside sales exemption may still qualify as an exempt employee under one of the other exemptions allowed by Section 13(a)(1) of the FLSA and the Part 541 regulations if all the criteria for the exemption is met.

Primary Duty

"Primary duty" means the principal, main, major, or most important duty that the employee performs. Determination of an employee's primary duty must be based on all the facts in a particular case, with the major emphasis on the character of the employee's job as a whole.

Making Sales

"Sales" includes any sale, exchange, contract to sell, consignment for sales, shipment for sale, or other disposition. It includes the transfer of title to tangible property, and in certain cases, of tangible and valuable evidences of intangible property.

Obtaining Orders or Contracts for Services or for the Use of Facilities

Obtaining orders for "the use of facilities" includes the selling of time on radio or television, the solicitation of advertising for newspapers and other periodicals, and the solicitation of freight for railroads and other transportation agencies. The word "services" extends the exemption to employees who sell or take orders for a service, which may be performed for the customer by someone other than the person taking the order.

Customarily and Regularly

The phrase "customarily and regularly" means greater than occasional but less than constant; it includes work normally done every workweek, but does not include isolated or one-time tasks.

Away from Employer's Place of Business

An outside sales employee makes sales at the customer's place of business, or, if selling door-to-door, at the customer's home. Outside sales does not include sales made by mail, telephone, or the Internet unless such contact is used merely as an adjunct to personal calls. Any fixed site, whether home or office, used by a salesperson as a headquarters or for telephonic solicitation of sales is considered one of the employer's

¶912.06

places of business, even though the employer is not in any formal sense the owner or tenant of the property.

Promotion Work

Promotion work may or may not be exempt outside sales work, depending upon the circumstances under which it is performed. Promotional work that is actually performed incidental to and in conjunction with an employee's own outside sales or solicitations is exempt work. However, promotion work that is incidental to sales made, or to be made, by someone else is not exempt outside sales work.

Drivers Who Sell

Drivers who deliver products and also sell such products may qualify as exempt outside sales employees only if the employee has a primary duty of making sales. Several factors should be considered in determining whether a driver has a primary duty of making sales, including a comparison of the driver's duties with those of other employees engaged as drivers and as salespersons, the presence or absence of customary or contractual arrangements concerning amounts of products to be delivered, whether or not the driver has a selling or solicitor's license when required by law, the description of the employee's occupation in collective bargaining agreements, and other factors set forth in the regulation.

(Source: Fact Sheet #17F: Exemption for Outside Sales Employees Under the Fair Labor Standards Act (FLSA))

.07 Minimum Wage

The FLSA minimum wage increased to $5.15 an hour on September 1, 1997.

Youth Subminimum Wage—Opportunity Wage

A subminimum wage—$4.25 an hour—is established for employees under 20 years of age during their first 90 consecutive calendar days of employment with an employer. Employers are prohibited from displacing employees in order to hire youth at the subminimum wage. Also prohibited are partial displacements such as reducing employees' hours, wages, or employment benefits.

Tip Credit

An employer may credit a certain amount of the tips received by tipped employees (e.g., waiters and waitresses) against the employer's minimum wage obligation when certain conditions are met. The law now sets the employer's cash wage obligation at not less than $2.13 an hour. However, if an employee's tips combined with the employer's cash wage of $2.13 an hour do not equal the minimum hourly wage, the employer must make up the difference.

Computer Exemption

The exemption from overtime pay for certain computer professionals now exempts these workers if they are paid at least $27.63 an hour. This replaces the former requirement that they be paid an hourly rate of at least $6\frac{1}{2}$ times the minimum wage.

Travel Time in Employer Vehicles

Time spent in home-to-work travel by an employee in an employee-provided vehicle, or in activities performed by an employee which are incidental to the use of the vehicle for commuting, is not "hours worked" and, therefore, does not have to be paid. This provision applies only if the travel is within the normal commuting area for the employer's business, and the use of the vehicle is subject to an agreement between the employer and the employee or the employee's representative.

.08 Minimum Wage Value Chart

Year	Value of the Minimum Wage	
	Nominal Dollars	2000 Dollars
1938	$0.25	$3.05
1939	0.3	3.72
1940	0.3	3.69
1941	0.3	3.51
1942	0.3	3.17
1943	0.3	2.99
1944	0.3	2.94
1945	0.4	3.83
1946	0.4	3.53
1947	0.4	3.09
1948	0.4	2.86
1949	0.4	2.89
1950	0.75	5.36
1951	0.75	4.97
1952	0.75	4.87
1953	0.75	4.84
1954	0.75	4.80
1955	0.75	4.82
1956	1	6.33
1957	1	6.13
1958	1	5.96
1959	1	5.92
1960	1	5.82
1961	1.15	6.62
1962	1.15	6.56
1963	1.25	7.03
1964	1.25	6.94
1965	1.25	6.83
1966	1.25	6.64
1967	1.4	7.22
1968	1.6	7.92
1969	1.6	7.51
1970	1.6	7.10
1971	1.6	6.80
1972	1.6	6.59
1973	1.6	6.21
1974	2	6.99
1975	2.1	6.72
1976	2.3	6.96
1977	2.3	6.54

¶912.08

Year	Nominal Dollars	2000 Dollars
1978	2.65	7.00
1979	2.9	6.88
1980	3.1	6.48
1981	3.35	6.35
1982	3.35	5.98
1983	3.35	5.79
1984	3.35	5.55
1985	3.35	5.36
1986	3.35	5.26
1987	3.35	5.08
1988	3.35	4.88
1989	3.35	4.65
1990	3.8	5.01
1991	4.25	5.37
1992	4.25	5.22
1993	4.25	5.06
1994	4.25	4.94
1995	4.25	4.80
1996	4.75	5.21
1997	5.15	5.53
1998	5.15	5.44
1999	5.15	5.32
2000	5.15	5.15

Source: Bureau of Labor Statistics.

.09 Investigations and Records

The Administrator (of the Wage and Hour Division of the Department of Labor) or his designated representatives may investigate and gather data regarding the wages, hours, and other conditions and practices of employment in any industry subject to this Act, and may enter and inspect such places and such records (and make such transcriptions thereof), question such employees, and investigate such facts, conditions, practices, or matters as he may deem necessary or appropriate to determine whether any person has violated any provision of this Act. (29 USC § 211(a))

Every employer subject to any provision of this Act or of any order issued under this Act shall make, keep and preserve such records of the persons employed by him and of the wages, hours and other conditions and practices of employment maintained by him. The employer shall preserve such records for such periods of time, and shall make such reports therefrom to the Secretary as he shall prescribe by regulation or order as necessary or appropriate for the enforcement of the provisions of this Act or the regulations or orders thereunder. (29 USC § 211(c))

Form of Records

No particular order or form of records is prescribed by the regulations. Every employer subject to any provisions of the Fair Labor Standards Act of 1938 is required to maintain records containing the information and data required by the specific Section of this part. The records may be maintained and preserved on microfilm or other basic source document of an automatic word or data processing memory provided that adequate projection or viewing equipment is available, that the reproductions are clear and identifiable by date or pay period and that extensions or transcriptions of the information required by this part are made available upon request. (29 CFR § 516.1)

Items Required

Every employer shall maintain and preserve payroll or other records containing the following information and data with respect to each employee:

- Name in full, as used for Social Security record keeping purposes, and on the same record, the employee's identifying symbol or number if such is used in place of name on any time, work or payroll records.
- Home address, including zip code.
- Date of birth, if under 19.
- Sex and occupation in which employed (sex may be indicated by use of the prefixes Mr., Mrs., Miss or Ms.). Employee's sex identification is related to the equal pay provisions of the Act which are administered by the Equal Employment Opportunity Commission.
- Time of day and day of week on which the employee's workweek begins (or for employees employed under Sec. 7(k) of the Act, the starting time and length of each employee's work period). If the employee is part of a workforce or employed in or by an establishment all of whose workers have a workweek beginning at the same time on the same day, a single notation of the time of the day and beginning day of the workweek for the whole workforce or establishment will suffice.
- Regular hourly rate of pay for any workweek in which overtime compensation is due.
  - Explain basis of pay by indicating the monetary amount paid on a per hour, per day, per week, per piece, commission on sales or other basis.
  - The amount and nature of each payment which is excluded from the "regular rate" (these records may be in the form of vouchers or other payment data).
- Hours worked each workday and total hours worked each workweek. A "workday" is any fixed period of 24 consecutive hours and a "workweek" is any fixed and regularly recurring period of seven consecutive workdays.
- Total daily or weekly straight-time earnings or wages due for hours worked during the workday or workweek, exclusive of premium overtime compensation.
- Total premium pay for overtime hours.
- Total additions to or deductions from wages paid each pay period including employee purchase orders or wage assignments. Also, individual employee records, the dates, amounts and nature of the items which make up the total additions and deductions.
- Total wages paid each pay period.
- Date of payment and the pay period covered by payment. (29 CFR § 516.2(a))

¶912.09

Records of Retroactive Payment of Wages

Every employer who makes retroactive payment of wages or compensation under the supervision of the Administrator of the Wage and Hour Division shall:

- Record and preserve, as an entry on the pay records, the amount of such payment to each employee, the period covered by such payment, and the date of payment.
- Prepare a report of each such payment on a receipt form provided by or authorized by the Wage and Hour Division, and preserve a copy as part of the records, deliver a copy to the employee and file the original, as evidence of payment by the employer and receipt by the employee, with the Administrator or an authorized representative, within 10 days after payment is made.

Employees Working on Fixed Schedules

With respect to employees working on fixed schedules, an employer may maintain records showing instead of the hours worked each day and each workweek the schedule of daily and weekly hours the employee normally works. Also,

- In weeks in which an employee adheres to this schedule, indicate by check mark, statement or other method that such hours were in fact actually worked by him, and
- In weeks in which more or less than the scheduled hours are worked, show the number of hours worked each day and each week. (29 CFR § 516.2(b))

Bona Fide Executive, Administrative, and Professional Employee (Including academic administrative personnel and teachers in elementary or secondary schools and outside sales employees)

With respect to each employee in a bona fide executive, administrative or professional capacity (including employees employed in the capacity of academic administrative personnel or teachers in elementary or secondary schools), or in outside sales, employers shall maintain and preserve records containing all the information and data required, except paragraphs (a)(6) through (10), and, in addition, the basis on which wages are paid in sufficient detail to permit calculation for each pay period of the employee's total remuneration for employment including fringe benefits and prerequisites. (This may be shown as the dollar amount of earnings per month, per week, per month plus commissions, etc., with appropriate addenda such as "plus hospitalization and insurance plan A," "benefits package B," "two weeks paid vacation," etc.) (29 CFR § 516.3)

Records to be Preserved for Three Years

Each employer shall preserve for at least three years:

- *Payroll records.* From the last date of entry, all payroll or other records containing the employee information and data required under any of the applicable sections of this part.
- *Certificates, agreements, plans, notices, etc.* From their last effective date, all written:
  - Collective bargaining agreements relied upon for the exclusion of certain costs.

— Collective bargaining agreements and any amendments or additions thereto.

— Plans, trusts, employment contracts, and collective bargaining agreements.

— Individual contracts or collective bargaining agreements. Where such contracts or agreements are not in writing, a written memorandum summarizing the terms of each such contract or agreement.

— Written agreements or memoranda summarizing the terms of oral agreements or understandings.

— Certificates and notices listed or named in any applicable section of this part.

- *Sales and purchase records.* A record of total dollar volume of sales or business and total volume of goods purchased or received during such periods (weekly, monthly, quarterly, etc.), in such form as the employer maintains records in the ordinary course of business. (29 CFR § 516.5)

Records to be Preserved for Two Years

Basic Employment and Earning Records

From the date of last entry, all basic time and earning cards or sheets on which are entered the daily starting and stopping time of individual employees, or of separate work forces, or the amounts of work accomplished by individual employees on a daily, weekly, or pay period basis (i.e., units produced) when those amounts determine in whole or in part the pay period earnings or wages of those employees.

Wage Rate Tables

From their last effective date, all tables or schedules of the employer which provide the piece rates or other rates used in computing straight-time earnings, wages or salary, or overtime pay computation.

Records of Additions to or Deductions from Wages

- Those records relating to individual employees referred to in § 516.2
- All records used by the employer in determining the original, operating and maintenance costs, and depreciation and interest charges, if such costs and charges are involved in the additions to or deductions from wages paid. (29 CFR § 516.6)

Place for Keeping Records and Their Availability for Inspection

Each employer shall keep the required records safe and accessible at the place or places of employment, or at one or more established central record keeping offices where such records are customarily maintained. Where the records are maintained at a central record keeping office, other than in the place or places of employment, such records shall be made available within 72 hours following notice from the Administrator or a duly authorized and designated representative. (29 CFR § 516.7)

Petitions for Exceptions

Submission of Petitions for Relief

Any employer or group of employers who, due to peculiar conditions under which they must operate, desire authority to maintain records in a manner other than required in this part, or to be relieved of preserving certain records for the period specified in this part, may submit a written petition to the Administrator requesting such authority, setting forth the reason therefore. (29 CFR § 516.9)

Exemptions

The provisions regarding minimum wages shall not apply with respect to:

- Any employee employed in a bona fide executive, administrative or professional capacity or in the capacity of outside salesman, except that an employee of a retail or service establishment shall not be excluded from the definition of an employee employed in a bona fide executive or administrative capacity because of the number of hours in his workweek which he devotes to activities not directly or closely related to the performance of executive or administrative activity, if less than 40 per centum of his hours worked in the workweek are devoted to such activities; or

- Any employee employed by any retail or service establishment, except an establishment or employee engaged in laundering, cleaning, or repairing clothing or fabrics or an establishment engaged in the operation of a hospital, institution, or school described in Section 3(s)(5), if more than 50 percent of such establishment's annual dollar volume of sales or goods or services is made within the state in which the establishment is located.

- Any employee employed by an establishment which is an amusement or recreational establishment, organized camp, or religious or nonprofit educational conference center, if it does not operate for more than seven months in any calendar year, or during the preceding calendar year, its average receipts for any six months of such year were not more than 33 ⅓ per centum of its average receipts for the other six months of such year.

- Any employee employed by an establishment which qualifies as an exempt retail establishment and is recognized as a retail establishment in the particular industry notwithstanding that such establishment makes or processes at the retail establishment the goods that it sells: provided, that more than 85 per centum of such establishment's annual dollar volume of sales of goods so made or processed is made within the state in which the establishment is located; or

- Any employee employed in the catching, taking, propagating, harvesting, cultivating, or farming of any kind of fish, or in conjunction with, such fishing operations.

- Any employee employed in agriculture if such employee is employed by an employer who did not, during any calendar quarter during the preceding calendar year, use more than five hundred man-days of agricultural labor if such employee is the parent, spouse, child, or other member of his employer's immediate family, if such employee is employed as a hand harvest laborer and is paid on a piece rate basis in an operation which has been, and is customarily and generally recognized as having been, paid on a piece rate basis in the region of employment, if such employee commutes daily from his permanent residence to the farm on which he is so employed, and has been employed in agriculture less than 13 weeks during the preceding calendar year; if such employee is 16 years of age or under and is employed as a hand harvest laborer, is paid on a piece rate basis in an operation which has been, and is customarily and generally recognized as having been, paid on a piece rate basis in the region of employment, is employed on the same farm as his parent or person standing in the place of his parent, and is paid at the same piece rate as employees over age 16 are paid on the same farm; or if such employee is principally engaged in the range production of livestock; or

- Any employee employed in connection with the publication of any weekly, semiweekly, or daily newspaper with a circulation of less than four thousand the major part of which circulation is within the county where published or counties contiguous thereto; or (Repealed) (relating to motion picture theater employees)

- Any switchboard operator employed by an independently owned public telephone company which has not more than seven hundred and fifty stations; or (Repealed) (relating to telegraph agency employees)

- Any employee employed as a seaman on a vessel other than an American vessel; or (Repealed) (relating to small logging crews) (Repealed) (relating to employees employed in growing and harvesting of shade-grown tobacco)

- Any employee on a casual basis in domestic service employment to provide baby-sitting services or any employee employed in domestic service employment to provide companionship services for individuals who (because of age or infirmity) are unable to care for themselves (as such terms are defined and delimited by regulations of the Secretary).

.11 Penalties

Any person who willfully violates any of the provisions shall upon conviction thereof be subject to a fine of not more than $10,000, or to imprisonment for not more than six months, or both. No person shall be imprisoned under this subsection, except for an offense committed after the conviction of such person for a prior offense under this subsection. Any employer who violates the provisions shall be liable to the employee or employees affected in the amount of their unpaid minimum wages, or their unpaid overtime compensation, as the case may be, and in an additional equal amount as liquidated damages. Any employer who violates the provisions shall be liable for such legal or equitable relief as may be appropriate to effectuate the purposes as enacted without limitation employment, reinstatement, promotion, and the payment of wages lost and an additional equal amount as liquidated damages. The Secretary is authorized to supervise the payment of the unpaid minimum wages or the unpaid overtime compensation owing to any employee, and the agreement of any employee to accept such payment shall upon payment in full constitute a waiver by such employee, of any right he may have under subSec. (b). (29 USC § 216)

Prohibited Acts

It shall be unlawful for any person to discharge or in any other manner discriminate against any employee because such employee has filed any complaint or instituted or caused to be instituted any proceeding under or related to this Act. (29 USC § 215(a)(3))

In FY 2002, the U.S. Department of Labor collected $175 million in back wages for 263,593 workers, the largest amount collected by the Department in 10 years. The Labor Department reports that its efforts at strong enforcement and compliance assistance programs are working to restore more wages and to protect the rights of workers.

.13 Fair Labor Standards Act Summary Charts

Exemptions from Both Minimum Wage and Overtime Pay

- Casual babysitters and persons employed as companions to the elderly or infirm.
- Seamen employed on foreign vessels.
- Employees engaged in fishing operations.
- Farm workers employed by anyone who used no more than 500 "man-days" of farm labor in any calendar quarter of the preceding calendar year.
- Switchboard operators of small telephone companies.
- Employees of certain individually owned and operated small retail or service establishments not part of a covered enterprise.
- Employees of certain seasonal amusement or recreational establishments.
- Outside sales persons (as defined in Department of Labor Regulations).
- Executive, administrative and professional employees.
- Employees of certain small newspapers.
- Teachers and academic administrative personnel in elementary and secondary schools.

Exemptions from Overtime Pay Provisions Only

- Transportation
  - Employees of railroads and air carriers
  - Taxi drivers
  - Certain employees of motor carriers
  - Seamen on American vessels
  - Local delivery employees paid on approved trip rate plans
  - Certain retail sellers
  - Certain highly paid commissioned employees of retail or service establishments
  - Auto drivers
  - Truck drivers
  - Trailer drivers
  - Farm implement operators
  - Boat operators
  - Aircraft salesworkers
  - Parts-clerks and mechanics servicing autos, trucks, or farm implements
  - Those employed by nonmanufacturing establishments primarily engaged in selling these items to ultimate purchasers
- Domestic service workers residing in the employers' residences
- Communications
  - Announcers

— News editors

— Chief engineers of certain nonmetropolitan broadcasting stations

- Employees of motion picture theaters
- Farmworkers

Nonagricultural Child Labor Provisions

- Fourteen is the minimum age for most nonfarm work.
- Youths 14 and 15 years old enrolled in an approved Work Experience and Career Exploration Program (WECEP) may be employed for up to 23 hours during the school week and three hours on school days (including during school hours).
- Youths 14 and 15 years old may work outside school hours in various non-manufacturing, non-mining, nonhazardous jobs under the following conditions:
  — No more than three hours in a school day, 18 hours in a school week, eight hours in a nonschool day, or 40 hours in a nonschool week.
  — Work may not begin before 7 a.m., nor end after 7 p.m., except from June 1st through Labor Day, when evening hours are extended to 9 p.m.
- Youths 16 and 17 years old may perform any nonhazardous job, for unlimited hours.
- Youths 18 years or older may perform any job, whether hazardous or not, for unlimited hours.
- At any age, youths may:
  — Deliver newspapers
  — Perform in radio, television, movie, or theatrical productions
  — Work for parents in their solely owned nonfarm business (except in manufacturing or on hazardous jobs)
  — Gather evergreens and make evergreen wreaths

Child Farm Labor Provisions

- Youths under 12 years old may perform jobs on farms owned or operated by parents or outside of school hours in nonhazardous jobs on farms not covered by minimum wage requirements with parents' written consent.
- Youths 12 and 13 years old may work outside of school hours in nonhazardous jobs, either with parents' written consent or on the same farm as the parents.
- Youths 14 and 15 years old may perform any nonhazardous farm job outside of school hours.
- Youths 16 years and older may perform any job, whether hazardous or not, for unlimited hours.
- Minors of any age may be employed by their parents at any time in any occupation on a farm owned or operated by their parents.

Violations Summary

- Violators of the child labor provisions are subject to a civil money penalty of up to $1,000 for each violation.

¶912.13

- Willful violations may be prosecuted criminally and the violator fined up to $10,000.
- It is a violation of FLSA to fire or in any other manner discriminate against an employee:
  — For filing a complaint
  — For participating in a legal proceeding under FLSA
- A second conviction may result in imprisonment.

Recovery of Back Wages

- An employee may file a private suit for back pay and an equal amount as liquidated damages, plus attorney's fees and court costs.
- An employee may not bring suit if he or she has been paid back wages under the supervision of the Wage-Hour Division of the Labor Department or if the Secretary of Labor has already filed suit to recover the wages.
- The Secretary of Labor may bring suit for back wages and an equal amount as liquidated damages.
- The Wage-Hour Division of the Labor Department may supervise payment of back wages.
- The Secretary of Labor may obtain an injunction to restrain any person from violating FLSA, including the unlawful withholding of proper minimum wage and overtime pay.
- A two-year statute of limitations applies to the recovery of back pay, except in the case of willful violation, in which case a three-year statute applies.

Records Required of Covered Employees of FLSA

- Date of payment and pay period covered.
- Total wages paid each pay period.
- Personal information, including employee's name, home address, occupation, sex and birth date (if under 19 years of age).
- Hour and day when workweek begins.
- Total hours worked each workday and each workweek.
- Total daily or weekly straight-time earnings.
- Regular hourly pay rate for any week when overtime is worked.
- Total overtime pay for the workweek.
- Deductions from or additions to wages.

.14 Computing Overtime Pay

Overtime must be paid at a rate of at least one and one-half times the employee's regular rate of pay for each hour worked in a workweek in excess of the maximum allowable in a given type of employment. Generally, the regular rate includes all payments made by the employer to or on behalf of the employee (excluding certain statutory exceptions). The following examples are based on a maximum 40-hour workweek.

Hourly rate (regular pay rate for an employee paid by the hour). If more than 40 hours are worked, at least one and one-half times the regular rate for each hour over 40 is due.

¶912.14

> *Example:* An employee paid $4.80 an hour works 44 hours in a workweek. The employee is entitled to at least one and one-half times $4.80, or $7.20, for each hour over 40. Pay for the week would be $192.00 for the first 40 hours, plus $28.80 for the four hours of overtime, which is a total of $220.80.

Piece rate. The regular rate of pay for an employee paid on a piecework basis is obtained by dividing the total weekly earnings by the total number of hours worked in the same week. The employee is entitled to an additional one-half times this regular rate for each hour over 40, plus the full piecework earnings.

> *Example:* An employee paid on a piecework basis works 45 hours in a week and earns $207. The regular rate of pay for that week is $207 divided by 45, or $4.60 an hour. In addition to the straight-time pay, the employee is entitled to $2.30 (half the regular rate) for each hour over 40.

Another way to compensate pieceworkers for overtime, if agreed to before the work is performed, is to pay one and one-half times the piece rate for each piece during the overtime hours.

The piece rate must be the one actually paid during non-overtime hours and must be enough to yield at least the minimum wage per hour.

Salary. The regular rate for an employee paid a salary for a regular or specified number of hour per week is obtained by dividing the salary by the number of hours for which the salary is intended to compensate.

If, under the employment agreement, a salary sufficient to meet the minimum wage requirement in every workweek is paid as straight time for whatever number of hours are worked in a workweek, the regular rate is obtained by dividing the salary by the number of hours worked each week.

> *Example:* Suppose an employee's hours of work vary each week and the agreement with the employer is that the employee will be paid $300 a week for whatever number of hours of work are required. Under this agreement, the regular rate will vary in overtime weeks. If the employee works 50 hours, the regular rate is $6 ($300 divided by 50 hours). In addition to the salary, half the regular rate, or $3 is due for each of the 10 overtime hours, for a total of $330 for the week. If the employee works 60 hours, the regular rate will be $5 ($300 divided by 60). In that case, an additional $2.50 is due for each of the 20 overtime hours, for a total of $350 for the week.

In no case may the regular rate be less than the minimum wage required by FLSA.

If a salary is paid on other than a weekly basis, the weekly pay must be determined in order to compute the regular rate and overtime. If the salary is for a half month, it must be multiplied by 24 and the product divided by 52 weeks to get the weekly equivalent. A monthly salary should be multiplied by 12 and the product divided by 52.

Hours Worked

During 2005, the U.S. Supreme Court rendered a decision relating to working time. The high court ruled that the workday includes the time employees spend walking from changing areas where protective equipment is donned to the production area, and the time walking back. Previously, the employer's practice had been to provide a limited pay

¶912.14

for workers to change into safety gear needed for their job, but the time spent walking through the plant to the work station was unpaid.

In writing the opinion for the Court, the Justices reported that they relied significantly on the interpretive regulations issued by the Labor Department. The government's interpretive bulletin Part 785, Hours Worked Under the Fair Labor Standards Act, clarifies what is compensable time for which employees should be paid, and what is non-compensable time for which employees need not be paid.

The regulations state that the employer must provide compensation to employees who are suffered or permitted to work. This means that an employee who performs work for the employer must receive pay. Listed below are common examples of work related activities that are considered working time for which employees should be compensated:

- Principle work activities
- Work performed on the job site or away from the job site
- Time spent on duty, working or not, where the employee is unable to use the time for his own purposes
- Stand-by time during brief shutdowns
- Rest periods of 20 minutes or less
- Show up time of 10 or 15 minutes
- On-call time where the employee is require to remain on the premises or liberty is restricted
- Training in regular duties or training to increase efficiency
- Participation in training programs required by the employer
- Travelling from one work site to another during work hours
- Make ready or preparatory work relating to principal activities
- Participation in fire or disaster drills
- Medical attention occurring at the employer's direction during work hours

Listed below are common examples of activities that are not considered working time and for which employees need not be compensated:

- Absence from work
- Nonworking time spent before or after work
- Changing clothes at the employee's convenience or at home
- Where an employee is relieved of duty
- Time spent waiting in line for a paycheck or to clock in or out
- Operation of the employer's vehicle for the commuting convenience of the employee
- Bona fide meal periods of 20 minutes or more are not considered as worktime
- Independent training elected by the employee outside of regular working hours where no productive work is performed
- Training not directly related to the employee's current job

- Voluntary participation in meetings outside of regular working hours where no productive work is performed
- Medical attention not at the direction of the employer or not during the employee's normal working hours
- Ordinary travel from home to work is not considered as worktime
- Time spent in travel after regular work hours is not counted as hours worked

The employer has a duty to manage the enterprise, to control work performed and to act to prevent work activity if it does not want work performed. Union agreements may define work activities that are compensable and noncompensable. Employees who are exempt from the Fair Labor Standards Act typically receive a weekly salary regardless of number of hours worked; see ¶ 913 of this chapter.

¶ 913 THE FAIR LABOR STANDARDS ACT—EQUAL PAY

.01 Minimum Wages

No employer having employees subject to any provisions of the Equal Pay Act shall discriminate, within any establishment in which such employees are employed, between employees on the basis of sex by paying wages to employees in such establishment at a rate less than the rate at which the employer pays wages to employees of the opposite sex for equal work on jobs the performance of which requires equal skills, effort, and responsibility, and which are performed under similar working conditions, except where such payment is made pursuant to a seniority system, a merit system, a system which measures earnings by quantity or quality of production, or a differential based on any other factor other than sex. However, an employer who is paying a wage rate differential in violation of this subsection shall not, in order to comply with the provisions of this subSec., reduce the wage rate of any employee. (29 USC § 206(d)(1))

For purposes of administration and enforcement, any amounts owing to any employee which have been withheld in violation of this subsection shall be deemed to be unpaid minimum wages or unpaid overtime compensation under the FLSA. (29 USC § 206(d)(3))

.03 Federal Regulations (29 CFR § 1620 et seq.)

The Equal Pay Act applies to executive, administrative, and professional employees who are normally exempted from the FLSA for most purposes by Section 13(a)(1) of that statute, and the Equal Pay Act covers all state and local government employees unless they are specifically exempted under Section 3(e)(2)(C) of the FLSA. The Equal Pay Act does not apply where the employer has no employees who are engaged in commerce, or in the handling of goods that have moved in commerce and the employer is not an enterprise engaged in commerce or in the production of goods for commerce. (29 CFR § 1620.1)

Coverage is not based on the amount of covered activity. The FLSA makes no distinction as to the percentage, volume, or amount of activities of either the employee or the employer which constitute being engaged in commerce or in the production of goods for commerce. Every employee whose activities in commerce or in the production of goods for commerce, even though small in amount, are regular and recurring is considered "engaged in commerce or in the production of goods for commerce." (29 CFR § 1620.6)

Definitions

Wage "Rate"

The term wage "rate," as used in the Equal Pay Act, refers to the standard or measure by which an employee's wage is determined and is considered to encompass all rates of wages, whether calculated on a time, commission, piece, job incentive, profit-sharing, bonus, or other basis. The term includes the rate at which overtime compensation or other special remuneration is paid as well as the rate at which straight time compensation for ordinary work is paid. It further includes the rate at which a draw, advance, or guarantee is paid against a commission settlement. Where a higher wage rate is paid to one gender than the other for the performance of equal work, the higher rate serves as a wage standard. When a violation of the Act is established, the higher rate paid for equal work is the standard to which the lower rate must be raised to remedy a violation of the Act. (29 CFR § 1620.12)

"Equal Work"

In general, the Equal Pay Act prohibits discrimination by employers on the basis of sex in the wages paid for "equal work on jobs the performance of which requires equal skill, effort and responsibility and which are performed under similar working conditions." The word "requires" does not connote that an employer must formally assign the equal work to the employee; the Equal Pay Act applies if the employer knowingly allows the employee to perform the equal work. The equal work standard does not require that compared jobs be identical, only that they be substantially equal.

"Male Jobs" and "Female Jobs"

Wage classification systems which designate certain jobs as "male jobs" and other jobs as "female jobs" frequently specify markedly lower rates for the "female jobs." Such practices indicate a pay practice of discrimination based on sex. It should also be noted that it is an unlawful employment practice under Title VII of the Civil Rights Act of 1964 to classify a job as "male" or "female" unless sex is a bona fide occupational qualification for the job.

Equal Pay Act Standards

The Equal Pay Act prohibits discrimination on the basis of sex in the payment of wages to employees for work on jobs which are equal under the standards which the Act provides. The rate of pay must be equal for persons performing equal work on jobs requiring equal skill, effort, and responsibility, and performed under similar working conditions. When factors such as seniority, education, or experience are used to determine the rate of pay, then those standards must be applied on a sex-neutral basis.

Job Content Controlling

Application of the equal pay standard is not dependent on job classifications or titles but rather, depends on actual job requirements and performance. For example, the fact that jobs performed by male and female employees may have the same total point value under an evaluation system in use by the employer does not in itself mean that the jobs concerned are equal according to the terms of the statute. Conversely, although the point values allocated to jobs may add up to unequal totals, it does not necessarily follow that the work being performed in such jobs is unequal when the statutory tests of the equal pay standard are applied. (29 CFR § 1620.13)

¶913.03

Testing Equality of Jobs

What constitutes equal skill, equal effort, or equal responsibility cannot be precisely defined. In interpreting these key terms of the statute, the broad remedial purpose of the law must be taken into consideration. The terms constitute separate tests, each of which must be met in order for the equal pay standard to apply. It should be kept in mind that "equal" does not mean "identical." Insubstantial or minor differences in the degree or amount of skill, or effort, or responsibility required for the performance of jobs will not render the equal pay standard inapplicable. On the other hand, substantial differences, such as those customarily associated with a difference in wage levels when the jobs are performed by persons of one sex only, will ordinarily demonstrate an inequality as between the jobs justifying differences in pay. (29 CFR § 1620.14)

Jobs Requiring Equal Skill in Performance

The jobs to which the equal pay standard is applicable are jobs requiring equal skill in their performance. Where the amount or degree of skill required to perform one job is substantially greater than that required to perform another job, the equal pay standard cannot apply, even though the jobs may be equal in all other respects. Skill includes consideration of such factors as experience, training, education, and ability. It must be measured in terms of the performance requirements of the job. Possession of a skill not needed to meet the requirements of the job cannot be considered in making a determination regarding equality of skill. The efficiency of the employee's performance in the job is not in itself an appropriate factor to consider in evaluating skill. (29 CFR § 1620.15)

Jobs Requiring Equal Responsibility

The equal pay standard applies to jobs the performance of which requires equal responsibility. Responsibility is concerned with the degree of accountability required in the performance of the job, with emphasis on the importance of the job obligation. Differences in the degree of responsibility required in the performance of otherwise equal jobs cover a wide variety of situations. (29 CFR § 1620.17)

Jobs Performed Under Similar Working Conditions

In order for the equal pay standard to apply, the jobs are required to be performed under similar working conditions. It should be noted that the EPA adopts the flexible standard of similarity as a basis for testing this requirement. In determining whether the requirement is met, a practical judgment is required in light of whether the differences in working conditions are the kind customarily taken into consideration in setting wage levels. The mere fact that jobs are in different departments of an establishment will not necessarily mean that the jobs are performed under dissimilar working conditions. (29 CFR § 1620.18)

Pay Differentials Claimed to Be Based on Extra Duties

Additional duties may not be a defense to the payment of higher wages to one sex where the higher pay is not related to the extra duties. The Commission will scrutinize such a defense to determine whether it is bona fide. For example, an employer cannot successfully assert an extra duties defense where:

- Employees of the higher paid sex receive the higher pay without doing the extra work;

- Members of the lower paid sex also perform extra duties requiring equal skill, effort, and responsibility;
- The proffered extra duties do not, in fact, exist;
- The extra task consumes a minimal amount of time and is of peripheral importance; or
- Third persons (i.e., individuals who are not in the two groups of employees being compared) who do the extra task as their primary job are paid less than the members of the higher paid sex for whom there is an attempt to justify the pay differential. (29 CFR § 1620.20)

Head of Household

Since a "head of household" or "head of family" status bears no relationship to the requirements of the job or to the individual's performance on the job, such a claimed defense to an alleged EPA violation will be closely scrutinized. (29 CFR § 1620.21)

Employment Cost Not a "Factor Other Than Sex"

A wage differential based on claimed differences between the average cost of employing workers of one sex as a group and the average cost of employing workers of the opposite sex as a group is discriminatory and does not qualify as a differential based on any "factor other than sex," and will result in a violation of the equal pay provisions, if the equal pay standard otherwise applies. (29 CFR § 1620.22)

Collective Bargaining Agreements Not a Defense

The establishment by collective bargaining or inclusion in a collective bargaining agreement of unequal rates of pay does not constitute a defense available to either an employer or to a labor organization. Any and all provisions in a collective bargaining agreement which provide unequal rates of pay in conflict with the requirements of the EPA are null and void and of no effect. (29 CFR § 1620.23)

Red Circle Rates

The term "red circle" rate is used to describe certain unusual, higher-than-normal wage rates which are maintained for reasons unrelated to sex. An example of a bona fide use of a "red circle" rate might arise in a situation where a company wishes to transfer a long-service employee who can no longer perform his or her regular job because of ill health to different work which is now being performed by opposite-gender employees. Under the "red circle" principle, the employer may continue to pay the employee his or her present salary, which is greater than that paid to the opposite-gender employees, for the work both will be doing. Under such circumstances, maintaining an employee's established wage rate, despite a reassignment to a less demanding job, is a valid reason for the differential, even though other employees performing the less demanding work would be paid at a lower rate, since the differential is based on a factor other than sex. (29 CFR § 1620.26)

¶ 914 ERGONOMICS

.01 OSHA Plan To Reduce Ergonomic Injuries

In 2001 Congress repealed OSHA's Ergonomics rule three months after it became effective. In 2002 OSHA unveiled a comprehensive plan to reduce ergonomic injuries via industry-targeted guidelines, tough enforcement measures, workplace outreach, advanced research, and dedicated efforts for immigrant workers. The first industry specific guidelines are being developed for nursing homes, grocery stores and poultry processing. OSHA enforcement will focus on industries' serious ergonomics problems that OSHA and DOL attorneys have successfully addressed in prior 5(a)(1) or General Duty clause cases.

.05 The Occupational Safety and Health Act of 1970 (OSH Act) (29 USC § 651 et seq.; 29 CFR 1900 to end)

Who is Covered

In general, the Act covers all employers and their employees in the 50 states, the District of Columbia, Puerto Rico, and other U.S. territories. Coverage is provided either directly by the federal Occupational Safety and Health Administration (OSHA) or by an OSHA-approved state job safety and health plan. Employees of the U.S. Postal Service also are covered.

The Act defines an employer as any "person engaged in a business affecting commerce who has employees, but does not include the United States or any state or political subdivision of a State." Therefore, the Act applies to employers and employees in such varied fields as manufacturing, construction, longshoring, agriculture, law and medicine, charity and disaster relief, organized labor, and private education.

The Act does not cover:

- Self-employed persons;
- Farms which employ only immediate members of the farmer's family;
- Industries in which other federal agencies, operating under the authority of other federal laws, regulate working conditions. This category includes most working conditions in mining, nuclear energy and nuclear weapons manufacture, and many aspects of the transportation industries; and
- Employees of state and local governments, unless they are in one of the states with OSHA-approved safety and health plans.

Basic Provisions/Requirements

The Act assigns OSHA two regulatory functions: setting standards and conducting inspections to ensure that employers are providing safe and healthful workplaces. OSHA standards may require that employers adopt certain practices, means, methods, or processes reasonably necessary and appropriate to protect workers on the job. Employers must become familiar with the standards applicable to their establishments and eliminate hazards.

Compliance with standards may include ensuring that employees have and use personal protective equipment when required for safety or health. Employees must comply with all rules and regulations that apply to their own actions and conduct.

Even in areas where OSHA has not set forth a standard addressing a specific hazard, employers are responsible for complying with the OSH Act's "general duty" clause. The general duty clause [Section 5(a)(1)] states that each employer "shall furnish . . . a place of employment which is free from recognized hazards that are causing or are likely to cause death or serious physical harm to his employees."

States with OSHA-approved job safety and health plans must set standards that are at least as effective as the equivalent federal standard. Most of the state-plan states adopt standards identical to the federal ones (three states, New Jersey, New York, and Connecticut, have plans which cover only public sector employees).

Federal OSHA Standards

Standards are grouped into four major categories: general industry (29 CFR 1910); construction (29 CFR 1926); maritime (shipyards, marine terminals, longshoring—29 CFR 1915-19); and agriculture (29 CFR 1928). While some standards are specific to just one category, others apply across industries. Among the standards with similar requirements for all sectors of industry are those that address access to medical and exposure records, personal protective equipment, and hazard communication.

- *Access to Medical and Exposure Records:* This regulation requires the employer to grant the employee access to any medical records the employer maintains with respect to that employee, including any records about the employee's exposure to toxic substances.

- *Personal Protective Equipment:* This standard, which is defined separately for each segment of industry except agriculture, requires employers to provide employees with personal equipment designed to protect them against certain hazards. This equipment can range from protective helmets to prevent head injuries in construction and cargo handling work, to eye protection, hearing protection, hard-toed shoes, special goggles for welders, and gauntlets for iron workers.

- *Hazard Communication:* This standard requires manufacturers and importers of hazardous materials to conduct hazard evaluations of the products they manufacture or import. If a product is found to be hazardous under the terms of the standard, the manufacturer or importer must so indicate on containers of the material, and the first shipment of the material to a new customer must include a material safety data sheet (MSDS). Employers must use these MSDSs to train their employees to recognize and avoid the hazards presented by the materials.

- *Employee Emergency Plans and Fire Prevention Plans:* This standard applies to employers covered by OSHA and applies to all emergency action plans required by a particular OSHA standard. The emergency action plan should be in writing except that such plans may be communicated orally in firms of 10 or fewer employees.

An emergency action plan should consist of the following elements:

— Emergency escape procedures and emergency route assignments,

— Procedures to be followed by employees assigned to operate critical plant operations prior to evacuation,

— Procedures to account for all employees after evacuation,

— Rescue and medical duties,

— The preferred means for reporting fires and other emergencies, and

— Names or job titles of persons who can be contacted for further information on the emergency plan.

In addition, the emergency action plan shall address the following:

— An alarm system shall be established to alert employees about an emergency.

— The emergency action plan shall establish types of evacuation needed in emergency circumstances.

— Designated employees shall be identified and provided training in carrying out the orderly emergency evacuation of employees.

— The employer shall review with each employee the plan or applicable portions at the time the plan is implemented, whenever employee responsibility changes, and whenever the plan is changed.

The employer also should prepare a fire prevention plan when required by a particular OSHA standard. The emergency action plan should be in writing except that such plans may be communicated orally in firms of 10 or fewer employees.

The fire prevention plan should consist of the following elements:

— A list of major workplace fire hazards, identification of their proper handling and storage procedures, potential ignition sources, applicable fire control procedures, and types of fire protection equipment or systems to control hazards,

— Names or job titles of personnel responsible to control fuel source hazards,

— Definition of housekeeping procedures to control accumulation of flammable or combustible waste material,

— Training for employees on fire hazards of materials in the work area,

— A review with each employee upon initial assignment those parts of the fire prevention plan that the employee must know in order protect him or herself in the event of an emergency.

The employer shall regularly and properly maintain equipment and systems installed on heat-producing equipment following proper procedures to prevent accidental ignition of combustible or flammable material. Such maintenance procedures shall be written and included in the fire prevention plan.

OSHA regulations cover such items as recordkeeping, reporting, and posting.

• *Recordkeeping:* Every employer covered by OSHA who has more than 10 employees, except for employers in certain low-hazard industries in the retail, finance, insurance, real estate, and service sectors, must maintain three types of OSHA-specified records of job-related injuries and illnesses.

— The OSHA Form 300 is an injury/illness log, with a separate line entry for each recordable injury or illness. Such events include work-related deaths, injuries, and illnesses other than minor injuries that require only first aid treatment and that do not involve medical treatment, loss of consciousness, restriction of work or motion, or transfer to another job. Each year, the employer must post a summary of the OSHA Form 300 on a Form 300A, which includes the previous year's injuries and illnesses, in the workplace from February through April.

¶914.05

— OSHA Form 301 is an individual incident report that provides added detail about each specific recordable injury or illness. A suitable insurance or workers' compensation form that provides the same details may be substituted for OSHA Form 301.

Employers with 10 or fewer employees and employers in statistically low-hazard industries (listed in 29 CFR 1904, Subpart B) are exempt from maintaining these records. Industries currently designated as low-hazard include: automobile dealers; apparel and accessory stores; eating and drinking places; most finance, insurance, and real estate industries; and certain service industries, such as personal and business services, medical and dental offices, and legal, educational, and membership organizations.

However, in one situation such employers must still keep these records. Each year, the Department of Labor's Bureau of Labor Statistics (BLS) conducts a national survey of workplace injuries and illnesses. Participants are selected by the individual states, and all employers selected for the survey, even those usually exempt from the record-keeping requirements, must maintain these records. Before the end of the year, OSHA notifies all selected employers to begin keeping records during the coming year. The state offices that selected the employers are available to help employers complete the forms.

- *Reporting:* Each employer, regardless of industry category or the number of its employees, must advise the nearest OSHA office of any accident that results in one or more fatalities or the hospitalization of three or more employees. The employer must so notify OSHA within eight hours of the occurrence of the accident. OSHA often investigates such accidents to determine whether violations of standards contributed to the event.

Voluntary Protection Program

The Voluntary Protection Program (VPP) is an OSHA initiative aimed at extending worker protection beyond the minimum required by OSHA standards. This program, along with others such as expanded on-site consultation services and full-service area offices, is a cooperative approach that, when coupled with an effective enforcement program, expands worker protection to help meet the goals of the OSH Act of 1970.

The VPP is designed to:

- Recognize the outstanding achievements of those who have successfully incorporated comprehensive safety and health programs into their total management systems;
- Motivate others to achieve excellent safety and health results in the same outstanding way; and
- Establish a relationship between employers, employees, and OSHA that is based on cooperation rather than coercion.

OSHA reviews an employer's VPP application and visits the worksite to verify that the safety and health program described is in effect at the site. OSHA conducts annual evaluations for Merit and Demonstration programs and triennial evaluations for Star programs. All participants must send their injury information annually to their OSHA regional offices. Sites participating in the VPP are not scheduled for programmed

¶914.05

inspections. However, OSHA handles any employee complaints, serious accidents, or significant chemical releases according to routine procedures.

An employer may apply for a VPP at the nearest OSHA regional office. If OSHA approves the written qualifications, it schedules an onsite review. The review team presents its findings in a report for the company's evaluation before submitting it to the Assistant Secretary for Occupational Safety and Health.

If the report is approved, the Assistant Secretary sends a letter to the employer informing him or her of the worksite's participation in the VPP, and the employer receives a certificate and flag at a ceremony held at or near the approved worksite. Employers at Star sites that are reapproved after triennial evaluation receive plaques at similar ceremonies.

The VPP is available in states under federal jurisdiction. Some states with their own safety and health programs have similar programs. Interested companies in these states should contact the appropriate state agency for more information.

Employee Rights

The Act grants employees several important rights. Among them are the right to complain to OSHA about safety and health conditions in their workplaces and have their identities kept confidential from employers, to contest the amount of time OSHA allows for correcting violations of standards, and to participate in OSHA workplace inspections.

Private sector employees who exercise their rights under OSHA can be protected against employer reprisal, as described in Section 11(c) of the OSH Act. Employees must notify OSHA within 30 days of the time they learned of the alleged discriminatory action. OSHA will then investigate, and if it agrees that discrimination has occurred, OSHA will ask the employer to restore any lost benefits to the affected employee. If necessary, OSHA can take the employer to court. In such cases, the worker pays no legal fees.

Compliance Assistance Available

Standards

The Federal Register is an excellent source of information on standards, since all OSHA standards are published there when made final, as are all amendments, corrections, insertions, and deletions. The Federal Register is published five days a week, and it is available in many public libraries. Annual subscriptions are available from the Superintendent of Documents, U.S. Government Printing Office (GPO), Washington, DC 20402. OSHA also provides copies of its Federal Register notices on its website.

Each year the Office of the Federal Register publishes all current regulations and standards in the Code of Federal Regulations (CFR), also available at many public libraries and from the GPO. OSHA's regulations and standards, which are collected in several volumes in Title 29 CFR, Parts 1900-1999, are also available on OSHA's Web page on standards. In addition, OSHA has a compliance assistance section on its website. For a fee, the GPO offers a data text-retrieval package in CD-ROM format that contains all OSHA standards, compliance directives, and standards interpretations.

Because states with OSHA-approved job safety and health programs adopt and enforce their own standards under state law, copies of these standards can be obtained from the individual states.

¶914.05

Consultation Assistance

Consultation assistance is available to employers who want help in establishing and maintaining safe and healthful workplaces.

On-site OSHA consultation assistance includes an opening conference with the employer to explain the ground rules for consultation, a walk through the workplace to identify specific hazards and to examine those aspects of the employer's safety and health program that relate to the scope of the visit, and a closing conference. Later, the consultant sends a report of findings and recommendations to the employer.

This process begins with the employer's request for consultation, which must include a commitment to correct any serious job safety and health hazards identified. The consultant will not report possible violations of OSHA standards to OSHA enforcement staff unless the employer fails or refuses to eliminate or control worker exposure to any identified serious hazard or imminent danger. Should this occur, OSHA may investigate and begin enforcement action. The employer must also agree to allow the consultant to confer freely with employees during the on-site visit.

Penalties/Sanctions

Every establishment covered by the Act is subject to inspection by OSHA compliance safety and health officers (CSHOs). These individuals, who are chosen for their knowledge and experience in occupational safety and health, are thoroughly trained in OSHA standards and in the recognition of occupational safety and health hazards. In states with their own occupational safety and health plans, state CSHOs conduct inspections.

OSHA conducts two general types of inspections, programmed and unprogrammed. Establishments with high injury rates receive programmed inspections, while unprogrammed inspections are used in response to fatalities, catastrophes, and complaints (which are further addressed by OSHA's complaint policies and procedures). Various OSHA publications and documents detail OSHA's policies and procedures for inspections.

Types of violations that may be cited and the penalties that may be proposed:

- *Other Than Serious Violation:* A violation that has a direct relationship to job safety and health, but probably would not cause death or serious physical harm. A proposed penalty of up to $7,000 for each violation is discretionary. A penalty for an other-than-serious violation may be adjusted downward by as much as 95 percent, depending on the employer's good faith (demonstrated efforts to comply with the Act), history of previous violations, and size of business. When the adjusted penalty amounts to less than $50, no penalty is proposed.

- *Serious Violation:* A violation where a substantial probability that death or serious physical harm could result and where the employer knew, or should have known, of the hazard. A mandatory penalty of up to $7,000 for each violation is proposed. A penalty for a serious violation may be adjusted downward, based on the employer's good faith, history of previous violations, the gravity of the alleged violation, and size of business.

- *Willful Violation:* A violation that the employer intentionally and knowingly commits. The employer either knows that what he or she is doing constitutes a violation, or is aware that a hazardous condition existed and has made no reasonable effort to eliminate it.

The Act provides that an employer who willfully violates the Act may be assessed a civil penalty of not more than $70,000 but not less than $5,000 for each violation. A proposed penalty for a willful violation may be adjusted downward, depending on the size of the business and its history of previous violations. Usually no credit is given for good faith.

If an employer is convicted of a willful violation of a standard that has resulted in the death of an employee, the offense is punishable by a court imposed fine or by imprisonment for up to six months, or both. A fine of up to $250,000 for an individual, or $500,000 for a corporation [authorized under the Omnibus Crime Control Act of 1984 (1984 OCCA), not the OSH Act], may be imposed for a criminal conviction.

- *Repeated Violation:* A violation of any standard, regulation, rule, or order where, upon reinspection, a substantially similar violation is found. Repeated violations can bring fines of up to $70,000 for each such violation. To serve as the basis for a repeat citation, the original citation must be final; a citation under contest may not serve as the basis for a subsequent repeat citation.

- *Failure to Correct Prior Violation:* Failure to correct a prior violation may bring a civil penalty of up to $7,000 for each day the violation continues beyond the prescribed abatement date.

Additional violations for which citations and proposed penalties may be issued:

- *Falsifying Records, Reports, or Applications:* Upon conviction, can bring a fine of $10,000 or up to six months in jail, or both.

- *Assaulting a CSHO:* This act, or otherwise resisting, opposing, intimidating, or interfering with a CSHO in the performance of his or her duties, is a criminal offense, subject to a fine of not more than $250,000 for an individual and $500,000 for a corporation (1984 OCCA) and imprisonment. Citation and penalty procedures may differ somewhat in states with their own OSH programs.

Appeals process:

- *Appeals by Employees:* If a complaint from an employee prompted the inspection, the employee or authorized employee representative may request an informal review of any decision not to issue a citation.

Employees may not contest citations, amendments to citations, penalties, or lack of penalties. They may contest the time allowed in the citation for abatement of a hazardous condition. They also may contest an employer's Petition for Modification of Abatement (PMA), which requests an extension of the abatement period. Employees who wish to contest the PMA must do so within 10 working days of its posting or within 10 working days after an authorized employee representative has received a copy.

Within 15 working days of the employer's receipt of the citation, the employee may submit a written objection to OSHA regarding the abatement date. The OSHA area director forwards the objection to the Occupational Safety and Health Review Commission, which operates independently of OSHA.

Employees may request an informal conference with OSHA to discuss any issues raised by an inspection, citation, notice of proposed penalty, or the employer's notice of intention to contest.

- *Appeals by Employers:* When issued a citation or notice of a proposed penalty, an employer may request an informal meeting with OSHA's area director to discuss the case. Employee representatives may be invited to attend the meeting. To avoid prolonged legal disputes, the area director is authorized to enter into settlement agreements that may revise citations and penalties.

- *Notice of Contest:* If the employer decides to contest the citation, the time set for abatement, or the proposed penalty, he or she has 15 working days from the time the citation and proposed penalty are received in which to notify the OSHA area director in writing. An orally expressed disagreement will not suffice. This written notification is called a "Notice of Contest."

  There is no specific format for the Notice of Contest. However, it must clearly identify the employer's basis for contesting the citation, notice of proposed penalty, abatement period, or notification of failure to correct violations. To better identify the scope of the contest, it also should identify the inspection number and citation number(s) being contested.

  A copy of the Notice of Contest must be given to the employees' authorized representative. If any affected employees are unrepresented by a recognized bargaining agent, a copy of the notice must be posted in a prominent location in the workplace, or else served personally upon each unrepresented employee.

- *Appeal Review Procedure:* If the written Notice of Contest has been filed within 15 working days, the OSHA area director forwards the case to the Occupational Safety and Health Review Commission (OSHRC). The Commission is an independent agency not associated with OSHA or the Department of Labor. The Commission assigns the case to an administrative law judge.

  The judge may disallow the contest if it is found to be legally invalid, or a hearing may be scheduled for a public place near the employer's workplace. The employer and the employees have the right to participate in the hearing; the OSHRC does not require that they be represented by attorneys.

  Once the administrative law judge has ruled, any party to the case may request a further review by OSHRC. Also, any of the three OSHRC commissioners may individually move to bring a case before the Commission for review. Commission rulings may be appealed to the U.S. Courts of Appeals.

- *Appeals in State Plan States:* States with their own occupational safety and health programs have their own systems for review and appeal of citations, penalties, and abatement periods. The procedures are generally similar to Federal OSHA's, but a state review board or equivalent authority hears cases.

Relation to State, Local, and Other Federal Laws

The agency covers all working conditions that are not addressed by safety and health regulations of another federal agency under other legislation. OSHA also has the authority to monitor the safety and health of federal employees.

Finally, OSHA is also responsible for administering a number of whistleblower laws relating to safety and health as described in the Whistleblower Protection section of this Guide.

(Source: Employment Law Guide, *www.dol.gov*)

¶ 915 HEALTH INSURANCE BENEFITS

.01 The Health Insurance Portability and Accountability Act of 1996

The Health Insurance Portability and Accountability Act of 1996 (HIPAA) protects working Americans and their families who have preexisting medical conditions or might suffer discrimination in health coverage based on a factor that relates to an individual's health. HIPAA's provisions place requirements on employer-sponsored group health plans, insurance companies and health maintenance organizations (HMOs). HIPAA provisions:

- Limit exclusions for preexisting conditions;
- Prohibit discrimination against employees and dependents based on their health status;
- Guarantee renewability and availability of health coverage to certain employers and individuals;
- Protect many workers who lose health coverage by providing better access to individual health insurance coverage.
- Promote the use of medical savings accounts.
- Simplify administration of health insurance.
- Provide privacy protections for health information (referred to as the Medical Privacy Rule).

Preexisting Condition Exclusions

Under HIPAA, a group health plan or a health insurance issuer offering group health insurance coverage may impose a preexisting condition exclusion with respect to a participant or beneficiary only if the following requirements are satisfied:

- A preexisting condition exclusion must relate to a condition for which medical advice, diagnosis, care or treatment was recommended or received during the 6-month period prior to an individual's enrollment date;
- A preexisting condition exclusion may not last for more than 12 months (18 months for late enrollees) after an individual's enrollment date; and
- This 12-(or 18-) month period must be reduced by the number of days of the individual's prior creditable coverage, excluding coverage before any break in coverage of 63 days or more.

Preexisting condition exclusions cannot be applied to pregnancy, regardless of whether the woman had previous coverage. In addition, a preexisting condition exclusion cannot be applied to a newborn, adopted child under age 18 or a child under 18 placed for adoption, as long as the child became covered under the health plan within 30 days of birth, adoption or placement for adoption, and provided the child does not incur a subsequent 63-day or longer break in coverage. States may impose stricter obligations on health insurance issuers.

HIPAA and COBRA Continuation Coverage

HIPAA makes two changes to the length of the COBRA continuation coverage period. Qualified beneficiaries who are determined to be disabled under the Social Security Act within the first 60 days of COBRA continuation coverage will be able to purchase an additional 11 months of coverage beyond the usual 18-month coverage period. This is a change from the old law which required that a qualified beneficiary be determined to be disabled at the time of the qualifying event to receive 29 months of COBRA continuation coverage.

This extension of coverage is also available to non-disabled family members who are entitled to COBRA continuation coverage. COBRA rules are also modified and clarified to ensure that children who are born or adopted during the continuation coverage period are treated as "qualified beneficiaries."

The Medical Privacy Rule at a Glance

The medical privacy rule implements certain privacy protections required by the Health Insurance Portability and Accountability Act of 1996. The standards appear at 45 CFR parts 160 and 164. Most covered entities must be in compliance by April 14, 2003.

Covered Entities

Public and private sector entities including health plans, health care clearing houses, and health care providers who conduct administrative or financial transactions electronically are subject to the rules. Certain business associates who serve the health care industry are also affected.

Information Protected

Covered information includes medical records or other data such as certain individually identifiable health information that may be used or disclosed in any form such as electronically, on paper, or orally.

New Patient Rights

Patients must be given a clear notice or explanation of how health information will be used or disclosed not later than the date of first service rendered. Prior consents, which provide equal or better protection, may be relied upon. In addition, patients will generally have the right to access their own medical information and may request amendment to records and restrictions in use. However, the covered entity does not have to comply with a requested restriction. A complaint procedure must be provided to resolve privacy violations.

Limits on Use and Release

Disclosures of health information should be limited to minimum amount necessary for specified purposes, and non-medical disclosures are permitted only upon a patient's written authorization. Disclosures for public health or law enforcement purposes are permitted when required or permitted by law.

Organizational Responsibilities

Covered organizations must adopt written privacy polices, designate a privacy officer, and conduct training for employees on the privacy policies.

¶915.01

Enforcement

The privacy rule is enforced by the Office of Civil Rights of the U.S. Health and Human Services Department. Civil and criminal penalties may be used when violations are found. Criminal penalties can go as high as $250,000 and 10 years.

Implementing HIPAA Privacy in the Personnel Office

Following the compliance deadline for the HIPAA medical privacy regulations, the health care industry implemented required procedures to protect patient health information. As a result, many employers are seeing the affect that the new privacy regulation has on numerous human resources practices. The far reaching impact of HIPAA affects nearly every employer even though many firms may not be defined as a covered entity under the regulation.

Under the HIPAA medical privacy regulation, health care providers and health plans can no longer release protected health information to employers unless certain conditions are met. As a result, the HIPAA regulation indirectly affects employer practices relating to employer contact with a physician and use of employee health information in employment settings.

HIPAA has an affect on employer practices relating to workers compensation, drug testing, physical exams, FMLA, maternity leaves, sick days, and health plan communications.

For example, many employers require an employee to return to work with a doctor's statement in the event of an absence of a specified number of days due to a medical reason. HIPAA now requires an employee authorization permitting such disclosures to the employer.

Listed below are several suggestions to employers for adapting human resources practices to accommodate the new HIPAA guidelines relating to disclosures of health information.

- Work with your organization's health plan administrator to insure that health plan documents are updated to reflect HIPAA requirements.
- Make sure that employees receive information about HIPAA amendments to the health plan.
- Disclosure of only summary health information to the employer is permitted for the purpose of obtaining bids for renewal of insurance services.
- Determine whether your organization can make adequate health plan decisions with this summary information.
- If more detailed information is desired, the employer must provide a certification to the health plan regarding safeguards taken to protect the privacy of health information received.

The employer will need to re-examine and re-define employment practices that involve use of employee health information.

- Employers using pre-employment physical exams or drug tests will need to update these policies to reflect the HIPAA requirements.
- Employer leave policies and practices relating to medical leaves FMLA, maternity leave, and attendance control need to be revised.
- Employer benefits such as disability pay plans or sick pay requiring use of a doctor's certification will need to be modified.

HIPAA regulations now require use of an authorization form that the employee signs to permit disclosure of health information to the employer. Even the common practice of asking the company benefits administrator to inquire about the status of an employee's health claim is affected by the authorization requirement. A valid authorization must meet requirements specified in the HIPAA regulation, so the employer is urged to carefully develop its authorization form or obtain professional assistance if needed. Disclosure of health information to the employer for workers compensation, OSHA, or other legally required purpose may be made without an authorization.

(Source: www.medicalprivacy.info)

The HIPAA Security Rule

The purpose of the HIPAA Security Rule is to define national standards for safeguards to protect the confidentiality, integrity, and availability of electronic protected health information. The standards appear at 45 CFR 164.302 through 164.318. The HIPAA Security Rule details standards for administrative, physical, and technical safeguards, as well as specifying certain organizational requirements and documentation guidelines relating to electronic protected health information.

The Security Rule applies to covered entities that include health plans, health care clearinghouses, and health care providers who transmit data electronically. In addition, firms that service the health care industry, referred to as business associates, are contractually obligated to establish security safeguards. Many employers are affected by HIPAA also. Employers who are health plan sponsors and receive protected health information will be required by the health plan to implement administrative, physical, and technical safeguards.

Security Standards—General Rules

Covered entities are responsible to ensure the confidentiality, integrity, and availability of the electronic protected health information which the organization creates, receives, maintains, or transmits to others. The organizations are responsible to anticipate threats and to take action to protect the data from such threats. A flexibility of approach is permitted. This means that a covered entity may implement security measures that reasonably and appropriately allow the entity to comply.

The HIPAA Security Standard details certain **required** actions must be implemented. In addition, certain **addressable** actions should be assessed and implemented as reasonable and appropriate. The HIPAA Security Rule consist of five mainsections, as summarized here.

Administrative Safeguards

The Security Rule requires the covered entity to establish a security management process. This means that the organization must implement policies and procedures to prevent, detect, contain, and correct security violations. "Required" administrative safeguards include: a risk analysis, implementation of risk management actions, development of a sanction policy, and conduct an information system activity review. The covered entity should identify the security official who will guide the security management process.

Where there is a health care clearinghouse function, this function must be isolated from the remainder of the organization. The covered entity should develop and make available a security incident report form with instructions for use by employees to report security incidents, and document the outcome to the incident. Covered entities are instructed to establish a contingency plan for responding to emergencies such as fire, vandalism, system failure, or natural disaster. The plan should address "required" components including: A data backup plan; a disaster recovery plan, and emergency mode operation plan.

The covered entity is "required" to periodically evaluate the extent to which security policies and procedures meet the requirements of the HIPAA Security Rule. Corrective actions may be taken based on the results of the evaluation. Additional addressable safeguards may be considered and implemented as necessary.

Physical Safeguards

The recommended and required physical safeguards are designed to provide facility access controls to limit physical access to the entity's electronic systems and the facility in which it is housed.

"Required" physical safeguards include the establishment of guidelines related to workstation use, workstation security, and device and media controls. The covered entity is responsible to establish guidelines for workstation use to promote reasonable security and safeguards in the handling of electronic protected health information. A second "required" physical safeguard is the establishment of guidelines for workstation security to promote reasonable safeguards for equipment and systems used in the handling of electronic protected health information. These guidelines should specify proper security precautions to protect systems and equipment. A third "required" physical safeguard is the establishment of guidelines to promote reasonable safeguards for device and media systems used in the handling of electronic protected health information. These guidelines shall specify proper security precautions to protect device and media systems and equipment. The device and media control procedure must define "required" disposal procedures and re-use procedures. Additional addrssable actions may be considered an implemented as appropriate.

Technical Safeguards

The goal of technical safeguards is to protect data by allowing access only by individuals or software programs that have been granted access rights to the information.

"Required" implementation specifications include use of a unique name and/or number for identifying and tracking user identity. This may be done by assigning to each user a password or log-on code. Other "required" elements include defining an emergency access procedure, developing audit controls that record and examine activity of hardware or software elements in an information system, and developing a procedure to verify that a person or entity seeking access to electronic protected health information is the one claimed. Additional optional addressable safeguards may be implemented as needed.

Organizational Requirements

The Organizational Requirements section of the regulation defines certain security requirements relating to business associates and to health plans. The covered entity must have a contract with the business associate which provides that the business associate will implement administrative, physical, and technical safeguards that reasonably and appropriately protect the health information held by the business associate.

A group health plan must ensure that its plan documents provide that the plan sponsor will use reasonable and appropriate safeguards to protect the health information received by the plan sponsor from the group health plan.

Policy and Documentation Requirements

The covered entity is required to implement reasonable and appropriate policies and procedures to comply with the standards and implementation specifications of the Security Rule. Policies may be updated and revised from time to time as necessary. The covered entity is responsible to document its policies in a written or electronic form. Likewise, any activity, action, or assessment required by the HIPAA Security Rule should be documented as well.

The covered entity's documentation practices must comply with the following "required" elements:

- Six-year retention of documentation,

- Assuring availability of documentation to those persons responsible for implementing the procedures.

- Reviewing its documentation periodically, and updating documentation as needed.

Compliance Date

The compliance date is April 20, 2005. Small health plans have a compliance date of April 20, 2006.

(Source: www.medicalprivacy.info)

.02 Health Care Costs

According to a Bureau of Labor Statistics report, "Employee Benefits in Private Industry, 2006," citing data from a national compensation survey, employer premiums for medical care plans averaged $617.18 a month per participant for family coverage and $266.50 a month for single coverage. Employer contributions were higher for those employees who were not required to contribute compared to those who contributed to premium costs, as shown below:

Contribution Category

Employee Contribution Not Required	Average Monthly Employer Premium	Percent of Participating Employees	
Single Coverage	$327.45	25	
Family Coverage	$788.53	13	

Employee Contribution Required	Average Monthly Employer Premium	Percent of Participating Employees	Avg. Mo. Employee Contribution
Single Coverage	$246.72	75	$76.05
Family Coverage	$592.38	87	$296.88

.03 The Women's Health and Cancer Rights Act of 1998

The Women's Health and Cancer Rights Act (Women's Health Act) includes important new protections for breast cancer patients who elect breast reconstruction in connection with a mastectomy.

Affect on Benefits

Under the Women's Health Act, group health plans, insurance companies and health maintenance organizations (HMOs) offering mastectomy coverage must also provide coverage for reconstructive surgery.

.04 Insurance Continuation Under COBRA

With the passage of the Consolidated Omnibus Budget Reconciliation Act in 1985, known as COBRA, federal law now provides that terminated employees and others who have lost insurance coverage for certain qualifying reasons may now be able to buy group insurance coverage for themselves and their families for limited periods of time.

When specified qualifying events occur, the employer is responsible to notify the eligible individual regarding insurance continuation rights under COBRA. On issues relating to spouse or dependents, the employee or dependent is responsible for notifying the employer that the qualifying event has occurred. Upon notice, the eligible individual has 60 days to accept coverage, and upon choosing coverage, the individual is required to make timely payment in order to received the continued insurance coverage.

Qualifying Events

Listed below are certain qualifying events that would cause, except for COBRA continuation coverage, an individual to lose health coverage.

Qualifying events for employees:

- Voluntary or involuntary termination of employment for reasons other than "gross misconduct"
- Reduction in the number of hours of employment

Qualifying events for spouses:

- Termination of the covered employee's employment for reasons other than "gross misconduct"
- Reduction in the number of hours of employment
- Covered employee becoming entitled to Medicare
- Divorce or legal separation of the covered employee
- Death of the covered employee

Qualifying events for dependent children:

- Termination of the covered employee's employment for reasons other than "gross misconduct"
- Reduction in the number of hours of employment
- Loss of dependent child status under plan rules
- Covered employee becoming entitled to Medicare
- Divorce or legal separation of the covered employee
- Death of the covered employee

COBRA provides the following general guidelines relating to periods of continued coverage:

Qualifying Events	Beneficiary	Term of Coverage
Termination Reduced hours	Employee Spouse Dependent child	18 months
Employee entitled to Medicare Divorce or legal separation Death of covered employee	Spouse Dependent child	36 months
Loss of "dependent child" status	Dependent child	36 months

In 2004, the U.S. Department of Labor updated its guidelines relating to the timing and content of notice of COBRA rights, and created a model notice for use by employers. Further information is available at www.dol.gov.

¶ 917 IMMIGRATION REFORM AND CONTROL ACT OF 1986

.01 Immigration Control and Discrimination Law

The Immigration Reform and Control Act of 1986 (IRCA) defines requirements relating to immigration and specifies limitations relating to employment of individuals who are not citizens of the United States. The law creates certain obligations for employers. Following the terrorist attacks of September 11, 2001, the federal government reorganized numerous federal agencies into the U.S. Department of homeland security. The Immigration and Naturalization service that administered the IRCA became the U.S. Citizenship and Immigration Service, a bureau of the Department of Homeland Security.

The IRCA prohibits anyone from hiring an illegal alien. However, the act contains special antidiscrimination rules:

- If a manager requests more or different employment-eligibility documents than are required under IRCA, or refuses to honor documents tendered that reasonably appear to be genuine, he or she will be subject to charges of discrimination.

- The Act also adds additional protection against employment discrimination for legal aliens. Employers with four or more employees may not discriminate on the basis of national origin or citizenship status.

- Be aware that seemingly neutral standards that are not supported by business necessity, such as lengthy residence requirements, preferred verification documents or restrictive language requirements, that in fact discriminate, may be treated by the government as intentional discrimination irrespective of the true motive.

- To avoid possible Civil Rights Act Title VII, age discrimination, and other discrimination suits, employers should avoid having applicants fill out the government's immigration form (Form I-9) during the application process. To do otherwise gives the employer access to information, such as age, that should not be used in the hiring decision. Instead, the employer could wait until the new employee reports for duty at the job site, before having him or her complete the Form I-9.

- Managers or supervisors that attempt to avoid problems under the Act by not hiring "foreign-looking" individuals may be violating the nondiscrimination provisions of Title VII.
- IRCA's ban against discrimination because of citizenship status applies to citizens, as well as to *intending* citizens.
- Citizenship status may be a basis for extending preference to an employee or job applicant over another individual who is an alien. The preference is limited, however, to instances where the two individuals are equally qualified.

.03 Employee Eligibility Verification Requirements

Congress reformed the immigration laws via passage of the Immigration Reform and Control Act of 1986 and the Immigration Act of 1990. Employers must verify the identity and employment eligibility of anyone hired and complete and retain the Employment Eligibility Verification Form I-9. Additionally, employers must not discriminate against individuals on the basis of national origin or citizenship, or require different documents from a particular individual.

In addition to traditional employers, the new requirements also apply to agricultural associations, agricultural employers and farm labor contractors who employ people, or recruit or refer people for a fee. Those who employ domestic help on a regular basis must also follow the requirement. Self-employed persons do not need to complete Form I-9 for themselves unless they are also employees of a business entity, such as a corporation or partnership, in which case the business entity is responsible for completion of the form.

Form I-9 must be completed when employers hire any person to perform labor or services for wages or other remuneration. Employers do not need to complete Form I-9 for persons hired before November 7, 1986 who are continuing their employment and have reasonable expectation of employment at all times. The form does not have to be completed for persons employed for casual domestic work in a private home on a sporadic, irregular or intermittent basis. The form does not have to be completed when an employer uses independent contractors or other persons who provide labor who are employed by a contractor providing contract services. However, employers cannot contract for the labor for an alien if they know the alien is not authorized to work in the United States.

.05 Form I-9 Requirements

Form I-9 was developed for verifying that persons are eligible to work in the United States, and it must be completed for everyone hired after November 6, 1986.

The law requires employers to:

- Ensure that employees fill out Section I of the form when they start work.
- Review documents establishing each employee's identity and eligibility to work.
- Properly complete Sec. 2 of the form.
- Retain the form for three years after the date the person begins work or one year after the employee's work is terminated, whichever is later.
- Make the form available for inspection to an officer of the United States Citizen and Immigration Service (USCIS), the Department of Labor, or the Office of

Special Counsel for Immigration Related Unfair Employment Practices upon request.

Antidiscrimination Provisions

- Employer cannot request more or different documents than required.
- Employer cannot refuse to honor documents which on their face appear genuine.

Document Fraud Prohibition Provisions

- To forge, counterfeit, alter or falsely make any document.
- To use, attempt to use, possess, obtain, accept, or receive any forged, counterfeit, altered or falsely made document.
- To use or attempt to use any document lawfully issued to a person other than the possessor.
- To accept or receive any document lawfully issued to a person other than the possessor.

Instructions for Completing Form I-9

Section 1

Employees fill out Section 1 at the time of hire when they begin work by filling in the correct information and signing and dating the form. Employees who cannot complete Section 1 by themselves may be assisted. When assistance is provided, it is noted in the Preparer/Translator block on the form. Employers are responsible for reviewing and ensuring that employees fully and properly complete Section 1.

Section 2

Employees must present an original document or documents that establish identity and employment eligibility within three business days of the date employment begins. Documents used in the process are categorized according to what they accomplish. Some documents establish both identity and employment eligibility (shown in List A reproduced below); some documents establish identity only (shown in List B below) and some documents establish employment eligibility only (shown below in List C). Employees can choose which document or documents they want to present from the lists of acceptable documents to establish their identity and employment eligibility.

Employers must examine the original document or documents presented and then fully complete Section 2. Since the documents must establish both identity and eligibility, employers must examine one document from List A or alternatively examine one document from both List B and List C. Section 2 requires the employer to record the title of the documents, issuing authority, document number and expiration date (if any). The employer must also fill in the date of hire and correct information in the certification block, then sign and date the Form I-9.

If employees are unable to present the required documents within three business days of the date of employment, they must show that they are obtaining the documents by presenting a receipt for the application for the documents within three business days. Remember, the employees must have indicated that they are already eligible to be employed in the United States by having checked an appropriate box in Section 1. When the individual provides a receipt showing that they have applied for a document evidencing eligibility, the employer must record the document title in Section 2 and write the word "receipt" and any document number in the "Document #" space. The employee must present the actual document within 90 days of the date employment begins. At that time, the employer should cross out the word "receipt" and any accompanying document number and insert the number from the actual document presented, then initial and date the change.

Future Expiration Dates

Future expiration dates may appear on the Form I-9 or on the employment authorization documents of aliens, including, among others, permanent residents, temporary residents, and refugees. USCIS includes expiration dates even on documents issued to aliens with permanent work authorization.

The existence of a future expiration date:

- Does not preclude continuous employment authorization.
- Does not mean that subsequent employment authorization will not be granted.
- Should not be considered in determining whether the alien is qualified for a particular position.

Reverifying Employment Authorization for Current Employees

When an employee's work authorization expires, you must reverify his or her employment eligibility. You may use Section 3 of the Form I-9 or, if Section 3 has already been used for a previous reverification or update, use a new Form I-9. If you use a new form, instead of filling out the form completely, you should write the employee's name in Section 1, complete Section 3, and retain the new form with the original. The employee must present a document that shows either an extension of the employee's initial employment authorization or new work authorization. If the employee cannot provide you with proof of current work authorization, you cannot continue to employ that person.

To maintain continuous employment eligibility, an employee with temporary work authorization should apply for new work authorization at least 90 days before the current expiration date. If the Service fails to adjudicate the application for employment authorization within 90 days, then the employee will be authorized for employment on Form I-688B for a period not to exceed 240 days. You must reverify on the Form I-9 not later than the date the employee's work authorization expires.

To reverify a rehired employee, you must do the following:

- Record the date of rehire;
- Record the document title, number, and expiration date (if any) of any document(s) presented;
- Sign and date Section 3; and
- If you are reverifying on a new form, write the employee's name in Section 1.
- If you rehire an employee who has previously completed a Form I-9, you may update on the employee's original Form I-9 or on a new Form I-9 if:
  — You rehire the employee within three years of the initial date of hire; and
  — The employee is still eligible to work on the same basis as when the original Form I-9 was completed.

¶917.05

To update, you must:

- Record the date of rehire;
- Sign and date Section 3; and
- If you are updating on a new form, write the employee's name in Section 1.

In all of the situations described above with respect to rehired employees, you always have the option of completing Sections 1 and 2 of a new Form I-9 instead of completing Section 3.

Minors (Individuals Under Age 18)

If a minor—a person under the age of 18—cannot present a List A document or an identity document from List B, the Form I-9 should be completed in the following way:

- A parent or legal guardian must complete Section 1 and write "Individual under age 18" in the space for the employee's signature;
- The parent or legal guardian must complete the "Preparer/Translator Certification" block;
- You should write "Individual under age 18" in Section 2, List B, in the space after the words "Document #"; and
- The minor must present a List C document showing his or her employment eligibility. You should record the required information in the appropriate space in Section 2.

Handicapped Employees (Special Placement)

If a person with a handicap, who is placed in a job by a nonprofit organization or as part of a rehabilitation program, cannot present a List A document or an identity document from List B, the Form I-9 should be completed in the following way:

- A representative of the nonprofit organization, or a parent or a legal guardian must complete Section 1 and write "Special Placement" in the space for the employee's signature;
- The representative, parent, or legal guardian must complete the "Preparer/Translator Certification" block;
- You should write "Special Placement" in Section 2, List B, in the space after the words "Document #"; and
- The handicapped employee must present a List C document showing his or her employment eligibility. You should record the required information in the appropriate space in Section 2.

Unlawful Discrimination

The Immigration and Nationality Act, as amended, and Title VII of the Civil Rights Act of 1964, as amended, prohibit employment discrimination. Employers with four or more employees are prohibited from discriminating against any person (other than an unauthorized alien) in hiring, discharging, or recruiting or referring for a fee because of a person's national origin, or in the case of a citizen or protected individual, because of a person's citizenship status. Employers with 15 or more employees may not discriminate against any person on the basis of national origin in hiring, discharge, recruitment, assignment, compensation, or other terms and conditions of employment. In practice, this means that employers must treat all employees the same when completing the

¶917.05

Form I-9. Employers cannot set different employment eligibility verification standards or require that different documents be presented by different groups of employees. Employees can choose which documents they want to present from the lists of acceptable documents. An employer cannot request that an employee present more or different documents than are required or refuse to honor documents which on their face reasonably appear to be genuine and to relate to the person presenting them. An employer cannot refuse to accept a document, or refuse to hire an individual, because a document has a future expiration date. For example, temporary resident aliens have registration cards and persons granted asylum have INS work authorization documents that will expire, but they are ordinarily granted extensions of their employment authorization, and they are protected by law from discrimination.

Generally, employers who have four or more employees cannot limit jobs to United States citizens to the exclusion of authorized aliens. Such a limitation may only be applied to a specific position when required by law, regulation, or executive order; when required by a federal, state, or local government contract; or when the Attorney General determines that United States citizenship is essential for doing business with an agency or department of the federal, state, or local government. On an individual basis, an employer may legally prefer a United States citizen or national over an equally qualified alien to fill a specific position. However, an employer may not adopt a blanket policy of always preferring a qualified citizen over a qualified alien. Verification of identity and employment eligibility is not required until an individual actually starts work. The Form I-9 should be completed at the same point in the employment process for all employees. Different procedures should not be established based on an individual's appearance, name, accent, or other factors.

Instructions for Recruiters and Referrers for a Fee

Under the Immigration and Nationality Act, as amended by the Immigration Act of 1990, it is unlawful for an agricultural association, agricultural employer, or farm labor contractor to hire, or to recruit or refer for a fee, an individual for employment in the United States without complying with the employment eligibility verification requirements. This provision applies to those agricultural associations, agricultural employers, and farm labor contractors who recruit persons for a fee and those who refer persons or provide documents or information about persons to employers in return for a fee. This limited class of recruiters and referrers for a fee must complete the Form I-9 when a person they refer is hired.

The Form I-9 must be fully completed within three business days of the date employment begins, or, in the case of an individual hired for less than three business days, at the time employment begins. Recruiters and referrers for a fee may designate agents, such as national associations or employers, to complete the verification procedures on their behalf. If the employer is designated as the agent, the employer should provide the recruiter or referrer with a photocopy of the Form I-9. However, recruiters and referrers are still responsible for compliance with the law and may be found liable for violations of the law. Recruiters and referrers for a fee must retain the Form I-9 for three years after the date the referred individual was hired by the employer. They must also make available Forms I-9 for inspection to a USCIS, DOL, or OSC officer.

¶917.05

.07 Lists of Acceptable Documents

List A

Documents that establish both identity and employment eligibility:

1. U.S. Passport (unexpired or expired)
2. Certificate of U.S. Citizenship (INS Form N-560 or N-561)
3. Certificate of Naturalization (INS Form N-550 or N-570)
4. Unexpired foreign passport, with I-551 stamp or attached INS Form I-94 indicating unexpired employment authorization
5. Alien Registration Receipt Card with photograph (INS Form I-151 or I-551)
6. Unexpired Temporary Resident Card (INS Form I-688)
7. Unexpired Employment Authorization Card (INS Form I-688A)
8. Unexpired Reentry Permit (INS Form I-327)
9. Unexpired Refugee Travel Document (INS Form I-571)
10. Unexpired Employment Authorization Document issued by the INS which contains a photograph (INS Form I-688B)

List B

Documents that establish identity:

1. Driver's license or ID card issued by a state or outlying possession of the United States, provided it contains a photograph or information such as name, date of birth, sex, height, eye color and address
2. ID card issued by federal, state, or local government agencies or entities provided it contains a photograph or information such as name, date of birth, sex, height, eye color and address
3. School ID card with a photograph
4. Voter's registration card
5. U.S. Military card or draft record
6. Military dependent's ID card
7. U.S. Coast Guard Merchant Marine Card
8. Native American tribal document
9. Driver's license issued by a Canadian government authority

For persons under age 18 who are unable to present a document listed above:

10. School record or report card
11. Clinic, doctor or hospital record
12. Day-care or nursery school record

List C

Documents that establish employment eligibility:

1. U.S. social security card issued by the Social Security Administration (other than a card stating it is not valid for employment)

2. Certification of Birth Abroad issued by the Department of State (Form FS-545 or Form DS-1350)

3. Original or certified copy of a birth certificate issued by a state, county, municipal authority or outlylng possession of the United States bearing an official seal

4. Native American tribal document

5. U.S. Citizen ID Card (INS Form I-197)

6. ID card for use of Resident Citizen in the United States (INS Form I-179)

7. Unexpired employment authorization document issued by the INS (other than those listed under List A)

¶ 918 PERSONAL RESPONSIBILITY AND WORK OPPORTUNITY RECONCILIATION ACT (PRWORA) OF 1996

.01 Employer New Hire Reporting Overview

All employers are required to report certain information on newly hired and rehired employees to a State Directory of New Hires. The new hire information provided by employers is compiled in a statewide directory. This directory is regularly compared with a database of individuals who are legally required to pay child support. When a match occurs, a notice is immediately sent to the child support obligor's employer, notifying the employer to withhold child support.

The new hire information is given to state agencies to compare with respective databases of applicants and recipients of various compensation and public assistance programs. This matching process will save taxpayers millions of dollars each year by preventing and detecting fraud in public assistance, unemployment benefits and workers' compensation programs.

Reporting Requirements

All employers will be required to report new hire information to the State Agency Directory within 20 days of the employees first day on the job. Businesses may choose to start reporting immediately or begin to make any programming or format changes necessary to comply with the new mandatory reporting requirements. A multi-state employer may choose to report all new hire information to a single state. Some payroll processing companies provide services to automatically report newly-hired employees.

What to Report

The six federally mandated data elements include:

- Federal Employer Identification Number
- Employee Social Security number
- Employer name
- Employee name
- Employer address
- Employee address

The employee's date of birth, salary, date of hire and state of hire are optional data elements that can be reported.

¶918.01

At the federal level, the Secretary of the Department of Health and Human Services has established and implemented safeguards with respect to the Federal Parent Locator Service to:

- Ensure the accuracy and completeness of information.
- Restrict access to confidential information to authorized persons and purposes.

How to Report

Any of the following formats that contain the required data elements may be used.

- Mail W-4, existing employer report, paper list or printouts
- Fax—Individual W4 forms or equivalent
- Magnetic tape
- Diskette
- Telephone
- E-Mail

Employers should make sure that all required information is included on the report. For employees with no Social Security number, reports should be held by the employer until a number is obtained. Incomplete or illegible reports will be returned for correction.

When to Report

Employers must report the required information for new or rehired employees within 20 days of their effective hire date. Only those new hires made since the employer's last reporting period should be included in future reports.

Multi-State Employers

Employers who have employees in more than one state may choose to report all new hires to one state. A business must notify the Office of the Secretary of Health and Human Services in writing to designate which state is the recipient of all new hire information. The single-state option also requires new hire information to be reported twice a month, not less than 12 and not more than 16 days apart. A business choosing to report to more than one state may elect to use any method of reporting acceptable in that state. However, each state's regulations must be observed. Mail the notification to the following address:

> Department of Health and Human Services
> Multistate Employer Registration
> Office of Child Support Enforcement
> Box 509
> Randallstown, MD 21133
> Fax: 1-410-277-9325
> Internet: http://www.acf.dhhs.gov/programs/cse/newhire/index.html

Privacy Issues

Security and privacy of new hire information are important issues for all those involved in the implementation of this nationwide program. Federal law requires all states to establish safeguards for confidential information handled by the State Directory of New

Hires. Once data are received by the State Directory, all data will be transmitted over secure and dedicated lines to the National Directory of New Hires.

¶ 919 INDEPENDENT CONTRACTOR STATUS

.01 Business Relationships

Four types of business relationships exist:

- Common-law employee
- Independent contractor
- Statutory employee
- Statutory nonemployee

.03 Employee Defined

The term "employee" includes every individual performing services if the relationship between him or her and the person for whom he or she performs such services is that of employer and employee. The term "employee" includes an officer of a corporation. The right to discharge is also an important factor indicating that the person possessing that right is an employer in addition to furnishing of tools and a place to work to the individual who performs the services for the employer. (Reg. § 31.3401(c)-1)

Description Immaterial

The designation or description of the relationship by the parties is immaterial. A director of a corporation in his capacity as such is not an employee of the corporation. (Reg. § 31.3401(c)-1(e))

Employer Defined

The term "employer" means any person for whom an individual performs or has performed any service, of whatever nature, as the employee of such person. (Reg. § 31.3401(d)-1(a))

Person Having Control Is Employer

If the person for whom the services are or were performed does not have legal control of the payment of the wages for such services, the term "employer" means the person having such control. (Reg. § 31.3401 (d)-1(f))

Employer Reporting Responsibility

It is a basic purpose to centralize in the employer the responsibility for withholding, returning, and paying the tax, and for furnishing statements of payroll reporting. (Reg. § 31.3401(d)-1(h))

Independent Contractor Defined

In general, if an individual is subject to the control or direction of another merely as to the result to be accomplished by the work and not as to the means and methods for accomplishing the result, he is not an employee.

.05 Common Law Factors—Determining Employee or Independent Contractor Status

Under the common law test, a worker is an employee if the person for whom he works has the right to direct and control him in the way he works, both as to the final results and as to the details of when, where, and how the work is to be done. The employer need not actually exercise control. It is sufficient that he has the right to do so. Both the Internal Revenue Service and the Social Security Administration have adopted common law concepts and developed "20 common law factors" for use in determining the nature of the relationship and the existence of the necessary control.

If the relationship of employer and employee exists, it is of no consequence whether the employee is designated as a partner, coadventurer, agent, independent contractor, or the like. Furthermore, all classes or grades of employees are included within the relationship of employer and employee. Thus, superintendents, managers, and other supervisory personnel are employees. Of the following 20 items, no single factor or small group of factors is conclusive evidence of the presence or absence of control. The weight to be given each factor is not always constant. The degree of importance of each factor may vary depending on the occupation and the reason for its existence. The 20 factors are as follows:

1. *Instructions.* A person who is required to comply with instructions about when, where, and how he is to work is ordinarily an employee.

2. *Training.* Training a person by an experienced employee, by correspondence, by required attendance at meetings, and by other methods indicates that the employer wants the services performed in a particular method or manner.

3. *Integration.* Integration of a person's services into the business operation generally shows that the person is subject to direction and control.

4. *Services rendered personally.* If the services must be rendered personally, the employer is interested in not only the result and method, but also the worker.

5. *Hiring, supervising and paying assistants.* Hiring, supervising, and paying assistants by the employer generally shows control over the employees on the job.

6. *Continuing relationship.* A continuing relationship between an individual and the person for whom the services are performed is a factor which indicates that an employer-employee relationship exists. Continuing services may include work performed at frequently recurring, though somewhat irregular, intervals, either on call of the employer or whenever the work is available. If the arrangement contemplates continuing or recurring work, the relationship is considered permanent even if the services are part-time, seasonal, or of short duration.

7. *Set hours of work.* The establishment of set hours of work by the employer is a factor indicating control. This condition bars the worker from being master of his own time, which is the right of the independent contractor.

8. *Full time required.* If a worker must devote full time to the business of an employer, the employer has control over the amount of time the worker spends working and impliedly restricts him from other gainful work. An independent contractor, on the other hand, is free to work when and for whom he chooses. Full time does not necessarily mean an 8-hour day or a 5-or 6-day week. Its meaning may vary with the intent of the parties, the nature of the occupation, and customs in the locality.

9. *Doing work on employer's premises.* Working on an employer's premises is not in itself an element of control. However, it does imply that the employer has control when the work is the kind that could be done elsewhere.

10. *Order or sequence set.* If a person must perform services in the order or sequence set by the employer, it shows that the worker is not free to follow other than the established routines and schedules of the employer.

11. *Oral or written reports.* Another element of control is the requirement of submitting regular oral or written reports to the employer. This action shows that the person is compelled to account for his actions.

12. *Payment by hour, week, month.* Payment by the hour, week, or month generally points to an employer-employee relationship, provided that this method of payment is not just a convenient way of paying a lump sum agreed upon as the cost of doing a job. The payment by a firm of regular amounts at stated intervals to a worker strongly indicates an employer-employee relationship. Payment made by the job or on a straight commission generally indicates that the person is an independent contractor.

13. *Payment of business and/or traveling expenses.* If a employer pays a person's business and/or traveling expenses, the person is ordinarily considered to be an employee. The employer, to be able to control expenses, must retain the right to regulate and direct the person's business activities. Conversely, a person who is paid on a job basis and who has to take care of all incidental expenses is generally an independent contractor. Since he is accountable only to himself for his expenses, he is free to work according to his own methods and means.

14. *Furnishing of tools, materials.* The fact that an employer furnishes tools, materials, etc., tends to show the existence of an employer-employee relationship. Such an employer can determine which tools the person is to use and, to some extent, in what order and how they shall be used. An independent contractor ordinarily furnishes his or her own tools. However, in some occupational fields, workers customarily furnish their own tools. They are usually small hand tools. Such a practice does not necessarily indicate a lack of control over the services of the worker.

15. *Significant investment.* Investment by a person in facilities he uses in performing services for another is a factor which tends to establish an independent contractor status. On the other hand, lack of investment indicates dependence on the employer for such facilities and, accordingly, the existence of an employer-employee relationship.

— Is investment real? Little weight can be accorded to a worker's investment in equipment if he buys it on time from the person for whom he does the work and if his equity in the equipment is small. The same is true if the worker purchases equipment from his employer on a time basis, but the employer retains title to the equipment, has the option of retaining legal ownership by paying the worker the amount of his equity in the equipment at any time before the equipment is fully paid for, requires its exclusive use in the operation of his business, and directs the worker in its use. Such investments are not "real."

— Is investment essential? An investment in equipment or premises not required to perform the services in question is not essential.

¶919.05

— Is investment adequate? Ownership by an individual of facilities adequate for the work and independent of the facilities of another points to an independent contractor relationship. Ownership of such facilities is an influential factor in letting the contract for service. The important point is the value of the investment compared to the total value of all the facilities provided for doing the work.

16. *Realization of profit or loss.* The individual who can realize a profit or suffer a loss as a result of services performed is generally an independent contractor, but the individual who does not realize a profit or loss is an employee. "Profit or loss" implies the use of capital by the individual in an independent business of his own. Payment on a piecework basis or the possibility of gain or loss from a commission arrangement is not considered profit or loss. Whether a profit is realized or loss suffered generally depends upon management decisions; that is, the one responsible for a profit or loss can use his own ingenuity, initiative, and judgment in conducting his business or enterprise. Opportunity for profit or loss may be established by one or more of a variety of circumstances, e.g., the individual:

— Hires, directs, and pays assistants;

— Has his or her own office, equipment, materials, or other work facilities;

— Has continuing and recurring liabilities or obligations, and success or failure depends on the relation of receipts to expenditures;

— Agrees to perform specific jobs for prices agreed upon in advance and pay expenses incurred in connection with the work; and

— Performs services that establish or affect the individual's business reputation and not the reputation of those who purchase the services.

17. *Working for more than one firm at a time.* A person who works for a number of persons or firms at the same time is generally an independent contractor because he or she is usually free from control by any of the firms.

18. *Making service available to general public.* The fact that a person makes his or her services available to the general public usually indicates an independent contractor relationship.

19. *Right to discharge.* The right to discharge is an important factor in indicating that the person possessing the right is an employer.

20. *Right to terminate.* An employee has the right to end his relationship with his employer at any time without incurring liability. An independent contractor usually agrees to complete a specific job, is responsible for its satisfactory completion and is legally obligated to make good for failure to complete the job. (Source: Rev. Rul. 87-41, 1987-1 CB 296)

.06 Court Factors Used For Determining an Individual as an Independent Contractor

The following factors were considered by district court:

• Whether the person rendering the service has an investment in his own equipment and tools.

- Whether the company receiving the benefit of the service has the right to control the manner and method of performance.
- The length of the relationship between the parties.
- The relationship the parties believed was created.
- Whether the custom in the industry was for the service to be performed as an employee or as an independent contractor.
- Whether the service rendered required special skills and training.
- Whether the person rendering the service incurred substantial cost to perform the services.
- Whether the person receiving the service had the right to dismiss without cause the person performing the service.
- Whether or not the person performing the services offers such services publicly and practices independently.
- Whether the service performed was an ancillary or an integral part of the recipient's business.
- Whether the person performing the service had the right to delegate duties to others.
- Whether the person performing the service had opportunity for profit from his managerial skills.
- Whether the person rendering the service risks a loss.

(*Jones, E.C. v. US*, 6/26/78, DC-TX, 43 AFTR 2d 79-521, 79-1 USTC)

.07 Employee v. Independent Contractor—Key Factors Summary

Characteristic	Indicators	
	Employee	**Independent Contractor**
Duration	Continuing relationship is intended at hire date	May exist whether work is performed at frequent but irregular intervals
Profit or loss	No effect	May make a profit or suffer loss
Right of discharge	Employee can be fired, generally at will	Independent cannot be fired if result meets specifications of contract
Industry custom/ norm	If industry norm is as employee	Whether industry norm is as an independent
Instructions	Employer has right to give on how, when, where	Right only regarding end product
Training	Trained to perform services in particular manner	Receives no training and uses own methods
Order of work	Sequence of work is controlled by employer	Sequence of work is controlled by independent contractor
On premise	Employee works on premise or designated route	Work is generally off premises or on different premises
Assistants	Help is provided by employer	Must be provided by contractor
Personally rendered services	Must render services personally	May subcontract out the services
Full-time work services	Employee normally works full-time for employer	Can work when and for whom he chooses
Expenses	Travel and entertainment are reimbursed	Travel and entertainment are not directly reimbursed
Remuneration	Paid by hour, week or month	Paid by job done or commission arrangement
Relationship believed	Where individual believed the relationship was as employee	Where individual believed the relationship was as an independent contractor
Investment in tools	Has no significant investment in tools	Has investment in tools
Costs to perform	Has no material costs to perform services	Incurs own costs to perform services
Public services	Services not available to the general public	Holds services out to the general public
Multiple parties	Works for one employer at a point in time	Provides services to many firms at the same time
Hours	Has specific hours of work	Controls own hours independently
Delegation of duties	Must be performed personally by individual	May be delegated

.09 FICA Statutory Employee Rules

In addition to common-law employees, the FICA provides for statutory employees, as follows:

- Agent drivers and commission drivers,
- Full-time life insurance salesmen,
- Home workers, and
- Traveling or city salesmen.

These four occupational groups are briefly covered in Reg. § 31.3121(d)-1. Workers in these four occupational groups are considered employees for FICA purposes only if they meet the following requirements:

- The contract of service contemplates that the worker will personally perform substantially all the work; and
- The worker has no substantial investment in facilities other than transportation facilities used in performing the work; and
- There is a continuing work relationship with the person for whom the services are performed.

Contract of Service

Work performed in these occupational groups is done under a contract of service. The term "contract of service" means the arrangement, oral or written, under which the work is done. This arrangement must contemplate that the worker will do substantially all the work.

Substantial Investment in Facilities

The words "substantial investment" refer to furnishing substantial facilities by the worker for conducting the business; they cannot be precisely defined. All the facts of each case must be considered.

Continuing Relationship

Work is considered to be of a continuing nature if it is regular or frequently recurring. Regular part-time work—for example, two days a week—is considered a continuing relationship. Regular seasonal employment is also work of a continuing nature. A single-job transaction, even though it takes a considerable period of time, is not generally a continuing relationship.

.11 Summary of Business Relationships' Tax Treatment

Type	Tax	Considerations
Common-law Employee	Social Security, W/H, Unemployment	• Have legal right to control what is to be done and how it is to be done. • Provide tools. • Have right to discharge. • Provide place to work.
Statutory Employee	Social Security, Unemployment	• Delivery driver of meats, fruits, vegetables, bakery, beverages, laundry; if driver is agent or paid commission.

Type	Tax	Considerations
	Social Security	• Life insurance sales agent selling primarily for one insurance company.
	Social Security	• Individual who works at home on materials supplied who must meet work specifications.
	Social Security, Unemployment	• Full-time salesperson who turns in orders. Goods sold must be merchandise for resale.
	Social Security, Unemployment	• If contract states or implies that almost all services are to be provided personally.
	Social Security, Unemployment	• The individual has little or no investment in the equipment used.
	Social Security, Unemployment	• The services are performed on a continuing basis.
Statutory Non-employee	No taxes withheld	• Substantially all payments are related to sales, not hours worked.
Direct Sellers or Licensed Real Estate Agents		• The services must be performed under a written contract establishing a contractual relationship. • Must be engaged in selling other than a permanent retail establishment. • Engaged in selling of consumer products to a buyer on a buy-sell basis for resale other than in a permanent retail establishment.
Leased	No taxes withheld	• Service corporation enters into contracts with subscribers for specific services to be provided. The contract states that the service corporation controls and directs the worker's services, has the right to discharge, reassign, and pays all employment taxes.
Independent Contractor	No taxes withheld File Form 1099-misc on amounts over $600/year	• Have right to control only the result of the work.

.12 Employee vs. Independent Contractor—Cost Difference

Assumptions:

	Employee	Contractor
Gross Wages:	$20,000	$20,000
FICA/Medicare:	1,530	0
State Unemployment, etc.:	540	0
Worker's Compensation:	200	0
Fringe Benefit Coverage:	200	0
Other- Medical, etc,:	160	0
Total	$22,630	$20,000
Employer Tax Rates:		
Federal Income tax rate:	27%	
State Income tax rate:	3%	

Comparison:

	Employee	Contractor
Total cost	$22,630	$20,000
(Less) Tax Savings	– 6,789	– 6,000
Net Cost to Business	= $15,841	= $14,000

.13 Employee vs. Independent Contractor—Section 530 Examination

Section 530 of the Revenue Act of 1978, which gave employers relief from the threat of a large retroactive employment tax liability for certain workers consistently treated as independent contractors, is amended, effective in 1997, to provide more clarity on the standards to be applied to this issue.

Background

Section 530 allowed employees to escape employment tax liability if the following conditions were met:

- Employer always treated the worker as an independent contractor;

- Employer filed all returns required (including information returns) for the worker for all periods after 1978 and the returns were consistent with independent contractor status; and

- Employer had a reasonable basis for treating the worker as an independent contractor.

- An employer was treated as having a reasonable basis if such treatment was in reasonable reliance on any of the following:

  — Judicial precedent, published rulings or technical advice or letter rulings to the employer;

  — A past IRS audit in which no assessment was made for improper treatment of the worker; or

  — A long-standing, recognized practice of a significant segment of the industry in which the individual worked.

1996 Amendments Change Section 530 Relief

Reliance on Prior Audit

In the past, employers could rely on a previous audit as a reasonable basis for treating workers as independent contractors even if the audit did not focus on employment tax issues. Under one provision that favors the IRS, employees will not be able to rely on a previous audit unless it included an examination for employment tax purposes of whether the worker involved or a similar worker was properly classified. Employers may still rely on audits that began before 1997, even though they were not related to employment tax matters.

Long-standing Practice

In determining whether an industry practice is long-standing enough for an employer to rely on in classifying workers, no fixed length of time will be required. In past the IRS had sought to require 10 years standing or that a practice was in existence before 1979.

Significant Segment of an Industry

In determining whether the industry practice was followed by a significant segment of the industry, no fixed percentage of the industry must be shown. In no case, however, will an employer be required to show that the practice is followed by more than 25 percent of the industry, not taking into account the employer itself.

Burden of Proof

Employers seeking to show reasonable reliance on one of the three factors of precedent, prior audit or industry practice, will have the burden only of establishing a prima facie case. If the employer cooperates with the IRS, the IRS will bear the burden of proving the employer wrong.

Later Reclassification Allowed

Although Section 530 requires consistent classification of workers from year to year before relief is granted, the Act clarifies that this consistency requirement is retrospective only. An employer may reclassify a worker as an employee and begin to pay employment taxes without compromising its independent contractor classification for prior years.

Relief Not Dependent on Employee Classification for Other Purposes

Prior to the Act, the IRS took the position that Section 530 is strictly a relief provision applicable to workers who would rightfully be classified as employees under the common law and the 20-factor test of Rev. Rul. 87-41, 1987-1 CB 296. The Act clarifies that an employer may take advantage of Section 530 rights and still maintain independent contractor classifications for other purposes.

IRS Required to Give Notice

The IRS will be required to notify employers of their rights under Section 530 as soon as an improper worker classification issue is raised in an audit.

Effective Dates

The rules apply to periods after December 31, 1996.

.17 Penalties for Treating Employees as Independent Contractors

Determination of Employer's Liability for Employment Taxes

If an employer fails to deduct and withhold any tax with respect to any employee by reason of treating such employee as not being an employee, the amount of the employer's liability for:

- Withholding taxes shall be determined as if the amount required to be deducted and withheld were equal to 1.5 percent of the wages paid to such employee.

- Employee social security tax shall be determined as if the taxes were 20 percent of the amount. (Code Sec. 3509)

Employer's Liability Increased Where Employer Disregards Reporting Requirements

- Substitute "three percent" for "1.5 percent" on withholding taxes above.

- Substitute "40 percent" for "20 percent" on social security above.

Failure to Collect and Pay Tax, or Attempt to Evade Tax

Any person required to collect and pay over any tax imposed who willfully fails to collect such tax, or willfully attempts in any manner to evade or defeat any such tax shall, in addition to other penalties provided by law, be liable to a penalty equal to the total amount of the tax evaded, or not collected for and paid over. The penalty for failure to collect and pay imposed under Code Sec. 6672 applies to trust fund taxes (taxes withheld from employees) only. Code Sec. 6672 does not apply to the employer's portion of payroll taxes. (Code Sec. 6672)

Penalties for Treating Employees As Independent Contractors; Employer Penalties Where Employer Incorrectly Treats Employee As Independent Contractor

Employer

If 1099 misc. issued	1.5% of wages paid	20% of employee's share of FICA
If no 1099 misc. issued	3% of wages paid	40% of employee's share of FICA

Employee

Remains liable for his share of FICA and income tax.

If income taxes and self-employment taxes were paid as an independent contractor, there will be no additional employee tax liability by being reclassified as an employee.

Employer Penalties Where Employer Intentionally Disregards Rules As Willful Neglect

The employer is liable for both parts of FICA income taxes on 20 percent of employee wages. If the employer obtains affidavit (Form 4669) from employees that they paid income tax and self-employment tax on their earnings, the employer is relieved of:

- The 20-percent income tax withholding.
- The employees' share of FICA taxes.

Section 6672

If employer is liable for underpaid employment taxes upon reclassification of contractor as employee, then:

- Employer is assessed penalty of 100 percent of taxes.
- Due to willful failure to collect or account for.

The penalty for failure to collect and pay imposed under Code Sec. 6672 applies to trust fund taxes (taxes withheld from employees) only. Code Sec. 6672 does not apply to the employer's portion of payroll taxes. An employer that cannot pay the full amount due may designate that partial payments are to be applied first to trust fund taxes and not to the employer's portion. The IRS must honor such designations unless the payment was obtained by levy or distraint. In practice, the IRS may not do so without taking the case to Appeals.

Payroll Period

The term "payroll period" means a period for which a payment of wages is ordinarily made to the employee by his employer, and the term "miscellaneous payroll period" means a payroll period other than a daily, weekly, biweekly, semimonthly, monthly, quarterly, semiannual, or annual payroll period. (Code Sec. 3401(b))

Employment Tax Liability Chart

The following rates apply where Forms 1099 were issued to the workers (Code Sec. 3509):

Year	FICA Rate Employer + Employee	Withholding
1981	6.65% + (6.65% × .20) = 7.98%	1.5%
1982	6.70% + (6.70% × .20) = 8.04%	1.5%
1983	6.70% + (6.70% × .20) = 8.04%	1.5%
1984	7.00% + (6.70% × .20) = 8.34%	1.5%
1985	7.05% + (7.05% × .20) = 8.46%	1.5%
1986-1987	7.15% + (7.15% × .20) = 8.58%	1.5%
1988-1989	7.51% + (7.51% × .20) = 9.01%	1.5%
1990-2002	7.65% + (7.65% × .20) = 9.18%	1.5%

The following rates apply where the employer disregards reporting requirements and does not issue Form 1099:

Year	FICA Rate Employer + Employees	Withholding
1981	6.65% + (6.65% × .40) = 9.31%	3.0%
1982	6.70% + (6.70% × .40) = 9.38%	3.0%
1983	6.70% + (6.70% × .40) = 9.38%	3.0%
1984	7.00% + (6.70% × .40) = 9.68%	3.0%
1985	7.05% + (7.05% × .40) = 9.87%	3.0%
1986-1987	7.15% + (7.15% × .40) = 10.01%	3.0%
1988-1989	7.51% + (7.51% × .40) = 10.51%	3.0%
1990-2002	7.65% + (7.65% × .40) = 10.71%	3.0%

¶ 920 EMPLOYMENT OF FOREIGN WORKERS

.01 Overview

Employers who wish to hire foreign workers to temporarily perform services or labor or to receive training may file an I-129 petition. The I-129 is mainly used for nonimmigrant categories; thus, in most cases, workers who enter the United States under this petition must depart the United States when their maximum period of stay has been reached. Form I-129 may also be used to petition for an extension of stay or change of status for certain nonimmigrants.

There are many categories of workers who are temporary visitors and who may be petitioned for on the I-129. These nonimmigrant classifications are symbolized by letters which generally correspond to the visas issued by the State Department. Only those categories incorporating employment or investment will be covered here.

To see the section of the Immigration and Nationality Act that applies to temporary worker categories, see § 101(a)(15). For the law applying to NAFTA categories, see § 214(e).

.02 Filing the I-129 Petition

USCIS Form I-129 consists of a basic petition and different supplements that apply to the various visa categories. In order to petition for a temporary worker, the prospective employer or agent must file Form I-129, Petition for Nonimmigrant Worker, and the appropriate supplement with the U.S. Citizenship and Immigration Services (USCIS) accompanied by the required payment, and initial evidence or documentation.

In some cases, the employer must get a certificate from the Department of Labor prior to filing the I-129. This process is described below in the appropriate categories.

Once the petition is approved, the employer or agent is sent a Notice of Approval, Form I-797. Approval of a petition does not guarantee visa issuance to an applicant. Applicants must also establish that they are admissible to the United States under provisions of the Immigration and Nationality Act (INA).

.03 Applying for the Visa

If the prospective worker (beneficiary) is outside of the country, he or she must apply for a visa. After the USCIS has approved the I-129 and sent notice to the consulate in the beneficiary's country, the beneficiary must file a visa application with the consulate. Some aliens may be visa- exempt. In those cases, the I-129 approval notice is sent to the port of entry (POE) where the beneficiary intends to apply for admission. For specific procedures on Visa Application Procedures, Required Documentation and Visa Ineligibility Waiver, please visit Visa Services at the Department of State.

If the beneficiary is already in the United States and is changing from one nonimmigrant status to another, a visa is not required. However, a visa may be required if the beneficiary subsequently leaves the United States and wishes to re-enter.

.04 Entry into the United States

Applicants should be aware that a visa does not guarantee entry into the United States. The U.S. Customs and Border Protection (CBP) has authority to deny admission at the port of entry to any applicant who is inadmissible under INA, even if the applicant has a visa. Also, the CBP, not the consular officer, determines the period for which the bearer of a temporary work visa is authorized to remain in the United States. At the port of entry, CBP officials issue Form I-94, Record of Arrival-Departure, which notes the length of stay permitted. The decision to grant or deny a request for extension of stay, however, is made solely by the USCIS.

.05 When to File

Petitions should be filed as soon as possible, but no more than six months before the proposed employment will begin or the extension of stay is required. If the petition is not submitted at least 45 days before the employment will begin, petition processing and subsequent visa issuance may not be completed before the alien's services are required or previous employment authorization ends.

Maximum Stay Information for Temporary Employment Visas

Class	Initial Stay	Extension of Stay
E-1	Two (2) years	Up to 2 years per extension. No maximum number of extensions, with some exceptions.
E-2	Two (2) years	Up to 2 years per extension. No maximum number of extensions, with some exceptions.

H-1B1	Up to 3 years	Increment of up to 3 years. Total stay limited to 6 years.
H-1B2	Up to 3 years	Increment of up to 3 years. Total stay limited to 6 years, with some exceptions.
H-1C	Up to 3 years	Total stay limited to 3 years.
H-2A and H-2B	Same as validity of labor certification, with maximum of 1 year. Same as validity of labor certification (increments of up to 1 year). Total stay limited to 3 years.	
H-3	Special Education Training-up to 18 months.	
	Other Trainee-up to 2 years Special Education Trainee-total stay limited to 18 months. Other Trainee-total stay limited to 2 years.	
L-1A	Coming to existing office-up to 3 years.	
	Coming to new office-up to 1 year. Increments of up to 2 years. Total stay limited to 7 years.	
L-1B	Coming to existing office-up to 3 years.	
	Coming to new office-up to 1 year One increment of up to 2 years. Total stay limited to 5 years.	
O-1 and O-2 P-1, P-2, P-3	Up to 3 years	Increments of up to 1 year and their support personnel. Individual athlete—up to 5 years.
	Athletic groups and Entertainment groups—up to 1 year. Individual athlete—Increments of up to 5 years. Total stay limited to 10 years.	
	Athletic groups and entertainment groups—Increments of 1 year.	
Q-1	Up to 15 months. Total stay limited to 15 months.	
	(Note: definition of each class of visa should display once only per chart)	
R-1 and R-2	Up to 3 years. Increments of up to 2 years. Total stay limited to 5 years.	
All other	Up to 1 year	Increments of up to 1 year

.06 Where to File

Generally, petitions are mailed to one of the USCIS service centers based on the place where the proposed employment or training will be conducted.

Certain exceptions apply:

- All H1C (nurses) Form I-129s are filed at the Vermont Service Center (VSC). If the person is a Canadian citizen applying for admission as an L-1 under the North American Free Trade Agreement, the petition may be filed at the port of entry when the person applies for entry.

- All TN (NAFTA) Form I-129s are filed at the Nebraska Service Center.

- Applications pertaining to E-1 or E-2 matters may be filed only at the Texas or California service centers. These petitions are to be filed at either (1) the Texas Service Center if the location of employment is in the areas previously covered by the Vermont and Texas service centers, or (2) the California Service Center if the location of employment is in the areas previously covered by the Nebraska and California service centers.

- If an alien currently in E-1 or E-2 status is requesting a change of status to another nonimmigrant classification, the application for change of status must be mailed to one of the USCIS service centers with jurisdiction over the new requested classification.

.07 Fees

Basic filing fees and other fees are defined by the USCIS. Information is available at www.uscis.gov.

(Source: United States Citizenship and Immigration Service (www.uscis.gov))

RETIREMENT

¶ 922 RETIREMENT CONSIDERATIONS

.01 Health Benefits Considerations for Retirees

Private-sector employers are not required to promise retiree health benefits. Employers that do offer retiree health benefits are not prevented by federal law from cutting or eliminating those benefits—unless they have made a specific promise to maintain them.

The key to understanding retiree health benefits lies in Plan Documents. The Summary Plan Description (SPD) is a summary of the terms of the plan. Employers are required to provide a copy to employees within 90 days after they become a participant in the plan.

For retirees, the SPD that was in effect at retirement is the controlling document. Retirees should save a copy of it. In addition, there may be formal written documents that outline health plan operations. These may include a collective bargaining agreement or an insurance contract.

If an employer has reserved the right in the SPD and controlling plan document to change the terms of the plan, an employee may lose coverage at any time during retirement. If an employer made a clear promise that employees will have specific health care benefits for a definite period of time or for life, and did not reserve the right to change the plan, an employee should be covered.

Plan Documents Need to be Reviewed

- Does the SPD or other plan documents promise that health benefits after retirement will continue at a specfied level for a certain period of time?

- If there is such language, how specific is it?

- If there is no specific language describing retiree health benefits in the plan documents, it is unlikely that coverage exists.

- Sometimes language covering retiree health benefits is included, but it is too vague to stand up to a test in the courts.

- Ambiguity can be an issue—some courts may not enforce what seems like clear "promise" language if the plan document contains general language reserving the employer's right to amend or terminate the plan.

- Some courts may take into account any informal communications that an employee and employer had concerning retiree health-care benefits, at least where the plan document and SPD are ambiguous.

.02 Early Retirement Concerns

- Any agreements or employer correspondence on early retirement should be carefully reviewed.

- Especially important are documents containing language regarding the duration of retiree health benefits.

- Records of meetings between employee and employer concerning an early retirement offer are important.

- Some courts will enforce the promises made with respect to early retirement offers even if the formal plan document, collective bargaining agreement or SPD contain language allowing the employer to terminate or amend the plan.

- Those facing early retirement may be able to protect themselves by negotiating a written contract that includes the specific terms of health-care benefits and the circumstances, if any, under which they may be changed.

- Employees are entitled to a copy of their SPD, which can be requested from their employer or from the Department of Labor at any time and received within 30 days for a reasonable copy charge. To obtain copies or other plan documents, a written request must be submitted to the employer.

(Source: Pension and Welfare Benefits Administration, Division of Public Affairs.)

.05 Selected Sources for Retirement Information

American Association of Retired Persons	800-424-3410
American Council of Life Insurers	202-624-2319
American Federation of Labor-Congress of Industrial Organizations	202-637-5000
American Federation of Teachers	202-879-4400
American Institute of Certified Public Accountants	888-777-7077
Commission on Saving and Investment in America	202-628-5900
Employee Benefit Research Institute	202-659-0670
Investment Company Institute	202-326-5800
National Education Association	202-833-4000
Pension and Welfare Benefits Administration, U.S. Dept. of Labor	202-219-8776
Pension Rights Center	202-296-3776
Social Security Administration	800-772-1213
TIAA/CREF	800-842-2776

¶ 923 RETIREMENT PLANS

.01 Retirement Plan Deduction

Tax savings are achieved by making retirement plan contributions for employer and employees. The net cost to the employer after factoring in the tax savings is as follows.

Assumptions:	Contribution Deductibility =100%
Yearly Retirement Plan Contribution:	$6,000 to Employer/$6,000 to Employees
Federal Income Tax Rate:	15%
State Income Tax Rate:	2%
Social Security Tax Rate:	6.20%
Medicare Tax Rate:	1.45%
Summary:	
Total Cost of Retirement Plan Contributions:	$12,000
Less Tax Savings	(2,040)
Net Cost to Business	$9,960

Benefits:

- Use the retirement plan as a form of "forced savings" to help insure there will be a retirement nest egg in the future.

- Immediate tax savings result since the dollar amount funded can be written off against other income.
- Income earned while in the retirement plan is not subject to current taxes. The compounding of this tax deferred money over the years grows significantly compared to saving outside the retirement plan.

Pre-tax Plan vs. Post-tax Plan

One should consider using a pre-tax savings plan to accumulate funds compared to saving with after-tax dollars. A pre-tax savings plan is an "income reduction" plan that allows one to deduct annual contributions from one's income, thus saving income taxes.

Advantages: Such a plan can cut the current tax bracket. The income from these investments compounds over time, tax-deferred while in the plan. A pre-tax savings plan should be viewed as a long-term plan.

Assumptions:	
Amount Contributed	$6,000
Amount Company Will Match	$6,000
Contributed Investment Rate of Return	12%
Initial Contribution age	35
Withdrawal Age	65
Penalty For Early Withdrawal	10%
Age Needed to Avoid Penalty	59½
Pre Tax Rate-of-Return	12%
Income Tax Rate	Federal 27%/State 1%
Estimated Tax Bracket At Withdrawal Date	15%

Pretax Savings Plan

Assumptions

1. Employer and employee each contribute $6,000 each year
2. The tax rate during the acumulation period is 28% (27% federal and 1% state)
3. Tax savings equal 28% of the sum of the $12,000 deposited each year and the earnings thereon each year
4. The deposits are assumed to be made at the end of the year and earn 12% compounded annually
5. The tax due if withdrawn early is 38% of the total amount (27% federal, 10% federal penalty, and 1% state)
6. At age 60, the tax due if withdrawn is 28% of the total amount (27% federal and 1% state)
7. At age 65, the tax due if withdrawn is 15% (15% federal and 0% state)

| | Pre-Tax Investing | | | | | Post Tax Investing | | | | Advantage or (Disadvantage) |
Age	Amount Deposited	Earnings at 12%	Total	Tax Due if Withdrawn	Total Net of Tax	Amount Deposited	Earnings at 12%	Less Tax at 28% (15% at age 65)	Total	of Pre-Tax Over Post-Tax
35	$12,000	$0	$12,000	$4,560	$7,440	$12,000	$0	$3,360	$8,640	($1,200)
36	$12,000	$1,440	$25,440	$9,667	$15,773	$12,000	$1,037	$3,650	$18,026	($2,254)
37	$12,000	$3,053	$40,493	$15,387	$25,106	$12,000	$2,163	$3,966	$28,224	($3,118)
38	$12,000	$4,859	$57,352	$21,794	$35,558	$12,000	$3,387	$4,308	$39,303	($3,744)
39	$12,000	$6,882	$76,234	$28,969	$47,265	$12,000	$4,716	$4,681	$51,338	($4,073)
40	$12,000	$9,148	$97,382	$37,005	$60,377	$12,000	$6,161	$5,085	$64,414	($4,037)
41	$12,000	$11,686	$121,068	$46,006	$75,062	$12,000	$7,730	$5,524	$78,619	($3,557)
42	$12,000	$14,528	$147,596	$56,087	$91,510	$12,000	$9,434	$6,002	$94,052	($2,542)
43	$12,000	$17,712	$177,308	$67,377	$109,931	$12,000	$11,286	$6,520	$110,818	($887)
44	$12,000	$21,277	$210,585	$80,022	$130,563	$12,000	$13,298	$7,083	$129,033	$1,530
45	$12,000	$25,270	$247,855	$94,185	$153,670	$12,000	$15,484	$7,696	$148,821	$4,849
46	$12,000	$29,743	$289,598	$110,047	$179,551	$12,000	$17,859	$8,360	$170,319	$9,231
47	$12,000	$34,752	$336,349	$127,813	$208,537	$12,000	$20,438	$9,083	$193,675	$14,862
48	$12,000	$40,362	$388,711	$147,710	$241,001	$12,000	$23,241	$9,867	$219,048	$21,953
49	$12,000	$46,645	$447,357	$169,995	$277,361	$12,000	$26,286	$10,720	$246,614	$30,747
50	$12,000	$53,683	$513,039	$194,955	$318,084	$12,000	$29,594	$11,646	$276,562	$41,523
51	$12,000	$61,565	$586,604	$222,910	$363,695	$12,000	$33,187	$12,652	$309,097	$54,598
52	$12,000	$70,392	$668,997	$254,219	$414,778	$12,000	$37,092	$13,746	$344,443	$70,335

	Pre-Tax Investing				Post Tax Investing				Advantage or (Disadvantage)	
Age	Amount Deposited	Earnings at 12%	Total	Tax Due if Withdrawn	Total Net of Tax	Amount Deposited	Earnings at 12%	Less Tax at 28% (15% at age 65)	Total	of Pre-Tax Over Post-Tax
53	$12,000	$80,280	$761,276	$289,285	$471,991	$12,000	$41,333	$14,933	$382,842	$89,149
54	$12,000	$91,353	$864,629	$328,559	$536,070	$12,000	$45,941	$16,224	$424,560	$111,510
55	$12,000	$103,756	$980,385	$372,546	$607,839	$12,000	$50,947	$17,625	$469,882	$137,957
56	$12,000	$117,646	$1,110,031	$421,812	$688,219	$12,000	$56,386	$19,148	$519,120	$169,099
57	$12,000	$133,204	$1,255,235	$476,989	$778,246	$12,000	$62,294	$20,802	$572,612	$205,634
58	$12,000	$150,628	$1,417,863	$538,788	$879,075	$12,000	$68,713	$22,600	$630,725	$248,350
59	$12,000	$170,144	$1,600,006	$608,002	$992,004	$12,000	$75,687	$24,552	$693,860	$298,144
60	$12,000	$192,001	$1,804,007	$505,122	$1,298,885	$12,000	$83,263	$26,674	$762,450	$536,436
61	$12,000	$216,481	$2,032,488	$569,097	$1,463,391	$12,000	$91,494	$28,978	$836,965	$626,426
62	$12,000	$243,899	$2,288,387	$640,748	$1,647,638	$12,000	$100,436	$31,482	$917,919	$729,719
63	$12,000	$274,606	$2,574,993	$720,998	$1,853,995	$12,000	$110,150	$34,202	$1,005,867	$848,128
64	$12,000	$308,999	$2,895,992	$810,878	$2,085,114	$12,000	$120,704	$37,157	$1,101,414	$983,700
65	$12,000	$347,519	$3,255,511	$488,327	$2,767,185	$12,000	$132,170	$21,625	$1,223,958	$1,543,226

.03 Summary of Retirement Plans by Features Chart

Following is a chart summary of retirement plans by features.

				Summary of Retirement Plans by Features				
IRA	Money Purchase	Profit Sharing	401(k)	Target Benefit	Defined Benefit	403(b)	457	Plan Features
X		X	X			X	X	Offers contribution flexibility
X	X	X	X	X	X			Contributions are deductible to employer
X	X	X	X			X	X	Plan features are easy to understand
X	X	X	X	X		X	X	Employer contributions are known
			X			X	X	Allows pre-tax employee contributions
X	X	X	X	X	X	X	X	Earnings of the plan are tax deferred
	X	X	X	X	X	X	X	Participants can also have an IRA
X	X	X	X	X	X	X	X	Participants can make voluntary after-tax contribution
		X	X	X		X		Distribution is available for hardships
	X	X	X				X	Forfeitures reduce employer contributions
				X	X			Favors large contributions for older participants
				X	X			Provides substantial benefits for employees near retirement
				X	X		X	Accelerated funding for those near retirement
					X			Participant knows retirement benefit
	X	X	X	X	X			Tax favored distribution is available
X	X	X	X	X	X	X	X	Participants can roll benefits to an IRA
X	X	X	X	X	X	X	X	Employer contributions are nontaxable to the participants
X	X	X	X	X	X	X	X	Earnings are not taxable to the employer
X	X	X	X			X	X	Administrative costs are minimal
X	X	X	X	X		X	X	Allows younger employees to accumulate substantial benefits
X	X	X	X	X	X			Favors contributions for younger participants
						X		Favors contributions for older participants
	X			X			X	"Guaranteed" contributions will be made for participants

.05 SIMPLES Savings Incentive Match Plan for Employees

Savings Incentive Match Plan for Employees of Small Employers—gives businesses with 100 or fewer employees an affordable way to offer retirement benefits through employee salary reductions and matching contributions (similar to those found in a 401(k) plan). SIMPLE retirement accounts can be either a part of a 401(k) plan or a plan that uses IRAs.

A SIMPLE plan is a start-up retirement savings plan for small employers who do not currently sponsor a retirement plan. Some advantages are as follows:

- Eligible employees can contribute up to $10,500 (for 2007) each year through convenient payroll deductions.

- Employers offer matching contributions equal to employee contributions (up to three percent of employee wages) or fixed contributions equal to two percent of employee wages.

SIMPLE plans eliminate many of the administrative costs associated with larger retirement plans. Model plan documents, employee notices and salary reduction agreements are available from the IRS.

Requirements

An employer that currently sponsors another retirement plan generally cannot sponsor a SIMPLE plan.

SIMPLE plans can be sponsored by most types of organizations, including C-corporations, S-corporations, partnerships, and sole proprietorships. Related employers (businesses under common control, for instance) are treated as a single employer.

A tax-exempt employer or governmental entity may start a SIMPLE plan as long as the basic requirements are met.

An added note for employers establishing a SIMPLE plan. When employers start these plans, they have two options as to where the contributions are deposited:

- The employer may choose the financial institution that will receive all contributions under the plan. In this case, employees will have a right to transfer contributions to a SIMPLE IRA at another financial institution without cost or penalty.

- Each employee may make the initial choice of financial institution to receive contributions. In this case, an employee does not have the right to transfer to another financial institution without cost or penalty.

Employees who are reasonably expected to receive at least $5,000 in compensation from their employer during a calendar year and who did so in any 2 preceding years must be eligible.

Employers can increase the number of employees eligible to participate by lowering the amount an employee must earn (for example, from $5,000 to $3,000) or by allowing all employees to participate regardless of how much they earn.

Employees covered by a collective bargaining agreement for which retirement benefits were part of good-faith bargaining may be *excluded* from SIMPLE plan participation.

Contributions

Employees contribute to SIMPLE plans by agreeing to a salary reduction from each paycheck; they can contribute up to $10,500 (for 2007) a calendar year.

Generally, contributing employees receive a matching contribution equal to their salary reduction contribution (up to three percent of their pay).

Alternatively, employers may contribute a "non-elective" or fixed contribution of two percent of pay for eligible employees.

Employers also may reduce the matching contribution amount to a limit of one percent of compensation, but certain restrictions apply to this choice.

Contributions are transferable to another SIMPLE IRA tax-free in a trustee-to-trustee transfer.

However, there is a two-year waiting period after the date the employee first enrolls in a SIMPLE plan to transfer tax-free his or her contribution to another IRA other than a SIMPLE IRA. Until this two-year period expires, any transfer from a SIMPLE IRA to an IRA other than a SIMPLE IRA will incur a 25 percent penalty.

All contributions made under a SIMPLE plan are fully vested—that is, all contributions by the employer and the employee immediately belong to the employee.

Employee Elections

SIMPLE plans operate on a calendar year basis, *except* that an employer may initially set up a SIMPLE plan effective as late as October 1 of the calendar year. Employees must be given the chance to enter into a SIMPLE plan salary reduction agreement at least once a year. Election periods must be at least 60-days long, and employees must receive notice about an upcoming enrollment opportunity prior to the election period.

Other Election Features

Each annual election period immediately precedes January 1 of that calendar year (i.e., November 2 to December 31), except that there is more flexibility with the election period requirement when a SIMPLE plan is initially established.

During the election period, employees can make a new salary reduction agreement or modify a prior agreement.

Employees must receive a copy of the plan's "summary description" when they receive notice about the election period.

Employees may elect to terminate their salary reduction contributions to a SIMPLE plan at any time. However, if they end a salary reduction agreement at a time other than a designated election period, employers may preclude them from participating again until the beginning of the next calendar year.

In certain cases, employees may also use the election period to select the financial institution they wish to receive their SIMPLE IRA contributions.

Notification Requirements

When employers give each year's notice about the enrollment period, they must do the following:

- Provide a copy of the summary description of the terms of the plan. This may be accomplished by providing a completed copy of IRS Forms 5304-SIMPLE or

5305-SIMPLE (including the financial institution's procedures for withdrawal), if the employer used these IRS-approved forms to establish its SIMPLE plan.

- Include information about the method the employer will use in contributing to employees' SIMPLE IRAs, for example, whether the method will be to match employee contributions up to three percent of their pay or another authorized method.

- Notify employees that they can choose their own financial institution to serve as trustee for their SIMPLE IRA. Or, if the employer chooses the financial institution to receive contributions for all employees under the SIMPLE plan, notify employees that they have the right to transfer contributions to a SIMPLE IRA at another financial institution without cost or penalty.

Employers may provide additional or longer periods of election time to their employees (for instance, extend the election period to 90 days or provide quarterly or semi-annual election periods).

There are substantial penalties for failure to notify employees before an election period.

Trustee Requirements

For SIMPLE plan purposes, only these institutions can be designated as trustees: banks, savings and loan associations, insured credit unions, insurance companies (that issue annuity contracts), or IRS-approved non-bank trustees.

Trustees must agree to do the following:

- Accept and deposit contributions.
- Prepare and provide the employer with a summary description each year that includes the following:
  - The name and address of the employer and trustee;
  - A description of eligibility requirements;
  - The benefits provided;
  - The time and method of making salary elections;
  - The procedure for and effects of withdrawals and rollovers (including the penalties for early withdrawals).

The requirement that the trustee provide the employer a summary description may be satisfied by providing the most recent copy of IRS Forms 5304-SIMPLE or 5305-SIM-PLE (if these forms are used to establish the SIMPLE plans), along with the financial institution's procedures for withdrawals and transfers. Timing is important, because substantial penalties maybe imposed and employers depend on receiving summary descriptions in time to notify employees of each year's election period.

There are three additional trustee requirements:

Within 30 days after the close of each calendar year, the trustee must provide each individual on whose behalf an account is maintained with a statement of the account balance and activity during the year.

The trustee reports SIMPLE IRA information to the IRS, the same as it does with any IRA account.

A trustee that is a "designated financial institution" by agreement with the employer also agrees to transfer, upon request, an individual's SIMPLE IRA balance to another IRA or SIMPLE IRA without cost or penalty to the participant.

For more information see IRS Form 5304-SIMPLE or Form 5305-SIMPLE; both include a model plan document, notice, and salary reduction agreement.

.06 SIMPLE Retirement Plan Advantages

Employees can elect to defer up to $10,500 (for 2007) of their compensation each year. Employers are required to either make a 2% contribution on behalf of all eligible employees (regardless of whether the employees elect to defer any of their own money), or match the deferral (up to 3% of the employee's compensation).

> **Example:** Taxpayer A and Taxpayer B own a small business and have three employees. The company sets up a SIMPLE IRA and elects a three percent match.

Participant	Earnings	Elective Deferral	3% Match
Taxpayer A (owner)	$ 100,000	$9,000	$3,000
Taxpayer B (owner)	80,000	9,000	2,400
Worker 1	60,000	9,000	1,800
Worker 2	20,000	500	500
Worker 3	42,000	0	0
	$302,000	27,500	$7,700

The two owners each elected to defer $9,000, and Worker 1 also did. Because Worker 2 elected to defer only $500, which is less than three percent of earnings, the company match is limited to $500. Worker 3 made no elective deferral and receives no company funding.

The total retirement benefit going to the two owners is $23,400 ($9,000 + $9,000 + $2,400 + $3000), counting both the elective deferrals and the three percent match. The company's out-of-pocket cost for the employees is only $2,300. Out of a total cost to the owners of $25,700, $23,400 goes into their own accounts.

SIMPLE IRA Calculation for Self Employed

Taxpayer A is a self-employed farmer with net self-employment income as shown on Schedule F of Form 1040 of $60,000 in 2007. He wants to contribute the maximum deductible amount to his retirement plan. The following table shows the difference in Taxpayer A's self-employment income for retirement plan contribution purposes, depending on whether he has a SIMPLE IRA, Keogh, or SEP.

	SIMPLE IRA	Keogh or SEP
Net Income per Schedule F	$60,000	$60,000
Deduction for SE Tax Only (Code Sec. 1402(a)(12))		
$60,000 × 15.3% × 1/2	(4,590)	(4,590)
Base for SE Tax and SIMPLE IRA	$55,410	$55,410
SE Tax Rate		15.3%
SE Tax		$ 8,478

	SIMPLE IRA	Keogh or SEP
Net Income per Schedule F		$60,000
One Half of SE Tax ($8,478 × 1/2)		(4,239)
Base for SEP and Keogh Contributions		$55,761

With a SIMPLE IRA and $60,000 of self-employment income from farming as reported on Schedule F, Taxpayer A could claim a total SIMPLE IRA deduction of $10,662 ($9,000 elective deferral + 3% employer match of $1,662 ($55,410 × 3%). Taxpayer A could contribute a maximum of $11,152 ($55,761 × 20%) for his own account to a SEP or Keogh.

Contributions made on behalf of employees are deductible on Schedule C (or Schedule F for farmers). A sole proprietor's contributions for himself or herself are deductible as an adjustment to income on Form 1040.

.07 SEPs—Simplified Employee Pensions

Simplified Employee Pensions—known as SEPs—represent an easy, low-cost retirement plan option for employers, which allow an employer to provide retirement benefits for employees without paying the start-up and operating costs of conventional plans.

SEPs allow an employer to establish and make contributions to IRAs. The two critical differences between SEP-IRAs and other IRAs are that:

SEP contributions are generally made by employers, not employees.

The amounts contributed to SEPs can be much larger than the amounts contributed to IRAs.

As a general rule, up to 25 percent of each employee's pay can be put into a SEP-IRA each year.

Employers who establish SEPs can do the following:

- Make tax deductible contributions to their own and their employees' IRAs.
- Omit or reduce contributions in years when contributions are unaffordable.
- Avoid the administrative costs and the reporting requirements of conventional plans.

Whether a SEP is appropriate for a business depends on the following factors:

- Revenue
- Firm size
- Ages of the business owner and employees
- Compensation needs of the business owner and employees

Advantages for the Employer

Contributions to a SEP are tax deductible and the business pays no taxes on the earnings on a SEP's investments.

Employers are not locked into making contributions in future years. The employer can decide each year whether to pay into the SEP and how much to contribute.

¶923.07

A SEP can be established and operated without the administrative expenses, consulting fees or commissions usually associated with maintaining a conventional retirement plan.

SEPs can be set up by sole proprietors, partnerships and corporations, including S corporations.

The employer can deduct contributions to a SEP for a previous tax year if the employer makes contributions by the due date of the employer's tax return, including any extensions.

Advantages for Employees

The money contributed to employees' SEP accounts, as well as the investment earnings, belongs to them—even if they stop working for the employer.

Employers' contributions to the SEP-IRA are not included in employees' income for income tax purposes.

Employees pay no taxes on the amounts in their SEP accounts until they start withdrawing the funds.

Employees can change the financial institution where their SEP is invested.

In case of an employee's death, the assets in a SEP will go to someone the employee has chosen.

SEP contributions can continue until employees retire, but they must start withdrawing assets from a SEP when they reach age 70½.

Establishing a SEP

An employer can set up a SEP by using the Internal Revenue Service's "Model SEP" agreement Form 5305-SEP:

- Decide the percentage of pay to contribute to the SEP. The contribution is limited to 25 percent of pay or $45,000* (for 2007), whichever is smaller. A uniform percentage of pay must be contributed for each employee.

    * This number is indexed for inflation each year.

- Fill out Internal Revenue Service Form 5305-SEP, a quarter-page form with six blank spaces. This form is not filed with the Internal Revenue Service.

- Set up an IRA at a financial institution to receive the SEP contributions. An IRA can be set up by or for the employees to receive the contributions made for them.

- Mail the SEP contributions to the financial institutions.

- Give employees eligible to be included in the SEP a completed copy of the Form 5305-SEP and the other documents and disclosures listed in the instructions, including an annual statement to each participating employee of the amounts contributed to their account for the year.

No other reporting or disclosure ordinarily is required.

Generally, any employee who performs services for certain affiliated or commonly controlled employers must be included in a SEP. However, there are five exceptions to this general rule. Employers may exclude from the SEP:

- Employees who have not worked for the company during three out of the last five years.

- Employees who earn less than $500* (for 2007) a year.

  * This number is indexed for inflation each year.

- Employees who have not reached age 21 during the calendar year for which contributions are made.

- Employees covered by a collective bargaining agreement, if retirement benefits were the subject of good-faith bargaining.

- Non-resident immigrants who do not earn U.S. source income from you.

Further Points to Consider

If the employees choose to do so, they may combine IRA and SEP contributions in one account. NOTE. Because SEP contributions make an individual an "active participant in a qualified plan" for IRA purposes, IRA contributions of certain employees may not be tax deductible.

All eligible employees must participate. An employer can set up an IRA for the employee at a financial institution and make the appropriate contribution.

The employer does not have to pay Social Security or federal unemployment compensation taxes on SEP contributions for employees.

However, employers in companies with Salary Reduction SEPs do have to pay Social Security taxes on their employees' pre-tax contributions. In addition, employees have to pay their portion of Social Security taxes.

SEP money can be withdrawn without penalty at age 59½. Earlier withdrawals are generally subject to a 10% additional income tax unless the participant comes under the following exceptions:

- Has unreimbursed medical expenses that exceed 7.5 percent of adjusted gross income (to the extent thereof).

- Distributions are not more than the cost of medical insurance.

- Distributions are received when the taxpayer is disabled.

- The recipient is the beneficiary of a decedent's IRA.

- Distributions are paid in an annuity over the taxpayer's lifetime or life expectancy.

- Distributions are not more than qualified higher education expenses.

- Distributions up to $10,000 that are used to buy, build, or rebuild a first home.

- Distributions are the return of contributions before the due date of the tax return.

- Distributions are the result of an IRS levy of the IRA.

¶ 924 RETIREMENT ACCOUNT DISTRIBUTION RULES

.01 Introduction

If you have helped clients plan for retirement, you know that complicated rules have regulated how money must be taken out of retirement savings plans. Recently, the IRS published new and simpler guidelines. Most advisers understand that contributions to the retirement savings plans, as well as the earnings on those contributions, are generally not taxed until the funds are taken out or distributed. Your client's money compounds and accumulates in the meantime—a great way to save for retirement. Thus, rule changes that allow your clients to keep money in plans longer should be examined in the context of your client's plans and objectives.

One of the key rules governing retirement savings plans requires the plan participant to begin taking minimum required distributions generally on April 1 following the year the participant reaches age 70½ or when he or she retires, if later.

While IRAs can use the new uniform distribution rules immediately without revising their governing documents, qualified retirement plans in which your client participates (401(k), profit-sharing, and other pension plans) will only operate under the new rules *if* the plan adopts an amendment to conform the terms of the plan to the new rules. The IRS has published a model amendment to make it easier for plan sponsors to do this. Your client will need to check with the plan administrator to find out whether the plan has adopted the amendment or intends to do so.

.03 Retirement Distributions Easier to Calculate

If your client's retirement money is in a tax-deferred account—whether it is an individual retirement account (IRA), a 401(k) plan, or another employer-sponsored qualified retirement plan—the IRS generally requires that the client start making withdrawals as soon as he or she reaches what it considers to be retirement age or face a 50 percent excise tax.

Of course, the client is free to withdraw all of the money in his or her plan account right away at retirement (without penalty), but only if he or she is willing to pay the full amount of the taxes due at ordinary income tax rates. Most retirees would rather withdraw from their retirement plans only what they need—or are required to withdraw—each year and allow the rest to keep growing in their tax-deferred accounts where the money can ultimately become part of their estate and pass to their heirs.

A "required minimum distribution" is the amount the IRS requires your client to start withdrawing from his or her retirement account each year, after the client retires or reaches age 70½ (depending on the type of plan).

Calculating Required Minimum Distributions Under the *New* Rules

The new rules call for one simple and uniform table to be used by most plan participants to determine the required minimum distributions that must be made during their lifetimes. This table provides a uniform distribution period for all participants who are the same age, and assumes uniformly—and quite generously—that each participant has a beneficiary who is younger by exactly 10 years. It is, in fact, based on an old table that was used when a plan participant had a significantly younger beneficiary. A participant determines his or her required yearly distribution by simply locating his or her current age on the table to obtain the distribution period, and then dividing that number into his or her account balance as of the end of the previous year. Under the new rules, IRA trustees are required to provide IRA owners with a statement of their year-end account balances at the close of each year.

New Uniform Distribution Period Table

The new rules' uniform distribution period table (shown below) for distributions made during your client's lifetime makes it far easier to calculate a required minimum distribution because the client:

- No longer needs to designate a beneficiary by his or her required beginning date;

- No longer needs to factor in his or her beneficiary's age to calculate required minimum distributions during the client's lifetime (unless required distributions can be reduced because the client has a spouse-beneficiary who is more than 10 years younger than the client);

- No longer needs to decide whether or not to recalculate the client's life expectancy each year to determine required minimum distributions; and

- No longer needs to satisfy a separate incidental death benefit rule. (This rule was intended to ensure that the present value of the benefits projected to go to the participant during his or her lifetime had to equal more than 50 percent of the present value of the cumulative projected benefits to be paid.)

This one uniform table that will be used by just about everyone is based on the joint life expectancies of an individual and a survivor 10 years younger, regardless of who they have named as a beneficiary or whether they have selected a beneficiary at all. Allowing the use of this table reflects the fact that the client's beneficiary elections are subject to change until the client's death. The designated beneficiary may ultimately be someone who is more than 10 years younger than the client. Of course, the beneficiary may also be less than 10 years younger—the table essentially gives the client the benefit of assuming a 10-year difference in order to streamline the calculation of required benefit payments. (If the client's beneficiary is the client's *spouse* who is more than 10 years younger, the distributions may be calculated using a table that specifically determines the client's joint life expectancies as a couple so that the client can benefit from the full difference in ages instead of being limited to the 10 years allowed by the table.)

Uniform Distribution Period Table for Determining Required Lifetime Minimum Distributions

Age of Individual	Number of Payout/ Distribution Years
70	27.4
71	26.5
72	25.6
73	24.7
74	23.8
75	22.9
76	22.0
77	21.2
78	20.3
79	19.5
80	18.7
81	17.9
82	17.1
83	16.3
84	15.5
85	14.8
86	14.1
87	13.8
88	12.7

Age of Individual	Number of Payout/ Distribution Years
89	12.0
90	11.4
91	10.8
92	10.2
93	9.6
94	9.1
95	8.6
96	8.1
97	7.6
98	7.1
99	6.7
100	6.3
101	5.9
102	5.5
103	5.2
104	4.9
105	4.5
106	4.2
107	3.9
108	3.7
109	3.4
110	3.1
111	2.9
112	2.6
113	2.4
114	2.1
115 and older	1.9

By using the uniform distribution period table as the standard table, most participants will be able to determine their required minimum distribution for each year based on just their current age and their account balance as of the end of the prior year. Although a change in beneficiaries used to have an impact on the participant's required minimum distribution, beneficiaries generally no longer matter, because the single table alone is now used to determine the distribution amounts. An important factor contributing to the impressive tax benefits provided under the new rules is the dramatic increase in the "life expectancy" period that the IRS is allowing participants to use in computing their required minimum distributions each year.

Annuity Contracts That Were Previously IRAs

If the client has an IRA, instead of withdrawing the required minimum distribution, the client can buy an annuity contract from an insurance company or financial institution with all or part of his or her IRA proceeds. If the client does this, however, the rules require that minimum payments under the annuity contract match the required minimum distributions from the client's IRA account that would have been required using the uniform distribution period table.

¶924.03

.05 What Is a "Required Beginning Date"?

"Required beginning date" is a technical term for the actual date on which the client is required by law to begin taking withdrawals of his or her required minimum distributions. Technically speaking, the Internal Revenue Code requires that the entire interest in a retirement plan be distributed (beginning no later than the participant's required beginning date) over no longer than the life of the participant or over the joint lives of the participant and a designated beneficiary.

Although the client may withdraw the entire balance in his or her retirement plan account on the client's required beginning date if desired, the client need not do so. That date represents the point at which you begin measuring the time period over which all of the client's account balance must be distributed. If the client takes more than his or her required minimum distribution, the client will pay taxes on the entire amount he or she receives (and the client may not credit the excess distributions toward future years' required distributions). If the client spreads the distribution out, however, he or she will be taxed only as the payments are made.

The client's required beginning date depends on the type of plan from which he or she is withdrawing retirement savings. How the date is determined depends on whether the client is withdrawing funds from a qualified retirement plan (401(k), profit-sharing, and pension) or an IRA.

Required Beginning Date for Qualified Retirement Plans

If the client is a participant in a qualified retirement plan, the required beginning date is April 1 of the calendar year following the later of (1) the calendar year in which the client reaches age 70½ or (2) the calendar year in which the client retires from his or her job with the employer maintaining the plan.

In other words, the client must be at least 70½ *and* retired before he or she will be *required* to take distributions from a qualified plan. By way of illustration, determine the year in which the client would attain age 70½ (six calendar months after the date of his or her 70th birthday); if the client is already retired on the date he or she reaches 70½, April 1 of the next year is the client's required beginning date. If the client is going to retire *after* age 70½ from the company that maintains his or her qualified plan, determine the year he or she plans to retire, and April 1 of the following year is the client's required beginning date.

There is one exception to this rule, and that is for owner-employees. If your client owns five percent or more of the business that maintains the client's qualified plan, he or she must determine the required beginning date the same way IRA owners do as described below.

Required Beginning Dates for IRAs (and Five-Percent-or-Greater Owner-Employees of the Company Which Sponsored the Qualified Plan)

For those clients who are IRA owners (or five-percent-or-greater owners of a business who participate in the business's plan), their required beginning date is April 1 of the calendar year following the calendar year in they reach age 70½, even if they have not retired. In other words, unlike most participants in employer-sponsored qualified plans, IRA owners (and five-percent-or-greater owner-employees participating in employer-sponsored qualified plans) trigger the required minimum distribution rules when they reach the age requirement of 70½—regardless of whether their employment continues beyond age 70½.

Required Beginning Date vs. the Client's Retirement Date

It may be obvious to advisers that the actual date on which the client retires should not be confused with what the distribution rules call the "required beginning date," which is the date on which distributions must begin. However, this difference may need to be explained to clients. Of course, in most cases involving qualified plans, the client's retirement date will help determine the "required beginning date" and the client should understand this as well.

Required Beginning Date vs. Date as of Which the Client Will Not Incur an Early Withdrawal Penalty

Clients may also confuse their "required beginning date" with the date on which they are *allowed* to start withdrawing money from a retirement savings account without an "early withdrawal penalty." The adviser may wish to explain that the Internal Revenue Code allows the client to start withdrawing without penalty at age 59½ (or earlier for a variety of specified need-based reasons, or if withdrawals are a series of substantially equal payments over the client's life or life expectancy, or the joint lives or life expectancies of the client and his or her designated beneficiary). On the client's "required beginning date," however, the client *must* start withdrawing some of his or her proceeds and start paying tax—and this may need to be reiterated for clarity.

.07 Greater Options for the Client's Heirs

Under the new IRS rules, distributions from retirement plans may be easier to manage, but the rules governing distributions to beneficiaries are still complex.

Distributions Tied to Your Client's Beneficiaries' Life Expectancies

The distribution period for the client's retirement savings plan *after the client's death* is generally measured by the life expectancy of the "designated beneficiary" at the end of the year following the client's death. If the client dies without a designated beneficiary, the distribution period is generally measured by the remaining life expectancy period immediately before the client's death. The client's designated beneficiary for purposes of calculating required minimum distributions is the person, persons, trust, or entity that (1) has been named by the client as a beneficiary before the client's death and (2) remains a beneficiary as of the September 30 of the year following the year of the client's death.

Death on or After the Client's Required Beginning Date

If the client dies on or after the required beginning date, all future required minimum distributions from the client's account would generally be calculated based on the life expectancy of the person who is the designated beneficiary. The designated beneficiary's life expectancy is calculated as of the year following the client's death. It is then reduced by one for each subsequent year. Similarly, if the client's sole beneficiary is a spouse and, subsequent to the client's death, that spouse also dies, the required minimum distributions after the spouse's death will be calculated by using the client's spouse's life expectancy as of the year of his or her death, reduced by one for each subsequent year. If the client's beneficiary is a trust, the life expectancy of the trust beneficiary will generally be used to determine required distributions. If there is no designated beneficiary as of the end of the year following the client's death, required minimum distributions will be calculated using the client's life expectancy as of the year of his or her death, reduced by one for each subsequent year.

The new rules also represent a substantial improvement for those participants who otherwise would have elected to have their life expectancy recalculated annually and who then die without a designated beneficiary. Under the old rules, since the participant's life expectancy, recalculated as of the date of death, would have to be zero, the entire account would have to be distributed within a year of his or her death. Under the new rules, however, distribution can be prolonged over the life expectancy of the participant as calculated immediately before death.

Death Before the Client's Required Beginning Date

If the client dies before his or her required beginning date, even if the client had already started withdrawing money from his or her account, the balance of the client's retirement plan must be either:

- Distributed (in accordance with regulations) over the client's life expectancy (measured immediately before the client's death) or the life expectancy of the client's designated beneficiary, with distributions beginning no later than one year after the date of the client's death (except that the client's surviving spouse may wait until the date the client would have attained age 70½ to begin taking required minimum distributions) or,
- If there is no designated beneficiary, distributed within five years of the end of the year of the client's death.

This new post-death distribution rule replaces the more restrictive provision in the old rules. The previous provision required that the client's entire benefit had to be distributed to any nonspouse beneficiary within five years of the client's death unless the client had specifically elected some other schedule. Now, the forced five-year pay-out rule has been replaced by the new life expectancy provision, which applies in all cases where the client has a designated beneficiary (spouse or nonspouse) and no other provision for distribution at the end of the year following the year of the client's death. Only if the client dies before the client's required beginning date without a designated beneficiary will the client's entire account balance have to be paid out within five years of the client's death.

The new rule allowing distribution over a designated beneficiary's life expectancy is now the default rule, meaning that it will apply when no provision is made to the contrary. However, the client is not the only one who can choose an alternative distribution provision for the client's account. An IRA or qualified plan can still require in its own controlling documents that the client's account balance be distributed within five years of the client's death, or can give the beneficiary the option to elect to have the five-year rule apply. This is another example of why it is wise to find out from the client's plan administrator what the client's plan documents *actually* allow, not just what they *could* allow.

Whether the client dies before, on, or after the client's required beginning date, the designated beneficiary whose life expectancy is used as a measure for minimum distributions from the client's account need not (in fact, under the new rules, cannot) be identified until September 30 of the year following the client's death. Thus, any beneficiary who receives his or her share in a lump sum or disclaims his or her share *before* that date will be ignored when calculating the required minimum distributions to be made after the client's death. The only factors that go into that calculation are (1) the life expectancy of each beneficiary who, on September 30 of the year following the year of the client's death, is still entitled to receive money from the client's account, and (2) the balance of the client's account on that date.

Life Expectancy Table for Beneficiaries

The uniform distribution period table now available to compute the client's required minimum distribution *is not* used to determine the life expectancy of a designated beneficiary. Instead, the ordinary single life table, and joint and last survivor table (in the case where the client's joint beneficiary is the client's spouse who is younger by more than 10 years) apply. The life-expectancy number obtained from the appropriate table when distributions first begin will be reduced by one for each subsequent year of distribution to calculate the payments that must be made to a beneficiary in each subsequent year.

Multiple Beneficiaries

If the client has more than one designated beneficiary and the client's account or benefit *is not* divided into separate accounts or shares for each beneficiary, the beneficiary with the shortest life expectancy is the "designated beneficiary" for calculating the payout period for all of the beneficiaries. If the client has more than one designated beneficiary and the client's account or benefit *is* divided into separate accounts or shares for each beneficiary, each beneficiary can use his or her own life expectancy to calculate individual required minimum distributions. These rules have not been changed except to the extent that designated beneficiaries are now not determined until September 30 of the year following the year of the participant's death.

Trusts as Beneficiaries

If a trust is a beneficiary of the client's retirement plan or IRA, the underlying beneficiary of the trust, instead of the trust itself, may be treated as the client's designated beneficiary for calculating the required minimum distributions. This is known as the "look-through" rule. In order for this to occur, the client must supply the administrator of the client's plan or the trustee of the client's IRA with written documentation of the underlying beneficiaries, and the beneficiaries must be individuals rather than organizations.

Since the final rules do not lock in the client's beneficiaries until September 30 of the year after the year of the client's death, the client or the client's executor presumably has until that date to submit the documentation needed for the look-through rule to apply. However, if the client's life expectancy is being determined using the joint life expectancy tables, this documentation should be delivered before the client's death. The final rules also clarify certain issues that had not been resolved by the old rules from 1987. For example, a testamentary trust named as a beneficiary is also eligible for the look-through rules. Further, if amounts are accumulated for the benefit of individuals holding a remainder interest in a qualified terminable interest property (QTIP) trust during the life of the income beneficiary of the trust, the remaindermen are to be considered beneficiaries for determining required minimum distributions.

¶924.07

Beneficiaries Are Easier to Change

Another very important change in the final rules involves the timing of the client's beneficiary selection. Under the old rules, the client had to designate a beneficiary by the client's required beginning date or the client's death, whichever came first. After that date, any change in the client's beneficiary could cause an increase in the amount of the client's required minimum distributions but would never result in a reduction. The IRS has replaced the old rule with new provisions that give the client—and the client's beneficiaries—greater flexibility. As noted previously, the new rules delay the deadline for finalizing the identity of the designated beneficiary until September 30 of the year following the client's death, which allows for both pre-death and post-mortem estate planning.

Permitting the beneficiary to be determined as late as September 30 of the year following the year of the client's death allows:

- The client, while alive, to change designated beneficiaries after the client's required beginning date without increasing the client's required minimum distribution, and

- The client's beneficiary to be changed after the client's death (for example, if one or more beneficiaries disclaim (refuse to accept their interest in the client's retirement plan or IRA) or is cashed out (takes his or her share of the money in a lump sum)).

This means that the client will have more time to designate a beneficiary without changing the amount of the client's required distributions. It also means that any beneficiary who receives his or her entire share of the benefit or disclaims his or her interest in the client's account between the date of the client's death and September 30 of the following year will no longer be considered a designated beneficiary. (Note that this does not mean that someone else can substitute a brand new beneficiary after the client's death for those the client had selected. While they have the power to affect their own distributions (by disclaiming or cashing out before required distributions are to begin), the beneficiaries the client selected cannot direct distributions to previously unnamed beneficiaries.) The change in the beneficiary rules obviously creates opportunities for estate planning that were unavailable under the old rules.

Beneficiary Rules Specific to IRAs

For an IRA, the new rules will allow the client to designate the client's surviving spouse as a beneficiary, and give the client's spouse the option either to keep the proceeds in the client's account or roll them over to his or her own IRA; or to disclaim any interest and allow the client's children (if named as secondary beneficiaries) to receive the account assets. This means that the tax-deferral aspect of the client's IRA can be extended over the life expectancies of the client's children instead of the shorter life expectancy of the client's spouse. If the client had tried this under the old rules, the required distributions for the client's children would have been calculated based on the life expectancy of the client's spouse, rather than on their own life expectancies. Under the new rules, so long as the client's spouse disclaims his or her interest between the date of the client's death and September 30 of the following year, it is as if the IRA proceeds went directly to the client's children, and on September 30, the applicable distribution period will be based on their life expectancies. This tactic can also be used with other secondary beneficiaries having a life expectancy longer than that of the client's spouse.

Timing of Designation of Beneficiaries

Under the new rules, determination of the designated beneficiary and calculation of the beneficiary's life expectancy generally are contemporaneous with commencement of required distributions to the beneficiary (by September 30 of the year following the client's death). Any prior designation of a beneficiary or beneficiaries is irrelevant for calculating distributions from individual accounts, unless the client have taken advantage of the special lifetime distribution period exception measured by the joint life expectancy of the client and the client's spouse who is more than 10 years the client's younger.

Thus, the identification of a designated beneficiary on September 30 of the client's first post-death year depends on the client's pre-death beneficiary elections as well as any post-death disclaimers or lump-sum distributions or cash outs.

Do the Client's Homework—Check the Client's Plan Rules and Beneficiaries

The new rules are not perfect, of course. While some of the required minimum distribution changes *may* apply to qualified retirement plans immediately, depending on whether a plan adopts the appropriate amendment, some plans may ultimately decide not to implement all of the rules relating to beneficiaries. Many retirement plans may not want to follow all of the new rules because that would mean taking on an increased administrative burden. IRAs are a different matter. The new rules are generally effective for IRAs without the necessity of adopting a special amendment. While restrictive terms in some IRAs may prevent participants from taking full advantage of *all* the possibilities now available under the new rules, in general, IRAs will be more flexible more quickly.

That being the case, the client may need to check out the rules that the client's plans follow. Upon retiring—and assuming the client wants to pass the account money to a younger generation, rather than to the client's spouse—the client may want to roll the money in the client's qualified plan into an IRA to ensure that the client can take advantage of the new beneficiary rules. The client should strongly consider the enhanced opportunities to use retirement accounts for estate planning without funneling these assets through the client's estate for purposes of probate. The client's financial advisors are in a position to advise the client on the specifics of the new rules and how they can be used to best advantage.

The generosity of the new rules should not lull the client into inactivity. The adviser can help make sure the client's beneficiary elections are properly made, including contingent beneficiaries, and filed with the client's plan administrator, the client's IRA sponsor or trustee, and the client's estate planner. You should also examine the client's IRA or plan documents or have someone else examine them, and make sure the terms of those documents will allow the client to dispose of the assets as intended and that they are drafted and administered so as to allow the client to take advantage of the new rules.

.09 Temporary Rules for Distributions from Defined Benefit Plans and Annuity Contracts

Introduction to Defined Benefit Plan Required Distributions

When the IRS published the final rules on minimum required distributions discussed above, it provided a number of changes to the old rules for taxing annuity payments from defined benefit plans. These rules were published in the form of temporary and proposed regulations in order to give practitioners and taxpayers an opportunity to provide commentary before these rules are finalized.

Even though the 2001 rules did not make any changes in the way the law is applied, they did make several important changes to the annuity distribution rules to simplify their administration. (The annuity distributions referred to in this section are typically payouts under a defined benefit pension plan. If the client purchases an annuity from the proceeds of an IRA, the annuity rules do not apply. Rather, the client's minimum distributions must be computed as if the annuity payments were annual IRA withdrawals.)

Basic Annuity Rules in Place Before Changes Made by Old Proposed Regulations or New Temporary Regulations

When determining the distribution period (in order to calculate the required minimum distribution and to determine whether the annuity payments equal that amount), the designated beneficiary will be the person who is the beneficiary on the *annuity starting dat* e, even if that date is after the required beginning date.

Next, there is no need for a "make-up" distribution for any annuity that starts on the required beginning date and that will be paid out over a fixed term of up to 20 years. Only accruals existing as of the end of the prior calendar year have to be considered when annuity payments start on the required beginning date. Any subsequent accruals figure in the next year's calculation.

The old rules permitted and the new rules continue to allow an increase in the client's annuity payments when the annuity is originally a joint and survivor annuity and the anticipated survivor dies. Under the old proposed regulations, and likewise under the new temporary rules, an increase is also permitted when the survivor is eliminated from a joint and survivor annuity because of a qualified domestic relations order (QDRO). And, in a further accommodation, a cash refund of paid-up premiums made to an insurance company because of the client's death will not be considered a violation of the requirement that annuity payments be nonincreasing.

.11 Changes Made by New Temporary Rules

The following includes some of the changes made by the new temporary regulations.

Annuity Payments for a Period Certain

Annuity payments are also permitted to be made for a period certain that is as long as the period under the uniform lifetime distribution table based on the employee's age in the year in which the annuity starting date occurs, regardless of who is the designated beneficiary. Further, the period does not change upon the death of the employee even if the remaining period certain is longer or shorter than the beneficiary's single life expectancy.

¶924.09

The same rule applies if the annuity also includes a life annuity or a joint and survivor annuity. If the sole beneficiary is the employee's spouse, if the spouse is more than 10 years younger than the employee, and if the annuity is only for a period certain and does not have a life contingent element, the period certain can only be as long as the joint life and last survivor expectancy of the employee and the employee's spouse.

Interpreting Minimum Distribution Incidental Benefits Requirements

Under these rules, if the survivor of a joint and survivor annuity is not the employee's spouse and if the survivor annuitant is more than 10 years younger then the employee, then the survivor portion must be less than 100 percent of the employee's benefit. In such a case, the survivor annuity must be reduced so that it does not exceed the employee's benefit multiplied by the percentage provided in the table in the regulations. However, the temporary regulations clarify that if the joint and survivor annuity also has a period certain, the reduction in survivor annuity is only required after the expiration of the period certain.

Changes Expanding Circumstances When Increasing Annuity Payments Are Permitted

Under the temporary regulations, an annuity purchased from an insurance company can increase annually by a constant percentage, provided that the initial payment is sufficiently larger than the total expected payments, determined without regard to these increases, and exceeds the account value being annuitized.

> **Note:** This minimum payment requirement, together with the adverse economic interests of the insurer and the annuity purchaser, effectively limits the constant percentage increase under the annuity to the assumed interest rate used in pricing the annuity.

Explicit Rules for Payment of Dividends Under Participating Annuity Contracts

Under the temporary regulations, a variation in the amount of the annuity payment (referred to as a dividend) or other payment resulting from favorable actuarial experience can be made provided that (1) the initial payment meets the minimum threshold described above, (2) actuarial experience is measured at least annually, and (3) the resulting dividend payment or other payment is either paid no later than the year following the year for which the actuarial experience is measured or is payable in the same form as the payment of the annuity over the remaining period of the annuity.

> **Note:** These requirements are intended to preclude backloading of the distribution stream through the use of conservative pricing assumptions where the actuarial gains with respect to those assumptions are deferred and paid on a later date. The definition of dividend or other payment resulting from actuarial gain is broad enough to encompass the contractual adjustment provided for in a variable annuity. Accordingly, the rules are that permitted payments that vary with the investment performance of underlying assets have been replaced with this more general construct.

.13 Provisions for Special Retirement Situations

Changes Made by New Temporary Rules

Annuity payments are also permitted to be made for a period certain that is as long as the period under the uniform lifetime distribution table based on the employee's age in the year in which the annuity starting date occurs, regardless of who is the designated beneficiary. Further, the period does not change upon the death of the employee even if the remaining period certain is longer or shorter than the beneficiary's single life expectancy.

The same rule applies if the annuity also includes a life annuity or a joint and survivor annuity. If the sole beneficiary is the employee's spouse, if the spouse is more than 10 years younger than the employee, and if the annuity is only for a period certain and does not have a life contingent element, the period certain can only be as long as the joint life and last survivor expectancy of the employee and the employee's spouse.

Roth IRA Conversions

The Roth IRA, the newest star in the world of tax savings, loses some of its sparkle with the introduction of the new minimum distribution rules. The heralded changes are less of a boon to Roth IRAs than to traditional IRAs because Roth IRAs have never been subject to the minimum distribution requirements imposed on traditional IRAs. And although a conversion of a traditional IRA to a Roth IRA may still offer some tax benefits, it will generally not be as helpful as it was before the publication of the new rules because a traditional IRA is now more tax beneficial than ever before. The client will have a lower required minimum distribution from all of the client's accounts. The client's heirs will be able to defer receipt and taxation of their benefits even under traditional IRAs. Furthermore, with planning, the acceleration of taxes can be avoided when using traditional IRAs.

On the other hand, the new rules do not detract from the desirability of establishing a new Roth IRA that does not involve a conversion. And if a client does decide to convert a traditional IRA, the new rules make it more likely now that he or she will be eligible to make a conversion. With the lower required distributions from traditional IRAs and retirement plans, more individuals will come under the $100,000 income limitation, making them eligible for Roth conversions.

Spousal Inherited IRAs

If the client's spouse is the sole beneficiary of the client's IRA, the spouse may continue under the new rules to treat it as the spouse's own IRA. If the client's IRA beneficiary is a trust, however, this option will not be available even if the underlying beneficiary is the client's spouse. The new rules also clarify additional requirements for a spouse who wishes to treat an inherited IRA as his or her own. An inherited IRA account can only be treated as the spouse's own IRA if the client's required minimum distributions have been made for the year of the client's death, if the client's spouse has an unlimited right of withdrawal from the account, and if the client's spouse is the only beneficiary of the account. According to the new rules, a spouse can make the election to treat an inherited IRA as his or her own simply by altering the terms of the IRA to designate the spouse as the IRA owner rather than its beneficiary. Alternatively, the spouse can roll over the participant's account into his or her own rollover IRA. If the spouse chooses the latter course, the new rules provide that the post-death required minimum distribution for a year (but *not* the required distribution for the year of the participant's death) can also be rolled over into that account.

Delaying Distributions

The new rules permit required minimum distributions from a retirement account to be delayed under limited circumstances. The client is now allowed a delay of up to 18 months while a domestic relations order (see below) is under review. Also, a delay is allowed while annuity payments from an annuity contract that was issued by a life insurance company that is involved in state insurer delinquency proceedings are reduced or suspended because of the state proceedings.

Qualified Domestic Relations Orders (QDROs)

The new rules provide that a former spouse who is entitled to any of the client's plan benefits under a QDRO will be treated as a surviving spouse for purposes of the required distribution rules. This new rule will apply no matter how many former spouses the client has. If the client's retirement benefit has been divided into separate accounts or shares, the distributions to the client and any alternate payee named in a QDRO must start as of the client's required beginning date. The amount of the required benefit payments will be determined separately; however, they will still be based on *the client's* life expectancy. This means that the alternate payee's required minimum distributions during the client's life will be based either on the client's life expectancy under the new table or, if the client's alternate payee is the client's former spouse who is more than 10 years younger, on the joint life expectancies.

(Source: *Retirement Savings Plans: Taking Advantage of the Minimum Distribution Rules,* 2nd Edition, Pub. 2003, CCH INCORPORATED.)

Chapter 10
Directories

Accounting Organizations Directory . . . . ¶ 1001
Federal Government Resources Directory . . . . ¶ 1002
State Agencies and Departments of Revenue . . . . ¶ 1003

¶ 1001 ACCOUNTING ORGANIZATIONS DIRECTORY

.01 AMERICAN INSTITUTE OF CERTIFIED PUBLIC ACCOUNTANTS (AICPA)

Main Office

1211 Avenue of Americas, New York, NY 10036-8775 888-777-7077

Internet . . . . www.aicpa.org

.02 FINANCIAL ACCOUNTING STANDARDS BOARD (FASB)

Main Office

401 Merritt 7, PO Box 5116, Norwalk, CT 06856-5116 203-847-0700

Internet . . . . www.fasb.org

.03 NATIONAL SOCIETY OF ACCOUNTANTS (NSA)

Main Office

1010 N Fairfax St, Alexandria, VA 22314 800-966-6679

Internet . . . . www.nsacct.org

.04 NATIONAL ASSOCIATION OF ENROLLED AGENTS

1120 Connecticut Ave NW, Ste 460, Washington, DC 20036-3922 . . . . 202-822-NAEA (6232)

Internet . . . . www.naea.org

.05 STATE SOCIETIES

AL Society of CPAs

1103 S Perry St, PO Box 5000, Montgomery, AL 36103 . . . . 334-834-7650 or 800-227-1711

Internet . . . . www.ascpa.org

AK Society of CPAs

341 W Tudor Rd, Ste 105, Anchorage, AK 99503 . . . . 907-562-4334 or 800-478-4334

Internet . . . . www.akcpa.org

AZ Society of CPAs

2120 N Central Ave, Ste 100, Phoenix, AZ 85004 . . . . 602-252-4144 or 888-237-0700

Internet . . . . www.ascpa.com

AR Society of CPAs

11300 Executive Center Dr, Little Rock, AR 72211-4352 . . . . 501-664-8739 or 800-482-8739

Internet . . . . www.arcpa.org

CA Society of CPAs

1235 Radio Rd, Redwood City, CA 94065-1217 . . . . 800-9CALCPA (922-5272)

Internet . . . . www.calcpa.org

CO Society of CPAs

7979 E Tufts Ave, Ste 1000, Denver, CO 80237-2845 . . . . 303-773-2877 or 800-523-9082

Internet . . . . www.cocpa.org

CT Society of CPAs

    845 Brook St, Bldg 2, Rocky Hill, CT 06067-3405 . . . . 860-258-4800 or 800-232-2232

    Internet . . . . www.cs-cpa.org

DE Society of CPAs

    3512 Silverside Rd, 8 The Commons,
    Wilmington, DE 19810 302-478-7412

    Internet . . . . www.dscpa.org

DC Institute of CPAs - (*see* Greater Washington Society of CPAs)

FL Institute of CPAs

    325 W College Ave, PO Box 5437,
    Tallahassee, FL 32314-5437 . . . . 850-224-2727 or 800-342-3197

    Internet . . . . www.ficpa.org

GA Society of CPAs

    3353 Peachtree Rd NE, Ste 400, Atlanta, GA 30326-1414 . . . . 404-231-8676 or 800-330-8889

    Internet . . . . www.gscpa.org

Greater Washington Society of CPAs

    1828 L St NW, Ste 900, Washington, DC 20036 202-204-8014

    Internet . . . . www.gwscpa.org

HI Society of CPAs

    900 Fort St Mall, Ste 850, PO Box 1754,
    Honolulu, HI 96806 808-537-9475

    Internet . . . . www.hscpa.org

ID Society of CPAs

    250 Bobwhite Ct, Ste 240, PO Box 2896, Boise ID 83701 208-344-6261

    Internet . . . . www.idcpa.org

IL CPA Society

    550 W Jackson, Ste 900, Chicago, IL 60661-5716 . . . . 312-993-0407 or 800-993-0407

    511 W Capitol, Ste 101, Springfield, IL 62704 . . . . 217-789-7914 or 800-572-9870

    Internet . . . . www.icpas.org

IN CPA Society

    8250 Woodfield Crossing Blvd, Ste 100,
    Indianapolis, IN 46240-4348 . . . . 317-726-5000 or 800-272-2054

    Internet . . . . www.incpas.org

IA Society of CPAs

    950 Office Pk Rd, Ste 300, W Des Moines, IA 50265-2548 . . . . 515-223-8161 or 800-659-6375

    Internet . . . . www.iacpa.org

KS Society of CPAs

    1080 SW Wanamaker Rd, Ste 200, PO Box 4291,
    Topeka, KS 66604-0291 785-272-4366

    Internet . . . . www.kscpa.org

KY Society of CPAs

    1735 Alliant Ave, Louisville, KY 40299 . . . . 502-266-5272 or 800-292-1754

    Internet . . . . www.kycpa.org

LA Society of CPAs

    2400 Veterans Blvd, Ste 500, Kenner, LA 70062 . . . . 504-464-1040 or 800-288-5272

    Internet . . . . www.lcpa.org

ME Society of CPAs
    153 US Rte 1, Ste 8, Scarborough, ME 04074-9053 . . . . 207-883-6090 or 800-660-2721
    Internet . . . . www.mecpa.org

MD Association of CPAs
    901 Dulaney Valley Rd, Ste 710, Towson, MD 21204-2683 800-782-2036
    Internet . . . . www.macpa.org

MA Society of CPAs
    105 Chauncy St, 10th Floor, Boston, MA 02111 . . . . 617-556-4000 or 800-392-6145
    Internet . . . . www.mscpaonline.org

MI Association of CPAs
    PO Box 5068, Troy, MI 48007-5068 248-267-3700
    Internet . . . . www.michcpa.org

MN Society of CPAs
    1650 W 82nd St, Ste 600, Bloomington, MN 55431 952-831-2707
    Internet . . . . www.mncpa.org

MS Society of CPAs
    306 Southampton Row, The Commons,
    Highland Colony Parkway, Ridgeland, MS 39157 . . . . 601-856-4244 or 800-772-1099
    Internet . . . . www.ms-cpa.org

MO Society of CPAs
    540 Maryville Centre Dr, Ste 200, PO Box 419042,
    St Louis, MO 63141 . . . . 314-997-7966 or 800-264-7966
    Internet . . . . www.mocpa.org

MT Society of CPAs
    33 S Last Chance Gulch, Ste 2B, Helena, MT 59601 406-442-7301
    Internet . . . . www.mscpa.org

NE Society of CPAs
    635 S 14th St, Ste 330, Lincoln, NE 68508 . . . . 402-476-8482 or 800-642-6178
    Internet . . . . www.nescpa.org

NV Society of CPAs
    5250 Neil Rd, Ste 205, Reno, NV 89502 . . . . 775-826-6800 or 800-554-8254
    Internet . . . . www.nevadacpa.org

NH Society of CPAs
    1750 Elm St, Ste 403, Manchester, NH 03104 603-622-1999
    Internet . . . . www.nhscpa.org

NJ Society of CPAs
    425 Eagle Rock Ave, Ste 100, Roseland, NJ 07068 973-226-4494
    Internet . . . . www.njscpa.org

NM Society of CPAs
    1650 University NE, Ste 450, Albuquerque, NM 87102 . . . . 505-246-1699 or 800-926-2522
    Internet . . . . www.nmcpa.org

NY State Society of CPAs
    3 Park Ave, 18th Floor, New York, NY 10016-5991 . . . . 212-719-8300 or 800-633-6320
    Internet . . . . www.nysscpa.org

NC Association of CPAs
    3100 Gateway Centre Blvd Morrisville NC 27560 . . . . 919-469-1040 or 800-722-2836
    Internet . . . . www.ncacpa.org

ND Society of CPAs

　　2701 S Colombia Rd, Grand Forks, ND 58201 . . . . 701-775-7100 or 877-637-2727

　　Internet . . . . www.ndscpa.org

OH Society of CPAs

　　535 Metro Pl S, PO Box 1810, Dublin, OH 43017-7810 . . . . 614-764-2727 or 800-686-2727

　　Internet . . . . www.ohioscpa.com

OK Society of CPAs

　　1900 NW Expressway, Ste 910,
　　Oklahoma City, OK 73118-1898 . . . . 405-841-3800 or 800-522-8261

　　Internet . . . . www.oscpa.com

OR Society of CPAs

　　10206 SW Laurel St, Beaverton, OR 97005-3209 . . . . 503-641-7200 or 800-255-1470

　　Internet . . . . www.orcpa.org

PA Institute of CPAs

　　1650 Arch St, 17th Floor, Philadelphia, PA 19103 . . . . .215-496-9272 or 888-CPA-2001

　　Internet . . . . www.picpa.org

RI Society of CPAs

　　45 Royal Little Dr, Providence, RI 02904 401-331-5720

　　Internet . . . . .www.riscpa.org

SC Association of CPAs

　　570 Chris Dr West, Columbia, SC 29169 . . . . 803-791-4181 or 888-557-4814

　　Internet . . . . www.scacpa.org

SD CPA Society

　　1000 N West Ave, Ste 100, PO Box 1798,
　　Sioux Falls SD 57101-1798 605-334-3848

　　Internet . . . . www.sdcpa.org

TN Society of CPAs

　　201 Powell Pl, Brentwood, TN 37027 . . . . 615-377-3825 or 800-762-0272

　　Internet . . . . www.tncpa.org

TX Society of CPAs

　　14651 Dallas Pkwy, Ste 700, Dallas, TX 75254-7408 . . . . 972-687-8500 or 800-428-0272

　　Internet . . . . www.tscpa.org

UT Association of CPAs

　　220 E Morris Ave, Ste 320, Salt Lake City, UT 84115 801-466-8022

　　Internet . . . . www.uacpa.org

VT Society of CPAs

　　100 State St, Ste 500, Montpelier, VT 05602 802-229-4939

　　Internet . . . . www.vtcpa.org

VA Society of CPAs

　　4309 Cox Rd, PO Box 4620, Glen Allen, VA 23058-4620 . . . . 804-270-5344 or 800-733-8272

　　Internet . . . . www.vscpa.com

WA Society of CPAs

　　902 140th Ave NE, Bellevue, WA 98005-3480 . . . . 425-644-4800 or 800-272-8273

　　Internet . . . . www.wscpa.org

WV Society of CPAs

　　900 Lee St E, Ste 1201, PO Box 1673,
　　Charleston, WV 25326 . . . . 304-342-5461 or 800-352-3855

　　Internet . . . . www.wvscpa.org

¶1001.05

WI Institute of CPAs

    235 N Executive Dr, Ste 200, PO Box 1010,
    Brookfield, WI 53005 . . . . 262-785-0445 or 800-772-6939

    Internet . . . . www.wicpa.org

WY Society of CPAs

    504 W 17th St, Ste 200, Cheyenne, WY 82001 307-634-7039

    Internet . . . . www.wyocpa.org

¶ 1002 FEDERAL GOVERNMENT RESOURCES DIRECTORY

.01 FEDERAL GOVERNMENT LISTING—GENERAL OFFICES

Agency for International Development

    Ronald Reagan Building, Washington, DC 20523-1000 202-712-4810

    Internet . . . . www.usaid.gov

Commodity Futures Trading Commission

    Three Lafayette Centre, 1155 21st St NW,
    Washington, DC 20581 202-418-5000

    Internet . . . . www.cftc.gov

Consumer Product Safety Commission

    4330 East-West Hwy, Bethesda, MD 20814 301-504-7923

    Internet . . . . www.cpsc.gov

Department of Agriculture

    1400 Independence Ave SW, Washington, DC 20250 202-720-2791

    Internet . . . . www.usda.gov

Department of the Air Force

    1690 Air Force Pentagon, Washington, DC 20330-1690 703-697-4110

    Internet . . . . www.af.mil

Department of the Army

    1500 Army Pentagon, Washington, DC 20310-1500 703-695-6547

    Internet . . . . www.army.mil

Department of Commerce

    1401 Constitution Ave NW, Washington, DC 20230 202-482-2000

    Internet . . . . www.doc.gov

Department of Defense

    1400 Defense Pentagon, Washington, DC 20301-1400 703-545-6700

    Internet . . . . www.defenselink.mil

Department of Education

    400 Maryland Ave SW, Washington, DC 20202 . . . . 202-401-2060 or 800-872-5327

    Internet . . . . www.ed.gov

Department of Energy

    1000 Independence Ave SW, Washington, DC 20585 . . . . 1-800-DIAL-DOE

    Internet . . . . www.energy.gov

Department of Health and Human Services

    200 Independence Ave SW, Washington, DC 20201 . . . . 202-619-0257 or 877-696-6775

    Internet . . . . www.hhs.gov

Department of Housing and Urban Development

    451 7th St SW, Washington, DC 20410 202-708-1112

    Internet . . . . www.hud.gov

Department of the Interior

    1849 C St NW, Washington, DC 20240 202-208-3100

    Internet . . . . www.doi.gov

Department of Justice

    950 Pennsylvania Ave NW, Washington, DC 20530-0001 202-353-1555

    Internet . . . . www.usdoj.gov

Department of Labor

    Francis Perkins Bldg, 200 Constitution Ave NW,
    Washington, DC 20210 . . . . 866-4-USA-DOL

    Internet . . . . www.dol.gov

Department of the Navy

    1200 Navy Pentagon, Rm 2E335,
    Washington, DC 20350-1200 703-697-9020

    Internet . . . . www.navy.mil

Department of State

    2201 C St NW, Washington, DC 20520 202-647-4000

    Internet . . . . www.state.gov

Department of Transportation

    400 Seventh St SW, Washington, DC 20590 202-366-4000

    Internet . . . . www.dot.gov

Department of the Treasury

    1500 Pennsylvania Ave NW, Washington, DC 20220 202-622-2000

    Internet . . . . www.treas.gov

Department of Veterans Affairs

    810 Vermont Ave NW, Washington, DC 20420 202-273-4900

    Internet . . . . www.va.gov

Enviromental Protection Agency

    1200 Pennsylvania Ave NW, Ariel Rios Bldg,
    Washington, DC 20460 202-272-0167

    Internet . . . . www.epa.gov

Equal Employment Opportunity Commission

    1801 L St NW, Washington, DC 20507 . . . . 202-663-4900 or 800-669-4000

    Internet . . . . www.eeoc.gov

Executive Office of the President

    Office of Administration

    725 17th St NW, Washington, DC 20503 202-395-2273

    The White House Office

    1600 Pennsylvania Ave NW, Washington, DC 20500 202-456-1414

    Internet . . . . www.whitehouse.gov

Export-Import Bank

    811 Vermont Ave NW, Washington, DC 20571 . . . . 202-565-3946 or 800-565-3946

    Internet . . . . www.exim.gov

Farm Credit Administration

    1501 Farm Credit Dr, McLean, VA 22102-5090 703-883-4000

    Internet . . . . www.fca.gov

Federal Communications Commission

    445 12th St SW, Washington, DC 20554 888-225-5322

    Internet . . . . www.fcc.gov

¶1002.01

Federal Deposit Insurance Corporation
    550 17th St NW, Washington, DC 20429-9990 800-759-6596
    Internet . . . . www.fdic.gov
Federal Emergency Management Agency
    500 C St SW, Washington, DC 20472 800-621-3362
    Internet . . . . www.fema.gov
Federal Housing Finance Board
    1625 Eye Street NW, Washington, DC 20006-4001 202-408-2500
    Internet . . . . www.fhfb.gov
Federal Maritime Commission
    800 N Capital St NW, Washington, DC 20573 202-523-5900
    Internet . . . . www.fmc.gov
Federal Mediation & Conciliation Service
    2100 K St NW, Washington, DC 20427 202-606-8100
    Internet . . . . www.fmcs.gov
Federal Reserve System Board of Governors
    20th St and Constitution Ave NW, Washington, DC 20551 202-452-3000
    Internet . . . . www.federalreserve.gov
Federal Trade Commission
    600 Pennsylvania Ave NW, Washington, DC 20580 202-326-2222
    Internet . . . . www.ftc.gov
Federal Transit Administration
    400 7th St SW, Washington, DC 20590 202-366-4043
    Internet . . . . www.fta.dot.gov
General Services Administration
    1800 F St NW, Washington, DC 20405 202-501-1231
    Internet . . . . www.gsa.gov
Government Accounting Office
    441 G St NW, Washington, DC 20548 202-512-3000
    Internet . . . . www.gao.gov
Government Printing Office
    732 N Capitol St NW, Washington, DC 20401 202-512-0000
    Internet . . . . www.gpo.gov
Internal Revenue Service — Hotlines
    Tax help line for individuals 800-829-1040
    Business and specialty tax line 800-829-4933
    Employer identification number applications 866-816-2065
    Refund hotline 800-829-1954
    Practitioner priority service (account inquiries) 866-860-4259
    Forms and publications 800-829-3676
    Internet . . . . www.irs.gov
    Taxpayer advocate's help line 877-777-4778
    Taxpayer advocacy panel 888-912-1227
    Estate & gift accounts line 866-699-4083
    EFTPS customer service 800-555-4477
    EFTPS enrollment forms 800-945-8400
    Exempt organization help line 877-829-5500
    Tele-tax system (recorded tax info) 800-829-4477

Automated extensions 888-796-1074

Abusive schemes hotline 866-775-7474

Report tax fraud 800-829-0433

Identity theft hotline 877-438-4338

TDD 800-829-4059

Extention to file tele-file system 888-796-1074

Pay tax using credit card . . . . 800-2PAY-TAX or 888-PAY-1040

Internet . . . . www.officialpayments.com or
www.pay1040.com

Office of professional responsibility (formerly Dir. of
Practice) 202-514-3365

International Trade Commission

500 E St SW, Washington, DC 20436 202-205-2000

Internet . . . . www.usitc.gov

Library of Congress

101 Independence Ave SE, Washington, DC 20540 202-707-5000

Internet . . . . www.loc.gov

Marine Corps

Headquarters of the U.S. Marine Corp.

2 Navy Annex, Washington, DC 20380 703-614-1034

Internet . . . . www.usmc.mil

National Archives and Records Administration

8601 Adelphi Rd, College Park, MD 20740-6001 866-272-6272

Internet . . . . www.archives.gov

National Endowment for the Humanities

1100 Pennsylvania Ave NW, Washington, DC 20506 800-634-1121

Internet . . . . www.neh.gov

National Labor Relations Board

1099 14th St NW, Washington, DC 20570-0001 202-273-1991

Internet . . . . www.nlrb.gov

National Science Foundation

4201 Wilson Blvd, Arlington, VA 22230 703-292-5111

Internet . . . . www.nsf.gov

Occupational Safety and Health Review Commission

1120 20th St NW, 9th Floor, Washington, DC 20036-3457 202-606-5383

Internet . . . . www.oshrc.gov

Office of Management & Budget

725 17th St NW, Washington, DC 20503 202-395-3080

Internet . . . . www.whitehouse.gov/omb

Office of Management & Budget — Office of Federal Procurement
Policy

725 17th St NW, Washington, DC 20503 202-395-3080

Internet . . . . www.whitehouse.gov/omb/procurement

Office of Personnel Management

1900 E St NW Washington DC 20415 202-606-1800

Internet . . . . www.opm.gov

Overseas Private Investment Corporation

1100 New York Ave NW, Washington, DC 20527 202-336-8400

Internet . . . . www.opic.gov

¶1002.01

Peace Corps

    1111 20th St NW, Washington, DC 20526 800-424-8580

    Internet . . . . www.peacecorps.gov

Pension Benefit Guaranty Corporation

    1200 K St NW, Washington, DC 20005-4026 202-326-4343

    Internet . . . . www.pbgc.gov

Postal Service Supplier Diversity Office

    475 L'Enfant Plaza W SW, Rm 3821,
    Washington, DC 20260 202-268-6578

Railroad Retirement Board

    844 N Rush St, Chicago, IL 60611-2092 . . . . 312-751-7139 or 808-800-0772

    Internet . . . . www.rrb.gov

Securities and Exchange Commission

    100 F Street NE, Washington, DC 20549 202-551-6551

    Internet . . . . www.sec.gov

Small Business Administration

    6302 Fairview Rd, Ste 300, Charlotte, NC 28210 800-827-5722

    Internet . . . . www.sba.gov

Smithsonian Institution

    PO Box 37012, SI Bldg, Rm 153, MRC 010,
    Washington, DC 20013-7012 202-633-1000

    Internet . . . . www.si.edu

Social Security Administration

    6401 Security Blvd, Baltimore, MD 21235 800-772-1213

    Internet . . . . www.ssa.gov

Surface Transportation Board

    1925 K St NW, Washington, DC 20423-0001 202-565-1500

    Internet . . . . www.stb.dot.gov

U.S. Tax Court

    400 2nd St NW, Washington, DC 20217 202-521-0700

    Internet . . . . www.ustaxcourt.gov

U.S. Postal Service

    475 L'Enfant Plaza SW, Washington, DC 20260-2200 800-275-8777

    Internet . . . . www.usps.gov

.03 FEDERAL GOVERNMENT OFFICES—SPECIALIZED LISTINGS

US DEPARTMENT OF COMMERCE

see various bureaus and offices listed

BUREAU OF INDUSTRY & SECURITY

of the U.S. Department of Commerce

    Internet . . . . www.bis.doc.gov

Director of Office of Export Enforcement

    14th Street and Constitution Ave NW, Washington, DC 20230 202-482-1208

Los Angeles Field Office-Office of Export Enforcement

    2601 Main St, Irvine, CA 92714-6299 949-251-9001

San Jose Field Office-Office of Export Enforcement

    96 N Third St, San Jose, CA 95112-5519 408-291-4204

Miami Field Office-Office of Export Enforcement
    200 E Las Olas Blvd, Ft Lauderdale, FL 33301 954-356-7540
Chicago Field Office-Office of Export Enforcement
    High Point Plaza, 4415 W Harrison St, Hillside, IL 60162 312-353-6640
Boston Field Office-Office of Export Enforcement
    10 Causeway St, Boston, MA 02222 617-565-6030
New York Field Office-Office of Export Enforcement
    1200 South Ave, Staten Island, NY 10314 718-370-0070
Dallas Field Office-Office of Export Enforcement
    525 S Griffin St, Dallas, TX 75202 214-767-9294
Washington Field Office-Office of Export Enforcement
    381 Elden St, Herndon, VA 20170 703-487-9300

DEPARTMENT OF LABOR

Bureau of Labor Statistics
    2 Massachusetts Ave NE, Washington, DC 20212-0001 202-691-5200
    Internet . . . . www.bls.gov
Employment & Training Adm
    Frances Perkins Building, 200 Consitution Ave NW,
    Washington, DC 20210 877-872-5627
    Internet . . . . www.doleta.gov
Employment Standards Adm-Office of Workers' Comp Prog
    200 Constitution Ave NW, Washington, DC 20210 202-693-4650
    Internet . . . . www.dol.gov/esa/owcp_org.htm
Occupational Safety & Health Adm
    200 Constitution Ave NW, Washington, DC 20210 800-321-6742
    Internet . . . . www.osha.gov

ECONOMIC DEVELOPMENT ADMINISTRATION

of the US Department of Commerce
    Internet . . . . www.osec.doc.gov/eda

ECONOMICS AND STATISTICS ADMINISTRATION

of the US Department of Commerce
    Internet . . . . www.esa.doc.gov

BUREAU OF THE CENSUS

of the US Department of Commerce
    4700 Silver Hill Rd, Washington, DC 20233-0001 301-763-4636
    Internet . . . . www.census.gov
Public Information Office
    Washington, DC 20233 301-763-3030

BUREAU OF ECONOMIC ANALYSIS

of the US Department of Commerce
    Internet . . . . www.bea.gov
Information
    1441 L St NW Washington DC 20230 202-606-9900

INTERNATIONAL TRADE ADMINISTRATION

of the US Department of Commerce

Internet . . . . www.ita.doc.gov

Trade Information Center 800-872-8723

Export Assistance Centers

Internet . . . . www.export.gov

Alabama

    950 22nd St N, Ste 707, Birmingham, AL 35203-5309 205-731-1331

Alaska

    431 W 7th Ave, Ste 108, Anchorage, AK 99501 . . . . : 907-271-6237

Arizona

    2901 N Central Ave, Ste 970, Phoenix, AZ 85012 602-640-2513

    120 N Stone Ave, Ste 200, Tucson, AZ 85701 520-670-5540

Arkansas

    425 W Capitol Ave, Ste 425, Little Rock, AR 72201 501-324-5794

California

    2100 Chester Ave, 1st Floor, Ste 166, Bakersfield, CA 93301 661-637-0136

    550 E Shaw Ave, Ste 155, Fresno, CA 93710 559-227-6582

    Cabazon Tribal Headquarters

    84-245 Indio Springs Pkwy, Indio, CA 92203 760-342-4455

    11150 W Olympic Blvd, Ste 975, Los Angeles, CA 90064 213-894-7104

    444 S Flower, 34th Floor, Los Angeles, CA 90071 310-235-8784

    411 Pacific St, Ste 316A, Montery, CA 93940 831-641-9850

    3300 Irvine Ave, Ste 307, Newport Beach, CA 92660 . . . . 949-660-1688 x153

    50 Acacia Ave, San Rafael, CA 94901 . . . . 415-485-6200 or 6209

    1301 Clay St, Ste 630N, Oakland, CA 94612 510-273-7350

    2940 Inland Empire Blvd, Ste 121, Ontario, CA 91764 909-466-4134

    1410 Ethan Way, Sacramento, CA 95825 916-556-7170

    6363 Greenwich Dr, Ste 230, San Diego, CA 92122 619-557-5395

    250 Montgomery St, 14th Floor, San Francisco, CA 94104 415-705-2300

    55 S Market St, Ste 1040, San Jose, CA 95113-2387 408-535-2757

    333 Panoma St, Port Hueneme, CA 93041 805-488-4844

Colorado

    1625 Broadway, Ste 680, Denver, CO 80202 303-844-6623

Connecticut

    213 Court St, Ste 903, Middletown, CT 06457-3382 860-638-6950

Delaware

    Serviced by Philadelphia PA District Office

    601 Walnut St, Curtis Center, Ste 580W, Philadelphia, PA 19106-3304 215-597-6101

District of Columbia

    Serviced by Baltimore MD Branch Office

    300 W Pratt St, Ste 300, Baltimore, MD 21201 410-962-4539

Florida

    5835 Blue Lagoon Dr, Ste 203, Miami, FL 33126 305-526-7425

    200 E Las Olas Blvd, Ste 1600, Ft Lauderdale, FL 33301 954-356-6640

    13805 58th St N, Ste 1-200, Clearwater, FL 33760 727-893-3738

    325 John Knox Rd, The Atrium Bldg, Ste 201, Tallahassee, FL 32303 850-942-9635

    PO Box 5115, Deltona, FL 32728-5115 407-968-8122

    3 Independent Dr, Jacksonville, FL 32202-5004 904-232-1270

¶1002.03

Georgia

75 Fifth St NW, Ste 1055, Atlanta, GA 30308   404-897-6090

111 E Liberty St, Ste 202, Savannah, GA 31401   912-652-4204

Hawaii

521 Ala Moana, Rm 214, Foreign Trade Zone #9, Honolulu, HI 96813   808-522-8040

Idaho

700 W State St, PO Box 83720, Boise, ID 83720   208-364-7791

Illinois

200 W Adams St, Ste 2450, Chicago, IL 60606   312-353-8040

605 Fulton Ave, Ste E103, Rockford, IL 61103 . . . .   815-987-8123 x105

28055 Ashley Cir, Ste 212, Libertyville, IL 60048   847-327-9082

1501 W Bradley Ave, Peoria, IL 61625   309-671-7815

Jobst Hall, Rm 141, Bradley University, 922 N Glenwood, Peoria, IL 61606   309-671-7815

Indiana

11405 N Pennsylvania St, Ste 106, Carmel, IN 46032   317-582-2300

Iowa

210 Walnut St, Ste 749, Des Moines, IA 50309   515-284-4590

Kansas

150 N Main St, Ste 200, Wichita, KS 67202-1305   316-263-4067

Kentucky

1600 World Trade Center, 333 W Vine St, Lexington, KY 40507   859-225-7001

601 W Broadway, Rm 634B, Louisville, KY 40202   502-582-5066

Louisiana

2 Canal St, Ste 2710, New Orleans, LA 70130   504-589-6546

One University Pl BE119H, Shreveport, LA 71115   318-676-3064

Maine

511 Congress St, Portland, ME 04101   207-541-7430

Maryland

300 W Pratt St, Ste 300, Baltimore, MD 21201   410-962-4539

Massachusetts

World Trade Center, 200 Seaport Blvd, Ste 307, Boston, MA 02210   617-424-5990

Michigan

8109 E Jefferson Ave, Ste 110, Detroit, MI 48214   313-226-3650

EMU Coll of Bus, 300 W Michigan Ave, Ste 306G, Owen Ypsilanti, MI 48197   734-487-0259

401 W Fulton St, Ste 349C, Grand Rapids, MI 49504   616-458-3564

250 Elizabeth Lake Rd, Ste 1300 W, Pontiac, MI 48341   248-975-9600

Minnesota

100 N 6th St, Ste 210C, Minneapolis, MN 55403   612-348-1638

Mississippi

175 East Capitol St, Ste 255, Jackson, MS 39201   601-965-4130

Missouri

8235 Forsyth Blvd, Ste 520, St Louis, MO 63105-1623   314-425-3302

2509 Commerce Tower, 911 Main, Kansas City, MO 64105   816-421-1876

Montana

University of MT, Gallagher Bus Bldg, Ste 257, Missoula, MO 59812   406-542-6656

Nebraska

13006 W Center Rd, Omaha, NE 68144   402-597-0193

Nevada

    400 South Fourth St, Ste 250, Las Vegas, NV 89101 702-388-6694

    One East First St, 16th Floor, Reno, NV 89501 775-784-5203

New Hampshire

    17 New Hampshire Ave, Portsmouth, NH 03801-2838 603-334-6074

New Jersey

    20 W State St, PO Box 820, Trenton, NJ 08625-0820 609-989-2100

    744 Broad St, Ste 1505, Newark, NJ 07102 973-645-4682

New Mexico

    1100 St. Francis Dr, PO Box 20003, Santa Fe, NM 87504-5003 505-231-0075

New York

    1305 Elmwood Ave, Ste 530, Buffalo, NY 14202 716-551-4191

    163 West 125th St, Ste 901, New York, NY 10027 212-860-6200

    33 Whitehall St, 22nd Floor, New York, NY 10004 212-809-2682

    400 Andrews St, Ste 710, Rochester, NY 14604 585-263-6480

    707 Westchester Ave, Ste 209, White Plains, NY 10604 914-682-6712

North Carolina

    342 N Elm St, Greensboro, NC 27401 336-333-5345

    521 E Morehead St, Ste 435, Charlotte, NC 28202 704-333-4886

    10900 World Trade Blvd, Ste 110, Raleigh, NC 27617 919-281-2750

North Dakota

    51 Broadway, Ste 505, Fargo, ND 58102 701-239-5080

Ohio

    One Cascade Plaza, 17th Floor, Akron, OH 44308 . . . . 800-621-8001 x.264

    36 E 7th St, Ste 2650, Cincinnati, OH 45202 513-684-2944

    600 Superior Ave E, Ste 700, Cleveland, OH 44114 216-522-4750

    401 N Front St, Ste 200, Columbus, OH 43215 614-365-9510

    300 Madison Ave, Toledo, Ohio 43604 419-241-0683

Oklahoma

    301 NW 63rd St, Ste 330, Oklahoma City, OK 73116 405-608-5302

    700 N Greenwood Ave, Ste 1400, Tulsa, OK 74106 918-581-7650

Oregon

    121 SW Salmon St, Ste 242, Portland, OR 97204 503-326-3001

Pennsylvania

    2 S George St, Cumberland House, PO Box 45, Millersville, PA 17555-0302 717-872-4386

    601 Walnut St, Curtis Center, Ste 580W, Philadelphia, PA 19106-3304 215-597-6101

    425 6th Ave, Ste 2950, Pittsburgh, PA 15219-1819 412-644-2800

Puerto Rico

    Centro Internacional de Mercadeo, Tower 11, Ste 702, Road 165, Guaynabo, PR 787-775-1992

Rhode Island

    One W Exchange St, Providence, RI 02903 401-528-5104

South Carolina

    7300 College St, MTC-Harbison Hall, 2nd Floor, Irms, SC 29063 803-738-1400

    1362 McMillan Ave, Ste 100, North Charleston, SC 29405 843-746-3404

    216 S Pleasantburg Dr, Ste 243, Buck Mickel Ctr, Greenville, SC 29607 864-250-8429

South Dakota

    Augustana College, Madsen Ctr, Rm 122, 2001 S Summit Ave,

    Sioux Falls, SD 57197 605-330-4265

¶1002.03

Tennessee

    22 North Front St, Ste 200, Memphis, TN 38103 901-544-0930

    211 Commerce St, Ste 100, Nashville, TN 37201-1802 615-259-6060

    17 Market Sq, Ste 201, Knoxville, TN 37902-1405 865-545-4637

Texas

    221 E 11th St, 4th Floor, PO Box 12428, Austin, TX 78711 512-916-5939

    15600 JFK Blvd, Ste 530, Houston, TX 77032 281-449-9402

    808 Throckmorton St, Fort Worth, TX 76102-6315 817-392-2673

    1450 Hughes Rd, Ste 220, Grapevine, TX 76051 817-310-3744

    1400 FM 1788, Rm 1303, Midland, TX 79707-1423 432-552-2490

    6401 S 36th St, Ste 4, McAllen, TX 78503 956-661-0238

    203 S St Mary St, Ste 360, San Antonio, TX 78205 210-228-9878

Utah

    9690 S 300W, Ste 331, Salt Lake City, UT 84070 801-255-1871

Vermont

    National Life Bldg, 6th Floor, Montpelier, VT 05620-0501 802-828-4508

Virgin Islands

    Serviced by PR Branch Office

    Tower 11, Ste 702, Road 165, Guavnabo, PR 787-775-1992

Virginia

    400 N 8th St, Ste 412, PO Box 10026, Richmond, VA 23240-0026 804-771-2246

    1100 N Glebe Rd, Ste 1500, Arlington, VA 22201 703-235-0331

Washington

    2601 Fourth Ave, Ste 320, Seattle, WA 98121 206-553-5615

    801 W Riverside Ave, Ste 100, Spokane, WA 99201 509-353-2625

    2601 4th Ave, Ste 310, Seattle, WA 98121 253-973-5386

West Virginia

    1116 Smith St, Ste 314, Charleston, WV 25301 304-347-5123

    Wheeling Jesuit Univ, 316 Washington Ave, Wheeling, WV 26003 304-243-5493

Wisconsin

    517 E Wisconsin Ave, Rm 596, Milwaukee, WI 53202 414-297-3473

Wyoming

    Serviced by Denver CO Office

    1625 Broadway, Ste 680, Denver, CO 80202 303-844-6623

MAJOR FEDERAL EXECUTIVE PROCUREMENT AGENCIES

Agriculture Department

    Mail Stop 9301, 300 7th St SW, Washington, DC 20024 202-720-9448

    Internet . . . . www.usda.gov/procurement

Air Force Department

    1060 Air Force Pentagon, Rm 5E271, Washington, DC 20330-1060 703-696-1103

    Internet . . . . www.selltoairforce.org

Army Department

    106 Army Pentagon, Washington, DC 20310-0106 703-697-2868

    Internet . . . . www.sellingtoarmy.info

Commerce Department

    1401 Constitution Ave NW, Washington, DC 20230 202-482-2000

    Internet . . . . www.commerce.gov

¶1002.03

Defense Department
      1000 Defense Pentagon, Washington, DC 20301-1000 703-588-8620
      Internet . . . . www.defenselink.mil

Defense Logistics Agency
      8725 John J. Kingman Blvd, Ste 2545, Fort Belvoir, VA 22060-6221   703-767-6200 or 877-DLA-CALL
      Internet . . . . www.dla.mil

Education Department
      400 Maryland Ave SW, Washington, DC 20202 800-872-5327
      Internet . . . . www.ed.gov

Energy Department
      1000 Independence Ave SW, Washington, DC 20585 . . . . 202-586-5000 or 800-342-5363
      Internet . . . . www.energy.gov

Environmental Protection Agency
      1200 Pennsylvania Ave NW, Mail Code 1230, Washington, DC 20460 202-564-4142
      Internet . . . . www.epa.gov/sadqfzsu

General Services Administration
      1800 F St NW, Washington, DC 20405 . . . . 202-501-1231 or 877-472-3779
      Internet . . . . www.gsa.gov

Health & Human Services Department
      200 Independence Ave SW, Washington, DC 20201 . . . . 202-619-0257 or 877-696-6775
      Internet . . . . www.hhs.gov

Housing & Urban Development Department
      451 7th St SW, Washington, DC 20410 202-708-1112
      Internet . . . . www.hud.gov

Interior Department
      1849 C St NW, Washington, DC 20240 202-208-3100
      Internet . . . . www.doi.gov

Justice Department
      950 Pennsylvania Ave NW, Washington, DC 20530 202-514-2000
      Internet . . . . www.usdoj.gov

Labor Department
      200 Constitution Ave NW, Washington, DC 20210 866-487-2365
      Internet . . . . www.dol.gov

Nat'l Aeronautics & Space Admin
      300 E St SW, Washington, DC 20546-0001 202-358-0000
      Internet . . . . www.nasa.gov

Navy Department
      720 Kennon St SE, Rm 207, Washington, DC 20374-5015 202-685-6485
      Internet . . . . www.hq.navy.mil/sadbu

State Department
      229 C St NW, Washington, DC 20520 202-647-4000
      Internet . . . . www.state.gov

Transportation Department
      400 7th St SW, Rm 9414 S-40, Washington, DC 20590 . . . . 202-366-1930 or 800-532-1169
      Internet . . . . osdbuweb.dot.gov

Treasury Department
      1500 Pennsylvania Ave NW, Washington, DC 20220 202-622-2000
      Internet . . . . www.ustreas.gov

¶1002.03

Veterans Affairs Department

    810 Vermont Ave NW, Washington, DC 20420 . . . . 202-565-8124 or 800-827-1000

    Internet . . . . www.va.gov

MINORITY BUSINESS DEVELOPMENT AGENCY

of the US Department of Commerce

    1401 Constitution Ave NW, Washington, DC 20230 888-324-1551

    Internet . . . . www.mbda.gov

OFFICE OF BUSINESS LIAISON

of the US Department of Commerce

    1401 Constitution Ave NW, Rm 5062, Washington, DC 20230 202-482-1360

    Internet . . . . www.osec.doc.gov/obl

OFFICE OF SECRETARY—DEPARTMENT OF COMMERCE

Office of Computer Services

    5285 Port Royal Rd, Springfield, VA 22161 703-487-4747

    Internet . . . . www.osec.doc.gov/ocs

PATENT AND TRADEMARK OFFICE

of the US Department of Commerce

    PO Box 1450, Alexandria, VA 22313-1450 . . . . 571-272-1000 or 800-786-9199

    Internet . . . . www.uspto.gov

SMALL BUSINESS ADMINISTRATION

SBA Hotline

    409 3rd St SW Washington DC 20416 800-827-5722

SBA Answer Desk

    6302 Fairview Rd, Ste 300, Charlotte, NC 28210 . . . . 800-U-ASK-SBA

    Internet . . . . www.sba.gov

SMALL BUSINESS DEVELOPMENT CENTERS

Internet . . . . www.sba.gov/sbdc

University of Alabama, Birmingham, AL 205-943-6750

University of Alaska/Anchorage, Anchorage, AK 907-274-7232

Maricopa County Community College, Tempe, AZ 480-731-8720

University of Arkansas, Little Rock, AR 501-324-9043

California Trade and Commerce Agency, Sacramento, CA 707-445-9720 x317

Office of Economic Development, Denver, CO 303-892-3864

University of Connecticut, Strorrs, CT 860-870-6370

University of Delaware, Newark, DE 302-831-2747

Howard University, Washington, DC 202-806-1550

University of West Florida, Pensacola, FL 850-473-7800

University of Georgia, Athens, GA 706-542-6762

University of Guam, Mangialo, Guam 671-735-2590

University of Hawaii, Hilo, HI 808-974-7515

Boise State University, Boise, ID 208-426-3799

Dept of Commerce & Community Affairs, Springfield, IL 217-524-5700

Economic Development Council, Indianapolis, IN 317-232-2464

Iowa State University, Ames, IA 515-294-2037
Fort Hays State University, Topeka, KS 785-296-6514
University of Kentucky, Lexington, KY 859-257-7668
University of Louisiana at Monroe, Monroe, LA 318-342-5506
University of Southern Maine, Portland, ME 206-780-4420
University of Maryland, College Park, MD 301-403-8300
University of Massachusetts, Amherst, MA 413-545-6301
Grand Valley State University, Grand Rapids, MI 616-331-7485
MN SBDC, St. Paul, MN 651-297-5773
University of Mississippi, University, MS 662-915-5001
University of Missouri, Columbia, MO 573-882-1348
Department of Commerce, Helena, MT 406-841-2746
University of Nebraska at Omaha, Omaha, NE 402-554-2521
University of Nevada in Reno, Reno, NV 775-784-1717
University of New Hampshire, Durham, NH 603-862-4879
Rutgers University, Newark, NJ 973-353-5950
Santa Fe Community College, Santa Fe, NM 505-428-1362
State University of New York, Albany, NY 518-443-5398
University of North Carolina, Raleigh, NC 919-715-7272
University of North Dakota, Grand Forks, ND 701-328-5375
Department of Development, Columbus, OH 614-466-5102
S.E. Oklahoma State University, Durant, OK 580-745-7577
Lane Community College, Eugene, OR 541-463-5250
University of Pennsylvania, Philadelphia, PA 215-898-1219
InterAmerican University, Hato Rey, PR 787-763-6811
Johnson & Wales, Providence, RI 401-598-2704
American Samoa Community College, Pago Pago, Samoa 011-684-699-4830
University of South Carolina, Columbia, SC 803-777-4907
University of South Dakota, Vermillion, SD 605-677-6256
MTSU, Murfreesbro, TN 615-849-9999
Dallas County Community College, Dallas, TX 214-860-5835
University of Houston, Houston, TX 713-752-8425
Texas Tech University, Lubbock, TX 806-745-3973
University of Texas at San Antonio, San Antonio, TX 210-458-2742
Salt Lake City Community College, Sandy, UT 801-957-3493
Vermont Technical College, Randolph Center, VT 802-728-9101
University of the Virgin Islands, St. Thomas, US VI 340-776-3206
George Mason University, Fairfax, VA 703-277-7727
Washington State University, Spokane, WA 509-358-7765
W Virginia Development Office, Charleston, WV 304-558-2960
University of Wisconsin, Madison, WI 608-263-7794
University of Wyoming, Laramie, WY 307-766-3505

SMALL BUSINESS LIAISONS

of the US Department of Commerce

      14th & Constitution Ave NW, Herbert C Hoover Bldg, Rm 6411,
      Washington, DC 20230 202-482-1472
      Internet . . . . www.osec.doc.gov/osdbu

¶1002.03

Committee for Purchase from People Who Are Blind or Severely Disabled
  1421 Jefferson Davis Highway,
  Jefferson Plaza 2, Ste 10800, Arlington, VA 22202-3259 703-603-7740
  Internet . . . . www.jwod.gov

Office of Electronic Government & Technology
  1802 F St NW, Washington, DC 20405 202-501-0202
  Internet . . . . www.estrategy.gov

House Small Business Committee
  2361 Rayburn House Office Bldg, Washington, DC 20515 202-225-5821
  Internet . . . . wwwc.house.gov/smbiz

International Franchise Association
  1501 K Street NW, Ste 350, Washington, DC 20005 202-628-8000
  Internet . . . . www.franchise.org

Minority Business Development Agency
  1401 Constitution Ave NW, Washington, DC 20230 . . . . 202-482-5061 or 888-324-1551
  Internet . . . . www.mbda.gov

National Minority Supplier Development Council
  1040 Avenue of the Americas, 2nd Floor, New York, NY 10018 212-944-2430
  Internet . . . . www.nmsdcus.org

Senate Small Business Committee
  428A Russell Senate Office Bldg, Washington, DC 20510 202-224-5175
  Internet . . . . sbc.senate.gov

SBA Office of Women's Business Ownership
  409 3rd St SW, 6th Floor, Washington, DC 20416 202-205-6673
  Internet . . . . www.onlinewbc.gov

TECHNOLOGY ADMINISTRATION

of the US Department of Commerce
    Office of Technology Policy
    1401 Constitution Ave NW, Washington, DC 20230 202-482-5687
    Internet . . . . www.technology.gov/otpolicy

NATIONAL INSTITUTE OF STANDARDS & TECHNOLOGY

of the US Department of Commerce
    Internet . . . . www.nist.gov

Director
  100 Bureau Dr, Stop 1000, Gaithersburg, MD 20899-1000 301-975-3080

Advanced Technology Program
  100 Bureau Dr, Stop 4701, Gaithersburg, MD 20899-4701 800-287-3863

Hollings Manufacturing Extension Partnership
  100 Bureau Dr, Stop 4800, Gaithersburg, MD 20899-4800 301-975-5020

Baldridge National Quality Program
  100 Bureau Dr, Stop 1020, Gaithersburg, MD 20899-1020 301-975-2036

General Inquiries
  100 Bureau Dr, Stop 1070, Gaithersburg, MD 20899-1070 301-975-6478

NATIONAL TECHNICAL INFORMATION SERVICE

of the US Department of Commerce
    Internet . . . . www.ntis.gov

¶1002.03

Customer Service

    5285 Port Royal Rd, Springfield, VA 22161 . . . . 703-605-6050 or 888-584-8332

FedWorld

    5285 Port Royal Rd, Springfield, VA 22161 703-605-6000

    Internet . . . . www.fedworld.gov

¶ 1003 STATE AGENCIES AND DEPARTMENTS OF REVENUE

.01 ALABAMA

AL Dept of Revenue

    50 N Ripley St, Montgomery, AL 36132 334-242-1170

    Internet . . . . www.ador.state.al.us

AL Development Office

    401 Adams Ave, 6th Floor, Montgomery, AL 36130 . . . . 334-242-0400 or 800-248-0033

    Internet . . . . www.ado.state.al.us

AL Dept of Econ & Comm Affairs

    401 Adams Ave, PO Box 5690,

    Montgomery, AL 36103-5690 334-242-5100

    Internet . . . . adeca.state.al.us

AL Dept of Finance

    600 Dexter Ave, Ste N-105, Montgomery, AL 36130 334-242-7160

    Internet . . . . www.finance.state.al.us

.02 ALASKA

AK Dept of Revenue

    333 W Willoughby Ave, 11th Floor, PO Box 110400,

    Juneau, AK 99811-0400 907-465-2300

    Internet . . . . www.revenue.state.ak.us

AK Dept of Comm & Econ Dev

    PO Box 110800, Juneau, AK 99811-0800 907-465-2500

    Internet . . . . www.dced.state.ak.us

AK Dept of Comm & Econ Dev — Div of Investments

    3032 Vintage Blvd, PO Box 34159, Juneau, AK 99803-4159 907-465-2510

    Internet . . . . www.dced.state.ak.us/investments

AK Dept of Comm & Econ Dev — Div of Corp, Bus, and Prof Licensing

    333 W Willoughby Ave, 9th Floor, PO Box 110808,

    Juneau, AK 99811-0808 907-465-2530

    Internet . . . . www.dced.state.ak.us/occ

.03 ARIZONA

AZ Dept of Revenue — Taxpayer Information & Assistance

    1600 W Monroe, PO Box 29086, Phoenix, AZ 85038-9086 602-255-3381

    Internet . . . . www.revenue.state.az.us

AZ Dept of Revenue — Forms

    1600 W Monroe, Phoenix, AZ 85007-2650 602-542-4260

AZ Dept of Commerce

    1700 W Washington, Ste 600, Phoenix, AZ 85007 602-771-1100

    Internet . . . . www.azcommerce.com

.04 ARKANSAS

AR Dept of Finance & Admin
  1509 W 7th, Little Rock, AR 72201 501-682-2242
  Internet . . . . www.arkansas.gov/dfa
AR Dept of Econ Development
  One State Capitol Mall, Little Rock, AR 72201 . . . . 501-682-1121 or 800-ARKANSAS
  Internet www.1800arkansas.com
Small & Minority Bus
  One State Capitol Mall, Little Rock, AR 72201 501-682-6105

.05 CALIFORNIA

CA Franchise Tax Board — Gen Info & Forms
  PO Box 942840, Sacramento, CA 94240-0040 800-852-5711
  Internet . . . . www.ftb.ca.gov
CA Franchise Tax Board — Tax Practitioner Hotline
  PO Box 1468, Sacramento, CA 95812-1468 916-845-7057
CA Technology Trade & Commerce Agency — Main Office
  1102 Q St, Ste 6000, Sacramento, CA 95814 916-322-1394
  Internet . . . . www.commerce.ca.gov
CA Technology Trade & Commerce Agency — Econ Dev
  1102 Q St, Ste 6000, Sacramento, CA 95814 916-322-8730
CA Technology Trade & Commerce Agency — Office of Small Bus
  1102 Q St, Ste 6000, Sacramento, CA 95814 916-322-5790
CA Technology Trade & Commerce Agency — Intl Trade & Invstmt
  1102 Q St, Ste 6000, Sacramento, CA 95814 916-324-5511
CA Dept Gen Servs Procurement
  707 3rd St, 2nd Floor, West Sacramento, CA 95605 . . . . 916-375-4400 or 800-559-5529
  Internet . . . . www.pd.dgs.ca.gov

.06 COLORADO

CO Dept of Revenue — Income Tax Info — Sales & Withholding
  1375 Sherman St, Denver, CO 80261 303-238-7378
  Internet . . . . www.revenue.state.co.us
CO Dept of Revenue — Automated Forms
  1375 Sherman St, Denver, CO 80261 303-238-3278
CO Office of Econ Dev & Int'l Trade
  1625 Broadway, Ste 2700, Denver, CO 80202 303-892-3840
  Internet . . . . www.state.co.us/oed
CU Business Advancement Ctr
  CU-BAC UCB 034, Boulder, CO 80309 303-492-8395
  Internet . . . . www.colorado.edu/cubac

.07 CONNECTICUT

CT Dept of Revenue -Taxpayer Services
  25 Sigourney St, Hartford, CT 06106-5032 . . . . 860-297-5962 or 800-382-9463
  Internet . . . . www.drs.state.ct.us
CT Dept Econ & Comm Dev
  505 Hudson St, Hartford, CT 06106-7106 860-270-8000
  Internet . . . . www.ct.gov/ecd

¶**1003.04**

CT Development Authority
>999 West St, Rocky Hill, CT 06067-3011 860-258-7800
>Internet . . . . www.ctcda.com

CT Econ Resource Ctr
>805 Brook St, Bldg 4, Rocky Hill, CT 06067-3405 . . . . 860-571-7136 or 800-392-2122
>Internet . . . . www.cerc.com

CT Business & Industry Association
>350 Church St, Hartford, CT 06103-1126 860-244-1900
>Internet . . . . www.cbia.com

.08 DELAWARE

DE Division of Revenue
>820 N French St, Wilmington, DE 19801 . . . . 302-577-8200 or 800-292-7826
>Internet . . . . www.state.de.us/revenue/default.shtml

DE Econ Dev Office
>99 Kings Hwy, Dover, DE 19901 302-739-4271
>Internet . . . . www.state.de.us/dedo/default.shtml

.09 DISTRICT OF COLUMBIA

DC Office of Tax & Revenue
>941 North Capitol St NE, 1st Floor,
>Washington, DC 20002 . . . . 202-727-4TAX
>Internet . . . . http://otr.cfo.dc.gov/otr/

.10 FLORIDA

FL Dept of Revenue — Taxpayer Services
>5050 W Tennessee St, Tallahassee, FL 32399-0100 . . . . 850-488-6800 or 800-352-3671
>Internet . . . . http://dor.myflorida.com/dor

FL Dept of Revenue — Service Center
>2410 Allen Rd, Tallahassee, FL 32312-2603 850-488-9719

Enterprise Florida Inc (EFI)
>390 N Orange Ave, Ste 1300, Orlando, FL 32801 407-316-4600
>Internet . . . . www.eflorida.com

.11 GEORGIA

GA Dept of Revenue — Taxpayer Services Div
>1800 Century Center Blvd NE, Atlanta, GA 30345-3205 . . . . 404-417-2400 or 877-622-8477
>Internet . . . . www.etax.dor.ga.gov/#

GA Dept of Revenue — Refunds
>1800 Century Center Blvd NE, Atlanta, GA 30345-3205 . . . . 404-656-6286 or 800-338-2389

GA Dept of Community Affairs
>60 Executive Pk S NE, Atlanta, GA 30329 . . . . 404-679-4940 or 800-359-4663
>Internet . . . . www.dca.state.ga.us

GA Dept of Admin Services
>200 Piedmont Ave, Ste 1804, West Tower,
>Atlanta, GA 30334-9010 404-656-5514
>Internet . . . . www.doas.state.ga.us

Bus Outreach Services — U GA Chicopee Complex
    1180 E Broad St, Athens, GA 30602-5412 706-542-7436
    Internet . . . . www.sbdc.uga.edu

.12 HAWAII

HI Dept of Taxation — Taxpayer Services
    PO Box 259, Honolulu, HI 96809-0259 808-587-4242
    Internet . . . . www.state.hi.us/tax/tax.html

HI Dept of Bus, Econ Dev & Tourism
    No. 1 Capitol Dist, Bldg 250, S Hotel St, PO Box 2359
    Honolulu HI 96804 808-586-2423
    Internet . . . . www.hawaii.gov/dbedt

HI State Procurement Office
    1151 Punchbowl St, Honolulu, HI 96813 808-587-4700
    Internet . . . . www.spo.hawaii.gov

.13 IDAHO

ID Tax Commission
    PO Box 36, Boise, ID 83722-0410 800-972-7660
    Internet . . . . tax.idaho.gov

ID Dept of Commerce
    700 W State St, PO Box 83720, Boise, ID 83720-0093 . . . . 208-334-2470 or 800-842-5858
    Internet . . . . www.idoc.state.id.us

.14 ILLINOIS

IL Dept of Revenue — Taxpayer Assis
    101 W Jefferson St, Springfield, IL 62702 . . . . 217-782-3336 or 800-732-8866
    Internet . . . . www.revenue.state.il.us

IL Dept of Revenue — Forms
    101 W Jefferson St, Springfield, IL 62702 800-356-6302

IL Dept of Commerce — Springfield
    620 E Adams St, Springfield, IL 62701 217-782-7500
    Internet . . . . www.commerce.state.il.us

IL Dept of Commerce — Chicago Office
    100 W Randolph St, Chicago, IL 60601 312-814-7179

.15 INDIANA

IN Dept of Revenue — Income Tax
    100 N Senate Ave, Indianapolis, IN 46240 317-232-2240
    Forms 317-615-2581
    Sales Tax 317-233-4015
    Withholding 317-233-4016
    Corporate 317-615-2662
    Internet . . . . www.in.gov/dor

IN Dept of Commerce
    One North Capitol Ave, Ste 700, Indianapolis, IN 46204 317-232-8800
    Internet . . . . www.in.gov/doc

IN Dev Finance Authority
>One North Capitol Ave, Ste 900, Indianapolis, IN 46204 317-233-4332
>Internet . . . . www.in.gov/idfa

.16 IOWA

IA Dept of Revenue & Fin — Taxpayer Services
>PO Box 10457, Des Moines, IA 50306-0457 . . . . 515-281-3114 or 800-367-3388
>Internet . . . . www.state.ia.us/tax
IA Dept of Econ Dev — Main
>200 E Grand Ave, Des Moines, IA 50309 515-242-4700
>Internet . . . . www.iowalifechanging.com
IA Dept of Econ Dev — Bus Dev Program
>200 E Grand Ave, Des Moines, IA 50309 515-242-4707

.17 KANSAS

KS Dept of Revenue — Taxpayer Assis & Forms
>Docking State Office Bldg, Rm 150, 915 SW Harrison St,
>Topeka, KS 66612 785-368-8222
>Internet . . . . www.ksrevenue.org
KS Dept of Commerce & Housing
>1000 SW Jackson, Ste 100, Topeka, KS 66612-1354 785-296-3481
>Internet . . . . www.kansascommerce.com
KS Dept of Commerce — Bus Dev
>1000 SW Jackson, Ste 100, Topeka, KS 66612-1354 785-296-5298
KS Dept of Commerce — Trade Dev
>1000 SW Jackson, Ste 100, Topeka, KS 66612-1354 785-296-4610
KS Dept of Commerce — Community Dev
>1000 SW Jackson, Ste 100, Topeka, KS 66612-1354 785-296-3004

.18 KENTUCKY

KY Revenue Cabinet — Taxpayer Assistance & General Info
>200 Fair Oaks Ln, Frankfort, KY 40620 502-564-4581
>Internet . . . . www.state.ky.us/agencies/revenue
KY Cabinet for Econ Dev
>Old Capitol Annex, 300 W Broadway, Frankfort, KY 40601 . . . . 502-564-7140 or 800-626-2930
>Internet . . . . www.thinkkentucky.com
KY Cabinet for Econ Dev — Div Sm & Minority Bus
>Old Capitol Annex, 300 W Broadway, Frankfort, KY 40601 800-626-2250
KY Cabinet for Econ Dev — Off Intl Trade
>2300 Capital Plaza Twr, 500 Mero St, Frankfort, KY 40601 502-564-5891
KY Cabinet for Econ Dev — Kentucky Procurement Assis
>Old Capitol Annex, 300 W Broadway, Frankfort, KY 40601 800-838-3266

.19 LOUISIANA

LA Dept of Revenue — Gen Info
>617 N 3rd St, PO Box 201, Baton Rouge, LA 70821 225-219-2448
>Internet . . . . www.rev.state.la.us
LA Dept of Revenue — Forms
>PO Box 201, Baton Rouge, LA 70821 225-219-2113

LA Dept of Revenue — Sales
　　PO Box 201, Baton Rouge, LA 70821 225-219-7356
LA Dept of Revenue — Withholding
　　PO Box 201, Baton Rouge, LA 70821 225-219-7318
LA Dept of Econ Dev — Main
　　1051 N 3rd St, PO Box 94185,
　　Baton Rouge, LA 70802-9185 . . . . 225-342-3000 or 800-450-8115
　　Internet . . . . www.lded.state.la.us

.20 MAINE

ME Revenue Services — General Info
　　24 State House Station, Augusta, ME 04333-0024 207-287-2076
　　Internet . . . . www.state.me.us/revenue
ME Revenue Services — Income Tax Division
　　24 State House Station, Augusta, ME 04333-0024 207-626-8475
ME Revenue Services — Forms
　　PO Box 9100, Augusta, ME 04332-9100 207-624-7894
ME Revenue Services — Corporate Tax
　　PO Box 1062, Augusta, ME 04332-1062 207-624-9670
ME Revenue Services — Withholding
　　PO Box 1061, Augusta, ME 04332-1061 207-626-8475
ME Revenue Services — Practitioner's Hotline
　　24 State House Station, Augusta, ME 04333-0024 207-624-8458
ME Revenue Services — Taxpayer Advocate
　　24 State House Station, Augusta, ME 04333-0024 207-624-9649
ME Dept of Econ & Comm Dev
　　59 State House Station, Augusta, ME 04333-0059 207-624-9800
　　Internet . . . . www.econdevmaine.com
Finance Authority of Maine
　　5 Community Dr, PO Box 949, Augusta, ME 04332-0949 . . . . 207-623-3263 or 800-228-3734
　　Internet . . . . www.famemaine.com

.21 MARYLAND

MD Comptroller Revenue Admin Div — Taxpayer Services
　　Comptroller of MD, Rev Adm Center, Taxpayer Service
　　Section, Annapolis, MD 21411 . . . . 410-260-7980 or 800-MD-TAXES
　　Internet . . . . www.marylandtaxes.com
MD Comptroller Revenue Admin Div — Practitioner Hotline
　　Comptroller of MD, Rev Adm Center, Taxpayer Service
　　Section, Annapolis, MD 21411 410-260-7424
MD Comptroller Revenue Admin Div — Income Tax Refund
　　Comptroller of MD, Rev Adm Center, Taxpayer Service
　　Section, Annapolis, MD 21411 . . . . 410-260-7701 or 800-218-8160
MD Dept of Bus and Econ Dev
　　217 E Redwood St, Baltimore, MD 21202 . . . . 410-767-6300 or 888-ChooseMD
　　Internet . . . . www.choosemaryland.org

.22 MASSACHUSETTS

MA Dept of Revenue — Customer Service Bureau

    PO Box 7010, Boston, MA 02204 . . . . 617-887-MDOR or 800-392-6089

    Internet . . . . www.mass.gov

MA Office of Minority & Women Bus Assis

    10 Park Plaza, Ste 3740, Boston, MA 02116 617-973-8692

    Internet . . . . www.somwba.state.ma.us

MA Dept of Bus & Tech—Office of Int'l Trade & Investment

    10 Park Plaza, Ste 4510, Boston, MA 02116 617-973-8650

    Internet . . . . www.mass.gov/moiti

MA Dept of Bus & Tech

    1 Ashburton Pl, Rm 2101, Boston, MA 02108 617-788-3637

    Internet . . . . www.mass.gov

MA Econ Dev Authority

    160 Federal St, Boston, MA 02110 . . . . 617-451-2477 or 800-445-8030

    Internet . . . . www.massdevelopment.com

MA Tech Dev Corp

    40 Broad St, Ste 818, Boston, MA 02109 617-723-4920

    Internet . . . . www.mtdc.com

MA Office of Bus Dev

    1 Ashburton Pl, Rm 2101, Boston, MA 02108 . . . . 877-BIZTEAM

    Internet . . . . www.state.ma.us/mobd

.23 MICHIGAN

MI Dept of Treasury — Gen Info

    Mich. Dept of Treasury, Lansing, MI 48922 517-373-3200

    Internet . . . . www.michigan.gov/treasury

MI Dept of Treasury — Income Tax Info & Refunds

    Mich. Dept of Treasury, Lansing, MI 48922 800-827-4000

MI Econ Dev Corp

    300 N Washington Sq, Lansing, MI 48913 . . . . 517-373-9808 or 888-522-0103

    Internet . . . . medc.michigan.org

MI Dept of Consumer & Industry Services

    611 W Ottawa, PO Box 30004, Lansing, MI 48909 517-373-1820

    Internet . . . . www.cis.state.mi.us

.24 MINNESOTA

MN Dept of Revenue — Taxpayer Help Line

    600 N Robert St, Mail Station 5510,
    St Paul, MN 55146-5510 651-296-3781

    Internet . . . . www.taxes.state.mn.us

MN Dept of Employment & Econ Dev — Small Bus Dev Ctr

    1st Nat'l Bank Bldg, 332 Minnesota St, Ste E200,
    St. Paul, MN 55101-1351 651-297-5770

    Internet . . . . www.deed.state.mn.us

MN Dept of Employment & Econ Dev — Communications Office

    1st Nat'l Bank Bldg, 332 Minnesota St, Ste E200,
    St. Paul, MN 55101-1351 651-642-0445

MN Small Dept of Employment & Econ Dev — Sm Bus Assis Office

    1st Nat'l Bank Bldg, 332 Minnesota St, Ste E200,

    St. Paul, MN 55101-1351 651-296-3871

.25 MISSISSIPPI

MS State Tax Commission — Taxpayer Assis

    PO Box 1033, Jackson, MS 39215-1033 601-923-7000

    Internet . . . . www.mstc.state.ms.us

MS Development Authority

    501 NW St, PO Box 849, Jackson, MS 39205 601-359-3449

    Internet . . . . www.mississippi.org

MS Secretary of State

    401 Mississippi St, PO Box 136, Jackson MS 39201 601-359-1350

    Internet . . . . www.sos.state.ms.us

.26 MISSOURI

MO Dept of Revenue — Taxpayer Services

    Harry S Truman State Office Bldg, 301 W High St,

    Jefferson City, MO 65101 573-751-4450

    Internet . . . . www.dor.mo.gov

MO Dept of Revenue — Indiv Income Tax

    PO Box 500, Jefferson City, MO 65105-0500 573-751-3505

MO Dept of Revenue — Sales Tax

    PO Box 840, Jefferson City, MO 65105-0840 573-751-2836

MO Dept of Revenue — Corp Income Tax

    PO Box 700, Jefferson City, MO 65105-0700 573-751-4541

MO Dept of Econ Dev — Admin Serv

    301 W High St, PO Box 1157, Rm 680,

    Jefferson City, MO 65102 573-751-4962

    Internet . . . . http://ded.mo.gov

MO Dept of Econ Dev — Div of Bus & Comm Serv

    Harry S Truman Bldg, 301 W High St, PO Box 118,

    Jefferson City, MO 65102 . . . . 573-522-4173 or 573-751-5098

MO Intl Marketing

    PO Box 630, 1616 Missouri Blvd,

    Jefferson City, MO 65102 573-751-4211

    Internet . . . . www.mda.mo.gov/Market/intmrkting.htm

.27 MONTANA

MT Dept of Revenue — Customer Service

    Sam W Mitchell Bldg, 125 N Roberts, 3rd Floor,

    PO Box 5805, Helena, MT 59604 406-444-6900

    Internet . . . . www.state.mt.us/revenue

MT Dept of Commerce — Census & Econ Info Ctr

    301 S Park Ave, PO Box 200505, Helena, MT 59620-0505 406-841-2740

    Internet . . . . ceic.commerce.state.mt.us

MT Dept of Commerce — Community Dev Block Grant

    301 S Park Ave, PO Box 200523, Helena, MT 59620-0523 406-841-2770

    Internet . . . . http://comdev.mt.gov/CDD_CDBG.asp

MT Dept of Commerce — Trade & Intl Relations

      301 S Park Ave, PO Box 200501, Helena, MT 59601 406-841-2757

.28 NEBRASKA

NE Dept of Revenue — Taxpayer Asst

      301 Centennial Mall S, PO Box 94818,
      Lincoln, NE 68509-4818 . . . . 402-471-5729 or 800-742-7474

      Internet . . . . www.revenue.state.ne.us

NE Dept of Econ Dev

      301 Centennial Mall S, PO Box 94666,
      Lincoln, NE 68509-4666 800-426-6505

      Internet . . . . www.neded.org

NE Dept of Econ Dev — Comm Dev Block Grant

      301 Centennial Mall S, PO Box 94666, Lincoln, NE 68509 402-471-3119

      Internet . . . . crd.neded.org/cdbg/index.htm

NE Dept of Econ Dev — Comm & Rural Dev

      301 Centennial Mall S, PO Box 94666,
      Lincoln, NE 68509-4666 402-471-3111

      Internet . . . . crd.neded.org

NE Dept of Econ Dev — Intl Trade & Investment Office

      301 Centennial Mall S, PO Box 94666,
      Lincoln, NE 68509-4666 800-426-6505

      Internet . . . . international.neded.org

NE Bus Dev Center — U of NE Omaha

      6001 Dodge St, College of Bus Adm, Roskens Hall Rm 415,
      Omaha, NE 68182-0248 402-554-2521

      Internet . . . . www.nbdc.unomaha.edu

NE Investment Finance Authority

      1230 O St, Ste 200, Lincoln, NE 68508-1402 . . . . 402-434-3900 or 800-204-NIFA

      Internet . . . . www.nifa.org

NE Econ Dev Corp

      1610 S 70th St, Ste 201, Lincoln, NE 68506 402-483-4600

      Internet . . . . www.nedcoloans.org

NE State Ombudsman

      PO Box 94604, Rm 807 State Capitol,
      Lincoln, NE 68509-4604 . . . . 402-471-2035 or 800-742-7690

      Internet . . . . www.unicam.state.ne.us/offices/ombud.htm

.29 NEVADA

NV Dept of Taxation — General Info

      1550 College Pkwy, Ste 115, Carson City, NV 89706 775-684-2000

      Internet . . . . tax.state.nv.us

NV Commission on Econ Dev — General Contact 800-336-1600

      Internet www.expand2nevada.com

NV Commission on Econ Dev — Carson City Office

      108 E Proctor St, Carson City, NV 89701 775-687-4325

NV Commission on Econ Dev — Las Vegas Office

      555 E Washington, Ste 5400, Las Vegas, NV 89101 702-486-2700

NV Dept of Bus & Industry
     555 E Washington Ave, Ste 4900, Las Vegas, NV 89101 702-486-2750
     Internet . . . . dbi.state.nv.us

.30 NEW HAMPSHIRE

NH Dept of Revenue Admin
     45 Chenell Dr, Concord, NH 03302-0457 . . . . 603-271-2191 or 800-735-2964
     Internet . . . . www.state.nh.us/revenue
NH Dept of Revenue Admin — Forms
     45 Chenell Dr, PO Box 457, Concord, NH 03302 603-271-2192
NH Dept of State
     State House Rm 204, Concord, NH 03301 603-271-3242
     Internet . . . . www.state.nh.us/sos
NH Bus Finance Authority
     2 Pillsbury St, Ste 201, Concord, NH 03301 603-415-0195
     Internet . . . . www.nhbfa.com
NH Dept of Resources & Econ Dev — Div of Econ Dev
     172 Pembroke Rd, PO Box 1856, Concord, NH 03302-1856 603-271-2591
     Internet . . . . www.nheconomy.com
NH Community Dev Fin Authority
     14 Dixon Ave, Ste 102, Concord, NH 03301 603-226-2170
     Internet . . . . www.nhcdfa.org/web/index.html
NH Sm Bus Dev Center
     U of NH, 110 McConnell Hall, 15 College Rd,
     Durham, NH 03824 603-862-2200
     Internet . . . . www.nhsbdc.org

.31 NEW JERSEY

NJ Division of Taxation — Customer Service
     Info & Pub, PO Box 281, Trenton, NJ 08695-0281 609-292-6400
     Internet . . . . www.state.nj.us/treasury/taxation
NJ Division of Taxation — Forms
     Info & Pub, PO Box 281, Trenton, NJ 08695-0281 800-323-4400
NJ Comm & Econ Growth Comm
     20 West State St, PO Box 820, Trenton, NJ 08625-0820 609-777-0885
     Internet . . . . www.state.nj.us/commerce
NJ Comm & Econ Growth Comm — Off of Sm Bus
     49 Bleeker St, Newark, NJ 07102 973-353-1927
     Internet . . . . www.njsbdc.com
NJ Comm & Econ Growth Comm — Urban Enterprise Zone
     20 West State St, Trenton, NJ 08625-0820 609-777-0885
     Internet . . . . www.state.nj.us/commerce/
                    about_uez_program.shtml
NJ Comm & Econ Growth Comm — Div Intl Trade
     20 West State St, Trenton, NJ 08625-0820 609-292-3860
     Internet . . . . www.state.nj.us/commerce/
                    about_intl_trade.shtml

NJ Econ Dev Authority

    PO Box 990, Trenton, NJ 08625-0990 609-292-1800

    Internet .... www.njeda.com

.32 NEW MEXICO

NM Dept of Taxation & Revenue

    1100 S St Francis Dr, PO Box 630,
    Santa Fe, NM 87504-0630 505-827-0700

    Internet .... www.state.nm.us/tax

NM Dept of Taxation & Revenue — Personal Income Tax

    1100 S St Francis Dr, PO Box 630, Santa Fe, NM 87504 505-827-0822

NM Econ Dev Dept

    1100 S St Francis Dr, Santa Fe, NM 87505 .... 505-827-0300 or 800-374-3061

    Internet .... www.edd.state.nm.us

NM Econ Dev Dept — Adm Services Div

    1100 S St Francis Dr, Santa Fe, NM 87504 505-827-0252

NM Econ Dev Dept — NM Film Office

    1100 S St Francis Dr, Santa Fe, NM 87504 505-827-9833

NM Econ Dev Dept — Science & Tech Div

    1100 S St Francis Dr, Santa Fe, NM 87504 505-827-0616

NM Econ Dev Dept — Trade Div

    1100 S St Francis Dr, Santa Fe, NM 87504 505-827-0278

.33 NEW YORK

NY Dept of Taxation — Taxpayer Assis

    WA Harriman Campus, Albany, NY 12227 .... 518-457-4242 or 800-225-5829

    Internet .... www.tax.state.ny.us

NY Bus Dev Corp

    50 Beaver St, Albany, NY 12207 800-923-2504

    Internet .... www.nybdc.com

Empire State Development — Business Dev

    30 S Pearl St, Albany, NY 12245 800-782-8369

    Internet .... www.empire.state.ny.us

.34 NORTH CAROLINA

NC Dept of Revenue — Ind Income Tax Div

    PO Box 25000, Raleigh, NC 27640-0640 877-252-4052

    Internet .... www.dor.state.nc.us

NC Dept of Revenue — Forms

    PO Box 25000, Raleigh, NC 27640 877-252-3052

NC Dept of Revenue — General Info

    PO Box 25000, Raleigh, NC 27640 919-733-8510

NC Tech Dev Authority

    2 Davis Dr, PO Box 13169,
    Research Triangle Park, NC 27709-3169 919-990-8558

    Internet .... www.nctda.org

NC Rural Econ Dev Center

    4021 Carya Dr, Raleigh, NC 27610 919-250-4314

    Internet .... www.ncruralcenter.org

Div of Purchase & Contract

    1305 Mail Service Center, Raleigh, NC 27699-1305 919-733-4544

    Internet   www.doa.state.nc.us/PandC

Small Bus & Tech Dev Ctr

    5 W Hargett St, Ste 600, Raleigh, NC 27601-1348 . . . . 919-715-7272 or 800-258-0862

    Internet . . . . www.sbtdc.org

Frank Hawkins Kenan Institute of Private Enterprise

    CB 3440 The Kenan Center, Chapel Hill, NC 27599-3440 919-962-8201

    Internet . . . . www.kenan-flagler.unc.edu/KI

.35 NORTH DAKOTA

ND Office of Tax Commissioner — Individuals

    600 E Boulevard Ave, Dept 127, Bismark, ND 58505-0599 701-328-3450

    Internet . . . . www.nd.gov/tax/index.html

ND Office of Tax Commissioner — Corporate

    600 E Boulevard Ave, Dept 127, Bismark, ND 58505-0599 701-328-2046

ND Office of Tax Commissioner — Sales

    600 E Boulevard Ave, Dept 127, Bismark, ND 58505-0599 701-328-3470

ND Dept of Econ Dev & Fin

    1600 E Century Ave, Ste 2, PO Box 2057,

    Bismark, ND 58502 701-328-5300

    Internet . . . . www.growingnd.com

Fargo Cass County Econ Dev Corp

    51 Broadway, Ste 500, Fargo, ND 58102 . . . . 701-364-1900 or 877-243-0821

    Internet . . . . www.fedc.com

.36 OHIO

OH Dept of Taxation — Ind Income Taxpayer Serv

    4485 Northland Ridge Blvd, Columbus, OH 43229 . . . . 614-387-0224 or 800-282-1780

    Internet . . . . www.state.oh.us/tax

OH Dept of Taxation — Sales Tax

    30 E Broad St, 20th Floor, Columbus, OH 43215 614-466-4810

OH Dept of Development

    77 S High St, PO Box 1001, Columbus, OH 43216-1001 800-848-1300

    Internet . . . . www.odod.state.oh.us

OH Dept of Dev — Small Bus Dev Center

    77 S High St, Columbus, OH 43215 614-466-2711

    Internet . . . . www.odod.state.oh.us/edd/osb/sbdc/

    default.htm

OH Dept of Dev — Minority Bus Prog

    77 S High St, Columbus, OH 43216 614-466-5700

.37 OKLAHOMA

OK Tax Commission — Individual Tax

    2501 N Lincoln Blvd, Oklahoma City, OK 73194 405-521-3160

    Internet . . . . www.oktax.state.ok.us

OK Tax Commission — Withholding

    2501 N Lincoln Blvd, Oklahoma City, OK 73194 405-521-3160

OK Tax Commission — Business Registration

    2501 N Lincoln Blvd, Oklahoma City, OK 73194 405-521-3279

OK Dept of Commerce — Main Office

    900 N Stiles, Oklahoma City, OK 73104 800-879-6552

    Internet . . . . www.okcommerce.gov

OK Rural Enterprises Inc

    PO Box 1335, Durant, OK 74702 800-658-2823

    Internet . . . . www.ruralenterprises.com

.38 OREGON

OR Dept of Revenue — Taxpayer Asst

    955 Center St NE, Salem, OR 97301 . . . . 503-378-4988 or 800-356-4222

    Internet . . . . www.oregon.gov/dor

OR Econ Dev Dept — Small Bus Council

    775 Summer St NE, Ste 200, Salem, OR 97301-1280 503-986-0123

    Internet . . . . www.oregon-smallbiz.com

OR Econ & Comm Dev Dept — Bus Dev Div

    775 Summer St NE, Ste 200, Salem, OR 97301-1280 503-986-0123

    Internet . . . . http://econ.oregon.gov

Office of Minority, Women, and Emerging Small Business

    350 Winter St NE, 2d Floor, PO Box 14480,

    Salem, OR 97309-0405 503-947-7976

    Internet . . . . egov.oregon.gov/DCBS/OMWESB

.39 PENNSYLVANIA

PA Dept of Revenue — Taxpayer Services

    4th & Walnut, Harrisburg, PA 17128-0101 717-787-8201

    Internet . . . . www.revenue.state.pa.us

PA Dept of Revenue — Business Tax

    4th & Walnut, Harrisburg, PA 17128 717-787-1064

PA DCED Entrepreneurial Assistance Dept

    Commonwealth Keystone Bldg, 400 North St, 4th Floor,

    Harrisburg, PA 17120-0225 . . . . 866-GO-NEWPA

    Internet . . . . www.newpa.com

PA DCED Sm Bus Advocate

    Commonwealth Keystone Bldg, 400 North St, 4th Floor,

    Harrisburg, PA 17120 717-783-2525

PA DCED Office of International Development

    Commonwealth Keystone Bldg, 400 North St, 4th Floor,

    Harrisburg, PA 17120 717-787-7190

PA DCED Center for Private Financing

    Commonwealth Keystone Bldg, 400 North St, 4th Floor,

    Harrisburg, PA 17120 717-783-1109

PA DCED Center for Bus Fin

    Commonwealth Keystone Bldg, 400 North St, 4th Floor,

    Harrisburg, PA 17120 717-787-7120

.40 RHODE ISLAND

RI Div of Taxation — Taxpayer Assis

    One Capitol Hill, Providence, RI 02908 401-222-1040

    Internet . . . . www.tax.state.ri.us

¶1003.40

RI Div of Taxation — Withholding

    One Capitol Hill, Providence, RI 02908 401-222-3911

RI Div of Taxation — Forms

    One Capitol Hill, Providence, RI 02908 401-222-1111

RI Div of Taxation — Corporate

    One Capitol Hill, Providence, RI 02908 401-222-1120

RI Div of Taxation — Estate Tax

    One Capitol Hill, Providence, RI 02908 401-222-3057

RI Div of Taxation — Sales / Excise

    One Capitol Hill, Providence, RI 02908 401-222-2950

RI Econ Dev Corp

    1 West Exchange St, Providence, RI 02903 401-222-2601

    Internet . . . . www.riedc.com

.41 SOUTH CAROLINA

SC Dept of Revenue — Taxpayer Assis

    301 Gervais St, PO Box 125, Columbia, SC 29214 803-898-5000

    Internet . . . . www.sctax.org

SC Dept of Revenue — Tax Refund

    301 Gervais St, Columbia, SC 29214 803-898-5300

SC Dept of Revenue — Forms 800-768-3676

SC Dept of Revenue — Corporate

    301 Gervais St, Columbia, SC 29214 803-898-5705

SC Dept of Commerce

    1201 Main St, Ste 1600, Columbia, SC 29201-3200 803-737-0400

    Internet . . . . www.sccommerce.com

Governor's Small & Minority Bus Prog

    1301 Gervais St, Ste 710, Columbia, SC 29201 . . . . 803-771-0131 x.102 or 866-340-7105

    Internet . . . . http://sc.gov

SC Jobs Econ Dev Authority

    1441 Main St, Ste 905, Columbia, SC 29201 803-461-3800

    Internet . . . . scjeda.net

.42 SOUTH DAKOTA

SD Dept of Revenue & Regulation

    445 E Capital Ave, Pierre, SD 57501-3185 605-773-3311

    Internet www.state.sd.us/drr2/revenue.html

Governor's Office of Econ Dev

    711 East Wells Ave, Pierre, SD 57501-3369 . . . . 605-773-3301 or 800-872-6190

    Internet . . . . sdreadytowork.com

University of SD - Business Research Bureau

    414 E Clark St Vermillion SD 57069 605-677-5287

    Internet . . . . www.usd.edu/brbinfo

.43 TENNESSEE

TN Dept of Revenue — Taxpayer Services Div

    Andrew Jackson Bldg, Rm 1200, Nashville, TN 37242-1099 . . . . 615-253-0600 or 800-342-1003

    Internet . . . . www.state.tn.us/revenue

TN Dept of Revenue — Forms
>Andrew Jackson Bldg, Rm 1200, Nashville, TN 37242-1099 1-800-342-1003

TN Dept of Econ & Comm Dev — Bus Services
>312 8th Ave N, 11th Floor, Nashville, TN 37243 615-741-1888
>Internet . . . . www.state.tn.us/ecd

.44 TEXAS

TX Comptroller of Public Accounts
>PO Box 13528, Capitol Station, Austin, TX 78711-3528 877-662-8375
>Internet . . . . www.window.state.tx.us

TX Office of the Governor — Econ Dev & Tourism
>PO Box 12428, Austin, TX 78711 512-463-2000
>Internet . . . . www.governor.state.tx.us/divisions/ecodev

.45 UTAH

UT State Tax Commission
>210 N 1950 W, Salt Lake City, UT 84134 . . . . 801-297-2200 or 800-662-4335
>Internet . . . . tax.utah.gov

UT Dept of Comm & Econ Dev — Main
>324 S State St, Ste 500, Salt Lake City, UT 84111 . . . . 801-538-8700 or 877-488-3233
>Internet . . . . goed.utah.gov

UT Dept of Comm & Econ Dev — Int Bus Dev Off
>324 S State St, Ste 500, Salt Lake City, UT 84111 801-538-8737

UT Dept of Comm & Econ Dev — Procurement Tech Asst Ctr
>324 S State St, Ste 500, Salt Lake City, UT 84111 . . . . 801-538-8775 or 800-999-UTAH

.46 VERMONT

VT Dept of Taxes — Taxpayer Assis
>133 State St, Montpelier, VT 05633-1401 . . . . 802-828-2720 or 866-828-2865
>Internet . . . . www.state.vt.us/tax

VT Dept of Taxes — Forms
>133 State St, Montpelier, VT 05633-1401 802-828-2515

VT Dept of Taxes — Business
>133 State St, Montpelier, VT 05633-1401 802-828-5723

VT Dept of Econ Dev
>National Life Bldg, Drw 20, Montpelier, VT 05620-0501 802-828-3080
>Internet . . . . www.thinkvermont.com

Agency of Commerce & Comm Dev
>National Life Bldg N, Drw 20, Montpelier, VT 05620 802-828-3211
>Internet . . . . www.state.vt.us/dca

.47 VIRGIN ISLANDS

Small Bus Dev Centers
>Nisky Center, Ste 702, St Thomas, VI 00802 340-776-3206
>Sunshine Mall, Ste 104, Frederiksted, St Croix, VI 00840 340-692-5270
>Internet . . . . http://rps.uvi.edu/SBDC

.48 VIRGINIA

VA Commonwealth — Dept Taxation — Income Tax

    3600 W Broad St, Ste 160, Richmond, VA 23230-4915 804-367-8031

    Internet . . . . www.tax.virginia.gov

VA Commonwealth — Dept Taxation — Business

    3600 W Broad St, Ste 160, Richmond, VA 23230-4915 804-367-8037

VA Dept of Bus Assis

    707 E Main St, Ste 300, PO Box 446,
    Richmond, VA 23219-0446 804-371-8200

    Internet . . . . www.dba.state.va.us

VA Commonwealth — Secretary of Finance

    Patrick Henry Building, PO Box 1475, 1111 E Broad St,
    Richmond, VA 23218 804-786-1148

    Internet . . . . www.finance.virginia.gov

VA Dept of Minority Bus Enterprise

    1111 E Main St, Ste 300, Richmond, VA 23219 . . . . 804-786-5560 or 800-223-0671

    Internet . . . . www.dmbe.state.va.us

.49 WASHINGTON

WA State Dept of Revenue — Taxpayer Info

    PO Box 47476, Olympia, WA 98504-7476 800-647-7706

    Internet . . . . www.dor.wa.gov

.50 WEST VIRGINIA

WV Tax Department — Taxpayer Services Div

    PO Box 3784, Charleston, WV 25337-3784 . . . . 304-558-3333 or 800-982-8297

    Internet . . . . www.state.wv.us/taxdiv

WV Small Bus Dev Center

    1900 Kanawha Blvd E, Bldg 6, Rm 652, Charleston, WV
    25305-0311 . . . . 304-558-2960 or 888-WVASBDC

    Internet . . . . www.wvsbdc.org

WV Dev Office

    Capitol Complex, Bldg 6, Rm 553,
    1900 Kanawha Blvd E, Charleston, WV 25305-0311 . . . . 304-558-2234 or 800-982-3386

    Internet . . . . www.wvdo.org

.51 WISCONSIN

WI Dept of Revenue — Forms

    PO Box 8949, Madison, WI 53708-8949 608-266-1961

    Internet . . . . www.dor.state.wi.us

WI Dept of Revenue — Income Tax

    PO Box 59, Madison, WI 53785-0001 608-266-2486

WI Dept of Revenue — Sales & Withholding

    PO Box 8902, Madison, WI 53708 608-261-6261

WI Dept of Revenue — Corp Hotline

    PO Box 8908, Madison, WI 53708-8908 608-266-1143

WI Dept of Commerce — Main Office

    201 W Washington Ave Madison WI 53703 608-266-1018

    Internet . . . . www.commerce.state.wi.us

¶1003.48

WI Dept of Commerce — Div of Bus Dev

    201 W Washington Ave, 5th Floor, PO Box 7970,
Madison, WI 53707-7970 . . . . 608-261-7710 or 267-9384

WI Dept of Commerce — Small Bus Ombdsmn

    201 W Washington Ave, Madison, WI 53707-7970 608-267-0297

WI Dept of Commerce — Bureau of Minority Bus Dev

    201 W Washington Ave, PO Box 7970,
Madison, WI 53707-7970 608-267-9550

WI Dept of Commerce — Div of Community Dev

    201 W Washington Ave, PO Box 7970,
Madison, WI 53707-7970 . . . . 608-264-7837 or 267-0766

WI Innovation Service Ctr — U WI—Whitewater

    402 McCutchan Hall, Whitewater, WI 53190 262-472-1365

    Internet . . . . academics.uww.edu/business/innovate

WI Bus Dev Finance Corp

    100 River Pl, Ste 1, PO Box 2717, Madison, WI 53701-2717 . . . . 608-819-0390 or 800-536-6799

    Internet . . . . www.wbd.org

WI Dept of Admin — State Bureau of Procurement

    PO Box 7867, Madison, WI 53707-7867 . . . . 608-264-7897 or 800-482-7813

    Internet . . . . vendornet.state.wi.us/vendornet

WI Housing & Econ Dev Authority

    201 W Washington Ave, Ste 700, PO Box 1728,
Madison, WI 53701-1728 . . . . 608-266-7884 or 800-334-6873

    Internet . . . . www.wheda.com

.52 WYOMING

WY Dept of Revenue

    Herschler Bldg, 2d Floor W, Cheyenne, WY 82002-0110 307-777-7961

    Internet . . . . revenue.state.wy.us

WY Business Council

    214 W 15th St, Cheyenne, WY 82002-0240 . . . . 307-777-2800 or 800-262-3425

    Internet . . . . www.wyomingbusiness.org

WY Business Council — Econ Dev Grant

    214 W 15th St, Cheyenne, WY 82002 307-777-2821

WY Business Council — Bus Permit

    214 W 15th St, Cheyenne, WY 82002 307-777-2843

WY Industrial Development Corporation

    232 E 2nd St, Ste 300, Casper, WY 82601 . . . . 307-234-5351 or 800-934-5351

    Internet . . . . www.widefrontier.com

A

Ability to Pay Valuation Method 405.10

Absolute Liquidity Ratio 663.09

Accounting Changes 116, 201

Accounting for Servicing Assets and
  Liabilities 214

Accounting Policies 202

Accounts Payable 601
. Budget 601.01
. Estimated Disbursements 601.02

Accounts Payable — Cash Disbursements
  Analysis 631.01

Accounts Payable — Maximizing Cash
  Retention 631.01

Accounts Receivable
. Aging by Percentages 602.09
. Aging Forward 602.10
. Assignment 101.01
. Bad Debt 103
. Cash Flow — Maximizing 631.01
. Collections Analysis 631.01
. Days Sales Outstanding Ratio 602.05
. Discounts 602.03
. Interest Cost Due to Billing Delay 602.17
. Interests on Receivables 602.01
. Non-Collection Cash Flow Requirements . . 602.14
. Percentage Uncollected 602.11
. Probability of Collection 602.15
. Turnover Ratio 663.09

Accumulated Earnings Tax 802.05

Acquisitions of Assets by Exchange 104

Adjusted Book Value Valuation Method . . . 405.05

Affirmative Action Requirements 909.15

Agency for Intl Development 1002.01

AICPA 1001.01

Alternative Minimum Tax for Corporation . . 802.03

American Institute of Certified Public Accountants—
  see AICPA

Annualized Yield 689.01

Annuities
. Exclusion Ratio 717.09
. Gross Income 717.05
. Overview 717.01
. Payout Provisions 717.05
. Penalty for Premature Withdrawal 717.07
. Units and Value 717.03

APB 2 245

APB 4 245

APB 6 279

APB 9 273

APB 10 . . . . 229, 230, 279

APB 12 . . . . 215, 217, 279

APB 14 210

APB 18 222

APB 21 235

APB 22 202

APB 23 229

APB 26 213

APB 28 237

APB 29 . . . . 104, 253

APB 30 . . . . 213, 273

ARB 43 . . . . 211, 217, 239, 263, 265

ARB 45 249

ARB 46 265

ARB 51 206

Asset Retirement Obligations 108, 290

Automobile
. Expenses 802.37
. Fixed and Variable Rate Allowance (FAVR) . 802.39
. Lease Valuation 802.41
. Standard Mileage Rates 802.41

Average Collection Period 663.09

Average Collection Period or Days to
  Receivable Ratio 403.07

B

Bad Debt Index Ratio 663.09

Bad Debts
. Collections-Reestablishing Account
    Previously Written Off 103.07
. Percentage-of-Outstanding-Receivables
    Method 103.04
. Percentage-of-Sales Method 103.03
. Write-off 103.06

Balance Sheet Analysis 403.03, 631.03

Banker's Rule 635.05

Bankruptcy/Solvency Indicator Ratios 663.01
. Business Valuation 403.07

Basic Earnings Per Share 221

Basis
. Basis of Home 811.55
. Basis Summary Chart 802.35

Bond Value
. Approximate Yield to Maturity 603.01
. Known Yield 603.03

Bonds — Accounting
. Convertible 107.11
. Interest Income and Discount Amortization . 107.05
. Issued with Detachable Stock Warrants . . 107.13
. Long-Term Investments in Debt Security
  Purchase 107.03
. Premium or Discount 107.04
. Recording Bond Issue 107.01
. Retirement Before Maturity 107.07
. Sale of Investment 107.09

Bonds — Investments **719**
. Government Bonds Type Chart 719.13
. Municipal Bond Ratings 719.03
. Overview 719.01
. Risks 719.08
. Tax Exempt vs. Taxable 719.09
. Terms 719.07
. Types 719.05
. Yield Charts 719.10
. Yields 719.09
. Zero Coupon 719.11

Bonus **605**

Breakeven
. Concepts 607.01
. Breakeven Point for Cash Flow 607.09
. Breakeven Point for Target Net Income 607.05
. Breakeven Point for Target Net Income —
  Dollars 607.06
. Breakeven Point — in Dollars 607.03
. Breakeven Point — in Units 607.07

Bureau of the Census **1002.03**

Bureau of Economic Analysis **1002.03**

Bureau of Industry & Security **1002.03**

Business Combination **203**
. Accounting Principles 105, 201
. Purchase Method 105.01

Business Entities—see also individual entities
. Buying-Selling Business 301
. Choice of Entity 303
. Corporations 303.02, 305
. Limited Liability Company 303.02, 309
. Partnerships 303.02, 307
. S-corporation 303.02, 313
. Sole Proprietorship 303.02, 311
. Franchising 317

Business Tax Issues **802**
. Payments 802.19
. Return of Excess 802.21

Business Valuation **401**
. Balance Sheet Analysis 403.03
. Combination of Methods 406.05
. Comparables 401.19

Business Valuation—continued
. Conventional Techniques—Validity 401.17
. Debt and Firm Value 401.27
. Definition of Value 401.03
. Factors 401.11, 407.19
. Financial Ratios 403.07
. Glossary 401.02
. Income Statement Analysis 403.05
. Methods 405
. Non-Financial Considerations 404
. Purposes 401.05
. Process 406
. Reasonable Compensation 401.35
. Report Presentation 406.07
. Sample Engagement Letter 406.07
. Steps 401.13
. Valuation and Risk 401.33

Buying-Selling Business **301**

C

Cafeteria Plan — Taxation **802.15**

Capital Gains Tax Rates **807.03**

Capitalized Value **651.17**

**Capitalized Value by Discounted Cash Flow
Method** **651.17**

Cash **609**

Cash Discounts **609.01**

Cash Flow
. Cash Flow Statement 109, 204
. Cash Flow Statement — Direct 109.01
. Cash Flow Statement — Indirect 109.03
. Cash Flow to Debt Ratio 663.01
. Cash Gap 611.11
. Cash Management—Baumol Approach . . . 611.03
. Cash Management—Investment Securities . 611.05
. Cash Management—Miller-Orr Approach . . 611.07
. For purchases of Fixed Asset 611.01
. Need to Support Sales Growth 611.02
. Short-Term Needs 611.09

Casualty Losses Taxation Chart **811.23**

Changing Prices **205**

Checklist for Incorporation **305.03**

Check -the-Box Regulations **303.02**

Child and Dependent Care Tax Credit **811.15**

Choice of Entity Chart **303.01**

Civil Rights Act of 1964, Title VII **909.01**

Clergy Housing Allowance Clarification Bill . . . **801**

College Funding — Investment Required **703**

Collection Ratio **663.09**

Commodity Futures Trading Commission . **1002.01**

Common Dollars **613**
. Converting Dollars to Common Dollars 613.01

Common Size Statements **614**

Common Stock Cash Flow Coverage Ratio . 663.03

Comparison of Up-Front Fees and Mortgage
Interest Rates Tables 691.31

Compensation Costs—Employer 907.02

Compound Interest 637

Consolidated Financial Statements 206

Construction Contracts — Percent of
Completion 111.01

Construction Contracts — Long-Term —
Accounting Standards 249

Consumer Credit Protection Act (CCPA) . . 908.05

Consumer Product Safety Commission . . . 1002.01

Contingencies 207

Contributions — Accounting Standards 209

Control Criteria 214

Convertible Debt—Accounting Principles 210

Corporate Tax 305.07, 802.01
. Accumulated Earnings Tax 802.05
. Alternative Minimum Tax 802.03
. Tax Rates 305.07, 802.01

Corporations 305
. Checklist for Incorporation 305.03
. Dividend Distributions 305.09
. Section 1244 Stock 305.11
. Tax 305.07
. Transfers of Property 305.05

Cost Basis of Home — Home Items 811.55

Cost of Capital 615
. Capital Asset Pricing Model 615.20
. Common Equity 615.05-615.19
. Cost of Common Equity 615.20
. Debt 615.02
. Preferred Stock 615.03
. Real Estate Method 615.21
. Weighted Average 617.23

Cost of Goods Manufactured Schedule 113

Coverage Ratios 663.03

Credit Cost 619.13

Credits 811
. Adoption. 811.37
. Child Tax Credit 811.39
. Child and Dependent Care Tax Credit 811.35
. Earned Income Credit 811.43
. Hope Scholarship Credit 811.41
. Lifetime Learning Credit 811.41
. Loan Comparisons 811.61
. Welfare-to-Work Credit 811.71
. Work Opportunity Credit 811.69

Current Assets and Current Liabilities 211

Current Assets to Total Debt Ratio 663.11

Current Asset Turnover Ratio 403.07, 663.21

Current Debt to Net Worth Ratio 663.21

Current Liabilities to Inventory
Ratio 403.07, 663.21

Current Ratio 663.09

D

Dates — Accumulated Days in a Year Chart . 617.01

Dates — Number of Days Between Dates
Chart 617.03

Days Coverage With No Revenue 663.09

Debt 619
. Cost of Debt 619.01
. Cost of Debt After Inflation and Taxes Tables . . . . .
. . . . 691.01
. Cost of Overall Debt Chart 619.06
. Credit 619.13-619.15
. Debt and Firm Value 401.27
. Debt Cash Flow Coverage Ratio 663.03
. Debt Extinguishment 213
. Debt Ratio 663.07
. Debt Repayment 619.09-619.11
. Debt to Equity Ratio 663.07
. Growth 633.02

Deductions 811
. Automobile 811.37, 811.39, 811.41
. Bad Debts 811.43
. Casualty Losses 811.23
. Dependent Tax Exemption 811.25
. Education Expense Deduction 811.25
. Employee Under Age 18, Example 811.45
. Entertainment 811.47, 811.49
. Health Insurance Deduction for the Self-
Employed 811.51
. Hobby Loss vs. Business Loss 811.53
. Home Deductions 811.55
. Home Office 811.55, 811.57, 811.59
. Meals 811.47
. Medical and Dental Expenses 811.17
. Medical Expense Deduction 811.19
. Medical Savings Account 811.63
. Moving Expenses 811.11
. NOL Carryovers 811.65
. Personal Exemption 811.15
. Property Taxes 811.21
. Purchase of Residence 811.53
. Rent vs. Own 811.51
. Schedule A 811.27
. Student Loan Interest Deduction 811.13
. Travel 811.67

Defense Department 1002.01

Deferred Compensation Contracts 215

De Minimis Fringe Benefits 802.13

Department of
. Agriculture 1002.01
. Air Force 1002.01
. Army 1002.01
. Commerce 1002.01
. Defense 1002.01
. Education 1002.01

Department of—continued

. Energy 1002.01
. Health and Human Services 1002.01
. Housing and Urban Development 1002.01
. Interior 1002.01
. Justice 1002.01
. Labor 1002.01, 1002.03
. Navy 1002.01
. State 1002.01
. Transportation 1002.01
. Treasury 1002.01
. Veterans Affairs 1002.01

Depletion **621**

Depreciation

. Accounting Standards 217
. Accumulated, Declining Balance Method . . . 623.18
. Accumulated, Double Declining Balance
    Method 623.19
. Accumulated, Sum of Years Digits Method . 623.20
. Capital Recovery 623.04-623.05
. Change in Accounting Estimate 116.02
. Composite Method 115.05
. Composite Rate of Depreciation 623.01
. Declining Balance 115.07, 623.10-623.14
. Depreciation Tax Effect 623.17
. Financial vs. Tax 115.01
. Fractional-Year Calculation 115.03
. Productive Output Method 623.16
. Service Hours Method 623.15
. Straight-Line Method of Depreciation 623.02
. Sum of Years Digits Method 623.07, 623.08
. Tangible Business Property 807.20
. 200 Percent Declining Balance Method 623.09
. Units of Production Method 623.06

Depreciation — Tax

. Business Use of Car 802.33
. Methods 802.33
. Section 1245 Depreciable Property 802.25
. Section 1250 Depreciable Property 802.27

Derivative Instruments and Hedging **218**

Development Stage Company **219**

Direct Costing **117**

Directories **1001**

. American Institute of Certified Public
    Accountants 1001.01
. Federal Government Offices — General
    Listing 1002.01
. Federal Government Offices — Specialized
    Listing 1002.03
. National Society of Accountants 1001.03
. State Agencies and Departments of Revenue . 1003
. State CPA Societies 1001.05

Disability —see Social Security Disability

Discounting —Continuous 651.03, 651.05

Discontinued Segments **119**

Discounted Future Earnings Valuation
Method **405.05**

Discrimination **909**

Discrimination—continued

. Age 909.17
. Disability 909.19
. Enforcement Procedures 911
. Handicap 909.19
. Investigating a Complaint 911.06
. National Origin 909.13
. Pregnancy 909.11
. Race or Color 909.03
. Religion 909.05
. Sex 909.07
. Sexual Harassment
. . Discrimination 909.09
. . State Anti-bias Laws 909.22
. Vietnam Veterans 909.21

Dividend Distributions **305.09**

Dividend Payout Ratio **663.11**

Dividend Yield Ratio **663.11**

Dividends **121**

Dollar Cost Averaging **705**

E

Earned Income Credit **811.43**

Earnings Per Share

. Accounting Standards 221
. Basic 123.05
. Financials 221
. Diluted 123.06, 123.07, 625.03
. Primary 625.01
. Retroactive Adjustments 123.03
. Weighted Average Shares Outstanding . . . 123.01

Earnings Power Ratio 403.07, 663.13

EBIT to Total Assets Ratio **663.01**

Economic Development Administration . . **1002.03**

Economic & Statistics Administration **1002.03**

Education Assistance **802.09**

EEOC and Equal Employment 911.01, 1002.01

EEOC — Interviewing Checklist **911.04**

EEOC—Investigations **911.06**

EEOC — Records, Notice Requirements . . . **911.03**

Effective Annual Rates for Different Periods
of Compounding Tables **691.05**

Employee Benefits **903**
. Fringe Benefits—Tax Savings 903.03
. Paid Time Off 903.08
. Pre-Tax Savings Plan 903.01

Employee Defined **919.03**

Employee Polygraph Protection Act of 1988
(EPPA) **908.06**

Employee Stock Ownership Plan **627**

Employee vs. Independent Contractor Sec.
530 Examination **919.13**

Employment Taxes
. Defined 907.03
. Deposit Requirement 909.05, 907.07, 907.11,
  907.13
. Safe Harbor/De Minimis Rules 907.09

Employment Wages and Withholding 907

Endowment Insurance 701.05

Entertainment Expenses 803.23, 803.25

Environmental Protection Agency 1002.01

Equal Employment Opportunity Commission—see
  EEOC

Equal Pay—see FLSA (Fair Labor Standards Act)

Equity Bond Formula 709.07

Equity Method Investment 222

Equity Ratio 663.07

Ergonomics 914

Error Corrections 116, 201

Estate and Gift Taxes
. Estate Tax Rates 805.05
. Gift Tax 805.01
. Gross Estate Defined 805.03
. State Death Tax Credit 805.07

Estate Planning
. Basics 707.01
. Business Owners 707.20
. Buy-Sell Agreements 707.21
. Estate Information Worksheet 707.03
. Power of Attorney 707.08
. Property Ownership 707.05
. Wills 707.07

Estimated Corporate Income Tax 305.07

Estimated Tax Payment Chart 811.09

Excess Earnings Valuation Method 405.05

Executive Office of the President 1002.01

Exit Activity Cost 141.12, 290

Expected Value 653.05

Expenses
. Accrued 125.01
. Computed from Balance Sheet Items 671.05
. Prepaid 125.03

Export-Import Bank 1002.01

F

Factorial 629

Fair Labor Standards Act—see FLSA

Fair Value Accounting 295

Family and Medical Leave Act 908.01

Farm Credit Administration 1002.01

FASB Interpretation 1 . . . . 201, 239

FASB Interpretation 4 271

FASB Interpretation 6 271

FASB Interpretation 8 211

FASB Interpretation 9 203

FASB Interpretation 18 229

FASB Interpretation 19 247

FASB Interpretation 20 201

FASB Interpretation 21 203

FASB Interpretation 23 247

FASB Interpretation 24 247

FASB Interpretation 26 247

FASB Interpretation 27 247

FASB Interpretation 30 253

FASB Interpretation 35 222

FASB Interpretation 39 . . . . 211, 255

FASB Interpretation 41 . . . . 211, 255

FASB Interpretation 46 . . . . 105.03

FASB Interpretation 47 . . . . 108, 290

FASB Interpretation 48 229

FASB Technical Bulletin 79-10 247

FASB Technical Bulletin 79-12 247

FASB Technical Bulletin 79-14 247

FASB Technical Bulletin 79-16 247

FASB Technical Bulletin 79-17 247

FASB Technical Bulletin 79-18 247

FASB Technical Bulletin 80-1 213

FASB Technical Bulletin 84-4 213

FASB Technical Bulletin 85-3 247

FASB Technical Bulletin 85-5 203

FASB Technical Bulletin 85-6 203

FASB Technical Bulletin 86-2 247

FASB Technical Bulletin 88-1 247

Federal Aquisition Regulation 1002.01

Federal Communications Commission . . . 1002.01

Federal Deposit Insurance Corporation . . . 1002.01

Federal Emergency Management Agency . 1002.01

Federal Government
. Offices — General Listing 1002.01
. Offices — Specialized Listing 1002.03

Federal Housing Finance Board 1002.01

Federal Maritime Commission 1002.01

Federal Mediation & Conciliation Service . 1002.01

**Federal Reserve System Board of
  Governors** 1002.01

Federal Trade Commission 1002.01

Federal Transit Administration 1002.01

Federal Unemployment Tax 907.11

50% Rule for Meal and Entertainment 811.47

Filing Requirements 811.05

Finance vs. Purchase vs. Straight Lease . . . 651.19

Financial Accounting Standards Board . . . 1001.02

Financial Analysis of a Business
. Balance Sheet 631.03
. Difficulties 631.05
. Difficulties — External Warning Signs 631.05
. Difficulties — Intermediate-Term Danger
   Signals 631.05
. Difficulties — Internal Warning Signs 631.05
. Difficulties — Long Term Danger Signals . . . 631.05
. Difficulties — Short-Term Danger Signals . . 631.05
. Difficulty Remedies 631.05
. Earnings Quality — Net Income 631.03
. Management Analysis 631.01
. Reporting 631.04

Financial Instruments 223

Financial Ratios—See Ratios

Financing Sources 693.03

Firing Fairly 911.05

Fixed Assets to Net Worth Ratio 663.11

Fixed Charge Coverage Ratio 663.03

**Fixed Expenses Given Any Known Amount
of Sale** 655.05

Flexible Spending Account, see also Flexible
Spending Arrangement 802.65

Flexible Spending Arrangement (FSA), see also
Flexible Spending Account 903.09

FLSA 912
. Definitions 912.01
. Employees Covered 912.05
. Enterprises Covered 912.03
. Equal Pay 913
. Exemptions 912.06
. Exemptions Regarding Minimum Wages . . . 912.13,
   913.01
. Fair Labor Standards Act Summary Charts . 912.13
. Hours Worked 912.01
. Investigations and Records 912.09
. Minimum Wage Values 912.08
. Overtime Pay/Overtime Rate 912.01, 912.14
. Prohibited Acts 912.11
. Regulations 913.03
. Summary Charts 912.13
. Workweek 912.01

**Foreclosure, Repossession, or
Abandonment — Tax** 807.13

Foreign Workers 920
. Applying for the Visa 920.03
. Employment of 920
. Entry into the United States 920.04

Foreign Workers—continued
. Filing the I-129 Petition 920.02, 920.05

Form I-9 . . . . 917.01
. Instructions 917.05
. Lists of Acceptable Documents 917.07
. Requirements 917.05
. Reverifying Current Employees 917.05

Franchising 317
. Business Format 317.09
. Code of Ethics 317.05
. Disclosure Rule 317.13
. Evaluation 317.07
. Fee — Journal Entries 126
. Franchising in the Economy 317.09
. International Franchise Association . 317.05, 317.07
. Investing in a Franchise 317.03
. Key Issues Checklist 317.11
. Legal Issues 317.13
. Overview 317.01
. Product and Trade Name 317.09

Fringe Benefits — Tax 802.13

Future Value 632

G

Gains and Losses 807
. Depreciation 807.20
. Tax Basis amd Holding Period of Like-Kind
   Property and Boot Received 807.10
. Treatment and Assumption of Liabilities . . . 807.11

General Accounting Office 1002.01

General Services Administration 1002.01

Generally Accepted Accounting Principles
. Accounting Changes 201
. Accounting Policies 202
. APB 2 245
. APB 4 245
. APB 6 279
. APB 9 273
. APB 10 . . . . 143, 144, 229, 230, 279
. APB 12 . . . . 215, 217, 279
. APB 14 210
. APB 17 231
. APB 18 222
. APB 21 235
. APB 22 202
. APB 23 229
. APB 26 213
. APB 28 237
. APB 29 . . . . 104, 253
. APB 30 . . . . 213, 273
. ARB 43 . . . . 211, 217, 239, 263, 265
. ARB 45 249
. ARB 46 265
. ARB 51 206
. Business Combinations 203
. Cash Flow Statement 109, 204
. Changing Prices 205
. Consolidated Financial Statements 206
. Contingencies 207

Generally Accepted Accounting Principles—
continued

. Contributions 209
. Convertible Debt 210
. Current Assets and Current Liabilities 211
. Debt Extinguishment 213
. Deferred Compensation Contracts 215
. Depreciation 217
. Derivative Instruments and Hedging 218
. Development Stage Company 219
. Earnings Per Share 221
. Equity Method Investment 222
. FASB Interpretation 1 . . . . 201, 239
. FASB Interpretation 4 271
. FASB Interpretation 6 271
. FASB Interpretation 8 211
. FASB Interpretation 9 203
. FASB Interpretation 18 229
. FASB Interpretation 19 247
. FASB Interpretation 20 201
. FASB Interpretation 21 203
. FASB Interpretation 23 247
. FASB Interpretation 24 247
. FASB Interpretation 26 247
. FASB Interpretation 27 247
. FASB Interpretation 30 253
. FASB Interpretation 39 . . . . 211, 255
. FASB Interpretation 41 . . . . 211, 255
. FASB Interpretation 46 . . . . 105.03
. FASB Interpretation 47 . . . . 108, 290
. FASB Interpretation 48 229
. FASB Technical Bulletin 79-10 247
. FASB Technical Bulletin 79-12 247
. FASB Technical Bulletin 79-14 247
. FASB Technical Bulletin 79-16 247
. FASB Technical Bulletin 79-17 247
. FASB Technical Bulletin 79-18 247
. FASB Technical Bulletin 80-1 213
. FASB Technical Bulletin 84-4 213
. FASB Technical Bulletin 85-3 247
. FASB Technical Bulletin 85-5 203
. FASB Technical Bulletin 85-6 203
. FASB Technical Bulletin 86-2 247
. FASB Technical Bulletin 88-1 247
. Financial Instruments 223
. Impairment of a Loan 225
. Impairment of Long-Lived Assets 227
. Income Taxes 229
. Installment Method of Accounting 230
. Intangible Assets 231
. Interest Capitalized 233
. Interest on Receivables and Payables 235
. Interim Financial Reporting 237
. Inventory 239
. Investment in Debt and Equity Securities 241
. Investment Held by Not-For-Profits 243
. Investment Tax Credit 245
. Leases 247
. Long-Term Construction Contracts 249
. Mortgage Banking 251
. Non-Monetary Transactions 253
. Offsetting/Setoffs 255
. Pension Plans 257
. Postretirement Benefits 259
. Product Financing Arrangements 261

Generally Accepted Accounting Principles—
continued

. Quasi-Reorganizations 265
. Real Property Taxes 263
. Related Party Transactions 269
. Research and Development 271
. Results of Operations 273
. Revenue Recognition 275
. Segment Reporting 277
. SFAS 2 271
. SFAS 5 . . . . 207, 141.13
. SFAS 6 211
. SFAS 7 219
. SFAS 13 247
. SFAS 15 285
. SFAS 22 247
. SFAS 23 247
. SFAS 27 247
. SFAS 28 247
. SFAS 29 247
. SFAS 34 233
. SFAS 42 233
. SFAS 43 211
. SFAS 45 . . . . 144.03
. SFAS 47 289
. SFAS 48 275
. SFAS 49 261
. SFAS 57 269
. SFAS 62 233
. SFAS 65 . . . . 218, 251
. SFAS 66 266
. SFAS 68 271
. SFAS 72 231
. SFAS 78 211
. SFAS 84 210
. SFAS 86 271
. SFAS 87 257
. SFAS 89 205
. SFAS 91 247
. SFAS 93 217
. SFAS 94 206
. SFAS 95 . . . . 109, 204
. SFAS 98 247
. SFAS 102 204
. SFAS 104 204
. SFAS 106 . . . . 257, 259
. SFAS 107 223
. SFAS 109 . . . . 229, 245
. SFAS 111 201
. SFAS 112 . . . . 257, 259
. SFAS 114 . . . . 225, 285
. SFAS 115 241
. SFAS 116 209
. SFAS 118 . . . . 207, 225, 285
. SFAS 121 227
. SFAS 122 251
. SFAS 123 . . . . 145.09, 223, 281, 283
. SFAS 124 243
. SFAS 125 214
. SFAS 127 213
. SFAS 128 221
. SFAS 129 279
. SFAS 130 273
. SFAS 131 277
. SFAS 132 . . . . 142.02, 237, 257, 259

Generally Accepted Accounting Principles—
continued
. SFAS 133 . . . . 120, 218, 223
. SFAS 134 251
. SFAS 135 257
. SFAS 136 209
. SFAS 137 218
. SFAS 138 218
. SFAS 139 . . . . 205, 227
. SFAS 140 . . . . 213, 214
. SFAS 141 . . . . 105, 203
. SFAS 142 231
. SFAS 143 . . . . 108, 290
. SFAS 144 . . . . 115.08, 119, 227, 273
. SFAS 145 213
. SFAS 146 . . . . 108, 141.12, 290
. SFAS 147 . . . . . 105.01, 115.08, 203, 227, 231
. SFAS 148 . . . . 145.09, 237, 283
. SFAS 149 218
. SFAS 150 223
. SFAS 151 . . . . 239, 253
. SFAS 152 266
. SFAS 153 . . . . 104, 239
. SFAS 154 . . . . 104, 201
. SFAS 155 . . . . 214, 218
. SFAS 156 214
. SFAS 157 . . . . 285, 290, 295
. SFAS 158 . . . . 142.01, 142.03, 257, 259
. SFAS Interpretation 1 201
. SFAS Interpretation 7 219
. SFAS Interpretation 14 207
. SFAS Interpretation 18 . . . . 229, 237
. SFAS Interpretation 43 266
. SFAS Interpretation 45 . . . . 141.13, 207
. SFAS Interpretation 46 206
. Stockholder's Equity 279
. Stock-Based Compensation 283
. Troubled Debt Restructuring 285
. Unconditional Purchase Obligations 289

Gift Tax 805.01

Government Printing Office 1002.01

Gross Margin Ratio 663.05

Gross Profit Ratios 663.13

**Gross-Up — for Employer's Payment of
Employee's Taxes** 685.03

Growth 633

H

Health Care Costs 915.02

Health Insurance Benefits 915
. Continuation under COBRA 915.04
. Health Insurance Portability and
Accountability Act 915.01
. Women's Health and Cancer Rights Act . . . 915.03

Health Reimbursement Arrangement (HRA) . 903.09

Health Savings Account (HSA) 903.09, 802.64

**Highly Compensated Participant in Cafeteria
Plans — Tax** 802.15

Hiring 904
. Application 904.07
. Background Checks 904.05
. Checklist 904.05
. Costs of 904.07
. Employment at Will 904.04
. Family Members 904.01
. Identification numbers 904.03

Home Expenses
. Home Deductions 811.55
. Home Office Deduction 811.51
. *Soliman* Case 811.51

Hospice Care — Medicare Coverage 509.09

Hospital Inpatient Reserve Days 509.09

I

Immigration Reform and Control Act of 1986 . . 917
. Employee Eligibility Verification
Requirements 917.03

Impairment of a Loan 225

Impairment of Long-Lived Assets 115.08, 227

Income
. Continuing Operations 127.05
. Deferred Revenues 127.01
. Financial vs. Tax 127.03
. Journal Entries 127
. Ratios 663.05

Income Statement Analysis 403.05

Income — Taxes—see Taxation

Incorporation 129

Independent Contractor Status 919
. Business Relationships 919.01
. Common Law Factors 919.05
. Cost Difference from Employee 919.12
. Court Factors 919.06
. FICA Statutory Employee Rules 919.09
. Key Factors Summary 919.07
. Penalties for Treating Employees as
Independent Contractors 919.17
. Safe Havens Under Section 530 . . . . 919.13
. Tax treatment 919.11

Indexes 634

Individual Returns 811
. Estimated Tax 811.09
. Filing Requirements 811.05
. Personal Exemptions 811.03
. Self Employment Taxes 811.07
. Standard Deductions 811.03
. Tax Rate Schedules 811.01

Installment Method of Accounting 230

**Installment Sale with Depreciation
Recapture, Example** 802.29

Insurance
. Business Interruption 721.07
. Cash Surrender Value—Journal Entry 130

Insurance—continued
. Cash Value Corridor 721.04
. Checklists 721.09
. Cost Savings 721.15
. Coverage Summary Analysis 721.09
. Co-Insurance 721.07
. Disability Insurance 721.13
. Employee Benefit Evaluation 721.02
. Endowment Insurance 701.05
. Estimating Lost Earnings Due to Death 721.19
. Health Insurance 721.11
. How Much Life Insurance Needed . . 701.05, 721.16
. Life Insurance 721.02, 721.16, 721.17
. Life Insurance Annual Review Checklist . . . 721.09
. Life Insurance as an Investment 721.17
. Life Insurance Techniques 721.02
. Long-Term 721.23
. Overview of Insurance Planning 721.01
. Overview of Types — Chart 701.05
. Planning Techiques 721.03
. Reasons for Insurance 701.05
. Taxation 721.05
. Term Life Insurance 701.05
. Unemployment Insurance Cost Reduction
    Checklist 721.09
. Universal Life Insurance 701.05
. Variable Life Insurance 701.05
. Whole Life Insurance 701.05

Intangible Assets **231**

Interest
. Accounting Principles 233, 235
. Banker's Rule 635.05
. Capitalized — Accounting Principles 233
. Capitalized — Assets Constructed for Self-
    Use 133.01
. Cash Proceeds On Discount 635.09
. Compound 637
. Discount of Promissory Note 635.14
. Discount Rate Versus Effective 635.13
. Effective Rate Computations 635.16-635.25
. Interest Rate Corresponding to Discount . . . 635.10
. Modified Merchant's Rule 635.07
. Period of Compounding — Other Than
    Annual 651.25
. Present Value of Simple Interest Note 635.08
. Rate Equivalent to Cash Discount Rate 635.15

Interim Financial Reporting **237**

Internal Rate of Return **651.21**

Internal Revenue Service **817**
. Hotlines 1002.01
. Internal Revenue Code 817.01
. Internal Revenue Bulletin 817.01
. Internal Revenue Terms and Abbreviations . 817.01
. Overview 817.01
. Treasury Department Regulations 817.01
. Treasury Decisions 817.01

International Trade Administration **1002.03**

International Trade Commission **1002.01**

Inventory
. Accounting Principles 116.01, 239
. Analysis 639.01

Inventory—continued
. Costs 639.01, 639.02
. Estimation Methods 639.03
. EOQ — Cost of Capital 639.08
. EOQ — Size/Volume Discounts 639.11
. Gross Profit Estimation Method 639.03
. Management 639.01
. Reorder Cycle 639.07
. Reorder Models 639.05
. Sell or Scrap Decisions 639.13
. Turnover Ratio 663.09

Inventory—Journal Entries
. Average Inventory Method 131.11
. Change in Accounting Principle 116.01
. Dollar-Value LIFO 131.09
. FIFO 131.07
. Gross Margin Method 131.13
. LIFO Retail Method 131.17
. Lower-of-cost-or-market 131.01
. Periodic Inventory System 131.03
. Perpetual Inventory System 131.05
. Retail Method 131.15

Investment
. After Age 50 . . . . 701.14
. Basics 701.01
. Debts and Equities Securities — Accounting
    Principles 241
. Dollar Cost Averaging 705
. Goals 701.01
. Growth by Instrument Chart 701.09
. Funding 701.02
. Held by Not-For-Profits — Accounting
    Principles 243
. Historical Rate of Return Chart 701.01
. Importance of Time Client Illustration 701.01
. Inflation 701.01
. Rental Property 724
. Return 701.17
. Risk—Market Decline 701.19
. Risk—Overview 701.15
. Small Gain Difference Chart 701.07
. Specific Goals 701.13
. Stock Market Declines 725.02
. Tax Credit 245
. Yields After Inflation and Taxes Chart 701.11

Investment Instruments
. Bonds 701.05
. Corporate Bonds 701.05
. Dividend Reinvestment Plans 701.05
. Life Insurance 721.17
. Limited Partnerships 701.05
. Municipal Bonds 701.05
. Mutual Funds 701.05, 723
. Stocks 701.05
. Survey of Instruments 701.05
. U.S.Treasury Bills, Bonds and Notes 701.05

Investment Mix
. Asset Allocation 709.01
. Diversification 709.06
. Fund Type 709.09
. Life Stage 709.11
. Model Portfolios 709.05

INV

Involuntary Conversions 807.12

IRA
. Five Year Investment Accumulation Chart . . 715.07

J

Journal Entries 101
. Accounts Receivable: Assignment 101
. Accounts Receivable: Bad Debt 103
. Acquisitions of Assets by Exchange 104
. Bad Debt — Percentage-of-Outstanding-
    Receivables Method 103.04
. Bad Debts — Collections-Reestablishing
    Account Previously Written Off 103.07
. Bad Debt — Percentage-of-Sales Method . . 103.03
. Bad Debt — Write-off 103.06
. Bonds — Convertible 107.11
. Bonds — Interest Income and Discount
    Amortization 107.05
. Bonds — Issued with Detachable Stock
    Warrants 107.13
. Bonds — Long-Term Investments in Debt
    Security Purchase 107.03
. Bonds — Premium Amortization of Bond
    Cost 107.01
. Bonds — Premium or Discount 107.04
. Bonds — Recording Bond Issue 107.01
. Bonds — Retirement Before Maturity 107.07
. Bonds — Sale of Investment 107.09
. Business Combination to Recognize
    Goodwill 105.03
. Business Combinations 203
. Business Combinations—
. . Pooling of Interests
. . . Methods Eliminated 105.01
. . . Purchase Method 105.01
. Cash Flow Statement 109
. Cash Flow Statement — Direct 109.01
. Cash Flow Statement — Indirect 109.03
. Construction Contracts—Long Term 111
. Cost of Goods Manufactured Schedule 113
. Depreciation 115
. Deprecation — Composite Method 115.05
. Depreciation—Declining Balance 115.07
. Depreciation — Financial vs. Tax 115.01
. Depreciation — Fractional-Year Calculation . 115.03
. Derivatives 120
. Direct Costing 117
. Discontinued Segments 119
. Dividends 121
. Earnings Per Share 123
. Earnings Per Share — Basic 123.05
. Earnings Per Share — Diluted 123.06, 123.07
. Earnings Per Share — Retroactive
    Adjustments for Stock Splits, Dividends, Reverse
    Splits 123.03
. Earnings Per Share — Weighted Average
    Shares Outstanding 123.01
. Error Corrections 116
. Expenses 125
. Expenses—Accrued 125.01
. Expenses—Prepaid 125.03
. Financial Instruments 120

Journal Entries—continued
. Franchise 126
. Income 127
. Income—Continuing Operations 127.05
. Income—Deferred Revenues 127.01
. Income—Financial vs. Tax 127.03
. Incorporation 129
. Insurance—Cash Surrender Value 130
. Interest Capitalized — Assets Constructed for
    Self-Use 133.01
. Inventory 131
. Inventory — Average Inventory Method . . . 131.11
. Inventory — Dollar-Value LIFO 131.09
. Inventory — FIFO 131.07
. Inventory — Gross Margin Method 131.13
. Inventory — LIFO Retail Method 131.17
. Inventory — Lower-of-Cost-or-Market 131.01
. Inventory — Perceptual Inventory System . . 131.05
. Inventory — Retail Method 131.15
. Investments — Equity Method for Long Term
    Investment 137.03
. Investments — Marketable Equity
    Securities 137.01
. Lease 140
. Leases — Capital 104.02, 140.03
. Leases — Operating 140.01
. Losses — Cumulative Benefit 139.05
. Losses — Interim Period 139.01
. Losses — Later Periods 139.03
. Notes 141
. Notes — Discount 141.11
. Notes — Interest Bearing 141.05
. Notes — Liabilities Estimated 141.06
. Notes — Long-Term Notes Payable 141.01
. Notes — Non-Interest Bearing 141.03
. Notes — Present Value 141.07
. Notes — Present Value with Interest 141.09
. Pension Plan 142
. Pension Plan — Defined Contribution 142.02
. Pensions — Defined Benefit 142.01
. Postretirement Plan — Defined Benefit 142.03
. Postretirement Plan — Defined Contribution . 142.04
. Product Costing 149.01
. Product Costing — Equivalent Units of
    Production 149.07
. Product Costing — Quantity Variation 149.09
. Product Costing — Volume Variation by Job
    Cost 149.11
. Retained Earnings 143
. Revenue Recognition 144
. Revenue Recognition — Cost Recovery
    Method 144.01
. Revenue Recognition — Franchise Fee
    Revenue 144.03
. Salary 116.03
. Stock 145
. Stock—Dividends 145.06
. Stock — Issuance of Capital Stock 145.01
. Stock — Issues Pursuant to Subscription . . 145.03
. Stock — Issuing Stock for Property 145.05
. Stock — Options 145.09
. Stock — Section 1244 . . . . 305.05
. Stock — Split 145.07
. Stock — Warrants 145.11
. Taxes 146

Journal Entries—continued

. Taxes — Rate Change or Law Change 146.01
. Treasury Stock 147
. Treasury Stock — Cost vs. Par Value 147.01
. Troubled Debt Restructuring 148
. Troubled Debt Restructuring — Discharge . . 148.01
. Troubled Debt Restructuring — Modification
    of Terms 148.03
. Work-in-Process Costing 149

Jury Service Protection **908.09**

L

**Labor-Management Reporting and
    Disclosure Act of 1959** **908.08**

Leases

. Accounting Standards 247
. Capital Leases 104.02, 140.03
. Capitalized Value 643.03, 643.15
. Effective Rate of Interest 643.01
. Lease Buyout Price 643.17
. Operating 140.01
. Versus Purchase 643.05-643.12

Leverage **644**
. Financial 644.09-644.11
. Financial and Operating Combined 644.13
. Financing with Preferred, Common Stock and
    Bonds 644.15, 644.21
. Operating 644.03, 644.07
. Ratios 663.07

Library of Congress **1002.01**

Like-Kind Exchanges **807.09, 724.01**

Limited Liability Company **303.02, 309**

Limited Partnerships
. Overview as Investment 701.05
. Types 701.05

**Line of Credit vs. Accounts Payable
    Extension** **645**

Liquidation Value Valuation Method **405.03**

Liquidity Ratios **403.07**

Loan Amortization Summaries
. Table Usage 649.03
. Tables 691.27

Loan Application Information Checklist . . . **693.05**

Loans **693**

Long Term Ratios **663.11**

Losses
. Cumulative Benefit 139.05
. Interim Period 139.01
. Later Periods 139.03

M

Management Rate of Return Ratio **663.13**

Margin of Safety **647**

Marginal Analysis
. Marginal Cost 646.05
. Marginal Revenue 646.03
. Overview 646.01

Marine Corps **1002.01**

Marital Status Determination by Employer . . **907.19**

Market Derived Valuation Method **405.07**

Market Equity to Debt Ratio **663.01**

Markup
. Based on Cost 655.06
. Gross Profit 655.06
. Selling Price 656.07
. Percentage to Cover Deductions 655.06

Material Requirement Planning **149.02**

Medical and Dental Expenses **811.17**

Medical Savings Account (MSA) **903.09**

Medicare **509**
. 2003 Legislation 509.01
. Basics 509.02
. Buying Medicare Part A and Part B 509.02
. Care Not Reasonable and Necessary 509.07
. Custodial Care 509.07
. Description of Four Parts 509.02
. Disabled and Under Age 65 . . . . 509.05
. Enrollment in Medicare-Managed Care
    Plans 509.03
. Intermediaries 509.02
. Medicare and Other Insurance 509.05
. Provider Sponsored Organizations 509.03
. Qualified Medicare Beneficiaries 509.02
. Quality Improvement Organizations . 509.02, 509.17
. Special Enrollment Period 509.15
. Specified Low-Income Medicare
    Beneficiaries 509.02
. Those Eligible for Hospital Insurance
    (Part A) 509.02
. Those Eligible for Medical Insurance
    (Part B) 509.02
. When Protection Ends for People 65 and
    Older 509.15

Medicare Hospital Insurance (Part A)
. Appealing Decisions Made by
    Intermediaries 509.17
. Appealing Decisions Made by Part A
    Providers 509.17
. Appealing Decisions Made by Peer Review
    Organizations 509.17
. Benefit Period Defined 509.09
. Care in Psychiatric Hospital 509.09
. Care Outside the US 509.09
. Christian Science Sanatarium 509.09
. Conditions for Hospital Inpatient Care Under
    Medicare 509.09
. Getting Medicare Part A Insurance 509.09
. Home Health Care 509.09
. Hospice Care 509.09
. Hospital Inpatient Reserve Days 509.09

Medicare Laboratory Services
. Ambulance Transportation 509.13

Medicare Laboratory Services—continued
. Blood 509.13
. Breast Cancer Screening 509.13
. Durable Medical Equipment 509.13
. Heart and Liver Transplants 509.13
. Kidney Dialysis/Transplants 509.13
. Medical Supplies 509.13
. Drugs and Biologicals 509.13
. Medicare Coverage Summary Chart 509.19
. Pap Smear Screening 509.13
. Portable Diagnostic X-rays 509.13
. Prostate Tests 509.13
. Prosthetic Devices 509.13
. Radiation Therapy 509.13

Medicare Medical Insurance (Part B)
. Appealing Decisions Made by Carriers on
  Part B 509.17
. Ambulatory Surgical Services 509.11
. Deductible and Coinsurance Amounts ... 509.11
. Doctor's Services Covered 509.11
. Doctor's Services Not Covered 509.11
. Dentist's Services 509.11
. Getting Part B 509.15
. Home Health Services 509.11
. Major Outpatient Hospital Services Covered . 509.11
. Optometrists' Services 509.11
. Partial Hospitalization for Mental Health ... 509.11
. Payments 509.15
. Rural Health Care Clinics 509.11
. Some Outpatient Hospital Services Not
  Covered 509.11

Medicare Modernization Act of 2003 ...... **509.01**

Medicare Part B — Payments
. Assignment Payment Method 509.15
. Doctors Who Do Not Accept Assignment ... 509.15
. Medicare Approved Amounts 509.15
. Participating Doctors and Suppliers ... 509.15
. Participating Providers 509.15
. Payment Examples 509.15
. Special Rule for Doctors Performing Elective
  Surgery 509.15

Medicare Part C — Medicare Advantage
. Appealing Decisions Made under Medicare
  Advantage Part C 509.17
. Program Rules 509.16
. Provider-Sponsored Organizations 509.03

**Medicare Part D—Voluntary Prescription
  Drug Benefit Program** **509.02**

Medigap Policies **509.05**

Minimum Wage **913.01, 912.07, 912.08, 912.13**

Minority Business Development Agency .. **1002.03**

Modified Merchants Rule **635.07**

Mortgages
. Adjustable Rate 649.01
. Banking Activities — Accounting Principles ... 251
. Loan Summary Tables 691.27
. Summary Amortization 649.03

Moving Expenses **811.11**

Mutual Funds
. Ex-distribution Date 723.04
. Investment Checklist 723.05
. Open Ended vs. Closed End 723.05
. Overview 723.01
. Performance 723.07
. Portfolio Strategy 723.09
. Pricing and Commissions 723.03
. Public Offering Price 723.03

N

**National Aeronautics & Space
  Administration** **1002.03**

**National Archives and Records
  Administration** **1002.01**

National Association of Enrolled Agents .. **1001.04**

National Endowment for the Humanities .. **1002.01**

**National Institute of Standards &
  Technology** **1002.03**

National Labor Relations Act **908.07**

National Labor Relations Board **1002.01**

National Science Foundation **1002.01**

National Society of Accountants **1001.03**

Net Income to Sales Ratio **403.07**

Net Income to Tangible Net Worth Ratio .. **403.07**

Net Operating Profit Ratio **663.13**

Net Profit to Sales Ratio **663.13**

Net Sales to Inventory Ratio **663.09**

Net Sales to Tangible Net Worth Ratio **403.07,
  663.05**

Net Worth to Total Liabilities Ratio ... **663.01**

Non-Monetary Transactions **253**

Notes
. Discount 141.11
. Interest Bearing 141.05
. Liabilites Estimated 141.06
. Long-Term Notes Payable 141.01
. Non-Interest Bearing 141.03
. Present Value 141.07
. Present Value with Interest 141.09

O

Occupational Safety and Health Act **914.05**

**Occupational Safety & Health Review
  Commission** **1002.01**

Office of Business Liason **1002.03**

Office of Federal Procurement Policy **1002.01**

Office of Management & Budget **1002.01**

Office of Personnel Management **1002.01**

Offsetting/Setoff — Accounting Principles **255**

Operating Expense Ratio 403.07, 663.05

Operating Ratio 403.07, 663.05

Opportunity Cost Analysis 648

OSHA
. Appeals 914.05
. Penalties/Sanctions 914.05
. Standards 914.05
. Whistleblower Protections 908.04

Overseas Private Investment Corporation . 1002.01

P

Paid Time Off 903.08

Partnerships
. Attributes 309.03
. Basis for Partnership Interest 309.07
. Checklist for Set-Up 309.05
. Definition 309.01
. Distributions 309.09
. Partner's Liabilities 309.13
. Partnership Changes 309.17
. Partnership Liabilities 309.15
. Partnership Liquidation 309.19

Passive Activity Gains and Losses 809
. Filling In Forms 809.05
. Form 8582 Comprehensive Example 809.01
. Worksheets 809.03

Past Due Ratio 663.09

Patent & Trademark Office 1002.03

Peace Corps 1002.01

Penalties, Tax
. Taxpayer 813.01

Pension Benefit Guaranty Corp 1002.01

Pension Plans —also see Retirement
. Coverage Chart 923.03
. Defined Benefit 142.01, 257
. Defined Contribution 142.02, 257

Performance Objectives 907.03

Periodic Average 681.05

Personal Exemptions, Standard Deductions,
and Taxable Income Brackets 811.03

Personal Responsibility and Work
Opportunity Reconciliation Act of 1996 918
. New Hire Reporting 918.01

Personal Service Corporation Tax Rate 305.07

Postal Service Supplier Diversity Office . . 1002.01

Postretirement Benefits 259

Power of Attorney 705.08

Present Value
. Annuities with Payments Increasing or
     Decreasing in Constant Amount . 651.11, 691.17
. Annuities with Payments Increasing or
     Decreasing in Constant Ratio . . . 651.13, 691.21

Present Value—continued
. Basic Concepts 651.01
. $1 Received at End of Period Tables 691.09
. Ordinary Annuity Decreasing in Constant
     Amount Tables 691.19
. Ordinary Annuity Decreasing in Constant
     Ratio Tables 691.23
. Ordinary Annuity Increasing in Constant
     Amount Tables 691.17
. Ordinary Annuity Increasing in Constant Ratio
     Tables 691.21
. Ordinary Annuity Table Usage 651.07
. Ordinary Annuity — Monthly Basis Table
     Usage 651.09
. Periodic Rent of an Annuity 651.08

Price Earnings
. Multiples Valuation Method 405.07
. Projections 713
. Ratio 663.13

Pricing 656
. Competitor Considerations 656.03, 656.06
. Product Considerations 656.05
. Segmenting Markets 656.04
. Sensitivity 656.02
. Strategies 656.01

Probability and Expected Value 653

Probability Range Expected Value 653.07

Product Costing 149.01

Product Financing Arrangements 261

Product Pricing 654, 656.05
. Formula 656.15
. Nonfinancial Considerations 654.02

Profit
. Analysis by Contribution Margin 655.04
. Business Profit Triangle 658
. Discount 655.07
. Fixed Expenses Given Any Known Amount of
     Sales 655.05
. Gross Profit Variation 655.01
. Growth vs. Debt 633.02
. Mark Downs 655.07
. Markups 655.06
. Profit Change by Price Cut 655.08
. Profit Analysis Per Product 655.03
. Rebate 655.07
. Rental Property Investment Return 655.08
. Required Sales Volume 655.15
. Sales Volume Change Required by Price
     Change 655.14
. Sales Volume Required to Recover Lost
     Profits 655.09
. Selling Price by Job Cost 656.11
. Selling Price — Markup Based on Cost 656.07
. Top Down Pricing for Service by Individual . . 656.09

Profitability Index 657

Profitability Ratios 663.13

Progressive Average 681.07

Projection 659

Property Tax Expenses **811.21**

Property Tax Expenses Deductions **811.21**

Proprietorship—Sole
. Definition 311.01
. Advantages vs. Disadvantages 311.03
. Formation 311.05
. Liquidation Schedule 311.07
. Start-Up Checklist 311.09

**Purchases Computed from Balance Sheet
Items** **671.03**

Q

Quick Accounts Receivable Ratio **663.09**

Quick Ratio **663.09**

R

Railroad Retirement Board **1002.01**

Random Numbers **661, 691.37**

Rate of Return on Common Stock Equity . . . **663.13**

Ratios
. Absolute Liquidity Ratio 663.09
. Accounts Payable Turnover 663.04
. Accountants Receivable Turnover Ratio . . . 663.09
. Assets Turnover 663.13
. Average Collection Period 403.07, 663.09
. Bad Debt Index 663.09
. Bankruptcy/Solvency Indicator Ratios 663.01
. Cash Flow to Debt Ratio 663.01
. Collection Ratio 663.09
. Common Stock Cash Flow Coverage 663.03
. Coverage Ratios 403.07, 663.03
. Current Assets and Current Liabilities 211
. Current Assets to Total Debt Ratio 663.11
. Current Asset Turnover Ratio 403.07, 663.21
. Current Debt to Net Worth Ratio . . . 403.07, 663.21
. Current Liabilities to Inventory Ratio . 403.07, 663.21
. Current Ratio 403.07, 663.09
. Days Coverage with No Revenue 663.09
. Debt Cash Flow Coverage 663.03
. Debt Ratio 663.07
. Debt to Equity Ratio 663.07
. Depreciation to Fixed Assets Ratio 663.05
. Dividend Payout Ratio 663.11
. Dividend Yield Ratio 663.11
. Earning Per Share Ratio 663.13
. Earnings Power Ratio 403.07, 663.13
. EBIT to Total Assets Ratio 663.01
. Equity Ratio 663.07
. Financial Ratios 403.07
. Finished Goods Turnover Ratio 663.09
. Fixed Assets to Net Worth Ratio 663.11
. Fixed Charge Coverage Ratio 663.03
. Gross Margin Ratio 663.05
. Gross Profit Ratios 403.07, 663.13
. Income Ratios 403.07, 663.05
. Inventory to Working Capital Ratio . . 403.07, 663.21
. Inventory Turnover Ratio 403.07, 663.09
. Leverage Ratios 663.07

Ratios—continued
. Liquidity Ratio 663.09
. Liquidity Ratios 403.07, 663.09
. Long Term Debt to Net Working Capital
    Ratio 403.07
. Long Term Ratios 663.11
. Management Rate of Return Ratio 663.13
. Market Equity to Debt Ratio 663.01
. Net Earnings to New Working Capital 663.21
. Net Income to Sales Ratio 403.07
. Net Income to Tangible Net Worth Ratio . . . 403.07
. Net Operating Profit Ratio 663.13
. Net Profit to Sales Ratio 663.13
. Net Sales to Inventory Ratio 663.09
. Net Sales to Tangible Net Worth Ratio 403.07,
    663.05
. Net Worth to Total Liabilities Ratio 663.01
. Operating Expense Ratio 403.07, 663.05
. Operating Profit Margin 403.07
. Operating Ratio 403.07, 663.05
. Past Due Ratio 663.09
. Preferred Stock Cash Flow Coverage 663.03
. Price Earnings 663.13
. Profit Margin 663.13
. Profitability Ratios 403.07, 663.13
. Quick Accounts Receivable Ratio 663.09
. Quick Ratio 663.09
. Rate of Return on Common Stock Equity . . . 663.13
. Raw Materials Turnover Ratio 663.09
. Repairs and Maintenance to Fixed Assets
    Ratio 663.05
. Repairs and Maintenance to Net Sales 663.05
. Retained Earnings to Total Assets 663.01
. Return on Equity 663.13
. Return on Total Assets 663.13
. Residual Income Ratio 663.19
. Return on Assets Employed 663.13
. Sales Acceptance Ratio 663.05
. Sales to Assets 663.01
. Sales to Receivables 403.07
. Sales to Total Operating Assets 403.07
. Stockholder's Equity to Total Assets 663.11
. Supplies Turnover Ratio 663.09
. Times Interest Earned Ratio 403.07, 663.03
. Total Asset Turnover 663.13
. Total Debt to Net Worth Ratio 663.11
. Total Fixed Charge Coverage Ratio 403.07
. Total Interest Coverage Ratio 403.07, 663.03
. Turnover of Total Operating Assets Ratio . . 663.13
. Work-in-Process Turnover Ratio 663.09
. Working Capital Changes Effect on Cash . . 688.04
. Working Capital — Permanent 688
. Working Capital Ratios 403.07, 663.21
. Working Capital to Total Assets Ratio 663.01
. Working Capital Turnover Ratio . . . 403.07, 663.21

Real Estate Valuation **403.09**

**Real Estate Valuation — Income
Capitalization Approach** **403.09**

**Real Property Taxes — Accounting
Standards** **263**

Record Retention Requirements **815**
. Business Tax Records 815.01
. Return Preparers 815.03

Refinancing 665

Related Party Transactions 269

Repairs and Maintenance to Fixed Assets
   Ratio 663.05

Repairs and Maintenance to Net Sales 663.05

Replacement Value Valuation Method 405.03

Research and Development 271

Residual Income Ratio 663.19

Residual Method, Example of Asset
   Purchase 807.06

Results of Operations 273

Retail Inventory Estimation Method 639.03

Retained Earnings 143

Retained Earnings to Total Assets Ratio . . . 663.01

Retirement—also see Pension Plans, Retirement Plans
. Considerations 922
. Deduction 923.01
. Distribution Rules 924
. Early Retirement Concerns 922.02
. Health Benefits 922.01
. Income After Inflation Chart 715.09
. Income Based on Various Principles Chart . 715.05
. Provisions for Special Retirement Situations . 924.13
. Retirement Plans 923
. Savings Incentive Match Plan for
    Employees 923.05
. SIMPLE Advantages 923.06
. Simplified Employee Pensions 923.07
. Sources of Information 922.05
. Summary of Features Chart 923.03
. Withdrawals of Savings Chart 715.04

Return on Assets Employed (ROAE) Ratio . 663.13

Return on Equity by Financial Performance . 663.15

Return on Investment 663.17, 667
. Age-Specific 639.15
. Average Book Method 667.09
. Capital Asset Sale 667.14
. Dupont Method 667.12
. Earning Power for Company 667.11
. Net Payback Method 667.05
. Original Book Method 667.07
. Payback Method 667.03
. Present Value of Dividend Growth 651.06
. Real Rate 667.13
. Simple 667.01

Return on Shareholder's Equity 663.17

Return vs. Risk vs. Time 701.15

Revenue Recognition
. Cost Recovery Method 144.01
. Franchise Fee Revenue 144.03

Revenue Valuation Methods 405.05

Risk by Investment Vehicle 701.15

Rule of 78 Factors 669

S

S Corporation
. Advantage and Disadvantages 313.03
. Definition 313.01
. ESBT 313.07
. Overview 313.13
. Tax Treatment of Shareholders 313.05

Sales 671

Sales Acceptance Ratio 663.05

Sales and Use Taxes 805.09

Sales Computed from Balance Sheet Items . 671.01

Sales Tax 673

Sales to Assets Ratio 663.01

Sales to Total Operating Assets Ratio 403.07

Sales Volume Change Required Given Sales
   Price Changes 655.14

Sales Volume Required to Recover Lost
   Profits 655.09

Savings and Investment Types 701.01

Savings Institutions 701.03

Savings Instruments 701.03
. Certificate of Deposit (CD) 701.03
. NOW Accounts 701.03
. Passbook Savings 701.03
. Savings Bonds 701.03
. Series EE Savings Bonds 701.03
. Series HH Savings Bonds 701.03
. U.S. Government Savings Bonds 701.03

Section 1244 Stock 305.11

Securities—also see Stock
. Convertible Stocks 725.09
. Index Tracking Stocks 725.16
. Indexes 725.07
. Initial Public Offerings 725.17
. Overview 725.01
. Stock—Bear Market 725.25
. Stock Exemptions From the Securities Act of
    1933 . . . . 725.11
. Stock Market Information 725.03
. Stock Options 725.13
. Stock Options—Employee 725.14
. Stock—Returns 725.06
. Stock Trading 725.15
. Types of Securities Orders 725.05

Securities and Exchange Commission . . . 1002.01

Segment Reporting 277

SFAS 2 271

SFAS 3 201

SFAS 5 . . . . 207, 141.13

SFAS 6 211

SFAS 7 219

SFAS 13 247

SFAS 15	285
SFAS 22	247
SFAS 23	247
SFAS 27	247
SFAS 28	247
SFAS 29	247
SFAS 34	233
SFAS 42	233
SFAS 43	211
SFAS 47	289
SFAS 48	275
SFAS 49	261
SFAS 57	269
SFAS 62	233
SFAS 65	251
SFAS 66	266
SFAS 68	271
SFAS 72	231
SFAS 73	201
SFAS 78	211
SFAS 84	210
SFAS 86	271
SFAS 87	257
SFAS 89	205
SFAS 91	247
SFAS 93	217
SFAS 94	206
SFAS 95	204
SFAS 98	247
SFAS 102	204
SFAS 104	204
SFAS 106	257, 259
SFAS 107	223
SFAS 109	229, 245
SFAS 111	201
SFAS 112	257, 259
SFAS 114	225, 285
SFAS 115	241
SFAS 116	209
SFAS 118	207, 225, 285
SFAS 121	227
SFAS 122	251
SFAS 123	145.09, 223, 281, 283
SFAS 124	243
SFAS 125	213
SFAS 127	213
SFAS 128	221
SFAS 129	279
SFAS 130	273
SFAS 131	273, 277
SFAS 132	142.02, 237, 257, 259
SFAS 133	120, 218, 223
SFAS 134	251
SFAS 135	257
SFAS 136	209
SFAS 137	218
SFAS 138	218
SFAS 139	205, 227
SFAS 140	213, 214
SFAS 141	105, 203
SFAS 142	231
SFAS 143	108, 290
SFAS 144	115.08, 119, 227, 273
SFAS 145	213
SFAS 146	108, 141.12, 290
SFAS 147	105.01, 115.08, 203, 227, 231
SFAS 148	145.09, 237, 283
SFAS 149	218
SFAS 150	223
SFAS 151	239, 253
SFAS 152	266
SFAS 153	104, 239
SFAS 154	104, 201
SFAS 155	214, 218
SFAS 156	214
SFAS 157	285, 290, 295
SFAS 158	142.01, 142.03, 257, 259
SFAS Interpretation 1	201
SFAS Interpretation 7	219
SFAS Interpretation 14	207
SFAS Interpretation 18	229, 237
SFAS Interpretation 43	266
SFAS Interpretation 45	141.13, 207
SFAS Interpretation 46	206
Share-based Payments	283
Simple Interest Tables	691.03

SFA

Simple Return on Investment 667.01

Small Business Administration 501, 1002.01, 1002.03
. Interest Rate Policy 501.02
. Loan Decision Considerations 501.01
. Loan Guaranty Program 501.03
. Loan Terms and Eligibility 501.01, 501.02
. Loan Types 501.03, 501.04, 501.05, 501.06
. Overview 501, 693.07
. Survey of Programs 501.03

Small Business Corporation (Section 1244) Defined 305.11

Small Business Development Centers . . . 1002.03

Smithsonian Institution 1002.01

Social Security Administration 1002.01
. Benefits for a Divorced Spouse 505.01
. Credits 505.03
. Full Benefits Age Chart 505.01
. Internet Service 510
. Maximum Wages Covered Chart 505.05
. Sign Up 505.01
. Summary Table 511.01
. Supplemental Security Income 502

Social Security Disability
. Claim Denials & Appeals 503.05
. Determination 503.03
. Eligibility 503.01
. For People With HIV Infection 503.01
. Government Pension Offset 503.06
. How Other Payments Affect Benefits 503.06
. Post Approval 503.06
. Process 503.03
. Rules for the Blind 503.03
. Ticket to Work and Work Incentive
   Improvement Act 503.06
. Work Requirements 503.01

Social Security — Earnings
. Rules under Senior Citizen Freedom to Work
   Act 505.03

Social Security — Supplemental Security Income (SSI)
. Continuing Disability Reviews (CDRs) 502.11
. Debt Collection 502.15
. Deeming 502.07
. Eligibility 502.03
. Fraud 502.13
. Living in Institution Impact 502.09
. Overview 502.01
. Sign Up 502.10
. SSI Disability 502.05

Social Security Retirement Benefits
. Basics and Decisions 505.01
. Delayed Retirement 505.01
. Early Retirement 505.01
. Increase for Delayed Retirement Chart . . . 505.01
. Internet Application 505.01
. Larger Benefits for Additional Work 505.04
. Personalized Benefit Estimate 505.01
. Spouse and Children Benefits 505.01
. Tables 505.05

Social Security Retirement Benefits—continued
. Taxability 505.04
. Working Recipients 505.03, 505.04

Social Security Survivors Benefits 507

Specified Low Income Medicare Beneficiaries (SLMB) 509.02

SSI Requirements 502.03

Standard Costs 674
. Overhead Rate 674.01

Standard and Poor's 500 Index 725.07

State Agencies and Departments of Revenue . 1003

State Societies 1001.05

Stock
. Bear Market 725.25
. Dividends 145.06
. Issuance of Capital Stock 145.01
. Issues Pursuant to Subscription 145.03
. Issuing Stock for Property 145.05
. Options 145.09
. Right Theoretical Value 676.01
. Right Value — Allocation of Cost 676.03
. Rights 676
. Selling 725.20
. Split 145.07
. Warrants 145.11

Stockholder's Equity 279

Stockholder's Equity to Total Assets Ratio . 663.11

Substantiation of Business Expenses 821

Sum of Series of Payments 677

Sum of Series of Payments with Constant Dollar Change 677.01

Sum of Series of Payments with Constant Percentage Change 677.03

Sunk Cost Analysis 678

Supplemental Security Income (SSI)—See Social Security Supplemental Security Income

Surface Transportation Board 1002.01

Survival Insurance—Social Security 507

T

Tables
. $10,000 Investment Earning 10% Extra Gain
   per Extra 1% of Interest per Year 701.07
. Actual Yield of Investment After Federal
   Taxes, After State Taxes and After
   Inflation 701.11
. Amount of Earnings Lost Before 65 Due to
   Death 721.19
. Annual Rate Given Vendor Discounts 609.01
. Bond Yields 719.10
. Comparison of Up-Front Fees and Mortgage
   Interest Rates 691.31
. Cost of Debt After Inflation 691.01
. Diversification of Investment Chart 709.06

Tables—continued

. Effective Annual Yield for Different Periods of
Compounding 691.05
. Future Value of $1 at End of Period 691.09
. Future Value of Ordinary Annuity of $1 per
Period 691.15
. Historical Rate of Return 701.01
. Impact of Time on IRA Investment of $2,000
per Year for Five Years 715.07
. Interest Factors for Rule of 78 . . . . 691.33
. Investment Risk by Vehicle 701.15
. Life Expectancy 721.21
. Loan Amortization Summaries 691.27
. Market Decline vs. Time Needed to
Recover 701.19
. Markups on Cost for Gross Profits 655.06
. Markups to Cover Deductions 655.06
. Monthly Income from Various Principles . . . 715.05
. Monthly Investment Required to Fund
College Expenses 703
. Mortgage Summary Amortization — Various
Rates 691.25
. Mortgage Summary Amortization — Given
Term 691.29
. New Issues of Corporations by Type of
Offering and Industry Group 1990-1996 . . 725.15
. Number of Days Between Dates 617.03
. Percent Change in Units Allowed to Maintain
Gross Profit Margin 691.35
. Percentage Gain Given Various Premium
Rates per $1,000 of Insurance 721.17
. Possible Value of $10,000 Investment in
Various Instruments 701.09
. Possible Value of $2,000 per Year Into IRA
Investments 715.02
. Present Value of $1 Received at End of
Period 691.07
. Present Value of Ordinary Annuity
Decreasing in Constant Amount 691.19
. Present Value of Ordinary Annuity
Decreasing in Constant Ratio 691.23
. Present Value of Ordinary Annuity Increasing
in Constant Amount 691.17
. Present Value of Ordinary Annuity Increasing
in Constant Ratio 691.21
. Present Value of Ordinary Annuity of $1 per
Period 691.11
. Present Value of Ordinary Annuity of $1 per
Year Based on Monthly Compounding of Nominal
Annual Rates 691.13
. Projected Price/Earnings Ratios for Given
Periods, for Given Projected Annual
Growth Rate 713
. Random Number Tables 691.37
. Return vs. Risk vs. Time 701.15
. Savings and Investment Types 701.01
. Simple Interest 691.03
. Specific Goals and Investment Required to
Reach Them 701.13
. Total of Savings Withdrawal for Given
Terms 715.04
. Value of Retirement Income After Inflation . . 715.09

Tax Annualized 679

Taxation

. Adoption 811.37
. Accumulated Earnings Tax 802.05
. Alternative Minimum Tax for Corporation . . . 802.03
. Allocation Rules for Applicable Asset
Acquisitions 807.05
. Amortization of Goodwill 807.07
. Automobile Expenses 802.37, 802.39, 802.41
. Automobile Fixed and Variable Rate
Allowance 802.39
. Automobile Lease Valuation 802.41
. Automobile Mileage Rates 802.41
. Bad Debts — Tax 811.43
. Basis Summary Chart 807.23
. Bonds — Tax Exempt vs. Taxable 719.09
. Business Tax Issues 802
. Cafeteria Plan — Taxation 802.15
. Capital Gains Tax Rates 807.03
. Casualty Losses Taxation Chart 811.23
. Child and Dependent Care Tax Credit 811.35
. Conversions 807.12
. Corporate Tax 802.01
. Deductibility Summary for Schedule A 811.27
. Deductions 811
. Dependent Care Assistance Plans 802.11
. Depreciation 115, 217, 807.15
. Depreciation — Auto 807.21
. Educational Assistance Plans — Tax 802.09
. Employee vs. Independent Contractor Sec.
530 Examination 919.13
. Employment Taxes — Defined 907.03
. Employment Taxes — Deposit Requirement   907.05,
907.07, 907.11, 907.13
. Employment Taxes — Safe Harbor/De
Minimis Rules 907.09
. Employment Wages and Withholding 907
. Entertainment Expenses 811.47, 811.49
. Estate and Other Taxes 805
. Estate Tax Rates Chart 805.05
. Estimated Tax Payment Chart 811.09
. Foreclosures, Repossession, or
Abandonment 807.13
. Fringe Benefits — Tax 802.13
. Gains and Losses 807
. Gift Tax 805.01
. Home Expenses 811.55
. Home Office Deduction . . . 811.55, 811.57, 811.59
. Income Taxes — Accounting Principles . . . 229
. Income — Financial vs. Tax 127.03
. Independent Contractor Status 919
. Individual Returns 811
. Like-Kind Exchanges 807.09
. Limited Liability Companies 802.07
. Medical and Dental Expenses 811.17
. Moving Expenses 811.11
. Passive Activity Gains and Losses 809
. Penalties, Tax 813.01
. Property Tax Expenses 811.21
. Real Property Cost Treatment Chart 811.21
. Reimbursements and Allowances 802.17
. S-Corporation — Tax Treatment of
Shareholders 313.05
. Section 1245 Depreciable Personal Property
Used in Trade or Business 807.17

Taxation—continued
. Section 1250 Depreciable Real Property of a
    Business or Trade 807.19
. State Death Taxes Chart 805.07
. State Sales and Use Taxes 805.09
. Tax Annualized 679
. Tax Audits 817
. Tax Positions — Uncertain 146.02
. Tax Rate Schedules 811.01
. Tax Withholding Deposits — Nonpayroll 907
. Taxpayer Penalties Chart 813.01
. Travel Expenses 811.67
. Unified Credit Against Gift Tax 805.01
. Withholding — Allowances 907.15
. Withholding — Benefits 907.17
. Withholding — Exemptions 907.19
. Withholding — From Pensions and
    Annuities 907.13
. Withholding — Included and Excluded
    Wages 907.01
. Withholding — On Eligible Rollover
    Distributions 907.13
. Withholding — On Nonperiodic Payments . . 907.13
. Withholding — On Periodic Payments 907.13
. Withholding — Penalties 907.21
. Withholding — Taxes for Employees —
    Record Keeping 907.23

Tax Audits—Substantiation of Expenses 821
. Business Expense Summary Chart 821.11
. Entertainment 821.05
. Evidence Rules 821.13
. Expenses Summary 821.02
. Gifts 821.07
. Listed Property 821.09
. Relief from Joint and Several Liability on Joint
    Return 821.15
. Travel 821.03
. Vehicles 821.01

Tax Legislation Highlights 801

Taxpayer Penalties Chart 813.01

Term Life Insurance 701.05

Times Interest Earned Ratio 403.07, 663.03

Total Debt to Net Worth Ratio 663.11

Total Fixed Charge Coverage Ratio 403.07

Total Interest Coverage Ratio 403.07, 663.03

Travel Expenses 811.67

**Treasury Department Regulations/
    Procedures** 817.01

Treasury Stock 147

Treasury Stock — Cost vs. Par Value 147.01

Trend Based on Moving Average 681.03

Trends 681
. Periodic Average 681.05
. Progressive Average 681.07
. Trend Based on Moving Average 681.03
. Trend Line — Projection 681.01

Troubled Debt Restructuring
. Accounting Principles 285
. Discharge 148.01
. Modification of Terms 148.03

Turnover of Total Operating Assets Ratio . . 663.13

U

Uncollectable Receivables 103

Unconditional Purchase Obligations 289

Unified Credit Against Gift Tax 805.01

**Uniformed Services Employment and
    Reemployment Rights Act (USERRA)** . . 908.03

United States Postal Service 1002.01

United States Tax Court 1002.01

Unit Investment Trusts 727

Universal Life Insurance 701.05

V

Valuation —see Business Valuation

Variable Life Insurance 701.05

Vehicle Business Use 682
. Recordkeeping 682.01

Venture Capital 683

**Voluntary Employees' Beneficiary
    Associations (VEBAs)** 903.07
. VEBAs—Form of WBT 903.07
. Welfare Benefit Trust 903.05

W

Wages 685
. Commissions 685.11
. Defined 907.01
. Determining Gross Wages When Net Wages
    Are Known 685.01
. Military Pay 907.02
. Minimum Wage 912.07
. Paid in Property 907.01
. Performance Appraisal 907.26
. Wages Benefits Estimate 685.05
. Withholding 907

Wasting Asset 687, 621.03

Wasting Asset — Value 687.01, 687.02

Welfare Reform —see Personal Responsibility and
    Work Opportunity

Whole Life Insurance 701.05

Withholding
. Allowances 907.15
. Benefits 907.17
. Exemptions 907.19
. From Pensions and Annuities 907.13
. Included and Excluded Wages 907.01

Withholding—continued
. On Eligible Rollover Distributions 907.13
. On Nonperiodic Payments 907.13
. On Periodic Payments 907.13
. Penalties 907.21
. Taxes for Employees—Record Keeping . . . 907.23
. Withholding Tax Rules Chart 907.23

**Worker Adjustment and Retraining
Notification Act (WARN)** **908.02**

Work-in-Progress Costing
. Product Costing 149.01
. Manufacturing — Material Requirement
. . . . Planning 149.02
. Job Order — Product Costing 149.03

Work-in-Progress Costing—continued
. Equivalent Units of Production 149.07
. Quantity Variation 149.09
. Volume Variation by Job Cost 149.11

Working Capital **688**
. Ratios 403.07, 663.01, 663.21

Y

Yield **689**

Z

Z-Score Analysis **663.01**